Contributors

Jay Ritter
University of Florida

Myron Scholes
*Stanford University and Chairman
of Oak Hill Platinum Partners*

Lemma Senbet
University of Maryland

William Sharpe
*Stanford University and cofounder
of Financial Engines*

Robert Shiller
Yale University

Laura Starks
University of Texas

Avanidhar Subrahmanyam
UCLA

Anjan Thakor
University of Michigan

Sheridan Titman
University of Texas

Greg Udell
Indiana University

Theo Vermaelen
INSEAD

Rohan Williamson
Georgetown University

Kent Womack
Dartmouth College

We are also grateful to the following individuals who shared their insights based on their experience practicing corporate finance. Our interviews with them appear in SMART PRACTICES VIDEOS and SMART ETHICS VIDEOS.

Beth Acton
*Vice President and Treasurer (former),
Ford Motor Company, currently
Chief Financial Officer, Comerica*

David Baum
*Cohead of M&A for the Americas,
Goldman Sachs*

Andy Bryant
*Executive Vice President of Finance
and Enterprise Systems, Chief
Financial Officer, Intel Corp.*

Beverly Caen
*Former Vice President, Instinet
Corporation*

David Childress
*Asset Liability Manager, Ford
Motor Co.*

Tom Cole
*Leveraged Finance Group,
Deutsche Bank*

John Eck
*President of Broadcast and Network
Operations, NBC*

Jay Goodgold
*Managing Director, Equities Division,
Goldman Sachs*

David Haeberle
*Chief Executive Officer,
Command Equity Group*

Jeff Kauffman
*Portfolio Manager, Managing
Director, Omega Advisors*

David Nickel
*Controller, Intel Communications
Group, Intel Corp.*

Jon Olson
Vice President of Finance, Intel Corp.

Frank Popoff
*Chairman of the Board (retired),
Dow Chemical*

Todd Richter
*Managing Director, Head of Equity
Healthcare Research, Bank of
America Securities*

Pam Roberts
*Executive Director of Corporate
Services, Cummins Inc.*

Paul Savastano
*Director of Information Technology,
Sprint Corp.*

Jackie Sturm
*Director of Finance for Technology
and Manufacturing, Intel Corp.*

Keith Woodward
*Vice President of Finance,
General Mills*

BRIEF CONTENTS

See Appendix C for a listing of Key Formulas used in the text.

CORPORATE FINANCE

CORPORATE FINANCE

Scott B. Smart
Indiana University

William L. Megginson
University of Oklahoma

Lawrence J. Gitman
San Diego State University

THOMSON
SOUTH-WESTERN

Australia · Canada · Mexico · Singapore · Spain · United Kingdom · United States

THOMSON

SOUTH-WESTERN

Corporate Finance

Scott B. Smart, William L. Megginson, Lawrence J. Gitman

Vice-President / Editorial Director:
Jack Calhoun

Vice-President / Editor-in-Chief:
Mike Roche

Executive Editor:
Mike Reynolds

Senior Developmental Editor:
Trish Taylor

Freelance Developmental Editor:
Joanne Butler

Production Editor:
Tamborah E. Moore

Senior Marketing Manager:
Charlie Stutesman

Senior Media Technology Editor:
Vicky True

Media Developmental Editor:
John Barans

Senior Media Production Editor:
Mark Sears

Manufacturing Coordinator:
Sandee Milewski

Production House:
G & S Typesetters, Inc.

Printer:
R.R. Donnelley, Willard, OH

Senior Design Project Manager:
Michelle Kunkler

Cover and Internal Designer:
Ramsdell Design, Cincinnati

Cover Images:
© PhotoDisc, Inc.

Library of Congress Control Number:
2002115168

ISBN: 0-03-0350-76-X (core text +
Student CD + InfoTrac package)

ISBN: 0-324-26960-9 (core text +
Student CD package)

ISBN: 0-324-27300-2 (core text)

To Dad, the first and best author in the family.

SBS

To my father, who made it all possible.

WLM

To Robin, my coauthor in life.

LJG

ABOUT THE AUTHORS

Scott B. Smart

Scott Smart has been a member of the finance department at Indiana University since 1990. He has published articles in scholarly journals such as the *Journal of Finance,* the *Journal of Financial Economics,* and the *Review of Economics and Statistics.* His research has been cited by the *Wall Street Journal, Business Week,* and other major newspapers and periodicals. Professor Smart holds a Ph.D. from Stanford University and has been recognized as a master teacher, winning more than a dozen teaching awards, all at the graduate level. His consulting clients include Intel and Unext.

William L. Megginson

Bill Megginson is Professor and Rainbolt Chair in Finance at the University of Oklahoma. He is also a voting member of the Italian Ministry of Economics and Finance's Global Advisory Committee on Privatization. He has published refereed articles in several top academic journals, including the *Journal of Economic Literature,* the *Journal of Finance,* the *Journal of Financial Economics,* the *Journal of Financial and Quantitative Analysis,* and *Foreign Policy.* Dr. Megginson has a Ph.D. in finance from Florida State University. He has visited 52 countries and has served as a privatization consultant for the New York Stock Exchange, the OECD, the IMF, the World Federation of Exchanges, and the World Bank.

Lawrence J. Gitman

Lawrence J. Gitman, professor of finance at San Diego State University, is a prolific textbook author and has published numerous articles in various finance-related journals. He is past president of the San Diego chapter of the Financial Executives Institute, the Midwest Finance Association, and the Academy of Financial Services. He also served as Vice President for Financial Education of the Financial Management Association. He received his bachelor's degree from Purdue University, his M.B.A. from the University of Dayton, and his Ph.D. from the University of Cincinnati.

PREFACE

WHY DO WE NEED ANOTHER M.B.A.-LEVEL CORPORATE FINANCE TEXT?

Change creates opportunity. New ideas, innovative technologies, and shifting tastes require successful purveyors of goods and services to respond to change or risk losing market share. Remember Lotus 1-2-3? The need to change is as pervasive in the market for textbooks and other forms of intellectual property as it is in "bricks and mortar" markets. In the textbook market, as in other markets, a widening gap between what customers need or want and what suppliers produce creates an opening for something new.

Our research of the core M.B.A. corporate finance market uncovered such an opening. The leading texts in this field undeniably have their strengths, but we sense a growing frustration from professors who feel that the books they have used for ten or fifteen years are stale, do not reflect the most current research contributions, do not adequately integrate current technology, and do not strike the appropriate balance between theory and practice. Professors who teach corporate finance at the M.B.A. level consistently tell us they want a book that has modern content, global integration, strong emphasis on practice, and cutting-edge technology. At the same time, however, they want a book that adds value along these dimensions while minimizing the costs of switching from the books they currently use. Well, here it is: a fresh, easy-to-use, thoroughly modern text that anchors student learning in the latest theory and practice of corporate finance.

OBJECTIVE AND PRIMARY GOALS OF TEXT

The overriding objective that guided our work in developing *Corporate Finance* was to create a focused, topically cutting-edge text grounded in modern theory. We wanted the book to have a truly global perspective and to reach students through the use of innovative and engaging technologies. Above all, our desire was that students would take away from the book a deeper understanding of the connection between financial theory and practice. To achieve these objectives, we focused our energies on five primary goals.

Goal 1: Focus on important topics. This goal drove the development of the overall text structure as well as the topics covered within each chapter. Using reviewer suggestions, our own classroom experience, and market research, including analysis of more than 150 M.B.A.-course syllabi, we designed the text to focus on what's really important to the practice of corporate finance. Throughout text development, we asked: Is this topic really important to the successful practice of corporate finance? Does coverage improve the M.B.A. student's chance of success? Is the topic purely academic, or does it provide the basis for important conceptual understanding that will improve the practice of corporate finance?

With this goal in mind, we designed a book that covers classic corporate finance concepts, such as risk and return, capital budgeting, and capital structure, as well as emerging theories that we feel are likely to have an impact in the business world as current students progress in their careers. Many of the themes in this book, as well as the overall organization of topics, will be familiar to professors with experience teaching this subject at the graduate or advanced undergraduate level. Even so, seasoned corporate finance instructors will discover something new here. It is our view that the best educational experience for students is one that not only allows them to learn the basic tools and techniques of corporate finance, but also exposes them to emerging discoveries from research. A glance at the references at the end of this book reveals the importance we place on financial scholarship. At the same time, we do not want to either intimidate or bore students with complicated and highly abstract theories. That leads to our second goal.

Goal 2: Present Cutting-Edge Theory in an Intuitively Appealing and Practical Manner. We feel it's important to expose M.B.A. students to the most current thinking in corporate finance. The art of doing this in an intuitively appealing and practical manner rests on the ability to synthesize, interpret, and communicate complex ideas in a way that readers can easily digest. We strive to provide students with a smooth bridge between theory and practice by highlighting examples in a feature that we call "Applying the Model." These illustrations, many of which use data from financial information sources accessible on the Internet, help students see how to put theory into action. Similarly, each chapter's Opening Focus relates a story from the business world that stresses the practical relevance of one or more of the chapter's main ideas.

Goal 3: Provide a Truly Global Perspective. It is clear that the financial world is shrinking. The move by more countries to capitalism, the rapid economic progress of many developing nations, and the increased role of financial markets among other forces all contribute to the ongoing globalization of business and finance. Rather than grouping international issues into a chapter or two, we incorporate a global perspective throughout the text. Every chapter has a unique feature that we call "Comparative Corporate Finance (CCF)," designed to highlight similarities and differences in corporate finance practices around the world. For example, Chapter 5's CCF examines historic returns on various types of investments in 16 different countries, and Chapter 7's CCF describes capital budgeting methods used in South Africa and the United Kingdom.

Another vehicle that we use to infuse international content throughout the book is the "Opening Focus" feature. More than half of these stories involve non-U.S. companies or markets. In Chapter 2, for instance, the Opening Focus explains the decision of the Deutsche Börse to drop Porsche from its M-Dax Index of midcap stocks because Porsche refused to comply with the exchange's demand that the company release quarterly financial statements. Chapter 14's Opening Focus describes the market's reaction to British Airways's decision to cut its dividend in the wake of the drop in air travel following September 11, 2001.

Most importantly, many chapters have extended coverage of international material, such as Chapter 11's discussion of research on law and finance and Chapter 16's coverage of venture capital markets around the world. The result is a book with a seamless international perspective that offers students a much broader view of the practice of corporate finance in a global economy than does any other corporate finance text.

Goal 4: Maintain High Reader Interest. We strongly believe that corporate finance can be presented in an interesting and engaging way. To maintain high reader interest, we use a relaxed, conversational writing style. Like most finance professionals, we are quantitatively oriented people, and we know that it is crucial for students to develop sharp quantitative skills to succeed in our field. Nevertheless, when we present mathematical topics, such as the variance of a portfolio of assets or pricing an option using Black and Scholes, we do more than simply present the equations along with "plug and chug" examples. We try to convey the intuition beneath the surface, urging readers to contemplate not just how an equation works, but also why it works. Writing clearly, incorporating real examples, and asking students to contemplate interesting questions are some of the ways that we try to make the quantitative material more approachable. But the most powerful tool we use to achieve this end is the book's technology package, Smart Finance.

Goal 5: Maximize the Pedagogical and Motivational Value of Technology. Too often we have experimented with technology in the classroom, only to find that somehow it impedes more than facilitates learning. At times the investment required to learn enough about a given technology to be able to use it effectively limits what students can learn about finance. In other cases, students focus too much on what a particular technology can do rather than what it should do. And of course, there is always the problem that a technology that we want to use in- or outside of class simply doesn't work.

We wanted to develop an integrated technology package that engaged, motivated, and at times entertained students, while helping them master financial concepts on their own time and at their own pace. We wanted to use technology to allow students to hear firsthand about exciting recent developments in financial research, and we wanted students to hear from business professionals why the material contained in the text is relevant after the final exam is over. We are confident that Smart Finance delivers on all counts. The flash animated concept reviews and problem solutions let students review some of the more difficult concepts at any time and as many times as they like. Nearly 100 short video interviews with leading scholars and practitioners give students access to "virtual guest speakers" and help build the bridge between theory and practice that we feel is so important. Tests with in-residence and online M.B.A. students as well as in executive M.B.A. programs have generated almost unanimous praise for these features. In fact, the most common complaint we have heard from students is, "Why can't we see more of this?" Play the CD that came with this text to see a sample of the rich content that students can access via the book's website.

ORGANIZATION OF THE TEXT

We carefully designed the text to meet our goals. It is divided into eight parts and contains 25 chapters. The eight part titles are:

Part 1:   Introduction
Part 2:   Valuation, Risk, and Return
Part 3:   Capital Budgeting
Part 4:   Capital Structure and Dividend Policy
Part 5:   Long-Term Financing
Part 6:   Options, Derivatives, and International Financial Management
Part 7:   Short-Term Financing Decisions
Part 8:   Special Topics

This structure evolved from a number of iterations based on reviewer feedback, practitioner comments, the structure of the leading texts in the field, and our own experiences teaching this course. Classroom tests using this structure confirm its effectiveness. Of course, those professors who prefer an alternative structure will find the text is flexible in that alternative sequences generally work well.

Part 1 includes three introductory chapters that provide background and review. Included are discussions of the scope of corporate finance, coverage of financial statement and cash flow analysis, and a chapter on present value. Because of differences in course prerequisites, some professors may assign these chapters and cover them in class while others may include them as review that students can use to confirm their understanding of those course prerequisites. The chapters have been developed to work well in both of these situations. Part 2 includes three chapters—one on bond and stock valuation and two on risk and return. These chapters together provide students with a solid understanding of risk, return, and value that serves as the conceptual base upon which subsequent discussions are built.

Part 3 includes three chapters devoted to capital budgeting processes and techniques, cash flow and capital budgeting, and risk in capital budgeting, including a discussion of the cost of capital. Part 4 on capital structure and dividend policy includes five chapters. They cover market efficiency; long-term financing; capital structure theory and taxes; nontax determinants of corporate leverage; and dividend policy. Part 5 includes three chapters on long-term financing. They focus on entrepreneurial finance and venture capital, investment banking and the public sale of equity securities, and long-term debt and leasing.

Part 6 includes four chapters—two on options (options basics and Black and Scholes and beyond), one on international financial management, and one on risk management and financial engineering. Part 7 contains two short-term chapters, one on strategic and operational financial planning and the other on short-term financial management. The final part, Part 8, includes two special topics chapters—one on mergers, acquisitions, and corporate control, and the other on bankruptcy and financial distress.

THE END RESULT

In the final analysis, a textbook must cover the topics that professors believe are important and it must do so using a level of rigor appropriate for its readers—in this case, graduate students. Beyond that, professors want a book that students can and will use as a resource to succeed in the classroom and in the workplace. We believe that we have created a text that delivers the best our profession has to offer in terms of modern theory and practice. *Corporate Finance* engages students, both in a linear fashion on the written page and interactively using the computer. We hope you'll try it. We are confident that if you do, both you and your students will be glad you did. Change is good.

ACKNOWLEDGMENTS

Most people realize that creating a textbook is a collaborative venture. What only reflective (and thankful) authors can truly appreciate is just how many people are involved in planning, writing, editing, producing, and launching a new book. In the paragraphs that follow, we thank the many people who made a significant and identifiable contribution to this book. Grouped together, the people directly involved with this "SMG Textbook Project" would make a full-strength army company, with the seven-figure operating budget to match. Add in the folks involved with the book's sales, production, and distribution, and the venture approaches battalion scale. Although only three people are listed as authors on the title page, we wish to acknowledge the debt we owe to those who have worked so closely with us.

First, we thank Mike Roche and Kristin Sandberg, who signed us to our original contract. Over the years, numerous other publishing company professionals have helped mold this book (and, with disturbing frequency, prodded the authors to deliver on time). This list includes Charlie Stutesman, Tamborah Moore, Trish Taylor, and, especially, Mike Reynolds. Our developmental editor, Joanne Butler, has combined great professional skill with amazing tact—and has never once referred to us (publicly at least) as prima donnas. Though we have worked with Kaila Wyllys of G&S Typesetters for only a few months, these have been truly dramatic and we have leaned very heavily on her expertise.

Several people made written contributions to the book and its supplements. We are particularly grateful to Lance Nail, David Whidbee, John Yeoman, Dubos Masson, and Richard Shockley for their written contributions to specific chapters, and to George Hettenhouse for his insightful reviews. We also thank Susan White for writing the Instructor's Manual and Solutions Manual; Harry Turtle, Peppi Kenny, Richard Gendreau, and Michael Alderson for the Test Bank; Joseph Vu for the Study Guide; and Dan Balan for the PowerPoint slides. Bill Reese not only provided valuable feedback to us about the book's strengths and weaknesses—in time for us to act on his recommendations—but also class tested the revised edition at Tulane University. Finally, Bill Megginson wishes to extend special thanks to the students in the five classes at the University of Oklahoma where he used early drafts of this book. Even though students received the text free of charge, they paid a price to help us remove errors from earlier drafts.

Technology is an extremely important part of this book, and we wish to express our deep appreciation to South-Western Publishing Company and Thomson Learning for their financial and professional support. In particular, we have been honored to work with technical professionals as competent and supportive as Thomson Learning's Vicky True and John Barans. Many other people have also contributed to creating what we believe to be an outstanding technology package. This list begins with Jack Koning, who made truly amazing contributions in developing the flash animations, and Don Mitchell, whose audio work made the animations come to life. Deryl Dale, Candace Decker, Rebecca Loftin, Neil Charles, Murray McGibbon, Andrew Ellul, Anne Kibler, Doug Hoffman, and Richard Fish all contributed their voices to the animations, and Rebecca Barrett and Joy Hudyma helped create the text's graphics.

Though it would be nice to pretend that our skills as authors are so advanced that we did not have to make repeated passes at writing the chapters you see today, in fact this book has benefited immeasurably from the feedback we have received from reviewers. We would like to thank the following people for their insightful comments and constructive criticism of the text:

John Affleck-Graves
University of Notre Dame

Ivan Brick
Rutgers University

Arturo Bris
Yale School of Management

James Cotter
Wake Forest University

Arnold Cowan
Iowa State University

Charles Cuny
Texas A&M University

Karen Denning
West Virginia University

Daniel Ebels
University of Michigan

Lawrence Glosten
Columbia University

John Graham
Duke University

John Hall
University of Arkansas at Little Rock

Joel Harper
Florida Atlantic University

Del Hawley
University of Mississippi

Praveen Kumar
University of Houston

David Lins
University of Illinois–Champaign

Roger Morin
Georgia State University

Charles Mossman
University of Manitoba

Jim Musumeci
Southern Illinois University–Carbondale

Narendar V. Rao
Oklahoma State University at Stillwater

Ramesh Rao
Texas Tech University

Patricia Ryan
Colorado State University

James Schallheim
University of Utah

James Seward
University of Wisconsin–Madison

Dennis Sheehan
Penn State University

Betty Simkins
Oklahoma State University

Mark Simonson
Arizona State University

Alex Tang
Morgan State University

Olaf Thorp
Babson College

Harry Turtle
Washington State University

Joseph Vu
DePaul University

Susan White
University of Maryland

The following people participated in a focus group meeting with the authors and provided detailed feedback on the manuscript. They also shared their classroom experiences, offering advice for improving the accessibility and user-friendliness of the text and support pieces.

William Reese
Tulane University

William Scott
Illinois State University

Michael Sullivan
University of Nevada–Las Vegas

Sorin Tuluca
Fairleigh Dickinson University

In order to develop a strong support package, market research was performed. We'd like to thank the following instructors for sharing their experience with support pieces and assisting us in the development of the test bank, instructors' manual, solutions manual, and PowerPoint presentation slides.

Shyam Bhandari
Bradley University

John Crocket
George Mason University

J. David Diltz
University of Texas–Arlington

Kenneth Kim
University of Wisconsin–Milwaukee

Hany Shawky
University at Albany

Tie Su
University of Miami

We would also like to thank Tom Arnold of Louisiana State University for class-testing some of the flash animations.

Last but certainly not least, the authors wish to thank their families and friends who provided invaluable support and assistance. We thank Kenneth Smart for proof-reading the manuscript. Finally, Susan Smart, Peggy Megginson, and Robin Gitman deserve much of the credit for bringing this book to fruition.

SBS, WLM, LJG
February 19, 2003

CONTRIBUTORS

A key feature of our book is that we integrate video clips of academics and finance professionals throughout the text. The following academics provided critical contributions to this text by explaining their important contributions to modern financial thought. Our interviews with them appear in SMART IDEAS VIDEOS and SMART ETHICS VIDEOS.

Anup Agrawal
University of Alabama

Franklin Allen
University of Pennsylvania

Ed Altman
New York University

Utpal Bhattacharya
Indiana University

Michael Brennan
UCLA

James Brickley
University of Rochester

Robert Bruner
University of Virginia

Jennifer Conrad
University of North Carolina

Francesca Cornelli
London Business School

David Denis
Purdue University

Diane Denis
Purdue University

Elroy Dimson
London Business School

Kenneth French
Dartmouth College

Jon Garfinkel
University of Iowa

Steven Kaplan
University of Chicago

Andrew Karolyi
Ohio State University

Laurie Krigman
Babson College

Scott Lee
Texas A&M University

Ike Mathur
Southern Illinois University at Carbondale

David Mauer
Southern Methodist University

Mitchell Petersen
Northwestern University

Manju Puri
Stanford University

Raghu Rajan
University of Chicago

Jay Ritter
University of Florida

Myron Scholes
*Stanford University and Chairman
of Oak Hill Platinum Partners*

Lemma Senbet
University of Maryland

William Sharpe
*Stanford University and cofounder
of Financial Engines*

Robert Shiller
Yale University

Laura Starks
University of Texas

Avanidhar Subrahmanyam
UCLA

Anjan Thakor
University of Michigan

Sheridan Titman
University of Texas

Greg Udell
Indiana University

Theo Vermaelen
INSEAD

Rohan Williamson
Georgetown University

Kent Womack
Dartmouth College

We are also grateful to the following individuals who shared their insights based on their experience practicing corporate finance. Our interviews with them appear in SMART PRACTICES VIDEOS and SMART ETHICS VIDEOS.

Beth Acton
*Vice President and Treasurer (former),
Ford Motor Company, currently
Chief Financial Officer, Comerica*

David Baum
*Cohead of M&A for the Americas,
Goldman Sachs*

Andy Bryant
*Executive Vice President of Finance
and Enterprise Systems, Chief
Financial Officer, Intel Corp.*

Beverly Caen
*Former Vice President, Instinet
Corporation*

David Childress
*Asset Liability Manager, Ford
Motor Co.*

Tom Cole
*Leveraged Finance Group,
Deutsche Bank*

John Eck
*President of Broadcast and Network
Operations, NBC*

Jay Goodgold
*Managing Director, Equities Division,
Goldman Sachs*

David Haeberle
*Chief Executive Officer,
Command Equity Group*

Jeff Kauffman
*Portfolio Manager, Managing
Director, Omega Advisors*

David Nickel
*Controller, Intel Communications
Group, Intel Corp.*

Jon Olson
Vice President of Finance, Intel Corp.

Frank Popoff
*Chairman of the Board (retired),
Dow Chemical*

Todd Richter
*Managing Director, Head of Equity
Healthcare Research, Bank of
America Securities*

Pam Roberts
*Executive Director of Corporate
Services, Cummins Inc.*

Paul Savastano
*Director of Information Technology,
Sprint Corp.*

Jackie Sturm
*Director of Finance for Technology
and Manufacturing, Intel Corp.*

Keith Woodward
*Vice President of Finance,
General Mills*

THE INSTRUCTIONAL PACKAGE

FOR INSTRUCTORS:

Instructor's Manual with Test Bank Prepared by Susan White, University of Maryland. Designed to support novice instructors and finance veterans alike, this comprehensive Instructor's Manual includes chapter overviews, lecture guides organized by section, enrichment exercises, PowerPoint notes, answers to concept review questions, answers to end-of-chapter questions, solutions for end-of-chapter problems, and the test bank. (0-030-35091-3)

Solutions Manual Prepared by Susan White, University of Maryland. Available to instructors and students alike, this comprehensive solutions manual provides step-by-step analysis of how to perform chapter exercises. (0-324-26073-3)

ExamView ExamView Computerized Testing Software contains all of the questions in the printed test bank. This program is an easy-to-use test creation software compatible with Microsoft Windows. Instructors can add or edit questions, instructions, and answers, and select questions randomly, by number, or by previewing them on the screen. Instructors can also create and administer quizzes online, whether over the Internet, a local area network (LAN), or a wide area network (WAN). (0-030350832)

PowerPoint Slides PowerPoint slides are available for use by students as an aid to note-taking and by instructors for enhancing their lectures. Available as a download from the product support Web site at http://smart.swcollege.com.

WebTutor WebTutor is an interactive, Web-based, student supplement on WebCT and/or BlackBoard that harnesses the power of the Internet to deliver innovative learning aids that actively engage students. The instructor can incorporate WebTutor as an integral part of the course, or the students can use it on their own as a study guide. Benefits to students include automatic and immediate feedback from quizzes and exams; interactive, multimedia-rich explanation of concepts; online exercises that reinforce what they've learned; flashcards for study of key terms. (0-030-35136-7)

FOR STUDENTS:

Study Guide   Prepared by Joseph Vu, DePaul University. This ancillary item includes brief chapter overviews, true/false and multiple choice questions, problem sets, and all answers to study guide questions. (0-030-35113-8)

Solutions Manual   Prepared by Susan White, University of Maryland. Available to instructors and students alike, this comprehensive solutions manual provides step-by-step analysis of how to perform chapter exercises. (0-324-26073-3)

PowerPoint Slides   PowerPoint slides are available for use by students as an aid to note-taking and by instructors for enhancing their lectures. Available as a download from the product support site at http://smart.swcollege.com.

YOUR BEST CHOICE FOR SOLID THEORETICAL COVERAGE

Use both theory and technology to achieve a new level of understanding in your corporate finance course. Smart, Megginson, and Gitman present a very focused, topically cutting edge MBA-level text anchored in modern theory. It provides a smooth bridge to the practice of finance in a global environment employing the most advanced financial and information technologies.

CHAPTER OPENER:

Set the stage with our Opening Focus feature. These timely examples highlight real companies and demonstrate the application of modern finance theory. The current and interesting stories will pique interest with readers and give them a jumping-off point for the topics being considered in each chapter.

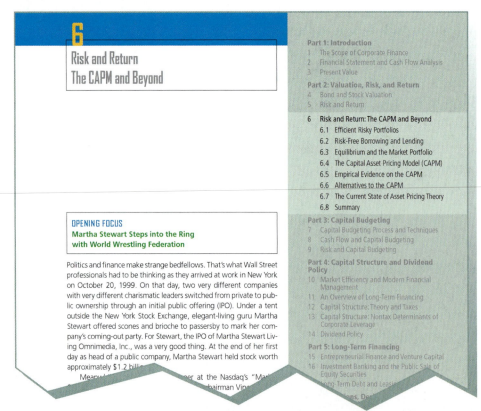

6

**Risk and Return
The CAPM and Beyond**

OPENING FOCUS
**Martha Stewart Steps into the Ring
with World Wrestling Federation**

Politics and finance make strange bedfellows. That's what Wall Street professionals had to be thinking as they arrived at work in New York on October 20, 1999. On that day, two very different companies with very different charismatic leaders switched from private to public ownership through an initial public offering (IPO). Under a tent outside the New York Stock Exchange, elegant-living guru Martha Stewart offered scones and brioche to passersby to mark her company's coming-out party. For Stewart, the IPO of Martha Stewart Living Omnimedia, Inc., was a very good thing. At the end of her first day as head of a public company, Martha Stewart held stock worth approximately $1.2 billi...

Meanw... ...er at the Nasdaq's "Mar... ...hairman Vin...

AND A TOTALLY INTEGRATED LEARNING PACKAGE.

CONCEPT REVIEW QUESTIONS:

Ensure retention of material before moving on in the chapter. Concept review questions offer opportunities for in-class discussion, quizzes, or self-study with brief questions at the end of each section.

or portfolio 8." By itself, Arrow International looks like a bad investment, offering relatively low returns and relatively high risk. But Arrow shines in a portfolio! ■

Concept Review Questions

1. Is the minimum variance portfolio always an efficient portfolio? Is an efficient portfolio always the minimum variance portfolio?

2. An efficient portfolio is one that maximizes expected return for any given level of risk. Is it equivalent to define an efficient portfolio as one that minimizes risk for any level of expected return?

3. What effect does expanding the types of assets included in the feasible set have on the efficient frontier?

4. Examine portfolio 10 in Table 6.1 and Figure 6.4. This portfolio contains equal investments in all four stocks. Why do you think it falls below the efficient frontier?

APPLYING THE MODEL:

Demonstrate the application of the concepts or theories with these examples sprinkled throughout each chapter. Applying the Model exercises often use data from companies that readers will recognize.

270   Part 3   Capital Budgeting

from the project will grow at a constant rate. For example, in valuing a large acquisition, many firms project cash flows from the target company for 5 to 10 years in the future. After that, they assume that cash flows will grow at a rate equal to the growth rate in gross domestic product (GDP) for the economy.[6]

APPLYING THE MODEL

Suppose that analysts at JDS Uniphase projected that their acquisition of SDL Inc. would generate the following stream of cash flows:

Year 1 $0.50 billion
Year 2   1.00 billion
Year 3   1.75 billion
Year 4   2.50 billion
Year 5   3.25 billion

In year 6 and beyond, analysts believed that cash flows would continue to grow at 5 percent per year. What is the terminal value of this investment? Recall that in Chapters 3 and 4, we learned that we can determine the present value of a stream of cash flows growing at a perpetual rate, g, by using the following formula:

$$PV_t = \frac{CF_{t+1}}{r - g}$$

the year-6 cash flow is 5 ... ore than in year 5, or $3.41 ...
numerator ... lso know that

COMPARATIVE CORPORATE FINANCE:

Observe similarities and differences in corporate finance practices around the world. The Comparative Corporate Finance feature offers a global perspective of key concepts in each chapter.

COMPARATIVE CORPORATE FINANCE

Investment Returns in 16 Countries

Table 5.2 shows real returns on common stocks, government bonds, and government bills from 1900 to 2000 for 16 different countries. Several robust patterns emerge from the table. First, in every country, the average annual return was lowest for bills and highest for common stocks, with bond returns falling in between. Second, the same pattern holds for standard deviations across countries. Bills exhibit the least year-to-year volatility, while stocks show the most variability. If we accept volatility as a measure of risk, this pattern makes sense because we expect riskier investments to pay higher returns over time. In other words, *investors seeking higher returns must generally accept more risk.*

Notice that in real terms, bills are not really risk-free investments. Remember, the real return on an investment approximately equals the nominal return minus the inflation rate. In France, Italy, and Japan, the average real return on bills falls below zero. Assuming that no one expects a negative return when investing, the negative average returns on bills suggest that investors in

these three countries encountered higher-than-expected inflation over time. A few countries sell government bonds that offer investors protection from this inflation risk. For example, in 1994 the U.S. government began selling Treasury Inflation Protection Securities (TIPS), which make coupon payments that fluctuate as the inflation rate moves. Because coupon and principal payments on TIPS rise and fall with the inflation rate, investors receive a risk-free real return, though, of course, the nominal return on TIPS varies over time.

By subtracting the average return on bills from the average equity return, we can estimate the equity risk premium in each country. The premium ranges from a high of 9.7 percent in Italy to a low of 3.2 percent in Denmark. The U.S. premium of 7.7 percent ties for seventh place among these nations. Keep in mind that these figures represent the historical equity risk premium in each country, which may or may not be a good forecast of the prospective risk premium in the future.

Table 5.2
Means and Standard Deviations of Real Returns on Asset Classes around the World, 1900–2000

Country	Common Stocks (%)		Government Bonds (%)		Government Bills (%)		Equity Risk Premium
	Mean Return	Standard Deviation	Mean Return	Standard Deviation	Mean Return	Standard Deviation	
Australia	9.0	17.7	1.9	13.0	0.6	5.6	8.4
Belgium		22.8	0.3	12.1	0.0	8.2	4.8
Canada	6.8		2.4	10	8	5.1	5.9
			3.3			6.4	
						11.4	

INTERNET RESOURCES:

Use web site addresses to access timely and relevant information that supports the chapter's contents.

4-11. Go to http://www.stockcharts.com/charts/YieldCurve.html, and click on the animated yield-curve graph. Answer the following questions:

a. Is the yield curve typically upward sloping, downward sloping, or flat?

b. Notice the behavior of the yield curve and the S&P 500 between July 28, 1998, and October 19, 1998. In August 1998, Russia defaulted on billions of dollars of foreign debt. Then, in late September came the news that at the behest of the Federal Reserve, 15 financial institutions would infuse $3.5 billion in new capital into hedge fund Long-Term Capital Management, which had lost nearly $2 billion in the previous month. Comment on these events as they related to movements in the yield curve and the S&P 500 that you see in the animation.

KEY TERMS:

These are bold faced when they first appear in the chapter. One can easily access the list of the key terms at the end of the chapter and the glossary at the end of the book.

> Corporations can obtain debt financing either by selling bonds (or other debt securities) directly to investors or by borrowing money from a commercial bank or other **financial intermediary.** The largest and most creditworthy firms raise large amounts of short-term funding by issuing **commercial paper** directly to investors in the **money market,** the market for debt instruments maturing in one year or less. Longer-term debt instruments include **notes** (debt with original maturities of less than seven years) and various types of corporate **bonds** (debt with original maturities of more than seven years). In addition to obtaining funds by issuing securities, most

SUMMARY:

See the whole chapter in a snapshot while quickly identifying key material. End of chapter summaries allow readers to gauge their comfort level with the material while identifying problem areas that might need additional review.

2.4 SUMMARY

- The four key financial statements are (1) the balance sheet, (2) the income statement, (3) the statement of retained earnings, and (4) the statement of cash flows. Notes describing the technical aspects of the financial statements are normally included with them.
- Depreciation is the most common noncash expense on income statements. To estimate cash flow from operations, add depreciation and other noncash charges back to net profit after taxes. A measure of cash flow that is important to financial analysts is free cash flow, the cash flow available to investors. Free cash flow equals

QUESTIONS AND PROBLEMS:

Using a diverse set of questions posed at differing levels (from simple review to challenging application), students can apply what they have learned and challenge themselves to refine their reasoning and analytical skills. An extensive selection of problems allows readers to apply what they have learned.

6-11. Consumers generally prefer low prices rather than high prices, yet we say that investors want to maximize the market price of risk (i.e., the slope of the *CML*). Explain this apparent paradox.

7-11. Contract Manufacturing, Inc., is considering two alternative investment proposals. The first proposal calls for a major renovation of the company's manufacturing facility. The second involves replacing just a few obsolete pieces of equipment in the facility. The company will choose one project or the other this year, but it will not do both. The cash flows associated with each project appear below, and the firm discounts project cash flows at 15 percent.

Year	Renovate	Replace
0	−$9,000,000	−$1,000,000
1	3,500,000	600,000

SMARTFinance

Smart Finance brings complex concepts to life. Through brief video clips and Flash animations, readers can explore theories with the individuals who helped define and develop them, gain insight into how CFOs make decisions, consider the ethical implications of key issues with an expert, and review key concepts and solutions to in-text problems.

To access Smart Finance, follow the instructions on the CD that is packaged with the book, or visit http://smartfinance.swcollege.com. The CD also includes a sample chapter of the features and a walkthrough animation that displays the features in more detail.

Smart Finance includes:

SMART IDEAS VIDEO:

Bring theory to life with leading academics and researchers explaining important concepts and theories from each chapter. Introduce your students to the person behind the theory or concept you are discussing!

SMART PRACTICES VIDEO:

Leaders in business and industry discuss how finance theory, as explained in the text, is used in practice on a daily basis. Interviewees include Presidents and CFOs of major corporations as well as corporate recruiters.

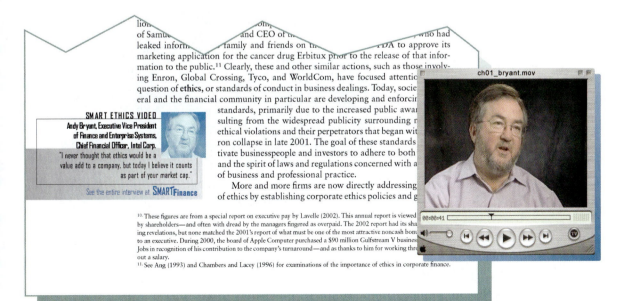

common. Even though the characteristics of stocks and bonds seem quite different, the principles involved in valuing debt and equity are much the same. However, applying those principles to equity securities can be quite challenging. Therefore, we begin with preferred stock, a security that resembles debt as much as it does equity.

PREFERRED STOCK VALUATION

SMART PRACTICES VIDEO
Todd Richter, Managing Director,
Head of Equity Healthcare Research,
Bank of America Securities
"The concepts of value, the things that
drive value, don't change."
See the entire interview at **SMARTFinance**

ch04_richter_clip01.mov
00:00:14

Neither a pure debt nor a pure equity instrument, preferred stock exhibits characteristics of both. Like bonds, preferred stocks usually pay investors a fixed cash flow stream over time. In addition, preferred shares usually promise to pay a dividend expressed as a percentage of par value, similar to a bond's coupon rate. However, if firms do not generate enough cash flow to meet preferred dividend payments, preferred stockholders, unlike bondholders, cannot force the firm into bankruptcy. In that sense, preferred stockholders are in a legal position similar to common shareholders, although preferred shares generally do not carry the right to vote. Most preferred stock is *cumulative,* which means that if a firm skips a preferred dividend payment, it cannot pay dividends to common shareholders until it makes up for all unpaid dividends to preferred shareholders. Finally, like equity, preferred stock typically has no fixed maturity date. For that reason, we treat preferred stock as a security with an infinite life in our valuation formulas.

In Chapter 3, you learned a shortcut for valuing a *perpetuity*—an annuity with an infinite life. To find today's value of a preferred stock, PS_0, we use Equation 3.10, the value of a perpetuity, discounting the preferred dividend, D_p, by the preferred stock's ...

SMART ETHICS VIDEO:

Do ethics matter? What are the consequences of unethical behavior? These video clips demonstrate the ways in which both academics and business executives see ethical conduct as crucial to the health of a firm's bottom line.

lion ... company ...
of Samuel ... and CEO of the ... who had leaked information ... family and friends on the ... FDA to approve its marketing application for the cancer drug Erbitux prior to the release of that information to the public.[11] Clearly, these and other similar actions, such as those involving Enron, Global Crossing, Tyco, and WorldCom, have focused attention on the question of **ethics,** or standards of conduct in business dealings. Today, society in general and the financial community in particular are developing and enforcing ...

SMART ETHICS VIDEO
Andy Bryant, Executive Vice President
of Finance and Enterprise Systems,
Chief Financial Officer, Intel Corp.
"I never thought that ethics would be a
value add to a company, but today I believe it counts
as part of your market cap."
See the entire interview at **SMARTFinance**

ch01_bryant.mov
00:00:41

... standards, primarily due to the increased public awareness resulting from the widespread publicity surrounding recent ethical violations and their perpetrators that began with the Enron collapse in late 2001. The goal of these standards is to motivate businesspeople and investors to adhere to both the letter and the spirit of laws and regulations concerned with all aspects of business and professional practice.

More and more firms are now directly addressing the issue of ethics by establishing corporate ethics policies and guidelines ...

[10]. These figures are from a special report on executive pay by Lavelle (2002). This annual report is viewed with interest by shareholders—and often with dread by the managers fingered as overpaid. The 2002 report had its share of interesting revelations, but none matched the 2001's report of what must be one of the most attractive noncash bonuses ever paid to an executive. During 2000, the board of Apple Computer purchased a $90 million Gulfstream V business jet for Steve Jobs in recognition of his contribution to the company's turnaround—and as thanks to him for working three years without a salary.

[11]. See Ang (1993) and Chambers and Lacey (1996) for examinations of the importance of ethics in corporate finance.

SMART CONCEPTS:

Animated concept review tutorials support each chapter and explain key topics step-by-step, offering readers the opportunity to review on their own time, at their own pace.

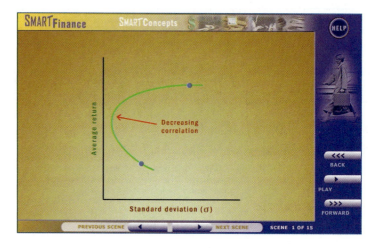

SMART SOLUTIONS:

Help sharpen problem-solving skills and master quantitative concepts with animated problems and solutions from each chapter. These solutions contain dynamic charts, graphs, and tables that help you see how to apply financial theory to a wide range of business problems. Smart Solutions not only illustrate the solution method, but also help readers develop intuition to identify the right tool to apply to a particular problem.

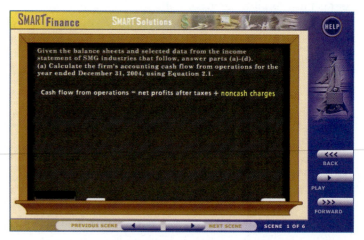

*The **new best** text and support package that employs the best technology to improve understanding and decision-making skills and provides experience using cutting-edge financial analysis tools and information sources.*

BRIEF CONTENTS

CONTENTS

Smart Practices Video
Tom Cole, Deutsche Bank, Leveraged Finance Group, page 2

Smart Concepts
page 7

Smart Practices Video
David Nickel, Controller for Intel Communications Group, Intel Corp., page 17

Smart Ethics Video
Andy Bryant, Executive Vice President of Finance and Enterprise Systems, Chief Financial Officer, Intel Corp., page 20

Smart Practices Video
Jon Olson, Vice President of Finance, Intel Corp., page 25

Smart Concepts
page 86

Smart Ethics Video
Kent Womack, Dartmouth College, page 87

Smart Solutions
Problem 3-27   page 103

Smart Solutions
Problem 3A-10   page 112

Smart Practices Video
Todd Richter, Managing Director, Head of Equity Healthcare Research, Bank of America Securities, page 132

Smart Concepts
page 136

PART 3: CAPITAL BUDGETING   225

Chapter 7: Capital Budgeting Process and Techniques   225

Opening Focus: Tantalized by Tantalum   225

Smart Concepts

page 429

Smart Solutions

Problem 12-3   page 438

Smart Ideas Video
Robert Bruner, University of Virginia, page 447

Smart Ideas Video
Sheridan Titman, University of Texas at Austin,
page 447

Chapter 16: Investment Banking and the Public Sale of Equity Securities   539

Smart Ideas Video
Manju Puri, Stanford University, page 517

Smart Ideas Video
Steven Kaplan, University of Chicago, page 519

Smart Practices Video
David Haeberle, Chief Executive Officer, Command
Equity Group, page 524

Smart Practices Video
David Baum, Co-head of M&A for Goldman Sachs
in the Americas, page 544

Smart Practices Video
Jay Goodgold, Managing Director, Equities Division,
Goldman Sachs, page 549

Smart Ethics Video
Jay Ritter, University of Florida, page 551

Smart Ideas Video
Jay Ritter, University of Florida, page 563

Smart Ideas Video
Jay Ritter, University of Florida, page 563

Smart Ideas Video
Ed Altman, New York University, page 595

PART 6: OPTIONS, DERIVATIVES, AND INTERNATIONAL FINANCIAL MANAGEMENT   621

Chapter 18: Options Basics   621

Chapter 19: Black and Scholes and Beyond   659

PART 7: SHORT-TERM FINANCING DECISIONS   763

Chapter 22: Strategic and Operational Financial Planning   763

Chapter 23: Short-Term Financial Management   791

PART 8: SPECIAL TOPICS 844

Chapter 24: Mergers, Acquisitions, and Corporate Control 844

Opening Focus: The Merger of Pharmacia and Upjohn—Why Mergers
Fail and How they Succeed 844

1

The Scope of Corporate Finance

OPENING FOCUS
Goldman Sachs and Airbus Go Public

Prior to May 1999, what did Wall Street's Goldman Sachs and Western Europe's Airbus Industries have in common? In addition to being highly successful and respected firms, Goldman and Airbus shared the distinction of being among the largest firms whose shares did *not* trade on a public stock exchange. Since its founding in 1869, Goldman Sachs had been organized as a partnership, and its tight-knit yet adaptable culture had long helped the firm prosper in competition with larger investment and commercial banks. Airbus Industries was organized in the 1970s as a consortium of mostly state-owned European aerospace companies. Though it had a much shorter history than that of Goldman Sachs, Airbus also prospered by offering a full line of state-of-the-art commercial aircraft. By 1999, Airbus rivaled long-time industry leader Boeing for dominance in aircraft manufacturing.

Despite its successful 130-year history, Goldman Sachs decided to reorganize as a corporation, and it sold stock to outside investors in an initial public offering (IPO) in May 1999. Fourteen months later, three of the main partners in the Airbus consortium created a new holding company, the European Aeronautic Defence and Space Company (EADS), to manage Airbus and its related businesses: As part of this reorganization, Airbus conducted its own IPO. Why would these two icons tamper with success by converting into publicly traded corporations after operating for so many years using different organizational forms?

The answer is that being a public corporation offers financial and operating benefits that over time tend to be decisive. For Goldman Sachs, the primary advantages were greater access to the huge amounts of capital modern investment banking required to be competitive and the need to have publicly traded stock for use in making acquisitions. It also did not hurt that, by turning illiquid partnership interests into publicly traded stock, Goldman's IPO made each of its 221 partners an average of $100 million richer! Airbus's owners also wished to attain better access to capital markets, but they decided to incorporate primarily for corporate governance reasons. By turning the consortium into a "regular" company, with a single board of directors and public shareholders to hold the firm accountable, the company hoped that the awkward negotiations that characterized decision making in a multinational consortium could be minimized.

By the summer of 2002, the financial community viewed both transformations as at least partial successes. Goldman Sachs had weathered the financial downturn of 2001–2002 much better than had most of its larger rivals, and the firm's stock price was up some 35 percent from its offering price three years before. The intermediate-term verdict on EADS was more nuanced. Prior to the terrorist attacks on September 11, 2001, Airbus had been on a roll—gaining market share from Boeing and announcing the launch of a massive new 550-seat jetliner, the A380. After the attacks, however, Airbus's operations suffered and by midsummer 2002, EADS's stock price was still 15 percent below its offering price. Most worrying, there were ongoing management struggles between the two controlling shareholders: France's Aerospatiale and Germany's Daimler Benz Aerospace. This nationalistic friction was exemplified by the fact that the company had co-CEOs, one French and one German. In spite of these troubles, Airbus remains one of the two premier commercial aircraft manufacturers, and both EADS and Goldman Sachs appear to have very promising futures.

Sources: Multiple articles, especially John Roussant, "Birth of a Giant," *Business Week* (July 10, 2000), pp. 170–176; Paul Betts, "EADS: Take-off Delayed by Squabbles in the Cockpit," *Financial Times* (November 16, 2001); and Emily Thornton, "Wall Street's Lone Ranger," *Business Week* (March 4, 2002), pp. 82–90. Stock prices are from the CNN Money (http://money.cnn.com) and Euronext Paris (http://www.euronext.com/en) websites.

1.1 WHAT IS CORPORATE FINANCE?

The example in the Opening Focus of dramatic change in the business structures of Goldman Sachs and Airbus Industries, two of the world's most successful and respected companies, provides important insights into the theory and practice of corporate finance. Companies everywhere must raise capital and use it with maximum efficiency, all the while balancing the competing objectives of corporate shareholders, managers, and other stakeholders. The importance (and status) of the finance function and the financial manager within business organizations has been rising steadily over the past two decades. Business professionals of all stripes have come to recognize that competent financial professionals can do more than just keep the books— they can create value in their own right. The principal focus of this textbook will be on the practicing financial manager, working as an integral part of the management team of a modern corporation. On the job, a financial manager must constantly apply the theoretical tools of finance to solve real business problems. As an introduction to what a financial manager's job entails, we begin this chapter with a description of the principal tasks and responsibilities that a finance professional employed by a large corporation might encounter.

SMART PRACTICES VIDEO

Tom Cole, Deutsche Bank, Leveraged Finance Group

"To be good at finance you have to understand how businesses work."

See the entire interview at **SMART**Finance

THE FIVE BASIC CORPORATE FINANCE FUNCTIONS

Although **corporate finance** can be defined generically as the science of managing money in a business environment, a more complete definition would emphasize that the practice of corporate finance involves five basic, related functions:

1. Raising capital to support a company's operations and investment programs (the **financing function**)
2. Selecting the best projects in which to invest the resources of the firm, based on each project's perceived risk and expected return (the **capital budgeting function**)
3. Managing the firm's internal cash flows and its mix of debt and equity financing (the **capital structure decision**) both to maximize the value of the debt and equity claims on the firm and to ensure the company can pay off its obligations when they come due (the **financial management function**)
4. Developing an ownership and corporate governance structure for the company that ensures the managers act ethically and in the interests of the firm's stakeholders, and particularly its stockholders (the **corporate governance function**)
5. Managing the firm's exposures to all types of risk, both insurable and uninsurable, in order to maintain the optimum risk-return trade-off and therefore maximize shareholder value (the **risk-management function**)

Throughout the world, corporations raise capital by selling debt (bonds and notes) and equity (stocks) claims against themselves, either directly to investors or indirectly to financial intermediaries such as commercial banks. Financial managers then allocate these funds to the most attractive investment opportunities. These same professionals also manage the firm's cash flows to ensure financial solvency and to minimize the resources needed to support a given level of corporate activity. Finally, financial managers must monitor and control all aspects of the firm's risk in order to maintain a balance of risk and return that is consistent with share-price maximization. In the following pages, we will provide a brief overview of the five principal functions of the modern financial manager.

Financing

Businesses raise money to support investment and other activities in one of two ways: either externally from investors (or creditors) or internally by retention and reinvestment of operating profits. Although both U.S. and non-U.S. companies raise the bulk of the funding they require each year internally, the external financing role will be the focus of this section—and indeed, of much of this book. As we discuss in the next section, sole proprietorships and partnerships face very limited external funding opportunities, but the choices for corporations are much richer. They can raise capital either by selling an ownership interest (**equity**), usually in the form of common or preferred stock, or by borrowing money (**debt**) from one or more creditors. When corporations are young and/or small, they usually must raise equity capital privately, either from acquaintances or from professional investors such as **venture capitalists,** who specialize in high-risk/high-return investments in rapidly growing entrepreneurial businesses. After a corporation **goes public** by conducting an **initial public offering (IPO)** of stock, it has the option of raising cash by selling additional stock in the future.

When a corporation sells securities to investors in exchange for cash, it raises capital in a **primary market transaction.** In such a transaction, money flows from investors to firms, and the firms invest the money they receive to exploit investment opportunities. On the other side of the transaction, investors holding the firm's securities can trade them with other investors. Trades between investors generate no new cash flow for the firm and are called **secondary market transactions.** Most stock (equity) market transactions involve secondary market trades, while a much larger fraction of all bond (debt) market transactions involve capital-raising primary offerings. Figure 1.1 details the dramatic growth in the total value of primary stock and bond

Figure 1.1
The Total Value of Primary (Capital-Raising) Corporate Security Issues, 1990–2001

This figure describes the growth in the volume of security offerings sold directly to investors through capital market issues around the world since 1990. Offerings by U.S. issuers typically account for two-thirds or more of the global total. These data are from the annual league tables (rankings of investment banks) published by Investment Dealers' Digest in early January, and include issues by corporations, housing finance authorities, and other nonsovereign issuers, but exclude government bond offerings and syndicated bank loans. The $4.08 trillion total for 2001 was a record.

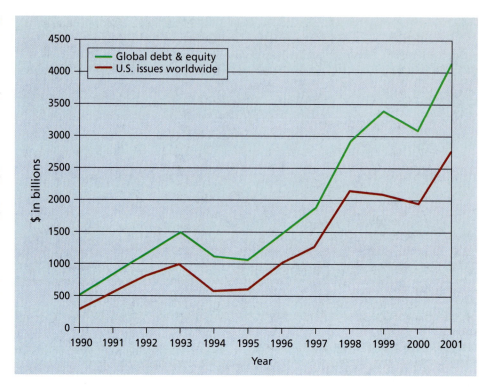

offerings sold by corporations and other entities over the 1990–2001 period. The total value of security offerings worldwide increased from $504 billion in 1990 to an astounding $4.08 *trillion* in 2001.

Figure 1.1 also points out the disproportionate importance of U.S. capital markets in global finance. Throughout the 1990–2001 period, U.S. issuers accounted for a surprisingly steady two-thirds share of the total value of securities issued by corporations around the world each year, though the mix of security issues changed dramatically from year to year. In 2001, for example, debt offerings accounted for an unusually high 91 percent of the $2.88 trillion total value of securities sold by U.S. issuers. To put these "market share" numbers in perspective, the United States represents only about one-quarter of world GDP and only about one-eighth of the total value of world trade (exports plus imports).

Corporations can obtain debt financing either by selling bonds (or other debt securities) directly to investors or by borrowing money from a commercial bank or other **financial intermediary**. The largest and most creditworthy firms raise large amounts of short-term funding by issuing **commercial paper** directly to investors in the **money market**, the market for debt instruments maturing in one year or less. Longer-term debt instruments include **notes** (debt with original maturities of less than seven years) and various types of corporate **bonds** (debt with original maturities of more than seven years). In addition to obtaining funds by issuing securities, most corporations borrow at least some money in the form of commercial loans directly from commercial banks. Nevertheless, the importance of bank financing, relative to capital market financing, as a source of general corporate funding has been declining for large U.S. corporations for several decades. However, bank financing remains important for smaller businesses.[1] Commercial banking also continues to be an impor-

---

[1] A very informative discussion of the changing role of commercial banking in American corporate financing is provided in Boyd and Gertler (1994). These authors show that although bank lending to corporations has indeed been declining in

tant source of financing in most of the world's other developed economies, as well as in virtually all developing countries.

Capital Budgeting

For two reasons, the capital budgeting function is arguably the single most important activity of the firm's financial managers. First, the scale of investments that managers evaluate in the capital budgeting process is usually quite large. Second, companies can prosper in a competitive economy only by seeking out the most promising new products, processes, and services to deliver to customers. Companies such as Intel, General Electric, Deutsche Telekom, and Toyota regularly make huge capital investments, the outcomes of which drive the value of their firms and the wealth of their owners. For these and other companies, the annual capital investment budget can run to several billion dollars, so the consequences of a flawed capital budgeting process are serious indeed.

The capital budgeting process, which is the focus of Chapters 7–9, breaks down into three steps: (1) identifying potential investments, (2) analyzing the set of investment opportunities, identifying those that will create shareholder value, and perhaps prioritizing them, and (3) implementing and monitoring the investments selected in step 2. The long-term success of almost any firm depends on mastering these three steps.

Financial Management

The finance function is charged with managing the firm's operating cash flows as efficiently and profitably as possible. A key element of this management process is the **capital structure decision,** or structuring the financial claims on the firm between debt and equity securities in order to maximize the market value of the firm. A second dimension to the financial management function is ensuring that firms have adequate working capital available to operate smoothly day to day. Managing working capital involves obtaining seasonal financing, building inventories sufficient to meet customer needs, paying suppliers, collecting from customers, and investing surplus cash, all while maintaining an adequate cash balance. Managing working capital effectively requires not only technical and analytical skills, but also people skills. Almost every component of working capital management involves building and maintaining relationships with customers, suppliers, lenders, and others.[2]

Corporate Governance

The existence of a corporate governance function is of overarching importance to the modern corporation. Good management does not develop in a vacuum. Instead, it results from a corporate governance system that hires and promotes qualified, honest people, and structures the financial incentives offered to employees in a way that motivates them to maximize firm value.

---

importance, the demand for other banking products and services (such as electronic funds transfers and risk-management products) has been increasing even more rapidly. Additionally, U.S. corporations remain the primary consumers of syndicated loans, which are large lines of credit arranged by consortiums of up to 200 commercial banks. According to Capital DATA Ltd.'s *Loanware* database, over $1.7 trillion worth of syndicated loans were arranged worldwide during 1999 (the total probably exceeded $2 trillion in 2000 and 2001), and U.S. borrowers accounted for over 60 percent of this total.

[2.] Graham and Harvey (2001) present one of the most comprehensive surveys yet published assessing what financial managers actually do and the tools they employ in making decisions. Mian (2001) looks specifically at the choice and replacement of the top financial executive in modern corporations, the chief financial officer (CFO). Mian's evidence makes clear that being a CFO offers little job security, as he finds that the external CFO succession (replacement) rate is markedly higher than that of the external chief executive officer (CEO). CFOs are also less likely to "die in their beds," as their (voluntary) retirement rate is much lower than that of CEOs.

This type of optimal corporate governance system is extremely difficult to develop in practice, not least because the incentives of stockholders, managers, and other stakeholders often conflict. A firm's stockholders certainly want managers to work hard and to protect shareholders' interests, but it is rarely in the interest of any *individual* stockholder to expend time and resources monitoring managers to see if they are acting appropriately. An individual stockholder who engaged in this activity would personally bear all the costs of monitoring management, but the benefit of his or her activities would accrue to all shareholders. This is a classic example of a **collective action problem** that is pervasive in most relationships between stockholders and managers. Likewise, managers may feel the need to increase the wealth of owners, but they also want to protect their own jobs. Managers rationally do not wish to work harder than necessary if others will reap most of the benefits. Finally, managers and shareholders may together decide to run a company in a way that benefits them at the expense of creditors or other stakeholders who do not generally have a direct say in corporate governance.

As you might expect, a variety of governance mechanisms designed to mitigate these problems have evolved over time. A strong board of directors is an essential element in any well-functioning governance system, because it is the board's duty to hire, fire, pay, and promote senior managers. The board must also develop *fixed* (salary) and *contingent* (bonus and stock-based) compensation packages that align the incentives of managers with those of shareholders. In addition, a firm's auditors play a governance role by certifying the validity of financial statements. In the United States, accounting scandals and concerns about auditors' conflicts of interest prompted the *Securities and Exchange Commission SEC* to require the CFOs of 688 large firms to personally certify their firms' earnings numbers.

Just as all companies struggle to develop an effective system of corporate governance, so do countries. Governments everywhere strive to establish legal frameworks for corporate finance that encourage the development of competitive businesses and efficient financial markets. For example, a legal system should permit efficiency-enhancing mergers and acquisitions but block business combinations that significantly restrict competition. It should provide protection for creditors and minority shareholders that limits the opportunities for managers or majority shareholders to expropriate wealth.

The financial systems that have developed in the United States, Western Europe, and Asia differ fundamentally from each other even though most of the nations making up the core of the world economy are capitalist democracies. Historically, the United States, Britain, and Canada have witnessed far more mergers and acquisitions (M&A's) than have other developed countries, but this is changing rapidly. As Figure 1.2 reveals, M&A activity worldwide surged between 1991 and 2000, before falling sharply in 2001. A substantial fraction of the growth in takeover activity has come from Europe. Roughly one-third of the total value of M&A's worldwide now involves European firms, and the total value of European M&A activity could well surpass that in the United States within a few years as continental firms adapt to the increasingly competitive business environment brought about by the adoption of the euro (€) and the increasing integration of the Atlantic economies.[3]

Risk Management

Historically, risk management has involved identifying a firm's risk exposures and using insurance products or self-insurance to manage those exposures. The risk-

---

[3.] An excellent discussion of how the political process has influenced corporate governance in the United States is provided in Roe (1997). For a comparison of corporate finance and governance in Japan, Germany, and the United States, see Prowse (1996). Also see the video clip from David Baum, head of M&A at Goldman Sachs, in Chapter 25.

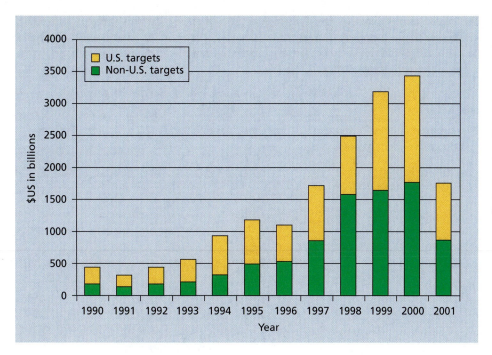

Figure 1.2
Global Value of Announced Mergers and Acquisitions, 1990–2001 ($US Billions)

Sources: *Thomson Financial Securities Data, as reported in "The Great Merger Wave Breaks,"* The Economist *(January 27, 2001), pp. 59–60; and Judy Radler Cohen, "Hoping for Recovery,"* Investment Dealers' Digest *(January 14, 2002), pp. 30–43.*

management function has now grown to encompass the identification, measurement, and management of all types of risk exposures. Common examples of these exposures include losses that can result from adverse interest rate movements, changes in commodity prices, and fluctuations in currency values. The techniques for managing these risks are among the most sophisticated of all corporate finance practices. The risk-management task begins with an attempt to quantify the sources and magnitudes of a firm's risk exposure and a decision on whether to simply accept these risks or to manage them.

Some risks are easily insurable, such as the risk of loss due to fire or flood damage, employee theft, or injury caused to customers by the company's products. Other corporate risks can be reduced through diversification. For example, rather than use a sole supplier for a key production input, a company might choose to contract with several suppliers, even if doing so means purchasing the input at slightly above the lowest attainable price. However, the focus of modern risk management is on the market-driven risks mentioned earlier, relating to interest rates, commodity prices, and currency values. Numerous derivative instruments have been developed over the past two decades for use in **hedging** (i.e., offsetting) many of the more threatening market risks. These financial instruments are called **derivatives** because they derive their value from another, underlying asset. The four principal derivative instruments are forwards, futures, options, and swaps, and we provide an in-depth discussion of their use in hedging various risks in Chapters 18–21 of this book.

Each of the five major finance functions will be discussed at length in this textbook, and we hope that every reader will come to share our respect for the knowledge, experience, and integrity that is required to become a successful corporate finance professional in today's world. We also hope each reader will come to share our excitement about the career opportunities corporate finance provides. Never before has finance been as fast paced, as technological, as international, as ethically challenging, or as rigorous as it is today, and these trends have helped make finance the most popular major for the roughly 100,000 students who graduate with MBAs from U.S. business schools each year. The jobs for which finance graduates can compete are

Smart Concepts
See the concept explained step-by-step at
SMARTFinance

extremely varied, both in the skills needed and in their long-run earnings potential. However, all these careers share a common necessity for understanding how value can be created by effective application of corporate finance functions.

Concept Review Questions

1. What are the five basic corporate finance functions? What is the general relationship between them?

2. Which of these functions might be considered "nontraditional"? Why do you think these functions have risen to prominence in recent years?

1.2 LEGAL FORMS OF BUSINESS ORGANIZATION

Companies exist so that people can organize to pursue profit-making ventures in a formal, legally secure manner. Although there are various ways to organize a company, only a handful of forms have proven viable, and variations of these legal forms are observed throughout the world. This section briefly examines how companies organize themselves legally and discusses the costs and benefits of each major form. We begin with the organizational forms available to businesses in the United States. After that, we briefly examine the most important organizational forms used by non-U.S. businesses.

BUSINESS ORGANIZATIONAL FORMS IN THE UNITED STATES

The three key legal forms of business organization in the United States have historically been the sole proprietorship, the partnership, and the corporation. These have recently been joined by a fourth type, the limited liability company, or LLC. The sole proprietorship is the most common form of organization. However, the corporation is by far the dominant form with respect to sales and total profits. In addition to these key forms, there are two very important "hybrid" organizational forms, the limited partnership and the S corporation. We will examine all these forms, beginning with the sole proprietorship.

Sole Proprietorships

As the name implies, a **sole proprietorship** is a business with a single owner. In fact, there is no legal distinction between the business and the owner. The business is the owner's personal property, it exists only as long as the owner lives and chooses to operate it, and all business assets belong to the owner personally. Furthermore, the owner/entrepreneur bears personal liability for all debts of the company and pays income taxes on the business's earnings. Sole proprietorships are by far the most common type of business in the United States, accounting for over 74 percent of all business tax returns filed each year. However, proprietorships receive less than 6 percent of business income and employ less than 10 percent of the work force.

Simplicity and ease of operation constitute the principal benefits of the proprietorship. However, this organizational form suffers from severe weaknesses that, in most cases, limit the firm's long-run growth potential. These include the following:

1. *Limited life.* By definition, a proprietorship ceases to exist when the founder dies or retires. Although the entrepreneur can pass the assets of the business on to his or her children (or sell them to a third party), most of what makes the business

valuable on a continuing basis, such as business contracts and relationships, are tied to the entrepreneur personally. Furthermore, changes in ownership of successful companies can trigger potentially devastating estate tax liabilities.

2. *Limited access to capital.* A proprietorship can obtain operating capital from only two sources: reinvested profits and personal borrowing by the entrepreneur. In practice, both of these sources are easily exhausted.

3. *Unlimited personal liability.* A sole proprietor is personally liable for all the debts of the business, including judgments awarded a plaintiff in a successful lawsuit. The United States is the most litigious society in history (each year some 20 *million* lawsuits are filed in state courts alone), and a single jury verdict can destroy a lifetime's accomplishments and impoverish even the most successful business family.

Partnerships

A (general) **partnership** is essentially a proprietorship with two or more owners who have joined together their skills and personal wealth. As in a sole proprietorship, there is no legal distinction between the business and its owners, each of whom can execute contracts binding on all the others, and each of whom is personally liable for all the debts of the partnership. This is known as **joint and several liability.** Though no legal requirement exists that requires the owners to formalize the terms of their partnership in a written partnership agreement, most partnerships create such a document. In the absence of a partnership agreement, the business dissolves whenever any one of the partners dies or retires. Furthermore, unless there is a partnership agreement specifying otherwise, each partner shares equally in business income and each has equal management authority. As with a proprietorship, partnership income is taxed only once, at the personal level.

In addition to the tax benefits and ease of formation that partnerships share with proprietorships, the partnership allows a large number of people to pool their capital and expertise to form a much larger enterprise. Partnerships enjoy more flexibility than proprietorships in that the business need not automatically terminate following the death or retirement of one partner. Industries in which partnerships are the dominant (or at least a very important) form of organization include accounting, consulting, engineering, law, and medicine.

The drawbacks of the partnership form resemble those of the sole proprietorship and include the following:

1. *Limited life.* The life of the firm can be limited, particularly if only a few partners are involved. Problems may also result from the instability inherent in long-term, multiperson business associations.

2. *Limited access to capital.* The firm is still limited to retained profits and personal borrowings.

3. *Unlimited personal liability.* This disadvantage is made all the worse by the fact that the partners are subject to joint and several liability.

As firms grow larger, the competitive disadvantages of the proprietorship and partnership forms tend to become extremely burdensome, so almost all successful companies eventually adopt the corporate organizational form. As discussed in the Opening Focus, the last major Wall Street investment banking partnership, Goldman Sachs, finally adopted the corporate form and executed an IPO in May 1999.

In many ways, a **limited partnership** combines the best features of the (general) partnership and the corporate organizational forms, in that most of the participants in the partnership (the limited partners) have the limited liability of corporate shareholders, but their share of the profits from the business is taxed as partnership income. In any limited partnership (LP), there must be one or more **general partners,** each of whom has unlimited personal liability. Because the general partners operate the business and they alone are legally exposed, the general partners usually receive a greater-than-proportional (based on their capital contribution) share of partnership income. The **limited partners,** however, must be totally passive. They contribute capital to the partnership, but they cannot have their names associated with the business, and they cannot take any active role in the operation of the business, even as employees. In return for this passivity, the limited partners do not face personal liability for the debts of the business. This means limited partners can lose their equity investment in the business, but successful plaintiffs (or the tax authorities) cannot look to the limited partners personally for payment of their claims. Best of all, limited partners share in partnership income, and that income is taxed only once, as ordinary personal income for the partners.

Limited partnerships are ideal vehicles for funding long-term investments that generate large noncash operating losses in the early years of the business, because these losses *flow through* directly to the limited partners. This means the limited partners can (under specified conditions) use the tax losses to offset taxable income from other sources. Disadvantages of LPs include illiquidity and difficulties with monitoring and disciplining the general partner(s). In some cases, registering an LP with the SEC allows secondary-market trading of partnership interests, reducing or eliminating the illiquidity problem.

Corporations

In U.S. law, a **corporation** is a separate legal entity with many of the economic rights and responsibilities enjoyed by individuals. A corporation can sue and be sued, it can own property and execute contracts in its own name, and it can be tried and convicted for crimes committed by its employees. This organizational form has several key competitive advantages over its competitors, including the following:

1. *Unlimited life.* Once created, a corporation has a perpetual life unless it is explicitly terminated.
2. *Limited liability.* The firm's shareholders cannot be held personally liable for the firm's debts.
3. *Separable contracting.* Corporations can contract individually with managers, suppliers, customers, and ordinary employees, and each individual contract can be renegotiated, modified, or terminated without affecting other stakeholders.
4. *Unlimited access to capital.* The company itself, rather than its owners, can borrow money from creditors, and it can also issue various classes of preferred and common stock to equity investors. Furthermore, the ownership claims themselves (shares of common stock) can be freely traded among investors without obtaining the permission of other investors if the corporation is a **public company.** This means that its shares are listed for trading in a public security market.

A corporation is a legal entity owned by the shareholders who hold its common stock. Shares of stock carry voting rights, and shareholders vote at an annual meeting to elect the **board of directors.** This board is then responsible for hiring and firing managers and setting overall corporate policies. The rules dictating voting procedures and other parameters of corporate governance appear in the firm's **corporate charter,** the legal document created at the corporation's inception to govern the firm's operations. The charter can be changed only by a vote of the shareholders. Also, in contrast to the practice in almost all other countries, incorporation in the United States is executed at the state rather than the national level and is governed primar-

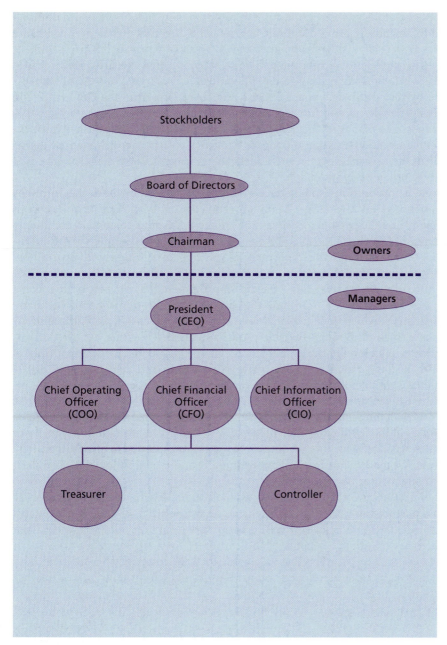

Figure 1.3
The Finance Function in the Organizational Structure of a Typical Large Corporation

ily by state rather than federal law. Nonetheless, all 50 states have broadly similar rules for incorporation and corporate governance, as described in Easterbrook and Fischel (1983). The top part of Figure 1.3 depicts the relationship among the important parties in a corporation.

Shareholders of common and preferred stock own the firm's equity securities, and are thus often called **equity claimants.** Though preferred stock appears in the stockholders' equity section of a firm's balance sheet, shareholders of preferred stock generally do not have the right to vote and bear less risk than shareholders of common stock. Therefore, we refer to common stockholders as the firm's ultimate owners.

Common stockholders vote periodically to elect the members of the board of directors and to amend the firm's corporate charter. The directors include key corporate personnel as well as outsiders, who are typically successful private businesspeople or executives of other major corporations. The **president** or **chief executive officer (CEO)** is responsible for managing day-to-day operations and carrying out the policies established by the board. The board expects regular reports from the CEO regarding the firm's current status and future direction. It is important to note the division between owners and managers in a large corporation, as shown by the dashed horizontal line in Figure 1.3. This separation leads to **agency costs,** the costs that arise due to the conflicts of interest between shareholders and managers. These costs are discussed in greater depth later in this chapter.

Although corporations dominate economic life around the world, this form has some competitive disadvantages. Many governments tax corporate income at both the company and the personal levels. In the United States, this treatment, commonly called the **double taxation problem,** is the single greatest disadvantage of the corporate form. To demonstrate the importance of this tax rule, Table 1.1 compares how $100,000 of operating income would be taxed for a corporation and for an otherwise-equivalent company organized as a partnership. Assume that the corporate income tax rate is 35 percent ($T_c = 0.35$) and that both the corporation's shareholders and the partnership's owners face personal tax rates of 40 percent ($T_p = 0.40$) on ordinary income received. Both partnership profits and dividend income are taxed in this way at the personal level in the United States. The $100,000 in partnership income is taxed once, at the personal level. The partners then have $100,000 \times (1 - 0.40) = $60,000 in disposable, after-tax income. In contrast, the corporation's operating income is first taxed at the corporate level, where federal taxes take a $100,000 \times 0.35 = $35,000 bite, and then again when the remaining $65,000 is distributed to shareholders in the form of cash dividends. These are taxed at the full marginal tax rate of 40 percent, leaving only $65,000 \times (1 - 0.40) = $39,000 in disposable, after-tax income. We ignore state taxes in our example, but they simply make the comparison more onerous for corporations.

The double taxation illustration shows that conducting a given business activity through a partnership rather than through a corporation can save the firm's owners 21 cents [($60,000 − $39,000) ÷ $100,000] in taxes on every dollar earned. Even given the massive, nontax benefits of the corporate form for most business activities, this tax "wedge" is a very heavy burden for U.S. companies to shoulder, and it is one that many other developed countries try to lighten for their limited liability corporations.

In contrast to a regular corporation, an **S corporation** (previously called a *Subchapter S corporation*) allows shareholders to be taxed as partners while still retaining their limited liability status as corporate stockholders. This type of company is

Table 1.1
Taxation of Business Income for Corporations and Partnerships

	Corporation	Partnership
Operating income	$100,000	$100,000
Corporate profits tax ($T_c = 0.35$)	(35,000)	0
Net income	$65,000	$100,000
Cash dividends or distributions	$65,000	$100,000
Personal tax on owner income ($T_p = 0.40$)	(26,000)	(40,000)
After-tax disposable income	$39,000	$60,000

an ordinary corporation (or *C corporation*), where the stockholders have elected to be treated as S corporation shareholders. To be eligible for S status, a firm must have 75 or fewer shareholders, the shareholders must be individuals or certain types of trusts (not corporations), the S corporation cannot issue more than one class of equity security, and it cannot be a **holding company.** This means it cannot hold a controlling fraction of the stock in another company.

If, however, a corporation can meet these requirements, then election of S corporation status allows the company's operating income to escape separate taxation at the corporate level.[4] Instead, each shareholder claims a proportionate fraction of total company profits as personal income and pays tax on this profit at his or her marginal tax rate. As with a limited partnership, S corporation status yields the limited liability benefit of the corporate form along with the favorable taxation of the partnership form. In addition, an S corporation can easily switch back to being a regular C corporation whenever company growth causes it to outgrow the 75-shareholder ceiling or if it needs to issue multiple classes of equity securities. Given the inherent flexibility of this type of organization, it is quite common for successful companies to begin life as S corporations and to retain S status until they decide to go public, which forces them to become regular corporations.

Limited Liability Companies

The limited liability company (LLC) combines the partnership's pass-through taxation with the S corporation's limited liability. All 50 U.S. states allow LLCs, which are very easy to set up. The IRS allows the LLC's owners to elect taxation as either a partnership or a corporation, and many states allow one-person LLCs as well as a choice of a finite or infinite life. Even though LLCs can be taxed as partnerships, their owners face no personal liability for the other partners' malpractice, making this type of company especially attractive for professional service firms. Given the limited liability feature and the flexibility of LLCs, we expect them to continue gaining significant "organizational market share" in coming years.

FORMS OF BUSINESS ORGANIZATION USED BY NON-U.S. COMPANIES

Although a comprehensive survey of international forms of business organization is beyond the scope of this chapter, this section will survey the most important organizational patterns observed in many industrialized economies. Even a cursory glance at non-U.S. systems shows strikingly universal patterns. In almost all capitalist economies, some form of joint stock, limited liability business structure exists—with freely tradable equity claims—and in most societies, these companies dominate economic life.

Limited Liability Companies in Other Industrialized Countries

Although pervasive, limited liability companies go by different names in different countries. In Britain, they are called public limited companies (PLC); in Germany, *Aktiengesellschaft* (AG); in France, *Société Générale;* and in Spain, Mexico, and elsewhere in Latin America, *Sociedad Anónima* (SA). While details vary, all of these structures are similar to the publicly traded corporations described previously. Key differences between international and U.S. companies revolve around tax treatment

---

[4.] According to the 2002 *Statistical Abstract of the United States,* over 53 percent (2.558 million of 4.849 million) of all corporations filing tax returns were S corporations in 1998, which indicates both the popularity of this organizational form and the relatively small *average* size of U.S. businesses.

of business income and the amount of information that publicly traded companies must disclose. Tax rules are typically, though not always, more punitive in the United States than abroad, while disclosure requirements are invariably greater for U.S. than for non-U.S. companies.

Many countries also make a distinction between limited liability companies meant to be traded publicly and those meant to be privately held. In Germany, *Gesellschaft mit beschränkten Haftung* (GmbH) are privately owned and unlisted limited liability stock companies; in France, these are called *Société à Responsibilité Limitée* (SARL). Private companies, and particularly family-owned firms, form the backbone of almost all market economies. For example, the German postwar "economic miracle" was not propelled by giant companies but rather by midsize, export-oriented companies that pursued niche market strategies at home and abroad. These *Mittelstand* (middle market) firms still account for some three-quarters of all German economic activity. A similar set of relatively small, entrepreneurial companies has helped propel Taiwan, Singapore, and other Asian nations to growth rates that until recently were consistently higher than those achieved in the West.[5]

State-Owned Enterprises and Privatization in Non-U.S. Economies

By far the biggest difference between the corporate organizational system of the United States and that of other countries is the almost total absence of **state-owned enterprises (SOEs)** in the United States. SOEs are companies owned and operated by the government that conduct business activities in areas outside what many would consider purely governmental affairs. As examples, the state has historically owned and operated the telephone, television, electric utility, airline, and railroad companies in many European countries, as well as throughout most of the developing world. The state has typically allowed little or no private-sector competition in these industries, and this has generally yielded relatively poor levels of service. Not surprisingly, the state still has great influence over many industrial sectors in the **transition economy** countries of Eastern Europe and the former Soviet Union.

However, the role of the state in economies around the world is being transformed by the spread of **privatization** programs, wherein the state sells off all or part of its holdings in SOEs to private companies or to individual private investors. Although the first major privatization program of the modern era was initiated by the (West) German government of Konrad Adenauer in the early 1960s, the Conservative government of Britain's Margaret Thatcher launched the current popularity of privatizations. In fact, these were called "denationalizations" until Thatcher gave them the more user-friendly name. After a tentative start, the Conservatives privatized all or part of the aerospace, telecommunications, automobile, airline, steel, oil and gas, electric and water utility, and air and seaport operating industries, raising over $80 billion in the process and transforming the role of the state in the British economy in little more than a decade. Prompted by the British success, governments around the world launched privatization programs that have to date raised over $1.2 trillion, with virtually all this money flowing to the selling governments rather than to the firms being privatized. Experts predict that privatization programs will continue to

---

5. Interestingly, a key feature of the corporate governance systems adopted by most of the dynamic Asian capitalist economies (including Japan, Korea, Taiwan, and Thailand) during their take-off phase was an explicit restriction on foreign (particularly American) ownership in key industries. Development of these sectors was considered to be so important that it could not be left in the hands of potential competitors, and the very high national savings rates and native entrepreneurial talent of these countries' citizens allowed this policy of excluding foreign direct investment to be successful. In contrast, Singapore and Hong Kong took exactly the opposite tack of welcoming foreign investment and achieved equally impressive growth rates, without the distortions inherent in a nationalistic investment and corporate ownership strategy.

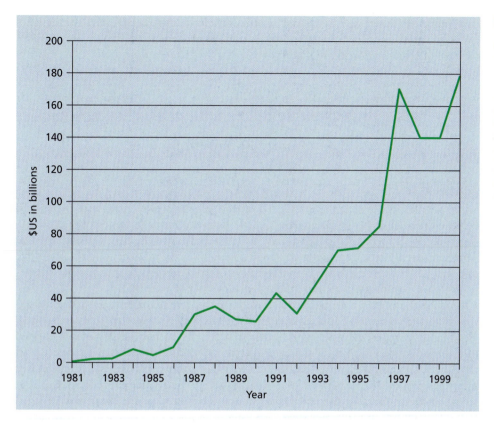

Figure 1.4
Annual Privatization Revenues for Divesting Governments World-wide, 1981–2000 (in $U.S. Billions)

Source: Privatisation International, *as reported in William L. Megginson and Jeffry M. Netter, "From State to Market: A Survey of Empirical Studies on Privatization,"* Journal of Economic Literature *39 (June 2001), pp. 321–389.*

raise over $100 billion per year for the foreseeable future. Figure 1.4 shows how much money governments raised through privatization programs between 1981 and 2000.[6]

Concept Review Questions

3. What are the costs and benefits of each of the three major organizational forms? Why do you think the various "hybrid" forms of business organization have proven so successful?

4. Comment on the following statement: Sooner or later, all successful private companies that are organized as proprietorships or partnerships must become corporations.

1.3 GOALS OF THE CORPORATE FINANCIAL MANAGER

In large publicly traded corporations, the owners are typically distinct from the managers. Traditionally, finance teaches that managers should act according to the interests of the firm's owners, its stockholders. In most cases, if the managers are successful in this endeavor, they will also achieve their own financial and professional objectives. In the sections that follow, we discuss what the proper goals of a corporate manager *should* be. We first evaluate profit maximization and then describe wealth

[6.] A brief history of privatization programs involving public share offerings is provided in Megginson, Nash, and van Randenborgh (1996). This paper also documents that the financial and operating performance of former state-owned enterprises improved significantly after they were privatized.

maximization. Next, we discuss the *agency costs* arising from potential conflicts between the goals of stockholders and the actions of management. Finally, we consider the role of ethics in corporate finance.

What Should a Financial Manager Try to Maximize?

What should a financial manager try to maximize: corporate profits, shareholder wealth, or something else? In the sections that follow, we hope to convince you that the proper objective for managers to pursue is shareholder wealth maximization.

Maximize Profit?

Some people believe that the manager's objective is always to maximize profits. To achieve the goal of profit maximization, the financial manager takes only those actions that are expected to make a positive contribution to the firm's overall profits. Thus, for each alternative being considered, the financial manager should select the one with the highest expected monetary return. From a practical standpoint, this objective would translate into maximizing earnings per share (EPS).

Although it seems a plausible objective for corporate managers, profit maximization suffers from several flaws. First, figures for earnings per share are inherently backward looking, reflecting what has happened in the past rather than what will happen in the future. Second, even if managers strive to maximize profits over a period of time, they should not ignore the timing of those profits. A large profit that arrives many years in the future may be less valuable than a smaller one earned today. Third, to maximize profits, the manager has to know how to measure them, and conventional barometers of profit rely on accounting principles rather than simply the measurement of cash flow. As the old saying goes, "You cannot pay your bills with earnings, only with cash."

Finally, and perhaps most decisively, focusing only on earnings ignores their variability, or risk. When comparing two investment opportunities, managers should not always choose the one they expect to generate the highest profits. They must consider the risks of the investments as well. A basic premise in corporate finance is that a trade-off exists between risk and return. *Risk and return are in fact the key determinants of share prices.* However, they affect share prices differently. Higher cash flow generally leads to higher share prices, while higher risk results in lower share prices. In general, stockholders are **risk averse,** meaning that they want to avoid risk and must be compensated (with a higher expected return) for the risks they accept.

Maximize Shareholder Wealth?

Modern finance asserts that the proper goal of the firm is to maximize the wealth of the stockholders, as measured by the market price of the firm's stock. A firm's stock price reflects the timing, magnitude, and risk of the *cash flows* that investors expect a firm to generate over time. When considering alternative strategies, financial managers should undertake only those actions that they expect will increase the firm's share price.

Why does finance preach the wisdom of share value maximization as the primary corporate objective? Why not focus instead on satisfying the desires of customers, employees, suppliers, creditors, or any other **stakeholders?** Both theoretical and empirical arguments exist to support our assertion that managers should focus on shareholder wealth maximization. A firm's shareholders are sometimes called its **residual claimants,** meaning that they can exert claims only on the firm's cash flows that remain after all other claimants are satisfied in full. It may help to visualize a queue with all the firm's stakeholders standing in line to receive their share of the firm's cash flows. Shareholders stand at the end of this line. If the firm cannot pay its employees, suppliers, creditors, and the tax authorities, then shareholders receive nothing. Shareholders earn a return on their investment only after other stakeholders' claims have been met. In other words, maximizing shareholder returns usually implies that the firm must also satisfy customers, employees, suppliers, creditors, and other stakeholders first.[7] Furthermore, by accepting their position as residual claimants, shareholders agree to bear most of the risk of running the firm. If firms did not operate with the goal of shareholder wealth maximization in mind, shareholders would have little incentive to accept the risks necessary for a business to thrive. To understand this point, consider how a firm would operate if it were run in the interests of its creditors. Would such a firm ever make risky investments, no matter how profitable, given that its creditors receive only a fixed return if this investment pays off? Only shareholders have the proper incentives to make risky, value-increasing investments.

SMART PRACTICES VIDEO
David Nickel, Controller for Intel Communications Group, Intel Corp.
"Finance's primary role is to try to drive the right business decisions to increase shareholder value."

See the entire interview at **SMARTFinance**

Focus on Stakeholders?

Although shareholder wealth maximization should be the primary goal of managers, in recent years many firms have broadened their focus to include the interests of other stakeholders. A firm with a stakeholder focus consciously avoids actions that would prove detrimental to stakeholders by damaging their wealth positions through the transfer of stakeholder wealth to shareholders. The goal is not so much to maximize stakeholder wealth as to preserve it. The stakeholder view is often considered part of the firm's "social responsibility" and is expected to provide long-run benefit to shareholders by maintaining positive stakeholder relationships. Such relationships should minimize stakeholder turnover, conflicts, and litigation. Clearly, the firm can better achieve its goal of shareholder wealth maximization with the cooperation of, rather than conflict with, its other stakeholders. In most cases, stakeholder wealth maximization is consistent with shareholder wealth maximization. But conflict between these two objectives is probably inevitable, and in that case the firm should ultimately be run in the shareholders' interests. Interestingly, even though American corporations are generally expected to act in a socially responsible way, they are rarely under binding legal or regulatory compunction to do so. The situation is much different in many Western European countries, where corporations are viewed as agents of social welfare almost as much as vehicles for private wealth creation.[8]

How Can Agency Costs Be Controlled in Corporate Finance?

The control of the modern corporation usually rests in the hands of professional, non-owner managers. We have seen that the goal of the financial manager should be to maximize the wealth of the owners of the firm; thus, managers can be viewed as agents of the owners who have hired them and given them decision-making authority to manage the firm for the owners' benefit. Technically, any manager who owns less than 100 percent of the firm's stock is to some degree an agent of the other owners.

[7.] Admittedly, this statement is overly simplistic, and conflicts of interest can exist between a firm's shareholders and its other constituents. Even so, from a legal perspective, shareholders profit only when the firm meets its contractual obligations to other stakeholders.

[8.] A positive take of the European "social market model" is provided in Hentzler (1992). A description and analysis of the role of stakeholders in U.S. financial management are provided in Cornell and Shapiro (1987).

COMPARATIVE CORPORATE FINANCE 1

The Growth of Stock Market Capitalization

The world's stock markets have increased phenomenally in value and importance during the past 20 years. This growth is revealed graphically in the figure, which traces the rise in the total value of the world's stock markets from 1983 to 2001, an 18-year period that saw total worldwide market capitalization increase from less than $3.4 trillion to about $27 trillion in December 2001. The market value of American stocks increased by almost seven times during this period, but non-U.S. mar-

kets experienced even faster growth. At its peak at the end of 1999, the total worldwide stock market capitalization of $35 trillion was roughly equal to world GDP. Trading volume, measured in dollars rather than in the number of shares traded, increased 26-fold from $1.23 trillion in 1983 to $31.56 trillion in 2000.

Sources: World Bank (http://www.worldbank.org) and World Federation of Exchanges (http://www.world-exchanges.org).

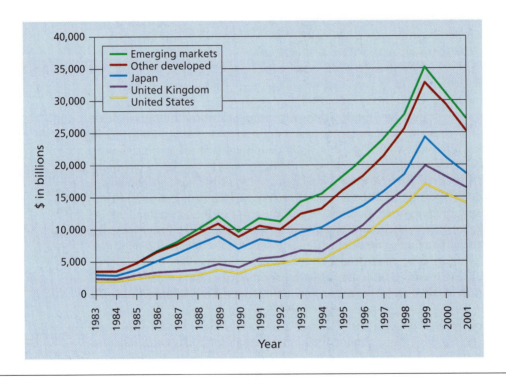

In practice, managers are also concerned with their personal wealth, job security, lifestyle, prestige, and perquisites such as country club memberships, limousines, and posh offices—provided at company expense, of course. Such concerns cause managers to pursue objectives other than shareholder wealth maximization. Shareholders recognize the potential for managers' self-interested behavior, and they use a variety of tools to limit this behavior. Financial economists recognize the *agency costs* caused by conflicts between the interests of shareholders and managers.

Types of Agency Costs

This conflict between the goals of a firm's owners and managers gives rise to managerial **agency problems,** which Jensen and Meckling (1976) define as costs arising from the likelihood that managers may place personal goals ahead of corporate goals. Shareholders can attempt to overcome these agency problems by (1) relying on market forces to exert managerial discipline, (2) incurring monitoring and bonding costs necessary to supervise managers, and (3) structuring executive compensation packages that align the interests of managers and stockholders.

Several market forces constrain the opportunistic behavior of a firm's managers. In recent years, large investors have become more active in management. This is particularly true for institutional investors such as mutual funds, life insurance companies, and pension funds, which often hold large blocks of a firm's stock. Institutional investor activists use their influence to put pressure on underperforming management teams, occasionally applying enough pressure to replace an existing CEO with a new one. An even more powerful form of market discipline is the hostile takeover. A **hostile takeover** involves the acquisition of one firm (the *target*) by another (the *acquirer*) through an open-market bid for a majority of the target's shares. By definition, a takeover attempt is hostile if the target firm's senior managers do not support (or, more likely, actively resist) the acquisition. The forces that drive hostile takeovers vary over time and from one acquisition to another, but poor financial performance is a common trait among targets of hostile bids. Bidders in hostile deals may believe that they can improve the value of the target company and thereby make a profit on their investment, by replacing incumbent management. Managers naturally see this as a threat and erect a variety of barriers to thwart potential acquirers. Nevertheless, the constant threat of a takeover provides additional motivation for management to act in the best interests of the firm's owners.

In addition to these market forces, other devices exist that encourage managers to behave in shareholders' interests or limit the consequences when managers misbehave. *Monitoring expenditures* pay for audits and control procedures that alert shareholders if managers pursue their own interests too aggressively.[9] *Bonding expenditures* protect against the potential consequences of dishonest acts by managers. Directors can make bonding expenditures, or managers can themselves make these expenditures to reassure the firm's directors of their benevolent intentions. This can be done, for example, by accepting a portion of their total pay in the form of delayed (and potentially forfeitable) compensation.

Use of Compensation Contracts to Control Agency Costs

One of the most popular, powerful, and expensive methods of overcoming agency costs and aligning managerial and stockholder interests is through the design of **executive compensation** contracts. The objective is to give managers the incentive to act in the best interests of the owners and to compensate them for such actions. In addition, the resulting compensation packages allow firms to compete for, hire, and retain the best managers available. For this reason, such pay packages are often called "golden handcuffs" because they tie good managers to the firm. Incentive compensation plans attempt to directly tie managerial wealth to the firm's share price. This primarily involves making outright grants of stock to top managers or, more commonly, giving them **stock options.** These give the manager the right to purchase stock at a fixed price, usually the market price of the stock at the time the manager receives the options. The key idea is that managers will have an incentive to take actions to maximize the stock price, because this will cause their wealth to increase along with that of the other shareholders.

Although experts agree that an effective way to motivate management is to tie compensation to performance, the execution of many compensation plans has been

[9.] But you may ask, "Who monitors the monitors?" In the wake of Enron's bankruptcy, Enron's auditor, Arthur Andersen, experienced the consequences of failing to alert shareholders to the company's problems. Arthur Andersen's audit clients abandoned the firm in droves, and many of the firm's partners quit. As this book was going into production, it was unclear whether Arthur Andersen would survive or not. In other words, the market imposed discipline on the auditors for their failure to impose discipline on Enron.

closely scrutinized in recent years. Individual and institutional investors, as well as the SEC, have publicly questioned the appropriateness of multi-million-dollar compensation packages (which include salary, bonus, and long-term compensation) that many corporate executives receive. For example, the highest-paid U.S. executives in 2001 were Larry Ellison of Oracle (total pay of $706.1 million) and Jozef Straus of JDS Uniphase ($150.3 million), but even the twenty-fifth highest-paid executive received $55.0 million in total pay.[10] The average total compensation for CEOs of large U.S. public companies surveyed by *Business Week* declined 16 percent in 2001, to $11.0 million. Average levels of CEO compensation in other developed countries tend to be much lower than this, a fact that critics of CEO pay in the United States do not miss.

While these sizable pay packages may be justified by exceptional increases in shareholder wealth, academic studies generally find only a modest (positive) relationship between CEO compensation and share price. These packages have also become extremely controversial, especially when managers of poorly performing companies still receive very large payouts. For example, while the U.S. stock market (especially Nasdaq) suffered one of its worst yearly declines in decades during 2000, the average total compensation of 365 CEOs at the companies in *Business Week*'s survey rose by 18 percent, to $13.1 million. Contributing to the publicity surrounding the annual survey of these awards is the relatively recent SEC requirement that publicly traded companies must disclose both the amount of and the method used to determine compensation to their highest-paid executives.

What Is the Importance of Ethics in Corporate Finance?

In recent years, the legitimacy of actions taken by certain businesses has received major media attention. Examples include the $100 million fine paid in early 2002 by Merrill Lynch to the State of New York for intentionally misleading investors with regard to buy and sell recommendations; the July 2002 arrest and charging of Adelphia founder, John Rigas, and his sons, Timothy and Michael, for looting about $2.3 billion from the cable-television company; and the June 2002 insider-trading arrest of Samuel Waksal, founder and CEO of the biotech firm ImClone Systems, who had leaked information to family and friends on the failure of the FDA to approve its marketing application for the cancer drug Erbitux prior to the release of that information to the public.[11] Clearly, these and other similar actions, such as those involving Enron, Global Crossing, Tyco, and WorldCom, have focused attention on the question of **ethics**, or standards of conduct in business dealings. Today, society in general and the financial community in particular are developing and enforcing ethical standards, primarily due to the increased public awareness resulting from the widespread publicity surrounding numerous ethical violations and their perpetrators that began with the Enron collapse in late 2001. The goal of these standards is to motivate businesspeople and investors to adhere to both the letter and the spirit of laws and regulations concerned with all aspects of business and professional practice.

More and more firms are now directly addressing the issue of ethics by establishing corporate ethics policies and guidelines

SMART ETHICS VIDEO

Andy Bryant, Executive Vice President of Finance and Enterprise Systems, Chief Financial Officer, Intel Corp.

"I never thought that ethics would be a value add to a company, but today I believe it counts as part of your market cap."

See the entire interview at **SMARTFinance**

---

[10] These figures are from a special report on executive pay by Lavelle (2002). This annual report is viewed with interest by shareholders—and often with dread by the managers fingered as overpaid. The 2002 report had its share of surprising revelations, but none matched the 2001's report of what must be one of the most attractive noncash bonuses ever paid to an executive. During 2000, the board of Apple Computer purchased a $90 million Gulfstream V business jet for Steve Jobs in recognition of his contribution to the company's turnaround—and as thanks to him for working three years without a salary.

[11] See Ang (1993) and Chambers and Lacey (1996) for examinations of the importance of ethics in corporate finance.

and by requiring employee compliance with them. Frequently, employees are required to sign a formal pledge to uphold the firm's ethics policies. Such policies typically apply to employee actions in dealing with all corporate stakeholders, including the public at large.[12] *Ethical behavior is therefore viewed as necessary for achievement of the firm's goal of owner wealth maximization.*

5. What are *agency costs?* Why do these tend to increase in severity as a corporation grows larger?

6. What are the relative advantages and disadvantages of using sophisticated management compensation packages to align the interests of managers and shareholders?

7. Why are ethics important in corporate finance? What is the likely consequence of unethical behavior by a corporation and its managers?

Concept Review Questions

1.4 SUMMARY

- The practice of corporate finance involves five basic, related sets of activities: financing, capital budgeting, financial management, corporate governance, and risk management.
- The three key legal forms of business organization in the United States are sole proprietorships, partnerships, and corporations. Sole proprietorships are most common, but corporations dominate economically. A new, fourth form, the limited liability company, has recently become popular due to its flexibility and favorable tax treatment.
- Limited liability companies exist in virtually every country, and those in developed countries share many of the same basic traits. Many countries also have a large number of state-owned enterprises, though most governments have launched privatization programs to sell their ownership stakes to private investors.
- The goal of the firm's managers should be to maximize shareholder wealth rather than maximize profits because the latter focuses on the past, not the future, ignores the timing of profits, relies on accounting values rather than future cash flows, and ignores risk. Shareholder wealth maximization is socially optimal because shareholders are residual claimants who profit only after all other claims are paid in full.
- Agency costs that result from the separation of ownership and control must be addressed satisfactorily for companies to prosper. These costs can be overcome (or at least reduced) by relying on the workings of the market for corporate control, incurring monitoring and bonding costs, and using executive compensation contracts that (theoretically) align the interests of shareholders and managers.

INTERNET RESOURCES

Note: *This textbook includes numerous Internet links throughout the text, both within the discussions and at the end of each chapter. Because some links will likely change or be elimi-*

[12.] Unfortunately, these steps are hardly enough. Enron had a detailed conflict-of-interest policy in place, but then waived it so that its executives could set up the special-purpose entities that subsequently caused Enron's failure. The result of a lack of effective ethics policies at Enron and numerous other firms has been an increased level of government oversight and regulation.

*nated during the life of this edition, please go to this book's website (http://smart.swcollege
.com) to obtain updated links in the event you encounter a dead link.*

http://money.cnn.com (CNN Money); http://www.yahoo.com (Yahoo!)—Among the best
   websites for general U.S. business information

http://www.ft.com (*Financial Times*)—One of the best websites for international business
   information

http://www.careers.com (CareerBuilder); http://www.monster.com (Monster); http://www
   .usnews.com (*U.S. News & World Report*); http://www.careers.wsj.com (WSJ Career
   Journal)—Websites for career-related facts and figures

http://www.witcapital.com (SoundView Technology); http://www.ameritrade.com (Ameri-
   trade); http://www.schwab.com (Charles Schwab); http://www.etrade.com (E*Trade);
   http://www.bankone.com (Bank One)—Excellent websites maintained by brokerage
   houses and Internet banking firms

KEY TERMS

agency costs	holding company
agency problems	hostile takeover
board of directors	initial public offering (IPO)
bonds	joint and several liability
capital budgeting function	limited partners
capital structure decision	limited partnership
collective action problem	money market
commercial paper	notes
corporate charter	partnership
corporate finance	president or chief executive officer (CEO)
corporate governance function	primary market transaction
corporation	privatization
debt	public company
derivatives	residual claimants
double taxation problem	risk averse
equity	risk-management function
equity claimants	S corporation
ethics	secondary market transactions
executive compensation	shareholders
financial intermediary	sole proprietorship
financial management function	stakeholder
financing function	state-owned enterprises (SOEs)
general partners	stock options
goes public	transition economy
hedging	venture capitalists

QUESTIONS

1-1.   Why must a financial manager have an integrated understanding of the five basic finance functions? Why is the corporate governance function considered a finance function? Has the risk-management function become more important in recent years?

1-2.   Enter the home page of the Careers in Business website (http://www.careers-in-
   business.com), and page through the finance positions listed and their corresponding
   salaries. What skill sets or job characteristics lead to the variation in salaries? Which
   of these positions generally require prior work experience?

1-3.   What are the advantages and disadvantages of the different legal forms of business organization? Could the limited liability advantage of a corporation also lead

to an agency problem? Why? What legal form would an upstart entrepreneur likely prefer?

1-4. Describe the differences between businesses in the United States and those in foreign countries with respect to taxation, financial disclosure, and ownership structure. Is privatization reducing or increasing these differences?

1-5. Can there be a difference between profit maximization and shareholder wealth maximization? If so, what could cause this difference? Which of the two should be the goal of the firm and its management?

1-6. Define a corporate *stakeholder*. Which groups are considered to be stakeholders? Would stockholders also be considered stakeholders? Compare the shareholder wealth maximization principle to the stakeholder wealth preservation principle in terms of economic systems.

1-7. What is meant by an "agency cost" or "agency problem"? Do these interfere with shareholder wealth maximization? Why? What mechanisms minimize these costs/problems? Are executive compensation contracts effective in mitigating these costs/problems?

1-8. Are ethics critical to the financial manager's goal of shareholder wealth maximization? How are the two related? Is the establishment of corporate ethics policies and guidelines, and requiring employee compliance with them, enough to ensure ethical behavior by employees?

PROBLEMS

Legal Forms of Business Organization

1-1. Calculate the tax disadvantage to organizing a U.S. business as a corporation versus as a partnership under the following conditions. Assume that all earnings will be paid out as cash dividends. Operating income (operating profit before taxes) will be $500,000 per year under either organizational form; the effective corporate profits tax rate is 36 percent ($T_c = 0.36$); and the average personal tax rate for the owners of the business is 45 percent ($T_p = 0.45$). Then, recalculate the tax disadvantage using the same income but with the maximum tax rates that existed prior to 1981. These rates were 50 percent ($T_c = 0.50$) on corporate profits and 70 percent ($T_p = 0.70$) on personal investment income.

Goals of the Corporate Financial Manager

1-2. Consider the following simple corporate example with one stockholder and one manager. There are two mutually exclusive projects in which the manager may invest and two possible manager compensation contracts that the stockholder may choose to employ. The manager may be paid a flat $300,000 or receive 10 percent of corporate profits. The stockholder receives all profits net of manager compensation. Which project maximizes shareholder wealth? Which compensation contract does the manager prefer if this project is chosen? Which project will the manager choose under a flat compensation arrangement? Under a profit-sharing arrangement? Which compensation contract aligns the interests of the stockholder and manager so that the manager will act in the best interest of the stockholder?

Project #1		Project #2	
Probability	Gross Profit	Probability	Gross Profit
33.33%	$ 0	50.0%	$600,000
33.33	3,000,000	50.0	900,000
33.33	9,000,000		

2

Financial Statement and Cash Flow Analysis

OPENING FOCUS

Porsche Removed from Stock Index for Inadequate Financial Reporting

How far would you go to make a point? On August 7, 2001, executives of the Deutsche Börse took the extraordinary step of voting to remove Porsche, the famous German sports car maker, from its M-Dax Index of midcap stocks. This ended a long standoff between Germany's main stock exchange and one of the country's most respected, and most profitable, companies. What offense did Porshce commit to warrant removal from the exchange's index? The company refused to comply with the Börse's requirement that companies in the index provide quarterly financial statesments. Porsche maintained that quarterly financial statements would only confuse shareholders seeking to analyze the performance of a firm operating in such a highly cyclical industry. Besides, Porsche had just been selected for inclusion in Morgan Stanley Capital International's (MSCI) index—arguably the most prestigious global stock index—and Porsche executives believed that this would increase worldwide demand for its shares. Given its recent high profitability, Porsche also had no need for external funding, and thus felt free to ignore the Börse's rules.

However, the Börse is certainly correct in demanding that German companies increase the frequency and transparency of their financial disclosures. Over the past decade, the percentage of Germany's adult population that owns shares has increased from less than 4 percent to more than 20 percent. This surge in stock ownership coincided with a dramatic increase in the number of companies "going public," or selling shares to the public for the first time. In 1997, the Deutsche Börse created the Neuer Markt as a venue for growth-oriented companies to sell stock, and in its first three years of existence, the Neuer Markt experienced rapid growth in both the number and value of listed companies. However, in March 2000, a series of accounting scandals, coupled with the global contraction in stock prices, launched an 18-month slide that wiped out more than

SMARTFinance

Use the learning tools at http://smartfinance.swcollege.com

90 percent of the value of stocks listed on the Neuer Markt. The Börse's new financial disclosure requirements were adopted as a response to the crisis in investor confidence these scandals had precipitated. They were also designed to persuade companies to abandon Germany's rather murky accounting rules in favor of more transparent international standards.

Source: Bettina Wassener, "Porsche Exits Deutsche Börse with Regret," *Financial Times* (August 8, 2001).

It is often said that accounting is the language of business. Corporate finance relies heavily on accounting concepts and language, but the primary focus of finance professionals and accountants differs significantly. Accountants apply *generally accepted accounting principles (GAAP)* to construct financial statements that attempt to portray fairly how a company has performed in the past. Accountants generally construct these statements using an **accrual-based approach,** which means that accountants record revenues at the point of sale and costs when they are incurred, not necessarily when a firm receives or pays out cash. In contrast, financial professionals use a **cash flow approach** that focuses their attention to a greater degree on current and prospective inflows and outflows of cash. This chapter describes how financial professionals use accounting information and terminology to analyze the firm's cash flows and financial performance. We begin with a brief review of the four major financial statements. Next, we use these statements to demonstrate some of the key concepts involved in cash flow analysis. We give special emphasis to the effect of depreciation and other noncash charges on cash flows and the various inflows and outflows of cash to the firm. Finally, we discuss the use of some popular financial ratios to analyze the firm's financial performance.

SMART PRACTICES VIDEO
Jon Olson, Vice President
of Finance, Intel Corp.
"At Intel, accounting is a fundamental requirement of a financial analyst."

See the entire interview at **SMARTFinance**

2.1 FINANCIAL STATEMENTS

Although our discussion in this chapter is based on U.S. accounting statements and conventions, the principles covered are actually quite general, because many national governments require public companies to generate financial statements based on widely accepted accounting rules. In the United States, these rules are the GAAP developed by the Financial Accounting Standards Board (FASB). The FASB is a nongovernmental, professional standards body that examines controversial accounting topics and then issues "rulings" that almost have the force of law, at least in terms of their impact on accounting practices. The SEC is responsible for regulating publicly traded U.S. companies, as well as the nation's stock and bond markets. Every other industrialized country also has an agency similar to the SEC, and most developed countries mandate that companies generate financial statements following international accounting standards (IAS). These are broadly similar to GAAP, although GAAP rules tend to place greater emphasis on public information disclosure than do IAS rules. The SEC has thus far adamantly insisted that all non-U.S. companies report results based on GAAP in order to sell their securities directly to U.S. investors. However, the corporate accounting scandals of 2001 and 2002 have tarnished the reputation of GAAP and enhanced that of IAS.

The four key financial statements required by the SEC are (1) the balance sheet, (2) the income statement, (3) the statement of retained earnings, and (4) the statement

of cash flows.[1] Our chief concern in this section is to review the information presented in these statements. Given the importance of cash flow in financial analysis, we provide in-depth coverage of the statement of cash flows in Section 2.2.

In what follows, we present the financial statements from the 2004 stockholders' report of the Global Petroleum Corporation (GPC). Though fictional, GPC's accounts are based on the actual statements of the five largest international petroleum companies. Three of these firms (BP Amoco, Royal Dutch Shell, and Total Elf Fina) are headquartered in Europe, and two are based in the United States (Exxon Mobil and Chevron Texaco).[2] The values constructed for GPC mirror those of a globally active oil company.

BALANCE SHEET

A firm's balance sheet presents a "snapshot" view of the company's financial position at a specific point in time. By definition, a firm's assets must equal the combined value of its liabilities and stockholders' equity. Phrased differently, either creditors or equity investors finance all a firm's assets. A balance sheet shows assets on the left-hand side and the claims of creditors and shareholders on the right-hand side. Both assets and liabilities appear in descending order of liquidity, or the length of time it will take for accounts to be converted into cash in the normal course of business. The most liquid asset, *cash*, appears first, and the least liquid, *fixed assets*, comes last. In a similar fashion, *accounts payable* represents obligations the firm must pay with cash within the next year, whereas the last entry on the right-hand side of the balance sheet, *stockholders' equity*, quite literally never matures.

Table 2.1 presents Global Petroleum Corporation's balance sheet as of December 31, 2004. As is standard practice in annual reports, the table also shows the prior year's (2003) accounts for comparison. *Cash and cash equivalents* are assets such as checking account balances at commercial banks that can be used directly as means of payment. *Marketable securities* represent very liquid, short-term investments, which financial analysts view as a form of "near cash." *Accounts receivable* represent the amount customers owe the firm from sales made on credit. *Inventories* include raw materials, work in process (partially finished goods), and finished goods held by the firm. The entry for *gross property, plant, and equipment* is the original cost of all real property, structures, and long-lived equipment owned by the firm. *Net property, plant, and equipment* represents the difference between this original value and *accumulated depreciation*—the cumulative expense recorded for the depreciation of fixed assets since their purchase. Governments allow companies to depreciate, or charge against taxable earnings, a fraction of a fixed asset's value each year to reflect a decline in the asset's economic value over time. The one fixed asset that is not

---

[1.] The SEC requires *publicly held corporations*—those whose stock is traded on either an organized securities exchange or the over-the-counter exchange and/or those with more than $5 million in assets and 500 or more stockholders—to provide their stockholders with an annual stockholders' report that includes these statements.

Whereas these statement titles are consistently used throughout the text, it is important to recognize that in practice, companies frequently use different statement titles. For example, General Electric uses "Statement of Earnings" rather than "Income Statement" and "Statement of Financial Position" rather than "Balance Sheet"; Bristol Myers Squibb uses "Statement of Earnings and Retained Earnings" rather than "Income Statement"; and Pfizer uses "Statement of Shareholders' Equity" rather than "Statement of Retained Earnings."

[2.] Interestingly, two of the three European companies (BP Amoco and Royal Dutch Shell) report their results in U.S. dollars, despite being headquartered in Europe, because international petroleum trading has traditionally been a dollar-based business—as is true for over half of all products traded internationally. Total Elf Fina's accounts are denominated in euros.

Table 2.1

Balance Sheet for Global Petroleum Corporation

Global Petroleum Corporation Balance Sheets at December 31, 2003 and 2004 ($ in millions)					
Assets	2004	2003	Liabilities and Stockholders' Equity	2004	2003
Current assets			Current liabilities		
Cash and cash equivalents	$ 440	$213	Accounts payable	$1,697	$1,304
Marketable securities	35	28	Notes payable	477	587
Accounts receivable	1,619	1,203	Accrued expenses	440	379
Inventories	615	530	Total current liabilities	$2,614	$2,270
Other (mostly prepaid expenses)	170	176	Long-term liabilities		
			Deferred taxes	$907	$793
Total current assets	$2,879	$2,150	Long-term debt	1,760	1,474
Fixed assets			Total long-term liabilities	$2,667	$2,267
Gross property, plant, and equipment	$9,920	$9,024			
			Total liabilities	$5,281	$4,537
Less: Accumulated depreciation	3,968	3,335	Stockholders' equity		
			Preferred stock	$30	$30
Net property, plant, and equipment	$5,952	$5,689	Common stock ($1 par value)	373	342
Intangible assets and others	758	471	Paid-in capital in excess of par	248	229
Net fixed assets	$6,710	$6,160	Retained earnings	4,271	3,670
Total assets	$9,589	$8,310	Less: Treasury stock	614	498
			Total stockholders' equity	$4,308	$3,773
			Total liabilities and stockholders' equity	$9,589	$8,310

depreciated is land, because it generally does not decline in value over time. Finally, *intangible assets* include items such as patents, trademarks, copyrights, or—in the case of petroleum companies—mineral rights entitling the company to extract oil and gas on specific properties. Although intangible assets are usually nothing more than legal rights, they are often extremely valuable, as the discussion of the market value of global brands in this chapter's Comparative Corporate Finance insert vividly demonstrates.

Now turn your attention to the right-hand side of the balance sheet. Current liabilities include *accounts payable,* amounts owed for credit purchases by the firm; *notes payable,* outstanding short-term loans, typically from commercial banks; and *accrued expenses,* costs incurred by the firm that have not yet been paid. Examples of accruals include taxes owed to the government and wages due employees.

In the United States and many other countries, laws permit firms to construct two sets of financial statements, one for tax purposes and one for reporting to the public. For example, when a firm purchases a long-lived asset, it can choose to depreciate this asset rapidly for tax purposes, resulting in large immediate tax write-offs and smaller tax deductions later. When the firm constructs financial statements for re-lease to the public, however, it may choose a different depreciaton method, perhaps

Assessing the Market Value of Global Brands

Rank	Brand	2001 Brand Value ($ in billions)	2000 Brand Value ($ in billions)	Percent Change	Country of Ownership
1	Coca-Cola	68.95	72.54	−5	U.S.
2	Microsoft	65.07	70.20	−7	U.S.
3	IBM	52.75	53.18	−1	U.S.
4	GE	42.40	38.13	11	U.S.
5	Nokia	35.04	38.53	−9	Finland
6	Intel	34.67	39.05	−11	U.S.
7	Disney	32.59	33.55	−3	U.S.
8	Ford	30.09	36.37	−17	U.S.
9	McDonald's	25.29	27.86	−9	U.S.
10	AT&T	22.83	25.55	−11	U.S.
11	Marlboro	22.05	22.11	0	U.S.
12	Mercedes	21.73	21.11	3	Germany
13	Citibank	19.01	18.81	1	U.S.
14	Toyota	18.58	18.82	−1	Japan
15	Hewlett-Packard	17.98	20.57	−13	U.S.
16	Cisco Systems	17.21	20.07	−14	U.S.
17	American Express	16.92	16.12	5	U.S.
18	Gillette	15.30	17.36	−12	U.S.
19	Merrill Lynch	15.02	NA	NA	U.S.
20	Sony	15.01	16.41	−9	Japan
21	Honda	14.64	15.25	−4	Japan
22	BMW	13.86	12.97	7	Germany
23	Nescafe	13.25	13.68	−3	Switzerland
24	Compaq	12.35	14.60	−15	U.S.
25	Oracle	12.22	NA	NA	U.S.

How much is a global brand name worth? Interbrand Corporation, a New York–based consulting firm, has been trying to answer this question for several years. The table details what this firm considers the 25 most valuable brands in 2001. The table also lists the values of these brands in 2000, which makes it clear that the global business environment declined considerably in 2001. The total brand values are large and are dominated by brands of U.S.-based companies. Although American companies are not required to disclose estimated brand values in their financial statements, large publicly traded British and Australian firms must do so. Brand values do, however, have a significant impact on U.S. accounting rules in one important area—accounting for the "goodwill" created when a firm is acquired by another company for more than the acquired firm's book value. This premium over book value represents the higher market (versus book) value of intangible as-

sets such as patents, copyrights, and trademarks, as well as brand names and business relationships that are not accounted for at all. Until 2001, goodwill was treated as an expense to be charged against the acquiring firm's earnings over a period of years. Now, however, the Financial Accounting Standards Board requires firms to periodically assess the fair value of assets that they purchase through acquisitions. If the fair value of those assets declines significantly over time, then firms must recognize "goodwill impairment," meaning that some of the value of their intangible assets has vanished. Charges arising from goodwill impairment can have a dramatic effect on reported earnings, as we will see in the opening focus to Chapter 8.

Source: Interbrand Corporation, as reported in Gerry Khermouch, "The Best Global Brands," *Business Week* (August 6, 2001), pp. 5–64.

one that results in higher reported earnings in the early years of the asset's life and lower earnings later. The **deferred taxes** entry on the balance sheet reflects the discrepancy between the taxes that firms actually pay and the tax liabilities they report on their public financial statements. **Long-term debt** represents debt that matures more than one year in the future. The stockholder's equity section provides information about the claims against the firm held by investors who own preferred and common shares. The **preferred stock** entry shows the historic proceeds from the sale of preferred stock ($30 million for GPC). Next, the amount paid in by the original purchasers of common stock is shown by two entries—common stock and paid-in capital in excess of par. The **common stock** entry equals the number of outstanding common shares times the **par value** per share. The par value of a share of stock is an arbitrary value with little or no economic significance. The entry, **paid-in-capital** in excess of par, equals the number of shares outstanding times the original selling price of the shares, net of the par value. Therefore, the combined value of common stock and paid-in-capital equals the proceeds the firm received when it originally sold shares to investors. **Retained earnings** are the cumulative total of the earnings that the firm has reinvested since its inception. It is important to recognize that retained earnings do not represent a reservoir of unspent cash. The retained earnings "vault" is empty because the firm has already reinvested the earnings in new assets. Finally, the **Treasury stock** entry records the value of common shares that the firm currently holds in reserve. Usually, Treasury stock appears on the balance sheet because the firm has reacquired previously issued stock through a share repurchase program.

GPC's balance sheet in Table 2.1 shows that the firm's total assets increased by $1,279 million, from $8,310 million in 2003 to $9,589 million in 2004. Other significant changes in GPC's balance sheet include sizable increases in cash, accounts receivable, and intangible assets, coupled with a massive $896 million increase in gross property, plant, and equipment. Balancing these increases in asset accounts is an increase of $393 million in accounts payable plus $601 million in new retained earnings. In other words, GPC financed increases in asset accounts mainly by borrowing more from suppliers (accounts payable) and by reinvesting profits (retained earnings). We will discover additional insights into these changes when we look more closely at the statement of cash flows.

Income Statement

Table 2.2 presents Global Petroleum Corporation's income statement for the year ended December 31, 2004. As with the balance sheet, GPC's income statement also includes data from 2003 for comparison.[3] In the vocabulary of accounting, income (also called *profit, earnings,* or *margin*) equals revenue minus expenses. GPC's income statement, however, has several measures of "income" appearing at different points on the statement. The first income measure is *gross profit,* the amount by which *sales revenue* exceeds the *cost of goods sold* (the direct material and labor cost of producing the goods sold). Next, various operating expenses, including selling expense, general and administrative expense, and depreciation expense, are deducted from gross profits.[4] The resulting *operating profit* of $1,531 million represents the profits earned from producing and selling products, although this amount does not include financial and tax costs. *Other income,* which includes interest earned on marketable

---

[3.] When reporting to shareholders, firms typically also include a **common-size income statement** that expresses all income-statement entries as a percentage of sales.
[4.] Depreciation expense can be, and frequently is, included in manufacturing costs—cost of goods sold—to calculate gross profits. Depreciation is shown as an expense in this text to isolate its impact on cash flows.

Table 2.2
Income Statement for
Global Petroleum
Corporation

Global Petroleum Corporation Income Statements for the years ended December 31, 2003 and 2004 ($ in millions)		
	2004	2003
Sales revenue	$12,843	$9,110
Less: Cost of goods sold[a]	8,519	5,633
Gross profit	$ 4,324	$3,477
Less: Operating and other expenses	1,544	1,521
Less: Selling, general, and administrative expenses	616	584
Less: Depreciation	633	608
Operating profit	$ 1,531	$ 764
Plus: Other income	140	82
Earnings before interest and taxes (EBIT)	$ 1,671	$ 846
Less: Interest expense	123	112
Pretax income	$ 1,548	$ 734
Less: Taxes		
Current	367	158
Deferred	232	105
Total taxes	599	263
Net income (net profit after tax)	$ 949	$ 471
Less: Preferred stock dividends	3	3
Earnings available for common stockholders	$ 946	$ 468
Less: Dividends	345	326
To retained earnings	$ 601	$ 142
Per-share data[b]		
Earnings per share (EPS)	$5.29	$2.52
Dividends per share (DPS)	$1.93	$1.76
Price per share	$76.25	$71.50

[a]Annual purchases have historically represented about 80 percent of cost of goods sold. Using this relationship, its credit purchases in 2004 were $10,274 and in 2003, they were $7,288.
[b]Based on 178,719,400 and 185,433,100 shares outstanding as of December 31, 2004 and 2003, respectively.

securities, is added to operating income to yield *earnings before interest and taxes* (*EBIT*) of $1,671 million. When a firm has no "other income," its operating profit and *EBIT* are equal. Next, $123 million of *interest expense*—representing the cost of debt financing—is subtracted from *EBIT* to find *pretax income* of $1,548 million.

The final step is to subtract taxes from pretax income to arrive at *net income,* or *net profits after taxes,* of $949 million. Note that GPC incurred a total tax liability of $599 million during 2004, but only the $367 million *current* portion must be paid immediately. Although the remaining $232 million in deferred taxes must be paid eventually, these are noncash expenses for year 2004. Net income is the proverbial "bottom line" and is the single most important accounting number for both corporate managers and external financial analysts. From its net income the firm paid $3 million in dividends on its $30 million of preferred stock outstanding during both 2003 and 2004. Dividing **earnings available for common stockholders** (net income net of preferred stock dividends) by the number of shares of common stock outstanding results in **earnings per share** (*EPS*). *EPS* represents the amount earned during the period on each outstanding share of common stock. Because there are 178,719,400

Table 2.3
Statement of Retained
Earnings for Global
Petroleum Corporation

Global Petroleum Corporation Statement of Retained Earnings for the Year Ended December 31, 2004 ($ in millions)		
Retained earnings balance (January 1, 2004)		$3,670
Plus: Net income (for 2004)		949
Less: Cash dividends (paid during 2004)		
Preferred stock	$ 3	
Common stock	345	
Total dividends paid		$ 348
Retained earnings balance (December 31, 2004)		**$4,271**

shares of GPC stock outstanding on December 31, 2004, its *EPS* for 2004 is $5.29, which represents a significant increase from the *EPS* of $2.52 GPC managed during 2003. The cash **dividend per share** (*DPS*) paid to GPC's common stockholders during 2004 is $1.93, up slightly from the dividend of $1.76 per share paid in 2003.

STATEMENT OF RETAINED EARNINGS

The statement of retained earnings reconciles the net income earned during a given year, and any cash dividends paid, with the change in retained earnings between the start and end of that year. Table 2.3 presents this statement for Global Petroleum Corporation for the year ended December 31, 2004. A review of the statement shows that the company began the year with $3,670 million in retained earnings and had net profits after taxes of $949 million, from which it paid a total of $348 million in preferred and common stock dividends, resulting in year-end retained earnings of $4,271 million. Thus, the net increase for GPC is $601 million ($949 million net income minus $348 million in dividends) during 2004.

Two aspects of the change in GPC's retained earnings between 2003 and 2004 merit explicit mention. First, note that 2004 was a very good year for GPC compared to 2003 in terms of increased sales and profits. GPC's net income more than doubled between 2003 and 2004, rising from $471 million to $949 million, so it is not surprising that the amount of earnings retained in the firm during 2004 ($601 million) was much larger than in 2003 ($142 million).[5] Second, note that while GPC increased its dividend payment to common shareholders from $326 million in 2003 to $345 million in 2004, this increase was far smaller proportionally than was the increase in net income. Another way to phrase this is to say that GPC's **dividend payout ratio**—the fraction of current earnings available for common stockholders paid out as dividends—declined from 69.7 percent ($326 million ÷ $468 million) in 2003 to 36.5 percent ($345 million ÷ $946 million) in 2004.

[5.] Also note that the two broadest measures of income (*EBIT* and net income) increased proportionally far more than did sales revenue. Whereas sales increased by 41 percent—from $9,110 million to $12,843 million—*EBIT* and net income increased by 98 percent and 101 percent, respectively. This suggests that the firm's extensive use of fixed-cost assets (refineries, pipelines, tankers, etc.) imparts to it a high degree of *operating leverage,* meaning that a given percentage increase (decrease) in sales yields a much larger percentage increase (decrease) in operating profits (same as *EBIT*). Even with higher taxes, this increased operating income also translates into higher net profits. Finally, note that the increased operating income is not a result of a higher profit margin *on each sale.* The gross profit margin per sales dollar (gross profit ÷ sales) declined from 38.2 percent in 2003 to 33.7 percent in 2004. As a result, GPC's gross profit increased by a smaller percentage than its sales did. *EBIT* and net income surged because GPC's operating, selling, general, administrative, and depreciation expenses remained largely unchanged between 2003 and 2004. Though not absolutely "fixed costs," these expense items increased very little during 2004, and this magnified the impact of the sales increase on *EBIT* and on net income.

Why did GPC effectively cut its dividend payout ratio in half during 2004? Although we defer an in-depth analysis of dividend policy until Chapter 14, we can quickly present the two most likely reasons for this change. First, GPC's managers may have concluded that the increase in 2004 sales and profits might be reversed during 2005 or subsequent years. In that case, GPC would either have to cut dividends or pay out an uncomfortably large fraction of earnings during 2005 — perhaps even more than the firm's net profits. Empirical research suggests that firms do have a "target" payout ratio, but this target is based on the level of sustainable, or "permanent," earnings. Thus, GPC's managers would be reluctant to increase dividends until they are convinced the firm's earnings have reached a permanently higher level. Second, managers typically follow a "partial adjustment" strategy when they change dividend payments. This means that even if GPC's managers are convinced earnings have permanently increased and they wish to keep the firm's long-term payout ratio at 2003's level of nearly 70 percent, they will only gradually raise the dividend payment each year until they reach the target payout ratio.

STATEMENT OF CASH FLOWS

The statement of cash flows provides a summary of a firm's cash flows over the year. This is accomplished by isolating the firm's operating, investment, and financing cash flows and reconciling them with changes in its cash and marketable securities during the year. GPC's statement of cash flows for the year ended December 31, 2004, is presented in Table 2.5. However, before we look at the preparation of this statement, it is helpful to understand how both noncash expenses, such as depreciation, and investments impact a firm's cash flow. We should also stress that other information presented in financial statements can be very useful to financial managers and analysts, and this is especially true about the "notes" to financial statements.

NOTES TO FINANCIAL STATEMENTS

A public company's financial statements will include detailed explanatory notes keyed to the relevant accounts in the statements. These notes provide detailed information on the accounting policies, calculations, and transactions underlying entries in the financial statements. For example, the notes to General Motors' 2001 financial statements cover 25 of the 50 pages in its annual report. Notes typically provide additional information about a firm's revenue recognition practices, income taxes, fixed assets, leases, and employee compensation plans. This information is particularly useful to professional security analysts. As they try to assess whether a firm's stock is under- or overvalued, analysts scour the notes to the firm's financial statements, looking for clues that will shed more light on the firm's past and future performance.

Concept Review Questions

1. Are balance sheets and income statements prepared with the same purpose in mind? How are these two statements different, and how are they related?

2. Which statements are of greatest interest to creditors, and which would be of greatest interest to stockholders?

3. Why are the notes to financial statements important to professional security analysts?

2.2 CASH FLOW ANALYSIS

Although the financial manager is interested in the information contained in the firm's accrual-based financial statements, the primary focus is on cash flows. Without adequate cash to pay obligations on time, to fund operations and growth, and to compensate owners, the firm will fail. The financial manager and other interested parties can gain insight into the firm's cash flows over a given period of time by both utilizing some popular measures of cash flow and analyzing the firm's statement of cash flows.

THE FIRM'S CASH FLOWS

Figure 2.1 illustrates the firm's cash flows. Note that the figure treats cash and marketable securities as perfect substitutes. Both cash and marketable securities represent a reservoir of liquidity that increases with *cash inflows* and decreases with *cash outflows*. Also note that the figure divides the firm's cash flows into (1) operating flows, (2) investment flows, and (3) financing flows. The **operating flows** are cash inflows and outflows directly related to the production and sale of the firm's products or services. **Investment flows** are cash flows associated with the purchase or sale of both fixed assets and business equity. Clearly, purchases would result in cash outflows, whereas sales would generate cash inflows. The **financing flows** result from debt and equity financing transactions. Taking on new debt (short-term or long-term) results in a cash inflow, whereas repaying existing debt represents a cash outflow. Similarly, the sale of stock results in a cash inflow, while the payment of cash dividends or repurchase of stock generates a cash outflow. In combination, the firm's operating, investment, and financing cash flows during a given period will affect the firm's cash and marketable securities balances. Two popular measures of cash flow are *cash flow from operations* and *free cash flow*.

Cash Flow from Operations

The financial manager's primary focus is on cash flows. To adjust the income statement to show *cash flow from operations,* all noncash charges must be *added back* to the firm's *net profits after taxes*. **Noncash charges,** such as depreciation, amortization, and depletion allowances, are expenses that appear on the income statement but do not involve an actual outlay of cash. Almost all firms list depreciation expense on their income statements, so we focus our attention on depreciation rather than amortization or depletion allowances, but they are treated in a similar fashion. A simple estimate of **cash flow from operations** often found in accounting textbooks is given in the following equation:[6]

> Cash flow from operations = net profits after taxes + depreciation   (Eq. 2.1)

Applying Equation 2.1 to the 2004 income statement for Global Petroleum Corporation yields a cash flow from operations of $1,582 million ($949 million net income + $633 million depreciation). This $1,582 million is the amount of cash generated by GPC's normal operating activities, and the firm's managers can use it to purchase additional assets, to repay debt, to pay dividends to GPC's shareholders, or

---

[6.] This formula is viewed as an accounting "estimate" because its accuracy is predicated on the assumption that inventories, accounts receivable, and accounts payable did not change over the period covered by this measure.

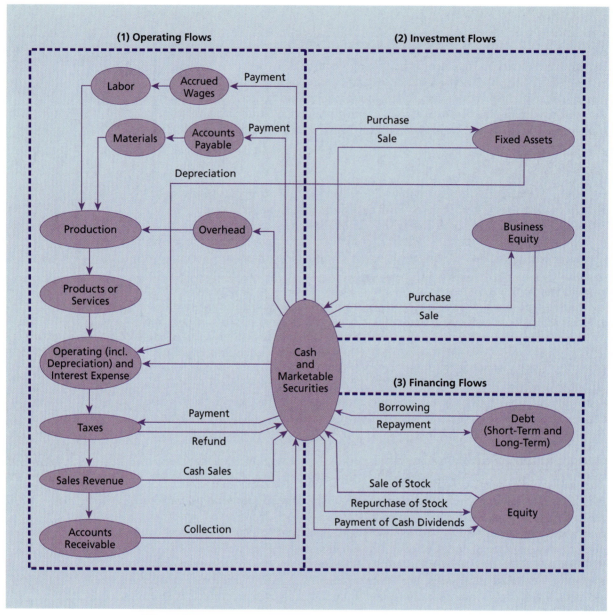

Figure 2.1
The Pattern of Cash Flows Through a Firm

to do all the above. This *internal cash flow* provides the bulk of net new financing for U.S. corporations every year, and the same is true in most other industrialized countries. External debt and equity financing, in contrast, usually account for less than one-third of new corporate funding.

Free Cash Flow

Although cash flow from operations is important, finance places more emphasis on the firm's free cash flow. **Free cash flow** (*FCF*) is the amount of cash flow available to investors—the providers of debt and equity capital. It represents the net amount of cash flow remaining after the firm has met all operating needs and paid for investments—both long-term (fixed) and short-term (current). Free cash flow for a given period can be calculated in two steps.

First, we find the firm's **operating cash flow** (**OCF**), which is defined by the following equation:

$$OCF = EBIT - \text{taxes} + \text{depreciation} \hspace{5em} \textbf{(Eq. 2.2)}$$

Substituting the values from GPC's 2004 income statement (from Table 2.2), we get GPC's operating cash flow:

$$OCF = \$1,671 - \$599 + \$633 = \$1,705$$

Comparing GPC's *OCF* of \$1,705 million to its *cash flow from operations* of \$1,582 million calculated earlier, the difference of \$123 million (\$1,705 million – \$1,582 million) represents interest expense. The accounting measure of cash flow from operations deducts interest expense, whereas the finance measure, operating cash flow, does not. The difference is subtle but important. In many settings, financial analysts want to separate the cash flows that a firm generates by producing goods and services from those associated with financing decisions. Clearly, interest is a cash expense that occurs because a firm chooses to finance part of its operations with debt rather than with equity, so financial analysts often ignore that item when assessing a firm's overall ability to generate cash.

Next, we convert operating cash flow to free cash flow (*FCF*). This is done by deducting the firm's net investments in fixed and current assets from operating cash flow as shown in the following equation:

$$FCF = OCF - \Delta FA - (\Delta CA - \Delta A/P - \Delta\text{accruals}) \hspace{3em} \textbf{(Eq. 2.3)}$$

where ΔFA = change in gross fixed assets,

ΔCA = change in current assets,

$\Delta A/P$ = change in accounts payable, and

$\Delta\text{accruals}$ = change in accrued liabilities.

Note that only spontaneous current liability changes are deducted from current assets to find the net change in short-term investment. From the preceding calculation, we know that GPC's *OCF* in 2004 was \$1,705 million. Using GPC's 2003 and 2004 balance sheets (Table 2.1), we can calculate the changes in gross fixed assets, current assets, accounts payable, and accruals between 2003 and 2004:

$$\Delta FA = \$9,920 - \$9,024 = \$896$$

$$\Delta CA = \$2,879 - \$2,150 = \$729$$

$$\Delta A/P = \$1,697 - \$1,304 = \$393$$

$$\Delta\text{accruals} = \$440 - \$379 = \$61$$

Substituting these values into Equation 2.3, we get the following:

$$FCF = \$1,705 - \$896 - (\$729 - \$393 - \$61)$$

$$= \$1,705 - \$896 - \$275$$

$$= \$534$$

Reviewing the second line of the *FCF* calculation above, we see that after subtracting $896 million in net fixed asset investment and $275 million in net current asset investment, GPC has free cash flow in 2004 of $534 million. During 2004, the firm therefore had $534 million available to pay investors who provide the firm with debt and equity financing. Free cash flow will be used in Chapter 4 to estimate the value of a firm. At this point, suffice it to say that *FCF* is an important measure of cash flow used by corporate finance professionals.

INFLOWS AND OUTFLOWS OF CASH

The statement of cash flows summarizes the inflows and outflows of cash during a given period. Table 2.4 classifies the basic inflows and outflows of cash for corporations. For example, if a firm's accounts payable increases by $1,000 during the year, this change would be an *inflow of cash*. If the firm's inventory increases by $2,500, the change would be an *outflow of cash*.

Table 2.4
The Inflows and Outflows of Corporate Cash

Inflows	Outflows
Decrease in any asset	Increase in any asset
Increase in any liability	Decrease in any liability
Net income (profit after tax)	Net loss
Depreciation and other noncash charges	Dividends paid
Sale of common or preferred stock	Repurchase or retirement of stock

A few additional points can be made with respect to the classification scheme in Table 2.4.

1. A *decrease* in an asset, such as the firm's inventory balance, is an *inflow of cash* because cash that has been tied up in the asset is released and managers can use it for some other purpose, such as repaying a loan. In contrast, an *increase* in the firm's inventory balance (or any other asset) is an *outflow of cash* because additional inventory ties up more of the firm's cash. Similar logic explains why an increase in any liability is an inflow of cash, and a decrease in any liability is an outflow of cash.
2. Our earlier discussion of cash flow from operations explains why net income and depreciation are considered cash inflows. The same logic suggests that a *net loss* (negative net profits after taxes) would be an outflow of cash. The firm must balance its losses with an inflow of cash—such as selling off some of its fixed assets (reducing an asset) or increasing external borrowing (increasing a liability). Note that a firm can have a *net loss* and still have positive cash flow from operations when depreciation and other noncash charges during the period are greater than the net loss. Therefore, the statement of cash flows treats net income (or net losses) and noncash charges as separate entries.

APPLYING THE MODEL

On June 30, 2002, and on March 31, 2002, Procter & Gamble Co. (P&G) (ticker symbol, PG) reported the following balances in certain current asset and liabilities accounts ($ in millions).

Account	June 30, 2002	March 31, 2002
Cash	$3,427	$3,061
Short-term investments	196	470
Accounts receivable	3,611	3,403
Inventory	3,456	3,772
Accounts payable	8,973	9,137
Short-term debt	3,731	5,993

In terms of current assets, short-term investments and inventory declined during the second quarter of 2002, providing an inflow of cash for P&G. Cash and accounts receivable increased during the quarter, representing a cash outflow. It may seem strange to think of an increase in cash balances as a use of cash, but that simply means that P&G used some of its cash flow to "invest in liquidity" rather than using the cash for another purpose. On the liabilities side, accounts payable and short-term debt declined, both representing an outflow of cash for P&G.

DEVELOPING THE STATEMENT OF CASH FLOWS

Accountants construct the statement of cash flows by using the income statement for a given year, along with the beginning- and end-of-year balance sheets. The procedure involves classifying balance sheet changes as inflows or outflows of cash; obtaining income statement data; classifying the relevant values into operating, investment, and financing cash flows; and presenting them in the proper format.[7] The statement of cash flows for the year ended December 31, 2004, for Global Petroleum Corporation appears in Table 2.5. Note that the statement assigns positive values to all cash inflows and negative values to all cash outflows. Notice under the investment activities section that the statement records the increase in *gross* fixed assets, rather than *net* fixed assets, as a cash outflow. Depreciation accounts for the difference between changes in gross and net fixed assets, but depreciation expense appears in the operating activities section of the statement. Thus, the focus on changes in gross fixed assets avoids double-counting depreciation in the statement. For a similar reason, the statement does not show a specific entry for the change in retained earnings as an inflow (or outflow) of cash. Instead, the factors that determine the change in retained earnings—profits or losses and dividends—appear as separate individual entries in the statement.

By adding up the items in each category—operating, investment, and financing activities—we obtain the net increase (decrease) in cash and marketable securities for the year. As a check, this value should reconcile with the actual change in cash and marketable securities for the year, which is obtained from the beginning- and end-of-year balance sheets.

By applying this procedure to GPC's 2004 income statement and 2003 and 2004 balance sheets, we obtain the firm's 2004 statement of cash flows (see Table 2.5). This statement shows that GPC experienced a $234 million increase in cash and marketable securities during 2004. Looking at GPC's 2003 and 2004 balance sheets in Table 2.1, we see that the firm's cash increased by $227 million and its marketable

---

[7.] For a description and demonstration of the detailed procedures for developing the statement of cash flows, see any recently published financial accounting text, such as Chapter 14 of *Corporate Financial Accounting*, 7th ed., by Warren, Reeve, and Fess (2002).

Global Petroleum Corporation Statement of Cash Flows for Year Ended December 31, 2004 ($ in millions)

Cash flow from operating activities		
Net income (net profit after tax)	$949	
Depreciation	633	
Increase in accounts receivable	(416)	
Increase in inventories	(85)	
Decrease in other current assets	6	
Increase in accounts payable	393	
Increase in accrued expenses	61	
Cash provided by operating activities		$1,541
Cash flow from investment activities		
Increase in gross fixed assets	($896)	
Increase in intangible and other assets	(287)	
Cash provided (consumed) by investment activities		($1,183)
Cash flow from financing activities		
Decrease in notes payable	($110)	
Increase in deferred taxes	114	
Increase in long-term debt	286	
Changes in stockholders' equity	(66)	
Dividends paid	(348)	
Cash provided (consumed) by financing activities		($ 124)
Net increase in cash and marketable securities		$ 234

securities increased by $7 million between December 31, 2003, and December 31, 2004. The $234 million net increase in cash and marketable securities from the statement of cash flows reconciles with the total change of $234 million in these accounts during 2004. GPC's statement of cash flows therefore reconciles with the balance sheet changes.

INTERPRETING THE STATEMENT

The statement of cash flows allows the financial manager and other interested parties to analyze the firm's cash flow over a period of time. Unusual changes in either the major categories of cash flow or in specific items may offer clues to problems that a firm may be experiencing. For example, an unusually large increase in accounts receivable and inventories resulting in major cash outflows may signal credit or inventory problems, respectively. Financial managers and analysts can also prepare a statement of cash flows developed from projected, or pro forma, financial statements. They use this approach to determine whether the firm will require additional external financing or whether it will generate excess cash that can be reinvested or distributed to shareholders.

Analysis of Global Petroleum Corporation's statement of cash flows for 2004 does not indicate major problems for the company. GPC used the $1,541 million of cash provided by operating activities primarily to purchase an additional $896 million in property, plant, and equipment and increase intangibles and other fixed assets by $287 million. Financing activities were basically a wash, with increases in deferred taxes and long-term debt contributing a combined cash inflow of $400 million. Roughly offsetting the inflows of cash from increased long-term debt and deferred taxes were outflows from a reduction of notes payable ($110 million), payment of common and preferred stock dividends ($348 million), and a net reduction in common stock outstanding of $66 million. In addition to cash provided by net income ($949 million) and depreciation ($633 million), major cash inflows were realized by increasing accounts payable ($393 million) and long-term debt ($286 million). The $1,183 million increase in fixed assets was unusually large, by recent historical standards, but consistent with the significant growth in revenue that occurred during 2004.

One financially encouraging step taken by GPC during 2004 was to increase its net working capital by $385 million. **Net working capital,** defined as current assets minus current liabilities, is a measure of the firm's overall liquidity; higher values reflect greater solvency, and vice versa. GPC's net working capital at the end of 2003 was −$120 million. As of December 31, 2004, GPC's net working capital had risen to a positive level of $265 million. GPC engineered this $385 million increase in net working capital by increasing its investment in current assets by $729 million while increasing its current liabilities by only $344 million. *Cash and marketable securities, accounts receivable,* and *inventories* increased by $234 million, $416 million, and $85 million, respectively, while the *other* current assets decreased by $6 million. Large increases occurred in two of the three categories of current liabilities—accounts payable ($393 million) and accrued expenses ($61 million)—and they were partially offset by a $110 million decline in notes payable. In general, it appears that GPC is growing and is managing its cash flows reasonably well.

---

4. How do depreciation and other noncash charges act as sources of cash inflow to the firm? Why does a depreciation allowance exist in the tax laws? For a profitable firm, is it better to depreciate an asset quickly or slowly for tax purposes? Explain.

5. What is *cash flow from operations?* Why do finance professionals prefer *operating cash flow (OCF)?* What is *free cash flow (FCF),* and how is it related to *OCF?*

6. Why is the financial manager likely to have great interest in the firm's statement of cash flows? What type of information can be obtained from this statement?

Concept Review Questions

2.3 ANALYZING FINANCIAL PERFORMANCE USING RATIO ANALYSIS

Analysis of a firm's financial statements is of interest to shareholders, creditors, and the firm's own management. In many cases, the constituents of a firm want to compare its financial condition to that of other similar firms, but doing so can be very tricky. For example, suppose you are introduced to a new acquaintance named Bill who tells you that he runs a company that earned a profit of $10 million last year. Would you be impressed by that feat? What if you knew that Bill's last name was Gates? Most people would agree that a profit of $10 million would be a great disappointment for Microsoft, the firm run by Bill Gates.

The point here is that the sales, profits, or almost any other item that appears on a firm's financial statements is difficult to interpret unless we have some way to put that number in perspective. To analyze financial statements, we need relative measures that in effect normalize size differences. Effective analysis of financial statements is thus based on the knowledge and use of *ratios* or *relative values*. **Ratio analysis** involves calculating and interpreting financial ratios to assess the firm's performance and status.

TYPES OF FINANCIAL RATIOS

Different constituents will focus on different types of financial ratios. The firm's creditors are primarily interested in ratios that measure the short-term liquidity of the company and its ability to make interest and principal payments. A secondary concern of creditors is the firm's profitability; they want assurance that the business is healthy and will continue to be successful. Both present and prospective shareholders are interested in ratios that measure the firm's current and future levels of risk and return, because these two dimensions directly affect the firm's share price. The firm's managers must be concerned with all aspects of the firm's financial situation, so they use all the ratios to generate an overall picture of the company's financial health. In addition, management uses ratios to monitor the firm's performance from period to period. The managers examine unexpected changes carefully to isolate developing problems.

An additional complication of ratio analysis is that for any given ratio, what is normal in one industry may be highly unusual in another. For example, by dividing a firm's net income by its sales, we obtain the net profit margin ratio. Net profit margins vary dramatically across industries. What might be considered an outstanding net profit margin in the retail grocery industry would look paltry in the software business. Therefore, when making subjective judgments about the health of a given company, analysts usually compare the firm's ratios to two benchmarks. First, analysts compare the financial ratios in the current year to previous years' ratios. By doing so, analysts hope to identify trends that they can use to evaluate the firm's prospects. Second, analysts usually compare the ratios of one company to those of other "benchmark" firms in the same industry or to an industry average obtained from a trade association or third-party provider.

We will use the 2004 and 2003 balance sheets and income statements for Global Petroleum Corporation, presented earlier in Tables 2.1 and 2.2, to demonstrate ratio calculations. We will delete the *millions* after GPC's values. Note that the ratios presented in the remainder of this chapter can be applied to nearly any company. Of course, many companies in different industries use ratios that are particularly focused on aspects peculiar to their industry.[8] We will cover the most common financial ratios, and we group them into five categories: *liquidity, activity, debt, profitability,* and *market* ratios.

LIQUIDITY RATIOS

The **liquidity** of a firm is measured by its ability to satisfy its short-term obligations *as they come due*. Because a common precursor to financial distress and bankruptcy is low or declining liquidity, liquidity ratios are good leading indicators of cash flow

---

[8.] For example, airlines pay close attention to the ratio of revenues to passenger miles flown. Retailers diligently track the growth in same-store sales from one year to the next.

problems. The two basic measures of liquidity are the *current ratio* and the *quick (acid-test) ratio*.

The **current ratio,** one of the most commonly cited financial ratios, measures the firm's ability to meet its short-term obligations. It is defined as current assets *divided* by current liabilities, and thus presents in ratio form what *net working capital* measures by *subtracting* current liabilities from current assets. The current ratio for GPC on December 31, 2004, is computed as follows:

$$\text{Current ratio} = \frac{\text{current assets}}{\text{current liabilities}} = \frac{\$2,879}{\$2,614} = 1.10$$

How high should the current ratio be? The answer depends on the type of business under consideration and on the costs and benefits of having too much versus too little liquidity. For example, a current ratio of 1.0 would be considered acceptable for a utility but might be unacceptable for a manufacturing firm. The more predictable a firm's cash flows, the lower the acceptable current ratio. Because GPC is in a business (oil exploration and development) with notoriously unpredictable annual cash flows, its current ratio of 1.10 indicates that GPC takes a fairly aggressive approach to managing its liquidity.

The **quick (acid-test) ratio** is similar to the current ratio except that it excludes inventory, which is usually the least-liquid current asset. The generally low liquidity of inventory results from two factors: (1) many types of inventory cannot be easily sold because they are partially completed items, special-purpose items, and the like; and (2) inventory is typically sold on credit, which means that it becomes an account receivable before being converted into cash. The quick ratio is calculated as follows:

$$\text{Quick ratio} = \frac{\text{current assets} - \text{inventory}}{\text{current liabilities}} = \frac{\$2,879 - \$615}{\$2,614} = 0.866$$

The quick ratio for GPC in 2004 is 0.866. The quick ratio provides a better measure of overall liquidity only when a firm's inventory cannot be easily converted into cash. If inventory is liquid, the current ratio is a preferred measure of overall liquidity. Because GPC's inventory is mostly petroleum and refined products, both of which can be readily converted into cash, the firm's managers will probably focus on the current ratio rather than the quick ratio.

ACTIVITY RATIOS

Activity ratios measure the speed with which various accounts are converted into sales or cash. Managers and outsiders use activity ratios as guides to assess how efficiently the firm manages assets such as inventory, receivables, and fixed assets, and the current liability, accounts payable.

Inventory turnover provides a measure of how quickly a firm sells its goods. GPC's 2004 *inventory turnover ratio* appears below:

$$\text{Inventory turnover} = \frac{\text{cost of goods sold}}{\text{inventory}} = \frac{\$8,519}{\$615} = 13.85$$

Notice that we used the ending inventory balance of $615 to calculate this ratio. If inventories are growing over time or exhibit seasonal patterns, analysts sometimes use the average level of inventory throughout the year rather than the ending balance to calculate this ratio. The resulting turnover of 13.85 is meaningful only when it is compared with that of other firms in the same industry or to the firm's past inventory turnover. An inventory turnover of 20.0 would not be unusual for a grocery store, whereas a common inventory turnover for an aircraft manufacturer would be 4.0. This value for GPC is in line with that for other oil and gas companies, and a bit above the firm's own historic norms.

Inventory turnover can be easily converted into an **average age of inventory** by dividing the turnover figure into 365—the number of days in a year. For GPC, the average age of inventory would be 26.4 days (365 ÷ 13.85). This result means that GPC's inventory balance turns over about every 26 days.

APPLYING THE MODEL

Inventory ratios, like most other financial ratios, vary a great deal from one industry to another. For example, for the four quarters ending March 30, 2002, Intel Corp. reported inventory of $2.48 billion and cost of goods sold of $13.56 billion. This implies an inventory turnover ratio for Intel of about 5.5, or an average age of inventory of about 66 days. With the rapid pace of technological change in the semiconductor industry, Intel cannot afford to hold inventory too long. In contrast, for the four quarters ending March 30, 2002, Robert Mondavi Corp., one of the few publicly traded wineries in the United States, reported cost of goods sold of $265.7 million and inventory of $417.1 million. This yields an inventory turnover ratio for Mondavi of just 0.64, or an average age of inventory of about 570 days. Clearly, the differences in these inventory ratios reflect differences in the economic circumstances of the industries. Whereas the value of semiconductors declines as they age, just the opposite occurs in the wine business, at least up to a point.

The **average collection period,** or average age of accounts receivable, is useful in evaluating credit and collection policies.[9] It is computed for GPC by dividing the firm's average daily sales into the accounts receivable balance. On average, it takes the firm 46.0 days to receive payment from a credit sale.

$$\text{Average sales per day} = \frac{\text{annual sales}}{365} = \frac{\$12,843}{365} = \$35.19$$

$$\text{Average collection period} = \frac{\text{accounts receivable}}{\text{average sales per day}} = \frac{\$1,619}{\$35.19} = 46.0 \text{ days}$$

The average collection period is meaningful only in relation to the firm's credit terms. If GPC extends 30-day credit terms to customers, an average collection period of 46.0 days may indicate a poorly managed credit or collection department, or both. The lengthened collection period could also be the result of an intentional relaxation of credit-term enforcement in response to competitive pressures. If the firm had extended 60-day credit terms, the 46.0-day average collection period would be quite

---

[9.] The average collection period is sometimes called the *days' sales outstanding (DSO)*. As with the inventory turnover ratio, the average collection period can be calculated using end-of-year accounts receivable or the average receivables balance for the year. The evaluation and establishment of credit and collection policies are discussed in Chapter 23.

acceptable. Clearly, additional information is required to evaluate the effectiveness of the firm's credit and collection policies.

Firms us the **average payment period** to evaluate their performance in repaying suppliers. It equals the firm's average daily purchases divided by the accounts payable balance. To calculate average daily purchases, an analyst may have to estimate the firm's annual purchases, often by taking a specified percentage of cost of goods sold. This estimate is necessary because annual purchases are not reported on a firm's published financial statements and are instead embodied in its cost of goods sold. In the case of GPC, its annual purchases in 2004 were estimated at 80 percent of cost of goods sold, as shown in footnote 1 to its income statement in Table 2.1. Using the annual purchase estimate of $10,274, GPC's average payment period indicates that the firm takes, on average, 60.3 days to pay its bills.

$$\text{Average purchases per day} = \frac{\text{annual purchases}}{365} = \frac{\$10,274}{365} = \$28.15$$

$$\text{Average payment period} = \frac{\text{accounts payable}}{\text{average purchases per day}} = \frac{\$1,697}{\$28.15} = 60.3 \text{ days}$$

In a fashion similar to the average collection period, the average payment period is meaningful only when viewed in light of the actual credit terms extended the firm by its suppliers. If GPC's suppliers, on average, extend 30-day credit terms, the firm's average payment period of 60.3 days indicates that the firm is generally slow in paying its payables. The fact that it takes GPC twice as long to pay its suppliers as the 30 days of credit they extended GPC could damage the firm's ability to obtain additional credit and raise the cost of any credit that it may obtain. On the other hand, if the average credit terms granted GPC by its suppliers were 60 days, its 60.3-day average payment period would be very good. It should be clear that an analyst would need further information to draw definitive conclusions from the average payment period with regard to the firm's overall payment policies.

The **fixed asset turnover** measures the efficiency with which a firm uses its fixed assets. The ratio tells analysts how many dollars of sales the firm generates per dollar of fixed asset investment. The ratio equals sales divided by net fixed assets:

$$\text{Fixed asset turnover} = \frac{\text{sales}}{\text{net fixed assets}} = \frac{\$12,843}{\$6,710} = 1.91$$

The fixed asset turnover for GPC in 2004 is 1.91. This means that the company turns over its net fixed assets 1.91 times a year; or stated another way, GPC generates almost $2 in sales for every dollar of fixed assets. As with other ratios, the "normal" level of fixed asset turnover varies widely from one industry to another.

An analyst, when using this ratio and the total asset turnover ratio described next, must be aware that the calculations use the *historical costs* of fixed assets. Because some firms have significantly newer or older assets than others do, comparing fixed asset turnovers of those firms can be misleading. Firms with newer assets will tend to have lower turnovers than those with older assets—which have lower book (accounting) values. A naive comparison of fixed asset turnover ratios for different firms might lead an analyst to conclude that one firm operates more efficiently than another, when in fact the firm that appears to be more efficient simply has older (i.e., more depreciated) assets on its books.

The **total asset turnover** ratio indicates the efficiency with which a firm uses *all* its assets to generate sales. Like the fixed asset turnover ratio, total asset turnover indicates how many dollars of sales a firm generates per dollar of asset investment. All other factors being equal, analysts favor a high turnover ratio because it indicates that a firm generates more sales (and hopefully more cash flow for investors) from a given investment in assets. GPC's total asset turnover in 2004 equals 1.34, calculated as follows:

$$\text{Total asset turnover} = \frac{\text{sales}}{\text{total assets}} = \frac{\$12,843}{\$9,589} = 1.34$$

DEBT RATIOS

Firms finance their assets from two broad sources, equity and debt. Equity comes from shareholders, whereas debt comes in many forms and from many different lenders. Firms borrow from suppliers, from banks, and from widely scattered investors who buy publicly traded bonds. *Debt ratios* measure the extent to which a firm uses money from creditors rather than shareholders to finance its operations. Because creditors' claims must be satisfied before firms can distribute earnings to shareholders, present and prospective investors pay close attention to the debts on a firm's balance sheet. Lenders share these concerns because the more indebted the firm, the higher the probability that the firm will be unable to satisfy the claims of all its creditors.

In general, the more debt a firm uses in relation to its total assets, the greater its financial leverage. Fixed-cost sources of financing, such as debt and preferred stock, create **financial leverage** that magnifies both the risk and the expected return on the firm's securities.[10] The more a firm borrows, the riskier its outstanding stock and bonds will be, and the higher the return will be that investors require on those securities. A detailed discussion of the impact of debt on the firm's risk, return, and value is included in Chapters 12 and 13. Here, we emphasize the use of debt ratios to assess the degree of a firm's indebtedness and its ability to meet the fixed payments associated with debt.

Broadly speaking, there are two types of debt ratios. One type focuses on balance sheet measures of outstanding debt relative to other sources of financing. The other type, known as the **coverage ratio,** focuses more on income statement measures of the firm's ability to generate sufficient cash flow to make scheduled interest and principal payments. Investors and credit-rating agencies use both types of ratios to assess a firm's creditworthiness.

The **debt ratio** measures the proportion of total assets financed by the firm's creditors. The higher this ratio, the greater is the firm's reliance on "other people's money" to finance its activities. The ratio equals total liabilities divided by total assets, and GPC's debt ratio in 2004 is 0.551, or 55.1 percent:

$$\text{Debt ratio} = \frac{\text{total liabilities}}{\text{total assets}} = \frac{\$5,281}{\$9,589} = 0.551 = 55.1\%$$

[10.] By *fixed cost* we mean that the cost of this financing source does not vary over time in response to changes in the firm's revenue and cash flow. For example, when a firm borrows money at a variable rate, the interest cost of that loan is *not* fixed through time, but the firm's obligation to make interest payments is "fixed" regardless of the level of the firm's revenue and cash flow.

This figure indicates that the company has financed over half of its assets with debt. A close cousin of the debt ratio is the **assets-to-equity (A/E) ratio,** sometimes called the **equity multiplier:**

$$\text{Assets-to-equity} = \frac{\text{total assets}}{\text{common stock equity}} = \frac{\$9,589}{\$4,278} = 2.24$$

Note that only common stock equity of $4,278 ($4,308 of total equity – $30 of preferred stock equity) is used in the denominator of this ratio. The resulting value indicates that GPC's assets in 2004 are 2.24 times greater than its equity This value seems reasonable given that the debt ratio shows that slightly more than half (55.1%) of GPC's assets in 2004 are financed with debt.

An alternative measure of the firm's leverage that focuses solely on the firm's long-term debt is the **debt-to-equity ratio,** calculated by dividing long-term debt by stockholders' equity. The 2004 value of this ratio for GPC is calculated as follows:

$$\text{Debt-to-equity ratio} = \frac{\text{long-term debt}}{\text{stockholders' equity}} = \frac{\$1,760}{\$4,308} = 0.409 = 40.9\%$$

GPC's long-term debts are therefore only 40.9 percent as large as its stockholders' equity. Note, however, that both the debt ratio and the debt-to-equity ratio use book values of debt, equity, and assets. Analysts should be aware that the market values of these variables may differ substantially from book values.

The **times interest earned ratio,** which equals earnings before interest and taxes divided by interest expense, measures the firm's ability to make contractual interest payments. A higher ratio indicates a greater capacity to meet scheduled payments. The times interest earned ratio for GPC equals 13.59, indicating that the firm could experience a substantial decline in earnings and still meet its interest obligations:

$$\text{Times interest earned} = \frac{\text{earnings before interest and taxes}}{\text{interest expense}} = \frac{\$1,671}{\$123} = 13.59$$

PROFITABILITY RATIOS

Several measures of profitability relate a firm's earnings to its sales, assets, or equity. *Profitability ratios* are among the most closely watched and widely quoted financial ratios. Many firms link employee bonuses to profitability ratios, and stock prices react sharply to unexpected changes in these measures.

The **gross profit margin** measures the percentage of each sales dollar remaining after the firm has paid for its goods. The higher the gross profit margin, the better. GPC's gross profit margin in 2004 was 33.7 percent:

$$\text{Gross profit margin} = \frac{\text{gross profit}}{\text{sales}} = \frac{\$4,324}{\$12,843} = 0.337 = 33.7\%$$

The **operating profit margin** measures the percentage of each sales dollar remaining after deducting all costs and expenses *other than* interest and taxes. As with the gross profit margin, the higher the operating profit margin, the better. This ratio is of interest because it tells analysts what a firm's bottom line looks like before deductions for payments to creditors and tax authorities. GPC's operating profit margin is 11.9 percent:

$$\text{Operating profit margin} = \frac{\text{operating profit}}{\text{sales}} = \frac{\$1,531}{\$12,843} = 0.119 = 11.9\%$$

The **net profit margin** measures the percentage of each sales dollar remaining after all costs and expenses, *including* interest, taxes, and preferred stock dividends, have been deducted. Net profit margins vary widely across industries. For example, consider two very profitable U.S. companies, Microsoft and Wal-Mart. For the quarter ending in June 2002, Microsoft reported a net profit margin of 21.0 percent, more than 6 times larger than the 3.4 percent net profit margin reported by Wal-Mart one month later. GPC's net profit margin of 7.4 percent is calculated as follows:

$$\text{Net profit margin} = \frac{\text{earnings available for common stockholders}}{\text{sales}}$$

$$= \frac{\$946}{\$12,843} = 0.074 = 7.4\%$$

Probably the most closely watched financial ratio of them all is earnings per share. The earnings per share represent the number of dollars earned on behalf of each outstanding share of common stock. The investing public closely watches *EPS* figures and considers them an important indicator of corporate success. Many firms tie management bonuses to meeting specific *EPS* targets. Earnings per share are calculated as follows:

$$\text{Earnings per share} = \frac{\text{earnings available for common stockholders}}{\text{number of shares of common stock outstanding}}$$

$$= \frac{\$946}{178.7} = \$5.29$$

The value of GPC's earnings per share on common stock outstanding in 2004 is $5.29.[11] This figure represents the dollar amount *earned* on behalf of each share outstanding. The amount of earnings actually *distributed* to each shareholder is the *dividend per share,* which as noted in GPC's income statement (Table 2.2), rose to $1.93 in 2004 from $1.76 in 2003.

The **return on total assets (*ROA*),** often called the *return on investment (ROI),* measures the overall effectiveness of management in generating returns to common stockholders with its available assets.[12] The return on total assets for GPC equals 9.9 percent:

$$\text{Return on total assets} = \frac{\text{earnings available for common stockholders}}{\text{total assets}}$$

$$= \frac{\$946}{\$9,589} = 0.099 = 9.9\%$$

A closely related measure of profitability is the **return on common equity (*ROE*),** which captures the return earned on the common stockholders' (owners') investment

---

[11.] All per-share values are stated strictly in dollars and cents; they are not stated in millions as are the dollar values used to calculate these and other ratios.

[12.] Naturally, all other things being equal, firms prefer a high *ROA*. However, as we will see later, analysts must be cautious when interpreting financial ratios. We recall an old Dilbert comic strip in which Wally suggests boosting his firm's *ROA* by firing the security staff. The reduction in expenses would boost the numerator while the reduction in security would lower the denominator.

in the firm. For a firm that uses only common stock to finance its operations, the *ROE* and *ROA* figures will be identical. With debt or preferred stock on the balance sheet, these ratios will usually be different. When the firm earns a profit, even after making interest payments to creditors and paying dividends to preferred stockholders, then the firm's use of leverage magnifies the return earned by common stockholders, and *ROE* will exceed *ROA*. Conversely, if the firm's earnings fall short of the amount it must pay to lenders and preferred stockholders, then leverage causes *ROE* to be less than *ROA*. For GPC, the return on common equity for 2004 is 22.1 percent, substantially above GPC's return on total assets:

$$\text{Return on common equity} = \frac{\text{earnings available for common stockholders}}{\text{common stock equity}}$$

$$= \frac{\$946}{\$4,278} = 0.221 = 22.1\%$$

Financial analysts sometimes conduct a deeper analysis of the *ROA* and *ROE* ratios using the **DuPont system,** which uses both income and balance sheet information to break the *ROA* and *ROE* ratios into component pieces. This approach highlights the influence of the net profit margin, total asset turnover, and financial leverage on a firm's profitability. In the DuPont formula, the return on total assets equals the product of the net profit margin and total asset turnover:

ROA = net profit margin $\times$ total asset turnover

By definition, the net profit margin equals earnings available for common stockholders divided by sales, and asset turnover equals sales divided by assets. When we multiply these two ratios together, the sales figure cancels, resulting in the familiar *ROA* measure:

$$ROA = \frac{\text{earnings available for common stockholders}}{\text{sales}} \times \frac{\text{sales}}{\text{total assets}}$$

$$= \frac{\$946}{\$12,843} \times \frac{\$12,843}{\$9,589} = 0.099 = 9.9\%$$

Naturally, the *ROA* value for GPC in 2004 obtained using the DuPont formula is the same value we calculated before, but now we can think of the *ROA* as a product of how much profit the firm earns on each dollar of sales and of the efficiency with which the firm uses its assets. Holding the net profit margin constant, an increase in total asset turnover would increase the firm's *ROA*. Similarly, holding total asset turnover constant, an increase in the net profit margin would increase *ROA*.

We can push the DuPont analysis one step further by multiplying the *ROA* times the ratio of *assets-to-equity* (*A/E*), or the *equity multiplier.* The product of these two ratios equals the return on equity. Notice that for a firm that uses no debt and has no preferred stock, the ratio of assets to equity equals 1.0, so the *ROA* equals the *ROE*. For all other firms, the ratio of assets to equity exceeds 1. It is in this sense that the ratio of assets to equity represents a leverage multiplier.

ROE = ROA $\times$ A/E

We can apply this version of the DuPont formula to GPC in 2004 to recalculate its return on common equity:

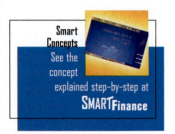

$$ROE = \underbrace{\text{net profit margin} \times \text{total asset turnover}}_{ROA} \times \text{equity multiplier}$$

$$= \frac{\$946}{\$12,843} \times \frac{\$12,843}{\$9,589} \times \frac{\$9,589}{\$4,278} = 0.074 \times 1.34 \times 2.24 = 0.221 = 22.1\%$$

Notice that for GPC, the ratio of assets to equity is 2.24, which means that GPC's return on common equity is more than twice as large as its return on total assets. Of course, using financial leverage has its risks. Notice what would happen if GPC's return on total assets were a negative number rather than a positive one. The financial leverage multiplier would cause GPC's return on common equity to be even more negative than its *ROA*.

The advantage of the DuPont system is that it allows the firm to break its return on common equity into a profit-on-sales component (net profit margin), an efficiency-of-asset-use component (total asset turnover), and a financial-leverage-use component (assets-to-equity ratio). Analysts can then study the impact of each of these factors on the overall return to common stockholders.[13]

MARKET RATIOS

Market ratios relate the firm's market value, as measured by its current share price, to certain accounting values. These ratios provide analysts with insight into how investors think the firm is performing. Because the ratios include market values, they tend to reflect on a relative basis the common stockholders' assessment of all aspects of the firm's past and expected future performance. Here we consider two popular market ratios, one that focuses on earnings and the other that considers book value.

The most widely quoted market ratio, the **price/earnings (P/E) ratio,** is often used as a barometer of a firm's long-term growth prospects. The P/E ratio measures the amount investors are willing to pay for each dollar of the firm's earnings. The price/earnings ratio indicates the degree of confidence that investors have in the firm's future performance. A high P/E ratio indicates that investors believe a firm will achieve rapid earnings growth in the future; hence, companies with high P/E ratios are referred to as *growth stocks*. Using the per-share price of $76.25 for Global Petroleum Corporation on December 31, 2004, and its 2004 *EPS* of $5.29, the P/E ratio at year-end 2004 is computed as follows:

[13.] Keep in mind that the ratios in the DuPont formula are interdependent and that the equation is just a mathematical identity. It is easy to draw questionable conclusions about lines of causality using the DuPont formula. For example, consider this farcical version of the formula:

$$ROE = \frac{\text{earnings available for common stockholders}}{\text{sales}} \times \frac{\text{sales}}{\text{assets}} \times \frac{\text{assets}}{\text{CEO age}} \times \frac{\text{CEO age}}{\text{common stock equity}}$$

In this equation, we might interpret the third term on the right as the efficiency with which a CEO of a given age manages the firm's assets. If a younger CEO could be found who could manage the same quantity of assets, then this ratio would increase, and holding all other factors constant, we might say that the firm's *ROE* would increase. This is clearly silly, but mathematically this expression does ultimately give you the firm's *ROE*.

$$\text{Price/earnings (P/E) ratio} = \frac{\text{market price per share of common stock}}{\text{earnings per share}} = \frac{\$76.25}{\$5.29}$$

$$= 14.41$$

This figure indicates that investors were paying $14.41 for each $1.00 of GPC's earnings. It is interesting to note that GPC's price/earnings ratio one year before (on December 31, 2003) had been almost twice as high at 28.37 ($71.50 per share stock price ÷ $2.52 earnings per share).

The **market/book (M/B) ratio** provides another assessment of how investors view the firm's past and, particularly, expected future performance. It relates the market value of the firm's shares to their book value. The stocks of firms that are expected to perform well—improve profits, grow market share, launch successful products, and so forth—typically sell at higher M/B ratios than those firms with less attractive prospects. Simply stated, firms that investors expect to earn high returns relative to their risk typically sell at higher M/B multiples than those expected to earn low returns relative to risk. To calculate the M/B ratio for GPC in 2004, we first need to find *book value per share* of common stock:

$$\text{Book value per share} = \frac{\text{common stock equity}}{\text{number of shares of common stock outstanding}}$$

$$= \frac{\$4,278}{178.7} = \$23.94$$

Market to book value is then computed by dividing this book value into the current price of the firm's stock:

$$\text{Market/book (M/B) ratio} = \frac{\text{market value per share of common stock}}{\text{book value per share of common stock}}$$

$$= \frac{\$76.25}{\$23.94} = 3.19$$

Investors are currently paying $3.19 for each $1.00 of book value of GPC's stock. Clearly, investors expect GPC to continue to grow in the future because they are willing to pay more than book value for the firm's shares.

---

7. Which of the categories and individual ratios described in this chapter would be of greatest interest to each of the following parties?
    a. Existing and prospective creditors (lenders)
    b. Existing and prospective shareholders
    c. The firm's management

8. How could the availability of cash inflow and cash outflow data be used to improve on the accuracy of the liquidity and debt coverage ratios presented previously? What specific ratio measures would you calculate to assess the firm's liquidity and debt coverage, using cash flow rather than financial statement data?

Concept Review Questions

9. Assume that a firm's total assets and sales remain constant. Would an increase in each of the ratios below be associated with a cash inflow or a cash outflow?

a. Current ratio
b. Inventory turnover
c. Average collection period

d. Average payment period
e. Debt ratio
f. Net profit margin

10. Use the *DuPont system* to explain why a slower-than-average inventory turnover could cause a firm with an above-average net profit margin and an average degree of financial leverage to have a below-average return on common equity.

11. How can you reconcile investor expectations for a firm with an above-average M/B ratio and a below-average P/E ratio? Could the age of the firm have any impact on this ratio comparison?

2.4 SUMMARY

- The four key financial statements are (1) the balance sheet, (2) the income statement, (3) the statement of retained earnings, and (4) the statement of cash flows. Notes describing the technical aspects of the financial statements are normally included with them.

- Depreciation is the most common noncash expense on income statements. To estimate cash flow from operations, add depreciation and other noncash charges back to net profit after taxes. A measure of cash flow that is important to financial analysts is free cash flow, the cash flow available to investors. Free cash flow equals operating cash flow less the firm's net investment in fixed and current assets.

- The statement of cash flows, in effect, summarizes the firm's cash flows over a specified period of time, typically one year. It presents cash flows divided into operating, investment, and financing flows. When interpreting the statement, an analyst typically looks at both the major categories of cash flow and the individual items of cash inflow and outflow to assess the reasonableness of the firm's cash flows over the given period.

- Financial ratios are a convenient tool for analyzing the firm's financial statements to assess its performance over the given period. A variety of financial ratios are available for assessing various aspects of a firm's liquidity, activity, debt, profitability, and market value. The DuPont system is often used to assess various aspects of a firm's profitability, particularly the returns earned on both the total asset investment and the owners' common stock equity in the firm.

INTERNET RESOURCES

Note: This textbook includes numerous Internet links throughout the text, both within the discussions and at the end of each chapter. Because some links will likely change or be eliminated during the life of this edition, please go to this book's website (http://smart.swcollege .com) to obtain updated links in the event you encounter a dead link.

http://www.sec.gov—SEC site containing the document search and retrieval engine, EDGAR; useful for obtaining up-to-date financial statements for publicly traded U.S. firms http://www.quicken.com—Can retrieve a fairly extensive ratio analysis of a given company by typing in a ticker symbol

http://www.yahoo.com—Contains a link to Yahoo! Finance for retrieval of recent financial statements and a wide variety of other financial information for any listed U.S. firm and many foreign firms

KEY TERMS

accrual-based approach
activity ratios
assets-to-equity (A/E) ratio
average age of inventory
average collection period
average payment period
cash flow approach
cash flow from operations
common stock
common-size income statement
coverage ratio
current ratio
debt ratio
debt-to-equity ratio
deferred
dividend payout ratio
dividend per share (DPS)
DuPont system
earnings available for common
    stockholders
earnings per share (EPS)
equity multiplier
financial leverage
financing flows
fixed asset turnover

free cash flow (FCF)
gross profit margin
inventory turnover
investment flows
liquidity
long-term debt
market/book (M/B) ratio
net profit margin
net working capital
noncash charges
operating cash flow (OCF)
operating flows
operating profit margin
paid-in-capital
par value
preferred stock
price/earnings (P/E) ratio
quick (acid-test) ratio
ratio analysis
retained earnings
return on common equity (ROE)
return on total assets (ROA)
times interest earned ratio
total asset turnover
Treasury stock

QUESTIONS

2-1. What information (explicit and implicit) can be derived from financial statement analysis? Does the standardization required by GAAP add greater validity to comparisons of financial data between companies and industries? Are there possible shortcomings to relying solely on financial statement analysis to value companies?

2-2. Distinguish between the types of financial information contained in the various financial statements. Which statements provide information on a company's performance over a reporting period, and which present data on a company's current position? What sorts of valuable information may be found in the notes to financial statements? Describe a situation in which the information contained in the notes would be essential to making an informed decision about the value of a corporation.

2-3. If you were a commercial credit analyst charged with the responsibility of making an accept/reject decision on a company's loan request, with which financial statement would you be most concerned? Which financial statement is most likely to provide pertinent information about a company's ability to repay its debt?

2-4.   What is *cash flow from operations?* How is it calculated? What benefit does the firm receive from the presence of "noncash charges"?

2-5.   What is *operating cash flow (OCF)?* How is it calculated? Why do financial managers prefer this measure of operating flows over the accountants' use of *cash flow from operations?*

2-6.   What is *free cash flow (FCF)?* How is it calculated from operating cash flow (OCF)? Why do financial managers focus attention on the value of *FCF?*

2-7.   Describe the common definitions of "inflows of cash" and "outflows of cash" used by analysts to classify certain balance sheet changes and income statement values. What three categories of cash flow are used in the statement of cash flows? To what value should the net value in the statement of cash flows reconcile?

2-8.   What precautions must one take when using ratio analysis to make financial decisions? Which ratios would be most useful for a financial manager's internal financial analysis? For an analyst trying to decide on which stocks are most attractive within an industry?

2-9.   How do analysts use ratios to analyze a firm's *financial leverage?* Which ratios convey more important information to a credit analyst—those revolving around the levels of indebtedness or those measuring the ability to meet the contractual payments associated with debt? What is the relationship between a firm's levels of indebtedness and risk? What must happen in order for an increase in financial leverage to be successful?

2-10. How is the *DuPont system* useful in analyzing a firm's *ROA* and *ROE?* What information can be inferred from the decomposition of *ROE* into contributing ratios? What is the mathematical relationship between each of the individual components (net profit margin, total asset turnover, and assets-to-equity ratio) and *ROE?* Can *ROE* be raised without affecting *ROA?* How?

PROBLEMS

Financial Statements

2-1.   Obtain financial statements for Microsoft for the last five years either from its website (http://www.microsoft.com) or from EDGAR online (http://www.sec.gov/edgar/searchedgar/webusers.htm). First, look at the statements without reading the notes. Then, read the notes carefully, concentrating on those regarding executive stock options. Do you have a different perspective after analyzing these notes?

Cash Flow Analysis

Smart Solutions
See the problem and solution explained step-by-step at
SMARTFinance

2-2.   Given the balance sheets and selected data from the income statement of SMG Industries that follow, answer parts (a)–(d).

   a. Calculate the firm's accounting *cash flow from operations* for the year ended December 31, 2004, using Equation 2.1.
   b. Calculate the firm's *operating cash flow (OCF)* for the year ended December 31, 2004, using Equation 2.2.
   c. Calculate the firm's *free cash flow (FCF)* for the year ended December 31, 2004, using Equation 2.3.
   d. Interpret, compare, and contrast your cash flow estimates in parts (a), (b), and (c).

SMG Industries Balance Sheets ($ in millions)

Assets	December 31 2004	December 31 2003
Cash	$ 3,500	$ 3,000
Marketable securities	3,800	3,200
Accounts receivable	4,000	3,800
Inventories	4,900	4,800
Total current assets	$16,200	$14,800
Gross fixed assets	$31,500	$30,100
Less: Accumulated depreciation	14,700	13,100
Net fixed assets	$16,800	$17,000
Total assets	$33,000	$31,800

Liabilities and Stockholders' Equity

	2004	2003
Accounts payable	$ 3,600	$ 3,500
Notes payable	4,800	4,200
Accruals	1,200	1,300
Total current liabilities	$ 9,600	$ 9,000
Long-term debt	$ 6,000	$ 6,000
Common stock	$11,000	$11,000
Retained earnings	6,400	5,800
Total stockholders' equity	$17,400	$16,800
Total liabilities and stockholders' equity	$33,000	$31,800

Income Statement Data (2004, $ in millions)

Depreciation expense	$1,600
Earnings before interest and taxes (EBIT)	4,500
Taxes	1,300
Net profits after taxes	2,400

2-3.   Classify each of the following items as an inflow (I) or an outflow (O) of cash, or as neither (N).

Item	Change ($)	Item	Change ($)
Cash	+600	Accounts receivable	−900
Accounts payable	−1,200	Net profits	+700
Notes payable	+800	Depreciation	+200
Long-term debt	−2,500	Repurchase of stock	+500
Inventory	+400	Cash dividends	+300
Fixed assets	+600	Sale of stock	+1,300

Analyzing Financial Performance Using Ratio Analysis

2-4.   Manufacturers Bank is evaluating Aluminum Industries, Inc., which has requested a $3 million loan, to assess the firm's financial leverage and risk. On the basis of the debt ratios for Aluminum, along with the industry averages and Aluminum's recent financial statements (which follow), evaluate and recommend appropriate action on the loan request.

Aluminum Industries, Inc. Income Statement for the Year Ended December 31, 2004

Sales revenue		$30,000,000
Less: Cost of goods sold		21,000,000
Gross profit		$ 9,000,000
Less: Operating expenses		
Selling expense	$3,000,000	
General and administrative expenses	1,800,000	
Lease expense	200,000	
Depreciation expense	1,000,000	
Total operating expense		$6,000,000
Operating profit		$3,000,000
Less: Interest expense		1,000,000
Net profit before taxes		$2,000,000
Less: Taxes (rate = 40%)		800,000
Net profits after taxes		$1,200,000

Aluminum Industries, Inc. Balance Sheet as of December 31, 2004

Assets		Liabilities and Stockholders' Equity	
Current assets		Current liabilities	
Cash	$ 1,000,000	Accounts payable	$ 8,000,000
Marketable securities	3,000,000	Notes payable	8,000,000
Accounts receivable	12,000,000	Accruals	500,000
Inventories	7,500,000	Total current liabilities	$16,500,000
Total current assets	$23,500,000	Long-term debt (including financial leases)	$20,000,000
Gross fixed assets (at cost)		Stockholders' equity	
Land and buildings	$11,000,000	Preferred stock (25,000 shares, $4 dividend)	$ 2,500,000
Machinery and equipment	20,500,000	Common stock (1 million shares, $5 par)	5,000,000
Furniture and fixtures	8,000,000	Paid-in capital in excess of par value	4,000,000
Gross fixed assets	$39,500,000	Retained earnings	2,000,000
Less: Accumulated depreciation	13,000,000	Total stockholders' equity	$13,500,000
Net fixed assets	$26,500,000	Total liabilities & stockholders' equity	$50,000,000
Total assets	$50,000,000		

Industry Averages	
Debt ratio	0.51
Debt-equity ratio	1.07
Times interest earned ratio	7.30

Use the following information for Problems 2-5 and 2-6.

Income Statements for the Year Ended December 31, 2004

	Heavy Metal Manufacturing (HMM)	Metallic Stamping Inc. (MS)	High-Tech Software Co. (HTS)
Sales	$75,000,000	$50,000,000	$100,000,000
− Operating expenses	65,000,000	40,000,000	60,000,000
Operating profit	$10,000,000	$10,000,000	$ 40,000,000
− Interest expenses	3,000,000	3,000,000	0
Earnings before taxes	$ 7,000,000	$ 7,000,000	$ 40,000,000
− Taxes	2,800,000	2,800,000	16,000,000
Net income	$ 4,200,000	$ 4,200,000	$ 24,000,000

Balance Sheets as of December 31, 2004

	Heavy Metal Manufacturing (HMM)	Metallic Stamping Inc. (MS)	High-Tech Software Co. (HTS)
Current assets	$ 10,000,000	$ 5,000,000	$ 20,000,000
Net fixed assets	90,000,000	75,000,000	80,000,000
Total assets	$100,000,000	$80,000,000	$100,000,000
Current liabilities	$ 20,000,000	$10,000,000	$ 10,000,000
Long-term debt	40,000,000	40,000,000	0
Total liabilities	$ 60,000,000	$50,000,000	$ 10,000,000
Common stock	$ 15,000,000	$10,000,000	$ 25,000,000
Retained earnings	25,000,000	20,000,000	65,000,000
Total common equity	$ 40,000,000	$30,000,000	$ 90,000,000
Total liabilities and common equity	$100,000,000	$80,000,000	$100,000,000

2-5. Use the DuPont system to compare the two heavy metal companies shown above (HHM and MS) during 2004. Which of the two has a higher return on common equity? What is the cause of the difference between the two?

2-6. Continuing with Problem 2-5, calculate the return on common equity of the software company, HTS. Why is this value so different from those of the heavy metal companies calculated in Problem 2-5? Compare the leverage levels between the industries. Which industry receives a greater contribution from return on total assets? Which industry receives a greater contribution from the financial leverage as measured by the assets-to-equity ratio? Can you make a meaningful DuPont comparison across industries? Why or why not?

2-7. Refer back to Problems 2-5 and 2-6, and perform the same analysis with real data. Download last year's financial data from Ford Motor Company (http://www2.ford.com), General Motors (http://www.gm.com), and Microsoft (http://www.microsoft.com). Which ratios demonstrate the greatest difference between Ford and General Motors? Which of the two is more profitable? Which ratios drive the greater profitability?

2-8. A common-size income statement for Aluminum Industries' 2003 operations follows. Using the firm's 2004 income statement presented in Problem 2-4, develop the 2004 common-size income statement and compare it to the 2003 statement. Which areas require further analysis and investigation?

Aluminum Industries, Inc. Common-Size Income Statement for the Year Ended December 31, 2003

Sales revenue ($35,000,000)		100.0%
Less: Cost of goods sold		65.9
Gross profit		34.1%
Less: Operating expenses		
Selling expense	12.7%	
General and administrative expenses	6.3	
Lease expense	0.6	
Depreciation expense	3.6	
Total operating expense		23.2
Operating profit		10.9%
Less: Interest expense		1.5
Net profit before taxes		9.4%
Less: Taxes (rate = 40%)		3.8
Net profits after taxes		5.6%

2-9. Use the following financial data for Greta's Gadgets, Inc., to determine the impact of using additional debt financing to purchase additional assets. Assume that an additional $1 million of assets is purchased with 100 percent debt financing with a 10 percent annual interest rate.

Greta's Gadgets, Inc.

Income Statement for the Year Ended December 31, 2004		Balance Sheet as of December 31, 2004	
Sales	$4,000,000	Current assets	$ 0
−Costs and expenses @90%	3,600,000	Fixed assets	2,000,000
Earnings before interest		Total assets	$2,000,000
& taxes	$400,000		
−Interest (.10 × $1,000,000)	100,000	Current liabilities	$ 0
Earnings before taxes	$ 300,000	Long-term debt @10%	1,000,000
−Taxes @40%	120,000	Total liabilities	$1,000,000
Net income	$ 180,000	Common stock equity	$1,000,000
		Total liabilities and	$2,000,000
		stockholders' equity	

  a. Calculate the current (2004) net profit margin, total asset turnover, assets-to-equity ratio, return on total assets, and return on common equity for Greta's.

  b. Now, assuming no other changes, determine the impact of purchasing the $1 million in assets using 100 percent debt financing with a 10 percent annual interest rate. Further, assume that the newly purchased assets generate an additional $2 million in sales and that the costs and expenses remain at 90 percent of sales. For purposes of this problem, further assume a tax rate of 40 percent. What is the effect on the ratios calculated in part (a)? Is the purchase of these assets justified on the basis of the return on common equity?

  c. Assume that the newly purchased assets in part (b) generate only an extra $500,000 in sales. Is the purchase justified in this case?

  d. Which component ratio(s) of the DuPont system is not affected by the change in sales? What does this imply about the use of financial leverage?

2-10. Tracey White, the owner of the Buzz Coffee Shop chain, has decided to expand her operations. Her 2004 financial statements follow. Tracey can buy two additional coffeehouses for $3 million, and she has the choice of completely financing these new coffeehouses with either a 10 percent (annual interest) loan or the issuance of new common stock. She also expects these new shops to generate an additional $1 million in sales.

Assuming a 40 percent tax rate and no other changes, should Tracey buy the two coffeehouses? Why or why not? Which financing option results in the better *ROE*?

Buzz Coffee Shops, Inc. 2004 Financial Statements

Balance Sheet		Income Statement	
Current assets	$ 250,000	Sales	$500,000
Fixed assets	750,000	−Costs and expenses @40%	200,000
Total assets	$1,000,000	Earnings before interest	
		and taxes (*EBIT*)	$300,000
Current liabilities	$ 300,000	−Interest expense	0
Long-term debt	0	Net profit before taxes	$300,000
Total liabilities	$ 300,000	−Taxes @40%	120,000
Common equity	$ 700,000	Net income	$180,000
Total liabilities and stock- holders' equity	$1,000,000		

2-11. The financial statements of Access Corporation for the year ended December 31, 2004, follow.

Access Corporation Income Statement for the Year Ended December 31, 2004

Sales revenue		$160,000
Less: Cost of goods sold[a]		106,000
Gross profit		$ 54,000
Less: Operating expenses		
Selling expense	$16,000	
General and administrative expense	10,000	
Lease expense	1,000	
Depreciation expense	10,000	
Total operating expense		$ 37,000
Operating profit		$ 17,000
Less: Interest expense		6,100
Net profit before taxes		$ 10,900
Less: Taxes @40%		4,360
Net profits after taxes		$ 6,540

[a]Access Corporation's annual purchases are estimated to equal 75 percent of cost of goods sold.

Access Corporation Balance Sheet as of December 31, 2004

Assets		Liabilities and Stockholders' Equity	
Cash	$ 500	Accounts payable	$ 22,000
Marketable securities	1,000	Notes payable	47,000
Accounts receivable	25,000	Total current liabilities	$ 69,000
Inventories	45,500	Long-term debt	$ 22,950
Total current assets	$ 72,000	Total liabilities	$ 91,950
Land	$ 26,000	Common stock[a]	$ 31,500
Buildings and equipment	90,000	Retained earnings	26,550
Less: Accumulated		Total liabilities and	$150,000
depreciation	38,000	stockholders' equity	
Net fixed assets	$ 78,000		
Total assets	$150,000		

[a]The firm's 3,000 outstanding shares of common stock closed 2004 at a price of $25 per share.

a. Use the preceding financial statements to complete the following table. Assume that the industry averages given in the table are applicable for both 2003 and 2004.

b. Analyze Access Corporation's financial condition as it relates to (1) liquidity, (2) activity, (3) debt, (4) profitability, and (5) market value. Summarize the company's overall financial condition.

Access Corporation's Financial Ratios

Ratio	Industry Average	Actual 2003	Actual 2004
Current ratio	1.80	1.84	_____
Quick (acid-test) ratio	.70	.78	_____
Inventory turnover	2.50	2.59	_____
Average collection period[a]	37 days	36 days	_____
Average payment period[a]	72 days	78 days	_____
Debt-to-equity ratio	50%	51%	_____
Times interest earned ratio	3.8	4.0	_____
Gross profit margin	38%	40%	_____
Net profit margin	3.5%	3.6%	_____
Return on total assets (ROA)	4.0%	4.0%	_____
Return on common equity (ROE)	9.5%	8.0%	_____
Market/book (M/B) ratio	1.1	1.2	_____

[a]Based on a 365-day year and on end-of-year figures.

2-12. Given the following financial statements, historical ratios, and industry averages, calculate the MBA Company's financial ratios for 2004. Analyze its overall financial situation both in comparison to industry averages and over the period 2002–2004. Break your analysis into an evaluation of the firm's liquidity, activity, debt, profitability, and market value.

MBA Company Income Statement for the Year Ended December 31, 2004

Sales revenue		$10,000,000
Less: Cost of goods sold[a]		7,500,000
Gross profit		$ 2,500,000
Less: Operating expenses		
Selling expense	$300,000	
General and administrative		
expense	650,000	
Lease expense	50,000	
Depreciation expense	200,000	
Total operating expense		1,200,000
Operating profit (EBIT)		$ 1,300,000
Less: Interest expense		200,000
Net profits before taxes		$ 1,100,000
Less: Taxes (rate = 40%)		440,000
Net profits after taxes		$ 660,000
Less: Preferred stock dividends		50,000
Earnings available for common stockholders		$ 610,000
Earnings per share (EPS)		$ 3.05

[a]Annual credit purchases of $6.2 million were made during the year.

MBA Company Balance Sheet as of December 31, 2004

Assets		Liabilities and Stockholders' Equity	
Current assets		Current liabilities	
Cash	$ 200,000	Accounts payable	$ 900,000
Marketable securities	50,000	Notes payable	200,000
Accounts receivable	800,000	Accruals	100,000
Inventories	950,000	Total current liabilities	$ 1,200,000
Total current assets	$ 2,000,000	Long-term debt (including	$ 3,000,000
Gross fixed assets	$12,000,000	financial leases)	
(at cost)		Stockholders' equity	
Less: Accumulated	3,000,000	Preferred stock (25,000 shares,	$ 1,000,000
depreciation		$2 dividend)	
Net fixed assets	$ 9,000,000	Common stock	600,000
Other assets	$ 1,000,000	(200,000 shares, $3 par)[a]	
Total assets	$12,000,000	Paid-in capital in excess of par	5,200,000
		Retained earnings	1,000,000
		Total stockholders' equity	$ 7,800,000
		Total liabilities and stock-	$12,000,000
		holders' equity	

[a]On December 31, 2004, the firm's common stock closed at $27.50.

Historical and Industry Average Ratios for MBA Company

Ratio	Actual 2002	Actual 2003	Industry Average 2004
Current ratio	1.40	1.55	1.85
Quick (acid-test) ratio	1.00	0.92	1.05
Inventory turnover	9.52	9.21	8.60
Average collection period[a]	45.0 days	36.4 days	35.0 days
Average payment period[a]	58.5 days	60.8 days	45.8 days
Fixed asset turnover	1.08	1.05	1.07
Total asset turnover	0.74	0.80	0.74
Debt ratio	0.20	0.20	0.30
Debt-to-equity ratio	0.25	0.27	0.39
Times interest earned ratio	8.2	7.3	8.0
Gross profit margin	0.30	0.27	0.25
Operating profit margin	0.12	0.12	0.10
Net profit margin	0.067	0.067	0.058
Return on total assets (ROA)	0.049	0.054	0.043
Return on common equity (ROE)	0.066	0.073	0.072
Earnings per share (EPS)	$1.75	$2.20	$1.50
Price/earnings (P/E) ratio	12.0	10.5	11.2
Market/book (M/B) ratio	1.20	1.05	1.10

[a]Based on a 365-day year and on end-of-year figures.

Smart Solutions
See the problem and solution explained step-by-step at
SMARTFinance

2-13.   Choose a company that you would like to analyze, and obtain its financial statements. Now, select another firm from the same industry, and obtain its financial data from the Internet. Perform a complete ratio analysis on each firm. How well does your selected company compare to its industry peer? Which components of your firm's *ROE* are superior, and which are inferior?

3

Present Value

OPENING FOCUS
Why Is a Lottery's "$315 Million Jackpot" Really Worth Only $170 Million?

The Powerball lottery is a game of chance in which participants pay one dollar for a lottery ticket, select six numbers, and then hope that the numbers selected will be picked in a random, televised drawing. The lottery is operated in the interests of 23 participating U.S. state governments, and over half of the total proceeds from ticket sales flow into the states' operating budgets. Remaining proceeds cover expenses and pay off lucky winners.

Even though the odds against winning these state-sponsored lotteries are astronomically high (so high, in fact, that cynics call the lottery "a tax on the stupid"), the lottery has proven to be very popular. The demand for lottery tickets rises to a near frenzy if several weeks pass without a winner, because the lottery jackpot grows over time until someone finally selects all six winning numbers. The last full week of December 2002 was such a period; after a week of near-record sales, the Powerball jackpot hit dizzying heights. Despite odds of more than 120,000,000 : 1 against winning, people dreamed of hitting the Christmas-day jackpot, which would pay them 30 annual checks of $10.5 million each. Based on this stream of payouts, Powerball officials touted their jackpot's value at $315 million (30 payments × $10.5 million = $315 million).

What few people noticed about this jackpot was the winner's option to exchange this stream of annual cash flows—which we will define in this chapter as a 30-year annuity due—for a single lump-sum payment of $170 million immediately. Why would anyone be willing to exchange a "$315 million jackpot" for a mere $170 million payment? Because the winner would receive $170 million right away rather than have to wait 30 years for lottery officials to dribble out the entire jackpot. With $170 million in hand, the winner could invest the money and earn interest on it. Clearly this means that having $170 million on hand today is more valuable than having it at some point in the future, but how much more valuable? Does the opportunity to earn interest mean that $170 million today is worth more than $315 million spread over 30 years?

The answer depends on the interest rate. To compare the $170 million lump sum payment to the $315 stream of payments, we must calculate the "present value" of the stream. For example, suppose an investor could earn 5 percent interest on a relatively safe investment such as U.S. government bonds. If that person invested $10 million today at 5 percent interest, he would have $10.5 million one year later. Thus, we can say that $10 million is the present value of a $10.5 million payment that arrives one year in the future. Similarly, by investing $8.23 million at 5 percent today, an investor would have $10.5 million after 5 years, so $8.23 million is the present value of a $10.5 million payment arriving in 5 years.

Applying this process to the entire cash flow stream, we can determine that, if the interest rate on an alternative investment is 5 percent, the present value of 30 annual $10.5 million payments (with the first payment arriving immediately) equals $169.5 million. Phrased differently, any investor who could earn 5 percent on low-risk investments should be almost indifferent between the $170 million lump sum and the "315 million jackpot." At interest rates above 5 percent, the lump sum becomes more attractive, and at interest rates below 5 percent, the stream of annual payments is more appealing.

Both as a profession and as an academic discipline, finance is primarily concerned with the *voluntary transfer of wealth* between individuals and across time. The transfer of wealth *between individuals,* which occurs in financial markets, can involve creditors lending money to borrowers in exchange for a promise of repayment with interest or investors purchasing an ownership claim in an entrepreneur's venture in exchange for a share in the venture's profits. Likewise, transferring wealth *across time* can take two forms. The first involves determining what the value of an investment made today will be worth at a specific future date, and the second determines the value today of a cash flow to be received at a specific date in the future. We refer to the first such computation as determining the **future value** of an investment and the second as determining the **present value** of a future cash flow.

Because these wealth transfers are voluntary "trades" of cash today for financial claims representing promises of greater payments in the future, the ability to execute these trades makes all parties better off. In the language of economics, the opportunity to borrow and lend using financial markets increases economic welfare because it helps both borrowers and savers, leaving no one worse off. By lending or investing money at a given interest rate, a saver can increase consumption in future periods by forgoing some consumption today. The opportunity to receive cash today in exchange for a promise to repay that cash plus interest in the future also makes borrowers better off. These borrowers might be individuals, such as new college graduates, who wish to obtain financing for new homes and are willing to commit substantial fractions of their future incomes to paying off these mortgages. Alternatively, "borrowers" might be entrepreneurs with great business plans and managerial talents who need equity financing to turn their dreams into solid businesses. Perhaps the most relevant example of how borrowing can improve personal welfare is to consider the bargain graduate students make with lenders. Students borrow (often sizable) sums of money to finance their educations, and the training they receive increases their lifetime earnings potential by more than enough to repay the debt. In sum, financial markets improve the welfare of savers, entrepreneurs, and ordinary citizens by allowing borrowing, lending, and investing to occur most efficiently.

We have several objectives in this chapter. The first is to introduce the concepts of future value and present value and to briefly describe how the opportunity to borrow and lend benefits everyone by allowing people with different consumption preferences to transact to their mutual benefit. Second, we will show how to compute future values, beginning with the simple process of computing the future value of a single investment made today, then examining increasingly complex cash flow streams. Third, we will demonstrate how to compute the present values of future cash flows, again beginning with a single cash flow and then examining streams of future cash flows. The chapter concludes with a presentation of some special applications of time value techniques that financial managers commonly employ. The chapter appendix presents several additional applications of time value techniques.

3.1 THE THEORY OF PRESENT VALUE

We have asserted that financial markets are economically valuable because they allow savers and borrowers to transact efficiently. We will try to illustrate the key ideas with a simple example.[1] Consider how financial interaction might improve the lots of two people who both have MBA degrees from the same school, but who are at much different stages in their careers. Sally Peak earned her MBA almost 30 years ago and is now a successful investment banker in her mid-50s. She hopes to work for another 10 years and then retire to a life of travel, comfort, and spoiling her grandchildren. Samuel Start has just graduated at the top of his class and has landed a well-paying job with a prestigious consulting firm. The future looks very bright for Samuel. He and his wife are eager to purchase a home and start a family even as they both begin promising careers.

How can financial markets meet the differing consumption preferences of Sally and Samuel? When we analyze these needs separately, the answer is obvious. Sally, now at the peak of her career, earns more than she consumes. In 10 years, however, she wishes to retire, living off her accumulated savings. Therefore, Sally would like to find an opportunity to lend or invest part of her current income at an attractive return so that she will have more income to consume when she retires. Samuel's situation is the mirror image of Sally's. Although his earnings *potential* is great, his current needs for income exceed his current earnings. Samuel would like to increase the amount of money he can spend today by borrowing. Further, because of his promising career prospects, Samuel would be considered an excellent credit risk by a potential lender.

Now assume that Sally and Samuel meet (perhaps at an alumni dinner) and begin discussing their financial plans and needs. A mutually beneficial financial exchange might emerge. Sally would agree to lend Samuel enough money today so that Samuel could buy a house, and Samuel would agree to repay this loan in full, with interest, over the next 10 years. As evidence of their agreement, the two parties would probably sign a contract disclosing the terms of the loan and establishing a repayment schedule. Assuming this contract met appropriate standards, the agreement would be legally enforceable, and either party would have recourse to the nation's courts in the event of a dispute. The agreement might even be written in such a way that Samuel would promise to make interest and principal payments to any investor who owned the contract, rather than specifically to Sally. This would allow Sally to sell the contract to a third party in case she did not wish to remain Samuel's creditor for the contract's full 10 years.

[1.] The basic ideas of time value and the net present value rule of investment were first presented by Irving Fisher (1930). Fisher's ideas were developed further and applied in a modern corporate setting by Hirshleifer (1958), Fama and Miller (1972), and Fama and Jensen (1985).

The transactions between Samuel and Sally accomplish several economic objectives. They allow Samuel to borrow against his future earnings in order to buy a house today. These trades also allow Sally to meet her savings objectives by making a relatively safe loan at an attractive interest rate. This will increase the amount of money she will have on hand when she retires. Because the loan is backed by a legally enforceable contract, each party enjoys protection from the other's exploitation. Finally, Sally's ability to sell the loan to another investor means that she has **liquidity,** the ability to resell her investment easily and at low cost. Both Sally and Samuel benefit from these exchanges, and the overall economy benefits as well because the money Sally saves today will be channeled into Samuel's productive investment.

We can, of course, generalize these basic principles of lending and borrowing. If there are a large number of savers and borrowers, then Sally and Samuel do not have to meet each other to achieve their separate objectives. As long as Sally finds a creditworthy borrower and Samuel finds a lender with surplus cash, Sally can profitably save for her retirement and Samuel can borrow enough to jump-start his personal and professional life. Once again, we can express this concept in economic terms: financial markets allow both savers and borrowers to achieve their desired pattern of intertemporal consumption, or consumption over time.

Our simple analogy can be pushed further, to eliminate the need for Sally to search for a borrower or for Samuel to search for a person willing to lend him money. Assume that companies called "banks" develop to serve the role of **financial intermediaries.** These companies eliminate the need for savers and borrowers to deal directly with each other; instead, both parties need deal only with the intermediaries. For example, banks can offer to pay savers interest on their "deposits" with the bank while simultaneously offering borrowers attractive rates of interest on a variety of loan products. As long as they charge borrowers a higher rate than they offer depositors, banks can realize a profit from this interest *spread* while meeting the financial needs of savers and borrowers. Savers have their choice of lending directly to a final borrower or lending to a financial intermediary (who then finds a final borrower), and borrowers have the same opportunity of borrowing directly from an ultimate saver or borrowing from an intermediary.

Competition between potential borrowers and lenders determines the market-wide interest rate, or **equilibrium interest rate.** This is the rate that "clears the market," equating total savings and investment within an economy. Competition also ensures that riskier borrowers—those who are more likely to be unable or unwilling to repay their loans—will have to pay a higher interest rate than will more creditworthy borrowers. We will see that this "pricing" of risk is fundamental to all financial decision making, by individuals as well as by firms. Companies evaluate prospective investment opportunities by assessing whether their expected return, adjusted for project risk, exceeds the firm's *required return.* This is the return the firm itself must promise debt and equity investors, which is also referred to as the corporation's *cost of capital,* or *opportunity cost.*

The fact that corporations receive their financing from financial markets also means that companies can follow the simple investment rule of accepting projects that maximize the value of the firm rather than accept projects that appeal to the consumption preferences of individual investors. As an illustration, consider the publicly traded Lambda Corporation, which has an opportunity to invest in a project that promises to pay off very handsomely—but not until several years in the future. Investors who trade in Lambda Corporation's securities value its shares by predicting what the firm's cash flows will be over time and then determining the present value of that stream today. This valuation process is called **capitalizing** a cash flow stream,

COMPARATIVE CORPORATE FINANCE

Save Money? Not Me; I'm an American.

This chapter presents the basic valuation rules that economic agents use in determining whether to save or consume their income. But just how different are the savings patterns of citizens in the major industrialized countries? As the chart shows, personal savings rates are strikingly different both between countries and within the same country at different points in time. France has the highest national savings rate (16%) among rich countries in 2001, followed by Belgium, Japan, and Italy. The ranking was somewhat different in 1991, when Italy was the thriftiest country with a savings rate approaching 20 percent. Although economists are divided about the determinants of varying national savings rates, systematic and enduring patterns exist, and

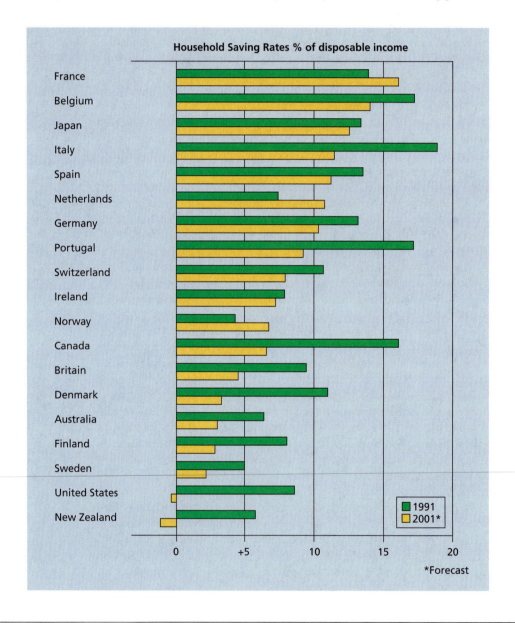

it seems likely that economic, demographic, and cultural factors all play important roles in explaining the international differences.

The chart also shows that savings rates declined between 1991 and 2001 for 16 of the 19 countries surveyed. For no country is this more true than the United States. While never high, the U.S. savings rate was at least a positive 8 percent in 1991; by 2001, the savings rate of American households had turned *negative*. What is going on here? Why did people stop saving during a decade that encompassed the longest economic expansion in U.S. history and that saw the stock market more than triple in value? An even more perplexing question is, how did American corporations finance the $8 trillion or so of capital investments they made between 1991 and 2001? There are several partial explanations

for this strange mix of a booming economy and a seemingly extravagant population. In part, the prosperity of the 1990s reduced the need for people to save as much out of their income, because the rising values of their homes and stock portfolios—the famous "wealth effect"—made it possible to finance future consumption with less saving from current income. Record inflows of foreign capital also helped fund the investment programs of U.S. corporations, as did the U.S government's switch from budget deficit to surplus during the late 1990s. These are all only partial answers, however. In truth, economists really do not understand why the U.S. savings rate has fallen so low or why the consequences of this decline have thus far been so muted.

Source: The Economist (January 20, 2001), p.107.

or determining the asset (capital) value today of a stream of future cash flows. We describe the specific techniques used to determine present values later in this chapter. For now, we simply need to state that market participants calculate the present value of a future cash flow by determining how much they would need to invest today, at a given interest rate, to equal that cash flow's value in the future. Because Lambda's investment project looks very profitable, the present value of the stream of future cash flows it will generate is greater than the cost of funding the investment today. We will define such a project as having a positive **net present value** (*NPV*), because the present value of the cash inflows (the future profits) exceeds the present value of the cash outflows (today's investment).

Assume that Lambda Corporation has two controlling shareholders, as well as many smaller investors who trade in its shares. The older of the controlling shareholders expects to retire in two years, but the other plans to continue working for a decade or more. In the absence of well-functioning financial markets, these two shareholders might disagree about whether the company should accept the attractive, but long-lived, project because the older shareholder wishes to maximize short-term returns while the other shareholder has a longer investment horizon. Financial markets eliminate this potential conflict because investors in the market will capitalize the investment project's expected value (i.e., the stock price will rise to reflect the value of the investment) as soon as the firm commits to making the investment. The controlling shareholder who wishes to retire in two years thus benefits from the investment because he can sell his shares immediately at a higher price. The other controlling shareholder naturally benefits as well because her shares, which she plans to retain, have increased in price by the net present value of the investment opportunity. This principle that corporations should accept all positive-*NPV* investment projects, regardless of which investors are financing those projects, is referred to as the **separation of investment and financing** decision rule. In following this rule, companies need to worry only about satisfying the impersonal demands of the financial market, not the personal preferences of investors.

In our discussion thus far, we have finessed a key principle of finance: a dollar received today is more valuable than a dollar (or euro, pound, franc, or yen) received in the future. The remainder of this chapter addresses this issue of **time value of money.** Section 3.2 describes how to compute the future value of a lump sum invested today at a given interest rate. The counterpart of computing future value is determining what the present value is today of a cash flow to be received in the future, if investors can earn a given return on investments of comparable risk. We present the technique for calculating the present value of a lump sum in Section 3.3. Sections 3.4 and 3.5 describe the procedures for calculating the future value and present value, respectively, of a stream of cash flows. Section 3.6 demonstrates some special applications of present and future value concepts.

Concept Review Questions

1. How do financial markets improve the financial prospects of both savers and borrowers? What is required for this to occur?

2. What does *net present value* mean? Why does the net present value rule allow the separation of investment and financing decisions?

3.2 FUTURE VALUE OF A LUMP SUM

THE CONCEPT OF FUTURE VALUE

By consuming less than 100 percent of their present income, investors can earn interest on their savings and thereby enjoy higher future consumption. A person who invests $100 today at 5 percent interest expects to receive $105 in one year, representing $5 interest plus the return of the $100 originally invested. In this example, we say that $105 is the *future value* of $100 invested at 5 percent for one year.

We can calculate the future value of an investment made today by applying compound interest over a specified period of time. **Compound interest** is interest earned both on the principal amount and on the interest earned in previous periods. **Principal** refers to the amount of money on which the interest is paid. To demonstrate these concepts, assume that you have the opportunity to deposit $100 into a risk-free account paying 5 percent interest. For simplicity, we will assume that interest compounds annually, though in later sections we show how to compute future values using semiannual, quarterly, and even continuous compounding periods.

At the end of one year, your account will have a balance of $105. This sum represents the initial principal of $100 plus 5 percent ($5) in interest. This future value is calculated as follows:

Future value at end of year 1 = $100 \times (1 + 0.05) = $105

If you choose to leave this money in the account for another year, you will be paid interest at the rate of 5 percent on the new principal of $105. In other words, 5 percent interest will be paid both on the original principal of $100 and on the first year's interest of $5. At the end of this second year, there will be $110.25 in your account, representing the principal at the beginning of year 2 ($105) plus 5 percent of the $105, or $5.25, in interest. The future value at the end of the second year is computed as follows:

Future value at end of year 2 = $105 \times (1 + 0.05) = $110.25

Substituting the first equation into the second one yields the following:

Future value at end of year 2 = $100 × (1 + 0.05) × (1 + 0.05)

$$= \$100 \times (1 + 0.05)$$

$$= \$110.25$$

Therefore, $100 deposited at 5 percent compound annual interest will be worth $110.25 at the end of two years. This represents two years' interest of 5 percent paid on the original $100 principal, plus 5 percent paid on the first year's $5 interest payment, or $0.25. It is important to recognize the difference in future values that results from compound versus simple interest. **Simple interest** is interest paid only on the initial principal of an investment, not on the interest that accrues in earlier periods. If the investment in our previous example pays 5 percent simple interest, then the future value in any year equals $100 plus the product of the annual interest payment times the number of years. In this case, its value would be only $110 at the end of year 2 [$100 + (2 × $5)], $115 at the end of year 3 [$100 + (3 × $5)], $120 at the end of year 4 [$100 + (4 × $5)], and so on. Although the difference between a $110 account balance after two years at simple interest and $110.25 at compound interest seems rather trivial, the difference quite literally grows exponentially over time. For example, with simple interest this account would have a balance of $250 after 30 years [$100 + (30 × $5)], but with compound interest the account balance would be $432.19 in 30 years.

THE EQUATION FOR FUTURE VALUE

Financial analysts routinely use compound interest, so throughout this book we generally use compound rather than simple interest. Equation 3.1 gives the general formula for calculating the future value, at the end of n years, of a lump sum invested today at an interest rate of r percent:

$$FV = PV \times (1 + r)^n \tag{Eq. 3.1}$$

where FV = future value of an investment,

PV = present value of an investment,

r = annual rate of interest paid,

n = number of periods (typically years) the present value is left on deposit.

The following Applying the Model illustrates an application of this equation by showing how you might use the concept of future value to evaluate an investment in a bank certificate of deposit (CD).

APPLYING THE MODEL

Assume that, in addition to having the opportunity to invest $100 into an open-ended savings account paying 5 percent interest, you also have the chance to invest $100 in a CD paying 6 percent interest. The difference is that you must leave your money in the CD for five years to earn the full 6 percent interest. If you withdraw the money early, you will face a substantial penalty. You would like to know how much your $100 CD investment will be worth at the end of five years. Substituting $PV = \$100$,

Figure 3.1
Time Line for $100
Invested for Five Years
at 6% Interest

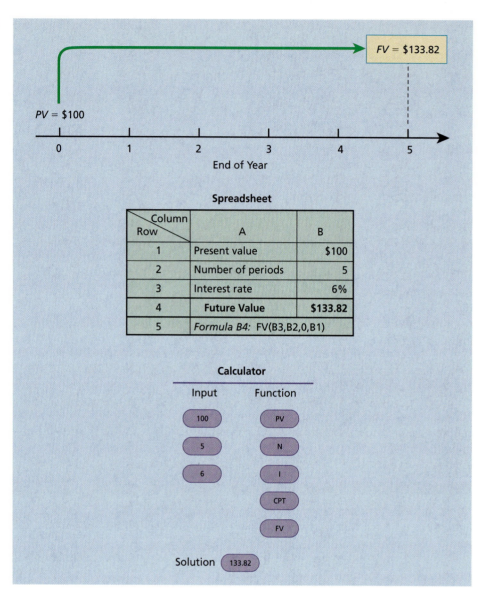

Figure 3.1
Time Line for $100 Invested for Five Years at 6% Interest

$r = 0.06$, and $n = 5$ into Equation 3.1 gives the future value at the end of year 5, expressed as FV:

$$FV = \$100 \times (1 + 0.06)^5 = \$100 \times (1.3382) = \$133.82$$

Your CD will have an account balance of $133.82 at end of the fifth year. This is presented graphically, as a **time line**, at the top of Figure 3.1.

In addition to algebra, there are three popular methods for simplifying future value calculations. One method is to use a future value factor (*FVF*) table, such as Table A1 in Appendix A. Such a table provides future value factors ($FVF_{r\%,n}$) for various interest rates (r) and holding periods (n). A portion of Table A1 is reproduced as Table 3.1.[2] To find the future value factor for 6 percent interest and a 5-year hold-

2. A complete table of future value factors is included in Appendix A of this text. Similarly, complete tables of other factors excerpted in this chapter are included in Appendix A.

Table 3.1
Format of a Future Value
Factor (*FVF*) Table

Period	Interest Rate (r)					
	1%	**2%**	**3%**	**4%**	**5%**	**6%**
1	1.010	1.020	1.030	1.040	1.050	1.060
2	1.020	1.040	1.061	1.082	1.102	1.124
3	1.030	1.061	1.093	1.125	1.158	1.191
4	1.041	1.082	1.126	1.170	1.216	1.262
5	1.051	1.104	1.159	1.217	1.276	1.338
6	1.062	1.126	1.194	1.265	1.340	1.419
7	1.072	1.149	1.230	1.316	1.407	1.504

ing period ($FVF_{6\%,5}$), we simply move across the interest rates on the horizontal axis of the table until we reach the column labeled "6%," and then move vertically down this column until we find the row labeled "Period 5." We find that $FVF_{6\%,5}$ is equal to 1.338, and this is the number we would multiply times $100 to compute FV_5. Not surprising, this matches the previous $FV_5 = \$133.80$ except for a small rounding difference.

A second and very popular method is to use a financial calculator. To compute *FV* in the example, you would simply input the number of years (5), the interest rate (6), the amount of the initial deposit ($100), and then calculate the future value of $133.82. A simplified financial calculator keypad showing the keystrokes and final value for this calculation for the TI BAII PLUS calculator is shown at the lower left of the time line in Figure 3.1.[3] The third popular method of simplifying time value calculations involves use of a financial spreadsheet such as Excel. Figure 3.1 shows a simplified spreadsheet illustrating the key inputs, the cell formula for the output, and the future value of $133.82.[4]

A GRAPHIC VIEW OF FUTURE VALUE

Remember that we measure future value at the *end* of the given period. The relationship between various interest rates, the number of periods interest is earned, and the future value of $1 appears in Figure 3.2. The figure shows that (1) the higher the interest rate, the higher the future value, and (2) the longer the period of time, the higher the future value. Note that for an interest rate of 0 percent, the future value always equals the present value ($1), but for any interest rate greater than zero, the future value is greater than the present value of $1.

---

3. Will a deposit made in an account paying compound interest (assuming compounding occurs once per year) yield a higher future value after one period than an equal-size deposit in an account paying simple interest? What about future values for investments held longer than one period?

4. How would (a) a *decrease* in the interest rate or (b) an *increase* in the holding period of a deposit affect its future value? Why?

Concept Review Questions

[3.] Calculator keystrokes using the same keypad will be included with all time lines in this chapter.
[4.] The format of Excel's future value formula is "=FV(*rate,nper,pmt,pv,type*)" where: *rate* = interest rate per period; *nper* = number of periods; *pmt* = the size of payments made each year in an annuity (in this case set to 0 because we are calculating the future value of a lump sum rather than of an annuity); *pv* = the present value or lump sum amount; *type* = a 0/1 variable (omitted in our example) that indicates whether payments occur at the beginning or at the end of each period.

If you enter this formula in Excel, it will generate the answer, −133.82. You can force Excel to produce a positive future value simply by inserting a minus sign in front of the FV equation.

Figure 3.2
The Power of Compound
Interest: Future Value of
$1 Invested at Different
Interest Rates

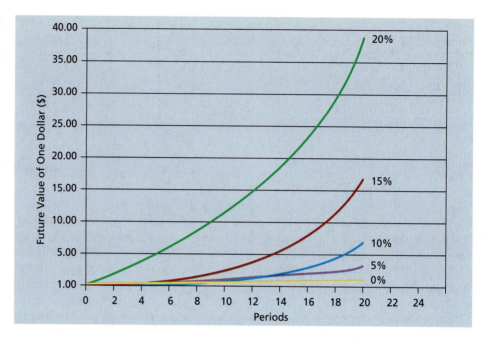

3.3. PRESENT VALUE OF A LUMP SUM

So far we have examined how to project the amount of cash that will build over time as an initial investment earns interest. Now we want to reverse that focus to ask what an investor would be willing to pay today in exchange for a lump-sum payment that arrives at some point in the future. In other words, we want to know the *present value* of the future payment. In the Opening Focus, we were trying to determine the present value of the lottery's 25-year *stream* of $11.8 million annual payments, assuming that a lottery winner could invest cash at an interest rate of 5 percent. In this section, we focus on the simpler problem of calculating the present value of a single future cash payment. In the previous section, we saw that the future value of a lump sum depended on the interest rate and on the amount of time that the money would earn that interest rate. Similarly, the present value depends largely on the investment opportunities of the recipient and the timing of the cash payment.

THE CONCEPT OF PRESENT VALUE

In finance, we use the term **discounting** to describe the process of calculating present values. Discounting answers this question: If I can earn *r* percent on my money, what is the most I would be willing to pay now for an opportunity to receive *FV* dollars *n* periods from today? This process is actually the inverse of compounding interest. Instead of finding the future value of present dollars invested at a given rate, discounting determines the present value of a future amount, assuming an opportunity to earn a given return (*r*), on the money.[5] To see how this works, suppose that some investment offers to pay you $300 one year from now. How much would you be willing to spend today to acquire this investment if you can earn 6 percent on an alternative in-

---

[5.] This interest rate is variously referred to as the *discount rate, required return, cost of capital, hurdle rate,* or *opportunity cost.*

vestment (of equal risk)? To answer this question, you must determine how many dollars would have to be invested at 6 percent today to have $300 one year from now. Let PV equal this unknown amount, and use the same notation as in the future value discussion:

$$PV \times (1 + 0.06) = \$300$$

Solving this equation for PV gives us the following:

$$PV = \frac{\$300}{(1 + 0.06)} = \$283.02$$

The present value of $300 one year from today is $283.02. That is, investing $283.02 today at a 6 percent interest rate would result in $300 at the end of one year. Therefore, you would be willing to pay no more than $283.02 for the investment that pays $300 in one year.

THE EQUATION FOR PRESENT VALUE

We can find the present value of a lump sum mathematically by solving Equation 3.1 for PV. In other words, the present value (PV) of some future amount (FV) to be received n periods from now, assuming an opportunity cost of r, is given by Equation 3.2:

$$PV = \frac{FV}{(1 + r)^n} = FV \times \left[\frac{1}{(1 + r)^n} \right] \qquad \text{(Eq. 3.2)}$$

The following Applying the Model illustrates the application of Equation 3.2, using a corporate investment opportunity as an example.

APPLYING THE MODEL

Pam Verity, the financial manager of the Wildcatter Oil Drilling Company, has been offered the chance to purchase the right to receive a $1,700 royalty payment eight years from now. The offer came from Sam Long, the owner of the Petroleum Land Management Company. Pam believes her company's opportunity cost should be 8 percent on investments of this level of risk. How much should she be willing to pay for the right to receive this royalty payment? Substituting $FV = \$1,700$, $n = 8$, and $r = 0.08$ into Equation 3.2 yields the following:

$$PV = \frac{\$1,700}{(1 + 0.08)^8} = \frac{\$1,700}{(1.85093)} = \$918.46$$

Pam finds that the present value of this $1,700 royalty payment is $918.46. If Sam offers this investment opportunity at a price of $918.46 or less, Pam should accept the offer; otherwise, she should reject it. At the top of Figure 3.3 is a time line describing this process graphically. ▮

As was the case with future values, there are three popular methods for simplifying present value calculations. One method is to use a present value factor (PVF)

Figure 3.3
Present Value of $1,700
to Be Received in 8 Years
at an 8% Discount Rate

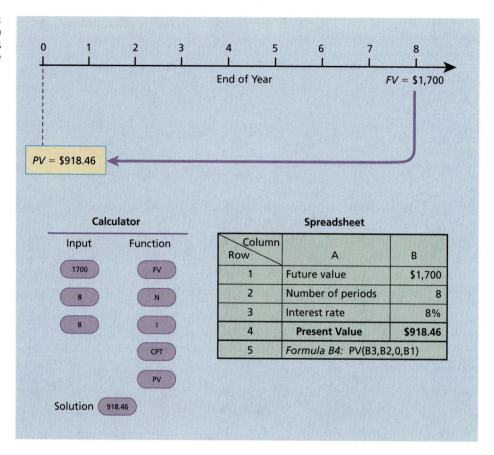

table, such as Table A2 in Appendix A. A portion of Table A2 appears below as Table 3.2. Present value factors for specific discount rates and compounding periods $(PVF_{r\%,n})$ are determined just as they were for future values. To find the relevant factor for the current example, $PV_{8\%,8}$, move across the top of the table until you reach the 8 percent column, then move down until you reach the row for 8 years. The table indicates that the present value of $1 discounted for 8 years at 8 percent equals $0.540. Multiply that figure by $1,700 to find the present value of the royalty payment, $918 (rounding to the nearest dollar). Using financial calculators or spread-

Table 3.2
Format of a Present Value Factor (*PVF*) Table

Period	\multicolumn{8}{c}{Interest Rate (*r*)}							
	1%	2%	3%	4%	5%	6%	7%	8%
1	0.990	0.980	0.971	0.962	0.952	0.943	0.935	0.926
2	0.980	0.961	0.943	0.925	0.907	0.890	0.873	0.857
3	0.971	0.942	0.915	0.889	0.864	0.840	0.816	0.794
4	0.961	0.924	0.888	0.855	0.823	0.792	0.763	0 735
5	0.951	0.906	0.863	0.822	0.784	0.747	0.713	0.681
6	0.942	0.888	0.837	0.790	0.746	0.705	0.666	0.630
7	0.933	0.871	0.813	0.760	0.711	0.665	0.623	0.583
8	0.923	0.853	0.789	0.731	0.677	0.627	0.582	0.540

sheets, as shown in the lower portion of Figure 3.3, are two other popular methods for simplifying present value calculations for a lump sum.[6]

A GRAPHIC VIEW OF PRESENT VALUE

For investors who expect to receive cash in the future, Figure 3.4 contains two important messages. First, the present value of a future cash payment declines the longer investors must wait to receive it. Second, the present value declines as the discount rate rises. Note that for a discount rate of 0 percent, the present value always equals the future value ($1). However, for any discount rate greater than zero, the present value falls below the future value.

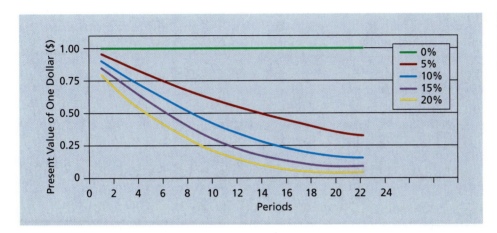

Figure 3.4
The Power of Discounting: Present Value of $1 Discounted at Different Interest Rates

5. How are the present value and the future value of a lump sum related—both definitionally and mathematically? Notice that for a given interest rate (r) and a given investment time horizon (n), $PVF_{r,n}$ and $FVF_{r,n}$ are inverses of each other. Why?

6. How would (a) an *increase* in the discount rate or (b) a *decrease* in the time period until the cash flow is received affect the present value? Why?

Concept Review Questions

3.4 FUTURE VALUE OF CASH FLOW STREAMS

Financial managers frequently need to evaluate *streams* of cash flows that occur in future periods. Though this is mechanically more complicated than computing the future or present value of a single cash flow, the same basic techniques apply. Two types of cash flow streams are possible: the mixed stream and the annuity. A **mixed stream** is a series of unequal payments reflecting no particular pattern, whereas an **annuity** is a stream of equal periodic (frequently annual) cash flows over a stated period of time. Either of these cash flow patterns can represent *inflows* of returns earned on investments or *outflows* of funds invested to earn future returns. Because certain shortcuts are possible when evaluating an annuity, we discuss mixed streams and annuities separately.

[6.] The format of the Excel function for present value is "$=PV(rate,nper,pmt,fv,type)$". The terms in the parenthesis have similar interpretations to those in the future value equation. Note that in the present value function, Excel produces an answer with the opposite sign to that of the value entered for the variable "fv." In other words, if a lump sum has a positive future value, Excel produces a negative estimate for the present value. You can change the sign of Excel's answer simply by putting a minus sign in front of the PV equation.

Finding the Future Value of a Mixed Stream

The future value of any stream of cash flows measured at the end of a specified year is merely the sum of the future values of the individual cash flows at that year's end. This future value is sometimes called the *terminal value*.

APPLYING THE MODEL

Assume that we wish to determine the balance in an investment account earning 9 percent annual interest, given the following five end-of-year deposits: $400 in year 1, $800 in year 2, $500 in year 3, $400 in year 4, and $300 in year 5. These cash flows appear on the time line at the top of Figure 3.5, which also depicts the future value calculation for this mixed stream of cash flows, followed by the financial calculator and spreadsheet solutions.

The future value of the mixed stream is $2,930.70.[7] Note that the first cash flow, which occurs at the end of year 1, earns interest for four years (end of year 1 to end of year 5); the second cash flow, which occurs at the end of year 2, earns interest for three years (end of year 2 to end of year 5); and so on. As a result of the 9 percent interest earnings, the five deposits, which total $2,400 before interest, have grown to more than $2,900 at the end of five years. ■

Letting CF_t represent the cash flow at the end of year t, the future value of an n-year mixed stream of cash flows (FV) can be expressed as shown in Equation 3.3:

$$FV = CF_1 \times (1 + r)^{n-1} + CF_2 \times (1 + r)^{n-2} + \cdots + CF_n \times (1 + r)^{n-n} \quad \textbf{(Eq. 3.3)}$$

Figure 3.5
Future Value at the End of Five Years of a Mixed Cash Flow Stream Invested at 9%

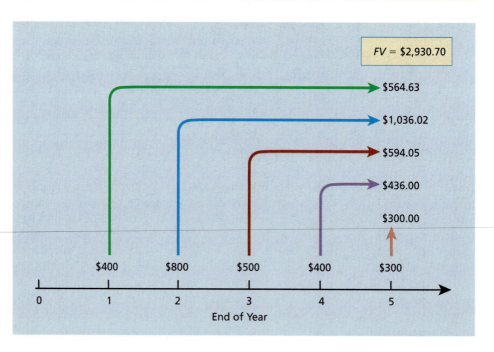

[7.] There is a $0.01 rounding difference between the future value given on the timeline compared to the future value calculation using a calculator or spreadsheet. As before, Excel reports the value $2,930.71 as a negative number because the FV function always reverses the signs of the cash flows and the final answer. Notice that to calculate the stream's present value (a necessary input in the FV formula), we use the NPV function rather than the PV function because the latter does not accommodate mixed cash flow streams.

Figure 3.5
(continued)

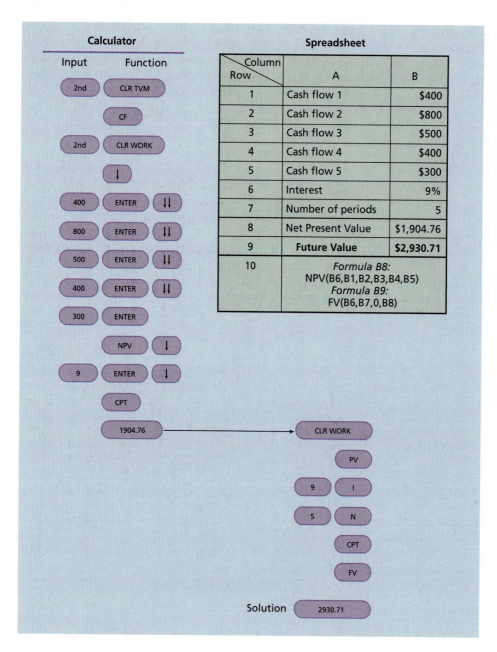

If we substitute the cash flows shown on the time line and the 9 percent interest rate into Equation 3.3, the values shown to the right of the time line would result. They would total $2,930.70.

We can simplify the notation for Equation 3.3, as shown in Equation 3.3a, by using the Greek summation symbol, Σ, as a shorthand way of saying that the future value of this n-year mixed stream is equal to the sum of the present values of individual cash flows from periods 1, 2, 3, . . . , n:

$$FV = \sum_{t=1}^{n} CF_t \times (1 + r)^{n-t}$$

(Eq. 3.3a)

Though summations economize on the notation needed to express most of the equations presented in this chapter, for clarity we present equations in their "non-condensed" format wherever possible, and we use the summation notation sparingly. Mathematical purists can use their imaginations to construct the more succinct formulations.

TYPES OF ANNUITIES

Before looking at future value computations for annuities, we distinguish between the two basic types of annuities: the ordinary annuity and the annuity due. An **ordinary annuity** is an annuity for which the payments occur *at the end of each period,* whereas an **annuity due** is one for which the payments occur *at the beginning of each period.* To demonstrate these differences, assume that you are attempting to choose the better of two annuities as a personal investment opportunity. Both are 5-year, $1,000 annuities, but annuity A is an ordinary annuity, and annuity B is an annuity due. Although the amount of each annuity totals $5,000, the timing of the cash flows differs; each cash flow arrives one year sooner with the annuity due than with the ordinary annuity. In fact, for any positive interest rate, *the future value of an annuity due is always greater than the future value of an otherwise identical ordinary annuity.*[8]

FINDING THE FUTURE VALUE OF AN ORDINARY ANNUITY

The future value of an ordinary annuity can be calculated using the same method demonstrated earlier for a mixed stream.

APPLYING THE MODEL

Assume that you wish to save money on a regular basis to finance an exotic vacation in five years. You are confident that, with sacrifice and discipline, you can force yourself to deposit $1,000 annually at the *end of each* of the next five years into a savings account paying 7 percent annual interest. This situation is depicted graphically at the top of Figure 3.6.

We can compute the future value (*FV*) of this annuity using Equation 3.3. We simply use the assumed interest rate (*r*) of 7 percent and plug in the known values of each of the five yearly (*n* = 5) cash flows (CF_1 to CF_5), as follows:

$$FV = CF_1 \times (1 + r)^{n-1} + CF_2 \times (1 + r)^{n-2} + \cdots + CF_n \times (1 + r)^{n-n}$$

$$FV = CF_1 \times (1 + r)^{5-1} + CF_2 \times (1 + r)^{5-2} + \cdots + CF_n \times (1 + r)^{5-5}$$

$$= \$1,000(1.07)^4 + \$1,000(1.07)^3 + \$1,000(1.07)^2 + \$1,000(1.07)^1 + \$1,000$$

$$= \$1,310.80 + \$1,225.04 + \$1,144.90 + \$1,070 + \$1,000 = \$5,750.74$$

The future value of the ordinary annuity is $5,750.74. The year-1 cash flow of $1,000 earns 7 percent interest for four years, the year-2 cash flow earns 7 percent interest for three years, and so on. ▪

Fortunately, a shortcut formula exists that simplifies the future value calculation of an ordinary annuity. Using the symbol *PMT* to represent the annuity's annual pay-

---

[8.] Because ordinary annuities arise frequently in finance, we use the term "annuity" throughout this book to refer to ordinary annuities unless otherwise specified.

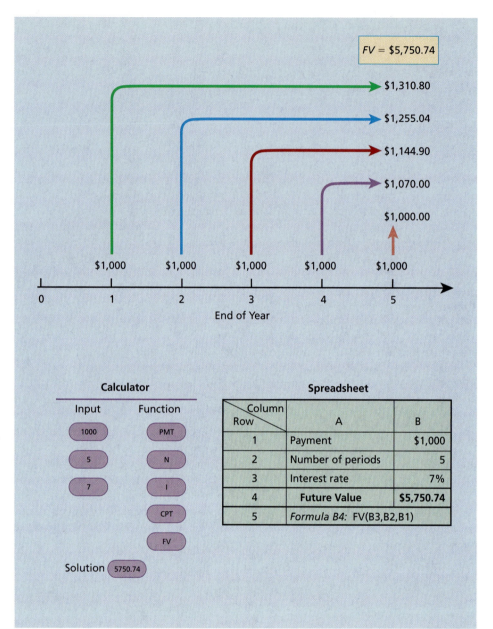

Figure 3.6
Future Value at the End of
Five Years of an Ordinary
Annuity of $1,000 Per
Year Invested at 7%

ment, Equation 3.4 gives the future value of an annuity that lasts for n years (FV), assuming an interest rate of r percent:

$$FV = PMT \times \left\{ \frac{[(1 + r)^n - 1]}{r} \right\} \qquad \text{(Eq. 3.4)}$$

APPLYING THE MODEL

We can demonstrate that Equation 3.4 yields the same answer we obtained in the previous model by plugging in the values, $PMT = \$1,000$, $n = 5$, and $r = 0.07$:

$$FV = \$1,000 \times \left\{ \frac{[(1.07)^5 - 1]}{0.07} \right\} = \$1,000 \times \left[\frac{(1.4026 - 1)}{0.07} \right]$$

$$= \$1,000 \times 5.7507 = \$5,750.74$$

Once again, we find the future value of this ordinary annuity to be $5,750.74. ∎

In addition to using algebra, we can use a table such as Table A3 in Appendix A that details future value factors for ordinary annuities at various interest rates for different holding periods. These are generically labeled $FVFA_{r\%,n}$; the factor corresponding to $r = 0.07$ and $n = 5$ equals $FVFA_{7\%,5}$, which equals 5.751. We can multiply this factor by the $1,000 to compute FV, which is $5,751. Two other popular methods for simplifying future value calculations for annuities involve the use of financial calculators or spreadsheets as demonstrated below the time line in Figure 3.6.[9]

FINDING THE FUTURE VALUE OF AN ANNUITY DUE

The calculations required to find the future value of an annuity due involve only a slight change to those already done for an ordinary annuity. How much money will you have at the end of five years if you deposit $1,000 annually at the *beginning of each* of the next five years into a savings account paying 7 percent annual interest? This scenario is graphically depicted at the top of Figure 3.7. Note that the ends of years 0 through 4 are respectively equivalent to the beginnings of years 1 through 5. The $6,153.29 future value of the annuity due is, as expected, greater than the $5,750.74 future value of the comparable ordinary annuity discussed in the preceding section. Because the cash flows of the annuity due occur at the beginning of the year, the cash flow of $1,000 at the beginning of year 1 earns 7 percent interest for five years, the cash flow of $1,000 at the beginning of year 2 earns 7 percent interest for four years, and so on. Comparing this to the ordinary annuity, it should be clear that each $1,000 cash flow of the annuity due earns interest for one more year than the comparable ordinary annuity cash flow. As a result, the future value of the annuity due is greater than the future value of the comparable ordinary annuity.

Because each cash flow of an annuity due earns an additional year of interest, the equation for the future value of an ordinary annuity, Equation 3.4, can be converted into an expression for the future value of an annuity due, FV (annuity due), simply by multiplying it by $(1 + r)$, as shown in Equation 3.5:

$$FV \text{ (annuity due)} = PMT \times \left\{ \frac{[(1 + r)^n - 1]}{r} \right\} \times (1 + r) \qquad \textbf{(Eq. 3.5)}$$

Equation 3.5 demonstrates that the future value of an annuity due always exceeds the future value of a similar ordinary annuity for any positive interest rate. The future value of an annuity due exceeds that of an identical ordinary annuity by a factor of 1 plus the interest rate. We can check this by comparing the results from the two different 5-year vacation savings plans presented previously. We determined that the future values of your ordinary annuity and annuity due at the end of year 5, given a 7 percent interest rate, were $5,750.74 and $6,153.29, respectively. Multiplying the future value of the ordinary annuity by 1 plus the interest rate yields the future value of the annuity due:

$$FV \text{ (annuity due)} = \$5,750.74 \times (1.07) = \$6,153.29$$

[9.] Notice that when calculating the future value of an ordinary annuity, Excel only requires three arguments in the FV formula: (1) the interest rate, (2) the number of periods or payments, and (3) the amount of each payment.

Figure 3.7
Future Value at the End of
Five Years of an Annuity
Due of $1,000 Per Year
Invested at 7%

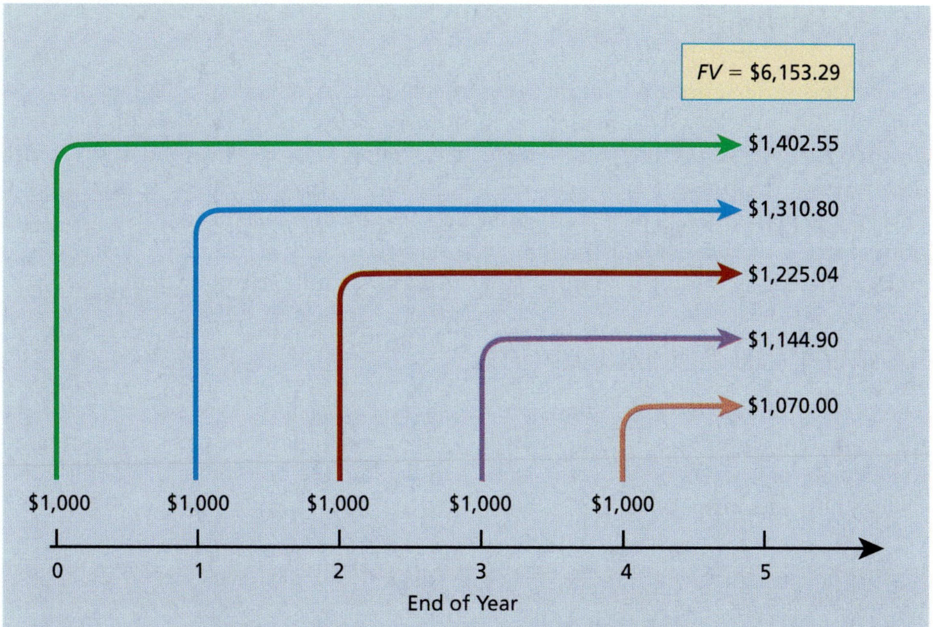

$FV = \$6,153.29$

$1,402.55

$1,310.80

$1,225.04

$1,144.90

$1,070.00

$1,000 $1,000 $1,000 $1,000 $1,000

| 0 | 1 | 2 | 3 | 4 | 5 |

End of Year

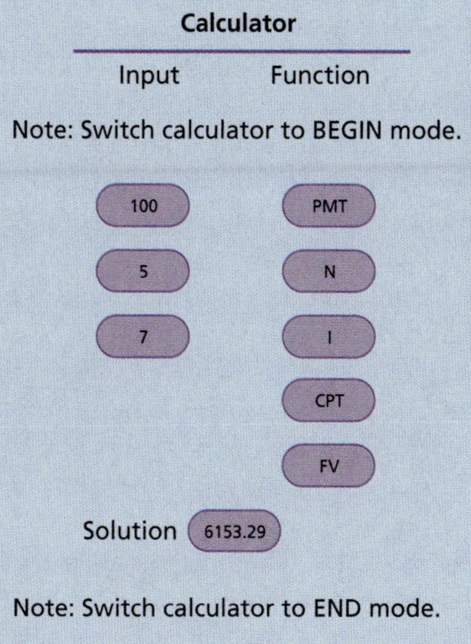

Calculator

Input   Function

Note: Switch calculator to BEGIN mode.

100   PMT

5   N

7   I

CPT

FV

Solution   6153.29

Note: Switch calculator to END mode.

Spreadsheet

Column Row	A	B
1	Payment	$1,000
2	Number of periods	5
3	Interest rate	7%
4	**Future Value**	**$6,153.29**
5	*Formula B4:* FV(B3,B2,B1,0,1)	

Because the cash flow of the annuity due occurs at the beginning of the period rather than at the end, its future value is greater. In our illustration, you would earn about $400 more with the annuity due and could enjoy a somewhat more luxurious vacation.

7. How would *the future value of a mixed stream of cash flows* be calculated, given the cash flows and applicable interest rate?

8. Differentiate between an *ordinary annuity* and an *annuity due*. How is the future value of an ordinary annuity calculated, and how (for the same cash flows) can it be converted into the future value of an annuity due?

Concept Review Questions

3.5 PRESENT VALUE OF CASH FLOW STREAMS

Many decisions in corporate finance require financial managers to calculate the present values of cash flow streams that occur over several years. In this section, we show how to calculate the present values of mixed cash flow streams and annuities. We also demonstrate the present value calculation for a very important cash flow stream known as a *perpetuity*. A perpetuity is a level (or growing) cash flow stream that continues forever. Perpetuities arise in many applications such as valuing a business as a going concern, or valuing a share of stock with no definite maturity date.

FINDING THE PRESENT VALUE OF A MIXED STREAM

The present value of any cash flow stream is merely the sum of the present values of the individual cash flows. In other words, we can apply the same techniques we used to calculate present values of lump sums to calculate the present values of all kinds of cash flow streams.

APPLYING THE MODEL

Assume that shortly after graduation you receive an inheritance that you use to purchase a small bed-and-breakfast inn as an investment (and a weekend escape). Your plan is to sell the inn after five years. The inn is an old mansion, so you know that appliances, furniture, and other equipment will wear out and need to be replaced or repaired on a regular basis. You estimate that these expenses will total $4,000 during year 1, $8,000 during year 2, $5,000 during year 3, $4,000 during year 4, and $3,000 during year 5, the final year of your ownership. For simplicity, assume that the expense payments will be made at the end of each year. Because you have some of your inheritance left over after purchasing the inn (the deceased was indeed generous), you want to set aside a lump sum today from which you can make annual withdrawals to meet these expenses when they come due, as shown in Figure 3.8. Suppose you can invest the lump sum in a bank account that pays 9 percent interest. To determine the amount of money you need to put in the account, you must calculate the present value of the stream of future expenses using 9 percent as the discount rate.

The present value of the mixed stream is $19,047.58. The present value factors corresponding to each annual cash flow can be determined using present value factor tables such as Table A2, using a financial calculator, or using an Excel spreadsheet. The more precise financial calculator and spreadsheet calculations are demonstrated below the time line in Figure 3.8. ■

As you no doubt suspect, there is a general formula for computing the present value of a stream of future cash flows. Continuing to let CF_t represent the cash flow at the end of year t, the present value of an n-year mixed stream of cash flows (PV) is expressed as Equation 3.6:

$$PV = \left[CF_1 \times \frac{1}{(1+r)^1} \right] + \left[CF_2 \times \frac{1}{(1+r)^2} \right] + \cdots + \left[CF_n \times \frac{1}{(1+r)^n} \right]$$

$$= \sum_{t=1}^{n} CF_t \times \frac{1}{(1+r)^t} \qquad \text{(Eq. 3.6)}$$

Figure 3.8
Present Value of a 5-Year
Mixed Stream Discounted
at 9%

(*continued on page 82*)

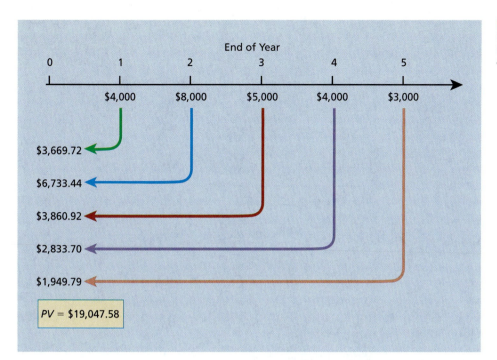

If we substitute the cash flows shown on the time line in Figure 3.8 and the 9 percent discount rate into Equation 3.6, we obtain the present value figure, $19,047.58.

FINDING THE PRESENT VALUE OF AN ORDINARY ANNUITY

The present value of an ordinary annuity can be found in a manner similar to that used for a mixed stream. Discount each payment and then add up each term to find the annuity's present value.

APPLYING THE MODEL

Assume that Braden Company, a producer of plastic toys, has been approached by its principal equipment supplier with an intriguing offer for a service contract. The supplier, the Extruding Machines Corporation (EMC), has offered to take over all of Braden's equipment repair and servicing for five years in exchange for a one-time payment today. Braden's managers know that their company spends $7,000 at the end of every year on maintenance, so EMC's service contract would reduce the Braden's cash outflows by this $7,000 annually for five years. Because these are equal annual cash benefits, Braden can determine what it should be willing to pay for the service contract by valuing it as a 5-year ordinary annuity with a $7,000 annual cash flow. If Braden requires a minimum return of 8 percent on all its investments, how much should it be willing to pay for EMC's service contract? The calculation of the present value of this annuity is depicted on the time line presented at the top of Figure 3.9, followed by the more precise financial calculator and spreadsheet solutions.

The present value of this ordinary annuity (EMC's service contract) is $27,948.97. This value was found using the same method used in the preceding section to find the present value of a mixed stream. Each end-of-year $7,000 cash flow is discounted back to time 0, and the present values of all five cash flows are summed to get the pres-

Figure 3.8
(continued)

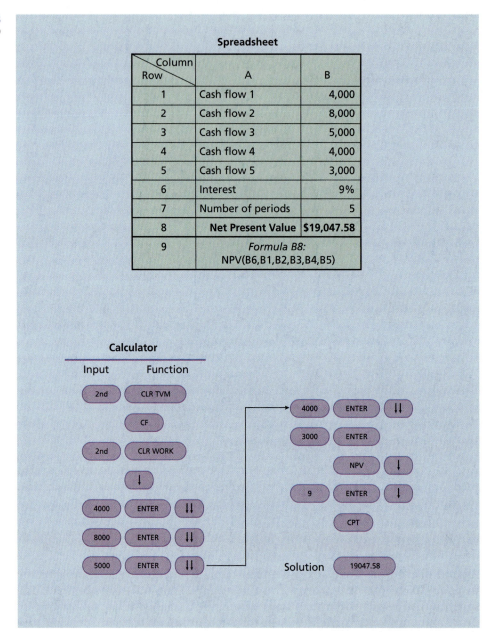

Spreadsheet

Row \ Column	A	B
1	Cash flow 1	4,000
2	Cash flow 2	8,000
3	Cash flow 3	5,000
4	Cash flow 4	4,000
5	Cash flow 5	3,000
6	Interest	9%
7	Number of periods	5
8	**Net Present Value**	**$19,047.58**
9	*Formula B8:* NPV(B6,B1,B2,B3,B4,B5)	

ent value of the annuity. Therefore, if EMC offers the service contract to Braden for a lump-sum price of $27,948.97 or less, Braden should accept the offer. Otherwise, Braden should continue to perform its own maintenance.

As was the case with the future value of an annuity, a shortcut formula is available to simplify the present value calculation for an annuity. Using the symbol PMT to denote the annual cash flow, the formula for the the present value of an n-year ordinary annuity (PV) appears in Equation 3.7:

$$PV = \frac{PMT}{r} \times \left[1 - \frac{1}{(1+r)^n} \right]$$ (Eq. 3.7)

Figure 3.9
Present Value of a 5-Year
Ordinary Annuity
Discounted at 8%

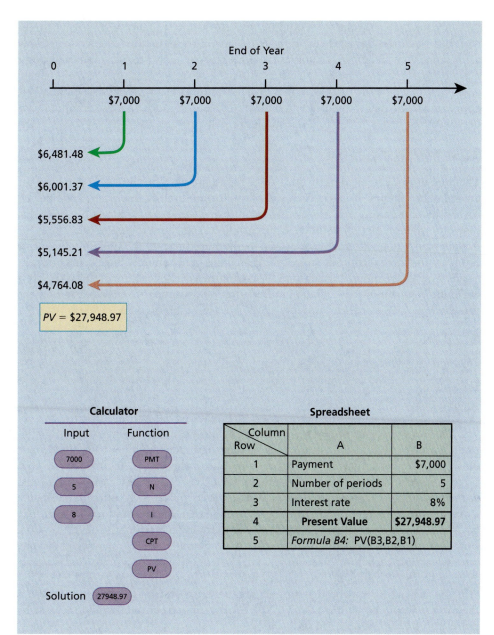

APPLYING THE MODEL

We can use Equation 3.7 to calculate the present value of the service contract EMC has offered to the Braden Company. Substituting in $n = 5$ years, $r = 0.08$, and $PMT = \$7,000$, we once again find the present value (PV) of this ordinary annuity to be $\$27,948.97$, as shown below:

$$PV = \frac{\$7,000}{0.08} \times \left[1 - \frac{1}{(1.08)^5} \right] = \frac{\$7,000}{0.08} \times [1 - 0.6806] = \$27,948.97$$

By now, you know these computations can be simplified using a table such as Table A4 in Appendix A that gives present value factors for ordinary annuities at various discount rates for different holding periods. Many students find it easier to understand Equation 3.7 when the right-hand side of the equation is expressed simply as the annual cash flow (PMT) times the present value factor for an annuity paying r percent for n years, or $PVFA_{r\%,n}$. From Table A4 we get $PVFA_{8\%,5} = 3.993$, which, when multiplied by the $7,000 annual cash flow, results in a present value of $27,951, approximately equal to the present value obtained using more precise computations demonstrated beneath the time line in Figure 3.9.

FINDING THE PRESENT VALUE OF AN ANNUITY DUE

The present value of an annuity due can be found in a fashion similar to that used for an ordinary annuity. Because each cash flow for an annuity due occurs one period earlier than for an ordinary annuity, an annuity due would have a larger present value than an ordinary annuity with the same cash flows, discount rate, and life. The value of the annuity due is found by the same method used to find the present value of an ordinary annuity except that each of the cash flows of the annuity due occurs one year earlier—at the beginning rather than the end of the year. The expression for the present value of an annuity due, shown in Equation 3.8, is similar to the equation for the present value of an ordinary annuity (PV) given in Equation 3.7.

$$PV(\text{annuity due}) = \frac{PMT}{r} \times \left[1 - \frac{1}{(1+r)^n} \right] \times (1+r) \qquad \textbf{(Eq. 3.8)}$$

It should be clear from a comparison of Equations 3.7 and 3.8 that the present value of an annuity due is merely the present value of a similar ordinary annuity multiplied by $(1 + r)$. To demonstrate, assume that the Braden Company in the previous illustration wishes to determine the present value of the 5-year, $7,000 service contract at an 8 percent discount rate, and assume that each of the cash flows occurs *at the beginning of the year*. To convert the service contract EMC offered the Braden Company into an annuity due, we simply assume that EMC would have had to pay its annual maintenance cost of $7,000 at the beginning of each of the next five years. Braden is still evaluating what amounts to a 5-year annuity; the company will just pay out each annual cash flow a year earlier. The present value of this annuity due is simply $(1 + r)$ times the value of the ordinary annuity: $PV(\text{annuity due}) = \$27,948.97 \times (1.08) = \$30,184.89$. If Braden paid its maintenance costs at the start of each year, the most it would be willing to pay EMC for the service contract would increase by more than $2,000 to $30,184.89.

FINDING THE PRESENT VALUE OF A PERPETUITY

A **perpetuity** is an annuity with an infinite life; it promises to pay the same amount at the end of every year forever. One of the first, and certainly the most famous, perpetuities in modern history was the massive "consol" bond issue sold by the British government after the Napoleonic Wars ended in 1815. This bond issue got its name from the fact that it consolidated all the existing British war debts into a single issue that paid a constant annual amount of interest into perpetuity. The issue itself never matured, meaning that the principal was never to be repaid.

Currently, not many corporations or governments issue perpetual bonds.[10] Perhaps

---

[10.] Some examples come close to being perpetuities. In July 1993, the Walt Disney Company sold $300 million of bonds that matured in the year 2093, 100 years after they were issued. The market dubbed these "Sleeping Beauty bonds" be-the simplest modern example of a perpetuity is preferred stock issued by corporations. Preferred shares promise investors a constant annual (or quarterly) dividend payment forever. Though "forever" seems a difficult time period to measure, we simply express the lifetime (n) of this security as infinity (∞), and modify our basic valuation formulation for an annuity accordingly. We wish to determine the present value of an annuity (PV) that pays a constant annual dividend amount (PMT) for a perpetual number of years ($n = \infty$) discounted at a rate r. Here, the Greek summation notation is helpful in expressing the formula in Equation 3.9:

$$PV = PMT \times \sum_{t=1}^{\infty} \frac{1}{(1 + r)^t} \qquad \text{(Eq. 3.9)}$$

Fortunately, Equation 3.9 also comes in a simplified version, which states that the present value of a perpetuity equals the annual, end-of-year payment divided by the discount rate. Equation 3.10 gives this straightforward expression for the present value of a perpetuity (PV):

$$PV = PMT \times \frac{1}{r} = \frac{PMT}{r} \qquad \text{(Eq. 3.10)}$$

APPLYING THE MODEL

Assume that you wish to find the present value of the dividend stream associated with a preferred stock issued by the Alpha and Omega Service Company. A&O, as the company is commonly known, promises to pay $10 per year on its preferred shares, and security analysts believe that the firm's business and financial risk merits a required return of 12.5 percent. Substituting the values $PMT = \$10$ per year and $r = 0.125$ into Equation 3.10, we find the following:

$$PV = \frac{\$10}{0.125} = \$80$$

The present value of A&O's preferred stock dividends, valued as an annuity with a perpetual life, is $80 per share. In other words, the right to receive $10 at the end of every year for an indefinite period is worth only $80 today if a person can earn 12.5 percent on investments of similar risk. The reason is that if the person had $80 today and earned 12.5 percent interest on it each year, $10 a year ($0.125 \times \$80$) could be withdrawn indefinitely without ever touching the initial $80. ■

Finding the Present Value of a Growing Perpetuity

As we have seen, perpetuities pay a constant periodic amount forever. However, few aspects of modern life are constant, and most of the cash flows we care about have a tendency to grow over time. This is true for items of income such as wages and salaries, dividend payments from corporations, and Social Security payments from governments.[11] Inflation is one, but only one, factor driving the increase in cash flows

---

cause their maturity matched the amount of time that Sleeping Beauty slept before being kissed by Prince Charming in the classic story.

[11.] Unfortunately, this is also true for expense items such as rent and utility expenses, car prices, and tuition payments.

over time. We must therefore examine how to adjust the present value of a perpetuity formula to account for expected growth in future cash flows. Suppose we want to calculate the present value (PV) of a stream of cash flows growing forever ($n = \infty$) at rate g. Given an opportunity cost of r, the present value of the **growing perpetuity** is given by equation 3.11, which is sometimes called the **Gordon Growth model:**[12]

$$PV = \frac{CF_1}{r - g} \qquad r > g \qquad \text{(Eq. 3.11)}$$

Note that the numerator in Equation 3.11 is CF_1, the first year's cash flow. This cash flow is expected to grow at a constant annual rate (g) from now to the end of time. The cash flow for any specific future year(t) can be determined by applying the growth rate (g) as follows:

$$CF_t = CF_1 \times (1 + g)^{t-1}$$

APPLYING THE MODEL

Assume that Gil Bates is a philanthropist wishing to endow a medical foundation with sufficient money to fund ongoing research. Gil is particularly impressed with the research proposal submitted by the Smith Cancer Institute (SCI). The Institure requests an endowment sufficient to cover its expenses for medical equipment. Next year these expenses will total $10 million, and they will grow by 3 percent per year in perpetuity afterwards. Assume that the Institute can earn an 11 percent return on Gil's contribution. How large must the contribution be to finance the Institute's medical equipment expenditures in perpetuity? Equation 3.11 tells us that the present value of these expenses equals $125 million computed as follows:

Smart Concepts
See the equation explained step-by-step.

SMARTFinance

$$PV = \frac{\$10,000,000}{0.11 - 0.03} = \frac{\$10,000,000}{0.08} = \$125,000,000$$

Note that Gil Bates would have to make an investment of only $90,909,090 ($10,000,000 ÷ 0.11, using Equation 3.10) to fund a nongrowing perpetuity of $10 million per year. The additional investment of almost $35 million is required to support the 3 percent annual growth in the payout to SCI. ■

Concept Review Questions

9. How would the present value of a mixed stream of cash flows be calculated, given the cash flows and an applicable required return?

10. Given the present value of an *ordinary annuity* and the applicable required return, how can this value be easily converted into the present value of an otherwise identical *annuity due*? What is the fundamental difference between the cash flow streams of these two annuities?

11. What is a *perpetuity,* and how can its present value be conveniently calculated? How do you find the present value of a growing perpetuity?

[12.] For this formula to work, the discount rate must be greater than the growth rate. When cash flows grow at a rate equal to or greater than the discount rate, the present value of the stream would be infinite.

3.6 SPECIAL APPLICATIONS OF TIME VALUE

Financial managers frequently apply future value and present value techniques to determine the values of other variables. In these cases, the future or present values are known, and the equations presented earlier are solved for variables such as the cash flow (*CF* or *PMT*), interest or discount rate (*r*), or number of time periods (*n*). Here we consider four of the more common applications and refinements: (1) compounding more frequently than annually; (2) stated versus effective annual interest rates; (3) the calculation of deposits needed to accumulate a future sum; and (4) loan amortization. This chapter's Appendix 3A goes further by describing how time value formulas and concepts can be used to determine interest or growth rates and the number of time periods.

COMPOUNDING MORE FREQUENTLY THAN ANNUALLY

In many applications, interest compounds more frequently than once a year. Financial institutions compound interest semiannually, quarterly, monthly, weekly, daily, or even continuously. This section explores how the present and future value techniques discussed earlier change if interest compounds more than once a year.

Semiannual Compounding

Semiannual compounding of interest involves two compounding periods within the year. Instead of the stated interest rate being paid once per year, one-half of the rate is paid twice a year. To demonstrate, consider an opportunity to deposit $100 in a savings account paying 8 percent interest with semiannual compounding. After the first six months, your account grows by 4 percent to $104. Six months later, the account grows by 4 percent once more to $108.16. Notice that after one year, the total increase in the account value is $8.16, or 8.16 percent. The return on this investment slightly exceeds the stated rate of 8 percent because semiannual compounding allows you to earn interest on interest during the year, increasing the overall rate of return. Table 3.3 shows how the account value grows every six months for the first two years. At the end of two years, the account value reaches $116.99.

Quarterly Compounding

As the name implies, **quarterly compounding** describes a situation in which interest compounds four times per year. An investment with quarterly compounding pays one-fourth of the stated interest rate every three months. Assume that after further investigation of your savings opportunities, you find an institution that will pay 8 percent interest compounded quarterly. After three months, your $100 deposit grows by 2 percent to $102. Three months later the balance increases 2 percent once more to

Period (months)	Beginning Principal (1)	Future Value Factor (2)	Future Value at End of Period [(1) × (2)] (3)
6	$100.00	1.04	$104.00
12	104.00	1.04	108.16
18	108.16	1.04	112.49
24	112.49	1.04	116.99

Table 3.3
The Future Value from Investing $100 at 8 Percent Interest Compounded Semiannually over Two Years

Table 3.4
The Future Value from
Investing $100 at
8 Percent Interest
Compounded Quarterly
over Two Years

Period (months)	Beginning Principal (1)	Future Value Factor (2)	Future Value at End of Period [(1) × (2)] (3)
3	$100.00	1.02	$102.00
6	102.00	1.02	104.04
9	104.04	1.02	106.12
12	106.12	1.02	108.24
15	108.24	1.02	110.40
18	110.40	1.02	112.61
21	112.61	1.02	114.86
24	114.86	1.02	117.16

Table 3.5
The Future Value from
Investing $100 at
8 Percent Interest for
Years 1 and 2 Given
Various Compounding
Periods

End of Year	Compounding Period		
	Annual	Semiannual	Quarterly
1	$108.00	$108.16	$108.24
2	116.64	116.99	117.16

$104.04. By the end of the year, the balance reaches $108.24. Compare that figure to the $108.16 you would earn with semiannual compounding. Table 3.4 tracks the growth in the account every three months for two years. At the end of two years, the account is worth $117.17.

Table 3.5 compares values for your $100 deposit at the end of years 1 and 2, given annual, semiannual, and quarterly compounding at the 8 percent rate. As you should expect by now, *the more frequently interest compounds, the greater the amount of money that accumulates.*

A General Equation

We can generalize the preceding examples in a simple equation. Suppose that a lump sum, denoted by *PV*, is invested at *r* percent for *n* years. If *m* equals the number of times per year that interest compounds, then the future value grows as shown in the following equation:

$$FV = PV \times \left(1 + \frac{r}{m}\right)^{m \times n} \qquad \text{(Eq. 3.12)}$$

Notice that if *m* = 1, Equation 3.12 reduces to Equation 3.1. The next several examples verify that this equation yields the same ending account values after two years as shown in Tables 3.3 and 3.4.

APPLYING THE MODEL

In previous discussions, we calculated the amount that you would have at the end of two years if you deposited $100 at 8 percent interest compounded semiannually and quarterly. For semiannual compounding, *m* = 2 in Equation 3.12; for quarterly compounding, $m = 4$. Substituting the appropriate values for semiannual and quarterly compounding into Equation 3.12 yields the following results:

For semiannual compounding:

$$FV = \$100 \times \left(1 + \frac{0.08}{2}\right)^{2\times2} = \$100 \times (1 + 0.04)^4 = \$116.99$$

For quarterly compounding:

$$FV = \$100 \times \left(1 + \frac{0.08}{4}\right)^{4\times2} = \$100 \times (1 + 0.02)^8 = \$117.17$$

These results agree with the values for FV_2 in Tables 3.3 and 3.4. If interest is compounded monthly, weekly, or daily, m would equal 12, 52, or 365, respectively. ■

Continuous Compounding

As we switch from annual, to semiannual, to quarterly compounding, the interval during which interest compounds gets shorter while the number of compounding periods per year gets larger. In principle, there is almost no limit to this process—interest could be compounded daily, hourly, or second by second. **Continuous compounding,** the most extreme case, occurs when interest compounds literally at every moment as time passes. In this case, m in Equation 3.12 would approach infinity, and Equation 3.12 converges to this expression:

$$FV \text{ (continuous compounding)} = PV \times (e^{r\times n}) \qquad \textbf{(Eq. 3.13)}$$

The number e is an irrational number, like the number π from geometry, which is useful in mathematical applications involving quantities that grow continuously over time. The value of e is approximately 2.7183.[13] As before, increasing the frequency of compounding, in this case by compounding as frequently as possible, increases the future value of an investment.

APPLYING THE MODEL

To find the value at the end of two years of your $100 deposit in an account paying 8 percent annual interest compounded continuously, we substitute $n = 2$, $PV = \$100$, and $r = 0.08$ into Equation 3.13:

$$FV \text{ (continuous compounding)} = \$100 \times (e^{0.08\times2}) = \$100 \times 2.7183^{0.16}$$
$$= \$100 \times 1.1735 = \$117.35$$

The future value with continuous compounding therefore equals $117.35, which, as expected, is larger than the future value of interest compounded semiannually ($116.99) or quarterly ($117.17).[14] ■

---

[13] In one of the more esoteric uses of the Internet, the first 2 million digits of the number e appear at the URL http://antwrp .gsfc.nasa.gov/htmltest/rjn_dig.html. Only the first million will be covered on the exam.

[14] The Excel function for continuous compounding is "=exp(argument)." For example, suppose you want to calculate the future value of $100 compounded continuously for five years at 8 percent. To find this value in Excel, first calculate the value of $e^{(.08\times5)}$ using "=exp(.08*5)" and then multiply the result by $100.

Stated versus Effective Annual Interest Rates

Both consumers and businesses need to make objective comparisons of loan costs or investment returns over different compounding periods. In order to put interest rates on a common basis for comparison, we must distinguish between *stated* and *effective annual interest rates*. The **stated annual rate** is the contractual annual rate charged by a lender or promised by a borrower. The **effective annual rate (EAR)**, also known as the *true annual return,* is the annual rate of interest actually paid or earned. The effective annual rate reflects the impact of compounding frequency, whereas the stated annual rate does not. We can best illustrate the differences between stated and effective rates with numerical examples.

Using the notation introduced earlier, we can calculate the effective annual rate by substituting values for the stated annual rate (r) and the compounding frequency (m) into Equation 3.14:

$$EAR = \left(1 + \frac{r}{m}\right)^m - 1 \qquad \text{(Eq. 3.14)}$$

We can apply this equation using data from preceding examples.

APPLYING THE MODEL

You wish to find the effective annual rate associated with an 8 percent stated annual rate ($r = 0.08$) when interest is compounded annually ($m = 1$); semiannually ($m = 2$); and quarterly ($m = 4$). Substituting these values into Equation 3.14 obtains the following results:

For annual compounding:

$$EAR = \left(1 + \frac{0.08}{1}\right)^1 - 1 = (1 + 0.08)^1 - 1 = 1.08 - 1 = 0.08 = 8.0\%$$

For semiannual compounding:

$$EAR = \left(1 + \frac{0.08}{2}\right)^2 - 1 = (1 + 0.04)^2 - 1 = 1.0816 - 1 = 0.0816 = 8.16\%$$

For quarterly compounding:

$$EAR = \left(1 + \frac{0.08}{4}\right)^4 - 1 = (1 + 0.02)^4 - 1 = 1.0824 - 1 = 0.0824 = 8.24\%$$

The results mean that 8 percent compounded quarterly is equivalent to 8.24 percent compounded annually. These values demonstrate two important points: (1) the stated and effective rates are equivalent for annual compounding, and (2) the effective annual rate increases with increasing compounding frequency.

Not surprisingly, the maximum effective annual rate for a given stated annual rate occurs when interest compounds continuously. The effective annual rate for this extreme case can be found by using the following equation:

$$EAR \text{ (continuous compounding)} = e^r - 1 \qquad \text{(Eq. 3.14a)}$$

For the 8 percent stated annual rate ($r = 0.08$), substitution into Equation 3.14a results in an effective annual rate of 8.33 percent, as follows:

$$e^{.08} - 1 = 1.0833 - 1 = .0833 = 8.33\%$$

At the consumer level in the United States, "truth-in-lending laws" *require disclosure* on credit cards and loans of the **annual percentage rate (APR)**. The *APR* is the *stated annual rate* found by multiplying the periodic rate by the number of periods in one year. For example, a bank credit card that charges 1.5 percent per month would have an *APR* of 18 percent (1.5% per month $\times$ 12 months per year). However, the actual cost of this credit card account can be determined by calculating the **annual percentage yield (APY)**, which is the same as the *effective annual rate*.[15] For the credit card example, 1.5 percent per month interest has an effective annual rate of $[(1.015)^{12} \times 1] = 0.1956$, or 19.56 percent. If the stated rate is 1.75 percent per month, as is the case with many U.S. credit card accounts, the *APY* is a whopping 23.14 percent. In other words, if you are carrying a positive credit card balance with an interest rate like this, pay it off as soon as possible!

DEPOSITS NEEDED TO ACCUMULATE A FUTURE SUM

Suppose that a firm or a person wishes to determine the annual deposit necessary to accumulate a certain amount of money at some point in the future. Assume that you want to buy a house five years from now and estimate that an initial down payment of $20,000 will be required at that time. You wish to make equal end-of-year deposits into an account paying annual interest of 6 percent, so you must determine what size annuity will result in a lump sum equal to $20,000 at the end of year 5. The solution can be derived from the equation for finding the future value of an ordinary annuity.

Earlier in this chapter, we found the future value of an *n*-year ordinary annuity (*FV*) by applying Equation 3.4. Solving that equation for *PMT*, in this case the annual deposit, we get equation 3.15:

$$PMT = \frac{FV}{\left\{ \dfrac{[(1 + r)^n - 1]}{r} \right\}} \qquad \text{(Eq. 3.15)}$$

Once this is done, we have only to substitute the known values of *FV*, *r*, and *n* into the right-hand side of the equation to find the annual deposit required.

APPLYING THE MODEL

We can demonstrate the calculation using the situation in which you wish to determine the equal annual end-of-year deposits required to accumulate $20,000 (*FV*) at the end of five years ($n = 5$), given an interest rate of 6 percent ($r = 6\%$), as follows:

$$PMT = \frac{\$20,000}{\left\{ \dfrac{[(1.06)^5 - 1]}{0.06} \right\}} = \$3,547.93$$

[15.] Note that the U.S. "truth-in-savings laws" *require disclosure* of the *APY* on savings deposits. Clearly, under current law, interest rates on savings are quoted in a more financially accurate way (*APY*) than are the rates charged on credit cards and loans (*APR*).

In addition to using algebra, you can use the future value annuity factor to calculate the amount of deposit. Note that the denominator of Equation 3.15 is equivalent to the future value factor for a 6 percent, 5-year annuity, which Table A3 shows as $FVFA_{6\%,5} = 5.637$. Dividing the future amount needed ($FV = \$20,000$) by this factor again gives (except for rounding) an annual cash flow of $3,547.99. The amount of the annual deposit can alternatively be found directly using either a financial calculator or spreadsheet, as shown below.

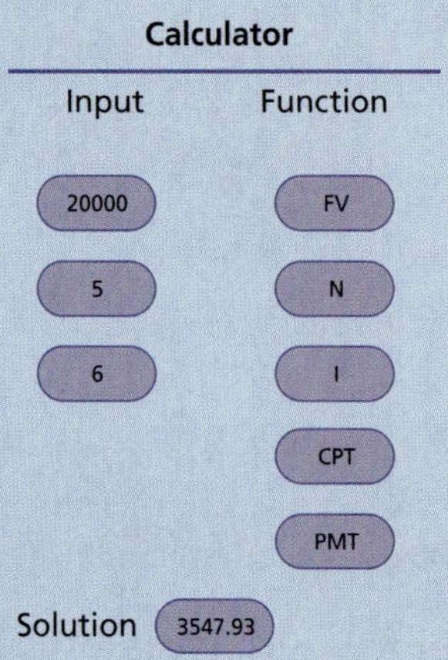

Calculator

Input	Function
20000	FV
5	N
6	I
	CPT
	PMT

Solution: 3547.93

Spreadsheet

Column / Row	A	B
1	Future value	$20,000
2	Number of periods	5
3	Interest rate	6%
4	**Payment**	**$3,547.93**
5	*Formula B4:* Pmt(B3,B2,0,B1)	

LOAN AMORTIZATION

Loan amortization refers to a situation in which a borrower makes equal periodic payments over time to fully repay a loan. For instance, with a conventional, 30-year home mortgage, the borrower makes the same payment each month for 30 years until the mortgage is completely repaid. To amortize a loan (i.e., to calculate the periodic payment that pays off the loan), you must know the total amount of the loan (the amount borrowed), the term of the loan, the frequency of periodic payments, and the interest rate. To be more specific, the loan amortization process involves finding a level stream of payments (over the term of the loan) with a present value equal to the amount borrowed. Lenders use a **loan amortization schedule** to determine these payments and the allocation of each payment to interest and principal.

For example, suppose that you borrow $25,000 at 8 percent annual interest for five years to purchase a new car. To demonstrate the basic approach, we first amortize this loan assuming that you make payments at the end of years 1 through 5. We will then modify the annual formula to compute the more typical monthly auto loan payments. To find the size of the annual payments, the lender determines the amount of a 5-year annuity discounted at 8 percent that has a present value of $25,000. This process is actually the inverse of finding the present value of an annuity.

Earlier, we found the present value (*PV*) of an *n*-year ordinary annuity using Equation 3.7. Solving this equation for *PMT*, the annual loan payment, we get Equation 3.16:

$$PMT = \frac{PV}{\left\{ \dfrac{1}{r} \times \left[1 - \dfrac{1}{(1+r)^n} \right] \right\}} \qquad \text{(Eq. 3.16)}$$

APPLYING THE MODEL

To find the annual payment required on the 5-year, $25,000 loan with an 8 percent annual rate, we have only to substitute the known values of *PV* = $25,000, *r* = 0.08, and *n* = 5 into the right-hand side of the equation:

$$PMT = \frac{\$25,000}{\left\{ \dfrac{1}{0.08} \times \left[1 - \dfrac{1}{(1.08)^5} \right] \right\}} = \$6,261.41$$

Five annual payments of $6,261.41 will thus be needed to fully amortize this $25,000 loan. ▪

As before, we can also calculate the annual cash flow (*PMT*) by recognizing that the denominator of Equation 3.16 is equal to the present value factor of an *r* percent, *n*-year annuity ($PVFA_{r\%,n}$). Because Table A4 shows $PVFA_{8\%,5} = 3.993$, we again determine that the payment required to fully amortize this loan is $6,260.96 (slight rounding difference) per year (*PMT* = $25,000 ÷ 3.993). The amount of the annual loan payment can alternatively be found directly using either a financial calculator or spreadsheet, as shown below.

Calculator

Input	Function
25000	PV
5	N
8	I
	CPT
	PMT

Solution   6261.41

Spreadsheet

Row \ Column	A	B
1	Present Value	$25,000
2	Number of periods	5
3	Interest rate	8%
4	**Payment**	**$6,261.41**
5	*Formula B4:* Pmt(B3,B2,B1)	

Table 3.6
Loan Amortization
Schedule for $25,000
Principal, 8 Percent
Interest, 5-Year
Repayment Period

End of Year	Loan Payment (1)	Beginning-of-Year Principal (2)	Payments Interest [0.08 × (2)] (3)	Payments Principal [(1) − (3)] (4)	End-of-Year Principal [(2) − (4)] (5)
1	$6,261.41	$25,000.00	$2,000.00	$4,261.41	$20,738.59
2	6,261.41	20,738.59	1,659.09	4,602.32	16,136.27
3	6,261.41	16,136.27	1,290.90	4,970.51	11,165.76
4	6,261.41	11,165.76	893.26	5,368.15	5,797.61
5	6,261.41	5,797.61	463.81	5,797.60	.01*

*This value should be zero, but due to rounding, an insignificant difference of 1 cent exists.

The allocation of each loan payment of $6,261.41 to interest and principal appears in columns 3 and 4 of the *loan amortization schedule* in Table 3.6. The portion of each payment representing interest (column 3) declines over the repayment period, and the portion going to principal repayment (column 4) increases. This pattern is typical of amortized loans; with level payments, the interest component declines as the principal falls, leaving a larger portion of each subsequent payment to repay principal.

Though computing amortized loan payments may seem a rather esoteric exercise, it is in fact the present value formulation that people use most frequently in their personal lives. In addition to calculating auto loan payments, it can be used to compute mortgage payments on a home purchase. These consumer loans typically require monthly payments, so we will now demonstrate how to do the amortization calculations using monthly rather than annual payments. First, Equation 3.16a is simply a modified version of Equation 3.16:

$$PMT = \frac{r}{[(1 + r)^n - 1]} \times (1 + r)^n \times PV \qquad \textbf{(Eq. 3.16a)}$$

Second, we can generalize this formula to more frequent compounding periods by dividing the interest rate by m and multiplying the number of compounding periods by m. This changes the equation as follows:

$$PMT = \frac{\dfrac{r}{m}}{\left[\left(1 + \dfrac{r}{m}\right)^{m \times n} - 1\right]} \times \left(1 + \frac{r}{m}\right)^{m \times n} \times PV \qquad \textbf{(Eq. 3.16b)}$$

APPLYING THE MODEL

We can use Equation 3.16b to calculate what our *monthly* car payment will be if we borrow $25,000 for five years at 8 percent annual interest. *PV* will again be the $25,000 amount borrowed, but the periodic interest rate ($r \div m$) will be 0.00667, or 0.667 percent per month (0.08 per year ÷ 12 months per year), and there will be $m \times n = 60$ compounding periods (12 months/year × 5 years = 60 months). Substituting these values into Equation 3.16b yields a monthly auto loan payment of $506.91:

$$PMT = \frac{\dfrac{0.08}{12}}{\left[\left(1 + \dfrac{0.08}{12}\right)^{12 \times 5} - 1\right]} \times \left(1 + \frac{0.08}{12}\right)^{12 \times 5} \times \$25{,}000$$

$$= \frac{0.00667}{[(1.00667)^{60} - 1]} \times (1.00667)^{60} \times \$25{,}000$$

$$= \$506.91$$

As a test of your command of the monthly payment formula, see if you can compute the monthly mortgage payment for a home purchased using a 30-year, \$100,000 loan with a fixed 7.5 percent annual interest rate. Note that there will be no fewer than 360 compounding periods (30 years × 12 months/year).[16]

---

12. What effect does increasing compounding frequency have on the (a) future value of a given deposit and (b) its *effective annual rate (EAR)*?

13. Under what condition would the stated annual rate equal the effective annual rate (*EAR*) for a given deposit? How do these rates relate to the *annual percentage rate (APR)* and *annual percentage yield (APY)*?

14. How would you determine the size of the annual end-of-year deposits needed to accumulate a given future sum at the end of a specified future period? What impact does the magnitude of the interest rate have on the size of the deposits needed?

15. What relationship exists between the calculation of the present value of an annuity and amortization of a loan? How can you find the amount of interest paid each year under an amortized loan?

Concept Review Questions

3.7 SUMMARY

- Financial managers can use future value and present value techniques to equate cash flows occurring at different times in order to compare decision alternatives. Managers rely primarily on present value techniques and commonly use financial calculators or spreadsheet programs to streamline their computations.
- The future value of a lump sum is found by applying compound interest to the present value (the initial investment) over the period of concern. The higher the interest rate and the further in the future the cash flow's value is measured, the higher its future value.
- The present value of a lump sum is found by discounting the future value at the given interest rate. It is the amount of money today that is equivalent to the given future amount, considering the rate of return that can be earned on the present value. The higher the interest rate and the further in the future the cash flow occurs, the lower its present value.

[16.] To find the solution, just enter the formula "=pmt(.00625,360,100000)" in Excel. The first argument in this function is the monthly interest rate, 7.5 percent divided by 12.

- The future value of any cash flow stream—mixed stream, ordinary annuity, or annuity due—is the sum of the future values of the individual cash flows. Future values of mixed streams are most difficult to find, whereas future values of annuities are easier to calculate because they have the same cash flow each period. The future value of an ordinary annuity (end-of-period cash flows) can be converted into the future value of an annuity due (beginning-of-period cash flows) by merely multiplying it by 1 plus the interest rate.
- The present value of a cash flow stream is the sum of the present values of the individual cash flows. The present value of a mixed stream is most difficult to find, whereas present values of annuities are easier to calculate because they have the same cash flow each period. The present value of an ordinary annuity can be converted to the present value of an annuity due by merely multiplying it by 1 plus the interest rate. The present value of an ordinary perpetuity—an infinite-lived annuity—is found by dividing the amount of the annuity by the interest rate.
- Some special applications of time value include compounding interest more frequently than annually, stated and effective annual rates of interest, deposits needed to accumulate a future sum, and loan amortization. The more frequently interest is compounded at a stated annual rate, the larger the future amount that will be accumulated and the higher the effective annual rate.
- The annual deposit needed to accumulate a given future sum is found by manipulating the future value of an annuity equation. Loan amortization—determination of the equal periodic payments necessary to fully repay loan principal and interest over a given time at a given interest rate—is performed by manipulating the present value of an annuity equation. An amortization schedule can be prepared to allocate each payment to principal and interest.

INTERNET RESOURCES

Note: *For updates to links, please go to the book's website at* http://smart.swcollege.com.

http://www.bankrate.com—Offers a variety of automated present and future value calculations, such as a loan amortization calculator and a tool that compares rebates and low-rate financing deals on automobiles

http://www.tcalc.com—Contains numerous financial calculators that can be purchased and added to a website

http://www.moneychimp.com—Can try the "How Finance Works" link to learn about many applications of present and future value mathematics; has a number of useful interactive graphs

http://www.financialplayerscenter.com—Provides helpful tutorials on time value concepts

KEY TERMS

annual percentage rate (APR)
annual percentage yield (APY)
annuity
annuity due
capitalizing
compound interest
continuous compounding
discounting

effective annual rate (EAR)
equilibrium interest rate
financial intermediaries
future value
Gordon growth model
growing perpetuity
liquidity
loan amortization

loan amortization schedule
mixed stream
net present value (*NPV*)
ordinary annuity
perpetuity
present value
principal

quarterly compounding
semiannual compounding
separation of investment and financing
simple interest
stated annual rate
time line
time value of money

QUESTIONS

3-1.   What is the importance for an individual of understanding time value of money concepts? For a corporate manager? Under what circumstance would the time value of money be irrelevant?

3-2.   From a time value of money perspective, explain why the maximization of shareholder wealth and the maximization of profits may not offer the same result or course of action.

3-3.   If a firm's required return were 0 percent, would time value of money matter? As these returns rise above 0 percent, what impact would the increasing return have on future value? Present value?

3-4.   What would happen to the future value of an annuity if interest rates fell in the late periods? Could the future value of an annuity factor formula still be used to determine the future value?

3-5.   What happens to the present value of a cash flow stream when the discount rate increases? Place this in the context of an investment. If the required return on an investment goes up but the expected cash flows do not change, would you be willing to pay the same price for the investment or would you pay more or less for this investment than before interest rates changed?

3-6.   Look at the formula for the present value of an annuity. What happens to the numerator as the number of periods increases? What distinguishes an annuity from a perpetuity? Why is there no future value of a perpetuity?

3-7.   What is the relationship between the variables in a loan amortization and the total interest cost? Consider the variables of interest rates, amount borrowed, down payment, prepayment, and term of loan in answering this question.

PROBLEMS

Future Value of a Lump Sum

3-1.   You have $1,500 to invest today at 7 percent interest compounded annually.

   a. How much will you have accumulated in the account at the end of the following number of years?
      1. Three years
      2. Six years
      3. Nine years
   b. Use your findings in part (a) to calculate the amount of interest earned in
      1. the first three years (years 1 to 3)
      2. the second three years (years 3 to 6)
      3. the third three years (years 6 to 9)
   c. Compare and contrast your findings in part (b). Explain why the amount of interest earned increases in each succeeding 3-year period.

Present Value of a Lump Sum

3-2. An Indiana state savings bond can be converted to $100 at maturity six years from purchase. If the state bonds are to be competitive with U.S. savings bonds, which pay 8 percent annual interest (compounded annually), at what price must the state sell its bonds? Assume no cash payments on savings bonds prior to redemption.

3-3. You just won a lottery that promises to pay you $1 million exactly 10 years from to-day. Because the $1 million payment is guaranteed by the state in which you live, op-portunities exist to sell the claim today for an immediate lump-sum cash payment.

    a. What is the least you will sell your claim for if you could earn the following rates of return on similar-risk investments during the 10-year period?
      1. 6 percent
      2. 9 percent
      3. 12 percent
    b. Rework part (a) under the assumption that the $1 million payment will be received in 15 rather than 10 years.
    c. Based on your findings in parts (a) and (b), discuss the effect of both the size of the rate of return and the time until receipt of payment on the present value of a future sum.

Future Value of Cash Flow Streams

3-4. Dixon Shuttleworth has been offered the choice of three retirement-planning invest-ments. The first investment offers a 5 percent return for the first 5 years, a 10 percent return for the next 5 years, and a 20 percent return thereafter. The second investment offers 10 percent for the first 10 years and 15 percent thereafter. The third invest-ment offers a constant 12 percent rate of return. Determine, for each of the given number of years, which of these investments is the best for Dixon if he plans to make one payment today into one of these funds and plans to retire in the following num-ber of years.

    a. 15 years
    b. 20 years
    c. 30 years

3-5. Robert Blanding's employer offers its workers a two-month paid sabbatical evry seven years. Robert, who just started working for the firm, plans to spend his sab-batical touring Europe at an estimated cost of $25,000. To finance his trip, Robert plans to make six annual deposits of $2,500 each, starting one year from now, into an investment account earning 8% interest.

    a. Will Robert's account balance in seven years be enough to pay for his trip?
    b. Suppose Robert increases his annual contribution to $3,150. How large will his account balance be in seven years?

3-6. Robert Williams is considering an offer to sell his medical practice, allowing him to retire five years early. He has been offered $500,000 for his practice and can invest this amount in an account earning 10 percent per year, compounded annually. If the practice is expected to generate the following cash flows, should Robert accept this offer and retire now?

End of Year	Cash Flow
1	$150,000
2	150,000
3	125,000
4	125,000
5	100,000

3-7. Gina Coulson has just contracted to sell a small parcel of land that she inherited a few years ago. The buyer is willing to pay $24,000 at closing of the transaction or will pay the amounts shown in the following table at the *beginning* of each of the next five years. Because Gina doesn't really need the money today, she plans to let it accumulate in an account that earns 7 percent annual interest. Given her desire to buy a house at the end of five years after closing on the sale of the lot, she decides to choose the payment alternative—$24,000 lump sum or mixed stream of payments in the following table—that provides the highest future value at the end of five years.

Mixed Stream	
Beginning of Year (t)	Cash Flow (CF_t)
1	$ 2,000
2	4,000
3	6,000
4	8,000
5	10,000

a. What is the future value of the lump sum at the end of year 5?

b. What is the future value of the mixed stream at the end of year 5?

c. Based on your findings in parts (a) and (b), which alternative should Gina take?

d. If Gina could earn 10 percent rather than 7 percent on the funds, would your recommendation in part (c) change? Explain.

3-8. For the following questions, assume an annual annuity of $1,000 and a required return of 12 percent.

a. What is the future value of an ordinary annuity for 10 years?

b. If you earned an additional year's worth of interest on this annuity, what would be the future value?

c. What is the future value of a 10-year annuity due?

d. What is the relationship between your answers in parts (b) and (c)? Explain.

3-9. Kim Edwards and Chris Phillips are both newly minted 30-year old MBAs. Kim plans to invest $1,000 per month into her 401(k) beginning next month, while Chris intends to invest $2,000 per month, but he does not plan to begin investing until 10 years after Kim begins investing. Both Kim and Chris will retire at age 67, and the 401(k) plan averages a 12 percent annual return, compounded monthly. Who will have more 401(k) money at retirement?

Present Value of Cash Flow Streams

3-10. Given the mixed streams of cash flows shown in the following table, answer parts (a) and (b):

	Cash Flow Stream	
Year	A	B
1	$ 50,000	$ 10,000
2	40,000	20,000
3	30,000	30,000
4	20,000	40,000
5	10,000	50,000
Totals	$150,000	$150,000

a. Find the present value of each stream, using a 15 percent discount rate.

b. Compare the calculated present values, and discuss them in light of the fact that the undiscounted total cash flows amount to $150,000 in each case.

3-11. As part of your personal budgeting process, you have determined that in each of the next five years you will have budget shortfalls. In other words, you will need the amounts shown in the following table at the end of the given year to balance your budget—that is, inflows equal outflows. You expect to be able to earn 8 percent on your investments during the next five years and wish to fund the budget shortfalls over these years with a single initial deposit.

End of Year	Budget Shortfall
1	$ 5,000
2	4,000
3	6,000
4	10,000
5	3,000

a. How large must the lump-sum deposit be today into an account paying 8 percent annual interest to provide for full coverage of the anticipated budget shortfall?

b. What effect would an increase in your earnings rate have on the amount calculated in part (a)? Explain.

3-12. Ruth Nail has just received two offers for her seaside home. The first offer is for $1 million today. The second offer is for an owner-financed sale with a payment schedule as follows:

End of Year	Payment
0 (Today)	$200,000
1	200,000
2	200,000
3	200,000
4	200,000
5	300,000

Assuming no differential tax treatment between the two options and that Ruth earns a rate of 8 percent on her investments, which offer should she take?

3-13. Melissa Gould wants to invest today in order to assure adequate funds for her son's college education. She estimates that her son will need $20,000 at the end of 18 years; $25,000 at the end of 19 years; $30,000 at the end of 20 years; and $40,000 at the end of 21 years. How much will Melissa have to invest in a fund today if the fund earns the following interest rate?

a. 6 percent per year with annual compounding

b. 6 percent per year with quarterly compounding

c. 6 percent per year with monthly compounding

3-14. Assume that you just won the state lottery. Your prize can be taken either in the form of $40,000 at the end of each of the next 25 years (i.e., $1 million over 25 years) or as a lump sum of $500,000 paid immediately.

a. If you expect to be able to earn 5 percent annually on your investments over the next 25 years, ignoring taxes and other considerations, which alternative should you take? Why?

b. Would your decision in part (a) be altered if you could earn 7 percent rather than 5 percent on your investments over the next 25 years? Why?

c. On a strict economic basis, at approximately what earnings rate would you be indifferent when choosing between the two plans?

3-15. For the following questions, assume an end-of-year cash flow of $250 and a 10 percent discount rate.

a. What is the present value of a single cash flow?

b. What is the present value of a 5-year annuity?

c. What is the present value of a 10-year annuity?

d. What is the present value of a 100-year annuity?

e. What is the present value of a $250 perpetuity?

f. Do you detect a relationship between the number of periods of an annuity and its resemblance to a perpetuity?

3-16. Use the following table of cash flows to answer parts (a)–(c). Assume an 8 percent discount rate.

End of Year	Cash Flow
1	$10,000
2	10,000
3	10,000
4	12,000
5	12,000
6	12,000
7	12,000
8	15,000
9	15,000
10	15,000

a. Solve for the present value of the cash flow stream by summing the present value of each individual cash flow.

b. Now, solve for the present value by summing the present value of the three separate annuities (one current and two deferred).

c. Which method is better for a long series of cash flows with embedded annuities?

3-17. Joan Wallace, corporate finance specialist for Big Blazer Bumpers, has been charged with the responsibility of funding an account to cover anticipated future warranty costs. Warranty costs are expected to be $5 million per year for three years, with the first costs expected to occur four years from today. How much will Joan have to place into an account today earning 10 percent per year to cover these expenses?

3-18. Landon Lowman, star quarterback of the university football team, has been approached about forgoing his last two years of eligibility and making himself available for the professional football draft. Talent scouts estimate that Landon could receive a signing bonus of $1 million today along with a 5-year contract for $3 million per year (payable at the end of the year). They further estimate that he could negotiate a contract for $5 million per year for the remaining seven years of his career. The scouts believe, however, that Landon will be a much higher draft pick if he improves by playing out his eligibility. If he stays at the university, he is expected to receive a $2 million signing bonus in two years along with a 5-year contract for $5 million per year. After that, the scouts expect Landon to obtain a 5-year contract for $6 million per year to take him into retirement. Assume that Landon can earn a 10 percent return over this time. Should Landon stay or go?

3-19. Matt Sedgwick, facilities and operations manager for the Birmingham Buffalo professional football team, has come up with an idea for generating income. Matt wants to expand the stadium by building skyboxes sold with lifetime (perpetual) season tickets. Each skybox will be guaranteed 10 season tickets at a cost of $200 per ticket per year for life. If each skybox costs $100,000 to build, what is the minimum selling price that Matt will have to charge for the skyboxes to break even, if the required return is 10 percent?

3-20. Log on to Hugh Chou's financial calculator web page (http://www.interest.com/ hugh/calc/simple.org), and look over the various calculator links available. Refer back to some of the earlier time value problems, and rework them with these calculators. Now, run through several numerical scenarios to determine the impact of changing variables on your results.

Special Applications of Time Value

3-21. You plan to invest $2,000 in an individual retirement arrangement (IRA) today at a *stated interest rate* of 8 percent, which is expected to apply to all future years.

a. How much will you have in the account at the end of 10 years if interest is compounded as follows?

1. Annually

2. Semiannually

3. Daily (assume a 360-day year)

4. Continuously

b. What is the effective annual rate (*EAR*) for each compounding period in part (a)?

c. How much greater will your IRA account balance be at the end of 10 years if interest is compounded continuously rather than annually?

d. How does the compounding frequency affect the future value and effective annual rate for a given deposit? Explain in terms of your findings in parts (a)–(c).

3-22. Jason Spector has shopped around for the best interest rates for his investment of $10,000 over the next year. He has found the following:

Stated Rate	Compounding
6.10%	Annual
5.90%	Semiannual
5.85%	Monthly

a. Which investment offers Jason the highest effective rate of return?

b. Now, assume that Jason wishes to invest his money for only six months and the annual compounded rate of 6.10 percent is not available. Which of the remaining investments should Jason choose?

3-23. Answer parts (a)–(c) for each of the following cases.

Case	Amount of Initial Deposit ($)	Stated Annual Rate, *r* (%)	Compounding Frequency, *m* (times/year)	Deposit Period (years)
A	2,500	6	2	5
B	50,000	12	6	3
C	1,000	5	1	10
D	20,000	16	4	6

a. Calculate the future value at the end of the specified deposit period.

b. Determine the effective annual rate (*EAR*).

c. Compare the stated annual rate (*r*) to the effective annual rate(*EAR*). What relationship exists between compounding frequency and the stated and effective annual rates?

3-24. Tara Cutler is newly married and is now preparing a surprise gift of a trip to Europe for her husband on their tenth anniversary. Tara plans to invest $5,000 per year until that anniversary and plans to make her first $5,000 investment on their first anniversary. If she earns an 8 percent rate on her investments, how much will she have saved for their trip if the interest is compounded in each of the following ways?

a. Annually

b. Quarterly

c. Monthly

3-25. John Tye has just been hired as the new corporate finance analyst at I-Ell Enterprises and has received his first assignment. John is to take the $25 million in cash received from a recent divestiture and use part of these proceeds to retire an outstanding $10 million bond issue and the remainder to repurchase common stock. However, the bond issue cannot be retired for another two years. If John can place the funds necessary to retire this $10 million debt into an account earning 6 percent compounded *monthly*, how much of the $25 million remains to repurchase stock?

3-26. Find the present value of a 3-year, $20,000 ordinary annuity deposited into an account that pays 12 percent interest, compounded *monthly*. Solve for the present value of the annuity in the following ways:

a. As three single cash flows discounted at the stated rate of interest

b. As three single cash flows discounted at the appropriate effective rate of interest

c. As a 3-year annuity discounted at the effective rate of interest

3-27. To supplement your planned retirement in exactly 42 years, you estimate that you need to accumulate $220,000 by the end of 42 years from today. You plan to make equal annual end-of-year deposits into an account paying 8 percent annual interest.

a. How large must the annual deposits be to create the $220,000 fund by the end of 42 years?

b. If you can afford to deposit only $600 per year into the account, how much will you have accumulated by the end of the forty-second year?

3-28. Determine the annual payment required to fund a future annual annuity of $12,000 per year. You will fund this future liability over the next five years, with the first payment to occur one year from today. The future $12,000 liability will last for four years, with the first payment to occur seven years from today. If you can earn 8 percent on this account, how much will you have to deposit each year over the next five years to fund the future liability?

3-29. Mary Sullivan, capital outlay manager for Waxy Widgets, has been instructed to establish a contingency fund to cover the expenses over the next two years (24 months) associated with repairing defective widgets from a new production process. Waxy Widgets' controller wants to make equal monthly cash deposits into this fund. If Mary faces the following monthly repair costs and has $1 million to start the fund today, what will be her *monthly payments* into the fund in order to assume that all repair costs will be covered? Mary will make her first payment one month from today, and the fund will earn 6 percent, compounded monthly.

Months	Repair Costs per Month
1–4	$500,000
5–12	250,000
13–24	100,000

3-30. Craig and LaDonna Allen are trying to establish a college fund for their son Spencer, who just turned three today. They plan for Spencer to withdraw $10,000 on his eighteenth birthday and $11,000, $12,000, and $15,000 on his subsequent birthdays. They plan to fund these withdrawals with a 10-year annuity, with the first payment to occur one year from today, and expect to earn an average annual return of 8 percent.

a. How much will the Allens have to contribute each year to achieve their goal?

b. Create a schedule showing the cash inflows (including interest) and outflows of this fund. How much remains on Spencer's twenty-first birthday?

3-31. Joan Messineo borrowed $15,000 at a 14 percent annual interest rate to be repaid over three years. The loan is amortized into three equal annual end-of-year payments.

a. Calculate the annual end-of-year loan payment.

b. Prepare a loan amortization schedule showing the interest and principal breakdown of each of the three loan payments.

c. Explain why the interest portion of each payment declines with the passage of time.

3-32. You are planning to purchase a building for $40,000, and you have $10,000 to apply as a down payment. You may borrow the remainder under the following terms: a 10-year loan with semiannual repayments and a stated interest rate of 6 percent. You intend to make $6,000 payments, applying the excess over your required payment to the reduction of the principal balance.

a. Given these terms, how long (in years) will it take you to fully repay your loan?

b. What will be your total interest cost?

c. What would your interest cost be if you made no prepayments and repaid your loan by strictly adhering to the terms of the loan?

3-33. Use a spreadsheet to create amortization schedules for the following five scenarios. What happens to the total interest paid under each scenario?

  a. Scenario 1:

     Loan amount: $1 million

     Annual rate: 5 percent

     Term: 360 months

     Prepayment: $0

  b. Scenario 2: Same as 1, except annual rate is 7 percent
  c. Scenario 3: Same as 1, except term is 180 months
  d. Scenario 4: Same as 1, except prepayment is $250 per month
  e. Scenario 5: Same as 1, except loan amount is $125,000

3-34. Go to the home page of the Bankrate.com (http://www.bankrate.com), and obtain current average mortgage rates. With this information, go to Hugh Chou's mortgage calculator (http://www.interest.com/hugh/calc/simple.org). Provide the requested variables to create an amortization schedule. Now, re-create the schedule with different prepayment amounts. What impact does the prepayment have on total interest and the term of the loan?

3-35. To analyze various retirement-planning options, check out the financial calculator at Bloomberg (http://www.bloomberg.com). Determine the effect of waiting versus immediate planning for retirement. What is the impact of changing interest-rate assumptions on your retirement "nest egg"?

3-36. For excellent qualitative discussions of the value of compounded interest on saving for future (retirement) obligations, see the following websites:

  http://www.prudential.com/retirement (Prudential Financial)

  http://www.vanguard.com (The Vanguard Group)

  http://www.fid-inv.com (Fidelity Investments)

  http://www.bloomberg.com (Bloomberg)

  What can you conclude about the timing of cash flows and future values available for retirement, considering the information provided on these websites?

APPENDIX 3A: ADDITIONAL APPLICATIONS OF TIME VALUE TECHNIQUES

As you have probably already guessed, there are a vast number of applications of time value techniques in modern finance. All are variations of the basic future value and present value formulas described in the text of Chapter 3. We expand our repertoire of computational methods in this appendix to discuss two of the most important specialized uses of time value techniques: determining (1) implied interest or growth rates and (2) the number of compounding periods.

IMPLIED INTEREST OR GROWTH RATES

Analysts often need to calculate the compound annual interest or *growth rate* (annual rate of change in values) of a series of cash flows. Because the calculations required for finding interest rates and growth rates, given known cash flow streams, are the same, this section refers to the calculations as those required to find interest or growth rates. We examine each of three possible cash flow patterns: lump sums, annuities, and mixed streams.

Lump Sums

The simplest situation is one in which a person wishes to find the interest or growth rate of a single cash flow over time. As an example, assume that you invested $1,000 in a stock mutual fund in December 1999 and this investment now, in December 2004, is worth $2,150. What was your compound annual rate of return over this 5-year period? As it happens, this is easy to determine, because we are unconcerned about the investment's value during any of the intervening years. We simply wish to determine what compound rate of return (r) converted a $1,000 investment ($PV$) into a future amount ($FV$) worth $2,150 in five years ($n$). Note that the number of years of growth (or interest) is the difference between the latest and earliest year number. In this case, n = 2004 - 1999 = 5 years. Although the period 1999 through 2004 includes six years, there are only five years of growth because the earliest year (1999) serves as the base year (i.e., time 0) and is then followed by five years of change: 1999 to 2000, 2000 to 2001, 2001 to 2002, 2002 to 2003, and 2003 to 2004. Finding r involves manipulating Equation 3.1 so that we have the value to be determined, in this case $(1 + r)^n$, on the left-hand side of the equation and the two known values, PV and FV, on the right-hand side of the equation, as shown in Equation 3.17:

$$(1 + r)^n = \frac{FV}{PV}$$

(Eq. 3.17)

Substituting in the known values, we obtain the following:

$$(1 + r)^5 = \frac{\$2,150}{\$1,000} = 2.150$$

This says that 1 plus the rate of return $(1 + r)$, compounded for five years (n = 5), equals 2.150. Our final step is to calculate the fifth root of 2.150, which can be done simply by raising 2.150 to the one-fifth power using the y^x key on a financial calculator, and then subtract 1:

$$r = (2.150)^{0.20} - 1 = 1.1654 - 1 = 0.1654 = 16.54\% \text{ per year}$$

A financial calculator or spreadsheet could be used to more directly solve for a growth or interest rate of a lump sum as demonstrated in the following example. (Note: The PV and FV values must be input with opposite signs.)

Calculator

Input	Function
1000	PV
−2150	FV
5	N
	CPT
	I

Solution: 16.54

Spreadsheet

Row \ Column	A	B
1	Present value	$1,000
2	Future value	−$2,150
3	Number of years	5
4	Interest rate	16.54%
5	Formula B4: RATE(B3,0,B1,B2)	

Annuities

Sometimes you may need to find the interest rate associated with an annuity, which represents the equal annual end-of-year payments on a loan. To demonstrate, assume that your friend John Jacobs can borrow $2,000 to be repaid in equal annual end-of-year amounts of $514.18 for the next five years. He wants to find the interest rate on the loan and asks you for assistance. You realize that he is really asking you an annuity valuation question, so you use a variant of the present value of an annuity formula shown in Equation 3.7:

$$PV = PMT \times \left\{ \frac{1}{r} \times \left[1 - \frac{1}{(1 + r)^n} \right] \right\}$$

You are trying to determine the interest rate (r) that will equate the present value of a 5-year annuity ($PV = \$2,000$) to a stream of five equal annual payments ($PMT = \$514.18$ per year). Because you know PV and PMT, you can rearrange Equation 3.7, putting the unknown value on the left-hand side and the known values on the right:

$$\left\{ \left[\frac{1}{r} \right] \times \left[1 - \frac{1}{(1 + r)^n} \right] \right\} = \frac{PV}{PMT} = \frac{\$2,000}{\$514.18} = 3.8897$$

Unfortunately, the term on the left-hand side is very difficult to solve directly, but there is an easy shortcut to obtain the solution. Equation 3.7 can also be expressed using present value factors as the annual cash flow (PMT) times the present value factor for an annuity paying r percent for n years, or $PVFA_{r\%,n}$, which is the unknown value on the left-hand side of the preceding equation. Substituting, we get the following:

$$PVFA_{r\%,5} = \frac{PV}{PMT} = \frac{\$2,000}{\$514.18} = 3.8897$$

We can then solve this equation by determining the appropriate 5-year $PVFA$ having a value of 3.8897. Table A4 in Appendix A shows that $PVFA_{9\%,5} = 3.890$, so we can tell John Jacobs that he is being charged about 9 percent on his loan.

A financial calculator or spreadsheet could be used to more directly solve for a growth or interest rate of an annuity as demonstrated in the following example. (Note: The PV and PMT values must be input with opposite signs.)

Calculator		
Input	Function	
2000	PV	
−514.18	PMT	
5	N	
	CPT	
	I	
Solution	9.00	

Spreadsheet		
Column / Row	A	B
1	Present value	$2,000
2	Payment	−$514.18
3	Number of periods	5
4	Interest rate	9.00%
5	Formula B4: RATE(B3,B2,B1)	

Mixed Streams

As demonstrated in the previous discussion, finding the unknown interest or growth rate for a lump sum or an annuity is relatively simple using the formulas presented here, present value tables, or a financial calculator or spreadsheet. Finding the unknown interest or growth rate for a mixed stream is very difficult to do using formulas or present value tables. It can be accomplished by using an iterative trial-and-error approach to find the interest rate that would cause the present value of the stream's inflows to just equal the present value of its outflows. This calculation is often referred to as finding the *yield-to-maturity* or *internal rate of return (IRR)*. A much more attractive way to make this type of calculation is to use a financial calculator or spreadsheet that has the IRR function built into it. With such an approach, an analyst can input (with all outflows input as negative numbers) all the cash flows—both outflows and inflows—and then use the IRR function to calculate the unknown interest rate. Because this approach is discussed and demonstrated in Chapter 4 with regard to bonds and in Chapter 7 with regard to its use in capital budgeting, detailed description of its application is not included here.

NUMBER OF COMPOUNDING PERIODS

Occasionally, for either a lump sum or an annuity, the financial analyst wishes to calculate the unknown number of time periods necessary to achieve a given cash flow goal. We briefly consider this calculation here for both lump sums and annuities.

Lump Sums

If the present (PV) and future (FV) amounts are known along with the interest rate (r), we can calculate the number of periods (n) necessary for the present amount to grow to equal the future amount. For example, assume that you plan to deposit $1,000 in an investment that is expected to earn an 8 percent annual rate of interest and you wish to determine how long it will take to triple your money (to accumulate $3,000). Stated differently, at an 8 percent annual interest rate, how many years (n) will it take for $1,000 ($PV$) to grow to $3,000 ($FV$)? This can be expressed simply by rearranging the basic future value formula, Equation 3.1, to express the unknown value, n, on the left-hand side and then plugging in the known values, FV, PV, and r:

$$FV = PV \times (1 + r)^n$$

$$(1 + 0.08)^n = \frac{FV}{PV} = \frac{\$3,000}{\$1,000} = 3.000$$

$$(1.08)^n = 3.000$$

Now what? How do we find the exponent value (n) that will turn 1.08 into 3.000? We do so by taking natural logarithms of both sides of this formula, and then expressing the unknown number of years (n) as a ratio of two log values, as follows:

$$\ln(1.08)^n = \ln(3.000)$$

$$n = \frac{\ln(3.000)}{\ln(1.08)} = \frac{1.0986}{0.0770} = 14.275$$

We thus find the number of years to be 14.275, which means that at an 8 percent annual rate of interest, it will take about 14.3 years for your $1,000 deposit to triple in value to $3,000. A financial calculator or spreadsheet could be used to more directly solve for the unknown number of periods for a lump sum, as demonstrated below:

Calculator

Input	Function
1000	PV
8	I
−3000	FV
	CPT
	N

Solution   14.275

Spreadsheet

Column / Row	A	B
1	Present value	$1,000
2	Interest rate	8%
3	Future value	−$3,000
4	**Number of periods**	**14.275**
5	*Formula B4:* Nper(B2,0,B1,B3)	

Annuities

Occasionally we want to determine the unknown life (n) of an annuity that is intended to achieve a specified objective, such as to repay a loan of a given amount (PV) with a stated interest rate (r) and equal annual end-of-year payments (PMT). To illustrate, assume that you can borrow $20,000 at a 12 percent annual interest rate with annual end-of-year payments of $3,000, and you wish to determine how long it will take to fully repay the loan's interest and principal. In other words, how many years (n) will it take to repay a $20,000 ($PV$), 12 percent ($r$), loan if the payments of $3,000 ($PMT$) are made at the end of each year? You have probably already deduced that this is similar to the problem we addressed earlier in this appendix of determining the unknown interest rate in an annuity, except now we know that $r = 12$ percent and are trying to determine the number of years (n). We once again rearrange the equation that expresses the present value of an annuity (PV) as the product of its payment (PMT) and the present value factor for an annuity paying r percent for n years ($PVFA_{r\%,n}$).

$$PVFA_{12\%,n} = \frac{PV}{CF} = \frac{\$20,000}{\$3,000} = 6.6667$$

We can solve this by finding the 12 percent $PVFA$ value in Table A4 that most closely corresponds to 6.667, which is between 14 years ($PVFA_{12\%,14} = 6.628$) and 15 years ($PVFA_{12\%,15} = 6.811$). Using a financial calculator or spreadsheet as shown below, we find the number of years to be 14.20, which means that you will have to repay $3,000 at the end of each year for 14 years and about $600 (0.20 × $3,000) at the end of 14.20 years in order to fully repay the $20,000 loan at 12 percent.

Calculator

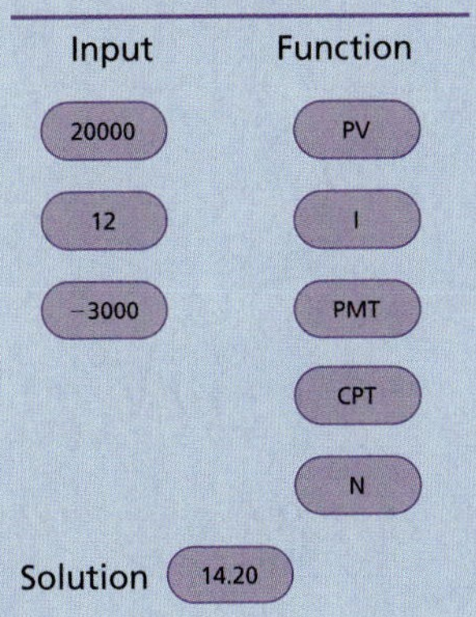

Input	Function
20000	PV
12	I
-3000	PMT
	CPT
	N

Solution   14.20

Spreadsheet

Column / Row	A	B
1	Present value	$20,000
2	Interest rate	12%
3	Payment	-$3,000
4	**Number of periods**	**14.20**
5	*Formula B4:* Nper(B2,B3,B1)	

3A1. How can you find the interest or growth rate for (a) a lump sum amount, (b) an annuity, and (c) a mixed stream?

3A2. How can you find the number of time periods needed to repay (a) a single-payment loan and (b) an installment loan requiring equal annual end-of-year payments?

Concept
Review
Questions

SUMMARY

- Implied interest or growth rates can be found using the basic future value equations for lump sums and annuities and require an iterative trial-and-error approach for mixed streams. Using a financial calculator or spreadsheet can greatly simplify these calculations.
- Given present and future cash flows and the applicable interest rate, the unknown number of periods can be found using the basic equations for future values of lump sums and annuities. Using a financial calculator or spreadsheet greatly simplifies these calculations.

PROBLEMS

Additional Applications of Time Value Techniques

3A-1. Find the rates of return required to do the following:

    a. Double an investment in 4 years

    b. Double an investment in 10 years

    c. Triple an investment in 4 years

    d. Triple an investment in 10 years

3A-2. You are given the series of cash flows shown in the following table.

	Cash Flows		
Year	A	B	C
1	$500	$1,500	$2,500
2	560	1,550	2,600
3	640	1,610	2,650
4	720	1,680	2,650
5	800	1,760	2,800
6		1,850	2,850
7		1,950	2,900
8			2,060
9			2,170
10			2,280

    a. Calculate the compound annual growth rate associated with each cash flow stream.

    b. If year-1 values represent initial deposits in a savings account paying annual interest, what is the annual rate of interest earned on each account?

    c. Compare and discuss the growth rate and interest rate found in parts (a) and (b), respectively.

3A-3. Determine the length of time required to double the value of an investment, given the following rates of return.

    a. 4 percent

    b. 10 percent

    c. 30 percent

    d. 100 percent

3A-4. You are the pension fund manager for Tanju's Toffees, and your CFO has just made a request of you. The CFO wants to know the minimum annual return required on the pension fund in order to make all required payments over the next five years and not diminish the current asset base. The fund currently has assets of $500 million.

a. Determine the required return if outflows are expected to exceed inflows by $50 million per year.

b. Determine the required return with the following fund cash flows.

End of Year	Inflows	Outflows
1	$55,000,000	$100,000,000
2	60,000,000	110,000,000
3	60,000,000	120,000,000
4	60,000,000	135,000,000
5	64,000,000	145,000,000

c. Consider the cash flows in part (b). What will happen to your asset base if you earn 10 percent? 20 percent?

3A-5. Jill Chew wishes to choose the best of four immediate retirement annuities available to her. In each case, in exchange for paying a single premium today, she will receive equal annual end-of-year cash benefits for a specified number of years. She considers the annuities to be equally risky and is not concerned about their differing lives. Her decision will be based solely on the rate of return she will earn on each annuity. The key terms of each of the four annuities are shown in the following table.

Annuity	Premium Paid Today	Annual Benefit	Life (years)
A	$30,000	$3,100	20
B	25,000	3,900	10
C	40,000	4,200	15
D	35,000	4,000	12

a. Calculate to the nearest 1 percent the rate of return on each of the four annuities Jill is considering.

b. Given Jill's stated decision criterion, which annuity would you recommend?

3A-6. Determine which of the following three investments offers you the highest rate of return on your $1,000 investment over the next five years.

Investment 1: $2,000 lump sum to be received in five years

Investment 2: $300 at the end of each of the next five years

Investment 3: $250 at the beginning of each of the next five years

a. Which investment offers the highest return?

b. Which offers the highest return if the payouts are doubled (i.e., $4,000, $600, and $500)?

c. What causes the big change in the returns on the annuities?

3A-7. Consider the following three investments of equal risk. Which offers the greatest rate of return?

End of Year	Investment		
	A	B	C
0	−$10,000	−$20,000	−$25,000
1	0	9,500	20,000
2	0	9,500	30,000
3	24,600	9,500	−12,600

3A-8. You plan to start saving for your son's college education. He will begin college when he turns 18 years old and will need $4,000 at that time and in each of the following three years. You will make a deposit at the end of this year in an account that pays 6 percent compounded annually, and an identical deposit at the end of each year, with the last deposit occurring when he turns 18. If an annual deposit of $1,484 will allow you to reach your goal, how old is your son now?

3A-9. Log on to MSN Money (http://www.investor.msn.com), and select five stocks to analyze. Use their returns over the last five years to determine the value of $1,000 invested in each stock five years ago. What is the compound annual rate of return for each of the five stocks over the 5-year period?

Smart Solutions
See the problem and solution explained step-by-step at
SMARTFinance

3A-10. The viatical industry offers a rather grim example of present value concepts. A firm in this business, called a viator, purchases the rights to the benefits from a life insurance contract from a terminally ill client. The viator may then sell claims on the insurance payout to other investors. The industry began in the early 1990s as a way to help AIDS patients capture some of the proceeds from their life insurance policies for living expenses.

Suppose a patient has a life expectancy of 18 months and a life insurance policy with a death benefit of $100,000. A viator pays $80,000 for the right to the benefit, and then sells that claim to another investor for $80,500.

a. From the point of view of the patient, this contract is like taking out a loan. What is the compound annual interest rate on the loan if the patient lives exactly 18 months? What if the patient lives 36 months?

b. From the point of view of the investor, this transaction is like lending money. What is the compound annual interest rate earned on the loan if the patient lives 18 months? What if the patient lives just 12 months?

4

Bond and Stock Valuation

OPENING FOCUS
Collateralizing Ziggy Stardust: Creating Bowie Bonds

What could 1970s glamour-rock icon David Bowie possibly have in common with the Prudential Insurance Company? Known through its advertising campaign as "the Rock," Prudential spent years cultivating an image of financial conservatism and security. Meanwhile, David Bowie was rising to stardom by releasing albums such as *The Rise and Fall of Ziggy Stardust and the Spiders from Mars,* and starring in cult films such as *The Man Who Fell to Earth.* Prudential and the orange-haired, androgynous Bowie seemed unlikely bedfellows. But in early 1997, Bowie made financial history by becoming the first rock star to issue bonds backed by the royalties on his albums. These "Bowie Bonds" promised to pay interest at a rate of 7.9 percent over 10 years using cash flow generated from the 25 albums that Bowie recorded prior to 1990. Recognizing the earning power of Bowie's music, Moody's Investor Services, one of the leading credit analysis firms in the world, assigned an investment-grade rating to the Bowie Bonds. Prudential purchased the entire bond issue for $55 million. For Prudential, the bonds offered an attractive interest rate (10-year Treasury bonds were paying about 6.4 percent interest at the time), as well as a substantial amount of free publicity. For Bowie, the transaction offered a way to immediately capture the present value ($55 million) of 10 years of future royalties. Other prominent musicians such as James Brown and the Isley Brothers soon followed suit by issuing their own royalty-backed bonds to investors. Even the famed wax museum in London, Madame Tussaud's, cashed in on the trend by selling bonds backed by future admissions.

Though they account for an almost infinitesimal fraction of the total bond market, Bowie Bonds illustrate a basic financial principle —the value of any financial instrument equals the present value of cash flows that investors expect the instrument to pay out over time. Asset-backed bonds, like the Bowie Bonds, distribute cash that is generated by the underlying assets. Some bonds, like Treasury bonds and ordinary corporate bonds, are backed only by the credibility of the entity that issues them. And some investments, such as common stock, offer only a vague promise to distribute cash to investors if the issuing firm generates sufficient cash flow. In each case, investors determine the value of the instrument by estimating the investment's future cash flows and discounting those cash flows to the present using an appropriate, risk-adjusted discount rate. This chapter explains how to apply that principle to value bonds and stocks.

Source: Kerry Capell, "Care to Buy Some David Bowie Bonds?" *Business Week* (International Edition, March 11, 2002).

In the popular imagination, "finance" is closely associated with markets for stocks, bonds, and other securities. References to the closing level of the Dow Jones Industrial Average, the Nikkei 225, the Financial Times Stock Exchange 100, and many other stock indexes form part of the daily routine for citizens of the world's largest economies, and most come to understand that these numbers can have a profound influence on their personal and professional lives. As more and more countries adopt market-oriented economic policies, the number of people whose lives are touched by security markets reaches into the billions. However, relatively few people understand the fundamental forces that determine security prices. Though we do not wish to understate the complexities of security valuation, a relatively straightforward framework exists that investors can use to value many types of financial assets, including bonds and stocks. This framework states that the value of any asset equals the present value of future benefits accruing to the asset's owner.

Our primary objective in this chapter is to describe the principal models commonly used to value debt and equity securities, beginning with the simplest discounted cash flow models. Why do corporate managers need to understand how to price bonds and stocks? First, firms must occasionally approach the bond and stock markets to raise capital for new investments. Understanding how investors in these markets value the firm's securities helps managers determine how to finance new projects. Second, firms periodically make investments by acquiring privately held companies, just as they unload past investments by selling divisions. In either case, knowing how the market values a firm guides a manager's expectations regarding the appropriate price for an acquisition or divestiture. Third, a company's stock price provides an external, independent performance assessment of top management, one that a diligent board of directors watches closely. Surely managers who will be judged (and compensated) based on the value of their firm's stock price need to understand the determinants of that price. Fourth, finance theory suggests that the objective of corporate management should be to maximize the stock price. How can managers take actions to maximize the stock price if they don't know what causes stock prices to be high or low?

This chapter presents an introduction to the process of security valuation. We begin by laying out the principles of valuation, principles that can be applied to a wide variety of valuation problems. Next, we use these principles by demonstrating simple methods for valuing bonds and stocks, making heavy use of the present value techniques covered in Chapter 3. These simple models enable analysts to make surprisingly accurate value estimates for several types of securities. However, when the simple models fail, analysts sometimes revert to rules of thumb or comparative valuation techniques to estimate security prices. We conclude the chapter with an overview of these comparative techniques, highlighting their strengths and weaknesses.

4.1 VALUATION FUNDAMENTALS

In a market economy, ownership of an asset confers the rights to the stream of benefits generated by the asset. These benefits may be tangible, like the interest payments on a government bond, or intangible, like the pleasure experienced from viewing a beautiful painting. Either way, *the value of any asset equals the present value of all its future benefits.* Finance theory focuses primarily on tangible benefits, typically the cash flows paid by an asset over time. The value of a bond equals the present value of future interest and principal payments to be paid by the borrower (issuer) to the lender (bondholder). The value of common stock equals the present value of future dividends and other cash payments that investors expect firms to distribute. The value of an apartment complex equals the present value of future rent payments net of the cost of operating and maintaining the property. In each case, the asset's worth is determined by the value today of the future benefits the asset is expected to convey to its owner.

This implies that pricing an asset requires knowledge of both its future benefits and the appropriate discount rate that converts future benefits into a present value. For some assets, such as U.S. government bonds, investors know what the future benefit stream will be with a high degree of certainty. For investments such as common stock, which give investors an ownership stake in a company, estimating the future benefit stream is quite challenging. Investors must consider how much cash the firm will generate now and in the future, how much of that cash the firm will reinvest to finance growth, and how much it will distribute to shareholders via dividends, share repurchases, or other means. Generally, *the greater the uncertainty about an asset's future benefits, the higher the discount rate investors will apply when discounting those benefits to the present.*

Consequently, the valuation process links an asset's risk and return to determine its price. Holding future benefits (returns) constant, an inverse relationship exists between risk and value. If two investments promise identical cash payments in the future, investors will pay a higher price for the one with the more credible promise. However, holding risk constant, a positive relationship exists between future benefits and value. Confronted with two equally risky assets, investors will pay more to acquire one of these if it offers higher future cash flows than the other. In equilibrium, riskier assets must offer higher returns to attract investors.[1]

The Fundamental Valuation Model

Chapters 5 and 6 present an in-depth analysis of the relationship between risk and return. For now, take as given the market's required rate of return on a specific investment. How does the market use that rate to determine the prices of different types of securities? Equation 4.1 expresses the fundamental valuation model mathematically as follows:

$$P_0 = \frac{CF_1}{(1+r)^1} + \frac{CF_2}{(1+r)^2} + \cdots + \frac{CF_n}{(1+r)^n} \qquad \text{(Eq. 4.1)}$$

[1.] This chapter emphasizes models that determine value by discounting future cash flows at an appropriate discount rate. In Chapter 18, we will examine a different approach to valuation known as *no-arbitrage pricing.* In essence, no-arbitrage pricing makes use of the fact that, in equilibrium, two assets that offer identical future benefit streams must sell for the same price. Otherwise, investors can make a risk-free profit by engaging in arbitrage, simultaneously buying and selling identical assets at different prices.

In this equation, P_0 represents the asset's price today (at time 0), CF_t represents the asset's expected cash flow at time t, and r is the required return—the discount rate that reflects the asset's risk. The letter n stands for the asset's life, the period over which it distributes cash flows to investors, usually measured in years. As you will see, n may be a finite number, as in the case of a bond that matures in a certain number of years, or it may be infinite, as in the case of a common stock with an indefinite life span. In either case, this equation provides us with a vehicle for valuing almost any type of asset. Consider the example in the following Applying the Model.

APPLYING THE MODEL

In the wake of the 1998 Master Settlement Agreement between state attorneys general and the tobacco industry, seven tobacco makers agreed to pay roughly $206 billion to the states over the next 25 years. States began to receive payments in 1999, but as the softening U.S. economy resulted in a reduction in state tax collections, many states looked for ways to cash in early on the tobacco lawsuit. "Tobacco bonds" were the solution. By selling the rights to their future tobacco settlement to investors who purchased tobacco bonds, states could capture the present value of future settlement proceeds immediately. Wisconsin closed its 2002–2003 budget shortfall by raising $1.6 billion in one such deal. How did the market determine the value of these tobacco bonds? Suppose that the settlement decreed that a particular state would receive $250 million per year for 20 years, and suppose that the market's required return on investments with this level of risk was 6.5 percent. The present value of this state's settlement proceeds was determined as follows:

$$P_0 = \frac{\$250 \text{ million}}{(1 + .065)^1} + \frac{\$250 \text{ million}}{(1 + .065)^2} + \cdots + \frac{\$250 \text{ million}}{(1 + .065)^{19}} + \frac{\$250 \text{ million}}{(1 + .065)^{20}}$$

$$= \$2.75 \text{ billion}$$

The state could sell bonds today worth $2.75 billion, using the settlement proceeds to repay bondholders over the next 20 years. In order to meet its needs for more immediate cash inflow, the state has effectively paid 6.5 percent annual interest to exchange its 20-year, $250 million annuity for an immediate $2.75 billion.   ■

With this simple framework in hand, we now turn to the problem of pricing bonds. Though bond-pricing techniques can get very complex, we will focus on "plain-vanilla" bonds, those that promise a fixed stream of cash payments over a finite time period. Among the largest issuers of such "fixed income" securities are national governments and large, multinational corporations.

Concept Review Questions

1. Why is it important for corporate managers to understand how bonds and stocks are priced?

2. Holding constant an asset's future benefit stream, what happens to the asset's price if its risk increases?

3. Holding constant an asset's risk, what happens to the asset's price if its future benefit stream increases?

4. Keeping in mind Equation 4.1, discuss how one might determine the price per acre of farmland in a particular region.

4.2 BOND VALUATION

BOND VOCABULARY

Bonds are debt instruments used by business and government to raise large sums of money, often from a diverse group of lenders. Though bonds come in many varieties, most bonds share certain basic characteristics. First, a bond promises to pay investors a fixed amount of interest, called the bond's **coupon.** Borrowers usually make coupon payments semiannually (every six months). Second, bonds typically have a limited life, or **maturity.** When the bond matures, the borrower repays investors a lump sum known as the bond's face value, or **par value,** often $1,000. Third, a bond's **coupon rate** is derived by dividing the bond's annual coupon payment by its par value. Fourth, a bond's **coupon yield** is obtained by dividing the bond's coupon by its current market price (which does not always equal its par value).[2] To illustrate, suppose that a firm issues a bond with a $1,000 par value and promises to pay investors $35 every six months over the life of the bond. The bond's *coupon* is $70 per year, and its *coupon rate* is 7 percent ($70 ÷ $1,000). If the current market value of this bond is $980, then its *coupon yield* is 7.14 percent ($70 ÷ $980).

Bonds can have a variety of additional features, such as a *call feature* that allows the issuer to redeem the bond at a predetermined price prior to maturity, or a *conversion feature* that grants bondholders the right to redeem their bonds for a predetermined number of shares in the borrowing firm. Chapter 17 discusses these and other features in detail. For now, we focus our attention on pricing ordinary bonds.

THE BASIC EQUATION (ASSUMING ANNUAL INTEREST)

Initially, for convenience, we will assume that bonds pay annual interest at a stated coupon rate, i, that M represents the bond's par or face value, that n is the number of years to the bond's maturity, and that r is the required return on the bond. As for any financial asset, the bond's price equals the present value of its future cash flows. The cash flows include two components: (1) the annual coupon, C, which equals the stated coupon rate, i, multiplied by M, the par value (that is, $C = i \times M$), received for each of the n years, and (2) the par value, M, received at maturity in n years. Equation 4.2 uses this notation to show that the bond's price is merely the sum of the present value of the interest cash flow stream plus the present value of its par value, typically $1,000.

$$\text{Price} = C \times \underbrace{\left[\frac{1}{(1+r)^1} + \frac{1}{(1+r)^2} + \cdots + \frac{1}{(1+r)^n} \right]}_{\substack{\text{Present value of} \\ \text{interest cash flows}}} + M \times \underbrace{\left[\frac{1}{(1+r)^n} \right]}_{\substack{\text{Present value of} \\ \text{par value}}} \quad \textbf{(Eq. 4.2)}$$

APPLYING THE MODEL

On January 1, 2004, Worldwide United had outstanding a $1,000 par value bond with a 9.125 percent coupon, which we will assume pays interest at the end of each

---

[2.] The *coupon yield* is but one of several important measures of a bond's return that goes by the term *yield*. Other common measures of a bond's return that use the word *yield* include *bond equivalent yield* and *yield to maturity*, both of which are discussed later in this section.

Figure 4.1
Time Line for Bond Valuation (Assuming Annual Interest) (Worldwide United 9⅛% Coupon, $1,000 Par Bond, Maturing at End of 2014; Required Return Assumed to Be 8%)

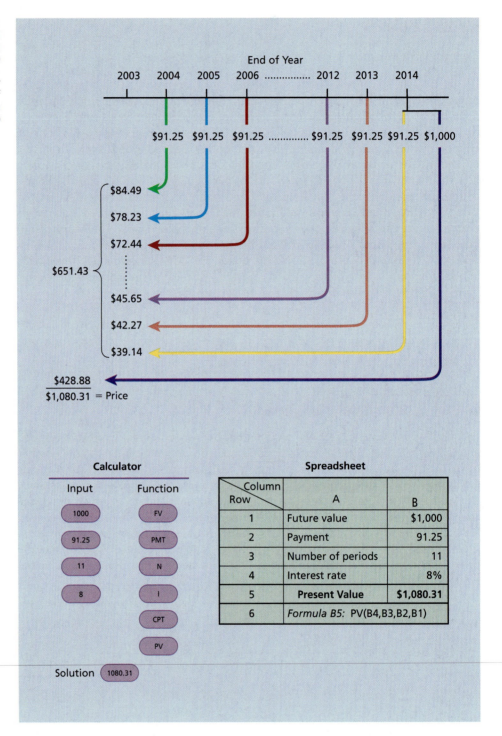

calendar year. The bond matures at the end of 2014—in exactly 11 years. In 2004, bonds of similar risk had a required return of 8 percent. The annual interest on this bond, C, is .09125 × $1,000 = $91.25. The bond's cash flows appear below the time line in Figure 4.1. Substituting these values into Equation 4.2, we get the following result:

$$\text{Price} = \$91.25 \times \left[\frac{1}{(1 + .08)^1} + \frac{1}{(1 + .08)^2} + \cdots + \frac{1}{(1 + .08)^{11}} \right]$$

$$+ \$1,000 \times \left[\frac{1}{(1 + .08)^{11}} \right]$$

$$= \$651.43 + \$428.88 = \$1,080.31$$

Figure 4.1 also shows how to obtain the same value using a financial calculator or spreadsheet. The Worldwide United bond sells at a *premium* of about $80 above its par value because the bond contractually pays 9.125 percent even though investors require only an 8 percent return at the time. As a result, investors will bid the bond price up to $1,080.31, at which point it will provide the required 8 percent return. ■

Again, we want to emphasize the fundamental lesson that the price of a bond equals the present value of its future cash flows. We now turn to a more in-depth development of the concepts underlying bond valuation, starting with a discussion of the simplest debt security possible, a pure discount bond.

Basic Bond Valuation

Pure discount instruments, such as U.S. Treasury bills, promise investors a single fixed payment on a specified future date. They make no intermediate interest payments, and therefore are sometimes called **zero-coupon bonds.** How can bonds that pay no interest be attractive investments? That's where the word *discount* comes into play. Investors purchase Treasury bills at a discount from their par value. If held to maturity, Treasury bills offer a dollar return equal to the difference between the par value and the purchase price. For example, an investor might purchase a Treasury bill maturing in six months for $9,800. When the bill matures, the U.S. Treasury pays $10,000, the par value of the bill, and the investor earns a $200 return. The percentage return on this investment is calculated as follows:

$$r = \frac{\$200}{\$9,800} = 0.0204 = 2.04\%$$

Of course, 2.04 percent represents the rate of return for six months, so we could state the percentage return on an annual basis in either of two ways. By multiplying the 6-month rate, denoted r_{6mo}, times 2, we obtain the simple-interest annual rate, 4.08 percent:

$$r_{simple} = r_{6mo} \times 2$$

$$= 0.0204 \times 2 = 0.0408 = 4.08\%$$

This is a simple-interest rate because it ignores the impact of compounding. Alternatively, we could obtain a compound annual rate, r_{ann}, as follows:

$$r_{ann} = (1 + r_{6mo})^2 - 1$$

$$= (1 + 0.0204)^2 - 1 = 0.0412 = 4.12\%$$

This rate represents the return that an investor would earn at the end of one year if she invested for six months at a rate of 2.04 percent and then reinvested the proceeds for another six months at the same rate. The rate slightly exceeds the simple-interest figure of 4.08 percent because this calculation takes into account the investor's opportunity to earn interest during the second half of the year on both the original principal and the interest from the first six months. To see how this works in practice, consider the following example from a Treasury bill auction.

The Treasury conducts periodic auctions of bills with maturities ranging from 4 to 26 weeks.[3] The following quote obtained from the Treasury website (http://www.treasury.gov) illustrates bill pricing in a typical auction:

182-day   07-25-2002   01-23-2003   1.675   1.713   99.153   912795LV1

The first entry indicates that this particular bill matures in 182 days, or about six months. The second item gives the date of the auction in which the bill was sold (July 25, 2002), and following that appears the bill's maturity date. The fourth and fifth entries in the quote are measures of the bond's yield, which we will discuss shortly, and the final item in the quote is the bill's CUSIP, essentially a tracking number that allows traders to communicate with each other about a specific security. Look at the next-to-last number in the quote, 99.153; it represents the market price of the bill (as determined by the auction) per $100 of par value. If an investor submitted a successful bid to purchase bills having a par value of $10,000, the purchase price for this order would be $9,915.30. If the investor purchases bills and holds them to maturity, the dollar return on that investment will be $84.70, the difference between the $10,000 par value and the purchase price. The percentage return is calculated as follows:

$$\frac{(\$10,000 - \$9,915.30)}{\$9,915.30} = 0.00854 = 0.85\%$$

However, this is a return over just six months. We could annualize this using simple interest as follows:

$$0.00854 \times \left(\frac{365}{182}\right) = 0.01713 = 1.713\%$$

Notice that this number, 1.713 percent, appears in the bond quotation shown previously. Bond traders call it the **bond equivalent yield,** and it is a simple-interest measure of an investor's annual return from holding a Treasury bill.[4] We can substitute

---

[3.] For many years, Treasury bills were available with maturities up to one year, but on February 27, 2001, the government auctioned its last 52-week Treasury bill. In general, the pace of Treasury debt offerings slowed dramatically near the turn of the century as the U.S. budget moved from deficit to surplus. The par value of a Treasury bill can be as low as $1,000, but larger denominations are also available. In mid-2002, the Treasury began selling its 10-year bonds quarterly rather than semiannually.

[4.] In this market, it is traditional to calculate one other measure of the bill's return, the **bank discount yield:**

$$\frac{(\$10,000 - \$9,915.30)}{\$10,000}\left(\frac{360}{182}\right) = .01675 = 1.675\%$$

Note that this number appears just before the bond equivalent yield in the price quote. For several reasons, this is a poor measure of an investor's return, but traders nonetheless use it to communicate with each other about current prices in the market. The important lesson here is not to memorize the differences between bond equivalent and bank discount yields, but to understand that the price of a Treasury bill is just the present value of the cash payment at maturity.

the second equation into the first and rearrange terms to arrive at a Treasury bill pricing formula that looks more like the generic present value pricing relationship given in Equation 4.1:

$$\frac{(\$10,000 - \$9,915.30)}{\$9,915.30} = 0.00854 = \frac{0.01713}{\left(\dfrac{365}{182}\right)}$$

$$\text{Price} = \frac{\$10,000}{\left[1 + 0.01713\left(\dfrac{182}{365}\right)\right]} = \$9,915.30$$

In other words, the price of the bond equals the $10,000 payment that it will make in six months, discounted using a 182-day interest rate. In this equation, the interest rate, 1.713 percent, is multiplied by the fraction of the year that will have elapsed at the bond's maturity date. This equation can be stated in a more general form:

$$\text{Price} = \frac{\text{Par}}{\left[1 + r\left(\dfrac{1}{2}\right)\right]} = \frac{\text{Par}}{\left(1 + \dfrac{r}{2}\right)}$$

where we have made the simplifying assumption that the bill matures in exactly one-half year (or that 2 is a sufficiently close approximation for $365 \div 182$). In this equation, r represents the market's required return on the bill, and we divide it by 2 because the bill matures in six months.[5] When conversing about current market conditions, Treasury bill traders will often refer to a bill's return rather than its price. It should be clear that if you know the bill's return, you can calculate its price, and vice versa. You can use the previous equation to price most pure discount bonds. Just discount the par value at an appropriate interest rate to obtain the price.

Valuing instruments that pay interest, such as Treasury notes and bonds, requires only a slight modification to the discount bond–pricing equation. Treasury notes and bonds resemble bills in that they receive backing by the full faith and credit of the U.S. government. However, unlike Treasury bills, notes and bonds make interest payments every six months, and they also have longer maturities than bills. It is a simple matter to modify the pricing equation for Treasury bills to fit the characteristics of notes or bonds:

$$\text{Price} = \frac{\dfrac{C}{2}}{\left(1 + \dfrac{r}{2}\right)^1} + \frac{\dfrac{C}{2}}{\left(1 + \dfrac{r}{2}\right)^2} + \frac{\dfrac{C}{2}}{\left(1 + \dfrac{r}{2}\right)^3} + \cdots + \frac{\dfrac{C}{2} + \$1,000}{\left(1 + \dfrac{r}{2}\right)^{2n}} \qquad \text{(Eq. 4.3)}$$

In this equation, C refers to the annual coupon payment, so $C/2$ represents the semi-annual payment. Note that in the last period, the bond makes its final coupon payment and repays the par value or principal (in this case, $1,000). As before, r represents the bond's yield, which you can think of as the market's required rate of return

[5.] Here's a pop quiz. Does the value r in this equation represent the simple-interest or compound-interest annual return? Because the equation calculates the 6-month rate by simply dividing the annual rate by 2, r is a simple-interest rate.

on this bond.[6] The bond matures in n years, so there are $2n$ semiannual payments. Simply stated, the price (or value) of a bond is the sum of the present value of interest payments and the present value of the par value, both discounted at the market's required return.

APPLYING THE MODEL

Suppose that six months ago the Treasury issued a new 5-year, $1,000 par value note with a 7 percent coupon rate. The bond just recently made its first interest payment, so the next one will be due in six months. Since the bond was first issued, market conditions have changed, and investors now require a return of 8 percent per year. What is the price of the bond? Given its coupon rate, the bond pays $70 in interest per year, or $35 every six months.

$$\text{Price} = \frac{\$35}{\left(1 + \frac{.08}{2}\right)^1} + \frac{\$35}{\left(1 + \frac{.08}{2}\right)^2} + \frac{\$35}{\left(1 + \frac{.08}{2}\right)^3} + \cdots + \frac{\$1,035}{\left(1 + \frac{.08}{2}\right)^9} = \$962.82$$

The bond has nine interest payments remaining (plus the principal repayment) and is worth $962.82.[7]   ■

In the example above, the bond's price was below its $1,000 par value. We say that a bond sells at a **discount** when its price is less than par value.[8] The bond sells at a discount because its coupon rate, 7 percent, offers a return lower than that currently required by the market, 8 percent. If investors demand an 8 percent return, the only way they can get it from a bond that pays 7 percent interest is to purchase the bond at a discount. At a price of $962.82, the bond offers a coupon yield of 7.27 percent ($70 ÷ $962.82), still not up to the 8 percent required return. For investors who purchase this bond and hold it to maturity, the total return will reflect both the interest payments and a capital gain of $37.18 when the Treasury repays the $1,000 principal. Combined, the interest payments and capital gain generate a return of 8 percent. The same logic can work in reverse. Suppose that the market's required return on this bond was 6 percent rather than 8 percent. When the market requires only a 6 percent return, a bond that pays 7 percent interest would be quite attractive. Investors would purchase this bond, driving its price above par value. In that case, the bond would sell for a **premium.** Substituting 6 percent for 8 percent in the equation above, you can verify that the market price of the bond would be $1,038.93.

How do you know what return the market "requires" for a particular bond? Your intuition probably tells you that the riskier the bond, the higher the rate of return the market will require, but putting that language into quantitative terms is a challenge.

[6.] Notice once again that this equation calculates the present value of payments arriving every six months by taking the annual interest rate (r) and dividing by 2 to get a semiannual rate. Therefore, the value r in this equation represents a simple-interest rate, the convention for quoting rates in the bond market. Remember that whenever we calculate an annual interest rate by multiplying a semiannual rate times 2 (or calculate a semiannual rate by dividing an annual rate by 2), we are dealing with simple rather than compound interest.

[7.] You can easily use Excel to calculate this number. First, enter the bond's nine payments in cells A1 through A9 on a spreadsheet. Next, in any empty cell, type the formula =NPV(.04,A1:A9), and Excel will produce the price of the bond. In the formula, .04 reflects the semiannual interest rate.

[8.] Because this bond trades below par value, it sells at a discount. It is not, however, a pure discount bond like a Treasury bill.

Chapters 5 and 6 explore the trade-off between risk and return in some depth, but for now we will make use of a convenient shortcut. Because Treasury bonds provide a known stream of cash flows, if you can observe the market price of a bond, you can infer what the market's required return must be. Suppose that a Treasury bond with par value of $1,000 matures in exactly 2.5 years and pays a 6 percent coupon. You look at the market and observe that the price of this bond is $988.63. Because this bond sells at a discount, you know that the market requires a return on the bond greater than 6 percent, the bond's coupon rate. But how much greater? Just use the bond-pricing equation to solve for the discount rate that equates the present value of the bond's cash flows to its current price:

$$\frac{\$30}{\left(1+\dfrac{r}{2}\right)^1} + \frac{\$30}{\left(1+\dfrac{r}{2}\right)^2} + \frac{\$30}{\left(1+\dfrac{r}{2}\right)^3} + \frac{\$30}{\left(1+\dfrac{r}{2}\right)^4} + \frac{\$1,030}{\left(1+\dfrac{r}{2}\right)^5} = \$988.63$$

By using a financial calculator or spreadsheet program, or by trial and error, you can solve this equation to find $r/2 = 0.0325$, so $r = 0.065$ or 6.5 percent. In this equation, the value of r is called the bond's **yield to maturity (YTM)**.[9] The yield to maturity of any bond is the discount rate that equates the present value of the bond's cash flows to its market price. For Treasury bonds, the yield to maturity measures the market's required return.

Valuing an ordinary corporate bond involves the same steps: write down the cash flows, determine an appropriate discount rate, and calculate the present value. The discount rate on a corporate bond should be higher than on a Treasury bond with the same maturity because corporate bonds carry **default risk,** the risk that the corporation may not make all scheduled payments. Bond traders often speak of the yield spread between Treasury bonds and corporate bonds. The **yield spread** is the difference in yield to maturity between two bonds or two classes of bonds with similar maturities. For example, suppose that a 1 percent yield spread exists between 10-year Treasury bonds and 10-year corporate bonds.[10] If the yield to maturity on 10-year Treasury bonds is 7 percent, then the yield to maturity on a 10-year corporate bond would be 8 percent. If you want to determine the price of a 10-year corporate bond with a 9 percent coupon, just solve the following equation:

$$\text{Price} = \frac{\$45}{\left(1+\dfrac{.08}{2}\right)^1} + \frac{\$45}{\left(1+\dfrac{.08}{2}\right)^2} + \frac{\$45}{\left(1+\dfrac{.08}{2}\right)^3} + \cdots + \frac{\$1,045}{\left(1+\dfrac{.08}{2}\right)^{20}}$$

$$= \$1,067.95$$

Bonds may seem like relatively safe investments, and in one sense they are. Investors who purchase Treasury bonds or high-quality corporate bonds can be fairly confident that promised cash payments will be made as scheduled. Even so, bond prices

---

[9.] A bond's yield to maturity is also called its internal rate of return (*IRR*). In Excel, you can calculate a bond's *YTM* using the =IRR function. See Problem 4-8 for an illustration.

[10.] The category "corporate bonds" encompasses a broad set of securities having a wide range of risks. Companies such as Moody's and Standard & Poor's have established rating systems for bonds that help investors evaluate the default risk of a particular bond. For the sake of this example, we have in mind relatively low-risk corporate bonds, those issued by large, profitable business enterprises. These bonds would carry the highest ratings from Moody's (Aaa) or Standard & Poor's (AAA). You can find up-to-date yield spreads for different classes of bonds at http://www.bondsonline.com.

can be quite volatile, and, for most bonds, that volatility is as important as default risk in determining the risk of investing in bonds.

BOND PRICES AND INTEREST RATES

The value of a bond in the marketplace changes constantly. One factor that can cause a bond's price to move is simply the passage of time. Whether a bond sells at a discount or a premium, its price will converge to par value (plus the final interest payment) as time elapses and the maturity date draws near. This is easy to understand if you imagine a bond that will mature in one day. The final cash flow of the bond is its par value plus the last coupon payment. If this final payment arrives just one day in the future, to determine the bond's price, you would simply discount this payment for one day. Therefore, the price and the final payment would be virtually identical. In addition to the mere passage of time, a variety of forces in the economy can cause movements in a bond's price. Whenever the required return on a bond changes, the bond's price changes in the opposite direction. You can see this inverse relationship between price and required return in the bond-pricing equation. The higher the bond's required return, the lower will be its price, and vice versa. How much a bond's price responds to changes in required returns depends on several factors, but among the most important is the bond's maturity.

Figure 4.2 shows how the prices of two bonds change as their required returns change. To focus on the effects of changes in required returns on bond prices, assume that both of these bonds are free of default risk. Both bonds pay a 6 percent coupon, but one matures in 2 years while the other matures in 10 years. As the figure shows, when the required return equals the coupon rate, 6 percent, both bonds trade at their $1,000 par value. However, as the required return increases, the bonds' prices fall. The rate of decline in the 10-year bond's price far exceeds that of the 2-year bond. Likewise, as the required return decreases, the prices of both bonds increase, but the

Figure 4.2
The Relationship between Bond Prices and Yields for Bonds with Differing Times to Maturity but the Same 6% Coupon Rate

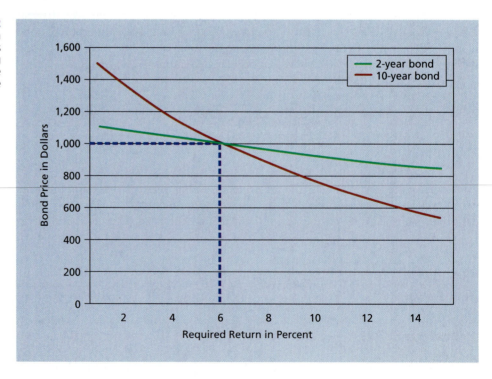

10-year bond's price increases much faster than that of the 2-year bond. The general point is that *the prices of long-term bonds display greater sensitivity to changes in interest rates than do the prices of short-term bonds.*[11]

Figure 4.2 illustrates that the most important risk for bond investors to consider is usually **interest rate risk,** the risk that changes in market interest rates will cause fluctuations in a bond's price. Changes in the required returns on bonds can occur as a result of economy-wide forces, such as increases in inflation, or of firm-specific factors, such as a decline in the creditworthiness of the borrower. The experience of France Telecom illustrates what can happen to corporate bonds when business conditions deteriorate. In an attempt to refinance its massive short-term debt obligations, France Telecom conducted the largest (at the time) corporate bond offering in history in March 2001 by selling the equivalent of $16.4 billion worth of bonds to investors around the world. France Telecom simultaneously issued bonds in three different currencies: U.S. dollars, euros, and British pounds. Days after successfully floating its bonds, France Telecom announced that it would not be able to retire as much short-term debt as it had originally anticipated, thereby signaling to the market that its cash flows were weaker than expected. Prices and yields of France Telecom bonds responded accordingly. For example, the required return on France Telecom's 5-year dollar bonds, issued with a 7.2 percent coupon, rose to about 8.5 percent. The following equation shows that this increase in the required return was associated with a decline in price of $52.07, or 5.2 percent, from the original $1,000 par value:

$$\frac{\$36}{\left(1 + \dfrac{.085}{2}\right)^1} + \frac{\$36}{\left(1 + \dfrac{.085}{2}\right)^2} + \cdots + \frac{\$1,036}{\left(1 + \dfrac{.085}{2}\right)^{10}} = \$947.93$$

Fortunately, the same effect can occur in reverse. Consider what might have happened if France Telecom's business had improved suddenly after the bond issue. Suppose that the bond market became convinced that France Telecom's brighter cash flow outlook lowered the risk of the 5-year bonds. If investors lowered their required return on these bonds to 6.5 percent, the price of the 5-year bonds would have risen to $1,029.48.

APPLYING THE MODEL

On February 15, 2000, the U.S. Treasury issued a 30-year bond paying a coupon rate of 6.25 percent on a par value of $1,000. The auction price of this bond was $987.71, resulting in a yield to maturity of 6.34 percent. In the ensuing 18 months, the U.S. economy weakened and interest rates fell. By the time the bond made its third interest payment, its *YTM* had fallen to about 5.50 percent. What was the bond's price?

After making 3 coupon payments, this bond had 57 payments remaining, 2 payments per year for the next 28.5 years. Use Equation 4.2 to calculate the price of the bond:

$$\frac{\$31.25}{\left(1 + \dfrac{.055}{2}\right)^1} + \frac{\$31.25}{\left(1 + \dfrac{.055}{2}\right)^2} + \frac{\$31.25}{\left(1 + \dfrac{.055}{2}\right)^3} + \cdots + \frac{\$1,031.25}{\left(1 + \dfrac{.055}{2}\right)^{57}} = \$1,107.31$$

[11] In certain unusual circumstances, there can be exceptions to this rule. For example, the prices of short-term bonds that sell at a deep discount can be more sensitive to interest-rate movements than the prices of bonds with longer maturities that sell at a premium. However, these special circumstances are rarely encountered in real bond markets.

Compared to its price when issued, the value of the bond had risen by nearly 11 percent in response to a decline in the required rate of return from 6.34 percent to 5.5 percent.   ■

You might argue that this entire discussion is irrelevant if an investor holds a bond to maturity rather than sells it. If the bond is held to maturity, there is a good chance that the investor will receive all interest and principal payments as promised, so any price decrease (or increase) that occurs between the purchase date and the maturity date is just a "paper loss." Though the tax code may ignore investment gains and losses until investors realize them, financial economists argue that losses matter whether investors realize them by selling assets or whether the losses exist only on paper. For example, when the France Telecom bond's value falls from $1,000 to $947.93, an investor holding the bond experiences an opportunity loss. Because the bond's price has fallen, the investor no longer has the opportunity to invest $1,000 elsewhere.

Thus far, we have maintained a simplifying assumption in our valuation models. You can see that assumption embedded in Equations 4.1 and 4.2. Both equations assume that a single discount rate, r, can be applied to determine the present value of cash payments made at any and all future dates. In other words, the models assume that investors require the same rate of return on an investment that pays cash 1 year from now and on one that pays cash 10 years from now. In reality, required rates of return depend on the exact timing of cash payments, as the next section illustrates.

ADVANCED BOND VALUATION — THE TERM STRUCTURE OF INTEREST RATES

A quick glance at actual prices and yields of bonds having different maturities reveals an important fact: yields vary with maturity. That is, if you examine the yield to maturity on a number of bonds that are similar (e.g., all Treasury bonds), except that they mature at different times, you will find that yields are not the same for short-term and long-term bonds. *The Wall Street Journal* and many other financial publications regularly display a graph that plots the relationship between *YTM* and maturity for a group of similar bonds. Finance professionals refer to this graph as the **yield curve,** and they call the relationship between yield to maturity and time to maturity the **term structure of interest rates.**

Figure 4.3 shows how the yield curve for U.S. government bonds looked at four different dates. Usually, long-term bonds offer higher yields than short-term bonds, and the yield curve slopes up. That was the case in January 1983 and in July 1993. However, the level of the yield curve was much higher in 1983 than in 1993. Differences in expected inflation rates in those two years largely explain why the yield curve was so much higher in 1983. In the 24 months just prior to January 1983, the annual rate of U.S. inflation had averaged about 6 percent. Assume that investors expected inflation to remain roughly at that level in the near term. Investors who purchased short-term Treasury bills in January 1983 earned a return of about 7.5 percent, slightly higher than the expected inflation rate. In contrast, in the 24 months prior to July 1993, the annual inflation rate averaged just under 3 percent. In July 1983, T-bills offered a return of roughly 3.75 percent, again just slightly above the level of expected inflation at that time. The general lesson here is that the yields offered by bonds must be sufficient to offer investors a positive **real return.** The real return on an investment

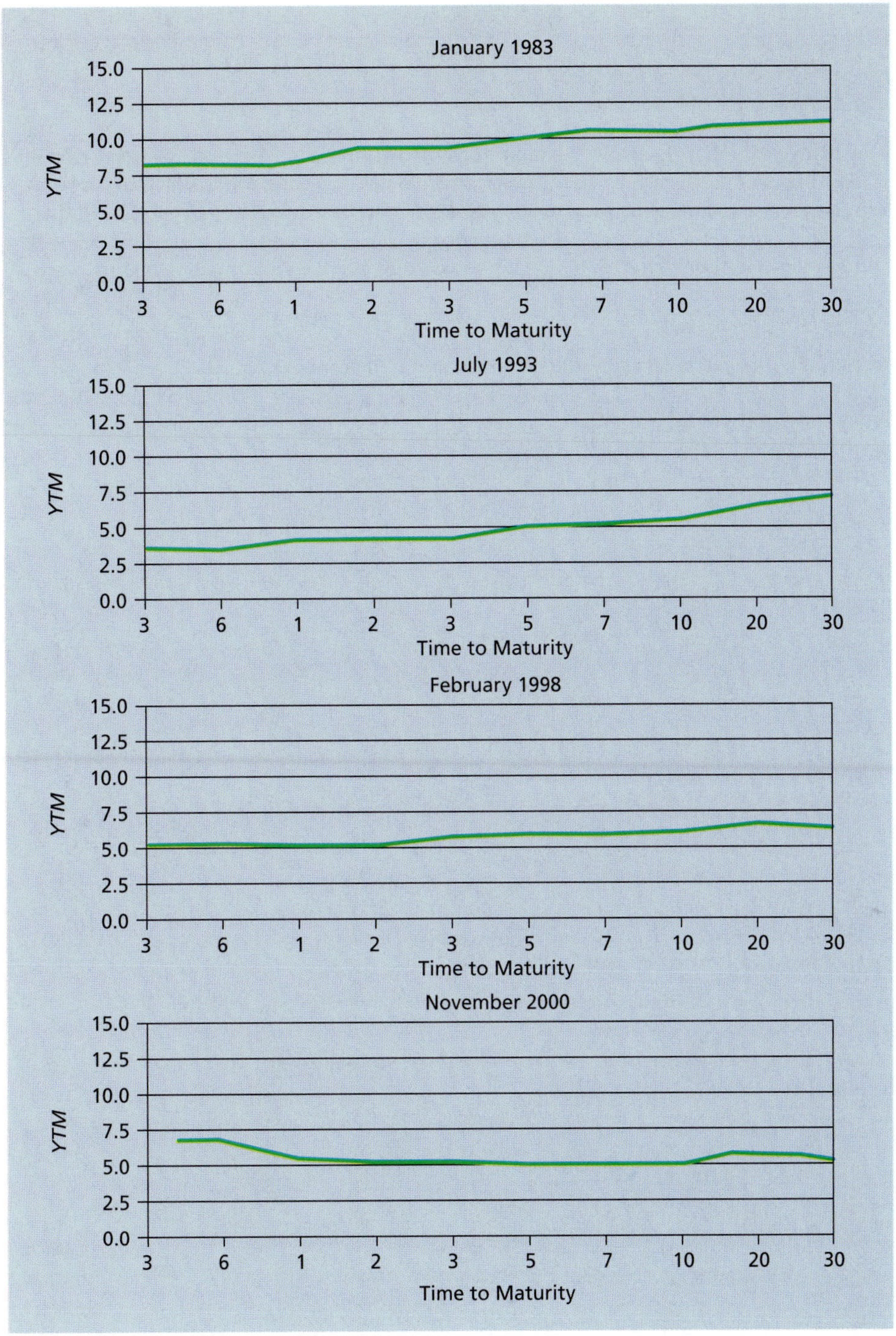

Figure 4.3
Yield Curves for U.S.
Government Bonds

approximately equals the difference between its stated or **nominal return** and the inflation rate.[12]

The other two graphs in Figure 4.3 illustrate that the shape of the yield curve can

---

[12.] Investors will be more concerned with the expected rate of inflation going forward than with the past inflation rate. We will discuss the relationship between expected inflation and returns in more depth in the next two chapters.

COMPARATIVE CORPORATE FINANCE

Is the Yield Curve a Good Economic Predictor?

Economists have known for many years that the slope of the yield curve—that is, the difference between yields on short-term and long-term Treasury securities—helps predict future economic growth in the United States. The same is true in many other countries, though the re-

liability of growth forecasts based on the yield curve varies internationally. The chart reports measures of the reliability of forecasts based on the yield curve in 11 different countries.

The forecasting models illustrated here are very

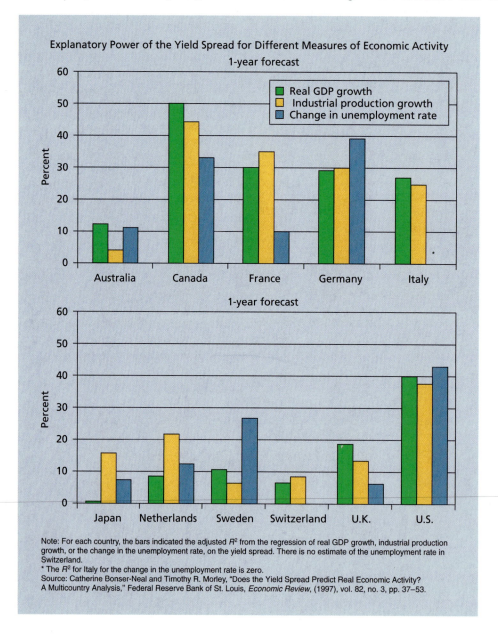

Note: For each country, the bars indicated the adjusted R^2 from the regression of real GDP growth, industrial production growth, or the change in the unemployment rate, on the yield spread. There is no estimate of the unemployment rate in Switzerland.
* The R^2 for Italy for the change in the unemployment rate is zero.
Source: Catherine Bonser-Neal and Timothy R. Morley, "Does the Yield Spread Predict Real Economic Activity? A Multicountry Analysis," Federal Reserve Bank of St. Louis, *Economic Review*, (1997), vol. 82, no. 3, pp. 37–53.

simple, even naive. The models use an ordinary linear regression in which the dependent variable is the percentage change in economic activity, and the independent variable is the difference between short-term and long-term bond rates. The three measures of economic activity studied here are the percentage change in real gross domestic product (GDP), the percentage change in industrial production, and the change in the unemployment rate. The height of the bars indicates the R-square value from each regression in each country. From statistics, remember that the R-square value measures how well the indepedent variable (the slope of the yield curve) predicts the dependent variable (changes in economic activity). For a perfect forecasting model, the R-square value equals 1.0. If the forecasting model is completely useless, the R-square value equals 0.0.

The chart indicates that the yield curve is most useful in predicting future economic activity in the United States and Canada. The yield curve's ability to predict economic activity is weaker, but still significant, in most European countries—the exception is Switzerland. The predictive power of the yield curve is also quite weak in Australia and Japan.

change over time. In February 1998, the yield curve was nearly flat, with yields on short-term and long-term bonds hovering around 5 percent. But by November 2000, the yield curve had inverted, with short-term yields lying slightly above long-term yields. Inverted yield curves typically occur prior to and during recessions.[13] In fact, Duke University economist Campbell Harvey (1993) argues that economic forecasts based on the slope of the yield curve perform as well as or better than many forecasts produced using complex statistical models. Research in this area shows that the yield curve works well as a predictor of economic activity, not only in the United States, but also in Canada, Germany, and other large industrialized economies.[14]

Economists have studied the yield curve intensely for several decades, trying to understand how it behaves and what it portends for the future. As a result of that research, we know that economic growth forecasts that include the slope of the yield curve perform well relative to forecasts that ignore the yield curve. Can the yield curve also tell us something about the direction in which interest rates are headed? The answer is a highly qualified yes. To understand the logic underlying the hypothesis that the slope of the yield curve might predict interest rate movements, consider the following example.

Russell wants to invest $1,000 for two years. He does not want to take much risk, so he plans to invest the money in U.S. Treasury securities. Consulting the Treasury website, Russell learns that 1-year Treasury bonds currently offer a 5 percent *YTM*, and 2-year bonds offer a 5.5 percent *YTM*. At first, Russell thinks that his decision about which investment to purchase is easy. He wants to invest for two years, and the 2-year bond pays a higher yield, so why not just buy that one? Thinking a bit more, Russell realizes that he could invest his money in a 1-year bond and reinvest the proceeds in another 1-year bond when the first bond matures. Whether that strategy will ultimately earn a higher return than that of simply buying the 2-year bond depends on what the yield on a 1-year bond will be one year from now. If, for example, the 1-year bond rate rises to 7 percent, then Russell will earn 5 percent in the first year and 7 percent in the second year, for a grand total of 12 percent (12.35 percent after compounding). Over the same period, the 2-year bond offers just 5.5 percent per year

---

[13.] One possible explanation for this phenomenon is that investors, faced with the prospect of a recession, anticipate that the weakening economy will lead to lower inflation, or perhaps deflation, in the long term. This may cause long-term interest rates to fall below short-term rates. Go to http://www.smartmoney.com/bonds/, and click the link for the "Living Yield Curve" to see how the yield curve has behaved in the United States since 1977.

[14.] See Bonser-Neal and Morley (1997).

Figure 4.4
The Expectations Theory

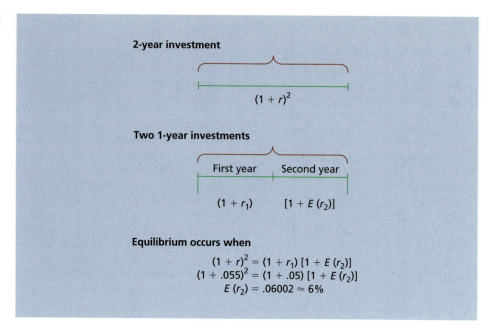

or 11 percent total (11.3 percent after compounding). Obviously, in this scenario, Russell earns more by investing in two 1-year bonds rather than one 2-year bond. But what if the yield on a 1-year bond is just 5 percent next year? In that case, Russell earns 10 percent over two years (or 10.25 percent after compounding), and he would be better off buying the 2-year bond. If next year's yield on the 1-year bond is about 6 percent, then Russell will earn approximately the same over the two years no matter which investment strategy he chooses.

This example illustrates the **expectations theory** of the term structure: in equilibrium, investors should expect to earn the same return whether they invest in long-term Treasury bonds or a series of short-term Treasury bonds. If the yield on 2-year bonds is 5.5 percent when the yield on 1-year bonds is 5 percent, then investors must expect next year's yield on a 1-year bond to be 6 percent. Suppose not. If they expected a higher yield than 6 percent, investors would be better off purchasing a series of 1-year bonds than they would be from buying the 2-year bond. Conversely, if investors expected next year's bond rate to be less than 6 percent, they would flock to the 2-year bond. Equilibrium occurs when investors' expectations are such that the expected return on a 2-year bond equals the expected return on two 1-year bonds. In this example, equilibrium occurs when investors believe that next year's interest rate will be 6 percent.

Figure 4.4 illustrates this idea. The first part of the figure shows that the value of $1 invested in one 2-year bond will grow to $(1 + r)^2$. In this expression, r represents the current interest rate on a 2-year bond. Next, the figure shows that investors expect $1 invested in a sequence of two 1-year bonds to grow to $(1 + r_1)[1 + E(r_2)]$. Here, r_1 represents the current 1-year bond rate, and $E(r_2)$ represents the expected 1-year bond rate in the second year. Equilibrium occurs when the two strategies have identical expected returns, or when the expected 1-year interest rate is about 6 percent.[15]

[15.] When we solve for the expected interest rate in year 2 that equates the returns on two 1-year investments to the returns on one 2-year investment, we are solving for the **forward interest rate**. Under the expectations theory, forward interest rates provide unbiased forecasts of future spot interest rates. That is, forward interest rates predict where interest rates are headed in the future.

The expectations theory says that when the yield curve is upward sloping—that is, when long-term bond yields exceed short-term bond yields—then investors must expect short-term yields to rise. According to the theory, only if investors expect short-term rates to rise will they be willing to forgo the higher current yield on a long-term instrument by purchasing a short-term bond. Conversely, when the yield curve inverts and short-term yields exceed long-term yields, investors must expect short-term rates to fall. Only then would investors willingly accept the lower yield on long-term bonds.

Unfortunately, the slope of the yield curve does not always provide a reliable signal of future interest rate movements, perhaps because the expectations theory ignores several factors that may be important to investors and that may influence the shape of the yield curve. The first factor is that investors may have a preference for investing in short-term securities. As we have seen, for a given change in the required return, the prices of long-term bonds fluctuate more than the prices of short-term bonds, so this added risk might deter some investors from investing in long-term bonds. To attract investors, perhaps long-term bonds must offer a return that exceeds the expected return on a series of short-term bonds. Therefore, when the yield curve slopes up, we cannot be sure whether this is the result of investors expecting interest rates to rise in the future, or simply a reflection of compensation for risk. The **liquidity preference theory** of the term structure recognizes this problem and states that the slope of the yield curve is influenced not only by expected interest rate changes, but also by the liquidity premium that investors require on long-term bonds.[16]

A second factor clouds the interpretation of the slope of the yield curve as a signal of interest rate movements if certain investors always purchase bonds with a particular maturity. For instance, pension funds that promise retirement income to investors, and life insurance companies that provide death benefits to policyholders, have very long-term liabilities. These companies may have a strong desire to invest in long-term bonds (the longest available in the market) to match their liabilities, even if long-term bonds offer low expected returns relative to a series of short-term bonds. Economists use the **preferred habitat theory** (or the *market segmentation theory*) to describe the effect of this behavior on the yield curve. If short-term bond rates exceed long-term rates, the cause might be that the demand for long-term bonds is very high relative to their supply. This demand drives up long-term bond prices and drives down their yields. If the investors purchasing long-term bonds have a strong preference to invest in those securities, despite their low yields, then the fact that the yield curve slopes down does not necessarily imply that investors expect interest rates to fall.[17]

Research on the yield curve continues.[18] It appears that the slope of the yield curve provides some information that is helpful in forecasting interest rates, but this information alone is not sufficient to generate forecasts with great accuracy. For now, the most important points are that bond prices derive from the present values of their

[16.] Note that whether long-term or short-term bonds are riskier depends on the investment horizon. For example, if you want to invest money for one year, then buying a 2-year bond is risky because you cannot be sure what price you will obtain when you sell the bond in one year. On the other hand, if you want to invest for two years, then buying a 1-year bond is risky because you cannot be sure what interest rate you will earn when you buy a new 1-year bond to replace the first bond when it matures. Therefore, the theoretical possibility exists that short-term bonds might have to offer a premium over long-term bonds if most investors in the market have long-term investment horizons. However, the weight of the evidence suggests that long-term bonds offer a risk premium.

[17.] Do you have a favorite place to go to enjoy a beer with your peers? Is the price of beer there the lowest price in town? If not, you are behaving according to the preferred habitat theory. You prefer to go to a particular establishment to socialize, even though you could buy the same beer at another location for less money. In the same way, some investors could prefer to invest in long-term bonds even though a series of short-term bonds might offer a higher expected return.

[18.] Backus, Foresi, Mozumdar, and Wu (2001) summarize some of the existing work on using the term structure to forecast interest rates and present a new approach of their own.

cash flows, and that prices of long-term bonds generally fluctuate more than those of short-term bonds in response to interest rate changes. We now turn our attention from pricing bonds to pricing stocks.

Concept Review Questions	
	5. What is the difference between the terms *coupon, coupon rate,* and *yield to maturity* for a bond?
	6. Why are bond prices and interest rates inversely related?
	7. What is the yield curve? What type of information does it provide?
	8. Briefly compare and contrast the three theories presented to explain yield-curve behavior. Which is generally accepted?

4.3 STOCK VALUATION

In this section, we examine valuation models for two types of stock: preferred and common. Even though the characteristics of stocks and bonds seem quite different, the principles involved in valuing debt and equity are much the same. However, applying those principles to equity securities can be quite challenging. Therefore, we begin with preferred stock, a security that resembles debt as much as it does equity.

PREFERRED STOCK VALUATION

Neither a pure debt nor a pure equity instrument, preferred stock exhibits characteristics of both. Like bonds, preferred stocks usually pay investors a fixed cash flow stream over time. In addition, preferred shares usually promise to pay a dividend expressed as a percentage of par value, similar to a bond's coupon rate. However, if firms do not generate enough cash flow to meet preferred dividend payments, preferred shareholders, unlike bondholders, cannot force the firm into bankruptcy. In that sense, preferred stockholders are in a legal position similar to that of common shareholders, although preferred shares generally do not carry the right to vote. Most preferred stock is *cumulative*, which means that if a firm skips a preferred dividend payment, it cannot pay dividends to common shareholders until it makes up for all unpaid dividends to preferred shareholders. Finally, like equity, preferred stock typically has no fixed maturity date. For that reason, we treat preferred stock as a security with an infinite life in our valuation formulas.

In Chapter 3, you learned a shortcut for valuing a *perpetuity*—an annuity with an infinite life. To find today's value of a preferred stock, PS_0, we use Equation 3.10 for the present value of a perpetuity, dividing the preferred dividend, D_P, by the required rate of return on the preferred stock, r_P:

$$PS_0 = \frac{D_P}{r_P}$$

APPLYING THE MODEL

Suppose that a particular preferred stock pays an annual dividend of $8. If the next dividend payment occurs in one year and the market's required return on this stock is 10 percent, then its price will be $80 ($8 ÷ 0.10). If you know the price of a preferred stock, you can easily determine its yield by dividing the dividend by the price.

As a source of capital for American industry, preferred stock has been in decline for at least six decades and now represents well under 5 percent of the net external financing for U.S. companies each year. This is at least partly due to tax factors. The U.S. tax code treats preferred dividends more like dividends on common stock than interest on bonds. Firms cannot treat preferred dividends as deductible business expenses as they can with interest payments on debt. Individuals face the same tax rate on preferred dividends and ordinary income (i.e., the tax rate that applies to preferred dividends is the same one that applies to wages). Because preferred shares offer a fixed dividend, the prospect of earning large capital gains (which are generally taxed at lower rates) on preferred stock is small relative to the potential for gains on common stock. Consequently, preferred stocks face a tax disadvantage relative to bonds at the corporate level, and a capital gain disadvantage relative to common stocks at the investor level.

Preferred stocks do enjoy one type of comparative tax advantage. In order to avoid taxing cash payments between corporate parents and subsidiaries, Congress has long allowed corporations who receive preferred dividends to exclude a large fraction of those receipts from corporate tax. For this reason, corporations have become the principal holders of preferred stock in the United States. Additionally, businesses sometimes issue new preferred stock as part of merger and acquisition transactions, especially when the company being purchased has preferred stock outstanding. In these cases, the acquiring firm often issues its own preferred shares to replace those previously issued by the target company. Acquirers commonly issue *convertible preferred stock*, shares that the holder can convert into a prespecified number of shares of common stock, in exchange for the common stock of the target firm.

Preferred stock also plays a key role in one other fairly small, but extremely influential area of American finance—venture capital financing. Venture capital firms raise and invest billions of dollars each year in private firms, usually with high growth potential. For a variety of reasons, venture capitalists frequently structure their investments in these high-risk, high-return companies in the form of convertible preferred stock.[19]

THE BASIC COMMON STOCK VALUATION EQUATION

Like the value of bonds and preferred stock, the value of a share of common stock equals the present value of all future benefits that investors expect it to provide. Unlike bonds, which have contractual cash flows, common stocks have cash flows that are noncontractual and unspecified. What are the benefits expected from a share of common stock? When you buy a share of stock, you may expect to receive a periodic dividend payment from the firm, and you probably hope to sell the stock at a future date for more than its purchase price. But when you sell the stock, you are simply passing the rights to future benefits to the buyer. The buyer purchases the stock from you in the belief that the future benefits, dividends and capital gains, justify the purchase price. This logic extends to the next investor who buys the stock from the person who bought it from you, and so on ad infinitum. Simply put, the value of common

[19.] Venture capital financing will be discussed more fully in Chapter 15. For more information and statistics on the venture capital industry, visit the National Venture Capital Association's website at http://www.nvca.org.

stock equals the present value of all future dividends that investors expect the stock to distribute.[20]

The easiest way to understand this argument is as follows. Suppose that an investor buys a stock today for price P_0, receives a dividend equal to D_1 at the end of one year, and immediately sells the stock for price P_1. The return on this investment is easy to calculate:

$$r = \frac{D_1 + P_1 - P_0}{P_0}$$

The numerator of this expression equals the dollar profit or loss, and dividing that by the purchase price converts the return into percentage form. Rearrange this equation to solve for the current stock price:

$$P_0 = \frac{D_1 + P_1}{(1 + r)} \qquad \text{(Eq. 4.4)}$$

This equation indicates that the value of a stock today equals the present value of cash that the investor receives in one year. But what determines P_1, the selling price at the end of the year? Use Equation 4.4 again, changing the time subscripts to reflect that the price next year will equal the present value of the dividend and selling price received two years from now:

$$P_1 = \frac{D_2 + P_2}{(1 + r)}$$

Now, take this expression for P_1 and substitute it back into Equation 4.4:

$$P_0 = \frac{D_1 + \dfrac{D_2 + P_2}{(1 + r)}}{(1 + r)} = \frac{D_1}{(1 + r)^1} + \frac{D_2 + P_2}{(1 + r)^2}$$

We have an expression that says that the price of a stock today equals the present value of the dividends it will pay over the next two years, plus the present value of the selling price in two years. Again we could ask, what determines the selling price in two years, P_2? By repeating the last two steps over and over, we can determine the price of a stock today, as shown in Equation 4.5:

$$P_0 = \frac{D_1}{(1 + r)^1} + \frac{D_2}{(1 + r)^2} + \frac{D_3}{(1 + r)^3} + \frac{D_4}{(1 + r)^4} + \frac{D_5}{(1 + r)^5} + \cdots \qquad \text{(Eq. 4.5)}$$

The price today equals the present value of the entire dividend stream that the stock will pay in the future. To calculate this price, an analyst must have two inputs:

[20] Firms can distribute cash directly to shareholders in forms other than dividends. For instance, many firms regularly buy back their own shares. Also, when an acquiring firm buys a target, it may distribute cash to the target's shareholders. In this discussion, we assume for simplicity that cash payments always come in the form of dividends, but the logic of the argument does not change if we allow for other forms of cash payments.

the future dividend amounts and the appropriate discount rate. Neither input is easy to estimate. The discount rate, or the rate of return required by the market on this stock, depends on the stock's risk. We defer a full discussion of how to measure a stock's risk and how to translate that into a required rate of return until Chapters 5 and 6. Instead, we will focus on the problem of estimating dividends. In most cases, analysts can formulate reasonably accurate estimates of dividends one year in the future. The real trick is to determine how quickly dividends will grow over time. Our discussion of stock valuation centers on three possible scenarios for dividend growth: zero growth, constant growth, and variable growth. We follow the dividend models with the presentation of the free cash flow approach for enterprise valuation.

ZERO GROWTH

The simplest approach to dividend valuation, the **zero growth model,** assumes a constant dividend stream. If dividends do not grow, then we can write the following equation:

$$D_1 = D_2 = \cdots = D$$

Plugging the constant value D for each dividend payment into Equation 4.5, you can see that the valuation formula simply reduces to the equation for the present value of a perpetuity:

$$P_0 = \frac{D}{r}$$

In this special case, the formula for valuing common stock is identical to that for valuing preferred stock.

APPLYING THE MODEL

Vulcan International (ticker symbol, VUL), manufacturer of rubber and foam products and bowling pins, paid a dividend of $0.20 per quarter, or $0.80 per year, without interruption from 1987 to 2002. Perhaps after 15 years of receiving the same dividend, investors believe that Vulcan will continue to pay this steady dividend indefinitely. What price would they be willing to pay for Vulcan stock?

The answer depends on Vulcan's required rate of return. If investors demand a 10 percent return on Vulcan stock, then the stock should be worth $0.80 ÷ 0.10, or $8 (making the simplifying assumption that the dividend is paid once per year).[21] In fact, for the past several years Vulcan stock has fluctuated between $30 and $40 per share. This implies one of two things: either investors require a rate of return on Vulcan stock that is much less than 10 percent, or they expect to receive higher cash distributions in the future than they have received in the past.

[21.] If you do not make this assumption, you can apply the same formula to quarterly dividends as long as you make an appropriate adjustment in the interest rate. For example, if investors expect a 10 percent effective annual rate of return on Vulcan stock, then they expect a quarterly return of $(1.10)^{.25} - 1$, or 2.41 percent. Using this figure, you can recalculate the stock price by dividing $0.20, the quarterly dividend, by 0.0241 to obtain $8.29. Why is Vulcan stock more valuable in this calculation? Because Vulcan's dividends arrive more often than once a year, the present value of the dividend stream is greater.

CONSTANT GROWTH

Of all the relatively simple stock valuation models that we consider in this chapter, the **constant growth model** probably sees the most use in practice. The model assumes that dividends will grow at a constant rate, g. If dividends grow at a constant rate forever, then we can calculate the value of that cash flow stream by using the formula for a growing perpetuity, given in Equation 3.11. Denoting next year's dividend as D_1, we can determine the value today of a stock that pays a dividend growing at a constant rate:[22]

$$P_0 = \frac{D_1}{r - g} \qquad \text{(Eq. 4.6)}$$

The constant growth model in Equation 4.6 is commonly called the **Gordon growth model**, after Myron Gordon, who popularized this formula during the 1960s and 1970s.

APPLYING THE MODEL

Few public companies have achieved a longer streak of uninterrupted increases in dividends than American National Insurance (ticker symbol, ANAT). An underwriter of life, health, and property and liability insurance products, American National increased its dividend every year from 1973 to 2002. Over this period, the company increased its dividend at an average annual rate of about 7.5 percent. Suppose that investors expect American National to pay $2.98 in dividends over the next year. Assuming investors expect the dividend to continue to grow at 7.5 percent indefinitely, what should be the price of American National's stock?

Suppose that investors require an 11 percent rate of return on American National Insurance stock. Substituting into the constant growth model, Equation 4.6, we obtain the following:

$$P_0 = \frac{\$2.98}{.110 - .075} = \$85.14$$

On July 29, 2002, American National Insurance shares closed on the Nasdaq at a price of $88, so we have underestimated the price a bit. If we either decrease the required return by 0.1 percent to 10.9 percent or add just 0.1 percent to our estimate of dividend growth, increasing it to 7.6 percent per year, then the model generates a price per share of $87.65.

Smart
Concepts
See the
concept
explained step-by-step at
SMARTFinance

We do not want to oversell the accuracy of the constant growth model. We based our calculations on a reasonable set of assumptions, using the long-run growth rate in dividends for g and the long-run rate of return on American National Stock for r. By making small adjustments to the dividend, the required rate of return, or the growth rate, we could easily obtain an estimate for American National Insurance stock that matches the current market price in July 2002. But we could also obtain a very differ-

---

[22.] To apply this equation, one must assume that $r > g$. Of course, some firms may grow very rapidly for a time, so that $g > r$ temporarily. We treat the case of firms that grow rapidly for a finite period later in the discussion. In the long run, it is reasonable to assume that r must eventually exceed g.

ent price with an equally reasonable set of assumptions. For instance, increasing the required rate of return from 11 percent to 11.5 percent and decreasing the dividend growth rate from 7.5 percent to 7.0 percent decreases the price to $66.22! Obviously, analysts want to estimate the inputs for Equation 4.6 as precisely as possible, but the amount of uncertainty inherent in estimating required rates of return and growth rates makes obtaining precise valuations very difficult.

Nevertheless, the constant growth model provides a useful way to frame stock-valuation problems, highlighting the important inputs and, in some cases, providing price estimates that seem fairly reasonable. But the model should not be applied blindly to all types of firms, especially not to those enjoying very rapid, albeit temporary, growth.

VARIABLE GROWTH

The zero and constant growth common stock valuation models just presented do not allow for any shift in expected growth rates. Many firms go through periods of relatively fast growth, followed by a period of more stable growth. Valuing the stock of such a firm requires a **variable growth model,** one in which the dividend growth rate can vary. Using our earlier notation and letting D_0 equal the last or most recent per share dividend paid, g_1 equal the initial (fast) growth rate of dividends, g_2 equal the subsequent (stable) growth rate of dividends, and N equal the number of years in the initial growth period, we can write the general equation for the variable growth model as follows:

$$P_0 = \underbrace{\frac{D_0(1 + g_1)^1}{(1 + r)^1} + \frac{D_0(1 + g_1)^2}{(1 + r)^2} + \cdots + \frac{D_N(1 + g_1)^N}{(1 + r)^N}}_{\substack{\text{Present value of} \\ \text{dividends during} \\ \text{initial growth period}}} + \underbrace{\left[\frac{1}{(1 + r)^N} \times \frac{D_{N+1}}{r - g_2}\right]}_{\substack{\text{Present value of} \\ \text{price of stock at end} \\ \text{of initial growth period}}} \quad \textbf{(Eq. 4.7)}$$

As noted by the labels, the first part of the equation calculates the present value of the dividends expected during the initial growth period, and the second part is the present value of the stock price calculated at the end of the initial growth period, which is found using the constant growth model. We can use an example to demonstrate the application of this model:

APPLYING THE MODEL

Imagine a food company that has developed a new fat-free ice cream. As the popularity of this product increases, the firm (unlike its customers) will grow quite rapidly, perhaps 20 percent per year. Over time, as the market share of this new food increases, the firm's growth rate will reach a steady state. At that point, the firm may grow at the same rate as the overall economy, perhaps 5 percent per year. Assume that the market's required rate of return on this stock is 14 percent.

To value this firm's stock, you need to break the future stream of cash flows into two parts. The first consists of the period of rapid growth, and the second is the constant growth phase. Suppose that the firm's most recent (year 0) dividend was $2 per share. You anticipate that the firm will increase the dividend by 20 percent per year for the next three years, and after that the dividend will grow at 5 percent per year indefinitely. The expected dividend stream looks like this:

Fast Growth Phase (g_1 = 20%)		Stable Growth Phase (g_2 = 5%)	
Year 0	$2.00	Year 4	$3.63
Year 1	2.40	Year 5	3.81
Year 2	2.88	Year 6	4.00
Year 3	3.46	Year 7	4.20

The value of the dividends during the fast growth phase is calculated as follows:

$$PV \text{ of dividends in fast growth phase} = \frac{\$2.40}{(1.14)^1} + \frac{\$2.88}{(1.14)^2} + \frac{\$3.46}{(1.14)^3}$$
$$= \$2.11 + \$2.22 + \$2.33 = \$6.66$$

The stable growth phase begins with the dividend paid four years from now. The final term of Equation 4.7 is actually Equation 4.6, which indicates that the value of a constant growth stock at time t equals the dividend a year later, at time $t + 1$, divided by the difference between the required rate of return and the growth rate. Applying that formula here means valuing the stock at the end of year 3, just before the constant growth phase begins:

$$P_3 = \frac{D_4}{r - g} = \frac{\$3.63}{.14 - .05} = \$40.33$$

Don't forget that $40.33 is the price of the stock three years from now. Today's present value equals $40.33 ÷ $(1.14)^3$ = $27.22. This represents the value today of all dividends that occur in year 4 and beyond. Putting the two pieces together, we get the following:

Total value of stock, P_0 = $6.66 + $27.22 = $33.88

This calculation is depicted on the time line in Figure 4.5. It can be more compactly shown in the following single algebraic expression:

$$P_0 = \frac{\$2.40}{(1.14)^1} + \frac{\$2.88}{(1.14)^2} + \frac{\$3.46 + \$40.33}{(1.14)^3} = \$33.88$$

The numerator of the last term contains both the final dividend payment of the fast growth phase, $3.46, and the present value *as of the end of year 3* of all future dividends, $40.33. The value of the firm's stock using the variable growth model is $33.88. The calculation of this value using a financial calculator or spreadsheet is shown below the time line in Figure 4.5.

How to Estimate Growth

By now it should be apparent that a central component in many stock-pricing models is the growth rate. Unfortunately, analysts face a tremendous challenge in estimating a firm's growth rate, whether that growth rate refers to dividends, earnings, sales,

Figure 4.5
Time Line for Variable
Growth Valuation

(*continued on page 140*)

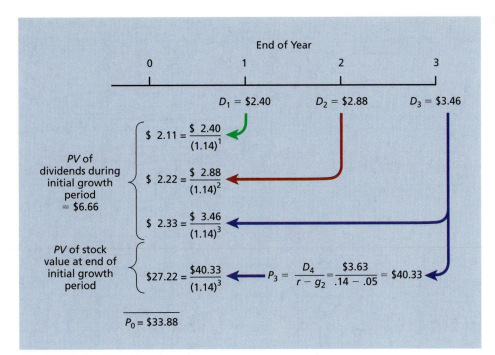

or almost any other measure of financial performance. A firm's rate of growth depends on several factors, but among the most important are the size of the investments
it makes in new and existing projects and the rate of return those investments earn.

A simple, but rather naive method for estimating how fast a firm will grow uses
information from financial statements. This approach acknowledges the importance
of new investments in driving future growth. First, calculate the magnitude of new
investments that the firm can make by determining its *retention rate, rr*, the fraction
of the firm's earnings that it retains. Second, calculate the firm's return on common
equity, *ROE*, to estimate the rate of return that new investments will generate. The
product of those two values is the firm's growth rate, *g*.

$$g = rr \times ROE \qquad \text{(Eq. 4.8)}$$

APPLYING THE MODEL

Simon Manufacturing traditionally retains 75 percent of its earnings to finance new
investments and pays out 25 percent as dividends. Last year, Simon's net income was
$44.6 million and the book value of its equity was $297.33 million, resulting in a return on common equity of 15 percent. Substituting into Equation 4.8 and multiplying
the retention rate by the return on common equity, we estimate Simon's growth rate:

$$g = 0.75 \times 0.15 = 0.1125$$

The resulting value is 11.25 percent.

An alternative approach to estimating growth rates makes use of historical data.
Analysts track a firm's sales, earnings, and dividends over several years in an attempt
to identify growth trends. But how well do growth rates from the past predict growth

Figure 4.5
(*continued*)

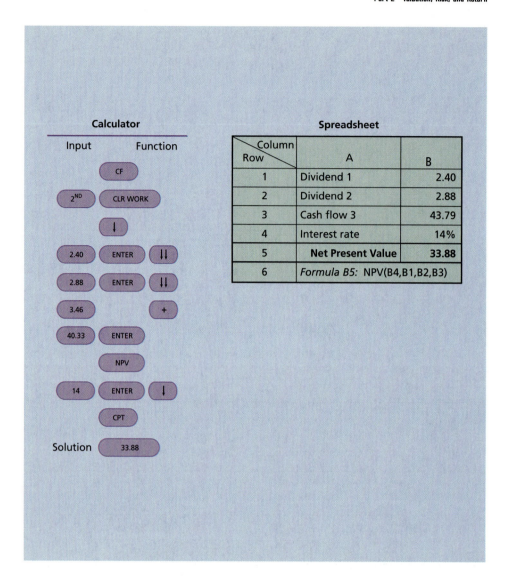

rates in the future? Unfortunately, the correlation between past and future growth rates for most firms is surprisingly low. Chan, Karceski, and Lakonishok (2003) report that future growth is almost completely unrelated to past growth—there is very little persistence in growth rates over time. They argue that analysts tend to be too optimistic about the future growth prospects of firms that have had high growth rates in the past.

That growth rates are largely unpredictable should not come as a great surprise. One of the most fundamental ideas in economics is that competition limits the ability of a firm to generate abnormally high profits for a sustained period of time. When one firm identifies a profitable business opportunity, people notice and entrepreneurs (or other companies) attempt to enter the same line of business. As more and more firms enter, profits (or the growth rate in profits) fall. At some point, if the industry becomes sufficiently competitive, profits will fall to such a low level that some firms will exit. As firms exit, profits for the remaining firms rise again. The constant pressure created by these competitive forces means that it is rare to observe a firm with a consistent, long-term growth trend. Perhaps one reason that companies such as Microsoft and Intel are so well known is that their histories of exceptional long-run growth are so uncommon.

Although it may be extremely difficult to predict how rapidly firms will grow, there can be no doubt that stock prices reflect the value of firms' growth opportunities. Consider the consumer products firm Procter & Gamble (P&G). In the summer of 2002, most analysts predicted that P&G would generate earnings of about $3.88 per share in 2003. Suppose that investors believed that P&G would stop reinvesting earnings to finance new investments and that P&G would simply distribute all its earnings to investors. If P&G could distribute $3.88 per share in perpetuity, and if the required return on P&G stock were 10 percent, then the price of P&G stock would be $38.80 ($3.88 ÷ 0.10). In fact, the price of P&G stock in the summer of 2002 fluctuated around $90. That price clearly implies that investors expect P&G to make new investments that will increase earnings and dividends over time.

We generalize this idea as follows. The price of any stock can be divided into two parts. The first part is the amount that investors would be willing to pay if a firm generated a constant annual earnings stream, E, in perpetuity and distributed it to investors. The second part represents the additional value associated with future growth opportunities, $PVGO$. Mathematically, this idea can be expressed as follows:

$$P_0 = \frac{E}{r} + PVGO$$

This equation indicates that the current stock price equals the present value of a perpetual earnings stream, plus the present value of growth opportunities, $PVGO$. For Procter & Gamble, the present value of growth opportunities in the summer of 2002 was about $51.20, the difference between the actual $90 stock price and $38.80, the present value of a constant earnings stream of $3.88 per share.

What If There Are No Dividends?

After seeing the different versions of the dividend growth models, students usually ask, "What about firms that don't pay dividends?" Though many large, well-established firms in the United States pay regular dividends, the majority of firms do not pay dividends at all. Of the more than 5,000 U.S. companies listed on the NYSE, AMEX, and Nasdaq, as many as 80 percent pay no cash dividends in a given year. Fama and French (2001) report that the percentage of U.S. firms paying cash dividends fell from 66.5 percent in 1978 to 20.8 percent in 1999. In part, this trend reflects a shift in the characteristics of U.S. public corporations. Specifically, the fraction of relatively young firms has risen with the boom of the initial public offering (IPO) market in the 1990s, especially in the technology sector. Younger firms with excellent growth prospects are traditionally less likely to pay dividends than are more mature firms. However, even controlling for the changing characteristics of listed firms, Fama and French report that the propensity for a given type of firm to pay dividends has fallen over time.

Can we apply the stock-valuation models covered thus far to firms that pay no dividends? Yes and no. On the affirmative side, firms that do not currently pay dividends may begin paying them in the future. In that case, we simply modify the equations presented earlier to reflect that the firm pays its first dividend, not in one year, but several years in the future. However, from an entirely practical standpoint, predicting when firms will begin paying dividends and what the dollar value of those far-off dividends will be is extremely difficult. Consider the problem of forecasting dividends for a company like Yahoo! Since its IPO in April 1996, Yahoo! has paid no cash dividends even though its revenues have increased from about $19 million to more than $700 million. Although the company reported a net loss in 2001, it was profitable in the three prior years. Is Yahoo! ready to start paying dividends, will it continue to reinvest income to finance growth, or will it be acquired by another firm? In all likelihood, investors will have to wait several years to receive Yahoo!'s first dividend, and there is no way to determine with any degree of precision when that dividend will arrive.

Perhaps firms that don't pay dividends will repurchase stock instead. In that event, we modify the valuation equations to focus on cash payments made to shareholders, whether the payments come in the form of dividends or share buybacks. However, Fama and French (2001) show that the firms that engage in share repurchases typically pay dividends. Repurchases apparently do not help us solve the valuation problem for no-dividend firms.

Analysts confronted with the problem of valuing firms that do not pay dividends have several alternative models at their disposal. Each of these models has strengths and weaknesses, and each should be applied with caution. Before discussing the details of those models, we want to comment on another question we hear frequently: What happens if a company never plans to pay a dividend, repurchase shares, or otherwise distribute cash to investors? Students point to a firm like Microsoft that has been in business for many years and certainly has sufficient cash flow to pay dividends. Don't thousands of investors buy and sell Microsoft shares every day with no expectation of ever receiving dividends? Our answer to this question is that for a stock to have value, there must be some expectation that the firm will distribute cash in some form to investors at some point in the future. That cash could come in the form of dividends or share repurchases. If the firm is acquired by another company for cash, the cash payment will come when the acquiring firm purchases the shares of the target. Investors must believe that they will receive cash at some point in the future. If you have a hard time believing this, we invite you to buy shares in the Smart, Megginson, & Gitman Corporation, a firm expected to generate an attractive revenue stream from selling its products and services. This firm promises never to distribute cash to shareholders in any form. If you buy shares, you will have to sell them to another investor later to realize any return on your investment. How much are you willing to pay for these shares?

Valuing the Enterprise—The Free Cash Flow Approach

One way to deal with the valuation challenges presented by a firm that does not pay dividends is to value the firm as a whole rather than try to value only the firm's shares. The advantage of this procedure is that it requires no assumptions about when or in what form (i.e., dividends or share repurchases) the firm distributes cash to stockholders. Instead, when using the free cash flow approach, we begin by asking, what is the total operating cash flow generated by a firm? Next, we subtract from the firm's operating cash flow the amount needed to fund new investments in both fixed assets and current assets. The difference is total **free cash flow** (*FCF*). Free cash flow represents the cash amount that a firm could distribute to investors after meeting all its other obligations. Note that we used the word *investors* in the previous sentence. Total free cash flow is the amount that the firm could distribute to *all types of investors*, including bondholders, preferred shareholders, and common stockholders. Once we have estimates of the *FCF*s that a firm will generate over time, then we can discount them at an appropriate rate to obtain an estimate of the total enterprise value.

But what do we mean by "an appropriate discount rate"? This is a subtle issue that will be discussed at much greater length in Chapter 9. To understand the main idea, recall that *FCF* represents the total cash available for all investors. We suspect that debt is not as risky as preferred stock, and preferred stock is not as risky as common stock. This means that bondholders, preferred shareholders, and common stockholders each have a different required return in mind when they buy the firm's securities. Somehow we have to capture these varying required rates of return to come up with a single discount rate to apply to free cash flow, the aggregate amount available for all three types of investors. The solution to this problem is known as the **weighted average cost of capital (WACC)**. The *WACC* is the after-tax weighted average required return on all types of securities issued by the firm, where the weights equal the percentage of each type of financing in the firm's overall capital structure. For example, suppose that a firm finances its operation with 50 percent debt and 50 percent equity. Suppose a firm pays an after-tax return of 8 percent on its outstanding debt, and suppose that investors require a 16 percent return on the firm's shares. The *WACC* for this firm would be calculated as follows:

$$WACC = (.50 \times 8\%) + (.50 \times 16\%) = 12\%$$

If we obtain forecasts of the *FCFs*, and if we discount those cash flows at a 12 percent rate, then the resulting present value is an estimate of the total value of the firm.

When analysts value free cash flows, they use some of the same types of models that we have used to value dividend streams. We could assume that a firm's free cash flows will experience zero, constant, or variable growth, and in each instance the procedures and equations would be the same as those introduced earlier for dividends, except we would now substitute *FCF* for dividends.

Recall that our goal in using the free cash flow approach was to develop a method for valuing a firm's shares without making assumptions about its dividends. The free cash flow approach begins by estimating the total value of the firm. To find out what the firm's shares are worth, V_S, we subtract from the total enterprise value, V_F, the value of the firm's debt, V_D, and the value of the firm's preferred stock, V_P. Equation 4.9 depicts this relationship:

$$V_S = V_F - V_D - V_P \hspace{3cm} \text{(Eq. 4.9)}$$

We already know how to value bonds and preferred shares, so this step is relatively straightforward. Once we subtract the value of debt and preferred stock from the total enterprise value, the remainder equals the total value of the firm's shares. Simply divide this total by the number of shares outstanding to calculate the value per share, P_0.

APPLYING THE MODEL

Had a good steak lately? One of the better-known purveyors of quality steak is Mortons of Chicago, operated by Mortons Restaurant Group (MRG). Its stock traded in the $20–$25 range in the first quarter of 2001. At the end of the year 2000, Mortons had debt with a market value of about $66 million, no preferred stock, and 4,148,002 shares of common stock outstanding. Its year-2000 free cash flow, calculated using the techniques presented in Chapter 2, was about $4.8 million. Its revenues and operating profits both grew at compound annual rates of about 14 percent between 1998 and 2000. Indeed, many consumers were returning to beef during that period. At the same time that the steak-house market was growing, competition was beginning to heat up. We assume that because of this competition, Mortons will experience about 14 percent annual growth in *FCF* from 2000 to 2004, followed by 7 percent annual growth thereafter, due to forecast competition as well as changing consumer tastes and preferences. A rough estimate of Mortons' *WACC* of 11 percent is deemed applicable in this valuation.

Mortons' forecast free cash flow for the fast growth period 2001 to 2004 and the year 2005, which begins the infinite-lived period of stable growth, are calculated in the following table.

End of Year	Growth Status	Growth Rate (%)	*FCF* Calculation	*FCF*
2000	Historic	—	Given	$4,800,000
2001	Fast	14	$4,800,000 \times (1.14)^1 =$	$5,472,000
2002	Fast	14	$4,800,000 \times (1.14)^2 =$	$6,238,080
2003	Fast	14	$4,800,000 \times (1.14)^3 =$	$7,111,411
2004	Fast	14	$4,800,000 \times (1.14)^4 =$	$8,107,009
2005	Stable	7	$8,107,009 \times (1.07)^1 =$	$8,674,499

Letting $D_t = FCF_t$ in Equation 4.7, and substituting $N = 4$, $r = .11$, and $g_2 = .07$, we can now estimate Mortons' enterprise value at the beginning of 2001, $V_{F\,2001}$:

$$V_{F2001} = \frac{\$5,472,000}{(1.11)^1} + \frac{\$6,238,080}{(1.11)^2} + \frac{\$7,111,411}{(1.11)^3} + \frac{\$8,107,009}{(1.11)^4}$$

$$+ \left[\frac{1}{(1.11)^4} \times \frac{\$8,674,499}{(.11 - .07)} \right]$$

$$= \$4,929,730 + \$5,062,966 + \$5,199,802 + \$5,340,338 + \$142,854,029$$

$$= \$163,386,865$$

Substituting Mortons' enterprise value of $163,386,865, its debt value, V_D, of $66 million, and its preferred stock value, V_P, of $0 into Equation 4.8, we get its total share value, V_S:

$$V_S = \$163,386,865 - \$66,000,000 - \$0 = \$97,386,865$$

Dividing the total share value by the 4,148,002 shares outstanding at the beginning of 2001, we get the per-share value of Mortons stock, P_{2001}.

$$P_{2001} = \frac{\$97,386,865}{4,148,002} = \$23.48 \text{ per share}$$

Our estimate of Mortons' total share value at the beginning of 2001 of $97,386,865, or $23.48 per share, is within its actual trading range of $20–$25 per share during the first quarter of 2001.[23]

[23.] Here's an interesting postscript for this example. As it was for many businesses, 2001 was a tough year for Mortons. The company experienced very significant declines in revenues, earnings, and cash flows, highlighting the difficulties we mentioned earlier in predicting how fast a firm will grow over time. By the first quarter of 2002, Mortons stock had fallen by roughly 75 percent, trading at times for less than $10 per share. However, some rather important investors felt that Mortons was a bargain at that price. The company received a number of acquisition bids from private investors. Mortons' board accepted an offer of $17 per share from the private equity group Castle Harlan, Inc. The board rejected a $17 per share offer from Carl Icahn after Castle responded by increasing its offer from $16 to $17. In fact, Castle raised its bid four times in response to bids from Icahn. The total offer was for $71.2 million for 66 restaurants that generated revenues of $233 million in 2001.

The free cash flow approach offers an alternative to the dividend discount model that is especially useful when valuing shares that pay no dividends. Security analysts have several alternative models at their disposal for estimating the value of shares, some of which do not rely on the discounted cash flow methods that we have studied thus far. We now take a look at some of those alternatives.

OTHER APPROACHES TO COMMON STOCK VALUATION

Practitioners employ many different approaches to value common stock. The more popular approaches include the use of book value, liquidation value, and some type of a price/earnings multiple.

Book Value

Book value refers to the value of a firm's equity shown on its balance sheet. Calculated using generally accepted accounting principles (GAAP), the book value of equity reflects the historical cost of the firm's assets, adjusted for depreciation, net of the firm's liabilities. Because of its backward-looking emphasis on historical cost figures, book value usually provides a conservative estimate of value. Book value does not incorporate information about a firm's potential to generate cash flows in the future and usually falls short of the market value of equity. An exception to this general rule occurs when firms experience financial distress. In some cases, such as when a firm's earnings prospects are very poor, the book value of equity may actually exceed its market value.

Liquidation Value

To calculate liquidation value, analysts estimate the amount of cash that would be left over if the firm's assets were sold and all liabilities paid. Liquidation value may be more or less than book value, depending on the marketability of the firm's assets and the depreciation charges that have been assessed against fixed assets. For example, an important asset on many corporate balance sheets is real estate. The value of raw land appears on the balance sheet at historical cost, but in many cases its market value is much higher. In that instance, liquidation value exceeds book value. In contrast, suppose that the largest assets on a firm's balance sheet are highly customized machine tools, purchased two years ago. If the firm depreciates these tools on a straight-line basis over five years, the value shown on the books would equal 60 percent of the purchase price. However, there may be little or no secondary market for tools that have been customized for the firm's manufacturing processes. If the firm goes bankrupt and the machine tools have to be liquidated, they may sell for much less than book value.

Price/Earnings and Price/Sales Multiples

The price/earnings (P/E) ratio reflects the amount investors are willing to pay for each dollar of earnings. The ratio simply equals the current stock price divided by annual earnings per share (*EPS*). The *EPS* used in the denominator of the P/E ratio may reflect either the earnings that analysts expect a firm to generate over the next year or earnings from the previous year.[24] An analyst using this method to value a stock might

---

[24.] Analysts refer to "leading" or "trailing" P/E ratios depending on whether the earnings number in the denominator is a forecast or a historical number.

proceed as follows. First, the analyst attempts to forecast what the firm's *EPS* will be in the next quarter or year. Second, the analyst tries to calculate a "normal" P/E ratio for that firm or industry. Third, the analyst obtains an estimate of the stock price by simply multiplying the earnings forecast times the P/E ratio.

Though P/E ratios are widely quoted in the financial press, interpreting them can be very difficult. Stock analysts frequently tie a firm's P/E ratio to its growth prospects, using logic similar to the following. Suppose one firm has a P/E ratio of 50 while another has a P/E of 20. Why would investors willingly pay $50 per dollar of earnings for the first company and only $20 per dollar of earnings for the second? One possibility is that investors expect the first firm's earnings to grow more rapidly than those of the second firm.

To see this relationship more clearly, look again at Equation 4.6, which indicates that the price of a stock depends on three variables: the dividend next period, the dividend growth rate, and the required rate of return on the stock. We can modify this formula by assuming that a firm pays out a constant percentage of its earnings as dividends. If we denote this payout percentage as d and next year's earnings per share as E_1, we can rewrite Equation 4.6 as follows:

$$P_0 = \frac{dE_1}{r - g}$$

where we replace the dividend next year in the numerator with the payout ratio times earnings next year. Now, divide both sides of this equation by E_1 to obtain the following:

$$\frac{P_0}{E_1} = \frac{d}{r - g}$$

On the left-hand side is the P/E ratio using next period's earnings. Notice that if the value of g increases, so does the P/E ratio. That provides some justification for the common notion that stocks with high P/E ratios have high growth potential. However, the equation illustrates that either an increase in the dividend payout or a decrease in the required rate of return will also increase the P/E ratio. Therefore, when comparing P/E ratios of different firms, one cannot conclude that the firm with the higher P/E ratio necessarily has better growth prospects. In addition, interpreting a P/E ratio is virtually impossible when the firm's earnings are negative or close to zero. For example, in May 2002, the A. T. Cross Company (ticker symbol, ATX), maker of fine writing instruments, had a P/E ratio of 740. Was Cross a company with phenomenal growth prospects, which justified an astronomical P/E ratio? Not likely. A better explanation is that the firm's EPS at the time was just $0.01. Even though A. T. Cross stock traded in the $7–$8 range, dividing that price by $0.01 resulted in a high P/E.

Despite the difficulties associated with P/E ratios, analysts frequently use them to make rough assessments of value. For instance, an analyst might calculate the average P/E ratio in a particular industry and then compare that average to the P/E ratio for a specific firm. If a particular stock's P/E ratio falls substantially above (below) the industry average, the analyst might suspect that the stock is overvalued (undervalued). In the same way, analysts sometimes look at the aggregate P/E ratio for the entire stock market to make judgments about whether stocks generally are over- or undervalued. Figure 4.6 shows the aggregate P/E ratio for U.S. stocks each month from 1900 through the first quarter of 2001 as calculated by Yale economist Robert Shiller. Over this period, the average market P/E ratio was a little less than 16. In his

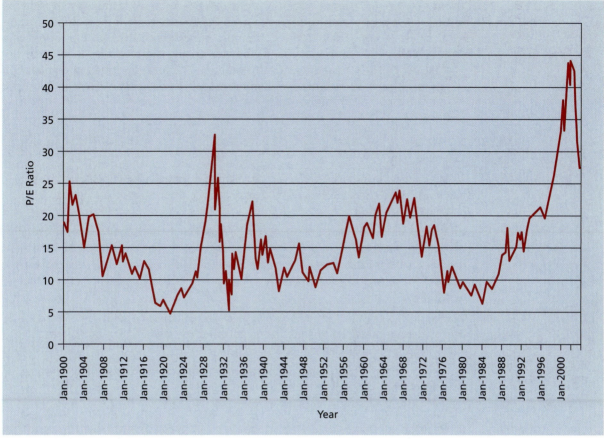

Figure 4.6
Aggregate Price/Earnings Ratio of the U.S. Stock Market (January 1900 through January 2002)

Source: Robert Shiller's home page, http://aida.econ.yale.edu/~shiller/data/ie_data.htm

book, *Irrational Exuberance,* Shiller argues that when the market P/E ratio is unusually high, as it was in the late 1920s and the late 1990s, stocks are overvalued and subsequent stock market returns are low, causing the market P/E to revert back toward its long-run average.[25]

When a private firm wants to convert to public ownership via an initial public offering, or when a private firm is the target in an acquisition, investment bankers examine P/E ratios of public firms with characteristics similar to those of the private company to estimate the value of the shares of the private company. For example, suppose that a firm that makes computer network security software wants to go public by selling 4 million shares in an IPO. The firm's projected earnings for the coming year are $1 million, or $0.25 per share. If investment bankers observe that the average P/E ratio for other networking software companies is 40, they would multiply that figure times the earnings per share to arrive at an estimate of $10 per share for the IPO. In the 1990s, many firms conducting IPOs were very young and had never generated any profit, making comparisons with P/E ratios of public firms impossible. As a result, analysts began to compare price/sales (P/S) ratios of similar public and private companies to determine the appropriate selling prices for shares of private

---

[25.] Whether stock market returns can be predicted using P/E ratios or any other information is an important topic to which we return in Chapter 10. For now, we will only say that the notion that stock returns are predictable is highly controversial.

firms. Because profit margins vary from industry to industry and from firm to firm, P/S ratios are even more difficult to interpret than P/E ratios. At best, both P/E and P/S ratios serve only as a rough guide for pricing shares. Professional securities analysts generally examine P/E and P/S ratios in conjunction with other valuation models to determine a reasonable price for a particular stock.

Concept Review Questions

9. What are the features that make preferred stock have more resemblance to bonds than to common stock?

10. In the 1990s, many finance professionals interpreted the booming stock market as a sign that investors were requiring lower future returns on common stocks than they had in the past. Explain.

11. Using a dividend forecast of $2.98, a required return of 11%, and a growth rate of 7.5 percent, we obtained a price for American National Insurance of $85.14. Holding all these assumptions fixed, what will the price of the stock be one year later? What price increase from the original value of $85.14 does your new estimate represent (in percentage terms)? Explain.

12. How can the free cash flow approach to valuing an enterprise be used to resolve the valuation challenge presented by firms that do not pay dividends? Compare and contrast this model to the dividend valuation models.

13. Why is it dangerous to conclude that a firm with a high P/E ratio will probably grow faster than a firm with a lower P/E ratio?

4.4 SUMMARY

- Conceptually, valuing either bonds or stock is quite straightforward: simply discount the stream of cash flows that will accrue to a security holder over that security's life, and the sum of the discounted cash flows is the security's current, or present, value.

- The appropriate discount rate to use to value a given bond or stock is based primarily on the risk of that security's cash flows. Payments on Treasury securities are discounted at a (default) risk-free rate; all other debt and equity securities are discounted at a higher rate to reflect their greater risk of nonpayment.

- Ordinary bonds make periodic fixed cash payments, called coupons, to investors. Bond prices move in the opposite direction of interest rates, and prices of long-term bonds are generally more sensitive to interest rate movements than are prices of short-term bonds.

- The term structure of interest rates is the relationship between time to maturity and yield to maturity on bonds having similar risk. A graphic representation of the term structure is called the yield curve. The slope of the yield curve is helpful in predicting future economic activity.

- Preferred stock has no maturity and pays a constant periodic dividend. Therefore, preferred shares can be valued using the formula for the present value of a perpetuity.

- Common stock is often very difficult to value, due to both the inherent difficulty of determining the "appropriate" risk-adjusted discount rate to use and the difficulty of estimating dividends (or other cash payments to shareholders) far into the future.

- Common stock valuation is much easier when dividends per share either are not growing or are growing at a constant rate. When dividends per share are expected to change their rate of growth one or more times in the future, stock valuation can become very complex.

- Discounting dividends to determine the stock price does not work very well for certain firms, particularly those that have no history of paying dividends. To value these firms, analysts may value free cash flows to determine the enterprise value, which can be reduced to total share value by deducting the value of all debt and preferred stock from the total enterprise value.

- Other approaches to valuing common stock include book value and liquidation value, both of which consider historic accounting values rather than future cash flows. More forward-looking, but simpler approaches involve use of P/E or P/S multiples.

INTERNET RESOURCES

Note: *For updates to links, please go to the book's website at* http://smart.swcollege.com

http://www.investinginbonds.com—Contains a wealth of information about markets for Treasury, corporate, and municipal bonds, including easy-to-read tutorials on bond basics, reading bond price quotations, and many other topics

http://www.bondmarkets.com—An extremely comprehensive site with extensive coverage of current events, policy issues, and research related to the bond markets; has an extensive list of links to other bond sites on the web

http://www.financenter.com—A consumer-oriented site offering various online financial calculators that allow you to calculate a bond's after-tax yield to maturity, the effect of interest rate movements on a bond's price, and many other figures

http://www.stockcharts.com/charts/YieldCurve.html—Offers a Java-animated yield curve juxtaposed to a plot of the S&P 500—an index of stock-price movements that includes 500 of the biggest and most important firms in the market; allows you to watch historical movements in stock and bond markets simultaneously

http://finance.yahoo.com—Can download historical price and dividend data for any firm by entering its ticker symbol

http://www.bondsonline.com—Provides an enormous amount of information on the bond markets

KEY TERMS

bank discount yield	free cash flow (*FCF*)
bond equivalent yield	Gordon growth model
constant growth model	interest rate risk
coupon	liquidity preference theory
coupon rate	maturity
coupon yield	nominal return
default risk	par value
discount	preferred habitat theory
expectations theory	premium
forward interest rate	real return

term structure of interest rates
variable growth model
weighted average cost of capital (*WACC*)
yield curve

yield spread
yield to maturity (*YTM*)
zero growth model
zero-coupon bonds

QUESTIONS

4-1. What is the relationship between the price of a financial asset and the return that investors require on that asset, holding other factors constant?

4-2. Define the following terms commonly used in bond valuation: (a) par value, (b) maturity date, (c) coupon, (d) coupon rate, (e) coupon yield, (f) yield to maturity (*YTM*), and (g) yield curve.

4-3. Under what circumstances will a bond's coupon rate exceed its coupon yield?

4-4. What is the difference between a pure discount bond and a bond that trades at a discount?

4-5. A firm issues a bond at par value. Shortly thereafter, interest rates fall. If you calculated the coupon rate, coupon yield, and yield to maturity for this bond after the decline in interest rates, which of the three values would be highest and which would be lowest? Explain.

4-6. Twenty-five years ago, the U.S. government issued 30-year bonds with a coupon rate of about 8 percent. Ten years ago, the U.S. government sold 5-year bonds with a coupon rate of about 5 percent. Suppose that the current coupon rate on newly issued 5-year Treasury bonds is 2.5 percent. For an investor seeking a low-risk investment maturing in five years, do the bonds issued 25 years ago with a much higher coupon rate provide a more attractive return than the new 5-year bonds? What about the 10-year bonds issued five years ago?

4-7. Describe how a bond's interest rate risk is related to its maturity.

4-8. Under the expectations theory, what does the slope of the yield curve reveal about the future path of interest rates?

4-9. If the yield curve is typically upward sloping, what would this imply about the long-term path of interest rates if the expectations theory were true?

4-10. Visit a website that posts an up-to-date yield curve. What is the current yield on long-term Treasury bonds? Next, using the web or the financial section of a newspaper, find the current prices of several outstanding preferred stocks. Make sure that the preferred shares you choose pay a fixed dividend and are not convertible into common stock. For each preferred stock, divide the current market price into the annual dividend that the stock pays. Compare this figure to the yield on long-term Treasuries. What should you expect to find?

4-11. Go to http://www.stockcharts.com/charts/YieldCurve.html, and click on the animated yield-curve graph. Answer the following questions:

a. Is the yield curve typically upward sloping, downward sloping, or flat?

b. Notice the behavior of the yield curve and the S&P 500 between July 28, 1998, and October 19, 1998. In August 1998, Russia defaulted on billions of dollars of foreign debt. Then, in late September came the news that at the behest of the Federal Reserve, 15 financial institutions would infuse $3.5 billion in new capital into hedge fund Long-Term Capital Management, which had lost nearly $2 billion in the previous month. Comment on these events as they related to movements in the yield curve and the S&P 500 that you see in the animation.

4-12. At http://www.nber.org/cycles.html, you can find the official beginning and ending dates for U.S. business cycles according to the National Bureau of Economic Research (NBER). For example, the NBER indicates that the U.S. economy was in recession from January 1980 to July 1980, from July 1981 to November 1982, and from July 1990 to March 1991. Next, go to http://www.smartmoney.com/onebond/index.cfm?story=yieldcurve, and click on the animation of the Living Yield Curve. Pause the animation at November 1978. Then, click one frame at a time until May 1980. Pause again at November 1981, and click one frame at a time until August 1982. Let the animation play again until you reach March 1989. What association do you notice between the shape of the yield curve and the NBER's dates for recessions?

4-13. Look again at the yield-curve animation from Question 4-12. Make a note of the overall level of the yield curve from about mid-1979 to mid-1982, and compare that to the level of the curve for most of the 1990s. What accounts for the differences in yield-curve levels in these two periods?

4-14. Explain why it is logical to value preferred stock by using the formula for the present value of a perpetuity.

4-15. The value of common stocks cannot be tied to the present value of future dividends because most firms don't pay dividends. Comment on the validity, or lack thereof, of this statement.

4-16. A common fallacy in stock market investing is assuming that a good company makes a good investment. Suppose we define a "good company" as one that has experienced rapid growth in the recent past. Explain the reasons why shares of "good companies" may or may not turn out to be "good investments."

4-17. Why is it not surprising to learn that firm growth rates rarely show predictable trends?

4-18. Why is the book value of equity typically less than the market value? Can you describe a scenario in which the liquidation value of equity would exceed its market value?

PROBLEMS

Valuation Fundamentals

4-1. A best-selling author decides to cash in on her latest novel by selling the rights to the book's royalties for the next four years to an investor. Starting in one month, the royalty stream will be $400,000, and that stream will decline at the rate of 5 percent per month for the next 11 months. Royalties in the second year will be $150,000 per month, followed by flat monthly royalties of $100,000 and $50,000 per month in the third and fourth years, respectively. If the investor requires a 0.5 percent return per month on this investment, what should he pay for the royalty stream?

Bond Valuation

4-2. A bond makes two $45 interest payments each year. Given that the bond's par value is $1,000 and its price is $1,050, calculate the bond's coupon rate and coupon yield.

4-3. A bond with a $1,000 par value makes semiannual interest payments. Its coupon rate is 8 percent and its coupon yield is 6 percent. What is the bond's price?

4-4. Calculate the price of a 5-year, $1,000 par value bond that makes semiannual payments, has a coupon rate of 8 percent, and offers a yield to maturity of 7 percent.

4-5. Recalculate the price of the bond in the previous problem, assuming a *YTM* of 9 percent. What is the relationship between the prices you have calculated in these two problems and the bond's par value? Explain.

Smart
Solutions
See the
problem and
solution explained step-by-step at
SMARTFinance

4-6. A bond pays a $100 annual coupon, and it matures in four years. If investors require a 10 percent return on this investment, what is the bond's price?

4-7. A bond pays a $100 annual coupon in two $50 semiannual installments. The bond matures in four years. If investors also require an annual return of 10 percent on this bond, should its price be higher than, lower than, or identical to the price of the bond in the previous problem? Use Equation 4.3 and let $r = 10\%$. What price do you obtain? Can you explain the apparent paradox?

4-8. A bond makes annual interest payments of $75. The bond matures in four years, has a par value of $1,000, and sells for $975.30. Calculate the *YTM* of this bond using a financial calculator or Excel as follows:

- Enter the price of the bond in cell A1, but enter the price as a *negative* number.
- Enter the four remaining payments that the bond makes in cells A2–A5.
- Enter the formula "=IRR(A1:A5, .05)" into any empty cell.
- The number .05 in the formula above simply represents a guess of what the *YTM* will turn out to be; Excel searches iteratively for the correct value, but you have to give Excel a starting value or guess to begin; it doesn't matter much whether the guess that you enter into the formula is a good one or not.
- The formula should calculate a *YTM* of 8.25 percent. (Hint: If you see only 8 percent when you enter the formula, be sure you use the "Format" command to force Excel to show you the additional numbers that occur after the decimal point.)

4-9. Repeat Problem 4-8, maintaining all the same assumptions except one. This time, assume that the bond pays $37.50 twice a year rather than one payment of $75. The bond will now make eight payments rather than four. Use a financial calculator or set up the spreadsheet following the same steps as before, and enter the formula "=IRR(A1:A9, .05)" in a blank cell. Excel will produce a value that equals the semiannual *YTM* (analogous to $r \div 2$ in our bond-pricing equations). To convert Excel's answer into annual terms, multiply it by 2 (note that this yields a simple-interest annual *YTM*—to get the effective annual *YTM*, you would square 1 plus the rate that Excel gives you, then subtract 1). Explain why the *YTM* in this problem does not equal 8.25 percent, the *YTM* in the previous problem.

4-10. A $1,000 par value bond offers a 6 percent coupon that it pays in two semiannual installments. The bond matures in five years. Its price is $1,019.50. What is its *YTM*?

4-11. A $1,000 par value bond offers a 2 percent coupon that it pays semiannually. The bond matures in eight years, and its price is $919.25. What is its *YTM*?

4-12. Two bonds make semiannual interest payments of $40. One bond matures in 2 years and the other matures in 10 years. Both bonds currently sell at par ($1,000), meaning that they offer a *YTM* of 8 percent. Calculate the price of each bond if the *YTM* drops to 6 percent, and then calculate the price of each bond if the *YTM* rises to 10 percent. Comment on the patterns that you observe.

4-13. Suppose that a 5-year Treasury bond with a $1,000 par value offers a coupon rate of 6 percent, paid semiannually. If the *YTM* on the bond is 6.5 percent, what is the bond's price?

4-14. In this problem, you will use yield spreads to calculate the price of a corporate bond with the same characteristics as the government bond in the previous question. Go to http://www.bondsonline.com, and click the link to "Corporate Bond Spreads." You will see a table that shows the additional *YTM* (over Treasuries) offered by bonds with different ratings at various maturities. The data in the table are expressed in basis points. For example, the number 50 means that the bond pays a *YTM* that is 0.50 percent higher than a comparable Treasury bond. Go to the column for 5-year bonds, and then go down to the row for bonds that carry the lowest rating that begins with an "A" (the seventh row of the table). Add the yield spread in that cell of the table to the 6.5 percent *YTM* from the previous problem and recalculate the

price. How large is the price difference between this bond and the risk-free Treasury bond in the previous problem?

Stock Valuation

4-15.   City Power & Light has preferred stock outstanding that pays an annual dividend of $8 per share. If investors demand a 10 percent return on this stock, what is the price?

4-16.   Suppose that a company's preferred shares sell for $33 and they pay an annual dividend of $4. What rate of return do investors require on these shares?

4-17.   Investors demand a 12 percent return on a particular preferred share that sells for $65. What is the annual dividend on this stock?

4-18.   Zenith Propulsion, Inc., is expected to pay a dividend next year of $2.45 per share. Investors think that Zenith will continue to increase its dividend by 5 percent each year for the foreseeable future. If the required rate of return on Zenith stock is 13 percent, what is Zenith's stock price?

4-19.   Refer to Problem 4-18. Investors expect Zenith to pay out 50 percent of its earnings as dividends. What is Zenith's price/earnings ratio (defined as current price divided by next year's earnings)?

4-20.   Refer to the previous two problems. Maintaining all the other assumptions, recalculate Zenith's stock price and P/E ratio if investors expect dividends to grow at 8 percent per year rather than at 5 percent.

4-21.   One year from today, investors anticipate that Groningen Distilleries Inc. stock will pay a dividend of $3.25 per share. After that, investors believe that the dividend will grow at 20% per year for three years before settling down to a long-run growth rate of 4%. The required rate of return on Groningen stock is 15%. What is the current stock price?

Smart Solutions
See the problem and solution explained step-by-step at **SMARTFinance**

4-22.   Yesterday, September 22, 2004, Wireless Logic Corp. (WLC) paid its annual dividend of $1.25 per share. Because WLC's financial prospects are particularly bright, investors believe that the company will increase its dividend by 20 percent per year for the next four years. After that, WLC will increase the dividend at a modest annual rate of 4 percent. Investors require a 16 percent return on WLC stock, and WLC always makes its dividend payment on September 22 of each year.

   a. What is the price of WLC stock on September 23, 2004?
   b. What is the price of WLC stock on September 23, 2005?
   c. Calculate the percentage change in price of WLC stock from September 23, 2004, to September 23, 2005.
   d. For an investor who purchased WLC stock on September 23, 2004, received a dividend on September 22, 2005, and sold the stock on September 23, 2005, what was the total rate of return on the investment? How much of this return came from the dividend, and how much came from the capital gain?
   e. What is the price of WLC stock on September 23, 2008?
   f. What is the price of WLC stock on September 23, 2009?
   g. For an investor who purchased WLC stock on September 23, 2008, received a dividend on September 22, 2009, and sold the stock on September 23, 2009, what was the total rate of return on the investment? How much of this return came from the dividend, and how much came from the capital gain? Comment on the differences between your answers to this question and your answers to part (d).

4-23.   Today's date is March 30, 2004. E-Pay, Inc., stock pays a dividend every year on March 29. The most recent dividend was $1.50 per share. You expect the company's dividends to increase at a rate of 25 percent per year through March 29, 2007. After that, dividends will increase at 5 percent year. Investors require a 14 percent return on E-Pay stock. Calculate the price of the stock on the following dates: March 30, 2004; March 30, 2008; and September 30, 2005.

4-24.   Roban Corporation is considering going public but is unsure of a fair offering price for the company. Before hiring an investment banker to assist in making the public

offering, managers at Roban have decided to make their own estimate of the firm's common stock value. The firm's CFO has gathered data for performing the valuation using the free cash flow valuation model.

The firm's weighted average cost of capital is 12 percent, and it has $1,400,000 of debt at market value and $500,000 of preferred stock at its assumed market value. The estimated free cash flows over the next five years, 2005 through 2009, are given below. Beyond 2009 to infinity, the firm expects its free cash flow to grow by 4 percent annually.

Year (t)	Free cash flow (FCF_t)
2005	$250,000
2006	290,000
2007	320,000
2008	360,000
2009	400,000

a. Estimate the value of Roban Corporation's entire company by using the *free cash flow approach.*

b. Use your finding in part (a), along with the data provided above, to find Roban Corporation's common stock value.

c. If the firm plans to issue 220,000 shares of common stock, what is its estimated value per share?

4-25. Assume that you have an opportunity to buy the stock of Pedal Systems, Inc., an IPO being offered for $13 per share. Although you are very much interested in owning the company, you are concerned about whether it is fairly priced. In order to determine the value of the shares, you have decided to apply the free cash flow approach to the firm's financial data that you've developed from a variety of data sources. The following table summarizes the key values you have compiled.

Free Cash Flow		
Year (t)	FCF_t	**Other Data**
2005	$ 750,000	Growth rate of FCF, beyond 2008 to infinity = 3%
2006	850,000	Weighted average cost of capital = 9%
2007	1,000,000	Market value of all debt = $2,500,000
2008	1,150,000	Market value of preferred stock = $1,200,000
		Number of shares of common stock outstanding = 1,000,000

a. Use the *free cash flow approach* to estimate Pedal Systems' common stock value per share.

b. Judging on the basis of your finding in part (a) and the stock's offering price, should you buy the stock?

c. Upon further analysis, you find that the growth rate in FCF beyond 2008 will be 4 percent rather than 3 percent. What effect would this finding have on your responses in parts (a) and (b)?

4-26. In the fall of 2001, analysts predicted that The Finish Line (ticker symbol, FINL), a specialty retailer offering athletic footwear and apparel, would generate earnings per share of $0.75 in the next 12 months. Finish Line stock was trading at about $10. Assuming that investors required a 10 percent return on Finish Line stock, calculate the present value of growth opportunities ($PVGO$ per share).

4-27. A firm follows a policy of paying out 50 percent of its earnings as dividends. Next year's earnings are expected to be $10 per share. The long-run growth rate of dividends for this firm is 5 percent, and investors require a 15 percent rate of return on the stock. What is the firm's P/E ratio?

5

Risk and Return

OPENING FOCUS
Why Buy Arab Bonds?

On March 5, 2002, an investment bank headquartered in the United Arab Emirates, Shuaa Capital, announced that it would create a new investment vehicle known as The Arab Income Fund (TAIF). As the words *income fund* in the title suggest, Shuaa intended to pool money from a wide range of investors to purchase dollar-denominated government bonds from at least seven different Arab nations: Saudi Arabia, Kuwait, Jordan, Algeria, Lebanon, Qatar, and Egypt. Ziad Makawi, executive director of the new fund, claimed that Shuaa expected to raise as much as $100 million from investors to get TAIF started.

What would prompt investors to allocate a portion of their savings to buy a stake in TAIF? Some Western observers might assume that shareholders of TAIF were driven by an ideological imperative to support Arab governments. Perhaps, but that was certainly not the marketing angle chosen by Makawi. Instead, he pitched the fund's diversification benefits, meaning that by purchasing shares in the fund, investors might simultaneously increase the return and decrease the risk of their total portfolios. In other words, Shuaa Capital hoped to attract investors in TAIF in precisely the same way that fund managers in the United States, and indeed around the world, do—by appealing to investors' desires for higher returns while assuaging their fears about risk.

But is it possible to increase returns and decrease risk at the same time? The answer depends on the definition of risk. If risk means volatility, the up-and-down movements of a given investment, then indeed it is possible to combine one investment with another in a way that reduces volatility and increases returns. A necessary condition for this happy circumstance to occur is a low degree of correlation between the two investments—that is, a tendency for their fluctuations to offset each other. In his appeal to investors, Ziad Makawi claimed that his fund's investments in Arab government bonds

would have low to negative correlation with other asset classes, such as stocks and bonds from other countries. In other words, Makawi's appeal was not to investors who held portfolios consisting of Arab investments exclusively, but to those whose investments were concentrated in the United States, Europe, and other parts of the world.

Source: "Shuaa Launches Fixed Income Fund," *Khaleej Times* (March 6, 2002).

What is it worth? is perhaps the most important question in finance. For an investor contemplating a stock purchase or a corporate manager weighing a proposal to build a new plant, placing a value on risky assets is fundamental to the decision-making process. The procedure for valuing a risky asset involves three basic steps: (1) determining the asset's expected cash flows, (2) choosing a discount rate that reflects the asset's risk, and (3) calculating the present value. Finance professionals apply these three steps, known as discounted cash flow (DCF) analysis, to value a wide range of real and financial assets. Chapter 3 introduced you to the rather mechanical third step of this process, converting a sequence of future cash flows into a single number reflecting an asset's present value. In this chapter and the next, we will emphasize the second step in DCF valuation—determining the appropriate discount rate.

Matching a discount rate to a specific asset requires answers to two critical questions. First, how risky is the asset, investment, or project that we want to value? Second, how much return should the project offer, given its risk? This chapter offers an answer to the first question, showing how different ways of defining and measuring risk apply to individual assets as compared to portfolios (collections of different assets). Some fluctuations in individual asset values cancel out in a portfolio, so investors should concern themselves only with those risks that remain, even in a well-diversified portfolio.

Building on this foundation, Chapter 6 provides a solution to the second problem, determining the required return for an asset with a particular risk level. If investors can easily eliminate part of an investment's risk through diversification, then the market should price (i.e., require a higher return for) only the undiversifiable component of risk. The capital asset pricing model (CAPM) proposes a specific way to measure this risk and to determine what compensation the market expects in exchange for that risk. By quantifying the relationship between risk and return, the CAPM supplies finance professionals with a powerful tool for determining the value of financial assets such as shares of stock, as well as real assets such as new plants and equipment. For their pathbreaking research on portfolio theory and the CAPM, Harry Markowitz and William Sharpe shared the 1990 Nobel Prize in economics (along with co-recipient Merton Miller).[1]

The CAPM's most basic insight, and indeed that of all asset pricing models, is that a trade-off exists between risk and return—to achieve higher returns, investors generally have to accept greater risks. From a purely theoretical perspective, it may seem logical that rewards and risk should be linked, but the notion that an unavoidable trade-off between the two exists is grounded in fact. In countries around the world, historical capital market data offer compelling evidence of a positive relationship between risk and return. It is to that evidence that we now turn.

[1.] DCF analysis is probably the most widely used financial valuation tool in corporate finance, but an alternative approach based on the principle of "no arbitrage" is used to value stock options and other assets with optionlike characteristics. The Nobel committee recognized the fundamental importance of both valuation paradigms when it awarded its 1997 prize in economics to Myron Scholes and Robert Merton, pioneers in the development of option-pricing theory.

5.1 RISK AND RETURN FUNDAMENTALS

A Historical Overview of Risk and Return

During the past 30 years, the percentage of U.S. households that own common stock, either directly as part of an investment portfolio or indirectly as part of their pension fund, has more than doubled to roughly 50 percent.[2] Although the level of stock ownership in most other Western countries is somewhat lower (15–30 percent in much of Western Europe, less in Japan, and *higher* than the U.S. level in Australia and Sweden), it has been rising even more rapidly in these countries over the past three decades. Why has this occurred? Why have investors throughout the developed world increasingly chosen to place their hard-earned savings in an investment vehicle that (1) is the most junior financial claim—meaning that if the firm goes bankrupt, all other claimants (creditors, vendors, employees) will be paid before money is distributed to stockholders; (2) does not promise a fixed, legally enforceable return to investors, but rather offers a relatively uncertain stream of cash dividend payments; and (3) has a history of great variability? In other words, why have seemingly rational investors chosen to put their money into risky stocks, given the availability of safer alternatives?

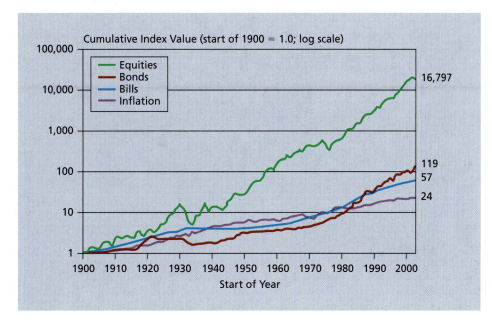

Figure 5.1
The Value of $1 Invested for 100 Years in Several U.S. Asset Classes

Source: Dimson and Marsh (2002).

Figure 5.1 provides much of the answer to this question, at least for U.S. investors. The figure compares the long-run performance of several types of investments during the twentieth century. The top line shows that the value of $1 invested in common stocks in 1900 would have grown to $16,797 by the year 2000. By comparison, a $1 investment in long-term government bonds would have grown to just $119 over the century. Remember, U.S. Treasury bonds receive backing by the full faith and

---

[2] The Investment Company Institute (ICI) reports that the percentage of U.S. households owning mutual funds, funds that pool contributions from many different investors to purchase financial assets, increased by a factor of 9 from 1980 to 2001. For this and other statistical data on the mutual fund industry in the United States, visit the ICI's website at http://www.ici.org.

credit of the U.S. government, making them among the safest long-term investments in the world. Even less risky are U.S. Treasury bills, which also enjoy the backing of the U.S. government but have shorter maturities than bonds. Because T-bills are short-term instruments, their prices do not fluctuate as much as Treasury bond prices do when interest rates change. Not surprisingly, T-bills offered even lower returns than bonds, with a $1 investment growing to just $57 over 100 years. The inescapable conclusion from Figure 5.1 is that common stocks provided superior returns during the last century compared to those of bonds and bills.

The bottom line in Figure 5.1 plots a consumer price index showing the cumulative inflation that occurred in the United States from 1900 to 2000. The line shows that prices rose by a factor of 24 during the century, meaning that the purchasing power of $1 in 1900 was equivalent to the purchasing power of $24 in 2000. Why do we include a plot of inflation in a graph focusing on investment returns? Because when people invest, they are sacrificing the opportunity to spend their money today in exchange for the opportunity to consume more in the future. Economists refer to the increase in purchasing power that an investment provides as its *real return*. An asset that merely keeps pace with inflation offers a real return of zero and fails to deliver increased future consumption for investors. For example, suppose that a boy born on January 1, 1900, received one share of stock in the Millennium Company from a generous relative and held it for a lifetime. Imagine that the price of this stock was $1 at the time. Over the next 100 years, the Millennium Company never paid a dividend, but its stock price steadily increased to $24 by January 1, 2000. What could our centenarian purchase if he sold his stock on his one-hundredth birthday? With the 24-fold rise in prices, one share of Millennium stock would buy no more or less than it did in 1900.

With the definition of a real return in mind, look again at Figure 5.1. Notice that the lines tracking Treasury bond and bill returns generally lie above the line tracing inflation, but not by much. Individuals who invested only in T-bills over the past century would have increased their purchasing power about 2.4 times ($57 ÷ $24 = 2.375), compared to an almost fivefold purchasing-power increase for those who invested in bonds ($119 ÷ $24 = 4.958). Both bills and bonds, therefore, provided a positive real return during the century, but the real returns on bonds and bills pale in comparison to the real return generated by common stocks. Investors who held stocks over the century would have increased their purchasing power almost 700 times ($16,797 ÷ $24 = 699.875). In light of this evidence, the rising tide of stock ownership is hardly surprising.

Table 5.1 looks at the data on long-term returns from another perspective. The first column of data shows the average annual real return on each type of investment over the century, and the second column gives the standard deviation of annual returns

Table 5.1
Real Returns on U.S.
Investments, 1900–2000

Asset	Mean Return (%)	Standard Deviation (%)	Highest Year (%)	Lowest Year (%)
Stocks	8.7	20.2	56.8	−38.0
Bonds	2.1	10.0	35.1	−19.3
Bills	1.0	4.7	20.0	−15.1
Inflation	3.3	5.0	20.4	−10.8

Source: Dimson and Marsh (2002).

for each asset type.[3] Recall from statistics that the standard deviation measures the dispersion of a random variable around its average, so we can interpret it as a measure of the uncertainty associated with each asset class. The third and fourth columns list the highest and lowest single-year real returns for each investment. A glance at the table reveals that higher returns on equity investments come at a price—higher volatility. Though the average real return on equity was 8.7 percent, the annual standard deviation of common stock returns was 20.2 percent, and the spread between the best (+56.8 percent) and worst (−38.0 percent) years was an astounding 94.8 percent! In other words, while investors historically earned higher returns on stocks than on other investments, the year-to-year fluctuations in stock returns was quite high. In contrast, the standard deviation of real T-bill returns was just 4.7 percent. Investors who opted for the relative certainty of T-bill returns earned very low real returns on average, just 1.0 percent per year.

SMART IDEAS VIDEO
Robert Shiller, Yale University
"The most famous example of a stock market bubble is the 1920s."
See the entire interview at **SMARTFinance**

By comparing the returns on the most and least volatile investments in Table 5.1, we can measure the equity **risk premium,** the difference in annual returns between common stocks and Treasury bills. During the twentieth century, the equity premium in the United States averaged 7.7 percent (8.7 percent returns on stocks minus 1.0 percent returns on T-bills).[4] To many, the size of the equity premium is a mystery. The 7.7 percent premium seems to imply that investors historically required a high degree of compensation to invest in stocks rather than T-bills. Financial economists refer to the surprisingly high equity premium in the United States as the **equity premium puzzle.** As the Comparative Corporate Finance insert explains, the U.S. equity risk premium lies well within the range observed in other industrialized countries.

SMART IDEAS VIDEO
Elroy Dimson, London Business School
"The worldwide average equity premium has been somewhere in the 4 to 5 percent range."
See the entire interview at **SMARTFinance**

APPLYING THE MODEL

As you will see throughout this text, the equity risk premium is an extremely important number in corporate finance. Analysts use the equity premium to project future investment returns, to calculate the cost of capital for firms, and to evaluate alternative investment proposals. For example, suppose that in October 2002, an investment banker is trying to place a value on a firm that her client is interested in acquiring. The analyst projects the firm's cash flows going forward and decides to discount them at a rate comparable to the return on the overall stock market. How can the analyst make a long-term projection of U.S. equity returns? By consulting

---

[3.] Table 5.1 also shows statistics for inflation. You can closely approximate the real return on an investment by subtracting the inflation rate from the nominal, or actual, return, which of course means that you can add the real return to the inflation rate to obtain the nominal return. For example, Table 5.1 shows that U.S. stocks earned an average annual real return of 8.7 percent, while inflation averaged 3.3 percent annually. The nominal average annual return on equities must therefore be roughly equal to the sum of these figures, 12.0 percent. A more precise definition of the real return is shown in the following equation:

$$\text{real rate} = \frac{(1 + \text{nominal rate})}{(1 + \text{inflation rate})} - 1$$

If we plug in 0.087 for the real rate and 0.033 for the inflation rate, we can solve for the nominal rate of 0.123, or 12.3 percent, very close to our 12.0 percent approximation.

[4.] One could also define the equity risk premium as the difference between average stock and bond returns. The rationale for defining the equity premium this way is that investors view both stocks and bonds as long-term investments, whereas T-bills are clearly short-term instruments. Though it is smaller because bonds pay higher returns than bills, the equity risk premium is still quite substantial using this definition.

COMPARATIVE CORPORATE FINANCE

Investment Returns in 16 Countries

Table 5.2 shows real returns on common stocks, government bonds, and government bills from 1900 to 2000 for 16 different countries. Several robust patterns emerge from the table. First, in every country, the average annual return was lowest for bills and highest for common stocks, with bond returns falling in between. Second, the same pattern holds for standard deviations across countries. Bills exhibit the least year-to-year volatility, while stocks show the most variability. If we accept volatility as a measure of risk, this pattern makes sense because we expect riskier investments to pay higher returns over time. In other words, *investors seeking higher returns must generally accept more risk.*

Notice that in real terms, bills are not really risk-free investments. Remember, the real return on an investment approximately equals the nominal return minus the inflation rate. In France, Italy, and Japan, the average real return on bills falls below zero. Assuming that no one expects a negative return when investing, the negative average returns on bills suggest that investors in

these three countries encountered higher-than-expected inflation over time. A few countries sell government bonds that offer investors protection from this inflation risk. For example, in 1994 the U.S. government began selling Treasury Inflation Protection Securities (TIPS), which make coupon payments that fluctuate as the inflation rate moves. Because coupon and principal payments on TIPS rise and fall with the inflation rate, investors receive a risk-free real return, though, of course, the nominal return on TIPS varies over time.

By subtracting the average return on bills from the average equity return, we can estimate the equity risk premium in each country. The premium ranges from a high of 9.7 percent in Italy to a low of 3.2 percent in Denmark. The U.S. premium of 7.7 percent ties for seventh place among these nations. Keep in mind that these figures represent the historical equity risk premium in each country, which may or may not be a good forecast of the prospective risk premium in the future.

Table 5.2
Means and Standard Deviations of Real Returns on Asset Classes around the World, 1900–2000

Country	Common Stocks (%)		Government Bonds (%)		Government Bills (%)		Equity Risk Premium
	Mean Return	Standard Deviation	Mean Return	Standard Deviation	Mean Return	Standard Deviation	
Australia	9.0	17.7	1.9	13.0	0.6	5.6	8.4
Belgium	4.8	22.8	0.3	12.1	0.0	8.2	4.8
Canada	7.7	16.8	2.4	10.6	1.8	5.1	5.9
Denmark	6.2	20.1	3.3	12.5	3.0	6.4	3.2
France	6.3	23.1	0.1	14.4	−2.6	11.4	8.9
Germany	8.8	32.3	0.3	15.9	0.1	10.6	8.7
Ireland	7.0	22.2	2.4	13.3	1.4	6.0	5.6
Italy	6.8	29.4	−0.8	14.4	−2.9	12.0	9.7
Japan	9.3	30.3	1.3	20.9	−0.3	14.5	9.6
The Netherlands	7.7	21.0	1.5	9.4	0.8	5.2	6.9
South Africa	9.1	22.8	1.9	10.6	1.0	6.4	8.1
Spain	5.8	22.0	1.9	12.0	0.6	6.1	5.2
Sweden	9.9	22.8	3.1	12.7	2.2	6.8	7.7
Switzerland	6.9	20.4	3.1	8.0	1.2	6.2	5.7
United Kingdom	7.6	20.0	2.3	14.5	1.2	6.6	6.4
United States	8.7	20.2	2.1	10.0	1.0	4.7	7.7

Source: Dimson and Marsh (2002).

Notes: Bond and bill statistics exclude 1922–1923 for Germany, and Swiss equity data begins in 1911. The equity risk premium is calculated as the difference between each country's mean return on common stock and its mean return on government bills.

A careful reader may notice one troubling pattern in the table. Thus far, we have used the standard deviation of returns as a proxy for risk, a practice that seems to work well when comparing one asset class to another. In every country, the data show a positive link between the standard deviation of returns and the average return when we compare bills to bonds or bonds to stocks. Can we extend this logic to compare one country to another? In Table 5.2, the country with the most volatile stock market over the last century was Germany, but the average return in Germany ranked only fifth among the 16 nations in the table. Similarly, the nation with the least volatile stock market was Canada, but 8 countries experienced lower average stock returns. Perhaps the positive relationship between risk and returns that holds from one asset class to another does not hold across national boundaries. Another explanation, and one to which we will return later in this chapter, is that the standard deviation of returns may not be an appropriate proxy for risk.

Table 5.1, the analyst sees that the premium on equities versus bonds averaged about 6.6 percent over the last 100 years. The yield on long-term Treasury bonds in October 2002 was roughly 4.0 percent, so adding the 6.6 percent equity premium to this figure yields a forecast for equity returns of 10.6 percent.[5] Using historical data is a common, but very rough approach for estimating the equity risk premium in the future. We discuss alternative methods in Chapter 9. ▪

The term "equity risk premium" seems to imply that stocks are riskier than bonds or bills, and certainly a comparison of the standard deviations of stock, bond, and bill returns in Tables 5.1 and 5.2 support that conclusion. However, those standard deviations are calculated using 1-year, holding-period returns. In other words, we calculate the rate of return assuming an investor buys stocks (or bonds or bills) at the beginning of each year and sells them at the end of the year. Repeating this process year after year generates a series of 1-year returns, and it is the standard deviation of that series that we report in the tables. However, it is possible to do these calculations using longer holding periods. For example, suppose that an investor buys stocks today and holds them for two years before selling. We can calculate the investor's average annual rate of return over this horizon and then repeat that calculation every two years. It turns out that the differences in volatility between stocks and other investments depend on the holding-period assumptions used to do the math.

Figure 5.2 illustrates this phenomenon using a 200-year sample of U.S. investment returns.[6] Assuming a 1-year holding period, the standard deviation of stocks is 2 (3) times greater than the standard deviation of bonds (bills). As the holding period increases, the standard deviation of all three investments declines, but it declines most rapidly for stocks. Using a 20-year holding period, stocks, bonds, and bills have nearly identical standard deviations, and at longer horizons stocks actually have a lower standard deviation than either bonds or bills.

So are stocks riskier than bonds? In the short run, the answer is absolutely yes. In the long run, it is harder to say. Relative to the risk of investing in bonds or bills, the risk of buying stocks declines rapidly over long periods of time, but we must temper that conclusion with an important observation. Even with 200 years of data to

---

[5.] This is an approximation. The exact formula is much like the one that links real returns to nominal returns and inflation:

$$\text{equity premium} = \frac{(1 + \text{equity return})}{(1 + \text{bond return})} - 1$$

Plugging in 0.066 for the equity premium and 0.040 for the bond return yields an equity return of 0.109 or 10.9 percent.

[6.] We thank Jeremy Siegel for granting permission to use this figure, which appears in the third edition of his book, *Stocks for the Long Run* (New York: McGraw-Hill, 2002).

Figure 5.2
The Standard Deviation of
Stocks, Bonds, and Bills
for Different Holding
Periods (1802–2001)

Source: Siegel (2002).

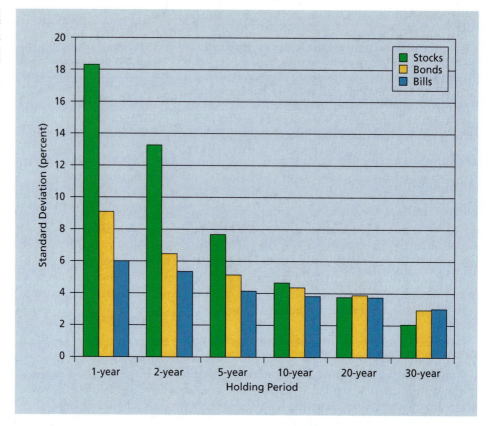

examine, we have fewer than seven independent (nonoverlapping) 30-year periods from which to draw conclusions. The data indicate that historically stocks and bonds have had a similar degree of risk for long holding periods, but we are hesitant to conclude that the next 200 years of data will reveal the same pattern.

RISK AVERSION

To understand why riskier investments offer a premium, it is necessary to make some assumptions describing the preferences and behavior of investors. Most financial models begin with the assumption that investors are **risk averse.** Risk aversion does not imply that investors always shun risk. Instead, risk aversion means that investors require compensation for taking risk. Here's a simple illustration that makes the point. Suppose that a friend offers you the following gamble. You roll a fair die. If the number six comes up, you win $6,000; otherwise, you win nothing. Your friend offers to let you play this game for a $1,000 fee. Would you play?

Assuming that the die is fair, the probability that you will roll a six and win $6,000 is one-sixth, or 16.67 percent. Thus, your expected payoff (or expected dollar return) from playing the game is calculated as follows:

Expected payoff = expected winnings − fee = (16.67% × $6,000) − $1,000 = $0

Statisticians refer to a gamble like this one as a **fair bet,** meaning that it offers an expected payoff of zero. Risk-averse investors will not accept this or any other fair bet because it exposes them to risk without offering (on average) any compensation in return. To persuade risk-averse investors to play this game, either the odds would have to be tilted in their favor (e.g., paying the $6,000 payoff for rolling either a five or a six), the payoff increased (e.g., paying $10,000 for rolling a six), or the entry fee reduced so that the expected payoff becomes positive.

We can extend this example to capital markets in a straightforward manner. The data in Table 5.1 illustrate that stocks outperform bonds on average, but the high standard deviation on stocks implies that sometimes they perform quite poorly. The years 2000–2001, for example, witnessed a decline in the value of most international stock indexes, while bonds generally posted above-average returns. Yet many investors persist in holding stocks in their investment portfolios. These investors presumably anticipate that stocks will continue to earn higher average returns than bonds, providing compensation for the higher risks associated with equity securities. Because the numbers in Table 5.1 show a consistent positive relationship between an asset's volatility and its average return, we conclude that the data are consistent with the hypothesis that investors are generally risk averse.

Of course, it is possible that some investors care only about the returns on their investments, totally disregarding risk. Investors of this type are said to be **risk neutral**, implying that they prefer investments with higher returns whether or not they entail greater risk. A risk-neutral investor would neither avoid nor accept our die-throwing gamble because it offers a zero expected return. But such an investor would accept the bet with only the slightest favorable modification, such as increasing the payoff from throwing a six in our hypothetical gamble from $6,000 to $6,001. Adding one dollar would generate a small, but positive expected payoff, and someone unconcerned with the risk of the proposition would roll the die. Similarly, a risk-neutral investor would be willing to buy stocks as long as they offer even a tiny premium over other investments, regardless of their risk.

Finally, we can define an almost pathological **risk-seeking** investor. A risk-seeking individual prefers to take risk and will be willing to invest in a risky asset when its expected return falls below that of a safer alternative. Risk-seeking investors may even purchase investments with negative expected returns. A risk-seeking investor might accept the die-throwing bet even if the payoff from rolling a six was just $4,000, resulting in a negative expected payoff. Risk-seeking investors would jump at the opportunity to buy stocks even if they offered lower returns than bonds. Clearly, the evidence on stock and bond returns does not support the notion that most people exhibit risk-seeking behavior when they invest their savings. Even so, examples of risk-seeking behavior easily come to mind. Lottery tickets and Las Vegas casinos give investors the opportunity to make high-risk "investments" with negative average returns.[7]

The most plausible explanation for the relationship between risk and return observed in capital markets is that investors are risk averse. High-risk investments must offer the prospect of high returns to attract investors. For a risk-averse investor, the ideal portfolio is the one that offers the most favorable trade-off between risk and return. The rest of this chapter deals with the search for that portfolio. That search begins with precise definitions of *risk* and *return*.

---

1. Is purchasing insurance an example of risk-averse, risk-neutral, or risk-seeking behavior? Explain.

2. If the real return on a risk-free investment is barely above zero, will a very cautious investor do almost as well to stuff his or her money inside a mattress rather than buy a Treasury bill (T-bill)?

Concept Review Questions

---

[7] One could argue that the negative return on gambling reflects its consumption value. After all, where else besides Las Vegas can you take in Wayne Newton and Julio Iglesias on the same night?

5.2 BASIC RISK AND RETURN STATISTICS

RETURN OF A SINGLE ASSET

The total gain or loss on an investment over a given period of time is called the investment's **return.** The return includes the change in the asset's values (either a gain or loss) plus any cash distributions such as dividends or interest payments. The mathematical expression for the return on an asset from time t to $t + 1$ is given by Equation 5.1:

$$R_{t+1} = \frac{P_{t+1} - P_t + CF_{t+1}}{P_t} \qquad \text{(Eq. 5.1)}$$

where P_{t+1} represents the asset's price at time $t + 1$, P_t is the price at time t, and CF_{t+1} is the cash flow paid by the asset at time $t + 1$. The numerator represents the dollar return on this investment from time t to time $t + 1$, and dividing through by the initial price of the asset, P_t, converts this dollar return into a fractional return. Multiplying this by 100 yields a percentage return. This equation measures returns after the fact, or *ex post.* But uncertainty about asset returns forms the very fabric of portfolio theory. Thus, we need a measure of an asset's *ex ante* expected return.

Estimating expected returns is very difficult, and we defer a more detailed discussion of that process to the next chapter. However, as a starting point, suppose that the past tells us something useful about the future. By observing returns on an investment or a group of similar investments over time (as in Table 5.1), we may surmise that the average return earned in the past provides a reasonable guess about the average return going forward.

A technical issue arises when using average historical returns to estimate expected returns. To illustrate the problem, look at the returns earned by a stock from 2001 to 2004:

Year	Return
2004	+12.2%
2003	+20.2%
2002	−18.2%
2001	+23.9%

What was the average annual return on this stock over these years? The simplest way to answer this question is to calculate the **arithmetic average return** by adding up the numbers in the second column and dividing the sum by 4, the number of observations. From 2001 to 2004, the arithmetic average return was 9.525 percent. An alternative approach is to calculate the **geometric average return.** The geometric average represents the compound annual return earned by an investor who bought and held the stock for four years. The geometric average of a series of annual returns over t years can be calculated using Equation 5.2:

$$\text{Geometric average return} = [(1 + R_1)(1 + R_2)(1 + R_3) \cdots (1 + R_t)]^{1/t} - 1 \qquad \text{(Eq. 5.2)}$$

Applying this formula to our example yields the following:

$$\text{Geometric average return} = [(1 + 0.122)(1 + 0.202)(1 - 0.182)(1 + 0.239)]^{1/4} - 1$$
$$= 0.081 \text{ or } 8.1\%$$

Notice that the arithmetic average exceeds the geometric average by about 1.4 percent. If returns vary through time, the geometric average will always fall below the arithmetic mean, and the difference between the two figures increases the greater the volatility in returns. For example, let us compare the arithmetic and geometric average real returns, as well as the standard deviation of returns, for common stock investments in Germany and Canada.[8]

Country	Geometric Average (%)	Arithmetic Average (%)	Standard Deviation (%)
Germany	3.6	8.8	32.3
Canada	6.4	7.7	16.8

In Germany, the arithmetic average return exceeds the geometric average by 5.2 percentage points, while in Canada the arithmetic average is just 1.3 percentage points higher than the geometric average. The reason for the discrepancy is that German stocks were much more volatile than Canadian equities over the past 100 years.

In Tables 5.1 and 5.2, we examined the equity risk premium by comparing the average returns on stocks and bills over 100 years. The returns in those tables are arithmetic averages. We know that stock returns display more volatility than bill returns do, so the difference between the arithmetic and geometric average returns for stocks will be much higher than the same difference for bills (just as the difference is higher for Germany than for Canada). Therefore, we will obtain a much higher estimate of the equity risk premium if we take the difference in arithmetic averages between stocks and bills than if we do the same calculation using geometric returns. For example, the U.S. equity premium (over bills) during the past century equals 5.8 percent using geometric means, but 7.7 percent using arithmetic averages.

But which number, the geometric or the arithmetic mean, serves as a better estimate of expected returns? Keep in mind that arithmetic and geometric means measure different things. The arithmetic mean is an estimate of the return one might expect, on average, in a single period. The geometric mean represents the average annual compound return one might expect after a series of repeated "draws" from a distribution of returns. Some economists recommend using the arithmetic mean when the holding period for the investment under consideration is very short, and the geometric mean when a long holding period applies. For now, we remain noncommittal on the choice of arithmetic versus geometric average returns to estimate expected returns, though we will return to this issue in Chapter 6.

RISK OF A SINGLE ASSET

Definitions of risk involve a degree of subjectivity. To most people, the term "risk" connotes the possibility of a bad outcome, perhaps earning a negative return on an investment, or worse, losing the entire sum of money invested. However, most financial models do not define risk strictly in terms of unfavorable outcomes. There are several reasons for this, but the simplest explanation arises from the properties of historical returns. An examination of the year-to-year returns earned by different types of investments yields an interesting symmetry. Those assets that earn the highest returns in good times often earn the lowest returns in bad times. Even recent history teaches that lesson. The Nasdaq Composite Index, a U.S. stock index heavily

---

[8.] *Source:* Dimson and Marsh (2002).

Figure 5.3
Histogram of Real Stock
Returns in the United
States (1900–2000)

Source: Dimson and Marsh
(2002).

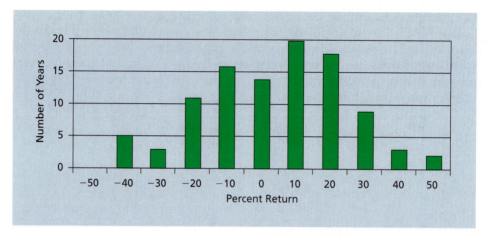

weighted with high-tech companies, rose 82 percent in 1999, but over the 31 months beginning in January 2000, the index declined by 68 percent. In contrast, the Standard & Poor's 500 Index (S&P 500), a collection of 500 large firms from a wide variety of industries, rose nearly 20 percent in 1999, and over the next 31 months, it fell by 36 percent.

Suppose we know that the returns offered by some investment follow a particular **probability distribution.** This distribution tells us what investment outcomes are possible and associates a probability with each outcome. Unfortunately, the probability distribution for almost any real-world investment cannot be known with certainty. However, by plotting a histogram showing the relative frequencies of different outcomes in the past, we can gain insight into the underlying, unknown distribution.

Figure 5.3 provides a histogram of annual real common stock returns in the United States from 1900 to 2000. You can see that stock returns tend to cluster near the middle of the histogram, with extremely good and bad years occurring infrequently. If you draw a smooth curve that just touches the top of each bar in the picture, you will generate a curve that is roughly bell shaped, like the familiar **normal distribution.** The normal distribution has several properties that make it useful in financial modeling. First, the distribution is symmetric about its mean, which implies that the probability of an outcome in the far right tail (e.g., very high returns) of the distribution matches the probability of an outcome in the far left tail (e.g., very low returns). The normal distribution's symmetry makes it easy to determine the probabilities of events that fall within certain ranges. For example, about 68 percent of the time a normally distributed random variable falls within one standard deviation of the mean, and about 95 percent of the time it falls within two standard deviations of the mean. Second, the normal distribution can be fully described by just two characteristics—its mean and variance (or equivalently, the standard deviation, the square root of variance). Assuming that the normal distribution provides a reasonable approximation for stock returns allows us to narrow the characteristics by which investors judge alternative investments to simply the mean and variance.

But does the normal distribution reasonably approximate returns on the assets available to investors in the real world? A glance at Figure 5.3 suggests that the approximation is a good one, though not perfect. One problem is that the histogram appears to be more "lumpy" than a normal curve. Even after 100 years of stock market history, there still may not be enough data to generate a perfectly smooth histogram. Beyond that, histograms of stock returns often exhibit an elongated right tail, indicating that very high returns occur more frequently than very low returns do.

This "right skewness" appears most dramatically when returns are measured over horizons of a year or more. In part, the skewness results from the limited liability protection afforded corporations. The minimum possible return on a share of common stock is −100 percent because a stock's price cannot fall below zero. On the other hand, there is no upper limit on a stock's return, resulting in the long right tail in return histograms.[9]

If we were to compare the histogram in Figure 5.3 to the same type of diagram for bond returns, the comparison would show that the likelihood of very low returns on stocks is greater than on bonds, but so is the likelihood of very high returns. If investments that offer a good chance of making a very high return also carry a substantial risk of very low returns, perhaps a reasonable way to define risk is to focus on the dispersion of returns. The most common measure of dispersion used as a proxy for risk in finance is the variance, or its square root, the standard deviation. The variance of a distribution equals the expected value of squared deviations from the mean. Suppose we treat the return on an investment as a random variable denoted R, with a mean, or expected value, of $E(R)$. Equation 5.3 gives the variance of returns for this investment, usually denoted by the Greek letter σ (sigma) squared, or σ^2:

$$\text{Variance} = \sigma^2 = E\{[R - E(R)]^2\} \qquad \text{(Eq. 5.3)}$$

where E stands for "expected value of."

If the range of possible returns for this investment is known, along with the probability attached to each possible outcome, then it is possible to calculate the variance using these probabilities. Consider the following hypothetical example. Suppose that a firm is involved in product liability litigation, and a decision in the case is expected today. If the firm's defense succeeds, its stock will rise 15 percent. You assess the probability of a successful defense to be 0.55. If the firm loses the case, its stock will drop 10 percent. Today's expected return and variance for this stock are calculated as follows:[10]

$$\text{Expected return} = 0.55(15\%) + 0.45(-10\%) = 3.75\%$$

$$\text{Variance} = 0.55(15\% - 3.75\%)^2 + 0.45(-10\% - 3.75\%)^2 = 154.7\%^2$$

Notice the peculiar units of measure in the variance calculation—percent squared! Rather than worry about how to interpret these admittedly odd units, simply take the square root and convert variance to standard deviation:

$$\text{Standard deviation} = \sigma = \sqrt{154.7\%^2} = 12.4\%$$

Though there may be special cases in which calculating the variance of returns for an investment using this probability-based approach makes sense, in most cases it is not feasible to list either the full set of returns that an investment might earn or their associated probabilities. Instead, financial analysts usually gather historical data and estimate the variance and standard deviation from these observations. In that case, we can use Equation 5.4 to calculate the variance:

---

[9] A distribution that allows for right skewness and more closely matches long-term historical return data is the lognormal distribution. Like the normal distribution, the lognormal distribution is fully described by its mean and variance.
[10] In the variance calculation, we are using percentage figures for returns rather than decimals—that is, 15 percent rather than 0.15. If we used decimals, the expected return and variance would be 0.0375 and .01547.

Table 5.3
Variance Calculation
for Cisco Systems

Month	Return	$(R\text{-mean})^2$	Month	Return	$(R\text{-mean})^2$
August 02	−0.083	0.010	October 99	0.079	0.004
July 02	−0.054	0.005	September 99	0.011	0.000
June 02	−0.116	0.018	August 99	0.092	0.005
May 02	0.077	0.003	July 99	−0.036	0.003
April 02	−0.135	0.023	June 99	0.182	0.027
March 02	0.186	0.028	May 99	−0.045	0.004
February 02	−0.279	0.088	April 99	0.041	0.001
January 02	0.093	0.006	March 99	0.120	0.010
December 01	−0.114	0.017	February 99	−0.123	0.020
November 01	0.208	0.036	January 99	0.202	0.034
October 01	0.389	0.138	December 98	0.231	0.045
September 01	−0.254	0.074	November 98	0.196	0.032
August 01	−0.150	0.028	October 98	0.019	0.000
July 01	0.056	0.001	September 98	0.132	0.013
June 01	−0.055	0.005	August 98	−0.145	0.027
May 01	0.134	0.013	July 98	0.040	0.000
April 01	0.074	0.003	June 98	0.217	0.040
March 01	−0.333	0.123	May 98	0.032	0.000
February 01	−0.367	0.149	April 98	0.071	0.003
January 01	−0.021	0.002	March 98	0.038	0.000
December 00	−0.201	0.048	February 98	0.045	0.001
November 00	−0.111	0.017	January 98	0.131	0.013
October 00	−0.025	0.002	December 97	−0.030	0.002
September 00	−0.195	0.045	November 97	0.052	0.001
August 00	0.049	0.001	October 97	0.122	0.011
July 00	0.030	0.000	September 97	−0.031	0.002
June 00	0.116	0.010			
May 00	−0.179	0.039	**Average (mean)**		
April 00	−0.103	0.015	return	0.018	
March 00	0.170	0.023	**Sum of squared**		
February 00	0.207	0.036	deviations		1.375
January 00	0.022	0.000	**N − 1**		59.000
December 99	0.201	0.033	**Variance**		0.023
November 99	0.205	0.035	**Standard deviation**		0.153

$$\text{Variance} = \sigma^2 = \frac{\sum_{t=1}^{N} (R_{it} - \overline{R}_i)^2}{N - 1} \qquad \text{(Eq. 5.4)}$$

where R_{it} represents the return on a particular investment i during period t and $\overline{R}_i$ represents the asset's sample mean return over the sample's N periods [replacing the unobservable expected return, $E(R)$].[11] As usual, the formula for standard deviation is simply the square root of the variance. Table 5.3 illustrates this calculation using monthly returns on Cisco Systems stock over the 5-year period ending August 1,

[11.] If you have the historical returns loaded into an Excel spreadsheet, you can use the formula "=var()" to calculate variance, or "=stdev()" to calculate standard deviation.

2002. First, calculate the average monthly return over this period, 0.018 or 1.8 percent. Next, subtract the mean return from each month's actual return and square the difference. Finally, add up these squared differences and divide by 59 (one less than the number of months in the sample) to obtain the variance, 0.023 percent squared. Taking the square root of this figure yields an estimate of Cisco's monthly standard deviation, 0.153 (15.3%). What does this figure mean? If we assume that Cisco's monthly returns are normally distributed, we can say that two-thirds of the time, Cisco's monthly return will fall within ±15.3 percent of its mean, and 95 percent of Cisco's monthly returns should fall within ±30.6 percent of the mean. Cisco is indeed a volatile stock!

---

3. Variance measures the dispersion of an investment's returns, both above and below the average. A measure of risk should focus only on the bad outcomes. Comment.

4. An investor purchases a share of stock for $20 on January 2, 2004, and sells it for $30 a year later. Is the rate of return on this investment 50 percent? What do you need to know to be sure?

Concept Review Questions

5.3 RISK AND RETURN FOR PORTFOLIOS

PORTFOLIO RETURNS

So far, we have seen only how managers and investors calculate the risk and return of single assets. The most valuable insights regarding the trade-off between risk and return come when we examine what happens when investors combine individual assets to form portfolios. Consider a simple portfolio consisting of just two assets. Denote the fraction (or weight) invested in each asset with w_1 and w_2.[12] The expected return on this portfolio is a simple weighted average of the expected returns of the two assets, $E(R_1)$ and $E(R_2)$, in the portfolio:

$$E(R_p) = w_1 E(R_1) + w_2 E(R_2) \qquad \text{(Eq. 5.5)}$$

Suppose the expected returns on assets 1 and 2 are 10 percent and 20 percent, respectively. If an investor creates a portfolio invested 30 percent in asset 1 and 70 percent in asset 2, the portfolio's expected return can be calculated as follows:

$$E(R_p) = 0.30(10\%) + 0.70(20\%) = 17\%$$

Notice that the equation for the portfolio's expected return is linear. The expected return on this portfolio increases at a constant rate as the proportion invested in asset 1 falls and the proportion invested in asset 2 rises. The general expression for the expected return of a portfolio with N assets is a natural extension of the two-asset case:

$$E(R_p) = w_1 E(R_1) + w_2 E(R_2) + w_3 E(R_3) + \cdots + w_N E(R_N) \qquad \text{(Eq. 5.6)}$$

[12.] At a broader level, you can think of w_1 and w_2 as representing the fraction of an investor's total wealth invested in two classes of assets. Note that the sum of w_1 and w_2 must be 1.0, but the individual weights can be either positive or negative. A negative value of w_1 means that the investor short sells the first asset. Short selling means borrowing the asset from someone else, selling it, and investing the proceeds in the second asset.

When estimating expected returns using historical averages, replace the terms $E(R_i)$ in the equation with $\overline{R}_i$.

Suppose that you want to invest one-third of your money in corporate bonds, one-third in large-firm stocks, and one-third in small-company stocks. You think that the expected return on each asset class is 6.1 percent, 13.0 percent, and 17.7 percent, respectively. What is the expected return on your portfolio?

$$E(R_p) = 0.333(6.1\%) + 0.333(13.0\%) + 0.333(17.7\%) = 12.3\%$$

PORTFOLIO VARIANCE—AN EXAMPLE

Determining the variance or standard deviation of a portfolio is a bit more complicated. First, look at Table 5.4. The table shows monthly returns on four stocks from 1999 to 2001. The first column of data lists returns for MeadWestvaco (Mead Corp.), a major producer and distributor of paper and wood products, including office and school supplies. The second column of data reports monthly returns on the stock of Boise Cascade, distributor of paper and building products and owner of more than 2 million acres of timberland in the United States. The next two columns contain returns for Nike, the well-known designer and marketer of athletic footwear and apparel, and Arrow International, producer of disposable catheters and related products for critical and cardiac care. Underneath the series of monthly returns appear each stock's average monthly return and standard deviation.

Notice that from 1999 to 2001, Nike stock earned the highest average monthly return, 2.06 percent, but also had the highest standard deviation, 14.53 percent. Boise Cascade stock produced the lowest returns, just 0.88 percent per month, but it was also much less volatile than Nike stock, with a standard deviation of 9.88 percent. Mead Corp. shares offered the second-highest monthly return at 1.11 percent, and it had volatility second only to Nike's. Arrow International's average monthly return was 1.08 percent, and it was the least volatile stock, with a standard deviation of 8.42 percent. Though there is not a one-for-one correspondence between stocks' average returns and standard deviations, this example offers some support for the notion that a trade-off exists between volatility and returns. However, you will soon see that a stock's standard deviation sometimes yields a misleading estimate of its risk.

The last two columns of Table 5.4 illustrate the monthly returns that an investor would have earned by forming portfolios of these stocks. One portfolio contains 50 percent of Mead stock and 50 percent of Boise Cascade, while the other contains equal amounts of Nike and Arrow International stock. Because you know that average monthly returns on Mead and Boise were 1.11 percent and 0.88 percent, respectively, you might guess that the monthly return on the Mead-Boise portfolio would fall in between these two figures. Exactly right! The return on a portfolio is just the weighted average of the returns of the stocks in the portfolio. Because this portfolio consists of equal amounts (50%) of each stock, then its return is 0.99 percent, exactly halfway between Mead's return and Boise's. Similarly, the average monthly return on the Nike-Arrow portfolio is 1.57 percent, exactly the midpoint between the returns of Nike and Arrow.

Look closely at the standard deviation of these portfolios, starting with the combination of Mead and Boise Cascade. Mead's standard deviation is 13.00 percent, and Boise's is 9.88 percent. Your intuition might suggest that an equally weighted

Table 5.4
Monthly Returns and Descriptive Statistics for Individual Stocks and Portfolios, 1999–2001

Date	Mead Corp.	Boise Cascade	Nike Inc.	Arrow International	50% Mead 50% Boise	50% Nike 50% Arrow
January 99	−2.35%	−3.02%	12.17%	−10.76%	−2.68%	0.71%
February 99	6.89%	3.33%	17.45%	−12.08%	5.11%	2.68%
March 99	1.03%	4.31%	8.18%	−12.21%	2.67%	−2.02%
April 99	37.11%	24.81%	7.80%	4.35%	30.96%	6.07%
May 99	−11.01%	−1.55%	−2.01%	13.02%	−6.28%	5.51%
June 99	11.71%	8.58%	4.20%	1.97%	10.14%	3.08%
July 99	−1.80%	−9.62%	−17.95%	4.83%	−5.71%	−6.56%
August 99	−8.60%	−6.13%	−10.10%	7.12%	−7.37%	−1.49%
September 99	−7.87%	0.58%	21.91%	−11.85%	−3.64%	5.03%
October 99	4.73%	−2.06%	−1.54%	6.11%	1.33%	2.29%
November 99	−0.40%	−2.98%	−17.86%	10.57%	−1.69%	−3.64%
December 99	21.72%	17.40%	8.01%	−3.13%	19.56%	2.44%
January 00	−14.24%	−12.65%	−8.20%	9.70%	−13.45%	0.75%
February 00	−19.17%	−15.72%	−37.50%	24.35%	−17.45%	−6.57%
March 00	16.70%	17.06%	39.76%	−20.57%	16.88%	9.60%
April 00	−0.36%	−6.29%	9.62%	8.76%	−3.33%	9.19%
May 00	−11.00%	−10.56%	−1.29%	−3.12%	−10.78%	−2.21%
June 00	−18.05%	−10.64%	−6.86%	1.52%	−14.35%	−2.67%
July 00	0.50%	6.76%	9.89%	1.87%	3.63%	5.88%
August 00	6.33%	8.14%	−9.57%	4.57%	7.24%	−2.50%
September 00	−12.82%	−10.59%	1.57%	2.11%	−11.70%	1.84%
October 00	23.80%	8.00%	−0.31%	10.82%	15.90%	5.26%
November 00	−8.05%	0.65%	6.73%	−7.60%	−3.70%	−0.44%
December 00	18.68%	16.97%	31.22%	1.30%	17.82%	16.26%
January 01	−3.27%	−2.07%	−1.42%	−7.18%	−2.67%	−4.30%
February 01	−9.19%	−2.58%	−29.03%	4.74%	−5.89%	−12.14%
March 01	−8.40%	−1.65%	4.15%	3.25%	−5.02%	3.70%
April 01	12.40%	11.40%	3.11%	0.93%	11.90%	2.02%
May 01	3.44%	0.77%	−1.70%	−1.33%	2.11%	−1.51%
June 01	−6.41%	0.20%	2.46%	2.32%	−3.11%	2.39%
July 01	9.51%	2.93%	13.24%	−3.80%	6.22%	4.72%
August 01	12.42%	1.38%	5.15%	−0.18%	6.90%	2.49%
September 01	−16.73%	−19.21%	−6.14%	1.33%	−17.97%	−2.40%
October 01	−3.03%	−3.19%	5.45%	2.01%	−3.11%	3.73%
November 01	15.83%	12.18%	7.35%	−0.38%	14.01%	3.49%
December 01	−0.10%	6.62%	6.36%	5.55%	3.26%	5.95%
Average monthly return	1.11%	0.88%	2.06%	1.08%	0.99%	1.57%
Standard deviation	13.00%	9.88%	14.53%	8.42%	11.12%	5.21%

portfolio of these stocks would have a standard deviation halfway between Mead's and Boise's, or 11.44 percent. In fact, the portfolio's standard deviation is a little less, 11.12 percent. But note that the portfolio's volatility still falls between that of Mead and Boise, as you anticipated.

Now, turn to the Nike-Arrow portfolio. Recalling that the standard deviations for Nike and Arrow are 14.53 percent and 8.42 percent, respectively, you conjecture that the standard deviation of a 50-50 portfolio should be about halfway between these two figures, 11.48 percent. Or perhaps, learning from the Mead-Boise example, you guess that the portfolio's standard deviation will be a bit less than the midpoint. In fact, the standard deviation is just 5.21 percent! The portfolio exhibits *less volatility than either of the stocks it contains*. More important, it achieves a substantial reduction in risk while still offering a return that exceeds the return on Arrow International. In other words, by choosing a portfolio containing both Nike and Arrow, instead of holding only Arrow stock, an investor simultaneously obtains higher returns and lower risk, the best of both worlds. How can this happen?

THE IMPORTANCE OF COVARIANCE

The risk reduction achieved in these portfolios occurs because fluctuations in one asset partially offset fluctuations in the other. This effect is especially dramatic in the Nike-Arrow portfolio because the best months for Nike stock were often the worst months for Arrow, and vice versa. Examine February and July 2001 for prominent examples of this phenomenon. In contrast, the best (worst) periods for Boise were typically periods in which Mead stock also performed well (poorly). September and November 2001 illustrate that tendency. In general, the risk of a portfolio of stocks will depend crucially on whether the components of the portfolio move together, as in the Mead-Boise case, or whether they tend to move in opposite directions, as Nike and Arrow did from 1999 to 2001.

In the concept of **covariance**, statistics provides a way to measure the co-movements of two random variables. Continuing to use the symbols R_1 and R_2 to represent returns on two different assets, the covariance of returns between them, denoted by σ_{12}, is given by Equation 5.7:

$$\text{Covariance }(R_1, R_2) = \sigma_{12} = E\{[R_1 - E(R_1)][R_2 - E(R_2)]\} \qquad \text{(Eq. 5.7)}$$

Remember that the terms $E(R_1)$ and $E(R_2)$ refer to the expected returns on the two assets. In virtually all practical applications, expected returns are unobservable, which means analysts have to estimate the expected return on each asset, often with the mean return from a sample of historical data. Given a sample of N periods during which returns on the assets are observed, the formula for covariance can be seen in Equation 5.8:[13]

$$\text{Covariance }(R_1, R_2) = \sigma_{12} = \frac{\sum_{t=1}^{N}(R_{1t} - \overline{R}_1)(R_{2t} - \overline{R}_2)}{N - 1} \qquad \text{(Eq. 5.8)}$$

Examine the numerator of this formula. Imagine that stocks 1 and 2 tend to move together, as did Mead and Boise Cascade in the previous example. When both stocks

---

[13.] Perhaps you are wondering why we divide by $N - 1$ here and in the variance formula when there are N observations in the sample. The reason is that estimating variance or covariance first requires estimating a mean, and you lose one degree of freedom in doing so. If you had the full population of returns for an investment, rather than just a sample, you could divide by N. Excel gives you the option, when calculating variance or standard deviation, to use formulas that are appropriate for either a sample or a population. In virtually all practical applications, the sample formula is appropriate. An unfortunate quirk of Excel is that its only formula for calculating covariance, "=covar()", divides by N and is, strictly speaking, inaccurate for a sample. However, in a reasonably large sample, dividing by N or $N - 1$ makes little difference.

experience above-average returns, both terms in parentheses will be positive, yielding a positive product when multiplied together. Similarly, when both stocks realize below-average returns, both terms in parentheses will be negative, again resulting in a positive product when multiplied. Thus, two assets that tend to move together will have a positive covariance (the covariance between Mead and Boise is 0.0114). Conversely, suppose the two stocks move in opposite directions, as did Nike and Arrow International. When Nike earns above-average returns, Arrow's will be below average. The product in the numerator will be negative. Likewise, if Arrow's returns are atypically high, Nike's will be unusually low, again resulting in a negative product. Consequently, two assets that tend to move in opposite directions will have a negative covariance (the covariance between Nike and Arrow is −0.0087). When two assets move independently—that is, when one asset's return yields no information about the other asset—then the covariance will be zero.

Covariance figures can be difficult to interpret because they depend on the units of measurement. A covariance calculation for stock returns will yield very different numerical results depending on whether the stock returns are measured in percentages, decimals, or dollars. Does the 0.0114 covariance between Mead and Boise indicate a strong or weak tendency for these two stocks to move together? A standardized measure, one that does not depend on units of measure, would help answer this question. Fortunately, the correlation coefficient is such a measure. Denoted by the Greek letter ρ (rho), the correlation coefficient between two random variables is shown in Equation 5.9:

$$\text{Correlation coefficient} = \rho_{12} = \frac{\sigma_{12}}{\sigma_1 \sigma_2} \qquad \text{(Eq. 5.9)}$$

The **correlation coefficient** standardizes the covariance measure by dividing it by the product of the standard deviations of each asset. Looking back at the formula for covariance, you can see that, like variance, it is measured in "percent-squared" units. Notice that the denominator of the correlation coefficient equation multiplies two figures together that are each measured in percentage units. Therefore, both the numerator and denominator are in "percent-squared" units that cancel each other out. The correlation coefficient is a unit-free measure of the co-movement of two assets, and it ranges between a maximum value of 1.0 and a minimum value of −1.0. If the correlation coefficient between two assets reaches 1.0, they exhibit *perfect positive correlation. Perfect negative correlation* occurs when the correlation coefficient between two assets is −1.0.

Apply this formula to compare the correlation between Mead and Boise Cascade to that of Nike and Arrow International:

$$\text{Mead/Boise correlation} = \frac{0.0114}{(0.13)(0.0988)} = 0.89$$

$$\text{Nike/Arrow correlation} = \frac{-0.0087}{(0.1453)(0.0842)} = -0.71$$

These figures indicate a fairly strong tendency for Mead and Boise returns to move together, not surprising given that they operate in some of the same industry segments, and a somewhat weaker tendency for Nike and Arrow to move in opposite directions. We would have predicted that Mead and Boise would display a high positive correlation, but the negative correlation between Arrow and Nike is quite unusual. Why would good times for Nike translate into bad times for Arrow, and vice versa? Perhaps when people are getting a lot of exercise, and spending plenty of money on Nike products, they are less likely to have heart attacks or other ailments that would make them customers of Arrow International![14]

VARIANCE OF A TWO-ASSET PORTFOLIO

In Table 5.4, you saw the monthly returns on two equally weighted portfolios, calculated by taking a 50-50 weighted average of the individual stock returns in each month. The portfolio containing Nike and Arrow International stock exhibited very low volatility, and now it should be apparent that the explanation for that phenomenon lies in the notion of covariance or correlation. In fact, the variance of any two-asset portfolio depends on three factors: the weight invested in each asset, w_i, the variance of each asset, s_i^2, and the covariance between the two assets, σ_{ij}. The variance of a two-asset portfolio is shown in Equation 5.10:

$$\text{Portfolio variance} = \sigma_p^2 = w_1^2\sigma_1^2 + w_2^2\sigma_2^2 + 2w_1w_2\sigma_{12} \qquad \text{(Eq. 5.10)}$$

Looking at the equation for the correlation coefficient, we can see that the covariance can be expressed as follows:

$$\sigma_{12} = \rho_{12}\sigma_1\sigma_2 \qquad \text{(Eq. 5.11)}$$

Plugging this new expression for covariance into the portfolio variance equation results in Equation 5.12:

$$\text{Portfolio variance} = \sigma_p^2 = w_1^2\sigma_1^2 + w_2^2\sigma_2^2 + 2w_1w_2\rho_{12}\sigma_1\sigma_2 \qquad \text{(Eq. 5.12)}$$

Notice the importance of the correlation between assets 1 and 2 in this expression. When ρ_{12} is positive, the third term in the equation is positive, leading to a higher overall portfolio variance. Conversely, if ρ_{12} is negative, the third term serves to reduce the variance of the portfolio.

APPLYING THE MODEL

What is the standard deviation for a portfolio containing 40 percent Nike and 60 percent Arrow International stock? Using the figures from Table 5.4 and the correlation coefficient between Nike and Arrow of -0.71, you can calculate the portfolio standard deviation in two steps. First, calculate the variance:

$$\sigma^2 = (.4)^2(.1453)^2 + (.6)^2(.0842)^2 + 2(.4)(.6)(-0.71)(.1453)(.0842)$$

$$= 0.00176$$

[14.] Although that story might appeal to someone with a dark sense of humor, we are skeptical. Common macroeconomic factors, such as changes in interest rates, inflation, and economic growth, should affect Nike and Arrow in similar ways, and those common factors tend to generate a positive correlation between most pairs of stocks. Statistics offers a simpler, and more likely, explanation for the negative correlation between Nike and Arrow. When we use a sample to estimate the value of some underlying parameter (like the correlation coefficient), it is always possible that by chance, we draw a very unusual sample. Indeed, if we use weekly data on Nike and Arrow shares from January 2001 to May 2002, the correlation between Nike and Arrow rises to 0.08. Even at that level, the correlation between the two stocks is very weak, but the example illustrates the difficulties analysts face when they estimate the statistical properties of stock returns using historical data.

Then, take the square root to obtain the standard deviation, .0419, or 4.19 percent. Notice that this portfolio has an even lower standard deviation than the 50-50 portfolio in the table.

The equation for portfolio variance allows quick recomputations if the portfolio weights change. Figure 5.4 plots the monthly return and standard deviation for many different combinations of (a) Mead-Boise and (b) Nike-Arrow. Notice that portfolios of Nike-Arrow trace out a backward-bending arc, while portfolios of Mead-Boise form an arc with much less curvature. This is the crux of diversification and the basis for the advice, "Don't keep all your eggs in one basket." The weaker the correlation between two assets, the greater the risk reduction achievable by holding a diversified portfolio of those assets. Figure 5.5 illustrates the point in a general setting with two assets, A and B. Note the change in the y-axis label. In this diagram, we presume that estimates of the expected returns on assets A and B are available (perhaps derived from historical average returns), enabling us to plot expected returns on portfolios. If these two investments are perfectly positively correlated ($\rho = +1.0$), then portfolios will lie along the straight line connecting A and B. If A and B are perfectly negatively correlated ($\rho = -1.0$), then portfolios of the two investments lie along the kinked line going from point A back to the y-axis, and then up to point B. The graph indicates that in this special case, one portfolio of assets A and B exists that has zero risk. Though it is virtually impossible to find two real-world stocks displaying perfect

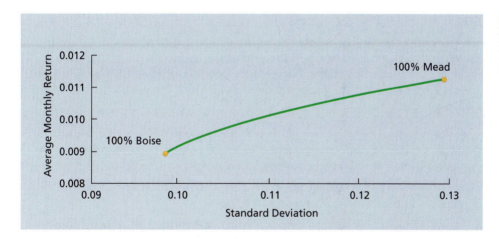

Figure 5.4(a)
Average Return and Standard Deviation for Portfolios of Mead and Boise Cascade

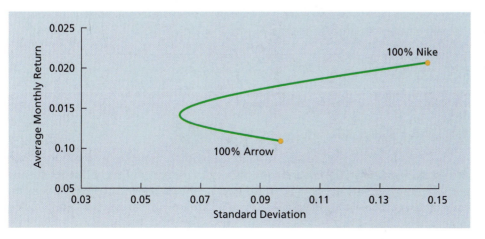

Figure 5.4(b)
Average Return and Standard Deviation for Portfolios of Nike and Arrow International

Figure 5.5
Portfolio Performance
with Different Values
of ρ

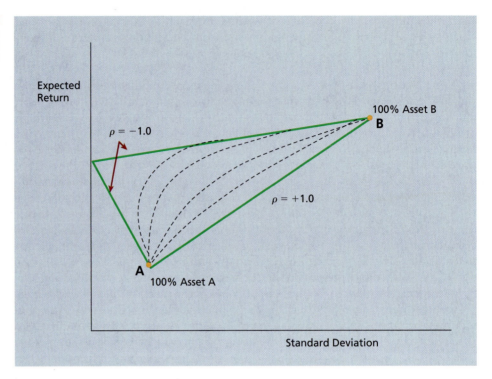

negative correlation, other types of securities can be constructed with this property. As you will see later in the text, option-pricing theory is built on precisely this logic: two risky assets can be combined to create a portfolio that is risk free. The dotted lines in Figure 5.5 illustrate intermediate cases in which the value of ρ falls between $+1.0$ and -1.0.

Concept Review Questions

5. If two assets are negatively correlated, when one has a positive return, the other will have a negative return. A portfolio of these assets will not make any money! Is this correct?

6. If you pick two stocks at random, would you guess that their returns would be positively correlated, independent, or negatively correlated? Why?

7. Imagine that two stocks have the same average return (10%) and the same standard deviation (30%). Would the average return on a 50-50 portfolio of these two stocks be equal to, greater than, or less than 10 percent? Would the portfolio standard deviation be equal to, greater than, or less than 30 percent?

5.4 SYSTEMATIC AND UNSYSTEMATIC RISK

WHAT DRIVES PORTFOLIO RISK?

A simple modification extends the variance equation to a portfolio with more than two assets. Remember, the equation for portfolio variance consists of three elements: portfolio weights, variances of individual assets, and covariances (or correlations) of pairs of assets. The variation equation for a portfolio with three stocks is expressed in Equation 5.13:

$$\sigma_p^2 = w_1^2\sigma_1^2 + w_2^2\sigma_2^2 + w_3^2\sigma_3^2 + 2w_1w_2\sigma_{12} + 2w_1w_3\sigma_{13} + 2w_2w_3\sigma_{23} \qquad \text{(Eq. 5.13)}$$

You can see the importance of the covariance between assets in a portfolio by applying this equation to an equally weighted portfolio of three stocks. With one-third of the portfolio invested in each security, the portfolio variance is calculated as follows:

$$\text{Portfolio variance} = \sigma_p^2 = \frac{1}{9}\sigma_1^2 + \frac{1}{9}\sigma_2^2 + \frac{1}{9}\sigma_3^2 + 2\left(\frac{1}{3}\right)\left(\frac{1}{3}\right)\sigma_{12}$$

$$+ 2\left(\frac{1}{3}\right)\left(\frac{1}{3}\right)\sigma_{13} + 2\left(\frac{1}{3}\right)\left(\frac{1}{3}\right)\sigma_{23}$$

Because the σ^2 terms are multiplied by $\frac{1}{9}$, each individual stock's variance contributes very little to the overall portfolio variance. Instead, the covariance terms receive more weight in the calculation. In a portfolio containing 10 assets, each individual stock's variance would be multiplied by $\frac{1}{100}$, receiving just 1 percent of the weight in the overall variance calculation. In general, the larger the number of securities in a portfolio, the less the individual variance terms matter and the greater the impact of the covariance terms. The following example demonstrates this point mathematically.

Consider an equally weighted portfolio consisting of a large number of securities denoted by N. The variance formula for this portfolio will have N distinct variance terms $(\sigma_1, \sigma_2, \ldots, \sigma_N)$ and $N^2 - N$ [or $N(N - 1)$] covariance terms $(\sigma_{12}, \sigma_{13}, \ldots, \sigma_{1N}, \sigma_{21}, \sigma_{23}, \ldots, \sigma_{2N}, \ldots, \sigma_{N1}, \sigma_{N2}, \ldots, \sigma_{N,N-1})$. Figure 5.6 places all the terms in a matrix, called the *variance-covariance matrix*. Each element on the main diagonal of this matrix represents the contribution to portfolio risk from an individual asset's variance. Because each of these terms is multiplied by $(\frac{1}{N})^2$ and because N is a large number, the terms contribute very little to the portfolio variance. Each covariance term is also multiplied by $(\frac{1}{N})^2$, but there are many more covariance terms, and collectively they largely determine the portfolio's variance.

A final illustration clarifies the main point. The matrix in Figure 5.6 contains N variance terms and $N(N - 1)$ covariance terms. Each variance and covariance term is multiplied by $(\frac{1}{N})^2$. Suppose that the average stock in this portfolio has a variance equal to s_{ave}^2, and across any pair of stocks, say, stock i and stock j, the average covariance is $\sigma_{ij,ave}$. Then the portfolio variance equation can be written as shown at the bottom of Figure 5.6.

As the number of stocks in the portfolio, N, becomes very large, the term σ_{ave}^2/N approaches zero, meaning that the average variance of individual stocks has no impact on portfolio variance. As N increases, the second term in the equation converges to just $\sigma_{ij,ave}$, indicating that what really determines the risk of a large portfolio is the average covariance between all pairs of securities. A portfolio consisting of securities that are, on average, only weakly correlated with each other will have a lower variance than a portfolio that consists of highly correlated securities.

Figure 5.7 plots the relationship between the number of securities in a portfolio and the portfolio's variance given by this equation. As the number of securities in the portfolio increases, the portfolio's variance declines. However, there is a limit to the risk reduction that can be achieved by adding more assets to the portfolio. The term $\sigma_{ij,ave}$ represents this limit. No matter how diversified a portfolio becomes, its variance cannot fall below the average covariance of securities in the portfolio. Financial economists give this type of risk special names: undiversifiable risk, systematic risk, or sometimes, market risk. Similarly, the proportion of risk that can be eliminated through diversification is called diversifiable risk, unsystematic risk, idiosyncratic

Figure 5.6
The Variance-Covariance Matrix and Portfolio Variance Equation for an Equally Weighted Portfolio of N Stocks

Variance-Covariance Matrix

Stock	1	2	3	$\cdots$	N
1	$\left(\dfrac{1}{N}\right)^2 \sigma_1^2$	$\left(\dfrac{1}{N}\right)^2 \sigma_{12}$	$\left(\dfrac{1}{N}\right)^2 \sigma_{13}$	$\cdots$	$\left(\dfrac{1}{N}\right)^2 \sigma_{1N}$
2	$\left(\dfrac{1}{N}\right)^2 \sigma_{21}$	$\left(\dfrac{1}{N}\right)^2 \sigma_2^2$	$\left(\dfrac{1}{N}\right)^2 \sigma_{23}$	$\cdots$	$\left(\dfrac{1}{N}\right)^2 \sigma_{2N}$
3	$\left(\dfrac{1}{N}\right)^2 \sigma_{31}$	$\left(\dfrac{1}{N}\right)^2 \sigma_{32}$	$\left(\dfrac{1}{N}\right)^2 \sigma_3^2$	$\cdots$	$\left(\dfrac{1}{N}\right)^2 \sigma_{3N}$
$\vdots$	$\vdots$	$\vdots$	$\vdots$	$\cdots$	$\vdots$
N	$\left(\dfrac{1}{N}\right)^2 \sigma_{N1}$	$\left(\dfrac{1}{N}\right)^2 \sigma_{N2}$	$\left(\dfrac{1}{N}\right)^2 \sigma_{N3}$	$\cdots$	$\left(\dfrac{1}{N}\right)^2 \sigma_N^2$

Portfolio Variance Equation

$$\sigma_p^2 = N\left(\frac{1}{N}\right)^2 \sigma_{\text{ave}}^2 + N(N-1)\left(\frac{1}{N}\right)^2 \sigma_{ij,\text{ave}}$$

$$\sigma_p^2 = \frac{\sigma_{\text{ave}}^2}{N} + \left(\frac{N-1}{N}\right)\sigma_{ij,\text{ave}}$$

Figure 5.7
The Effect of Diversification on Portfolio Variance

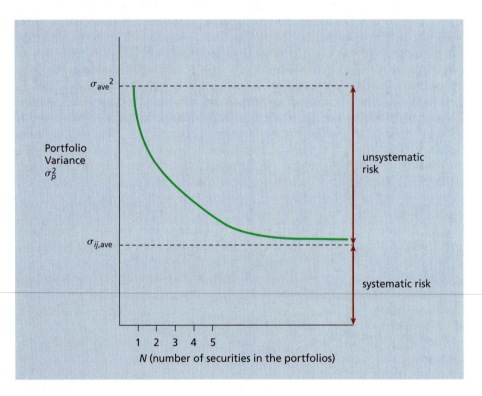

risk, or unique risk. Here, we refer to nondiversifiable risk as **systematic risk** and diversifiable risk as **unsystematic risk.**

In real-world terms, what exactly is systematic risk? This is a difficult question to answer, and we explore it in more depth in the next chapter. However, systematic risks are those that are common across all types of securities. Fluctuations in GDP, inflation, or interest rates might fit into this category, and so might certain political factors. For example, the legal system governing investors and markets in a given country can also influence systematic risk because that system determines the level of protection given to minority shareholders, creditors, and ordinary investors. In stock markets it is impossible, and perhaps even undesirable, to create a totally level playing field among different types of investors. However, when investors perceive that the legal system protects their interests when they trade, and hence trading is less risky, their willingness to trade increases and the returns they require for bearing risk decline.

Because unsystematic risk can be eliminated through diversification, the market does not reward investors for bearing unsystematic risk. Undiversified portfolios must therefore be suboptimal because they expose investors to unsystematic risk without offering higher returns as compensation. To see this point more clearly, imagine two investors, Antonin and Stephen. Both are contemplating the purchase of shares of stock in a new company, but Antonin already holds a diversified portfolio, and Stephen does not yet have any investments in his portfolio. Imagine that Antonin and Stephen share the same expectations regarding this company's future, in the sense that they have identical forecasts for the cash flows that the company's stock will generate. They also expect the shares of such a new firm to be quite volatile. Which of them will be willing to pay a higher price for the shares?

For Antonin, an investment in this company entails less risk than for Stephen, because the contribution of the stock to the risk of Antonin's overall portfolio is small. For Stephen, the investment in this stock represents his entire portfolio, and he has no other investments to dampen the stock's fluctuations. In other words, this stock will be much riskier from Stephen's perspective because he holds an undiversified portfolio. Therefore, given that both investors expect the same cash flows from the stock, Antonin will be willing to pay a higher price to acquire it (because he discounts those cash flows at a lower rate than Stephen does). In equilibrium, the market-clearing price of the stock will rise to a level at which it offers a return reflecting its systematic risk, not its overall volatility.

SMART ETHICS VIDEO
Utpal Bhattacharya, Indiana University
"The cost of equity goes up if insider trading laws are not enforced."

See the entire interview at SMARTFinance

APPLYING THE MODEL

In Table 5.1 we saw that the average annual real return on a portfolio of U.S. stocks over the last 100 years was 8.7 percent. If we add to that the 3.3 percent average inflation rate, we have a rough estimate of the average nominal return on a portfolio of stocks—12 percent per year. According to Table 5.1, the standard deviation of this portfolio's return was 20.2 percent (the standard deviation is slightly higher in nominal terms).

Let's compare those numbers to the data reported in Table 5.4 for Boise Cascade. Its average monthly return (admittedly, over a much shorter time period) was 0.88%. With compounding, that translates into an annual return of 11.1 percent. Notice, however, that Boise's monthly standard deviation was 9.88 percent. By multiplying the monthly standard deviation by the square root of 12, we convert it into an annualized figure of 34.2 percent.[15] What this comparison reveals is that although

---

[15] To convert a monthly standard deviation into an annualized figure, recognize that:

Monthly variance $\times$ 12 = annual variance

If we take the square root of both sides we have

Monthly standard devation $\times \sqrt{12}$ = annual standard deviation.

Boise's average return is a little lower than the average return on a portfolio of U.S. stocks, Boise's standard deviation is much higher (almost 70% higher) than that of the portfolio. An investor who holds only Boise stock accepts much higher volatility than an investor who holds a portfolio, but the market does not compensate the Boise investor with higher average returns. In other words, the market does not reward an investor for bearing Boise's unsystematic risk.

MEASURING THE SYSTEMATIC RISK OF AN INDIVIDUAL SECURITY

The previous section demonstrated two important facts. First, the formula for the variance of a portfolio shows that each security contributes to a portfolio's risk through two channels, the security's own variance and its covariance with all other securities in the portfolio. In diversified portfolios, only the second channel matters. This implies that a stock's variance may be a poor measure of its risk. The variance of a stock captures its total volatility, some of which is idiosyncratic and some of which is systematic. Second, because diversification eliminates unsystematic risk, the market provides no reward for bearing it. As a consequence, though we still expect to see a positive relationship in the market between risk and return, we can longer be confident that a positive relationship will exist between returns on individual assets and their variances. Again, a stock's variance captures both its systematic and unsystematic fluctuations, but only the systematic component should be correlated with returns.

We need a new measure for the risk of an individual asset, one that captures only the systematic component of its volatility. Remember, the primary contribution to portfolio risk from a single asset comes from its covariance with all the other assets in the portfolio. Imagine that an investor holds a fully diversified portfolio, literally a portfolio containing some of every asset available in the market. How would this investor determine the contribution of a single security to the risk of the overall portfolio? One way to do that would be to measure the covariance between a single asset and the portfolio. Recall, though, the difficulties associated with interpreting covariance calculations. A standardized measure would be preferable, and finance theory gives us just such a measure in the concept of **beta**:

$$\beta_i = \frac{\sigma_{im}}{\sigma_m^2} \qquad\qquad \textbf{(Eq. 5.14)}$$

The beta of a particular asset, β_i, equals the covariance of the asset's returns with the returns on the overall portfolio divided by the portfolio's variance. As you will see in the next chapter, the portfolio we refer to here is known as "the market portfolio," a value-weighted portfolio of all available assets.[16] In a security's beta, we have a standardized measure of its covariance with all other assets, or a measure of its systematic risk. If the market rewards only systematic risk, and if beta captures the systematic risk of an individual asset, then we should observe a positive relationship between betas and returns in the market.

Notice that the formula for an asset's beta closely resembles that of the correlation coefficient:

---

[16] The term "value-weighted" means that the fraction invested in a particular security is equal to that security's total market value as a percentage of the market value of all securities. For example, if the total market value of all securities in the market is $10 trillion and the total market value of a certain company's stock equals $100 billion, then the fraction of that stock in a value-weighted portfolio would be 0.01, or 1 percent.

$$\beta_i = \frac{\sigma_{im}}{\sigma_m^2} = \frac{\sigma_{im}}{(\sigma_m)(\sigma_m)}$$

$$\rho_{im} = \frac{\sigma_{im}}{\sigma_i \sigma_m}$$

The equations are identical except that the denominator of the correlation coefficient multiplies the standard deviations of the asset and the market, whereas the denominator of the beta formula squares the standard deviation of the market. This small adjustment to the denominator makes the interpretation of beta a little different from that of the correlation coefficient. First, unlike ρ, beta has no maximum or minimum value. Second, beta indicates how much the individual asset's return moves, on average, when the market moves by 1 percent. For example, if a stock has a beta of 1.5, when the market return increases by 1 percent, the stock return will increase by 1.5 percent, again on average.

APPLYING THE MODEL

Now that we have a new measure of a stock's risk, how does it compare to the measure we started with, standard deviation? Comparing the monthly returns on each of the four stocks listed in Table 5.4 to returns on the overall stock market, suppose you calculate the following statistics:

Stock	Covariance with Market
Mead	0.0031
Boise	0.0026
Nike	0.0011
Arrow	−0.0003

If the variance of market returns were 0.0028, then the betas of the stocks are as follows:

Mead	1.11	Boise	0.93	Nike	0.39	Arrow	−0.11

These figures contain several surprises. First, based on comparison of the standard deviations of each stock in Table 5.4, we concluded that Nike was the riskiest security. Comparing the betas, however, we find that Nike appears to be less risky than either Mead or Boise Cascade. Remember the dramatic risk reduction achieved in the Nike-Arrow portfolio. Apparently, much of the volatility of Nike and Arrow, at least over the 1999–2001 period, was unsystematic—that is, uncorrelated with the broader market. Thus, Nike and Arrow contribute very little risk to a portfolio.

The second surprise is that Arrow's beta is actually negative, though just barely. This is surprising because over long periods of time, economic booms tend to lift returns on all types of stocks, and recessions tend to lower them. To find a security that usually blossoms when the market swoons (and vice versa) is something of an anomaly. Though it is theoretically possible for a stock to have a negative beta, Arrow's −0.11 beta could be the result of drawing an unusual sample from the record of historical returns.

The third surprise is found in the relationship between the betas and the returns of these four companies. If the market rewards investors only for bearing systematic risk, and if beta measures systematic risk, then we might expect to see a positive relationship between beta and returns. In this case, Nike delivered the highest return but had a relatively low beta. Nike's standard deviation was the highest of the group, so we might be tempted to conclude that market returns are more strongly correlated with total risk (standard deviation) than with systematic risk (beta). For a variety of reasons, such a conclusion would be premature at this point.

LIMITATIONS OF BETA

The example in the preceding Applying the Model suggests that estimates of beta may not yield perfect measures of the systematic risk exposure of specific stocks, and that at best an imprecise link exists between beta and returns. Nike stock had the highest returns, but Nike also had the next-to-smallest beta. If beta provides a good measure of systematic risk, and if a positive correlation exists between systematic risk and returns, then the Nike figures present something of an anomaly. Using data from more than three years to examine the link between beta and returns might make this anomaly vanish. And certainly it makes sense to examine more than four companies before drawing any firm conclusions about the relationship between beta and returns. Nevertheless, this simple example suggests that the search for a measure of the systematic risk of an individual stock may not end with beta.

Chapter 6 explores the relationship between beta and expected returns in greater depth. For now, the important point is that a stock's variance (or standard deviation) measures its total risk, but total risk contains both systematic and unsystematic components. Only the systematic part is priced in the market. Beta is one way to measure the systematic risk of an asset.

8. Would you expect a portfolio consisting only of U.S. stocks to have a higher or lower variance than a portfolio consisting of stocks from the United States, Japan, the United Kingdom, France, and Germany?

9. Suppose you track the stock of an Internet company and notice it swinging wildly from month to month. You do some research on the Internet and find several sites reporting relatively low betas for this firm. Is this possible, or are the websites miscalculating?

10. Go to http://www.quicken.com. Type in the ticker symbol for Nike (NKE) in the box labeled "Enter symbol," and click "Go." On the next screen, click "Fundamentals," and you'll see Quicken's estimate of Nike's stock beta using the most recent five years of data. Compare that figure to what we obtained, and do the same for the other three stocks (ticker symbols, ARRO, BCC, and MWV). What effect does estimating the beta over this 5-year period have relative to the estimates obtained from 1999 to 2001?

5.5 SUMMARY

- Historically, in the United States and in most other countries, stocks have earned higher average returns than bonds, but stock returns have also been more volatile. However, the difference between the volatility of stock and bond returns depends on the investment horizon. The longer the horizon, the smaller the difference between the volatility of stock and bond returns.

- When individuals save and invest money, they want to increase their purchasing power over time, so the most relevant measure of an investment's return is its real return.
- Most investors are risk averse, which means that they expect compensation for bearing risk.
- The return of an asset measures the amount by which it increases an investor's wealth over time. When calculating average returns from historical data, an analyst must decide whether to compute the arithmetic or geometric average. The geometric average will generally be lower than the arithmetic average.
- Risk can be defined in many ways, including the chance of a loss or the dispersion of returns around the average. Sophisticated financial models recognize that a better measure of risk captures an investment's contribution to the overall variability of a portfolio. This is the only type of risk that the market should reward; we call it systematic risk.
- The systematic risk of any asset depends on its covariance with other assets. One measure of systematic risk is beta, which equals the ratio of the covariance of an asset's returns with the overall market's return divided by the variance of the market's returns.

INTERNET RESOURCES

Note: *For updates to links, please go to the book's website at* http://smart.swcollege.com

http://www.yahoo.com—One of the best websites for obtaining historical stock return data. Problem 5-8 gives step-by-step instructions on how to download this information into an Excel spreadsheet, but you must do the analysis. This site is also useful for selecting securities based on logical statements.

http://www.money.cnn.com/markets (CNN Money)—Useful for obtaining up-to-the-minute market-pricing data

http://www.nyse.com (The New York Stock Exchange)—Useful for obtaining up-to-the-minute market-pricing data and general market information

http://www.nasdaq.com (National Association of Securities Dealers Automated Quotation system)—Useful for obtaining up-to-the minute OTC market-pricing and other market information

http://www.londonstockexchange.com (The London Stock Exchange)—Useful in obtaining current London Stock Exchange market-pricing and other market information

http://www.marketguide.com/home.asp (Multex Investor)—For information on investing in specific securities

http://www.wallstreetcity.com (Wall Street City)—For information on investing in specific securities and programs for searching for securities meeting various criteria

http://www.standardandpoors.com (Standard & Poor's [publisher of COMPUSTAT])—For a fee, provides a wealth of data on U.S. and/or international assets

http://www.ibbotson.com (Ibbotson Associates)—For a fee, provides a wealth of historical data on various financial assets

http://www.datastream.com (Datastream and Thomson Financial)—For a fee, provides a wealth of data on various financial assets

http://www.bloomberg.com (Bloomberg)—For a fee, provides pricing, return, and many other types of data on various financial assets

KEY TERMS

arithmetic average return
beta
correlation coefficient
covariance
equity premium puzzle
fair bet
geometric average return
normal distribution

probability distribution
return
risk averse
risk neutral
risk premium
risk-seeking
systematic risk
unsystematic risk

QUESTIONS

5-1. Why are investors more concerned with the real returns than the nominal returns on their investments?

5-2. You observe that the price of some financial asset falls, but you do not believe that the expected future cash flows from the investment have changed. After the price decline, what has happened to the asset's expected return?

5-3. Why must a corporate manager consider the risk of a project as well as its return?

5-4. What is meant by the term "risk premium"? Why must riskier assets offer a risk premium?

5-5. How does risk affect the decision-making process of risk-averse and risk-neutral individuals?

5-6. Risk-neutral investors would never buy insurance products, but risk-averse investors would. Explain.

5-7. Given a series of historical returns on some investment, what is the relationship between the arithmetic and geometric average returns obtained from this series? Why is this important when comparing average returns on alternative investments?

5-8. An investor purchases a bond at par value. The bond pays a coupon rate of 8 percent, and for simplicity, assume that the firm pays interest just once per year. The investor holds the bond for one year and sells it just after it makes its first coupon payment. Will the investor's total return on this investment equal 8 percent? Why or why not?

5-9. Describe two measures of the risk of an investment discussed in this chapter. How do these measures differ?

5-10. What is the basis for the claim that, relative to other investments, stocks are not as risky in the long run as they are in the short run?

5-11. Suppose that returns on two stocks are perfectly negatively correlated, so the correlation coefficient is −1.0. Does this imply that whenever the price of one security goes up, the price of the other security goes down?

5-12. Under what circumstances can you construct a risk-free portfolio with only risky securities? What would be the required return on such a portfolio?

5-13. Explain why covariance matters more than variance in determining the risk of a large portfolio.

5-14. Suppose that a portfolio consists of 10 stocks. In the equation defining the variance of this portfolio,
  a. how many terms will be linked to the variance of the individual stocks in the portfolio?
  b. how many terms will be linked to the covariance between pairs of assets in the portfolio? (Hint: See Figure 5.6.)

5-15. What is the basis for saying that the variance of an individual asset is not a good measure of that asset's risk?

5-16. What comprises total risk, and how is it measured? Of the two components of total risk, which one can be eliminated? What is the remaining risk, and how is it measured?

5-17. Explain why the curve in Figure 5.7 does not reach all the way down to the x-axis.

5-18. Why do we say that the only risk that the market rewards with higher expected returns is systematic risk?

5-19. What is the logic behind the claim that a stock's beta provides a better measure of its systematic risk than its standard deviation does?

PROBLEMS

Risk and Return Fundamentals

5-1. Would a risk-averse person accept a gamble that offered a 50 percent chance of making $1,000 and a 50 percent chance of losing $1,000? Why or why not? Would a risk-seeking person accept the gamble?

5-2. A particular gamble offers a 50 percent chance of winning $1,000 and a 50 percent chance of losing $900. Can you say for sure whether or not a risk-averse person would accept this gamble? Why or why not? What would a risk-neutral person do?

5-3. Return to the dice-throwing example of a fair bet on page 162 of Section 5.1. If we think about the $1,000 entry fee as the price of playing the game, what is the expected percentage return on this investment? Calculate the expected percentage return on the game if the entry fee is reduced to $900. Repeat the calculation if the entry fee equals $800. What general relationship does this reveal between the price of an asset and its expected return (holding expected future cash flows constant)?

Basic Risk and Return Statistics

5-4. On January 3, 2004, you purchased 100 shares of stock for $45 per share. On January 3, 2005, you received a dividend of $2 per share, and then you immediately sold your shares at a price of $48 per share. What was your dollar return on this investment? What was your percentage return?

5-5. In the first two and one-half years of the twenty-first century, the S&P 500 Index fell by about one-third. Suppose the long-run arithmetic average return on the S&P 500 is 12 percent per year in nominal terms. At that rate, how many years would it take the S&P 500 to recover its losses? How would your answer change if you decided to use the geometric average return rather than the arithmetic average? Assume that the geometric average nominal return is 9 percent.

5-6. In the first two and one-half years of the twenty-first century, the Nasdaq Composite Index fell by about two-thirds. Suppose that the long-run arithmetic average return on the Nasdaq Composite is 15 percent per year in nominal terms. At that rate, how many years would it take the index to recover its losses? How would your answer change if you decided to use the geometric average return rather than the arithmetic average? Assume that the geometric average nominal return is 10 percent.

5-7. Calculate the expected return and standard deviation for an investment with the following probability distribution:

Return (%)	Probability (%)
−10	20
5	20
10	20
15	30
25	10

5-8. You are weighing the risk and return characteristics of a particular investment. You believe that the return of this investment can be characterized by the probability distribution that follows:

Return (%)	Probability (%)
−16	12.5
−8	12.5
0	12.5
4	12.5
8	12.5
12	12.5
16	12.5
32	12.5

  a. Calculate the expected return and standard deviation for this investment.

  b. Suppose that the returns listed in the first column are not points on a probability distribution (in other words, ignore the probabilities in the second column). Instead, imagine that they are the actual returns earned by this investment over the last eight years. Calculate the arithmetic average return and the standard deviation using this 8-year sample. Comment on any differences between your answers to this question and those in part (a).

  c. Next, suppose we list 100 different possible outcomes for an investment's returns, each of which might occur with probability of 1 percent, and we ask you to calculate the expected return and standard deviation using that probability distribution. Conceptually, how would your answers change if we ask you to calculate the expected return and standard deviation using 100 years' worth of historical returns?

5-9. Calculate the covariance and correlation coefficient for two assets with the following returns over the past year.

Month	Asset #1	Asset #2
Jan.	0.05	0.02
Feb.	0.10	0.06
Mar.	−0.02	−0.11
Apr.	0.01	0.09
May	0.07	0.08
June	−0.12	−0.06
July	0.03	0.04
Aug.	0.08	0.11
Sep.	−0.05	−0.01
Oct	−0.07	−0.04
Nov.	0.04	0.05
Dec.	0.00	0.01

Smart
Solutions
See the
problem and
solution explained step-by-step at
SMARTFinance

5-10. Go to http://www.yahoo.com, and click the link labeled "Finance." (Note: Consult this text's website [http://smart.swcollege.com] if you suspect that links may have changed after the text was printed.) The next screen asks you to enter a ticker symbol; type in "PHM" (the ticker symbol for Pulte Homes, a home building and financial services company), and hit "Get." After clicking the "Get" button, you will see very current information about this stock, as well as a number of additional links to explore. Start by clicking "Historical Prices." At the top of the next page, you are given several choices about the time period over which you want to collect data. In the "Start" boxes, enter "Jan, 02, 99." In the "End" boxes, type in "Jan, 02, 02." Also click "Monthly" to indicate that you want monthly data rather than daily or weekly. Next, click the link "Get Data." You will then see a table containing 37 months of data for this company (you can ignore the dividends for now). The table gives you the price at the beginning and end of each month, as well as the high and low prices during the month. It also tells you how many shares were traded during the month. The final column contains the "Adjusted Close," a price that reflects dividend payments, stock dividends, or stock splits. By using this adjusted close, you can calculate the return from one month to the next just by calculating the percentage difference in prices. For example, the closing price in June 1999 was $22.69, and the next month it was $22.32. The percentage return during that period was -1.63 percent [($22.32 - $22.69) ÷ $22.69]. Click the link labeled "Download Spreadsheet Format" below the table, and save the file when prompted. This should save the data in a comma-delimited file (with the .csv file extension), which you can open in Excel.

    a. Using the series of adjusted closing prices, calculate the return for Pulte Homes stock in each month.

    b. Using the "=average()" function in Excel, calculate the average monthly return.

    c. What is the geometric average monthly return?

    d. Using the functions "=var()" and "=stdev()" in Excel, calculate the variance and standard deviation of monthly returns.

5-11. Repeat the steps in Problem 5-10 to obtain monthly data for Toll Brothers, Inc. (ticker symbol, TOL).

    a. Calculate the monthly return, variance, and standard deviation for Toll Brothers stock.

    b. Calculate the covariance and correlation coefficient between Pulte Homes and Toll Brothers. Are these two stocks strongly or weakly correlated over this period? Can you explain why? (Hint: Look for the "Profile" link on Yahoo! to read about Toll Brothers' business.)

    c. Follow the instructions in problem 5-10 once more to download historical data for two more companies: Unocal Corp. (ticker symbol, UCL) and Maxwell Shoe (ticker symbol, MAXS). Use the adjusted closing prices to calculate monthly returns for each stock, and then calculate the correlation coefficient. Based on what you can learn online about each firm's industry (again, look at the company profiles on Yahoo!), can you provide an explanation for the magnitude of the correlation coefficient? Do you believe that if people spend more time walking than driving, they buy more shoes and less oil? What else might explain the correlation coefficient that you found?

Risk and Return for Portfolios

5-12. You observe the following returns on two different stocks over the past several years:

Year	Stock 1 (%)	Stock 2 (%)
1996	5	3
1997	25	14
1998	−8	1
1999	13	9
2000	12	13
2001	1	−1
2002	−17	2
2003	−5	11
2004	46	20

    a. Calculate the arithmetic average return for each stock over these nine years.

    b. Calculate the geometric average return for each stock over the same period.

    c. Compare your answers to parts (a) and (b), and explain the general points that these calculations illustrate.

    d. For each stock, calculate the value of $1,000 invested at the beginning of 1996, assuming that you hold the stock until the end of 2004.

    e. Calculate the standard deviation of returns for each stock, and then calculate the covariance and correlation coefficient between stock 1 and stock 2. (Hint: Be sure to use $N - 1$ in the denominator because you are using a sample of data.)

    f. Using the historical arithmetic average return for each stock as an estimate of its expected return, calculate the expected return and standard deviation for a portfolio consisting of 35 percent stock 1 and 65 percent stock 2.

5-13. Use the data you obtained for problems 5-10 and 5-11 to calculate the standard deviation of the following portfolios:

100% Pulte Homes	100% Unocal
100% Toll Brothers	100% Maxwell Shoe
50% Pulte, 50% Toll Brothers	50% Unocal, 50% Maxwell Shoe

Comment on your findings.

5-14. Asset 1 has an expected return of 10 percent and a standard deviation of 20 percent. Asset 2 has an expected return of 20 percent and a standard deviation of 50 percent. The correlation coefficient between the two assets is 0.0. Calculate the expected return and standard deviation for each of the following portfolios, and plot them on a graph:

Portfolio	% Invested in Asset 1	% Invested in Asset 2
A	100	0
B	75	25
C	50	50
D	25	75
E	0	100

Now, repeat the calculations above, changing just one assumption. Suppose the standard deviation of asset 1 equals zero. In other words, asset 1 pays a risk-free (because it never varies) return of 10 percent. How does the graph of the expected return and standard deviation for various portfolios change in this case?

Systematic and Unsystematic Risk

5-15. You hold a portfolio consisting of N different stocks. The average variance of a stock in your portfolio is 0.16 (remember, variance is measured in units of "percent squared"—the average standard deviation would be 0.4 or 40%), and the average covariance between a pair of stocks in your portfolio is 0.12.

a. Calculate the variance and standard deviation of your portfolio if $N = 5$.
b. Repeat these calculations assuming that $N = 10$ and $N = 100$. What lesson do these calculations illustrate?

5-16. Suppose that you form an equally weighted portfolio of 100 different stocks.

a. In the equation defining the variance of this portfolio, how many terms appear representing the variance of individual stocks?
b. What weight is associated with each variance term when calculating the portfolio's variance?
c. How many terms are there in the portfolio variance equation representing the covariance or correlation between a pair of stocks?

5-17. Calculate the standard deviation of the following three-asset portfolio.

Smart
Solutions
See the
problem and
solution explained step-by-step at
SMARTFinance

Statistic	Asset 1	Asset 2	Asset 3
Standard deviation	30%	25%	10%
Correlation with 1	1.00	0.75	0.25
Correlation with 2	0.75	1.00	0.40
Correlation with 3	0.25	0.40	1.00
Portfolio weight	50%	30%	20%

5-18. You observe that the standard deviation of a particular stock is 40 percent per year, while the standard deviation on a broad market index is 25 percent per year. If the correlation coefficient between the stock and the market index is 0.8, what is the stock's beta?

5-19. Repeat the analysis from problem 5–18, assuming that the individual stock's standard deviation is 60 percent rather than 40 percent per year. Holding the market's standard deviation and the correlation between the market and the stock fixed at 25 percent and 0.8, respectively, how does an increase in a stock's standard deviation affect its beta? Repeat the problem one more time, assuming that the stock's standard deviation is just 15 percent.

Risk and Return: The CAPM and Beyond

OPENING FOCUS
Martha Stewart Steps into the Ring with World Wrestling Federation

Politics and finance make strange bedfellows. That's what Wall Street professionals had to be thinking as they arrived at work in New York on October 20, 1999. On that day, two very different companies with very different charismatic leaders switched from private to public ownership through an initial public offering (IPO). Under a tent outside the New York Stock Exchange, elegant-living guru Martha Stewart offered scones and brioche to passersby to mark her company's coming-out party. For Stewart, the IPO of Martha Stewart Living Omnimedia, Inc., was a very good thing. At the end of her first day as head of a public company, Martha Stewart held stock worth approximately $1.2 billion.

Meanwhile, just around the corner at the Nasdaq's "Market Site," World Wrestling Federation company chairman Vince McMahon hoped to spoil Martha's party as he posed for photos with other company executives. Standing next to a life-size cutout of one of the firm's most recognized characters, "The Undertaker," McMahon nervously waited to gauge the market's reception of his company. Reviled by his critics as a promoter of cultural decay, McMahon founded the World Wrestling Federation in 1980 and built it into a multifaceted entertainment company with revenues exceeding $250 million. And in contrast to his company's main product, there was nothing fake about the money he made that day. By that afternoon, McMahon's stock had a market value of $1.4 billion.

Though it might seem difficult to find two companies with less in common, in fact, the fortunes of investors who purchased shares in either McMahon's company or Stewart's were nearly identical after October 20. The following chart tracks the value of $1 invested in each company for 21 months after the first-day close. Except for a few months during the spring of 2000, the two lines move almost perfectly in sync. How can we explain that phenomenon? Can selling books and magazines illustrating how to make the perfect

The Value of a
$1 Investment in World
Wrestling Federation and
Martha Stewart Living
Omnimedia

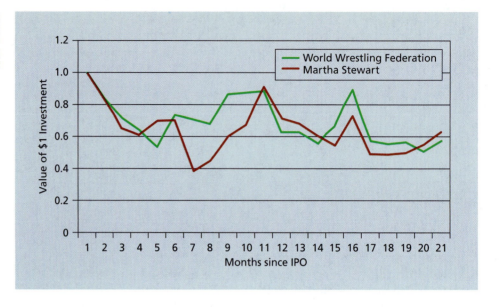

wedding cake really compare to attracting viewers to watch oversized men in tights in headlocks?

An alternative explanation is that the chart illustrates that certain risk factors affect all types of stocks at the same time. In finance, asset pricing models attempt to quantify these risk factors and to price them—that is, to determine how much return investors expect for exposure to systematic sources of risk. So no matter the industry in which you plan to begin your career, read on.

Source: Dean Bonham, "Martha Stewart Should Pin the WWF," *Pittsburgh Post-Gazette,* Scripps Howard News Service (November 28, 1999).

Chapter 5 introduced the basic elements of portfolio theory, starting with the simple observation that investments that have offered the highest average returns historically have also displayed the greatest volatility. The positive relationship between returns and volatility seen in the historical data makes sense in a world populated by risk-averse investors. If riskier investments did not offer the prospect of higher returns, they could not survive in the market. But as a measure of risk, total volatility (as measured by the variance or standard deviation of returns) has serious flaws. Investors can easily eliminate some asset-return fluctuations through diversification. Systematic risk, the volatility that cannot be diversified away, concerns investors most. Asset pricing models attempt to quantify systematic risk. More important, these models attempt to determine the rate of return that investors expect as compensation for bearing systematic risk. If we know the return that the market requires on a given asset, then we have critical information necessary to determine the asset's price.

For decades, beta stood alone as the most popular metric for an investment's systematic risk. *Beta,* as defined in Chapter 5, measures the sensitivity of an investment's returns to fluctuations in the overall market. Investments with below-average levels of systematic risk have betas below 1.0, and those with above-average systematic risk have betas greater than 1.0. Put another way, high-beta investments increase the systematic risk exposure of a portfolio, while low-beta investments decrease it. If investors concern themselves only with systematic risk, and if beta measures that risk accurately, then we should anticipate a positive relationship between beta and returns. This is the crux of the *capital asset pricing model (CAPM)*.

This chapter traces the development of the CAPM, explaining its intellectual foundations as well as its practical impact. Though it enjoys widespread use in corporate finance today, the CAPM has come under a variety of attacks since it first appeared in the mid-1960s. We explain how these criticisms led to modifications of the original CAPM, as well as to entirely new approaches to asset pricing. We conclude with a discussion of the current state of the "CAPM controversy" and descriptions of the leading alternatives to the CAPM.

6.1 EFFICIENT RISKY PORTFOLIOS

THE EFFICIENT FRONTIER WITH TWO ASSETS

Are some portfolios better than others? For risk-averse investors, the answer is clearly yes. Recall the portfolios we examined containing different combinations of Nike and Arrow International shares in Figure 5.4(b). An investor holding a portfolio consisting entirely of Arrow shares could unambiguously improve the portfolio's performance by selling some Arrow shares and using the proceeds to buy Nike stock. By doing so, the investor increases the portfolio's return while simultaneously decreasing its standard deviation, at least up to a point. In this example, diversification achieves two goals at once—increasing portfolio returns and decreasing portfolio volatility.

Figure 6.1 illustrates this phenomenon for two generic stocks, A and B. Stock A has a lower expected return and a lower standard deviation than stock B. The curve connecting A and B, called the **feasible set,** plots the expected return and standard deviation for all possible portfolios of these two stocks. By glancing at the figure, we can

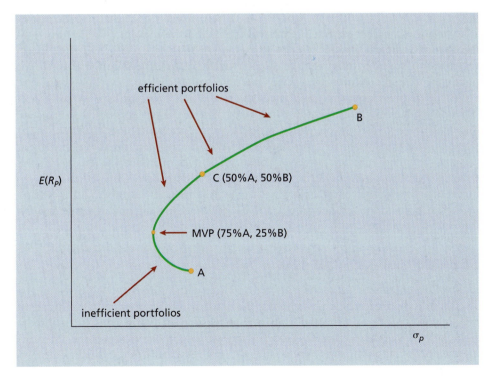

Figure 6.1
Expected Return and Standard Deviation for Portfolios of Two Assets

Source: Dimson and Marsh (2002).

conclude that the correlation between the returns for A and B falls below 1.0—otherwise, portfolios of A and B would lie on a straight, upward-sloping line connecting the two points. Likewise, because the arc connecting A and B does not bend all the way back to the y-axis, the correlation between A and B exceeds −1.0. Figure 6.1 therefore illustrates an intermediate case, one that you might observe by picking any pair of stocks at random.

Because the arc initially bends backward toward the y-axis, an investor can construct a portfolio of A and B that has less volatility than either A or B. By trial and error (or by using calculus), you can find the combination of A and B shares that results in the portfolio marked MVP, the **minimum variance portfolio.** No other combination of assets A and B yields a portfolio with a lower standard deviation. For the sake of illustration, suppose that investing 75 percent in A and 25 percent in B results in the MVP. How can an investor use this information?

Examine the two segments of the arc separated by the point MVP. An investor allocating money between A and B should avoid buying shares in company A exclusively because another portfolio that offers a higher return for the same level of volatility exists on the arc. The same statement could be made for any portfolio lying on the upward-sloping portion of the arc, from A to MVP. At any point on this segment, another portfolio exists with the same standard deviation and a higher expected return. Therefore, all portfolios lying on the segment from A to MVP (i.e., all portfolios with less than 25 percent invested in B) are **inefficient portfolios.** We say that a portfolio is inefficient if it offers a lower expected return than another portfolio with the same standard deviation. Faced with the investment opportunities portrayed in Figure 6.1, an investor who knows that the MVP contains 25 percent of stock B reasons that 25 percent is the minimum rational investment in stock B. Any smaller investment in B results in an inefficient portfolio.

By the same token, all portfolios lying on the segment connecting MVP and B qualify as **efficient portfolios.** A portfolio is efficient if it offers the highest expected return among the group of portfolios with equal or less volatility. In other words, if you mark any point on the arc from MVP to B, you will notice that no other portfolio promises a higher expected return without adding more volatility. The terms **efficient set** and **efficient frontier** refer to all the points on the arc from MVP to B. Investors want to hold portfolios that lie on the efficient frontier because those portfolios maximize expected returns for any given level of volatility.

If the minimum rational investment in asset B is 25 percent, can we say that a portfolio containing 50 percent B would be even better? Not necessarily. The answer depends on the investor's tolerance for risk. A 50-50 portfolio plots on Figure 6.1 at point C. This portfolio provides a higher expected return than the MVP, but only at the cost of higher volatility. Some very risk-averse investors might decide that C's additional return was inadequate compensation for the extra risk, while other investors might take the opposite view. Portfolio theory says that no investor should choose an inefficient portfolio (lying between A and MVP), but choosing among efficient portfolios involves subjective assessments that vary from one investor to another.

THE EFFICIENT FRONTIER WITH MANY ASSETS

Figure 6.2 generalizes these concepts to a market with more than two investments. The arc and the area beneath it represent the new feasible set. Each point underneath the arc corresponds to a specific security. The feasible set simply consists of all possible portfolios of these assets. As before, the upward-sloping portion of the arc forming the northwest boundary of the feasible set is the efficient frontier. Inefficient port-

Figure 6.2
The Efficient Frontier with
Many Assets

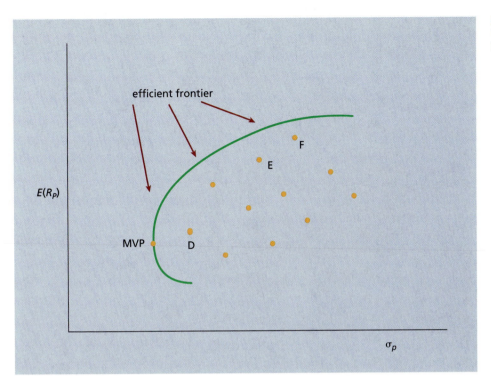

folios in this figure include points such as D, E, and F. For each of these assets, a portfolio on the frontier exists offering a higher expected return for the same risk.

We must make two important points here. First, in describing the feasible set and efficient frontier in Figures 6.1 and 6.2, we have often used the terms "stock" or "share" to describe the individual investments available to investors. However, the important lessons of portfolio theory apply to the full universe of investment classes, not just to common stocks. For example, the feasible set consists not only of portfolios that might be formed by purchasing shares in companies listed on the New York Stock Exchange, but also portfolios that include assets such as corporate and government bonds, real estate, and even exotic investments such as precious metals or art. Furthermore, there is no reason to restrict the feasible set to domestic investments. It also includes stocks and bonds that trade in foreign countries. Chapter 5 demonstrated that diversification reduces portfolio risk, and that lesson applies here. *The broader the range of investments included in the feasible set, the greater the risk reduction achievable through diversification.* Figure 6.3 illustrates the point by showing hypothetical efficient frontiers for different feasible sets encompassing an expanding array of investment choices.

A second important lesson to glean from this section relates to the concepts of systematic and unsystematic risk from Chapter 5. Examine point D in Figure 6.2. Because D lies beneath the efficient frontier, another asset or portfolio exists that dominates D, meaning that it offers a higher return for the same volatility. If that is the case, you might ask, how can asset D survive in the market if no one wants to own it? The answer is subtle. Although it would not be wise for an investor to hold asset D in isolation, it does not follow logically that investors will avoid D entirely. In fact, investors may need to hold some fraction of their wealth in D to construct a portfolio that lies on the efficient frontier. For example, suppose that asset D exhibits very low correlation with the other assets in the feasible set. Adding such an asset to a

Figure 6.3
The Effect of Expanding
the Feasible Set on the
Efficient Frontier (EF)

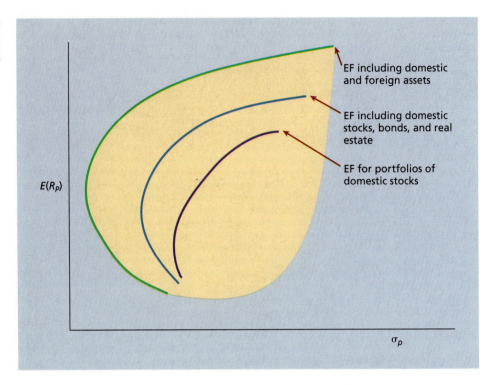

EF including domestic
and foreign assets

EF including domestic
stocks, bonds, and real
estate

EF for portfolios of
domestic stocks

$E(R_P)$

σ_p

portfolio reduces the portfolio's level of systematic risk. In that case, investors will be willing to hold asset D as part of their portfolios even if it offers a relatively low return.[1]

APPLYING THE MODEL

A few simple calculations illustrate the main points to take away from this section. Chapter 5 examined the risk-and-return characteristics of two different portfolios, one containing shares of Mead Corp. and Boise Cascade, and the other made up of shares of Nike and Arrow International. Table 6.1 calculates the expected monthly return and standard deviation for 16 different portfolios consisting of various combinations of these four stocks.[2] Figure 6.4 plots the expected return and standard deviation for each portfolio. Notice how closely the shape of the set in this figure resembles those shown in Figures 6.2 and 6.3. You could trace the boundary of this set by drawing lines connecting

[1] In other words, the risk of a portfolio that contains asset D is less than it would be if asset D were removed. Insurance provides a more concrete example of this phenomenon. Because fire and casualty insurance companies price their policies to make a profit, the average purchaser of fire insurance loses money. As a consequence, purchasers of fire insurance can expect negative returns on their policies, on average. Is it irrational to buy fire insurance? Absolutely not. A fire insurance policy pays off big at precisely the time that the value of an investor's home declines sharply (i.e., when the home is reduced to ashes). For most people, a home represents a significant fraction of total wealth. Because the correlation between the return on a home and the return on a fire insurance policy is negative, combining them in a portfolio makes sense. Fire insurance reduces overall portfolio risk, even though most individuals can expect to lose money on the fire insurance component of their portfolios.

[2] The data for these calculations come from Table 5.4.

Table 6.1
Expected Return (per month) and Standard Deviation for Various Portfolios

| Portfolio Number | Percentage Invested in Each Stock | | | | Portfolio Characteristics | |
	Boise Cascade	Mead Corp.	Nike	Arrow International	Expected Return (per month)	Standard Deviation
1	0	0	0	100	1.08	8.42
2	50	0	0	50	0.98	5.34
3	25	0	25	50	1.28	4.37
4	0	0	50	50	1.57	5.12
5	0	25	50	25	1.58	8.14
6	10	10	70	10	1.75	10.99
7	5	5	85	5	1.91	12.70
8	0	0	100	0	2.06	14.53
9	0	50	0	50	1.09	6.95
10	25	25	25	25	1.28	7.31
11	20	20	40	20	1.44	8.17
12	50	0	50	0	1.47	10.93
13	0	50	50	0	1.59	11.88
14	100	0	0	0	0.88	9.88
15	50	50	0	0	0.99	11.12
16	0	100	0	0	1.11	13.00

Note: Portfolios 3 through 8 are efficient portfolios.

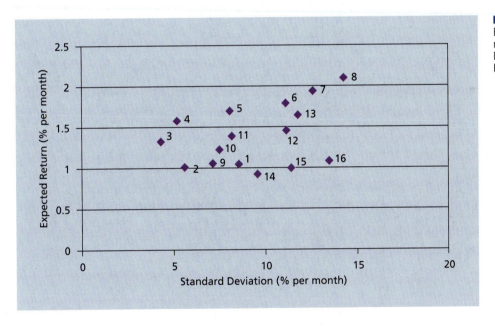

Figure 6.4
Expected Return (per month) and Standard Deviation for Various Portfolios

portfolios 2 through 8 in the figure, and the upward-sloping portion of that boundary (including portfolios 3, 4, and 8) would roughly trace out the efficient frontier.

Take a moment to examine a few inefficient portfolios lying beneath the efficient frontier. Portfolio 9, for example, is clearly inferior to portfolios 3 and 4, both of which offer higher returns and lower standard deviations than portfolio 9. For the same reason, portfolio 5 dominates portfolios 11–12 and 14–16.

Portfolio 1, consisting entirely of Arrow International stock, falls well below the efficient frontier. Does that mean that investors should stay away from Arrow stock? Not at all. Notice that portfolios 3 and 4, both of which lie on the efficient fronteir, contain significant investments in Arrow. Arrow's returns are negatively correlated with returns on each of the other three stocks, so when investors mix Arrow shares with other stocks, the resulting portfolios benefit from diversification. Notice that the portfolios containing no Arrow shares fall below the frontier, again with the exception of portfolio 8.[3] By itself, Arrow International looks like a bad investment, offering relatively low returns and relatively high risk. But Arrow shines in a portfolio! ■

Concept Review Questions

1. Is the minimum variance portfolio always an efficient portfolio? Is an efficient portfolio always the minimum variance portfolio?

2. An efficient portfolio is one that maximizes expected return for any given level of risk. Is it equivalent to define an efficient portfolio as one that minimizes risk for any level of expected return?

3. What effect does expanding the types of assets included in the feasible set have on the efficient frontier?

4. Examine portfolio 10 in Table 6.1 and Figure 6.4. This portfolio contains equal investments in all four stocks. Why do you think it falls below the efficient frontier?

6.2 RISK-FREE BORROWING AND LENDING

PORTFOLIOS OF RISKY AND RISK-FREE ASSETS

By plotting the expected return and standard deviation for portfolios of two or more assets, we have seen that these portfolios define a set with a curved boundary. The lower the correlation between the assets in the portfolio, the more this boundary curves back toward the y-axis. Now we introduce a new possibility. What happens if investors can add a risk-free investment to their portfolios?

By definition, the expected return equals the actual return on a risk-free investment. That is, investors holding this asset get exactly the return they expected when they bought it. There is no uncertainty about what return the asset will generate. In reality, no investment is completely free of risk, but an investment such as a U.S. Treasury bill comes very close to that ideal. Keep in mind that when they buy U.S. T-bills, investors lend money to the government, albeit on a very short-term basis.

For now, assume that a truly risk-free investment exists. Denoting its return by R_f, we can write the following equations:

$$E(R_f) = R_f \text{ (this means that the actual return is exactly what was expected)}$$

$$\text{Var}(R_f) = \sigma_{R_f}^2 = 0$$

$$\text{Std. dev. } (R_f) = \sigma_{R_f} = 0$$

---

[3] Investors wanting to create a portfolio with the highest possible expected return have just one choice—invest everything in the stock with the highest expected return, Nike. However, that conclusion will change in the next section when we allow investors to borrow and lend when forming portfolios.

Imagine that an investor currently holds a diversified mutual fund of risky securities with an expected return equal to $E(R_{MF})$ and a variance of σ^2_{MF}. We can treat this mutual fund as a single asset. Now, form a portfolio by investing w_{R_f} percent in the risk-free asset and w_{MF} percent in the mutual fund. You can derive the expected return and variance of this new, two-asset portfolio using the standard equations for any two-asset portfolio:

$$E(R_p) = w_{R_f}R_f + w_{MF}R_{MF}$$

$$\text{Var}(R_p) = \sigma^2_p = (w_{R_f})^2\sigma^2_{R_f} + (w_{MF})^2\sigma^2_{MF} + 2(w_{R_f})(w_{MF})\text{Cov}(R_f,R_{MF})$$

Because the risk-free asset's return has no variance, $\sigma^2_{R_f} = 0$. Likewise, if the risk-free return is constant, it cannot covary with any other asset, so $\text{Cov}(R_f, R_{MF}) = 0$. Therefore, the equation for the variance of a portfolio consisting of a risky asset and a risk-free asset reduces to the following:

$$\text{Var}(R_p) = \sigma^2_p = (w_{MF})^2\sigma^2_{MF}$$

Taking the square root to obtain the standard deviation of this portfolio results in the following:

$$\sigma_p = w_{MF}\sigma_{MF}$$

The standard deviation of this two-asset portfolio increases linearly as the fraction invested in the risky asset increases. Geometrically, that means that portfolios of risky and risk-free assets lie along the straight line shown in Figure 6.5. Point A in the figure represents a portfolio invested 50 percent in the risk-free asset and 50 percent

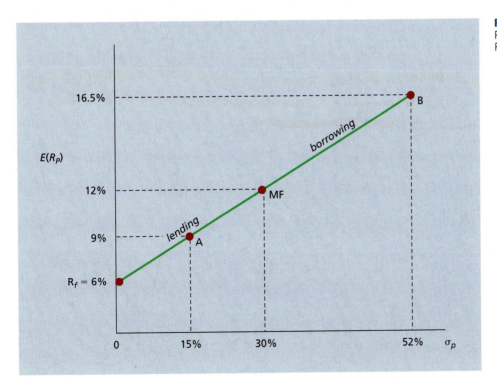

Figure 6.5
Portfolios of Risky and Risk-Free Assets

in the risky asset. But what about point B? How can investors form portfolios of risky and risk-free assets that lie above and to the right of the risky asset, *MF*?

The answer is that investors can borrow money and invest the proceeds in risky assets. Consider an individual who has $1,000 to invest. Assume that the risk-free asset pays 6 percent and the expected rate of return on the mutual fund she wants to buy is 12 percent, with a standard deviation of 30 percent. She could put all of her money in the risky asset and reach point *MF* in the figure, she could put all of it in the risk-free asset and reach point R_f, or she could buy some of both and reach an intermediate point such as point A. But what if she can borrow money at 6 percent interest? By borrowing money and investing the proceeds in the risky asset, she can increase the fraction of her portfolio invested in *MF* to more than 100 percent. In other words, she invests all of her own money *plus* borrowed funds in the risky security. For instance, if she borrows $750 and invests it, she effectively invests 175 percent of her initial wealth in *MF*. The expected return on her portfolio is shown in the following equation:

$$E(R_p) = -0.75(6\%) + 1.75(12\%) = 16.5\%$$

The first term in this equation, $-0.75\,(6\%)$, reflects the fact that borrowing is just the opposite of lending. The investor borrows an amount equal to 75 percent of her initial wealth. The minus sign indicates that her return on these borrowed funds will be negative—she has to pay 6 percent interest on the amount she borrows. However, she reinvests the $750 (plus her own $1,000) in the mutual fund that has a higher expected return. Because the mutual fund's expected return exceeds the interest rate on her loan, she expects to magnify her rate of return relative to what she could earn using only her own money. In this case, her expected return is 16.5 percent.

Of course, the downside to all this is the risk that the *actual return* on the mutual fund may turn out to be less than expected. Suppose that the mutual fund earns a 0 percent return. At the end of the year, the total value of her portfolio will be just what it was at the beginning, $1,750. Of this total, however, $795 belongs to the lender ($750 principal and $45 interest). Our investor, who began the year with $1,000, now has just $955, a loss of 4.5 percent. The general pattern that this numerical example illustrates is that the return on a portfolio financed with borrowed money fluctuates more than the return on the portfolio's underlying assets, as demonstrated by the following calculations.

If the mutual fund's return is	her return is
18%	27 %
12	16.5
6	6
0	−4.5
−6	−15

To see how volatile this portfolio is, just use the equation for standard deviation:

$$\sigma_p = w_{MF}\sigma_{MF} = 1.75(30\%) = 52.5\%$$

The lesson here is straightforward. *The greater the amount of money invested in the risky asset, the higher will be the expected return and risk of the portfolio. The greater the investment in the risk-free asset, the lower will be the portfolio's risk and return.*

FINDING THE OPTIMAL PORTFOLIO

The opportunity to borrow and lend at the risk-free rate fundamentally changes an investor's portfolio-selection problem. In a world with only risky assets, risk-averse investors search for portfolios that lie on the efficient frontier, then select from that set the portfolio that best matches their tolerance for risk. Though all investors can rule out many portfolios as inefficient (e.g., those underneath the frontier), there can be no agreement on which of the portfolios on the frontier is best. It is a matter of individual taste.

Figure 6.6 demonstrates how adding a risk-free asset alters the picture. The graph shows the familiar feasible set and efficient frontier. Point R_f on the vertical axis indicates the return available on the risk-free security. In this world, any investor can form a portfolio consisting of the risk-free asset and any other risky portfolio. For instance, the line marked L_1 represents all portfolios that an investor might create by combining the risk-free asset with risky portfolio X. Notice that some of these portfolios lie outside the old feasible set, meaning that the availability of risk-free securities opens up new investment opportunities.

The portfolios that lie along line L_1 are inferior to those on line L_2, formed by combining the risk-free asset with risky portfolio Y. For any portfolio on line L_1, a portfolio exists on line L_2 that has the same standard deviation and a higher expected return. But other portfolios exist that dominate those on line L_2. Only when investors reach line L_3, combining the risk-free asset with risky portfolio M, have they maximized the expected return on their portfolio for a given standard deviation. In other words, *line L_3 defines a new efficient frontier.* Risky portfolios X and Y, which lie along the old efficient frontier in a world without a risky asset, are no longer efficient. To reach this new efficient frontier, investors first search for the point of

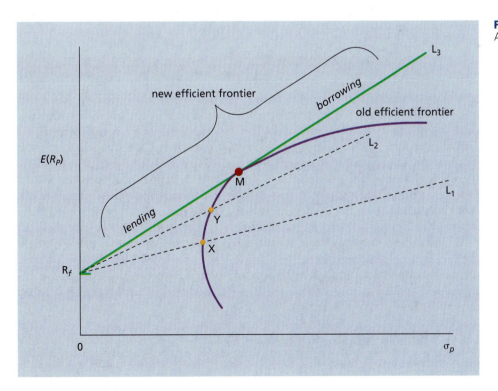

Figure 6.6
A New Efficient Frontier

Figure 6.7
Finding the Optimal
Portfolio

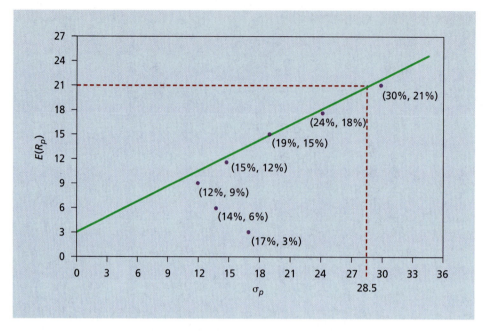

tangency on the line connecting the risk-free asset to the old efficient frontier. That is, investors endeavor to determine the composition of portfolio M. Next, investors allocate their wealth between portfolio M and the risk-free asset according to their risk preferences. This amounts to deciding where on the line they want their portfolios to lie. Investors who are very risk averse will invest heavily in the risk-free asset, thereby locating their portfolios near the y-axis. Investors who are less risk averse will allocate more of their money to the risky asset, perhaps even borrowing money to structure a portfolio lying to the right of point M.[4]

APPLYING THE MODEL

Suppose that Rachel can borrow or lend at the risk-free rate of 3 percent. She needs to decide which of seven risky portfolios she should hold in combination with a position in the risk-free asset. Figure 6.7 plots the standard deviation and expected return of each portfolio. To determine which portfolio is best, she draws a line from the risk-free rate to each dot in the figure and chooses the line with the highest slope. As the figure indicates, the portfolio with a standard deviation of 19 percent and an expected return of 15 percent maximizes the slope. Investing money in any of the other portfolios is irrational. They offer lower returns for any level of risk than can be achieved by choosing a portfolio on this line.

To see this point more clearly, it is useful to derive the equation of the line in Figure 6.7. Two points in the figure, the first at coordinates [$\sigma_p = 0\%$, $E(R) = 3\%$] and the second at [$\sigma_p = 19\%$, $E(R) = 15\%$], determine this line. Its slope equals the difference in expected returns divided by the difference in standard deviations between the two points:

[4.] Economists refer to this process of first finding portfolio M and then deciding how to allocate funds between M and the risk-free asset as the **two-fund separation principle.** When a risk-free asset exists, the optimal strategy for all investors is to invest some money in M and some in the risk-free security. The only thing that changes from one investor to another is how much to invest in each type of asset.

Slope $= (15\% - 3\%) \div (19\% - 0\%) = 0.632$

Because the intercept occurs at the risk-free rate, the equation of the line is as follows:

$$E(R_p) = 3\% + \left(\frac{15\% - 3\%}{19\%} \right) \sigma_p = 0.03 + 0.632\sigma_p$$

The terms $E(R_p)$ and σ_p in this equation refer to the expected return and standard deviation of a portfolio lying on the line. Every portfolio on this line reflects some mixture of the risk-free asset and the "optimal" risky portfolio. Investors can alter the mix of risky and risk-free assets according to their own tolerance for risk.

Suppose that Rachel, who has a very high tolerance for risk, reasons that she should hold the risky portfolio with the highest expected return (i.e., the one appearing in the top right portion of the figure). This portfolio offers a return of 21 percent, much higher than the "optimal" portfolio identified previously. Rachel might ask, "If I don't mind the fact that this portfolio has a standard deviation of 30 percent, why would I bother investing in something with a lower expected return?"

Another approach exists that allows Rachel to construct a portfolio with the same expected return, 21 percent, but with less risk. Start by determining how to create a portfolio of the risk-free asset and the "optimal" portfolio to achieve a 21 percent return. Let w represent the fraction invested in the risk-free asset, leaving $(1 - w)$ to be invested in the optimal portfolio:

$$E(R_p) = 21\% = w(3\%) + (1 - w)(15\%)$$

$$w = -0.5 = -50\%$$

Rachel should borrow an amount equal to 50 percent of her wealth, allowing her to invest 150 percent in the optimal portfolio. What will be the standard deviation of this new portfolio? It equals the standard deviation of the risky portfolio times the fraction invested in that portfolio:

$$\sigma_p = 1.5(19\%) = 28.5\%$$

Figure 6.7 highlights the advantage of this portfolio. By borrowing funds and investing them in the optimal risky portfolio, Rachel achieves her target expected return, but with a standard deviation of 28.5 percent rather than 30 percent.   ■

Before going on, let us summarize what we know so far. Because all risky assets are not perfectly correlated, investors should diversify. Diversification allows investors to eliminate unsystematic risk. Some diversified portfolios will perform better than others in the sense of providing higher expected returns for the same standard deviation. We call these efficient portfolios. However, if investors can borrow and lend at the risk-free rate, then from the entire feasible set of risky portfolios, one portfolio will emerge that maximizes the return that investors can expect for a given standard deviation. This is the **optimal risky portfolio.** All investors will want to hold this portfolio, and they will adjust their investments in this portfolio and the risk-free asset to achieve the combination of expected return and standard deviation that best suits their individual preferences.

How do you go about finding that optimal risky portfolio? We have good news and bad news for you. The good news is that although the mathematics of solving for the optimal portfolio gets a little complex, many software packages can do the computations for you. The bad news is that you have to provide the software with a set of inputs that in themselves present a challenge. Specifically, to determine the composition of the optimal portfolio, you need to know the expected return and standard deviation for every risky asset, as well as the covariance between every pair of assets. Even taking the simple approach of estimating these quantities using historical data involves a lot of number crunching.

As we will see later in this chapter, the *capital asset pricing model (CAPM)* tells us the composition of the optimal portfolio from a theoretical standpoint. Recognizing that everyone engages in the same search for an optimal portfolio, the CAPM makes certain assumptions about investors' information to derive its prediction for the composition of that portfolio. Those assumptions lead to a novel and practical way to assess the expected return of any risky asset by using beta to measure its sensitivity to the optimal portfolio.

Concept Review Questions

5. If the covariance between two risky assets is zero, portfolios of these two assets will lie along a backward-bending curve. The covariance between a risky and a risk-free asset is zero, yet portfolios of these two assets lie along a straight line. Explain.

6. Explain how investors can use leverage (i.e., borrowed money) to increase both the expected return and the risk of their portfolios.

7. How does an investor's portfolio-selection problem change when risk-free borrowing and lending is possible?

8. Explain the following statement: With risk-free borrowing and lending, there is only one optimal risky portfolio, but there are still many efficient portfolios.

6.3 EQUILIBRIUM AND THE MARKET PORTFOLIO

THE MARKET PORTFOLIO

The preceding analysis suggests that all investors should search for the composition of the optimal portfolio. That search begins when investors form estimates of the expected returns, standard deviations, and covariances for all risky assets in the economy. Think for a moment about how investors might arrive at these estimates. First, they might look at the historical record to see how asset prices moved in the past. To conduct this analysis, they will use one of the websites providing historical data on stock returns or purchase the data directly from a vendor, such as the Center for Research on Securities Prices. Second, they may examine other sources of public information, such as documents available from the Securities and Exchange Commission's EDGAR database (http://www.sec.gov/edgar.shtml). Third, they could listen to the opinions of analysts in the media or subscribe to one of the popular investment newsletter services. The point is, in their search for the optimal portfolio, investors will sift through more or less the same information sources to arrive at their estimates of expected returns, standard deviations, and covariances.

Recognizing that most investors have access to similar types of information, economists ask what happens if all investors reach the same conclusions from their analyses. That is, if all investors have access to the same information, perhaps their estimates of the inputs needed to solve for the optimal portfolio are identical. Although it is clearly true that differences of opinion exist from one investor to another, economists adopt the assumption of **homogeneous expectations** as a way to consider how the market will reach equilibrium.

If all investors agree on the risk-and-return characteristics of specific assets, then they will all agree on the shape of the efficient frontier. Given knowledge of the risk-free rate, every investor will find the same point of tangency with the efficient frontier—that is, the same optimal portfolio. Because that portfolio allows investors to maximize expected return for any level of standard deviation, all investors want to hold it.

In economics, equilibrium occurs in a market when the market price equates the quantity demanded and supplied of a good. If all investors want to hold the same portfolio, then equilibrium requires that to be the portfolio supplied by the market. Economists refer to this portfolio, designated by point M in Figure 6.6, as the market portfolio. In theory, the **market portfolio** literally consists of every available asset, with each asset weighted by its market value relative to the total market value of all assets. In practice, no such portfolio exists, but we can approximate it with a value-weighted, diversified portfolio of many different assets, such as the Standard & Poor's 500 Stock Index.

THE CAPITAL MARKET LINE

Under the assumption of homogeneous expectations, portfolio M in Figure 6.6 receives a special designation, the market portfolio. Similarly, the line connecting point M to the risk-free rate, L_3, is referred to as the **capital market line** (**CML**). The *CML* quantifies the relationship between the expected return and standard deviation for portfolios consisting of the risk-free asset and the market portfolio, using Equation 6.1:

$$E(R_p) = R_f + \left\{ \frac{[E(R_m) - R_f]}{\sigma_m} \right\} \sigma_p \qquad \text{(Eq. 6.1)}$$

This equation indicates that the expected return on any portfolio, $E(R_p)$, equals the risk-free rate, plus a premium that depends on the portfolio's risk, σ_p. The term R_p measures the risk premium on the market portfolio relative to its standard deviation. Sometimes called the reward-to-risk ratio, or the **market price of risk,** this term is what investors try to maximize as they search for the optimal risky portfolio. Risk-averse investors want as much reward as they can obtain for a given level of risk.

The *CML* defines the efficient frontier when investors have homogeneous expectations and can borrow and lend at the risk-free rate. Investors should hold no portfolios other than those located on the *CML*. But what does this imply regarding the expected return and risk for individual assets? The capital asset pricing model, to which we now turn, answers this question.

9. Do investors want to maximize or minimize the market price of risk? Why?

10. Refer to the equation for the *CML*. Is it possible to construct a portfolio such that σ_p exceeds σ_m? How?

Concept Review Questions

6.4 THE CAPITAL ASSET PRICING MODEL (CAPM)

THE SECURITY MARKET LINE

The basic CAPM was developed almost simultaneously during the mid-1960s by William Sharpe (1964), John Lintner, and Jan Mossin (1966) and was quickly embraced by academic researchers. Finance practitioners took somewhat longer to accept the model, but it was ultimately hailed almost universally as a simple and powerful tool for anyone interested in investments or in the workings of capital markets. The reason for this enthusiasm is not hard to find—for the first time, researchers and practitioners alike had a model that generated testable predictions about the risk-and-return characteristics of individual assets by specifying how they would covary with the market portfolio.

The formal development of the CAPM requires several assumptions about investors and markets. Rather than present a detailed list of these assumptions, we present the logic of the CAPM as it flows from the material we have covered so far.

1. Investors are risk averse and require higher returns on riskier investments.
2. Because investors can diversify, they care only about the systematic risk of any investment. The market offers no reward for bearing unsystematic risk.
3. Some portfolios are better than others. Portfolios that maximize expected return for any level of risk are efficient portfolios.
4. If investors can borrow and lend at the risk-free rate, then there exists a single risky portfolio that dominates all others. Only portfolios consisting of the risk-free asset and the optimal risky portfolio are efficient.
5. If investors have homogeneous expectations, they will agree on the composition of the optimal portfolio and unanimously demand it. In equilibrium, the optimal portfolio will be the market portfolio.
6. The central insight of the CAPM is that if all investors hold the market portfolio, when they evaluate the risk of any specific asset, they will be concerned with the covariance of that asset with the overall market. The implication is that any measure of an asset's systematic risk exposure must capture how it covaries with the rest of the market. An asset's beta provides a quantitative measure of this risk, and therefore the CAPM predicts a positive, linear relationship between expected return and beta.

The **capital asset pricing model (CAPM)** says that the expected return on a specific asset, $E(R_i)$, equals the risk-free rate plus a premium that depends on the asset's beta, β_i, and the expected risk premium on the market portfolio, $E(R_m) - R_f$:

$$E(R_i) = R_f + \beta_i[E(R_m) - R_f] \qquad \text{(Eq. 6.2)}$$

$$\beta_i = \frac{\sigma_{im}}{\sigma_m^2}$$

Recall that beta measures an asset's sensitivity to a broader portfolio, in this case the market portfolio. The higher the beta of a security, the greater the security's exposure to systematic risk and the higher the expected return it must offer investors. Though there are three variables on the right-hand side of the CAPM equation—R_f, β_i, and $E(R_m)$—only beta changes from one security to the next. For that reason, ana-

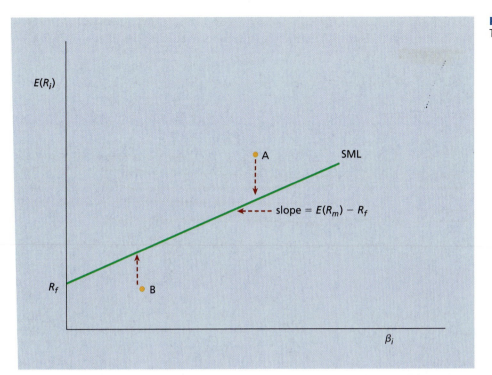

Figure 6.8
The Security Market Line

lysts classify the CAPM as a **single-factor model,** meaning that just one variable explains differences in returns across securities.

Figure 6.8 plots the CAPM equation on a diagram with the expected return on the y-axis and beta on the x-axis. The intercept of this line is R_f, and its slope is $E(R_m) - R_f$. According to the CAPM, the equilibrium expected returns of all securities must plot on this line, called the **security market line** (**SML**). An asset that offered an expected return above the line, like asset A, would be underpriced. Investors would snap up this stock, driving its price up and driving its expected return down until it reached the line. Conversely, if an asset's expected return fell below the line, as depicted by point B, then it would be overpriced. Investors would divest their holdings of this asset, driving its price down and its expected return up.

Smart Concepts
See the concept explained step-by-step at
SMARTFinance

APPLYING THE MODEL

Suppose that the risk-free rate is 5 percent and the expected return on the market portfolio is 13 percent. If a particular stock has a beta of 1.5, what is its expected return?

$$E(R) = 5\% + 1.5(13\% - 5\%) = 17\%$$

Because this stock has a relatively high beta, its expected return exceeds the expected return of the market portfolio. What if the stock had a beta of 1.0?

$$E(R) = 5\% + 1.0(13\% - 5\%) = 13\%$$

In this case, the stock displays average systematic risk, so its expected return equals the market portfolio's return. Finally, suppose that you could find a stock with a beta of 0.0:

$$E(R) = 5\% + 0.0(13\% - 5\%) = 5\%$$

Here the expected return equals the risk-free rate. Does that mean that this stock is identical to a Treasury bill? Not exactly. An investor who buys a Treasury bill and holds it to maturity earns a certain, nominal return. Not so with a zero beta stock. The realized return on the stock is not locked in like the return on a T-bill. However, if the stock has a zero beta, it has zero exposure to systematic risk and its returns fluctuate independently of market returns. Because the stock carries no systematic risk, it can offer an equilibrium expected return equivalent to a risk-free government security.

Estimating Betas

As the CAPM gained wider acceptance in the business community, a cottage industry developed, with firms offering proprietary estimates of beta for virtually all listed common stocks in the U.S. markets. Today you can find estimates of betas in many public and university libraries by looking in sources such as the *Value Line Investment Survey*, or you can find them online at sites such as Yahoo! Finance (http://www.finance .yahoo.com) or Quicken (http://www.quicken.com). Even so, you may want to construct your own estimates using the most up-to-date data available. Here's how to do it.

From Yahoo! Finance we downloaded a series of recent weekly returns on two stocks, as well as a market index. Figure 6.9 shows scatterplots comparing the weekly returns on these stocks to the weekly return on the S&P 500 Index. Version A of the figure plots weekly returns on The Sharper Image, a retailer specializing in luxury consumer goods, against the weekly return on the S&P 500 Index. Version B replaces The Sharper Image returns with returns on ConAgra Foods, the largest food-service supplier and the second-largest food retailer in North America. Part A shows a positive correlation between returns on The Sharper Image and the market index. Whether returns on the market are correlated with returns on ConAgra is difficult to say from visual inspection of Part B. The lines drawn through each figure are regression lines estimated using Excel. Recall from statistics that regression analysis identifies a line through a series of data points that minimizes the sum of squared errors or distances between the points and the line. The slope of the regression line indicates how much impact changes in one variable have on another.

In this instance, the slope of the regression lines indicates the extent to which movements in individual stocks are associated with movements in the overall market. In other words, the regression line's slope equals the stock's beta.[5] Notice that the regression line appears much steeper for The Sharper Image than for ConAgra— that is, The Sharper Image has a higher beta. The general tendency is for The Sharper Image stock to perform very well (poorly) when the overall stock market is up (down). In contrast, returns on ConAgra stock display much less sensitivity to market movements, as indicated by its low beta of 0.11. But these patterns make perfect sense. ConAgra produces food, and people have to eat in good times and bad. The

---

[5] Sometimes, rather than use actual returns to generate these plots, analysts use net returns or excess returns. That is, the *y*-axis would plot the actual return on a stock net of the risk-free rate, and the *x*-axis would show the net return on the market index.

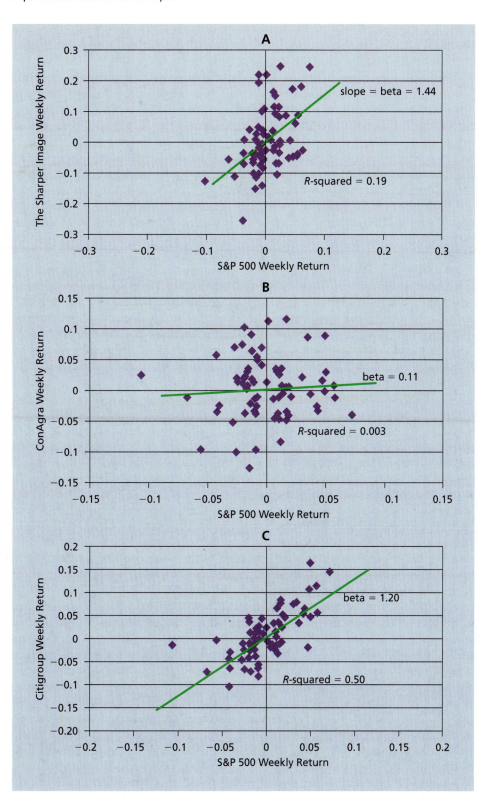

Figure 6.9
Scatterplots of Weekly Returns for Sharper Image, ConAgra, and Citigroup, and the S&P 500 Index

Sharper Image sells vibrating chairs, brushes that use ozone to reduce pet odors, and handheld body-fat analyzers, among other unusual products. People indulge in these products much more in good times than in bad.

Estimating a regression line yields additional information besides the beta of a stock. Typically, the regression output produced by a program includes a variety of other statistics about the regression. One of the most useful of these statistics is the regression R-squared value. The R-squared measures "goodness of fit" and ranges from a minimum value of 0 percent (if there is no relationship between two variables) to 100 percent (if one variable is perfectly linked to another). In the present context, the R-squared value indicates the percentage of variability in the stock's return that can be explained by variability in the market's return. The R-squared values in Figure 6.9 show that fluctuations in the market account for about 19 percent of the movements in The Sharper Image and virtually none of the movements in ConAgra. At least over this sample period, ConAgra stock moved more or less independently of the overall market.

But what does this mean? The volatility of any stock contains two components—systematic and unsystematic risk. The systematic component reflects the extent to which the stock moves with the market, and the unsystematic part results from random fluctuations in the stock that are unrelated to (or unexplained by) the market. The regression R-squared, therefore, gives an indication of the percentage of an asset's volatility that is systematic. Given the R-squared values in Figure 6.9, we can say that a larger fraction of The Sharper Image's volatility reflects systematic risk, compared to that of ConAgra.

The Sharper Image has a higher absolute level of systematic risk (i.e., a higher beta) and a higher fraction of systematic risk (i.e., a higher R-squared) than ConAgra does. That need not always be the case. As an analogy, there are more cellular phone users in the United States than in Finland, but the fraction of the population that uses cellular phones in Finland is greater than in the United States. In the same way, a stock might have a very high (low) beta, but the fraction of its total volatility associated with market movements could still be relatively low (high). Part C of Figure 6.9 shows the scatterplot and regression line for Citigroup, a financial services holding company. At 1.20, Citigroup's beta falls between the betas of The Sharper Image and ConAgra, but the regression R-squared shows that systematic risk represents a larger proportion of total risk for Citigroup than for either of the other two firms. According to the CAPM, the beta, not the R-squared, determines a stock's expected return, but the R-squared value nonetheless provides useful information.

To conclude this section, we mention some of the thorny issues encountered when estimating betas. To obtain the estimates in Figure 6.9, we used weekly data for each stock and for the market index, but we could have used data gathered at other frequencies as well (e.g., daily, monthly, or quarterly). The factors determining which type of data to use are somewhat subjective. For instance, from statistics we learn that larger samples often yield better estimates. But in the context of a financial market, collecting a larger sample may necessitate gathering data from more distant time periods. We collected 74 *weekly* observations spanning 1.5 years to form our beta estimates. Had we gathered the same number of *monthly* observations, our data would have covered more than 6 years. Over time, companies often change the mix of industries in which they compete by acquiring new businesses and divesting old ones. Consequently, data drawn from several years past may not reflect the current risks of a particular stock. Why not use 74 daily observations then? Illiquidity presents a problem when using daily data. Many stocks do not trade each and every day. On the average business day, slightly less than 2 percent of NYSE-listed stocks and about

If Emerging Market Returns Are Uncorrelated, Why Do They Always Seem to Crash Together?

Most empirical studies that measure the degree of correlation between the returns of national stock markets find relatively low correlation coefficients. The figure below is a good example, as it presents correlations and betas with the world equity portfolio for 48 developed (d) and emerging (e) markets based on data through the early 1990s. More recent studies show much the same pattern of low return correlation, both between emerging and developed markets and between emerging markets themselves. How, then, can we explain the disturbingly common phenomenon that emerging markets always seem to move together—sharply downward—during times of global economic stress? This circumstance occurred in December 1994, when Mexico surprised the world with a sharp (and bungled) devaluation; in July 1997, when the devaluation of the Thai Baht triggered

devaluations throughout east Asia; and again in 1998, when Russia defaulted on its external debts. In all three cases, seemingly minor and localized financial crises precipitated huge losses for investors in almost all emerging markets. Many commentators refer to this as financial contagion, meaning that the financial virus of panic can rapidly, and irrationally, spread from sick to healthy countries once a single nation causes investors to lose confidence. Although researchers have not conclusively proven that contagion actually occurs, the risk of investing in emerging markets is, unfortunately, undeniable. As you might expect, investing in emerging markets would be rational only if expected returns are commensurately high, and over many time periods this has in fact been true.

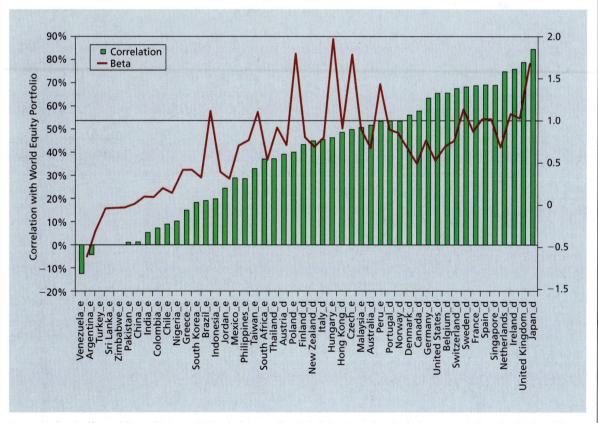

Source: Stephen Godfrey and Ramon Espinosa, "A Practical Approach to Calculating Costs of Equity for Investments in Emerging Markets," *Journal of Applied Corporate Finance* 9 (Fall 1996), pp. 80–89.

10 percent of Nasdaq stocks do not trade at all. On days when no trading occurs, it is impossible to measure the return on the stock in the same way that it is hard for homeowners to know the value of their homes unless they sell them. Deciding which type of data to use when estimating a beta requires evaluating the trade-off between having the most up-to-date information about a stock (which argues for high-frequency data) against having a large sample of returns (which argues for low-frequency data). Practitioners using the CAPM in business and researchers testing the model both confront these trade-offs.

Concept Review Questions

11. Why does an underpriced asset lie above the security market line?

12. Running a regression with an individual asset's return as the dependent variable and the market's return as the independent variable yields two estimates of systematic risk: beta and R-squared. Explain how these relate to systematic risk and how they differ from each other.

13. You run regressions on two different stocks. One stock has a higher beta, and the other has a higher R-squared. Which stock would have a higher expected return according to the CAPM?

6.5 EMPIRICAL EVIDENCE ON THE CAPM

Since William Sharpe published his seminal paper on the CAPM, researchers have subjected the model to numerous empirical tests. Early on, most of these tests seemed to support the CAPM's main predictions. Over time, however, evidence mounted indicating that the CAPM had serious flaws. In this section, we briefly describe the most important findings from empirical tests of the CAPM, and in the sections that follow, we describe how asset pricing theory has evolved beyond the CAPM.

Testing the CAPM poses several challenges to researchers. First, the CAPM makes predictions about a variable that is inherently unobservable—the expected return on an asset. There is no database that measures the returns that investors expect when they trade securities. Researchers testing the CAPM must therefore invoke the assumption of **rational expectations,** which means that even if investors make mistakes when they form assessments about expected returns, their errors are not systematic. In other words, if investors are not right all the time, they are at least correct on average. By assuming that investors have rational expectations, researchers can use realized historical returns as a proxy for expected returns.[6]

A second challenge arises because the CAPM is a one-period model. That is, the model describes the way that investors form expectations one period ahead, but it does not address how those expectations might change from one period to the next. Similarly, the CAPM treats a security's beta as a constant, but researchers testing the model must contend with the possibility that betas can change over time as firms invest in new industries, alter their capital structures, or take other actions that can cause betas to change. Furthermore, the CAPM does not even specify what unit of time corresponds to "one period." The model offers researchers no guide about whether they should run their tests using daily, weekly, monthly, or even annual historical returns.

[6.] Miller (1999) recounts the merciless ribbing that he and his corecipients (Harry Markowitz and William Sharpe) of the Nobel Prize in economics endured when they accepted their award in Stockholm. The physicists and chemists present at the awards ceremony were amused to hear Miller admit that the basic unit of their research, the expected return on an asset, could not be observed.

The third problem confronting empirical studies of the CAPM relates to the risk-free rate. Intuitively, we know that no investment is truly risk free like the investment contemplated in the CAPM, and the returns on the closest real-world proxies for the risk-free asset (e.g., Treasury securities) fluctuate over time rather than remain constant as the CAPM assumes. In addition, the CAPM is silent on whether researchers should use short-term Treasury bills or long-term Treasury bonds as a proxy for the risk-free rate.

The fourth and perhaps the most difficult problem that tests of the CAPM face involves the market portfolio. Recall that in the CAPM, the market portfolio is a value-weighted combination of every asset in the economy. The CAPM assumes that every asset in the economy is tradable, so investors who want to hold "the market" can easily do so. In practice, there is no index or other mechanism that allows investors to hold every asset in the economy in just the right proportion. Empirically, researchers have to use a proxy for the market portfolio, calculating individual security betas by calculating their covariance relative to this proxy. This implies that whether a test rejects or fails to reject the CAPM's predictions, researchers can never be certain whether their results truly reflect the model's strengths and weaknesses, or whether the results simply reflect the difficulties of measuring betas when the market portfolio is unobservable. And just as betas can fluctuate over time, so too can the expected risk premium on the market portfolio, further confounding empirical tests.

These difficulties notwithstanding, scholars have published dozens, perhaps hundreds of tests of the CAPM over the last four decades. To put these studies in context, we must first clarify which of the model's predictions one could test. First, the model says that the relationship between betas and expected returns is linear, that the security market line (*SML*) should be a straight line rather than a curve. The model predicts that the slope of this line equals the expected risk premium on the market portfolio, and the line's intercept should equal the risk-free rate. Second, the CAPM asserts that no factor other than beta should be systematically related to expected returns. This means that if one were to run a regression with returns as the dependent variable and with a host of independent variables (including the stock's variance, its dividend yield, the company's historical growth rate, and so on), the only independent variable that should display a significant correlation with returns is beta.

One of the earliest tests was conducted by Black, Jensen, and Scholes (1972). Their study found a positive relationship between beta and returns, just as the CAPM predicted. However, the difference in returns between high-beta and low-beta stocks was not as large as they expected. Put differently, the authors found that the *SML* was "too flat." A year later, Fama and MacBeth (1973) reported the disquieting result that the relationship between beta and returns was unstable. From one 5-year period to the next, betas seemed to fluctuate almost randomly, hardly comforting for practitioners using historical beta estimates to formulate investment strategies or to estimate the cost of capital for a corporation.

More than a decade later, more evidence of the CAPM's shortcomings emerged. Roll (1988) demonstrated that even with the benefit of hindsight, the CAPM could explain no more than 40 percent of the cross-sectional variation in stock returns. In Roll's "best-case scenario," more than half of the difference between stocks that earned high returns and those that earned low returns was still a mystery. In a series of papers in the early 1990s, Eugene Fama and Ken French (1992, 1996, 2002) argued that two other factors did a much better job explaining why some stocks earned higher returns than others. These factors were the size of the firm (as measured by its market capitalization) and the firm's book-to-market value ratio. Fama and French discovered that small firms earned consistently higher average returns than large firms, and similarly, firms with high book-to-market ratios earned higher returns than firms with low book-to-market ratios did. Controlling for these two effects, Fama and French found almost no relationship between beta and returns. In other words, the *SML* was not just "too flat"; it was completely flat.[7]

Where does all of this leave us? From an academic point of view, the answer is uncertain. The empirical and theoretical shortcomings of the CAPM are by now well documented, and though the literature offers several alternative asset pricing models, none has emerged as the CAPM's clear heir apparent. As a matter of practice, however, the CAPM still reigns supreme in the corporate finance realm. Graham and Harvey (2001) show that corporations use the CAPM more than any other model to estimate the cost of equity capital. Likewise, professionals in the investment field do not neglect the CAPM. Most brokerage and investment advisory firms still offer estimates of betas as part of their service package. Whether that will be the case in another 10 or 20 years is anyone's guess. To prepare you for that uncertain future, we now briefly review two of the leading alternatives to the CAPM—arbitrage pricing theory (APT) and the Fama-French three-factor model (F-F).

Concept Review Questions

14. What does it mean to say that early tests of the CAPM discovered that the *SML* was "too flat"?

15. Suppose that, on average, individuals become more risk averse during recessions and less risk averse during economic booms. How might this complicate tests of the CAPM?

6.6 ALTERNATIVES TO THE CAPM

ARBITRAGE PRICING THEORY

The earliest theory to receive widespread support as an alternative to the CAPM was the **arbitrage pricing theory** (**APT**), developed in the mid-1970s by Stephen Ross (1976, 1977). Mathematically and intuitively more challenging than the CAPM, the APT begins with the notion that financial markets are frictionless. Investors can buy or sell short any of a large number of assets that trade in this market. **Short-selling** is a transaction in which an investor sells borrowed assets that must be returned to the lender of the assets at a later date. In the simplest case, short sales are made in an attempt to profit from an expected decline in a given asset's value.[8] The APT assumes that all investors know that returns on specific assets follow this simple relationship:

$$R = \alpha + \beta_1(\text{risk factor 1}) + \beta_2(\text{risk factor 2}) + \beta_3(\text{risk factor 3}) + \cdots$$
$$+ \text{random error}$$

[7.] Financial theorists made major improvements to the CAPM after it first appeared in 1964. Brennan (1970) developed a version of the CAPM that incorporated the possibility that investors might have to pay taxes on their returns. Mayers (1972) modified the model to allow for nontradable assets such as human capital. Merton (1973) extended the CAPM to a multiperiod setting, while Breeden (1979) refocused the CAPM on investors' consumption opportunities rather than wealth per se. Adler and Dumas (1983) added a global slant to the debate with their international asset pricing model. But critics of the CAPM were working on the theoretical dimension, too. Roll (1977) offered the best-known theoretical critique of the CAPM, arguing that the CAPM is not testable as long as the true market portfolio is unobservable.

[8.] In Section 6.2, we discussed how lending and borrowing in combination with the minimum variance portfolio can be used to create a new efficient frontier. As an alternative to borrowing at the risk-free rate, an investor could sell the risk-free asset—assumed to be a 6 percent Treasury bill in the earlier example—short and thereby effectively borrow risk-free money at a 6 percent T-bill rate. Therefore, short-selling a T-bill is equivalent to borrowing at the T-bill rate.

Unlike the CAPM, which is a single-factor model, the APT posits that asset returns are driven by a group of different factors. The APT specifies neither the identity nor the number of these factors (except for the restriction that the number of assets available must be much larger than the number of factors). The risk factors represent sources of systematic risk that cannot be diversified away. For example, unexpected fluctuations in oil prices, interest rates, inflation, exchange rates, or economic growth might be candidates for risk factors. Even fluctuations in the market portfolio could represent a significant risk factor, just as is the case in the CAPM. The APT leaves the identification of these factors as an empirical matter for researchers to sort out.

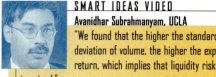

SMART IDEAS VIDEO
Avanidhar Subrahmanyam, UCLA
"We found that the higher the standard deviation of volume, the higher the expected return, which implies that liquidity risk is priced."

See the entire interview at **SMARTFinance**

In the world of the APT, each asset can be affected by each risk factor. That is, each firm has its own set of "factor betas," just as each stock has its own beta in the CAPM. Also like the CAPM, each risk factor is associated with a risk premium. For example, if fluctuations in oil prices represent a source of systematic risk, then stocks that are sensitive to that factor will have to pay investors higher returns as compensation. This relationship can be summarized as follows:

$$\overline{R}_i - R_f = \beta_{i1}(\overline{R}_1 - R_f) + \beta_{i2}(\overline{R}_2 - R_f) + \beta_{i3}(\overline{R}_3 - R_f) + \cdots + \beta_{in}(\overline{R}_n - R_f)$$

(Eq. 6.3)

The left-hand side of this equation represents the risk premium on a particular asset. The betas reflect that particular asset's sensitivity to each of the factors, and the terms in parentheses stand for the risk premium associated with each factor.[9] You can see that if there is only one factor, the market factor, then this equation reduces to something that looks just like the CAPM.

Recall that the APT offers no guidance about what factors should be important, or even how many factors should be included in Equation 6.3. Empirical work on the APT suggests that between two and five factors are linked to stock returns, but interpreting these factors can be tricky. If we observe, for example, that the difference between long-term and short-term bond yields is correlated with stock returns, we are left wondering why this is so. Is the correlation a sign of some deep, causal economic relationship, or is it a statistical fluke? Without additional theory, it is impossible to say, because the APT itself is silent on the question.

One avenue of empirical research that offers hope of yielding interpretable results is the **observable variables approach.** This involves estimating which macroeconomic variables significantly influence security prices. The foremost study adopting this approach is presented by Chen, Roll, and Ross (1986). They test whether unanticipated movements in various macroeconomic variables are risks that are priced in the stock market. They find that security prices are significantly related to (1) changes in industrial production, (2) the yield spread between long- and short-term interest rates (interpreted as a business-cycle proxy), (3) the yield spread between low- and high-grade bonds (interpreted as a proxy for overall business risk in the economy), and (4) changes in expected and unexpected inflation—though this is highly significant only during periods of pronounced inflation volatility. Perhaps most intriguing are the

---

[9.] Technically, each term in parentheses represents the expected risk premium on a security with a beta equal to 1.0 for a particular factor and betas equal to 0.0 for all the other factors.

variables that the authors find are not significant. After they account for the macroeconomic factors, they find that the return on the overall stock market itself is not significant and there is no significant relationship between stock returns and aggregate consumption. Unfortunately, more recent tests using this approach have proven less successful.

THE FAMA-FRENCH (F-F) MODEL

We have already mentioned the criticisms leveled at the CAPM by Eugene Fama and Ken French in their series of papers beginning in the early 1990s. It is one thing to criticize a theoretical model, but it is another thing entirely to suggest an alternative. Fortunately, Fama and French did both. Fama and French (1992, 1996, 2002) sought to explain "the cross section of expected returns," or why some stocks earned higher average returns than others. They make two key points in attacking the CAPM and presenting their alternative. The first point is that two factors, the size of a firm and the ratio of the book value of its equity to its market value, are systematically related to returns. Looking back through the historical record, Fama and French found that small firms earned higher returns than large firms, even after holding beta constant, and firms with high book-to-market ratios (*value stocks*) outperformed firms with low book-to-market ratios (*glamour stocks*). The second point is that after controlling for firm size and market-to-book ratio, beta has little or no impact on returns. Why then did early tests of the CAPM indicate that high-beta stocks earned higher returns than low-beta stocks? Perhaps high-beta stocks tend to be small firms with high book-to-market ratios. Fama and French argue that if you look at a group of firms of similar size (and similar book-to-market ratio), within that group, high-beta stocks earn about the same returns as low-beta stocks.

The mathematical expression of the **Fama-French (F-F) model** looks very much like the APT with three factors:

$$R_i - R_f = \alpha + \beta_{i1}(R_m - R_f) + \beta_{i2}(R_{small} - R_{big}) + \beta_{i3}(R_{high} - R_{low}) \qquad \textbf{(Eq. 6.4)}$$

The risk premium on stock i equals a constant term, α, plus a risk premium that depends on the stock's sensitivity to each factor, and the risk premium associated with each factor. The term β_{i1} is the sensitivity of stock i to the market factor, and $(R_m - R_f)$ is the familiar risk premium on the market. β_{i2} is the stock's sensitivity to the size factor and $(R_{small} - R_{big})$ is the added expected return on small stocks compared to large stocks. Finally, β_{i3} represents the stock's sensitivity to the book-to-market factor, with $(R_{high} - R_{low})$ representing the book-to-market risk premium. If the Fama-French model explains the cross section of expected returns, then the average value of α should be close to zero.

What really distinguishes the Fama-French approach from both the CAPM and the APT is that it is an entirely empirical attempt to model asset prices. Fama and French do not derive their pricing equation from a rigorous theoretical model as the other asset pricing models do; neither do they offer mathematical arguments for why these three factors (as opposed to some other set of factors) predict returns. Certainly, one can tell plausible stories to explain why small firms are riskier than large firms, or why firms with high book-to-market ratios are riskier than low book-to-market firms. For instance, a firm with very dim prospects, teetering on the edge of financial disaster, would probably have a very small market capitalization. That same firm might have a significant amount of equity "on the books" either from external financing raised in the past or from accumulated profits from earlier periods. In that case, the firm would not only be small, but would have a high book-to-market ratio. Such a firm would indeed be very risky and would be priced by the market to reflect a high expected return.[10]

But critics of Fama and French have their own stories. According to the three-factor model, a firm with a low book-to-market ratio is less risky and will offer lower returns than a firm with a high ratio. But what sorts of firms often have low book values and high market values (i.e., a low book-to-market ratio)? New firms, especially those in high-technology industries, often fit this description. In the late 1990s, stocks in the Internet sector had astronomical market values relative to their book values. Critics of Fama-French say that it is hard to conceive that investors viewed these as low-risk firms. Interestingly, some critics of the Fama-French model do not dispute the claim that a positive correlation exists between returns and book-to-market ratios, but they offer a different interpretation of that fact. Perhaps investors become too pessimistic about some firms, driving down their market values and pushing up their book-to-market ratios. Over time, investors learn that they underestimated these firms, and they drive prices back up. The reverse happens for low book-to-market firms, generating the positive correlation observed in the historical data.

---

16. Over time, firms with high book-to-market ratios earn higher returns than firms with low book-to-market ratios do. Offer two interpretations that might explain this pattern.

17. In what sense is it reasonable to say that the Fama-French model is really an application of arbitrage pricing theory?

Concept Review Questions

6.7 THE CURRENT STATE OF ASSET PRICING THEORY

What is the state of asset pricing theory early in the twenty-first century? Theory provides us with several competing models to describe asset returns, but unfortunately, no clear leader among those models has emerged. Even so, there are several valuable conclusions that we can draw based on the material in this chapter and Chapter 5. First, investors demand compensation for taking risk because they are risk averse. This fact in itself is important to keep in mind as you think about market valuations. To see why, imagine that a cultural shift takes place, and investors generally become less risk averse. Why might this occur? Over time, more and more investors learn the basic facts presented in Table 5.1. In the United States, stocks have generally outperformed safer investments such as bonds by a wide margin, at least in the last 70+ years. Of course, there is no guarantee that the same pattern will emerge in the next 70 years, but presented with the historical evidence, many investors may become more comfortable with the idea of investing in stocks. Remember, the percentage of the population that owns stock has been increasing over time, in the United States and abroad. What is the implication of a decline in the population's aversion to risk? As

---

[10.] Students sometimes find it counterintuitive that a firm with poor prospects would be priced to offer a high return. It may help to think of junk bonds. When firms with outstanding debt get into financial trouble, their bonds may slip from investment grade to the junk category. As this happens, the price on the bonds declines, but the yield on the bond (interest paid divided by price) rises. An investor who buys such a bond earns a very high rate of return if the firm survives long enough to meet its debt obligations.

risk aversion decreases, the compensation that a risky investment must offer to attract investors declines. As more and more investors invest in stocks, market prices rise and expected returns fall. Many commentators attribute part of the remarkable bull market in U.S. stocks in the 1990s to declining risk aversion among U.S. investors.

Second, there is widespread agreement that systematic risk drives returns. At a minimum, this tells us that investors should hold diversified portfolios rather than invest a large fraction of their wealth into just a few securities. This is important advice to remember as you begin your career. Over time, you may accumulate stock options or other forms of equity in your employer. Holding a large fraction of your financial wealth in the firm for which you work is very risky, as Enron employees discovered in late 2001. This situation results in an undiversified financial portfolio, which is highly correlated with your most valuable asset—your own human capital.

As a sidebar, we will point out here that when it comes to diversification, what is good for individual investors is not necessarily good for firms. While it is clearly advisable for investors to hold diversified portfolios, it does not logically follow that firms should invest in many different industries to diversify their holdings. An individual can diversify across many different industries at very low cost, perhaps by following a strategy as simple as investing in mutual funds. For a firm, diversification is much more costly. One way that firms often diversify is by acquiring existing businesses. But when one firm buys another, the acquirer must usually pay a significant premium over the target's market value to gain control. Furthermore, managers who are very successful at operating a firm in one line of business may be less successful in other industries. There may also be a kind of managerial capacity constraint that makes it difficult for firms to manage many different businesses at once. The bottom line is that because investors can diversify at low cost on their own, there is no reason for them to pay a premium for firms to diversify on their behalf. In fact, recent research in finance documents just the opposite, that investors tend to place lower values on diversified firms than on those that are more focused.[11]

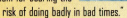

Third, you can measure systematic risk in several different ways depending on the asset pricing model you choose. In the CAPM, beta captures the systematic risk of any investment. In the APT or the Fama-French three-factor model, each asset will have several betas capturing the asset's sensitivity to each of the factors. The CAPM and the APT provide a theoretical apparatus that explains why assets are priced in a particular way, while the Fama-French approach is purely empirical. On the other hand, the CAPM and the Fama-French model tell you what factors influence returns, but you have to guess which factors count in the APT (or rely on the lessons from past research). And while the CAPM presumes that just one systematic risk factor drives returns, the APT and the Fama-French model allow for several independent factors. In the end, each model has its advantages and disadvantages.

[11.] Servaes (1996) documents that diversified firms traded at a substantial discount during the 1960s, a finding corroborated in the 1980s by Lang and Stulz (1994). Lins and Servaes (1999) find that diversified firms in the United Kingdom and in Japan trade at 15 percent and 10 percent discounts, respectively, relative to undiversified firms. Rajan, Servaes, and Zingales (2000) attribute the discount to inefficient allocation of resources across divisions of diversified firms. Comment and Jarrell (1995), Denis, Denis, and Sarin (1997), Lamont and Polk (2001), Whited (2001), and Bernardo and Chowdhry (2002) examine other elements of this diversification discount.

Fourth, despite its flaws, the CAPM is still widely used in practice in both corporate finance and investment-oriented jobs. Understanding how to estimate and interpret expected returns using the CAPM is part of the required tool kit for business school graduates. Perhaps in time, finance theory will provide an indisputably superior model to the CAPM that will make its way into practice. Until then, we muddle through. As Richard Roll observed in his 1988 presidential address to the American Finance Association, "The immaturity of our science is illustrated by the conspicuous lack of predictive content about some of its most intensely interesting phenomena, particularly changes in asset prices." We still have far to go before we catch up with the predictive ability of the physical sciences, but at least we are closer than we were before Harry Markowitz explained portfolio theory to us in 1952.

---

18. Summarize the lessons of asset pricing theory that go beyond specific asset pricing models such as the CAPM, APT, and Fama-French.

Concept Review Question

6.8 SUMMARY

- Finance teaches that markets reward investors for bearing risk, but only systematic risk. Asset pricing models attempt to measure systematic risk and to quantify the trade-off between systematic risk and returns.
- Some portfolios are better than others. In general, risk-averse investors should only hold efficient portfolios, portfolios that maximize expected returns for any level of risk.
- If investors can borrow and lend at the risk-free rate, then a unique, efficient risky portfolio exists. Investors must first attempt to learn the composition of this portfolio. Then they can divide their wealth between the efficient risky portfolio and the risk-free asset according to their own risk preferences.
- Under certain conditions, the optimal risky portfolio is the market portfolio, a value-weighted combination of all the assets in the economy.
- The CAPM predicts a linear, positive relationship between expected returns and betas. The beta measures the systematic risk exposure of a particular asset. The graphical representation of the relationship between expected returns and beta is called the security market line.
- Early empirical tests offered some support for the CAPM, but the weight of the evidence now suggests that the CAPM offers at best an incomplete explanation of why some assets earn higher average returns than others do.
- Two leading alternatives to the CAPM are the APT and the Fama-French three-factor model. Neither has completely supplanted the CAPM, especially in the corporate finance realm, where the CAPM sees widespread use.

INTERNET RESOURCES

Note: *For updates to links, please go to the book's website at* http://smart.swcollege.com

http://www.yahoo.com—One of the best websites for obtaining historical stock return data. Problem 5-10 in Chapter 5 gives step-by-step instructions on how to download this information into an Excel spreadsheet, but you must do the analysis. Also useful for selecting securities based on logical statements.

http://www.money.cnn.com/markets (CNN Money)—Useful for obtaining up-to-the-minute market-pricing data

http://www.nyse.com (The New York Stock Exchange)—Useful for obtaining up-to-the-minute market-pricing data and general market information

http://www.nasdaq.com (National Association of Securities Dealers Automated Quotation system)—Useful for obtaining up-to-the minute OTC market-pricing and other market information

http://www.londonstockexchange.com (The London Stock Exchange)—Useful in obtaining current London Stock Exchange market-pricing and other market information

http://www.marketguide.com/home.asp (Multex Investor)—For information on investing in specific securities

http://www.wallstreetcity.com (Wall Street City)—For information on investing in specific securities and programs for searching for securities meeting various criteria

http://www.standardandpoors.com (Standard & Poor's [publisher of COMPUSTAT])—For a fee, provides a wealth of data on U.S. and/or international assets

http://www.ibbotson.com (Ibbotson Associates)—For a fee, provides a wealth of historical data on various financial assets

http://www.datastream.com (Datastream and Thomson Financial)—For a fee, provides a wealth of data on various financial assets

http://www.bloomberg.com (Bloomberg)—For a fee, provides pricing, return, and many other types of data on various financial assets

KEY TERMS

arbitrage pricing theory (APT)
capital asset pricing model (CAPM)
capital market line (*CML*)
efficient frontier
efficient portfolios
efficient set
Fama-French (F-F) model
feasible set
homogeneous expectations
inefficient portfolios

market portfolio
market price of risk
minimum variance portfolio
observable variables approach
optimal risky portfolio
rational expectations
security market line (*SML*)
short-selling
single-factor model
two-fund separation principle

QUESTIONS

6-1.   Define the terms "feasible set" and "efficient set."

6-2.   Why is the efficient frontier generally a curved arc rather than a straight line?

6-3.   Suppose that you adopt the rule of investing only in portfolios that have the minimum level of risk possible at a given expected return. If you follow this rule, will you always hold an efficient portfolio? (Answer this question assuming that only risky assets are available—there is no risk-free asset.)

6-4. Suppose that there are only two risky assets to invest in. One offers a higher return than the other, but it also has a higher standard deviation. Will one of these assets always lie on the efficient frontier? Will one of these assets always be inefficient if held alone?

6-5. Suppose that the rate of inflation is negatively correlated with the rate of return in the stock market. A few years ago, the U.S. Treasury began issuing inflation-indexed bonds, bonds that pay a variable interest rate that rises and falls with the inflation rate. Explain what effect this new security has had on the feasible set available to investors.

6-6. Why is the relationship between expected return and standard deviation for portfolios of risky and risk-free assets linear?

6-7. Suppose that you have a friend who likes to invest in technology stocks. "Sure, they're risky," he says, "but the technology sector can go up 50 percent in a year. You'll never achieve that kind of return with a diversified portfolio." How should you respond?

6-8. In Japan, interest rates on short-term government bonds have been just over 0 percent in the last several years. If you could borrow and lend at a risk-free rate of 0 percent, would using borrowed money to finance part of your portfolio still increase the risk of your position?

6-9. Refer to Figure 6.1. Suppose that a risk-free rate was available in this diagram, and that the risk-free rate was at a level such that the tangent line from R_f to the efficient frontier went through point C. From that level, if the risk-free interest rate rises, what happens to the composition of the optimal portfolio?

6-10. How does the homogeneous expectations assumption lead to the conclusion in the CAPM that the optimal risky portfolio is the market portfolio?

6-11. Consumers generally prefer low prices rather than high prices, yet we say that investors want to maximize the market price of risk (i.e., the slope of the *CML*). Explain this apparent paradox.

6-12. According to the CAPM, is it possible in equilibrium for an asset with a variance greater than zero (i.e., an asset other than the risk-free asset) to have an expected return below the risk-free rate?

6-13. Suppose that stock A has a higher variance than stock B. According to the CAPM, can stock A survive in the market if its expected return is lower than that for stock B?

6-14. Suppose that a mutual fund has a beta equal to 0.75. Is it necessarily the case that the standard deviation of returns on the fund is less than the standard deviation of market returns?

6-15. Suppose that investors generally become less risk averse. What effect would this have on stock prices and on expected returns?

6-16. If an asset lies above the *SML*, is it underpriced or overpriced? Why?

6-17. Is the expected return on a stock with a beta = 2.0 twice the expected return on a stock with a beta = 1.0?

6-18. Stock A has a beta of 1.5, and stock B has a beta of 1.0. Using concepts from portfolio theory and the CAPM, determine whether each of the following statements is true or false.

   a. Stock A is more volatile (has a higher variance) than stock B.
   b. Stock A has a higher expected return that stock B.
   c. The expected return on stock A is 50 percent higher than the expected return on the market portfolio.
   d. In a regression with the individual stock's return as the dependent variable and the market's return as the independent variable, the *R*-squared value is higher for stock A than it is for stock B.

6-19. In a regression using an asset's returns as the dependent variable, y, and returns on a market index as the independent variable, x, interpret both the regression slope coefficient and the regression R^2 value.

6-20. Beta estimates may be obtained from data gathered at different frequencies (daily, weekly, monthly, etc.) Explain the trade-offs analysts confront when choosing the data's frequency.

6-21. What problems do researchers encounter when trying to test the validity of the CAPM?

6-22. What evidence supporting the CAPM have researchers found?

6-23. What data would you need to estimate the cost of capital for a particular company using the CAPM? What data would you need to do the same analysis using the Fama-French model?

6-24. Describe what each of the following pairs of asset pricing models has in common, as well as how they differ:

    a. APT and CAPM   **b.** CAPM and F-F   **c.** F-F and APT

PROBLEMS

The following problems require you to download monthly returns on several stocks from the Yahoo! website. Step-by-step instructions for gathering this data may be found in Problem 5-10 in Chapter 5.

Risk-Free Borrowing and Lending

6-1. Following the instructions given in Chapter 5 (see Problem 5-10), go to Yahoo! Finance and download monthly returns from February 1, 1996, through November 1, 2001, for Intel Corp. (INTC) and Advanced Micro Devices (AMD). Calculate the average monthly return and standard deviation for each company, as well as the covariance between them. Using these historical estimates, plot the expected return and standard deviations for the following portfolios of Intel and AMD:

%AMD	%Intel
100	0
90	10
80	20
70	30
60	40
50	50
40	60
30	70
20	80
10	90
0	100

6-2. Refer to your plot in Problem 6-1. Which of these portfolios is the minimum variance portfolio (MVP)? Which of these portfolios is efficient?

6-3. Repeat the analysis of Problem 6-1, downloading monthly returns for Pfizer Corp. (ticker symbol, PFE) and using those rather than AMD's returns to form portfolios with Intel. Comment on the differences in the two plots.

6-4. Refer to Table 6.1 and Figure 6.4. Suppose that you can borrow and lend at the risk-free rate of 0.5 percent per month. Under these circumstances, which risky portfolio is optimal to hold in combination with the risk-free asset?

6-5. Repeat Problem 6-4 with a risk-free rate of 1.3 percent per month.

6-6. The expected return on a particular stock is 15 percent, and its standard deviation is 38 percent. The risk-free return is 4 percent. Calculate the expected return and standard deviation on the following portfolios:

% Risky	% Risk-Free	E(R)	Standard Deviation
75	25	_____	_____
50	50	_____	_____
25	75	_____	_____
150	−50	_____	_____

6-7. You have the following data on three different risky assets:

	Asset A	Asset B	Asset C
Expected return %	10	14	12
Standard deviation %	20	40	30

Correlation coefficient between A & B = 0.5; A & C = 0.1; B & C = −0.35.

a. Calculate the expected return and standard deviation for each of the following portfolios:

% in A	% in B	% in C	E(R)	Standard Deviation
100	0	0	_____	_____
0	100	0	_____	_____
0	0	100	_____	_____
50	50	0	_____	_____
50	0	50	_____	_____
0	50	50	_____	_____
10	40	50	_____	_____
30	30	40	_____	_____
40	20	40	_____	_____
50	40	10	_____	_____
0	75	25	_____	_____

b. Considered in isolation, which asset lies on the efficient frontier?
c. Which of the portfolios are efficient, and which are inefficient?

6-8. If the market has an expected return of 13 percent and a standard deviation of 28 percent, and the risk-free rate is 5 percent, explain how you can construct a portfolio with an expected return of 20 percent. What will be the standard deviation of this portfolio?

6-9. Refer to the numbers given in Problem 6-8. Explain how you can create a portfolio with a standard deviation of 16 percent. What will be the expected return on this portfolio?

Smart Solutions See the problem and solution explained step-by-step at SMARTFinance

Equilibrium and the Market Portfolio

6-10. You must allocate your wealth between two securities. Security 1 offers an expected return of 10 percent and has a standard deviation of 30 percent. Security 2 offers an expected return of 15 percent and has a standard deviation of 50 percent. The correlation between the returns on these two securities is 0.25.

a. Calculate the expected return and standard deviation for each of the following portfolios, and plot them on a graph:

% Security 1	% Security2	E(R)	Standard Deviation
100	0	_____	_____
80	20	_____	_____
60	40	_____	_____
40	60	_____	_____
20	80	_____	_____
0	100	_____	_____

b. Based on your calculations in part (a), which portfolios are efficient and which are inefficient?

c. Suppose that a risk-free investment is available that offers a 4 percent return. If you must divide your wealth between the risk-free asset and one of the risky portfolios in the table above, which risky portfolio would you choose?

d. Repeat your answer to part (c) assuming that the risk-free return is 8 percent rather than 4 percent. Can you provide an intuitive explanation for why the optimal risky portfolio changes?

e. Now suppose that you can short-sell (i.e., or borrow to purchase) either security, investing the proceeds in the other. Calculate the expected return and standard deviation of the following portfolios and add them to your graph in part (a).

% Security 1	% Security 2	$E(R)$	Standard Deviation
140	40	_____	_____
120	20	_____	_____
−20	120	_____	_____
−40	140	_____	_____

6-11. In this problem, you will use several Excel features to map out a portfolio frontier. Once again, assume that there are two stocks available in the market with the following characteristics:

Stock	$E(R)$	Standard Deviation
1	12%	35%
2	18%	60%

Correlation coefficient = 0.15

Follow these instructions to create an Excel data table that will allow you to rapidly calculate the expected return and standard deviation for a large number of portfolios of these two assets. By plotting these figures, you can see the portfolio frontier.

a. Starting in cell A2 and going down to cell A5, type in the following numbers:

−.50
−.49
−.48
−.47

You can see that the pattern is to decrease the number in increments of 0.01 as you move down the column. Highlight all four numbers and grab the lower corner of the highlighted rectangle. As you drag the corner down, Excel will recognize the pattern and fill out the rest of the column (or you can use a formula to accomplish this task). Stop when cells A2 through A202 are full, with numbers that begin with −.50 and increase until you reach the value 1.50 in cell A202. The numbers in this column represent the fraction of the portfolio invested in the first stock. Because this value ranges from −.50 to 1.50, this problem will allow short-selling (i.e., or borrowing to purchase). That is, the investor can take a short position of up to 50 percent of his or her wealth, investing the proceeds in the other stock.

b. In cell B1, type an Excel formula that will calculate the standard deviation of a portfolio consisting of these two stocks. This formula will use a cell reference to A1 instructing Excel to look in column A for the portfolio weight to place in stock 1. Note that so far, cell A1 is empty. Type the following formula in cell B1:

=((A1^2)*(0.35^2)+((1−A1)^2)*(0.60^2)+2*A1*(1−A1)*0.35*0.60*0.15)^.5

c. In cell C1, type an Excel formula that will calculate the expected return of a portfolio consisting of these two stocks. Again, this formula will reference cell A1 to tell Excel where to find the percentage invested in stock 1. Type the following formula in cell C1:

=A1*0.12+(1−A1)*0.18

d. Now, to create the data table, highlight the entire rectangle from cell A1 to cell C202. Once this is highlighted, select the "Data" menu and choose "Table." In the blank space that says "Column input cell," type "A1" and hit OK. Excel will automatically calculate the standard deviation (in column B) and the expected return (in column C) for every possible portfolio.

1. What is the minimum variance portfolio?
2. For an investor to create an efficient portfolio, what is the minimum rational investment in security 1?
3. If an investor is willing to endure a portfolio standard deviation of 35 percent, how much can the investor increase the portfolio expected return by diversifying rather than by holding security 1 alone?

e. Finally, click the chart wizard, and select "XY Scatter" as the type of graph you want to create. Tell Excel that the data series are in columns ranging from cells B2:C202. Add titles and headers if you like; then, produce the graph in a separate sheet.

6-12. The stock of Adams Teleped Corp. offers an expected return of 8 percent and has a standard deviation of 55 percent. Shares of Feldman Cosmetics, Inc., have an expected return of 13 percent and a standard deviation of 40 percent. The correlation coefficient between the two assets' return is -0.2.

a. Plot each stock on a graph with standard deviation on the x-axis and expected return on the y-axis.

b. Calculate the expected return and standard deviation of the following portfolios, and add them to the graph from part (a):

% Adams	% Feldman	E(R)	Standard Deviation
100	0	_____	_____
80	20	_____	_____
60	40	_____	_____
50	50	_____	_____
40	60	_____	_____
20	80	_____	_____
0	100	_____	_____

c. Now suppose that the investor can short-sell (i.e., borrow to purchase) Adams shares and invest the proceeds in Feldman stock. Calculate and plot (on the same graph) the expected return and standard deviation of the following portfolios:

% Adams	% Feldman	E(R)	Standard Deviation
−10	110	_____	_____
−30	130	_____	_____
−50	150	_____	_____

d. Can the situation depicted in this problem persist in a general equilibrium setting? That is, can one stock survive in the market when another stock with a lower standard deviation offers a higher expected return?

The Capital Asset Pricing Model (CAPM)

6-13. The risk-free asset pays 5 percent, the market portfolio's expected return is 13 percent, and its standard deviation is 35 percent. What is the slope of the capital market line?

6-14. The expected return on a particular asset is 10 percent, and its beta is 1.5. The risk-free return is 2 percent, and the expected return on the market portfolio is 14 percent. Does this asset lie on, above, or below the security market line? Explain.

6-15. A particular stock has a beta of 1.2 and an expected return of 10.2 percent. The expected risk premium on the market portfolio is 6 percent. What is the expected return on the market portfolio?

6-16. If a stock has a beta of 1.5 and the standard deviation of the market is 30 percent, what is the covariance between the stock and the market?

Smart
Solutions
See the
problem and
solution explained step-by-step at
SMARTFinance

6-17.   Assume that the expected risk premium on the market portfolio is 8 percent and the risk-free rate is 5 percent. If an asset has an expected return of 15 percent, what is its CAPM beta?

Alternatives to the CAPM

6-18.   Suppose that you believe three risk factors drive stock returns: unexpected changes in oil prices, unexpected shifts in GDP, and unexpected movement in the overall stock market. The risk premium for bearing oil-price risk is 4 percent, the risk premium for bearing GDP risk is 5 percent, and the risk premium for bearing market risk is 6 percent. A particular firm's fortunes are very sensitive to oil prices, meaning that its "oil-price beta" is 2.0. Its GDP beta is 0.5, and its market beta is 1.0. If the risk-free rate is 3 percent, what is the expected return on this stock?

6-19.   Suppose that the expected risk premium on small stocks relative to large stocks is 6 percent, and the expected risk premium on low book-to-market stocks relative to high book-to-market stocks is 4 percent. Also assume that the expected risk premium on the overall stock market relative to the risk-free rate is 5 percent. A particular stock has a market beta of 0.8, a size beta of 0.2, and a book-to-market beta of 0.4. If the risk-free rate is 4 percent, what is the expected return on this stock according to the Fama-French model?

7

Capital Budgeting Process and Techniques

OPENING FOCUS
Tantalized by Tantalum

On January 9, 2002, the *Financial Times* reported a 53 percent increase in the stock price of Tertiary Minerals PLC (London Stock Exchange ticker symbol, TYM). The market was apparently reacting to an independent report that one of Tertiary's major investments could generate an internal rate of return of 33 percent over several years. Specifically, the analysis referred to Tertiary's opportunity to extract tantalum, a metal used in cell phones and other electronic devices, from deposits located on the southwest coast of Finland. One month later, the company's shares jumped another 58 percent on news that it won a 5-year license to explore tantalum reserves in Saudi Arabia.

Tantalized by tantalum? A firm's investments in capital assets, whether in the form of physical plant and equipment or intangible assets such as brands, trademarks, and patents, are largely responsible for creating and maintaining its competitive advantage. Financial markets monitor firms' investment decisions very closely, and share prices reflect investors' beliefs about the likely success or failure of these endeavors.

For example, consider what happened to the stock of BHP Billton, an Australian natural resources firm, when it announced on April 4, 2002, plans to open a new iron ore mine in the Pilbara region of Western Australia. An analyst at Credit Suisse First Boston projected that BHP would spend $213 million to open the mine, and that the project would generate a net present value of about $400 million, equivalent to just under A$0.13 (Australian dollars) per BHP common share. Dealers with two Australian financial services firms, Macquarie Equities and JB Were Stockbroking, echoed the view that the investment would create value for BHP shareholders, an opinion that traders on the Australian Stock Exchange apparently shared. BHP stock rose slightly less than 1 percent, or about A$0.08 on news of the pending investment.

When managers, analysts, and investors evaluate the major investments that firms undertake, they have several tools at their disposal to help them determine whether the investments benefit or harm shareholders. Two of the most widely used investment evaluation techniques are the net present value and internal rate of return methods. Read on to learn how to apply these techniques to the investment decision process.

Sources: "BHP Billton Higher after New Iron Ore Project Approval," *AFX News Limited* (April 4, 2002); "Europower Boosted by Approach," *Financial Times* (January 9, 2002); "Tertiary Tantalizes Investors," *Investors Chronicle* (February 8, 2002).

On a daily basis, firms make decisions that have financial consequences. Some decisions, such as extending credit to a customer or ordering inventory, have consequences that are short-lived. Moreover, managers can reverse these short-term actions with relative ease. In contrast, some decisions that managers face have a long-term impact on the firm and can be very difficult to unwind once started. Major investments in plant and equipment fit this description, but so might spending on advertising designed to build brand awareness and loyalty among consumers. The terms **capital investment** and **capital spending** refer to investments in these kinds of long-lived assets, and the term **capital budgeting** refers to the process of identifying which of these investment projects a firm should undertake.

The capital budgeting process involves three basic steps:

1.   Identifying potential investments
2.   Analyzing the set of investment opportunities, identifying those that will create shareholder value, and perhaps prioritizing them
3.   Implementing and monitoring the investment projects selected in step 2

The capital budgeting process begins with an idea and ends with implementation and monitoring. Ideas for investment projects can come from virtually anywhere within the firm. Marketing may propose that the firm spend money to reach a new class of customers. Operations may want to modernize equipment to realize production efficiencies. Engineering may seek resources to engage in research and development designed to improve existing products or create new ones. Information Systems may want to upgrade the firm's computer network to enable more efficient information sharing across functional areas and physical locations. Each group will undoubtedly have a compelling story to justify spending money on its pet project. The firm will analyze each proposal, approving some and rejecting others.

Once a project gains approval, the attention of financial managers turns to implementation. It is probably safe to say that managers, especially financial managers, devote a significant fraction of their time to step 3, implementing and monitoring investments that the firm has decided to make. When firms undertake a capital investment, they almost always do so with a specific budget outlining the financial objectives and constraints of that investment. Financial managers work to ensure that project managers adhere to budget guidelines, and they help track a project's success over time to determine if an investment's initial promises were realized.

Without understating the importance of step 1 (which we discuss in Chapter 9) and step 3, our focus in this chapter is on the second stage of the process, evaluating the merits of investment proposals. In practice, firms use many different techniques to justify their capital investments, ranging from simple to sophisticated. We will describe several of these techniques, highlighting their strengths and weaknesses. In the end, the preferred technique for evaluating most capital investments is one that we have already seen—net present value.

7.1 A CAPITAL BUDGETING PROBLEM

Firms use a variety of techniques to evaluate capital investments. Some techniques involve very simple calculations and are easy to grasp intuitively. Other things being equal, people generally prefer tools that are simple to use and easy to understand, and that accounts for the popularity of some capital budgeting methods, such as the *payback rule* (defined later). Unfortunately, when comparing simple capital budgeting methods to more complex ones, other things are decidedly not equal. More complex tools such as the *internal rate of return (IRR), net present value (NPV),* or the *profitability index (PI)* generally lead to better decisions because they take into account issues such as the time value of money, risk, and the supremacy of cash flow over accounting measures of profit, factors neglected or ignored by simpler methods. Moreover, the net present value approach provides a direct estimate of the increase or decrease in shareholder value resulting from a particular investment. Managers who seek to maximize shareholder value must therefore understand not just how to use the more complex techniques, but also the logic that explains why some methods are better than others. As challenging as that may sound, there is no reason to worry. We have already seen these tools at work in valuing bonds and stocks, and now we will simply apply the discounted cash flow apparatus to real assets such as plant and equipment.

We will apply each of the decision techniques in this chapter to a single, simplified business problem facing Global Wireless Incorporated, a (fictitious) U.S.-based worldwide provider of wireless telephony services. Unlike most sectors of the U.S. economy, the global wireless industry was growing rapidly in early 2003. Americans were signing up for cellular phone service at the rate of one person every 1.5 seconds, and subscribers were spending more time on their cell phones than ever before. In the spring of 2003, the typical cell phone customer used around 450 minutes per month as compared to about 70 minutes per month two years earlier. Wireless carriers scrambled to attract and retain customers in this growing market. According to customer surveys, the number-one reason for selecting a given carrier (or for switching to a new one) was the quality of service. Customers who lost calls as they commuted to work or traveled from one business location to another were apt to switch if another carrier offered fewer service interruptions.

Against this backdrop, Global Wireless was contemplating a major expansion of its wireless network in two different regions. Figure 7.1 depicts the projected cash inflows and outflows of each project over the next five years. By investing $250 million, Global Wireless could add up to 100 new cell sites to its existing base in Western Europe, giving it the most comprehensive service area in that region. Company analysts projected that this investment would generate net after-tax cash inflows at the end of each year that would grow over the next five years as outlined below:

Initial outlay	−$250 million
Year 1 inflow	$35 million
Year 2 inflow	$80 million
Year 3 inflow	$130 million
Year 4 inflow	$160 million
Year 5 inflow	$175 million

Alternatively, Global Wireless could make a much smaller investment to establish a toehold in a new market in the southeastern United States. For an initial investment of $50 million, Global Wireless believed it could create a southeastern net-

Figure 7.1
Global Wireless
Investment Proposals

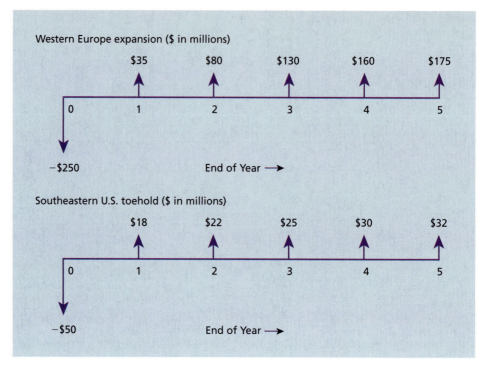

work with its hub centered in Atlanta, Georgia. The projected end-of-year cash flows associated with this project were as follows:

Initial outlay	−$50 million
Year 1 inflow	$18 million
Year 2 inflow	$22 million
Year 3 inflow	$25 million
Year 4 inflow	$30 million
Year 5 inflow	$32 million

Which investment should Global Wireless make? If the company could undertake both investments, should it do so? If it can make only one investment, which one is better for shareholders? We will see how different capital budgeting techniques would lead to different investment decisions, starting with the simplest approach, the payback method.

7.2 PAYBACK ANALYSIS

THE PAYBACK DECISION RULE

The payback method is the simplest of all capital budgeting decision tools. It enjoys widespread use, particularly in small firms. Firms using the payback approach typically define a minimum acceptable payback period. The **payback period** is the amount of time it takes for a given project's cumulative net cash inflows to recoup the initial investment. If a firm decides that it wants to avoid any investment that does not "pay for itself" in three years or less, then the payback decision rule is to accept projects with a payback period of three years or less and reject all other investments. If several projects satisfy this condition, then firms may prioritize investments based on which ones achieve payback more rapidly. The decision to use three years as the cutoff point is somewhat arbitrary, and there are no hard-and-fast guidelines that establish what the "optimal" payback period should be. Nevertheless, suppose that Global Wireless uses three years as its cutoff when doing payback analysis. What investment decision would it make?

The investment to expand the wireless network in Western Europe requires an initial outlay of $250 million. According to the firm's cash flow projections, this project will bring in just $245 million in its first three years, so the firm would reject the investment. The toehold investment in the southeastern U.S. project requires just $50 million. In its first two years, this investment generates $40 million in cash flow, and by the end of year 3, it produces a cumulative cash flow of $65 million. Thus, the project earns back the initial $50 million at some point during the third year. A rough estimate of the project's payback period is 2.4 years (because the project reaches the payback point after $10 million in cash flow in year 3, and $10 million equals 40 percent of the $25 million in total cash flows earned in year 3). In any case, investing in the southeastern U.S. project clearly meets the firm's minimum requirement of a payback period of three years or less, so Global Wireless would undertake the investment. ■

Pros and Cons of the Payback Method

Simplicity is the main virtue of the payback approach. Once a firm estimates a project's cash flows, it is a simple matter of addition to determine when the cumulative net cash inflows equal the initial outlay. The intuitive appeal of the payback method is strong. It sounds reasonable to expect a good investment to pay for itself in a fairly short period of time. Furthermore, by requiring projects to earn back the initial cash outlay within a few short years, the payback approach appears to take into account the time value of money, at least in a rough sense. Some managers say that establishing a short payback period is one way to account for a project's risk. Projects that take longer to pay off are intrinsically riskier than those that recoup the initial investment more quickly. Career concerns may also lead managers to prefer the payback rule. Particularly in large companies, managers rotate quite often from one job to another. To obtain promotions and to enhance their reputations, managers may want to make investments that will enable them to point to success stories at each stage of their careers. A manager who expects to stay in a particular position in the firm for just two or three years may prefer to undertake investments that recover costs quickly rather than projects that have payoffs far into the future. In that case, selecting projects based on how quickly they meet the payback requirement offers considerable appeal to someone trying to build a career.

Despite these apparent virtues, the payback method suffers from several serious problems. First, the payback cutoff period is simply an arbitrary choice with little or no connection to shareholder value maximization. How can we be sure that accepting projects that pay back within three years maximizes shareholder wealth rather than accepting projects that pay back within two years or four years? Second, the way that the payback method accounts for the time value of money is crude in the extreme. The payback method assigns a 0 percent discount rate to cash flows that occur before the cutoff point. That is, if the payback period is three years, then cash flows that occur in years 1, 2, and 3 receive equal weight in the payback calculation. Beyond the cutoff point, the payback method implicitly assigns an infinite discount rate to all future cash flows. In other words, cash flows in year 4 and beyond receive zero weight (or have zero present value) in today's decision to invest or not invest.[1] Third, using the payback period as a way to control for project risk is equally crude. Finance teaches that riskier investments should offer higher returns. If it is true, as managers sometimes argue, that riskier projects have longer payback periods, then the payback rule simply rejects all such investments, whether or not they offer higher returns in the long run. Managers who naively follow the payback rule will tend to underinvest in long-term projects that could offer substantial rewards for shareholders. Fourth, if career concerns lead managers to favor projects with very quick payoffs, then firms should adjust the way that they evaluate employees. Firms could reduce incentives for managers to focus on short-term successes by rewarding them for their efforts in meeting short-term goals of long-term projects (e.g., staying on budget, meeting revenue forecasts), as well as for long-term results.

DISCOUNTED PAYBACK

The **discounted payback** rule is essentially the same as the payback rule except that in calculating the payback period, managers discount cash flows first. In other words, the discounted payback method calculates how long it takes for a project's discounted cash flows to recover the initial investment. This represents a minor improvement over the simple payback method in that it does a better job of accounting for the time value of cash flows that occur within the payback cutoff period. As with the ordinary payback rule, discounted payback totally ignores cash flows that occur beyond the cutoff point.

APPLYING THE MODEL

Suppose that Global Wireless uses the discounted payback method, with a discount rate of 18 percent and a cutoff period of three years. The following schedules show the present values of each project's cash flows during the first three years.[2] For example, $29.7 million is the present value of the $35 million that the Western Europe investment is expected to earn in its first year, $57.4 million is the present value of the $80 million that the project is expected to earn in its second year, and so on.

Present Value	Western Europe Project ($ in millions)	Southeastern U.S. Project ($ in millions)
PV of Year 1	29.7	15.2
PV of Year 2	57.4	15.8
PV of Year 3	79.1	15.2
Cumulative PV	166.2	46.2

You can see that neither investment satisfies the condition that the discounted cash flows recoup the initial investment in three years or less, so Global Wireless would reject both projects. ■

---

[1] We know that the present value of a future cash flow becomes smaller and smaller as we discount at higher and higher interest rates. Discounting at an infinite interest rate results in a future cash flow having zero present value.

[2] We are assuming here that the first year's cash flows occur one year after the initial investment, that the second year's cash flows occur two years after the initial investment, and so on.

PROS AND CONS OF DISCOUNTED PAYBACK

The discounted payback rule offers essentially the same set of advantages and disadvantages of ordinary payback analysis. The primary advantage is simplicity. Discounted payback does correct the payback rule's problem of implicitly applying a 0 percent discount rate to all cash flows that occur before the cutoff point. However, like the ordinary payback rule, the discounted payback approach ignores cash flows beyond the cutoff point, in essence applying an infinite discount rate to these cash flows. In the final analysis, though it represents a marginal improvement over the simplest version of the payback rule, discounted payback analysis is likely to lead managers to underinvest in profitable projects with long-run payoffs.

1. What factors account for the popularity of the payback method? 2. What are the major flaws of the payback and discounted payback approaches?	**Concept Review Questions**

7.3 ACCOUNTING-BASED METHODS

ACCOUNTING RATE OF RETURN

For better or worse, managers in many firms focus as much on how a given project will influence reported earnings as on how it will affect cash flows. Managers justify this focus by pointing to the positive (negative) stock-price response that occurs when their firms beat (fail to meet) earnings forecasts made by Wall Street securities analysts. Managers may also pay more attention to the accounting-based earnings of a project than they pay to its cash flows because their compensation is based on meeting accounting-based performance measures such as earnings-per-share or return-on-assets targets. Consequently, many firms decide whether or not to invest in a given project based on the rate of return the investment will earn on an accounting basis.

Companies have many different ways of defining a *hurdle rate* for their investments in terms of accounting rates of return. Almost all these metrics involve two steps: (1) identify the net income associated with the project in each year of its life, and (2) measure the amount of invested capital, as shown on the balance sheet, devoted to the project in each year. Given these two figures, a firm may calculate an **accounting rate of return** by dividing net income by the book value of assets, either on a year-by-year basis or by taking an average over the project's life. Companies will usually establish some minimum rate of accounting return that projects must earn before they can be funded. When more than one project exceeds the minimum standard, firms prioritize projects based on their accounting returns, investing in projects with higher returns first.

APPLYING THE MODEL

Suppose that it is the practice at Global Wireless to calculate a project's accounting rate of return by taking the project's average contribution to net income and dividing by its average book value. Global Wireless ranks projects based on this measure and accepts those that offer an accounting rate of return of at least 25 percent. So far, we have been given the cash flows from each of the two projects that Global Wireless is evaluating. Chapter 8 discusses in more depth the differences between cash flow and net income, but for now we will simplify by assuming that we can determine each project's contribution to net income by subtracting depreciation from cash flow each year. We will assume that the company depreciates fixed assets on a straight-line basis over five years, so the Western Europe project will have an annual depreciation charge of $50 million (one-fifth of $250 million), and the southeastern U.S. project will have an annual depreciation charge of $10 million. These assumptions yield the following net income figures for the next five years:

Year	Western Europe Project ($ in millions)	Southeastern U.S. Project ($ in millions)
1	−15	8
2	30	12
3	80	15
4	110	20
5	125	22

The Western Europe project begins with a book value of $250 million and after five years of depreciation has a book value of $0. Therefore, the average book value of that project is $125 million. The project's average net income equals $66 million [(−$15 + $30 + $80 + $110 + $125) ÷ 5], so its average accounting rate of return is an impressive 52.8 percent ($66 ÷ $125). The same steps applied to the southeastern U.S. project yield an average book value of $25 million, an average net income of $15.4 million, and an accounting rate of return of 61.6 percent. On the basis of this analysis, Global Wireless should be willing to invest in either project, but it would rank the southeastern U.S. investment above the Western Europe expansion. ■

Pros and Cons of the Accounting Rate of Return

Though many firms use accounting-based metrics to evaluate capital investments, these techniques have serious flaws. First, as the preceding Applying the Model demonstrates, the decision about what depreciation method to use has a large impact on both the numerator and the denominator of the accounting rate of return formula. Second, this method makes no adjustment for project risk or for the time value of money. Third, investors should be more concerned with the market value than the book value of the assets that a firm holds. After five years, the book value of Global Wireless's investment (in either project) is zero, but the market value will almost certainly be positive, and may be even greater than the initial amount invested. Fourth, as explained in Chapter 2, finance theory teaches that investors should focus on a company's ability to generate cash rather than on its net income. Fifth, the choice of the 25 percent accounting return hurdle rate is essentially arbitrary. This rate is not based on rates available on similar investments in the market, but instead reflects a purely subjective judgment on the part of management.

By now you may have noticed some common themes in our discussion of pros and cons of different approaches to capital budgeting. Each of the methods discussed thus far fails to properly account for the time value of money. None of these methods deals adequately with differences in risk from one investment to another, and none factors all the cash flows of a project into the decision-making process. We now turn our attention to a method that solves all these difficulties and therefore enjoys widespread support from both academics and businesspeople.

Concept Review Questions

3. Why do managers focus on the impact that an investment will have on reported earnings rather than on the investment's cash flow consequences?

4. What factors determine whether the accounting rate of return on a given project will be high or low in the early years of the investment's life? In the latter years?

7.4 NET PRESENT VALUE

NET PRESENT VALUE CALCULATIONS

Calculating the **net present value** (**NPV**) of an investment project is relatively straight-forward. First, write down the net cash flows that the investment will generate over its life. Second, discount these cash flows at an interest rate that reflects the degree of risk inherent in the project. The resulting sum of discounted cash flows equals the project's net present value. The *NPV* decision rule says to invest in projects when the net present value is greater than zero:[3]

$$NPV = CF_0 + \frac{CF_1}{(1 + r)^1} + \frac{CF_2}{(1 + r)^2} + \frac{CF_3}{(1 + r)^3} + \cdots + \frac{CF_N}{(1 + r)^N} \qquad \text{(Eq. 7.1)}$$

$NPV > \$0$ invest

$NPV < \$0$ do not invest

In this expression, CF_t represents net cash flow in year t, r is the discount rate, and N represents the life of the project. The cash flows in each year may be positive or negative, though we usually expect projects to generate cash outflows initially and cash inflows later on. For example, suppose that the initial cash flow, CF_0, is a negative number representing the outlay necessary to get the project started, and suppose that all subsequent cash flows are positive. In this case, the *NPV* decision rule says that firms should invest when the present value of future cash inflows exceeds the initial project cost. That is, $NPV > \$0$ occurs when the following occurs:

$$-CF_0 < \frac{CF_1}{(1 + r)^1} + \frac{CF_2}{(1 + r)^2} + \frac{CF_3}{(1 + r)^3} + \cdots + \frac{CF_N}{(1 + r)^N}$$

Why does the *NPV* rule generally lead to good investment decisions? Remember that the firm's goal in choosing investment projects is to maximize shareholder wealth. Conceptually, the discount rate, r, in the *NPV* equation represents an opportunity cost, the highest rate of return that investors can obtain in the marketplace on an investment with risk equal to the risk of the specific project. When the *NPV* of a cash flow stream equals zero, that stream of cash flows provides a rate of return exactly equal to shareholders' required return. Therefore, when a firm can find a project with a positive *NPV*, the project offers a return that exceeds shareholders' expectations.

[3.] What about investments with $NPV = \$0$? A zero *NPV* represents a kind of wealth-creation breakeven point. That is, when an investment's *NPV* is positive, a firm creates wealth for its shareholders, and when the *NPV* is negative, the firm destroys wealth by undertaking the project. When the *NPV* is zero, investing neither creates nor destroys wealth, so shareholders are indifferent to whether the firm accepts or rejects the project.

A firm that consistently finds positive-*NPV* investments will consistently surpass shareholders' expectations and will enjoy a rising stock price. Conversely, if the firm makes an investment with a negative *NPV*, the investment will disappoint shareholders. A firm that regularly makes negative-*NPV* investments will see its stock price lag as it persists in generating lower-than-required returns for stockholders.

We can develop an analogy, drawing on what we already know about valuing bonds, to drive home the point about the relationship between stock prices and the *NPV* rule. Suppose that at a given point in time, investors require a 5 percent return on 5-year Treasury bonds. Of course, this means that if the U.S. Treasury issues 5-year, $1,000 par value bonds paying an annual coupon of $50, the market price of these bonds will be $1,000, exactly equal to par value.[4]

$$\$1,000 = \frac{\$50}{1.05^1} + \frac{\$50}{1.05^2} + \cdots + \frac{\$1,050}{1.05^5}$$

Now apply *NPV* logic. If an investor purchases one of these bonds for $1,000, the *NPV* equals zero because the bond's cash flows precisely satisfy the investor's expectation of a 5 percent return.

$$NPV = \$0 = -\$1,000 + \frac{\$50}{1.05^1} + \frac{\$50}{1.05^2} + \cdots + \frac{\$1,050}{1.05^5}$$

Next, imagine that in a fit of election-year largesse, the U.S. Congress decrees that the coupon payments on all government bonds will double, so this bond now pays $100 in interest per year. If the bond's price remains fixed at $1,000, this investment's *NPV* will suddenly switch from zero to positive:

$$NPV = \$216.47 = -\$1,000 + \frac{\$100}{1.05^1} + \frac{\$100}{1.05^2} + \cdots + \frac{\$1,100}{1.05^5}$$

Of course, the bond's price will not remain at $1,000. Investors will quickly recognize that at a price of $1,000 and with a coupon of $100, the return offered by these bonds substantially exceeds the required rate of 5 percent. Investors will flock to buy the bonds, rapidly driving up bond values until prices reach the point at which buying bonds becomes a zero-*NPV* investment once again.[5] In the new equilibrium, the bond's price will rise by $216.47, exactly the amount of the *NPV* that was created when Congress doubled the coupon payments:

$$NPV = \$0 = -\$1,216.47 + \frac{\$100}{1.05^1} + \frac{\$100}{1.05^2} + \cdots + \frac{\$1,100}{1.05^5}$$

The same forces drive up a firm's stock price when it makes a positive-*NPV* investment, as shown in Figure 7.2. In the figure, we depict a firm that investors believe will pay an annual dividend of $4 in perpetuity. If investors require a 10 percent return on this firm's stock, the price will be $40.[6] What happens if the firm makes a new investment? If the return on this investment is greater than 10 percent, it will have a

[4] Though Treasury bonds pay interest semiannually, we assume annual interest payments here to keep the example simple.
[5] Recall that in Chapter 6, we said that an underpriced stock would lie above the security market line. The same thing is happening here. At a price of $1,000, the bond is underpriced if Congress raises the bond's coupon to $100. The price of the bond rises, and its expected return falls.
[6] Remember that the price of a stock that pays a constant dividend in perpetuity equals the annual dividend divided by the required rate of return—in this case, $4 ÷ 0.10 = $40.

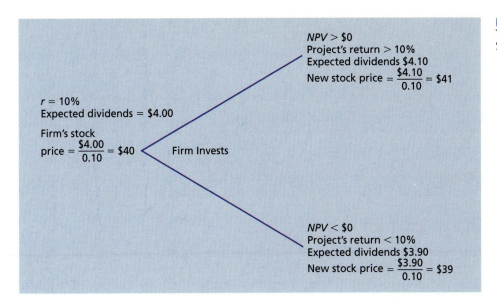

Figure 7.2
The *NPV* Rule and
Shareholder Wealth

positive *NPV*. Investors will recognize that the firm has made an investment that exceeds their expectations, and investors will raise their forecast of future dividends, perhaps to $4.10 per year. At that level, the new stock price will be $41. The same thing happens in reverse if the firm makes an investment that earns a return below 10 percent. At that rate, the project has a negative *NPV*. Shareholders recognize that this investment's cash flows fall below their expectations, so they lower their estimates of future dividends to $3.90 per year. As a consequence, the stock price falls to $39.

Now apply this thought process to Global Wireless. Suppose that its shareholders demand an 18 percent return on their shares. According to the principles we discussed in Chapter 4, the price of Global Wireless stock will reflect the value of all future cash distributions that investors expect from the company, discounted at a rate of 18 percent. But what if Global Wireless discovers that it can make an investment that offers a return substantially above 18 percent? By definition, such an investment has a positive *NPV*, and by undertaking it, Global Wireless will increase the price of its stock as investors come to realize that the company will be able to distribute higher-than-anticipated cash flows as a result of the investment opportunity. How far will the stock price rise? Simply divide the project's *NPV* (which represents the amount of wealth the project creates) by the number of outstanding shares. The result is the amount by which Global Wireless's stock price should increase.

APPLYING THE MODEL

What are the *NPV*s of each of the investment opportunities now facing Global Wireless? Discounting each project's cash flows at 18 percent yields the following results:[7]

$$NPV_{\text{Western Europe}} = -\$250 + \frac{\$35}{(1.18)^1} + \frac{\$80}{(1.18)^2} + \frac{\$130}{(1.18)^3} + \frac{\$160}{(1.18)^4} + \frac{\$175}{(1.18)^5}$$

$$= \$75$$

[7.] Of course, you can do this calculation in Excel using the "=*NPV*" function. Imagine that you have all the Western Europe project's cash flows in column A of a spreadsheet, with the initial outlay in row 1, the first year's inflow in row 2, and so on. In any blank cell, type the formula "=NPV(0.18,A2:A6) + A1." Excel will return the value $75.26, which represents the *NPV* of the project. Notice that the *NPV* function contains as its first argument the discount rate, and fol-

$$NPV_{\text{Southeastern U.S.}} = -\$50 + \frac{\$18}{(1.18)^1} + \frac{\$22}{(1.18)^2} + \frac{\$25}{(1.18)^3} + \frac{\$30}{(1.18)^4} + \frac{\$32}{(1.18)^5}$$

$$= \$25.7$$

Both projects increase shareholder wealth, so both are worth undertaking. However, if the company can make only one investment, it should choose to expand its presence in Western Europe because that investment increases shareholder wealth by $75 million, whereas the southeastern U.S. investment increases wealth by one-third as much. If Global Wireless has 100 million shares of common stock outstanding, accepting the Western Europe project should increase the stock price by $0.75, while accepting the southeastern U.S. investment would increase the stock price by almost $0.26. ▪

Pros and Cons of *NPV*

The net present value method solves all the problems we have identified with the payback and discounted payback rules, as well as problems associated with decision rules based on the accounting rate of return. First, the *NPV* rule focuses on cash flow, not accounting earnings. Second, when properly applied, the net present value method makes appropriate adjustments for the time value of money. Third, the decision rule to invest when *NPV*s are positive and to refrain from investing when *NPV*s are negative reflects the firm's need to compete for funds in the marketplace rather than an arbitrary judgment of management. Fourth, the *NPV* approach offers a relatively straightforward way to control for differences in risk among alternative investments. Cash flows on riskier investments should be discounted at higher rates. Fifth, the *NPV* method incorporates all the cash flows that a project generates over its life, not just those that occur in the project's early years. Sixth, the *NPV* gives a direct estimate of the change in shareholder wealth resulting from a given investment.

Though we are enthusiastic supporters of the *NPV* approach, especially compared to the other decision methods examined thus far, we must acknowledge that the *NPV* rule suffers from a few weaknesses. Relative to alternative capital budgeting tools, the *NPV* rule seems less intuitive to many users. When you hear that Global Wireless's southeastern U.S. project has an *NPV* of $25.7 million, does that seem more or less intuitive than learning that the investment pays back its initial cost in 2.4 years or that it earns an accounting return of 61.6 percent? Though the mathematics of an *NPV* calculation could hardly be called sophisticated, it is still easier to calculate a project's payback period than its *NPV*.

There is one other subtle drawback to the *NPV* rule, a drawback that results from the inability to incorporate the value of managerial flexibility when calculating a project's *NPV*. What we have in mind when we use the term "managerial flexibility" are options that managers can exploit after an investment has been made to increase its value. For example, if a firm makes an investment that turns out better than expected, managers have the option to expand that investment, making it even more valuable. Conversely, if a firm invests in a project that does not generate as much positive cash flow as anticipated, then managers have the option to scale back the investment and redeploy resources to more productive uses. The *NPV* method (like every

---

lowing that are the cash flows from year 1 to year 5 (contained in rows 2–6). By design, Excel's *NPV* function assumes that the first cash flow listed in the function (in this case, the cash flow in cell A2) occurs one year after the initial investment. We add the initial cash outflow, contained in cell A1, as a separate argument to get the total project *NPV*. Remember, the numerical value in cell A1 equals −$250, so by adding a negative number, we are subtracting the initial cash outflow from the present value of the cash inflows in years 1–5. Excel's *NPV* function assumes that the project's cash flows are equally spaced through time and occur at the end of each period.

other method studied in this chapter) does a poor job of capturing the value of managerial flexibility, or the value of options open to managers to improve the returns on investments after they have been made. To incorporate the value of these options into the analysis requires a highly sophisticated approach that relies on the principles of option pricing. We offer a brief introduction to valuing investments with option-like characteristics in Chapter 9, but defer an in-depth discussion of that technique until Chapter 19.

Though most large corporations use the *NPV* method, perhaps in conjunction with other capital budgeting tools, to make major investment decisions, the *NPV* rule has a close cousin that sees even more widespread use. This cousin, known as the *internal rate of return*, uses essentially the same mathematics as *NPV* does in evaluating a project's merits. The output of internal rate of return analysis is a single, intuitively appealing number representing the return that an investment earns over its life. In most cases, the internal rate of return yields investment recommendations that are in agreement with the *NPV* rule, although important differences between the two approaches arise when ranking alternative projects.

---

5. If a project has an *NPV* of $1 million, what does that mean?

6. At a given point in time, why might the discount rates used to calculate the *NPVs* of two competing projects differ?

Concept Review Questions

7.5 INTERNAL RATE OF RETURN

FINDING A PROJECT'S *IRR*

As methods for evaluating investment projects, payback, discounted payback, and accounting rate of return all suffer from common problems—a complete or partial failure to make adjustments for the time value of money and for risk. Alternative methods exist that correct these shortcomings, and perhaps the most popular and most intuitive of these alternatives is known as the **internal rate of return** (*IRR*) method. An investment's internal rate of return is analogous to a bond's *yield to maturity (YTM)*, a concept we introduced in Chapter 4. Recall that the *YTM* of a bond is the discount rate that equates the present value of the bond's future cash flows to its market price. The *YTM* measures the compound annual return that an investor earns by purchasing a bond and holding it until maturity (provided that all payments are made as promised and that interest payments can be reinvested at the same rate). In a similar vein, the *IRR* of an investment project is the compound annual return on the project, given its up-front costs and subsequent cash flows.

A project's *IRR* is the discount rate that makes the net present value of all project cash flows equal to zero:

$$NPV = \$0 = CF_0 + \frac{CF_1}{(1+r)^1} + \frac{CF_2}{(1+r)^2} + \frac{CF_3}{(1+r)^3} + \cdots + \frac{CF_N}{(1+r)^N} \quad \textbf{(Eq. 7.2)}$$

To find a project's *IRR*, we must begin by specifying the project's cash flows. Next, using a financial calculator, spreadsheet, or even trial and error, we find the discount rate that equates the present value of cash flows to zero. Once we have the *IRR* in hand, we compare it to a prespecified hurdle rate established by the firm. The hurdle

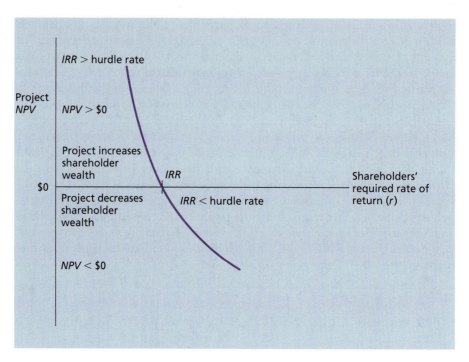

rate represents the firm's minimum acceptable return for a given project, so the decision rule is to invest only if the project's *IRR* exceeds the hurdle rate.

But where does the hurdle rate come from? How do firms decide whether to require projects to exceed a 10 percent hurdle or a 20 percent hurdle? The answer to this question provides insight into another advantage of *IRR* over capital budgeting methods that focus on a project's payback period or accounting return. A company should set the hurdle rate at a level that reflects market returns on investments that are just as risky as the project under consideration. For example, if the project at hand involves expanding a chain of fast-food restaurants, then the hurdle rate should reflect the returns that other fast-food businesses offer investors in the marketplace. Therefore, the *IRR* method, like the *NPV* method, establishes a hurdle rate or a decision criterion that is *market based,* unlike the payback and accounting-based approaches that establish arbitrary thresholds for investment approval. In fact, for a given project, the hurdle rate used in *IRR* analysis should be the discount rate used in *NPV* analysis.

Figure 7.3 illustrates the relationship between the *NPV* and *IRR* for a typical project. By "typical," we mean a project with cash flows that begin with an initial outflow that is followed by a series of inflows. In this case, the *NPV* declines as the discount rate used to calculate the *NPV* increases. Not all projects have this feature, as we will soon see. The line in Figure 7.3 plots the *NPV* of a project at various discount rates. When the discount rate is relatively low, the project has a positive *NPV.* When the discount rate is high, the project has a negative *NPV.* At some discount rate, the *NPV* of the project will equal zero, and that rate is the project's *IRR.*

APPLYING THE MODEL

Suppose that Global Wireless requires its analysts to calculate the *IRR* of all proposed investments, and the company agrees to undertake only those investments that offer an *IRR* exceeding 18 percent, a rate that Global Wireless believes to be an industry standard. Calculating the *IRR* for each of Global Wireless's potential investments involves solving these two equations:

$$0 = -\$250 + \frac{\$35}{(1 + r_{WE})^1} + \frac{\$80}{(1 + r_{WE})^2} + \frac{\$130}{(1 + r_{WE})^3} + \frac{\$160}{(1 + r_{WE})^4} + \frac{\$175}{(1 + r_{WE})^5}$$

$$0 = -\$50 + \frac{\$18}{(1 + r_{SE})^1} + \frac{\$22}{(1 + r_{SE})^2} + \frac{\$25}{(1 + r_{SE})^3} + \frac{\$30}{(1 + r_{SE})^4} + \frac{\$32}{(1 + r_{SE})^5}$$

The numerical values in these equations come from each project's cash flow estimates, and the terms r_{WE} and r_{SE} represent the *IRR* for the Western Europe and southeastern U.S. investments, respectively. Solving these expressions yields the following: [8]

$$r_{WE} = 27.8\%$$

$$r_{SE} = 36.7\%$$

Because both investments exceed the hurdle rate of 18 percent, Global Wireless would like to undertake both projects. But what if it can invest in only one project or the other? Should the company invest in the southeastern U.S. project because it offers a higher *IRR* than the alternative? ■

ADVANTAGES OF THE *IRR* METHOD

The question of how to rank investments that offer different *IRR*s points to an important weakness of this method. However, before getting into the problems associated with *IRR* analysis, we will discuss the advantages that make it one of the most widely used methods for evaluating capital investments.

First, the *IRR* makes an appropriate adjustment for the time value of money. The value of a dollar received in the first year is greater than the value of a dollar received in the second year, and even cash flows that arrive several years in the future receive some weight in the analysis (unlike payback, which totally ignores distant cash flows). Second, the hurdle rate itself can be based on market returns obtainable on similar investments. This takes away some of the subjectivity that creeps into other analytical methods, like the arbitrary threshold decisions that must be made when using payback or accounting rate of return, and it allows managers to make explicit, quantitative adjustments for differences in risk across projects. Third, because the "answer" that comes out of an *IRR* analysis is a rate of return, its meaning is easy for both financial and nonfinancial managers to grasp intuitively. As we will see, however, the intuitive appeal of the *IRR* approach has its drawbacks, particularly when ranking investments with different *IRR*s. Fourth, the *IRR* technique focuses on cash flow rather than on accounting measures of income.

Though it represents a substantial improvement over payback or accounting return analysis, the *IRR* technique has its own set of quirks and problems that should concern analysts. Some of these problems arise from the mathematics of the *IRR* calculation, but other difficulties come into play only when companies must discriminate between **mutually exclusive projects.** That is, when several investments exceed

---

[8.] Here's how to use Excel to solve for the *IRR*. Put the numbers for the Western Europe project in column A of a spreadsheet, and put the numbers for the southeastern U.S. project in column B. In row 1, type in the cash outflow for each project, entering the values as negative numbers. In rows 2–6 of the spreadsheet, enter the cash inflows in each year. Then, in any empty cell, type "=*IRR*(A1:A6, 0.10)" to calculate the *IRR* of the Western Europe project. The cells A1:A6 contain the relevant cash flows, and the value "0.10" is just a starting value that Excel uses to begin searching for the *IRR*. Likewise, enter the formula "=*IRR*(B1:B6, 0.10)" in any empty cell to calculate the *IRR* of the southeastern U.S. investment.

the hurdle rate, but only a subset of those can be undertaken at any given time, how does the firm choose? It turns out that the intuitive approach, selecting those projects with the highest *IRR*s, can lead to bad decisions in certain cases.

PROBLEMS WITH THE INTERNAL RATE OF RETURN

There are two classes of problems that analysts encounter when evaluating investments using the *IRR* technique. The first class might be described as "mathematical problems," which are difficulties in interpreting the numbers that one obtains from solving an *IRR* equation. For example, consider a simple project with cash flows at three different points in time:

$$CF_0 \qquad\qquad CF_1 \qquad\qquad CF_2$$

0	1	2

$$\text{years} \rightarrow$$

CF_0 is the immediate cash flow when the project begins, and CF_1 and CF_2 are cash flows that occur at the end of years 1 and 2, respectively. Note that conceptually the values of CF_0, CF_1, and CF_2 could be either positive or negative. Solving for this project's *IRR* means setting the net present value of all these cash flows equal to zero:

$$NPV = \$0 = CF_0 + \frac{CF_1}{(1 + r)^1} + \frac{CF_2}{(1 + r)^2}$$

Notice that this equation involves terms such as r and r^2. In other words, this is a quadratic equation in terms of r. We know that solving a quadratic equation can result in a variety of possible outcomes, including (1) a unique solution, (2) multiple solutions, and (3) solutions involving imaginary numbers. The following examples illustrate some of the problems that may arise when interpreting solutions to an *IRR* equation.

Lending and Borrowing

A firm establishes a hurdle rate of 20 percent for new investments. Consider two projects with cash flows occurring at just two dates—now and one year from now.

Project	Cash Flow Now	Cash Flow in One Year	IRR	NPV (20%)
1	−$100	+$150	50%	+$25
2	+ 100	− 150	50	− 25

The first project displays the familiar pattern of an initial cash outflow followed by a cash inflow. Most investment projects probably fit this profile. But the second project begins with a cash inflow followed by a cash outflow. What kinds of projects in the real world follow this pattern of cash inflows at the start and cash outflows downstream? Think of a firm that is cutting timber in a forest. The timber is cut and sold immediately at a profit, but when harvesting is complete, the company must replant the forest at considerable expense. Consider an optional warranty sold with a new car. The firm receives payment up front but must pay claims later on. The third column shows that the internal rate of return is 50 percent on both project 1 and project 2. Are these projects equally desirable? It should be intuitive to you that project 1 is superior because it generates net cash inflows over time, while project 2 generates net cash outflows. Indeed, the *NPV*s bear this out, as project 1 generates a positive $25 *NPV*, whereas project 2 yields a negative $25 *NPV*.

The problem we are confronting here is known as the **lending versus borrowing problem.** We can think of project 1 as analogous to a loan. Cash flows out today in exchange for a larger amount of cash in one year. When we lend money, a higher interest rate, or a higher internal rate of return, is preferable, other things held constant. In contrast, project 2 is analogous to borrowing money. We receive cash up front but have to pay back a larger amount later. When borrowing money, a lower interest rate, or a lower *IRR* is preferred, other factors held constant. Therefore, we can modify the internal rate of return decision rule as follows:

1. When projects have initial cash outflows and subsequent cash inflows, invest when the project *IRR* exceeds the hurdle rate.
2. When projects have initial cash inflows and subsequent cash outflows, invest when the project *IRR* falls below the hurdle rate.

Figure 7.4 illustrates this situation. The *NPV* of project 1 falls as the discount rate rises, as we would normally expect. Therefore, if the firm's hurdle rate is below the project's *IRR*, then the project has a positive *NPV*; but if the hurdle rate is above the *IRR*, the project has a negative *NPV*. Thus, following the usual rule of accepting projects when the *IRR* exceeds the hurdle rate makes sense. Notice that the *NPV* of project 2 actually rises as the discount rate rises. This counterintuitive relationship holds because the firm is essentially borrowing money in project 2. The higher the rate at which the firm discounts the amount it will have to repay, the lower the present value of that payment and the higher the *NPV* of the project. In this case, it makes sense to accept projects only when the *IRR* falls short of the firm's hurdle rate.

Multiple *IRRs*

A second difficulty with the *IRR* method can occur when a project's cash flows alternate between negative and positive values—that is, when the project generates an alternating series of net cash inflows and outflows. In that case, there may be more than one solution to the *IRR* equation. As an example, consider a project with the following stream of cash flows:

Year	*CF* ($ in millions)
0	+100
1	−460
2	+791
3	−602.6
4	+171.6

Admittedly, this project has a rather strange sequence of alternating net cash inflows and outflows, but it is not hard to think of real-world investments that generate cash flow streams that flip back and forth like this. For example, think about high-technology products. A new product costs money to develop. It generates plenty of cash for a year or two, but it quickly becomes obsolete. Obsolescence necessitates more spending to develop an upgraded version of the product, which then generates cash again. The cycle continues indefinitely.

Figure 7.5 plots the *NPV* of this cash flow stream at various discount rates. Notice that there are several points on the graph at which the project *NPV* equals zero. In other words, there are several *IRRs* for this project, including 0 percent, 10 percent, 20 percent, and 30 percent. How does one apply the *IRR* decision rule in a situation such as this? Suppose that the hurdle rate for this project is 15 percent. Two of the four *IRRs* on this project exceed the hurdle rate, and two fall below the hurdle rate. Should the firm invest or not? The only way to know for sure is to check the *NPV*.

Figure 7.4
Lending versus Borrowing

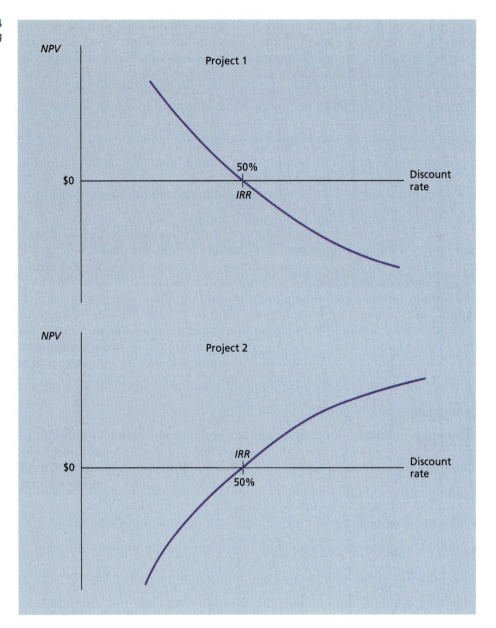

On the graph, we see that at a discount rate of 15 percent, the project's *NPV* is positive, so the firm should invest.

The general rule of thumb here is that the maximum number of *IRR*s that a project can have equals the number of sign changes in the cash flow stream. Therefore, in the typical project with cash outflows up front and cash inflows later on, there is just one sign change, and there will be at most one *IRR*. In the previous example, there are four sign changes in the cash flow stream and four different *IRR*s. *In the event that you have to evaluate a project with more than one sign change in the cash flows, beware of the multiple IRR problem.*

No Real Solution

Occasionally, when you enter the cash flows from a particular investment into a calculator or spreadsheet, the computer may send you an error message indicating that

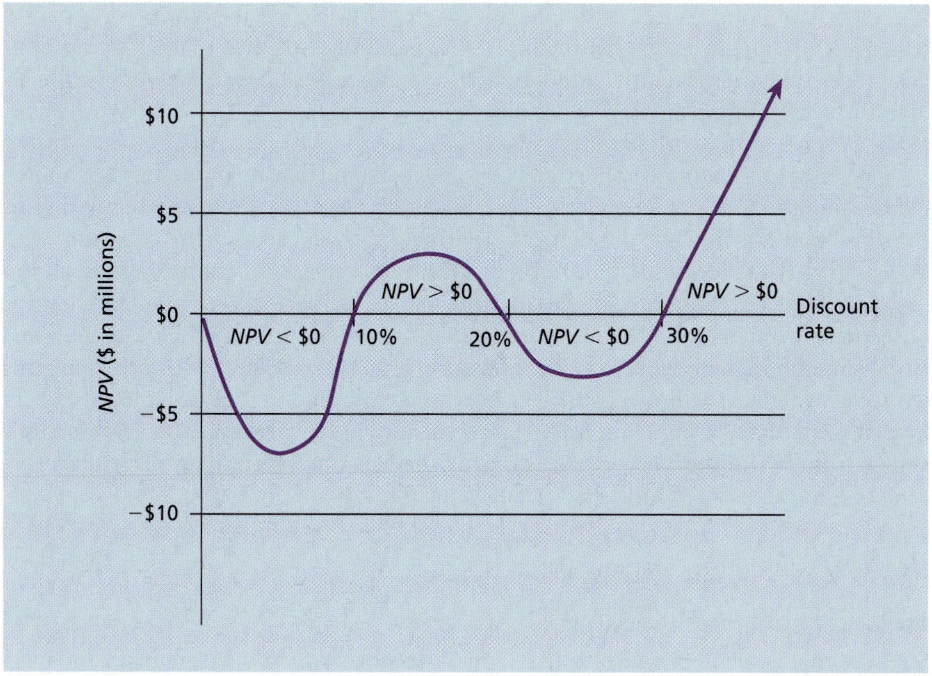

Figure 7.5
Multiple *IRR*s

there is no solution to the problem. For some cash flow patterns, it is possible that there is no real discount rate that equates the project's *NPV* to zero. In these cases, the only solution to the *IRR* equation involves imaginary numbers, hardly something that we can compare to a firm's hurdle rate.

APPLYING THE MODEL

When we first looked at the Global Wireless Western Europe expansion project, we examined cash flows over a 5-year project life. Let's modify the example a little. Suppose that the project life is six years rather than five, and in the sixth year the firm must incur a large negative cash outflow. The modified cash flow projections now look like this:

Year	Western Europe Project ($ in millions)
0	−250
1	35
2	80
3	130
4	160
5	175
6	−355

When we attempt to calculate the *IRR* for this stream of cash flows, we find that Excel (or our financial calculator) returns an error code. The problem is that for this stream of cash flows, there is no real solution to the *IRR* equation. That is, there is no (real) interest rate at which the present value of cash flows equals zero. If we cannot determine the *IRR* of this project, how can we determine whether the project meets the firm's hurdle rate of 18 percent? In this particular example, the magnitudes of the cash outflows at the beginning and end of the modified project are such that intuition suggests that Global Wireless should not invest. However, it is possible to generate scenarios in which no solution to the *IRR* equation exists, and the pattern of cash flows over time is sufficiently complex that it is difficult to decide whether or not to invest based on intuition. ◼

The last three examples illustrate various problems that analysts may encounter when using the *IRR* decision rule. These problems are all mathematical in nature in the sense that they involve difficulties in getting a solution to the *IRR* equation or in interpreting the solution that you obtain. Although we do not want to diminish the importance of watching out for these problems, we suspect that in practice they are of secondary importance. We mean that most investment projects that you will evaluate using the *IRR* method will probably have a unique solution with little ambiguity about whether the project involves borrowing or lending (because most projects involve cash outflows up front followed by cash inflows). However, the *IRR* method suffers from two additional problems that arise when analysts have to prioritize projects, or choose between mutually exclusive projects.

IRR, *NPV*, AND MUTUALLY EXCLUSIVE PROJECTS
The Scale Problem

Suppose that a friend promises to pay you $2 tomorrow if you lend him $1 today. If you make the loan and your friend fulfills his end of the bargain, you will have made an investment with a 100 percent *IRR*.[9] Now consider a different case. Your friend asks you to lend him $100 today in exchange for $150 tomorrow. The *IRR* on that investment is 50 percent, exactly half the *IRR* of the first example. Both of these loans offer very high rates of return. Assuming that you trust the friend to repay you in either case, which investment would you choose if you could choose only one? The first investment increases your wealth by $1, and the second increases your wealth by $50. Even though the rate of return is lower on the second investment, most people would prefer to lend the larger amount because of its substantially greater payoff.

The point of these examples is not to tempt you to enter the loan-shark business, but rather to illustrate the scale problem inherent in *IRR* analysis. When choosing between mutually exclusive investments, we cannot conclude that the one offering the highest *IRR* necessarily provides the greatest wealth-creation opportunity. When several alternative investments offer *IRR*s that exceed a firm's hurdle rate, choosing the investment that maximizes shareholder wealth involves more than picking the project with the highest *IRR*. For example, take another look at the investment opportunities faced by Global Wireless, opportunities that vary dramatically in scale.

APPLYING THE MODEL

Here again are the *NPV* and *IRR* figures for the two investment alternatives.

Project	IRR	NPV (18%)
Western Europe	27.8%	$75.0 million
Southeastern U.S.	36.7	25.7 million

If we had to choose just one project, and we ranked them based on their *IRR*s, we would choose to invest in the southeastern U.S. project. But we have also seen that the Western Europe project generates a much higher *NPV*, meaning that it creates

---

[9.] The *IRR* is 100 percent per day in this example, which is not a bad return if you annualize it.

more wealth for Global Wireless shareholders. The *NPV* criterion tells us to expand in Western Europe rather than in the southeastern United States. Why the conflict? The scale of the Western Europe expansion is roughly 5 times that of the southeastern U.S. project. Even though the southeastern U.S. investment provides a higher rate of return, the opportunity to make a much larger investment (an investment that also offers a return well above the firm's hurdle rate) is more attractive. ■

Fortunately for analysts who prefer to use the *IRR* method, there is a resolution to the scale problem. The solution involves calculating the *IRR* for a hypothetical project, a project with cash flows equal to the difference in cash flows between the large-scale (Western Europe) and small-scale (southeastern U.S.) investments. Call this the **incremental project.** The logic of this approach is as follows. We already know that both investments have *IRR*s that exceed the hurdle rate, but due to limitations on money or managerial talent, we can invest in only one of them. But we can think of the Western Europe investment as consisting of two investments rolled into one. The Western Europe project equals the sum of the southeastern U.S. project and the incremental project. If we examine the incremental project's *IRR* and find that it also exceeds our hurdle rate, then by accepting the Western Europe project, we are essentially making two investments, not just one. In accepting the Western Europe project, it is as if we are accepting one project with cash flows identical to those of the southeastern U.S. investment and another with cash flows equal to those of the incremental project.

Year	Incremental *CF* [Western Europe − Southeastern U.S.] ($ in millions)
0	−200
1	17
2	58
3	105
4	130
5	143

The *IRR* of this cash flow stream equals 25.8 percent. Because this exceeds the 18 percent hurdle rate, we conclude that we would like to accept the incremental project AND the southeastern U.S. project, but of course, the only way to do both is to accept the Western Europe project!

The Timing Problem

Managers of public corporations often receive criticism for neglecting long-term investment opportunities for the sake of meeting short-term financial performance goals. We prefer to remain noncommittal on whether corporate managers as a rule put too much emphasis on short-term performance. However, we agree with the proposition that a naive reliance on the *IRR* method can lead to investment decisions that sometimes favor investments with short-term payoffs over those that offer returns over a longer horizon. The Applying the Model illustrates the problem we have in mind.

APPLYING THE MODEL

A company wants to evaluate two investment proposals. The first involves a major effort in new product development. The initial cost is $1 billion, and the company expects the project to generate relatively meager cash flows in the first four years, followed by a big payoff in year 5. The second investment is a significant marketing campaign to attract new customers. It too has an initial outlay of $1 billion, but it generates significant cash flows almost immediately and lower levels of cash in the later years. A financial analyst prepares cash flow projections and calculates each project's *IRR* and *NPV* as shown in the following table (the firm uses 10 percent as its hurdle rate):

Cash Flow	Product Development ($ in millions)	Marketing Campaign ($ in millions)
Initial Outlay	−1,000	−1,000
Year 1	0	450
Year 2	50	350
Year 3	100	300
Year 4	200	200
Year 5	1,500	100
Technique		
IRR	14.1%	15.9%
NPV (10%)	$184.44	$122.44

The analyst observes that the first project generates a higher *NPV*, whereas the second offers a higher *IRR*. Bewildered, he wonders which project to recommend to senior management. ■

Even though both projects require the same initial investment and both last for five years, the marketing campaign generates more cash flow in the early years than the product development proposal. Therefore, in a relative sense, the payoff from product development occurs later than the payoff from marketing. We know from our discussion of interest-rate risk in Chapter 4 that when interest rates change, long-term bond prices move more than short-term bond prices do. The same phenomenon is at work here. Figure 7.6 plots the *NPV* of each investment at different discount

Figure 7.6
The Timing Problem

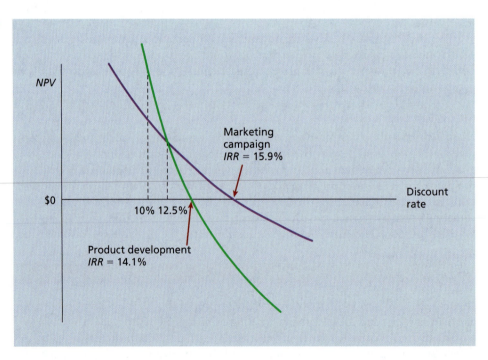

rates. The pattern created is called an **NPV profile.** Notice that one line, the line plotting *NPV*s for the product development idea, is much steeper than the other. In simple terms, this means that the *NPV* of that investment is much more sensitive to the discount rate than the *NPV* of the marketing campaign is.

Each investment's *IRR* appears in Figure 7.6 where the *NPV* lines cross the *x*-axis. Figure 7.6 shows that both *IRR*s exceed the hurdle rate of 10 percent and that the marketing proposal has the higher *IRR*. The two lines intersect at a discount rate of 12.5 percent. At that discount rate, the *NPV*s of the projects are equal. At discount rates below 12.5 percent, product development, which has a longer-term payoff, has the higher *NPV*. At discount rates above 12.5 percent, the investment in marketing offers a larger *NPV*. Given that the required rate of return on investments for this particular firm is 10 percent, the firm should choose to spend the $1 billion on product development. However, if the firm bases its investment decision solely on achieving the highest *IRR*, it will choose the marketing proposal instead.

Summarizing, we can say that when the timing of cash flows is very different from one project to another, the project with the highest *IRR* may or may not have the highest *NPV*. As in the case of the scale problem, the timing problem can lead firms to reject investments that they should accept. We want to emphasize that this problem (and the scale problem) occurs only when firms must choose between mutually exclusive projects. In the previous example, if the firm could invest in both projects, it should.

When firms must prioritize projects, leaving some acceptable projects on the table, there are two ways they can avoid falling into the timing trap. First, using *NPV* will lead to the correct decision when evaluating projects with very different cash flow patterns over time. Second, analysts can look at the incremental cash flows on the long-term project compared to those on the short-term project, the same technique we used before to deal with the *IRR*'s scale problem. For example, calculating the incremental cash flows on the product development idea compared to the marketing campaign by subtracting the marketing campaign cash flows from those associated with product development, we obtain the following:

Smart Concepts

See the concept explained step-by-step at

SMARTFinance

	[Product Development − Marketing Campaign]
Cash Flow	**($ in millions)**
Year 0	0
Year 1	−450
Year 2	−300
Year 3	−200
Year 4	0
Year 5	1,400

The *IRR* of this incremental cash flow stream is 12.5 percent. Because the *IRR* on the incremental project exceeds the firm's hurdle rate (10 percent), it makes sense to invest in product development.

---

7. Describe how the *IRR* and *NPV* approaches are related.

8. If the *IRR* for a given project exceeds a firm's hurdle rate, does that mean that the project necessarily has a positive *NPV*? Explain.

9. How can the *IRR* be used to choose from two mutually exclusive projects the project with the higher *NPV*?

Concept Review Questions

7.6 PROFITABILITY INDEX

CALCULATING THE PROFITABILITY INDEX

A final capital budgeting tool that we want to discuss is the **profitability index** (**PI**). Like the *IRR*, the profitability index is a close cousin of the *NPV* approach. Mathematically, the *PI* equals the ratio of the present value of a project's cash flows, excluding the initial cash outflow (the initial investment), divided by the initial cash outflow.

$$PI = \frac{\dfrac{CF_1}{(1+r)^1} + \dfrac{CF_2}{(1+r)^2} + \cdots + \dfrac{CF_N}{(1+r)^N}}{CF_0} \qquad \text{(Eq. 7.3)}$$

The decision rule to follow when evaluating investment projects using the *PI* is to invest when the *PI* is greater than 1.0 (i.e., when the present value of cash flows exceeds the initial cash outflow) and to refrain from investing when the *PI* is less than 1.0. Notice that if the *PI* is above 1.0, the *NPV* must be greater than zero. That means that the *NPV* and *PI* decision rules will always yield the same investment recommendation when we are simply trying to give a thumbs up or thumbs down to a single project.

APPLYING THE MODEL

To calculate the *PI* for each of Global Wireless's investment projects, calculate the present value of cash flows from years 1–5 and then divide by the initial cash outflow to obtain the following result:

Project	PV of CF (1–5) ($ in millions)	Initial Outlay ($ in millions)	PI
Western Europe	325.0	250	1.3
Southeastern U.S.	75.7	50	1.5

Because both projects have a *PI* greater than 1.0, both are worthwhile. However, notice that if we rank projects based on the *PI*, the southeastern U.S. project looks better. ◼

Because the *NPV*, *IRR*, and *PI* methods are so closely related, they share many of the same advantages relative to payback or accounting rate of return analysis, and there is no need to reiterate those advantages here. However, it is worth pointing out that the *PI* and the *IRR* share an important flaw. Both suffer from the scale problem described earlier. Recall that our *NPV* calculations suggested that the Western Europe project created more value for shareholders than the southeastern U.S. endeavor, whereas the *IRR* and *PI* comparisons suggest just the opposite project ranking. The reason that the *IRR* and *PI* analyses identify the southeastern U.S. project as the superior investment is that they do not take into account the differences in scale between the two projects. For the southeastern U.S. project, the *PI* indicates that project inflows exceed the initial cash outflow by 50 percent on a present value basis. The present value of cash flows for the Western Europe investment exceeds the initial cash outflow by just 30 percent. But the Western Europe project is much larger, and as our *NPV* figures reveal, it generates considerably more wealth for Global Wireless stockholders.

When we encountered the scale problem before, we found that it could be solved by looking at the *IRR* of an incremental project. In the same way, we can modify our analysis using the *PI* to solve its scale problem. First, calculate the incremental cash flows on the Western Europe investment relative to the southeastern U.S. investment. Next, take the present value of these incremental cash flows in years 1–5. Finally, divide this present value by the incremental initial cash outflow. If the profitability index on the incremental project exceeds 1.0, then invest in the larger project.

[Western Europe − Southeastern U.S.]

Year	Incremental CF ($ in millions)	PV (18%)
0	−200	−200.0
1	17	14.4
2	58	41.7
3	105	63.9
4	130	67.0
5	143	62.5

$$PI = \frac{\$14.4 + \$41.7 + \$63.9 + \$67.0 + \$62.5}{\$200.0} = 1.25$$

Because the *PI* of the incremental project equals 1.25, we should choose the Western Europe expansion proposal.

THE PROFITABILITY INDEX AND CAPITAL RATIONING

At several points in this chapter, we have asked the following question: If a firm must choose between several investment opportunities, all of which are worth taking, how does the firm prioritize projects? We have seen that the *IRR* and *PI* methods sometimes rank projects differently than the *NPV* does, though it is often possible to reconcile differences in the recommendations of each method by examining incremental cash flows between projects.

There is a fundamental question that we have avoided until now. If the firm has many projects with positive *NPV*s (or investments with acceptable *IRR*s), why not accept all of them? One possibility is that the firm simply does not have enough money to finance all its attractive investment opportunities. But surely large, publicly traded firms could raise money by issuing new shares to investors and use the proceeds to undertake any and all appealing investments?

If you watch firms closely over a period of time, you will notice that most do not issue new shares very often. As Chapter 11 discusses more fully, firms seem to prefer to finance investments with internally generated cash flow and will only infrequently raise money in the external capital markets by issuing new equity. There are several possible reasons for this apparent reluctance to issue new equity. First, when firms announce their intention to raise new equity capital, they may send an unintended negative signal to the market. Perhaps investors will interpret the announcement as a sign that the firm's existing investments are not doing very well. Perhaps investors will see the decision to issue new shares as an indication that managers believe the firm's stock is overvalued. In either case, investors may react negatively to this announcement, causing the stock price to fall. Undoubtedly, managers will try to persuade investors that the funds being raised will be invested in profitable projects, but convincing investors that this is the true motive for the issue will be an up-hill struggle.[10]

A second reason why managers may avoid issuing new equity is that by doing so, they dilute their ownership stake in the firm (unless they participate in the offering by purchasing some of the new shares). A smaller ownership stake means that managers control a shrinking block of votes, raising the potential of a corporate takeover or other threat to their control of the firm.

In conversations with senior executives, we often hear a third reason why firms do not fund every investment project that looks promising. Behind every idea for a new investment is a person, someone who may have an emotional attachment to the idea or a career-building motivation for proposing the idea in the first place. Upper-level managers are wise to be a little skeptical of the cash flow forecasts they see on projects with favorable *NPV*s or *IRR*s. It is a given that every cash flow forecast will prove to be wrong, but if the forecasting process is unbiased, half the time forecasts will be too pessimistic, and half the time they will be too optimistic. Which half is likely to surface on the radar screen of a CFO or CEO in a large corporation? Rationing capital is one mechanism by which senior managers impose discipline on the capital budgeting process. By doing so, they hope to weed out some of the investment proposals with an optimistic bias built into the cash flow projections.

Whatever the motivation for their behavior, managers cannot always invest in every project that offers a positive *NPV*. In such an environment, **capital rationing** occurs. Given a set of attractive investment opportunities, managers must choose a combination of projects that maximizes shareholder wealth, subject to the constraint of limited funds. In this environment, ranking projects using the *PI* can be very useful. Once managers rank projects, they select the investment with the highest *PI*. If the total amount of capital available has not been fully exhausted, then managers invest in the project with the second-highest *PI*, and so on until no more capital remains to invest. By following this routine, managers will select a portfolio of projects that in aggregate generates a higher *NPV* than any other combination of projects.[11]

Table 7.1 illustrates this technique. A particular firm has five projects to choose from, all of which have positive *NPV*s and *IRR*s that exceed the firm's hurdle rate of 12 percent. Notice that the first project has the highest *IRR* and the highest *PI*, but project 5 has a larger *NPV*. This is again the familiar scale problem. Suppose that this firm can invest no more than $300 million this year. What portfolio of investments maximizes shareholder wealth?

Notice that there are several combinations of projects that satisfy the constraint of investing no more than $300 million. If we begin by accepting the project with the highest *PI*, then continue to accept additional projects until we bump into the $300 million capital constraint, we will invest in projects 1, 2, and 3. With these three projects, we have invested just $250 million, but that does not leave us with enough capital to entertain either project 4 or 5. The total *NPV* obtainable from the first three projects is $170.8 million. No other combination of projects that satisfies the capital

---

[10.] Take another look at the Opening Focus involving Tertiary Minerals PLC. Its stock price shot up after an independent report calculated a 33 percent *IRR* for the company's tantalum project in Finland. Which do you think investors find more credible, a statement by the firm that its investments will pay off handsomely, or the same report produced by an independent third party?

[11.] We are simplifying a bit here. Sorting projects according to the *PI* and selecting from that list until capital runs out may not maximize shareholder wealth when capital is rationed not only at the beginning of an investment's life, but also in all subsequent periods. This method can also lead to suboptimal decisions when projects are interdependent—that is, when one investment is contingent on another. In these situations, more-complex decision tools, such as integer programming, may be required.

	Projects ($ in millions)				
Year	1	2	3	4	5
0	−70	−80	−100	−150	−200
1	30	30	40	50	90
2	40	35	50	55	80
3	50	55	60	60	80
4	55	60	65	90	110
NPV	$59.2	$52.0	$59.6	$38.4	$71.0
IRR	44%	36%	36%	23%	28%
PI	1.8	1.6	1.6	1.3	1.4

Table 7.1
Capital Rationing and the
Profitability Index

constraint yields a higher aggregate *NPV*. For example, investing in projects 3 and 5, thereby using up the full allotment of $300 million in capital, generates a total *NPV* of just $130.6 million. Likewise, investing in projects 1, 2, and 4, another combination that utilizes all $300 million in capital, generates an aggregate *NPV* of $149.6 million.

---

10. How are the *NPV*, *IRR*, and *PI* approaches related?

11. Why doesn't choosing the project with the highest *PI* always lead to the best decision?

**Concept
Review
Questions**

7.7 WHICH TECHNIQUES DO FIRMS ACTUALLY USE?

In a recent survey of 392 chief financial officers (CFOs), Graham and Harvey (2001) studied the capital budgeting methods that companies use to make real investment decisions. They asked CFOs to indicate how frequently they used several capital budgeting methods by ranking them on a scale ranging from 0 (never) to 4 (always). The techniques CFOs use most often are *NPV* (score, 3.08) and *IRR* (score, 3.09), with roughly 75 percent of CFOs indicating that they always or almost always use these techniques. A 25-year-old study by Gitman and Forrester (1977) found that only 9.8 percent of large firms used *NPV* as a primary capital budgeting tool, so Graham and Harvey's results clearly illustrate that the popularity of the *NPV* approach has grown over time. Interestingly, the popularity of the *NPV* approach is correlated both with the size of the firm and the educational background of its CFO. Large, publicly traded firms run by CFOs with an MBA are much more likely to rely on the *NPV* method than are small, private firms headed by CFOs without an MBA.

Third on the list of most frequently used capital budgeting tools is the payback method. Small firms in particular use the payback approach almost as often as they use *NPV* and *IRR*. Older CFOs and those without MBA degrees also tend to make decisions based on payback analysis much more frequently than other CFOs do. Most CFOs reported that they rarely used discounted payback, accounting rate of return, or the profitability index when making investment decisions. The Comparative Corporate Finance insert compares Graham and Harvey's results to similar studies

SMART PRACTICES VIDEO
**Beth Acton, Vice President and Treasurer
of Ford Motor Co. (former)**
"We look at capital investments in a very similar fashion whether they're routine or large investments."

See the entire interview at **SMARTFinance**

In a survey of companies listed on the Industrial Sector of the Johannesburg Stock Exchange, Hall (2000) finds that two-thirds of responding South African firms use discounted cash flow techniques to make capital budgeting decisions. Specifically, 32.3 percent of these firms report that they believe that the *IRR* method is the best tool for evaluating capital investments, 16.9 percent say that *NPV* is their preferred tool, and 16.9 percent rely on discounted payback. Moreover, the importance of these techniques in the investment decision process rises with the size of the firm. Among the smallest South African firms in the survey, just over 14 percent calculate

the *IRR* or *NPV* of their investment projects, but 75 percent of the largest firms do.

A study published in Lumby (1991) reports similar patterns among U.K. firms, with 54 percent using discounted cash flow techniques. The same positive relationship between firm size and the tendency to use discounted cash flow analysis that exists in South Africa also emerges in the United Kingdom.

Sources: J. H. Hall, "An Empirical Investigation of the Capital Budgeting Process," working paper, University of Pretoria (2000); L. Lumby, *Investment Appraisal and Investment Decisions,* 4th ed. (London: Chapman & Hall, 1991).

conducted in South Africa and the United Kingdom. All these papers point to the preeminence of discounted cash flow analysis in making investment decisions around the world.

7.8 SUMMARY

- The capital budgeting process involves generating, reviewing, analyzing, selecting, and implementing long-term investment proposals that are consistent with the firm's strategic goals.
- Though simplicity is a virtue, the simplest approaches to capital budgeting do not always lead firms to make the best investment decisions.
- Capital budgeting techniques include the payback period, discounted payback period, and accounting rate of return, which are less-sophisticated techniques because they do not explicitly deal with the time value of money and are not tied to the firm's wealth-maximization goal. More-sophisticated techniques include net present value (*NPV*), internal rate of return (*IRR*), and profitability index (*PI*). These methods often give the same accept-reject decisions, but do not necessarily rank projects the same.
- Using the *IRR* approach can lead to poor investment decisions when projects have cash flow streams alternating between net inflows and outflows. The *IRR* technique may provide suboptimal project rankings when different investments have very different scales or when the timing of cash flows varies dramatically from one project to another.
- The profitability index suffers from the same scale problem as the *IRR* approach. The profitability index is most useful in capital rationing situations.

INTERNET RESOURCES

Note: *For updates to links, please go to the book's website at* http://smart.swcollege.com

http://www.teachmefinance.com/—A site that has definitions and examples of many finance concepts, including most of the capital budgeting tools discussed in this chapter

http://clinton3.nara.gov/pcscb/—Contains a report by the President's Commission to Study Capital Budgeting, a group created in 1997 and asked to evaluate capital budgeting techniques used by other governments and the private sector

KEY TERMS

accounting rate of return	internal rate of return (*IRR*)
capital budgeting	lending versus borrowing problem
capital investment	mutually exclusive projects
capital rationing	net present value (*NPV*)
capital spending	*NPV* profile
discounted payback	payback period
incremental project	profitability index (*PI*)

QUESTIONS

7-1. Can you name some industries where the payback period is unavoidably long?

7-2. In statistics, you learn about Type I and Type II errors. A Type I error occurs when a statistical test rejects a hypothesis when the hypothesis is actually true. A Type II error occurs when a test fails to reject a hypothesis that is actually false. We can apply this type of thinking to capital budgeting. A Type I error occurs when a firm rejects an investment project that would actually enhance shareholder wealth. A Type II error occurs when a firm accepts a value-decreasing investment, an investment it should have rejected.

   a. Describe the features of the payback rule that could lead to Type I errors.

   b. Describe the features of the payback rule that could lead to Type II errors.

   c. Which error do you think is more likely to occur when firms use payback analysis? Does your answer depend on the length of the cutoff payback period? You can assume a "typical" project cash flow stream, meaning that most cash outflows occur in the early years of a project.

7-3. Which of the two types of errors—Type I or Type II (described in Question 7-2)—is more likely to occur when firms use the discounted payback approach?

7-4. Holding the cutoff period fixed, which method has a more severe bias against long-lived projects, payback or discounted payback?

7-5. For a firm that uses the *NPV* rule to make investment decisions, what consequences result if the firm misestimates shareholders' required returns and consistently applies a discount rate that is "too high"?

7-6. "Cash flow projections more than a few years out are not worth the paper they're written on. Therefore, using payback analysis, which ignores long-term cash flows, is more reasonable than making wild guesses as one has to do in the *NPV* approach." Respond to this comment.

7-7. "Smart analysts can massage the numbers in *NPV* analysis to make any project's *NPV* look positive. It is better to use a simpler approach like payback or accounting rate of return that gives analysts fewer degrees of freedom to manipulate the numbers." Respond to this comment.

7-8. In what way is the *NPV* consistent with the principle of shareholder wealth maximization? What happens to the value of a firm if a positive-*NPV* project is accepted? If a negative-*NPV* project is accepted?

7-9. A particular firm's shareholders demand a 15 percent return on their investment, given the firm's risk. However, this firm has historically generated returns in excess of shareholder expectations, with an average return on its portfolio of investments of 25 percent.

    a. Looking back, what kind of stock-price performance would you expect to see for this firm?

    b. A new investment opportunity arises, and the firm's financial analysts estimate that the project's return will be 18 percent. The CEO wants to reject the project because it would lower the firm's average return and therefore lower the firm's stock price. How do you respond?

7-10. What are the potential faults in using the *IRR* as a capital budgeting technique? Given these faults, why is this technique so popular among corporate managers?

7-11. Why is the *NPV* considered to be theoretically superior to all other capital budgeting techniques? Reconcile this result with the prevalence of the use of *IRR* in practice. How would you respond to your CFO if she instructed you to use the *IRR* technique to make capital budgeting decisions on projects with cash flow streams that alternate between inflows and outflows?

7-12. Outline the differences between *NPV*, *IRR*, and *PI*. What are the advantages and disadvantages of each technique?

7-13. Under what circumstances will the *NPV*, *IRR*, and *PI* techniques provide different capital budgeting decisions? Are these differing results found in analysis of independent or mutually exclusive projects? Why are the differences found in one type of project analysis and not the other?

7-14. Under what conditions would you use the *NPV* technique over the *PI* technique when they offer conflicting solutions? How can both techniques be consistent with shareholder wealth maximization and offer differing results?

7-15. What is the only relevant decision for independent projects if an unlimited capital budget exists? How does your response change if the projects are mutually exclusive? How does your response change if the firm faces *capital rationing*?

PROBLEMS

Payback Analysis

7-1. Suppose that a 30-year Treasury bond offers a 4 percent coupon rate, paid semiannually. The market price of the bond is $1,000, equal to its par value.

    a. What is the payback period for this bond?

    b. With such a long payback period, is the bond a bad investment?

    c. What is the discounted payback period for the bond? What general principle does this example illustrate regarding a project's life, its discounted payback period, and its *NPV*?

7-2. The cash flows associated with three different projects are as follows:

Cash Flows	Alpha ($ in millions)	Beta ($ in millions)	Gamma ($ in millions)
Initial Outflow	−1.5	−0.4	−7.5
Year 1	0.3	0.1	2.0
Year 2	0.5	0.2	3.0
Year 3	0.5	0.2	2.0
Year 4	0.4	0.1	1.5
Year 5	0.3	−0.2	5.5

a. Calculate the payback period of each investment.

b. Which investments does the firm accept if the cutoff payback period is three years? Four years?

c. If the firm invests by choosing projects with the shortest payback period, which project would it invest in?

d. If the firm uses discounted payback with a 15 percent discount rate and a 4-year cutoff period, which projects will it accept?

e. One of these almost certainly should be rejected, but might be accepted if the firm uses payback analysis. Which one?

f. One of these projects almost certainly should be accepted (unless the firm's opportunity cost of capital is very high), but might be rejected if the firm uses payback analysis. Which one?

Accounting-Based Methods

7-3. Kenneth Gould is the general manager at a small-town newspaper that is part of a national media chain. He is seeking approval from corporate headquarters (HQ) to spend $20,000 to buy some Macintosh computers and a laser printer to use in designing the layout of his daily paper. These computers will replace outmoded equipment that will be kept on hand for emergency use.

HQ requires Kenneth to estimate the cash flows associated with the purchase of new equipment over a 4-year horizon. The impact of the project on net income is derived by subtracting depreciation from cash flow each year. The project's average accounting rate of return equals the average contribution to net income divided by the average book value of the investment. HQ accepts any project that (1) returns the initial investment within four years (on a cash flow basis), and (2) has an average accounting rate of return that exceeds the cost of capital of 15 percent. The following are Kenneth's estimates of cash flows:

	Year 1	Year 2	Year 3	Year 4
Cost Savings	$7,500	$9,100	$9,100	$9,100

a. What is the payback period of this investment?

b. If the computers are depreciated on a straight-line basis over four years, what is the average contribution to net income across all four years?

c. What is the average book value of the investment?

d. What is the average accounting rate of return?

e. Critique the company's method for evaluating investment proposals.

Net Present Value

7-4. Calculate the net present value (NPV) for the following 20-year projects. Comment on the acceptability of each. Assume that the firm has an opportunity cost of 14 percent.

a. Initial cash outlay is $15,000; cash inflows are $13,000 per year.

b. Initial cash outlay is $32,000; cash inflows are $4,000 per year.

c. Initial cash outlay is $50,000; cash inflows are $8,500 per year.

7-5. Michael's Bakery is evaluating a new electronic oven. The oven requires an initial cash outlay of $19,000 and will generate after-tax cash inflows of $4,000 per year for eight years. For each of the costs of capital listed, (1) calculate the NPV, (2) indicate whether to accept or reject the machine, and (3) explain your decision.

a. The cost of capital is 10 percent

b. The cost of capital is 12 percent.

c. The cost of capital is 14 percent.

7-6. Using a 14 percent cost of capital, calculate the NPV for each of the projects shown in the following table and indicate whether or not each is acceptable.

	Project A	Project B	Project C	Project D	Project E
Initial cash outflow (CF_0)	$20,000	$600,000	$150,000	$760,000	$100,000
Year (t)			Cash Inflows (CF_t)		
1	$3,000	$120,000	$18,000	$185,000	$ 0
2	3,000	145,000	17,000	185,000	0
3	3,000	170,000	16,000	185,000	0
4	3,000	190,000	15,000	185,000	25,000
5	3,000	220,000	15,000	185,000	36,000
6	3,000	240,000	14,000	185,000	0
7	3,000		13,000	185,000	60,000
8	3,000		12,000	185,000	72,000
9	3,000		11,000		84,000
10	3,000		10,000		

7-7. Scotty Manufacturing is considering the replacement of one of its machine tools. Three alternative replacement tools—A, B, and C—are under consideration. The cash flows associated with each are shown in the following table. The firm's cost of capital is 15 percent.

	A	B	C
Initial cash outflow (CF_0)	$95,000	$50,000	$150,000
Year (t)		Cash Inflows (CF_t)	
1	$20,000	$10,000	$58,000
2	20,000	12,000	35,000
3	20,000	13,000	23,000
4	20,000	15,000	23,000
5	20,000	17,000	23,000
6	20,000	21,000	35,000
7	20,000	—	46,000
8	20,000	—	58,000

a. Calculate the *NPV* of each alternative.
b. Using *NPV*, evaluate the acceptability of each tool.
c. Rank the tools from best to worst, using *NPV*.

Smart Solutions
See the problem and solution explained step-by-step at
SMARTFinance

7-8. Erwin Enterprises has 10 million shares outstanding with a current market price of $10 per share. There is one investment available to Erwin, and its cash flows are provided below. Erwin has a cost of capital of 10 percent. Given this information, determine the impact on Erwin's stock price and firm value if capital markets fully reflect the value of undertaking the project.

Initial cash outflow = $10,000,000

Year	Cash Inflow
1	$3,000,000
2	4,000,000
3	5,000,000
4	6,000,000
5	9,800,000

Internal Rate of Return

7-9. For each of the projects shown in the following table, calculate the internal rate of return (*IRR*).

	Project A	Project B	Project C	Project D
Initial cash outflow (CF_0)	$72,000	$440,000	$18,000	$215,000
Year (t)		Cash Inflows (CF_t)		
1	$16,000	$135,000	$7,000	$108,000
2	20,000	135,000	7,000	90,000
3	24,000	135,000	7,000	72,000
4	28,000	135,000	7,000	54,000
5	32,000	—	7,000	—

7-10. William Industries is attempting to choose the better of two mutually exclusive projects for expanding the firm's production capacity. The relevant cash flows for the projects are shown in the following table. The firm's cost of capital is 15 percent.

	Project A	Project B
Initial cash outflow (CF_0)	$550,000	$358,000
Year (t)	Cash Inflows (CF_t)	
1	$110,000	$154,000
2	132,000	132,000
3	165,000	105,000
4	209,000	77,000
5	275,000	55,000

a. Calculate the *IRR* for each of the projects.
b. Assess the acceptability of each project based on the *IRR*s found in part (a).
c. Which project is preferred, based on the *IRR*s found in part (a)?

7-11. Contract Manufacturing, Inc., is considering two alternative investment proposals. The first proposal calls for a major renovation of the company's manufacturing facility. The second involves replacing just a few obsolete pieces of equipment in the facility. The company will choose one project or the other this year, but it will not do both. The cash flows associated with each project appear below, and the firm discounts project cash flows at 15 percent.

Year	Renovate	Replace
0	−$9,000,000	−$1,000,000
1	3,500,000	600,000
2	3,000,000	500,000
3	3,000,000	400,000
4	2,800,000	300,000
5	2,500,000	200,000

a. Rank these investments based on their *NPV*s.
b. Rank these investments based on their *IRR*s.
c. Why do these rankings yield mixed signals?
d. Calculate the *IRR* of the incremental project. Reconcile your answer to this question with those from parts (a) and (b).

7-12. Consider a project with the following cash flows and a firm with a 15 percent cost of capital.

End of Year	Cash Flow
0	−$20,000
1	50,000
2	−10,000

a. What are the two *IRR*s associated with this cash flow stream?
b. If the firm's cost of capital falls between the two *IRR* values calculated in part (a), should it accept or reject the project?

7-13.   A certain project has the following stream of cash flows:

Year	Cash Flow
0	$ 17,500
1	− 80,500
2	138,425
3	− 105,455
4	30,030

a. Fill in the following table:

Cost of Capital (%)	Project NPV
0	_____
5	_____
10	_____
15	_____
20	_____
25	_____
30	_____
35	_____
50	_____

b. What is this project's *IRR*?

c. Describe the conditions under which the firm should accept this project.

Profitability Index

7-14.   Evaluate the following three projects, using the profitability index. Assume a cost of capital of 15 percent.

	Project		
	Liquidate	Recondition	Replace
Initial cash outflow	−$100,000	−$500,000	−$1,000,000
Year 1 cash inflow	50,000	100,000	500,000
Year 2 cash inflow	60,000	200,000	500,000
Year 3 cash inflow	75,000	250,000	500,000

a. Rank these projects by their *PI*s.

b. If the projects are independent, which would you accept according to the *PI* criterion?

c. If these projects are mutually exclusive, which would you accept according to the *PI* criterion?

7-15.   Consider the same projects from Problem 7-14, and further assume that these three projects are the only three available for investment. Now apply the *NPV* criterion for the capital budgeting decision.

a. Rank these projects according to their *NPV*s.

b. If the projects are independent, which do you accept?

c. If the projects are mutually exclusive, which do you accept?

d. Does your answer to part (c) match your answer to part (c) from Problem 7-14? Explain this result.

7-16.   You have a $10 million capital budget and must make the decision about which investments your firm should accept for the coming year. Use the following information on three mutually exclusive projects to determine which investment your firm should accept. The firm's cost of capital is 12 percent.

	Project 1	Project 2	Project 3
Initial cash outflow	−$4,000,000	−$5,000,000	−$10,000,000
Year 1 cash inflow	1,000,000	2,000,000	4,000,000
Year 2 cash inflow	2,000,000	3,000,000	6,000,000
Year 3 cash inflow	3,000,000	3,000,000	5,000,000

a. Which project do you accept on the basis of *NPV*?

b. Which project do you accept on the basis of *PI*?

c. If these are the only investments available, which one do you select?

7-17. Use the information from Problem 7-16, and again make the appropriate capital budgeting decision assuming a $10 million capital budget. Now assume that another independent project is available to you. This new project has a cost of $5 million, with an *NPV* of $1.5 million. Given the availability of this new project, which of the mutually exclusive projects do you accept? Is the *NPV* or *PI* the better technique in this situation? Why?

Which Techniques Do Firms Actually Use?

7-18. Both Old Line Industries and High Tech, Inc., use the *IRR* to make investment decisions. Both firms are considering investing in a more efficient $4.5 million mail-order processor. This machine could generate after-tax savings of $2 million per year over the next three years for both firms. However, due to the risky nature of its business, High Tech has a much higher cost of capital (20%) than does Old Line (10%). Given this information, answer parts (a)–(c).

a. Should Old Line invest in this processor?

b. Should High Tech invest in this processor?

c. Based on your answers in parts (a) and (b), what can you infer about the acceptability of projects across firms with different costs of capital?

7-19. Butler Products has prepared the following estimates for an investment it is considering. The initial cash outflow is $20,000, and the project is expected to yield cash inflows of $4,400 per year for seven years. The firm has a 10 percent cost of capital.

a. Determine the *NPV* for the project.

b. Determine the *IRR* for the project.

c. Would you recommend that the firm accept or reject the project? Explain your answer.

7-20. Reynolds Enterprises is attempting to evaluate the feasibility of investing $85,000, CF_0, in a machine having a 5-year life. The firm has estimated the *cash inflows* associated with the proposal as shown below. The firm has a 12 percent cost of capital.

End of Year (*t*)	Cash Inflows (CF_t)
1	$18,000
2	22,500
3	27,000
4	31,500
5	36,000

a. Calculate the payback period for the proposed investment.

b. Calculate the *NPV* for the proposed investment.

c. Calculate the *IRR* for the proposed investment.

d. Evaluate the acceptability of the proposed investment using *NPV* and *IRR*. What recommendation would you make relative to implementation of the project? Why?

7-21. Sharpe Manufacturing is attempting to select the best of three mutually exclusive projects. The initial cash outflow and after-tax cash inflows associated with each project are shown in the following table.

Cash Flows	Project X	Project Y	Project Z
Initial cash outflow (CF_0)	$80,000	$130,000	$145,000
Cash inflows (CF_t), years (t) = 1–5	27,000	41,000	43,000

a. Calculate the payback period for each project.

b. Calculate the *NPV* of each project, assuming that the firm has a cost of capital equal to 13 percent.

c. Calculate the *IRR* for each project.

d. Summarize the preferences dictated by each measure, and indicate which project you would recommend. Explain why.

7-22. Wilkes, Inc., must invest in a pollution-control program in order to meet federal regulations to stay in business. There are two programs available to Wilkes: an all-at-once program that will be immediately funded and implemented and a gradual program that will be phased in over the next three years. The immediate program costs $5 million, whereas the phase-in program will cost $1 million today and $2 million per year for the following three years. If the cost of capital for Wilkes is 15 percent, which pollution-control program should Wilkes select?

Smart
Solutions
See the
problem and
solution explained step-by-step at
SMARTFinance

7-23. A consumer product firm finds that its brand of laundry detergent is losing market share, so it decides that it needs to "freshen" the product. One strategy is to maintain the current detergent formula, but to repackage the product. The other strategy involves a complete reformulation of the product in a way that will appeal to environmentally conscious consumers. The firm will pursue one strategy or the other, but not both. Cash flows from each proposal appear below, and the firm discounts cash flows at 13 percent.

Year	Repackage	Reformulate
0	−$3,000,000	−$25,000,000
1	2,000,000	10,000,000
2	1,250,000	9,000,000
3	500,000	7,000,000
4	250,000	4,000,000
5	250,000	3,500,000

a. Rank these investments based on their *NPV*s.

b. Rank these investments based on their *IRR*s.

c. Rank these investments based on their *PI*s.

d. Do these rankings yield mixed signals?

e. Calculate the *IRR* of the incremental project. Reconcile your answer to this question with those from parts (a) and (b).

7-24. Lundblad Construction Co. recently acquired 10 acres of land and is weighing two options for developing the land. The first proposal is to build 10 single-family homes on the site. This project would generate a quick cash payoff as the homes are sold over the next two years. Specifically, Lundblad estimates that it would spend $2.5 million on construction costs immediately, and it would receive $1.6 million as cash inflows in each of the next two years.

The second proposal is to build a strip shopping mall. This project calls for Lundblad to retain ownership of the property and to lease space for retail businesses that would serve the neighborhood. Construction costs for the strip mall are also about $2.5 million, and the company expects to receive $350,000 annually (for each of 50 years, starting one year from now) in net cash inflows from leasing the property. Lundblad's cost of capital is 10 percent.

a. Rank these projects based on their *NPV*s.

b. Rank these projects based on their *IRR*s.

c. Rank these projects based on their *PI*s. Do these rankings agree with those based on *NPV* or *IRR*?

    d. Why do *NPV* and *IRR* methods yield mixed signals in this case?

    e. Which project should Lundblad choose? Calculate the *IRR* of the incremental project to verify your answer.

    f. Which project should Lundblad choose if its cost of capital is 13.5 percent? 16 percent? 20 percent?

8

Cash Flow and Capital Budgeting

OPENING FOCUS

JDS Uniphase: How to Lose $50 Billion without Really Trying

How can one firm lose $50 billion in a single year? That's a question that shareholders of JDS Uniphase, a U.S.-Canadian producer of fiber-optic components for high-speed Internet networks, may have been asking themselves in the summer of 2001 just after the company reported what was then the largest fiscal-year loss in corporate history. As might be expected from a company with joint headquarters in California and Ottawa, JDS Uniphase had shares that traded simultaneously on the Nasdaq (ticker symbol, JDSU) and on the Toronto Stock Exchange (ticker symbol, JDU). Shares in both markets dropped on news of the enormous loss. However, there were several puzzles surrounding the company's earnings release and the market's reaction to it. First, JDS shares dropped about 12 percent, resulting in a decline in the firm's market value of less than $2 billion. Second, fiscal-year revenues for JDS were $3.2 billion. How could a company with just over $3 billion in revenue lose $50 billion? And if the firm really lost $50 billion, why did its market value drop by just a fraction of that amount?

One explanation for the market's relatively modest response to JDS's announcement is that the market had long anticipated bad news from the company. It was no secret that business conditions for optical components had been deteriorating throughout the year. In fact, JDS stock had been on a long slide for several months leading up to the company's fiscal year-end, a slide that wiped out about $25 billion of the company's total market value. Even so, a decline of that magnitude was still only half of $50 billion.

Perhaps a better explanation, both for the magnitude of the loss relative to revenues and for the market's reaction to the news, is that JDS Uniphase did not really lose $50 billion in cash. In fact, the vast majority of its losses resulted from writing down "goodwill" linked to acquisitions the company had completed in the previous two years.

JDS typically acquired firms by exchanging JDS shares for shares in the target company rather than by paying for target-firm shares with cash. For example, in its July 2000 purchase of a competitor, SDL Inc., JDS Uniphase exchanged $41 billion of its own stock for control of SDL. The book value of SDL's equity, the total shareholders' equity shown on SDL's balance sheet, was much less than the value that JDS paid. Accounting standards required JDS to report the $39 billion difference between what it paid for SDL stock and the book value of the stock as goodwill. Those same standards required JDS Uniphase to write down the value of this goodwill (and goodwill from several other deals) as the market value of its own stock fell over the following year. The result was almost $45 billion in noncash expenses, generating the enormous fiscal-year loss reported in July 2001. Surprisingly, if one ignores all of JDS's noncash expenses in the fourth quarter, the company generated a small positive cash flow for the period.

Analysts debated how to evaluate JDS write-offs. Some argued that in the JDS-SDL stock swap, firms had simply traded one piece of overvalued paper for another and that the goodwill that JDS had to add to its balance sheet (and then subsequently write down) was a meaningless accounting convention. "Earnings is about accountants; cash is why you're in business," said Arnie Berman, a strategist for SoundView Technology Group. Mark Cheffers, CEO of an accounting consultancy firm, commented, "The valuation community essentially follows the sunk-costs perspective. If an asset's no longer viable as a producer of ongoing earnings, then it's worth nothing. You made a bad decision. Get over it." Anthony Muller, CFO for JDS Uniphase, expressed a similar view in a conference call with analysts: "This goodwill results from our acquiring good companies when valuations were high. But keep in mind that while we purchased highly valued shares, we were also in effect selling highly valued shares at the same time. Had these transactions been done at different times when valuations were lower with exactly the same share exchange ratios, the goodwill amounts would have been considerably smaller."

But other analysts disagreed. They pointed out that there was an opportunity cost associated with these stock swaps. JDS might have sold its shares on the open market when the price was high and invested the money elsewhere. Had JDS simply put the money in investment-grade bonds, the bonds would have earned a positive rate of return, enabling JDS to acquire SDL later on better terms. But what would the market's reaction have been a year earlier if JDS had attempted to sell $41 billion of its shares on the open market rather than swap them for shares in SDL? Surely the price of JDS stock would have dropped sharply. And how would the market have reacted if JDS announced its intentions to invest the proceeds from the stock sale in bonds? Would JDS shareholders see this decision in a positive or negative light?

In finance, cash is king. When firms evaluate investment opportunities, managers must carefully examine the cash flow consequences of each investment. Analysts know to look for certain types of cash flows whether they are analyzing a complex project on a grand scale, such as an acquisition, or an investment as commonplace as replacing old equipment. Likewise, a common set of principles determines which cash flows managers should count and which they should ignore when valuing almost any investment.

Sources: "Huge Tech Write-Offs Raising Questions," *Investors Business Daily* (November 29, 2001); "More about JDS Uniphase and That Goodwill Write-Down," *The San Francisco Chronicle* (August 7, 2001).

Chapter 7 described various capital budgeting techniques that analysts use when evaluating and ranking investment proposals. Each of the examples in Chapter 7 began with a sequence of cash flows, though we did not discuss the origins of those cash flow figures. This chapter describes procedures for determining a project's relevant cash flows, the inputs for the capital budgeting decision tools from Chapter 7. We begin with an overview of the kinds of cash flows that may appear in almost any type of investment. An extended capital budgeting example follows. Next, we demonstrate how to deal properly with the problem of inflation in capital budgeting problems. Then we discuss special problems and situations that frequently arise in the capital budgeting process. The chapter concludes with a brief discussion of the human element in capital budgeting.

8.1 TYPES OF CASH FLOWS

CASH FLOW VS. ACCOUNTING PROFIT

When accountants prepare financial statements for external reporting, they have a very different purpose in mind than financial analysts have when they evaluate the merits of an investment. Accountants want to produce financial statements that fairly and accurately represent the state of a business at a particular point in time, as well as over a period of time. Given this purpose, accountants measure the inflows and outflows of a business's operations on an accrual basis rather than on a cash basis. For example, accountants typically credit a firm for earning revenue once a sale is made, even though customers may not pay cash for their purchases for several weeks or months. Similarly, accountants typically will not record the full cost of an asset as an expense if they expect the asset to confer benefits to the firm over a long period of time. The best example of this approach is depreciation. If a firm spends $1 billion on an asset that it plans to use over 10 years, accountants may count only one-tenth of the purchase price, or $100 million, as a current-year depreciation expense.

For capital budgeting purposes, financial analysts focus on *incremental* cash inflows and outflows. In part, this emphasis simply recognizes that no matter what earnings a firm may show on an accrual basis, it cannot survive for long unless it generates cash to pay its bills. If a firm purchases an asset for $500 million, and if the purchase contract requires an immediate payment, then the firm must come up with $500 million in cash even if it plans to deduct only a portion of the purchase price each year as depreciation expense. The importance placed on cash flow in capital budgeting also reflects the time value of money. If a firm sells a product for $1,000, the value of that sale is greater if the customer pays immediately rather than 30 or 90 days in the future.

Much of this chapter focuses on which cash flows to include in calculating a project's *NPV*, but we should also mention an important category of cash flows that should be excluded—financing cash flows. When calculating a project's *NPV*, analysts should ignore the costs of raising the money to finance the project, whether those costs come in the form of interest expense from debt financing or dividend payments to equity investors. It may seem counterintuitive to ignore an item, such as interest expense, that appears on the income statement but it is necessary to do so because financing costs are fully captured in the process of discounting a project's future cash flows to the present. In previous chapters we have seen that the present discounted value of a cash flow is less than its future value. When analysts discount a project's future cash flows, they are taking into account the opportunity that investors have to invest in other firms. Therefore, if an analyst deducted items flowing to investors, such as dividend and interest payments, the analyst would, in effect, double count the financing costs of the investment.

Analysts should measure all cash flows of a project on an after-tax basis. Remember, when deciding whether an investment is worth taking or not, we must determine whether the cash flows of the project are sufficient to meet or exceed shareholders' expectations. The firm can only distribute after-tax cash flows to investors, and thus, only after-tax cash flows are relevant in the decision process. The tax consequences associated with a particular investment can be very complex, in part because cash flows from a single investment may fall under several tax jurisdictions (local, state, national, international, etc.). An examination of all the nuances of the tax code is well beyond the scope of this book, but we will offer simplified illustrations of the principles involved in measuring after-tax cash flows. The most important of these principles is that financial managers should measure the after-tax cash flows of a given investment by using the firm's **marginal tax rate.** The marginal tax rate equals the percentage of taxes owed on an incremental dollar of income. Usually, a firm's marginal tax rate exceeds its average tax rate, which equals total taxes paid divided by total pretax income. Throughout this chapter, we will assume that the marginal tax rate equals 40 percent.

A second tax-related principle relevant for measuring cash flows is that analysts cannot entirely ignore noncash expenses such as depreciation when projecting cash flows, because noncash expenses reduce taxable income, and therefore they reduce cash tax payments. There are two ways to calculate cash flows that take this effect into account. First, we can add noncash expenses back to after-tax earnings. Second, we can ignore noncash expenses when calculating after-tax earnings, and then add back the tax savings created by noncash deductions.[1]

APPLYING THE MODEL

Let's take a look at two ways to treat noncash expenses to obtain cash flow numbers for a simple project. Suppose that today a firm spends $30,000 in cash to purchase a fixed asset that it plans to fully depreciate on a straight-line basis over three years. Using this machine, the firm produces 10,000 units of some product each year. The product sells for $3 and costs $1 to make. The following is an income statement for a typical year of this project:

Sales	$30,000
Less: Cost of goods	10,000
Gross profit	$20,000
Less: Depreciation	10,000
Pretax income	$10,000
Less: Taxes (40%)	4,000
Net income	$ 6,000

How much cash flow does this project generate in a typical year? There are two ways to arrive at the answer. First, take net income and add back depreciation, for which there was no cash outlay:

Cash flow = net income + depreciation

$$= \$6,000 + \$10,000 = \$16,000$$

---

[1] Deriving accurate cash flow numbers from real financial statements issued by real companies is considerably more complex than the following simple example might lead you to believe.

Second, calculate after-tax net income ignoring depreciation expense, and then add back the tax savings generated by the depreciation deduction:

Sales	$30,000	
Less: Cost of goods	10,000	
Pretax income	$20,000	
Less: Taxes (40%)	8,000	
After-tax income	$12,000	
Plus: Depreciation tax savings	4,000	(40% × $10,000)
Total cash flow	$16,000	

DEPRECIATION

The largest noncash item for most investment projects is depreciation. Analysts must know the magnitude and timing of depreciation deductions for a given project because these deductions affect the amount of taxes that the firm will pay. Treating depreciation properly is complicated by the fact that the law allows firms to use several different depreciation methods. For example, in the United States and the United Kingdom, firms can (and do) keep separate sets of books, one for tax purposes and one for financial reporting purposes, using different depreciation methods for each set. As a result, most U.S. and U.K. firms use accelerated depreciation methods for tax purposes and straight-line depreciation for financial reporting. In contrast, in nations such as Japan, Sweden, and Germany, the law requires that the income that firms report to the tax authorities be substantially the same as the income they report to investors. Naturally, firms in these countries want to enjoy the tax benefits of accelerated depreciation, so they depreciate assets using methods such as double-declining balance or sum-of-the-years' digits almost exclusively.[2] Because we are interested in the cash flow consequences of investments, and because depreciation only affects cash flow through taxes, we will consider only the depreciation method that a firm uses for tax purposes when determining project cash flows.

Table 8.1 illustrates the tax depreciation allowed in the United States on various classes of equipment. The Tax Reform Act of 1986 set forth a **modified accelerated cost recovery system (MACRS),** which defined the allowable annual depreciation deductions for various classes of assets. Automobiles used for business purposes fall under the 3-year class, computer equipment is part of the 5-year class, and most manufacturing equipment is part of the 7-year class. A quick glance at the table reveals that U.S. tax laws allow firms to take larger depreciation deductions in the early years of an asset's life. The cash flow impact of this system is to accelerate the tax benefits associated with depreciation.[3]

[2.] The International Forum on Accountancy Development (IFAD) maintains a website where you can find a brief overview of accounting standards in 62 different countries, all benchmarked against international accounting standards (IAS). See Internet Resources in this chapter.

[3.] That is, the tax benefits accrue faster than would be the case under straight-line depreciation. An observant reader of Table 8.1 will notice that the law grants four years of depreciation deductions on the 3-year asset class, six years of deductions for assets in the 5-year class, and so on. There appears to be one "extra year" of depreciation for each asset class because the first year's deduction reflects an assumption that, on average, investments in fixed assets are in service for just one-half of the first year. The last half-year of depreciation deductions for an asset falling in the N-year class occurs in year $N + 1$. Special rules apply to real estate assets. In general, land is not depreciable. The law does allow depreciation deductions for structures, with the depreciable life of the structure depending on whether it is a commercial or residential property.

Table 8.1
Tax Depreciation
Schedules by Asset Class

Year(s)	3-Year	5-Year	7-Year	10-Year	15-Year	20-Year
1	33.33	20.00	14.29	10.00	5.00	3.75
2	44.45	32.00	24.49	18.00	9.50	7.22
3	14.81	19.20	17.49	14.40	8.55	6.68
4	7.41	11.52	12.49	11.52	7.70	6.18
5		11.52	8.93	9.22	6.93	5.71
6		5.76	8.93	7.37	6.23	5.28
7			8.93	6.55	5.90	4.89
8			4.45	6.55	5.90	4.52
9				6.55	5.90	4.46
10				6.55	5.90	4.46
11				3.29	5.90	4.46
12					5.90	4.46
13					5.90	4.46
14					5.90	4.46
15					5.90	4.46
16					2.99	4.46
17–20						4.46
21						2.25

Notes: U.S. tax depreciation allowed for various MACRS asset classes. Figures represent the percentage of asset value depreciable in each year.

FIXED ASSET EXPENDITURES

Many capital budgeting decisions involve the acquisition of a fixed asset. The cost of this investment often appears as the initial cash outflow for a project (assuming that the firm pays the full purchase price in one cash payment). Additional factors that influence the cash consequences of fixed asset acquisitions include installation costs and proceeds from sales of existing fixed assets.

In many cases, the cost of installing new equipment can be a significant part of a project's initial outlay. Firms combine the asset's purchase price and its installation cost to arrive at the asset's depreciable tax basis. Though depreciation itself is not a cash outflow, we have seen that depreciation deductions affect future cash flows by lowering taxes. Depreciation deductions influence taxes through another channel when firms sell old fixed assets. Specifically, when a firm sells an old piece of equipment, there will be a tax consequence of the sale if the selling price exceeds or falls below the old equipment's book value. If the firm sells an asset for more than its book value, the firm must pay taxes on the difference. If a firm sells an asset for less than its book value, then it can treat the difference as a tax-deductible expense.

APPLYING THE MODEL

Electrocom Manufacturing purchased $100,000 worth of new computers three years ago. Now it is replacing these machines with newer, faster computers. Because computers qualify as 5-year equipment under MACRS depreciation rules, the company has depreciated 71.20 percent of the old machines' cost, leaving a book value of

$28,800. Electrocom sells its old computers to another firm for $10,000. This allows Electrocom to report a loss on the sale of $18,800. Assuming that Electrocom's business is otherwise profitable, it can use this loss to shelter other sources of current income, resulting in a tax savings of $7,520, or 40 percent of $18,800.   ▪

Working Capital Expenditures

Consider a retail firm evaluating the opportunity to open a new store. Part of the cost of this investment involves expenditures on fixed assets such as shelving, cash registers, and merchandise displays, but stocking the store with inventory constitutes another important cost. A portion of this cost may be deferred if the firm can purchase inventory from suppliers on credit. By the same token, cash inflows from selling the inventory may be delayed if the firm sells to customers on credit.

Just as a firm must account for cash expenditures on fixed assets, it must also weigh the cash inflows and outflows associated with changes in **net working capital.** Net working capital equals the difference between current assets and current liabilities. Frequently, the term **working capital** is used to refer to what is more correctly known as "net working capital." An increase in net working capital represents a cash outflow. Notice that net working capital increases if current assets rise (e.g., if the firm buys more inventory) or if current liabilities fall (e.g., if the firm pays down accounts payable). Therefore, any increase in a current asset account or any decrease in a current liability account results in a cash outflow.[4] Similarly, a decrease in net working capital represents a cash inflow. Net working capital decreases when current assets fall (as when a firm sells inventory) or when current liabilities increase (as when the firm borrows from suppliers). A decrease in any current asset or an increase in any current liability results in a cash outflow.

APPLYING THE MODEL

Have you ever noticed the cottage industries that temporarily spring up around certain big events? Think about the booths that open in shopping malls near the end of each year and sell nothing but calendars. Suppose that you are evaluating the opportunity to operate one of these booths from November to January. You begin by ordering (on credit) $15,000 worth of calendars. Your suppliers require a $5,000 payment on the first day of each month starting in December. You anticipate that you will sell 30 percent of your inventory in November, 60 percent in December, and 10 percent in January. You sell entirely on a cash basis. You also plan to keep $500 in the cash register until you close up shop on February 1. Your balance sheet at the beginning of each month looks like this:

[4.] Of course, one important current asset account is cash. It may seem counterintuitive to argue that if the balance in the cash account increases, then that should be treated as a cash outflow. However, consider again the example of a new retail store. If the company opens a new store, a small amount of cash will have to be held in that store for transactions purposes. Holding fixed the amount of cash that the firm maintains in all of its other stores and in its corporate accounts, opening a new store requires a net increase in the firm's cash holdings. If the firm did not open the new store, then it could invest the cash that it would have held in reserve in the new store in a different project. Likewise, consider what happens if the company decides to close one of its stores. The cash kept in reserve at that location can be redeployed for another use, so reducing cash at that store represents a cash inflow to the firm as a whole. As we will see in Chapter 23, cash management tools have become so sophisticated today that few investments require significant changes in cash holdings. Changes in the other working capital items, such as inventory, receivables, and payables, typically have a much larger cash flow impact than changes in cash balances.

	Oct. 1	Nov. 1	Dec. 1	Jan. 1	Feb. 1
Cash	$0	$ 500	$ 500	$ 500	$ 0
Inventory	0	15,000	10,500	1,500	0
Accounts payable	0	15,000	10,000	5,000	0
Net working capital	0	500	1,000	− 3,000	0
Monthly net working capital change	NA	+ 500	+ 500	− 4,000	+ 3,000

The cash flows associated with changes in net working capital are as follows:

$500 cash outflow from October to November
$500 cash outflow from November to December
$4,000 cash inflow from December to January
$3,000 cash outflow from January to February

   Notice that at the start of November, purchases of inventory are entirely on credit, so the increase in inventory is exactly offset by an increase in accounts payable. The only working capital cash outflow occurs because you must raise $500 to put in the cash register. During November, sales reduce your inventory by $4,500 (inflow), but you have to pay suppliers $5,000 (outflow). You still have the same amount in the cash register as before, $500, so on net you have an outflow of $500, exactly equal to the increase in net working capital from the prior month. During the month of December, sales reduce your inventory by $9,000 (inflow), and you pay $5,000 to suppliers (outflow). That leaves you with cash inflow of $4,000, equal to the decrease in net working capital during the month. By February 1, sales reduce your inventory by the remaining $1,500 in calendars (inflow), you empty $500 from the cash register (inflow), and you pay the last $5,000 to suppliers (outflow). The net effect is a $3,000 cash outflow during January.[5]

TERMINAL VALUE

Some investments have a well-defined life span. The life span may be determined by the physical life of a piece of equipment, by the length of time until a patent expires, or by the period of time covered by a leasing or licensing agreement. Often, however, investments have an indefinite life. When JDS Uniphase acquired SDL in a stock swap, it was undoubtedly the case that JDS managers expected SDL's assets to continue to generate cash flow for a very long period of time.

   When managers invest in an asset with a long life span, they typically do not construct cash flow forecasts more than 5 to 10 years into the future. One reason they give for this behavior is that forecasts more than 5 to 10 years in the future have so much error that the fine detail entailed in an item-by-item cash flow projection is not very meaningful. Instead, managers project detailed cash flow estimates for 5 to 10 years, then calculate a project's **terminal value** as of some future date. The terminal value is a number intended to reflect the value of a project at a given future point in time, and there are a number of ways to estimate this value.

   Perhaps the most common approach to calculate terminal value is to take the final year of cash flow projections and make an assumption that all future cash flows

---

[5.] Notice that we are only looking at the working capital cash flows associated with this project. We have not considered any fixed asset investment up front. We are not considering the profits from selling calendars at a markup, nor the labor costs of operating the booth.

from the project will grow at a constant rate. For example, in valuing a large acquisition, many firms project cash flows from the target company for 5 to 10 years in the future. After that, they assume that cash flows will grow at a rate equal to the growth rate in gross domestic product (GDP) for the economy.[6]

APPLYING THE MODEL

Suppose that analysts at JDS Uniphase projected that their acquisition of SDL Inc. would generate the following stream of cash flows:

Year 1 $0.50 billion
Year 2   1.00 billion
Year 3   1.75 billion
Year 4   2.50 billion
Year 5   3.25 billion

In year 6 and beyond, analysts believed that cash flows would continue to grow at 5 percent per year. What is the terminal value of this investment? Recall that in Chapters 3 and 4, we learned that we can determine the present value of a stream of cash flows growing at a perpetual rate, g, by using the following formula:

$$PV_t = \frac{CF_{t+1}}{r - g}$$

We know that the year-6 cash flow is 5 percent more than in year 5, or $3.41 billion. Put that figure in the numerator of the equation. We also know that $g = 5$ percent. Suppose that JDS Uniphase discounted the cash flows of this investment at 10 percent. Using the formula above, we can determine that the present value, *as of year 5*, of cash flows in years 6 and beyond equals the following:

$$PV_5 = \frac{\$3.41}{0.10 - 0.05} = \$68.20$$

This means that the terminal value, the value of the project at the end of year 5, equals $68.20 billion. To determine the entire value of the project, just discount this figure along with all the other cash flows at 10 percent to obtain a total value of $48.67 billion:[7]

$$\frac{\$0.50}{1.1^1} + \frac{\$1.00}{1.1^2} + \frac{\$1.75}{1.1^3} + \frac{\$2.50}{1.1^4} + \frac{\$3.25}{1.1^5} + \frac{\$68.20}{1.1^5} = \$48.67$$

Given this set of assumptions, it is not hard to see why JDS might be willing to part with $41 billion worth of stock to acquire SDL Inc. ■

[6.] We should emphasize that when companies assume that an investment's cash flows will grow at some rate in perpetuity, the rate of growth in GDP, either in the local economy or the world economy, serves as a maximum potential long-run growth rate. Why? If an investment generates cash flows that grow forever at a rate that exceeds the growth of GDP, then eventually that one investment becomes the entire economy.

[7.] Notice that this is the gross present value, not the *NPV*, because we are not deducting any up-front cost for acquiring SDL. Recall that JDS parted with $41 billion of its own stock. This $41 billion is not a cash outlay, but that does not mean that JDS acquired SDL for free. As mentioned in the Opening Focus, JDS incurred an opportunity cost by issuing shares to buy SDL rather than selling the shares for cash or using them for another purpose. The exact magnitude of this opportunity cost is difficult to determine because we cannot know exactly how much money the company might have raised had they tried to sell the same number of shares that they exchanged to acquire SDL. We will return to the concept of opportunity costs shortly.

Notice in the preceding example that the terminal value was very large relative to all the other cash flows. If we discount the terminal value for five years at 10 percent, we find that $42.35 billion of the project's total $48.67 billion present value comes from the terminal value assumptions. Those proportions are not uncommon for long-lived investments, illustrating just how important estimates of terminal value can be in assessing an investment's merit. Analysts must think very carefully about the assumptions they make when calculating terminal value. For example, the growth rate used to calculate a project's terminal value does not always equal the long-run growth rate of the economy. A factory with fixed capacity might offer zero growth in cash flows, or growth that just keeps pace with inflation, once the firm hits the capacity constraint.

Several other methods enjoy widespread application in terminal value calculations. One method calculates terminal value by multiplying the final year's cash flow estimate by a market multiple such as a price-to-cash-flow ratio for publicly traded firms with characteristics similar to those of the investment. For example, the last specific cash flow estimate for the SDL acquisition was $3.25 billion in year 5. JDS Uniphase might observe that the average price-to-cash-flow ratio for companies in this industry is 20. Multiplying $3.25 billion by 20 results in a terminal value estimate of $65 billion, quite close to the estimate obtained from the perpetual growth model. One hazard in using this approach is that market multiples fluctuate through time, which means that when year 5 finally arrives, even if SDL generates $3.25 billion in cash flow as anticipated, the market may place a much lower value on that cash flow than it did when the acquisition originally took place.

Other approaches to this problem use an investment's book value or its expected liquidation value to estimate the terminal value figure. Using book value is most common when the investment involves physical plant and equipment with a limited useful life. In such a case, firms may plausibly assume that after a number of years of depreciation deductions, the asset's book value will be zero. Depending on whether the asset has fairly standard characteristics that would enable other firms to use it, its liquidation value may be positive or it may be zero.[8] Some assets may even have negative terminal values if disposing of them entails substantial costs. Projects that involve the use of substances hazardous to the environment fit this description. When an investment has a fixed life span, part of the terminal value or terminal cash flow may also include recovery of working capital investments. When a retail store closes, for example, the firm realizes a cash inflow from liquidating inventory.

INCREMENTAL CASH FLOW

We have seen that many investment problems have similar types of cash flows that analysts must estimate: initial outlays on fixed assets, working capital outlays, operating cash flow, and terminal value. But in a broader sense, there is only one type of cash flow that matters in capital budgeting analysis—incremental cash flow. To rephrase the oath that witnesses take in television courtroom dramas, analysts must focus on "all incremental cash flow and nothing but incremental cash flow." Determining which cash flows are incremental and which are not for a given project can become complicated at times.

Consider, for example, the incremental cash flows associated with a student's decision to pursue an MBA degree. Many of the incremental outflows are fairly obvi-

---

[8.] Asplund (2000) estimates that firms can expect to recover no more than 20–50 percent of the original purchase cost of a new machine once it has been installed. This is true even for assets with reasonably active secondary markets.

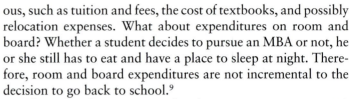

ous, such as tuition and fees, the cost of textbooks, and possibly relocation expenses. What about expenditures on room and board? Whether a student decides to pursue an MBA or not, he or she still has to eat and have a place to sleep at night. Therefore, room and board expenditures are not incremental to the decision to go back to school.[9]

The cash inflows associated with an investment in an MBA degree are more difficult to estimate. For most students, obtaining an MBA degree offers the opportunity to earn higher pay after graduation than they earned before returning to school. Furthermore, most students hope that their salary trajectory will be steeper after obtaining an MBA. That is, students expect that their pay will increase at a faster rate than it otherwise would have had they not obtained an MBA. The net cash flow equals the difference in the salary that a student would earn with an MBA versus the salary that would be earned without an MBA, after taxes of course.

APPLYING THE MODEL

Norman Paul makes $60,000 per year working as an engineer for an auto manufacturer, and he pays taxes at a flat rate of 35 percent. He expects salary increases each year of about 5 percent. Lately, Norm has been thinking about going back to school to earn an MBA. A few months ago he spent $1,000 to enroll in a Graduate Management Admission Test (GMAT) study course. He also spent $2,000 visiting various MBA programs in the United States. From his research on MBA programs, Norm has learned a great deal about the costs and benefits of the degree. At the beginning of each of the next two years, his out-of-pocket costs for tuition, fees, and textbooks will be $35,000. He expects to spend roughly the same amount on room and board in graduate school that he spends now. At the end of two years, he anticipates that he will receive a job offer with a salary of $90,000, and he expects that his pay will increase by 8 percent per year over his career (about the next 30 years). The schedule of incremental cash flows for the next few periods, excluding the salary that Norm gives up if he goes back to school (more on that later), looks like this:

Year 0	−$35,000
Year 1	− 35,000
Year 2	+ 15,503

Notice that Norm's cash outflows do not include the money he has already spent on the GMAT review course and on visits to MBA programs. These are **sunk costs,** costs that have already been spent and are not recoverable if Norm decides to keep working rather than go back to school. The cash inflow figure for year 2 requires some explanation. Had Norm stayed at his current job for the next two years rather than go back to school, his pay would have increased to $66,150. Therefore, the difference between that figure and his $90,000 post-MBA salary represents a net cash inflow of $23,850. Assuming that Norm pays about 35 percent of his earnings in taxes, the after-tax inflow would be $15,503. In year 3, Norm expects to earn 8 percent more, or $97,200, compared to what he would have earned at his old job, $69,458. The

---

9. Of course, there may be a difference between money spent on housing and food depending on whether the person is a student or a working professional. The difference in spending would be an incremental cash flow, but it could be an incremental inflow (if these costs are lower in graduate school) or an outflow (if the MBA program is located in a city with a high cost of living).

after-tax cash inflow in year 3 equals $18,032. If you carry these steps out for 30 years, you will quickly see that the MBA has a substantial positive *NPV* at almost any reasonable discount rate. ■

Incremental cash flows show up in surprising forms. One type of incremental cash outflow that firms must be careful to measure when launching a new product is called **cannibalization.** This simply means that when a firm introduces a new product, some of the new product's sales may come at the expense of the firm's existing products. In the food products industry, sales of a low-fat version of a popular product may reduce sales of the original (presumably, high-fat) version. Firms must be careful to consider the incremental cash outflows from existing product sales that are cannibalized by a newer product.[10]

Opportunity Costs

We made a number of simplifying assumptions in the preceding Applying the Model example. For instance, we assumed that Norm received his pay in a lump sum each year and that he faced a flat tax rate. Of course, the incremental salary that Norm earns arrives monthly, and his higher earnings may be taxed at a higher rate. All these effects are easy to account for, although the calculations become a bit more tedious.

However, there is one major error in our analysis of Norm's investment problem. We ignored a significant opportunity cost. Undertaking one investment frequently means passing on an alternative. In capital budgeting, the **opportunity costs** of one investment are the cash flows on the alternative investment that the firm (or in this case, the individual) decides not to make. If Norm did not attend school, he would earn $60,000 ($39,000 after taxes) the first year and $63,000 ($40,950 after taxes) the second year. This is Norm's *opportunity cost* of getting an MBA, and it is just as important in the overall calculation as his out-of-pocket expenses for tuition and books. Though it is still true, given the assumptions of our example, that the *NPV* of an MBA is positive, the value of the degree falls substantially once we recognize opportunity costs. As every MBA student knows, opportunity costs are real, not just hypothetical numbers from a textbook. Directors of MBA programs all over the world know that MBA applications are countercyclical. That is, the number of students applying to MBA programs rises during economic downturns and falls during booms. The most plausible explanation of this phenomenon is that potential MBA students face higher opportunity costs when the economy is strong.

What kinds of opportunity costs do businesses encounter in capital budgeting problems? We have seen one example in the JDS Uniphase acquisition of SDL Inc. JDS issued $41 billion worth of stock to acquire the shares of SDL. As we noted earlier, some "experts" indicated that the cash flow consequence of this transaction was nil. Firms just traded pieces of paper, and no one paid or received cash. This ignores JDS's opportunity cost. Though it may be true that JDS could not have raised $41 billion in cash had it attempted to sell the same number of shares that it gave to SDL shareholders in the acquisition, JDS certainly could have raised a substantial amount of cash from a stock sale. The amount of cash that JDS gave up by issuing shares to pay for the acquisition, rather than selling them, is the opportunity cost of the acquisition.

Probably the most common type of opportunity cost encountered in capital budgeting problems involves the alternative use of an asset owned by a firm. Suppose that

Smart Concepts
See the concept explained step-by-step at **SMARTFinance**

[10.] On a capital budgeting exam problem, one of our students mentioned that a firm needed to be wary that its new product should not "cannibalize the existing sales force." Needless to say, that's not the kind of cannibalization that we have in mind, although should it occur, it would certainly represent an incremental cash outflow.

a company owns raw land that it purchased some years ago in anticipation of an expansion opportunity. Now the firm is ready to expand by building new facilities on the raw land. Even though the firm may have paid for the land many years ago, using the land for expansion entails an incremental opportunity cost. The opportunity cost is the cash that could be raised if the firm sold the land or leased it for another purpose. That cost should be factored into the *NPV* calculation for the firm's expansion plans.

In the next section, we work through an extended example of a capital budgeting project, illustrating how to apply the principles from this section to calculate the project's cash flows each year. Before getting into the details, we want to remind you of the big picture. Cash flows are important because they are necessary to calculate a project's *NPV*, and estimating the *NPV* is important because it provides an estimate of the increase or decrease in shareholder value that will occur if the firm invests. McConnell and Muscarella (1985) demonstrate the connection between capital investment decisions and shareholder value by showing that stock prices rise on average when firms publicly announce significant new capital investment programs. This suggests that, on average, firms invest in positive *NPV* projects. The Comparative Corporate Finance insert offers evidence supporting this big picture that what matters is not just the amount of investment that firms undertake but how efficiently they invest.

SMART ETHICS VIDEO
Scott Lee, Texas A&M University
"We have found evidence that the market punishes firms that were involved in defense procurement fraud."

See the entire interview at **SMARTFinance**

Concept Review Questions

1. Why do we consider *changes* in net working capital associated with a project to be cash inflows or outflows rather than the absolute level of working capital?

2. For what kinds of investments would terminal value account for a substantial fraction of the total project *NPV*, and for what kinds of investments would terminal value be relatively unimportant?

3. A real estate development firm owns a fully leased 40-story office building. A tenant recently moved its offices out of 2 stories of the building, leaving the space temporarily vacant. If the real estate firm considers moving its own offices into this 40-story office building, what cost should it assign for the space? Is the cost of the vacant space zero because the firm paid for the building long ago, a cost that is sunk, or is there an incremental opportunity cost?

4. Suppose that an analyst makes a mistake and calculates the *NPV* of an investment project by discounting the project's contribution to net income each year rather than by discounting its cash flows. Would you expect the *NPV* based on net income to be higher or lower than the *NPV* calculated using cash flows?

8.2 CASH FLOWS FOR CLASSICALTUNES.COM

Classicaltunes.com is a (fictitious) profitable Internet-based music club selling classical-music CDs to its membership.[11] The company is considering a proposal to expand its music selection to include jazz recordings. Management believes that many lovers of classical music also enjoy jazz, and so the company has a built-in clientele for the new music offerings. If the company decides to undertake this project, it will

---

[11.] Some might say that because Classicaltunes.com is a profitable Internet-based firm, it must be fictitious.

COMPARATIVE CORPORATE FINANCE

Is a High Investment Rate Good for a Nation's Economic Health?

Most people would accept as a given that a high investment rate, measured as capital investment spending as a percentage of GDP, is strongly correlated with rapid growth in industrial production and overall employment. As the table below illustrates, no such strong relationship exists for industrialized countries over the period 1980 to 2000. The industrialized country with the highest investment rate, Japan, indeed saw industrial production increase rapidly between 1980 and 1990, but industrial production barely rose in the following decade, and total employment declined by more than 2 percent between 1980 and 2000. Similarly, the large continental European economies of France, Germany, and Italy had about-average investment rates throughout the 1980–2000 period, but industrial production grew more slowly than the average for all industrial countries, and all three nations experienced large net employment *declines* over these two decades. Country-specific factors help explain the exceptional

performance of two of the smaller countries in the table, Ireland and Norway. Ireland adopted an explicit open-market strategy after 1980 and attracted large net inflows of foreign direct investment over the next two decades—with a spectacular payoff in industrial production plus a more muted, but still significant, increase in employment. Norway benefited from an investment boom resulting from exploration and development of massive North Sea petroleum deposits. However, by far the best-performing large economy was that of the United States. Despite having a below-average investment rate throughout this period, industrial production increased by 84 percent and employment increased by 46 percent between 1980 and 2000. The moral is clear: How efficiently capital is invested is far more important to a nation's economic health than is the absolute level of investment.

Source: International Financial Statistics Yearbook 2001 (Washington, D.C.: International Monetary Fund).

Country	Capital Investment Spending (as a % of GDP)			Industrial Production Index (1995 = 100)			Total Employment (1995 = 100)		
	1980	1990	2000[a]	1980	1990	2000[a]	1980	1990	2000[a]
United States	23.5	18.0	21.4	69.7	86.5	128.5	77.2	93.4	112.4
Canada	19.7	20.7	20.5	71.8	88.8	119.5	114.1	112.6	120.6
Japan	32.4	32.8	25.9	71.4	105.3	106.4	92.9	101.7	90.9
France	25.0	23.4	20.5	89.6	100.4	115.5	132.6	113.6	97.2
Germany	25.1	24.6	22.6	86.8	103.2	113.5	103.3	100.0[b]	85.9[b]
Ireland	27.8	21.0	23.9	32.7	62.1	159.8	107.4	90.7	114.5
Italy	27.0	22.2	20.5	82.2	93.5	108.2	123.9	107.7	99.7
Spain	23.2	25.4	24.1	80.5	96.9	119.3	94.7	104.5	120.2
Norway	28.3	23.3	21.5	55.1	86.5	110.4	92.1	97.7	102.8
Sweden	21.3	21.3	17.9	74.5	87.8	115.5	133.3	124.7	99.1
Switzerland	28.5	28.3	21.5	79.7	97.0	121.1	122.6	119.4	94.7
United Kingdom	17.6	20.2	17.8	76.7	94.1	105.0	101.0	102.5	107.4
Industrial country average	**23.5**	**22.6**	**22.0**	**75.0**	**95.2**	**115.4**	**95.6**	**102.4**	**102.4**

[a] Or most recent year, usually 1999.
[b] Employment index for Germany: 1990 = 100 and data end in 1994.

begin selling jazz-music CDs next month when its new fiscal year begins. The company accepts projects with positive *NPV*s, and it uses a 10 percent discount rate to calculate *NPV*.

Up-front costs associated with the investment include $50,000 in computer equipment (which falls under the MACRS 5-year asset class) and $4,500 in inventory ($2,500 of which is purchased on credit). For transactions purposes, the firm plans to increase its cash balance by $1,000 immediately. The firm does not expect to begin selling CDs until the new fiscal year begins, though it is entitled to take the first half-year of MACRS depreciation in the current fiscal year. Currently, the average selling price of Classicaltunes.com's CDs is $13.50, and company executives believe that CD prices will increase over time at a 2 percent annual rate. Classicaltunes.com knows that some of its suppliers will sell CDs on credit. In addition to relying on this trade credit, the firm expects to finance this investment using cash flow generated from its existing classical-music business.

Like most new business ventures, this one will not be profitable immediately. Managers expect unit sales volume to increase rapidly in the first few years before reaching a long-run stable growth rate. As sales volume increases, the firm expects gross profit margins to widen slightly. The firm does allow credit sales to customers with excellent payment histories. Expanding sales volume will require increases in current assets, as well as additional spending on fixed assets. Classicaltunes.com pays taxes at a 40 percent rate.

Table 8.2 shows various projections for the jazz-music CD project. The top two lines list anticipated selling prices and unit volumes in each of the next six years. Un-

Table 8.2
Projections for Classicaltunes.com's Jazz-Music CD Proposal

Year	0	1	2	3	4	5	6
Price per unit	$13.50	$13.77	$14.05	$14.33	$14.61	$14.91	$15.20
Units	0	4,000	10,000	16,000	22,000	24,000	25,000
Abbreviated Projected Income Statements							
Revenue	$ 0	$55,080	$140,454	$229,221	$321,482	$357,722	$380,080
− Cost of goods sold	0	41,861	105,341	169,623	234,682	259,349	273,657
Gross profit	$ 0	$13,219	$ 35,113	$ 59,598	$ 86,800	$ 98,373	$106,423
− SG&A expenses	0	8,262	19,664	29,799	35,363	35,772	38,008
− Depreciation	10,000	18,000	13,800	14,280	23,872	25,208	18,512
Pretax profit	−$10,000	−$13,043	$ 1,649	$ 15,519	$ 27,565	$ 37,393	$ 49,903
Abbreviated Projected Balance Sheets							
Cash	$ 1,000	$ 2,000	$ 2,500	$ 3,000	$ 3,200	$ 3,300	$ 3,500
Accounts receivable	0	4,590	11,705	19,102	26,790	29,810	31,673
Inventory	4,500	7,344	18,727	30,563	42,864	47,696	50,677
Current assets	$ 5,500	$13,934	$32,932	$52,665	$ 72,854	$ 80,806	$ 85,850
Gross P&E	$50,000	$60,000	$65,000	$90,000	$130,000	$145,000	$155,000
− Accumulated depreciation	10,000	28,000	41,800	56,080	79,952	105,160	123,672
Net P&E	$40,000	$32,000	$23,200	$33,920	$ 50,048	$ 39,840	$ 31,328
Total assets	$45,500	$45,934	$56,132	$86,585	$122,902	$120,646	$117,178
Accounts payable	$ 2,500	$ 4,320	$11,016	$17,978	$ 25,214	$ 28,057	$ 29,810

derneath that appears a series of projected income statements for the next six years. Top-line revenue simply equals the product of expected selling price and unit volume each year. The figures for cost of goods sold and selling, general, and administrative expenses (SG&A) reflect management's belief that costs as a percentage of sales will fall slightly as volume increases. Depreciation expense each year is determined by spending on fixed assets and the MACRS schedule for 5-year equipment.

Beneath the income statement appears a series of balance sheets. Each shows the project's total asset requirements (including both current and fixed assets) as well as the financing available from suppliers in the form of accounts payable. As mentioned previously, any additional financing the project requires will come from internally generated funds from the classical-music CD side of the business.

To determine whether this is an investment opportunity worth taking, we will determine the project's cash flows through time and discount them at 10 percent to calculate the project's *NPV*. As part of this calculation, we will have to estimate the value of the endeavor beyond the sixth year. In other words, we will have to estimate the project's terminal value.

YEAR 0 CASH FLOW

The firm will have cash outlays of $50,000 for computer equipment immediately. MACRS rules allow the firm to take a depreciation deduction of 20 percent, or $10,000, in the first year. Because the company has no other expenses or revenues, the project's incremental pretax profit this year is −$10,000. However, the $10,000 loss does not represent a cash outflow because it derives entirely from a noncash depreciation expense. Assuming that this expense can be deducted from the firm's classical-music CD profits, the expense will save Classicaltunes.com $4,000 in taxes (40% × $10,000). The firm purchases $4,500 in inventory and sets up a cash account with an initial balance of $1,000. Accounts payable totaling $2,500 are used to finance a portion of these outlays, resulting in an initial working capital investment of $3,000 ($4,500 inventory + $1,000 cash − $2,500 accounts payable). Therefore, the net cash flow for year 0 is shown as follows:

Increase in gross fixed assets	−$50,000
Tax savings	4,000
Initial working capital investment	− 3,000
Net cash flow	−$49,000

YEAR 1 CASH FLOW

Notice in Table 8.2 that gross plant and equipment (P&E) increases by $10,000 in year 1. This means that Classicaltunes.com has purchased $10,000 in additional computer equipment or other fixed assets. Depreciation in the first full year of operation equals $18,000, the difference between accumulated depreciation in year 1 and year 0. That figure combines a depreciation charge of 32 percent of the initial $50,000 investment in fixed assets ($16,000) and a deduction of 20 percent of the current-year $10,000 investment in fixed assets ($2,000).

With sales volume increasing, the firm also makes additional investments in working capital. Cash balances increase by $1,000, receivables rise by $4,590, and inventories go up by $2,844. Partially offsetting the increase in current assets is an increase in accounts payable of $1,820. Therefore, net working capital increases by $6,614, a net cash outflow for the firm.

At a sales volume of 4,000 units in its first year of operation, the jazz-music CD business earns a pretax loss of $13,043. To convert this figure into cash flow, we must make two adjustments. First, if Classicaltunes.com can charge this loss against profits in its other operations, then the loss will generate tax savings of $5,217 (40% × $13,043). Second, we need to add depreciation expense back into the pretax loss because depreciation involves no cash outlay. Together, these adjustments result in a net operating cash inflow of $10,174 (−$13,043 + $18,000 + $5,217).

Combining each source of cash flow, we can determine the net cash flow for the project's first full year:

Increase in gross fixed assets	−$10,000
Change in working capital	− 6,614
Operating cash inflow	10,174
Net cash flow	−$ 6,440

YEAR 2 CASH FLOW

We can simply repeat the steps we followed in year 1 to determine cash flow for year 2. First, gross fixed assets increase by $5,000. Depreciation for year 2 is $13,800 (again, the difference between accumulated depreciation in year 2 and year 1). The depreciation in year 2 equals the sum of allowable depreciation on assets purchased up front (19.20% × $50,000), assets purchased in year 1 (32% × $10,000), and assets purchased in year 2 (20% × $5,000).

Sales continue to rise in year 2, requiring a large investment in working capital. Total current assets increase by $18,998, but accounts payable rises by $6,696. The net increase in working capital equals $12,302 and results in a cash outflow.

In year 2, the firm earns a small pretax profit of $1,649. After taxes of $660 are deducted, the net earnings amount to $989. Add to that figure the depreciation expense of $13,800 to arrive at operating cash inflow of $14,789. The following are the total net cash flows in year 2:

Increase in fixed assets	−$5,000
Change in working capital	−12,302
Operating cash inflow	14,789
Net cash flow	−$2,513

Table 8.3 illustrates the annual net cash flows for the jazz-music CD project all the way through the sixth year. As you can see, project cash flows do not turn from negative to positive until the fifth year. If we take the NPV of the stream of cash flows shown in Table 8.3, it is clear that the project will not generate a positive NPV. However, just because the year-by-year cash flow projections end in year 6 does not mean that the project ends at that time. To complete our analysis, we must estimate the project's terminal value.

Terminal Value

We will produce two different terminal value estimates for this project. In the first, we assume that by year 6 the project has reached a steady state, meaning that cash flows will continue to grow at 2 percent per year indefinitely. In the second, we assume that the firm sells its investment at the end of year 6 and receives a cash payment equal to the project's book value.

In year 6, the project generates a net cash inflow of $35,163. Assuming that cash flows beyond the sixth year grow at 2 percent per year, and discounting those cash flows at 10 percent, we can determine the terminal value of the project *as of the end of year 6* as follows:

Table 8.3
Annual Cash Flow Estimates for Classicaltunes.com

	Year 0	Year 1	Year 2	Year 3	Year 4	Year 5	Year 6
New fixed assets	−$50,000	−$10,000	−$ 5,000	−$25,000	−$40,000	−$15,000	−$10,000
Change in working capital	− 3,000*	− 6,614	− 12,302	− 12,771	− 12,953	− 5,109	− 3,291
Operating cash flow	4,000	10,174	14,789	23,591	40,411	47,644	48,454
Net cash flow	−$49,000	−$ 6,440	−$ 2,513	−$14,180	−$12,542	$27,535	$35,163

* Represents the initial working capital investment.

$$\text{Terminal value} = \frac{\$35,866}{0.10 - 0.02} = \$448,325$$

Notice that the numerator of this expression is 2 percent greater than the cash flow in year 6. Remember, when valuing a stream of cash flows that grows at a perpetual rate, the *value today* equals *next year's cash flow* divided by the difference between the discount rate and the growth rate. Thus, to determine the terminal value in year 6, we must use the cash flow in year 7 in the numerator.

As a second approach, assume that the terminal value of the project simply equals the book value at the end of year 6. At that time, the firm owns fixed assets worth $31,328. If the firm liquidates its current assets and pays off outstanding trade credit, it will generate an additional $56,040 in cash. The terminal value equals the sum of these two items, $87,368. Notice that this value is just one-fifth of the value we obtained using the perpetual growth model. The magnitude of that difference should not surprise us too much. In general, a profitable, growing business will have a market value that exceeds its book value.

Jazz-Music CD Project *NPV*

Putting all this together, we arrive at two different estimates of the project's *NPV*, depending on which estimate of terminal value we use. Assuming that this business will continue to increase profits forever, we arrive at the following *NPV*:

$$NPV = -\$49,000 - \frac{\$6,440}{1.1^1} - \frac{\$2,513}{1.1^2} - \frac{\$14,180}{1.1^3} - \frac{\$12,542}{1.1^4} + \frac{\$27,535}{1.1^5}$$

$$+ \frac{\$35,163 + \$448,325}{1.1^6} = \$213,862$$

On the other hand, if we assume that the terminal value is only equal to book value after six years, then we arrive at the following *NPV*:

$$NPV = -\$49,000 - \frac{\$6,440}{1.1^1} - \frac{\$2,513}{1.1^2} - \frac{\$14,180}{1.1^3} - \frac{\$12,542}{1.1^4} + \frac{\$27,535}{1.1^5}$$

$$+ \frac{\$35,163 + \$87,368}{1.1^6} = \$10,111$$

In this example, the project yields a positive *NPV* no matter which terminal value estimate we choose, so investing will increase shareholder wealth. However, in many real-world situations, especially those involving long-lived investments, the "go" or "no-go" decision will depend critically on terminal value assumptions. It is not at all uncommon for the perpetual growth approach to yield a positive *NPV* while the book value approach shows a negative *NPV*. In that case, managers have to think more deeply about the long-run value of their enterprise.

Concept Review Questions

5. Embedded in the analysis of the jazz-music CD proposal is an assumption about how Classicaltunes.com's customers will behave when they are able to choose from a new set of CDs. What is that assumption?

6. What other ways might Classicaltunes.com estimate the terminal value of this project?

7. Suppose that Congress passes a new MACRS schedule that reclassifies computers as 3-year equipment rather than 5-year equipment. In general, what impact would this legislation have on the project's *NPV*?

8.3 CASH FLOWS, DISCOUNTING, AND INFLATION

At least since World War II, inflation has been a pervasive element of the macro-economic environment in most countries. Inflation rates can vary dramatically across countries and across time for a given country. There are several ways to deal with inflation in capital budgeting analysis, but a simple way to characterize the proper treatment of inflation is as follows. If inflation is in the numerator, be sure that it is also in the denominator. If the numerator ignores inflation, so too must the denominator.

In Chapter 5, we commented on the difference between the nominal rate of return and the real rate of return on an investment. The *nominal return* reflects the actual dollar return, whereas the *real return* measures the increase in purchasing power gained by holding a certain investment. In general, when the inflation rate is high, so too will be the nominal rate of return offered by various investments because investors will demand a return that not only keeps pace with inflation, but also offers a positive real return.

APPLYING THE MODEL

Imagine that a movie ticket today costs $10. If you have $1,000, you have the power to watch 100 movies. Now suppose that you put $1,000 in a mutual fund that earns a 23 percent nominal return over the next year. Suppose also that the inflation rate for that year was 6 percent. By the end of the year, each movie ticket costs $10.60. Your money has grown to $1,230, so you have just enough to purchase 116 movie tickets. In other words, your purchasing power increased by 16 percent during the year, which represents your real return on the mutual fund.   ■

Remember that we formalized the relationship between the nominal rate of return, the inflation rate, and the real rate through the following equation: [12]

[12.] Students may be more familiar with the expression that says that the nominal rate equals the real rate plus the inflation rate. If you multiply out the terms in Equation 8.1, you will see that the nominal rate equals the real rate, plus the inflation rate, plus the product of the real rate and the inflation rate. When both the real rate and the inflation rate are very small, their product is close to zero. In that case, the nominal rate is approximately equal to the inflation rate plus the

(1 + nominal rate) = (1 +inflation rate) × (1 + real rate)

We can rearrange the terms to solve for the real interest rate:

$$\text{real rate} = \left(\frac{1 + \text{nominal rate}}{1 + \text{inflation rate}} \right) - 1 \qquad \textbf{(Eq. 8.1)}$$

Plugging in the figures from our movie ticket example in the preceding Applying the Model, we find that the real interest rate is just a little more than 16 percent:

$$\text{real rate} = \left(\frac{1 + .23}{1 + .06} \right) - 1 = 0.1604 = 16.04\%$$

In most cases, when firms establish a discount rate for capital budgeting purposes, the discount rate reflects then-current market rates of return. As we have seen, embedded in market interest rates is an assumption about inflation, or more precisely, an estimate of expected inflation. Therefore, if we use a market interest rate in the denominator of an *NPV* calculation, we must be careful that the cash flow estimates in the numerator are **nominal cash flows,** which reflect the same inflation rate that the interest rate does. We refer to this as Inflation Rule 1.

Inflation Rule 1—When we discount cash flows at a nominal interest rate, embedded in the discount rate is an estimate of expected inflation. We must employ the same inflation assumption when forecasting project cash flows.

APPLYING THE MODEL

Refer again to Table 8.2. Notice that two factors cause the project's revenues to rise over time. The first factor is that the average price of a CD increases 2 percent each year. In this example, 2 percent is the underlying inflation rate, meaning that all prices rise, on average, 2 percent per year. The second factor causing revenues to rise is the increase in sales volume. Multiplying price times quantity gives us revenue in *nominal terms*—that is, the actual dollar revenue figure that the firm expects to generate each year. Because the cash flow projections for the project include a 2 percent inflation rate, the discount rate used to calculate the *NPV* should be the nominal rate. As long as the 10 percent discount rate used by Classicaltunes.com reflects current market returns, the company is treating inflation properly. It is discounting nominal cash flows with a nominal discount rate. ■

Occasionally, cash flow projections for a project may be stated in *real* terms. **Real cash flows** reflect current prices only and do not incorporate upward adjustments for expected inflation. When project cash flows are stated in real terms, the proper discount rate to use in calculating the *NPV* is the real rate.

APPLYING THE MODEL

An alternative way to construct Table 8.2 would be to use the current-year price of CDs, $13.50, all the way through the analysis. If we took that approach, being care-

---

real rate. The quality of this approximation declines as either the real rate or the inflation rate increases. For instance, in our movie ticket example in the preceding Applying the Model, the real rate plus the inflation rate equals 22 percent, while the nominal rate equals 23 percent.

ful to use current-year labor costs, current-year prices for fixed assets, and so on, then we would be stating cash flows in real terms. For example, if we calculate revenues in all future years using today's CD price of $13.50, we find that real revenues are about 2 percent lower in year 1 than the figure shown in Table 8.2. In year 2, real revenues are about 4 percent less than the number given in Table 8.2. In general, to convert nominal cash flows into real cash flows, we "discount" the nominal figures by the rate of inflation. By doing so, we restate cash flows in a manner that reflects today's prices, not prices in the future that have risen due to inflation. With cash flows stated in real terms, the real rate is the appropriate discount rate to use. From Equation 8.1, we can calculate the real rate for Classicaltunes.com:

$$\text{real rate} = \left(\frac{1 + 0.10}{1 + 0.02}\right) - 1 = 0.0784 = 7.84\%$$

Using a real rate to discount real cash flows should result in the same project *NPV* as using a nominal rate to discount nominal cash flows. To demonstrate this, we have restated all the project's cash flows in real terms in the following equations. For example, the net cash flow in year 1 of −$6,440 has been restated in real terms by deflating the nominal cash figure by the inflation rate:

$$\frac{-\$6,440}{1.02} = -\$6,314$$

Similarly, we restate the nominal cash flow in year 2 into real terms as follows:

$$\frac{-\$2,513}{1.02^2} = -\$2,415$$

Converting cash flows in every year (except the cash flows that occur immediately) from nominal to real terms and then discounting at the real rate of 7.84 percent yields the following *NPV*:[13]

$$NPV = -\$49,000 - \frac{\$6,314}{1.0784^1} - \frac{\$2,415}{1.0784^2} - \frac{\$13,362}{1.0784^3} - \frac{\$11,587}{1.0784^4} + \frac{\$24,939}{1.0784^5}$$

$$+ \frac{\$31,224 + \$398,100}{1.0784^6} = \$213,862$$

When cash flow figures for a particular project ignore the effects of inflation (i.e., when cash flows are in real terms), it is necessary to discount those cash flows at a rate that also excludes the impact of inflation—the real rate. This leads to Inflation Rule 2.

Inflation Rule 2—When project cash flows are stated in real rather than in nominal terms, the appropriate discount rate is the real rate.

Discounting real cash flows at a real interest rate should yield the same *NPV* as discounting nominal cash flows at a nominal rate. Errors occur when firms discount real cash flows using a nominal interest rate, or when firms discount nominal cash flows using a real discount rate. Figure 8.1 illustrates four possible scenarios in which

---

[13] Notice that we are once again using the perpetual growth approach to estimate the project's terminal value. In addition, the equation shows a discount rate of 7.84 percent, but in reality we are using 7.8431 percent to get exactly the same *NPV* figure as we obtained before. Using 7.84 percent makes the *NPV* in this case look a little larger than it was before, but that is simply a rounding error.

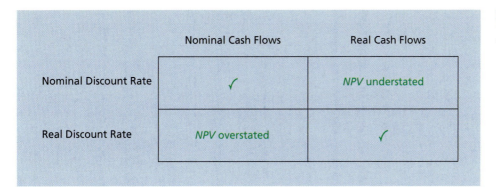

Figure 8.1
Capital Budgeting
and Inflation

firms can choose to project cash flows in nominal or in real terms and to discount those cash flows using a nominal or real discount rate. As long as both cash flows are either in real terms or in nominal terms, firms obtain the correct *NPV*. However, if firms project nominal cash flows, which increase over time due to inflation, and discount those cash flows using a real rate, then they will overstate the project's *NPV*. This bias will lead firms to accept projects that they should in fact reject. Just the opposite happens when firms discount real cash flows, which are not adjusted upward for inflation, using a nominal discount rate. The resulting *NPV* understates the project's true contribution to shareholder value, and firms may be misled into rejecting projects that they should accept.

> **8.** Look back at the cash flow projections for Classicaltunes.com's jazz-music CD project. Are the depreciation deductions stated in nominal or in real terms?
>
> **9.** Can you think of a project for which it might be easier to project real cash flows than to project nominal cash flows?

Concept Review Questions

8.4 SPECIAL PROBLEMS IN CAPITAL BUDGETING

Though our objective in writing this book was to give it the most real-world focus possible, real business situations are more complex and occur in more varieties than any textbook can reasonably convey. In this section, we examine common business decisions with special characteristics that make them a little more difficult to analyze than the examples we have covered thus far. We will see that while the analysis may require a little more thinking, the principles involved are the same ones discussed throughout this chapter and Chapter 7.

EQUIPMENT REPLACEMENT AND EQUIVALENT ANNUAL COST

Assume that a firm must purchase an electronic control device to monitor its assembly line. Two types of devices are available. Both meet the firm's minimum quality standards, but they differ in three dimensions. First, one device costs less than the other. Second, the cheaper device requires higher maintenance expenditures. Third, the less expensive device does not last as long as the more expensive one, so it will have to be replaced sooner. The sequence of expected *cash outflows* (we have omitted the negative signs for convenience) for each device are as follows:

Device	End of Year				
	0	1	2	3	4
A	$12,000	$1,500	$1,500	$1,500	$ 0
B	14,000	1,200	1,200	1,200	1,200

Notice that the maintenance costs do not rise over time. This means either that the expected rate of inflation equals zero, in which case the nominal discount rate and the real discount rate are one and the same, or that we have ignored inflation in making the projections. In the latter case, we must be careful to discount cash flows at the real rate.[14] Suppose that this firm uses a real discount rate of 7 percent. Following is the NPV of each stream of cash flows:

Device	NPV
A	$15,936
B	18,065

Purchasing and operating device A seems to be much cheaper than using device B (remember that we are looking for a lower NPV because these are cash outflows). But this calculation ignores the fact that using device A will necessitate a large replacement expenditure in year 4, one year earlier than device B must be replaced. We need a way to capture the value of replacing device B less frequently than device A.

One way to do this is to look at both machines over a 12-year time horizon. Over the next 12 years, the firm will replace device A four times and device B three times. At the end of the twelfth year, both machines have to be replaced, and thus begins another 12-year cycle. Table 8.4 shows the streams of cash flows over the cycle. Notice that in years in which the firm must replace one of the devices, it must pay both the maintenance cost on the old device (to keep it running through the year) and the purchase price of the new device. Following is the present value (using a 7% discount rate) of cash flows over the entire 12-year period:

Device	NPV
A	$48,233
B	42,360

Taking into account the greater longevity of device B, it is the better choice.

An alternative approach to this problem is called the **equivalent annual cost (EAC) method.** The EAC method begins by calculating the present value of cash flows for each device over its lifetime. We have already seen that the NPV for operating device A for three years is $15,936, and the NPV for operating device B for four years is $18,065. Next, the EAC method asks, what annual expenditure over the life of each machine would have the same present value? That is, the EAC solves each expression as follows:

$$\$15,936 = \frac{X}{1.07^1} + \frac{X}{1.07^2} + \frac{X}{1.07^3} \qquad X = \$6,072$$

$$\$18,065 = \frac{Y}{1.07^1} + \frac{Y}{1.07^2} + \frac{Y}{1.07^3} + \frac{Y}{1.07^4} \qquad Y = \$5,333$$

In the first equation, the variable X represents the annual cash flow from a 3-year annuity that has the same present value as the actual purchase and operating costs of device A. If the firm purchases device A and keeps replacing it every three years for the indefinite future, the firm will incur a sequence of cash flows over time with the

---

[14.] Of course, we could restate the cash flows, building in an inflation assumption, then discount the cash flows at the nominal interest rate.

Table 8.4
Operating and
Replacement Cash Flows
for Two Devices

	Device	
Year	A	B
0	$12,000	$14,000
1	1,500	1,200
2	1,500	1,200
3	13,500	1,200
4	1,500	15,200
5	1,500	1,200
6	13,500	1,200
7	1,500	1,200
8	1,500	15,200
9	13,500	1,200
10	1,500	1,200
11	1,500	1,200
12	1,500	1,200
NPV (7%)	$48,233	$42,360

Note: At the end of 12 years, the firm would have to replace equipment regardless of whether it chooses device A or B; thus, a new 12-year cycle begins.

same present value as a perpetuity of $6,072. In other words, $6,072 is the equivalent annual cost of device A. Likewise, in the second equation, Y represents the annual cash flow from a 4-year annuity with the same present value as the purchase and operating costs of device B. If the firm buys device B and replaces it every four years, then the firm will incur a sequence of cash flows having the same present value as a perpetuity of $5,333. The firm should choose the machine with the lower EAC, device B.

Our approaches for solving the problem of choosing between equipment with unequal lives both assume that the firm will continue to replace worn-out equipment with similar machines for a long period of time. That may not be a bad assumption in some cases, but many times new technology makes old equipment obsolete. For example, suppose that the firm in our example believes that in three years a new electronic device will be available that is more reliable, less costly to operate, and longer lived. If this new device becomes available in three years, the firm will replace whatever device it is using at the time with the newer model. Furthermore, the superior attributes of the new model imply that the salvage value for the old devices will be zero. How should the firm proceed?

Knowing that it will replace the old device with the improved device in three years, the firm can simply discount cash flows for three years:

$$NPV_A = \$12,000 + \frac{\$1,500}{1.07^1} + \frac{\$1,500}{1.07^2} + \frac{\$1,500}{1.07^3} = \$15,936$$

$$NPV_B = \$14,000 + \frac{\$1,200}{1.07^1} + \frac{\$1,200}{1.07^2} + \frac{\$1,200}{1.07^3} = \$17,149$$

In this case, the best device to purchase is A rather than B. Remember that B's primary advantage was its longevity. In an environment in which technological developments make old machines obsolete, longevity is not much of an advantage.

Excess Capacity

Firms often operate at less than full capacity. In such situations, managers encourage alternative uses of the excess capacity because they view it as a free asset. Although it may be true that the marginal cost of using excess capacity is zero in the very short run, using excess capacity today may accelerate the need for more capacity in the future. When that is so, managers should charge the cost of accelerating new capacity development against the current proposal for using excess capacity.

Imagine a retail department store chain with a regional distribution center in the southeastern United States. At the moment, the distribution center is not fully utilized. Managers know that in two years, as new stores are built in the region, the firm will have to invest $2 million (cash outflow) to expand the distribution center's warehouse. A proposal surfaces to lease all the excess space in the warehouse for the next two years at a price that would generate cash inflow of $125,000 per year. If the firm accepts this proposal, it will have no excess capacity. In order to hold inventory for new stores coming on line in the next few months, the firm will have to begin expansion immediately. The incremental investment in this expansion is the difference between investing $2 million now versus investing $2 million two years from today. The incremental cash inflow is, of course, the $125,000 lease cash flows that are received today and one year from today. Should the firm accept this offer? Assuming a 10 percent discount rate, the NPV of the project is shown as follows:

$$NPV = \$125,000 - \$2,000,000 + \frac{\$125,000}{1.1^1} + \frac{\$2,000,000}{1.1^2} = -\$108,471$$

Notice that we treat the $2 million investment in the second year as a cash inflow in this expression, because by building the warehouse today, the firm avoids having to spend the money two years later. Even so, the NPV of leasing excess capacity is negative. However, a clever analyst might propose a counteroffer derived from the follow equation:

$$NPV = X - \$2,000,000 + \frac{X}{1.1^1} + \frac{\$2,000,000}{1.1^2} = \$0$$

The value of X represents the amount of the lease cash inflow (one received today and the other received in one year) that would just make the firm indifferent to the proposal. Solving the equation, we see that if the lease cash inflows are $181,818, the project NPV equals zero. Therefore, if the firm can lease its capacity for a price above $181,818, it should do so.

Concept Review Questions

10. Under what circumstance is the use of the equivalent annual cost method to compare substitutable projects with different lives clearly more efficient computationally than using multiple investments over a common period where both projects terminate in the same year?

11. In almost every example so far, firms must decide to invest in a project immediately or not at all. But suppose that a firm could invest in a project today or it could wait one year before investing. How could you use NPV analysis to decide whether to invest now or later?

12. Can you articulate circumstances under which the cost of excess capacity is zero? Think about why the cost of excess capacity normally is not zero.

8.5 THE HUMAN FACE OF CAPITAL BUDGETING

This chapter illustrates which cash flows analysts should discount and which cash flows they should ignore when valuing real investment projects. Though there are relatively simple rules of thumb that guide managers in this task, executing these rules well in practice is obviously a challenge. Deciding which costs are incremental and which are not, incorporating the myriad tax factors that influence cash flows, and measuring opportunity costs properly are all much more complex in practice than we or anyone else can convey in a textbook. The nuances of capital budgeting are best learned through practice.

There is another factor that makes real-world capital budgeting more complex than textbook examples—the human element. Neither the ideas for capital investments nor the financial analysis evaluating them occurs in a vacuum. Almost any investment proposal important enough to warrant a thorough financial analysis has a champion behind it, someone who believes that the project is a good idea, or at least that the project will advance the individual's own career. When companies allocate investment capital across projects or across divisions, they must recognize the potential for an optimistic bias to creep into the numbers. This bias can arise through intentional manipulation of the cash flows to make an investment look more attractive, or it may simply arise if the analyst calculating the *NPV* is also the cheerleader advocating the project in the first place.

One way that companies attempt to control for this bias is by putting responsibility for analyzing an investment proposal under an authority independent from the individual or group proposing the investment. For example, it is common in large firms for a particular group to have the responsibility of conducting the financial analysis required to value any potential acquisition targets. In this role, financial analysts play a kind of gatekeeper role, protecting shareholders' interests by steering the firm away from large negative-*NPV* investments. Naturally, these independent analysts face intense pressure from the advocates of each project to portray the investment proposal in its best possible light. Consequently, financial experts need to know more than just which cash flows count in the *NPV* calculation. They also need to have a sense of what is reasonable when forecasting a project's profit margin and its growth potential. Analysts must also prepare to defend their assumptions, explaining why their (often more conservative) projections do not line up with those offered by the managers advocating a certain investment.

Many experienced managers will say that they have never seen an investment with a negative *NPV*. In saying this, they do not mean that all investments are good investments, but rather that all analysts know enough about *NPV* analysis to know how to make any investment look attractive. Small adjustments to cash flow projections and discount rates can often sway a project's *NPV* from negative to positive. In this environment, another skill comes into play in determining which project receives funding. We might refer to this skill as storytelling, as opposed to number crunching. Most good investments have a compelling story behind them, a reason, based on sound economic logic, that the investment's *NPV should be* positive. The best financial analysts can not only provide the numbers to highlight the value of a good investment but can also explain why the investment makes sense, highlighting the competitive opportunity that makes one investment's *NPV* positive and another one's negative. We will return to this storytelling element of capital budgeting in Chapter 9.

SMART IDEAS VIDEO
Raghu Rajan, University of Chicago
"Capital budgeting is not just about estimating cash flows and discount rates, but is also a lot about horse trading."

See the entire interview at **SMARTFinance**

Concept Review Question

13. What role does the human factor play in the capital budgeting decision process? Could it cause a negative-*NPV* project to be accepted?

8.6 SUMMARY

- Certain types of cash flow are common to many different kinds of investments. These include fixed asset cash flow, working capital cash flow, operating cash flow, and terminal cash flow.
- The costs of financing an investment, such as interest paid to lenders and dividends paid to shareholders, should not be counted as part of a project's cash outflows. The discount rate captures the financing costs, so deducting interest expense and dividends from a project's cash flows would be double counting.
- To find working capital cash flow, calculate the change in working capital from one period to the next. Increases in working capital represent cash outflows, while decreases in working capital represent cash inflows.
- To find operating cash flow, calculate after-tax net income and add back any non-cash expenses.
- To find terminal value, or terminal cash flow, employ one of several methods, including the perpetual growth model and the use of book value.
- Only the incremental costs associated with a project should be included in *NPV* analysis. The analyst should avoid including sunk costs.
- Opportunity costs should be included in cash flow projections.
- Discount nominal cash flows at a nominal rate, and real cash flows at a real rate. Failure to match the type of cash flow with the correct discount rate will either overstate or understate the value of a project.
- When evaluating alternative equipment purchases with unequal lives, determine the equivalent annual cost of each type of equipment and choose the one that is least expensive.
- When confronted with proposals to use excess capacity, think carefully about the true cost of that capacity. It is rarely zero.
- When analyzing capital budgeting projects, it is important to consider human factors and make sure that the project, in addition to having a positive *NPV*, makes sense.

INTERNET RESOURCES

Note: *For updates to links, please go to the book's website at* http://smart.swcollege.com

http://www.ifad.net/content/ie/ie_f_gaap_frameset.htm—An excellent comparison of accounting standards for different countries

http://clinton3.nara.gov/pcscb/—An interesting report prepared in 1999 for President Clinton, outlining capital budgeting trends and practices in both the public and private sectors

http://www.quicken.com/taxes/investing/marginal/yahoo—Can be used for personal investment decisions by calculating your own marginal tax rate

http://www.secondarymarket.com—Site can be searched by registered users for used equipment in many different industrial sectors; can use market prices of used equipment to form estimates of salvage value or terminal value for a long-lived project

KEY TERMS

cannibalization
equivalent annual cost (EAC) method
marginal tax rate
modified accelerated cost recovery
    system (MACRS)
net working capital

nominal cash flows
opportunity costs
real cash flows
sunk costs
terminal value
working capital

QUESTIONS

8-1.   In capital budgeting analysis, why do we focus on cash flow rather than accounting profit?

8-2.   To finance a certain project, a company must borrow money at 10 percent interest. How should it treat interest payments when it analyzes the project's cash flows?

8-3.   Does depreciation affect cash flow in a positive or negative manner? From a net present value perspective, why is accelerated depreciation preferable? Is it acceptable to utilize one depreciation method for tax purposes and another for financial reporting purposes? Which method is relevant for determining project cash flows?

8-4.   In what sense does an increase in accounts payable represent a cash inflow?

8-5.   List several ways to estimate a project's terminal value.

8-6.   What are the tax consequences of selling an investment asset for more than its book value? Does this have an effect on project cash flows that must be accounted for in relevant cash flows? What is the effect if the asset is sold for less than its book value?

8-7.   Why must incremental after-tax cash flows rather than total cash flows be evaluated in project analysis?

8-8.   Differentiate between sunk costs and opportunity costs. Which of these costs should be included in incremental cash flows, and which should be excluded?

8-9.   Before entering graduate school, a student estimated the value of earning an MBA at $300,000. Based on that analysis, the student decided to go back to school. After completing the first year, the student ran the *NPV* calculations again. How would you expect the *NPV* to look after the student has completed one year of the program? Specifically, what portion of the analysis must be different than it was the year before?

8-10. Punxsutawney Taxidermy Inc. (PTI), operates a chain of taxidermy shops across the Midwest, with a handful of locations in the South. A rival firm, Heads Up Corp., has a few Midwestern locations, but most of its shops are located in the South. PTI and Heads Up decide to consolidate their operations by trading ownership of a few locations. PTI will acquire four Heads Up locations in the Midwest, and in exchange will relinquish control of its Southern locations. No cash changes hands up front. Does this mean that an analyst working for either company can evaluate the merits of this deal by assuming that the project has no initial cash outlay? Explain.

8-11. True or False: If a company's practice is to calculate project *NPV*s using nominal cash flows and a nominal discount rate, it must have a forecast for expected inflation. However, if the company discounts real cash flows at the real rate, developing an inflation forecast is unnecessary.

8-11. Explain why the *EAC method* helps firms evaluate alternative investments with unequal lives.

8-12. Why isn't excess capacity free?

Smart Solutions
See the problem and solution explained step-by-step at
SMARTFinance

PROBLEMS

Types of Cash Flows

8-1. Calculate the present value of depreciation tax savings on a depreciable asset with a purchase price of $5 million and zero salvage value, assuming a 10 percent discount rate, a 34 percent tax rate, and the following type of depreciation:

  a. The asset is depreciated over a 3-year life according to Table 8.1.
  b. The asset is depreciated over a 7-year life according to Table 8.1.
  c. The asset is depreciated over a 20-year life according to Table 8.1.

8-2. A certain piece of equipment costs $32 million plus an additional $2 million to install. This equipment qualifies under the 5-year MACRS category. For a firm that discounts cash flows at 12 percent and faces a tax rate of 34 percent, what is the present value of depreciation tax savings associated with this equipment? By how much would that number change if the firm could treat the $2 million installation cost as a deductible expense rather than include it as part of the depreciable cost of the asset?

8-3. The government is considering a proposal to allow even more-accelerated depreciation deductions than specified by MACRS.

  a. For which type of company would this change be more valuable, a company facing a 10 percent tax rate or one facing a 30 percent tax rate?
  b. If companies take larger depreciation deductions in the early years of an investment, what will the impact be on reported earnings? On cash flows? On project *NPV*s? How do you think the stock market might respond if the tax law changes to allow more-accelerated depreciation?

8-4. Taylor United is considering overhauling its equipment to meet increased demand for its product. The cost of equipment overhaul is $3.8 million plus $200,000 in installation costs. The firm will depreciate the equipment modifications under MACRS using a 5-year recovery period. Additional sales revenue from the overhaul should amount to $2.2 million per year, and additional operating expenses and other costs (excluding depreciation) will amount to 35 percent of the additional sales. The firm has an ordinary tax rate of 40 percent. Answer the following questions about Taylor United for each of the next six years.

  a. What additional earnings before depreciation and taxes will result from the overhaul?
  b. What additional earnings after taxes will result from the overhaul?
  c. What incremental operating cash flows will result from the overhaul?

8-5. Wilbur Corporation is considering replacing a machine. The replacement will cut operating expenses by $24,000 per year for each of the five years the new machine is expected to last. Although the old machine has a zero book value, it has a remaining useful life of five years. The depreciable value of the new machine is $72,000. Wilbur will depreciate the machine under MACRS using a 5-year recovery period and is subject to a 40 percent tax rate on ordinary income. Estimate the incremental operating cash flows attributable to the replacement. Be sure to consider the depreciation in year 6.

8-6. Advanced Electronics Corporation is considering purchasing a new packaging machine to replace a fully depreciated packaging machine that will last five more years. The new machine is expected to have a 5-year life and depreciation charges of $4,000 in year 1; $6,400 in year 2; $3,800 in year 3; $2,400 in both year 4 and year 5; and $1,000 in year 6. The firm's estimates of revenues and expenses (excluding depreciation) for the new and old packaging machines are shown in the following table. Advanced Electronics is subject to a 40 percent tax rate on ordinary income.

	New Packaging Machine		Old Packaging Machine	
Year	Revenue	Expenses (excluding depreciation)	Revenue	Expenses (excluding depreciation)
1	$50,000	$40,000	$45,000	$35,000
2	51,000	40,000	45,000	35,000
3	52,000	40,000	45,000	35,000
4	53,000	40,000	45,000	35,000
5	54,000	40,000	45,000	35,000

a. Calculate the operating cash flows associated with each packaging machine. Be sure to consider the depreciation in year 6.

b. Calculate the incremental operating cash flows resulting from the proposed packaging machine replacement.

c. Depict on a time line the incremental cash flows found in part (b).

8-7. Premium Wines, a producer of medium-quality wines, has maintained stable sales and profits over the past eight years. Although the market for medium-quality wines has been growing by 4 percent per year, Premium Wines has been unsuccessful in sharing this growth. To increase its sales, the firm is considering an aggressive marketing campaign that centers on regularly running ads in major food and wine magazines and running TV commercials in large metropolitan areas. The campaign is expected to require an *annual* tax-deductible expenditure of $3 million over the next five years. Sales revenue, as noted in the following income statement for 2004, totaled $80 million. If the proposed marketing campaign is not initiated, sales are expected to remain at this level in each of the next five years, 2005–2009. With the marketing campaign, sales are expected to rise to the levels shown in the sales forecast table for each of the next five years; cost of goods sold is expected to remain at 75 percent of sales; general and administrative expense (exclusive of any marketing campaign outlays) is expected to remain at 15 percent of sales; and annual depreciation expense is expected to remain at $2 million. Assuming a 40 percent tax rate, find the relevant cash flows over the next five years associated with Premium Wines' proposed marketing campaign.

Premium Wines
Income Statement
for the year ended December 31, 2004

Sales revenue		$80,000,000
Less: Cost of goods sold (75%)		60,000,000
Gross profits		$20,000,000
Less: Operating expenses		
General and administrative expense (15%)	$12,000,000	
Depreciation expense	2,000,000	
Total operating expense		$14,000,000
Net profits before taxes		$ 6,000,000
Less: Taxes (rate = 40%)		2,400,000
Net profits after taxes		$ 3,600,000

Premium Wines
Sales Forecast

Year	Sales Revenue
2005	$82,000,000
2006	84,000,000
2007	86,000,000
2008	90,000,000
2009	94,000,000

8-8. Barans Manufacturing is developing the incremental cash flows associated with the proposed replacement of an existing stamping machine with a new, technologically advanced one. Given the following costs related to the proposed project, explain whether each would be treated as a *sunk cost* or an *opportunity cost* in developing the incremental cash flows associated with the proposed replacement decision.

a. Barans would be able to use the same dies and other tools, which had a book value of $40,000, on the new stamping machine that it used on the old one.

b. Barans would be able to link the new machine to its existing computer system in order to control its operations. The old stamping machine did not have a computer control system. The firm's excess computer capacity could be leased to another firm for an annual fee of $17,000.

c. Barans would have to obtain additional floor space to accommodate the larger new stamping machine. The space that would be used is currently being leased to another company for $10,000 per year.

d. Barans would use a small storage facility to store the increased output of the new stamping machine. The storage facility was built by Barans at a cost of $120,000 three years earlier. Because of its unique configuration and location, it is currently of no use to either Barans or any other firm.

e. Barans would retain an existing overhead crane, which it had planned to sell for its $180,000 market value. Although the crane was not needed with the old stamping machine, it would be used to position raw materials on the new stamping machine.

8-9. Blueberry Electronics is exploring the possibility of producing a new handheld device that will serve both as a basic PC with Internet access and as a cell phone. Which of the following items are relevant for the project's analysis?

a. Research and development funds that the company has spent working on a prototype of the new product.

b. The company's current-generation product has no cell phone capability. The new product would therefore make the old one obsolete in the eyes of many consumers. However, Blueberry expects that other companies will soon bring to market products combining cell phone and PC features, and these will also reduce sales on Blueberry's existing products.

c. Costs of ramping up production of the new device.

d. Increases in receivables and inventory that will occur as production increases.

Cash Flows for Classicaltunes.com

8-10. New York Pizza is considering replacing an existing oven with a new, more sophisticated oven. The old oven was purchased three years ago at a cost of $20,000, and this amount was being depreciated under MACRS using a 5-year recovery period. The oven has five years of usable life remaining. The new oven being considered costs $30,500, requires $1,500 in installation costs, and would be depreciated under MACRS using a 5-year recovery period. The old oven can currently be sold for $22,000 without incurring any removal or cleanup costs. The firm pays taxes at a rate of 40 percent on both ordinary income and capital gains. The revenues and expenses (excluding depreciation) associated with the new and the old machines for the next five years are given in the following table.

	New Oven		Old Oven	
Year	Revenue	Expenses (excluding depreciation)	Revenue	Expenses (excluding depreciation)
1	$300,000	$288,000	$270,000	$264,000
2	300,000	288,000	270,000	264,000
3	300,000	288,000	272,000	264,000
4	300,000	288,000	271,000	264,000
5	300,000	288,000	270,000	264,000

    a. Calculate the initial cash outflow associated with replacement of the old oven by the new one.

    b. Determine the incremental cash flows associated with the proposed replacement. Be sure to consider the depreciation in year 6.

    c. Depict on a time line the relevant cash flows found in parts (a) and (b) associated with the proposed replacement decision.

8-11. Speedy Auto Wash is contemplating the purchase of a new high-speed washer to replace the existing washer. The existing washer was purchased two years ago at an installed cost of $120,000; it was being depreciated under MACRS using a 5-year recovery period. The existing washer is expected to have a usable life of five more years. The new washer costs $210,000 and requires $10,000 in installation costs; it has a 5-year usable life and would be depreciated under MACRS using a 5-year recovery period. The existing washer can currently be sold for $140,000 without incurring any removal or cleanup costs. To support the increased business resulting from purchase of the new washer, accounts receivable would increase by $80,000, inventories by $60,000, and accounts payable by $116,000. At the end of five years, the existing washer is expected to have a market value of zero; the new washer would be sold to net $58,000 after removal and cleanup costs and before taxes. The firm pays taxes at a rate of 40 percent on both ordinary income and capital gains. The estimated *profits before depreciation and taxes* over the five years for both the new and the existing washer are shown in the following table.

	Profits before Depreciation and Taxes	
Year	New Washer	Existing Washer
1	$86,000	$52,000
2	86,000	48,000
3	86,000	44,000
4	86,000	40,000
5	86,000	36,000

    a. Calculate the initial cash outflow associated with the replacement of the existing washer with the new one.

    b. Determine the incremental cash flows associated with the proposed washer replacement. Be sure to consider the depreciation in year 6.

    c. Determine the terminal cash flow expected at the end of year 5 from the proposed washer replacement.

    d. Depict on a time line the relevant cash flows associated with the proposed washer-replacement decision.

8-12. TransPacific Shipping is considering replacing an existing ship with one of two newer, more efficient ones. The existing ship is three years old, cost $32 million, and is being depreciated under MACRS using a 5-year recovery period. Although the existing ship has only three years (years 4, 5, and 6) of depreciation remaining under MACRS, it has a remaining usable life of five years. Ship A, one of the two possible replacement ships, costs $40 million to purchase and $8 million to outfit for service. It has a 5-year usable life and will be depreciated under MACRS using a 5-year recovery period. Ship B costs $54 million to purchase and $6 million to outfit. It also has a 5-year usable life and will be depreciated under MACRS using a 5-year recovery period. Increased investments in net working capital will accompany the decision to acquire ship A or ship B. Purchase of ship A would result in a $4 million increase in net working capital; ship B would result in a $6 million increase in net working capital. The projected *profits before depreciation and taxes* with each alternative ship and the existing ship are given in the following table.

	Profits before Depreciation and Taxes		
Year	Ship A	Ship B	Existing Ship
1	$21,000,000	$22,000,000	$14,000,000
2	21,000,000	24,000,000	14,000,000
3	21,000,000	26,000,000	14,000,000
4	21,000,000	26,000,000	14,000,000
5	21,000,000	26,000,000	14,000,000

The existing ship can currently be sold for $18 million and will not incur any removal or cleanup costs. At the end of five years, the existing ship can be sold to net $1 million before taxes. Ships A and B can be sold to net $12 million and $20 million before taxes, respectively, at the end of the 5-year period. The firm is subject to a 40 percent tax rate on both ordinary income and capital gains.

a. Calculate the initial outlay associated with each alternative.
b. Calculate the operating cash flows associated with each alternative. Be sure to consider the depreciation in year 6.
c. Calculate the terminal cash flow at the end of year 5 associated with each alternative.
d. Depict on a time line the relevant cash flows associated with each alternative.

8-13. The management of Kimco is evaluating replacing their large mainframe computer with a modern network system that requires much less office space. The network would cost $500,000 (including installation costs) and would generate $125,000 per year in operating cash flows (accounting for taxes and depreciation) over the next five years due to efficiency gains. The mainframe has a remaining book value of $50,000 and would be immediately donated to a charity for the tax benefit. Kimco's cost of capital is 10 percent and tax rate, 40 percent. On the basis of *NPV*, should management install the network system?

8-14. Pointless Luxuries Inc. (PLI) produces unusual gifts targeted at wealthy consumers. The company is analyzing the possibility of introducing a new device designed to attach to the collar of a cat or dog. This device emits sonic waves that neutralize airplane engine noise, so that pets traveling with their owners will enjoy a more peaceful ride. PLI estimates that developing this product will require up-front capital expenditures of $10 million. These costs will be depreciated on a straight-line basis for five years. PLI believes that it can sell the product initially for $250. The selling price will increase to $260 in years 2 and 3 before falling to $245 and $240 in years 4 and 5, respectively. After five years the company will withdraw the product from the market and replace it with something else. Variable costs are $135 per unit. PLI forecasts sales volume of 20,000 units the first year, with subsequent increases of 25 percent (year 2), 20 percent (year 3), 20 percent (year 4), and 15 percent (year 5). Offering this product will force PLI to make additional investments in receivables and inventory. Projected end-of-year balances appear in the following table.

	Year 0	Year 1	Year 2	Year 3	Year 4	Year 5
Accounts receivable	$0	$200,000	$250,000	$300,000	$150,000	$0
Inventory	0	500,000	650,000	780,000	600,000	0

The firm faces a tax rate of 34 percent. Assume that cash flows arrive at the end of each year, except for the initial $10 million outlay.

a. Calculate the project's contribution to net income each year.
b. Calculate the project's cash flows each year.
c. Calculate two *NPV*s, one using a 10 percent discount rate and one using 15 percent.
d. A PLI financial analyst reasons as follows: "With the exception of the initial outlay, the cash flows from this project arrive in more or less a continuous stream rather than at the end of each year. Therefore, by discounting each year's cash flow

for a full year, we are understating the true *NPV*. A better approximation is to move the discounting six months forward (e.g., discount year-1 cash flows for six months, year-2 cash flows for 1.5 years, and so on), as if all the cash flows arrive in the middle of each year rather than at the end." Recalculate the *NPV* (at 10% and 15%) maintaining this assumption. How much difference does it make?

8-15. TechGiant Inc. (TGI) is evaluating a proposal to acquire Fusion Chips, a young company with an interesting new chip technology. This technology, when integrated into existing TGI silicon wafers, will enable TGI to offer chips with new capabilities to companies with automated manufacturing systems. TGI analysts have projected income statements for Fusion five years into the future. These projections appear in the income statements that follow, along with estimates of Fusion's asset requirements and accounts payable balances each year. These statements are designed assuming that Fusion remains an independent, stand-alone company. If TGI acquires Fusion, analysts believe that the following changes will occur.

1. TGI's superior manufacturing capabilities will enable Fusion to increase its gross margin on its existing products to 45 percent.
2. TGI's massive sales force will enable Fusion to increase sales of its existing products by 10 percent above current projections (for example, if acquired, Fusion will sell $110 million, rather than $100 million, in 2005). This increase will occur as a consequence of regularly scheduled conversations between TGI salespeople and existing customers and will not require added marketing expenditures. Operating expenses as a percentage of sales will be the same each year as currently forecasted (ranges from 10% to 12%). The fixed asset increases currently projected through 2009 will be sufficient to sustain the 10 percent increase in sales volume each year.
3. TGI's more efficient receivables and inventory management systems will allow Fusion to increase its sales as previously described without making investments in receivables and inventory beyond those already reflected in the financial projection. TGI also enjoys a higher credit rating than Fusion, so after the acquisition, Fusion will obtain credit from suppliers on more favorable terms. Specifically, Fusion's accounts payable balance will be 30 percent higher each year than the level currently forecast.
4. TGI's current cash reserves are more than sufficient for the combined company, so Fusion's existing cash balances will be reduced to $0.
5. Immediately after the acquisition, TGI will invest $50 million in fixed assets to manufacture a new chip that integrates Fusion's technology into one of TGI's best-selling products. These assets will be depreciated on a straight-line basis for eight years. After five years, the new chip will be obsolete, and no additional sales will occur. The equipment will be sold at the end of year 5 for $1 million. Before depreciation and taxes, this new product will generate $20 million in (incremental) profits the first year, $30 million the second year, and $15 million in each of the next three years. TGI will have to invest $3 million in net working capital up front, all of which it will recover at the end of the project's life.
6. Both companies face a tax rate of 34 percent.

Fusion Chips
Income Statements
($ in thousands for years ended December 31)

	2005	2006	2007	2008	2009
Sales	$100,000	$150,000	$200,000	$240,000	$270,000
− Cost of goods sold	60,000	90,000	120,000	144,000	162,000
Gross profit	$ 40,000	$ 60,000	$ 80,000	$ 96,000	$108,000
− Operating expenses	12,000	17,250	22,000	25,200	27,000
− Depreciation	12,000	18,000	24,000	28,800	32,400
Pretax income	$ 16,000	$ 24,750	$ 34,000	$ 42,000	$ 48,600
− Taxes	5,440	8,415	11,560	14,280	16,524
Net income	$ 10,560	$ 16,335	$ 22,440	$ 27,720	$ 32,076

Assets and Accounts Payable
($ in thousands on December 31)

	2004	2005	2006	2007	2008	2009
Cash	$ 400	$ 400	$ 525	$ 600	$ 600	$ 600
Accounts receivable	6,000	7,000	10,500	14,000	16,800	18,900
Inventory	10,000	12,500	18,750	25,000	30,000	33,750
Total current assets	$16,400	$ 19,900	$ 29,775	$ 39,600	$ 47,400	$ 53,250
Plant and equipment						
Gross	$80,000	$113,000	$166,500	$226,000	$283,200	$336,900
Net	50,000	71,000	106,500	142,000	170,400	191,700
Total assets	$66,400	$ 90,900	$136,275	$181,600	$217,800	$244,950
Accounts payable	$ 7,500	$ 13,500	$ 20,250	$ 27,000	$ 32,400	$ 36,450

Note: The 2004 figures represent the balances currently on Fusion's balance sheet.

a. Calculate the cash flows generated by Fusion as a stand-alone entity in each year from 2005 to 2009.

b. Assume that by 2009, Fusion reaches a "steady state," which means that its cash flows will grow by 5 percent per year in perpetuity. If Fusion discounts cash flows at 15 percent, what is the present value as of the end of 2009 of all cash flows that Fusion will generate from 2010 forward?

c. Calculate the present value as of 2004 of Fusion's cash flows from 2005 forward. What does this *NPV* represent?

d. Suppose that TGI acquires Fusion. Recalculate Fusion's cash flows from 2005 to 2009, making all the changes previously described in items 1–4 and 6.

e. Assume that after 2009 Fusion's cash flows will grow at a steady 5 percent per year. Calculate the present value of these cash flows as of 2009 if the discount rate is 15 percent.

f. Ignoring item 5 in the list of changes, what is the *PV* as of 2004 of Fusion's cash flows from 2005 forward? Use a discount rate of 15 percent.

g. Finally, calculate the *NPV* of TGI's investment to integrate its technology with Fusion's. Considering this in combination with your answer to part (f), what is the maximum price that TGI can pay for Fusion? Assume a discount rate of 15 percent.

8-16. A project generates the following sequence of cash flows over six years:

Year	Cash Flow ($ in millions)
0	−59.00
1	4.00
2	5.00
3	6.00
4	7.33
5	8.00
6	8.25

a. Calculate the *NPV* over the six years. The discount rate is 11 percent.

b. This project does not end after the sixth year, but instead will generate cash flows far into the future. Estimate the *terminal value*, assuming that cash flows after year 6 will continue at $8.25 million per year in perpetuity, and then recalculate the investment's *NPV*.

c. Calculate the *terminal value*, assuming that cash flows after the sixth year grow at 2 percent annually in perpetuity, and then recalculate the *NPV*.

d. Using market multiples, calculate the *terminal value* by estimating the project's market value at the end of year 6. Specifically, calculate the terminal value under the assumption that at the end of year 6, the project's market value will be 10 times greater than its most recent annual cash flow. Recalculate the *NPV*.

Cash Flows, Discounting, and Inflation

8-17. Sherry Bishop of Thayer Industries is considering investing in a capital project that costs $1.2 million and is expected to generate after-tax operating cash flows of $500,000 in the first year and decline by $100,000 per year until the final year of the project's life in five years. Assume that Thayer's nominal discount rate for this project is 12 percent and the annual inflation rate is 3 percent.

    a. Calculate the project's *NPV*, assuming that cash flows given in the problem are in nominal terms. Would you accept this project?

    b. Calculate the real values of future cash flows.

    c. Recalculate the project's *NPV*, using the real cash flows and the appropriate real discount rate. Does your accept/reject decision change from your decision in part (a)?

8-18. A certain investment will require an immediate cash outflow of $4 million. At the end of each of the next four years, the investment will generate cash inflows of $1.25 million.

    a. Assuming that these cash flows are in nominal terms and the nominal discount rate is 10.25 percent, calculate the project's *NPV*.

    b. Now assume that the expected rate of inflation is 5 percent per year. Recalculate the project's cash flows in real terms, discount them at the real interest rate, and verify that you obtain the same *NPV*.

8-19. The engineers in the aircraft manufacturing division of a diversified conglomerate want the firm to fund a certain investment proposal. The investment will require an initial outlay of $75 million and will generate the following net cash inflows over five years:

Smart Solutions
See the problem and solution explained step-by-step at SMARTFinance

Year	Cash Inflow ($ in millions)
1	10
2	20
3	20
4	30
5	40

This project will compete for funds with one proposed by the company's consumer products division. The alternative project requires an initial $55 million outlay and will generate the following net cash inflows over five years:

Year	Cash Inflow ($in millions)
1	10
2	12
3	14
4	20
5	25

In the airline division, it is common practice to state all project cash flows in nominal terms, whereas in the consumer products division, all cash flows are stated in real terms. The expected rate of inflation is 5 percent, and the required real rate of return on investments in both divisions is 8 percent. Which project should the firm accept if it can accept only one?

Problems in Capital Budgeting

8-20. Semper Mortgage wishes to select the best of three possible computers, each expected to meet the firm's growing need for computational and storage capacity. The three computers—A, B, and C—are equally risky. The firm plans to use a 12 percent cost of capital to evaluate each of them. The initial outlay and annual cash flows over the life of each computer are shown in the following table.

Initial Outlay (CF₀)	Computer A $50,000	Computer B $35,000	Computer C $60,000
Year (t)		Cash Inflows (CFₜ)	
1	$7,000	$ 5,500	$18,000
2	7,000	12,000	18,000
3	7,000	16,000	18,000
4	7,000	23,000	18,000
5	7,000	—	18,000
6	7,000	—	—

a. Calculate the *NPV* for each computer over its life. Rank the computers in descending order based on *NPV*.

b. Use the *equivalent annual cost (EAC)* approach to evaluate and rank the computers in descending order based on the EAC.

c. Compare and contrast your findings in parts (a) and (b). Which computer would you recommend that the firm acquire? Why?

8-21. Seattle Manufacturing is considering the purchase of one of three mutually exclusive projects for improving its assembly line. The firm plans to use a 14 percent cost of capital to evaluate these equal-risk projects. The initial outlay and annual cash flows over the life of each project are shown in the following table.

Initial Outlay (CF₀)	Project X $156,000	Project Y $104,000	Project Z $132,000
Year (t)		Cash Inflows (CFₜ)	
1	$34,000	$56,000	$30,000
2	50,000	56,000	30,000
3	66,000	—	30,000
4	82,000	—	30,000
5	—	—	30,000
6	—	—	30,000
7	—	—	30,000
8	—	—	30,000

a. Calculate the *NPV* for each project over its life. Rank the projects in descending order based on *NPV*.

b. Use the *equivalent annual cost (EAC)* approach to evaluate and rank the projects in descending order based on the EAC.

c. Compare and contrast your findings in parts (a) and (b). Which project would you recommend that the firm purchase? Why?

8-22. As part of a hotel renovation program, a company must choose between two grades of carpet to install. One grade costs $22 per square yard, and the other, $28. The costs of cleaning and maintaining the carpets are identical, but the less expensive carpet must be replaced after six years, whereas the more expensive one will last nine years before it must be replaced. Which grade should the company choose? The relevant discount rate is 13 percent.

8-23. Gail Dribble is a financial analyst at Hill Propane Distributors. Gail must provide a financial analysis of the decision to replace a truck used to deliver propane gas to residential customers. Given its age, the truck will require increasing maintenance expenditures if the company keeps it in service. Similarly, the market value of the truck declines as it ages. The current market value of the truck, as well as the market value and required maintenance expenditures for each of the next four years appears below.

Year	Market Value	Maintenance Cost
Current	$7,000	$ 0
1	5,500	2,500
2	3,700	3,600
3	0	4,500
4	0	7,500

The company can purchase a new truck for $40,000. The truck will last 15 years and will require end-of-year maintenance expenditures of $1,500. At the end of 15 years, the new truck's salvage value will be $3,500.

a. Calculate the *equivalent annual cost (EAC)* of the new truck. Use a discount rate of
9 percent.

b. Suppose that the firm keeps the old truck one more year and sells it then rather than sells it now. What is the opportunity cost associated with this decision? What is the present value of the cost of this decision as of today? Restate this cost in terms of year-1 dollars.

c. Based on your answers to (a) and (b), is it optimal for the company to replace the old truck immediately?

d. Suppose that the firm decides to keep the truck for another year. Next, Gail must analyze whether replacing the old truck after one year makes sense or whether the truck should stay in use another year. As of the end of year 1, what is the present value of the cost of using the truck and selling it at the end of year 2? Restate this answer in year-2 dollars. Should the firm replace the truck after two years?

e. Suppose that the firm keeps the old truck in service for two years. Should it replace it rather than keep it in service for the third year?

8-24. A firm that manufactures and sells ball bearings currently has excess capacity. The firm expects that it will exhaust its excess capacity in three years, at which time it will spend $5 million, which represents the cost of equipment as well as the value of depreciation tax shields on that equipment, to build new capacity. Suppose that this firm can accept additional manufacturing work as a subcontractor for another company. By doing so, the firm will receive net cash inflows of $250,000 immediately and in each of the next two years. However, the firm will also have to spend $5 million two years earlier than originally planned to bring new capacity on line. Should the firm take on the subcontracting job? The discount rate is 12 percent. What is the minimum cash inflow that the firm would require (per year) to accept this job?

9

Risk and Capital Budgeting

OPENING FOCUS
Flat Panel Manufacturer Falls Flat

Without a doubt, NXT PLC, a U.K. firm specializing in audio and speech technologies, can boast of major technological breakthroughs that may change the way consumers interact with media. NXT's SoundVu technology is an excellent example. SoundVu enables the production of completely transparent, ultrathin audio speakers that, in principle, can be used in a wide array of products, such as televisions, cell phones, and handheld computer devices. Like most high-tech firms, NXT has seen its share of ups and downs in the stock market. From 1994, when the company first acquired its exclusive license to a flat panel loudspeaker technology, until mid-1998, NXT shares substantially outperformed London's FTSE 250 stock index, but since then the ride has been a rocky one. The company saw its stock price fall by more than 70 percent in the fall of 1998, reach new heights the next winter, and fall to a new low during the summer of 2001.

Therefore, it could not have been good news when, on September 29, 2001, Merrill Lynch decided to downgrade its rating of NXT stock from "buy" to "accumulate." The stock fell almost 10 percent on that announcement, completing a precipitous drop of more than 70 percent in just one month. Merrill Lynch cited NXT's higher weighted average cost of capital, among other factors, as an explanation for its decision to lower estimates of the company's intermediate-term value.

The weighted average cost of capital plays a central role in many capital budgeting decisions. For many types of investments, the weighted average cost of capital is the discount rate that firms should use when calculating project *NPV*s. Holding constant a project's cash flows, a higher weighted average cost of capital implies a lower *NPV*. Putting this in practical terms, if Merrill Lynch and others believed that NXT faced a higher cost of capital in the fall of 2001 than they had previously thought, then they would place a lower

SMARTFinance
Use the learning tools at http://smartfinance.swcollege.com

value on NXT's existing assets, as well as any future investments that might be available to NXT.

Source: "Stockwatch—NXT Weak; Broker Merrill Lynch Cuts Rating as FY Disappoints," *AFX News Limited,* http://afxpress.com (September 28, 2001).

This chapter concludes our coverage of capital budgeting. Chapter 7 preached the virtues of *NPV* analysis, and Chapter 8 showed how to generate the cash flow estimates required to calculate a project's *NPV*. This chapter focuses on the risk dimension of project analysis. To calculate an *NPV*, an analyst must evaluate the risk of a project and decide what discount rate adequately reflects the opportunity costs of investors who are willing to invest in the project. In many cases, the best place to discover clues for solving this problem is the market for the firm's securities. The chapter begins with a discussion of how managers can look to the market to calculate a discount rate that properly reflects the risk of firms' investment projects. Even when managers are confident that they have estimated project cash flows carefully and chosen a proper discount rate, they want to perform additional analysis to understand the sources of a project's risk. Such tools include break-even analysis, sensitivity analysis, simulation, and decision trees, all covered in the middle part of this chapter. The chapter concludes with two sections—one on real options and the other on strategy —that describe the sources of value in investment projects and illustrate how *NPV* analysis can sometimes understate the value of certain kinds of investments.

9.1 CHOOSING THE RIGHT DISCOUNT RATE

COST OF EQUITY

What discount rate should managers use to calculate a project's *NPV*? This is a very difficult question indeed, undoubtedly the source of heated discussions when firms evaluate capital investment proposals. Conceptually, when a firm establishes a project's discount rate, the rate should reflect the opportunity costs of investors who can choose to invest either in the firm's project or in similar projects undertaken by other firms. This is a rather roundabout way of saying that a project's discount rate must be high enough to compensate investors for the project's risk. One implication of this statement is that if a firm undertakes many different kinds of investment projects, each of which may have a different degree of risk, managers err if they apply a single, firmwide discount rate to each investment. In principle, the appropriate discount rate to use in *NPV* calculations can vary from one investment to another as long as risks vary across investments.

To simplify things a little, we consider a firm that finances its operations using only equity and invests in only one industry. Because the firm has no debt, its investments must provide returns sufficient to satisfy just one type of investor, common stockholders. Because the firm invests in only one industry, we may assume that all its investments are *equally risky*. Therefore, when calculating the *NPV* of any project that this firm might make, its managers can use the required return on equity, often called the *cost of equity*, as the discount rate. If the firm uses the cost of equity as its discount rate, by definition, any project with a positive *NPV* will generate returns that exceed shareholders' required returns.

To quantify shareholders' expectations, managers must look to the market. Recall from Chapter 6 that according to the CAPM, the expected or required return on any security equals the risk-free rate plus the security's beta times the expected market risk premium:

$$E(R_i) = R_f + \beta_i[E(R_m) - R_f]$$ (Eq. 9.1)

Managers can estimate the return that shareholders require if they know (1) their firm's stock beta, (2) the risk-free rate, and (3) the expected market risk premium. Graham and Harvey (2001) show that managers actually do use the CAPM to compute their firm's cost of equity this way.

APPLYING THE MODEL

Carbonlite Inc. manufactures bicycle frames that are both extremely strong and very light. Carbonlite, which finances its operations 100 percent with equity, is evaluating a proposal to build a new manufacturing facility that will enable the firm to double its frame output within three years. Because Carbonlite sells a luxury good, its fortunes are very sensitive to macroeconomic conditions, and its stock has a beta of 1.5. Carbonlite's financial managers observe that the current interest rate on risk-free government bonds is 5 percent, and they believe that the expected return on the overall stock market will be about 11 percent per year in the future. Given this information, Carbonlite should calculate the NPV of the expansion proposal using a discount rate of 14 percent:

$$E(R) = 5\% + 1.5(11\% - 5\%)$$
$$= 14\%$$

To reiterate, Carbonlite can use its cost of equity capital, 14 percent, to discount cash flows because we have assumed both that the company has no debt on its balance sheet and that undertaking any of Carbonlite's investment proposals will not alter the firm's risk. If either assumption is invalid, then the cost of equity is not the appropriate discount rate.   ■

In the preceding example, Carbonlite's stock beta is 1.5 because sales of premium bicycle frames are highly correlated with the state of the economy. Carbonlite's investment in new capacity is therefore riskier than an investment in new capacity by a firm that produces a product with sales that are relatively insensitive to economic conditions. For example, managers of a food-processing company might apply a lower discount rate to an expansion project than Carbonlite's managers would because the stock of a food processor would have a lower beta. The general lesson is that the same type of capital investment project (such as capacity expansion, equipment replacement, or new product development) may require different discount rates in different industries. The level of systematic risk varies from one industry to another, and so too should the discount rate used in capital budgeting analysis.

Several other factors affect betas, which in turn affect project discount rates. One of the most important factors is a firm's cost structure, specifically its mix of fixed and variable costs. In general, holding all other factors constant, the greater the im-

portance of fixed costs in a firm's overall cost structure, the more volatile will be its cash flows and the higher will be its stock beta. **Operating leverage** measures the tendency of the volatility of operating cash flows to increase with fixed operating costs. Mathematically, the definition of operating leverage can be expressed as follows:

$$\text{Operating leverage} = \frac{\Delta EBIT}{EBIT} \div \frac{\Delta \text{sales}}{\text{sales}} \qquad \text{(Eq. 9.2)}$$

where *EBIT* means "earnings before interest and taxes" and the symbol Δ means "change in." In accounting, *operating profits* typically equal the firm's *EBIT*. Operating leverage equals the percentage change in earnings before interest and taxes divided by the percentage change in sales. When a small percentage increase (decrease) in sales leads to a large percentage increase (decrease) in *EBIT*, the firm has high operating leverage. The connection between operating leverage and the relative importance of fixed and variable costs is easy to see in the following example.

APPLYING THE MODEL

Carbonlite Inc. uses robotic technology to paint its finished bicycle frames, whereas its main competitor, Fiberspeed Corp., offers customized, hand-painted finishes to its customers. Robots represent a significant fixed cost for Carbonlite, but its variable costs are quite low. Fiberspeed has very low fixed costs, but it has high variable costs due to the time and effort expended painting frames by hand. Both firms sell their bike frames at an average price of $1,000 apiece. Last year each firm made a profit of $1 million on sales of 10,000 bicycle frames, as shown in Table 9.1. Suppose that next year both firms experience a 10 percent increase in sales volume to 11,000 frames, holding constant all the other figures. Carbonlite's fixed costs do not change, and its *EBIT* will increase by $600 ($1,000 price minus $400 variable costs) per additional frame sold. Carbonlite's *EBIT* will increase 60 percent from $1 million to $1.6 million, while Fiberspeed's *EBIT* will grow from $1 million to $1.3 million, an increase of just 30 percent. Because Carbonlite has higher fixed costs and lower variable costs, its profits increase more rapidly in response to a given increase in sales than Fiber-

Item	Carbonlite	Fiberspeed
Fixed cost per year	$5 million	$2 million
Variable cost per bike frame	$400	$700
Sale price per bike frame	$1,000	$1,000
Contribution margin[a] per bike frame	$600	$300
Last year's sales volume	10,000 frames	10,000 frames
EBIT[b]	$1 million	$1 million

Table 9.1
Financial Data for Carbonlite Inc. and Fiberspeed Corp.

[a] *Contribution margin* is the sale price per unit minus the variable cost per unit. In this case:
  Carbonlite: $1,000 − $400 = $600 per bike
  Fiberspeed: $1,000 − $700 = $300 per bike
[b] *EBIT* equals sales volume times the contribution margin minus fixed costs. In this case:
  Carbonlite: (10,000 × $600) − $5,000,000 = $1,000,000
  Fiberspeed: (10,000 × $300) − $2,000,000 = $1,000,000

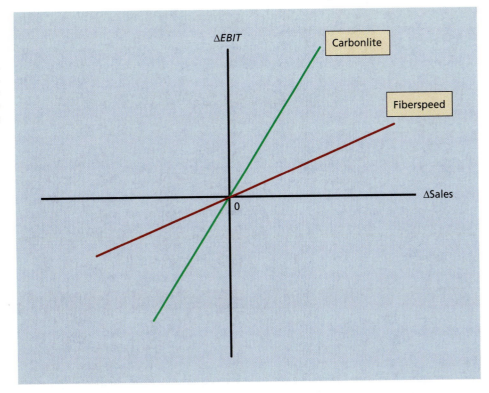

speed's profits do. In short, Carbonlite has more operating leverage. Figure 9.1 shows this graphically. The figure shows two lines, one tracing out the relationship between sales growth (from the base of 10,000 bicycles per year) and *EBIT* growth (from the $1 million *EBIT* base) for Carbonlite, and the other illustrating the same linkage for Fiberspeed.[1] Because of its higher operating leverage, Carbonlite has a much steeper line than Fiberspeed does. Even though Carbonlite and Fiberspeed compete in the same industry, they may use different discount rates in their capital budgeting analysis because operating leverage increases the risk of Carbonlite's cash flows relative to Fiberspeed's.

We have seen that Carbonlite's sales are very sensitive to the business cycle because the firm produces a luxury item. We have also observed that Carbonlite's profits are quite sensitive to sales changes due to high operating leverage. Both of these factors contribute to Carbonlite's relatively high stock beta of 1.5 and its correspondingly high cost of equity of 14 percent. One other factor looms large in determining whether firms have high or low stock betas. Remember that Carbonlite's financial structure is 100 percent equity. In practice, it is much more common to see both debt and equity on the right-hand side of a firm's balance sheet. When firms finance their operations with debt and equity, the presence of debt creates **financial leverage**, which leads to a higher stock beta. The effect of financial leverage on stock betas is much the same as the effect of operating leverage. When a firm borrows money, it creates a fixed cost

[1] These comparisons are based on a reference point of 10,000 bikes per year sold for $1,000 per bike and *EBIT* of $1 million. All changes described and shown in Figure 9.1 assume these points of reference in each case. Clearly, the sensitivity of these values to change will vary depending on the point of reference utilized.

Table 9.2
The Effect of Financial Leverage on Shareholder Returns

Account	Firm A	Firm B
Assets	$100 million	$100 million
Debt	$ 0	$ 50 million
Equity	$100 million	$ 50 million
When Return on Assets Equals 20 Percent		
EBIT	$20 million	$20 million
Less: Interest	0	(.08 × $50 million) = 4 million
Cash to equity	$20 million	$16 million
ROE	$20 million/$100 million = 20%	$16 million/$50 million = 32%
When Return on Assets Equals 5 Percent		
EBIT	$5 million	$5 million
Less: Interest	0	(.08 × $50 million) = 4 million
Cash to equity	$5 million	$1 million
ROE	$5 million/$100 million = 5%	$1 million/$50 million = 2%

that it must repay whether sales are high or low.[2] As was the case with operating leverage, an increase (decrease) in sales will lead to sharper increases (decreases) in earnings for a firm with financial leverage compared to a firm that has only equity on its balance sheet.

Table 9.2 illustrates the effect of financial leverage on the volatility of a firm's cash flows, and hence on its beta. The table compares two firms, A and B, which are identical in every respect except that Firm A finances its operations with 100 percent equity, and Firm B uses 50 percent long-term debt with an interest rate of 8 percent and 50 percent equity. For simplicity, we assume that neither firm pays taxes. Firms A and B sell identical products at the same price, they both have $100 million in assets, and they face the same production costs. Suppose that over the next year both firms generate EBIT equal to 20 percent of total assets, or $20 million. Firm A pays no interest, so it can distribute all $20 million to its shareholders, a 20 percent return on their $100 million investment. Firm B pays 8 percent interest on $50 million for a total interest cost of $4 million. After paying interest, Firm B can distribute $16 million to shareholders, but that represents a 32 percent return on their investment of $50 million. Conversely, suppose that the firm earns EBIT equal to just 5 percent of its assets, or $5 million. Firm A pays out all $5 million to its shareholders, a return of 5 percent. Firm B pays out $4 million in interest, leaving just $1 million for shareholders, a return of only 2 percent. Therefore, in periods when business is very good, shareholders of Firm B earn higher returns than shareholders of Firm A, and the opposite happens when business is bad.

The inclusion of debt as part of a firm's capital structure complicates discount-rate selection in two ways. First, as just shown, debt creates financial leverage, which increases a firm's stock beta relative to the value that it would be if the firm financed

[2.] Note that even if a firm enters a loan agreement with a variable interest rate, the cost of repaying the debt does not generally vary with sales. In that sense, even a loan with a variable interest rate creates a fixed expense with respect to sales.

investments only with equity. Second, when a firm issues debt, it must satisfy two groups of investors rather than one. Cash flows generated from capital investment projects must be sufficient to meet the return requirements of both bondholders and stockholders. Therefore, a firm that issues debt cannot discount project cash flows using only its cost of equity capital. It must choose a discount rate that reflects the expectations of both investor groups. Fortunately, finance theory offers a way to find that discount rate.

WEIGHTED AVERAGE COST OF CAPITAL (*WACC*)

In Chapter 5, we learned that the expected return on a portfolio of two assets equaled the weighted average of the expected returns of each asset in the portfolio. We can apply that idea to the problem of selecting an appropriate discount rate for a firm that has both debt and equity in its capital structure. Imagine that Lox-in-a-Box Inc., a chain of kosher fast-food stores, has outstanding $100 million worth of common stock on which investors require a return of 15 percent. In addition, the firm has outstanding $50 million in bonds that offer a 9 percent return.[3] What rate of return must the firm earn on its investments to satisfy both groups of investors?

The answer lies in a concept known as the **weighted average cost of capital** (**WACC**). Let the letters D and E represent the *market value* of the firm's debt and equity securities, respectively, and let r_d and r_e represent the rate of return that investors require on bonds and shares. The *WACC* is the simple weighted average of the required rates of return on debt and equity, where the weights equal the percentage of each type of financing in the firm's overall capital structure.[4]

$$WACC = \left(\frac{D}{D + E} \right) r_d + \left(\frac{E}{D + E} \right) r_e \qquad \text{(Eq. 9.3)}$$

Plugging in the values from our example, we find that the *WACC* for Lox-in-a-Box equals 13 percent:

$$WACC = \left(\frac{\$50}{\$50 + \$100} \right) \times 9\% + \left(\frac{\$100}{\$50 + \$100} \right) \times 15\% = 13\%$$

How can Lox-in-a-Box managers be sure that a 13 percent return on its investments will satisfy the expectations of both bondholders and shareholders? There are two ways to see the answer. First, imagine that a wealthy investor decides to purchase all the outstanding debt and equity securities of Lox-in-a-Box. Two-thirds of the investor's portfolio would consist of Lox-in-a-Box stock, with an expected return of 15 percent, and one-third of the portfolio would contain the firm's bonds, with an ex-

---

[3.] The return we have in mind here is the yield to maturity (*YTM*) on the firm's bonds. Unless the bonds sell at par, the coupon rate and the *YTM* will be different, but the *YTM* provides a better measure of the return that investors who purchase the firm's debt can expect. If the probability that the firm will default on its debt is nontrivial, then the *YTM* actually overstates the expected return on the firm's bonds. For now, we will keep things simple by assuming that the likelihood of default is very low, so the *YTM* provides a close approximation to the expected return on debt.

[4.] As a practical matter, firms in many countries can deduct interest payments to bondholders when they calculate taxable income. If a firm's interest payments are tax deductible, and if the corporate tax rate equals T_c, we have the following:

$$WACC = \left(\frac{D}{D + E} \right)(1 - T_c) r_d + \left(\frac{E}{D + E} \right) r_e$$

We will address this important adjustment later in this chapter after we have fully developed the key concepts.

Table 9.3
Cash Distributions to
Lox-in-a-Box Investors

Total cash flow available to distribute (13% × $150 million)	$19.5 million
Less: Interest owed on bonds (9% × $50 million)	4.5 million
Cash available to shareholders ($19.5 million − $4.5 million)	$15.0 million
Rate of return earned by shareholders ($15 million ÷ $100 million)	15 %

pected return of 9 percent. Relying on the portfolio theory concepts covered in Chapter 5, we can conclude that expected return on this wealthy investor's portfolio would be 13 percent. If the firm invests only in those projects that have positive NPVs, projects offering returns in excess of 13 percent, it will generate returns that exceed the investor's expectations.

Here's a second way to verify that the $WACC$ is the proper hurdle rate for Lox-in-a-Box. Suppose that the company invests in a project that earns exactly 13 percent and therefore has a zero NPV if the company uses the $WACC$ as its hurdle rate. Lox-in-a-Box has $150 million in assets. A project that offers a 13 percent return will generate $19.5 million in cash flow each year (13% × $150 million). Suppose that the company distributes this cash flow to its investors. Will they be satisfied? Table 9.3 illustrates that the cash flow the company generates is just enough to meet the expectations of bondholders and stockholders. Bondholders receive $4.5 million, or exactly the 9 percent return they expected when they purchased bonds. Shareholders receive $15 million, representing a 15 percent return on their $100 million investment in the firm's shares.

The $WACC$ is a figure of critical importance to almost all firms. Firms that use the $WACC$ to value real investments know that a higher $WACC$ means that investments have to pass a higher hurdle before they generate shareholder wealth. If an event beyond the firm's control increases the firm's $WACC$, both its existing assets and its prospective investment opportunities become less valuable. The Comparative Corporate Finance insert borrows from a PricewaterhouseCoopers consulting report to demonstrate the importance of the $WACC$ to managers around the world.

Firms can modify the $WACC$ formula to accommodate more than two sources of financing. For instance, suppose that a firm raises money by issuing equity, E, long-term debt, D, and preferred stock, P. Denoting the required return on each security with r_e, r_d, and r_p, we can determine the following $WACC$ for this firm (still ignoring taxes):

$$WACC = \left(\frac{E}{E + D + P}\right)r_e + \left(\frac{D}{E + D + P}\right)r_d + \left(\frac{P}{E + D + P}\right)r_p$$

APPLYING THE MODEL

The S. D. Williams Company has 1 million shares of common stock outstanding, which currently trade at a price of $50 per share. The company believes that its stockholders require a 15 percent return on their investment. The company also has $47.1 million (par value) in 5-year, fixed-rate notes with a coupon rate of 8 percent and a yield to maturity of 7 percent. Because the yield on these bonds is less than the coupon rate, they trade at a premium. The current market value of the 5-year notes is $49 million. Finally, the company has 200,000 outstanding preferred shares, which pay an $8 annual dividend and currently trade for $80 per share. What is the company's $WACC$? Begin by calculating the market value of each security. S. D. Williams

COMPARATIVE CORPORATE FINANCE

The Cost of Capital in India

In December 1999, PricewaterhouseCoopers (PwC) conducted a survey of leaders in the business and financial communities in India to determine the forces that influenced the cost of capital in India. Some of the study's more interesting findings included the following:

- When asked to rank the importance of cost of capital and six other factors from most to least important in determining corporate value, managers of Indian firms ranked cost of capital first, ahead of other factors such as sales growth, working capital efficiency, and corporate taxes (see chart below).
- Firms in India used the CAPM more frequently than any other method to determine their cost of equity.
- The most common approach to estimate the CAPM beta was to use data from weekly stock returns over a period of three years.
- Almost all respondents reported using the yield on 10-year government bonds to proxy for the CAPM's

risk-free rate. In 1999, this rate was almost 11 percent, roughly twice as high as seen in Western industrialized economies at the time.

- Estimates of the cost of equity capital in India average about 20 percent.
- Inflation expectations in India provided a partial explanation for the high cost of capital in that country. In late 1999, Indian managers expected future inflation to be in the 5–7 percent range.
- During the 1990s, firms in India reduced their reliance on debt and increased their reliance on equity.
- In 1999, the average Indian firm's capital structure consisted of approximately 40 percent debt and 60 percent equity.
- The WACC for Indian companies falls in the 15–20 percent range, and the average WACC for U.S. firms falls in the 8–12 percent range.

Ranking of Important Value Drivers by Managers in Several Countries
(1 corresponds to the highest level of importance, 7 to the lowest level)

Factor	India	Hong Kong	U.K.	Australia
Profit margin	1	1	1	1
WACC	1	3	2	2
Sales growth	4	2	2	3
Fixed capital efficiency	1	4	4	4
Working capital efficiency	6	4	4	4
Corporate tax rate	7	7	6	7
Time period until positive returns	5	6	7	5

has $50 million in common stock, $49 million in long-term debt, and $16 million in preferred stock, for a total capitalization of $115 million. Next, determine the required rate of return on each type of security. The rates on common stock, long-term debt, and preferred stock are 15 percent, 7 percent, and 10 percent, respectively. Plug all these values into the WACC equation to obtain 10.9 percent:

$$WACC = \left(\frac{\$50}{\$115}\right)0.15 + \left(\frac{\$49}{\$115}\right)0.07 + \left(\frac{\$16}{\$115}\right)0.10 = 0.109 = 10.9\%$$

Now we have seen two approaches for determining the correct discount rate to apply to capital budgeting problems. An all-equity firm should discount project cash flows using the cost of equity, and a firm that uses both debt and equity (common and possibly preferred stock) should discount cash flows using the WACC. Both recom-

mendations are subject to the important proviso that the firm makes investments in only one line of business, or stated differently, that the firm discounts cash flows using the *WACC* only when the project under consideration is very similar to the firm's existing assets. For example, if managers at Lox-in-a-Box believe that the firm should vertically integrate by investing in a salmon-fishing fleet, they should not discount cash flows from that investment at the firm's *WACC*. The risks of salmon fishing hardly resemble those of running a fast-food chain, and it is the latter that are reflected in the firm's *WACC*. Evaluating investments that deviate significantly from a firm's existing investments requires a different approach. To understand this approach, we need to revisit the CAPM to see how it is related to the *WACC*.

Connecting the *WACC* to the CAPM

The CAPM states that the required return on any asset is directly linked to the asset's beta. By now we are used to thinking about betas of shares of common stock, but there is nothing about the CAPM that restricts its predictions to shares. When a firm issues bonds or preferred stock, the required returns on those securities should reflect their systematic risks (i.e., their betas) just as the required returns on the firm's common shares do. Because both preferred stock and bonds generally make fixed, predictable cash payments over time, measuring the rate of return that investors require on these securities is relatively easy, even without knowing their betas. For preferred stock, the dividend yield (dividend ÷ price) provides a good measure of required returns, and for debt, the yield to maturity does the same. However, this does not rule out the possibility that we could estimate the beta of a share of preferred stock or of a bond. Calculating the beta of a preferred share or a bond is no different than calculating the beta of common stock—just estimate the covariance between returns on the security of interest and returns on the market and divide by the variance of the market's returns.

Remember, though, that returns on preferred shares and bonds are generally not as sensitive to the market's up-and-down movements as returns on common stocks are. This implies that the beta on a firm's bonds, for example, will be low relative to the beta of its shares. A lower beta translates into a lower expected return, but that is exactly what we should expect. Bonds, because they are less risky than stocks, offer lower expected returns.

APPLYING THE MODEL

Suppose that an analyst gathers monthly returns on the bonds of a large corporation. Because interest rates and bond prices fluctuate from month to month, bond returns fluctuate too. The analyst calculates the covariance between returns on the bonds and returns on a diversified portfolio of securities, then divides by the variance of returns on the portfolio to obtain an estimate of the bond's beta. The number obtained is 0.1. Assuming that the risk-free rate of interest equals 5 percent and the expected return on the market portfolio equals 15 percent, the analyst estimates the required return on the bonds using the CAPM equation:

$$r_d = 5\% + 0.1 \times (15\% - 5\%) = 6\%$$

The number 0.1 equals the **debt beta.** Not surprisingly, the debt beta is very close to zero because the bond's returns are not highly correlated with the market portfolio. Of course, there is another way to estimate the debt beta. Suppose that the analyst observes that a firm's bonds offer a yield to maturity of 6 percent. Making the same assumptions as before about the risk-free rate (5%) and the expected return on the market (15%), the analyst could estimate the debt beta indirectly by solving this equation:

$$6\% = 5\% + \beta_d(15\% - 5\%)$$

$$\beta_d = 0.1$$

The preceding example illustrates that applying the concept of beta to a bond, a share of preferred stock, or any other asset is no different from applying it to common stock. *Any asset that generates cash flows has a beta, and that beta establishes the required return on the asset through the CAPM.* This allows us to establish a link between the CAPM and the WACC as follows. Recall that the WACC represents the rate of return that a company must earn on its investments to satisfy both bondholders and stockholders:

$$WACC = \left(\frac{D}{D + E}\right)r_d + \left(\frac{E}{D + E}\right)r_e$$

However, the CAPM establishes a direct link between required rates of return on debt and equity and the betas of these securities. That connection leads to the following relationship for the asset's beta, β_A:

$$\beta_A = \left(\frac{D}{D + E}\right)\beta_d + \left(\frac{E}{D + E}\right)\beta_e \qquad \text{(Eq. 9.4)}$$

Equation 9.4 states that the beta of a firm's assets equals the weighted average of the firm's debt and equity betas.[5] What is an **asset beta?** It is simply a measure of the systematic risk of a real asset, or the covariance of the cash flows generated by that asset divided by the variance of cash flows from the market portfolio. Suppose that a company owns a factory that it uses to produce tires. The cash flows of this operation will vary due to changes in the business cycle and other factors. The factory's asset beta measures the systematic risk of the cash flow stream generated by the factory.

The asset beta on the left-hand side of Equation 9.4 represents a measure of the risk of a physical asset. The terms on the right-hand side illustrate how the risk of the asset is allocated between debt and equity investors. For instance, suppose that a firm has manufacturing assets with a beta of 1.0. If the firm is financed entirely with equity, then we have the following:

$$\beta_A = 1.0 = \left(\frac{\$0}{\$0 + E}\right)\beta_d + \left(\frac{E}{\$0 + E}\right)\beta_E = \beta_E$$

---

[5] Again, we are just applying a basic concept from portfolio theory. If an investor holds a portfolio of two securities, then the beta of the portfolio equals the weighted average of the betas of the securities in the portfolio. Hamada (1972) was the first to rigorously demonstrate how equity betas could be converted into asset betas, and vice versa.

When there are no bondholders, shareholders bear all the risk associated with the firm's assets, so the asset beta and the equity beta both equal 1.0. However, suppose that the same firm decides to raise 20 percent of its money by issuing relatively safe bonds with a beta of 0.1. The assets of this firm have not changed, so the asset beta still equals 1.0. The firm's bonds are substantially less risky than the firm's assets, and equity holders must therefore bear all the residual risk. Using the previous equation and substituting 0.1 for the debt beta and 0.2 and 0.8 for the fractions of debt and equity financing, respectively, we find the following:

$$\beta_A = 1.0 = (0.2)(0.1) + (0.8)\beta_E$$
$$\beta_E = \frac{1.0 - (0.2)(0.1)}{0.8} = 1.225$$

Compared to the all-equity firm, the firm with 20 percent debt has a much higher equity beta. That is exactly what we should have expected given our previous discussion of the effects of financial leverage on equity betas. There is a kind of "law of conservation of risk" at work here. The fundamental risk of a firm depends on the risk of the assets in which it chooses to invest. This is what the asset beta captures. The firm can allocate that risk between different types of investors any way that it sees fit. If a firm chooses to offer investors a security such as a bond that has relatively low risk, it does not change the fact that the firm's underlying assets are still risky. If bondholders are not bearing this risk, then that task must fall to shareholders. The more promises a firm makes to provide investors with a "safe" return (i.e., the more debt it issues), the greater the uncertainty surrounding the returns that the firm will be able to provide to shareholders.

It is easy to see the effect of leverage on equity betas if we make the assumption that the debt beta equals zero. Given that assumption, rearranging terms in Equation 9.4 yields the following:

$$\beta_E = \beta_A\left(1 + \frac{D}{E}\right) \qquad \text{(Eq. 9.5)}$$

Once again, we can see in this equation that if the firm has zero debt, the asset beta equals the equity beta. For firms that use debt, the term $\left(1 + \dfrac{D}{E}\right)$ will be greater than 1.0, which in turn means that $\beta_E > \beta_A$. Holding the asset beta, the risk of the firm's assets, constant, the more money the firm raises by issuing debt, the greater its financial leverage and the higher its equity beta.

After such a long digression on linkages between the WACC and the CAPM, it is worthwhile to stop and recall our original objective—to find the right discount rate for capital budgeting projects. When a new project is very similar to a firm's existing projects, managers should discount cash flows using the WACC. However, the WACC does not apply when a firm is considering a project outside its normal line of business or when a firm has many different lines of business under one corporate umbrella. In the latter case, the WACC represents the required rate of return on the firm's "average" investment, but some divisions of a company may be inherently riskier than others. Applying the WACC to all projects will tend to overstate the NPVs of projects that are more risky than average and understate the NPVs of projects that are less risky than average. Managers can solve this problem by focusing their attention on the asset betas of specific projects, sometimes called **project betas.**

ASSET BETAS AND PROJECT DISCOUNT RATES

General Electric Corp. (ticker symbol, GE) is a diversified conglomerate with significant investments in industries as wide ranging as lighting, aircraft engine manufacturing, broadcasting, and financial services. Suppose that GE's WACC equals 13 percent. When GE evaluates a proposal to replace existing equipment in its aircraft engine division, it should not necessarily calculate the NPV using a 13 percent discount rate, because engine manufacturing may be more or less risky than the average GE investment. The WACC tells GE that on average it must earn 13 percent across all its investments to keep its investors happy, but GE should discount its most risky investments at rates above 13 percent and its least risky investments at lower rates. Similarly, if GE decides to invest in a brand-new line of business, it should not use its WACC as the hurdle rate for that investment. Instead, for every investment that it makes, GE must assess the underlying risk of the investment and establish a discount rate appropriate for that risk level. To do this, GE should measure the asset betas of different investments.

As an example, suppose that GE decides to diversify into oil and gas production. How can GE managers determine an appropriate rate with which to discount cash flows from new investments in this industry? The answer is that GE's managers should look to the market. By looking at characteristics of existing oil and gas firms whose securities trade in the market, GE analysts can gain considerable insight into the risks and required returns in this industry.

As a starting point, GE managers should look for firms that compete in just one industry—oil and gas production. A firm that competes in a single line of business is called a **pure play,** so GE wants to find pure play firms in the oil and gas business. Two such firms are Berry Petroleum Co. (ticker symbol, BRY) and Forest Oil Corp. (ticker symbol, FST). Table 9.4 lists several characteristics of these two firms (as of March 2002) that should be of interest to analysts at GE. Note that even though both companies produce oil and gas, the equity beta of Forest Oil (0.90) is almost 40 percent higher than the equity beta of Berry Petroleum (0.65). If both of these firms operate in the same industry, why are their stock betas so different? One possibility is that the companies use different production technologies with different degrees of operating leverage. Another is that the companies make different financing decisions, with one firm using more debt than the other. Indeed, Table 9.4 shows that Forest obtains 39 percent of its financing from debt and Berry borrows just 14 percent of the money it needs to do business. Even if the underlying risks of the two firms are identical—that is, even if their asset betas are equal—Forest's greater use of financial leverage will result in a higher stock beta. Besides, GE is not interested in the risk of Berry Petroleum and Forest Oil shares, because the investment GE plans to make is

Table 9.4
Data for Berry Petroleum
and Forest Oil[a]

	Berry Petroleum	Forest Oil
Stock beta	0.65	0.90
Debt (D) proportion	0.14	0.39
Equity (E) proportion	0.86	0.61
D/E ratio	0.16	0.64
Asset beta[b]	0.56	0.55

[a]Data taken from Value Line Investment Survey.
[b]Using Equation 9.4 and assuming debt beta = 0.00.

not a purchase of oil and gas stocks. Rather, GE plans to invest in assets required to produce oil and gas, so GE managers need to know the asset beta for this industry.

We will make two assumptions to simplify this example. First, we will assume that the debt of both companies has very little risk, so their debt betas equal zero. Second, we will ignore taxes for now. Given the information in the table, we can use Equation 9.4 to calculate the asset betas, β_A, for each firm:

For Berry Petroleum: $\beta_A = (0.14)(0) + (0.86)(0.65) = 0.56$

For Forest Oil: $\beta_A = (0.39)(0) + (0.61)(0.90) = 0.55$

The calculations show that despite the rather large differences in equity betas between the two companies, Berry and Forest have nearly identical asset betas. That should not be too surprising because they make very similar investments with similar risks and rewards. The differences in the equity betas apparently are driven by differences in leverage between these two firms. The asset beta calculations for these firms take away the effects of leverage to reveal striking similarities in the firms' underlying risks. When we remove the effects of leverage on an equity beta in this way, we are calculating a figure that analysts sometimes refer to as an **unlevered equity beta.** Therefore, *when a firm uses no leverage, its equity beta equals its asset beta,* so an unlevered beta simply tells us how risky the equity of a company might be if it used no leverage at all.[6]

An analyst at GE might calculate asset betas for many other firms in this industry, starting with each firm's equity beta and unlevering it if necessary. Next, the analyst might take an average across all those firms to arrive at a final asset beta estimate. This is a measure of the risk of the assets in which GE plans to invest. The next step is to incorporate GE's own capital structure into the analysis by "relevering" the asset beta. In other words, once GE estimates the oil and gas asset beta, it must adjust this beta upward if GE's capital structure contains both debt and equity. With this "relevered beta" in hand, the analyst calculates the appropriate project discount rate using the CAPM.

APPLYING THE MODEL

To determine the appropriate discount rate for a proposed investment in oil and gas production, a financial manager at GE calculates asset betas for several pure play firms in the industry and averages them to arrive at an industry asset beta of 0.55. Next, the analyst recognizes that GE's capital structure consists of 20 percent debt and 80 percent equity (implying a debt/equity ratio of 0.25) and determines the following relevered project beta:

$$\beta_{GE} = \beta_A\left(1 + \frac{D}{E}\right) = 0.55(1 + 0.25) = 0.69$$

---

[6] In mid-1996, Conrail was the target of takeover bids from two rivals, Norfolk Southern and CSX. For an extended illustration of how the investment bank Lazard Frères & Co. used the concepts of levered and unlevered betas to calculate the *WACC* in its valuation of Conrail, see Thompson (2000).

Suppose that the risk-free rate of interest equals 6 percent and the expected risk premium on the market equals 7 percent. By plugging these figures, as well as the relevered project beta, into the CAPM equation, the analyst obtains the rate of return that a GE shareholder would require on this oil and gas investment—10.83 percent:

$$E(R) = 6\% + 0.69(7\%) = 10.83\%$$

There is still one more necessary step to find the right discount rate for GE's investment in this industry. The analyst should calculate a project *WACC* (sometimes called a divisional *WACC* in reference to the firm's oil and gas division) using Equation 9.3. For instance, suppose equity makes up 80 percent of GE's financing, with debt accounting for the remaining 20 percent. Suppose also that investors expect a return of 6.5 percent on GE's bonds (just over the risk-free rate). The project *WACC* equals

$$WACC_{project} = 10.83\%(80\%) + 6.5\%(20\%) = 9.96\%$$

We do not want to overstate the precision of this process. Calculating the discount rate requires several steps, each of which involves estimating an uncertain number. If the GE analyst arrives at a figure of 9.96 percent for the oil and gas discount rate, as shown in the preceding Applying the Model example, the report might show that the appropriate discount rate should be "between 9 and 11 percent." There is certainly room to argue around this figure, but notice that it is less than the *WACC* of 13 percent we assumed for GE.

Summarizing the main lessons of this section, we offer the following rules about finding the right discount rate for an investment project:

1. When an all-equity firm invests in an asset similar to its existing assets, the cost of equity is the appropriate discount rate to use in *NPV* calculations.
2. When a firm with both debt and equity invests in an asset similar to its existing assets, the *WACC* is the appropriate discount rate to use in *NPV* calculations.
3. In conglomerates, the *WACC* reflects the return that the firm must earn on average across all its assets to satisfy investors, but using the *WACC* to discount cash flows of a particular investment leads to mistakes. The reason for this is that a particular investment may be more or less risky than the firm's average investment, requiring a higher or lower discount rate than the *WACC*.
4. When a firm invests in an asset that is different from its existing assets, it should look for pure play firms to find the right discount rate. Firms can calculate an industry asset beta by unlevering the betas of pure play firms. Then it must relever the industry asset beta based on the acquiring firm's existing capital structure. Given the relevered industry asset beta, firms can determine an appropriate discount rate using the CAPM.[7]

Nothing in the real world is as simple as it is portrayed in textbooks. One important item that we have neglected thus far is the effect of taxes on project discount rates. In the United States and many other countries, corporations must pay taxes on their earnings, but interest payments to bondholders are tax deductible. The opportunity to deduct interest payments reduces the after-tax cost of debt and changes the *WACC* formula:

[7.] Though this advice is theoretically unimpeachable, Graham and Harvey (2001) document the curious fact that most real managers use the firm's own discount rate for all capital budgeting projects, even for those that are in industries different from the firm's core business.

$$WACC = \left(\frac{D}{D + E}\right)(1 - T_c)r_d + \left(\frac{E}{D + E}\right)r_e \qquad \text{(Eq. 9.6)}$$

where T_c is the marginal corporate tax rate. The equation linking asset and equity betas changes in a similar fashion. Maintaining an earlier assumption that the debt beta equals zero, we can define the relationship between asset betas and equity betas this way:

$$\beta_E = \beta_A\left[1 + (1 - T_c)\frac{D}{E}\right] \qquad \text{(Eq. 9.7)}$$

Fortunately, the four main lessons listed previously do not change when we add taxes to the picture. Only the calculations change. When a firm is making an "ordinary" investment, it can use Equation 9.6 to determine its after-tax *WACC* to serve as the discount rate in *NPV* calculations. Alternatively, when a firm makes an investment in a new line of business, it can use Equation 9.7 to calculate asset betas for pure play firms to arrive at an industry asset beta. As before, once analysts have an industry beta in hand, they simply relever it if necessary to reflect their own firm's capital structure; then they plug the beta into the CAPM to find the right discount rate for the investment.

A NOTE ON THE EQUITY RISK PREMIUM

When managers use the CAPM to determine the discount rate for an investment project, they must know three things: (1) the project or asset beta, (2) the risk-free rate, and (3) the expected risk premium on the market portfolio. In Chapter 6, we demonstrated how to use regression analysis to estimate the beta of a share of stock, and in this chapter we have shown how to use the betas of the firm's securities to estimate its asset beta. Measuring the risk-free rate is a straightforward exercise that involves nothing more complex than obtaining current market rates on government bills or bonds. Now we briefly turn our attention to measuring the expected risk premium on the market portfolio.

Recall that in the CAPM, the market portfolio is a value-weighted combination of all assets in the economy. At present, we are unaware of any market index that attempts to incorporate every type of asset. When using the CAPM, most practitioners and academics use the returns on a broad-based stock index as a proxy for the true market portfolio. Accordingly, rather than try to estimate the expected risk premium on the market portfolio, analysts usually focus on the expected equity risk premium, the difference in expected returns between a portfolio of common stocks and a risk-free asset such as a Treasury bond.

Chapter 5 demonstrated that in the United States and many other countries, average returns on stocks exceed average returns on government bonds over long time periods. During the twentieth century, the average real return on stocks outpaced the average real return on U.S. Treasury bills by 7.7 percent per year. But in the CAPM, what matters is not the actual equity risk premium from the past, but the expected equity risk premium looking forward. Though many analysts trust the historical evidence and simply plug in a figure close to 8 percent for the term $E(R_m - R_f)$, a naive reliance on long-run historical averages may not be the best approach for estimating the expected risk premium. Getting an unbiased estimate is important because an error in the risk premium translates directly into an error in a project's discount rate, and hence its *NPV*.

One variable that analysts can use for a forward-looking estimate of the risk premium is the market's aggregate earnings yield ($E \div P$), or just the reciprocal of the price-to-earnings ratios. For example, to calculate the earnings yield for the S&P 500, just add up the earnings of all 500 companies and divide by the aggregate market value of these firms. Corporate earnings fluctuate with the business cycle, so analysts usually try to smooth out, or normalize, these temporary effects before using the earnings yield to estimate the risk premium. In the United States, the long-run average value of the earnings yield is about 7 percent, not far from the (geometric) average real return on stocks. It should not be surprising that the earnings yield is closely related to the real return on stocks. After all, stocks represent a claim on the earnings of firms. In mid-2002, the normalized earnings yield on U.S. stocks was between 4 and 5 percent. To many experts, this figure signals lower future returns on stocks than the historical record might suggest.

A second forward-looking method for estimating the equity risk premium makes use of the dividend growth model from Chapter 4. Recall that the dividend growth model calculates the present value of a perpetual dividend stream that grows at a constant rate, g:

$$P_0 = \frac{D_1}{r - g}$$

Rearranging this equation a little shows that the required return on the stock equals the sum of the dividend yield and the dividend growth rate:

$$r = \frac{D_1}{P_0} + g$$

To use this model to estimate the equity risk premium, we must think of the equation in aggregate, macroeconomic terms. In other words, r represents the (real) required return on the stock market rather than the required return on a specific stock. The ratio $D_1 \div P_0$ represents the aggregate dividend yield, and g represents the (real) growth rate of aggregate dividends. Fama and French (2002) show that from 1872 to 1950, the expected equity risk premium derived from this model almost exactly matches the actual risk premium measured using average historical returns (a little more than 4 percent), but from 1950 to 2000, the average real return on equities was much higher than the dividend growth model predicted. Fama and French conclude that fundamental indicators such as growth rates in dividends and earnings all point to an expected equity risk premium below the long-run historical average premium.[8]

Perhaps the most direct forward-looking approach is simply to gather forecasts of the equity premium made by experts. Yale economist Ivo Welch did just that by surveying finance and economics professors in 1998 and again in 2001. Welch (2001) reports that the average equity premium forecast declined considerably from 1998 to 2001, a period in which U.S. stocks earned low average returns. In 2001, the average forecast of the 1-year equity premium was 3.4 percent, in contrast to 5.8 percent in the 1998 survey. When Welch asked professors in 2001 for a forecast of the arith-

[8] Ritter (2001) argues that the expected equity risk premium could be as low as 1 percent due to two factors. First, Ritter concurs with Fama and French that real equity returns in the future are likely to be lower than they have been in the past. Second, he observes that the real return on inflation-indexed bonds in the United States has risen. A decline in real equity returns coupled with an increase in real, risk-free returns squeezes the equity risk premium from both ends.

metic average equity premium over the next 30 years, their average prediction was 5.5 percent, in contrast to 7.1 percent in the 1998 survey.[9]

All three forward-looking indicators—the earnings yield, the dividend growth model, and the consensus of academic experts—point toward a future equity risk premium that is lower than the average historical premium.

Concept Review Questions

1. Why is using the cost of equity to discount project cash flows inappropriate when a firm uses both debt and equity in its capital structure?

2. Two firms in the same industry have very different equity betas. Offer two reasons why this could occur.

3. For a firm considering expansion of its existing line of business, why is the *WACC* rather than the cost of equity the preferred discount rate if the firm has both debt and equity in its capital structure?

4. The cost of debt, r_d, is generally less than the cost of equity, r_e, because debt is a less risky security. A naive application of the *WACC* formula might suggest that a firm could lower its cost of capital (thereby raising the *NPV* of its current and future investments) by using more debt and less equity in its capital structure. Give one reason why using more debt might not lower a firm's *WACC* even if $r_d < r_e$.

5. Explain the difference between a levered and an unlevered equity beta.

9.2 A CLOSER LOOK AT RISK

Thus far, the only consideration we have given to risk when doing capital budgeting analysis is selecting the right discount rate. But it would be simplistic to say that, given a set of project cash flows, once an analyst has discounted those cash flows using a risk-adjusted discount rate to determine the *NPV*, the analyst's work is done. Managers generally want to know more about a project than just its *NPV*. They want to know the sources of uncertainty in the project as well as the quantitative importance of each source. Managers need this information to decide whether a project requires additional analysis, such as market research or product testing. Managers also want to identify a project's key value drivers so they can closely monitor these factors after an investment is made. In this section, we explore several techniques that give managers deeper insights into the uncertainty structure of capital investments.

BREAK-EVEN ANALYSIS

When firms make investments, they do so with the objective of making a profit. But another objective that sometimes enters the decision process is avoiding losses. Managers often want to know what is required for a project to break even. **Break-even analysis** can be couched in many different ways. For instance, when a firm introduces a new product, it may want to know the level of sales at which incremental net income

---

[9.] Graham and Harvey (2002) survey chief financial officers and obtain average estimates of the equity risk premium ranging from 3.0 to 4.7 percent.

turns from negative to positive. Evaluating a new product launch over several years, managers might ask what growth rate in sales the firm must achieve to reach a project *NPV* of zero. When considering a decision to replace old production equipment, a firm might calculate the level of production volume needed to generate cost savings equal to the cost of the new equipment.

APPLYING THE MODEL

Take another look at Table 9.1, which shows price and cost information for Carbonlite Inc. and Fiberspeed Corp. How many bicycle frames must each firm sell to achieve a break-even point with *EBIT* equal to zero? We can obtain the answer by dividing fixed costs by the **contribution margin,** sale price per unit minus variable cost per unit:

Carbonlite break-even point = $5,000,000 ÷ ($1,000 − $400) = 8,333 frames

Fiberspeed break-even point = $2,000,000 ÷ ($1,000 − $700) = 6,667 frames

Figure 9.2 illustrates the break-even point (BEP) for each firm. Despite its $600 contribution margin, Carbonlite's high fixed costs result in a break-even point at higher sales volume than Fiberspeed's break-even point. This should not surprise us, as we already know that Carbonlite's production process results in higher operating leverage than Fiberspeed's. ■

The popularity of break-even analysis among practitioners arises in part because it gives managers very clear targets. From break-even calculations, managers can derive specific targets for different functional areas in the firm (e.g., produce at least 10,000 units, gain at least a 5 percent market share, hold variable costs to no more than 65 percent of the selling price). As always, we encourage managers to use break-

Figure 9.2a
Break-Even Point for
Carbonlite

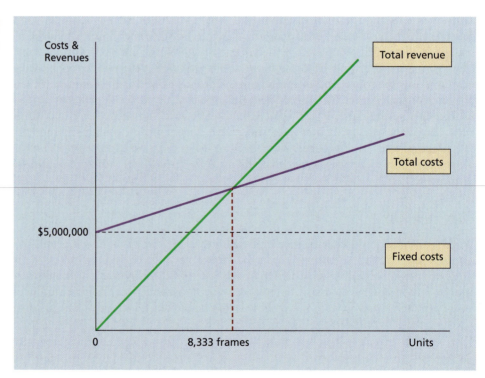

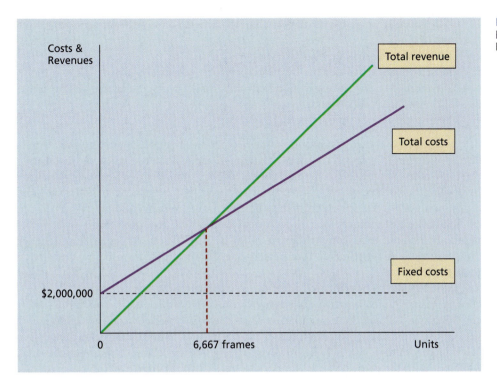

Figure 9.2b
Break-Even Point for Fiberspeed

even analysis in the context of net present values rather than earnings. A project that reaches the break-even point in terms of net income may destroy shareholder value because it does not recover the firm's cost of capital.

SENSITIVITY ANALYSIS

Most capital budgeting problems require analysts to make many different assumptions before arriving at a final *NPV*. For instance, forecasting project cash flows may require assumptions about the selling price of output, costs of raw materials, market share, and many other unknown quantities. In **sensitivity analysis,** managers have a tool that allows them to explore the importance of each individual assumption, holding all other assumptions fixed, on the project's *NPV*. To conduct a sensitivity analysis, firms establish a "base-case" set of assumptions for a particular project and calculate the *NPV* based on those assumptions. Next, managers allow one variable to change while holding all others fixed, and they recalculate the *NPV* based on that change. By repeating this process for all the uncertain variables in an *NPV* calculation, managers can see how sensitive the *NPV* is to changes in baseline assumptions.

Imagine that Greene Transportation Incorporated (GTI) has developed a new skateboard equipped with a gyroscope for improved balance. GTI's estimates indicate that this project has a positive *NPV* of $236,000 under the following base-case assumptions:

1. The project's life is five years.
2. The project requires an up-front investment of $7 million.
3. GTI will depreciate the initial investment on a straight-line basis for five years.
4. One year from now, the skateboard industry will sell 500,000 units.
5. Total industry unit volume will increase by 5 percent per year.
6. GTI expects to capture 5 percent of the market in the first year.

7. GTI expects to increase its market share by one percentage point each year after year 1.
8. The selling price will be $200 in year 1.
9. The selling price will decline by 10 percent per year after year 1.
10. All production costs are variable and will equal 60 percent of the selling price.
11. GTI's tax rate is 30 percent.
12. The appropriate discount rate is 14 percent.

Under the base-case assumptions, the project has a small (relative to the $7 million investment), positive *NPV*, but GTI managers may want to explore how sensitive the *NPV* is to changes in the assumptions. Analysts often begin a sensitivity analysis by developing both pessimistic and optimistic forecasts for each of the model's important assumptions. These forecasts may be based on subjective judgments about the range of possible outcomes, or on historical data drawn from the firm's past investments. For example, a firm with historical data available on output prices might set the pessimistic and optimistic forecasts at one standard deviation below and above their expected price.

Table 9.5 shows pessimistic and optimistic forecasts for several of the *NPV* model's key assumptions. Next to each assumption is the project *NPV* that results from changing one and only one assumption from the base-case scenario. For example, if GTI can sell its product for $225 rather than $200 per unit the first year, the project *NPV* increases to $960,000. If, however, the selling price is less than expected, at $175 per unit, the project *NPV* declines to −$488,000. A glance at Table 9.5 reveals that small deviations in market-share assumptions generate very large *NPV* changes, whereas changes in market-size figures have less impact on *NPV*s.

Table 9.5
Sensitivity Analysis of the Gyroscope Skateboard Project (dollar values in thousands except price)

NPV	Pessimistic	Assumption	Optimistic	NPV
−$558	$8,000	initial investment	$6,000	$1,030
−$343	450,000 units	market size in year 1	550,000 units	$815
−$73	2% per year	growth in market size	8% per year	$563
−$1,512	3%	initial market share	7%	$1,984
−$1,189	0%	growth in market share	2% per year	$1,661
−$488	$175	initial selling price	$225	$960
−$54	62% of sales	variable costs	58% of sales	$526
−$873	−20% per year	annual price change	0% per year	$1,612
−$115	16%	discount rate	12%	$617

SCENARIO ANALYSIS AND MONTE CARLO SIMULATION

Smart Concepts
See the concept explained step-by-step at
SMARTFinance

Scenario analysis is just a more complex variation on sensitivity analysis. Rather than adjust one assumption up or down, analysts conduct scenario analysis by calculating the project *NPV* when a whole set of assumptions changes in a particular way. For example, if consumer interest in GTI's new skateboard is low, the project may achieve a lower market share and a lower selling price than originally anticipated. If production volume falls short of expectations, cost as a percentage of sales may also be higher than expected.

Developing realistic scenarios requires a great deal of thinking about how an *NPV* model's assumptions are related to each other. Analysts must ask questions such as, if the market doesn't grow as fast as we expect, which other of our assumptions will also probably be wrong? As with sensitivity analysis, firms often construct a base-case scenario along with more optimistic and pessimistic ones. For instance, consider a worst-case scenario for GTI's new skateboard. Suppose that Murphy's Law kicks in and every pessimistic assumption from Table 9.5 becomes reality. In that case, the project *NPV* is a disastrous negative $4.9 million. On the other hand, if all the optimistic assumptions turn out to be correct, then the *NPV* rises to $11.7 million. Neither of these outcomes is particularly surprising. If everything goes wrong, the company should expect an extremely negative *NPV*, and it should expect just the opposite if the project does better than predicted in every possible way. These scenarios are still useful in that they illustrate the range of possible *NPV*s.

An even more sophisticated variation on this theme is **Monte Carlo simulation.** In a simulation, analysts specify a range or a distribution of potential outcomes for each of the model's assumptions. For example, a simulation might specify that GTI's skateboard price is a random variable drawn from a normal distribution with a mean of $200 and a standard deviation of $30. Similarly, the analyst could dictate that the skateboard might achieve an initial market share anywhere between 1 percent and 10 percent, with each outcome being equally likely (i.e., a uniform distribution). It is even possible to specify the degree of correlation between key variables. The model could be structured in such a way that when the demand for skateboards is unusually high, the likelihood of obtaining a high price increases.

Analysts enter all the assumptions about distributions of possible outcomes into a spreadsheet. Next, a simulation software package begins to take random "draws" from these distributions, calculating the project's cash flows (and perhaps its *NPV*) over and over again, perhaps thousands or tens of thousands of times. After completing these calculations, the software package produces a large amount of statistical output, including the distribution of project cash flows (and *NPV*s) as well as sensitivity figures for each of the model's assumptions.

The use of Monte Carlo simulation has grown dramatically in the last decade because of steep declines in the costs of computer power and simulation software.[10] Unfortunately, misuse of simulation analysis has grown as well. Perhaps the most common misuse involves the calculation and misinterpretation of a distribution of project *NPV*s. If managers use a computer to generate a distribution of *NPV*s, they should discount cash flows using the risk-free rate. Why not use the cost of capital? Remember that the purpose of discounting cash flows at the cost of capital is to take into account the uncertainty of expected project cash flows. When a simulation package calculates an *NPV*, the cash flows in the numerator represent just one outcome drawn from a large distribution of possible outcomes, not the expected value. Therefore, plotting an entire distribution of *NPV*s and looking at the mean and variance of that distribution is, in a sense, double-counting risk. A better approach is to calculate *NPV*s using the risk-free rate. A distribution of *NPV*s generated by discounting at the risk-free rate is free of any prior risk adjustment, so the volatility of that distribution to some degree measures the risk of the project.

However, interpreting a distribution of *NPV*s calculated using the risk-free rate has its own problems. For example, if analysts look at the variance of such a distribution to draw inferences about risk, they ignore the opportunities of shareholders

---

[10] Just a few of the companies that we know have used Monte Carlo simulation include Merck, Intel, Procter & Gamble, General Motors, Pfizer, Owens-Corning, and Cummins Engine. For an account of how Merck uses simulations, see Nichols (1994).

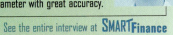
to eliminate some of the risk through diversification.[11] Moreover, the simulated distribution of one project's *NPV*s can be artificially reduced by joining one project with another and rerunning the simulation. If an examination of *NPV* distributions is part of a firm's project approval process, then employees will soon learn to propose joint projects that have less volatility than stand-alone investments.

The bottom line is that simulation is a powerful, effective tool when used properly. Using simulation to explore the distribution of a project's cash flows, and the major sources of uncertainty driving that distribution, is very sensible, but be wary of distributions of *NPV*s produced by a simulation program.

Decision Trees

Most important investment decisions involve much more complexity than simply forecasting cash flows, discounting at the appropriate rate, and investing if the *NPV* exceeds zero. In the real world, managers face a sequence of future decisions that influence an investment's value. These decisions might include whether to expand or abandon a project, whether to alter a marketing program, when to upgrade manufacturing equipment, and, most important, how to respond to actions of competitors. A **decision tree** is a visual representation of the choices that managers face over time with regard to a particular investment. Sketching out a decision tree is somewhat like thinking several moves ahead in a game of chess. The value of decision trees is that they force analysts to think through a series of "if-then" statements that describe how they will react as the future unfolds.

Imagine that Trinkle Foods Limited of Canada has invented a new salt substitute, branded Odessa, which it plans to sell in consumer snack foods such as potato chips and crackers. The company is trying to decide whether to spend 5 million Canadian dollars (C$) to test-market a new line of potato chips flavored with Odessa in Vancouver, British Columbia. Depending on the outcome of that test, Trinkle may spend an additional C$50 million one year later to launch a full line of snack foods across Canada. If consumer acceptance in Vancouver is high, the company predicts that its full product line will generate net cash inflows of C$12 million per year for 10 years.[12] If consumers in Vancouver respond less favorably, Trinkle expects cash inflows from a nationwide launch to be just C$2 million per year for 10 years. Trinkle's cost of capital equals 15 percent.

Figure 9.3 shows the decision tree for this problem. Initially, the firm can choose to spend the C$5 million on test-marketing or not. If Trinkle goes ahead with the market test, it estimates the probability of high and low consumer acceptance to be 50 percent. Once the company sees the test results, it will decide whether to invest C$50 million for a major product launch.

The proper way to work through a decision tree is to begin at the end and work backward to the initial decision. Suppose that one year from now Trinkle learns that the Vancouver market test was successful. At that point, the *NPV* (in millions of Canadian dollars) of launching the product can be determined as follows:

$$NPV = -C\$50 + \frac{C\$12}{1.15^1} + \frac{C\$12}{1.15^2} + \frac{C\$12}{1.15^3} + \cdots + \frac{C\$12}{1.15^{10}} = C\$10.23$$

[11.] Note that calculating a single *NPV* using the *WACC* or another appropriate discount rate does not suffer from this problem because the discount rate selected depends on the project's beta, a measure of its systematic risk.

[12.] Note that the test begins immediately, the C$50 million investment starts one year later, and the stream of C$12 million annual cash inflows begins one year after that.

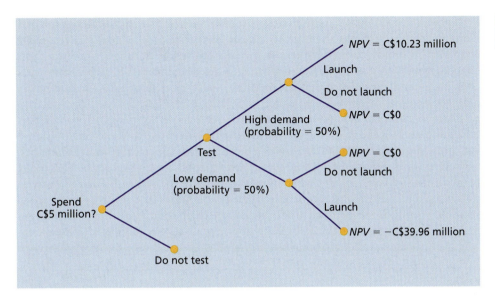

Figure 9.3
Decision Tree for Odessa
Investment

Clearly, Trinkle will invest if it winds up in this part of the decision tree, but what if initial test results are unfavorable and it launches the product? In that situation, the following NPV (in millions of Canadian dollars) results:

$$NPV = -\text{C\$}50 + \frac{\text{C\$}2}{1.15^1} + \frac{\text{C\$}2}{1.15^2} + \frac{\text{C\$}2}{1.15^3} + \cdots + \frac{\text{C\$}2}{1.15^{10}} = -\text{C\$}39.96$$

The best decision to make if the initial test does not go well is to walk away. After the test has been done, its cost is a sunk cost. Therefore, as of time 1, the NPV of doing nothing is zero.

Now we have a set of simple "if-then" decision rules that come from the decision tree. If initial test results indicate high consumer acceptance of Odessa, Trinkle should go ahead with the full product launch to capture a positive NPV of C\$10.23 million. On the other hand, if initial results show that consumers do not particularly like foods flavored with Odessa, Trinkle should not invest the additional C\$50 million.

Finally, with this information in hand, we can evaluate today's decision about whether or not to spend the C\$5 million on testing. Recall that we calculated the NPVs in terms of year-1 dollars—that is, as of the date of the decision whether or not to launch the product nationwide. In terms of today's Canadian dollars (in millions), the expected NPV of conducting the market test is determined as follows:

$$NPV = -\text{C\$}5 + 0.5\left(\frac{\text{C\$}10.23}{1.15}\right) + 0.5\left(\frac{\text{C\$}0}{1.15}\right) = -\text{C\$}0.55$$

Spending the money for market testing does not appear to be worthwhile. However, there is a very subtle flaw in our analysis. Can you spot it? At the present time, when Trinkle must decide whether or not to invest in test-marketing, it does not know what the results of the test will be. One year later, when the firm chooses whether or not to invest C\$50 million for a major product launch, it knows a great deal more. If Odessa is a big success in Vancouver, the risk that it will flop elsewhere in Canada may be very low. If so, does it make sense to use a discount rate of 15 percent when calculating the NPV of the product launch decision? Even a one-point reduction in the discount rate from 15 percent to 14 percent would be sufficient to change Trinkle's decision about test-marketing.

Though decision trees are useful tools for sharpening strategic thinking, the previous example illustrates their most serious flaw. The risk of many investments changes as you move from one point in the decision tree to another. Worse, analysts have no obvious way to make adjustments to the discount rate to reflect these risk changes. That makes it very difficult to know whether the final *NPV* obtained from a decision tree is the correct one.

Another practical difficulty in using decision trees is determining the probabilities for each branch of the tree. Unless firms have a great deal of experience making similar "bets" over and over again, estimating these probabilities is more an art than a science. How does Trinkle Foods know that the probability of a successful Vancouver market test equals 50 percent? Why not 80 percent or 10 percent? The only way to form even remotely reliable estimates of these probabilities is to rely on experience—your experience or the experience of others. For example, large pharmaceutical companies have enough experience investing in potential drug compounds to make reasonable estimates of the odds that any particular drug will ever make it to market.

Concept Review Questions

6. Why would a project that reaches the break-even point in terms of net income potentially be bad for shareholders?

7. Which variable do you think would be more valuable to examine in a project sensitivity analysis—the growth rate of sales or the allowable depreciation deductions each year? Explain.

8. You work for an airline that is considering a proposal to offer a new, nonstop flight between Atlanta and Tokyo. Senior management asks a team of analysts to run a Monte Carlo simulation of the project. Your job is to advise the group on what assumptions they should put in the simulation regarding the distribution of the ticket price your airline will be able to charge. How would you go about this task?

9. Why might the discount rate vary as you move through a decision tree?

9.3 REAL OPTIONS

WHY *NPV* DOESN'T ALWAYS GIVE THE RIGHT ANSWER

Only a few decades ago, the net present value method was essentially absent from the world of corporate practice. Today, it has become the standard tool for evaluating capital investments, especially in very large firms. Even so, *NPV* can systematically overstate or understate the value of certain types of investments. These systematic errors occur because the *NPV* method is essentially static. That is, *NPV* calculations do not take into account actions by managers to increase the value of an investment once it has been made. When managers can react to changes in the environment in ways that alter an investment's value, we say that the investment has an embedded **real option.** A real option is the right, but not the obligation, to take a future action that changes an investment's value. We will present an in-depth analysis of how option-pricing techniques can be used to improve capital budgeting processes in Chapters 18 and 19, so only an overview can be presented here. Hopefully, this will be enough to convince you that identifying and valuing—even if only conceptually—the real options embedded in most capital investment projects can help managers make better investment decisions.[13]

[13.] Brennan and Schwartz (1985) wrote the pathbreaking paper showing how option-pricing concepts can be used to describe embedded real options. They apply option-pricing theory to the operation of a mine and describe optimal decision

A simple example shows where *NPV* can go wrong. Suppose that you are bidding on the rights to extract oil from a proven site over the next year. You expect extraction costs from this field to run about $18 per barrel. Currently, oil sells for $16 per barrel. You know that oil prices fluctuate over time, but you do not possess any unique ability to predict where the price of oil is headed next. Accordingly, you assume that the price of oil follows a **random walk,** meaning that your best estimate of the future price of oil is just today's price. How much would you bid?

An *NPV* analysis would tell you not to bid at all. If your best forecast of the future price of oil is $16 per barrel, then you cannot make money when extraction costs are $18 per barrel. The expected *NPV* of this investment is negative no matter how much oil you can pump out of the ground.

A real options approach to the problem yields a different answer. If you own the rights to extract oil, you are not obligated to do so without regard to the price of your output. You reason that you will pump oil only when the market price is high enough to justify incurring the extraction costs. Predicting exactly when the price of oil will be high enough to make pumping profitable is impossible, but historical price fluctuations persuade you that the price of oil will be higher than extraction costs at least some of the time. Therefore, extraction rights at this site are worth more than zero.[14]

The oil-extraction problem is analogous to the test-marketing problem in the previous section. In both cases, managers have an option to choose whether to spend additional resources at a future date. These options add to a project's value in a way that *NPV* analysis, because of its static approach to decision making, cannot capture. In general, we can say that the value of a project equals the sum of two components— the part captured by *NPV* and the remaining value of real options.

Project value = *NPV* ± option value

The *NPV* may either understate or overstate a project's value depending on whether the proposed investment creates or destroys future options for the firm. In the oil drilling example, buying extraction rights creates an option, the option to pump or not to pump oil in the future, and the *NPV* understates the investment's value. It is easy to imagine projects that eliminate options rather than creating them. For instance, if the firm signs a long-term contract to supply a refinery with a certain quantity of crude oil each month, then it loses flexibility in the extraction decision.

Like Monte Carlo simulation, real options analysis is growing in popularity in many industries. We defer a full-blown discussion of the real options approach to capital budgeting to a later chapter. Instead, we now turn to a description of common types of real options encountered in capital budgeting decisions.

Types of Real Options

Expansion Options

What do companies do when one of their investments becomes a huge success? They look for new markets in which to expand that investment. For instance, in recent years DVD technology has gained enormous popularity. Not surprisingly, consumers can rent DVDs in video stores, grocery stores, and many other places where they were recently unavailable. The same is true for DVD players. The number of retail outlets

---

rules regarding when to open a closed mine or shut down a mine that is currently operating. Seventeen years later, Moel and Tufano (2002) showed that managers do indeed seem to make decisions about opening and closing mines in the manner predicted by Brennan and Schwartz.

[14.] To determine exactly how much these rights are worth, we have to use techniques covered in later chapters.

selling DVD players has expanded dramatically. It is even possible in many major airports to rent a DVD player and a movie to watch during your flight.

Naturally, companies invest in expansion only for their most successful investments. As mentioned in the decision-tree problem, the risk of expanding an already-successful project is much less than the risk when the project first begins. An NPV calculation misses both of these attributes—the opportunity to expand or not depending on initial success, and the change in risk that occurs when the initial outcome is favorable.

Abandonment Options

Just as firms have the right to invest additional resources to expand projects that enjoy early success, they also may withdraw resources from projects that fail to live up to short-run expectations. In an extreme case, a firm may decide to withdraw its entire commitment to a particular project and exercise its *option to abandon.*

In legal systems that provide limited liability to corporations, shareholders have the ultimate abandonment option. A firm may borrow money to finance its operations, but if it cannot generate cash flow sufficient to pay back its debts, shareholders can declare bankruptcy and turn over the company's assets to lenders and walk away. Though declaring bankruptcy is not what shareholders hope for when they invest, it offers shareholders considerable protection against personal liability for a firm's debts. Put another way, investors who buy shares are willing to pay a little more because of the option to abandon (in this case, the *default option*) than they would be willing to pay without that option.

Share value = NPV + value of default option

Consider the same situation from the perspective of lenders. When they commit funds to a corporation, lenders know that the borrower may default and their ability to recover their losses does not extend to shareholders' personal assets. We could even say that when an investor buys a bond from a corporation, the investor is simultaneously selling an option to the firm—the option to default. Notice that this option to default is essentially absent in U.S. Treasury securities. Suppose that a Treasury bond and a corporate bond offer the same interest payments to investors. Which one would sell at a higher price?

Corporate bond value = Treasury bond value − value of firm's default option

Abandonment options crop up in expected places, and it is important for managers to recognize whether a given investment has an attached abandonment option or grants another party the right to abandon. Consider refundable and nonrefundable airline tickets. With a refundable ticket, the traveler has the right to abandon travel plans without incurring a penalty. Such a ticket is more valuable than one that requires a traveler to pay a penalty if plans change.

Follow-on Investment Options

A follow-on investment option is similar to an expansion option. It entitles a firm to make additional investments should earlier investments prove to be successful. The difference is that the subsequent investments are more complex than a simple expansion of the earlier ones.

Hollywood offers an excellent example of follow-on options. Did you know that the rights to movie sequels are sometimes bought and sold before the original movie is completed? By purchasing the right to produce a sequel, a studio obtains the opportunity to make an additional investment should the first film become a commercial success.

Flexibility Options

The final types of options that have recently come to prominence in capital budgeting analyses are collectively known as flexibility options. Three examples illustrate the nature of flexibility options. First, Kulatilaka (1993) describes how the ability to use multiple production inputs creates option value. An example of this *input flexibility* is a boiler that can switch between oil or gas as a fuel source, enabling managers to switch from one type of fuel to another as prices change. Second, Trigeorgis and Mason (1987), Triantis and Hodder (1990), and Baldwin and Clark (1992) demonstrate the value of a flexible production technology capable of producing (and switching between) a variety of outputs using the same basic plant and equipment. This type of *output/operating flexibility* creates value when output prices are volatile.

Finally, McLaughlin and Taggart (1992) and Kogut and Kulatilaka (1994) document the option value of maintaining excess production capacity that managers can utilize quickly to meet peaks in demand. Though costly to purchase and maintain, this *capacity flexibility* can be quite valuable in capital-intensive industries subject to wide swings in demand and long lead times for building new capacity. Kogut and Kulatilaka's paper is especially important because it studies the profit opportunities a multinational company can exploit if it has the excess capacity needed to move production around the world in response to real exchange rate movements.

The Surprising Link between Risk and Real Option Values

Up to now, every valuation problem covered in this text satisfies the following statement: Holding other factors constant, an increase in an asset's risk decreases its price. If two bonds offer the same coupon, but investors perceive one to be riskier than the other, the safer bond will sell at a higher price. If two investment projects have identical cash flows, but one is riskier, analysts will discount the cash flows of the riskier project at a higher rate, resulting in a lower *NPV*.

A surprising fact is that this relationship does not hold for options. For an explanation, we go back to the oil-extraction problem. The current price of oil is $16 per barrel, and extraction costs at a particular site are $18. The expected future price of oil is the same as the current price, $16, so an *NPV* calculation would say that this investment is worthless.

Consider two different scenarios regarding the future price of oil. In the low-risk scenario, the price of oil in the future will be $18 or $14, each with probability of one-half. This means that the expected price of oil is still $16. However, both an *NPV* and an options analysis would conclude that bidding on the rights to this site is not a good idea because the price of oil will never be above the extraction cost.

Next, think about the high-risk scenario. The price of oil may be $22 or $10 with equal probability, so again we have an expected price of $16. If the price turns out to be $10, extracting the oil clearly does not make sense. But if the price turns out to be $22, extracting oil generates a profit of $4 per barrel. Therefore, a real options analysis would say that bidding at least a little for the right to extract the oil is a sensible decision.

Why does more risk lead to higher option values? Notice in the two previous scenarios that the payoff from extracting oil is the same no matter how low the price goes. At a price of $14 and at a price of $10, an oil producer would simply decline to incur

SMART PRACTICES VIDEO

Andy Bryant, Executive Vice President of Finance and Enterprise Systems, Chief Financial Officer, Intel Corp.

"Option theory was always used to show why we should do something. I never saw an analysis that said why we should not do something."

See the entire interview at **SMARTFinance**

extraction costs. A huge decline in the price of oil is no more costly than a small decline. On the other hand, the payoffs on the upside increase, the higher the price of oil goes. In other words, options are characterized by asymmetric payoffs. When the price of oil is extremely volatile, the potential benefits if prices rise are quite large. At the same time, if oil prices fall precipitously, there is no additional cost relative to a slight decline in prices. In either case, the payoff is zero.

Concept Review Questions	**10.** Give a real-world example of an *expansion option* and an *abandonment option*. **11.** We know that riskier firms must pay higher interest rates when they borrow money. Explain this using the language of real options.

9.4 STRATEGY AND CAPITAL BUDGETING

COMPETITION AND *NPV*

Finance textbooks tend to focus on the mechanics of project evaluation—how to calculate an *NPV* or *IRR*, how to estimate cash flows, how to select the right discount rate, and so on. This emphasis on technique is not entirely misplaced. Knowing how to apply quantitative discipline to the project selection process is very important. Nevertheless, experienced managers rarely make major investment decisions solely on the basis of *NPV* calculations. The best managers have a well-honed intuition that tells them why a particular project should or should not be a good investment. Their business acumen helps them recognize projects that will create shareholder value, even if the *NPV* numbers from financial analysts are negative, and to avoid investments that will destroy value, even when the *NPV* calculations are positive.[15]

No textbook can adequately substitute for the invaluable experience of making many investment decisions over several years, watching some of them succeed and some of them fail. However, there are certain common characteristics shared by projects that enhance shareholder value, and in this section we give you some guidance on how to identify these characteristics.

Recall some of the most basic lessons from microeconomics about a perfectly competitive market. In such a market, there are many buyers and sellers trading a homogeneous product or service. Because every agent in the market is small relative to the market as a whole, everyone behaves as a price taker. Competition and the lack of entry or exit barriers for sellers ensures that the product's market price equals the marginal cost of producing it, and no firm earns pure economic profit.[16]

[15.] One of the authors of this textbook had a humbling (but also awe-inspiring) lesson in the intuitive powers of good managers. On a consulting assignment for a Fortune 100 corporation, the author was asked to evaluate the assumptions of a firm's *NPV* calculations for a major acquisition. After gathering thousands of data points and running a week or two of simulations, the author was prepared to present his work to the chief financial officer (CFO). "From my work, I can tell you what the probability is that this acquisition will ever be profitable for your company," claimed the intrepid author. "But I already know that," the CFO responded. In a fit of hubris, the author challenged, "OK, tell me what you think that probability is." After hearing the CFO's response, the author had to admit that after several weeks of work, he had arrived at exactly the same probability estimate that the CFO had reached intuitively.

[16.] Remember that the notion of "economic profit" is very different from accounting profit. If a firm makes a zero economic profit, it earns just enough to pay competitive prices for the labor and capital that it employs to produce a good or service.

In a market with zero economic profits, the *NPV* of any investment equals zero because every project earns just enough to recover the cost of capital: no more and no less.

Therefore, if we want to form an intuitive judgment about whether or not an investment proposal should have a positive *NPV* (before actually calculating the *NPV*), we have to identify ways in which the project deviates from the perfectly competitive ideal. For instance, if the proposal calls for production of a new good, is there something about this good that clearly differentiates it from similar goods already in the market? If the new product is genuinely unique, will the firm producing this good be able to erect some kind of entry barrier that will prevent other firms from producing their own nearly identical versions of the product, thereby competing away any pure economic profits?

Competitive advantages of this sort can come in many forms. One firm may have superior engineering or R&D talent that generates a continuous stream of innovative products. Another may excel at low-cost manufacturing processes. Still another may create a sustainable competitive advantage through its unique marketing programs. The main point is that if any project is to have a positive *NPV*, advocates of that project ought to be able to articulate the project's competitive advantage even before "running the numbers." No matter how positive the project's *NPV* appears to be on paper, if no one can explain its main competitive advantage in the market, the firm should probably think twice about investing. Similarly, when an investment proposal has a compelling story explaining its competitive edge but the *NPV* numbers come out negative, it may be worth sending the financial analysts back to their desks to take a second look at their assumptions.[17]

Strategic Thinking and Real Options

We conclude this chapter with a return to the topic of real options. The technical aspects of calculating the real option value of a given project (which we cover later in this book) can be quite complex. Real options techniques are still relatively new and are used extensively by only a handful of firms in a few industries. Though we expect an increasing number of firms to include real options analysis as part of their standard capital budgeting approach, we claim that just thinking about a project from a real options perspective can be valuable, even if coming up with a dollar value for a real option proves to be elusive.

Investments generally have real option value as long as they are not "all-or-nothing" bets. Almost all investments fit this description. Managers usually have opportunities to make decisions subsequent to the initial investment that can increase or decrease its value. These decisions can create (or perhaps destroy) an investment's option value. To maximize an investment's option value, or at least to recognize that value, managers should try to describe up front, before the firm commits to an investment, all the subsequent decisions they will make as events unfold. In other words, managers must articulate their strategy for a given investment. This strategy will consist of a series of statements like these:

- If sales in the first year exceed our expectations, then we will commit another $50 million to ramp up production.

[17.] We want to emphasize here that we still believe the numbers are extremely important. Our point is that the numbers and the intuition should line up. When they are in conflict, managers need to think hard about whether the NPV model is in error or whether the project lacks a true competitive advantage. These conflicts can also result from human factors as explained in Chapter 8, Section 8.5.

- If consumers enjoy sending and receiving e-mail on their cell phones, then we will be prepared to invest additional resources so that our cell phones will be capable of performing other tasks on the Internet.
- If our MP3 player cannot hold as many songs as the leading model, the unit must weigh at least two ounces less than the market leader, or we will not commit the resources necessary to manufacture it.

This series of "if-then" statements is necessary to value a real option, but it also has intangible value in that it forces managers to think through their strategic options before they invest. Identifying a real option is tantamount to identifying future points at which it may be possible for managers to create and sustain competitive advantages.

Concept Review Question	**12.** Why must manager intuition be part of the investment decision process regardless of a project's *NPV* or *IRR*? Why is it helpful to think about real options when making an investment decision?

9.5 SUMMARY

- All-equity firms can discount their "standard" investment projects at the cost of equity. Managers can estimate the cost of equity using the CAPM.
- The cost of equity is influenced by a firm's operating leverage as well as its financial leverage.
- Firms with both debt and equity in their capital structures can discount their "standard" investments using the weighted average cost of capital or *WACC*.
- The *WACC* equals the weighted average of the cost of each source of financing used by a firm, with the weights equal to the proportion of the market value of each source of financing.
- The *WACC* and the CAPM are connected in that the cost of debt and equity (and any other financing source) are driven by the betas of the firm's debt and equity.
- When a firm wants to make an "unusual" investment, an investment outside its normal line of business, it should try to estimate the asset beta for this industry using pure play firms.
- To estimate the asset beta for a different industry, analysts first must unlever the equity beta of the pure play firm that uses debt. Then, the analyst must relever the industry asset's beta based on its existing capital structure.
- A variety of tools exist to assist managers in understanding the sources of uncertainty of a project's cash flows. These tools include break-even analysis, sensitivity analysis, scenario analysis, Monte Carlo simulation, and decision trees.
- The value of many investments includes not just the *NPV*, but also the investment's option value. As a static analytical tool, *NPV* misses the value of management's ability to alter an investment's value in response to environmental changes that may occur after an investment is made.
- Types of real options include the option to expand, the option to abandon, the option to make follow-on investments, and flexibility options.
- An investment's option value, unlike its *NPV*, increases as risk increases.
- For an investment to have a positive *NPV*, it should have a competitive advantage, something that distinguishes it from the economic ideal of perfect competition.

- Valuing an investment's option value requires strategic thinking. Articulating the strategy may be as important as calculating the option value.

INTERNET RESOURCES

Note: *For updates to links, please go to the book's website at http://smart.swcollege.com*

http://www.quicken.com—Contains information relevant to calculating the *WACC*, including equity betas, total market value of equity, and debt/equity ratios

http://valuation.ibbotson.com—A fee-based site with cost-of-capital estimates for more than 300 industries

http://www.stern.nyu.edu/~adamodar—Website of NYU professor Aswath Damodaran; contains downloadable data sets with levered and unlevered industry betas as well as industry-level estimates of the cost of capital

KEY TERMS

asset beta	project beta
break-even analysis	pure play
contribution margin	random walk
debt beta	real option
decision tree	scenario analysis
financial leverage	sensitivity analysis
Monte Carlo simulation	unlevered equity beta
operating leverage	weighted average cost of capital (*WACC*)

QUESTIONS

9-1.   Explain when firms should discount projects using the cost of equity. When should they use the *WACC* instead? When should they use neither?

9-2.   If a firm takes actions that increase its operating leverage, we might expect to see an increase in its equity beta. Why?

9-3.   Firm A and Firm B plan to raise $1 million to finance identical projects. Firm A finances the project with 100 percent equity, while firm B uses a 50-50 mix of debt and equity. The interest rate on the debt equals 7 percent. At what rate of return on the investment (i.e., assets) will the rate of return on equity be the same for Firms A and B? (*Hint:* Think through Table 9.2.)

9-4.   Why do you think it is important to use the market values of debt and equity rather than book values to calculate a firm's *WACC*?

9-5.   Assuming that there are no corporate income taxes, what is the connection between a firm's *WACC* and its asset beta?

9-6.   What is the relationship between the size of a firm's debt beta and the total amount of debt the firm borrows?

9-7.   Suppose that two firms have identical asset betas but very different equity betas. Why might this be so?

9-8.   Many high-tech companies use the following compensation strategy to attract key talent. They offer a relatively low base salary (low relative to what employees with a given level of experience and training might earn in another industry), but they augment this below-market salary with large incentive-pay packages including cash bonuses and stock options. Presumably, there is a trade-off at work in the labor market such that high-tech firms could attract the same employees by offering a higher base and lower incentive pay. Which of these two strategies would lead to a higher stock beta, assuming other factors are held constant?

9-9. What is the relationship between the equity risk premium and the aggregate value of the stock market? If the equity risk premium declined suddenly (holding all other factors constant), what would happen to the value of the stock market?

9-10. In what sense could one argue that if managers make decisions using break-even analysis, they are not maximizing shareholder wealth? How can break-even analysis be modified to solve this problem?

9-11. Explain the differences between *sensitivity analysis* and *scenario analysis*. Offer an argument for the proposition that scenario analysis offers a more realistic picture of a project's risk than sensitivity analysis does.

9-12. In Chapter 8, we discussed how one might calculate the *NPV* of earning an MBA. Suppose that you are asked to do a sensitivity analysis on the MBA decision. Which of the following factors do you think would have a larger impact on the degree's *NPV*?

   a. The ranking of the school you choose to attend
   b. Your choice of a major
   c. Your GPA
   d. The state of the job market when you graduate

9-13. Suppose that you wanted to model the value of an MBA degree with decision trees. What would such a decision tree look like?

9-14. If you decide to invest in an MBA, what is your abandonment option? Your follow-on investment option?

9-15. Your company is selling the mineral rights to several hundred acres of land it owns that are believed to contain silver deposits. The current price of silver is $5 per ounce, but of course, future prices are uncertain. Would you expect the mineral rights to sell for more or less if investors believe that silver prices will be more volatile in the future than they have been in the past? Explain.

PROBLEMS

Choosing the Right Discount Rate

9-1. Krispy Kreme Doughnuts (KKD) has a capital structure consisting almost entirely of equity.

   a. If the beta of KKD stock equals 1.6, the risk-free rate equals 6 percent, and the expected return on the market portfolio equals 11 percent, what is KKD's cost of equity?
   b. Suppose that a 1 percent increase in expected inflation causes a 1 percent increase in the risk-free rate. Holding all other factors constant, what will this do to the firm's cost of equity? Is it reasonable to hold all other factors constant? What other part of the calculation of the cost of equity is likely to change if expected inflation rises?

9-2. Follow the instructions given in Problem 5-10 at the end of Chapter 5, and download historical stock-price data for the pharmaceutical industry giant, Merck (ticker symbol, MRK). Be sure to check the box indicating that you want monthly data, and use September 1, 1996, as your start date and September 1, 2002, as your ending date.

Retrieve data from Yahoo! and download it into an Excel spreadsheet (the file downloads in comma delimited format with a .csv file extension, but once you have the data, save it as an Excel file with the familiar .xls file extension). Repeat this process using exactly the same settings (e.g., monthly data using the same starting and ending dates) and the ticker symbol SPY, which stands for Standard & Poor's Depository Receipts, commonly called Spiders. Returns on Spiders will closely approximate returns on the S&P 500 index, our proxy for the market portfolio in this problem.

a. Calculate the monthly return on Merck by dividing the adjusted close in any particular month by the adjusted closing price the previous month and subtracting 1. This should yield 71 monthly returns for Merck (you can calculate returns in only 71 of the 72 months because of the need to have the previous month's price to calculate the current month's return).

b. Calculate the monthly return on the S&P 500 Index the same way. Paste the returns on the S&P and the returns on Merck into a single spreadsheet (use the "Paste-Special-Values" sequence in Excel).

c. You will run a regression in Excel using the returns on Merck as the dependent, or Y variable, and returns on the S&P 500 as the independent, or X variable. There are two ways to do this. You can use the data analysis function under the tools menu (you may have to first click "Add ins" under the tools menu and then check the box labeled "Analysis ToolPak"). Click "Tools—Data Analysis Regression" to set up the regression. Type in the cell range containing Merck returns for the input Y range, and type in the cell range containing the S&P returns for the input X range. Leave all the other boxes unchecked, except the one that places the output in a new worksheet. After you run the regression, your output will look something like this:

Summary Output

Regression	Statistics
Multiple R	0.298342
R-squared	0.089008
Adjusted	0.075805
Standard	0.086325
Observations	71

ANOVA

	df	SS	MS	F	Significance F
Regression	1	0.050239	0.050239	6.741628	0.011501
Residual	69	0.514192	0.007452		
Totals	70	0.564431			

	Coefficient	Standard Error	t Statistic	P-value	Lower 95%	Upper 95%
Intercept	0.006603	0.010306	0.640716	0.523829	−0.013957	0.027164
X Variable 1	0.525503	0.202392	2.596465	0.011501	0.121743	0.929263

The other way to estimate a regression in Excel is to use the "=linest function." We refer the reader to Excel's help feature for more information on that function.

The figure to the right of the label "X Variable 1" is the slope of the regression line, and it represents Merck's equity beta. Does it surprise you that Merck would have an equity beta less than 1.0? What economic rationale can you give for this finding?

d. Suppose that the risk-free rate is 5 percent and the expected return on the market is 10 percent. What is Merck's cost of equity? Assuming Merck's capital structure is virtually 100 percent equity, what is its WACC?

e. Now go back and repeat the steps necessary to download monthly data for General Electric (ticker symbol, GE). Calculate monthly returns on GE stock as before, pair them up with monthly returns on the S&P 500 Index, and using regression analysis, estimate GE's beta. Given that GE is a highly diversified conglomerate, what would you expect GE's beta to be before estimating it? Does your estimate confirm your intuition?

Smart Solutions
See the problem and solution explained step-by-step at
SMART Finance

9-3. In its 2001 annual report, The Coca-Cola Company reported sales of $20.09 billion for fiscal year 2001 and $19.89 billion for fiscal year 2000. The company also reported operating income (roughly equivalent to *EBIT*) of $5.35 billion and $3.69 billion in 2001 and 2000, respectively. Meanwhile, arch rival PepsiCo, Inc. reported sales of $26.94 billion in 2001 and $25.48 billion in 2000. PepsiCo's operating profit was $4.03 billion in 2001 and $3.82 billion in 2000. Based on these figures, which company had higher operating leverage?

9-4. Firm 1 has a capital structure with 20 percent debt and 80 percent equity. Firm 2's capital structure consists of 50 percent debt and 50 percent equity. Both firms pay 7 percent interest on their debt. Finally, suppose that both firms have invested in assets worth $100 million. Calculate the return on equity for each firm, assuming the following:

a. The return on assets is 3 percent.
b. The return on assets is 7 percent.
c. The return on assets is 11 percent.

What general pattern do you observe?

9-5. Return to the figures in Problem 9-4. The stock of Firm 1 has a beta of 1.0, and the stock of Firm 2 has a beta of 1.375. The risk-free rate of interest equals 4 percent, and the expected return on the market portfolio equals 12 percent. Calculate the *WACC* for each firm. You may assume there are no taxes.

Smart Solutions
See the problem and solution explained step-by-step at
SMART Finance

9-6. Recalculate the *WACC* figures from Problem 9-5, assuming that the firms face a marginal tax rate of 34 percent. Explain how taking taxes into account changes your answer.

9-7. The risk-free rate equals 5 percent, and the expected risk premium on the market portfolio equals 6 percent. A particular company has bonds outstanding that offer investors a yield to maturity of 6.5 percent. What is the debt beta?

9-8. Refer to the numbers in Problem 9-7. The company also has common stock outstanding (with market value equal to its bonds outstanding) with an expected return of 15 percent. What is the firm's *WACC*? What is the beta of the firm's assets? You may assume there are no taxes.

9-9. A firm's assets have a beta of 1.0. Assuming that the debt beta equals 0.0 and that there are no taxes, calculate the firm's equity beta under the following assumptions:

a. The firm's capital structure is 100 percent equity.
b. The capital structure is 20 percent debt and 80 percent equity.
c. The capital structure is 40 percent debt and 60 percent equity.
d. The capital structure is 60 percent debt and 40 percent equity.
e. The capital structure is 80 percent debt and 20 percent equity.

Do you believe that the assumption of a zero debt beta is equally valid for each of these capital structures? Why or why not?

9-10. A diversified firm with investments in many industries is considering investing in the fast-food industry. Looking at data on publicly traded fast-food companies, an analyst discovers the following information for McDonald's Corporation and Wendy's International Inc.

	Equity β	D/E
McDonald's	0.70	1.00
Wendy's	0.40	0.45

In addition, the analyst has the following information from financial markets:

- The risk-free rate of interest is 5 percent.
- The expected return on the market portfolio is 10 percent.
- The debt beta for McDonald's and Wendy's is zero.
- The corporate tax rate is 34 percent.

Calculate the asset beta for McDonald's and Wendy's, and illustrate how these could be used to calculate the discount rate for an investment in the fast-food business.

9-11. Suppose that the aggregate dividend yield on stocks is 3 percent and is constant over time. The long-term (real) growth rate of aggregate dividends is 2.5 percent. What is the expected real return on equities?

A Closer Look at Risk

9-12. Alliance Pneumatic Manufacturing, a specialty machine-tool producer, has fixed costs of $200 million per year. Across all the firm's products, the average contribution margin equals $1,200. What is Alliance's break-even point in terms of units sold?

9-13. Turn to the figures in Table 9.5. Determine which of the following has the greater impact on the *NPV* of the gyroscope skateboard project—an increase in the selling price of 10 percent (compared to the base case) or an increase in the size of the market of 10 percent in year 1.

10

Market Efficiency and Modern Financial Management

OPENING FOCUS

Markets React Quickly to Inadvertent Employment Report

The employment report released by the U.S. Department of Commerce at 8:30 A.M. on the first Friday of every month is perhaps the most intently watched and influential of all the economic statistics released by the federal government. A report showing rapid employment growth and declining unemployment often indicates that the Federal Reserve Board will feel pressure to tighten monetary policy and raise interest rates. Conversely, a weak job report typically signals a slowing economy, declining interest rates, and a less-restrictive monetary policy. The connection between the employment report and Federal Reserve actions, combined with the influence of interest rates on economic activity and asset prices, means that bond and stock prices often react dramatically to surprises contained in the Commerce Department's report.

Imagine the Commerce Department's embarrassment when the October 1998 employment report was inadvertently posted on an internal working section of the department's Internet site on Thursday morning, November 5, rather than on Friday, November 6. Almost instantly, a financial analyst at a large brokerage firm noted the statistic, contacted a Commerce Department spokesperson for verification, and then disseminated the number to the brokerage firm's customers and the business news media. Within minutes of its discovery, the number had been broadcast worldwide, and its impact (it showed a smaller than expected monthly rise in employment) on interest rates and financial asset prices had been felt in full. During the rest of Thursday, the Commerce Department struggled to disclose all the supplementary data that typically accompanies the headline employment numbers and to determine how such a breach of security could have occurred. The lesson for financial markets, however, was clear. Significant information will immediately affect financial markets, even if the information is unexpectedly released at the "wrong" time. The Commerce Department also learned its lesson, and no comparable premature information disclosure has occurred since 1998 (at least through December 2002).

In this chapter, we turn our attention from product markets to purely financial ones and try to answer one question of overriding importance: Can financing activities create value for a company in the same way that investment activities can? Our study of capital budgeting implied that product markets are less than perfectly competitive. Casual observation of real industries around the world supports this conclusion. Many products are manufactured by a relatively small number of firms, which frequently do not compete head-to-head on price in all markets. In addition, firms that invest in research and development do so because they believe that R&D will give them sole access to new investment opportunities. Positive *NPV* investment opportunities derive from these market imperfections.

Do financial markets offer creative financial managers the same positive-*NPV* investment opportunities as imperfectly competitive product markets? We will argue in this chapter that they usually do not, for several reasons. First, although there are obvious differences between financial markets in the types of securities traded, the currencies in which the securities are denominated, and the trading rules of each market, financial assets are nonetheless much more similar to each other than are real assets. To see this, simply consider how vast a range of items the term "manufactured goods" covers. This category includes items as dissimilar to one another as paper clips are to commercial aircraft. In contrast, the array of financial assets is more limited, and most financial assets share common characteristics. By comparing the prices of similar financial assets, investors can identify and exploit pricing discrepancies, ensuring that similar assets offer similar expected returns.

Second, the sheer size and transparency of modern money and capital markets should make financial markets more competitive than markets for other goods and services. Financial asset prices are set by open auction in large, competitive arenas that are typically governed by rules designed to make the auction process as fair and open as possible. An excellent example of this is the foreign exchange market, which is perhaps the closest thing to a perfectly competitive market in the world today. The trading volume in this market is over $1.6 trillion *per day*, and there are literally thousands of traders dealing in the largest currencies. The size, sophistication, and low trading costs of this market ensure that all currencies will be perfect substitutes for each other. This means that if traders can exchange 1 U.S. dollar ($) for 2 Swiss francs (SF) or for 100 Japanese yen (¥), then SF1 must also be worth ¥50. If any deviation from this pricing relationship occurs, arbitrageurs will observe and act on the deviation instantly. No comparable arbitrage process can ensure that the relative pricing of American, Swiss, and Japanese scientific instruments will always stay the same in every market worldwide.

A third distinction between financial and real asset markets relates to the number of people studying and reporting on individual products. Perhaps several hundred business and professional reporters will comment on the technical merits of the products offered by large companies such as IBM, Shell Oil, or Toyota Motors, but thousands of financial analysts worldwide routinely offer opinions regarding the investment merits of the debt and equity securities issued by these companies. Furthermore, the rapid growth of electronic media during the past two decades has caused an explosion in the total volume of financial information available to investors. As the cost of obtaining reliable financial information has fallen, the demand for it has risen accordingly.

In summary, financial markets differ from product and factor markets in that financial assets are more easily comparable with each other, they are usually traded in larger and more-competitive arenas, pricing errors are easier to identify and exploit, and financial asset classes are studied more intensively by a larger number of analysts. Does this imply that there is no gain to be made from creative financing strategies? Not necessarily, but it does imply that there will be fewer opportunities to profit from clever financing strategies than from smart capital investment spending, and that the former will be generally less profitable. It also implies that those financial value-creating opportunities that do exist will involve searching out areas of financial markets that are less than perfectly competitive.

Concept Review Questions	**1.** Suppose that traders can exchange 1 U.S. dollar ($) for 2 Swiss francs (SF) or for 100 Japanese yen (¥). Explain how arbitrage ensures that SF1 will be worth ¥50. Then, describe a comparable arbitrage process for a manufactured product (i.e., machine tools). Which process seems more realistic?
	2. Describe how the Internet might push the market for airline tickets closer to the theoretical ideal of perfect competition. How might the Internet have the same impact on the stock market?

10.1 WHAT IS AN EFFICIENT FINANCIAL MARKET?

DEFINITIONS OF EFFICIENCY

So far, we have couched our discussion of financial markets in terms of how competitive they are compared to product markets. Although this is obviously important, analysts and researchers are actually more interested in the informational efficiency of financial markets. **Informational efficiency** refers to the tendency (or lack thereof) for prices in a market to rapidly and fully incorporate new, relevant information. This definition is somewhat different from more familiar economic notions of efficiency. **Allocative efficiency** means that markets channel resources to their most productive uses, while **operational efficiency** determines whether markets produce outputs at the lowest possible cost. These are vital measures of the economic utility of markets, but for financial markets, informational efficiency is more important because it is more basic. Informationally efficient capital markets incorporate all relevant information into financial asset prices, which in turn helps ensure that economically promising investment projects receive funding.[1]

The concept of informationally efficient capital markets is also one of the most important and influential contributions that financial economics has made to modern economic thought. The **efficient markets hypothesis (EMH)**, as formally presented by Eugene Fama in 1970, has already revolutionized financial thought, practice, and regulation.[2] The EMH asserts, with beguiling simplicity, that financial asset prices

---

[1.] Although these three forms of efficiency usually go hand in hand, a financial market *can* be operationally efficient without being informationally efficient, and vice versa. For example, a nation's banking system may extend credit to borrowers at a very low cost in terms of labor and overhead expense, yet still price the loans much too high or too low based on the true creditworthiness of the borrower. The distinction between the informational and allocative efficiency of a financial market is less clear-cut. Even though a market must be informationally efficient to allocate capital to its highest and best (most profitable) use, the converse does not necessarily apply. The securities of a monopolist can be priced quite rationally in a financial market, offering investors only a normal return on their investments, even if the monopolist is earning unjustifiably large economic profits.

[2.] Furthermore, this model's soul mate in economic thought, the rational expectations hypothesis, has transformed the way people view macroeconomic policymaking. Indeed, the worldwide adoption of market-oriented economic policies during

fully reflect all available information. What do we mean by the phrase "all available information"? The answer to that question varies and defines three distinct versions of the efficient markets hypothesis, which we will discuss further.

The rest of Section 10.1 and all of Section 10.2 examine the impact that the efficient markets hypothesis has had on modern finance. Those seeking only a brief description of the three "forms" of market efficiency originally presented by Fama (1970) can read the remainder of this section, then skip over to Section 10.4, which discusses the implications of market efficiency for practicing financial managers. Students interested in examining the impact of the EMH on financial thought and practice should read Sections 10.2 and 10.3 as well. Section 10.2 discusses empirical tests of the EMH, while Section 10.3 presents the contrary evidence marshaled by researchers who are less convinced of the informational efficiency of financial markets. In recent years, many of these scholars have advanced an alternative to market efficiency known as behavioral finance. **Behavioral finance** asserts that because traders in financial markets are human beings, they are subject to all the foibles and fads that bedevil human judgment in other spheres of life. Moreover, behaviorists claim that human errors do not simply "cancel out" in markets. Instead, these errors cause prices to deviate far from "fundamental value" in ways that arbitrage does not eliminate, at least not immediately. Here we present only a brief overview of the evidence for and against the EMH. The references in the text and footnotes will guide the interested reader to academic sources and survey articles describing how the EMH has altered financial thought. It is a fascinating story.

THE THREE FORMS OF MARKET EFFICIENCY

The EMH presents three increasingly stringent definitions of efficiency, based on what information market prices reflect. In markets characterized by **weak-form efficiency,** asset prices incorporate all information from the historical price record. In other words, prices in a weak-form efficient market incorporate all information about price trends or repeating patterns that may have occurred in the past. This seemingly innocuous proposition implies that trading strategies based on analyses of historical pricing trends or relationships cannot consistently yield market-beating returns. Prices in a weak-form efficient market will be unpredictable and will change only in response to the arrival of new information. In technical terms, this means that prices follow a **random walk,** a deliciously descriptive phrase meaning that prices wander aimlessly, with no connection to past price changes and no tendency to return to a mean value over time.[3] Equation 10.1 expresses this mathematically: the expected price of an asset next period, $E(P_t)$, is equal to today's price, P_0, plus a random error, e_t, which has an expected value of zero.

$$E(P_t) = P_0 + e_t \qquad \text{(Eq. 10.1)}$$

---

the past 20 years is based on an intellectual acceptance of the idea that markets efficiently process information and then allocate resources to their highest and best use (or at least markets allocate capital more efficiently than do government bureaucrats).

[3] The CFO of a sporting goods company once told us that his company's stock always performed exceptionally well during the Summer Olympics because the games caused an increase in demand for his firm's products. Without a doubt, seasonal demand patterns exist for many kinds of products, but this is hardly a surprise to financial markets. Even though this firm's stock might have performed well during previous Olympic years, imagine what would happen if investors expected the pattern to repeat over time. Investors would buy the shares in the spring, before the Summer Olympics began. Buying pressure in the spring would cause the stock price to increase several weeks or months before the summer. Seeing this, investors might purchase shares even farther ahead of the next Olympics, and eventually the seasonal pattern would simply disappear. See Ritter (1996) for an amusing account of this dynamic in futures markets.

A modified version of the random walk model recognizes that stock prices do not move entirely at random. Rather, prices move randomly around a long-term trend. The trend represents a stock's expected return, which as we have seen is driven by the stock's systematic risk. For stock that pays no dividends, we can express this "random walk with drift" mathematically as follows:

$$E(\Delta P_t) = E(R) + e_t$$

where $E(\Delta P_t)$ is the expected price change next period, $E(R)$ is the expected return, and e_t is again a random error term.[4]

The second form of market efficiency is called **semistrong-form efficiency.** This version of the EMH asserts that asset prices incorporate *all publicly available information.* There is both a "stock" and a "flow" aspect to the information-processing capabilities of semistrong-form efficient markets. First, the *level* of asset prices should correctly reflect all pertinent historical, current, and predictable future information that investors can obtain from public sources. Second, asset prices should *change* fully and instantaneously in response to the arrival of relevant new information. The key point about this form of efficiency is that it requires only that prices reflect information that can be gleaned from *public* sources (e.g., newspapers, press releases, computer databases).

In markets characterized by **strong-form efficiency,** asset prices reflect *all* information, public and private. This is an extreme form of market efficiency because it implies that important company-specific information will be fully incorporated in asset prices with the very first trade after the information is generated. For example, a firm's stock price should increase immediately after the board of directors votes for a dividend increase and before the firm publicly announces the increase. In strong-form efficient markets, most insider trading would be unprofitable, and there would be no benefit to ferreting out information on publicly traded companies, because any data morsel so obtained would already be reflected in stock and bond prices. Like semistrong-form efficiency, strong-form efficiency also implies that there is both a stock and flow aspect to a market's information-processing abilities. Table 10.1 describes the three forms of market efficiency and summarizes the key implications of each form.

OVERVIEW OF THE EMPIRICAL EVIDENCE ON MARKET EFFICIENCY

Ultimately, whether financial markets are informationally efficient is an empirical question. For more than a quarter of a century, the efficient market hypothesis enjoyed overwhelming support among financial economists. However, in recent years a large body of empirical evidence challenging the EMH has accumulated, causing many former "true believers" to take a fresh look at the efficiency question. Adding to this disquiet, there have been several dramatic recent examples of markets surging for an extended period, then collapsing suddenly, the so-called bubble phenomenon. Figure 10.1 details the most recent "boom-and-bust" cycle, the rise in U.S. technology stock prices from January 1998 to March 2000 and their ruinous decline thereafter. The Nasdaq Composite Index tripled over the 3-year period leading up to March 2000, while the Goldman Sachs Internet Index increased by *600 percent.* Be-

---

[4.] An old metaphor used to describe a random walk is a drunk person staggering aimlessly in a field. The best place to start looking for this person is the last place he was seen. The analogous metaphor for a random walk with drift is a drunk person on the side of a hill. We expect to find this person at the bottom of the hill, but exactly what path he takes to the bottom is unpredictable.

Table 10.1
Forms of Informational
Market Efficiency

Form of Efficiency	Definition	Example
Weak form	Financial asset (stock) prices incorporate *all historical information* into current prices; future stock prices cannot be predicted based on an analysis of past stock prices.	Nothing of value is to be gained by analyzing past stock price changes, since this doesn't help you predict future price changes—renders "technical analysis" useless.
Semistrong form	Stock prices incorporate *all publicly available information* (historical and current); there will not be a delayed response to information disclosures.	The relevant information in an SEC filing will be incorporated into a stock price as soon as the filing is made public.
Strong form	Stock prices incorporate *all information*—private as well as public; prices will react as soon as new information is generated, rather than as soon as it is publicly disclosed.	Stock prices will react to a dividend increase as soon as the firm's board of directors votes—and before the board announces its decision publicly.

cause there was no comparable rise and fall in "dot.com" company earnings during this period, many have concluded that this and other recent market collapses have been the result of exploding **price bubbles.** Subscribers to behavioral finance argue that bubbles occur when investors irrationally bid prices to unsustainable levels. When investors finally realize their errors, prices fall dramatically (and perhaps suddenly). If bubbles do in fact occur, they would constitute direct evidence against market efficiency.

Not surprisingly, the debate between behaviorists and those who believe strongly in market efficiency has triggered a surge in research during the past 10 years. In this chapter, we present an overview of more than 30 years of research on market efficiency, breaking our survey into two main sections. The next section (10.2) adopts an

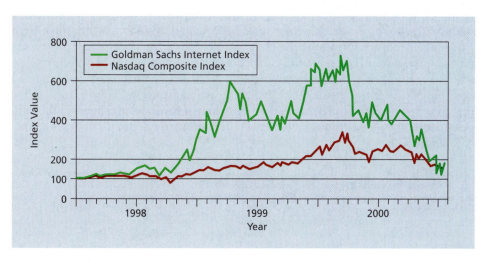

Figure 10.1
Rational Market Valuation or Price Bubble? Nasdaq and Internet Stock Prices, January 1998 to January 2001

Source: "The Party's Over: A Survey of Corporate Finance," *The Economist* (January 27, 2001), p.14, fig. 6.

updated version of the classification scheme used by Eugene Fama when he surveyed the existing literature himself in 1991. Instead of relying on the original "forms" of market efficiency, Fama (1991) classified empirical tests of market efficiency into three categories: (1) tests for return predictability; (2) event studies (or tests for rapid price adjustment); and (3) tests for private information. Though we discuss some of the classic empirical tests Fama describes, we focus on papers published since 1991. Section 10.3 then summarizes the evidence supporting the behavioral finance critique of market efficiency. We present our own assessment of the validity of the market efficiency hypothesis at the beginning of Section 10.4. Those wishing only an overview can skip to that section.[5]

Concept Review Questions

3. Describe the differences between *allocative* efficiency, *operational* efficiency, and *informational* efficiency.

4. Many people criticize the efficient markets hypothesis as unrealistic but do not then describe what the absence of efficiency would imply. Give a specific example of how a semi-strong-form *inefficient* market would react to new information. Does this seem realistic?

5. There is frequently an upward drift in the stock price of a firm that will eventually become the target of a takeover attempt prior to the announcement of the bid itself. What do you think causes this drift, and is this phenomenon consistent with market efficiency?

10.2 EMPIRICAL EVIDENCE ON MARKET EFFICIENCY (OPTIONAL)

TESTS FOR RETURN PREDICTABILITY

Much of the research on market efficiency has examined the validity of the weak-form efficiency prediction that past price changes do not predict future changes, or that prices follow a random walk. We refer to papers that study this aspect of market efficiency as *tests for return predictability*. We further classify these tests into four categories. First, tests of simple trading rules examine whether an investor can construct a consistently profitable trading strategy based on observed trends in very recent stock returns.[6] Second, tests of the effectiveness of technical analysis examine whether it is profitable to buy or sell stocks based on historical pricing "patterns" identified by stock analysts. Third, some tests for return predictability study whether there is an exploitable tendency for stock-price changes to continue from one period to the next or, conversely, to reverse direction each period. Trading rules based on return continuations are often called either **momentum strategies** or **underreaction strategies,** and those based on reversals are called **overreaction strategies.** Fourth, tests of the performance of newly issued shares examine whether firms issuing shares to the public underperform stock market indexes over the next several years.

[5.] If you skip the material in Sections 10.2 and 10.3, you should make time to read one of the recent survey articles on market efficiency. These include Bernard, Thomas, and Abarbanell (1993); Ball (1995); Lee and Verbrugge (1996); and Bernstein (1999), who support market efficiency. Shefrin (2001) and Heaton and Korajczyk (2002) put a more favorable emphasis on behavioral research.

[6.] To be more precise about what we mean by the term "profitable" here, market efficiency tests usually ask whether a given trading strategy earns higher returns than some benchmark, where the benchmark is the "normal" or "expected" return from investing in securities of a given risk level.

Simple Trading Rule Tests

Prior to the 1950s, most experts believed that perceptive investors could identify patterns in stock prices that could be exploited through an appropriate trading strategy. It therefore came as quite a surprise when Maurice Kendall (1953) documented that stock-price changes were essentially uncorrelated with each other. This means that simply knowing that a stock price fell yesterday does not tell you anything useful about what it will do today or tomorrow and also implies that daily stock returns are unpredictable. Subsequent studies by Roberts (1959), Fama (1965), and Jensen and Benington (1970) supported Kendall's conclusion and found that stock prices seemed to follow a random walk.

The lack of persistence in price trends identified by the early finance researchers meant that a strategy of buying recent winners and selling recent losers would not be profitable. Fama and Blume (1966) tested a number of more sophisticated **filter rules,** such as "buy a stock after it has increased by x percent, and don't sell it until it has decreased by y percent." They found that none of these strategies generated significant profits, particularly after accounting for trading costs. This evidence altered the professional consensus and led many people to conclude that trading rules based on such strategies were not worth pursuing in either U.S. or international stock markets.[7] In fact, the view that stock prices moved almost randomly took hold so strongly that the relatively small number of subsequent papers that documented predictable patterns in stock returns was dubbed "the anomalies literature."

Another way to test whether stock prices follow a random walk is to measure whether returns are serially correlated (i.e., correlated from one period to the next). Positive serial correlation means there is a consistent tendency for positive (negative) stock returns in one period to be followed by positive (negative) returns in another, while negative correlation means that positive returns in one period tend to be followed by negative returns in the next. Lo and MacKinlay (1988) developed a unique and innovative method of testing for serial correlation in stock returns by exploiting the fact that the variance of uncorrelated stock returns should increase in direct proportion to the sampling interval (monthly variances should be 4 times larger than weekly variances). They found strong evidence that weekly stock returns are positively correlated, and thus reject the random walk hypothesis.[8] On the other hand, more-recent studies by Richardson and Smith (1994) and others cast doubt on the empirical significance of the serial correlation studies.

If trading strategies based on filter tests and serial correlation do not yield consistent profits, what about other mechanical trading strategies? In the early 1980s, researchers discovered several "anomalies" that seemed to offer investors the opportunity to earn large profits. These included the day-of-the-week effect (Gibbons and Hess 1981), the small-firm effect (Banz 1981), and the January effect (Keim 1983). Gibbons and Hess documented significantly negative abnormal returns for stocks on Mondays, while Banz found significantly positive excess returns on very small (low market capitalization) stocks. Keim pointed out that small stocks earned particularly high returns relative to large stocks in the first few trading days of January. In each case, it seemed that investors could exploit the anomaly through a relatively simple trading strategy. For example, if returns are, on average, lower on Mondays than during the rest of the week,

SMART IDEAS VIDEO

Laura Starks, University of Texas

"Stock prices of small firms tend to be increasing during the first four days of January, a puzzle called the January effect."

See the entire interview at **SMARTFinance**

[7]. International markets are examined by Ojah and Karemera (1999) and Lee, Gleason, and Mathur (2000), among others.
[8]. Lo and MacKinlay (1990) later found a tendency of large stock portfolio returns to lead those of small stock portfolios. This finding was verified by other researchers, including Conrad and Kaul (1988, 1989).

wouldn't it pay an investor (or a mutual fund) to short-sell stocks on Friday afternoons and then repurchase them at a lower price on Tuesday mornings?

The published research that explicitly examines the profitability of such trading strategies often shows that they do not yield excess profits.[9] There are several reasons for this. First, strategies designed to exploit pricing anomalies generally involve a great deal of trading. For example, to exploit the size effect, investors would have to buy a portfolio of the smallest, most illiquid stocks in the market. Strategies that require a great deal of trading naturally generate high transactions costs that eat away most or all of the gross profits from implementing the strategy. Second, some anomalies seem to disappear once they have been identified. Fama (1991) documented that the January effect diminished after Keim's 1983 discovery. Several other anomalies have suffered a similar fate.

A third, rather technical, reason that anomalies may not yield abnormally high trading profits is best illustrated with an example. Suppose that we could document that high-tech stocks earned higher average returns than stocks in the retail sector. Could we call this an anomaly, a violation of efficient markets that investors should exploit to earn abnormally high profits? By now, your financial intuition should be sufficiently developed that you can easily spot the error in our claim. High-tech stocks are likely to be riskier than retail stocks, and in equilibrium they should earn higher returns. But how much higher? Should a portfolio of tech stocks outperform a retail portfolio by 1 percent per year on average? Is 3 percent per year a more reasonable figure? To answer these questions, we need an asset pricing model. Such a model enables us to determine the differences in risk and expected returns between the high-tech and retail portfolios.

Suppose that we use the CAPM to form judgments about the risks and expected returns of the two portfolios, and suppose that given the differences in the betas of the two portfolios, the CAPM predicts that high-tech stocks should earn 2 percent higher returns on average than retail stocks. We look at the historical data and find that tech stocks outperform retail stocks by 4 percent per year, and a new anomaly is born. Our findings suggest that investors should short-sell retail stocks and use the proceeds to buy shares in high-tech firms. Doing so generates abnormally high profits.

For better or worse, there is an alternative interpretation that we must consider. Perhaps the 4 percent premium on high-tech stocks is not an example of market inefficiency, but a failure of the CAPM instead. After all, the CAPM is just a model, and models are prone to errors. Perhaps the CAPM understates the true expected return on high-tech stocks (or overstates the expected return on retail stocks). If we had a more accurate asset pricing model at our disposal, then it might predict that high-tech stocks should outperform retail companies by 4 percent per year, and there would be no anomaly to discuss.

Financial economists refer to this dilemma, first identified by Roll (1977), as the **joint hypothesis problem.** It is almost unavoidable that tests of the EMH are joint tests of market efficiency and the particular asset pricing model used to conduct the test. When an anomaly appears, it may be the result of market inefficiency or of a deficient asset pricing model. For example, Ritter and Chopra (1989) found that the size of the January effect was very sensitive to the choice of stock index used in the test. The current standard in market efficiency research is to use several different asset pricing models to test the robustness of potential anomalies. For most anomalies, reasonable changes in the asset pricing model used to form the benchmark "expected returns" cause the abnormal returns to shrink or to vanish entirely.

---

[9] An important exception to this assertion is the study by Lakonishok and Smidt (1988). They find that several seasonal anomalies yield statistically significant, though quite small, trading profits.

Tests for the Effectiveness of Technical Analysis

The term **technical analysis** describes an investing approach in which analysts search for profitable trading strategies based on recurring patterns in stock prices. Historically, analysts pored over stock charts to identify most of these patterns, and they described them with graphical phrases such as "head and shoulders" or "double tops." Not surprisingly, the investment community began to refer to practitioners of technical analysis as **chartists.** Today, technical analysis involves sophisticated statistical and mathematical tools, as well as computing-intensive tools such as genetic algorithms. Even so, the goal of technical analysis has not changed—to find ways to identify and profit from recurring patterns in prices.

Academic finance has long ridiculed technical analysis because it violates even the weak form of market efficiency, and most early research supported the conclusion that technical analysis was of little value to investors. More recently, however, charting has gained at least a little respect, largely due to the work of Brock, Lakonishok, and LeBaron (1992). These authors tested whether an investor following any of the more popular technical trading rules would have earned excess returns over the 90-year period from 1897 to 1986. Surprisingly, they found that trading rules based on long moving averages of 50, 150, and 250 trading days did in fact outperform the Dow Jones Industrial Average (DJIA). Sullivan, Timmerman, and White (1999) re-examined this issue using a new methodology that allowed them to test nearly *8,000* possible technical trading rules. They also learned that certain trading rules outperformed the DJIA over the 1897–1986 sample period. On balance, however, their evidence contradicts the usefulness of technical analysis and supports weak-form market efficiency. First, they show that the strategies identified in their study do not generate profits after transactions costs. Most telling, they find that none of the trading rules that worked in the 1897–1986 period (or in any subperiod) were profitable versus the DJIA during the following decade.

Lo, Mamaysky, and Wang (2000) examine the usefulness of technical analysis from a different perspective. Rather than test whether technical trading rules yield excess profits to investors, they ask whether any of the standard pricing patterns can be identified *statistically* (rather than visually) and, if so, whether this provides any useful new information. Applying their methodology to a large sample of U.S. stock returns from 1962 to 1996, they find that several technical patterns are in fact observed much more frequently than chance would predict. The four most frequently observed patterns are described in Figure 10.2. "Double tops" and "double bottoms" occur almost four times more frequently than chance alone would suggest, while "head and shoulders" and "inverse head and shoulders" show up three times more often than they should.

Though certainly intriguing, these results do not necessarily amount to a clear violation of market efficiency. Lo, Mamaysky, and Wang themselves acknowledge that identifying recurring patterns does not mean that trading on these patterns would be profitable. In fact, the results presented by previous researchers explicitly show that technical trading rules *do not* generate excess profits when applied out of sample or when realistic transactions costs are accounted for. Market efficiency survives another round.

Tests for Stock Market Underreaction and Overreaction

One of the key predictions of the efficient markets hypothesis is that stock prices should react rapidly and *fully* to new information. Several empirical studies have tested this proposition by examining the completeness of the market's reaction to specific corporate news announcements, and two types of seemingly anomalous patterns

Figure 10.2

The Most Common Technical Analysis Patterns Observed in Stock Prices

These graphs visually describe the four most common patterns in U.S. stock prices over the period 1982 to 1996. The graphs express stock price on the vertical (y) axis and trading days on the horizontal (x) axis.

Source: Andrew W. Lo, Harry Mamaysky, and Jiang Wang, "Foundations of Technical Analysis: Computational Algorithms, Statistical Inference, and Empirical Implementation," *Journal of Finance* 55 (August 2000), pp. 1705–1765.

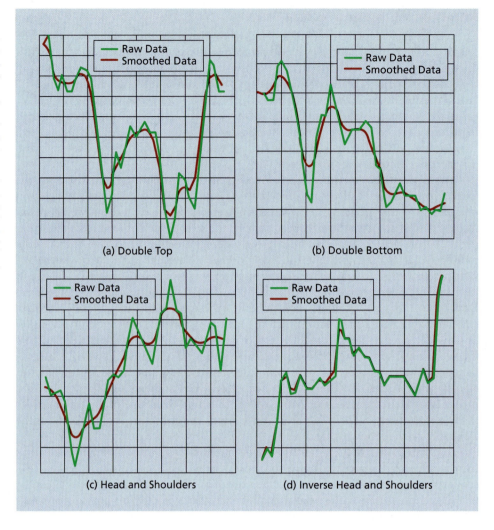

have emerged. One group of studies finds evidence that prices **underreact** to announcements such as dividend initiations and omissions (Michaely, Thaler, and Womack 1995). This means that stock prices on average react positively to, for example, a dividend initiation, but then a positive, ongoing reaction continues over the next several months. This gives rise to a pattern known as stock-price *momentum,* since positive initial returns are followed by more positive returns in the intermediate term. A related group of momentum studies examines whether stocks that perform very well or very poorly in one period (day, month, year, multiyear period) continue to do so in subsequent periods.

The opposite of underreaction to corporate news announcements or prior period returns is **overreaction.** Several studies have examined whether a positive (negative) average reaction to a corporate announcement such as listing of a firm's stock on a new exchange (Dharan and Ikenberry 1995) is generally followed by negative (positive) returns on that stock in subsequent months. Table 10.2 lists several of the most important corporate announcements that researchers have studied. This table indicates whether abnormal returns in a given study are positive or negative before, during, and after the event in question.

Table 10.2
Signs[a] of Long-Term Pre-Event, Announcement, and Long-Term Postevent Returns for Various Long-Term Return Studies

Event	Long-Term Pre-Event Return	Announcement Return	Long-Term Postevent Return
Initial public offerings (IPOs) (Ibbotson 1975; Loughran and Ritter 1995)	Not available	+	−
Seasoned equity offerings (Loughran and Ritter 1995)	+	−	−
Mergers (acquiring firm) (Asquith 1983; Agrawal, Jaffe, and Mandelker 1992)	+	0	−
Dividend initiations (Michaely, Thaler, and Womack 1995)	+	+	+
Dividend omissions (Michaely, Thaler, and Womack 1995)	−	−	−
Earnings announcements (Ball and Brown 1968; Bernard and Thomas 1990)	Not available	+	+
New exchange listings (Dharan and Ikenberry 1995)	+	+	−
Share repurchases (open market) (Ikenberry, Lakonishok, and Vermaelen 1995; Mitchell and Stafford 2000)	0	+	+
Share repurchases (tenders) (Lakonishok and Vermaelen 1990; Mitchell and Stafford 2000)	0	+	+
Proxy fights (Ikenberry and Lakonishok 1993)	−	+	− (or 0)
Stock splits (Dharan and Ikenberry 1995; Ikenberry, Rankine, and Stice 1996)	+	+	+
Spin-offs (Miles and Rosenfeld 1983; Cusatis, Miles, and Woolridge 1993)	+	+	+ (or 0)

[a]A plus sign (+) indicates that the study found positive abnormal returns, a negative sign (−) indicates negative abnormal returns, and a zero (0) indicates no abnormal returns.
Source: Table 1 from Eugene Fama, "Market Efficiency, Long-Term Returns, and Behavioral Finance," *Journal of Financial Economics* 49 (1998), pp. 283–306.
Note: This table summarizes the empirical literature, through 1998, on long-term returns to stockholders around various corporate events. Many of these studies claimed to identify statistically significant long-term over- or underreaction to specific events under the control of corporate managers, such as stock offerings, exchange listings, and dividend initiations.

Evidence of underreaction or overreaction would refute the efficient markets hypothesis because this would imply that a mechanical trading rule would yield excess profits. For example, if stock prices underreact to dividend initiations or omissions, an investor could exploit this by simply purchasing all stocks that initiate dividend payments and short-selling all stocks that omit dividends. If such a strategy yielded positive abnormal returns, semistrong-form market efficiency would be violated because the strategy uses publicly available information to "beat the market."

Underreaction Tests. Underreaction tests fall into several categories. First, some studies have examined whether stock prices underreact to important but infrequent corporate events. These include the aforementioned dividend initiations and omissions, seasoned equity offerings (Loughran and Ritter 1995), stock splits (Ikenberry, Rankine, and Stice 1996; Desai and Jain 1997), share repurchases (Lakonishok and Vermaelen 1990; Mitchell and Stafford 2000), and spin-offs of corporate divisions to investors (Miles and Rosenfeld 1983). As Table 10.2 indicates, most of these actions were announced by corporate managers after an extended period of strong stock-price performance, and most had positive announcement-period and post-announcement-period abnormal returns. The exceptions to this are seasoned equity offerings (positive returns prior to announcement; negative returns at and subsequent to announcement) and dividend omissions, which have negative abnormal returns through the entire period from prior to the omission announcement to years thereafter. These studies suggest that an investor could follow a profitable trading rule of buying the stocks of firms announcing stock splits, dividend increases, share repurchases, and spin-offs, and short-selling the stocks of firms announcing equity issues and dividend omissions.

The second type of underreaction study tests whether stock prices tend to systematically underreact to certain types of routine information disclosures, particularly earnings announcements and recommendations by security analysts. In one of the first such studies, Bernard and Thomas (1990) document that stock prices do not fully incorporate the information embodied in both positive and negative "earnings surprises." They find that a trading strategy of buying the stocks of firms with significant, unanticipated earnings increases over the prior year and selling firms with unexpected earnings decreases consistently yields abnormal returns over the subsequent year. In a later study, Bernard, Thomas, and Abarbanell (1993) find larger abnormal returns for small- and medium-size firms (where they reach 11% and 9.5%, respectively) than for large firms. In other words, investors do not seem to realize that very good (bad) earnings news this quarter will be followed by good (bad) earnings news in subsequent quarters, so stock prices continue to drift up (down) for several months. One recent paper of this genre is a study of brokerage recommendations by Kent Womack (1996), who documents modest but significant (+2.4%) postevent drift after broker buy recommendations and much larger (−9.1%) and longer-lasting drift following sell recommendations.

The third type of underreaction study examines whether buying previous period "winners" or selling prior period "losers" is profitable. Jegadeesh and Titman (1993) find that buying stocks that have increased in price in the recent past and selling those that have performed poorly yields significant abnormal profits over 3- to 12-month holding periods. They also confirm Bernard and Thomas's findings regarding the profitability of a momentum strategy based on earnings. Chan, Jegadeesh, and Lakonishok (1996) attempt to determine why momentum strategies work. They rule out stock-specific factors such as market risk, size, and book-to-market value effects, and instead conclude that it is simply a case of market participants (including secu-

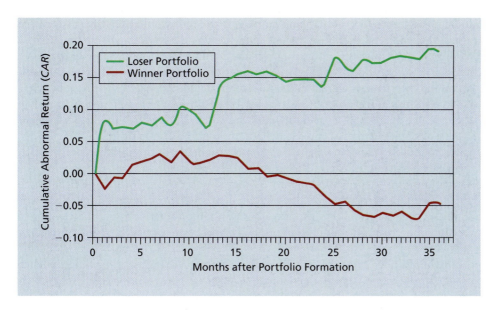

Figure 10.3
Potential Returns from Pursuing an "Over-reaction" Strategy

This figure documents the average 3-year (36-month) return achievable from purchasing a portfolio of extreme "losers" (the 35 stocks with the worst 3-year return prior to portfolio formation) and extreme "winners" (the 35 stocks with the best 3-year return) over the period January 1933 to December 1980.

Source: Werner F. M. DeBondt and Richard Thaler, "Does the Stock Market Overreact?," *Journal of Finance* 40 (July 1985), pp. 793–805.

rity analysts) responding only gradually to new information. Moskowitz and Grinblatt (1999) argue that momentum is mostly an industry-level phenomenon. They show that an industry-based momentum trading strategy is profitable, though they point out that such an undiversified trading portfolio (concentrated in one industry) would be quite risky. However, Lewellen (2002) finds strong evidence of momentum even in diversified portfolios.

Overreaction Tests. One of the most important early tests of market overreaction was a study by DeBondt and Thaler (1985). Their results indicate that portfolios of prior extreme "losers" dramatically outperform prior extreme "winners," even though the latter are more risky. Dubbed the value stock phenomenon, because stocks in the "loser" portfolio trade at low prices relative to earnings, dividends, and other measures of fundamental value, this effect cumulates to the point that, 36 months after portfolio formation, the prior-period losing stocks have earned 25 percent more than the winners. DeBondt and Thaler's principal results appear in Figure 10.3. Studies by Jegadeesh (1990) and Jegadeesh and Titman (1993) also test trading strategies based on stock-price overreaction, and find seemingly massive profit opportunities.

Though the profitable trading opportunities offered by an overreaction investing strategy appear impressive, many people remain unconvinced that stock markets overreact at all. These skeptics make three key points. First, studies by McQueen (1992) and Jones (1993) show that the price reversals documented by DeBondt and Thaler were much larger during the Depression and World War II than in any other period.[10] Ball, Kothari, and Shanken (1995) find that the DeBondt and Thaler results were distorted by some very large (up to 3500%!) percentage gains on some very low-priced stocks. Second, the potential profits identified by the overreaction studies are simply too large to be credible. If real, such simple trading strategies should have been

---

[10.] Cox and Peterson (1994) cast further doubt on the validity of DeBondt and Thaler's overreaction hypothesis. Cox and Peterson show that much of the daily "bounce back" in stock prices following large (10% or more) 1-day price declines is caused by liquidity and bid-ask spread effects, not by market irrationality. Furthermore, they document that even this pattern of overreaction has disappeared since 1987. Conrad and Kaul (1993) also find that U.S. stock prices do not overshoot, and Baytas and Cakici (1999) present similar findings for international stock markets.

adopted by at least a few mutual fund managers, and thus would have left a discernible trace in the empirical literature, but no evidence of this exists.[11] Most telling, Fama (1998) points out that the empirical evidence documents a roughly equal number of examples of stock-price overreactions as underreactions. This is what you would expect to find by chance if a great many talented researchers pored over the same database (the historical record of U.S. stock prices) searching for anomalies.

Fama also makes the case that most of the under- and overreaction tests are very sensitive to slight changes in empirical methodology and that many of the conclusions drawn from these studies are based on equally weighted returns. In other words, studies that examine underreaction to corporate events place the same weight on the observations of a very small company as they do on returns for a large firm in the sample. When researchers use value-weighted returns, most of the anomalous over- and underreaction evidence disappears. A final point about assessing the validity of over- and underreaction studies is in order. The proper test of such a trading strategy is not whether it yields profits when applied to historical returns, but whether it yields profits when applied out of sample. By this measure, there is less-compelling evidence that stock prices consistently over- or underreact in a way that violates market efficiency. Beyond that, even if trading strategies based on the value phenomenon or on momentum generate abnormal profits on average, investors are not necessarily over- or underreacting irrationally to information. Brav and Heaton (2002) develop a model in which investors are fully rational but lack complete information. In this world, anomalies can exist even if investors do not suffer from the psychological biases described in behavioral finance research.

Tests of Long-Run Returns to Firms Issuing Common Stock

As early as 1975, academic researchers (Ibbotson 1975) began to document the strange result that initial public offerings were, on average, significantly **underpriced.** This means that an investor who purchased the typical IPO at the offering price and sold the stock at the end of the first day's trading earned an *initial return* that averaged around 15 percent. Not a bad return for a 1-day investment! Though such a large return seems hard to square with market efficiency, several special characteristics of the IPO market suggest that these returns are not entirely at odds with efficient markets. First, the median initial returns (around 6%) documented by Ibbotson, Sindelar, and Ritter (1994) and others were much lower than the mean returns. Second, there is almost always excess demand for the most underpriced (and hence most profitable) IPOs, so investors generally cannot buy as many shares in these deals as they want. However, investors are more likely to receive large share allocations in IPOs that are overpriced.[12] In other words, it may be very difficult in practice for an investor to earn the "average return" that researchers calculate when they study IPOs. These factors led many financial economists to conclude that IPO underpricing did not present a major challenge to market efficiency.

This contented state of affairs ended abruptly with Jay Ritter's (1991) study documenting that investors who purchased shares in newly public companies *after* the IPO earned significantly negative abnormal returns over the next several years. In fact,

---

[11.] The literature on mutual fund investment performance is surveyed later in this subsection, but there is little evidence that managers of these funds can consistently beat the market. In fact, a well-known academic, Richard Roll (1994), argues from personal experience as a multi-billion-dollar mutual fund manager that real trading strategies based on overreaction and other anomalies do not yield excess returns.

[12.] This leads to what is known as the **winner's curse,** since an investor who "wins" by achieving a goal of purchasing a full allotment of stock actually loses because the stock thus purchased immediately declines in price. The moral here: Be careful what you ask for, as you may get it!

such an investment strategy left investors with 44 percent less wealth than they would have had by simply buying the market portfolio. Such a large negative excess return, if robust, would directly contradict weak-form efficiency, as it begs the question: Why do investors keep buying shares in IPOs when the average return is so bad? This anomaly became even more puzzling when Loughran and Ritter (1995, 2000) and Spiess and Affleck-Graves (1995) also documented negative average long-run returns following seasoned equity offerings. These were similar in magnitude to the negative IPO returns, and they raised the same perplexing question about why investors continue to buy newly issued stock.

Several authors have cast doubt on the validity and/or interpretation of these findings of negative long-run returns to firms issuing common stock. Brav and Gompers (1997) find that only the smallest IPOs not backed by venture capital firms underperform. Venture capital–backed firms and larger IPOs do not underperform. Furthermore, Brav, Geczy, and Gompers (2000) find that small firms generally, and not firms that issue equity to the market, are the ones who underperform the market. Finally, Gompers and Lerner (2000) show that there was no evidence of poor long-term performance for IPO stocks in the period before the formation of Nasdaq in 1972.

The response to this challenge to the EMH has indeed been impressive, though it is unclear both whether a separate new-issue effect exists and whether this constitutes a de facto violation of market efficiency. This is one of the most important challenges to the EMH, and it is likely to remain hotly debated for years to come.

Tests for Rapid Price Adjustment

In one of the most influential empirical articles in financial economics, Fama, Fisher, Jensen, and Roll (1969) presented the first **event study,** which examined how stock markets respond to new information releases. Their study analyzed the market's response to stock splits. In a stock split, firms distribute new shares to existing shareholders, which causes a decline in the stock price. For example, in a 2-for-1 split, shareholders receive one new share for every existing share they own, and the stock price drops by roughly 50 percent. The innovation of this study was to line up the companies in *event time* rather than in calendar time. For every company, the researchers assigned day 0 to the date the stock split was executed, day -1 to the trading day before the split date, day $+1$ to the trading day immediately following the split, and so on.[13] This allowed them to calculate the average return for each event day simply by summing up all the sample returns from, for example, day -1 to day $+5$, and then dividing by the number of observations. The study results, which appear in Figure 10.4, show that firms that choose to split their stock do so after an extended period during which their stock earns above-market returns. After the split, however, the stock earns returns roughly equal to those of the overall market. This suggests that markets are efficient because investors who buy shares after split announcements do not earn above-market returns. The event study soon became one of the key tools empirical researchers used to study how the stock market reacted to many different corporate events, such as security issues or merger announcements.

In this section, we examine tests of the EMH that focus on whether prices adjust rapidly to news, grouping studies into two categories. First, *event studies* examine whether prices of stocks and other financial assets adjust fully and rapidly to new in-

---

[13.] Fama, Fisher, Jensen, and Roll (FFJR) actually used monthly, rather than daily, stock return data because only monthly data were available in the late-1960s. However, because we are discussing FFJR as the paradigm of event studies, and because most post-1980 event studies have employed daily data, we will use the term "event day" even in our discussion of FFJR's results.

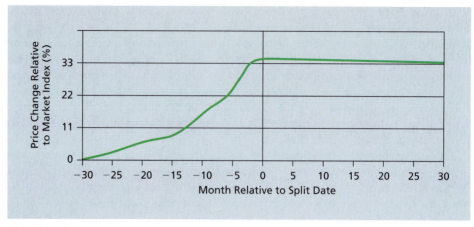

Figure 10.4
The First Event Study—Stock Splits

This figure describes the average stock price response to the "event" of a stock split where a company distributes, say, two shares to investors for every one share they already own (a 2-for-1 stock split). The stock prices are lined up in "event time," where the month of the stock split is defined as 0. Because all of the information in the stock split is incorporated into stock prices by the event date, there is on average no tendency for prices to change after the split.

Source: Eugene F. Fama, Lawrence Fisher, Michael C. Jensen, and Richard Roll, "The Adjustment of Stock Prices to New Information," *International Economic Review* 10 (February 1969), pp. 1–21, as presented in Ray Ball, "The Theory of Stock Market Efficiency: Accomplishments and Limitations," *Journal of Applied Corporate Finance* 8 (Spring 1995), pp. 4–17.

formation. The second category is a rather amorphous group of studies that examine whether (and how) financial markets rationally process all available information. Included in this group are tests of how markets process rumors, unexpected announcements with uncertain outcomes, and news about additions and deletions of shares from major stock indexes.

Event Studies

As empirical tools, event studies have several major strengths. Consider the advantages of using the event study approach to determine how the market reacts to dividend increases. When a particular firm announces that it will pay higher dividends, its stock price may rise or fall because the price is affected by many factors other than the dividend announcement. However, when researchers look at dividend-announcement days for a large number of firms (lining up their returns in event time), much of the random noise in returns cancels out, leaving the one characteristic that the firms all have in common—the reaction to the dividend announcement. Furthermore, by examining announcement returns on a single day (or over just a few days), researchers finesse the joint hypothesis problem. No matter what asset pricing model researchers use in their tests, the expected return on a single day will be close to zero, and therefore a bad asset pricing model cannot impart a large bias to the test.[14] Finally, by analyzing returns after the event, researches can determine whether stock prices drift up or down. This tests the market efficiency prediction that prices should respond quickly and fully to new information.

[14.] The vagaries of event study methodology have been explored at length in numerous studies. See especially Brown and Warner (1980, 1985). Reassuringly, these studies show that event studies are quite robust to changes in the specific return-generating process used to calculate expected returns and to the event interval examined, provided that an event date can be precisely identified.

Event studies have dramatically advanced our understanding of how stockholders view dividend payments, security issues, takeover bids, and myriad other internal and external financial events. A very important example of the potential impact of this methodology is the Bradley, Desai, and Kim (1988) event study of the returns to both bidding and target firms in cash tender offers (takeover bids) over the period 1963–1984. This study documents that the increase in the combined value of bidder and target firms' stocks (the synergistic gain) averaged a virtually constant 7.4 percent throughout this 22-year period, but that the split of the total synergistic gain shifted steadily in favor of the target during the three subperiods of the study (1963–1968, 1968–1980, and 1981–1984). Just as important, stock prices responded instantaneously and completely to the tender-offer announcements.

Many other authors have used event studies to answer important corporate finance questions. The key point of this research is that, with some important exceptions, event studies tend to support market efficiency, revealing that stock prices respond quickly and completely to news.

Tests of Rational Information Processing

In addition to carrying out event studies, numerous researchers have examined whether financial markets process current information in a rapid and *rational* manner. Taken together, these studies provide indirect evidence largely supportive of semistrong-form market efficiency. Pound and Zeckhauser (1990) study the response to takeover rumors published in the "Heard on the Street" column of the *Wall Street Journal*. They find that the market responds efficiently, in that a simple trading rule based on buying rumored takeover targets yields no excess returns. They also document that these rumors are usually incorrect, because only 18 of the 42 sample companies received takeover bids within one year, and only 2 received bids within 50 days. On the other hand, numerous researchers have documented a significant run-up in the stock prices of firms that in fact do become targets of takeover bids. Whether this results from insiders trading on nonpublic information (which is illegal) or from perceptive analysis of public documents such as SEC filings, or both, is still not clear.[15]

Several authors examine whether the phenomenon of significant positive stock-price responses for companies that are chosen for inclusion in the S&P 500 Index—or one of the other popular indexes—is compatible with market efficiency. As do earlier researchers, Dhillon and Johnson (1991) document a positive stock-price effect resulting from the inclusion announcement. Unlike previous researchers, however, they find no evidence that this price increase dissipates in the months after inclusion, as predicted by the price-pressure hypothesis.[16] Finally, Ederington and Lee (1993) examine the impact of scheduled macroeconomic news announcements on interest rate and foreign exchange futures contract prices. They examine futures markets because they open for trading 10 minutes before the 8:30 A.M. time when these an-

---

[15.] Jarrell and Poulsen (1989) find that much of this run-up can be explained by market participants analyzing several sources of legitimate information, such as the forms potential acquirers must file with the SEC when they accumulate more than 5 percent of a firm's stock. While noncommittal regarding the cause of this run-up, Schwert (1996) shows that it is unrelated to the subsequent takeover premium offered by a bidder. In other words, bidders must pay a premium both for the firm itself and for the prebid run-up.

[16.] This hypothesis, presented most clearly by Harris and Gurel (1984), suggests that stocks are not perfect substitutes for each other and implies that a share's inclusion in an index leads to a temporary surge in trading volume and stock price. This occurs because investors rebalance their index-linked portfolios to include the new index component. Once this demand has been met, volume slows and the stock's price falls back to its original level. This would be incompatible with market efficiency because a trading strategy of shorting stocks immediately after announcement of their inclusion (after prices rise) and then closing out the position after prices readjust would yield excess profits. Interestingly, a study of the S&P 500 Index using post–October 1989 data by Lynch and Mendenhall (1997) documents just such a pattern.

nouncements are made, whereas stock markets do not open until 9:30. These authors document both that several types of macroeconomic announcements significantly impact interest rate and foreign exchange contracts, and that the bulk of the price adjustment to a major announcement occurs *within the first minute* of trading, although volatility remains substantially higher than normal for at least 15 minutes after the announcement. On balance, these tests of rational information processing support the conclusion suggested by the event study evidence—markets respond rapidly and completely to most types of new information releases.

TESTS FOR PRIVATE INFORMATION

In place of tests of strong-form market efficiency, Fama's 1991 survey article suggested the phrase "tests for private information." Implied in this is an examination of whether someone, such as a corporate insider or a particularly perceptive mutual fund manager, could earn excess returns by trading on private (nonpublic) information. We categorize these tests into three groups and review them below.

Tests of the Profitability of Insider Trading

The most direct test of strong-form market efficiency is whether corporate insiders can earn abnormal profits when they trade in their own firms' securities. As you surely suspect, studies document that insiders do earn excess returns on these trades, contrary to strong-form market efficiency. The studies differ, however, on the critical issue of whether outside investors can earn excess profits by mimicking insider trades after they are publicly disclosed. Jaffe (1974) reports that outsiders can profit from mimicking trades, which constitutes a rejection of semistrong-form efficiency. However, Seyhun (1986) argues that real investors cannot learn about and trade on insider trades as quickly as Jaffee assumes they can. Using actual information-release dates, Seyhun shows that outside investors cannot profit by mimicking the announced trades of corporate insiders. In a subsequent study, Seyhun and Bradley (1997) also show that insiders frequently sell shares of their firms' stock prior to filing for bankruptcy protection and make significant abnormal profits on these transactions.

The previous three studies thus represent a rejection of strong-form market efficiency, though Seyhun's work does support semistrong-form efficiency. Intriguing, related efficiency questions are whether and how quickly private information is incorporated into market prices through the act of trading. In her study of traders convicted of illegal trading on nonpublic information, Lisa Meulbroek (1992) documents that the abnormal return surrounding insider trades averages 3 percent per day. Combining all cases of known insider trading prior to takeover bids, she finds that almost half the pretakeover run-up in the target firm's stock price occurs on days when insiders illegally trade. This clearly shows that markets incorporate some nonpublic information into stock prices.[17]

Tests of Mutual Fund Investment Performance

In our experience, students approach the notion of market efficiency with a great deal of skepticism. Surely, smart investors can beat the market if they work hard enough.

[17.] Though it is not a test of market efficiency, the survey of insider trading laws and enforcement around the world provided in Bhattacharya and Daouk (2001) shows that insider trading is a severe problem in almost every market outside the United States and a few other advanced industrial countries. Insider trading is so severe in Mexico, in fact, that Bhattacharya, Daouk, Jorgenson, and Kehr (2000) find that stock prices do not react *at all* to company-specific news announcements. All the information content of the announcement had been embedded in stock prices due to insider trading beforehand.

Research on the performance of professionally managed mutual funds offers perhaps the most compelling evidence that outguessing the market is extremely challenging. More than 30 years ago, Sharpe (1966) and Jensen (1968) reported negative net returns for the majority of mutual fund managers. Net returns in this context equal gross returns minus fund operating costs. Jensen's model for assessing mutual fund performance has been used by many subsequent researchers:

$$R_{pt} - R_{ft} = \alpha_p + \beta_p(R_{mt} - R_{ft}) + u_{pt} \qquad \text{(Eq. 10.2)}$$

where $R_{pt} - R_{ft}$ = the excess return, above the risk-free rate R_{ft}, on a managed portfolio,

β_p = the beta of the portfolio during period t,

$R_{mt} - R_{ft}$ = the excess return on the market portfolio during period t,

α_p = the regression "alpha" or intercept term, and

u_{pt} = an error term.

In this framework, the product of a fund's beta times the risk premium on the market, $\beta_p(R_{mt} - R_{ft})$, measures the fund's expected return given its risk. Therefore, testing for superior investment performance (i.e., for returns that reflect more than just compensation for risk) reduces to a test of whether the intercept term, α_p, is significantly greater than zero. To this day, even casual discussions of a mutual fund's performance will often be couched as "What is the fund's alpha?" Jensen found that the funds in his sample had negative alphas, meaning that they did not even match the market return. Since Sharpe documented a similar result, the received wisdom within the finance profession (at least within academia) was that mutual fund managers, on average, could not beat the stock market on a risk-adjusted basis.[18]

Following publication of the Sharpe and Jensen studies, a veritable cottage industry emerged to assess the investment performance of mutual fund managers. Most of these studies separate managerial investment performance into two components: **selectivity** (stock-picking ability) and **timing** (the ability to time market turns—getting in before upturns and getting out before crashes). Several important studies claim to document superior mutual fund performance, at least before fund expenses are deducted to calculate a net return to fund investors. These include Bjerring, Lakonishok, and Vermaelen (1983), Cumby and Modest (1987), Ippolito (1989), Edelen (1999), and Wermers (2000). Both Edelen and Wermers show that a key factor depressing measured returns for mutual fund managers is their need to maintain sizable holdings of cash and marketable securities so that they can meet withdrawal demands from fund investors. These nonstock holdings reduce measured returns by about 1 percent on average.

Naturally, some mutual fund managers will beat the market over a given period of time, even if the average fund manager does not. An important question for researchers and investors alike is whether the performance of a fund persists over time, or whether fund performance, like stock prices, fluctuates randomly. Hendricks, Patel, and Zeckhauser (1993) find that the relative performance of no-load, growth-

---

[18.] We add the modifier "on a risk-adjusted basis" because if a fund beats the market simply by investing in very risky stocks, the higher return does not reflect superior stock-selection ability by the manager. Instead, the higher return merely compensates investors for the extra risk they take when investing in the fund.

oriented mutual funds persists in the near term, with the strongest evidence being found for a 1-year evaluation horizon. They also present provocative findings that an investor who pursues an investment strategy of buying the funds managed by "hot hands" and avoiding funds managed by "icy hands" (the evil twin of hot hands) will earn risk-adjusted abnormal returns as high as 6 percent per year. Goetzmann and Ibbotson (1994) and Carpenter and Lynch (1999) also present evidence that successful mutual fund managers tend to earn above-average returns in subsequent periods. On the other hand, Carhart (1997) disputes these results. He finds, as do Pástor and Stambaugh (2002), that individual fund managers who follow a momentum strategy do not earn excess returns.

The studies finding superior (or at least break-even) mutual fund performance have also been attacked on several other fronts by defenders of market efficiency. In perhaps the best such retort, Malkiel (1995), whose books have popularized the notion that stock prices follow a random walk, points out two critical biases in most of the tests showing superior performance. The first and most serious is the *survivorship bias*. This involves examining the returns over, say, the period 1982–1991 of mutual funds that are still in existence in 1991 and comparing the returns on these funds to those of the S&P 500 or some other index. By definition, such a strategy involves examining only surviving, successful funds and ignores funds with seemingly equal promise in 1982 that earned subpar returns and were closed down (or merged) by their managers over the next decade. As Table 10.3 clearly shows, this survivorship bias dramatically overstates the returns earned by mutual fund managers. Funds that were closed between 1982 and 1992 earned lower returns than those that survived. Therefore, if researchers begin their analysis by looking only at the funds that survived (which is clearly something that an investor choosing a fund in 1982 could not do), they overstate the average fund's performance. The second bias Malkiel documents is the tendency of mutual fund management companies to privately launch a large number (say, 10) of "incubator" funds, and then after a few years to publicly launch those 2 or 3 funds that have been the most successful. The 7 or 8 poorly per-

Table 10.3
Differences in Rates of Return of Surviving and Nonsurviving Mutual Funds

Year	Total Funds in Existence		Total Number of Funds Surviving until 1992		Funds That Did Not Survive until 1992			T-test for Difference between Means of Surviving and Nonsurviving Funds
	Mean Return	Number	Mean Return	Number	Mean Return	Number	Mortality Rate	
1982	25.03	331	26.03	272	20.42	59	17.8	3.09
1983	20.23	353	21.66	296	12.80	57	16.1	7.15
1984	−2.08	395	−1.25	331	−6.39	64	16.2	3.67
1985	27.17	431	28.10	371	21.42	60	13.9	5.77
1986	13.39	511	14.39	425	8.45	86	16.8	6.29
1987	0.47	581	0.92	489	−1.91	92	15.8	3.04
1988	14.44	686	15.48	586	8.35	100	14.6	7.54
1989	23.99	720	24.91	639	16.73	81	11.3	7.57
1990	−6.27	724	−6.00	685	−11.07	39	5.4	4.07

Source: Burton G. Malkiel, "Return from Investing in Equity Mutual Funds 1971 to 1991," *Journal of Finance* 50 (June 1995), pp. 549–572.

forming funds are shut down, so their returns are not included in the "stellar" fund averages. Once these two biases are accounted for, Malkiel finds that mutual funds underperform the S&P 500 even before deducting transaction costs and load fees; their net return (after fees and expenses) is far worse.[19]

Like many other MBA students, your first reaction to this litany of academic studies favoring market efficiency is probably disbelief. What about Peter Lynch, Warren Buffet, George Soros, or the other investment gurus whose performances have become part of Wall Street lore?[20] Or, for that matter, if mutual fund managers actually subtract value from the portfolios they manage, why have they been so successful over the past decade that today there are more mutual funds than there are stocks listed on the New York Stock Exchange? Gruber (1996) argues that there is enough persistence in fund performance over time that sophisticated investors can earn higher returns than they could earn on a passive, buy-and-hold strategy. Although it is indeed difficult to deny that a few individuals and funds have long-term performance that seems inexplicably high, this is actually what you would expect as a result of the survivorship bias discussed earlier.

To see this, consider the following exercise. At the beginning of a decade (say, the year 2000), survey all 5,000 currently active mutual fund managers and ask each to pick a basket of stocks that he or she expects to outperform the S&P index over the coming year. Market efficiency predicts that by chance, roughly half of the managers will pick a portfolio that outperforms the S&P in 2000, and half will underperform. Those that outperform the index in 2000 are asked to try again in 2001, and so on as long as they continue to beat the market. By the end of the decade, the original 5,000 managers will be whittled down to a mere 5. Put differently, 5 of 5,000 managers can be expected to outperform the market 10 years in a row merely by chance, but these 5 will be the ones who are lionized as investment gurus.[21] Potential consumers of investment advice should ask themselves why an investment guru is offering to sell "unbeatable" investment advice. If the investment strategy being peddled truly yields superior returns, why let the world in on the secret? It would make far more sense for the guru to form a private investment fund and to exploit the strategy in secret. The important question is not whether some investors beat the market over long periods of time, but whether the number of these very successful investors relative to the total population of professionals trying to beat the market is higher than random chance would predict. Affirmative evidence to that question is relatively scarce.

Tests of Pension Fund and Hedge Fund Investment Performance

Somewhat surprising, the investment performance of pension funds has attracted far less attention than has that of mutual funds, even though pension funds exercise

---

[19.] Several other studies also find that mutual fund managers have average investment performance records that are dominated by the S&P 500 Index. See, for example, Grinblatt and Titman (1989) and Elton, Gruber, Das, and Hlavka (1993).

[20.] Actually, the investment advice of even recognized gurus is less valuable than commonly imagined. Desai and Jain (1995) show this dramatically in their study of the returns an investor would have earned if he or she had followed the buy recommendations made by the most widely respected money managers each year, as published in *Barron's,* over the period 1968 to 1991. These recommendations earn significant abnormal returns of 1.91 percent between the time they are made and the date they are published (a period of about 14 days), but the abnormal returns are essentially zero for 1- to 3-year postpublication holding periods. And remember, these managers are believed to be the best of the best. A more general study by Graham and Harvey (1996) examining the value of a sample of 237 investment newsletter strategies over the period 1980–1992 reaches a similar conclusion.

[21.] Greene and Smart (1999) documented this pattern in a *Wall Street Journal* stock-picking contest in which 100 professional investors picked stocks that they expected to beat the market over a 6-month period. After six months, those contestants who beat the market were invited to try again. Market efficiency predicts that 50 analysts would beat the market in the first round, 25 would do so in the second round, and so on. In fact, 53 analysts succeeded in the first round and 27 did in the second round. The pros' success rate is statistically indistinguishable from the outcome predicted by the efficient markets hypothesis.

In this chapter's Opening Focus, we saw how the U.S. stock market reacted quickly to a premature employment report from the Department of Commerce. It should not surprise you that the U.S. stock market is not the only one that responds to these announcements. Becker, Finnerty, and Friedman (1995) studied the reaction of the U.K. equity market to U.S. news announcements and found that the U.K. market moved quickly in response to news from across the Atlantic Ocean. The U.S. government typically releases key macroeconomic statistics at 8:30 A.M. Eastern Standard Time (EST), which corresponds to 1:30 P.M. Greenwich Mean Time (GMT). Although the government intentionally releases this information before the U.S. stock markets open, analysts can measure the impact of the news by comparing the market's opening level on the day of an important announcement to its close the previous day (the *overnight return*). Measuring the impact of these announcements on U.K. stocks is easier because the London Stock Exchange is active at that time.

The first row of the table below shows the correlation between the overnight return on the S&P 500 and the return on the Financial Times Stock Exchange 100 Index (FTSE) from 1:30 to 2:00 P.M. GMT on days with and without macroeconomic news announcements. Not surprising, these returns are highly correlated (0.63) on announcement days and are relatively uncorrelated (0.056) on other days. The second row calculates the variance of FTSE returns from 1:30 to 2:00 on announcement and nonannouncement days. Notice that in the half hour around U.S. news announcements, the variance of the FTSE index is more than five times higher than it is during the same half hour on days with no news. However, the difference in volatility on days with and without announcements vanishes just one-half hour later (third row), suggesting that the FTSE response to U.S. news is indeed very rapid.

The linkages that exist when stock markets around the world are efficient create headaches for mutual fund managers. A standard practice in the mutual fund industry is to calculate the price at which investors can buy or sell fund shares (the net asset value, or *NAV*), using market closing prices. Mutual fund managers who invest in overseas markets must contend with the fact that markets around the world open and close at different times, and this creates a "stale price" problem that smart investors can exploit to earn arbitrage profits. Consider, for example, the case of a U.S. mutual fund that invests in Japanese stocks. The Japanese market closes each day at 1:00 A.M. EST, several hours before the U.S. market opens. During the U.S. trading day, news develops that will influence stock prices in Japan when trading resumes. If the news is good, investors can purchase shares in the Japanese mutual fund at prices that reflect the previous day's close. Or, if the news is bad, investors can sell shares in the fund, putting their money into a safe investment, such as a money market fund, until the next good news arrives.

The events of October 28 and 29, 1997, illustrate the problem fund managers face. On October 28, stock markets around the world fell precipitously, especially in Asia. At the end of the trading day in Asia, U.S. fund managers calculated the *NAV*s of their funds using the closing prices in Japan, Hong Kong, and so on. A few hours after the Asian markets closed, the U.S. market rallied, rising more than 10 percent in the morning, and closing up about 4.5 percent for the day. This signaled to investors that Asian markets would likely reopen higher, and investors in droves took the opportunity to buy shares of Asian-focused mutual funds at the now-stale *NAV*s. As expected, Asian markets followed the U.S. rally on October 29, and some investors earned returns of 8–9 percent on a single day. Goetzmann, Ivkovic, and Rouwenhorst (2001) estimate that this type

Impact of U.S. Macroeconomic News Announcements on FTSE Index		
Statistic	Days without Announcements	Days with Announcements
Correlation between U.S. overnight return and FTSE 1:30–2:00 P.M. GMT return	0.056	0.630
Variance of FTSE returns from 1:30 to 2:00 P.M. GMT	0.264	1.445
Variance of FTSE returns from 2:00 to 2:30 P.M. GMT	0.510	0.475

of arbitrage beats a buy-and-hold strategy by roughly 20 percent per year, while Greene and Hodges (2002) show that the trades of arbitrageurs dilute returns for passive investors in international mutual funds by as much as 1 percent per year.

Sources: Kent G. Becker, Joseph E. Finnerty, and Joseph Friedman, "Economic News and Equity Market Linkages between the U.S. and U.K.," *Journal of Banking and Finance* 19 (1995), pp. 1191–1210; William N. Goetzmann, Zoran Ivkovic, and K. Geert Rouwenhorst, "Day Trading International Mutual Funds: Evidence and Policy Solutions," *Journal of Financial and Quantitative Analysis* 36 (September 2001), pp. 287–309; Jason T. Greene and Charles W. Hodges, "The Dilution Impact of Daily Fund Flows on Open-end Mutual Funds," *Journal of Financial Economics* 65 (July 2002), pp. 131–158.

control over more assets. Brinson, Hood, and Beebower (1986) demonstrate that investment policy (the percentage allocation of funds to different asset classes) is far more important than investment strategy in explaining the cross-sectional variation in fund returns. They also document that active management yields an average total return 1.10 percent per year *less* than that achievable with a passive strategy of buying the market index. On the other hand, Coggin, Fabozzi, and Rahman (1993) find that the best pension fund managers produce risk-adjusted excess returns 6 percent higher than those achieved by the poorest fund managers.

One of the most interesting types of professionally managed investment funds to reach prominence in recent years is the **hedge fund.** These differ from U.S. mutual funds in their organizational structure (most are partnerships instead of corporations), in their extensive use of performance-based compensation, in their generally higher appetites for risk taking, and in their being largely unregulated. In the first major empirical study of hedge funds, Ackermann, McEnally, and Ravenscraft (1999) not only document these differences between hedge funds and mutual funds, but also test whether their sample of 906 hedge funds outperforms mutual funds over the period 1988 to 1995. They show that hedge funds consistently outperform mutual funds, but not standard market indexes.

In summary, there is no unambiguous answer to the question of whether professionally managed funds are able to achieve investment returns comparable to that achievable with a naive buy-and-hold investment strategy. Even this lack of conclusive evidence, however, amounts to damning fund managers with faint praise, because the evidence that they can achieve significantly positive *net* returns (after deducting fees and expenses) for fund shareholders is relatively scarce. The mutual, pension, and hedge fund performance studies therefore do little to disprove the semistrong form of the efficient market hypothesis.

Tests of the Stock-Picking Abilities of Security Analysts

The final empirical studies we survey in this section are those that examine whether security analysts and investment newsletter writers demonstrate superior stock-picking abilities. Many students have heard that the *Value Line Investment Survey* has a reputation for selecting stocks that subsequently outperform the market portfolio, and there is some empirical evidence to support this belief (Stickel 1985). The question for market efficiency is whether this is a common phenomenon: Can security analysts make recommendations that consistently beat the markets? There is some evidence that they can. For example, Womack (1996) documents that brokerage recommendations do embody valuable information for which a brokerage firm should be compensated. Additionally, Barber, Lehavy, McNichols, and Trueman (2001; hereafter

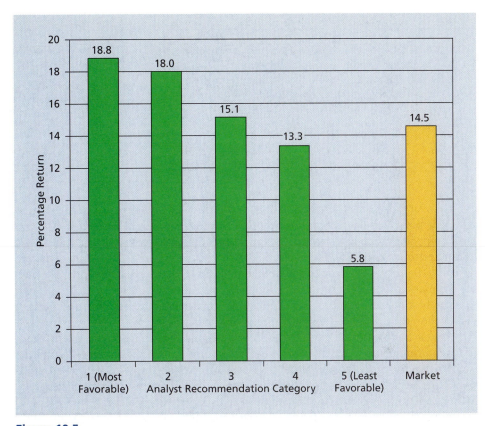

Figure 10.5
Can Security Analysts Beat the Market? Returns Earned by Portfolios Formed on the Basis of Consensus Analyst Recommendations, 1986–1996

This figure describes annualized geometric mean percentage returns an investor could earn by forming portfolios based on changes in the consensus of analyst recommendations of individual stocks from 1986 to 1996. The consensus forecast is generated using Zacks' Recommendation Database, *which details the recommendations made by analysts at top-tier brokerage firms. The specific trading strategy detailed in the figure involves buying a stock that is moved into a more favorable category and short-selling a stock that is moved to a less favorable category.*

Source: Brad Barber, Reuven Lehavy, Maureen McNichols, and Brett Trueman, "Can Investors Profit from the Prophets? Security Analyst Recommendations and Stock Returns," *Journal of Finance* 56 (April 2001), pp. 531–563.

BLMT) show that investors who followed the consensus advice of the 4,340 analysts (and 361,620 individual recommendations) covered in the *Zacks Recommendation Database* from 1985 to 1996 earned excess profits of more than 4 percent per year. The specific strategy in the BLMT study is to buy a stock when analysts move it into a more favorable recommendation category and to short-sell a stock when it moves into a less-favorable category. The annual returns on buying and selling stocks that move between the five recommendation categories are presented in Figure 10.5, along with the average annual return on the market portfolio.

On its face, the BLMT study seems to provide striking evidence in favor of security analysts' stock-selection ability, and in contradiction to market efficiency. The catch is that very high portfolio turnover, of up to *400 percent* per year, is required to achieve these returns. Trading costs make this strategy far less profitable. Using a comprehensive and bias-free database covering analysts' recommendations from 1980 to 1996, Metrick

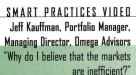

SMART PRACTICES VIDEO
Jeff Kauffman, Portfolio Manager, Managing Director, Omega Advisors
"Why do I believe that the markets are inefficient?"

See the entire interview at **SMARTFinance**

(1999) finds no significant evidence of stock-picking ability. Additionally, Metrick finds no evidence of abnormal short-run performance persistence, or hot hands, among the analysts studied.[22]

An interesting question that is also related to the stock-picking ability of analysts is whether they **herd** together by following each others' recommendations. Obviously, few analysts would admit to such behavior, as this would beg the question why anyone would pay for such secondhand advice. Nonetheless, there is substantial theoretical and empirical evidence that herding behavior is very common among newsletter writers. Graham (1999) finds that several types of analysts are likely to herd on *Value Line*'s recommendations, and Welch (2000) shows that the buy and sell recommendations of analysts have a significant positive influence on the next two analysts to publish forecasts. Finally, Chang, Cheng, and Khorana (2000) find that herding behavior is so extreme in Korea and Taiwan that macroeconomic information has more impact on stock prices than does stock-specific information.

On balance, there seems to be little empirical evidence to suggest that the advice offered by security analysts allows investors to consistently beat the market portfolio of stocks. Together with the other empirical evidence surveyed in this section, the EMH appears quite undamaged. Before reaching this conclusion, however, we must weigh the evidence marshaled against market efficiency by the acolytes of behavioral finance.

Smart Concepts

See the concept explained step-by-step at **SMARTFinance**

Concept Review Questions

6. What are the strongest pieces of evidence in support of the EMH? Against it?

7. The "Super Bowl Predictor" suggests that the stock market will rise during a year when a former-NFL professional football team wins the Super Bowl, and will fall when a former-AFL team wins. This predictor has correctly forecast the stock market's actual performance almost 90 percent of the time during the past three decades, far better than most human forecasters. What do you think explains this superior predictive performance, and is it consistent with market efficiency?

8. How would you implement a negative earnings momentum strategy? Would this be easier or more difficult than implementing a positive earnings momentum strategy?

9. Describe how you would construct an event study to test the stock market reaction to CEO resignations, and to examine whether the market reaction is different for voluntary versus involuntary resignations.

10. Several academic researchers have suggested that legalizing insider trading would improve market efficiency by more rapidly incorporating private information into market prices. What do you think would be the costs and benefits of such a legal change?

10.3 THE BEHAVIORAL FINANCE CRITIQUE OF MARKET EFFICIENCY (OPTIONAL)

The EMH has long held sway among financial professionals (especially academics), both because it provided a logical, internally consistent theoretical model of how markets work and because empirical evidence weighed in its favor. However, the past 10 years have seen the rise of a group of respected economists who reject the EMH

[22.] In a September 2002 working paper, BLMT update their study of the performance of analysts' recommendations and find that "the years 2000–2001 were disasters." Stocks that analysts ranked as least favorable outperformed stocks ranked most favorable by more than 20 percentage points per year. Even so, for the entire 1986–2001 period, stocks ranked in the highest category outperformed those in the lowest category by a little less than 12 percent per year.

as a defensible model of investor behavior and security market performance. Because these economists draw many of their insights from the findings of psychological research, they have become known as *behaviorists* and their collective research is called behavioral finance.

The behavioral finance attack on market efficiency has occurred on two levels. First, behaviorists interpret the empirical evidence surveyed in Section 10.2 much differently than do believers in market efficiency, who for brevity we will refer to as "true believers" throughout this discussion.[23] Whereas true believers interpret the evidence on stock market over- and underreaction as minor anomalies caused by random chance, behaviorists perceive this body of research as proof that markets are irrational. Behaviorists have made a persuasive case that financial markets in general, and stock markets in particular, are simply too volatile for prices to be based on rational valuations. Second, behaviorists believe that investors are emotional creatures who process financial information in systematically biased ways. They suggest that this flawed cognitive process in fact causes investors to overreact to some types of financial information and underreact to others.

We examine the behavioral finance critique of market efficiency in the following three sections. The first surveys the empirical evidence that behaviorists have stressed in their critique of the EMH. The second section briefly describes the theoretical underpinnings of behavioral finance and discusses the biases that are believed to color investor behavior. In the final section, we present our own assessment of the relative merits of behavioral finance and market efficiency.

BUBBLES, FADS, AND CASCADES: THE EMPIRICAL EVIDENCE ON BEHAVIORAL FINANCE

Few objective observers would disagree with the proposition that financial asset prices tend to be highly volatile. Behaviorists go a step further and claim that financial markets are *irrationally* volatile and are prone to recurring bubbles, fads, and information cascades. Bubbles and fads are easily understood, but a cascade occurs when a piece of "information" rapidly travels through a large group of market participants, influencing many peoples' trading behavior and being accepted as correct—whether it is or not. All three of these phenomena, if they in fact exist, are inconsistent with market efficiency.

One of the most respected behavioral economists, Robert Shiller, makes the case in his best-selling book *Irrational Exuberance* that stock prices are not determined rationally. Serendipitously for Shiller, his book hit the stores in March 2000, just as the Nasdaq market's nearly 75 percent swoon was commencing. Figure 10.6 is reproduced from this book and shows the relationship between U.S. stock prices and earnings from 1871 to 2000, as well as the price/earnings ratio of the S&P Composite Index over the 1881–2000 period. Although stock prices have risen to very high levels before, only to fall back shortly thereafter, Shiller argues that the enormous rise in valuations since 1990 is both unprecedented in scale and unexplained by any comparable increase in corporate sales and profits.

The figures and tables presented in Shiller's book are actually popularized and updated representations of academic research he and others have been publishing for many years. Shiller (1979) launched what has been called the **variance bounds** litera-

---

[23.] To someone trying to objectively weigh the merits of the EMH and behavioral finance, this tendency to interpret the same empirical evidence in fundamentally different ways is disconcerting. The best example of this can be seen by comparing the studies cited in Appendix A of Daniel, Hirshleifer, and Subrahmanyam (1998) with the virtually identical list of papers cited in Table 1 of Fama (1998), which we have reproduced here as Table 10.2. Since these are arguably the best academic papers respectively supporting and refuting behavioral finance, it is easy to see why a professional consensus has to date been very hard to reach.

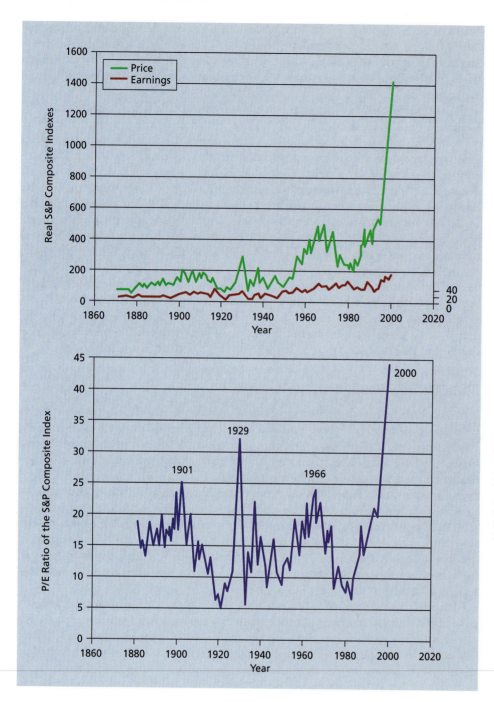

Figure 10.6
Is This Rational Pricing? Stock Prices versus Earnings and Price-Earnings Ratios For U.S. Stocks, 1871–2000

Real (inflation-corrected) S&P Composite Stock Price Index, monthly, January 1871 through January 2000 (upper series), and real S&P Composite earnings (lower series), January 1871 to September 1999.

Source: Author's calculations using data from S&P Statistical Service; U.S. Bureau of Labor Statistics; Cowles and Associates, *Common Stock Indexes;* and Warren and Pearson, *Gold and Prices.*

Price-earnings ratio, monthly, January 1881 to January 2000. Numerator: real (inflation-corrected) S&P Composite Stock Price Index. Denominator: moving average over preceding ten years of real S&P Composite earnings. Years of peaks are indicated.

Source: Robert J. Shiller, *Irrational Exuberance* (Broadway Books; New York, 2000), p. 6, fig. 1.1; p. 8, fig. 1.2.

ture with his observation that long-term interest rates vary far more than they should, given the actual fluctuations in short-term interest rates. In later studies, Shiller and others developed tests to determine whether the observed variance in real stock prices can be explained by *ex post* (after the fact) variations either in the real dividend series or in the discount rates used by investors to compute the present value of the dividend series.[24] These authors visually and statistically compare the time series of ob-

[24.] See also Shiller (1981), Grossman and Shiller (1981), LeRoy and LeRoy (1991), and Campbell and Ammer (1993).

served prices with the series of "perfect foresight" prices, defined as the discounted value of actual future period real dividends. When the variance of actual stock prices exceeds the maximum rational variation (the *variance bound*) in perfect foresight prices, these authors conclude that stock prices are too volatile to have been produced by rational investors.

These studies have been attacked on both theoretical and econometric grounds by Kleidon (1986), Kothari and Shanken (1992, 1993), and others. Ackert and Smith (1993) show that when the definition of "dividends" is expanded to include stock repurchases and cash takeover payments made to shareholders, corporate cash distributions to shareholders roughly double during the postwar period. With this new definition of "dividend payments," variance bounds tests no longer reject market efficiency. There is also a rather surreal aspect to the proposition that estimates of future cash flows and stock prices *can* be too variable. At face value, this literature seems to imply that investors in, say, early 1933 should have been able to foresee the eventual triumph of democratic capitalism over depression, fascism, and communism—and thus should never have allowed stock prices to decline by 86 percent from their 1929 peak. On the other hand, a behaviorist could ask a true believer to explain how the devaluation of the Thai baht in July 1997 could prompt a regionwide economic meltdown, or how the subsequent Russian default and devaluation (in August 1998) could precipitate a global financial crisis. Neither country represented a meaningful fraction of total world GDP.

THEORETICAL UNDERPINNINGS OF BEHAVIORAL FINANCE

It is one thing to marshal empirical evidence against the EMH, as the behaviorists have certainly done, and something else entirely to develop a full-blown theoretical model to replace it. Although there is not yet a fully developed model of behavioral finance, behaviorists have at least explained how markets might be less than fully efficient. One track of this development has sought to explain how biases in human cognition can cause individual investors to misprice financial assets. The thrust of this research has been to explain investor under- and overreaction to specific information announcements. The second track of theoretical research seeks to explain how these irrational *individual* valuations can affect overall *market* valuations. In other words, even if individual investors make bad valuation decisions, why don't arbitrageurs or other more rational investors act swiftly to correct any observed mispricing of assets?

Daniel, Hirshleifer, and Subrahmanyam (1998; hereafter DHS) propose a theory of securities market under- and overreaction to corporate news announcements that is based on two well-documented psychological biases: **overconfidence** and **biased self-attribution.** Investors are overconfident in the sense that they believe they are better informed about the true state of a company's affairs than is in fact the case. Investors with biased self-attribution will interpret the arrival of new private information supporting their existing beliefs as important confirmatory evidence, but will tend to disregard contradictory new evidence as being random noise. As Figure 10.7 demonstrates, these two biases interact to make investors systematically misinterpret corporate information releases.

Regardless of whether the news is positive or negative, overconfidence causes investors to overreact to new information. As the true state of affairs is revealed over time, investors' beliefs will fall back toward rational valuation, and this causes price changes to reverse over time. In other words, prices will rise (fall) after initially falling below (rising above) "true value." The self-attribution bias has the opposite effect; it causes investors to underreact to public information signals that contradict

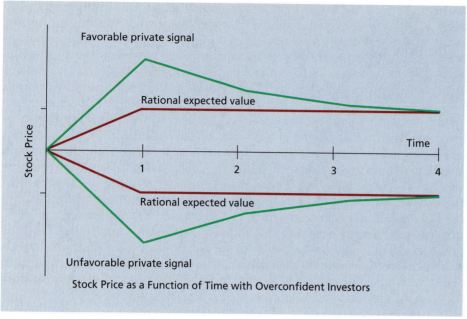

Figure 10.7

A Theoretical Explanation of Overreaction and Underreaction

*This figure shows how stock prices can theoretically overreact to some corporate news announce-
ments and underreact to others. When firms announce good news, stock prices should react to
the Rational Expected Values on the top part of this figure. But because investors are overconfident,
in the sense that they believe they have more accurate private information about a firm's real
value than is in fact the case, they drive stock prices above their rational values immediately after
receiving the information signal (the good news). Over time, investors realize their mistake, which
means that stock prices will drift back to their rational values in later periods. This series of price
changes induces overreaction in stock prices, with a subsequent reversal as time passes. The bottom
part of this figure shows the pattern that would result from a negative initial price signal.*

Source: Kent Daniel, David Hirshleifer, and Avindhar Subrahmanyam, "Investor Psychology and Under and Overreactions," *Journal of Finance* 53 (December 1998), pp. 1839–1882.

their existing beliefs. For example, suppose that an investor who expects a stock to
perform poorly receives information contradicting this belief. At first, the investor
discounts the value of this information. Over time, as more good news emerges, the
investor's opinion gradually changes from negative to positive. If many investors behave this way, stock prices will respond gradually to new information, rising slowly
in response to good news and falling slowly after bad news. In other words, the self-
attribution bias leads to "continuation" or momentum in stock prices, just the opposite effect of overconfidence.[25]

Even if this theory of individual investor decision making is correct, why don't
investors who do not suffer from these biases arbitrage away any asset mispricing
that is induced? Behaviorists point to the **noise trader theory** of asset pricing. Shleifer
and Summers (1990) suggest that markets are populated by two types of investors.

[25.] For a humorous (but very informative) assessment of how behavioral finance notions are likely to influence economic
thought over the next two decades, see Thaler (2000). Among his predictions are two: *Homo Economicus* will begin losing IQ points (will become less than perfectly informed) and will become a slower learner. Additionally, Barber and Odean
(2002) present striking evidence of overconfidence in their study of online investors. These (mostly young and male) investors generally had been very successful, telephone-based traders prior to going online, but once they began trading
over the Internet, their trading increased dramatically and their performance began to trail the overall market by 3 percent annually. Barber and Odean (2000) show that, without regard to whether investors trade online or over the phone,
the most active traders earn the lowest net returns. They argue that these investors trade too much because they are overconfident in their ability to pick winning stocks.

First, rational **arbitrageurs** are traders who seek to exploit small pricing differences by purchasing an asset when it is undervalued and reselling it when it is overvalued. These traders accurately assess the true risks and expected returns offered by all securities. Second, **noise traders** (or liquidity traders) trade based on beliefs or sentiments that are not fully justified by fundamental news. The activities of noise traders cause prices to diverge from fundamental valuations, but the rational arbitrageurs have a limited capacity to exploit pricing errors. Two types of risk prevent arbitrageurs from driving prices back to fundamental value immediately. The first is fundamental risk, or the chance that the overall market may go up or down during the coming period. The second is the unpredictability of the future resale price. Even if an asset is overpriced today, the actions of noise traders may cause the asset to become even more overpriced in the future.

DeLong, Shleifer, Summers, and Waldmann (1990a) further develop a model of how extended deviations of prices from fundamental values can develop. They present a model of a financial market in which noise traders affect prices, thereby directly increasing the risk for rational speculators who might otherwise be tempted to trade against them. Finally, a more recent paper by Shleifer and Vishny (1997), titled "The Limits to Arbitrage," argues that the (riskless, instantaneous) arbitrage process that efficient-markets theorists always assume will enforce rational pricing is in fact capital-intensive, extremely risky, and an art form practiced by a very small number of investment professionals. Because of this, they argue that arbitrage will become ineffective in extreme situations, such as when prices diverge widely from fundamental values. Unfortunately, this is the time when financial markets rely most heavily on arbitrage to ensure rational pricing.

ASSESSING BEHAVIORAL FINANCE AND MARKET EFFICIENCY

An unbiased observer must come away from a reading of the behavioral literature more than a little impressed. In particular, behaviorists present persuasive evidence that price bubbles occur, and somewhat less-compelling evidence that the U.S. stock market was grossly overvalued near the turn of the century. On balance, however, we believe that investors and managers are wise to take the efficient markets hypothesis very seriously. Even though the quantity of evidence challenging the EMH has grown in recent years, stock prices, and prices of other financial assets, are still largely unpredictable. Strategies to beat the market generate transactions costs, which are a certainty, in pursuit of returns that are quite uncertain.

In addition, even if we accept the notion that there is some degree of predictability in stock prices, the finance profession is far from understanding *why* this is so. The theory behind the efficient markets hypothesis is logically consistent and has stood the test of time very well. With a few notable exceptions, behavioral finance offers no specific theory to counter the EMH. Instead, behavioral finance provides an admittedly puzzling set of empirical facts, with a collection of fairly loosely knit stories that might explain the data. Perhaps the puzzles of behavioral finance will be solved by the development of a new asset pricing model or some other theory that relies on rational economic agents rather than on cognitive biases. Until behaviorists offer a consistent, testable alternative to the efficient market model, we will remain skeptical of irrationality as the cause of anomalies in financial markets.

Finally, proponents of any important pricing anomaly must explain how it has remained stable in the face of the explosive growth in the size, sophistication, liquidity, and technical efficiency of financial markets during the past two decades. When billions of dollars are committed to arbitraging bond-pricing errors as small as a few

basis points, it seems inconceivable that deviations from fundamental valuation as gross as those implied by the behavioral finance literature could long endure.

On the other hand, this chapter offers a tribute to the intellectual impact behavioral finance research has had and is likely to continue having on our profession. Behavioral finance has provided by far the strongest challenge to the EMH in the last three decades and has won many converts in academia and business. An unscientific poll of our colleagues suggests that the consensus in favor of the EMH is not as strong as it was a decade ago, though we believe that the majority of financial economists (in academia at least) lean toward the efficient markets view.

---

11. Evaluate your driving skill as better than average, average, or worse than average. Take a poll of friends and relatives, asking the same question. What percentage of people put themselves into each group, and what does this say about the tendency of people to be overconfident? By definition, can the majority of drivers be better than average?

12. How could the existence of irrational or "noise" traders make the process of arbitrage risky for rational investors?

13. Gather a group of friends and try this experiment. Invite each person to write down a number between 0 and 100 without showing the number to anyone else. You, as the moderator of the experiment, will collect the pieces of paper and calculate the average of these numbers. Next, you will divide the average number by 2. The person who wrote down a number closest to this final value wins a $10 prize. If there is a tie, the proceeds should be equally divided among the winners. If everyone is rational, what number should everyone write down? If some people do not behave rationally (because they do not think carefully enough about the rules of the game), how does that change the strategy of a rational player?

Concept Review Questions

10.4 WHAT DOES MARKET EFFICIENCY IMPLY FOR CORPORATE FINANCING?

We have surveyed the academic research on market efficiency and reached a highly nuanced conclusion that modern financial markets tend to be informationally efficient, most of the time. What specifically does this imply for the practice of financial management? Perhaps the simplest way to summarize efficiency's lesson for practicing managers is to paraphrase Lincoln's dictum about citizens in a democracy: "You can't fool all the people (investors) all of the time." Therefore, you as a manager might as well assume that you are facing informed, active market participants who will not be fooled by financial gimmicks or "creative accounting." This has specific implications for managerial practices with regard to accounting choices, financing choices, and selection of a corporate strategy for communicating with investors.

How Do Markets Process Accounting and Other Information Releases?

Financial managers tend to devote a great deal of energy and attention to selecting different accounting policies, such as whether to use last-in, first-out (LIFO) or first-in, first-out (FIFO) inventory accounting techniques in financial statement reporting. The logic of market efficiency, buttressed by substantial empirical evidence, suggests this managerial obsession is misplaced, for two reasons. First, unless an accounting change affects cash flows, investors will not be concerned with its impact on a company's income statement or balance sheet. Second, if the accounting change merely involves the release of previously disclosed information in a new form, investors can be assumed to have already calculated the new information on their own.

A striking example of the ambiguous role of accounting information involves the disclosure of the largest net losses ever reported by an American corporation. In 1992, a change in FASB reporting requirements forced General Motors Corporation

to charge off a massive $20.8 billion against net income to account for the present value of future health benefits for its retirees. The resulting net loss for GM for fiscal year 1992 was several times larger than any net loss ever reported by any other public company. What was the stock-price response to this monumental flood of red ink? Virtually nothing. Because investors could readily estimate the present value of GM's pension liabilities, the repackaging of this information as a charge against current income revealed nothing new about either the size or the risk of GM's cash flows, and thus did not affect its stock price. This type of situation occurred again in March 2002, when AOL Time Warner announced a new record loss of $54 billion resulting from a write-off of goodwill. Since analysts had known for some time that (1) AOL had grossly overpaid for many of the companies it had acquired and (2) that a large write-off of these excessive acquisition payments was in the works, the actual stock-price response to the announcement of the specific amount was negligible.

This irrelevance thesis can be overdone, of course. Financial statements do convey vital information, and changes in reporting requirements that affect a firm's cash flows or its ability to borrow can dramatically impact share valuation. In addition, when corporate earnings announcements convey new information about current business conditions and/or future earnings prospects, the stock-price reaction can be very dramatic. Finally, an efficient market is not immune to fraud. As this book was going to press, U.S. courts were trying to determine whether WorldCom, Enron, and their accountants perpetrated a fraud against investors. We do not wish to imply that markets can always see through every accounting sleight of hand, but we do think markets are quite sophisticated in this regard. After all, one of the reasons that these bankruptcies were so newsworthy was that they were so unusual.

How Do Markets Respond to Corporate Financing Announcements?

Yet another common but unproductive managerial fixation, according to the EMH, is the attempt by managers to "time" security issues. Several academic studies, which we survey in later chapters, show that managers on average announce new seasoned equity issues *after* a period during which their firm's stock prices have experienced unusually large increases in value. Another widely noted tendency is an unwillingness to issue new equity at a time when stock prices are believed to be "too low." Both of these behavioral tendencies imply that managers believe they know better than the market what the value of their stock "should" be. To the extent that managers have inside information about the firm's prospects that has not yet been disclosed, this might be true. In the more common case where managers think they are more perceptive than investors and can predict when stock prices will naturally adjust, the EMH suggests that they are simply being delusional.

Because investors know that managers *may* have superior information about their firm's prospects, there is a clear danger that investors will interpret all managerial actions as being based on inside information, even when managers are not better informed. For example, the announcement of an equity issue conveys to investors that management thinks the firm's current stock price is too high, while announcement of a debt issue or share repurchase program conveys management's belief that the stock price is too low. In fact, investors may interpret an announcement of any

financing event as a signal that the firm will experience a cash flow shortfall of some kind. Investors are not omniscient, but their interpretations are, on balance, surprisingly accurate. Studies by Hansen and Crutchley (1990) and others have shown that firms that raise cash through security issues do experience earnings shortfalls in subsequent quarters, and the larger the earnings decline, the more capital must be raised. Additionally, investors differentiate between announcements of public security offers, to which they usually react negatively, and privately placed security issues, which are viewed much more favorably. In other words, investors react to all aspects of new financing announcements as though the terms and type of security selected convey useful information.

How Can Managers Devise a Corporate "Communications" Policy?

Given that we have shown that investors respond vigorously to security-issuance announcements, yet often react with indifference to accounting-change announcements, how should managers ensure that investors do not misinterpret their intentions or react to essentially meaningless events? Put differently, how can a manager devise a value-maximizing communication strategy that will credibly (and accurately) convey both positive and negative information to investors and other stakeholders, and also interpret the signals conveyed by these same parties? We suggest that managers develop their strategy with the following four principles in mind: (1) assume that your words and actions have consequences; (2) assume that loose lips sink corporate ships; (3) consider honesty to be the best policy; and (4) listen to your stock price.

Assume That Your Words and Actions Have Consequences

As our discussion of financing events makes clear, market participants will react to actions you as a manager take or to statements you make, so be careful what you do and say. You should thus try to predict how investors will interpret any particular news announcement and be ready to respond appropriately if the actual reaction is other than what you expected. This is true for both good and bad news. Needlessly withholding good news (i.e., a dividend increase) can lead to the impression that you were sitting on this information until you and other insiders had the opportunity to profit by trading on it.[26] The same is true for bad news. For instance, if you learn that quarterly earnings are less than the market was expecting, your wisest strategy will usually be to disclose this news immediately, along with an unbiased assessment of whether you believe the earnings decline is likely to be temporary or permanent. Withholding bad news does not prevent the market from reacting if the news is about a predictable event, such as a quarterly earnings announcement, and the appearance of withholding can itself cause the stock-price reaction to be worse than necessary.

Assume That Loose Lips Sink Corporate Ships

The opposite sin to withholding information that should be disclosed is to discuss publicly information that should be kept private, or to prematurely disclose sensitive information. For example, it is almost always unwise (and sometimes illegal) to publicly discuss ongoing merger negotiations, planned security offerings, actual or potential corporate litigation, or personnel issues of almost any kind.[27]

---

[26] Since, as we have shown, there are many studies documenting the pervasiveness of insider trading, such a suspicion is not necessarily a sign of paranoia. In any case, even paranoids (investors) have enemies (unscrupulous managers).

[27] One important exception to this general rule involves the announcement of layoffs. Here, it is almost always best to make *all* the bad news public as soon as legally permissible, both for the sake of those who will be asked to leave and for those who will be asked to stay.

Most corporate managers have also learned not to comment on earnings forecasts (except in the most innocuous manner) made by outside analysts, as this is usually a no-win situation for the executive involved. If the manager confirms an analyst's forecast of unexpectedly high earnings, and earnings actually end up less than predicted, the manager will incur the wrath of investors who purchased stock on the belief that profits would be higher. On the other hand, a manager who acts conservatively and supports a forecast of lower earnings risks alienating investors who sold their stock based on the executive's statements, only to be surprised by higher-than-predicted earnings.

Consider Honesty to Be the Best Policy

Although this mandate sounds naive, it is actually a core prediction of the efficient markets hypothesis, because investors will rationally form beliefs concerning the trustworthiness of corporate managers based on their observed behavior. Managers who convey good and bad information honestly and do not try to fool the market with accounting gimmicks or other misleading strategies will be believed, while managers with reputations for deception will be viewed skeptically. The same is true regarding a manager's reputation for maximizing shareholder wealth. Investors will tend to support managers with a history of acting in the shareholders' best interests and will oppose managers who put their own interests ahead of those of the shareholders. In other words, though stock *prices* lack memories, stock market *investors* have long memories regarding managerial performance and honesty.

Listen to Your Stock Price

Most of our discussion thus far has dealt with how managers should convey information to investors, but market efficiency also implies that managers should listen to what the markets are telling them in return. Managers should view financial markets as vast information processors that generate unbiased assessments of corporate performance. Managers who disregard market signals do so at their peril. There are essentially two types of information that markets convey to managers: (1) reactions to specific corporate announcements and (2) movements in the firm's stock price relative to the overall market over extended periods of time. Both can be very informative to the alert manager.

Consider first the stock-price reaction to a specific corporate announcement. For example, assume you announce that your firm is planning to acquire another company at a price per share that is 40 percent higher than the target's closing stock price yesterday. If your firm's stock price rises in response to this announcement, you should feel reassured that the market believes the takeover is a wise step and that you negotiated a fair price for the acquisition. If, on the other hand, your firm's stock price falls on the acquisition announcement, you should realize either that the market believes the acquisition is unwise or that your firm is paying too much, or both. Even though this decline is typically what happens to bidding-firm share prices, particularly in mergers paid for with bidding-firm stock, managers often refuse to accept the market's assessment that they acted foolishly. Alas, the weight of empirical evidence is on the side of investors rather than that of bidding-firm managers.

An equally common conflict between managers and investors occurs when executives have articulated a business strategy that seems brilliant to them, yet the firm's stock price languishes. The natural tendency is for managers to bemoan the idiocy of investors, but it would usually be more appropriate for the managers to rethink their strategy's objectives and/or implementation. Unfortunately, examples of unwise corporate strategies pursued with heedless passion abound, and include the conglomer-

ate merger frenzy of the 1960s and the "financial supermarket" craze of the 1980s. Of course, the converse is also true. Managers who pursue an unconventional or unpopular strategy can draw comfort if investors bid up their firms' stock values, even if their colleagues and competitors view the strategy with befuddlement. In either case, a wise manager should not ignore what the market says about strategic moves.

---

14. Why do you think the average stock-price response to private security placements is significantly positive, while the average response to almost all public security issues is significantly negative?

15. What should a manager do when he or she firmly believes that a particular corporate strategy is wise, even though the stock market has clearly indicated disapproval of this strategy?

Concept Review Questions

10.5 SUMMARY

- In comparison to product markets, financial markets tend to be much more competitive and efficient because the assets traded tend to be commodity-like and very similar.
- Efficiency can be defined several ways. An allocatively efficient market ensures that capital is invested very productively, and an operationally efficient market is one where outputs are produced at the lowest possible input cost. Financial economists are most concerned with the informational efficiency of financial markets, which refers to how quickly and fully asset prices incorporate relevant new information.
- In weak-form efficient markets, prices reflect all information available in the record of historical prices, while semistrong-form efficient markets reflect all publicly available information, whether historic or current. In strong-form efficient markets, prices reflect all information—private as well as public.
- The efficient markets hypothesis has been extensively tested, and empirical research has generally found that the major Western stock and bond markets are weak-form and semistrong-form efficient, but not strong-form efficient. In particular, the efficacy of crude forms of "technical analysis" is easily rejected. However, the evidence against more-sophisticated trading rules, such as "momentum strategies," is less overwhelming, and people with access to "inside" (nonpublic) information can earn excess profits by trading on this knowledge.
- Though some empirical studies document that certain types of financial asset returns are partly predictable, the extent of predictability is modest, and the predictability itself need not be inconsistent with market efficiency.
- Most empirical studies find that asset prices respond fully and nearly instantaneously to the release of relevant new information. On the other hand, it is much more difficult to test whether prices always are "accurate" in the sense that they rationally reflect fundamental value at all times.
- Research in behavioral finance argues that market participants make systematic errors in valuing assets due to cognitive problems such as overconfidence and self-attribution bias. If these cognitive biases are widespread, they can cause prices of financial assets to deviate from fundamental value for long periods of time.
- Market efficiency research offers several lessons for practicing financial managers. For example, it suggests that managers should not try to "fool" markets by manipulating earnings numbers or through other accounting gimmicks, as investors will usually see through these games.

- Managers should be very careful in making public utterances. If a public statement is required, however, it is imperative that managers speak truthfully.

INTERNET RESOURCES

Note: *For updates to links, please go to the book's website at* *http://smart.swcollege.com*

http://www.dfafunds.com/The_Firm/About_Dimensional/Philosophy/philosophy.html—Dimensional Fund Advisors, a professional money management company with roughly $35 billion under management, has an investment philosophy firmly rooted in the philosophy of efficient markets. The website explains how this philosophy shapes the company's investment strategies and offers an interesting piece by Eugene Fama on the impact of behavioral finance.

http://www.vanguard.com/bogle_site/sp20011021.html—John C. Bogle founded Vanguard, the giant mutual fund company, and introduced the first indexed mutual fund for individual investors in 1975. Index funds represent a "passive" approach to investing in which a fund does not try to select winners and losers, but rather holds a broad basket of stocks to mimic the returns on an index like the S&P 500. At this site you can read one of Bogle's speeches offering his evidence on the superiority of indexing over an "active" approach to selecting stocks.

KEY TERMS

allocative efficiency	overconfidence
arbitrageurs	overreaction
behavioral finance	overreaction strategies
biased self-attribution	price bubbles
chartists	random walk
efficient markets hypothesis (EMH)	selectivity
event study	semistrong-form efficiency
filter rules	strong-form efficiency
hedge fund	technical analysis
herd	timing
informational efficiency	underpriced
joint hypothesis problem	underreact
momentum strategies	underreaction strategies
noise trader theory	variance bounds
noise traders	weak-form efficiency
operational efficiency	winner's curse

QUESTIONS

10-1.   In what way does *informational efficiency* impact corporate finance and investment decisions? In an efficient market, can a corporate manager enhance shareholder value through changes in financial reporting that have no impact on a company's cash flows?

10-2.   Distinguish between allocational, operational, and informational efficiency. Does the existence of one of these efficiencies imply that the other two exist? Explain.

10-3.   List and describe the three forms of informational efficiency. What is the implication for technical analysis under each of these forms?

10-4.   What is a *random walk*, and how does it relate to weak-form efficiency?

10-5.   If stock returns follow a random walk with trend, does this mean that investing in stocks is akin to gambling?

10-6.   Explain why market efficiency implies that "the stock of an exceptionally well-run company will not necessarily be an exceptionally good investment."

10-7.   What types of information are reflected in asset prices under the assumption of semi-strong-form efficiency? How is this different from strong-form efficiency?

10-8.   Comment on the profitability of trading on inside information in capital markets that are strong-form efficient. What about the profitability of trading on public information?

10-9.   Over the long term, stocks of high-tech companies tend to earn higher returns than stocks of public utilities. Does this violate market efficiency?

10-10.   Distinguish between the types of empirical tests of market efficiency. How does each type actually test market efficiency?

10-11.   One investor follows a strategy of buying a stock whenever it hits a 52-week low and holding it for a year before selling it. Another investor follows a strategy of buying a stock whenever it hits a 52-week high and holding it for a year before selling it. Suppose that the first investor's portfolio outperforms the second investor's portfolio over time. Is this inconsistent with efficient markets? Why or why not?

10-12.   What is an asset-pricing anomaly? Discuss the "January effect," and explain why it represents an anomaly. In particular, explain why it is difficult to argue that this anomaly is merely a manifestation of the *joint hypothesis problem.*

10-13.   Explain why the efficient markets hypothesis says that analysts should not be able to predict future stock returns based on recurring patterns observed in past stock returns.

10-14.   Discuss the difference between overreaction and underreaction to information events. Which of the two is related to a *momentum strategy?* How is a momentum strategy applied to investing?

10-15.   What is an *event study* designed to test?

10-16.   Do empirical studies support, or reject, the notion that corporate insiders earn abnormal profits on their trades? What about outside investors who mimic their trades? What forms of market efficiency, if any, are supported by these studies?

10-17.   In terms of mutual fund performance assessment, what is the meaning of the term "alpha"? Historically, have actively managed mutual funds exhibited positive or negative alphas, on average? What do these results imply about market efficiency?

10-18.   What other empirical results have been documented regarding the relationship between active mutual fund performance and market efficiency? What conclusion does Burton Malkiel draw about the performance of actively managed mutual funds?

10-19.   Suppose that you study the performance of 50 equity mutual funds over the past 10 years. Does the efficient markets hypothesis predict that none of these 50 funds will have a positive *alpha?* What predictions about alpha does the efficient markets hypothesis offer?

10-20.   Have security analysts generally been able to offer valuable stock-picking advice? If they could, why would this pose a challenge to the efficient markets hypothesis?

10-21.   What is an asset price "bubble"? Do you think the rapid rise, and even more rapid subsequent fall, in Nasdaq stock market prices between 1998 and 2000 is evidence of a pricing bubble? Why or why not?

10-22.   What is *behavioral finance?* Describe the two key cognitive biases that investors are prone to, according to behaviorists. How might these biases explain stock market over- and underreaction?

10-23.   What are *noise traders?* Briefly describe how these traders might cause stock prices to deviate from rational fundamental values for long periods.

10-24. Describe how Robert Shiller concluded that American capital markets are too volatile to be rational. Do you agree with this assessment? Why or why not?

10-25. What empirical evidence do defenders of market efficiency offer to counter the behavioral finance challenge?

10-26. Briefly describe the four principles of external communications strategy that a corporate manager should consider.

10-27. Why should a corporate manager "listen to his or her stock price"? If capital markets are efficient and if a company's stock price lags behind those of its peer group, what message should be inferred by the manager?

PROBLEMS

What Is an Efficient Financial Market?

10-1. The stock of Ultrasound Communications Company (UCC) is listed for trading on the Euronext-Paris stock exchange. For the past several weeks, UCC's stock price has remained around €35.00 per share. Assume that a competitor, Broadband Telephony Company (BTC), announces that it wishes to acquire UCC in an all-cash tender offer for €60.00 per share. BTC also announces that it is willing to pay this price for all UCC's shares tendered to it under the offer, and BTC says that UCC's managers support the takeover attempt. If the tender offer is successful, a merger will be effected in three months' time, and UCC will cease to exist as a separate company. Thus, its stock will be delisted from the exchange.

a. What price do you think UCC's stock will sell for immediately after this announcement?

b. Draw a figure illustrating the likely evolution of UCC's stock price over the next three months.

c. Suppose rather than offering cash, that BTC offers to exchange four of its own shares (which recently traded for €15.00 each) for each outstanding share of UCC. However, after this announcement, BTC shares drop to €12.00. Answer parts (a) and (b) again under this new scenario.

10-2. You want to measure the cumulative abnormal return (CAR) on a particular stock over a period of time. Assume that the stock has a beta of 1.0, so its expected return equals the market's expected return. Each day, you calculate the return on the stock and subtract the return on the market that day to get the daily abnormal return. As time passes, you simply add these daily abnormal returns together to get the CAR.

a. Fill in the missing values in the following table.

Day	Stock Return (%)	Market Return (%)	Daily Abnormal Return	CAR
1	2.0	1.8	————	————
2	−0.35	0.1	————	————
3	0.25	−0.15	————	————
4	0.65	0.75	————	————
5	−0.53	−0.49	————	————

b. Next, suppose that you gather a sample of stocks that just reported higher earnings-per-share figures than most analysts had anticipated. You calculate the CAR for each company over the 30 days preceding the earnings announcement. You continue to follow these firms for the next 30 days, keeping track of the CARs each day. The following three figures plot the average CAR across all stocks in your

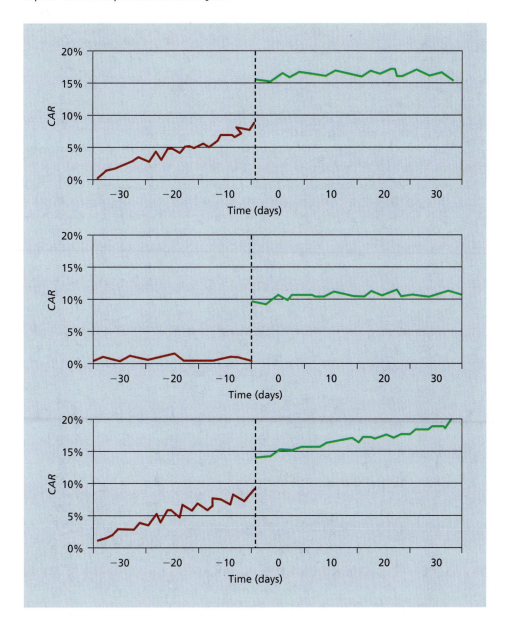

sample for the 30 days prior to and the 30 days after the earnings announcement. One of these graphs is inconsistent with the notion that markets are efficient. Identify that graph, and explain why it violates market efficiency. Also explain why the other two graphs do not necessarily violate market efficiency.

Empirical Evidence on Market Efficiency (Optional)

10-3.   You have been asked to assess the performance, relative to that of the overall stock market, of several mutual fund managers over the past year. During the past year, the risk-free interest rate was 3.0 percent ($R_f = 0.03$) and the return on the S&P 500 Index was 10 percent ($R_m = 0.10$). The following table details each mutual fund's portfolio beta, measured return over the past year, and the management fee charged by each manager.

Fund	Portfolio Beta	Return (%)	Management Fee (%)
Aggressive Growth	1.60	14.5	1.25
Conservative Income	0.90	11.0	0.75
Contrarian	0.40	5.6	1.00

a. Compute Jensen's *alpha* for each fund, both before accounting for the fund manager's fee and on a net basis.

b. Discuss whether each fund manager created value (outperformed the market index) for investors.

10-4. In the 1994 business best-seller, *Built to Last,* James Collins and Jerry Porras described lessons that all corporate managers should learn by studying a set of "Visionary Companies." In the book's first chapter, the authors plotted a graph showing that, over the long term, a $1 investment in a portfolio of visionary firms substan-

Source: James C. Collins and Jerry I. Porras, *Built To Last: Successful Habits of Visionary Companies* (New York: HarperCollins, 1994).

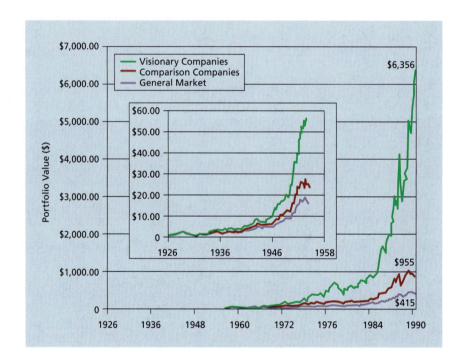

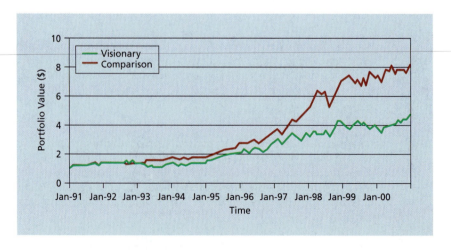

tially outperformed a $1 investment in either a portfolio of comparison firms from the same industries or the broad market index. We reproduce that graph below, as well as an updated graph showing the performance of visionary and comparison companies during the 1990s. What are the lessons about market efficiency to be gleaned from these diagrams?

10-5. Each day, the *Wall Street Journal* lists stocks that have reached a 52-week low. A sample of firms appearing on that list on September 4, 2002, appears below. Also shown is the closing price of each stock nine trading days later on September 18.

Firm	9/4/2002	9/18/2002
AAR	$ 6.11	$ 5.05
Albertsons	24.96	25.38
Alcoa	23.14	20.93
American Safety Ins.	8.05	8.05
Ameron International	46.79	47.61
Ashland	27.76	28.62
ATS	1.88	2.05
Boise Cascade	25.85	24.55
Footstar	10.11	10.42
Ford Motor	11.05	10.26
Goodyear	12.87	10.94
Grubb & Ellis	1.30	2.13
Heico	10.09	10.83
Hitachi	51.35	54.13
JLG Industries	8.61	8.71
Longview Fibre	6.15	7.20
Manulife Financial	22.29	21.62
National Semiconductor	15.18	11.93
Oakley	9.70	10.62
Oakwood Homes	1.60	1.70
PCW	1.60	1.44
Sothebys	9.40	7.43
SPS Technologies	27.50	28.03
Stillwater Mining	7.31	6.43
TECO Energy	15.84	15.31
Teradyne	12.19	11.05
Three-Five Systems	5.29	5.20
U.S. Steel	13.13	12.04
ValuCity	1.99	1.90
Vishay Intertechnology	13.37	10.31

  a. What fraction of these stocks increased after hitting their 52-week lows, and what fraction continued to decline? Is this consistent with what we would expect if prices follow a *random walk*?

  b. Assuming no dividend payments, calculate the percentage return on each stock from September 4 to September 18. Next, calculate the return on an equally weighted portfolio of these stocks by simply calculating the average return across all firms. Does this return seem consistent with market efficiency? Why or why not?

  c. Over the same period, the return on the Nasdaq Composite Index was −1.27 percent. Does this change your answer to part (b)?

10-6. As a simple test of whether stock prices move randomly, go to Yahoo! (http://www.yahoo.com) and download a few weeks of daily returns for a particular stock. Yahoo! gives you the stock's high, low, and closing prices each day. If stock prices display momentum, then we might expect the closing price to be equal to either the high or the low price for the day. Why? Compare the closing price each day to the day's high price, the day's low price, and the midpoint of the high and low prices. What does this tell you about the tendency of stock prices to move randomly?

Smart Solutions
See the problem and solution explained step-by-step at
SMARTFinance

10-7. The Super Bowl indicator predicts that the stock market will decline in a year follow-ing a Super Bowl victory by a team from the old American Football League (AFL) and that the market will otherwise rise. The table below indicates the signal that this indi-cator gave to investors in each year from 1967 to 2001, as well as the returns on the Dow Jones Industrial Average (DJIA) in the 12 months after the outcome of the Super Bowl had been determined.

Year	Super Bowl Indicator	Subsequent DJIA (%)
2001	sell	−3.7
2000	buy	3.6
1999	sell	8.8
1998	sell	8.9
1997	buy	24.3
1996	buy	25.4
1995	buy	36.8
1994	buy	4.7
1993	buy	13.7
1992	buy	3.2
1991	buy	13.4
1990	buy	9.7
1989	buy	16.3
1988	buy	9.0
1987	buy	−6.9
1986	buy	30.1
1985	buy	33.1
1984	sell	11.2
1983	buy	3.8
1982	buy	34.9
1981	sell	−15.4
1980	sell	12.9
1979	sell	6.7
1978	buy	9.0
1977	sell	−20.7
1976	sell	−3.7
1975	sell	31.6
1974	sell	−14.1
1973	sell	−9.9
1972	buy	2.9
1971	sell	5.6
1970	sell	13.0
1969	sell	−14.1
1968	buy	7.7
1967	buy	0.1

a. Calculate the compound annual percentage return on the DJIA over this period.
b. Suppose that you have followed the Super Bowl indicator every year since 1967. Specifically, when the indicator directed you to buy stocks, you held a portfolio that earned a return comparable to that of the DJIA. In years when the indicator suggested that you should sell stocks, you put your money in Treasury bills earn-ing 4 percent. Calculate the compound annual rate of return on this strategy.
c. The New England Patriots, an AFC team, won the Super Bowl in 2002. How did U.S. stocks fare in that year?
d. Is this phenomenon inconsistent with market efficiency? Would you advise inves-tors to follow this indicator going forward?

10-8. KPN NV, is a telecommunications company in the Netherlands. The following table lists the monthly closing price, the monthly return, and the previous month's return from November 1998 to September 2002. Calculate the correlation coefficient between each month's return and the previous month's return. Are your findings consistent with market efficiency?

Date	Price	Return (%)	Previous Month's Return (%)
Sep-02	5.08	−7.3	19.1
Aug-02	5.48	19.1	0.0
Jul-02	4.6	0.0	8.2
Jun-02	4.6	8.2	−6.4
May-02	4.25	−6.4	−10.5
Apr-02	4.54	−10.5	7.0
Mar-02	5.07	7.0	−1.3
Feb-02	4.74	−1.3	−5.1
Jan-02	4.8	−5.1	10.7
Dec-01	5.06	10.7	18.4
Nov-01	4.57	18.4	43.0
Oct-01	3.86	43.0	−8.8
Sep-01	2.7	−8.8	−39.1
Aug-01	2.96	−39.1	−14.1
Jul-01	4.86	−14.1	−39.0
Jun-01	5.66	−39.0	−27.2
May-01	9.28	−27.2	31.3
Apr-01	12.75	31.3	−22.2
Mar-01	9.71	−22.2	−24.4
Feb-01	12.48	−24.4	48.5
Jan-01	16.51	48.5	−16.9
Dec-00	11.12	−16.9	−35.3
Nov-00	13.38	−35.3	−4.3
Oct-00	20.69	−4.3	−20.0
Sep-00	21.62	−20.0	−26.5
Aug-00	27.03	−26.5	−18.1
Jul-00	36.76	−18.1	−1.6
Jun-00	44.88	−1.6	−9.9
May-00	45.6	−9.9	−11.3
Apr-00	50.6	−11.3	−10.8
Mar-00	57.05	−10.8	49.6
Feb-00	63.97	49.6	−10.2
Jan-00	42.76	−10.2	72.8
Dec-99	47.63	72.8	9.0
Nov-99	27.57	9.0	14.6
Oct-99	25.3	14.6	−2.2
Sep-99	22.08	−2.2	0.7
Aug-99	22.57	0.7	−5.1
Jul-99	22.42	−5.1	0.0
Jun-99	23.62	0.0	13.9
May-99	23.62	13.9	8.1
Apr-99	20.74	8.1	−23.7
Mar-99	19.19	−23.7	−6.4
Feb-99	25.15	−6.4	10.6
Jan-99	26.87	10.6	17.2
Dec-98	24.3	17.2	8.9
Nov-98	20.74	8.9	31.2

The Behavioral Finance Critique of Market Efficiency (Optional)

10-9.   In September 2001, the month of the terrorist attacks on New York and Washington, D.C., the American Stock Exchange Airline Index fell 47 percent. However, from the end of September to the end of March the next year, the index rose 55 percent.

   a. How might behavioral finance explain this pattern of returns?

   b. From September 30, 2001, through September 19, 2002, the return on the airline index was negative 44 percent. Does this seem consistent with your answer to part (a)? From a behavioral point of view, does it appear that investors over- or underreacted to the events of September 11, 2001?

11

An Overview of Long-Term Financing

OPENING FOCUS

So You Think the U.S. Has a Stock Market–Based Corporate Finance System?

Most people would accept as a given that the U.S. system of corporate finance is based squarely on the nation's stock markets. It is certainly true that the New York Stock Exchange and Nasdaq markets are the largest (and some would say the most efficient) in the world, and that U.S. investors, managers, and government policymakers all pay very close attention to stock prices. In one crucial sense, however, it is incorrect to say that the United States has a stock market–based financial system, because very few established American companies raise capital by selling new stock in any given year. In fact, as the figure below makes clear, on net, U.S. firms retire more equity than they issue in many years, and the deficit has exceeded −$100 billion several times since 1995. Three reasons explain why the net equity statistics frequently turn negative. First, corporate acquisitions paid for with cash, which often total as much as $1 trillion per year, remove the stock of the acquired company from the market. Second, U.S. corporations repurchase over $100 billion worth of their own shares each year, which also removes stock from the market. Third, only a small fraction of large U.S. corporations sell new common stock in a given year. In fact, many of these companies have not sold any new stock for several decades.

Why then is the United States considered a stock market–based economy if equity issues are such an unimportant overall source of new capital? The answers are surprising and revealing. First, the stock market is an extremely important source of funding for one key group of firms, entrepreneurial growth companies. Each year, these firms raise billions in new equity capital through initial public offerings (IPOs), capital that enables them to grow rapidly. Second, and more important, U.S. stock markets play a central role in the American system of "corporate governance." This refers to the system of laws, institutions, and practices that determine how a public company is run, and in whose interest. One of the key governance roles

U.S. New Equity
Financing, 1990–2000

Source: "The Party's Over:
A Survey of Corporate
Finance," *The Economist*
(January 27, 2001), p. 11.

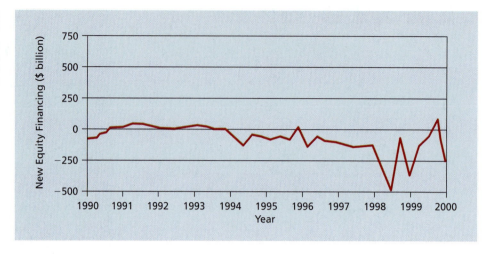

assigned to stock markets is to serve as arenas for corporate control contests, which in plain English usually means mergers and acquisitions. So, the next time someone asks you if the United States has a corporate financial system based on stock markets, you can answer with a ringing "yes, but . . ."

This chapter introduces the primary instruments that companies around the world use for long-term financing, and it examines key patterns observed in corporate financial systems. The basic instruments are similar worldwide and include common stock, preferred stock, and long-term debt. However, significant differences exist across countries in terms of how corporations use these instruments and in the degree to which firms rely on capital markets rather than financial intermediaries for funding. For example, the corporate financial systems of industrialized countries with legal systems based on English common law—such as Canada, the United States, Britain, and Australia—are characterized by large, highly liquid stock and bond markets. Other industrialized countries, particularly those in continental Europe with legal systems based on German or French civil law, have much smaller capital markets and rely primarily on commercial banks for corporate financing. Despite these differences in financial systems, corporations the world over display certain common tendencies. Perhaps the most important of these regularities is the near universal reliance on internally generated cash flow (retained earnings) as the dominant source of new financing.

We begin this chapter with a brief survey of the principal instruments used in corporate finance around the world. We then describe the critical choices companies make regarding their use of internal versus external financing, and their reliance on capital markets versus financial intermediaries for external funding. The final section examines the key role that **corporate governance** plays in modern finance. As foreshadowed in the Opening Focus, a nation's corporate governance system encompasses its body of commercial law, but also includes the institutions, regulations, and practices that influence how (and in whose interest) managers run companies. The effectiveness of a country's corporate governance system influences both national productivity and the financial performance of individual companies.

11.1 THE BASIC INSTRUMENTS OF LONG-TERM FINANCING

Debt and equity constitute the two main sources of corporate long-term financing. Equity capital represents an ownership interest that is junior to debt, sometimes called a residual claim. Debt capital represents a legally enforceable claim with cash flows that either are fixed or vary according to a predetermined formula. These basic financial instruments exist in most countries, and the rights and responsibilities of the holders of these instruments are very similar worldwide. This section examines common stock, the most junior ownership claim.

COMMON STOCK

Table 11.1 details the stockholders' equity accounts of Halogen Actuated Lighting (HAL). As of December 31, 2004, HAL had only common stock outstanding. During 2004, the company paid off the $247 million of preferred stock it had outstanding at the end of 2003 and did not issue any new preferred stock in replacement. Several terms that appear in the stock accounts require an explanation, beginning with par value. As discussed in Chapter 2, common stock can be sold with or without **par value,** which in the United States is a rather archaic phrase having little real economic significance. Because many states prohibit firms from selling shares at a price below par value, there is a clear incentive to set this value low. For this reason, HAL follows a standard convention of setting par value quite low, at $0.20 per share, so that it is unlikely ever to prove a binding constraint.[1]

	2004	2003
Preferred stock, par value $0.01 per share	—	$ 247
Shares authorized: 150,000,000		
Shares issued: (2003) 2,546,011		
Common stock, par value $0.20 per share	$14,248	12,400
Shares authorized: 4,687,500,000		
Shares issued: (2004: 1,913,513,218; 2003: 1,893,940,595)		
Retained earnings	30,142	23,784
Less: Treasury stock, at cost	20,114	13,800
Shares: (2004: 190,319,489; 2003: 131,041,411)		
Less: Employee benefits trust, at cost (shares, 2003: 20,000,000)	—	1,712
Less: Accumulated gains and losses not affecting		
retained earnings	662	295
Total stockholders' equity	$23,614	$20,624

Table 11.1
Stockholders' Equity Accounts for HAL December 31, 2004, and 2003 ($ in millions)

At the end of 2004, HAL had 4,687,500,000 **shares authorized,** meaning that the firm's stockholders have given HAL's board of directors the right to sell up to this number of shares without further stockholder approval.[2] At that time, there were 1,913,513,218 **shares issued** and outstanding (compared with 1,893,940,595 at year-

---

[1.] Outside the United States par values are often higher because it is common practice for firms to quote dividend payments and other cash distributions as a percentage of par value.

[2.] Though we have changed the names and dates in this example, the numbers for HAL are real. Following Stanley Kubrick in *2001: A Space Odyssey,* the data for our mythical company HAL actually come from recent financial reports for International Business Machines Corporation (IBM).

end 2003), with a total par value of $382,702,644 ($0.20/share × 1,913,513,218 shares). The total book value of common stock equals $14,248 million, so we can calculate the amount of **additional paid-in capital,** or capital in excess of par value, that HAL received for these shares as $13,865 million ($7.25 per share). This equals the difference between the $14,248 million book value and the $383 million par value. Since HAL's stock price was $126.39 per share at the end of December 2004, we can determine that HAL's **market capitalization** on that date was $241.86 billion ($126.39/share × 1,914,000,000 shares outstanding).

In addition to the shares that were outstanding at the end of 2004, HAL has been aggressively repurchasing its shares in the open market for several years. The company repurchased 51 million shares worth $5.3 billion in 2004 and 61 million shares worth $6.7 billion in 2003. The stock repurchased during these two years was held as **treasury stock,** with a book value of $20,114 million on December 31, 2004. HAL holds these shares as part of its employee stock-purchase plan.

Finally, HAL's accounts show that the firm has retained earnings of $30,142 million at year-end 2004. This represents the cumulative amount of profits that the firm has reinvested over the years. Don't be fooled by the $30.1 billion balance of this account. Retained earnings do not represent a pool of cash that the firm can use should a need for cash arise. Retained earnings simply reflect earnings that HAL reinvested in previous years.

Common Stockholders as Residual Claimants

Because common stockholders own the firm, they generally retain all the important decision rights concerning what the firm does and how it is governed. However, shareholders cannot receive cash distributions from the company unless the firm first pays what it owes to its creditors and preferred shareholders. Because shareholders hold the right to receive only the cash flow that remains after all other claims against the firm have been satisfied, they are sometimes called **residual claimants.** Obviously, holding the most junior claim on a firm's assets and cash flows is very risky. For this reason, common stockholders generally expect to earn a higher, though more variable, return on their investment than do creditors or preferred shareholders.

Stockholder Voting Rights

As residual claimants, stockholders have several important rights, the most important of which is the right to vote at any shareholders' meeting.[3] Most U.S. corporations have a single class of common stock outstanding, and every shareholder has the same rights and responsibilities. Most U.S. corporations also have a **majority voting system,** which allows each shareholder to cast one vote per share for each open position on the board of directors. It stands to reason that the owners (or owner) of 50.1 percent of the firm's stock can decide every contested issue and can elect the people they want to become directors. In practice, an investor or group of investors can control most corporate elections, even if they own less than 50.1 percent of the outstanding shares, because many investors do not vote at all.

A large number of states, including California, Illinois, and Michigan, require corporations to use a **cumulative voting system** to elect directors, unless shareholders explicitly vote for a majority system. Other states permit cumulative voting if the corporation's charter allows it. This system gives to each share of common stock a num-

---

[3.] U.S. public corporations must hold a general shareholders' meeting at least once per year. Additionally, special shareholders' meetings may be held to allow stockholders to vote on especially important questions, such as approving corporate mergers, divestitures, or major asset sales.

ber of votes equal to the total number of directors to be elected. The votes can be given to *any* director(s) the stockholder desires. Minority shareholders have a better chance of electing at least some directors under a cumulative voting system because they can concentrate all their votes on just one contested board seat.

APPLYING THE MODEL

Trish Corporation is in the process of electing five new directors. Each of the top five vote getters earns a seat on the board. The existing management has a slate of five candidates running for board seats. They control 79 of the firm's 100 shares outstanding. Amy, a disgruntled shareholder, owns the other 21 outstanding shares. Because they control more than half the outstanding shares, the firm's managers and their allies can elect all five directors under a *majority voting system*. Under a *cumulative voting system*, management would have 395 votes to allocate among these candidates (79 shares × 1 vote per share × 5 board seats), whereas Amy would have 105 votes (21 shares × 1 vote × 5 board seats). If Amy casts all of her 105 votes for herself, she will be assured of winning a seat, because there is no way that the firm's managers can allocate their 395 votes to prevent Amy from being one of the top five vote getters in the election. ■

U.S. companies will occasionally have two or more outstanding classes of stock, usually with differential voting rights. In these cases, corporate insiders will generally concentrate their holdings in the superior voting-share class and ordinary investors will hold relatively more of the inferior voting-share class. This dual-class capital structure is much more common in many other countries than it is in the United States, at least partly because both the New York Stock Exchange and the SEC have actively discouraged American companies from adopting such a structure.[4]

Proxies and Proxy Contests

Because most shareholders who own small amounts of stock do not attend the annual meeting to vote, they may sign a **proxy statement** giving their votes to another party. The firm's incumbent managers generally receive most of the stockholders' proxies, partly because managers can solicit them at company expense. Occasionally, when the ownership of the firm is widely dispersed, outsiders may attempt to gain control by waging a **proxy fight.** They attempt to solicit a sufficient number of votes to unseat existing directors. In their study of 97 proxy contests, Ikenberry and Lakonishok (1993) find that firms targeted for the proxy fights generally experience poor financial performance leading up to the proxy battle. More recently, Mulherin and Poulsen (1998) study the effects of 270 proxy contests and report that these clashes usually benefit shareholders, especially when the targeted firm is ultimately acquired by another company.

A significant fraction of stockholders routinely fail to exercise their right to vote. In some cases, brokers and banks that hold shares in "street name" on behalf of their

---

[4.] For most of its modern history, the NYSE automatically delisted any firm that adopted a dual-class capital structure and also refused to list any company with such a capitalization. The exchange was forced to back off this policy in 1986, when General Motors adopted a two-class structure as part of its acquisitions of Hughes and EDS. Two years later, however, the SEC issued a ruling prohibiting publicly traded companies from adopting a dual-class structure, though the ruling did allow firms going public with such a structure to retain it. Academic papers have examined dual-class capitalizations in the United States (Lease, McConnell, and Mikkelson 1983; DeAngelo and DeAngelo 1985); Israel (Levy 1983); Canada (Jog and Riding 1986); Italy (Zingales 1994); the United Kingdom (Megginson 1990); and Sweden (Bergstrom and Rydqvist 1990).

clients are allowed to vote, and they almost always side with management. Bethel and Gillan (2002) show that when managers submit a proposal for a shareholder vote, and when they believe that the outcome of that vote will be close, they can craft the proposal in a way that maximizes the votes cast by brokers and banks. Therefore, managers have a limited ability to manipulate the proxy process to obtain outcomes favorable to their own interests.

Rights to Dividends and Other Distributions

A firm's board of directors decides whether to pay dividends or not. Most U.S. corporations that pay dividends pay them quarterly, while the common practice in other developed countries is to pay dividends semiannually or annually. Firms usually pay dividends in cash, but they may also make dividend payments using stock or (on rare occasions) merchandise. Common stockholders have no guarantee that the firm will pay dividends, but shareholders come to expect certain payments based on the historical dividend pattern of the firm. The dividend decision and its impact on firm valuation have perplexed researchers for decades, and we examine it in detail in Chapter 14.

Just as shareholders have no guarantee they will receive dividends, they have no assurance they will receive any cash settlement in the event that the firm is liquidated. Due to limited liability, however, shareholders cannot lose more than they invest in the firm. Moreover, the common stockholder can receive unlimited returns through dividends and through the appreciation in the value of his or her holdings. In other words, although nothing is guaranteed, the *possible* rewards for providing equity capital can be considerable.

Preferred Stock

Preferred stock investors hold claims that are in most respects senior to those held by common stockholders. The firm promises preferred stockholders a fixed periodic return, stated either as a percentage or as a dollar amount. To use the example of HAL presented in Table 11.1, during 2004 the firm retired the single class of preferred stock it had outstanding at year-end 2003. These were Series A shares, with a 7.5 percent dividend yield, on which HAL paid total cash dividends of $20 million in 2003. Since HAL sold the preferred shares for approximately $100 per share, these had a total book value of $247 million, and each preferred share received cash dividends of $7.50 per year. As with common stock, the HAL preferred stock class had a very small par value ($0.01 per share), and there were far more shares authorized (150 million) than were actually issued (2,546,011). Firms generally do not issue large quantities of preferred stock.

Although it is not uncommon to find industrial firms issuing preferred stock, it is most often issued by public utilities, by acquiring firms in merger transactions, or by firms that wish to attract corporate rather than individual investors. As we will discuss in Chapter 15, venture capitalists also typically structure their investments in entrepreneurial growth companies as convertible preferred stock, which means that the preferred shares can be converted into a fixed number of common shares at the option of the holder. Historically, public utilities in the United States have been highly regulated, with state agencies exercising some control over the rates that utilities can charge for their services. Some elements of the rate-setting process give utilities the incentive to issue a hybrid security, one that counts as equity capital and thus increases the firm's credit rating and its debt capacity but at the same time does not carry as high a required rate of return as common stock does. This is why so many utilities raise capital by issuing preferred stock. Firms sometimes issue preferred stock in connection with mergers and acquisitions to capture certain tax advantages that arise when one company buys another's assets. A large fraction of the dividends that corporations holding preferred shares receive are tax deductible, so corporations rather than individuals own much of the preferred stock that is issued in the United States.

The rights of preferred stockholders resemble those of creditors in some respects, but in other ways they resemble the rights of common stockholders. For example, preferred shareholders, like lenders, receive periodic cash payments that are contractually specified and do not vary with the profits of the firm (except when profits are so low that the firm defaults and creditors receive less than they were promised). Preferred investors also hold a claim that is senior to that of common stock, just as lenders do. However, unlike lenders, who can force a firm into bankruptcy if it fails to make scheduled interest and principal payments, preferred stockholders cannot force the firm into bankruptcy if it skips a preferred dividend payment. Like common stockholders, preferred investors hold claims with no fixed maturity date and a lower priority than lenders' claims if the firm is liquidated. Preferred shareholders typically do not have the voting rights that common stockholders enjoy.

LONG-TERM DEBT

Because we provide in-depth coverage of long-term debt in Chapter 17, we will present only the briefest sketch of its key features here, beginning with the various methods of classifying these financial instruments.

The simplest classification of debt instruments is based on their maturities. **Short-term debt** matures in one year or less, and **long-term debt** matures in more than one year. Analysts also classify debt according to its seniority status. As stated earlier, debt is always a senior claim to equity, meaning that interest payments must be made before any dividends can be paid, and in the event of corporate bankruptcy, all debt claims must be paid in full before anything can be distributed to equity investors. There can, however, also be differences in seniority status among a firm's debt claims. **Subordinated debt** securities, for example, are junior claims to senior debt and are entitled to receive interest or principal payments only if the senior debt claims have been paid in full. Naturally, subordinated debt offers a higher interest rate than does senior debt as compensation for its greater risk.

Still another means of classifying debt is whether the debt is secured or unsecured. Most corporate borrowing from banks and other financial intermediaries is **secured debt,** meaning that the loan is backed by **collateral** that creditors can seize in the event of default. A loan secured by real property is usually called a **mortgage,** while loans extended for the purchase of transportation equipment are often structured as **equipment trust receipts.** Perhaps surprising, most of the publicly traded bonds issued by American corporations are **debentures,** meaning that the bonds are backed only by the general faith and credit of the borrowing company. In many other developed countries, virtually all corporate borrowing is secured, and the corporate bond market is typically quite small.

We may also classify debt instruments based on whether they pay fixed-rate or floating-rate interest. For example, most publicly traded debt securities issued by U.S. corporations promise fixed-coupon interest payments, meaning that they promise an unchanging series of interest payments (usually semiannual) over the life of the bond. A corporation that issues a 10-year, 8 percent coupon rate debenture with a $1,000 principal value promises purchasers of this bond that the firm will make 20 equal semiannual coupon payments of $40 each ($80 per year) for 10 years, at the end of which time the firm will repay the $1,000 principal to the investor.

Although U.S. debentures typically have fixed-coupon interest rates, most bank loans obtained by both U.S. and non-U.S. corporations are **floating-rate instruments,** which means that the interest rate charged on the loan periodically changes to reflect changes in market interest rates. For example, the interest rates on most large **syndicated bank loans** (loans that are funded by a large number of commercial banks, called a syndicate) fluctuate with a market rate known as **LIBOR,** the London interbank offered rate.

APPLYING THE MODEL

On June 17, 2002, China-based Grace Semiconductor Manufacturing Corp. announced that it had reached an agreement to borrow $830 million (U.S. currency) from a group of Chinese banks. The maturity of the loan was set at five years, and the interest rate equaled LIBOR plus a spread of 1.8 percentage points. If at the time of the loan agreement the LIBOR rate was about 2 percent, then the rate on Grace Semiconductor's loan would be 3.8 percent. In addition, the rate would change periodically as determined by the loan agreement with the syndicate.   ■

We can further classify corporate bonds by noting whether they are convertible or callable. Most bonds issued by American corporations are **callable,** meaning that the issuing corporation has the right to force investors to sell the bonds back to the firm at the firm's discretion. This right becomes valuable for corporations when market interest rates decline because it gives the corporation the right to refinance its long-term fixed rate, borrowing at a lower interest rate. Obviously, what is good for the issuing corporation is bad for the investor, so callable bonds have to offer higher interest rates than otherwise equivalent noncallable debt. Furthermore, most bonds are protected from being called during the first several years after they are issued, and corporations usually must pay a **call premium** (frequently set at one year's additional interest) to call bonds after the protection period ends.

Some corporate bonds grant investors the right to exchange their bonds for shares of stock rather than cash. Called **convertibles,** these bonds offer investors the seniority (relative to equity) of a debt instrument and the potential for much higher returns if the underlying stock rises in value. Convertible bonds usually grant investors the right to exchange one bond for a fixed number of shares. Because the number of shares per bond is fixed, the value of the conversion option rises as the price of the underlying stock does. Because the option to convert bonds into shares is valuable, convertible bonds pay lower interest rates than otherwise similar nonconvertible bonds.

SMART IDEAS VIDEO
David Mauer, Southern Methodist University
"What is the short-term market price reaction to call events?"

See the entire interview at **SMARTFinance**

APPLYING THE MODEL

On May 28, 2002, Nikon Corp. announced that it would sell convertible bonds worth ¥10 billion to one of its strategic business partners, Intel Corp. Nikon, one of Japan's leading manufacturers of photolithography equipment used to make semiconductors, said that its bonds would grant Intel the right to buy Nikon shares at a price of ¥1,857. That represented a premium of almost 30 percent over Nikon's then-current stock price of ¥1,429. Aside from the strategic business reasons for Intel to make this deal, the bonds offered the company an attractive trade-off. If Nikon's shares performed well, Intel could convert the bonds to shares and earn a substantial profit. If

Nikon's shares lagged, Intel could hold the bonds and receive the cash payments due until the bonds were scheduled to mature in 2007. ■

Finally, we can distinguish those debt instruments that can be traded among investors, called securities, from those that are essentially loan products offered by financial intermediaries. In our previous discussions, we have used the terms "loan," "bond," and "debt instrument" more or less interchangeably. However, the terms and conditions imposed upon a company borrowing from a financial intermediary in the form of loans or lines of credit are often quite different from those that would be imposed if the same company sold (issued) debt securities directly to investors using the public capital markets. As will be discussed in greater detail in Chapter 17, a bank generally imposes **loan covenants** on a borrower in an attempt to protect its investment. **Positive covenants** specify what borrowers *must* do, such as provide audited financial statements and maintain minimum debt coverage ratios, while **negative covenants** specify what the borrowing firm *must not* do, such as sell assets without the bank's approval or borrow additional senior debt. Additionally, banks are usually willing and able to monitor a borrower's operating and financial performance over the life of the loan and can intervene when a problem emerges.[5]

As an example of the choices that large corporations have regarding their borrowing needs, Table 11.2 demonstrates the short- and long-term debt accounts for HAL at the end of 2004. This table reveals that HAL has several borrowing patterns typical of most large U.S. companies. First, the book value of HAL's short-term debt of $11,188 million is comparable in amount to its long-term debt of $15,567 million. Second, a large fraction of the short-term borrowing takes the form of **commercial paper**. This is a type of short-term instrument that is sold directly to corporate and individual investors and is usually held to maturity. Commercial paper is almost always supported by a standby borrowing arrangement with a commercial bank.[6] Third, HAL has several different borrowing programs in place that are not being tapped to the full, including various bank loan arrangements and note-issuance facilities. In other words, the company has substantial unused borrowing capacity that it could draw on very quickly. Fourth, the company has numerous publicly traded debentures outstanding with varying maturities, interest rates, and even currencies. As one of the world's best-known and most respected corporations, HAL has virtually unlimited access to capital markets around the world.

In this section, we have described the major types of financial instruments that companies use to raise long-term financing, but the number of variations on each of these types is truly astonishing. Finnerty and Emery (2002) identify 80 distinct securities that have been introduced in the United States since 1970. Each of these securities is designed to fill a specific gap in the market. For example, catastrophe bonds distribute interest and principal payments that vary according to whether or not the issuer, an insurance company, experiences losses of a certain magnitude from a nat-

Smart Concepts
See the concept explained step-by-step at **SMARTFinance**

[5.] Public security issues also contain positive and negative covenants, but since there are usually a large number of small investors for any single bond issue, these covenants are very difficult to monitor and enforce. Although an agent (trustee) is appointed to represent the investors' interests, it remains true that less corporate monitoring will generally be undertaken with publicly issued debt than with intermediated borrowing.

[6.] According to U.S. Federal Reserve Board statistics, American companies had over $1.6 *trillion* worth of commercial paper outstanding at year-end 2001, of which some $310 billion was issued by nonfinancial corporations such as HAL. By early April 2002, however, the total amount of commercial paper outstanding had fallen by over $150 billion, with all the decline coming from nonfinancial borrowers. In order to be exempt from registration as a publicly issued "security," commercial paper must have an original maturity of 270 days or less, and most real issues have much shorter maturities. The **Eurocommercial paper** market has been growing very rapidly during the past decade, although the total amount outstanding ($260 billion in early 2002) is still less than one-fifth of that in the United States.

Table 11.2
Short- and Long-Term
Debt of HAL, December 31, 2004, and 2003
($ in millions)

Short-Term Debt		2004	2003
Commercial paper		$ 4,809	$ 3,521
Short-term loans		1,564	3,975
Long-term debt: Current maturities		4,815	2,709
Total		$11,188	$10,205

Long-Term Debt		2004	2003
	Maturities	Amount	Amount
U.S. dollars Debentures:			
6.22%	2027	$ 500	$ 500
6.5%	2028	700	700
7%	2025	600	600
7%	2045	150	150
7.125%	2096	850	850
7.5%	2013	550	550
8.375%	2019	750	750
Notes: 6.3% average	2005–2014	2,772	2,933
Medium-term note program: 5.8% average	2005–2014	3,620	4,305
Other: 6.8% average	2005–2012	828	1,092
		$11,320	$12,430
Other currencies (average interest rate in parentheses)			
Euros (4.4%)	2005–2008	$ 3,042	$ 3,042
Japanese yen (1.1%)	2005–2014	4,749	4,845
Canadian dollars (5.8%)	2005–2008	441	302
Swiss francs (4.0%)	2005–2006	151	231
Other (6.1%)	2005–2014	726	275
		$20,429	$21,125
Less: Net unamortized discount		47	45
Less: Current maturities		4,815	2,709
Total		$15,567	$18,371

ural disaster, such as a hurricane or an earthquake. Insurance companies sell these bonds to redistribute some of the risk of their product portfolios. For investors, catastrophe bonds offer unique diversification benefits because the occurrence of natural disasters is not highly correlated with other sources of financial risk (e.g., interest rate movements, currency movements, business cycles). Another recent financial product innovation, called zero-premium exchangeable notes (ZENS), involved Reliant Energy and Time Warner, as described in the Applying the Model.

APPLYING THE MODEL

In September 1999, Reliant Energy issued 30-year notes with a payout tied to the price of Time Warner stock. Reliant Energy granted buyers the right to sell their notes back to the firm for 95 percent of the value of Time Warner stock. Reliant promised to pay investors at maturity cash equal to the greater of (1) the value of Time Warner stock or (2) the original principal amount of the ZENS. The ZENS also offered investors a relatively low coupon rate, and Reliant could defer interest payments for up to five years if necessary (skipped interest payments would compound over time). For investors, ZENS offered the opportunity to profit from long-term appreciation in Time Warner stock without accepting the risk of a steep decline in those shares. By issuing ZENS, Reliant could monetize its existing holdings of Time Warner shares without actually giving up ownership of those shares.   ■

---

1. What relationship would you expect between the interest rate offered on a callable bond and the call premium?

2. Most large Japanese corporations hold their annual shareholders' meeting on the same day and require voting in person. What does this practice say about the importance and clout of individual shareholders in Japanese corporate finance?

**Concept
Review
Questions**

11.2 THE BASIC CHOICES IN LONG-TERM FINANCING

Companies the world over face the same basic financing problem: how to fund those projects and activities the firm needs to undertake if it is to grow and prosper. This section examines the choices firms face in selecting among financing alternatives, particularly the choices regarding internal versus external financing. The next section surveys key issues related to the choice between financing via capital markets versus through financial intermediaries.

The Need to Fund a Financial Deficit

Corporations everywhere are net dissavers, which is an economic way of saying they demand more financial capital for investment and for making payments to investors than they supply in the form of retained profits. Corporations must close this **financial deficit** by borrowing or by issuing new equity securities. Every major firm confronts four critical financing decisions on an ongoing basis:

1. How much capital must the company raise each year?
2. How much of this must be raised externally rather than through retained profits?
3. How much of the external funding should be raised through borrowing from a bank or another financial intermediary, and how much capital should be raised selling securities directly to investors?
4. What proportion of the external funding should be structured as common stock, preferred stock, or long-term debt?

The answer to the first question depends on the capital budgeting process of a particular firm, as discussed in Chapters 7–9. A company must raise enough capital to fund all its positive-*NPV* investment projects and to cover its working capital needs. The true financing decision begins with question 2, the choice between internal versus external finance.

The Choice between Internal versus External Financing

At first glance, the internal/external choice seems to be a decision that firms can make mechanically. A company's managers might approximate external funding needs by subtracting cash dividend payments from the firm's **cash flow from operations** (net income plus depreciation and other noncash charges), with the difference between

Table 11.3
Sources and Uses of Funds for U.S. Nonfinancial Corporations

Sources and Uses of Funds, Billions of Current Dollars

	2000	1999	1998	1997	1996	1995	1994	1992	1990	1985	1980
Uses of funds											
Capital expenditures	1,021	907	847	784	685	666	593	439	430	381	262
Direct investment abroad	110	137	128	84	77	91	79	42	35	14	20
Net acquisition of financial assets	404	482	148	197	295	310	172	82	73	197	105
Total uses	1,535	1,503	1,091	1,046	1,051	1,036	824	563	538	592	387
Internal sources of funds											
Profit after tax	410	372	338	345	310	286	253	166	141	103	116
− Dividends	(264)	(248)	(238)	(219)	(201)	(178)	(158)	(134)	(118)	(72)	(45)
+ Consumption of fixed capital	667	622	583	540	506	474	445	391	371	323	159
+ Foreign earnings retained abroad	89	70	66	59	60	59	39	45	51	26	19
+ Inventory valuation adjustment	−16	−9	21	7	3	−18	−12	−3	−13	0	−42
Total internal sources	887	806	764	732	678	623	567	465	432	380	207
External sources of funds											
Increase in nonmarket liabilities	387	404	215	175	313	215	152	89	120	278	139
Net funds raised in markets	294	338	151	152	80	169	90	72	64	102	83
Net new equity issues	−153	−143	−267	−114	−70	−58	−45	27	−63	−85	10
Credit market instruments	447	482	418	266	149	227	135	45	127	186	73
Statistical discrepancy[a]	−33	−8	−24	−32	−25	22	15	−63	−78	−168	−42
Total external sources = Financial deficit	648	697	330	314	373	413	257	98	106	212	180
Percent of Total (Total Sources = Total Uses)											
Internal financing as % total	58	54	70	70	65	60	69	83	80	64	54
Financial deficit as % total	42	46	30	30	35	40	31	17	20	36	46
Financial market financing as % total	19	20	13	16	8	17	11	13	12	17	21
Net equity issues as % total	−10	−10	−24	−11	−7	−6	−5	5	−12	−14	3

Source: Board of Governors of the Federal Reserve System, as reported in the *Statistical Abstract of the United States,* various issues.
[a]Calculated as the amount needed to make total sources of funds equal total uses. This is small in recent years, but significant before 1994.

this internally generated funding and the firm's total financing needs equaling the external financing requirement. The decision is not simple, however, because management may wish to build up or reduce working capital stocks over time and because dividend policy is not fixed, except in the very short term. Nonetheless, it is basically true that the total amount of net external financing a firm requires each year is a residual amount, calculated as the difference between the firm's total capital needs and its cash flow from operations (net of dividend payments). Not surprising, the residual nature of external funding needs implies that this figure will be highly variable from year to year for individual companies. As Table 11.3 makes clear, external funding is also a highly variable figure for the U.S. corporate sector as a whole, and the same is true for most other developed economies. In the aggregate, the amount of external funding that U.S. firms required to cover their financial deficit between 1980 and 2000 fluctuated from about $98 billion to almost $700 billion.

There are several other important regularities to be observed in the external financing data presented in Table 11.3. For example, external funding needs tend to peak at the ends of economic expansions and bottom out during recessions. Intuitively, this makes sense because firms invest little during recessions and much during expansions. The second key pattern that Table 11.3 reveals is that internal cash flow is the dominant source of corporate funding in the United States. Businesses regularly finance two-thirds to three-quarters of all their capital spending needs internally. Over time, other countries have also moved in the same direction. Whereas European corporations relied quite heavily on external funding as recently as the 1970s, the corporate sectors of Western European nations now meet the majority of their total funding needs internally. Japanese corporations still meet up to half of their total financing needs externally, primarily through bank borrowing, but this still implies far lower dependence on external funding than was the case prior to the 1980s.

OTHER FINANCING CHOICES

Once a company has determined how much capital it needs to raise externally, it must then confront the next two financing decisions: whether to raise money through financial intermediaries or through the sale of securities, and how to allocate the money required between debt and equity. Our discussion of the choice between equity and debt financing will be deferred until Chapters 12 and 13, where we examine the firm's capital structure decision. The remainder of this chapter will describe the firm's choice between intermediated and capital market financing and the need for effective corporate governance. We begin by examining the role intermediaries play in the corporate finance systems of the United States and other countries. We then detail the rapidly growing role of capital markets in funding corporate activities around the world. Finally, we describe what corporate governance means and discuss why it has assumed such prominence in corporate finance the world over.

---

3. Why do you think corporations maintain a fixed dividend payment and thus make net external financing the "residual" financial choice, rather than the other way around? In other words, why don't firms make dividends the residual?

4. Why do you think that corporations around the world rely so heavily on internally generated funds for investment capital? Why do you think firms sometimes simultaneously increase dividends and sell securities?

Concept Review Questions

11.3 THE ROLE OF FINANCIAL INTERMEDIARIES IN FUNDING CORPORATE INVESTMENT

Should a corporation care whether it raises capital by selling securities to investors in public capital markets or by dealing more directly with a financial intermediary such as a commercial bank? Because money is a commodity, a bank's money and an investor's money should seemingly be perfect substitutes. In reality, however, a corporation's choice between intermediated and security market financing significantly influences its postfinancing ownership structure, financial flexibility, and repayment burden. On a broader scale, whether a country emphasizes intermediary or capital market–based financing also influences the key features of the corporate finance system that nation develops. Before analyzing this issue, however, we should formally define what a financial intermediary is and briefly describe what services it provides.

WHAT IS A FINANCIAL INTERMEDIARY, AND WHAT DOES IT DO?

A **financial intermediary** (**FI**) is an institution that raises capital by issuing liabilities against itself—for example, in the form of demand or savings deposits. The intermediary then pools the funds raised and uses these to make loans to borrowers or, where allowed, to make equity investments in nonfinancial firms. Borrowers repay the intermediary and have no direct contact with the individual savers who actually funded the loans. In other words, both borrowers and savers deal directly with the intermediary, which specializes in credit analysis and collection, even as it offers financial products tailored to the specific needs of both borrowers and savers.

Intermediaries provide a variety of financial services to corporations, but the most important is **information intermediation.** In financial markets, it is very difficult for investors either to assess the true creditworthiness of borrowers prior to lending them money or to monitor the subsequent use of the funds so borrowed. Faced with these informational asymmetries, investors will either choose not to lend at all or will do so only at high interest rates. To overcome this problem, a commercial bank or other FI can become a **corporate insider,** trusted with confidential information about the borrowing firm's operations and opportunities and interacting with corporate managers on an ongoing basis. If successful, the bank will become well positioned to first assess, then meet, the firm's evolving financial needs.[7]

In many countries, intermediaries also play an extremely important corporate governance role, distinct from their activities in granting credit and monitoring loan repayment. Commercial banks, in particular, frequently help set operating and financial policies of firms they have invested in by serving on corporate boards and monitoring the performance of senior managers. In countries such as Germany, where banks can both directly own large equity stakes and vote the shares they hold in trust for individual customers, financial institutions wield tremendous economic power. And in countries with a long tradition of state ownership of corporate assets, state-owned banks are usually the chosen vehicle for exercising financial control. For political and historical reasons, however, the United States has chosen to effectively prohibit commercial banks from exercising a corporate governance role, even as it has discouraged other intermediaries (insurance companies, pension funds, mutual funds, etc.) from actively monitoring and disciplining corporate management.[8]

[7.] Petersen and Rajan (1994) document the value of banking relationships, particularly to small firms. Other academic researchers present similar findings.

[8.] For a description of these rules and a discussion of their impact, see Grundfest (1990), Black (1992), Jensen (1993), Bhide (1993), and especially, Roe (1990, 1997). La Porta, López-de-Silanes, and Shleifer (2000) detail both the extensiveness of government ownership of commercial banks around the world and the negative impact this has on profitability and efficiency.

The Role of Financial Intermediaries in U.S. Corporate Finance

Americans have a long history of distrusting concentrated private economic power, and this has dramatically influenced U.S. financial regulations. In response to public opinion, policymakers have discouraged the growth of large intermediaries (especially commercial banks), in part by imposing on them severe geographical restrictions. Existing geographical restrictions were codified into national law when Congress passed the **McFadden Act** in 1927, which prohibited interstate banking. After numerous failed attempts to repeal the McFadden Act over the years, a bill allowing full interstate branch banking was finally approved by Congress in July 1994. This prompted an acceleration of the trend toward consolidation of the banking industry. The number of independent U.S. banks declined from 11,461 to 8,256 between October 1992 and December 2000, primarily through mergers.

The second pivotal law affecting American FIs was the **Glass-Steagall Act,** which was passed in 1933 in response to perceived banking abuses during the Great Depression. This legislation mandated the separation of investment and commercial banking, thereby prohibiting commercial banks from underwriting corporate security issues, providing security brokerage services to their customers, or even owning voting equity securities on their own account. Banking's corporate financing role was thus effectively restricted to making commercial loans and to providing closely related services, such as leasing. As with the McFadden Act, there were repeated attempts to repeal Glass-Steagall, and these finally succeeded when Congress passed the **Gramm-Leach-Bliley Act** in November 1999.

Nonbank FIs play important roles in American corporate finance, both as creditors and as equity investors. Insurance companies not only provide much of the long-term financing for large real estate development and factory construction, but also directly own roughly 5 percent of all publicly traded corporate equity. Specialized finance companies such as General Electric Credit Corporation and General Motors Acceptance Corporation have carved out very successful niches as secured lenders for major equipment purchases. However, public and private pension funds have emerged in recent years as by far the single most important class of equity investor in the United States, and these institutions have assumed the role of activist monitors of corporate managers.

Perhaps the most interesting U.S. nonbank financial intermediaries are the institutional venture capital firms, which we examine in depth in Chapter 15. These companies have enjoyed remarkable success over the years in identifying, financing, and nurturing to maturity many of today's best-known high-technology companies—including Intel, Microsoft, Dell, Amgen, Cisco Systems, Sun Microsystems, and more recently, Yahoo!, Amazon.com, and eBay.

The Corporate Finance Role of Non-U.S. Financial Intermediaries

In markets outside the United States, commercial banks typically play much larger roles in corporate finance. In most countries, a relative handful of very large banks service most large firms, and the size and competence of these banks give them tremendous influence over corporate financial and operating policies. This power is further strengthened by the ability of most non-U.S. banks to underwrite corporate security issues and to make direct equity investments in commercial firms. Most Western countries allow commercial banks to act as true **merchant banks** capable of providing the full range of financial services. These services include (1) payment and cash management services; (2) short-, intermediate-, and long-term commercial lending; (3) trade and project finance; (4) securities underwriting; and (5) direct private placement of

Table 11.4
The World's Largest Companies in 2001, Ranked by Assets, Are Commercial Banks

Bank Name	Country	Total Assets Amount	Total Assets Rank[a]	Stockholders' Equity Amount	Stockholders' Equity Rank[a]	Market Capitalization Amount	Market Capitalization Rank[b]
Mizuho Holdings[c]	Japan	$1,304,342	1	$49,908	14	$ 46,874	94
Citigroup[d]	U.S.	902,210	2	66,206	5	260,796	5
Deutsche Bank	Germany	882,541	3	25,827	46	47,401	92
Bank of Tokyo-Mitsubishi	Japan	716,934	4	23,082	54	54,129	78
J. P. Morgan Chase & Co.	U.S.	715,348	5	42,338	21	97,014	34
HSBC Holdings	Britain	674,381	7	45,608	18	115,611	24
Hypovereinsbank	Germany	672,692	8	18,397	83	25,839	188
UBS	Switzerland	671,118	9	27,666	40	66,227	57
BNP Paribas	France	651,590	10	20,291	70	38,940	124
Bank of America Corp	U.S.	642,191	11	47,628	16	95,197	36
Credit Suisse	Switzerland	609,335	13	25,271	48	54,483	76
Sumitomo Bank[e]	Japan	537,783	14	14,660	112	9,368	511
ABN AMRO Holdings	Netherlands	509,949	15	11,757	144	28,719	171
Credit Agricole	France	502,903	16	24,215	51	na[f]	—
Industrial & Commercial Bank China	China	482,980	17	22,653	58	Government owned	—
Norinchukin Bank	Japan	480,199	18	17,712	87	na	—
Royal Bank of Scotland	Britain	478,019	19	34,531	30	61,736	65
Barclays	Britain	472,322	20	19,699	74	49,792	85
Dresdner Bank	Germany	453,927	22	12,228	138	24,531	200
UFJ Holdings[g]	Japan	439,020	24	15,284	105	26,854	181
Commerzbank	Germany	431,549	26	11,757	144	13,525	355
Société Générale	France	427,999	27	12,850	130	25,202	193
Sakura Bank	Japan	413,750	29	17,363	89	47,746[h]	91
Fortis	Belgium	411,290	31	14,267	114	17,426	nr[i]
Bank of China	China	382,727	33	19,748	73	Government owned	—
Westdeutsche Landesbank	Germany	375,574	34	8,287	197	Government owned	—
Santander Central Hispano Group	Spain	327,588	36	18,854	76	43,057	109
Lloyds TSB Group	Britain	325,619	37	14,545	113	55,079	75
Rabobank	Netherlands	321,947	38	13,870	121	na	—
Intesabci	Italy	311,949	39	11,495	152	23,440	205
China Construction Bank	China	305,854	41	13,875	120	Government owned	—
Abbey National	Britain	305,317	42	10,203	165	24,532	199

Notes: Total assets, stockholders' equity (capital) and stock market capitalization for the 32 international commercial banks with total assets exceeding $300 billion. All amounts are in millions of U.S. dollars. This table's rankings are based on total asset and stockholders' equity data from "Fortune Global 500: The World's Largest Corporations," *Fortune* (July 23, 2001), and use the most recent data available, usually year-end 2000. Market capitalization data are from "The Business Week Global 1000: The World's Most Valuable Companies," *Business Week* (July 9, 2001), and are based on market values as of May 31, 2001.

[a]Rank within Fortune's Global 500 listing of the world's largest corporations.
[b]Rank within Business Week's Global 1000 listing of the world's most valuable companies.
[c]Formed by merger of Dai-Ichi Kangyo Bank, Fuji Bank, and Industrial Bank of Japan, September 2000.
[d]Data for entire group, including Travelers Insurance and Salomon Smith Barney, as well as Citibank.
[e]Acquired by Sakura Bank in April 2001.
[f]Not available.
[g]Formed by merger of Sanwa Bank, Tokai Bank, and Toyo Trust & Banking, April 2001.
[h]Market value for Sumitomo Mitsui Banking Corp, formed after Sakura acquired Sumitomo, April 2001.
[i]Not ranked.

equity capital. Whereas the United States, Britain, and a few other nations have promoted the development of a security market–based corporate finance system, most other advanced countries have chosen to emphasize intermediated systems. A listing of the 32 largest banks in the world in 2001 is provided in Table 11.4. As you can see, the ranking based on assets is heavily tilted in favor of European and, especially, Japanese banks. Several U.S. banks rank highly based on stockholders' equity (capital) or market value, however, and are among the world's most profitable FIs.

Most non-U.S. banks also have far greater power vis-à-vis corporate borrowers than American banks do, and they play more-central roles in the resolution of client-firm bankruptcy or financial distress.[9] Although this may seem bad for borrowers, research on Japanese banking relationships during the 1980s suggests just the opposite. Given their positions as creditors and investors, Japanese banks were far more willing to continue lending money to financially distressed borrowers than were U.S. banks. The ability of these banks to intervene directly in a troubled firm's operations also meant they were often able to get involved in time to avert disaster. Unfortunately, the perilous state of financial health of most Japanese banks today suggests they are no longer capable of playing such a valuable role as corporate monitor. In fact, several of these banks may not even survive as independent entities themselves.

---

5. What factors might lead to better information intermediation by a financial intermediary as compared to a public financial market?

6. How do you think a bank's incentives change if it is allowed to hold the equity securities of firms in addition to offering them loans?

7. Compare the intermediation services performed by a small community bank and a large corporate pension fund. What do they have in common, and what are their major differences?

**Concept
Review
Questions**

11.4 THE EXPANDING ROLE OF SECURITIES MARKETS IN THE GLOBAL ECONOMY

No trend in modern finance is as clear or as transforming as the worldwide shift toward corporate reliance on securities markets rather than intermediaries for external financing. We begin this section by documenting this global trend toward market-based financing and then look specifically at security issuance in U.S. capital markets. We conclude by describing security-issue patterns in other advanced countries.

Overview of Securities Issues Worldwide

Table 11.5 presents summary information from the *Investment Dealers' Digest* on **primary security issues** worldwide, and for the United States alone, for the years 1990–2001. Primary issues actually raise capital for firms and are thus distinct from **secondary offerings,** where an investor sells his or her holdings of existing securities. The total value of primary issues around the world in 2001 was a record $4.075 tril-

---

[9.] The effect of differential bankruptcy procedures on observed national capital structure patterns is examined in Rajan and Zingales (1995).

Table 11.5
Worldwide Securities Issues, 1990–2000

Type of Security Issue	2001	2000	1999	1997	1995	1993	1990
Worldwide offerings	$ 4,075	$ 3,268	$ 3,288	$ 1,816	$1,066	$1,503	$ 504
[debt & equity]	(16,748)	(14,659)	(21,724)	(15,669)	(9,305)	(9,969)	(7,574)
Global debt (2000–01)	3,610	2,624	1,114	635	385	479	184
International debt							
(1990–99)	(14,033)	(10,827)	(4,122)	(4,066)	(2,548)	(2,701)	(1,376)
Eurobonds	—	946	1,069	475	280	388	172
		(3,858)	(3,893)	(2,804)	(1,840)	(2,162)	(1,213)
Yankee bonds (2000–01)	36	47	302	150	45	59	13
Foreign bonds (1990–99)	(84)	(112)	(2,706)	(1,177)	(237)	(270)	(81)
International common stock	148	335	139	34	21	19	7
[excluding US][a]	(1,659)	(2,662)	(817)	(302)	(242)	(309)	(132)
U.S. issuers worldwide[b]	2,880	1,958	2,103	1,196	700	1,049	313
[debt & equity]	(12,269)	(15,686)	(17,115)	(11,644)	(6,807)	(7,378)	(6,141)
All debt[c]	2,618	1,726	—	—	—	—	—
	(11,271)	(7,824)					
Straight corporate debt[d]	1,209	744	713	726	417	386	109
	(4,423)	(2,986)	(7,601)	(9,098)	(4,562)	(3,637)	(1,016)
High-yield corporate debt	76	43	95	114	28	55	1
	(261)	(196)	(434)	(769)	(153)	(345)	(7)
Collateralized securities	935	488	579	378	155	475	175
	(1,623)	(1,201)	(3,027)	(1,557)	(709)	(1,285)	(4,542)
Convertible debt and	103	56	40	15	9	15	5
preferred stock	(210)	(161)	(143)	(83)	(57)	(162)	(43)
Common stock[e]	126	223	175	119	82	86	14
	(559)	(955)	(1,069)	(1,341)	(1,159)	(1,374)	(362)
Initial public offerings[e]	37	73	64	44	30	41	5
	(106)	(429)	(531)	(625)	(572)	(707)	(174)

Notes: This table details the total value, in billions of U.S. dollars, and number (in parentheses) of securities issues worldwide (including the United States) for selected years in the period 1990–99. The data are taken from early-January issues of the *Investment Dealers' Digest.*
[a]Capital-raising private-sector offers; does not include privatization issues.
[b]From 1998, all figures include Rule 144A offers on U.S. markets.
[c]Includes mortgage-backed securities (MBS), asset-backed securities (ABS), and municipal bonds.
[d]Years 1999–2001 are long-term straight debt only. Before 1999, figures are for investment-grade debt.
[e]Excludes closed-end fund. Data for 1990–2000 are not comparable to 2001 due to definition change.

lion. Worldwide security offerings were $1.066 trillion in 1995 and less than $400 billion as recently as 1988. The 10-fold increase in the value of security market financing between 1988 and 2001 was not matched by a remotely comparable increase in world trade, investment, or economic activity, but is instead a reflection of the power of the trend toward the "securitization" of corporate finance. **Securitization** involves the repackaging of loans and other traditional bank-based credit products into securities that can be sold to public investors.

Security Issues by U.S. Corporations

Besides rapid recent growth, another major trend that can be observed from these data is the relatively steady fraction of worldwide security offerings accounted for by U.S.

issuers. American issues represented 70.7 percent ($2,880 billion of $4,075 billion) of the worldwide total value of security offerings in 2001, and U.S. issuers have sold between 62 percent and 74 percent of the global total every year since 1990. Looking more closely at the statistics for the United States alone, we can identify several other trends that are working to transform American finance. First, companies issue far more debt than equity each year. During 2001, American corporations issued $2,618 billion in straight (nonconvertible) debt, $103 billion in convertible debt and preferred stock, $125 billion in common stock, and a mere $33 billion in nonconvertible preferred stock (not listed in Table 11.5). Straight debt therefore represented almost 91 percent of the total capital raised by U.S. companies through public security issues during 2001. The $126 billion in common stock issued in 2001 represented a mere 4.4 percent of the capital-raising total. Even though this fraction was unusually small, equity issues always account for a very small share of the total amount of capital raised through public security issues in the United States. And remember that these are all gross issue amounts; once the value of stock removed from public markets through mergers and stock repurchases is accounted for, net equity issues are often negative. Add in the roughly $2 trillion in syndicated bank loans that American companies arrange each year, and it becomes clear that firms needing to raise capital externally greatly prefer to issue debt rather than common or preferred stock.

Second, the relative insignificance of new equity issues as a financing source for U.S. corporations is further accentuated by the fact that **initial public offerings (IPOs)**, excluding closed-end investment funds, accounted for over one-fourth ($37 billion of the $126 billion total) of common stock issued by companies in 2001 (and accounted for almost one-third of total issues in previous years). Initial public offerings involve the first public sale of stock to outside investors and are discussed in depth in Chapter 16. IPOs, as well as subsequent **seasoned** issues, must be registered with the SEC, and virtually all companies choose to list their stock on one of the organized exchanges so that investors can easily buy or sell the stock. America's IPO market is easily the world's largest and most liquid source of equity capital for small, rapidly growing firms, and most observers consider it a key national asset.

Non-U.S. Security Issues

We can also identify a number of patterns in the international security-issuance data presented in Table 11.5. First, the Eurobond market is by far the largest security market outside the United States, with the foreign bond market ranking second (neither category is listed separately for 2001). A **Eurobond** issue is a single-currency bond sold in several countries simultaneously,

SMART ETHICS VIDEO
Kent Womack, Dartmouth College
"It's very easy for analysts to have conflict of interest problems."

See the entire interview at SMARTFinance

whereas a **foreign bond** is an issue sold by a nonresident corporation in a single foreign country, and denominated in the host country's currency. A dollar-denominated bond issued by an American corporation and sold to European investors is an example of a Eurobond; and a Swiss franc–denominated bond sold in Switzerland by a Japanese corporate issuer is an example of a foreign bond. As in most years, **Yankee bonds** sold by foreign corporations to U.S. investors are the single largest category of foreign bond issue, with Swiss (Heidi bonds) and Japanese (Samurai) foreign bonds the next largest.

International issuers placed $946 billion in Eurobonds in 2000 (figures for Eurobond sales in 2001 are not listed separately). This was over three times the 1995 level, but was a slight decline from 1999's record volume of $1,069 billion. Corporate issues represent 57 percent of this total value ($540 billion), while issues from U.S. federal agencies and non-U.S. governments account for an additional 24 percent

COMPARATIVE CORPORATE FINANCE

What Do Private Pension Funds and Capital Markets Have in Common?

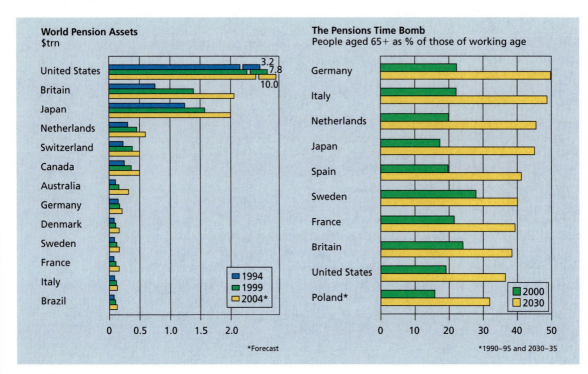

World Pension Assets
$trn

United States   3.2 / 7.8 / 10.0
Britain
Japan
Netherlands
Switzerland
Canada
Australia
Germany
Denmark
Sweden
France
Italy
Brazil

■ 1994
■ 1999
□ 2004*

0   0.5   1.0   1.5   2.0

*Forecast

The Pensions Time Bomb
People aged 65+ as % of those of working age

Germany
Italy
Netherlands
Japan
Spain
Sweden
France
Britain
United States
Poland*

■ 2000
□ 2030

0   10   20   30   40   50

*1990–95 and 2030–35

Source: The Economist (May 20, 2000), p. 127.   *Source: The Economist* (February 3, 2001), p. 54.

Although not obvious at first glance, there is in fact a strong link between the size of a nation's capital markets and the type of pension system covering most of that nation's citizens. Countries that rely primarily on a privately financed, or "funded," pension system tend also to have large capital markets, partly because most of the annual pension fund contributions are invested in the nation's stock and bond markets. As the chart on the left demonstrates, the countries with funded pension systems—particularly the United States, Britain, Japan, the Netherlands, and Switzerland—also hold the bulk of the world's pension fund assets. Most other developed countries, especially the large continental European nations, rely almost exclusively on state-run, "pay-as-you-

go" pension systems, where a younger generation of employed workers supports an older generation of retirees. These unfunded systems are coming under severe strain, for two reasons. First, as the chart on the right indicates, declining birth rates in all these countries are causing the average age of the population to rise rapidly, thus reducing the ratio of employed workers to retirees. Second, most of these countries offer very generous payments to pensioners, which can only be supported by equally high taxes on workers. Most countries with pay-as-you-go systems are attempting to switch to a funded system—or at least increase the role of private financing in pensions—but these charts make clear how difficult this transition will be.

($225 billion). American corporate issuers account for less than 10 percent of today's Eurobond totals, though dollar-denominated Eurobonds are still the most common. This is a dramatic change from the early and mid-1980s, when American firms accounted for roughly half of total Eurobond issue volume, and issued almost as much debt internationally as in the domestic bond market. This is largely because shelf registration (discussed in Chapter 16) has lowered bond issue costs for U.S. borrowers in their home market.

A second pattern observable in international finance is that **international common stock** issues raised $148 billion in 2001, somewhat less than 2000's $335 billion record, but up dramatically from the $82 billion total in 1995. These are equity issues that are sold in more than one country by nonresident corporations.[10] Although this total has grown steadily over the years, it is small by American standards, and over half of the total is usually **Yankee common stock** issued by foreign firms in the U.S. market.

To summarize, the growth in international security issues has kept pace with that in the United States, though this growth has probably impacted non-U.S. economies more because it began from a much smaller base. This is particularly true for the countries of continental Europe, which over the past decade have become very acquainted with a phenomenon long associated with U.S. financial markets: large numbers of mergers and acquisitions.

The Worldwide Surge in Mergers and Acquisitions

Figure 11.1 details the total value of mergers and acquisitions around the world from 1990 to 2001. The global value of M&A hovered around $500 billion from 1990– 1993. By 1998, it had increased sevenfold to $2.5 trillion, and reached more than $3.4 trillion in 2000 before dropping sharply to $1.75 trillion in 2001. No comparable period in financial history saw as dramatic an increase in takeover activity as did the 1992–2000 period, and 2000's record $3.46 trillion in announced takeover deals equaled almost 10 percent of world GDP. The fraction of each year's total accounted for by U.S. versus European transactions fluctuated between 40 percent and 65 percent over the decade, with European deals outpacing U.S. acquisitions in the early 1990s, and American transactions predominating later. Acquisitions with U.S. targets had a total value of $825.7 billion in 2001 (versus $1.8 trillion in 2000), whereas deals involving European targets had a total value of $551.6 billion (versus $1.0 trillion in 2000). M&A activity outside Europe and the United States represents less than 10 percent of the worldwide total most years.

What accounts for this amazing increase in takeover activity in Europe and the United States? Although the root industrial and economic causes of takeover waves are still poorly understood, two things are clear. First, takeover waves tend to occur during periods of rising stock market valuations, and our discussions earlier in this book show that stock market valuations in Europe and America surged during the 1990s. Second, mergers and acquisitions appear to be an unavoidable side effect of increasing reliance on capital markets for financing. This is true even though, as we have seen, relatively little new common stock is issued each year by the corporations of any major Western country, because bond and stock markets tend to develop together. As the size, liquidity, and efficiency of public bond markets increase, the demand for firm-specific information disclosure also increases, and the national regulatory agencies set up to police capital markets tend to grow in size and effectiveness. The increasing efficiency and trustworthiness of markets in turn promotes both the rise of sophisticated institutional investors and the spread of an "investment culture"

[10.] It should be noted that the international common stock figure does not include proceeds from privatization issues, which are typically not capital-raising events because the government is merely selling off existing shares. Total privatization proceeds (including asset sales) reached a record $180 billion in 2000, with two-thirds of this total being raised in Europe. This fell to $54 billion in 2001.

Figure 11.1
Total Value of Announced U.S. Mergers and Acquisitions, 1990–2001

Source: Judy Radler Cohen, "M & A: Hoping for Recovery," *Investment Dealers' Digest* (January 14, 2002), pp. 29–43, and previous *IDD* issues.

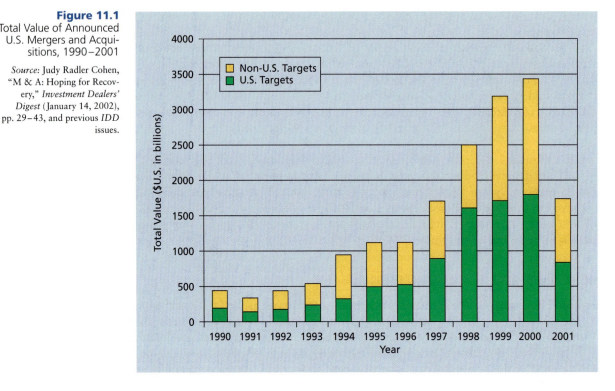

among a nation's citizenry. These factors work to promote the growth of all capital markets, equity as well as debt.

In order for a nation's capital markets to grow, however, an effective system of corporate governance must be in place. As mentioned in the Opening Focus, a nation's corporate governance system is the set of laws, regulations, institutions, and practices that determine how a public company will be governed and how control of a company can be contested. Academic research has now clearly documented how important effective corporate governance is in explaining both individual company performance and national economic achievement. We conclude this chapter by very briefly discussing what this research implies for practicing financial managers.

Concept Review Questions

8. What patterns are observed in U.S. security issues each year? How do these patterns compare to those in international security issues?

9. Why do you think that mergers and acquisitions have grown so rapidly during the past decade? If stock market valuations do not grow as rapidly over the next 10 years, what impact will this have on the total value of M&A's?

11.5 LAW AND FINANCE: THE IMPORTANCE OF CORPORATE GOVERNANCE

A nation's system of corporate governance encompasses both private- and public-sector institutions. Important private-sector institutions include stock exchanges and accounting firms, whereas the public sector provides a nation's legal and regulatory systems. All these players and forces interact to determine how responsibly a country's business firms are run and whether managers of these corporations are held accountable to a legitimate authority. Most students are not surprised to learn that a nation's regulatory regime significantly influences the size and efficiency of its capital markets. After all, history influences a citizenry's attitude toward business enterprise, and financial regulations arise naturally in democratic societies as a means of balancing the often conflicting rights of corporations and individuals. Most advanced industrial countries have well-established financial regulatory systems, and these are often used as models by developing and transition countries wishing to set up a regulatory regime.

What most students are surprised to learn is that the single most important determinant of the size of a country's capital markets is something much more basic than its regulatory framework: the legal tradition on which a nation's commercial code is based. In an important recent stream of academic papers, La Porta, López-de-Silanes, Shleifer, and Vishny (1997, 1998, 2000, 2002; hereafter LLSV), Shleifer and Vishny (1997), Levine (1997), Demirgüç-Kunt and Maksimovic (1998), and many others have developed what has come to be called the "Law and Finance" model of economic growth. This model states that the most important factor in determining capital market development is the degree of legal protection afforded to outside (noncontrolling) investors, and that this in turn depends largely on whether a country has a legal system based on English common law or another legal tradition.

Countries that were once part of the British Commonwealth—such as Australia, Canada, India, New Zealand, the United States, and Britain itself—afford great protection to external creditors and minority shareholders, who are thus willing to invest their capital in public companies. Managers always have an incentive to expropriate investors' wealth, but the legal protections offered by English common law temper these incentives and give investors legal recourse if they are wronged. Over time, countries with common-law systems have evolved large stock and bond markets, characterized by **atomistic** stock and bond ownership structures, with large numbers of individual investors and low levels of ownership concentration in most public firms. In other words, capital markets have grown large because investors are willing to accept small ownership and creditor positions in public companies.

The other three major Western legal traditions, or families, are German law, Scandinavian law, and French civil law. LLSV (1998) describe the key rules within each legal family that pertain to the rights and duties of investors. They conclude that French civil law offers by far the weakest legal protections to outside investors, while German law and Scandinavian law fall between the civil and common-law systems. Table 11.6 is derived from LLSV (1997) and details the impact of a nation's legal family on the size of its capital markets, on its economic growth rate, and on the incentive for a citizen to become an entrepreneur. This last variable is proxied by the number of domestic firms per 1 million people. The last three columns of Table 11.6 present summary measures of a nation's tradition of law and order, as well as the effectiveness of the legal system in protecting the rights of outside investors.

The results presented in Table 11.6 are striking. English common-law countries have much larger public equity and debt markets than do countries with other legal systems. Common-law countries also demonstrate much higher entrepreneurial tendencies, with an average of 35.45 domestic firms per million citizens in these countries versus 27.26 and 16.79 firms per million people, respectively, in countries with a tradition of Scandinavian law and German law, and only 10.00 in countries with civil-law traditions. It is not clear whether entrepreneurs are able to start companies more easily in common-law countries than in others because the laws are more encouraging or because the entrepreneurs are better able to attract external financing, or both. Although the relationship between legal tradition and average economic growth rate over the 1970–1993 period is not as clear-cut, the empirical evidence surveyed in

Table 11.6
Law and Finance—An English Common-Law System Promotes Capital Market Growth

Country (1)	External Capital-ization/ GDP (2)	Debt/ GDP (3)	GDP Growth Rate (4)	Domestic Firms/ Population (5)	Rule of Law (6)	Anti-director Rights (7)	Creditor Rights (8)
Australia	0.49	0.76	3.06%	63.55	10.00	4	1
Canada	0.39	0.72	3.36	40.86	10.00	4	1
Israel	0.25	0.66	4.39	127.60	4.82	3	1
United Kingdom	1.00	1.13	2.27	35.68	8.57	4	4
United States	0.58	0.81	2.74	30.11	10.00	5	1
English-origin average	0.60	0.68	4.30%	35.45	6.46	3.39	3.11
Belgium	0.17	0.38	2.46%	15.59	10.00	0	2
France	0.23	0.96	2.54	8.05	8.98	2	0
Greece	0.07	0.23	2.46	21.60	6.18	1	1
Italy	0.06	0.55	2.82	3.91	8.33	0	2
Spain	0.17	0.75	3.27	9.71	7.80	2	2
French-origin average	0.21	0.45	3.18%	10.00	6.05	1.76	1.58
Austria	0.06	0.79	2.74%	13.87	10.00	2	3
Germany	0.13	1.12	2.60	5.14	9.23	1	3
Japan	0.62	1.22	4.13	17.78	8.98	3	2
Korea	0.44	0.74	9.52	15.88	5.35	2	3
Switzerland	0.62	—	1.18	33.85	10.00	1	1
German-origin average	0.46	0.97	5.29%	16.79	8.68	2.00	2.33
Denmark	0.21	0.34	2.09%	50.40	10.00	3	3
Finland	0.25	0.75	2.40	13.00	10.00	2	1
Norway	0.22	0.64	3.43	33.00	10.00	3	2
Sweden	0.51	0.55	1.79	12.66	10.00	2	2
Scandinavian-origin average	0.30	0.57	2.42%	27.26	10.00	2.50	2.00
Sample average (44 countries)	0.44	0.59	3.79%	21.59	6.85	2.44	2.30

Source: Rafael LaPorta, Florencio López-de-Silanes, Andrei Shleifer, and Robert Vishny, "Legal Determinants of External Finance," *Journal of Finance* 52 (July 1997), pp. 1131–1150.

Notes: This table details the relationship between the type of legal system upon which a country's commercial code is based and the size of that nation's capital markets for selected countries in 1994. Column 2 of this table is the ratio of the stock market capitalization held by minority (non-controlling) shareholders to GDP, and column 3 provides a similar measure for private-sector debt (bank loans and bonds). Column 4 presents the country's average annual GDP growth rate over 1970–1993, and column 5 is the ratio of the number of domestic firms in a country to its population, in millions. Columns 6–8 present summary measures of the law-and-order traditions in a country (column 6) and of how well its legal code protects the rights of shareholders (column 7) and creditors (column 8). In all three cases, the higher the rating, the better the legal protection accorded investors. Countries with English common-law systems, presented first in this table, provide the best legal protections for investors, and thus have the largest stock and bond markets. French civil-law countries provide the poorest legal protection for outside investors, and thus tend to have very small capital markets. German and Scandinavian legal systems fall between these two extremes.

Levine (1997) shows that capital market development and economic growth are indeed positively related.

What does the Law and Finance research imply for practicing financial managers in different countries? A lot more than might at first seem obvious. A key implication of this research is that corporate ownership is likely to be much less concentrated in

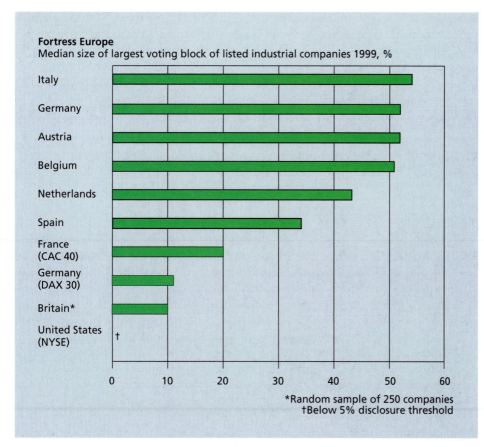

Fortress Europe
Median size of largest voting block of listed industrial companies 1999, %

*Random sample of 250 companies
†Below 5% disclosure threshold

Figure 11.2
Ownership Structure and
Corporate Governance
in Continental Europe

This figure details the median size of the largest voting block of shares in several European countries, as well as in the United States, in 1999. In Italy, the country with the most-concentrated ownership structures, a single block of shares controls 54 percent of the voting stock in the typical publicly listed industrial company. Majority block holdings are also the norm in Germany, Austria, and Belgium; and concentrated ownership is prevalent in the Netherlands, Spain, and France. On the other hand, the largest single shareholder owns less than 5 percent of the voting stock in the typical American and Japanese (not listed) listed industrial company.

Source: "Lean, Mean and European: A Survey of European Business," *The Economist* (April 29, 2001), p. 12.

common-law countries than in other advanced economies, and the evidence is consistent with this prediction. Figure 11.2 presents the median size of the largest voting block of shares in a random sample of 250 publicly traded industrial companies from nine European countries and the United States. In Italy, Germany, Austria, and Belgium, a single investor or a single block of shareholders controls a majority of the voting stock in the typical public company. In the Netherlands and Spain, the largest voting block controls 43 and 33 percent of the voting shares, respectively. Although France's 20 percent median voting block seems small by comparison, this figure is only for the companies that make up the CAC 40 Index, which are 40 of the nation's largest public companies. The median voting blocks for the common-law countries Britain and the United States are much lower.

Who belongs to the voting blocks in Figure 11.2? Overwhelmingly, these are members of a firm's founding family, and the reason they must retain such concentrated ownership long after the founder's death relates directly to the legal system in place. In civil-law and German-law countries, families must retain concentrated ownership either to ensure they retain managerial control of the firm or to protect themselves from expropriation at the hands of incumbent managers, or both. There is thus a clear cost to continental European families in terms of less-than-optimal wealth diversification, since founding families in Britain and America tend to divest their concentrated ownership stakes in favor of other investments once the founding generation passes away. There is also an economic efficiency loss to these countries, because the need to preserve concentrated ownership discourages companies from making new public security issues, particularly stock offerings, which in turn lowers the rate at which companies can grow. The good news is that ownership structures have become much less concentrated in continental Europe since the mid-1990s, and this is likely to continue apace with the capital market growth. The practicing financial manager must, however, still understand how the corporate governance system of the nation he or she is operating in affects the firm's ability to raise external capital—and on what terms.

10. What impact do you think a nation's regulatory framework has on its corporate governance system? What does this imply for the newly democratic counties in Central and Eastern Europe?

11. Why should a nation's legal tradition have such a strong influence on the size of its capital markets? Why do you think the effect is similar for stockholders and bondholders?

11.6 SUMMARY

- The three basic instruments of long-term financing are much the same in all market economies: common stock, preferred stock, and long-term debt. The way these instruments are used and the degree to which corporations rely on capital markets rather than financial intermediaries for funding differs between countries.
- In almost all market economies, internally generated funds (primarily retained earnings) are the dominant source of funding for corporate investment. External financing is used only when needed, and then debt is almost always preferred to equity financing. The difference between a firm's total funding needs and its internally generated cash flow is referred to as its financial deficit.
- Financial intermediaries are institutions that raise funds by selling claims on themselves (often in the form of demand deposits, or checking accounts) and then use those funds to purchase the debt and equity claims of corporate borrowers. They thus break—or intermediate—the direct link between final savers and borrowers that exists when companies fund their investment needs by selling securities directly to investors.
- Though financial intermediaries are essential to the smooth running of the U.S. economy, FIs play a relatively small direct role in financing American corporations. This is especially true of large, multinational firms. Intermediaries remain very important in the corporate financial systems of most other nations, however.
- The total volume of security issues has surged eight-fold in 11 years—reaching $4.08 trillion worldwide in 2001—but U.S. corporate issuers routinely account for two-thirds of the worldwide total. U.S. commercial banks are relatively small (though extremely profitable) by world standards.
- Recent academic research has shown that an effective system of corporate governance significantly impacts the financial performance of individual companies, and entire economies. The legal tradition upon which a country's commercial code is based has been shown to be especially important. Countries with legal systems based on English common law tend to have larger stock and bond markets than do countries with other legal systems.

INTERNET RESOURCES

Note: *For updates to links, please go to the book's website at http://smart.swcollege.com*

http://www.ipo.com—Offers up-to-date information on three types of new equity financing: venture capital, IPOs, and seasoned equity offerings; has a calendar of upcoming financing events

http://marketrac.nyse.com/mt/index.html—A portion of the NYSE site offering an exceptional virtual tour of the exchange floor, showing which stocks trade at each "post" and numerous up-to-date trading statistics for each stock

KEY TERMS

additional paid-in capital	long-term debt
atomistic	majority voting system
call premium	market capitalization
callable	McFadden Act
cash flow from operations	merchant bank
collateral	mortgage
commercial paper	negative covenants
convertibles	par value
corporate governance	positive covenants
corporate insider	primary security issues
cumulative voting system	proxy fight
debenture	proxy statement
equipment trust receipt	residual claimants
Eurobond	seasoned
Eurocommercial paper	secondary offering
financial deficit	secured debt
financial intermediary (FI)	securitization
floating-rate instruments	shares authorized
foreign bond	shares issued
Glass-Steagall Act	short-term debt
Gramm-Leach-Bliley Act	stock split
information intermediation	subordinated debt
initial public offering (IPO)	syndicated bank loan
international common stock	treasury stock
LIBOR	Yankee bond
loan covenants	Yankee common stock

QUESTIONS

11-1. What role does par value play in the pricing and sale of common stock by the issuing corporation? Why do most firms assign relatively low par values to their shares?

11-2. How can you find the initial proceeds per share received by an issuer of common stock if you know the number of shares issued, the par value per share, and the total additional paid-in capital?

11-3. Assuming you know the number of authorized shares, the number of issued shares, and the amount of treasury stock held by the corporation, how could you find the number of outstanding shares? How does a firm typically end up with treasury stock?

11-4. Why are common stockholders known as residual claimants? What does this imply about the risk and required return on common stock relative to other security classes?

11-5. Distinguish between majority and cumulative voting structures. Which is more advantageous to minority shareholders?

11-6. What is a proxy fight? Why does the existing management have an advantage in a proxy fight?

11-7. Why is preferred stock often referred to as a hybrid of common stock and debt? Why do U.S. corporations generally prefer to receive preferred stock dividends rather than debt interest payments from other corporations as a source of investment income?

11-8. Discuss the basic rights and features of preferred stock. Include in your discussion the topics of seniority of claims relative to other securities, voting rights, callability, and convertibility.

11-9. Why do subordinated debts pay higher interest rates than senior debts? Is most corporate debt from banks and other intermediaries unsecured or secured?

11-10. List and describe the various types of secured debt that constitute corporate borrowing. What mechanisms can be attached to debentures in order to reduce their default risk?

11-11. How are the interest rates typically set on debentures? On loans obtained by both U.S. and non-U.S. corporations? What market rate is typically used to price syndicated bank loans?

11-12. Why are corporate bonds issued by most U.S. companies callable? Does the inclusion of this feature by the corporation have a cost? Is there a cost to the company of issuing convertible rather than straight bonds?

11-13. How are restrictive covenants used to protect debt holders' investments? Why is the monitoring of these covenants different for intermediated and for public debt?

11-14. What are the key features and costs of commercial paper? What are zero-premium exchangeable notes (ZENS)? What is their appeal?

11-15. How should a corporation estimate the amount of financing that must be raised externally during a given year? Once that amount is known, what other decision must be made?

11-16. What is the dominant source of capital funding in the United States? Given this result and the fact that most corporations are net dissavers, what decisions must most managers face in order to address this financial deficit?

11-17. Define the term "financial intermediary." What role do financial intermediaries play in U.S. corporate finance? How does this compare to the role of non-U.S. financial intermediaries?

11-18. Discuss the U.S. banking system regulations that have had a major impact on the development of the U.S. financial system. In what ways has the U.S. system been affected (positively and negatively) by these regulations?

11-19. Differentiate between a U.S. commercial bank and the merchant banks found in other developed countries. How have these differences affected the securities markets in the United States versus those in other developed countries?

11-20. What are the general trends regarding public security issuance by U.S. corporations? Specifically, which security type is most often sold to the public? What is the split between initial and seasoned equity offerings?

11-21. Distinguish between a Eurobond, a foreign bond, and a Yankee bond. Which of these three represents the greatest volume of security issuance?

11-22. How does the corporate governance function of financial intermediaries differ between the United States and most other countries?

11-23. How would you describe the recent levels of M&A activity in the United States and elsewhere? What accounts for this change in activity?

11-24. List and briefly discuss the roles played by the key institutions and legal/regulatory systems that make up a nation's system of corporate governance. Apart from legal tradition, which influence do you think is the most important?

11-25. Why does a nation's legal tradition have such a large impact on the size of its capital markets? Do you think that a nation can really change its legal tradition, even if doing so would promote capital market development?

11-26. How does the concentration of corporate ownership differ between common-law and other countries? Why? What implication do these differences have on the corporate financial manager's ability to raise funds?

PROBLEMS

The Basic Instruments of Long-Term Financing

11-1. How many shares are needed to elect two directors out of a slate of seven if a firm has 10 million shares outstanding and uses cumulative voting in its election?

Smart Solutions
See the problem and solution explained step-by-step at **SMARTFinance**

11-2. Schrell Corporation has 1,700,000 shares of voting common stock outstanding. Recent board actions and their dismal outcomes have raised the ire of many shareholders. A major group of dissident shareholders that controls 600,000 shares of the common stock wishes to change the composition of the firm's seven-member board to improve the quality of the firm's governance. Management effectively controls the other 1,100,000 shares, many through proxies granted them by shareholders. Management's slate of directors for the upcoming election includes all of the existing directors. The dissident shareholders want to obtain as much representation as possible in the upcoming election of all seven directors.

  a. If the firm has a *majority voting system,* how many directors can the dissident group of shareholders elect?

  b. If the firm has a *cumulative voting system,* how many directors can the dissident shareholders elect?

  c. If the dissident shareholders decide to wage a *proxy fight* to obtain additional votes, how many additional votes would they need to gain voting control of the board (i.e., control four of seven votes) under majority voting? Under cumulative voting?

11-3. The equity section of the balance sheet for Lopez Digital Entertainment follows:

Common stock, $0.50 par $ 545,000
Paid-in capital surplus   5,229,000
Retained earnings   7,649,000

  a. How many shares has the company issued?

  b. What is the book value per share?

  c. Suppose that Lopez Digital has made only one offering of common stock. At what price did it sell shares to the market?

11-4. Go to the website for Gateway, Inc. (http://www.gateway.com), one of the major direct marketers of personal computers and related products and services. Click successively on "About Us," "Investor Relations," and "Annual Reports," and then on the most recent "Complete Report" and find within it the "Consolidated Balance Sheets." Use the statement to answer the following questions.

  a. How much preferred stock did Gateway have outstanding at the statement date?

  b. How many shares of common stock was Gateway authorized to issue? What is its par value?

  c. How many shares of common stock has Gateway issued? How much did the firm raise from the initial sale of its common stock?

  d. How many shares of common stock did Gateway hold in its treasury at the statement date?

  e. How many shares of common stock did Gateway have outstanding at the statement date?

f. How much retained earnings did Gateway have at the statement date? By how much did this value change from the previous year? What does this change represent?

The Basic Choices in Long-Term Financing

11-5. Meltzer Electronics estimates that its total financing needs for the coming year will be $34.5 million. The firm's required financing payments on its debt and equity financing during the coming fiscal year will total $12.9 million. The firm's financial manager estimates that operating cash flows for the coming year will total $33.7 million and that the following changes will occur in the accounts noted.

Account	Forecast Change
Gross fixed assets	$8.9 million
Change in current assets	+2.3 million
Change in accounts payable	+1.3 million
Change in accrued liabilities	+0.8 million

a. Use Equation 2.3 and the data provided to estimate Meltzer's *free cash flow* in the coming year.

b. How much of the free cash flow will the firm have available as a source of new internal financing in the coming year?

c. How much external financing will Meltzer need during the coming year to meet its total forecast financing need?

11-6. Last year Guaraldi Instruments Inc. conducted an IPO, issuing 2 million common shares with a par value of $0.25 to investors at a price of $15 per share. During its first year of operation, Guaraldi earned net income of $0.07 per share and paid a dividend of $0.005 per share. At the end of the year, the company's stock was selling for $20 per share. Construct the equity account for Guaraldi at the end of its first year in business, and calculate the firm's market capitalization.

12

Capital Structure: Theory and Taxes

OPENING FOCUS

Korea Tries to *Reduce* Chaebol Debt-to-Equity Ratios to 200 Percent

During December 1998, Korea's recently elected Kim Dae Jong government brokered a series of deals wherein the country's leading industrial groups, the Chaebol, would "trade" subsidiaries in order to rationalize industrial structures and ultimately reduce pervasive excess capacity. For example, Samsung Group agreed to swap its newly built automobile-producing subsidiary with Daewoo in exchange for the latter's consumer-electronics group. In addition to reducing overcapacity, the government was trying to force the Chaebol to adopt policies that would reduce the crushing load of domestic and external debt. By late 1998, this debt had reached a nearly incredible debt-to-equity ratio of over 400 percent (four dollars of debt for each dollar of equity), a level almost 10 times as high as that observed in typical Western firms.

Although Chaebol companies have long been characterized by high leverage (roughly a 200% debt-to-equity level), total indebtedness exploded following the onset of the Asian economic crisis in July 1997. As economic growth, sales, and profits all slowed dramatically, the Chaebol initially maintained headlong capital investment programs—funded with borrowed funds. This rapid debt buildup was rendered even more burdensome by the fact that much of the Chaebol debt was denominated in dollars, whereas most of their cash flows were in Korean won, which depreciated by over 50 percent versus the dollar during 1997 and 1998.

From 1998 to 2002, the Chaebol indeed responded to the Korean government's "tough love" strategy, though not always in the manner hoped for. Creditors forced the breakup (and partial sale to foreigners) of both Daewoo and Hyundai, and several of the smaller Chaebol were forced into bankruptcy. However, the Samsung Group turned the financial crisis into an opportunity to effect a much-needed restructuring. The company cut its workforce by 40 percent, sold off underperforming divisions, and used the proceeds to reduce

the dollar value of its debt from $95 billion in 1997 to $75 billion in 1998 (the Korean won value of its debt was reduced by far more). The company also focused its marketing efforts on a successful campaign to become a purveyor of high-quality branded electronics, rather than remain a commodity supplier. These steps allowed Samsung to triple its net income, and double its stockholders' equity, between the fiscal years 1997 and 2000. Even with this improvement, however, Samsung's total debts of $84.8 billion were almost three times larger than its $28.9 billion in stockholders' equity.

Sources: "South Korean Restructuring: Cut to Fit," *The Economist* (December 12, 1998), p. 66; John Thornhill, "Wake-up Call Comes amid Reform Fatigue," *Financial Times* (May 8, 2001), Survey—Asia Banking, Finance and Investment, p. 1; Jay Solomon, "Seoul Survivors: Back from the Brink, Korea Inc. Wants a Little Respect," *Wall Street Journal* (June 13, 2002), p. A1; and Samsung's corporate website (http://www.samsung.com).

In previous chapters, we have argued that the value of a firm equals the present value of the cash flows generated by its investments. In this chapter and the next, we examine whether the way in which a firm divides its cash flows between different types of investors can have an independent impact on value. That is, can the mix of debt and equity securities that a firm issues to fund its operations affect that company's total market valuation? First posed by Franco Modigliani and Merton Miller (1958), the capital structure question continues to fascinate and bedevil finance professionals today. After four decades of intense research, financial commentators would probably answer the question cautiously, perhaps with "Yes, the firm's capital structure choices can influence total firm value, but the firm's investment decisions impact total value far more." Although the finance profession understands a great deal more about the decision to use debt or equity than it did when Modigliani and Miller conducted their seminal research, there are still many unsolved puzzles to explore. Furthermore, even though finance theory has had a major impact on the practices of corporations in areas such as capital budgeting and valuation, the connections between theory and practice seem much weaker in the area of capital structure.

Accordingly, this chapter begins with the facts. Over the last half century, researchers have documented a number of consistent patterns related to capital structure, patterns that occur in countries all over the world. We begin by listing some of these regularities. The purpose of this listing is to make clear what facts a theory of corporate leverage must explain. We then provide an overview of the four major theoretical models of capital structure. Next, we present the original Modigliani and Miller (M&M) capital structure theory, which yielded the revolutionary conclusion that in a frictionless market, capital structure is *irrelevant*. Next, we explain why incorporating taxes into the M&M framework may lead to a dramatically different conclusion—that an optimal (that is, value-maximizing) capital structure exists for every company. This chapter concludes with a discussion of other tax-based capital structure theories, and Chapter 13 presents several nontax determinants of corporate leverage. That chapter also discusses how a firm's asset characteristics, production technology, and business environment impact its optimal capital structure. Chapter 13 concludes with a checklist that managers can use in making real leverage decisions.

12.1 CAPITAL STRUCTURE PATTERNS OBSERVED WORLDWIDE

Research on the capital structure issue establishes a set of key facts that any viable theory of capital structure must explain. Some of these facts will strike you as quite intuitive, but others are more surprising. In broad brush strokes, capital structure research documents the following.

1. **Capital structures have pronounced industry patterns that transcend national borders.** In all developed countries, certain industries have high debt-to-equity ratios, whereas other industries employ little or no long-term debt financing. Highly levered industries include utilities, transportation, and many capital-intensive manufacturing sectors, while firms in the service, mining, and high-technology industries generally use little or no debt. These patterns are very strong, suggesting that an industry's optimal asset mix, plus the variability of its operating environment, significantly influences the capital structures chosen by firms in that industry anywhere in the world.[1] Table 12.1 illustrates these industry patterns using data on large U.S. firms. The table lists several leverage ratios for each firm, some of which use book values of debt and equity and others of which use market values. A glance at the table reveals a clear tendency for firms in different industries to use different levels of debt. For example, the high-tech firms listed at the top of the table use almost no debt, whereas firms in industries such as auto manufacturing and utilities use a great deal more. The final column in the table shows the market value of equity divided by its book value. The market-to-book ratios vary a great deal from one firm to another, but you can see that these ratios tend to fall as you move down the table. Firms with high market-to-book ratios use less debt than firms with low market-to-book ratios.

SMART IDEAS VIDEO

Mitchell Petersen, Northwestern University

"When firms structure their business, they need to think about trading off operating and financial leverage."

See the entire interview at **SMARTFinance**

2. **Capital structures vary across countries.** Table 12.2 shows three measures of leverage (also called *gearing* in some countries) for 7 developed (the G7) and 10 developing countries. In which countries do firms rely heavily on debt? The answer depends on whether we examine total debt or long-term debt and on whether we measure debt relative to assets using book values or market values. Looking at the book value of all forms of debt, firms in Japan, Italy, France, Germany, and South Korea appear to use more debt than firms in the United Kingdom, Canada, Brazil, Mexico, and many other countries. However, if we focus only on the long-term component of debt, the leverage of German firms does not seem particularly high in comparison with that of firms in other countries. Indeed, on a market-value basis, German companies use less long-term debt than firms in any other developed economy. Even though the leverage rankings of different countries change depending on what measure of leverage we use to create them, Table 12.2 does show that, on average, firms in developing countries borrow less than firms in developed countries do.[2] Why leverage ratios vary so much across countries is an unsolved puzzle. In part, differences in leverage may reflect differences in the industrial composition of national economies, but historical, institutional, and even cultural factors all probably play a part, as does a nation's reliance on capital markets versus banks for corporate financing.[3]

3. **Leverage ratios appear to be inversely related to the perceived costs of financial distress.** Both across industries and across countries, the larger the perceived costs

---

[1.] The classic article documenting these relationships is by Bradley, Jarrell, and Kim (1984). More recent articles documenting similar relationships include those by Long and Malitz (1985), Titman and Wessels (1988), Smith and Watts (1992), Gaver and Gaver (1993), Alderson and Betker (1995), and Hovakimian, Opler, and Titman (2001). A historical listing of average U.S. capital structures, by industry, is provided in Table 14 of Bernanke and Campbell (1988), while a very thorough survey of the non-tax-related capital structure literature through 1990 is provided in Harris and Raviv (1991).

[2.] For book value data, see Rutterford (1988), Sekely and Collins (1988), Frankel [Japan] (1991), Rajan and Zingales [G7 countries] (1995), and Booth, Aivazian, Demirgüç-Kunt, and Maksimovic [10 developing countries] (2001). Market value leverage ratios are presented in Rajan and Zingales (1995), Shin and Park [Korea] (1999), Booth et al. (2001), and de Miguel and Pindado [Spain] (2001).

[3.] The importance of a nation's reliance on capital markets versus financial intermediaries for external corporate financing was first discussed rigorously by Mayer (1990), and evidence of its importance in Japanese capital structure decisions is presented in Prowse (1990) and Anderson and Makhija (1999). Shin and Park (1999) provide similar evidence for Korea's Chaebol.

Table 12.1
Debt Ratios for Selected U.S. Corporations in 2002

Company	Industry	Debt to Total Assets		Long-Term Debt to Total Capital[b]		Market-to-Book Ratio[c]
		Book Value	Market Value[a]	Book Value	Market Value	
Microsoft	Computer software	0	0	0	0	5.54
Cisco Systems	Computer systems	0	0	0	0	3.94
Intel	Semiconductors	0.03	0.01	0.03	0.01	4.03
Dell Computer	Computer hardware	0.04	0.01	0.10	0.01	14.87
IBM	Computer hardware	0.27	0.16	0.40	0.11	5.54
Exxon Mobil	Integrated petroleum	0.07	0.04	0.09	0.03	3.72
Chevron Texaco	Integrated petroleum	0.25	0.16	0.21	0.08	2.71
Johnson & Johnson	Pharmaceuticals	0.08	0.02	0.08	0.01	7.32
Merck	Pharmaceuticals	0.23	0.08	0.30	0.04	7.18
Eli Lilly	Pharmaceuticals	0.32	0.06	0.31	0.03	8.54
AOL Time Warner	Entertainment, media	0.11	0.29	0.13	0.29	0.74
Walt Disney	Entertainment, media	0.21	0.27	0.28	0.25	1.92
Coca-Cola	Consumer products	0.12	0.04	0.10	0.02	12.85
Procter & Gamble	Consumer products	0.45	0.12	0.49	0.07	10.13
Duke Energy	Electricity trading	0.29	0.46	0.49	0.39	1.73
United Technologies	Aerospace	0.18	0.12	0.34	0.11	3.76
Boeing	Aerospace	0.25	0.27	0.50	0.24	3.65
Lockheed Martin	Aerospace	0.28	0.20	0.53	0.19	4.33
Alcoa	Aluminum production	0.24	0.21	0.38	0.20	2.58
Wal-Mart	Retailing	0.27	0.08	0.35	0.06	7.01
Kroger	Retailing	0.46	0.36	0.71	0.34	4.49
Southwest Airlines	Airline	0.15	0.12	0.25	0.12	3.13
AMR	Airline	0.35	0.78	0.65	0.73	0.60
Delta Air Lines	Airline	0.36	0.77	0.69	0.75	0.82
SBC Communications	Telecommunications	0.26	0.20	0.35	0.14	3.53
BellSouth	Telecommunications	0.39	0.23	0.45	0.17	3.18
Verizon Communications	Telecommunications	0.36	0.36	0.58	0.26	3.63
American Electric Power	Electric utility	0.31	0.54	0.54	0.36	1.62
Southern Company	Electric utility	0.35	0.37	0.51	0.30	2.32
General Electric	Conglomerate	0.40	0.44	0.59	0.17	5.38
Georgia Pacific	Forest products	0.49	0.69	0.68	0.55	1.19
General Motors	Auto manufacturing	0.51	0.84	0.89	0.83	4.12
Ford Motor Company	Auto manufacturing	0.60	0.84	0.96	0.84	4.24

Source: Firm-specific data taken from each company's financial information at http://money.cnn.com on June 12, 2002.

Notes: This table presents book value and market value leverage ratios for 33 of the most valuable publicly traded U.S. corporations in July 2002. Companies are listed beginning with the industry with the lowest leverage (computer software) and ranging through to the industry with the highest leverage (automobile manufacturing).

[a] Total liabilities (book value) divided by the market value of equity plus the book value of debt.

[b] Long-term debt (book value) divided by the sum of the market value of equity plus the book value of long-term debt.

[c] Per share price of company stock divided by the per share book value of shareholders' common equity.

Country	Number of Firms	Total Debt to Total Assets (book value, %)	Long-Term Debt to Total Capital (book value, %)	Long-Term Debt to Total Capital (market value, %)
G7				
United Kingdom	608	0.54	0.28	0.35
Canada	318	0.56	0.39	0.35
United States	2,580	0.58	0.37	0.28
Japan	514	0.69	0.53	0.29
Italy	118	0.70	0.47	0.46
France	225	0.71	0.48	0.41
Germany	191	0.73	0.38	0.23
Developing				
Brazil	49	0.30	0.10	N/A
Mexico	99	0.35	0.14	N/A
Zimbabwe	48	0.42	0.13	0.26
Malaysia	96	0.42	0.13	0.07
Jordan	38	0.47	0.12	0.19
Thailand	64	0.49	N/A	N/A
Turkey	45	0.59	0.24	0.11
Pakistan	96	0.66	0.26	0.19
India	99	0.67	0.34	0.35
South Korea	93	0.73	0.49	0.64

Sources: Raghuram G. Rajan and Luigi Zingales, "What Do We Know about Capital Structure? Some Evidence from International Data," *Journal of Finance* 50 (December 1995), pp. 1421–1460; Laurence Booth, Varouj Aivazian, Asli Demirgüç-Kunt, and Vojislav Maksimovic, "Capital Structures in Developing Countries," *Journal of Finance* 56 (February 2001), pp. 87–130.

Notes: Book and market value leverage measures for nonfinancial companies from the G7 group of industrialized countries and 10 developing countries. The G7 results are from Rajan and Zingales (1995) and are based on data for 1991 reported in the *Global Vantage* database. The developing-country results are from Booth et al. (2001) and are based on data for varying periods from 1980 to 1991, depending on the country, as reported by the World Bank.

of bankruptcy and financial distress, the less debt firms use. For example, when the principal assets of a company are intangible (e.g., brands, intellectual property), the costs of financial distress are much higher than when the principal assets are physical commodities that can be pledged as collateral and sold by lenders in the event of default. Therefore, firms with high-value intangible assets use less debt than firms that invest in more tangible assets.[4]

4. Within industries, leverage varies inversely with profitability. Regardless of the industry in question, the most profitable companies typically borrow the least.[5] Although this may not seem surprising at first, the pattern raises some deep questions. For example, in many countries, debt financing enjoys a tax advantage in that firms

[4.] Documentation of the importance of bankruptcy costs in influencing capital structure decisions is provided in Titman (1984), Maksimovic and Titman (1991), and Pulvino (1999), as well as in the articles cited in Footnote 1.

[5.] See Myers (1993), Fama and French (1998), Shyam-Sunder and Myers (1999), Graham (1996, 2000), Fama and French (2002), and especially Baker and Wurgler (2002) for evidence of the literature on the relationship between leverage and profitability.

Figure 12.1
Book Value Leverage
Measures for U.S. Non-
financial Corporations,
1951–1996

*This figure plots the aver-
age book value of equity
to total capital, long-
term debt to total capital,
short-term debt to total
capital, and preferred
stock to total capital ratios
for U.S. nonfinancial firms
over the period 1951–
1996.*

Source: Eugene F. Fama and
Kenneth R. French, "The Corporate Cost of Capital and the
Return on Corporate Investment," *Journal of Finance* 54
(December 1999), pp. 1939–
1967, fig. 2.

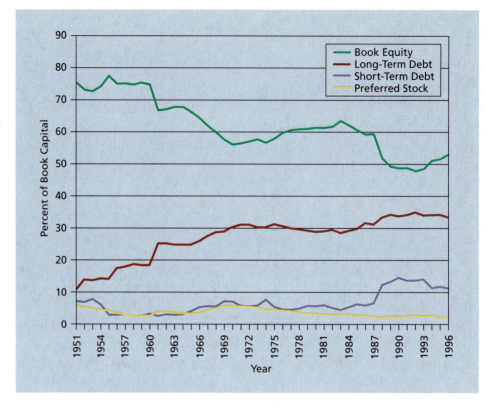

can deduct interest payments before paying taxes. This suggests that, others things
being equal, profitable firms should use *more* leverage than unprofitable firms use because by borrowing money, profitable companies shelter a larger proportion of their
cash flows from taxes.

**5. Corporate and personal taxes influence capital structures, but taxes alone cannot
explain differences in leverage across firms, industries, or countries.** Taxes certainly
matter, but are not decisive. For example, U.S. corporations apparently used no less
debt prior to the introduction of the income tax in 1913 than they did either after
it was introduced or when corporate and personal tax rates peaked during World
War II. In fact, U.S. book value debt ratios reached their lowest point in modern history during World War II and have risen slowly but inexorably ever since. Figure 12.1
shows that, on a book value basis, equity's (debt's) share in the capital structures of
U.S. firms declined (rose) steadily during the second half of the twentieth century. In
contrast, market value leverage ratios show no similar long-term trend.[6] Figure 12.2
indicates that the market value share of equity (debt) fell (rose) from 1951 to 1973,
but the trend subsequently reversed. These gradual changes in leverage seem at odds
with the sudden changes in tax laws (and hence, sudden changes in the tax advantages
of debt) that have occurred over the last 50 years.[7] On the other hand, research has

---

[6.] Though this figure ends with data from 1996, the sharp rise in market valuations for U.S. firms since then suggests that
market leverage ratios have declined significantly during the past five years.

[7.] For historical information on U.S. capital structure measures, see Taggart (1985), Bernanke and Campbell (1988), Barclay, Smith, and Watts (1995), and Fama and French (1999). Evidence regarding the impact of taxes on corporate financing decisions is presented in Wedig, Hassan, and Morrisey (1996), Graham (1996, 2000), Fama and French (1998), Calegari (2000), and Graham and Harvey (2001), though these papers do not all yield consistent stories.

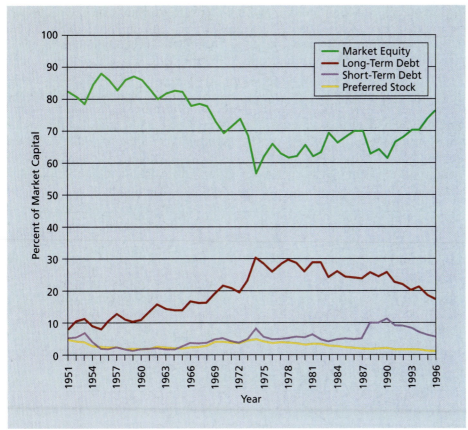

Figure 12.2
Market Value Leverage
Measures for U.S.
Nonfinancial
Corporations,
1951–1996

This figure plots the average market value of equity to total capital, long-term debt to total capital, short-term debt to total capital, and preferred stock to total capital ratios for U.S. nonfinancial firms over the period 1951–1996.

Source: Eugene F. Fama and Kenneth R. French, "The Corporate Cost of Capital and the Return on Corporate Investment," *Journal of Finance* 54 (December 1999), pp. 1939–1967, fig. 1.

shown that increases in corporate income tax rates are associated with increased debt usage by corporations in most countries and that decreases in the personal tax rates on equity income relative to those on interest income are associated with decreased corporate debt usage.[8]

6. Existing shareholders invariably consider leverage-increasing events to be "good news" and leverage-decreasing events to be "bad news." An empirical regularity that surprises most students is that the stock market generally responds favorably when firms take actions that increase leverage. Almost every published empirical study shows that stock prices rise when a company announces leverage-increasing events, such as debt-for-equity exchange offers, debt-financed share repurchase programs, and debt-financed cash tender offers to acquire control of another company.[9] On the other hand, leverage-decreasing events such as equity-for-debt exchange offers, new stock offerings, and acquisition offers involving payment with a firm's own shares are almost always associated with share price declines.[10]

[8.] See Fung and Theobald (1984), Hamada and Scholes (1985), and Ang and Megginson (1990).

[9.] The first major paper documenting this phenomenon was by Masulis (1980). Subsequent articles showing similar results include those by Dann (1981), Mikkelson and Partch (1986), and Travlos (1987). While Eckbo (1986) shows that "plain-vanilla" bond offerings yield insignificant abnormal returns to shareholders, James (1987) and Lummer and McConnell (1989) document that announcements of bank loans are associated with positive abnormal shareholder returns for corporate borrowers.

[10.] See Dann and Mikkelson (1984), Asquith and Mullins (1986), Linn and Pinegar (1988), Shah (1994), Loughran and Ritter (1995), and Spiess and Affleck-Graves (1995).

7. Corporations that are forced away from a preferred capital structure tend to return to that structure over time. This forced departure from a preferred debt ratio has occurred frequently in recent years, particularly for U.S. corporations that have taken on large amounts of new debt to finance (or defend against) takeovers of other companies or to fund major new ventures. The first priority of these companies after the transactions are completed usually becomes paying down the debts incurred to a more comfortable level.[11] More generally, there is evidence that corporations like to operate within **target leverage zones** and will issue new equity when debt ratios get too high and will issue debt (or repurchase equity) if they fall too low. However, the single best predictor of new equity issues is the recent trend in stock prices. Companies tend to issue equity following unusually large increases in their stock prices and essentially refuse to issue new equity after share prices have fallen.[12]

Concept Review Questions	**1.** In most countries, firms in high-tech industries are almost all intangible-asset rich rather than fixed-asset rich. What impact do you think the continued growth of these industries will have on average leverage ratios in the future? **2.** If the government decided to increase the tax rate on retained corporate earnings, what impact do you think this would have on observed corporate leverage over time? Why? What impact would increases in personal tax rates on dividend and interest income likely have? **3.** Leverage-decreasing actions such as stock-financed takeover bids reduce shareholder wealth, on average, yet these events occur regularly. How do you reconcile these actions with running a corporation in the shareholders' best interests?

12.2 AN OVERVIEW OF CAPITAL STRUCTURE THEORIES

Not surprising, devising a single theory to explain all the phenomena previously described is extremely difficult. Nonetheless, four major theoretical models of capital structure choice have been developed, and we will introduce each one in turn and then discuss them in more depth in subsequent sections and in Chapter 13.

The Trade-off Model

In the **trade-off model** of capital structure, managers choose the mix of debt and equity that strikes a balance between the tax advantages of debt and the various costs of using leverage. Because interest payments to lenders are tax deductible, when a firm uses more leverage, it reduces the percentage of cash flows that tax authorities capture. However, the more a firm borrows, the higher is the probability that the firm will encounter financial distress and its associated costs in the future. For example, consider the costs that an airline might face if the public believed that the firm was on the brink of bankruptcy. Customers worried that the airline would attempt to avert

---

[11.] The most dramatic example of this phenomenon has occurred in leveraged buyouts, as the debt levels of newly private companies are often extremely high. See, in particular, Muscarella and Vetsuypens (1990). Furthermore, Fischer, Heinkel, and Zechner (1989) and Hovakimian et al. (2001) document that corporate security-issuance patterns indicate firms have preferred leverage ratio ranges that they return to over time with new debt and equity issues, though the interpretation of this evidence is disputed by Shyam-Sunder and Myers (1999).

[12.] This pattern is documented by Marsh (1982) for British firms, and by Asquith and Mullins (1986) and Korajczyk, Lucas, and McDonald (1991) for U.S. companies. On a prospective basis, Hansen and Crutchley (1990) show that firms tend to issue new stock immediately before they experience significant earnings declines, suggesting these issues are at least partly made to cover a cash flow shortfall resulting from lower-than-expected earnings.

bankruptcy by cutting maintenance expenditures might choose a different carrier. Employee turnover might increase as pilots, mechanics, and flight attendants defected to competing airlines with more-secure finances. Therefore, when a firm chooses its capital structure, it must weigh the tax savings of debt against the expected costs of financial distress.

THE PECKING ORDER HYPOTHESIS

A very strong challenger has emerged during the past two decades as the shortcomings of the simple trade-off model have become apparent. The **pecking order hypothesis,** developed by Stewart Myers and his coauthors, begins with two assumptions.[13] First, managers are better informed about the investment opportunities faced by their firms than are outside investors (an asymmetric information assumption). Second, managers act in the best interests of *existing* shareholders. Myers demonstrates that under these conditions, a firm will sometimes forgo positive-*NPV* projects if accepting them means the firm will have to issue new equity at a price that does not reflect the true value of the company's investment opportunities. This in turn provides a rationale for firms to value **financial slack,** such as large cash and marketable security holdings or unused debt capacity.

This model explains three key empirical patterns. First, debt ratios and profitability tend to be inversely related. In other words, as the pecking order hypothesis would predict, when firms are profitable and generate enough cash to fund investment needs, they do not borrow just to capture the tax advantage of debt. Second, markets react negatively to new equity issues, and managers seem to issue equity only when they either have no choice (following an unexpected earnings decline) or feel the firm's shares are overvalued. Third, the pecking order hypothesis explains why firms hold vast amounts of cash and marketable securities. Whereas the trade-off theory explains observed corporate debt *levels* fairly well, the pecking order theory offers an apparently superior explanation for observed capital structure *changes,* especially those involving security issues.

APPLYING THE MODEL

Several of the world's largest and most profitable automobile manufacturers had truly enormous cash and marketable security holdings during the late 1990s. In particular, both Ford and Toyota had cash holdings in excess of $20 billion in 1998. The companies claimed that they needed large cash reserves to exploit acquisition opportunities and to guard against insolvency during an economic downturn. Recent events provide some support for both contentions. Auto companies did, in fact, spend many billions on mergers and joint ventures over the past five years, and the new decade brought much tougher economic times. By mid-summer 2002, only Toyota and General Motors retained cash holdings in excess of $10 billion; the cash and marketable securities holdings of most other companies had been cut by as much as half from their late-1990s peak.

THE SIGNALING MODEL OF CORPORATE FINANCIAL STRUCTURE

A third capital structure theory is the **signaling model.** As in the pecking order model, the signaling theory assumes that managers know more about a firm's prospects than

---

13. See Myers (1984, 1993), Myers and Majluf (1984), and Shyam-Sunder and Myers (1999).

investors do. In the absence of any compelling evidence to the contrary, investors assign an "average" valuation to each firm. However, a manager who knows that his
firm's true value is much greater than investors think it is wants to communicate his
knowledge to the market. Naturally, a manager of a less-valuable firm would also like
to persuade investors that her firm is undervalued too, so investors will remain skeptical of what managers say. The only way for a manager to convince investors of the
true value of his firm is to send a costly signal that is hard for the manager of a less-
valuable firm to mimic. One such signal is issuing debt. As we have seen before, issuing debt raises the odds of financial distress and its associated costs. Investors know
this, so when they observe a firm issuing debt, they interpret that as a credible signal
that the firm's managers must expect future cash flows sufficient to avoid financial
distress. Managers of lower-quality firms will not mimic this signal because of the
higher costs of financial distress. Investors respond to the signal by bidding up the
share prices of debt-issuing firms.

THE MANAGERIAL OPPORTUNISM HYPOTHESIS

Malcolm Baker and Jeffrey Wurgler (2002) offer one of the newest and most intuitively appealing theories to explain the debt-equity choice, the **managerial opportunism hypothesis.** They argue that firms attempt to time the market by issuing equity when share values are high and by issuing debt when share prices are low. As
a consequence, a firm's capital structure simply reflects the cumulative effects of its
managers' past attempts to issue equity opportunistically. Baker and Wurgler find
evidence that the firms with high leverage are those that raised
capital when their stock prices were low, whereas firms with
low leverage are those that raised capital when their share prices
were high. They also cite the findings of other studies that support their theory, the most important of which is the survey by
Graham and Harvey (2001) in which corporate CFOs report
that the level of stock prices influences their decisions to issue
equity or not.

**Concept
Review
Questions**

4. Table 12.1 shows that debt ratios vary from one industry to another. How might the
trade-off model explain this? Specifically, given that the tax deductibility of interest applies to firms in all industries, if high-tech firms use less debt than automobile manufacturers, then the *trade-off model* indicates that the expected costs of financial distress
must be greater for high-tech firms. Why might this be so?

5. Stock prices respond favorably to leverage-increasing events and unfavorably to
leverage-decreasing events. Furthermore, research indicates that firms issuing equity exhibit below-average long-run stock performance. Explain how these two facts relate to
the *managerial opportunism hypothesis.*

12.3 THE MODIGLIANI & MILLER CAPITAL STRUCTURE IRRELEVANCE PROPOSITIONS

We now turn our attention to the original Modigliani & Miller (hereafter, M&M) argument that capital structure decisions cannot affect firm value. It is very important
for students to understand how and why M&M arrived at their famous capital struc-

ture irrelevance conclusion, even though we believe that M&M's primary conclusion that capital structure is irrelevant is incorrect. We believe, as do most financial economists, that capital structure *is not* irrelevant. Nevertheless, the M&M argument has enormous value for two reasons. First, understanding the conditions under which capital structure is irrelevant helps managers disentangle what is and what is not important about real-world capital structure decisions. Specifically, M&M argue that capital structure matters only to the extent that financial markets are not perfect. Therefore, managers need to know what kinds of market imperfections exist and how to adjust the firm's capital structure to exploit them. Second, the logic of the M&M argument rests on the principle of no arbitrage, a principle that drives many important concepts in finance, from the determination of exchange rates to option pricing. Seeing how this principle applies to the capital structure decision will clarify its use in other areas throughout the book.

In their original 1958 article, M&M set out to provide "an operational definition of the cost of capital and a workable theory of investment" that would be solidly based on the principle of market value maximization. In attempting to develop such a model, they also showed that capital structure could not affect firm value in a world with perfect markets.

Assumptions of the M&M Capital Structure Model

Modigliani & Miller begin by making several assumptions about capital markets and about firms, assumptions designed to simplify the analysis and to focus it entirely on the potential valuation effects of leverage. For instance, M&M assume that capital markets are frictionless, meaning that neither firms nor investors pay taxes on earnings or on the securities they buy and sell. Similarly, transactions costs are zero in a frictionless market. M&M presume that investors can borrow and lend at the same rate that corporations can. Finally, M&M focus their attention on firms that are identical in every respect except for capital structure. Importantly, in the following examples, we will examine the capital structure decisions of two firms with identical business risk and identical expected operating cash flows over time. Of course, it is impossible to find two identical firms in the real world, but you can think of firms operating in the same industry as a way to grasp the M&M assumptions intuitively.

Proposition I

To arrive at **Proposition I,** the famous "irrelevance proposition," we must imagine that a company is operating in a world of frictionless capital markets, but also in a world where there is uncertainty about corporate revenues and earnings. Let us assume that a company is expected to earn operating profits (net operating income) averaging NOI each period for the foreseeable future. We will denote the market value of this firm's debt as D, its equity as E, and the total value of its outstanding securities as V, where $V = E + D$. The last expression simply says that the value of a firm equals the combined value of all the securities the firm issues. Finally, given the risk of this firm's profits, its weighted average cost of capital ($WACC$) is r. M&M's Proposition I then asserts the following:

$$V = (E + D) = \frac{NOI}{r} \qquad \text{(Eq. 12.1)}$$

meaning, *the market value of any firm is independent of its capital structure and is given by capitalizing its expected net operating income at the rate r.*

M&M proved their proposition using an **arbitrage** argument. In economics, arbitrage is the process of buying a good in one market at a low price, and then reselling it in another market where the identical good is selling at a higher price. Since arbitrage promises infinite profits, it is a powerful force ensuring that the same assets must sell for the same price in two different markets. M&M demonstrate that an arbitrage opportunity exists if the market value of the combined debt and equity of a levered firm differs from that of an otherwise identical all-equity firm. This is easiest to show with an example.

Computing Returns to Levered and Unlevered Shareholders

Consider two firms, Unleverco and Leverco, which are equally risky and have the same level of expected operating profit, $100,000 per year. Furthermore, assume that the required return on the firm's assets, r, is 10 percent, implying that the total market value of each firm is $1 million ($100,000 operating profit ÷ 0.10 required return). Unleverco has no debt outstanding. Instead, it has 20,000 shares of stock, each of which should be worth $50.[14] Remember, too, that because Unleverco has no debt, the required return on its shares equals the required return on its assets, 10 percent. We denote the required return on unlevered shares as r_u. Leverco, on the other hand, began life as an all-equity firm, but it recently issued debt and used the proceeds to retire shares. Assume it issued $500,000 worth of debt at a promised interest rate of 6 percent per year and used the proceeds of this issue to repurchase half of its outstanding equity. This means Leverco purchased 10,000 shares at $50 each.[15] It therefore has 10,000 shares remaining that should also be worth $50 each, for a total of $500,000.

But what return can Leverco's shareholders expect on their levered shares? As we will see, M&M's Proposition II could tell us directly, but instead, let's reason through to the answer. Recall that Leverco will earn $100,000 in operating profits, from which it must pay $30,000 in interest on its outstanding debt (0.06 × $500,000). This leaves $70,000 for the firm's 10,000 shareholders, or $7 per share. Given that Leverco's shares sell for $50 each, the expected return on its shares must be 14 percent ($7 ÷ $50). We will refer to this as r_l, the required return on levered equity. Table 12.3 summarizes what the financial values *should* be for our two firms in a world where M&M's assumptions hold.

Now that we know what the market values of the securities of Unleverco and Leverco should be, let's see how an arbitrageur (one who engages in arbitrage) could profit *from any other valuation*. Let us assume, as most authors did prior to 1958, that investors are willing to pay a premium price for the shares of levered firms. This is exactly the same as saying that investors would accept "too low" an expected return, r_l, on levered equity, so let's say that Leverco's shares are selling to yield a 12.5 percent expected return. This implies a market valuation for Leverco's equity of $560,000 ($70,000 net income ÷ 0.125 required return) or $56 per share. Added to the market value of the firm's debt ($500,000), this implies a total market valuation

---

[14.] You can derive the $50 stock price in two ways. First, divide the total value of the firm, $1 million, by the number of shares outstanding, 20,000. The result is the price per share, $50. Alternatively, divide the total expected operating income, $100,000, by the number of shares to get earnings per share of $5. Remember that the required return on these shares is 10 percent, so the market price per share must be $50.

[15.] To keep this analysis clearly focused on pure capital structure changes, it is vital to assume that any money raised through the issuance of debt be used strictly to retire outstanding equity, and vice versa. This keeps the total value of the firm's assets constant, and allows one to examine financial changes in isolation.

Table 12.3
Equilibrium Expected Values for Firms Unleverco and Leverco

	Unleverco	Leverco
Net operating income (NOI)	$100,000	$100,000
Less: Interest paid (0.06 × D)	0	30,000
Net income [NOI − (0.06 × D)]	$100,000	$ 70,000
Required return on assets (r)	0.10	0.10
Total firm value (NOI ÷ r)	$1,000,000	$1,000,000
Required return on equity (r_u or r_l)	0.10	0.14
Market value of equity (E)	$1,000,000	$500,000
Interest rate on debt (r_d)	0	0.06
Market value of debt (D)	0	$500,000

for Leverco of $560,000 + $500,000 = $1,060,000, while Unleverco's market value remains $1 million. These "disequilibrium" relative valuations are summarized in Table 12.4.[16]

Proving Proposition I Using "Homemade Leverage"

How can an individual investor exploit these valuations to earn an arbitrage profit? To understand this process, remember that the two firms in question are virtually identical and must therefore have the same business and operating risk. Remember also that investors can borrow or lend on their own account at 6 percent. This allows them to adjust their own portfolios to achieve any desired leverage position. Therefore, an individual investor who currently owns, say, 1 percent of Leverco's outstanding stock expects to earn a 12.5 percent return on that investment, or 0.125 × $5,600 = $700. The investor could earn an arbitrage profit from the following transactions:

1. Sell all the Leverco shares currently owned (1% × 10,000 = 100 shares), receiving $56 per share, for a total of $5,600.

Table 12.4
Disequilibrium Expected Values for Firms Unleverco and Leverco Allowing Arbitrage

	Unleverco	Leverco
Net operating income (NOI)	$100,000	$100,000
Less: Interest paid (0.06 × D)	0	30,000
Net income [NOI − (0.06 × D)]	$100,000	$ 70,000
Required return on assets for firms in this risk class (r)	0.10	0.0943
Total firm value (NOI ÷ r)	$1,000,000	$1,060,000
Required return on equity (r_u or r_l)	0.10	0.125
Market value of equity (E)	$1,000,000	$560,000
Interest rate on debt (r_d)	0	0.06
Market value of debt (D)	0	$500,000

[16.] You may wonder how we obtained the 9.43 percent required return on assets for Leverco in this table. We began with the assumption that the total market value of Leverco was $1,060,000. Simply divide that figure into the company's operating profits, $100,000, to obtain the required return on assets.

2. Borrow $5,000, an amount equivalent to 1 percent of Leverco's debt (1% × $500,000 = $5,000), promising to pay 6 percent interest, or $300 per year (0.06 × $5,000).

3. Use $10,000 of the proceeds from steps 1 and 2 to purchase 1 percent (200 shares) of Unleverco's stock at $50 per share (0.01 × 20,000 shares × $50/share = $10,000). Ignore for now the $600 remaining from steps 1 and 2 ($5,600 + $5,000 − $10,000).

What has our investor/arbitrageur accomplished with this series of transactions? The investor initially held 1 percent of the stock of a company with a capital structure containing equal proportions of debt and equity. In other words, the individual held a small levered equity position. Steps 1–3 transformed this into an equally risky levered equity stake (also 1%) in the all-equity firm Unleverco, but now the leverage is all on personal account. Using **homemade leverage,** or borrowing on personal account, the investor has constructed a portfolio consisting of $10,000 worth of Unleverco's stock ($5,000 purchased with the proceeds from selling Leverco stock, plus $5,000 purchased with borrowed funds). The investor also has $5,000 in personal borrowings, on which $300 annual interest must be paid. The investor thus has constructed a personal levered position (50% debt and 50% equity) in the stock of an unlevered firm. Because the Unleverco stock should earn 10 percent, or $1,000 per year, the net return to this new portfolio is $1,000 − $300 = $700 per year, exactly the same return expected on the original 1 percent stake in Leverco's shares.

But our intrepid arbitrageur is still not through. There is still $600 remaining because only $10,000 of the $10,600 raised in steps 1 and 2 has been invested. Let's assume this is invested back into Leverco stock to earn 12.5 percent, or 0.125 × $600 = $75. This brings the total return from the arbitrage transactions to $700 + $75 = $775, which exceeds the return on the original 1 percent stake in Leverco's stock, for no additional risk. Such an arbitrage opportunity is a money machine that will force prices back into line. Equilibrium can be reestablished only when the expected return on Leverco's stock rises to 14 percent, yielding a total equity value of $500,000 and a total Leverco market value of $1 million.

What if the expected return on Leverco's shares was originally set *too high,* say at 16 percent? In this case, arbitrage would proceed in the opposite direction. An investor/arbitrageur would sell Unleverco shares and then purchase 1 percent of *both* the equity and the debt of Leverco to create an equally low-risk portfolio that has a higher expected return than Unleverco shares alone. In other words, the investor would "unwind" Leverco's indebtedness by lending (buying bonds) on personal account. The key point in all these examples is that under the assumption of the M&M model, the profit-maximizing activities of individual investors/arbitrageurs will force M&M's Proposition I to hold. Whether a company uses leverage or not will have no impact on its total market value.

Proposition II

So far, we have dwelled almost exclusively on M&M's Proposition I and have barely mentioned their second famous proposition, which specifies what the expected return on levered equity must be for market equilibrium to hold. This is no oversight; we place greater relative emphasis on Proposition I because it is more fundamental. In fact, if you accept Proposition I, you have also accepted Proposition II, because it follows logically. We will demonstrate this but will first define Proposition II. Remember that the required return on the firm's assets is r, the interest rate on its debt is r_d, and the market value of its debt and equity is D and E, respectively. **Proposi-**

tion II asserts that the expected return on a levered firm's equity, r_l, is a linear function of that firm's debt-to-equity ratio:

$$r_l = r + (r - r_d)\frac{D}{E} \qquad\qquad \textbf{(Eq. 12.2)}$$

Notice that if we hold the required return on assets and the required return on debt constant, this equation says that the required return on levered equity rises as the debt-to-equity ratio rises. With a little rearranging, we can write Equation 12.2 this way:

$$r = r_l\left(\frac{E}{D + E}\right) + r_d\left(\frac{D}{D + E}\right)$$

Does this look familiar? It should. It's the expression for a firm's weighted average cost of capital (WACC), a concept we introduced in Chapter 9. Recall that the WACC is the discount rate that the firm uses to value its investments in real assets, and it is also the return that satisfies the return requirements of stockholders and bondholders. One way to interpret Proposition II is to say that when the proposition holds, the WACC is independent of a firm's capital structure. In other words, in the equations above, the term r is a constant. But if the WACC is independent of capital structure, then so is the value of the firm, because the WACC is the rate we use to convert the firm's perpetual stream of cash flow into its current market value. Hence the connection between Propositions I and II.

The previous paragraph is counterintuitive on at least two fronts. First, if we examine the WACC equation, it seems as though any adjustment to the terms on the right-hand side must result in a change on the left-hand side. In other words, the equation seems to say that changes in capital structure will affect the WACC. M&M Proposition II says that the WACC is not influenced by changing the mix of debt and equity because changes in leverage cause an offsetting change in the required return on equity that leaves the WACC, or the return on assets, unchanged. We can see this by comparing our two hypothetical firms. Unleverco uses no debt and has a required return on equity of 10 percent, identical to its required return on assets. Suppose that the managers of Unleverco decide to reduce the percentage of equity in their firm's capital structure from 100 percent to 50 percent. In other words, managers want to mimic the capital structure of Leverco. We have already seen that the required return on Leverco's equity must be 14 percent if the interest rate is 6 percent. Plug in these values to confirm that Unleverco's WACC will remain at 10 percent even if the firm changes its capital structure:

$$r = 14\%(50\%) + 6\%(50\%) = 10\%$$

If capital structure is irrelevant (if Proposition I holds), Proposition II tells us what the required return on levered equity must be to maintain a constant total firm value (or a constant WACC). As Figure 12.3 shows, the cost of equity will rise continuously as firms substitute debt for equity, but the weighted average cost of capital remains constant.

The second counterintuitive element of Proposition II is that firms cannot lower their cost of capital by substituting low-cost debt for high-cost equity. A common

Figure 12.3
M&M Proposition II
Illustrated—The Cost of
Equity, Cost of Debt, and
Weighted Average Cost
of Capital for a Firm in a
World without Taxes

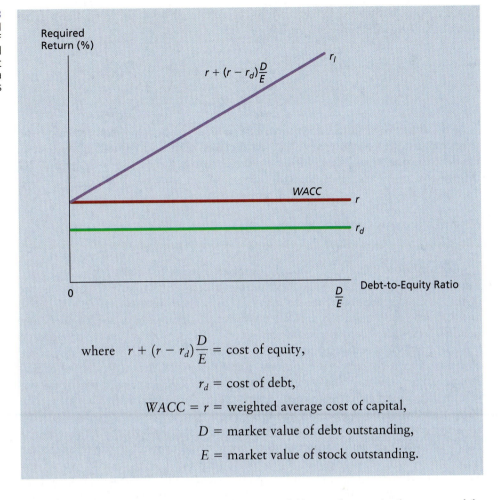

where $r + (r - r_d)\dfrac{D}{E}$ = cost of equity,

r_d = cost of debt,

WACC = r = weighted average cost of capital,

D = market value of debt outstanding,

E = market value of stock outstanding.

mistake that students often make is to reason as follows. The required return on debt is less than the required return on equity because debt is a less-risky instrument (true enough). Therefore, a firm can lower its average cost of capital by issuing bonds and repurchasing shares. Replacing a security with a high required return with a security with a lower required return must lower the average cost of financing the firm's operations. Right? Wrong—at least in an M&M world. As a firm replaces equity with debt, the required return on the remaining equity increases just fast enough that the weighted average cost of capital under the new capital structure is the same as it was under the old one.

**Concept
Review
Questions**

6. Explain how *Propositions I and II* are different, as well as what they have in common.

7. What is the difference between levered and unlevered equity? If you believe that Intel Corp., a widely followed company with very little debt, should include more debt in its capital structure, what actions could you take in an M&M world that would have a similar impact?

8. In their original article, M&M demonstrated, by using the analogy of trying to create value by separating whole milk into separate streams of "cream" and "skim milk," that repackaging a firm's operating cash flows into debt and equity streams cannot create value. How does this analogy relate to Proposition I? Can separating whole milk into cream and skim components create value? Why or why not?

12.4 THE M&M CAPITAL STRUCTURE MODEL WITH CORPORATE AND PERSONAL TAXES

The easiest way to demonstrate the impact of corporate income taxes is to refer back to the two firms, Unleverco and Leverco, used to develop capital structure irrelevance in perfect markets. We will use the same logic Modigliani and Miller used in their 1963 "modified" capital structure model, which explicitly incorporated a tax on corporate profits.

THE M&M MODEL WITH CORPORATE TAXES

Absent taxes, each of the firms in Table 12.3 has assets with a market value of $1 million. Unleverco has financed these assets completely with equity, whereas Leverco uses 50 percent equity and 50 percent debt, yielding a debt-to-total capital ratio of 50 percent. Each firm generates $100,000 in net operating income (NOI) each year. The entire stream goes to Unleverco's shareholders, while Leverco must pay $30,000 in interest on its debt ($500,000 with a 6% interest rate), leaving $70,000 for its shareholders. Into this idealized world, let's introduce a tax on corporate profits at a rate of 35 percent ($T_c = 0.35$). This yields income statements for Unleverco and Leverco as given in Table 12.5. Note that the total income (earnings and interest) paid to private investors (stockholders and bondholders) is higher by $10,500 ($75,500 − $65,000) for Leverco than for Unleverco. Put another way, by using debt, Leverco reduces the government's tax claim on the firm's earnings, while Unleverco's capital structure choice maximizes the government's take.

We can now compute the value of Unleverco (V_U), using the basic M&M valuation formula used before, modified to discount net income (NI) rather than net operating income. We can also assume that investors still require a 10 percent return on the firm's assets, so $r = 0.10$ as before. This yields the following:

$$V_U = \frac{[NOI(1 - T_c)]}{r} = \frac{NI}{r} = \frac{\$65,000}{0.10} = \$650,000 \qquad \text{(Eq. 12.3)}$$

Therefore, the introduction of a 35 percent corporate profits tax causes an immediate $350,000 reduction in the market value of our all-equity company, Unleverco. This represents a pure wealth transfer from Unleverco's shareholders to the government.

Figure 12.4 illustrates the impact of taxes on firm value by using a series of pie charts. Panel A represents the situation in the original M&M world of no taxes. In

	Unleverco	Leverco
Net operating income (NOI)	$100,000	$100,000
Less: Interest paid ($0.06 \times D$)	0	30,000
Taxable income [$NOI − (0.06 \times D)$]	$100,000	$ 70,000
Less: Tax at 35% ($T_c = 0.35$)	35,000	24,500
Net income (NI)	$ 65,000	$ 45,500
Total income to private investors (interest + net income)	$ 65,000	$ 75,500
Value of tax shield each period ($T_c \times 0.06 \times D = 0.35 \times$ interest)	0	$ 10,500

Table 12.5
Income Statements for Unleverco and Leverco with Corporate Income Taxes

Figure 12.4
Pie Chart Models of
Capital Structure with and
without Corporate
Income Taxes

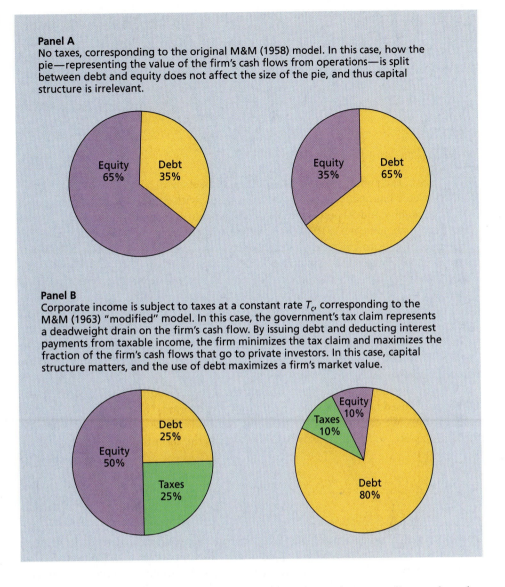

Panel A
No taxes, corresponding to the original M&M (1958) model. In this case, how the pie—representing the value of the firm's cash flows from operations—is split between debt and equity does not affect the size of the pie, and thus capital structure is irrelevant.

Panel B
Corporate income is subject to taxes at a constant rate T_c, corresponding to the M&M (1963) "modified" model. In this case, the government's tax claim represents a deadweight drain on the firm's cash flow. By issuing debt and deducting interest payments from taxable income, the firm minimizes the tax claim and maximizes the fraction of the firm's cash flows that go to private investors. In this case, capital structure matters, and the use of debt maximizes a firm's market value.

this case, capital structure is irrelevant, because no matter how you slice up the value of the firm (the overall pie) between debt and equity claimants, its overall size (value) remains constant. When we introduce corporate income taxes into the M&M model, the value of the firm to private investors is not independent of capital structure. The amount of debt the firm issues determines the size of the government's tax slice of the pie. The more the firm borrows, the smaller is the government's claim, and therefore the larger are the claims held by private investors. Panel B of Figure 12.4 illustrates this point. At the limit, the government's slice (its tax claim) is eliminated completely when the firm finances its operations entirely through debt and pays all its earnings in the form of interest.

DETERMINING THE PRESENT VALUE OF DEBT TAX SHIELDS

Equation 12.3 reveals that corporate taxes cause a reduction in the value of an unlevered firm (compared to its value in a zero-tax environment). How can we modify

our valuation formula to reflect the increase in firm value that results from adding leverage to the capital structure? If we assume that the debt is permanent (the firm will always renew it at maturity), the interest deduction represents a perpetual tax shield equal to the tax rate times the amount of interest paid ($T_c \times r_d \times D = 0.35 \times 0.06 \times \$30,000 = \$10,500$ each year). To find the present value of this perpetuity, we capitalize this stream of benefits at r_d, the rate of interest charged on the firm's debt. With these assumptions, we can compute the present value of the interest tax shields as follows:

$$PV \text{ interest tax shields} = \frac{(T_c \times r_d \times D)}{r_d} = T_c \times D = 0.35(\$500,000)$$
$$= \$175,000$$

(Eq. 12.4)

In other words, the present value of interest tax shields on (perpetual) debt is equal to the tax rate times the face value of the debt outstanding. Therefore, the value of our levered firm, V_L, is equal to the value of Unleverco plus the present value of the interest tax shields:

$$V_L = V_U + PV \text{ tax shield} = V_U + T_c D = \$650,000 + \$175,000 = \$825,000$$

(Eq. 12.5)

What a deal! In essence, the government has given Leverco's shareholders a $175,000 subsidy to employ debt financing rather than equity. But this cannot represent equilibrium. If a 50 percent debt-to-capital ratio increases total firm value by $175,000 over that of an otherwise equivalent unlevered firm, and each additional $1 of debt increases value by $0.35, then the *optimal* leverage ratio for any firm is embarrassingly obvious: 100 percent debt! This is the result M&M arrived at in 1963, though they never quite said so, and this result more than any other lessened initial acceptance of their propositions. How could the theory be correct if it predicted that firms should be so highly levered?

Smart Concepts
See the concept explained step-by-step at SMARTFinance

THE M&M MODEL WITH CORPORATE AND PERSONAL TAXES

For 14 years after the second M&M paper was published, finance researchers and practitioners were in a quandary. Their best theoretical models said capital structure was either irrelevant or should be set at 100 percent debt, but the capital structures of most firms fell in between these extremes. Then Miller (1977) himself offered an explanation for the puzzle. Debt levels had averaged between 30 percent and 40 percent of total capital for several decades (except during the Depression), in spite of the fact that corporate tax rates had varied from zero (prior to 1913) to over 50 percent (in the 1950s) during the same period. He pointed out that legislators had almost invariably changed corporate and personal tax rates at the same time and in the same direction.[17] Miller developed a more sophisticated model that incorporated both corporate and personal taxes. From this model, Miller provided the following formula

[17.] For a listing of U.S. corporate and personal tax rates during the twentieth century, see Table 1.6 of Taggart (1985). As do others, Beatty (1995) provides empirical evidence that the stock market values financial policies (i.e., employee stock ownership plans) that minimize corporate tax payments.

for computing the gains from using leverage, G_L, both for individual companies and for the corporate sector as a whole:

$$G_L = \left[1 - \frac{(1 - T_c)(1 - T_{ps})}{(1 - T_{pd})} \right] D \qquad \text{(Eq. 12.6)}$$

where T_c = tax rate on corporate profits, as before,

T_{ps} = personal tax rate on income from stock (dividends and capital gains),

T_{pd} = personal tax rate on income from debt (interest income),

D = market value of a firm's outstanding debt.

This is, in fact, a very general formulation. In a no-tax world ($T_c = T_{ps} = T_{pd} = 0$), the gains from leverage equal zero and the original M&M irrelevance proposition holds. In a world with only corporate income taxes ($T_c = 0.35$; $T_{ps} = T_{pd} = 0$), the 100 percent optimal debt result again obtains. If, however, personal tax rates on interest income are sufficiently high, and personal tax rates on equity income are sufficiently low, the gains to corporate leverage can be dramatically reduced, or even offset entirely. To see this, assume for a moment, as Miller did, that personal taxes on equity income are zero ($T_{ps} = 0$). This is not as wild as it might sound, as U.S. investors pay capital gains taxes only upon realization, and taxes on some equity investments can be skipped entirely with careful estate planning. Investors can also choose non-dividend-paying stocks to avoid personal taxes on equity income. With this assumption, we can plug into the gain-from-leverage formula the (approximate) top U.S. corporate and personal income tax rates ($T_c = 0.35$ and $T_{pd} = 0.40$):

$$G_L = \left[1 - \frac{(1 - 0.35)(1 - 0.0)}{(1 - 0.4)} \right] D = (-0.083)D$$

With this set of tax rates, the "gain" from leverage is actually negative! In some cases, the effects of corporate and personal taxes may exactly offset each other. If the personal tax on equity income is 7.7 percent, the gain from leverage is zero and capital structure is again irrelevant.

APPLYING THE MODEL

To illustrate how personal and corporate taxes interact to determine the net gains from leverage, consider a situation in which the corporate tax rate is 35 percent, the personal tax rate on interest income is 40 percent, and the personal tax rate on capital gains is 20 percent. Suppose that a firm finances its operations entirely with equity. In a particular year, this firm earns net operating income of $1 million, or $650,000 after taxes. Rather than pay out this profit as a dividend, the firm retains it, resulting in a total capital gain of $650,000 for shareholders. Given the capital gains tax rate of 20 percent, shareholders experience an after-tax gain of $520,000 (0.8 × $650,000).

Next, imagine that this firm had financed its operations entirely with debt rather than equity. This means that the entire $1 million operating profit would flow to bondholders in the form of interest and would escape corporate taxes entirely. However, bondholders receiving the interest would have to pay $400,000 in personal

taxes, resulting in an after-tax gain of $600,000. Because this net gain is higher than in the case of all-equity financing, the tax code still offers firms an incentive to use leverage, but the magnitude of that incentive is reduced by the fact that personal taxes on interest income exceed personal taxes on capital gains. By changing the corporate and personal tax rates, legislators change the relative merits of debt and equity financing. For instance, lowering the corporate tax rate from 35 percent to 25 percent in this example would erase the tax advantage of debt.   ■

Naturally, the importance of interactions between personal and corporate tax rates in determining the relative merits of debt and equity is not limited to firms in the United States. As the Comparative Corporate Finance insert on the next page shows, countries the world over must choose capital structures keeping in mind the influence of corporate and personal taxes. Increasingly, the personal tax element matters most.

BOND MARKET EQUILIBRIUM WITH CORPORATE AND PERSONAL TAXES (ADVANCED MATERIAL)

As important as Miller's (1977) gain-from-leverage model is, however, the most important contribution of his paper is to make clear what the interaction of corporate and personal taxes implies for the equilibrium level of interest rates in a market economy. Consider what happens immediately after corporate income taxes are first introduced into a previously untaxed economy. Whereas firms had been indifferent to whether they issued debt or equity, now income destined for shareholders has become worth only $(1 - T_c)(NOI)$, and interest paid to bondholders escapes corporate taxation entirely. This means that firms have a massive incentive to borrow, and as more and more firms increase their borrowing, interest rates will rise. Equilibrium occurs when the tax advantages of the interest deduction are completely offset by higher interest rates. This occurs when pretax, nominal interest rates are **grossed up,** or increased to provide a given after-tax yield, from r_d to $r_d \div (1 - T_c)$. At that point, individual firms are again indifferent to whether they issue debt or equity, but the equilibrium level of debt in the economy is far higher than in the no-tax case.

You have probably noticed that we have not said anything yet about personal taxes due on interest income received by investors. Wouldn't taxable investors also demand that the rate paid to them be grossed up as compensation for taxes due? The answer is yes, but it is not that simple. The reason why interest rates are not bid up immediately is explained by Miller in two additional, and quite realistic, assumptions about capital market participants. First, he assumes the existence of a sizable group of investors who do not have to pay tax on interest income. Real-world examples of such investors include university endowment funds, certain trust funds, and corporate and public-sector pension funds. Second, he assumes that ordinary investors who are subject to personal income tax can choose to invest in **municipal bonds,** which are low risk and free from personal tax. Municipal bonds, whose interest is exempt from federal income tax, are issued by U.S. state and local governments. These bonds pay an interest rate of r_0, which is equal to the after-tax return on similar-risk corporate bonds, or $(1 - T_{pd})r_d$.

Given these assumptions, we can graphically represent the relationship between D, the total amount of corporate bonds outstanding in an economy (shown on the horizontal axis of Figure 12.5), and the level of interest rates (shown on the vertical axis of Figure 12.5). The horizontal line labeled $r_s(D)$ is the supply curve for corporate bonds (debt). As we previously argued, corporations have an incentive to issue debt as long as equilibrium interest rates are less than or equal to this interest rate. The upward-sloping line $r_d(D)$ is the demand curve for debt, and requires some explanation. Immediately after the imposition of corporate and personal income taxes,

COMPARATIVE CORPORATE FINANCE

Is the State Withering Away? No, Based on Government Spending Levels

Given the large volume of privatization worldwide and the spread of market-based economic policies, it is easy to conclude that the economic role of the government in the affairs of developed nations is declining, and the figure below seems to support that view. Government spending as a percentage of nominal GDP declined between 1995 and 2000 for every country on the list except Japan. However, this is a very recent trend. In the prior decades, government spending had been rising steadily in all countries. Between 1965 and 1997, government spending as a percentage of GDP increased by 17 percentage points for Italy, 13 points for Canada, 11 points for France, 10 points for Japan, 6 points for Britain, and

4 points for Germany and the United States. To meet the demands for increased spending, taxes have also increased significantly since the 1960s. Almost without exception, however, Western democratic governments have *decreased* tax rates for corporations even as they increased effective personal income tax rates. The reason for favoring corporate over individual taxpayers is simple: corporations are mobile and will often move their operations to countries with more favorable tax regimes, but few individuals have that option.

Source: OECD in Washington, no. 25, Organization for Economic Co-operation and Development (March–April 2001).

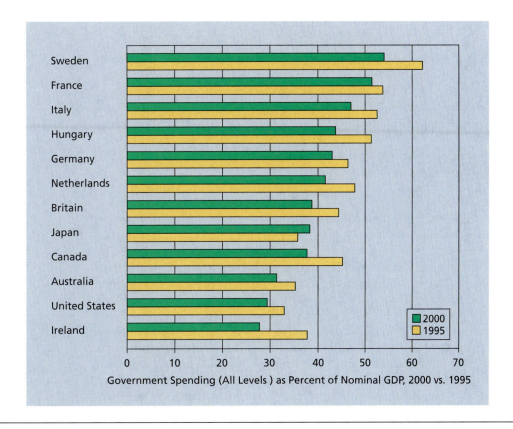

Government Spending (All Levels) as Percent of Nominal GDP, 2000 vs. 1995

the interest rate would be at point r_0. Here, corporations have a huge incentive to issue debt, tax-exempt investors are willing to buy debt (lend money) at this rate, and taxable investors shun taxable corporate debt in favor of tax-free municipal bonds.

This is not equilibrium, however, because corporations still have the incentive to issue more debt. As this occurs, we move farther and farther out (to the right) on the flat portion of curve $r_d(D)$, until all tax-exempt demand for bonds has been met. What

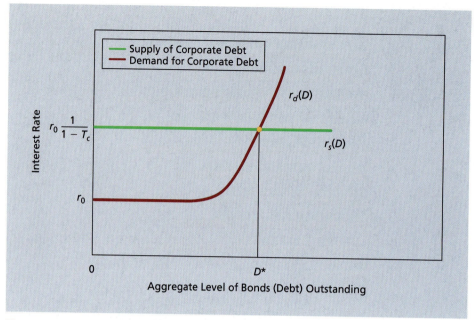

Figure 12.5
Bond Market Equilibrium in the Miller (1977) Model

The horizontal line in this figure represents the supply curve of corporate bonds (debt). This line intersects the y-axis at the point at which the interest rate on corporate bonds exactly offsets debt's corporate tax advantage. The upward sloping line represents the demand curve for debt and indicates that bonds must offer higher rates to attract investors from higher tax brackets. Equilibrium occurs at D*. At that point, the only investors holding corporate bonds are tax-exempt investors and taxable investors facing a personal tax rate on interest income less than or equal to the corporate tax rate. Investors with personal tax rates above the corporate tax rate would choose to hold municipal bonds rather than taxable corporate bonds. D* is the aggregate level of debt in the economy, but for any particular company, there is no net advantage to using debt or equity.

then? Corporations can no longer issue debt at rate r_0, but debt is still cheaper than issuing equity [r_d is still below $r_0 \div (1 - T_c)$]. Companies must therefore entice taxable investors to purchase debt, beginning with those investors in the lowest tax brackets, by offering interest rates high enough to compensate them for the taxes they will have to pay. Once that demand is exhausted, corporations will raise rates further to entice investors in the next tax bracket, and so on until the marginal interest rate paid has been grossed up to equal $r_0 \div (1 - T_c)$. At this point, represented as D^*, corporations are again indifferent to whether they issue debt or equity, and capital market equilibrium is reestablished. To phrase this differently, the first corporations to issue bonds after passage of the Income Tax Amendment to the U.S. Constitution in 1913 were able to issue debt at unusually low rates [between r_0 and $r_0 \div (1 - T_c)$]. But from that time forward, Miller argued, equilibrium interest rates fully reflected investor tax rates, and capital structure has been irrelevant, from a tax standpoint, ever since.

Although few people suggest that the Miller model perfectly describes reality, the model is both intuitively appealing and supported by some (but not all) empirical research. For example, over long periods of time, U.S. tax-exempt municipal bonds have generally offered nominal yields that equal 65–80 percent of the yield on corporate bonds of comparable risk and maturity. This suggests that the personal tax rate of the marginal bond investor has fluctuated between 20 percent and 35 percent. Further support for the need to consider both personal and corporate income taxes in economic models comes from research using data from countries such as Great Britain, which have *imputation* or split-rate tax systems. These systems seek to partially off-

Figure 12.6
Rates of Corporate and Personal Income Taxes in Selected OECD Countries

Source: Organization for Economic Cooperation and Development, *OECD in Washington,* No. 25 (March–April 2001).

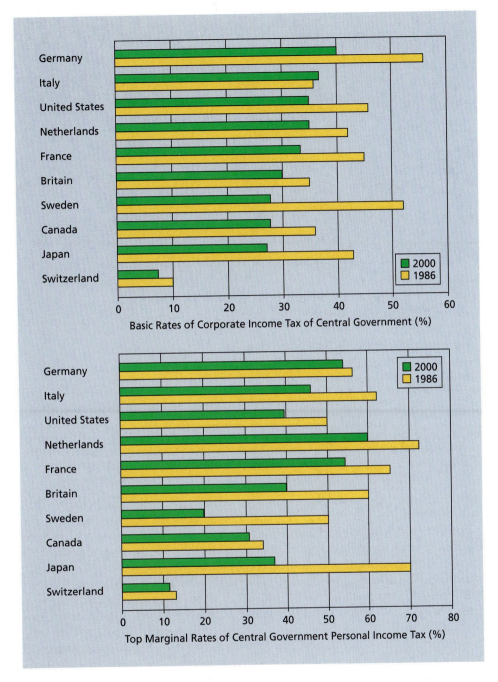

set the tax incentive for corporate debt by giving investors a tax credit for corporate taxes paid on dividends received. Corporate and personal tax rates for several Western countries are presented in Figure 12.6.

Academic research suggests that tax changes that penalize equity income (i.e., increasing taxes on dividends and capital gains) are associated with increases in aggregate debt ratios, whereas the reverse is true for changes that reduce effective tax rates on equity income. Only the arrogant among us, however, would claim anything like a precise understanding of exactly how taxes influence corporate decision making. It

is extremely difficult to estimate the incremental effects of even something as important as a change in corporate tax rates on a complex, $10 trillion economy like that of the United States. It is nearly impossible to estimate the overall effects of corporate taxes in the $35 trillion world economy.

OTHER TAX-BASED MODELS OF CAPITAL STRUCTURE

Following Miller, several authors developed tax-based extensions of the basic capital structure models. The most important of these, by DeAngelo and Masulis (1980), incorporates nondebt tax shields (NDTS) as substitutes for debt in corporate financial structures. Their **nondebt tax shields hypothesis** states that companies with large amounts of depreciation, investment tax credits, R&D expenditures, and other nondebt tax shields should employ less debt financing than otherwise equivalent companies with fewer such shields. Plausible as this hypothesis is, however, early research found just the reverse.[18] Leverage seemed to be directly, not inversely, related to the availability of NDTS. This was interpreted as evidence that assets that generated such tax shields could also be used as collateral for additional debt, so firms rich in tangible assets were able to use higher levels of (secured) debt. This **secured debt hypothesis** has been supported both theoretically and empirically. More recent research has been able to measure the separate effects of NDTS and assets that can be collateralized, and provides support for both the secured debt and the nondebt tax shields hypotheses.[19]

---

9. M&M suggested that "real-world considerations," primarily institutional constraints on high leverage, would prevent firms from approaching 100 percent debt levels. Do you find this convincing? Why or why not?

10. Over time, an increasing percentage of common stock has been held by institutional investors, especially pension funds, which are effectively untaxed on their investment income. What do you think this trend implies for corporate leverage?

11. In 1964, Britain adopted a corporation taxation system with separate company-level taxation of corporate operating income and personal taxation of distributed profits (dividends). After 1964, debt levels increased in Britain. Offer an explanation of this phenomenon.

Concept Review Questions

12.5 A CHECKLIST OF HOW TAXES SHOULD IMPACT CAPITAL STRUCTURE

Although our discussion in this chapter should have made clear that the impact of taxes on corporate leverage is often complex, we can at least summarize three predictions that various researchers have made and that empirical research has tended to support. We will state each formally and then describe the expected relationship more conversationally. Other things equal, and assuming (as is generally true around the

---

[18.] See Bradley, Jarrell, and Kim (1984) and Titman and Wessels (1988).

[19.] The secured debt hypothesis is generally credited to Scott (1977). MacKie-Mason (1990) was the first to show a strong tax impact on the marginal security issuance decision, and Hovakimian et al. (2001) provide supporting evidence. On the other hand, Graham (1996, 2000) shows that established corporations tend to use debt much more conservatively than seems rational strictly from a tax perspective. Additionally, Fama and French (1998) can find no direct evidence of a tax effect in measured leverage ratios of U.S. corporations, after adjusting for other firm-specific influences.

world) that interest is a tax-deductible expense for corporations but that dividend payments are not, the following relationships should hold:

1. **The higher the corporate income tax rate, T_c, the higher will be the equilibrium leverage level economywide.** Put differently, an increase in T_c should cause debt ratios to increase for most firms.
2. **The higher the personal tax rate on equity-related investment income—that is, dividends and capital gains, T_{ps}—the higher will be the equilibrium leverage level.** Put simply, an increase in T_{ps} should cause debt ratios to increase.
3. **The higher the personal tax rate on interest income, T_{pd}, the lower will be the equilibrium leverage level.** That is, an increase in T_{pd} should cause debt ratios to fall.

These relationships have proven quite robust across time and across tax regimes, though one should always bear in mind our cautionary tale about disentangling the true impact of tax rates and systems in complex, modern economies. Given democratic demands for government services, taxes will always be a feature of business environments everywhere. The challenge for government policymakers is to minimize the distortive effects of taxes on corporate and personal decision making. The challenge for corporate financial managers is to make financing decisions that maximize the value of the firm for any given taxation regime.

12.6 SUMMARY

- Corporate debt ratios can be measured in various ways, but "capital structure" ratios measure the ratio of a firm's long-term or permanent debt to its equity capital. More problematic is the need to express leverage ratios in terms of both book value and market value, because each type of measure is appropriate for some purposes, but not for others. We usually focus on market value capital structure ratios.
- Several regularities are observed in capital structure patterns around the world. In general, industries rich in fixed assets and/or those with assets that retain their value in bankruptcy, tend to have high leverage, while industries rich in intangible assets tend to have low levels of indebtedness. This is particularly true for industries where research and development spending is important.
- Though firms in the same industries tend to exhibit similar debt levels in all countries, there are also significant differences in average leverage levels between countries. In those countries where bankruptcy laws favor creditors, especially Britain and Germany, market-value leverage levels tend to be lower than in nations where debtors enjoy greater bankruptcy protection.
- In one of the core papers of scientific finance, Franco Modigliani and Merton Miller (1958) showed that capital structure is irrelevant in a world of frictionless capital markets. This means that the leverage choice cannot affect firm valuation. In the years since 1958, most of the assumptions used to derive this model have been successfully weakened, thus retaining the irrelevance result, but the assumptions of no taxation and cost-free bankruptcy have been shown to be essential.
- In a world with only company-level taxation of operating profits and tax-deductible interest payments, the optimal corporate strategy is to use the maximum possible leverage. This minimizes the government's claim on profits in the form of taxes and maximizes the amount of income flowing to private investors.

- When corporate profits are taxed at both the corporate and personal levels (with taxes on interest and dividends received), the benefits to high levels of corporate leverage are much reduced, and may be completely negated. In this more "realistic" world of multiple taxes and other market imperfections, such as transactions costs to issuing securities, it is unclear whether an "optimal" debt level exists for the average firm in any given nation.

INTERNET RESOURCES

Note: *For updates to links, please go to the book's website at* *http://smart.swcollege.com*

http://www.cfoeurope.com/199809g.html—An article from CFO Europe that discusses the impact of the Modigliani and Miller propositions from a CFO's perspective

http://www.taxsites.com/international.html—A site providing country-specific tax information for dozens of countries, as well as links to a wide variety of tax-related sites.

KEY TERMS

arbitrage
financial slack
grossed up
homemade leverage
managerial opportunism hypothesis
municipal bonds
nondebt tax shield hypothesis

pecking order hypothesis
Proposition I
Proposition II
secured debt hypothesis
signaling model
target leverage zones
trade-off model

QUESTIONS

12-1.   What are the industrial and national capital structure patterns exhibited globally? What factors seem to be driving these patterns?

12-2.   What is the observed relationship between debt ratios and profitability and the perceived costs of financial distress? Why does the relationship between leverage and profitability imply that capital structure choice is residual in nature?

12-3.   How influential are corporate and personal taxes on capital structure? Historically, have changes in American tax rates greatly affected debt ratios?

12-4.   How do stock prices generally react to announcements of firms' changes in leverage? Why is this result perplexing and seemingly contradictory given your answer to Question 12-2?

12-5.   Briefly describe each of the four major models of capital structure choice. Which of these models are based on an assumption of asymmetric information between managers and outside investors?

12-6.   Explain the concept of *financial slack* within a capital structure framework. Why has this concept added credibility to the *pecking order hypothesis* over the agency cost/tax shield *trade-off model* of capital structure choice?

12-7.   According to the *pecking order hypothesis,* what is the purpose of maintaining financial slack? How does this relate to the assumption in this hypothesis of asymmetric information?

12-8. How does the *signaling model* of financial structure differ from the pecking order model with respect to the assumption of asymmetric information?

12-9. What is the basic conclusion of the original Modigliani and Miller *Proposition I?* What argument do M&M offer as a defense of this conclusion? How is "homemade leverage" used within this argument?

12-10. Following from the conclusion of Proposition I, what is the crux of M&M *Proposition II?* What is the natural relationship between the required returns on debt and equity that results from Proposition II?

12-11. In what way did M&M change their conclusion regarding capital structure choice with the additional assumption of corporate taxes? In this context, what composes the difference in value between levered and unlevered firms?

12-12. By introducing personal taxes into the model for capital structure choice, how did Miller alter the previous M&M conclusion that 100 percent debt is optimal? What happens to the gains from leverage if personal tax rates on interest income are significantly higher than those on stock-related income?

12-13. What is the implication about the equilibrium level of interest rates offered by Miller in his model? Address the concept of interest rates that are *grossed up* in your answer.

12-14. List and describe the three predictions made by academic researchers regarding the impact of taxes on corporate leverage. Have these predictions been supported empirically?

PROBLEMS

Capital Structure Patterns Observed Worldwide

12-1. Go to Yahoo! and download recent balance sheets for Microsoft, Merck, Archer Daniels Midland, and General Mills (ticker symbols MSFT, MRK, ADM, and GIS, respectively). Calculate several debt ratios for each company and comment on the differences that you observe in the use of leverage. What factors do you think account for these differences?

The Modigliani & Miller Capital Structure Irrelevance Propositions

12-2. An unlevered company operates in perfect markets and has net operating income of $250,000. Assume that the required return on assets for firms in this industry is 12.5 percent and that the firm issues $1 million worth of debt with a required return of 5 percent and uses the proceeds to repurchase outstanding stock.

   a. What is the market value and required return of this firm's stock before the repurchase transaction?

   b. What is the market value and required return of this firm's remaining stock after the repurchase transaction?

12-3. Assume that capital markets are perfect. A firm finances its operations with $50 million in stock with a required return of 15 percent and $40 million in bonds with a required return of 9 percent. Assuming that the firm could issue $10 million in additional bonds at 9 percent, using the proceeds to retire $10 million worth of equity, what would happen to the firm's *WACC*? What would happen to the required return on the company's stock?

12-4. A firm operates in perfect capital markets. The required return on its outstanding debt is 6 percent, the required return on its shares is 14 percent, and its *WACC* is 10 percent. What is the firm's debt-to-equity ratio?

12-5. Assume that two firms, U and L, are identical in all respects except that Firm U is debt free and Firm L has a capital structure that is 50 percent debt and 50 percent equity by market value. Further suppose that the assumptions of the Modigliani & Miller capital structure irrelevance proposition hold (no taxes or transactions costs, no bankruptcy costs, etc.) and that each firm will have net operating income of $800,000. If the required return on assets, r, for these firms is 12.5 percent and risk-free debt yields 5 percent, calculate the following values for both Firm U and Firm L: (1) total firm value, (2) market value of debt and equity, and (3) required return on equity. Then, recompute these values, assuming that the market mistakenly assigns Firm L's equity a required return of 15 percent, and *describe* the arbitrage operation that will force Firm L's valuation back into equilibrium.

12-6. Hearthstone Corp. and The Shaky Image Co. are companies that compete in the luxury consumer goods market. The two companies are virtually identical, except that Hearthstone is financed entirely with equity and The Shaky Image uses equal amounts of debt and equity. Suppose that each firm has assets with a total market value of $100 million. Hearthstone has 4 million shares of stock outstanding worth $25 each. Shaky has 2 million shares outstanding, and it also has publicly traded debt with a market value of $50 million. Both companies operate in a world with perfect capital markets (no taxes, etc.). The *WACC* for each firm is 12 percent. The cost of debt is 8 percent.

   a. What is the price of Shaky stock?
   b. What is the cost of equity for Hearthstone? For Shaky?
   c. Suppose that you want to buy 1 percent of the outstanding Shaky shares, but you do not like the fact that Shaky uses leverage. Assuming that you can borrow and lend at 8 percent, show how you can trade on your own account to unwind the effects of Shaky's leverage.
   d. Suppose that you want to buy 1 percent of the outstanding Hearthstone shares, but you wish that the firm's managers were not so conservative, refraining entirely from issuing debt. Demonstrate how you can trade on your own account to create an investment in Hearthstone that is equivalent in terms of risk and return to buying 1 percent of Shaky's shares.

12-7. In the mid-1980s, Michael Milken and his firm, Drexel Burnham Lambert, made the term "junk bonds" a household word. Many of Drexel's clients issued junk bonds (bonds with low credit ratings) to the public to raise money to conduct a leveraged buyout (LBO) of a target firm. After the LBO, the target firm would have an extremely high debt-to-equity ratio, with only a small portion of equity financing remaining. Many politicians and members of the financial press worried that the increase in junk bonds would bring about an increase in the risk of the U.S. economy because so many large firms had become highly leveraged. Merton Miller disagreed. See if you can follow his argument by assessing whether each of the statements below is true or false:

   a. The junk bonds issued by acquiring firms were riskier than investment-grade bonds.
   b. The remaining equity in highly leveraged firms was more risky than it had been before the LBO.
   c. After an LBO, the target firm's capital structure would consist of very risky junk bonds and very risky equity. Therefore, the risk of the firm would increase after the LBO.
   d. The junk bonds issued to conduct the LBO were less risky than the equity they replaced.

The M&M Capital Structure Model with Corporate and Personal Taxes

12-8. Within the M&M framework of corporate taxes but no personal taxes, determine the present value of the interest tax shield of Herculio Mining, as well as the total value of the firm. Herculio has net operating income of $5 million; there is $50 million of debt outstanding with a required rate of return of 6 percent; the required rate of return on the industry is 12 percent; and the corporate tax rate is 40 percent.

12-9.   Using the information from Problem 12-8, determine the gain from leverage if personal taxes of 20 percent on stock income and 30 percent on debt income exist.

12-10. An all-equity firm is subject to a 30 percent tax rate. Its total market value is initially $3,500,000. There are 175,000 shares outstanding. The firm announces a program to issue $1 million worth of bonds at 10 percent interest and to use the proceeds to buy back common stock. Assume that there is no change in costs of financial distress and that the debt is perpetual.

   a. What is the value of the tax shield that the firm acquires through the bond issue?
   b. According to Modigliani & Miller, what is the likely increase in market value per share of the firm after the announcement, assuming efficient markets?
   c. How many shares will the company be able to repurchase?

12-11. Intel Corp. is a firm that uses almost no debt and had a total market capitalization of about $125 billion in June 2002. Assume that Intel faces a 35 percent tax rate on corporate earnings. Ignoring all elements of the decision except corporate tax savings, by how much could Intel managers increase the value of the firm by issuing $50 billion in bonds (which would be rolled over in perpetuity) and simultaneously repurchasing $50 billion in stock? Why do you think that Intel has not taken advantage of this opportunity?

12-12. Refer to Problem 12-11. Suppose that the personal tax rate on equity income faced by Intel shareholders is 10 percent, and the personal tax rate on interest income is 40 percent. Recalculate the gains to Intel from replacing $50 billion of equity with debt.

12-13. Soonerco has $15 million of common stock outstanding, net operating income of $2.5 million per year, and $15 million of debt outstanding with a required return (interest rate) of 8 percent. The required rate of return on assets in this industry is 12.5 percent, and the corporate tax rate is 35 percent. Within the M&M framework of corporate taxes but no personal taxes, determine the present value of the interest tax shield of Soonerco, as well as the total value of the firm. Finally, determine the gain from leverage if personal tax rates exist in the form of 15 percent on stock income and 25 percent on debt income.

13

Capital Structure: Nontax Determinants of Corporate Leverage

OPENING FOCUS
$8.68 Billion Kraft IPO Helps Philip Morris Pay Off Acquisition Debt

A distinctive feature of modern corporate finance in most advanced economies over the past decade has been the explosion in the number and size of corporate takeovers. In the majority of large acquisitions, the buyer pays for the target's shares with cash, using borrowed funds to finance the deal. Funding takeovers with borrowed money can dramatically increase the acquiring firm's leverage ratios, as a series of recent deals involving Philip Morris Company illustrates. In December 2000, Philip Morris purchased Nabisco Holdings Corporation for $18 billion in cash and raised over $12 billion through the issuance of short- and intermediate-term debt securities. Though Philip Morris borrowed this money itself, it channeled the acquisition through its wholly owned Kraft Foods Inc. subsidiary and then merged Nabisco with Kraft after completing the acquisition. Although this acquisition made good strategic sense, it burdened Philip Morris with an extremely high total debt-to-equity ratio of 2.05 and a long-term debt-to-equity ratio of 1.26. Both ratios were far higher than the historical norm for Philip Morris, or for comparable firms in its industry, prompting analysts to question what steps the firm might take to reduce its leverage.

The answer was not long in coming. In early 2001, Philip Morris announced plans for its subsidiary, Kraft Foods Inc., to sell a minority stake in a transaction called an **equity carve-out.** Then, in June 2001, Kraft executed the second-largest initial public offering in U.S. history, raising $8.68 billion through the sale of 280 million shares at $31 each. Although the IPO reduced Philip Morris's total ownership interest in Kraft by about 15 percent, Philip Morris's voting power over Kraft was only reduced to 97.7 percent because Kraft had a dual-class share structure and offered only low-vote shares in the IPO. Kraft's new shareholders prospered after the IPO; the company's shares rose approximately 30% from June 2001 to December 2002, outperforming the S&P 500 index by almost 50 percent.

Kraft used the proceeds of the IPO to pay off the $9 billion loan

Philip Morris had extended to it as part of the Nabisco acquisition. Philip Morris then used the cash to pay off much of its own borrowing related to the Nabisco takeover. The net result of all these transactions was that Philip Morris first became a heavily indebted company in order to finance an important corporate acquisition, but then reduced its leverage back to reasonable levels within seven months by selling a minority stake in one of its subsidiaries. Many other companies have pursued similar strategies during the acquisitions boom of the past decade.

Sources: The CNN Money website (http://money.cnn.com) provided narrative information about the Nabisco acquisition and the Kraft IPO; the Securities and Exchange Commission's EDGAR database (http://www.sec.gov/edgar .shtml) provided in-depth financial data.

At the start of this second chapter on corporate capital structure, we are very much like readers of a mystery novel at the midpoint of the book. We know the mystery that must be solved (how and why corporate leverage impacts firm valuation), and we know that it is a difficult case (in a world of perfect markets, capital structure is irrelevant; but in the real world, firms act as though leverage is important indeed). Further, we know which suspects have already been cleared of the crime (corporate and personal taxes influence debt levels, but neither causes nor prevents corporate leverage) and which suspects remain to be interrogated. Our job in this chapter is to systematically question the remaining suspects and examine the forensic capital structure evidence in our effort solve the mystery of corporate leverage. The list of suspects includes bankruptcy costs, the agency costs of debt and equity, and the characteristics of a firm's assets.

As we saw in Chapter 12, under the assumptions of the M&M theory, capital structure is irrelevant. We also saw that corporate income taxes, viewed in isolation, give corporations a strong incentive to employ financial leverage, but that things are much less clear-cut when personal income taxes are also considered. On balance, we concluded that corporate and personal taxes influence, but do not in themselves explain, the variation in leverage ratios observed in the U.S. or other modern economies. If taxes do not explain why firms and investors pay attention to capital structure, then what does? To see how capital structure *can* be relevant, we simply need to turn the M&M assumptions around. If leverage does matter, markets must be imperfect in some way. Examples of market imperfections that could influence capital structures include the following: (1) there must be significant costs to bankruptcy or financial distress; (2) there must be significant costs to negotiating and enforcing contracts between managers, stockholders, and creditors; (3) a firm's investment opportunities must be related to the firm's use of leverage; or (4) it must be costly for the firm to credibly convey relevant information about its current operations or future prospects. This chapter will consider each of these possibilities, beginning with bankruptcy and financial distress.

13.1 COSTS OF BANKRUPTCY AND FINANCIAL DISTRESS

It seems obvious that the threat of bankruptcy might make some firms reluctant to use debt financing. In the real world, overly indebted companies can be severely penalized if they cannot service their debts, and managers of bankrupt firms usually face bleak career prospects.[1] As Table 13.1 shows, tens of thousands of businesses (and many times more individuals) file for bankruptcy protection in the United States each year. Practical experience suggests that a bankrupt company's security holders, even

---

[1.] The first study to clearly show that bankruptcy is costly for firms is by Altman (1984). Later, Gilson (1989) and Gilson and Vetsuypens (1993) also document that bankruptcy can be similarly painful for individual managers—Enron notwithstanding (its top executives all sold large amounts of stock before the firm collapsed).

Table 13.1
Bankruptcy Petitions Filed and Pending in the United States, by Type and Chapter

Item	1985	1990	1993	1995	1996	1997	1998	1999	2000
Total filed	364,535	725,484	918,734	858,104	1,042,110	1,316,999	1,429,451	1,391,964	1,276,922
Business[a]	66,651	64,688	66,428	51,288	52,938	53,993	50,202	39,934	36,910
Nonbusiness[b]	297,885	660,796	852,306	806,816	989,172	1,263,006	1,379,249	1,352,030	1,240,012
Voluntary	362,939	723,886	917,350	856,991	1,040,915	1,315,782	1,428,550	1,391,130	1,276,146
Involuntary	1,597	1,598	1,384	1,113	1,195	1,217	901	834	776
Chapter 7[c]	244,650	505,337	638,916	581,390	712,129	917,274	1,015,453	993,414	885,447
Chapter 9[d]	3	7	9	12	10	9	5	3	8
Chapter 11[e]	21,425	19,591	20,579	13,221	12,859	11,159	9,613	8,684	9,947
Chapter 12[f]	NA	1,351	1,434	904	1,063	1,006	845	829	732
Chapter 13[g]	98,452	199,186	257,777	262,551	316,024	387,521	403,501	389,004	380,770
Section 304[h]	6	12	19	26	24	29	34	30	18
Total pending	608,945	961,919	1,183,009	1,090,446	1,169,112	1,331,290	1,389,917	1,401,862	1,400,416

Source: Statistical Abstract of the United States 2001, U.S. Department of Commerce (Washington, D.C.).

Notes: Covers only bankruptcy cases filed under the *Bankruptcy Reform Act of 1978.* Bankruptcy is defined as the legal recognition that a company or individual is insolvent and must restructure or liquidate. Petitions "filed" means the commencement of a proceeding through the presentation of a petition to the clerk of the court. "Pending" is a proceeding in which the administration has not been completed.

[a]Business bankruptcies include those filed under chapters 7, 9, 11, or 12.
[b]Bankruptcies include those filed under chapters 7, 11, or 13.
[c]Chapter 7: liquidation of nonexempt assets of businesses or individuals.
[d]Chapter 9: adjustment of debts of a municipality.
[e]Chapter 11: individual or business reorganization.
[f]Chapter 12: adjustment of debts of a family farmer with regular income, effective November 26, 1986.
[g]Chapter 13: adjustment of debts of an individual with regular income.
[h]Chapter 11, U.S.C., Section 304: cases ancillary to foreign proceedings.

supposedly protected senior bondholders, can lose their entire investment in a firm. Surely, then, differing costs of bankruptcy and financial distress between industries can cause firms in one industry to employ less debt than do comparable firms in other industries, right?

Before reaching this conclusion, we need to clearly explain what we mean (and what we do not mean) by the term **bankruptcy costs.** Bankruptcy costs are distinct from the decline in firm value that leads to financial distress in the first place. Poor management, unfavorable movements in input and output prices, and recessions are examples of events that can push a firm into bankruptcy, but they are not examples of bankruptcy costs. Instead, bankruptcy costs refer to direct and indirect costs of the bankruptcy process itself. In the United States, a firm becomes bankrupt when it comes under the supervision of the federal government's bankruptcy courts and ceases to operate as a separate, independently contracting legal entity. The court can then choose either to liquidate the firm and distribute the money received to the firm's creditors to satisfy their claims, or to reorganize the firm's operations and finances, thereby allowing it to reemerge from bankruptcy as a new company. In theory, the firm's original shareholders lose their entire investment in either case, and ownership of the firm (or the firm's remaining assets) will pass to bondholders and other creditors. These investors then become the firm's new stockholders. The process of reorganizing a firm and negotiating the terms of the reorganization with the firm's managers, shareholders, and creditors consumes resources. Bankruptcy costs, then, refer to the resource-consumption aspect of bankruptcy.

The Importance of Bankruptcy Costs

Bankruptcy is a legal process involving the reorganization of financial claims and the transfer of corporate ownership; it is not a "cremation" (Haugen and Senbet 1978). Even if a firm is liquidated, its assets will not disappear but will instead be employed by a new owner. Bankruptcy is the *result* of economic failure, not the cause, and the decline in firm value and loss of jobs commonly associated with the event of bankruptcy is actually what pushes the firm into bankruptcy court in the first place. In fact, think about what a bankruptcy filing actually means for a firm's shareholders; it means they are exercising their **option to default** on the company's debt. As we have seen, this is a key benefit of the corporate form of organization. Absent this limited liability feature, shareholders would have to pay off the firm's creditors out of their own pockets instead of simply handing creditors the company's assets in bankruptcy court.

Therefore, unless the *process* of bankruptcy imposes costs on a company that a similarly distressed, nonbankrupt firm would not have to bear, the mere possibility of falling into bankruptcy cannot significantly influence capital structure decision making. Similarly, a firm cannot consider financial leverage itself as something to avoid unless debt financing somehow makes encountering financial distress more painful for a levered company than it would be for an all-equity company. The following example demonstrates that the mere prospect of bankruptcy does not imply that capital structure decisions will influence a firm's value. Only if the bankruptcy process is costly does capital structure become value relevant, a scenario we develop in a subsequent example.

APPLYING THE MODEL

Both the Low-Debt Parking Company and the High-Debt Parking Company have 1-year contracts to manage identical parking lots for the scenic resort town of Falling Rivers. The value of these parking contracts depends on economic conditions in Falling Rivers during the coming year. If the recent economic boom continues, Falling Rivers will attract large numbers of visitors. However, if a recession occurs, the number of visitors will fall drastically. The probability that the expansion will continue is the same as the probability of a recession, 50 percent.

If the boom continues, each company will earn a management fee (net of the costs of operating the lots) of $900,000. If a recession occurs, however, each will earn a net fee of just $200,000.

Each company financed its purchase of the parking-management contract from the City of Falling Rivers in part with borrowed money, which must be repaid with interest when the parking contracts expire in one year. At maturity, Low-Debt will owe $106,000 in principal and interest, while High-Debt will owe $270,000. If there is a recession, High-Debt will be unable to pay its creditors in full and will file for bankruptcy. If there are no costs to the bankruptcy process, High-Debt's stockholders will lose their investment, and the firm's creditors will receive the $200,000 cash flow. Assume that High-Debt's stockholders require a return of 11.54 percent and its bondholders expect a return of 8 percent. Both stockholders and bondholders of Low-Debt are willing to accept slightly lower returns because the firm uses leverage more sparingly. Low-Debt's stockholders require an 11 percent return, and its bondholders require 6 percent. The following table details the payoffs to security holders of both firms under the additional assumption that neither firm pays taxes.

	Low-Debt Parking Company		High-Debt Parking Company	
Item	Expansion (probability = 0.5)	Recession (probability = 0.5)	Expansion (probability = 0.5)	Recession (probability = 0.5)
Cash flow at contract expiration	$900,000	$200,000	$900,000	$200,000
Debt-service payment (interest and principal)	106,000	106,000	270,000	200,000
Distributions to stockholders	794,000	94,000	630,000	0

To value the equity, E, and debt, D, claims of these two firms, we first compute the expected value of the payoffs to each investor group and then find the present value of the payoffs using the required returns to discount cash flows. The value, V, of the firm is then the sum of equity and debt values, $V = E + D$.

$$E_{\text{Low-Debt}} = [(0.5 \times \$794,000) + (0.5 \times \$94,000)] \div 1.11$$

$$= \$444,000 \div 1.11 = \$400,000$$

$$D_{\text{Low-Debt}} = [(0.5 \times \$106,000) + (0.5 \times \$106,000)] \div 1.06$$

$$= \$106,000 \div 1.06 = \$100,000$$

$$V_{\text{Low-Debt}} = \$400,000 + \$100,000 = \$500,000$$

$$E_{\text{High-Debt}} = [(0.5 \times \$630,000) + (0.5 \times \$0)] \div 1.1154$$

$$= \$315,000 \div 1.1154 = \$282,407^2$$

$$D_{\text{High-Debt}} = [(0.5 \times \$270,000) + (0.5 \times \$200,000)] \div 1.08$$

$$= \$235,000 \div 1.08 = \$217,593$$

$$V_{\text{High-Debt}} = \$282,407 + \$217,593 = \$500,000$$

[2.] We are actually using a discount rate of 11.541 percent here. You can double-check that given the percentages of debt and equity used by each firm, and given the required return on each firm's debt and equity, the weighted average

Because both firms have the same total market value, we can conclude that cost-less bankruptcy will not affect a firm's market value. Therefore, the fact that High-Debt's financing strategy makes bankruptcy more likely does not affect the value of the firm, and capital structure is irrelevant. It is worth noting that High-Debt's bond-holders have a *promised* return of more than 24 percent $[(270,000 - 217,593) \div 217,593]$ but an *expected* return of only 8 percent, so the possibility of partial default is priced into the bonds today. ■

In fact, bankruptcy is a costly process, and those costs can influence a firm's capital structure decisions. Consider three channels through which bankruptcy costs could have an impact on a firm's mix of debt and equity. First, if the process of bankruptcy entails deadweight costs—such as cash payments to lawyers, accountants, or advisers—then firms will have a strong incentive to minimize leverage to reduce the likelihood of going bankrupt. Second, bankruptcy costs are important if encountering financial distress would reduce demand for a firm's products or increase its costs of production. Third, bankruptcy costs matter if financial distress would give the firm's managers, operating as agents of the firm's shareholders, perverse operating or financial incentives to take actions likely to reduce overall firm value. As you might imagine, empirical research indicates that all these costs do arise and do significantly impact observed leverage ratios.

APPLYING THE MODEL

To demonstrate the effect of costly bankruptcy on capital structure decision making, we again use the assumptions made in the previous Applying the Model for Low-Debt Parking Company and High-Debt Parking Company, with one change. We now assume that if there is a recession and High-Debt is forced to file for bankruptcy, the process will be contentious and costly. Instead of receiving the full $200,000 terminal cash flow as in the costless bankruptcy case, High-Debt's creditors will receive only $120,000. In other words, the conflicts between High-Debt's stockholders and bond-holders (and their lawyers) consume $80,000 of value. The cash flows to the stock-holders and bondholders of Low-Debt Parking and High-Debt Parking in one year are detailed in the following table.

| | Low-Debt Parking Company | | High-Debt Parking Company | |
| | Expansion (probability = 0.5) | Recession (probability = 0.5) | Expansion (probability = 0.5) | Recession (probability = 0.5) |
Item				
Cash flow at contract expiration	$900,000	$200,000	$900,000	$200,000
Debt-service payment (interest and principal)	106,000	106,000	270,000	120,000
Distributions to stockholders	794,000	94,000	630,000	0

When we recompute the stock and bond values for each firm, it becomes clear that if the process of bankruptcy involves real costs, these reduce the current value of

---

cost of capital for managing parking lots is 10 percent. Does it surprise you that High-Debt's *WACC* is the same as Low-Debt's?

a highly levered firm. For High-Debt Parking Company, costly bankruptcy reduces overall firm value by \$37,037 (\$500,000 − \$462,963).[3]

$$E_{\text{Low-Debt}} = [(0.5 \times \$794,000) + (0.5 \times \$94,000)] \div 1.11$$

$$= \$444,000 \div 1.11 = \$400,000$$

$$D_{\text{Low-Debt}} = [(0.5 \times \$106,000) + (0.5 \times \$106,000)] \div 1.06$$

$$= \$106,000 \div 1.06 = \$100,000$$

$$V_{\text{Low-Debt}} = \$400,000 + \$100,000 = \$500,000$$

$$E_{\text{High-Debt}} = [(0.5 \times \$630,000) + (0.5 \times \$0)] \div 1.1154$$

$$= \$315,000 \div 1.1154 = \$282,407$$

$$D_{\text{High-Debt}} = [(0.5 \times \$270,000) + (0.5 \times \$120,000)] \div 1.08$$

$$= \$195,000 \div 1.08 = \$180,556$$

$$V_{\text{High-Debt}} = \$282,407 + \$180,556 = \$462,963$$

ASSET CHARACTERISTICS AND BANKRUPTCY COSTS

Intuitively, it seems clear that certain firms should be able to weather financial distress better than others. For example, if you wish to purchase a commodity item (i.e., raw flour) or use a service (i.e., printing a set of business cards) only once, you would care little whether the specific company you purchased that good or service from remained in business after your transaction. On the other hand, if you are contemplating the purchase of a large new computer system, or are choosing which airplane manufacturer's equipment to purchase, the long-term viability of the supplier becomes very important. As a general rule, therefore, producers of sophisticated products or services will have an incentive to use less debt than will firms producing nondurable goods or basic services. It is more important for producers of durable goods to assure customers that their firms will be able to provide ongoing service, warranty and repair work, and product improvements.[4] Based on this logic, it is not surprising that Table 12.1 showed that companies such as Intel, IBM, United Technologies, and Boeing use leverage very sparingly.

SMART IDEAS VIDEO
Robert Bruner, University of Virginia
"The case of Revco illustrates the principle of too much or too little debt."

See the entire interview at **SMARTFinance**

A firm's asset characteristics also influence its willingness to risk financial distress by using large amounts of debt. Companies whose assets are mostly tangible and have well-established secondary markets should be less fearful of financial distress than companies whose assets are mostly intangible. Therefore, trucking companies, airlines, construction firms, pipeline companies, and railroads can all employ relatively more debt than can companies with few, if any, tangible assets, such as pharmaceutical manufacturers, food distributors (what is the collateral value of week-old tomatoes?), or pure service companies. Once again, Table 12.1 verifies this logic; Delta

SMART IDEAS VIDEO
Sheridan Titman, University of Texas at Austin
"It seems to be the case that the product-market strategies of firms to a large extent dictate how firms are financed."

See the entire interview at **SMARTFinance**

[3.] A careful reader may notice that we have fudged a bit in this example. The risk of costly bankruptcy means that bondholders should no longer be willing to accept an 8 percent return. However, the general point is that bankruptcy costs siphon resources away from the firm's investors and in so doing, reduce the value of the firm.

[4.] This point is made most clearly in Titman (1984) and Maksimovic and Titman (1991).

Air Lines and AMR have much higher leverage ratios than do Merck and Eli Lilly. Financial distress can be particularly damaging to firms that produce research and development–intensive goods and services, for two reasons. First, most of the expenses incurred in producing the good or service are sunk costs, which have already been made and which can be recovered only with a long period of profitable sales. Second, "cutting-edge" goods and services typically require ongoing research and development spending to ensure market acceptance, and a bankrupt or impoverished firm will be unable to finance such spending. Further, intangible assets such as patents and trademarks are extremely valuable and are unlikely to survive financial distress or bankruptcy intact. Microsoft, Intel, and Cisco Systems are three classic examples of companies that invest massive sums in R&D in order to produce cutting-edge products and services, and Table 12.1 shows that all three firms are essentially debt free!

Financial distress can also dramatically increase the costs of production for many companies. Suppliers may be unwilling to extend credit to a company perceived as too risky, or may do so only under very restrictive conditions. The firm may be unable to attract business partners for joint ventures or risk-sharing developmental projects. Perhaps most important of all, a highly indebted firm may be unable to attract talented new employees and may well see its best people leave for more-promising careers elsewhere.[5] After all, these workers are generally the most mobile. Any firm that is dependent on the creativity, loyalty, and stability of its workforce is thus particularly vulnerable to leverage-induced financial distress and can be expected to employ less debt than other firms.

The Asset Substitution Problem

One major problem associated with financial distress is that it provides otherwise-trustworthy managers with perverse, but rational, incentives to play a variety of financial and operating "games," mostly at bondholders' expense. Two such games, asset substitution and underinvestment, are particularly important and potentially damaging. Both typically begin when a company first encounters financial difficulties and its managers realize the firm will probably not fulfill its obligations to creditors.

To illustrate how **asset substitution** works, assume that a firm has bonds with a face value of $10 million outstanding that mature in 30 days. These bonds were issued years ago when the firm was prospering, but since then the firm has fallen on hard times. The company's operations are currently unprofitable due to an unexpected economic slowdown, though the firm's managers believe the firm can be profitable again once the economy picks up. In spite of its difficulties, the firm still has $8 million in cash on hand that it can invest in one of two projects. Alternatively, the firm can simply hold the cash in reserve to partially repay the bond issue in 30 days. The first investment opportunity is a low-risk project requiring an $8 million investment that will pay off $8.15 million in 30 days with virtual certainty. This is a monthly return of 1.88 percent, or annual return of almost 25 percent. In other words, it is a positive-*NPV* project that will increase firm value, but it does not earn a return high enough to fully redeem the maturing bonds.

[5.] One of this book's authors experienced these problems personally when he worked for a large manufacturing firm experiencing financial distress. Suppliers refused to deliver merchandise on credit, shippers refused to deliver finished goods unless they were paid in advance, and it became extremely difficult to replace departing employees (of which there were many). Perhaps the most dramatic examples of the financial problems caused by this company's distress were the cash discounts the firm offered its customers for prompt payment. The interest rates implied by these discounts sometimes exceeded 50 percent per year.

How Important Is R&D Spending to Modern Economies?

This chapter discusses the influence of a firm's research and development spending on its capital structure and shows that, other things equal, firms that invest large sums of money in research and development typically employ relatively little debt. Casual observation suggests that R&D spending is an extremely important source of innovation and growth for many U.S. corporations, as well as for the United States as a nation. In fact, U.S. corporations, governments, and universities spent some $243.5 billion on R&D in 1999, or about 2.44 percent of GDP. This chart puts that into international perspec-

tive by showing the ratio of R&D spending to GDP for 25 advanced and developing countries. Though the United States ranks first in the total amount of R&D spending, it ranks only seventh among industrialized economies in the fraction of GDP spent on R&D. Not surprising, developing and transition economies invest relatively less in R&D than do developed countries.

Source: World Competitiveness Yearbook 2001, International Institute for Management Development, Lausanne, Switzerland (http://www.imd.ch/wcy).

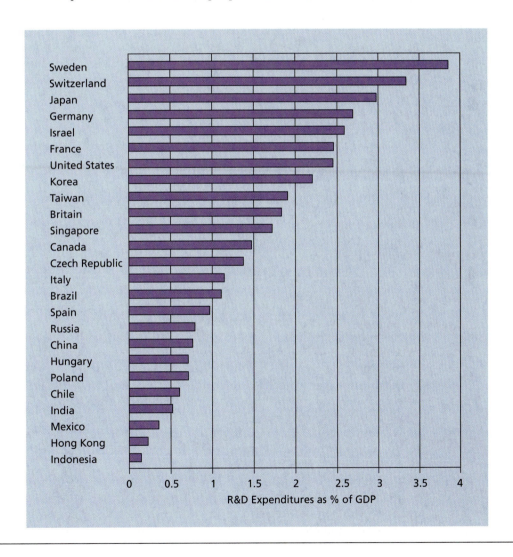

The second investment opportunity (given the code name Project Vegas) is basically a gamble. It also requires an investment of $8 million and offers a 40 percent chance of a $12 million payoff and a 60 percent chance of a $4 million payoff. Because its expected value is only $7.2 million, Vegas is a negative-*NPV* project that the firm's managers would reject if the firm did not have debt outstanding. However, if Vegas succeeds, the project's $12 million payoff will allow the company to fully pay off the bonds and pocket a $2 million profit.

Consider the incentives that managers face. Clearly, bondholders want the managers either to select the low-risk project or retain the firm's cash in reserve. But this is manifestly not in the interests of the firm's shareholders. Because they will lose control of the firm unless they can pay off the creditors' claims in full when they mature, shareholders are effectively "playing with the bondholders' money," and they thus want managers to accept Project Vegas. If successful, the project will yield enough for shareholders to pay off the creditors and retain ownership of the firm. On the other hand, if Project Vegas is unsuccessful, the shareholders will simply hand the firm over to bondholders after defaulting on the maturing bonds, precisely the same outcome that would happen if the firm played it safe. Shareholders have everything to gain and nothing to lose from this strategy, and their agent (the manager) controls the firm's investment policy until default actually occurs. As we will see, bondholders can use restrictive covenants that offer some protection from wealth expropriation by a firm's managers, but these only partially solve the problem.

The Underinvestment Problem

The second game set up by financial distress is **underinvestment.** This also arises when a firm's managers realize default is likely but still control investment policy until default actually occurs. Once more using the example of the firm on the verge of bankruptcy, assume that the firm gains access to a very profitable, but short-lived, investment opportunity. In this case, a longtime supplier offers the company the opportunity to purchase the supplier's excess inventory at a dramatically discounted price, provided that the firm can pay for the inventory immediately with cash. The additional components will cost $9 million today but will allow the firm to increase production and profitability dramatically during the next 30 days. In fact, the firm will be able to sell the additional production so profitably that in 30 days managers expect to have the $10 million cash on hand needed to pay off the maturing bond issue. However, because the firm has only $8 million in cash on hand today, the firm's shareholders must contribute the additional $1 million needed to buy the supplier's inventory. Accepting this project would maximize overall firm value and would clearly benefit the bondholders, but the shareholders would rationally choose not to accept the project because they would have to finance the investment while all the benefit would accrue to the bondholders.[6] In other words, this **debt overhang** problem prevents the financing of newly arriving, positive-*NPV* projects because the benefits would accrue to existing creditors rather than to the shareholders who finance the new project.

An all-equity firm would not be vulnerable to either of these two games associated with financial distress. Managers would always choose the project maximizing firm value in the first example, and would always contribute cash for positive-*NPV* projects in the second example. Because these costs of financial distress are related to conflicts of interest between two groups of security holders, they are also referred to as *agency costs* of the relationship between bondholders and stockholders.

[6.] This incentive problem associated with leverage is first described theoretically in Myers (1977), and the empirical significance of debt's role in limiting growth by firms with poor investment opportunities is documented in Lang, Ofek, and Stulz (1996).

DIRECT AND INDIRECT COSTS OF BANKRUPTCY

Finally, if the process of bankruptcy is itself sufficiently costly, firms have a reason to limit financial leverage in order to minimize the possibility of being forced into the bankruptcy courts. To make clear how this might be possible, we need to differentiate between the direct and indirect costs of bankruptcy. **Direct costs of bankruptcy** are out-of-pocket cash expenses directly related to bankruptcy filing and administration. Document printing and filing expenses, as well as professional fees paid to lawyers, accountants, investment bankers, and court personnel are all examples of direct bankruptcy costs. These can run to several million dollars per month for complex cases. However, empirical research indicates that direct costs are much too small, relative to the prebankruptcy market value of large firms, to provide an effective deterrent to the use of debt financing.[7] In addition, when firms evaluate the merits of using debt, the expected bankruptcy costs become important. In other words, if the direct costs for a given firm are $10 million and the probability of bankruptcy is 10 percent, then the expected bankruptcy costs would be just $1 million.

Indirect bankruptcy costs, as the name implies, are expenses or economic losses that result from bankruptcy but are not cash expenses spent on the process itself. These include the diversion of management's time while bankruptcy is underway, lost sales during and after bankruptcy, constrained capital investment and R&D spending, and the loss of key employees after a firm becomes bankrupt. Even though indirect bankruptcy costs are inherently difficult to measure, empirical research clearly suggests they are quite significant.[8] Recent studies have presented five key findings. First, firms entering bankruptcy have lower sales in the years after filing than they were expected to have based on an extrapolation of prebankruptcy sales growth rates. This evidence supports the intuitive notion that customers may be reluctant to deal with firms close to or mired in bankruptcy proceedings. Second, managers of bankrupt firms lose their jobs much more frequently than do managers of nonbankrupt firms, and the pay of those managers who retain their jobs falls dramatically. Third, U.S. courts frequently deviate from the absolute priority rules that are supposed to govern wealth distributions among security holders. Fourth, bankruptcy costs are much higher in the United States than in other advanced countries, and court decisions generally favor managers over creditors in determining when to liquidate a company. Finally, bankruptcy reduces a firm's debt levels far less than might be expected, and far less than is usually needed, leaving many firms vulnerable to reentering bankruptcy a second or even third time.

Other studies provide indirect evidence that firms facing higher bankruptcy risk use less debt. Researchers have documented three key findings about this relationship. First, companies with highly variable earnings use less debt than do those with more stable profits. Second, the observed leverage ratios across industries are systematically related to that industry's investment opportunities in the way we would expect. Capital-intensive industries with few growth options tend to be highly levered, while technology-based industries with many growth options employ relatively little debt.[9] Third, leverage ratios appear to be directly related to the ease with which a firm's as-

---

[7] For evidence that the direct costs of bankruptcy are usually of essentially trivial magnitude for large firms, see Warner (1977).

[8] Altman (1984) provides the best direct *empirical* evidence to date that the indirect costs of financial distress are large enough to discourage excessive use of financial leverage. Lang and Stulz (1992), Opler and Titman (1994), and Phillips (1995) present evidence that high leverage can weaken a firm's industrial competitiveness.

[9] One of the most interesting recent studies of this kind is by Goyal, Lehn, and Racic (2002). They argue that defense contractors enjoyed tremendous growth opportunities in the early 1980s under the Reagan administration, but many of these opportunities vanished a decade later with the end of the Cold War. The authors find that defense firms used less debt in the 1980s and more in the 1990s.

Figure 13.1
The Agency Cost/Tax
Shield Trade-Off Model
of Corporate Leverage

*This model describes the
optimal level of debt for a
given firm as a trade-off
between the tax benefits
of corporate borrowing
and the increasing bank-
ruptcy costs that come
from additional
borrowing.*

Source: Stewart C. Myers,
"The Capital Structure Puzzle,"
Journal of Finance 39 (July
1984), pp. 575–592.

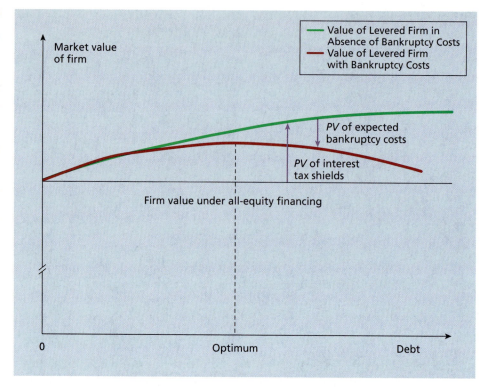

sets can pass through bankruptcy without losing value. Clearly, bankruptcy costs significantly influence capital structure decisions in complex ways. This allows us to expand the basic valuation formula first presented in Chapter 12 to express the value of a levered firm, V_L, in terms of the value of an unlevered firm, V_U, the present value of the benefits from debt and nondebt tax shields, and the present value of expected bankruptcy costs:

$$V_L = V_U + PV \text{ tax shields} - PV \text{ bankruptcy costs} \qquad \text{(Eq. 13.1)}$$

One can begin to understand why this is referred to as the trade-off model, because it assumes that managers trade off the tax-related benefits of increasing leverage against the bankruptcy and agency costs that grow progressively worse as leverage rises. Figure 13.1 describes how bankruptcy costs and tax benefits of leverage interact for a typical firm to determine its optimal debt level. Starting from a capital structure with no debt, managers can increase firm value by replacing equity with debt, thus shielding more cash flow from taxation. In the absence of bankruptcy costs, managers would maximize firm value by borrowing as much as possible, a situation represented by the green line in Figure 13.1. The red line shows how bankruptcy costs alter this conclusion. As a firm borrows more, it increases the probability that it will go bankrupt, and therefore expected bankruptcy costs rise with leverage. At some point, the additional tax benefit from issuing more debt is exactly offset by the increase in expected bankruptcy costs. When that occurs, the red line reaches a maximum and managers have found the mix of debt and equity that maximizes the value of the firm.

International Differences in Bankruptcy Costs

Although we discuss U.S. and international bankruptcy procedures in depth in Chapter 25, a very brief description of institutional details is warranted here. There are similarities in the bankruptcy codes of all advanced economies, but in many ways the differences between these codes are the most important factors in explaining capital structure variations.[10] In the United States, there are two principal types of bankruptcy filings. A **Chapter 7** filing is an application for **liquidation** of the firm's assets and distribution of the proceeds according to the **absolute priority rule,** whereby secured creditors are paid first, then unsecured creditors, then preferred shareholders, and finally common stockholders. A **Chapter 11** filing is a petition for **reorganization** of the firm's liabilities with the implied intent that the reorganized company will continue to operate as an independent business. Provided certain tests are met, each type of bankruptcy filing can be made either by the firm's managers in a voluntary filing, or by the firm's creditors in an involuntary filing. Once a bankruptcy court judge accepts a petition, the court issues an order barring creditors from further prosecution of claims, except as allowed by the court itself. The bankruptcy judge thus effectively becomes the ultimate authority over a company once it enters the court's protection.

Although most major Western countries make a broadly similar distinction between liquidation and reorganization, they differ substantially regarding the rights of creditors during bankruptcy and regarding which party holds the initiative as the process unfolds. In most countries, the judge has the right to appoint a **trustee** to replace the firm's current management team and to oversee liquidation or reorganization, but the countries differ greatly in how often courts appoint trustees. In many European countries, a trustee will generally be appointed unless there is a compelling reason to do otherwise. U.S. bankruptcy law, on the other hand, generally allows corporate managers to remain in control of the firm during reorganization, particularly if there was a voluntary filing. This gives corporate managers significant incentives to file for Chapter 11 voluntarily and then to propose reorganization plans quickly. This not only allows managers to remain in charge, but also gives them the freedom to operate the firm without ongoing collection pressure from creditors.

The results of this debtor bias in U.S. bankruptcy laws have sometimes been disastrous for creditors. Barred from legally enforcing their claims, creditors may be forced to watch as corporate managers operate a bankrupt firm in the interest of managers, employees, and shareholders. The saga of Eastern Airlines is particularly instructive. Had the airline been liquidated immediately after it filed for bankruptcy protection in 1991, creditors would probably have received over 90 cents for each dollar of their claims, and perhaps would have been made entirely whole. Instead of liquidating Eastern, however, the bankruptcy judge handling Eastern's case allowed the airline to operate for almost two more years, at the end of which time the company was essentially worthless. Creditors received less than 10 cents per dollar of their claims. Managers and employees, of course, enjoyed an additional two years of compensation, and shareholders were effectively able to "roll the dice" with the bondholders' money.

Because most other Western countries strike the balance between creditor and debtor rights in bankruptcy more in favor of the former, creditors have less reason to fear an effective expropriation of their wealth in the event that the borrower encoun-

---

[10.] The discussion in this section draws heavily on the material presented in Table VII of Rajan and Zingales (1995). More in-depth coverage of European bankruptcy procedures, as well as an analysis of the implications of the laws' varying terms on corporate financial incentives, is provided in Kaiser (1996).

ters financial distress. Naturally, creditors are thus more willing to lend money to corporate borrowers at attractive rates. Conversely, corporate managers in these countries have more reason to fear financial distress, because there is a much greater chance that they will be quickly fired in the event of default than is likely for their American counterparts. At the margin, this should encourage the managers of non-U.S. firms to use less debt financing than do the managers of similar U.S. companies, and this pattern should be especially noticeable in countries where the bankruptcy laws most favor creditors over debtors. As we will see later, this is what seems to occur.

Concept Review Questions

1. As late as the nineteenth century, people who could not (or would not) pay their debts would be sent to debtors' prison, often for many years. What do you think was the primary rationale for the laws mandating such punishment, and what effect do you think this had on personal borrowing?

2. Revisit the example of the High-Debt and Low-Debt companies. Both the required return on equity and the required return on debt are higher for High-Debt than for Low-Debt. Given this fact, how can the cost of capital for both firms be 10 percent?

3. Suppose that an individual borrows from a bank to buy a new car. A few months later, the borrower realizes that he will have to default on this loan in a few months and the bank will repossess the car. What kind of underinvestment problem might occur here?

4. Suppose that a commercial bank experiences losses on some of its loans and as a result approaches the brink of insolvency. What kinds of asset substitution problems might arise? How might bank regulators try to prevent these problems?

13.2 AGENCY COSTS AND CAPITAL STRUCTURE

An **agency cost theory of financial structure** is put forward by Michael Jensen and William Meckling (1976), and few papers in the history of financial economics have had a comparable impact on how we view issues of corporate control, capital structure, or financial contracting. Jensen and Meckling observe that when an entrepreneur owns 100 percent of the stock of a company, there is no separation between corporate ownership and control. In plain English, this means that the entrepreneur bears all the costs, and reaps all the benefits, of her actions. Once the entrepreneur sells a fraction of the firm's stock to outside investors, she bears only a fraction of the cost of any actions she takes that reduce the value of the firm. This gives the entrepreneur a clear incentive to, in Jensen and Meckling's tactful phrasing, "consume perquisites" (goof off, purchase a corporate jet, frequently tour the firm's plant in Hawaii, become a regular "business commentator" on television, etc.). By selling off a stake in her company, the entrepreneur lowers the cost of engaging in such activity as illustrated in the following example.

APPLYING THE MODEL

Suppose that the founder of a software company sells a 60 percent stake in her firm to outside investors through an initial public offering of common stock. Next, she uses $80,000 of the IPO proceeds to purchase a luxurious, hand-carved mahogany desk for her office. Assuming that this desk does nothing more to make the firm more efficient or profitable than a much cheaper desk would do, the expenditure lowers the value of the firm by roughly $80,000. The reduction in the entrepreneur's shares is just $32,000, equal to the product of the cost of the desk and the entrepreneur's fractional ownership stake (40 percent). In general, if the entrepreneur sells a fraction, α, of the firm's shares to outside investors, she bears just $(1 - \alpha)$ of the cost of any perquisites she consumes. The higher the value of α, the lower the cost to a manager of consuming corporate resources.

This illustrates a nice deal for the entrepreneur, right? Not in an efficient market. Informed investors expect the entrepreneur's performance to change after they purchase their stake α in the firm, and they will thus only pay a price per share that fully reflects the expected decline in firm value that will result from the entrepreneur's consumption of "perks." In other words, the entrepreneur is charged in advance for the perks she is expected to consume after the equity sale, so the entrepreneur once again bears the full costs of her actions. Furthermore, society suffers because these **agency costs of (outside) equity** reduce the market value of corporate assets by $(1 - \alpha)$ times the expected value of entrepreneurial perquisite consumption. We are therefore at an impasse. Selling stock to outside investors creates agency costs of equity, which are borne solely by the entrepreneur, but which also harm society by reducing the value of corporate assets and discouraging additional entrepreneurship. On the other hand, selling external equity is vital for entrepreneurs and to society at large. Selling shares to outside investors allows firms to pursue growth opportunities that would exhaust an entrepreneur's personal wealth, and it permits entrepreneurs to diversify their portfolios.

Using Debt to Overcome the Agency Costs of Outside Equity

Jensen and Meckling (1976) point out that using debt financing can help overcome the agency costs of external equity in two ways. First, using debt, by definition, means that less external equity will have to be sold to raise a given dollar amount of external financing. If agency costs of outside equity rise more than proportionally as α increases, then economizing on the amount of outside equity sold will reduce the deadweight agency costs of the manager/stockholder relationship. The second, and more important, effect of employing outside debt rather than equity financing is that it reduces the scope for excessive managerial perquisite consumption. The burden of having to make regular debt-service payments serves as a very effective tool for disciplining entrepreneurs. With debt outstanding, the cost of excessive perk consumption might well include the entrepreneur losing control of her company following default. In Jensen and Meckling's words, external debt serves as a **bonding mechanism** for managers to convey their good intentions to outside shareholders. Because taking on debt validates a manager's willingness to risk losing control of her firm if she fails to perform effectively, shareholders are willing to pay a higher price for the firm's shares.

You may think this is all esoteric theory, but consider for a minute just how important the agency costs of equity are for a large, publicly traded U.S. corporation. Managers and directors of most Fortune 500 companies collectively own less than 5 percent of their company's shares, yet they reap considerable financial and nonfinancial benefits from controlling a large, prestigious organization. The typical CEO of such a company makes over $9.1 *million* per year in salary, bonuses, and stock options, and some directors receive fees and services worth as much as $100,000 per year for attending fewer than a dozen meetings (Lavelle 2002).

Now, consider what you as an individual shareholder can do to discipline management if you become dissatisfied with the performance of one of the companies in which you have invested. Unfortunately, very little. Even if you represent an institutional investor with a $10 million stake in a large company, your shares represent a tiny fraction of the total outstanding, and management can usually ignore you with impunity. You can vote against management at the annual shareholders' meeting, but the question again becomes, so what? You can sell your shares on the open market, but if management's actions have driven down their market price, who suffers when you sell at a loss? Finally, you can try to sue management for malfeasance, but this is extremely hard to prove because of the **Business Judgment Rule.** This legal doctrine gives directors broad legal discretion to use their business judgment and protects boards of directors from shareholder second-guessing in all but obvious cases of abuse. Although an active takeover market offers you as a shareholder some protection from an entrenched management team, this has proven to be an uncertain and costly disciplining mechanism.

The point of the previous discussion is not to berate inept management teams, but to make clear that agency costs for managers and stockholders are real and are very difficult to reduce effectively. One way the firm can control these costs is to issue debt. This accomplishes two things. First, it subjects managers to direct monitoring by the public capital market.[11] If investors have a negative view of management's competence, they will charge a high interest rate on the money they lend to the firm, or they will insist on restrictive bond covenants to constrain management's freedom of action, or both. Second, debt effectively limits management's ability to reduce firm value through incompetence or perquisite consumption. If management is unable to operate the firm well enough to at least cover interest and principal payments, the firm will be forced into bankruptcy, the bondholders will take control of the firm, and the offending managers will be invited to seek employment elsewhere. By choosing to issue debt, managers voluntarily accept this risk of being replaced, which reduces the agency costs of the manager/stockholder relationship.

Agency Costs of Outside Debt

If debt is such an effective disciplining device, why then don't firms use "maximum debt" financing? The answer is that there are also agency costs of debt. To understand these, keep in mind that as the fraction of debt in a firm's capital structure increases, bondholders begin taking on an increasing fraction of the firm's business and operating risk. However, shareholders and managers still control the firm's investment and operating decisions. This gives managers a variety of incentives to expropriate bondholder wealth for the benefit of themselves and other shareholders. The easiest way to do this would be to float a bond issue, then pay out the money raised to shareholders as a dividend. After default, the bondholders would be left with an empty corporate shell, and limited liability would prevent the bondholders from trying to collect directly from shareholders.[12]

Another way the shareholders can separate bondholders from their wealth is to borrow money on the promise that it will be used to finance a "safe" investment, and then actually invest in a risky project (such as Project Vegas). If lenders are convinced their money will be employed prudently, they will accept a lower interest rate. There-

---

[11.] The logic of using capital market financing requirements as a means of disciplining management is expressed most clearly in Easterbrook (1984).

[12.] Kalay (1982) describes how bondholders protect themselves from firms paying excessive dividends, and Bernando and Talley (1996) examine the perverse investment incentives that outstanding debt can engender for corporate managers who are acting in their shareholders' interest.

fore, if managers and stockholders can find enough naive bondholders, they can borrow at a "safe" interest rate and then make high-risk/high-return investments. If these investments are successful, shareholders can fully repay bondholders and pocket any excess project returns. If the project is unsuccessful, shareholders simply default and bondholders take whatever remains. This game of promising to accept a safe project, then accepting a risky project after securing low-cost financing is often called **bait and switch,** and it can be devastating for bondholders.

As you might imagine, very few naive bondholders are still around, since wisdom comes from survived pain. The surviving, skeptical bond investors take steps to effectively prevent managers from playing these games with their money. The most effective preventive steps bond investors can take involve writing very detailed covenants into bond contracts, which constrain borrowers' actions and limit their ability to expropriate bondholder wealth. Unfortunately, these covenants make bond agreements costly to negotiate and enforce, and may also prevent managers from making value-increasing investments.[13] For example, consider what might happen if a bond covenant limits a firm's ability to issue additional debt of equal or greater seniority (one of the most common covenants). Managers might then pass up value-increasing investments if financing them would require the firm to issue new bonds. Other covenants restrict dividend payments, even for very profitable firms.

In any case, the **agency costs of debt** are real, and they become more important as a firm's leverage ratio increases. Consequently, firms must weigh the benefits of leverage in reducing the agency costs of outside equity against the agency costs of debt.

THE AGENCY COST/TAX SHIELD TRADE-OFF MODEL OF CORPORATE LEVERAGE

Jensen and Meckling's (1976) model predicts that managers of an individual firm, starting from an all-equity position, will substitute bonds for stock in the firm's capital structure in order to reduce the agency costs of equity. As this process continues, however, the agency costs of debt begin to rise at an increasing rate. The firm's optimal (value-maximizing) debt-to-equity ratio is reached at the point where the agency cost of an additional dollar of debt issued exactly equals the agency cost of the dollar of equity retired.

We are now ready to tie together all the threads of the modern agency cost/tax shield trade-off theory of corporate capital structure. This model expresses the value of a levered firm in terms of the value of an unlevered firm, adjusted for the present values of tax shields, bankruptcy costs, and the agency costs of debt and equity, as follows:

$$V_L = V_U + PV \text{ tax shields} - PV \text{ bankruptcy costs}$$
$$+ PV \text{ agency costs of outside equity} - PV \text{ agency costs of outside debt}$$

(Eq. 13.2)

This model provides an intuitively attractive explanation of how capital structures should be set by real corporations. Unfortunately, the individual components of the model are difficult to estimate. This means that although the trade-off model in Equation 13.2 may be theoretically sound, it is difficult to implement in practice. For example, if we want to calculate the optimal capital structure for Microsoft, what do we need to know? The value of the debt tax shield is relatively easy to obtain. Looking

---

[13.] See Macquieira, Megginson, and Nail (1998) for a description of the impact of certain types of bond covenants on the securities of firms involved in stock-swap mergers.

at historical bankruptcy cases, we might derive estimates of the direct and indirect costs of bankruptcy for Microsoft, and we might even estimate the probability that Microsoft would be thrust into bankruptcy given a certain degree of leverage. But how much value would Microsoft create by reducing the agency costs of equity by issuing bonds, and at what debt level would the agency costs of debt outweigh these benefits? Empirical research in finance offers support for the trade-off model, modified to include agency costs of debt and equity, but the model is not sufficiently developed to offer precise recommendations for the optimal capital structures of individual firms. At least not yet.

<table>
<tr>
<td>

**Concept
Review
Questions**

</td>
<td>

5. Think of some rather gaudy corporate perks given to managers, such as a plush office, a company jet, or a luxury box at professional sporting events. How might managers justify these as value-maximizing corporate expenditures that benefit the shareholders?

6. Overinvestment is another type of agency problem in which managers invest in nega-tive-*NPV* projects to increase the size of the firm (as measured by sales or assets). Explain how debt constrains this behavior.

7. Can you think of a retailing analogy of the "bait-and-switch" investment strategy described in this section? Why are these admittedly effective techniques not used more frequently? (Hint: Consider the importance of reputation.)

</td>
</tr>
</table>

13.3 THE PECKING ORDER HYPOTHESIS OF CORPORATE CAPITAL STRUCTURE

Although the trade-off model has to be considered the "mainstream" choice as the dominant capital structure theory today, there are several embarrassing regularities in observed corporate behavior that it has difficulty explaining. Three real-world patterns are particularly hard to reconcile with even the most sophisticated trade-off model. First, within virtually every industry, the most profitable firms have the lowest debt ratios. This is exactly the opposite of what a tax-effect trade-off model would predict, because more-profitable firms can take greater advantage of the tax shield that leverage provides. Second, leverage-increasing events, such as stock repurchases and debt-for-equity exchange offers, are almost invariably associated with positive abnormal returns for a company's stockholders, while leverage-decreasing events lead to stock-price declines. According to the trade-off model, these events should both net out to zero abnormal returns, because some firms will be below their "optimal" debt level when they increase leverage while others will be above the optimum. Third, firms issue debt securities frequently, but seasoned equity issues are very rare, as we saw in Chapter 11. In fact, few large U.S. companies issue new stock as frequently as once per decade, and non-U.S. firms are even less inclined to sell new equity issues. Furthermore, announcements of new issues of seasoned equity are invariably greeted with a large decline in the firm's stock price—sometimes equal to one-third or more of the value of the new offering.

ASSUMPTIONS UNDERLYING THE PECKING ORDER HYPOTHESIS

How do we account for these perplexing facts about observed capital structures? One answer to this question was put forward by Stewart Myers (1984) when he proposed the pecking order theory of corporate capital structure. This model is based on the three empirical patterns that the trade-off theory has trouble explaining, plus four

other observations about corporate financial behavior. First, Myers noted that dividend policy is "sticky." Managers tend to maintain a stable per-share dividend payment, and will neither increase nor decrease dividends in response to temporary fluctuations in current profits.[14] Second, firms prefer internal financing (retained earnings and depreciation) to external financing of any sort, debt or equity. Third, if a firm must obtain external financing, it will choose to issue the safest security first. Finally, as a firm is required to obtain more external financing, it will work down the pecking order of securities, beginning with very safe debt, then progressing through risky debt, convertible securities, preferred stock, and finally, common stock as a last resort. The pecking order model thus focuses on the motivations of the corporate manager.

In its crudest form, this pecking order theory has been in circulation for many years, but was largely ignored by modern economists because it seemed to be based on irrational, value-decreasing corporate behavior that financial natural selection should have excised long before. And, indeed, the simple pecking order model presumes severe market imperfections, such as very high transactions costs, uninformed investors, and managers who are completely insensitive to the firm's stock market valuation. These assumptions are hard to accept as accurate portraits of modern capital markets. Myers provides a firmer justification for the pecking order theory, based on asymmetric information, in a paper with Nicholas Majluf. Myers and Majluf (1984) make two key (and plausible) assumptions about corporate managers. First, they assume a firm's managers know more about the company's current earnings and investment opportunities than do outside investors. Second, they assume managers act in the best interests of the firm's *existing* shareholders.

Why are these two assumptions crucial? The asymmetric information assumption implies that managers who develop or discover a marvelous new positive-*NPV* investment opportunity are unable to convey that information to outsiders because the managers' statements will not be believed. After all, every management team has an incentive to announce wondrous new projects, and investors are unable to verify these claims until long after the fact. Investors will thus assign a low average value to the stocks of all firms and will buy new equity issues only at a large discount from what the stock price would be without informational asymmetries. Corporate managers understand these problems, and in certain cases will refuse to accept positive-*NPV* investments if this would entail issuing new equity, as this would give too much of the project's value to the new shareholders at the expense of the old.

What a dilemma! Investors cannot trust managers, so investors place a low value on common stocks. Managers are thus forced to forgo valuable projects because they cannot credibly convey their private information to existing shareholders. Furthermore, information problems in financial markets are caused by human nature, and thus cannot be resolved through reductions in trading costs or other capital market innovations. What is the solution to this pervasive problem of modern corporate finance? According to Myers and Majluf, the solution is for corporations to retain sufficient *financial slack* to be able to fund positive-*NPV* projects internally.

Financial slack includes a firm's cash and marketable securities holdings, as well as unused debt capacity. Firms with sufficient financial slack will never have to issue equity securities to finance investment projects and are thus able to finesse information problems between managers and investors. In addition, the optimal investment rule of accepting all positive-*NPV* investments without worrying about how to

---

[14] This is one of the most constant phenomena in all of finance. In fact, corporate managers are as intent on maintaining stable nominal dividend payments today as they were when Lintner (1956) first documented this behavior in the 1950s. We discuss dividend policy at length in Chapter 14.

finance them is once again in force, because managers can accept all positive-NPV projects without harming existing shareholders. Perhaps most important, this model provides an explanation for the observed pattern of profitable firms retaining their earnings as equity and building up their cash reserves. These firms are building both financial slack and financial flexibility. An extreme example of this is provided by Microsoft, which had cash and marketable securities holdings worth over $38 billion in 2002.

The pecking order model also explains stock market reactions to leverage-increasing and leverage-decreasing events. Because firms with valuable investment opportunities find a way to finance their projects internally, or use the least risky securities possible if they have to obtain financing externally, the only firms that will issue equity are those with managers who consider the firm's shares to be overvalued. Investors understand these incentives, and also realize that managers are better informed about a firm's prospects than they are. Investors thus always greet the announcement of a new equity issue as "bad news," as a sign that management considers the firm's shares to be overvalued.[15]

In addition to explaining the negative stock market response to leverage-decreasing transactions, and the positive response to leverage-increasing events, the pecking order model provides a rationale for the development of financial intermediaries, based on the pervasiveness of the informational asymmetry between corporate managers and shareholders. Not all companies with positive-NPV investment opportunities will be lucky enough to have financial slack on hand to finance these projects. Young, entrepreneurial growth companies are especially likely to have more valuable investment projects than they can finance through retained earnings, and these companies are also the most prone to experience serious informational asymmetry problems. Banks, venture capitalists, and other financial intermediaries effectively overcome these information problems by becoming corporate "insiders" through repeated contact with the firm's managers and by having proprietary access to the firm's financial statements and operating plans. As mutual trust between management and the intermediary develops, the intermediary can assess and meet the company's financial needs. The intermediary is also in a position to monitor managerial performance and to directly intervene in the firm's operations if necessary. This helps explain the pattern of bank-related corporate financing observed in most advanced countries.

LIMITATIONS OF THE PECKING ORDER THEORY

Unfortunately, the pecking order theory cannot explain all the capital structure regularities observed in practice. For example, it suffers in comparison with the trade-off theory in its inability to explain how taxes, bankruptcy costs, security-issuance costs, and an individual firm's investment opportunities influence that company's actual debt ratio. Furthermore, the theory ignores significant agency problems that can arise when a firm's managers accumulate so much financial slack that they become immune to market discipline. Nonetheless, the pecking order hypothesis seems to explain certain aspects of observed corporate behavior better than other models do, and this is particularly true of corporate financing choices and market responses to security issues (Fama and French 2002).

[15.] This works in reverse, too. The CFO of a Fortune 500 company with billions in cash reserves told us that his company wanted to distribute some of the cash to investors, but management did not want to force investors to pay taxes on high dividend payments, and they were reluctant to repurchase shares because they thought the firm's stock was overvalued.

Concept
Review
Questions

8. What other explanation might there be for the most profitable firms having the lowest leverage, other than that offered by the pecking order theory?

9. Do you think that allowing firms to make a rights issue—sell stock only to their existing shareholders, perhaps at a below-market price—would negate the importance of the informational asymmetry problem described by Myers and Majluf?

10. How do you think the pecking order theory might rationalize the existence of financial intermediaries such as commercial banks?

13.4 SIGNALING AND OTHER ASYMMETRIC INFORMATION MODELS OF CORPORATE LEVERAGE

Beginning in the late 1970s, Ross (1977) and others developed a signaling model of corporate capital structure based on asymmetric information problems between well-informed managers and poorly informed outside shareholders. These models are based on the idea that corporate executives with favorable inside information about their firms have an incentive to convey this information to outside investors in order to increase the firm's stock price. Managers cannot simply announce that they have good news because shareholders will be properly skeptical about such statements.

How Signaling with Capital Structure Can Convey Information

One solution to this problem is for managers of high-value firms (i.e., firms with good news to convey) to *signal* this information to investors by taking some action, or adopting some financial policy, that is prohibitively costly for less-valuable firms to mimic. As used in the finance and economics literature, a **signal** is an action that imposes significant costs on the sender in order to credibly convey information to uninformed outsiders (usually, investors). The cost of the signal makes it credible. For example, suppose that managers of a particular firm have inside information that one of the firm's investments will generate spectacular cash flows in the future. Managers cannot simply hold a press conference to announce this, because any management team can make such a claim in the news media. Instead, managers of the firm could adopt a heavily leveraged capital structure. This capital structure commits the firm to paying out large cash sums to bondholders, a move that a firm with a less-favorable cash flow outlook would be foolish to imitate. In equilibrium, firms that want to signal good news to the market and thereby raise the value of their shares, take on more leverage. Less-valuable companies are unwilling to assume as much debt because they are much more likely to fall into bankruptcy, with all its attendant costs. This allows investors to differentiate between high- and low-value firms simply by observing their capital structures.

Empirical Evidence on Capital Structure Signaling Models

Even though signaling models have intuitive appeal, they enjoy less empirical support than either the trade-off or pecking order theories. As we have seen, leverage ratios are *inversely* related to profitability in almost every industry. Signaling models predict a positive relationship. Furthermore, the signaling model predicts that companies rich

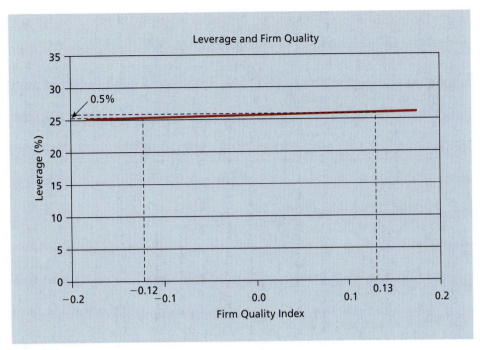

Figure 13.2

The Economic Significance of Signaling with Corporate Leverage Choices

This figure shows the relationship between leverage and firm quality, as measured by abnormal earnings (profit changes from the previous period), or by the Firm Quality Index. The signaling model of corporate leverage predicts that increasing leverage should be positively correlated with an increasing Firm Quality Index. The evidence here shows that this theory garners statistically significant support, but the economic importance of signaling is trivial. This figure shows that moving from the 10th percentile of abnormal earnings in the sample (those firms whose earnings decreased by 12 percent) to the 90th percentile (those whose earnings increased by 13 percent) raised the predicted leverage ratio by only 0.5 percentage points.

Source: Michael J. Barclay, Clifford W. Smith, and Ross L. Watts, "The Determinants of Corporate Leverage and Dividend Policies," *Journal of Applied Corporate Finance* 7 (Winter 1995), pp. 4–19.

in growth options and other intangible assets should employ more debt than mature firms rich in tangible assets because growth companies have more-severe information asymmetry problems, and thus greater need to signal. As we know, exactly the opposite pattern is observed. Asset-rich companies use far more debt than do growth companies. Even in those research studies that present a best-case scenario for signaling theory, the bottom line is discouraging. Barclay, Smith, and Watts (1995) examine signaling models empirically and find they receive support that is statistically significant, but economically trivial. "High-quality" firms do employ more leverage than do "low-quality" ones, after controlling for other factors, but the differences in leverage are very small. As Figure 13.2 illustrates, after firms are ranked based on their recent earnings performance, the difference in leverage ratios between the best and worst firms was negligible.

Signaling models will surely be refined further in the future, and an emerging literature that ties capital structure to specific characteristics of firms' product and factor markets shows a great deal of promise.[16] For now, however, we must look primarily to the trade-off and the pecking order theories for clues about how managers make capital structure choices.

[16.] Harris and Raviv (1991) provide a thorough review of these and other information-based leverage models.

13.5 DEVELOPING A CHECKLIST FOR CAPITAL STRUCTURE DECISION MAKING

Having surveyed the most important theoretical models of corporate leverage and assessed the empirical support for each, we are now in a position to present a tentative summary of what we know about capital structure decision making in the real world. Table 13.2 summarizes the results of over 20 empirical capital structure studies re-

Table 13.2
A Checklist for Capital Structure Decision Making

Variable	Description	Documented Relationship between Variable and Leverage
Firm- and Industry-Specific Operating and Financial Variables		
Profitability	Level of corporate profits	Negative
Market-to-book (MTB) ratio	Market value of firm divided by book value of assets; proxy for growth options	Negative
Earnings volatility	The variability of corporate earnings over time	Negative
Nondebt tax shields	Presence and amount of noninterest tax shields	Negative
Effective tax rate	Effective marginal corporate income tax rate actually faced (not statutory rate)	Positive
Regulation	Is the firm operating in a regulated industry?	Positive
Size	Firm size, measured by assets or sales	Positive
Asset tangibility	Tangible assets as fraction of total assets (similar, but opposite to MTB)	Positive
Growth rate	Rate of growth in firm sales or assets	Ambiguous: Positive Negative
Ownership Structure Variables		
Insider share ownership	Percentage of firm stock owned by officers and directors	Ambiguous: Positive Negative
Managerial entrenchment	Is the management team able to deter internal or external challenges to their tenure?	Negative
Macroeconomic and Country-Specific Variables		
Creditor power in bankruptcy	Do nation's bankruptcy laws support rights of creditors over corporate debtors?	Negative
Corporate income tax rate	Statutory rate of tax on corporate profits	Positive
Personal income tax rate, equity	Statutory personal tax rate on equity income	Negative
State ownership	Is firm a state-owned enterprise?	Positive

Note: This table summarizes the empirically documented relationship between leverage and several operating, financial, ownership structure, tax, and country-specific variables.

garding the relationship between corporate leverage and several operating, owner-ship, and macroeconomic variables. We do not cite the specific articles in this table, as most have already been cited elsewhere, but a complete listing is available upon request. The first line of the table shows that researchers have documented a negative relationship between firm/industry profitability and leverage, meaning that the more profitable a firm or industry is, the lower its leverage will tend to be, holding other things equal. The rest of the table describes the link between leverage and other fac-tors in a similar fashion. The studies surveyed cover a number of different time pe-riods and countries, and in total they offer a fairly complete picture of what we know of how corporate managers actually set capital structures and how investors value the choices made. The independent (explanatory) variables listed in the table fall into three categories: (1) firm- or industry-specific operating and financial variables, (2) ownership structure variables, and (3) macroeconomic and country variables.

We should not, however, overstate our ability to explain the actual steps that corporate managers take in setting their firms' leverage levels. Graham and Harvey's (2001) survey of corporate financial practices, which shows a clear connection be-tween finance theory and practice in the area of capital budgeting, finds little evidence that managers establish capital structures in ways that resemble the models we have discussed here. That may change in time. After all, the widespread use of *NPV* analy-sis in capital budgeting did not occur immediately after the technique was first rec-ommended. Historically, financial theories find their way into practical application gradually (with the possible exception of derivative-pricing theories, which have a much more rapid impact on practice). In any event, Table 13.2 presents the most cur-rent and best evidence regarding corporate leverage decisions we can provide to cor-porate managers.

THE RELATIONSHIP BETWEEN LEVERAGE AND FIRM- AND INDUSTRY-SPECIFIC OPERATING AND FINANCIAL VARIABLES

Profitability

The first section of Table 13.2 summarizes the relationship between financial lever-age and firm- or industry-level characteristics. As predicted by the pecking order the-ory, highly profitable firms tend to use less debt than do less-profitable ones. We do not know the exact reason for the negative leverage/profitability relationship. Is it that highly profitable firms can fund most of their investment projects using retained earnings? Is it that highly profitable firms tend to be rich in growth options that firms must finance with equity rather than debt? Or, is it that more-profitable firms have higher equity market values than less-profitable ones, thus mechanically driving down the market value debt-to-equity ratio? All three explanations probably have some validity.

Market-to-Book Ratio

In addition to studying profitability, empirical studies document a fairly clear nega-tive relationship between leverage and the market-to-book (MTB) ratio. Economists interpret the market-to-book ratio as a measure of the value of a firm's growth op-tions, options that often depend on intangible rather than tangible fixed assets. The negative MTB/leverage relationship verifies one of the more consistent predictions of capital structure models. Other proxies for growth options, such as advertising or re-search and development expenditures as a percentage of sales, also tend to vary in-versely with leverage.

Earnings Volatility

The negative relationship between leverage and earnings volatility verifies the importance of bankruptcy costs in capital structure decision making. The more volatile are a firm's cash flows, the greater the likelihood that earnings in any given period will fail to cover debt-service payments, and the greater the likelihood that the firm will default on its debts. Firms in industries such as mining and petroleum exploration, which often experience wildly fluctuating sales and profits, tend to issue less debt than do firms with less-volatile revenue streams and fewer fixed-cost production technologies.

Nondebt Tax Shields

The negative relationship between leverage and the presence and amount of nondebt tax shields (NDTS) confirms the prediction made by DeAngelo and Masulis (1980). Common sense suggests that firms with unused depreciation allowances, tax loss carryforwards, investment tax credits, and other tax credits or deductions have less incentive to shelter corporate profits from income taxes by paying interest on borrowed funds. Nondebt tax shields substitute for interest tax shields, so firms with high NDTS have lower leverage ratios than other firms. Although earlier, cross-sectional capital structure studies found a positive relationship between NDTS and leverage, more-recent studies that examine the relationship between marginal security-issuance decisions and the presence of NDTS offer strong support for the DeAngelo and Masulis thesis.

Effective Tax Rate

The next variable in Table 13.2, the effective marginal tax rate, is in many ways the inverse of NDTS, because it measures the tax rate charged on the next dollar of pre-tax corporate income. Firms with unused NDTS face a low (perhaps even zero) marginal tax rate. The greater is a firm's marginal tax rate, the stronger its incentive to find ways to shelter income from taxes. Recent empirical studies find convincing evidence of a positive relationship between leverage and the marginal tax rate. The results linking NDTS and marginal tax rates to leverage ratios generally support the trade-off model.

Regulation

Although relatively few empirical studies examine the relationship between leverage and industry regulation, the work that exists suggests that firms in regulated industries use more debt. Industries such as banking, electric power generation, transportation, and telecommunications have historically been subject to stringent regulation, and firms in these industries have higher debt ratios than do unregulated firms. There appear to be several reasons for this tendency. Regulation tends to reduce competition and business risk in an industry, so there is less variability in the earnings streams of regulated firms and thus less danger of the firm encountering financial distress. Investors often believe that regulation involves at least a partial government guarantee that the government will not allow regulated firms to go bankrupt. This implicit insurance makes it feasible for regulated firms to use more leverage.

Recent years have witnessed a sea of change in political ideology in most Western countries, in favor of deregulating many industries, which offers researchers a golden opportunity to test capital structure theories. As countries simultaneously deregulate these industries and open them to competition, we should observe dramatic reductions in leverage ratios of surviving firms. The evidence regarding the deregulation of the U.S. telecommunications industry presented in Barclay, Smith, and Watts (1995) is consistent with this prediction.

Size

Although most capital structure theories make no prediction about the relationship between leverage and firm size, empirical evidence strongly suggests that larger firms borrow more than do smaller ones. This positive relationship between size and leverage could be due to the likelihood that larger, more-established firms have better access to debt capital markets than do less well known smaller firms. Perhaps larger companies control a more diversified pool of assets, resulting in less-variable revenue and earnings streams compared to those of small firms, or perhaps larger firms have fewer growth opportunities to pursue. For whatever reason, larger firms tend to employ more leverage in their capital structures than do smaller firms.

Asset Tangibility

The positive relationship between asset tangibility, defined as tangible assets as a fraction of total assets, and leverage appears in row 8 of Table 13.2. The empirical results support the idea that firms rich in tangible assets use more debt than do firms that invest more heavily in intangibles.

Growth Rate

The final operating/financial variable summarized in Table 13.2 is the relationship between leverage and the firm's growth rate. The empirical evidence here is mixed. Two empirical studies find a positive relationship between growth and leverage, and two find a significant negative relationship. Because the most recent studies find a negative relationship, we tend to lean toward that interpretation of the evidence. The results presented in Lang, Ofek, and Stulz (1996) are especially persuasive as they find that only firms with poor investment opportunities find growth to be hampered by leverage. For firms with better investment opportunities and fewer agency problems between managers and shareholders, the growth/leverage relationship is insignificantly positive. In general, therefore, we conclude that firms that are growing rapidly tend to have less debt in their capital structures than do slower-growing firms, and vice versa.

THE RELATIONSHIP BETWEEN LEVERAGE AND OWNERSHIP STRUCTURE VARIABLES

Although capital structure studies have historically focused on the relationship between leverage and firm- or industry-specific operating or financial variables, several recent studies have examined how a firm's ownership structure influences its capital structure. The relationship between leverage and two ownership variables has received particular attention: officer and director (insider) ownership and the degree to which a firm's current management team is entrenched in office.

Insider Share Ownership

Unfortunately, the empirical results regarding the leverage/insider ownership relationship remain ambiguous. One important recent study by Berger, Ofek, and Yermack (1997) is specifically designed to examine the importance of managerial entrenchment incentives on corporate leverage. This work documents a significant positive relationship, while two other recent studies find that managerial ownership and debt levels are inversely related. In one sense, this ambiguity is not surprising, because there are two potentially offsetting effects of insider shareholdings. On the one hand, a manager/owner with a large holding of stock in his firm would have much to fear from excessive corporate leverage, because both his human and financial capital could be put at risk if the firm encounters financial distress. On the other hand, a manager wishing to protect her tenure in office could do so by substituting debt for equity in her company's capital structure, because this would maximize the voting power of her own stockholdings. At present, empirical research cannot determine which of these two effects dominates.

Managerial Entrenchment

The evidence on the relationship between leverage and managerial entrenchment is much more clear-cut, thanks mostly to Berger, Ofek, and Yermack (1997). These authors show that entrenched management teams prefer to employ little debt, even when this policy is harmful to the firm's shareholders. Intriguingly, the authors find that when an unexpected event, such as a takeover attempt, reduces the perceived entrenchment of a management team, those managers respond in a value-maximizing way by increasing debt and thus committing themselves to distribute more cash flow to investors going forward. In summary, entrenched managers opt for the easy life of a low-debt capital structure, while management teams subject to effective monitoring/disciplining by shareholders employ more leverage.

THE RELATIONSHIP BETWEEN LEVERAGE AND MACROECONOMIC AND COUNTRY-SPECIFIC VARIABLES

A significant body of research compares capital structure policies in different countries. We briefly summarize the key lessons this literature has taught us concerning how a nation's bankruptcy laws, tax policies, and attitudes toward state ownership of corporate assets affect the capital structure decisions made by that country's managers. Although much research remains to be done, the key findings of the current studies are surprisingly clear-cut.

Creditor Power in Bankruptcy

In what is probably the single most influential international capital structure study yet published, Rajan and Zingales (1995) document that one important determinant of a country's average corporate leverage level is the relative power of creditors in bankruptcy court. They show that the two Group of Seven (G7) countries with bankruptcy laws most favorable to creditors, Germany and Great Britain, also have the lowest average market-value corporate debt levels. Though a clear cause-and-effect relationship between creditor power and low leverage cannot be established, these results persuasively suggest that such a relationship exists and influences corporate decision making. When corporate managers know that creditors will have great power over them in the event of financial distress, they are much less likely to tempt fate by borrowing excessively. Conversely, managers in countries like the United States, where the bankruptcy laws tend to favor debtors over creditors, are more willing to adopt a highly leveraged capital structure.

Corporate and Personal Income Tax Rates

Somewhat surprising, given the prominent role that taxes play in capital structure theory, relatively few studies have attempted to estimate the impact of tax-rate changes on leverage decisions. One instance in which estimating the impact of a tax change is relatively straightforward occurs when a country switches from one system of taxing corporate and personal income to a new one. Although this seems a highly unlikely event to most people, Great Britain changed taxation systems no less than four (arguably, six) times between 1947 and 1973, and two of the studies underlying

Table 13.2 examine one or more of these British tax changes. As expected, increases in the corporate income tax rate are associated with increases in average corporate leverage, and vice versa. The same relationship holds for increases in the personal tax rate on equity income (dividends and capital gains).

State Ownership

The final country-specific variable, whether or not a company's stock is owned wholly or in part by the national government, is one that is probably alien to most American readers of this text, but is surely well known to international readers. Most state-owned enterprises are heavily indebted, at least partly because they cannot raise equity capital from private investors. Furthermore, several recent empirical studies of the effect that privatization had on the operating and financial policies of formerly state-owned enterprises indicate that privatization led to a reduction in leverage levels.[17] We therefore conclude that state-owned enterprises tend to use more debt than do otherwise comparable privately owned firms.

Concept Review Questions	**13.** Why do you think managers of highly profitable firms allow the leverage ratios to decline during profitable periods (due to profit retention) rather than pay higher cash dividends and keep leverage high? **14.** If nondebt tax shields (NDTS) substitute for interest charges, why do real estate investment trusts and other firms rich in real estate (which generate large amounts of depreciation and other NDTS) also have very high leverage ratios?

13.6 SUMMARY

- In addition to corporate and personal taxation of income, several characteristics of a firm's asset structure, operating environment, investment opportunities, and ownership structure significantly influence the level of debt that firm will choose to have.
- Firms with large amounts of tangible assets, such as buildings, transportation equipment, and general-purpose machine tools, tend also to use a large amount of debt in their capital structures. These assets can pass fairly easily through bankruptcy with their values intact. In contrast, firms that rely more on intangible assets, such as brand names and research and development spending, tend to use very little financial leverage.
- Creditors know that corporate managers, who operate their firms in the interests of shareholders, have incentives to try to expropriate creditor wealth by playing a series of "games" with the firm's investment policy. Asset substitution is one such game. It involves promising to purchase a safe investment asset to obtain an interest rate reflecting this risk, and then substituting a higher risk asset promising a higher expected return. Creditors protect themselves from these games through a variety of techniques, especially by inserting covenants into loan agreements.
- There are several important agency costs inherent in the relationship between corporate managers and outside investors and creditors. In some cases, using financial leverage can help overcome these agency problems; in others, use of leverage ex-

---

[17.] Megginson, Nash, and van Randenborgh (1994) examine privatizations mainly in developed countries, and Boubakri and Cosset (1998) examine sales in developing countries. More-recent studies also find that leverage declines after privatization.

acerbates the problems. The modern trade-off theory of corporate leverage predicts that a firm's optimal debt level will be set by trading off the tax benefits of increasing leverage against the increasingly severe agency costs of heavy debt usage.

- Two competing theories have been put forth in recent years to explain observed corporate leverage levels. The pecking order theory predicts that managers will operate their firms in such a way as to minimize the need to secure outside financing—for example, by retaining profits to build up financial slack. These same managers will use the safest source of funding, usually senior debt, when they must secure outside financing. The signaling theory predicts that managers will select their firms' leverage levels in order to signal that the firm is strong enough to employ high debt and still fund its profitable investment opportunities.

- Most of the empirical research cited in this chapter tends to support the trade-off theory of corporate leverage over the pecking order or signaling theories, though enough remains unanswered to temper our enthusiasm in crowning a champion.

INTERNET RESOURCES

Note: *For updates to links, please go to the book's website at http://smart.swcollege.com*

http://www.quicken.com; http://www.yahoo.com; http://www.sec.gov—Three sites from which you can download leverage figures for specific companies and compare them to figures for firms in the same industry as well as firms in other industries

http://www.bondsonline.com—A site that offers a wealth of information regarding bonds

http://www.standardandpoors.com—A site with information on bond ratings and the latest changes to ratings on outstanding bonds

KEY TERMS

absolute priority rule	debt overhang
agency cost theory of financial structure	direct costs of bankruptcy
agency costs of (outside) equity	equity carve-out
agency costs of debt	indirect bankruptcy costs
asset substitution	liquidation
bait and switch	option to default
bankruptcy costs	reorganization
bonding mechanism	signal
Business Judgment Rule	trustee
Chapter 11	underinvestment
Chapter 7	

QUESTIONS

13-1. Aside from corporate and personal taxes, what factors affect the relationship between firm value and the use of leverage?

13-2. Empirically, what does research say regarding the three principal nontax factors that influence capital structure decisions? Specifically, what are the general relationships between these factors and the level of leverage employed by firms?

13-3.   Why do a firm's stockholders hold a valuable "default option"? Why might this option induce stockholders to employ high levels of financial leverage?

13-4.   All else equal, which firm would face a greater level of financial distress, a software-development firm or a hotel chain? Why would financial distress costs affect the firms so differently?

13-5.   Describe how managers of firms that have debt outstanding and face financial distress might jeopardize the investments of creditors with the "games" of asset substitution and underinvestment.

13-6.   Differentiate between direct and indirect costs of bankruptcy. Which of the two is generally more significant?

13-7.   What empirical results have been documented regarding indirect bankruptcy costs? What have other empirical studies shown regarding the relationship between the risk of bankruptcy and levels of leverage?

13-8.   What are some of the differences in U.S bankruptcy laws and those in place internationally? What incentives do these differences provide for U.S. managers? For their peers in most other countries?

13-9.   What is meant by the use of external debt as a bonding mechanism for managers? In what way does this bonding mechanism reduce the agency costs of external equity? How can restrictive covenants in bonds be both an agency cost of debt and a way to prevent agency costs of debt?

13-10.   What are the trade-offs in the agency cost/tax shield trade-off model? How is the firm's optimal capital structure determined under the assumptions of this model? Does empirical evidence support this model?

13-11.   What is the main premise underlying the pecking order theory of capital structure? What is the "pecking order" of sources of financing? Why is dividend policy so important to this model? How does the concept of financial slack relate to this model?

13-12.   How and what type of information is conveyed in a signaling model of capital structure? According to this model, how should leverage affect the market value of firms? Does empirical evidence support this model?

13-13.   Outline the empirically defined relationships between leverage and firm- or industry-specific operating and financial variables. In general, which of the models of capital structure are supported by these results?

13-14.   What capital structure choices might managers seeking to entrench themselves choose? How does this decision relate to the bonding mechanism discussed earlier?

13-15.   A CFO says that her firm chooses a capital structure that allows it to maintain a credit rating of AA. She reasons that a credit rating of AAA would be too conservative, but anything less than AA would be too risky. What capital structure model does this firm appear to follow?

PROBLEMS

Costs of Bankruptcy and Financial Distress

13-1.   Using the data presented in Table 13.1, compute the following ratios for the years provided:

   a. Business versus nonbusiness bankruptcy filings
   b. Voluntary versus nonvoluntary bankruptcy filings
   c. Liquidations (Chapters 7 and 13 of the Bankruptcy Code) versus reorganizations (Chapter 11) as a percentage of total filings

13-2. Using the ratios computed in Problem 13-1, discuss whether the following statements are true or false:

    a. There is a trend toward more business bankruptcy filings and fewer nonbusiness bankruptcy filings over time.

    b. The total number of bankruptcies filed for and pending does not appear to be sensitive to business conditions, but instead has been increasing steadily over time.

    c. Reorganization filings represent a fairly constant percentage of total filings over time.

13-3. Assume that you are the manager of a financially distressed corporation with $1.5 million in debt outstanding that will mature in two months. Your firm currently has $1 million cash on hand. Assuming that you are operating the firm in the shareholders' best interests and that debt covenants prevent you from simply paying out the cash to shareholders as cash dividends, what should you do?

13-4. Using the data from Problem 13-3, assume that you are offered the opportunity to invest in either of the two projects described below.

    Project 1: the opportunity to invest $1 million in risk-free Treasury bills, with a 4 percent annual interest rate

    Project 2: a high-risk gamble, which will pay off $1.6 million in two months if successful (probability = 0.4), but will only pay $400,000 if unsuccessful (probability = 0.6)

    a. Compute the expected payoff for each project, and state which one you would adopt if you were operating the firm in the shareholders' best interests? Why?

    b. Which project would you accept if the firm were unlevered? Why?

    c. Which project would you accept if the company were organized as a partnership rather than a corporation? Why?

13-5. A firm has the choice of investing in one of two projects. Both projects last one year. Project 1 requires an investment of $11,000 and yields $11,000 with a probability of 0.5 and $13,000 with a probability of 0.5. Project 2 also requires an investment of $11,000 and yields $5,000 with a probability of 0.5 and $20,000 with a probability of 0.5. The firm is capable of raising $10,000 of the investment required through a bond issue carrying an annual interest rate of 10 percent. Assuming that the investors are concerned only about expected returns, which project would stockholders prefer? Why? Which project would bondholders prefer? Why?

13-6. An all-equity firm has 100,000 shares outstanding worth $10 each. The firm is considering a project requiring an investment of $400,000 and has an *NPV* of $50,000. The company is also considering financing this project with a new issue of equity.

    a. What is the price at which the firm needs to issue the new shares so that the existing shareholders are indifferent to whether the firm takes on the project with this equity financing or does not take on the project?

    b. What is the price at which the firm needs to issue the new shares so that the existing shareholders capture the full benefit associated with the new project?

13-7. You are the manager of a financially distressed corporation that has $5 million in loans coming due in 30 days. Your firm has $4 million cash on hand. Suppose that a long-time supplier of materials to your firm is planning to exit the business but has offered to sell your company a large supply of material at a bargain price of $4.5 million—but only if payment is made immediately in cash. If you choose not to acquire this material, the supplier will offer it to a competitor, and your firm will have to acquire the materials at market prices totaling $5 million over the next few months.

    a. Assuming that you are operating the firm in shareholders' best interests, would you accept the project? Why or why not?

    b. Would you accept this project if the firm were unlevered? Why or why not?

   c. Would you accept the project if the company were organized as a partnership? Why or why not?

Agency Costs and Capital Structure

Smart Solutions
See the problem and solution explained step-by-step at
SMARTFinance

13-8. Using the data in Problem 12-8 on pages 439 and 440, compute the value of Herculio Mining, assuming that the present value of bankruptcy costs are $10 million.

13-9. Slash and Burn Construction Company currently has no debt and expects to earn $10 million in net operating income each year for the foreseeable future. The required return on assets for construction companies of this type is 12.5 percent, and the corporate tax rate is 40 percent. There are no taxes on dividends or interest at the personal level. Slash and Burn calculates that there is a 10 percent chance that the firm will fall into bankruptcy in any given year, and if bankruptcy does occur, it will impose direct and indirect costs totaling $12 million. If necessary, use the industry required return for discounting bankruptcy costs.

   a. Compute the present value of bankruptcy costs for Slash and Burn.
   b. Compute the overall value of the firm.

13-10. Using the data from Problem 13-9, calculate the value of Slash and Burn Construction Company, assuming that the firm's shareholders face a 25 percent personal tax rate on equity income.

13-11. Assume that the managers of Slash and Burn Construction Company, described in Problem 13-9, are weighing two capital structure alteration proposals. Proposal 1 involves borrowing $20 million at an interest rate of 6 percent and using the proceeds to repurchase an equal amount of outstanding stock. With this level of debt, the likelihood that Slash and Burn will fall into bankruptcy in any given year increases to 15 percent, and if bankruptcy occurs, it will impose direct and indirect costs totaling $12 million. Proposal 2 involves borrowing $30 million at an interest rate of 8 percent, also using the proceeds to repurchase an equal amount of outstanding stock. With this level of debt, the likelihood of Slash and Burn falling into bankruptcy in any given year rises to 25 percent, and the associated direct and indirect costs of bankruptcy, if it occurs, increase to $20 million. For each proposal, calculate both the present value of the interest tax shields and the overall value of the firm, assuming that there are no personal taxes on debt or equity income.

Developing a Checklist for Capital Structure Decision Making

13-12. Go to the home page for Ford Motor Company (http://www.ford.com), and search for its most recent annual report to shareholders. Within this report, find management's discussion and analysis of financial condition and results of operations. Find management's discussion about liquidity and capital resources about halfway through the report. How large a cash position does Ford hold? How large is this cash position relative to Ford's overall capital structure (also found in the annual report)? Does this indicate a preference for or against financial slack by Ford's management?

14

Dividend Policy

OPENING FOCUS
British Airways Cuts Dividend to Preserve Cash during Airline Crisis

To say that the period immediately following the September 11, 2001, terrorist attacks on the World Trade Center and Pentagon was a difficult one for the world's airlines would be a serious understatement. Traffic on all the major airlines fell precipitously, and almost all were forced to cut both staff and schedules quite severely. Within weeks of the attack, two major European carriers—Swissair and Sabena—filed for bankruptcy protection, and several other international carriers appeared on the brink of following suit. The threat to the viability of the U.S. airline industry was so severe, in fact, that the major carriers successfully lobbied the U.S. Congress for an unprecedented $15 billion bailout package. Even with this financial lifeline, U.S. carriers announced job cuts of over 120,000 people in the weeks following September 11.

British Airways (BA) faced all these pressures and more during the fall of 2001, especially because most of BA's scheduled flights were international rather than domestic, and these had suffered the largest drops in demand following the attacks. The following figure shows how the stock price for British Airways (ticker symbol, BAV) fared compared to the overall UK stock market (UKX) in the weeks and months after September 11. In response to the financial pressures weighing on the firm, British Airways took the unprecedented step in early October 2001 of suspending its interim (semiannual) dividend payment, which it normally paid in December, and announcing that its full-year dividend payment for fiscal year 2002 was in serious jeopardy. This dividend suspension was very traumatic for BA because the company had taken great pride in paying a dividend every six months since its privatization in 1987. Over the years, its dividend payment had increased steadily and stood at $1.82 per share for fiscal year 2001. In line with industry norms, this payment represented over 57 percent of BA's net profits for 2001. But with massive financial losses looming and job cuts of 7,000 employees al-

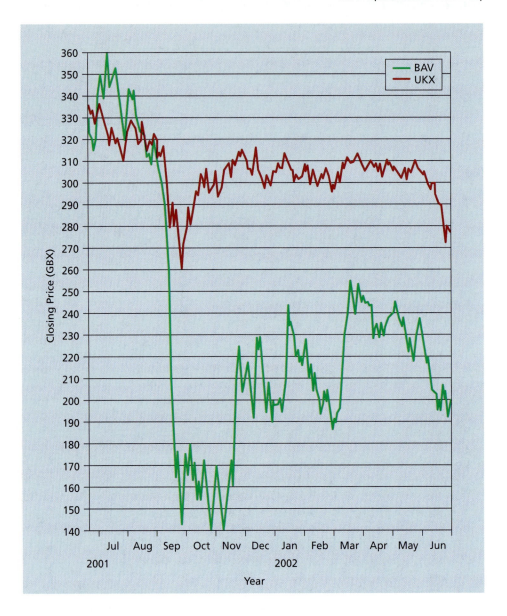

ready announced, BA's managers felt there was no alternative to eliminating dividend payments. Because the chief executive officer had already announced he would take a salary cut and the firm had told the British government it might need a bailout package similar to that given to the American airline industry, the firm was fighting for financial survival.

Sources: Kevin Done and Cathy Newman, "BA's Dividend Warning Signals Trouble," *Financial Times* (October 7, 2001), p. 10; and data from http://money.cnn.com and the BA website (http://www.britishairways.com).

A firm's *dividend policy* refers to its choice of whether to pay shareholders a cash dividend, how large the cash dividend should be, and how frequently it should be distributed. In a broader sense, dividend policy also encompasses decisions such as whether to distribute cash to investors via share repurchases or specially designated dividends rather than regular dividends, and whether to rely on stock rather than cash distributions. Though there are numerous elements in the dividend decision, modern corporations still struggle with the same issues that, according to Lintner (1956), occupied managers in the 1950s. Managers must decide if the firm should maintain its current dividend or change it. Managers tend to increase regular dividends only when they expect future cash flow sufficient to pay the dividends and meet the firm's other financial needs. Firms must also weigh the stock market's reaction to changes in dividend policy. Influencing that reaction are factors such as the level of a firm's dividends, the volatility of the dividend stream over time, and the income taxes that investors must pay when they receive dividends. As you might expect, the many dimensions of this problem make dividend policy decisions quite difficult, at least for some firms.

In addition to these firm-level issues regarding dividend policy, two recent trends in the aggregate dividend decisions of U.S. firms interest us. The first of these is the phenomenal growth in both the number of firms implementing **share repurchase programs** and in the total value of these programs. A company announcing a share repurchase program states that it will buy some of its own shares over a period of time. In executing a repurchase program, the firm distributes some of the cash it has accumulated to investors who wish to sell their shares. Therefore, dividends and share repurchases are alternative means by which firms distribute cash to investors. In fact, aggregate share repurchases in the United States often exceed aggregate dividends.

The second, dramatic trend in corporate dividend policy is the very sharp decline in the percentage of publicly traded U.S. companies that pay any dividends at all. As Panel A of Figure 14.1 demonstrates, the percentage of all publicly traded firms paying dividends was four times greater in the 1950s than it is today. Panel B of the figure breaks this out by exchange. Additionally, those firms that do pay dividends pay out a lower fraction of their earnings now than in the past. Stated differently, companies have a lower *propensity* to pay dividends today than in years past. As we will see, both of these patterns appear to reflect the changing nature of publicly listed companies in the United States, as increasing numbers of young, rapidly growing technology companies that consume more cash than they generate have "gone public" over the past three decades.

Our objective in this chapter is to answer two basic questions. First, does dividend policy matter? Can managers increase or decrease the total market value of a firm's securities by changing its dividend payments? Second, if dividend policy does matter, what factors determine a firm's optimal dividend policy? Before attacking these questions, however, we will provide a brief overview of the fundamentals of dividend payments, defining the key terms and discussing the basic issues corporate managers everywhere must face in setting dividend policies. Section 14.2 provides an overview of dividend payment patterns around the world as a way of motivating a modern theory of dividends. Section 14.3 develops this theory by describing the significance of dividends in a world without market frictions such as taxes and trading costs. You will not be surprised to hear that in such a world, dividend policy is irrelevant. Section 14.4 describes how real-world market imperfections affect actual dividend policy decisions. Section 14.5 presents a summary of the predictions of the current "mainstream" model of dividend policy and also presents a checklist that practicing managers can use to set dividend policies for their firms.

14.1 DIVIDEND FUNDAMENTALS

In Chapter 4, we argued that the value of a share of stock equals the present value of cash flows that the shareholder receives over time. Even if a company is not paying dividends (or repurchasing shares) today, its market value reflects the likelihood either that the firm will pay dividends in the future or that it will be acquired in the future by another company at a price that reflects a higher stream of dividend payments.

Figure 14.1
The Fraction of Publicly
Traded U.S. Firms Paying
Cash Dividends,
1926–1999

*This figure details the
percentage of all publicly
traded firms in the United
States that paid regular
cash dividends over
the period 1926–1999.
Panel A of the figure
shows this for all publicly
traded firms, and Panel B
breaks this out by
exchange from 1962
(AMEX) and 1972
(Nasdaq) onward.*

Source: Eugene F. Fama and
Kenneth R. French, "Disap-
pearing Dividends: Changing
Firm Characteristics or Lower
Propensity to Pay?" *Journal of
Applied Corporate Finance* 14
(Spring 2001), pp. 67–79.

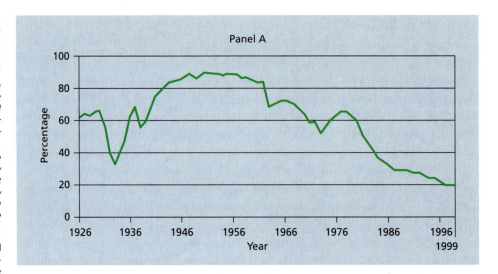

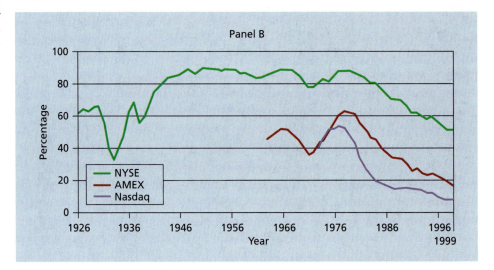

To provide an understanding of the fundamentals of dividend policy, we discuss the
procedures for paying cash dividends and the factors affecting dividend policy.

CASH DIVIDEND PAYMENT PROCEDURES

In the United States, as in most countries, shareholders do not have a legal right to
receive dividends. Instead, a firm's board of directors must decide whether to pay
dividends. The directors usually meet to evaluate the firm's recent financial performance and future outlook and to determine whether and in what amount dividends
should be paid. The payment date of the cash dividend, if one is declared, must also
be established.

Most U.S. firms that pay cash dividends do so once every quarter, whereas corporations in other industrialized countries commonly pay dividends annually or semiannually. Firms adjust the size of their dividends periodically, but not necessarily every
quarter. For example, among the roughly 1,100 U.S. firms that paid dividends continuously from 1997 to 2001, just over 30 percent changed their dividend once per
year, on average. About 13 percent of these firms maintained a constant dividend dur-

ing this 5-year span, and about 24 percent changed their dividend more frequently than once per year. Only 4 of the 1,100 firms changed their dividend every quarter.[1] These figures suggest that firms maintain a constant dividend until significant increases or decreases in earnings justify changing the dividend.

Relevant Dates

If a firm's directors declare a dividend, they also set the dividend record and payment dates. The day the firm releases this information to the public is the **announcement date.** All persons whose names are recorded as stockholders on the **date of record** receive the declared dividend at a specified future time. The stockholders who own shares on this *record date* are often referred to as *shareholders of record*. Due to the time needed to make bookkeeping entries when a stock is traded, the stock begins selling **ex dividend** several business days prior to the date of record. Purchasers of a stock selling ex dividend do not receive the current dividend. Ignoring general market fluctuations, the stock's price should drop by approximately the amount of the declared dividend on the ex-dividend date. For example, suppose a stock that pays a $1 dividend sells for $51 just before going ex dividend. Once the ex-dividend date passes, the price should drop to $50 in the absence of any other news affecting the stock. However, the average ex-dividend day price drop in the United States and many other countries is significantly less than 100 percent of the value of the dividend payment, partly due to what appears to be a personal tax effect. The **payment date** is generally set a few weeks after the record date. The payment date is the actual date on which the firm mails the dividend payment to the holders of record.

APPLYING THE MODEL

On April 25, 2002, Bausch & Lomb announced that it would cut its quarterly dividend payment in half, from $0.26 per share to $0.13. The dividend would be paid to shareholders of record as of June 3, and the stock would trade ex dividend as of May 30. The firm's directors set the payment date at July 1. On news of the dividend cut, Bausch & Lomb shares fell $1.26, or 3.4 percent. When the ex-dividend date arrived, Bausch & Lomb shares fell an additional $0.19. Notice two key patterns in this example. First, the large decline in Bausch & Lomb shares occurred on the announcement date, more than one month before the stock went ex dividend. Investors apparently interpreted the company's decision to cut dividends as a signal that Bausch & Lomb would be less profitable than they previously believed it would be. Second, the decline in Bausch & Lomb stock on the ex-dividend date was more than the dividend amount. In addition to the fact that on May 31, shareholders no longer had the right to the $0.13 dividend, there must have been other unfavorable news that pushed the stock down a little bit more.   ▪

External Factors Affecting Dividend Policy

Before discussing the basic types of dividend policies, we should briefly consider some of the practical factors involved in formulating a value-maximizing policy (theoretical issues will be discussed in later sections). These include legal constraints, contractual constraints, internal constraints, the firm's growth prospects, and owner considerations.

Most U.S. states prohibit corporations from paying out as cash dividends any

---

[1.] Author's calculations are from Compustat, excluding closed-end mutual funds, real estate investment trusts (REITs), and other investment companies.

Table 14.1
Calculating the Maximum
Amount a Firm Can Pay
in Cash Dividends

Alpha Corporation's Stockholders' Equity	
Common stock at par	$100,000
Paid-in capital in surplus of par	200,000
Retained earnings	140,000
Total stockholders' equity	$440,000

portion of the firm's "legal capital," which is measured by the par value of common stock. Other states define legal capital to include not only the par value of the common stock, but also any paid-in capital in excess of par. States establish these *capital-impairment restrictions* to provide a sufficient equity base to protect creditors' claims. The example presented for the Alpha Corporation in Table 14.1 will clarify the differing definitions of capital.

In states where the firm's legal capital is defined as the par value of its common stock, Alpha could pay out $340,000 ($200,000 paid-in capital in excess of par + $140,000 retained earnings) in cash dividends without impairing its capital. In states where the firm's legal capital includes all paid-in capital, the firm could pay out only $140,000 (the value of retained earnings) in cash dividends. An earnings requirement limiting the amount of dividends to the sum of the firm's present and past earnings is sometimes imposed. In other words, Alpha cannot pay more in cash dividends than the sum of its most recent and historic retained earnings. However, *laws do not prohibit the firm from paying more in dividends than its current earnings.*

If a firm has overdue liabilities or is legally insolvent or bankrupt (if the fair market value of its assets is less than its liabilities), most states prohibit cash dividends. In addition, the Internal Revenue Service prohibits firms from accumulating earnings to reduce the owners' taxes. A firm's owners must pay income taxes on dividends when received, but the owners pay no tax on capital gains until they sell the stock. A firm may retain a large portion of earnings to delay the payment of taxes by its owners. If the IRS can determine that a firm has accumulated excess earnings to allow owners to delay paying ordinary income taxes, it may levy an **excess earnings accumulation tax** on any retained earnings above a specified amount. This rarely occurs in practice, however.

Restrictive provisions in loan agreements sometimes constrain a firm's ability to pay cash dividends. Generally, these constraints prohibit cash dividends until the firm achieves a certain level of earnings, or they may limit dividends to a certain dollar amount or percentage of earnings.[2] Constraints on dividend payments help protect creditors from losses due to insolvency. If a firm violates one of these contractual restrictions, creditors generally have the right to demand immediate repayment on their loans.

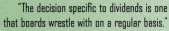

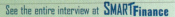
TYPES OF DIVIDEND POLICIES

The following sections describe three basic dividend policies, though one should bear in mind that the constant nominal dividend policy predominates in every major economy. A particular firm's cash dividend policy may incorporate elements of each policy type.

[2.] Specific bond covenant constraints on dividend payment policy are discussed in depth in Smith and Warner (1979) and Kalay (1982).

Constant Payout Ratio Policy

One type of dividend policy that is only rarely adopted by firms is a constant payout ratio. The **dividend payout ratio,** calculated by dividing the firm's cash dividend per share by its earnings per share, indicates the percentage of each dollar earned that is distributed to the owners. With a **constant payout ratio dividend policy,** the firm establishes that a certain percentage of earnings is paid to owners in each dividend period. The problem with this policy is that if the firm's earnings drop or if a loss occurs in a given period, the dividends may be low or even nonexistent, and will in any case be as volatile as the firm's earnings.

Constant Nominal Payment Policy

Another type of dividend policy, the **constant nominal payment policy,** is based on the payment of a fixed-dollar dividend in each period. Often, firms using this policy increase the regular dividend once a *proven* increase in earnings has occurred. Under this policy, a firm almost never cuts dividends unless it faces a true crisis.[3]

Firms that pay a steady dividend may build their policy around a **target dividend payout ratio.** Under this policy, the firm attempts to pay out a certain percentage of earnings, but rather than let dividends fluctuate, it pays a stated dollar dividend and adjusts it toward the target payout slowly as proven earnings increases occur. This is known as a *partial-adjustment strategy,* and it implies that at any given time, many firms will be in a transition between two dividend payment levels.

Low-Regular-and-Extra Policy

Some firms establish a **low-regular-and-extra policy** paying a low regular dividend, supplemented by an additional cash dividend when earnings warrant it. If earnings are higher than normal in a given period, the firm may pay this additional dividend, which is designated an **extra dividend** or a **special dividend.** By designating the amount by which the dividend exceeds the regular payment as an extra dividend, the firm avoids giving shareholders false hopes. The use of the "extra" or "special" designation is more common among companies that experience temporary shifts in earnings.[4] For example, in late 2002, interest rates on residential mortgages declined to the lowest level in 35 years, and as a result, many homeowners refinanced their loans. The refinancing boom resulted in a sharp increase in fees earned by banks and other financial institutions active in the mortgage market, and many of these companies paid special dividends as a way to distribute some of this cash to investors.

OTHER FORMS OF DIVIDENDS

In addition to paying cash dividends, firms often employ three other methods of distributing either cash or securities to investors: stock dividends, stock splits, and share repurchases.

Stock Dividends

A **stock dividend** is the payment to existing owners of a dividend in the form of stock. For example, if a firm declares a 20 percent stock dividend, it will issue 20 new shares

---

[3.] The Fall 2001 issue of the *Journal of Portfolio Management* described a unique variant of a constant dividend payment strategy. The Smith Company is a private investment company whose primary objective is to provide a constant stream of real dividend payments to approximately 100 members of the Smith family. In other words, the company aims to pay out an inflation-adjusted dividend stream with constant purchasing power over time.

[4.] Evidence that investors are quite savvy about interpreting the information in these dividends is presented in Brickley (1983), Lie (2000), and DeAngelo, DeAngelo, and Skinner (2000).

for every 100 shares that an investor owns. Often, firms pay stock dividends as a replacement for, or a supplement to, cash dividends.[5] Keep in mind that a stock dividend does not necessarily increase the value of an investor's holdings. If a firm pays a 20 percent stock dividend, and nothing else about the firm changes, then the number of outstanding shares increases by 20 percent and the stock price drops by 20 percent. The net effect on shareholder wealth is neutral. Shareholders receiving stock dividends also maintain a constant proportional share in the firm's equity.

Stock Splits

Stock splits have an effect on a firm's share price similar to that of stock dividends. When a firm conducts a stock split, its share price declines because the number of outstanding shares increases. For example, in a 2-for-1 split, the firm doubles the number of shares outstanding. As in the case of a stock dividend, intuition suggests that stock splits should not create value for shareholders. After all, if someone offers to give you two $5 bills in exchange for one $10 bill, you are no better off.

We have often stated that managers should strive to increase stock prices, not decrease them. In the case of a stock split (or stock dividend), if the decrease in share prices is proportional to the change in shares outstanding, the net effect on shareholder wealth is zero (ignoring the administrative costs of doing the split). Managers nevertheless decide to engage in stock splits because they believe that if the price per share gets too high, some investors (especially individual investors) will no longer trade the stock. A stock split also has no effect on the firm's capital structure; it simply increases the number of shares outstanding and reduces the stock's per-share par value.

APPLYING THE MODEL

Since going public in March 1986, Microsoft has split its stock eight times, most recently on March 26, 1999. Just before the last stock split, Microsoft shares traded for about $178 per share. After the 2-for-1 split, the shares dropped to $92.[6] An investor who purchased a single Microsoft share in its IPO in 1986 would own 144 Microsoft shares today. Put another way, taking Microsoft's stock performance since its IPO as given, if the company had never split its stock, the price by June 2002 would have been almost $8,000 per share. ■

Though most stock splits increase the number of shares outstanding, firms sometimes conduct **reverse stock splits,** in which the firm replaces a certain number of outstanding shares with just one new share. For example, in a 1-for-2 split, one new share replaces two old shares; in a 2-for-3 split, two new shares replace three old shares; and so on. Firms initiate reverse stock splits when their stock is selling at a very low price, perhaps so low that the exchange on which the stock is listed threatens to delist the stock.

APPLYING THE MODEL

In the wake of the collapse of Internet company stock prices, the Nasdaq began to drop firms that failed to meet its minimum price requirement. Nasdaq gave many firms a reprieve after the September 11, 2001, terrorist attacks, but by the beginning

---

[5.] Though hardly rare in the United States, stock dividends are much more commonly observed in Britain, where they are called "scrip dividends." These are discussed at length in Lasfer (1997) and Ang, Blackwell, and Megginson (1991).

[6.] Notice that Microsoft shares did not fall by 50 percent as we would expect in a 2-for-1 split. This is a common pattern that presents something of a puzzle to financial economists. Investors seem to view stock splits as good news, even though a split does nothing but change the number of shares outstanding.

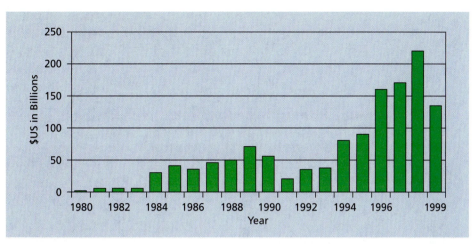

Figure 14.2
Market Value of Share Repurchase Announcements, 1980–1999

This figure plots the total value of share repurchase programs announced by U.S. companies over the period 1980–1999.

Source: Gustavo Grullon and David L. Ikenberry, "What Do We Know about Stock Repurchases?" *Journal of Applied Corporate Finance* 13 (Spring 2000), pp. 31–51, fig. 1.

of 2002, Nasdaq warned firms that they had four months to comply with the exchange's rules. Among them was the requirement to sustain a stock price in excess of $1 per share for at least 30 consecutive days. Former Internet darlings such as Razorfish Inc. and Rare Medium Group Inc. asked shareholders to accept reverse splits ranging from 1-for-10 to 1-for-30 to avoid being removed from Nasdaq.

Share Repurchases

U.S. firms have dramatically increased repurchases of their own outstanding common stock in recent years, particularly since 1982. In that year, an SEC ruling clarified when companies could and could not repurchase their shares without fear of being charged with insider dealing or price manipulation. Figure 14.2, taken from a recent study by Grullon and Ikenberry (2000), illustrates the dramatic growth in repurchases. The practical motives for stock repurchases include obtaining shares to be used in acquisitions, having shares available for employee stock option plans, and retiring shares. From a broader perspective, the rising importance of share repurchases implies that they enhance shareholder value, perhaps because they are a tax-advantaged method of distributing corporate cash. Though it is not clear exactly what managers are trying to achieve through repurchases, frequently mentioned rationales include (1) sending a *positive signal* to investors in the marketplace that management believes that the stock is undervalued, (2) reducing the number of shares outstanding and thereby raising earnings per share (*EPS*), and (3) providing a temporary floor for the stock price, which may have been declining. The last two of these rationales have logical flaws. Reducing the number of shares outstanding will indeed lead to an increase in *EPS*, assuming net income remains constant or increases, but for this alone to increase value, *EPS* must increase proportionally more than the percentage reduction in shares outstanding. It is equally unclear exactly how "creating a floor" under a stock price creates value if it is achieved using the firm's own money for repurchases.

To see the tax advantages of share repurchases, consider a firm that is weighing the choice of distributing $2 million as a cash dividend or as a share repurchase. If the firm pays a cash dividend, the shareholders must pay ordinary income taxes on the dividend.[7] However, if the firm buys back $2 million worth

SMART IDEAS VIDEO
Scott Lee, Texas A&M University
"Generally associated with repurchase announcements is a fairly strong market response."

See the entire interview at **SMARTFinance**

[7.] As this book went to press, President Bush sent a major tax package to Congress that includes a provision that effectively eliminates double taxation of stock dividends. If passed, the tax law would no longer make dividends taxable to their recipient.

Figure 14.3
Average Stock
Market Reaction to
Share Repurchase
Announcements

*Plot of cumulative mean
rates of return for com-
mon stocks over a 121-
day period around the an-
nouncement of a tender
offer to repurchase com-
mon stock (143 observa-
tions). The figure shows
that stock prices increased
on average by about 15%
in response to tender of-
fer announcements*

Source: Larry Y. Dann, "Common Stock Repurchases: An
Analysis of Returns to Bondholders and Shareholders,"
Journal of Financial Economics
9 (June 1981), pp. 113–138,
fig. 1.

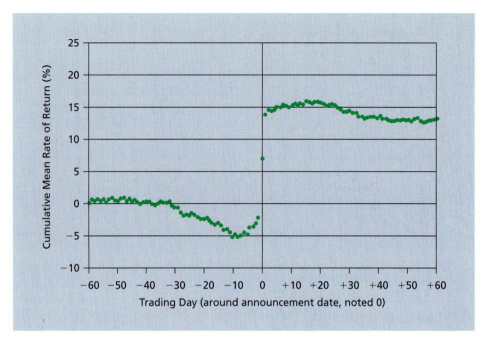

of its shares, the total tax bite will almost certainly be much lower for several reasons. Only the shareholders who choose to sell must pay taxes. For them, only a fraction of the proceeds from the stock sale will be taxable (i.e., the capital gain), and the tax rate on capital gains is less than that on dividends. If the share repurchase results in an increase in the firm's stock price, shareholders who do not sell out can defer paying taxes on their gains indefinitely.

There are several methods that companies use to repurchase shares. The most common approach is called an "open-market share repurchase," in which, as the name implies, firms simply buy back their shares by transacting in the open market. A second share repurchase method is called a "tender offer," or "self-tender." Firms using this approach announce their intentions to buy back a certain number of their outstanding shares at a premium over the current market price. Figure 14.3 shows that the market reaction to self-tender announcements is generally quite positive.

The phenomenal recent growth in repurchases in the United States significantly complicates our discussion in this chapter, because it blurs exactly what we mean by "dividend payout." Repurchases today are roughly equal in total value to ordinary cash dividends, so we should probably talk about corporate payout policy as encompassing both dividends and share repurchases because both represent regular cash distributions from corporations to their shareholders.[8] Additionally, empirical research documents that dividends and repurchases are complements in that companies paying high cash dividends also tend to be the companies most likely to repurchase their shares. In the following sections, we will thus adopt the convention of referring to "payout policy" when we are talking about both types of cash distributions and will

---

[8.] Michaely and Allen (2002) point out that an even broader definition of "payout" would encompass cash payments for shares acquired by bidding firms in mergers and acquisitions. Because the acquired firm will disappear as a separate entity after the merger, cash payments by the acquirer to the target's stockholders are effectively the same as a liquidating cash dividend. In recent years, cash payments in mergers have exceeded the combined value of share repurchases and ordinary cash dividends, which means that the total cash payout from the corporate sector significantly exceeds the total net profits of U.S. companies every year. This "excess payout" must be financed by new security issues (roughly one-third equity, two-thirds debt) and net borrowing from financial institutions.

use the narrower term "dividend policy" when we are discussing just the payment of cash dividends.

Having surveyed the basic mechanics and issues surrounding dividend payments, we can now look more closely at the economically interesting questions about dividends, such as why firms pay dividends at all and how capital markets value dividends.

SMART IDEAS VIDEO

Laurie Krigman, Babson College

"After they announce repurchase programs, some firms wait up to six months before they start repurchasing."

See the entire interview at **SMARTFinance**

---

1. What do you think the typical stock market reaction is to the announcement that a firm will increase its dividend payment? Why?

2. Assume you are the sole owner of a profitable private U.S. corporation. What do you think would be the most tax-efficient method of receiving ownership income (via salary, perks, retained earnings, or dividends)?

3. Why should we expect a firm's stock price to decline by approximately the amount of the dividend payment on the ex-dividend date?

4. Well-diversified investors are willing to tolerate great volatility in the prices of stocks they own. Do you think they value a constant dividend payment even though the underlying corporate profits on which dividends are ultimately based are highly variable?

Concept Review Questions

14.2 PATTERNS OBSERVED IN PAYOUT POLICIES WORLDWIDE

Similar to our discussion of capital structure, we find that summarizing observed dividend payment and share repurchase patterns around the world makes clear exactly what a viable theory of payout policy must explain. The following stylized facts reveal remarkable similarities in the dividend policies observed worldwide, but equally fascinating differences also exist.

Payout Patterns Observed

1. Payout policies show distinct national patterns. As shown in Table 14.2, companies headquartered in countries with legal systems based on English common law generally have higher cash dividend payout ratios than do companies headquartered in countries with civil-law systems. British, Australian, Singaporean, and South African firms have especially high payout ratios, whereas U.S. firms are near the global average.[9] French and Italian firms tend to have lower payouts than do other Western companies, and companies headquartered in developing countries typically have very low

---

[9] Having the United States fall in the midrange of national payout policies actually represents a very significant change from the traditional pattern. American companies have historically ranked near the top of the dividend payout league, but this has changed over the past decade for three reasons. First, as noted, share repurchases have grown dramatically in recent years; including these with cash dividends would once again make the United States a high-payout country. Second, as shown by Fama and French (2001), a far lower fraction of publicly traded U.S. firms pay dividends today than in the past—and those that do pay dividends pay out less than in previous eras. Third, European and Japanese companies have significantly increased their payout ratios since the early 1990s. Historical differences in the financial management of Anglo-American and other developed-country firms are discussed in Kester (1992), Rajan and Zingales (1995), and Prowse (1992). This picture is significantly different when one looks at payout policy (including share repurchases) rather than just dividends. Though these are now legal in most developed countries, only the United States has witnessed a dramatic surge in the total value of repurchases. When both dividends and repurchases are included, the United States once more becomes a high-payout country; in fact, by this definition, the payout ratio of the U.S corporate sector has been increasing rather than decreasing since the early 1990s.

Table 14.2
Dividend Payout Measures
for OECD and Selected
Developing Countries

Country	Number of Firms	Dividends to Cash Flow (%)	Dividends to Earnings (%)	Dividends to Sales (%)
Civil-Law Systems				
Belgium	33	11.77%	39.38%	1.09%
Denmark	75	6.55	17.27	0.71
Finland	39	8.08	21.27	0.77
France	246	9.46	23.55	0.63
Germany	146	12.70	42.86	0.83
Italy	58	9.74	21.83	0.92
Japan	149	13.03	52.88	0.72
Netherlands	96	11.29	30.02	0.74
Norway	50	10.74	23.91	0.98
Spain	33	15.77	30.45	1.04
Sweden	81	5.59	18.33	0.78
Switzerland	70	10.38	25.30	0.98
Civil-Law Median	**33**	**9.74%**	**25.11%**	**0.83%**
Common-Law Systems				
Australia	103	22.83%	42.82%	2.22%
Canada	236	8.00	19.78	0.78
Hong Kong	40	35.43	45.93	7.51
Malaysia	41	15.29	37.93	3.12
Singapore	27	22.28	41.04	2.14
South Africa	90	16.16	35.62	1.90
United Kingdom	799	16.67	36.91	1.89
United States	1,588	11.38	22.11	0.95
Common-Law Median	**40**	**18.28%**	**37.42%**	**2.02%**
Sample Median	**39**	**11.77%**	**30.02%**	**0.98%**

Sources: Rafael LaPorta, Florencio López-de-Silanes, Andrei Shleifer, and Robert W. Vishny, "Agency Problems and Dividend Policies around the World," *Journal of Finance* 55 (February 2000), pp. 1–33.
Note: This table classifies countries by legal origin (civil law versus common law) and presents three measures of average dividend payout for the firms from each country.

dividend payouts, if they pay dividends at all. Many factors influence these patterns, but clearly the nation's legal system is an important factor. This factor also underlies other differences, such as differences in capital market size and efficiency. Common-law countries that rely heavily on capital markets for corporate financing tend to observe higher dividend payments than do continental European and other countries that rely more on intermediated financing.[10] Not surprising, countries with a strong socialist tradition or those with a long history of state involvement in the economy tend to discourage dividend payments to private investors.[11]

2. Payout policies have pronounced industry patterns, and these are the same worldwide. In general, large, profitable firms in mature industries tend to pay out much

[10.] In-depth discussions of the difference between the financial objectives of U.S. and Japanese firms are provided in Berglöf and Perotti (1994), Frankel (1991), and Kaplan and Minton (1994). LaPorta, López-de-Silanes, Shleifer, and Vishny (2000) document the importance of common-law versus civil-law codes in explaining differences in dividend payout.
[11.] Three recent studies document that state-owned enterprises that are privatized significantly increase (or initiate) dividend payouts after divestment. See Megginson, Nash, and van Randenborgh (1994), Boubakri and Cosset (1998), and D'Souza and Megginson (1999).

Table 14.3
Dividend Payout Ratios for Selected U.S. Industries

Industry	Simple Average Payout Ratio (%)	Weighted Average Payout Ratio (%)
Biotechnology	0	0
Airlines	0.3	0.2
Computer software	1.5	0.8
Semiconductors	6.8	5.8
Computer hardware	14.0	14.3
Transportation: commercial	15.0[a]	12.0[a]
Insurance: property & casualty	19.5	18.6
Aerospace & defense	28.0	34.1
Paper & forest products	28.0[a]	25.2[a]
Telecommunications	39.3	41.1
Household nondurables	40.5	40.4
Metals: industrial	46.0[a]	36.4[a]
Pharmaceuticals	46.5	46.2
Banking	47.3	46.0
Basic chemicals	47.7[a]	51.7[a]
Foods & nonalcoholic beverages	51.3[a]	73.2[a]
Autos & auto parts	52.3	50.4
Electric utilities	64.5	67.6
Alcoholic beverages & tobacco	69.5	70.4
Oil & gas production & marketing	75.3	73.3
Natural gas distribution	96.3	70.0

Source: Standard & Poor's Corporation, *Industry Reports,* Various issues (January–July 2001).
Notes: This table describes average dividend payout ratios for the four largest (based on sales) companies in selected U.S. industries. The simple average ratio gives equal weight to all four firms in an industry, whereas the weighted average weights firms by their most recent annual sales.
[a]Average based on three firms instead of four, due to extremely high payout ratios (over 125%) resulting from very low (or negative) levels of earnings for one firm.

larger fractions of their earnings than do firms in younger, rapidly growing industries, and utility companies have very high dividend payouts in almost every country. The most important influences on payout decisions appear to be industry growth rate, capital investment needs, profitability, earnings variability, and asset characteristics (the mix between tangible and intangible assets).[12] In the United States, an industry's average payout ratio (dividends plus repurchases) is negatively related to the richness of its investment opportunities and positively related to the degree to which the industry is regulated. Table 14.3 lists average dividend payout ratios for several U.S. industries.

3. Within industries, dividend payout tends to be directly related to asset intensity and the presence of regulation, but is inversely related to growth rate. Companies with tangible assets as a large fraction of total value tend to have higher dividend payouts than those companies with intangible assets as a large fraction of total market value. Furthermore, regulated companies (particularly utilities) pay out more of their earnings than do nonregulated companies. The relationship between dividend payout and growth rate is equally clear. Rapidly growing firms hoard cash and select zero or very low dividend payouts. As these companies mature, dividend payouts typically in-

[12.] Four recent empirical studies document these relationships. See Smith and Watts (1992), Gaver and Gaver (1993), Barclay, Smith, and Watts (1995), and Fama and French (2002). The survey results detailed in Baker, Farrelly, and Edelman (1985) offer further support for these interindustry dividend patterns.

Table 14.4
Dividend Ratios for Selected U.S. Corporations in 2002

Company	Industry	Annual Dividend per Share ($)	Dividend Yield (%)	Payout Ratio (%)	Market-to-Book Ratio[a]
Microsoft	Computer software	0	0	0	5.54
Cisco Systems	Computer systems	0	0	0	3.94
Dell Computer	Computer hardware	0	0	0	14.87
IBM	Computer hardware	0.60	0.8	13.8	5.54
Intel	Semiconductors	0.08	0.4	42.1	4.03
Exxon Mobil	Integrated petroleum	0.92	2.4	42.2	3.72
ChevronTexaco	Integrated petroleum	2.80	3.2	75.7	2.71
Johnson & Johnson	Pharmaceuticals	0.82	1.4	44.6	7.32
Eli Lilly	Pharmaceuticals	1.24	2.1	48.1	8.54
Merck	Pharmaceuticals	1.40	2.7	44.6	7.18
AOL Time Warner	Entertainment, media	0	0	0[b]	0.74
Walt Disney	Entertainment, media	0.21	1.0	190.9	1.92
Duke Energy	Electricity trading	1.10	3.8	43.0	1.73
Coca-Cola	Consumer products	0.80	1.5	50.0	12.85
Procter & Gamble	Consumer products	1.52	1.7	73.4	10.13
United Technologies	Aerospace	0.98	1.4	25.9	3.76
Boeing	Aerospace	0.68	1.6	19.9	3.65
Lockheed Martin	Aerospace	0.44	0.7	NM[b]	4.33
Alcoa	Aluminum production	0.60	1.9	57.1	2.58
Wal-Mart	Retailing	0.30	0.5	20.1	7.01
Kroger	Retailing	0	0	0	4.49
Southwest Airlines	Airline	0.02	0.1	3.2	3.13
AMR	Airline	0	0	0[b]	0.60
Delta Air Lines	Airline	0.10	0.4	NM[b]	0.82
SBC Communications	Telecommunications	1.08	3.4	50.5	3.53
BellSouth	Telecommunications	0.76	2.4	55.9	3.18
Verizon Communications	Telecommunications	1.54	3.8	700.0	3.63
American Electric Power	Electric utility	2.40	5.9	77.2	1.62
Southern Company	Electric utility	1.34	5.1	74.0	2.32
General Electric	Conglomerate	0.72	2.4	50.7	5.38
Georgia Pacific	Forest products	0.50	1.9	NM[b]	1.19
General Motors	Auto manufacturing	2.00	3.4	113.0	4.12
Ford Motor Company	Auto manufacturing	0.40	2.4	NM[b]	4.24
Caterpillar	Construction equipment	1.40	2.8	60.3	2.52

Source: Dividend data taken from each company's financial information on http://money.cnn.com on June 12, 2002.

Notes: This table presents the annual dividend payment, as well as dividend yield and payout ratios, for 34 of the most valuable publicly traded U.S. corporations in June 2002. Companies are listed beginning with the industry with the lowest leverage and ranging through to the industry with the highest leverage.

[a]Per-share price of company stock divided by the per-share book value of shareholders' common equity.
[b]Indicates company had negative net income for fiscal year in question.

crease. Table 14.4 reports dividend ratios for 34 large U.S. companies. Rapidly growing and/or high-technology companies, such as Microsoft, Cisco, and Dell, pay no dividends; slower-growing, less-technology-centered firms, such as Chevron Texaco, Procter & Gamble, and Caterpillar, pay out more than half of their net profits.

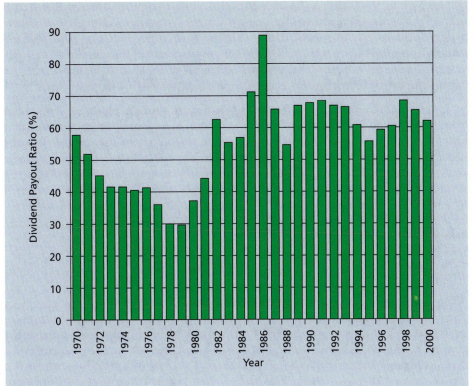

Figure 14.4
Aggregate Dividend
Payout Ratio for the U.S.
Corporate Sector, 1970–
2000

*Source: Statistical Abstract of
the United States*, U.S. Department of Commerce, various
issues (1972–2001).

4. Firms maintain constant nominal dividend payments per share for significant periods of time. Put another way, companies everywhere tend to "smooth" dividend payments, and these payments show far less variability than do the corporate profits on which they ultimately are based.[13] In the terminology introduced in Section 14.2, firms follow a policy of constant nominal dividend payments (regular dividends), with partial adjustments being made as earnings change over time. Managers will not increase per-share dividends until they believe that "permanent" earnings have increased enough to support a higher dividend level. Even then, managers will gradually increase dividend payments to reach a new equilibrium payment. Likewise, corporate managers will try to maintain constant per-share dividend payments, even in the face of temporary net losses, until it becomes clear that earnings will not revive. Managers will then reduce, but rarely eliminate, dividend payments and will make the full downward adjustment in one large cut.[14] Figure 14.4 shows the aggregate dividend payout ratio for the U.S. corporate sector from 1970 to 2000.

5. The stock market reacts positively to dividend (and share repurchase) initiations and increases and has a strong negative reaction to decreases or eliminations. When a company announces either its first regular cash dividend payment (an initiation) or an increase in its existing per-share dividend, that company's stock price typically in-

---

[13.] This is one of the first important empirical regularities to be documented in the dividend literature, in that it was suggested by the work of Lintner (1956) and then documented by Fama and Babiak (1968). The empirical importance of dividend smoothing is addressed in Garrett and Priestley (2000).

[14.] The extreme reluctance of managers to reduce or eliminate dividends is documented in DeAngelo and DeAngelo (1990) and DeAngelo, DeAngelo, and Skinner (1992).

creases by 1 to 3 percent. A similar response occurs when firms announce share repurchase programs.[15] However, the market punishes firms that cut or eliminate their dividends. Investors understand that managers smooth dividends, and stockholders' reactions to dividend changes reflect rational assessments of managerial signals. Investors seem to believe that dividend increases imply that management expects higher earnings in the future, whereas decreases imply declining earnings prospects.

6. Taxes influence payout policies, but taxes neither cause nor prevent companies from initiating dividend payments or share repurchases. It might seem obvious that levying income taxes on investors who receive dividend payments would reduce the demand for dividends and thus prompt corporations to retain a larger share of their profits. In the extreme, very high tax rates should cause corporations to stop paying dividends entirely. Plausible though these arguments may be, they are not supported by empirical evidence; in fact, some studies show that dividend payouts actually increase following tax increases. Furthermore, U.S. corporations paid dividends long before the adoption of the personal income tax on dividends in 1936, and they continued paying dividends even when marginal tax rates increased to over 90 percent.[16] In fact, the dividend payout ratios of U.S. companies have shown little sensitivity to changes in taxation regimes, at least since 1929. There is a bit more evidence that the favorable taxation of capital gains over dividend income promoted the growth of share repurchases in the United States over the past two decades, but at most, taxes seem to have had a second-order effect. In particular, share repurchases accelerated after the Tax Reform Act of 1986, but this law actually reduced the tax penalty on dividend income more than on capital gains.

7. In spite of intensive research, it is unclear exactly how dividend payments affect the required return on a firm's common stock. Some asset-pricing models predict that stocks with high dividend yields must offer higher pre-tax returns than stocks with lower dividend yields do. The intuition behind this prediction is simple. Suppose two stocks are identical except that one pays a higher dividend than the other. Because dividends are taxed at a higher rate than capital gains are, the after-tax return will be lower on the high-dividend stock. In equilibrium, we might expect investors to require a higher pre-tax return on the high-dividend stock to compensate them for the extra tax liability they incur. Although some empirical research supports this prediction, other studies contradict it, and the net effect of dividend taxes on the valuation of corporate equity remains an unsolved puzzle.

8. Changes in transactions costs or in the technical efficiency of capital markets seem to have very little impact on dividend payments. Some theories suggest that the presence of transactions costs causes investors to value dividends. Dividends put cash in

[15.] Dividend initiations were first studied in Asquith and Mullins (1983); Ghosh and Woolridge (1988) and Healy and Palepu (1988) were the first to examine dividend omissions. The magnitude of the price response to share repurchase announcements is much larger when firms engage in a tender offer for their own shares, paying a premium price for a limited time to repurchase a limited number of shares. In most cases, firms repurchase shares by purchasing them in the open market, and it is when that type of program is announced that the price response is similar to what occurs when firms increase their dividends.

[16.] Poterba (1987) provides a detailed listing of dividend tax rates on aggregate dividend payout ratios in the United States for the period 1929–1986. The most striking aspect of this data is that dividend payouts have been so stable for so many decades, in spite of dramatic changes in marginal tax rates, investment incentives, and economic growth rates. Eades, Hess, and Kim (1984) also document that four major U.S. tax-law changes over the period 1977–1987 had very little impact on dividend valuation—as measured using ex-dividend-day returns—and Barclay (1987) documents that dividends were paid, and were apparently valued much the same as today, in the pretax years of the early 1900s. Finally, Christie and Nanda (1994) show that the federal government's unexpected imposition of an undistributed profits tax in 1936 produced an *increase* in share prices and in dividend payments because it forced reluctant managers to pay out as dividends cash they would rather have retained in the firm.

investors' hands without requiring them to pay brokerage commissions or other transactions costs. If transactions costs do create an investor preference for dividends, the steep decline in transactions costs in recent years should have been accompanied by a steep decline in dividends. Though it is true that the percentage of companies paying dividends has declined recently, aggregate dividend payments have not. If we broaden our focus to include all forms of cash payments to shareholders, then corporations today pay out an even higher fraction of total profits than in the past.

9. Ownership matters. One of the most enduring dividend regularities, both in the United States and around the world, is that private or closely held companies rarely pay any dividends at all, whereas publicly traded companies are more likely to pay out substantial fractions of their earnings as dividends each year.[17] In almost every country and every industry, firms with tightly knit control coalitions tend to have very low dividend payouts, and companies with more diffuse ownership structures tend to have higher payouts.

OVERVIEW OF THE AGENCY COST/CONTRACTING MODEL OF DIVIDENDS

As was true for capital structure, it is very hard to conceive of a single theoretical model that can explain all the empirical regularities previously described. Nonetheless, several theoretical models have been developed, and each has garnered some empirical support. In this chapter, we will concentrate on one of these, the **agency cost/contracting model of dividends** (or simply, the agency cost model). We also very briefly introduce the agency cost model's principal competitor, the signaling model of dividend payments.

The agency cost model assumes that dividend payments arise as an attempt to overcome the agency problems that result when there is a separation of corporate ownership and control. In privately held companies with tight ownership coalitions, there is little or no separation between ownership and control. Because agency problems in these firms are minimal, dividends are unnecessary. Even after a company goes public, it rarely commences dividend payments immediately because ownership tends to remain quite concentrated for a number of years after the IPO. Eventually, however, ownership becomes widely dispersed as the firm raises new equity capital and as original stockholders/owners diversify their holdings. As ownership becomes more dispersed, few investors have the incentive or the ability to monitor and control corporate managers, and agency problems become more important. These problems are especially severe in large, slowly growing firms that generate large quantities of free cash flow. The natural tendency of corporate managers is to spend this cash flow (calling it "investment," of course) rather than to pay it out to shareholders. Investors understand these incentives and will pay a low price for manager-controlled firms that hoard cash. On the other hand, shareholders are willing to pay higher prices for stock in companies with more responsive management teams. Managers who wish to maximize firm value will thus begin paying dividends in order to commit themselves to paying out free cash flow; by doing this, managers overcome the agency costs associated with retaining excess cash in the firm. This model thus explains why announcements of dividend initiations or increases are associated with stock-price increases. Other aspects of the model help explain cross-sectional variations in dividend payments based on industry growth rates, firm size, or asset characteristics.

[17.] This relationship is documented in Walker and Petty (1978) and in Dwyer and Lynn (1989). Lipson, Macquieira, and Megginson (1998) examine the reasons why managers of newly public companies decide to take the essentially irreversible step of initiating regular cash dividend payments.

APPLYING THE MODEL

The agency cost model predicts that dividend-paying firms will be older and larger than firms that do not pay dividends. It also predicts that dividend payers have fewer growth opportunities. The data for U.S. firms confirm these predictions. If we compare U.S. firms that pay dividends to firms that do not, we find that dividend payers are more than 10 times larger and grow half as fast as nonpayers. Almost 75 percent of dividend-paying firms have been in existence at least 16 years, whereas only 30 percent of nonpayers have operating histories that long.

	Dividend Payers	Nonpayers
Market cap ($ in millions)	$5,825	$481
Sales growth (%)	9.7	18.8
Firms 8 years old or younger (%)	19	57
Firms 16 years old or older (%)	72	30

Note: Figures determined by author's calculations and Compustat. Dividend payers are firms that paid dividends in 1997, and nonpayers are those that did not. Market capitalization is as of 1997. Sales growth is the compound annual growth rate in sales from 1997 to 2000 for the average firm in each group. Firm age is calculated based on the number of years of data available on Compustat.

Grullon, Michaely, and Swaminathan (2002) report that firms that increase dividends subsequently become less profitable and less risky, while the opposite happens to firms that cut dividends. Similarly, dividend-increasing firms subsequently cut back on capital spending, and dividend-decreasing firms increase capital expenditures. All these results are broadly consistent with the agency cost model. When a firm has many profitable investment opportunities to exploit, it reinvests more cash and distributes less to investors. When a firm's investment opportunities dim, it pays higher dividends rather than reinvest its cash in negative-NPV projects.

The competing **signaling model of dividends** assumes that managers use dividends to convey positive information to poorly informed shareholders.[18] Cash dividend payments are costly both to the paying firms, as this reduces the amount of money the firm can use for investment, and to shareholders receiving the dividends, as they will have to pay taxes on the dividends received. This means that only the "best" (most profitable) firms can afford to pay dividends, in the sense that they can bear the cost of these payments. Weaker firms cannot mimic the dividend payments of strong firms, so dividends help investors solve an asymmetric information problem—distinguishing between high-quality and low-quality firms. Like the agency cost model, the signaling model predicts that stock prices should rise (fall) in response to dividend increases (cuts). However, the signaling model also predicts that firms with high growth opportunities will pay higher dividends, contrary to the empirical evidence. Finally, many observers think that the "tax cost" of signaling with dividends is implausibly high. That is, when firms distribute cash by paying dividends rather than by repurchasing shares, they impose an additional tax burden on investors. Firms who want to signal that they have excellent future prospects should be able to find another sig-

---

[18.] The real "grandfather" of all signaling models in economics is that of Akerlof (1970). Pivotal subsequent signaling models in economics include those of Spence (1973) and Riley (1979). The first significant application of signaling theory in the finance literature (in a capital structure setting) was by Leland and Pyle (1977). In recognition of their contributions in this and other areas, Akerlof and Spence were awarded (along with Joseph Stiglitz) the 2001 Nobel Prize in economics. The first major dividend signaling paper was by Bhattacharya (1979). Important subsequent signaling models were developed in Miller and Rock (1985), John and Williams (1985), Ambarish, John, and Williams (1987), Williams (1988), John and Lang (1991), and Noe and Rebello (1996).

naling mechanism that weaker firms cannot mimic but that does not cause investors to pay higher taxes.

Before describing a model that explains dividend policy in the "real world," however, we must examine the role of dividend policy in a world of perfect and frictionless capital markets. Such a model was first presented in Miller and Modigliani (1961), and as with capital structure, resulted in the notion of irrelevance.

---

5. How do the industrial patterns observed for dividend payouts compare to the patterns observed for capital structures? For example, are industries characterized by high dividend payouts also characterized by high leverage?

6. Can you provide an answer to the following question: If high-dividend stocks offer a higher expected (and required) return than low-dividend stocks due to higher personal taxes levied on the former, why don't corporations simply reduce dividend payments and thus lower their cost of capital?

7. What is the basis of the argument that transactions costs provide a reason for firms to pay dividends, and what light has the steep decline in transactions costs in recent years shed on this argument?

**Concept
Review
Questions**

14.3 PAYOUT POLICY IRRELEVANCE IN A WORLD WITH PERFECT CAPITAL MARKETS

In a world of frictionless capital markets, payout policy cannot affect the market value of the firm. Value derives solely from the inherent profitability of the firm's assets and the competence of its management team. Even though markets are not perfect, describing how dividend payments or share repurchases affect firm valuation in frictionless markets allows us to say more conclusively under what conditions dividend policy *will* matter in a world with frictions such as taxes, transactions costs, information asymmetries, and other market imperfections. Because, in a frictionless world, there would be little difference between cash dividends and share repurchases, we will analyze only cash dividend payments in this section in the interest of simplicity.

The notion that dividends are irrelevant may seem to be a contradiction. After all, we argued in Chapter 4 that the value of stock was equal to the present value of the dividends that the stock would pay over time. If cash dividends are the only source of value to market participants, how do we arrive at a dividend irrelevance result? As was the case for capital structure, the answer to this question is that the economic value of a firm will always be derived solely from the operating profits the firm is currently generating and will continue to generate in the future as its investments unfold. As long as the firm accepts all positive-*NPV* investment projects and has *costless* access to capital markets, it can pay any level of dividends it desires each period. But if a firm pays out its earnings as a dividend, it must issue new shares to raise the cash required to fi-nance its ongoing investment projects. A company can thus choose to retain all its profits and finance its investments with internally generated cash flow, or that same company can pay out all its earnings as dividends and raise the cash needed for investment by selling new shares. As usual, this principle is best explained with an example.

Consider two firms, Retention and Payout, that today (time 0) are the same size, are in the same industry, and have access to the same investment opportunities. Both companies have assets worth $20 million that will generate a net cash inflow of $2 million next year (time 1), thus providing a return on investment of 10 percent. Furthermore, assume that the return required by investors, r, is 10 percent per year for both companies, and that each company is presented with the opportunity to invest $2 million in a positive-$NPV$ project at time 1. Assume also that each firm currently has 1 million shares outstanding, implying that each firm's share price is $20 ($P_0 = $20). The managers of firm Payout want to distribute all the firm's earnings as dividends, but they also intend to finance the company's $2 million investment opportunity by issuing as many new shares as necessary. The managers of firm Retention would rather not pay dividends, preferring instead to retain the firm's net cash inflow for use in funding the planned $2 million investment program. Can each management team pursue its preferred strategy and still have the market values of the two firms be identical at the end of the period?

Yes. To see how, we first examine Retention's strategy and then Payout's. Retention's managers decide to retain the $2 million ($2 per share) profit the firm earns at time 1 in order to internally finance the $2 million investment project. Therefore, total dividends paid (and dividends per share) at time 1 are zero, and the market value of the firm is equal to the $20 million beginning value plus the $2 million in reinvested earnings plus the net present value of the investment opportunity. For simplicity, we will assume for now that the project's NPV is positive but small enough to be ignored. The value of Retention at time 1 is therefore equal to $22 million ($20 million + $2 million), which is equal to $22 per share ($P_1 = $22), because the firm did not have to issue any new shares to finance its investment opportunity. Plugging these values into our basic valuation equation from Chapter 4 verifies that Retention shareholders indeed earn the 10 percent return on investment they expected:

$$r_1 = \left[\frac{D_1 + P_1 - P_0}{P_0}\right] = \left[\frac{\$0 + \$22 - \$20}{\$20}\right] = 10\%$$

We can extend this example indefinitely into the future. In each period, firm Retention commits to reinvesting all its annual profits (10% return on assets) in new productive assets. Shareholders earn their return by seeing the value of their shares increase by 10 percent each year. No new shares are ever issued, so the number of outstanding shares remains fixed at 1 million over time..

So far, so good, but what about firm Payout? This firm's managers decide to pay out as a $2 per-share dividend the net cash flow of $2 million, so they must raise the $2 million needed to finance the investment project by selling new shares. But how many shares must they sell? To answer that, we must reason through what the price of Payout's shares will be next year (time 1). After it distributes the dividend, Payout will have assets worth $20 million, exactly the amount that it started with one year earlier. With 1 million shares outstanding, the share price will still be $20, so Payout must issue 100,000 new shares at $20 each to raise the $2 million it needs to undertake its investment opportunity. After the company issues new shares and invests the proceeds, Payout's total market value will equal $22 million ($20 per share × 1.1 million shares outstanding). Therefore, at time 1, the market value of Payout, $22 million, is identical to the market value of Retention. Once again, we can verify that Payout's original shareholders earned exactly the rate of return they expected, the same return earned by Retention's investors:

$$r_1 = \left[\frac{D_1 + P_1 - P_0}{P_0}\right] = \left[\frac{\$2 + \$20 - \$20}{\$20}\right] = 10\%$$

As was the case earlier, we can repeat this process indefinitely into the future. Each year, Payout distributes all of its net cash flow as a dividend, and the firm issues new shares to finance new investment opportunities.

We have shown that the time-1 market capitalization of Retention equals that of Payout even though they follow radically different dividend policies. Retention has 1,000,000 shares outstanding worth $22 each, while Payout has 1,100,000 shares outstanding worth $20 each. Because both companies have an aggregate value of $22 million, we can conclude that dividend policy is irrelevant in determining the value of a firm, at least when markets are frictionless. But what if investors in Retention prefer that the company pay out earnings rather than reinvesting them, or what if shareholders in Payout prefer that the company reinvest earnings rather than issuing new shares? We can reinforce the notion that dividend policy is irrelevant by demonstrating that investors can "unwind" the dividend policy decisions of firms. In the end, what is true for the firm as a whole is true for each of its investors. Dividend policy is irrelevant.

APPLYING THE MODEL

Consider two investors, Sharon and Ozzy. At time 0, Sharon owns an 11 percent (110,000 shares) stake in Retention, while Ozzy holds an 11 percent stake (also 110,000 shares) in Payout. At the end of the year, Sharon receives no dividend, but she still owns 11 percent of Retention's outstanding shares, which are now worth $22 each. Ozzy, however, receives a dividend payment of $220,000, but because Payout issues 100,000 shares to finance its investment opportunity, the shares Ozzy owns now represent only a 10 percent ownership stake in Payout (110,000 ÷ 1,100,000).

If either Sharon or Ozzy is unhappy with the dividend policy of the firm in which she or he has invested, either can "unwind" that policy. For example, suppose Sharon would like to receive a dividend. At the end of the year, Sharon could sell 10,000 of her shares for $22 each, generating a cash inflow of $220,000, exactly equal to the dividend that Ozzy received on his investment. After selling a portion of her shares, Sharon would own just 10 percent of the outstanding equity of Retention, exactly equal to the ownership stake that Ozzy holds in Payout.

Conversely, suppose that Ozzy would prefer that Payout did not pay dividends. The solution to Ozzy's problem is simple. When he receives the $220,000 dividend, he could simply reinvest the money by purchasing 11,000 new shares in Payout. That would bring his total ownership stake to 121,000, or 11 percent of Payout's outstanding shares (121,000 ÷ 1,100,000). In other words, Ozzy's position is just like Sharon's. ■

This may seem rather complex, but the essential points of these examples are really quite simple. Investors are indifferent about whether (1) the firm retains earnings to fund positive-NPV investments or (2) the firm distributes cash dividends and sells new shares to finance new investments. In either case, shareholders' returns are determined by the cash flows generated by the firm's investments and not by how the firm distributes those cash flows. In the absence of taxes, transactions costs, or any other market friction, investors do not care whether they earn returns in the form of dividends (as Payout's shareholders do) or capital gains (as Retention's shareholders do).

Smart Concepts
See the concept explained step-by-step at

Concept Review Questions

8. Imagine a firm that has an "intermediate" dividend policy compared to Payout and Retention. This firm pays out half its earnings to shareholders, and finances new investment partially through new share issues and partially through retained profits. Describe how dissatisfied shareholders in this firm could "unwind" the dividend policy if they preferred either higher or lower dividends.

9. Around the world, utilities generally have the highest dividend payouts of any industry, yet they also tend to have massive investment programs to finance through external funding. How do you reconcile high payouts and large-scale security issuance?

10. Managers of slow-growing, but profitable firms (i.e., tobacco companies) *should* pay out these high earnings as dividends. What might they choose to do instead?

14.4 THE EFFECTS OF MARKET IMPERFECTIONS ON PAYOUT POLICY IRRELEVANCE

Few of us have ever transacted in frictionless capital markets, so our next task is to examine how robust the dividend irrelevance propositions are under more realistic market conditions. Our final goal will be to determine whether a given firm has an "optimal" (value-maximizing) dividend policy and, if so, how that policy should be set. As we proceed, you may notice a puzzling fact: almost all the real-world issues we incorporate—such as taxes, transactions costs for issuing new securities, and uncertainty about a firm's investment opportunities—argue *against* the payment of cash dividends. Yet, U.S. corporations pay out over half of their annual earnings in most years, and non-U.S. firms also regularly pay out substantial fractions of their earnings. We will show that the factors of agency costs, informational asymmetries, and ownership structure do a better job of explaining dividend policies than do arguments based on taxes or market frictions such as trading costs. In other words, dividends do not exist to overcome changing technical problems with markets and tax regimes; dividends exist to overcome unchanging human problems with trust, communication, and commitment.

PERSONAL INCOME TAXES AND DIVIDEND IRRELEVANCE

When the personal tax rate on dividends is higher than the tax rate on capital gains, we have an unambiguous result: firms should retain all earnings, and shareholders should reap their investment returns in the form of capital gains resulting from stock appreciation. To see this, note that personal taxes reduce the after-tax value of dividends relative to capital gains, so firms should not pay dividends as long as dividends are taxed at a higher rate. Any distribution from the firm should be through a share repurchase program because this offers investors the choice of receiving cash in a tax-favored form (as a capital gain) or forgoing the cash altogether by not selling shares and thus seeing their share values increase as their proportionate ownership increases.

What if a large capital gains tax is imposed? Will that reestablish dividend policy irrelevance? (Before reading on, see if you can reason through to an answer.) Apparently, imposing a capital gains tax at a rate equal to the dividend tax rate will again make investors indifferent to whether they receive taxable dividends or taxable capital gains, but this will happen only if the tax on stock appreciation is levied every period, regardless of whether the shares are sold or not. Such a levy is called a **wealth tax;** although never employed in the United States, such a tax has been tried in Norway and some other Western European countries. Capital gains taxes are almost always paid only at *realization* (when the shares are actually sold), and a tax payment delayed is a tax payment rendered less painful. Furthermore, in the United States and other countries, stock-related capital gains taxes can often be escaped entirely if shares are passed on to an investor's heirs at his or her death. Therefore, investors generally have a tax preference for capital gains over cash dividends, even if the nominal tax rates for both types of income are the same.[19] Debt financing enjoys a tax advantage relative to equity in most industrialized countries, but retained earnings almost always enjoy a significant tax preference relative to dividend payments. In summary, almost all real-world dividend taxation systems discourage the payment of cash dividends. We must look elsewhere for a reason for dividends to exist.

What is the empirical evidence regarding the impact of taxes on dividend payments? Researchers have employed two principal methodologies to study tax effects. The first method is to employ a variant of the capital asset pricing model (CAPM) to see if investors demand a higher pretax return on high-dividend-paying stocks than they do on stocks paying a low dividend, as would be expected if investors paid a higher effective tax rate on cash dividend income than on capital gains income. Studies using this approach show mixed results. Despite the empirical findings, proponents of a tax-effect model have great difficulty explaining why rational corporate managers would ever pay cash dividends if doing so resulted in a higher pretax required return. Apparently, managers could increase stock prices and thus lower the firm's cost of capital simply by cutting dividend payouts. The survival of dividend payments in modern economies therefore suggests that the tax-effect models of dividend valuation must be missing something important.

The second method used is to examine the average change in a firm's stock price on its ex-dividend day. Prior to this day, an investor who owns the stock is entitled to receive the next dividend payment. If an investor buys the stock after it goes ex dividend, the dividend is paid to the former owner. Consider the problem faced by a taxable investor who holds a stock and wants to sell it near an ex-dividend date. The investor faces a choice between selling the stock before the ex-dividend date at the higher cum-dividend (with dividend) price, thus earning a return in the form of a capital gain, or waiting until the stock goes ex dividend, selling the stock at a lower price, and receiving a return in the form of cash dividends. If stock prices fall by the full amount of the dividend payment, the investor would prefer to sell shares before they go ex dividend. By selling the shares and realizing a capital gain rather than receiving a dividend, the investor earns higher after-tax returns. The only circumstances under which this investor would be indifferent about whether to take the dividend or the capital gain is if the ex-dividend price drop is less than the dividend payment. In that case, the higher pretax return from receiving the dividend offsets the tax disadvantage of dividends. The empirical observation that stock prices fall on ex-dividend days by significantly less than the amount of the dividend (on average, by about 60–70 cents on the dollar) has often been interpreted as evidence of a tax effect in dividend valuation.[20]

APPLYING THE MODEL

Three months ago, you purchased a share of stock for $20. Today that share sells for $22, a gain of 10 percent. The stock will pay a $2 dividend in a few days, and the ex-dividend date is tomorrow. Suppose you want to sell the stock, and you face a 33 per-

---

[19.] Bell and Jenkinson (2002) describe an interesting example in Britain where just the opposite was true—an important class of investors had a tax preference for dividends over retained earnings. Prior to a change in the law in 1997, British pension funds and other tax-exempt investors could effectively receive a refund on personal income taxes withheld by the paying corporation on net dividends paid to stockholders. After the law was changed, the authors document a significant decline in the valuation of dividend income among those (high-yield) shares that should be most attractive to tax-exempt investors.

[20.] Modern ex-dividend studies trace their roots to Elton and Gruber (1970). Subsequent papers include those by Lakonishok and Vermaelen (1983, 1986), Eades, Hess, and Kim (1984, 1994), Kalay and Subrahmanyan (1984), Heath and Jarrow (1988), and Bell and Jenkinson (2002).

cent tax rate on dividend income and a 20 percent tax rate on capital gains. If you sell today, you earn an after-tax profit of $1.60 ($2 capital gain minus $0.40 in taxes). That represents an 8 percent return on your original $20 investment. If you sell tomorrow, your after-tax return depends on how far the price drops when the stock goes ex dividend. If the price drops by the full $2, then you earn no capital gain and your after-tax profit equals $1.34 ($2 dividend minus $0.66 in taxes), or 6.7 percent. Clearly, in this scenario your after-tax return is higher if you sell the stock before it goes ex dividend. However, suppose the stock price drops by just $1 when it goes ex dividend. In that case, if you wait to sell the stock you receive a $1 capital gain (worth $0.80 after taxes) and a $2 dividend (worth $1.34 after taxes), for an after-tax return of $2.14, or 10.7 percent. In that case, it pays to wait for the dividend. Only when the stock price falls by $1.675 on the ex-dividend date would you be indifferent about whether to sell immediately or wait until the dividend is paid.   ■

Although ex-dividend-day studies show plausible average results, there is reason to be suspicious of these studies as definitive evidence of differential tax effects, particularly because transactions costs must be very high for a pure tax effect to occur. The reason is that tax-free traders have an incentive to buy stocks just before they go ex dividend if the traders expect the price to decline by less than the dividend. For example, suppose a stock is about to pay a $2 dividend and traders expect the price to drop $1.67 on the ex-dividend date because of differential tax rates applied to capital gains and dividends. As the previous example demonstrated, a taxable investor presented with these figures would be indifferent about whether to sell the stock immediately or wait until it goes ex dividend, but a tax-free investor would be anything but indifferent. Such an investor could purchase the stock at $22, receive the $2 dividend, and then resell the stock immediately afterwards for $20.33, generating a one-day profit of $0.33. If the transactions costs associated with this strategy are greater than $0.33 per share, then "dividend arbitrage" is not profitable, and the differential tax treatment of capital gains and dividends determines the size of the ex-dividend-day price decline. However, currently in U.S. markets the per-share cost of a round-trip trade can be as low as a few pennies, and in that case the actions of tax-free investors should increase the ex-dividend-day price decline to almost the full amount of the dividend.

Another conceptual flaw in these ex-dividend studies is their inability to explain why relative ex-dividend-day price drops have not increased (become closer to matching the nominal dividend payment) over time as tax-free investors have risen to prominence in modern stock markets. Because institutional investors currently account for as much as 90 percent of average trading volume on the New York Stock Exchange, and because these investors face very low trading costs, it is not clear why a differential tax effect that is relevant only for certain individual investors should exist in the market.

Finally, share repurchases pose a problem for those who believe that personal taxes on dividends affect share prices. When investors participate in a firm's share repurchase program, most of the cash they receive escapes personal taxation because U.S. tax law treats the money as a return of capital. For those investors who experience a capital gain when they sell their shares, only the gain is taxable and even then it is taxed at a lower rate than dividend income is. In other words, share repurchases seemingly provide an alternative, tax-advantaged method of distributing cash to investors.[21]

[21.] Numerous studies document significant, positive abnormal returns to shareholders at the announcement of repurchase programs. The first two of these are by Dann (1981) and Vermaelen (1981). Subsequent articles examining share repurchases include those by Ikenberry, Lakonishok, and Vermaelen (1995), Guay and Harford (2000), Lie (2000), and Jagannathan, Stephens, and Weisbach (2000).

Why don't more companies substitute share repurchase programs for cash dividend payments? There are three answers to this question. First, as we have seen, many U.S. companies *have* been repurchasing their shares for several years, and increasing numbers of non-U.S. companies are beginning to do so as their national laws allow. Second, Fama and French (2001) point out that the firms that initiate share repurchase programs are the same companies that also make large cash dividend payments. In the grammar of economics, this means that firms seem to treat repurchases and cash dividends as *complements* rather than *substitutes*. Finally, the IRS has the power to rule that a given company's share repurchase program is merely an attempt to avoid taxes, and it can impose the higher personal income tax rates on all income received by investors under the program. In other words, companies that adopt routine share repurchase programs in lieu of dividend payments can theoretically be imposing large supplemental tax liabilities on their shareholders. The actual importance of this rule in deterring repurchases is questionable, however, because the IRS almost never invokes it.

On balance, incorporating personal taxes into our model does not help us understand why firms pay dividends. Tax effects can, however, explain some of the patterns we observe, such as the rise in share repurchase programs in the United States and other industrialized countries.

TRANSACTIONS COSTS AND DIVIDEND IRRELEVANCE

If personal taxes cannot explain observed dividend payments, what about transactions costs of issuing and trading stocks? Positive trading costs affect expected dividend payouts in two, potentially offsetting ways. First, if investors find it costly to sell just a few shares to generate cash (i.e., to create homemade dividends), then they might pay a premium for stocks that habitually pay dividends. Regular cash dividend payments are a costless way to receive a cash return on an investor's stock portfolio, and this cash could be used either for consumption or for rebalancing the investor's portfolio. A serious flaw in this argument, however, is that it suggests dividend payments should be highest in undeveloped markets with very high transactions costs. In reality, dividend payments are highest in countries with liquid, low-cost stock markets—such as Britain, Germany, and Australia—and are low or nonexistent in most developing countries. Furthermore, a transactions-cost argument cannot easily explain why aggregate dividend payouts in the United States have remained fairly high, even as U.S. stock markets have become vastly more efficient and the costs of trading have declined dramatically.

The second effect of transactions costs on dividend payments is unambiguously negative. This relates to a corporation's need to replace cash paid out as dividends with cash obtained through new share sales. Remember that our dividend-irrelevance result depends critically on a company being able to fund its investment either by retaining corporate profits or paying out profits as dividends and replacing this cash by issuing new shares. As long as share issues are costless, investors will be indifferent about whether to receive returns in the form of capital gains (on non-dividend-paying shares) or as cash dividends on shares. If issuing securities entails large costs, however, all parties should prefer a full-retention strategy, and no corporation should ever both pay dividends and raise funds for investment by issuing new stock.[22] Because many large corporations do just that, it is obvious that transactions costs alone do not explain observed dividend policy.

[22.] Interestingly, an important dividend theory paper, Easterbrook (1984), suggests that corporations pay dividends precisely because this will force them into the capital market for financing (rather than rely solely on internal financing), where investors have the incentive and ability to monitor and discipline corporate management.

The Residual Explanation for Dividend Payments

The previous discussion suggests another possible explanation of observed dividend payments. Might they simply be a residual, the cash left over after corporations have funded all their positive-*NPV* investments? This would help explain why firms in rapidly growing industries retain almost all their profits while firms in mature, slow-growing industries tend to have very high dividend payouts. It would also explain the "life-cycle" pattern of dividend payments for individual firms where young companies that are growing rapidly rarely pay any dividends, but those same companies typically change to a high-payout strategy once they mature and their growth rate slows.

The residual explanation for dividends probably has some merit, but it suffers from one massive empirical problem. Dividend payments simply are not as variable as they would be if firms were viewing them as residuals from cash flow. In fact, dividend payments are the most stable of any cash flow into or out of a firm, and all available evidence suggests that corporate managers smooth dividends and are very cautious about changing established dividend payout levels. Clearly, the residual theory is not the sole explanation of observed dividend payments.

Dividends as a Transmitter of Information

Sooner or later, many who study the dividend puzzle recognize that firms may pay dividends to convey information to investors. Managers, who have a better understanding of the firm's true financial condition than shareholders do, can convey this information to shareholders through the dividend policy managers select. Dividend payments have what accountants call "cash validity," meaning that these payments are believable and are hard for weaker firms to duplicate. Phrased in economic terms, in a world that is characterized by informational asymmetries between managers and investors, cash dividend payments serve as a credible transmitter of information from corporate insiders (officers and directors) to the company's shareholders. Viewed this way, every aspect of a firm's dividend policy conveys significant new information.

What Type of Information Is Being Transmitted?

When a company begins paying dividends (a dividend initiation), the company is conveying management's confidence that the firm is now profitable enough to both fund its investment projects and pay out cash. Investors and managers know that cutting or eliminating dividend payments once they begin results in a very negative market reaction, so dividend initiations send a strong signal to the market about management's assessment of the firm's long-term ability to generate cash.

The same logic applies to dividend increases. Because everyone understands that dividend cuts are to be avoided at almost all costs, the fact that management is willing to increase dividend payments clearly implies that it is confident profits will remain high enough to support the new payment level. Dividend increases therefore suggest a *permanent* increase in the firm's normal level of profitability—or, phrased somewhat differently, dividends change only when the level of *permanent earnings* changes.[23] Unfortunately, this logic applies even more forcefully to dividend decreases. Because all concerned understand that dividend cuts are perceived as being very bad

---

[23.] Two recent papers by Lee (1995, 1996) discuss the relative importance of temporary versus permanent earnings changes in explaining dividend changes. In another recent paper, Hines (1996) documents the intriguing fact that American multinational companies appear to pay dividends on foreign profits at rates that are three times higher than the payout rates on their domestic profits, though why they do this is unclear.

news, managers will reduce dividend payments only when they have no choice, such as when there is a cash flow crisis or when the financial health of the firm is declining and no turnaround is in sight. Therefore, it is no surprise that when managers do cut dividends, the market reaction is often very severe.

What Is the Empirical Support for an Informational Role for Dividends?

There is much empirical support for the informational role of dividend payments, beginning with John Lintner's (1956) classic article documenting that corporate managers approach dividend decisions with great care and with the idea that the level of dividend payments selected will become a fixed expense of the company for the foreseeable future. Lintner shows that managers are far more concerned with *changing* an established per-share dividend payment than they are with finding the theoretically "correct" level of dividend payout (what fraction of profits should be paid out each period). A later study by Fama and Babiak (1968) documents that managers do in fact have target payout ratios in mind and that dividend payments track the course of corporate profits quite closely over time. However, Fama and Babiak also show that managers employ a *partial adjustment* strategy in adjusting dividend payments to changes in corporate profits, wherein an increase in profit levels will not be fully reflected in a higher equilibrium dividend until several quarters have elapsed. This strategy allows management to become confident that profits have permanently increased before fully committing to higher dividend payments. Naturally, over time, knowledge of this corporate behavior pattern is incorporated into investor perceptions of dividend policy changes.

However, two important recent empirical studies contradict the idea that dividend increases (decreases) imply that managers believe earnings will be higher (lower) in the future. DeAngelo, DeAngelo, and Skinner (1996) find virtually no support for the earnings-forecasting hypothesis. Instead, they find that dividends are not reliable signals of future profitability because managers are overoptimistic about actual future earnings growth and make only modest cash commitments when they increase dividends. As if this evidence were not bad enough for the earnings-forecasting hypothesis, a study by Benartzi, Michaely, and Thaler (1997) indicates that managers do not even try to forecast future earnings when they change dividend levels. Instead, firms alter dividends in response to past changes in earnings; dividend changes convey no useful information about future earnings prospects. There is essentially no correlation between a dividend change one year and earnings changes in subsequent years. The authors answer the question asked in their paper's title, "Do Changes in Dividends Signal the Future or the Past?," by concluding that dividends signal what *has* happened, rather than what *will* happen.

THE FREE CASH FLOW HYPOTHESIS: DIVIDEND PAYMENTS AS SOLUTIONS TO AGENCY PROBLEMS

The free cash flow hypothesis offers yet another solution to the dividend puzzle. This hypothesis was first developed by Michael Jensen (1986) and has since been refined in many other studies, including recent works by Dewenter and Warther (1998), Lie (2000), and Fenn and Liang (2001). The free cash flow hypothesis is based squarely on the agency problems resulting from the separation of ownership and control observed in large public companies. When firms are small and growing rapidly, they not only have tight ownership structures, but also tend to have a great many profitable investment opportunities. These growth firms can profitably employ all the cash flow they generate internally, and thus have no reason to pay cash dividends. In time, successful growth firms establish secure, often dominant, market positions and begin to generate operating cash flows that are much larger than the remaining positive-*NPV* investment opportunities open to them. Jensen defines free cash flow as any cash flow in excess of that needed to fund all positive-*NPV* projects. Managers of firms with free cash flow *should* begin to pay dividends to ensure that they will not invest the free cash flow in negative-*NPV* projects. However, managers may prefer to retain cash and spend it because of the increased status attained from running a larger (though not necessarily more valuable) company.

Jensen asserts that if managers are given the proper incentives, they will initiate dividend payments as soon as the firm begins generating free cash flow. Managerial contracts that tie compensation to the firm's stock-price performance are designed to ensure that managers disgorge free cash flow rather than invest it unwisely. The larger the free cash flow generated, the larger the dividend payout should be. This is the essential prediction of what is commonly termed the agency cost/contracting model of dividend payments, which was introduced in Section 14.2. The central predictions of this model are threefold. First, it predicts that dividend initiations and increases should be viewed as good news by investors and thus should lead to stock-price increases upon announcement. Second, the agency cost model predicts that firms (and industries) that generate the largest amounts of free cash flow should also have the highest dividend payout ratios. Finally, this model predicts that managerial compensation contracts will be designed to entice managers to pursue a value-maximizing dividend policy, and that these contracts will be effective. The empirical patterns observed in dividend payment policies around the world, described in Section 14.2, are all consistent with these predictions.

Concept Review Questions

11. During the late 1960s, the top marginal personal income tax rate on dividends received by British investors reached 98 percent, yet dividend payouts actually *increased*. How might you justify this empirical fact?

12. Why is it difficult for a firm with weaker cash flows to mimic a dividend increase undertaken by a firm with stronger cash flows?

14.5 A CHECKLIST FOR DIVIDEND PAYMENTS UNDER THE AGENCY COST MODEL OF DIVIDENDS

As we have seen, the agency cost model explains cash dividend payments as value-maximizing attempts by managers of certain companies to minimize the agency costs resulting from the separation of ownership and control. The severity of these agency problems is, in turn, a function of the firm's *investment opportunity set* and its *ownership structure*. The investment opportunity set encompasses the industry the firm operates in, the company's size, the capital intensity of the firm's production process, the free cash flow generated, and the availability of positive-*NPV* investment opportunities to the firm. Ownership structure refers to the number of shareholders, the size of each investor's holdings, and the presence or absence of an active investor willing and able to directly monitor corporate management. Other factors that influence dividend payments include transactions costs, taxes, and two characteristics of a firm's home country: its legal system and the importance of capital markets relative to financial intermediaries.

COMPARATIVE CORPORATE FINANCE

Dividend Policies of the Largest Non-U.S. Public Companies

Company Name	Country	Industry	Market Value May 31, 2001 ($US in billions)	Dividend Payout Ratio (%)	Dividend Yield (%)	P/E Ratio
Royal Dutch Shell	Netherlands/ UK	Petroleum	216	34	2.1	16
BP	*Britain*	*Petroleum*	*200*	*39*	*2.3*	*17*
Vodafone Group	Britain	Telecommunications	175	34	0.8	43
NTT DoCoMo	Japan	Telecommunications	193	0	0	75
GlaxoSmithKline	Britain	Pharmaceuticals	169	53	1.7	31
Nokia	Finland	Mobile phone manufacturing	136	31	0.8	39
Toyota Motor	Japan	Automobiles	130	20	0.6	33
HSBC Holdings	Britain	Banking	116	63	3.5	18
Novartis	Switzerland	Pharmaceuticals	110	35	1.3	27
TotalFinaElf	*France*	*Petroleum*	*108*	*49*	*2.9*	*17*
Nippon Telegraph & Telephone	*Japan*	*Telecommunications*	*100*	*N/M*	*0.7*	*−89*
China Mobile (Hong Kong)	*China*	*Telecommunications*	*90*	*0*	*0*	*41*
Deutsche Telekom	*Germany*	*Telecommunications*	*88*	*47*	*3.6*	*13*
AstraZeneca	Britain	Pharmaceuticals	83	41	1.5	27
Nestle	Switzerland	Food & beverages	80	38	1.5	25
Sony	Japan	Electronics	71	150	0.3	499
Vivendi Universal	France	Consumer products	70	70	2.0	35
Allianz	Germany	Insurance	69	25	0.7	35
Telefonica	*Spain*	*Telecommunications*	*68*	*0*	*0*	*31*
Roche Holdings	Switzerland	Pharmaceuticals	67	19	0.7	27
UBS	Switzerland	Banking	66	27	1.7	16
ING Groep	*Netherlands*	*Banking*	*64*	*46*	*2.4*	*19*
France Telecom	*France*	*Telecommunications*	*64*	*46*	*2.3*	*20*
Royal Bank of Scotland Group	Britain	Banking	62	32	2.0	16
Telecom Italia	*Italy*	*Telecommunications*	*61*	*129*	*2.8*	*46*

As this table shows, the dividend policies of the world's most valuable companies are becoming increasingly similar—regardless of the country in which the companies are headquartered. Privatized companies, which are indicated with *italics*, have led the way in promoting high dividend payments by publicly traded, non-U.S. firms, especially because these are usually some of the largest and most valuable companies in most national markets.

Source: "The Business Week Global 1000," *Business Week* (July 9, 2001).

DEVELOPING A CHECKLIST FOR DIVIDEND POLICY

In this section, we summarize what managers need to know about dividends. The following list summarizes the predictions of the agency cost model about the relationship between corporate-level variables and expected dividend payout. The second column shows the impact on dividend payout of an increase in each firm-level variable in the first column.

Firm-Level Variable	Impact of Increase on Dividend Payout
Asset growth rate	Reduce
Positive-NPV investment opportunities	Reduce
Capital intensity of the production process	Increase
Free cash flow generated	Increase
Number of individual shareholders	Increase
Relative "tightness" of ownership coalition	Reduce
Size of largest block holder	Reduce

In addition to firm-level variables, macroeconomic and national financial variables also influence equilibrium dividend payments. The predictions of the agency cost/contracting model concerning these variables are detailed in the following list. Again, the second column shows the impact on dividend payout of an increase in each macroeconomic variable in the first column.

Macroeconomic Variable	Impact of Increase on Dividend Payout
Transactions costs of security issuance	Increase
Personal tax rates on dividend income	Reduce
Personal tax rates on capital gains income	Increase
Importance of institutional investors	Reduce
Corporate governance power of institutional investors	Reduce
Capital market relative to intermediated (bank) financing	Increase

14.6 SUMMARY

- One of the most enduring features of corporate finance around the world is that publicly traded corporations almost invariably choose to pay regular cash dividend payments to their shareholders. Further, these payments are generally a constant absolute amount per period ($0.25 per share), rather than a constant fraction (25%) of the firm's profits. In the United States, dividends are usually paid on a quarterly basis, but are paid annually or semiannually in most other countries.
- There are striking regularities in the patterns of dividend payments observed across countries and industries. Among developed countries, dividend payout ratios (dividends as a fraction of corporate profits) tend to be highest in British Commonwealth countries, whereas payouts are much smaller in France and Italy. Payouts by U.S. and other continental European companies tend to fall between these two extremes. However, the same industries (utilities, transportation firms)

have high dividend payouts in all countries, and certain other industries (high-technology, health sciences) have low dividend payouts in all countries.

- In the United States, and increasingly in other countries, corporations frequently choose to repurchase shares on the open market rather than pay (or in addition to paying) ordinary cash dividends, at least partly because repurchases are subject to lower effective tax rates for most individual investors. In recent years, repurchases by U.S. corporations have exceeded $100 billion per year, and ordinary (cash) dividend payments have been around $250 billion annually.

- Stock splits and stock dividends are used by companies that wish to reduce the per-share price of their stock in the open market. In a 2-for-1 stock split, for example, one new share is distributed for every existing share an investor holds, and the price of the stock falls by roughly half.

- In a world without market imperfections, dividend policy is irrelevant in the sense that it cannot affect the value of a firm. However, the fact that many firms pay dividends is something of a puzzle because most real market imperfections (such as taxes) argue against paying cash dividends.

- One theory of dividend policy assumes that dividend payments serve to reduce agency costs between corporate managers and external investors by committing the firm to pay out excess profits, thereby preventing the managers from consuming the profits as perquisites or wasting them on unwise capital investments (such as unrelated corporate acquisitions). Most of the empirical evidence supports this agency cost model of dividends over the competing signaling model, which predicts that managers use dividend payments to convey information to investors about the firm's expected future earnings.

- In addition to ownership considerations, several other aspects of a firm's operating and regulatory environment seem to influence dividend payouts. Other things equal, closely held corporations operating in a high-growth industry where large ongoing capital investments are needed to compete will have lower dividend payouts than will widely held firms in slow-growing or highly regulated industries.

INTERNET RESOURCES

Note: For *updates to links, please go to the book's website at* http://smart.swcollege.com

http://www.ex-dividend.com—Lists recent stock splits and dividend changes; includes record dates, ex-dividend dates, and payment dates

htttp://www.ise.ie—Site of the Irish Stock Exchange lists; includes, among many other interesting facts, the set of stocks going ex dividend in the near future

KEY TERMS

agency cost/contracting model of dividends
announcement date
constant nominal payment policy
constant payout ratio dividend policy
date of record

dividend payout ratio
ex dividend
excess earnings accumulation tax
extra dividend
low-regular-and-extra policy

payment date   stock dividend
reverse stock splits   stock split
share repurchase programs   target dividend payout ratio
signaling model of dividends   wealth tax
special dividend

QUESTIONS

14-1. How does dividend policy interact with capital structure policy to affect a firm's investment decisions? How might a firm's sources and cost of capital be affected by dividend policy?

14-2. What do record date, ex-dividend date, and payment date mean with regard to dividends? Why would you expect the price of a stock to drop by the amount of the dividend on the ex-dividend date? What rationale has been offered for why this does not actually occur?

14-3. What justifies a low-dividend payout policy? When should firms adopt a high-dividend payout policy?

14-4. Why do capital markets (and therefore corporate managers) have a preference for fixed or increasing dividends? What is the usual reward to firms who maintain such a policy?

14-5. Compare and contrast the three dividend policies discussed in the chapter. Of the three policies, which is rarely observed in practice? Why?

14-6. Is the low-regular-and-extra dividend policy appropriate for firms in all industries? Why? Would this policy be more appropriate for an automobile manufacturer or a medium-sized bank? Why?

14-7. In what ways may stock repurchases enhance shareholder value? Why is a repurchase preferred over cash dividends for most investors who pay taxes?

14-8. What is the clear capital market reaction to dividend cuts or omissions?

14-9. What is the basic premise of the agency cost model of dividend policy? How does this model differ from the signaling model of dividend policy with respect to the motivation of managers for paying/increasing dividends?

14-10. How do Miller and Modigliani (M&M) arrive at their conclusion that dividend policy is irrelevant in a world of frictionless capital markets? Why is the assumption of fixed investment policy crucial to this conclusion?

14-11. What impact does the introduction of personal income taxes on dividend income have on the dividend-irrelevance conclusion of M&M? What is the impact of transactions costs?

14-12. According to the residual theory of dividends, how does a firm set its dividend? With which dividend policy is this theory most compatible? Does it appear to be empirically validated?

14-13. In what way may managers use dividends to convey pertinent information about their firms in a world of informational asymmetry? Why would a manager choose to convey information via dividend policy? Does empirical evidence support or refute the informational role of dividends?

14-14. Why do firms with more-diverse shareholder bases typically pay higher dividends than private firms or public firms with more-concentrated ownership structures? How are fixed dividends used as a bonding (commitment) mechanism by managers of firms with dispersed ownership structures and large amounts of free cash flow?

14-15. What is the expected relationship between dividend payout levels and the growth rate and availability of positive-*NPV* projects under the agency cost model of dividends? What about the expected relationship between dividend payout and the diffusion of firm shareholders? Free cash flow? Consider a firm such as Microsoft awash in free cash flow, positive-*NPV* projects available, and a relatively diffuse shareholder base in an industry with increasing competition. Does either the agency model or signaling model adequately predict the dividend policy of Microsoft? Which does the better job?

PROBLEMS

Dividend Fundamentals

14-1. What are alternative ways in which investors can receive a cash return from their investment in the equity of a company? From a tax standpoint, which of these would be preferred, assuming that everybody pays a 30 percent tax on income and capital gains? What are the pros and cons of paying out cash dividends?

14-2. Global Utilities Company (GUC) follows a policy of paying out 60 percent of its net income as cash dividends to its shareholders each year. The company plans to do so again this year, during which GUC earned $50 million in net profits after tax. If the company has 25 million shares outstanding and pays dividends quarterly, what is the company's nominal dividend payment per share each quarter?

14-3. Using the data for Global Utilities Company presented in Problem 14-2 and assuming that GUC's stock price is $42 per share immediately before its ex-dividend date, what is the expected price of GUC stock on the ex-dividend date if there are no personal taxes on dividend income received?

14-4. Use your findings for Global Utilities Company from Problems 14-2 and 14-3 and assume that an investor purchased GUC stock a year ago at $38. The investor, who faces a personal tax rate of 40 percent on dividend income and 20 percent on capital gains, plans to sell the stock very soon. Transactions costs are negligible.

   a. Calculate the after-tax return this investor will earn if she sells GUC stock at the current $42 stock price prior to the ex-dividend date.
   b. Calculate the after-tax return the investor will earn if she sells GUC stock on the ex-dividend date, assuming that the price of GUC stock falls by the dividend amount on the ex-dividend date.
   c. By how much must the price of GUC stock be expected to fall on the ex-dividend date in order for this investor to be indifferent (in terms of after-tax net return) to whether she sells before or after the ex-dividend date?

14-5. Samuel Prudent is a shareholder in the Slow Growth Manufacturing Company (SGMC). The current price of SGMC's stock is $66 per share, and there are 1 million shares outstanding. Samuel owns 10,000 shares, or 1 percent of the stock, which he purchased one year ago for $60 per share. Assume that SGMC makes a surprise announcement that it plans to repurchase 100,000 shares of its own stock at a price of $70 per share. In response to this announcement, SGMC's stock price increases $2 per share, from $66 to $68, but this price is expected to fall back to $67 per share after the repurchase is completed. Assume that Samuel faces marginal personal tax rates of 30 percent on dividend income and 15 percent on capital gains.

   a. Calculate Samuel's (realized) after-tax return from his investment in SGMC shares, assuming that he chooses to participate in the repurchase program and all of the shares he tenders are purchased at $70 per share.

   b. How many shares will Samuel be able to sell if all SGMC's shareholders tender their shares to the firm as part of this repurchase program and the company purchases shares on a pro rata basis?

   c. What fraction of SGMC's total common equity will Samuel own after the repurchase program is completed if he chooses not to tender his shares?

Patterns Observed in Payout Policies Worldwide

14-6. Go to the home page of Microsoft (http://www.microsoft.com), and link to its financial reports page. Download the most recent annual report, and observe the capital investment and dividend policies of Microsoft. Now, do the same for ExxonMobil (http://www2.exxonmobil.com). Which of the two firms appears to have the higher-growth, positive-*NPV* investment opportunities? Which pays the higher relative dividend? Do these results support the agency cost model? The signaling model?

14-7. Go to the home page for Dogs of the Dow (http://www.dogsofthedow.com), look at the year-to-date figures, and observe the dividend yields of the 30 stocks of the Dow Jones Industrial Average. Which industries contain the higher-dividend-yielding stocks, and which contain the lower-yielding stocks? Are there differences in the growth prospects between the high- and low-yielding stocks? Is this what you expected? Explain.

14-8. A publicly traded firm announces a decrease in its dividend with no other material information accompanying the announcement. What inside information is this announcement likely to convey, and what is the expected stock-price impact due to the market's assimilation of this information?

Payout Policy Irrelevance in a World with Perfect Capital Markets

14-9. Quixotic Caitlin Card Company currently has assets of $100 million and a required return of 20 percent on its 10 million shares outstanding. The firm has an opportunity to invest in positive-*NPV* (minimal) projects that will cost $20 million and is trying to determine if it should withhold this amount from dividends payable to finance the investments or if it should pay out the dividends and issue new shares to finance the investments. Show that the decision is irrelevant in a world of frictionless markets. What happens if a personal income tax of 40 percent is introduced into the model?

14-10. Assume that two unlevered firms operate in the same industry, have identical assets worth $50 million that yield a net profit of 15 percent per year, and have 2 million shares outstanding. Further assume that each firm has the opportunity to invest an amount equal to its net income each year in (slightly) positive-*NPV* investment projects. The Alpha Company wishes to finance its capital spending through retained earnings. The Omega Company wishes to pay out 100 percent of its annual earnings as cash dividends and to finance its investments with a new share offering each year. There are no taxes or transactions costs to issuing securities.

   a. Calculate the overall and per-share market value of the Alpha Company at the end of each of the next three years. What return on investment will this firm's shareholders earn?

   b. Describe the specific steps that the Omega Company must take today (end-of-year 0) and at the end of each of the next three years if it is to both pay out all of its net income as dividends and still grow its assets at the same rate as that of the Alpha Company.

c. Calculate the number and per-share price of shares that the Omega Company must sell today and at the end of each of the next three years if it is to both pay out all of its net income as dividends and still grow its assets at the same rate as that of the Alpha Company.

d. Assuming that you currently own 20,000 shares (1 percent) of Omega Company stock, compute the fraction of the company's total outstanding equity that you will own three years from now if you do not participate in any of the share offerings the firm will make during this holding period.

14-11. Kilgore Chemical Inc. traditionally pays an annual dividend equal to 25 percent of its earnings. Investors anticipate that the next dividend, due in one year, will be $2 per share. The company has 2 million shares outstanding. Investors expect earnings to grow at 6 percent in perpetuity, and they require a return of 10 percent on their shares. Use the Gordon growth model (see Equation 4.6) to calculate Kilgore's stock price today.

14-12. Refer to Problem 14-11. Suppose Kilgore Chemical announces a new dividend policy. Henceforth, it will distribute all of its earnings as dividends, but each year it will issue new shares to pay for investments that previously would have been financed with retained earnings. What effect does this change in policy have on Kilgore's current stock price? Assume that markets are frictionless.

Smart Solutions

See the problem and solution explained step-by-step at **SMARTFinance**

Entrepreneurial Finance and Venture Capital

OPENING FOCUS
Amazon.com Redefines Electronic Commerce and Stock Volatility

Since its founding in July 1994, Amazon.com has emerged as one of the prototypical companies of the Internet age. Billed from inception as "Earth's Biggest Bookstore," Amazon.com quickly established itself as the premier online marketer of published materials, offering several million titles in a variety of languages. After it began expanding its online offerings in 1999 to include music, auctions, toys, electronics, travel, and other products and services, Amazon.com changed its slogan to claim that it had Earth's Biggest Selection™. Few could doubt this claim, since Amazon.com's customers in 220 countries ordered no less than 37.5 million items online during the 2001 Christmas season alone, and in the 12 months ending on September 30, 2002, the company's sales reached $3.62 billion.

In addition to becoming a poster child for savvy electronic marketing, Amazon.com also offers a classic example of creative corporate finance. Launched with a $10,000 cash investment and a $15,000 loan by Jeffrey Bezos, the company's founder and CEO, Amazon.com's early growth was fueled in part by credit card loans drawn on Mr. Bezos's personal account. One year after Amazon.com went "online" in July 1995, the company secured private equity funding from Silicon Valley's top venture capital firm (Kleiner Perkins Caufield & Byers), and in May 1997, the firm executed one of the splashiest initial public offerings of a very splashy decade. Within one year of its IPO, and less than four years after its inception, Amazon.com had annual revenues of $175 million and a market capitalization of over $7 billion. Investors who purchased Amazon's stock at its IPO price of $18 per share experienced a 1-year return of over 400 percent, and the private equity investors (whose weighted average share purchase price was a mere $0.56 per share) received an astronomical total return of over 15,000 percent!

Amazon.com's stock peaked in December 1999 at $107 per share ($1,280 per share after adjusting for three stock splits). This gave the firm a market capitalization of over $33 billion, in spite of the fact that it had never reported a single quarterly profit since inception (and did not until the fourth quarter of 2001). The stock price then began a long slide, hitting bottom at $5.51 per share in late September 2001, before rebounding to $21 by January 2003.

The brief, but exciting, history of Amazon.com offers a classic case study of the promise and perils of financing entrepreneurial growth companies. Venture capitalists facilitated Amazon.com's rapid early development, and the company later obtained a large chunk of pure risk capital through a very successful IPO. Nevertheless, Amazon.com's evolution as a public company has been marked by an extremely high level of stock-price volatility, and the company faces the ongoing challenge of sustaining and financing rapid growth.

Sources: The information on Amazon.com cited in this chapter is drawn from a variety of sources, including the prospectus for the company's IPO, the firm's own now-famous website (http://www.amazon.com), the websites of CNN Money (http://money.cnn.com) and Quicken (http://www.quicken.com), and various published reports.

The past quarter century has been kind to finance generally, but no area of our profession has prospered quite as much as the field of **entrepreneurial finance.** From the proliferation of venture capital investors, to the boom and bust in Internet-related IPOs, the financial performance of **entrepreneurial growth companies** (**EGCs**) offered spectacular theater over the past decade. In this chapter, we examine the particular challenges faced by financial managers of EGCs and the ways that venture capitalists (VCs) help meet these challenges. The topic is an important one, even for students who are not aspiring venture capitalists. Formerly the near-exclusive domain of small, highly specialized venture capital limited partnerships, the financing of EGCs now affects professionals working for mutual funds, pension funds, and even Fortune 500 manufacturing concerns. Increasingly, large corporations have internal venture capital units charged with financing, nurturing, and growing new business opportunities. Companies such as Merck, Intel, Microsoft, Cisco Systems, and General Electric spend billions each year investing in EGCs. Deciding which EGCs to invest in, as well as how to structure and monitor those investments, presents a difficult problem. By studying how VCs approach these issues, we will learn lessons that extend well beyond the venture capital industry.

15.1 THE CHALLENGES OF FINANCING ENTREPRENEURIAL GROWTH COMPANIES

How does entrepreneurial finance differ from "ordinary" finance? Entrepreneurial growth companies differ from large, publicly traded firms in four important ways. First, EGCs often achieve compound annual growth rates of 50 percent or more in sales and assets. Though it is somewhat counterintuitive, companies growing that rapidly usually consume more cash than they generate because growth requires ongoing investments in fixed assets and working capital. In fact, there is an old saying that the leading causes of death for young firms are (1) not enough customers and (2) too many customers. Too many customers, or very rapid growth, can lead to bankruptcy if firms do not have adequate financing in place. Privately owned EGCs almost always plan to convert to public ownership, either through an initial public offering (IPO) or by selling out to a larger firm. Once they become publicly traded, EGCs tend to rely on external equity funding much more than do older, larger firms. In other words, EGCs grow rapidly and require a great deal of cash, much of which must be obtained externally.

Second, the most valuable assets of many of these firms are often patents and other (intangible) intellectual property rights, which we know are inherently difficult

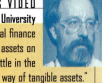

SMART IDEAS VIDEO
Greg Udell, Indiana University
"Firms that access venture capital finance typically have loads of intangible assets on their balance sheets and very little in the way of tangible assets."

See the entire interview at SMARTFinance

to finance externally. This poses a huge challenge to those professionals charged with obtaining adequate funding on attractive terms. Third, many entrepreneurial growth companies seek to commercialize highly promising but untested technologies, and this inevitably means that both the risk of failure and the potential payoff from success are dizzyingly high. Fourth, EGCs must attract, motivate, compensate, and retain highly skilled technical and entrepreneurial talent in a way that minimizes claims on the firm's current cash flow (which is often severely constrained) but also provides maximum incentives to achieve success.

The distinctive features of entrepreneurial finance imply that EGCs will rely heavily on equity financing and that financial contracting between these companies and their financiers will be fraught with informational asymmetries. Although this imperative to finance growth opportunities with equity arises in most technology- and knowledge-based companies, mature firms obtain the bulk of the equity funding they need each year by reinvesting profits. But entrepreneurial growth firms, with their extremely rapid growth in assets and cash flow that is often negative, typically must rely on outside equity financing, the scarcest and most expensive type of funding. Further, because most of these firms are privately held, they lack access to public stock markets and rely instead on private equity financing. Private equity generally means either capital investments by current owners or funding by professional venture capitalists.

We should point out that the vast majority of firms, even those that subsequently emerge as EGCs, begin life on a modest scale and with little or no external equity financing besides that provided by the founder's friends and family. This is what Bhide (1992) calls "bootstrap finance." Only after entrepreneurs exhaust these sources of personal equity can they expect to obtain debt financing from banks or other financial institutions. Table 15.1 describes the results of an empirical study examining the sources of start-up capital for a sample of 132 companies founded during 1987. The table shows that personal equity financing and institutional loans con-

Table 15.1
Sources of Start-up Capital for a Sample of 132 Companies

Capital Sources[a]	Mean Percentage	Standard Deviation
Equity		
Personal equity	35.6	40.8
Partnerships	5.2	17.9
Issuance of stock	3.2	14.5
Miscellaneous	2.7	13.6
	46.7	
Debt		
Institutional loans	43.8	40.5
Loans from individuals	5.3	19.1
Issuance of bonds	1.1	8.6
Miscellaneous	2.7	12.8
	52.9	

Source: Richard B. Carter and Howard E. Van Auken, "Personal Equity Investment and Small Business Financial Difficulties," *Entrepreneurship: Theory and Practice* 15 (Winter 1990), pp. 51–60.
[a]Capital sources are stated as percentages of the total start-up capital. Means do not add to 100%, due to rounding.

stitute the two most important sources of start-up capital, accounting for almost 80 percent of funds raised.

15.2 VENTURE CAPITAL FINANCING IN THE UNITED STATES

Defined broadly, *venture capital* has been a fixture of Western civilization for many centuries. In this context, the decision by Spain's Ferdinand and Isabella to finance the voyage of Christopher Columbus can be considered one of history's most profitable venture capital investments (at least for the Spanish). However, modern **venture capital**—defined as a professionally managed pool of money raised for the sole purpose of making actively managed direct equity investments in rapidly growing private companies—is a modern financial innovation. Until recently, only the United States had an active venture capital market.[1] This is changing rapidly, as many countries have experienced rapid growth in venture capital financing over the past five years.

Gompers and Lerner (2001) trace the birth of America's venture capital industry to the American Research and Development Company (ARDC) that began operating in Boston shortly after the end of World War II. As often happens with pioneers, ARDC had to invent the practices of modern venture capital and made many unprofitable investments in its early years. However, ARDC more than made up for its early mistakes with a single, spectacularly successful investment in Digital Equipment. Through the late 1970s, the total pool of venture capital was quite small, and most of the active funds were sponsored either by financial institutions (e.g., Citicorp Venture Capital) or nonfinancial corporations (e.g., Xerox). Most of the money raised by these funds came from their corporate backers and from wealthy individuals or family trusts. There are two features of early venture capital funds that we still observe today: (1) these funds' investments were mostly intermediate-term, equity-related investments targeted at technology-based private companies and (2) the venture capitalists played a unique role as active investors, contributing both capital and expertise to portfolio companies. Also, from the very start, VCs looked to invest in those rare companies with the potential of going public or being acquired at a premium within a few years, and which offered investment returns of 25–50 percent per year.

A fundamental change in the U.S. venture capital market occurred during the late 1970s. Two seemingly unrelated public policy innovations contributed to this change. First, Congress lowered the top personal income tax rate on capital gains from 35 percent to 28 percent in 1978, thereby increasing the return to entrepreneurship. Second, the Labor Department adopted its "Prudent Man Rule" in 1979, effectively authorizing pension fund managers to allocate a moderate fraction of fund assets to private equity investments. While neither of these changes appears revolutionary, their effect on venture capital funding was dramatic. Total venture capital funds raised in-

---

[1] Two older, though still frequently cited, articles describe the "classic" venture capital process in detail. See Tybejee and Bruno (1984) and Gorman and Sahlman (1989). A more recent description of the venture capital investment process is provided by the National Venture Capital Association, "The Venture Capital Industry: An Overview" (http://www.nvca .org/def.html).

creased from $68.2 million in 1977 to $978.1 million in 1978 (both figures are in 1987 dollars). A further capital gains tax reduction in 1981 contributed to venture capital funding growth from $961.4 million in 1980 to $5.1 billion in 1983. Funding then remained in the $2–$5 billion range for the rest of the 1980s. After falling to $1.3 billion in 1991, venture capital funding began a steady climb to a record $106.8 billion in 2000 before falling back to $40.6 billion during 2001.

TYPES OF VENTURE CAPITAL FUNDS

In discussing venture capital, we must carefully differentiate between institutional venture capital funds and angel capitalists. **Institutional venture capital funds** are formal business entities with full-time professionals dedicated to seeking out and funding promising ventures, while **angel capitalists** (or *angels*) are wealthy individuals who make private equity investments on a more ad hoc basis. A vibrant market for "angel capital" exists and routinely provides over $50 billion per year in total equity investment to private businesses in the United States.[2] Until very recently, angel capitalists provided far more total investment to entrepreneurial companies each year than did institutional venture capital firms. Nonetheless, we focus on the latter group throughout this text because these firms operate nationally and provide the performance benchmark against which all private equity investment is compared.

There are four categories of institutional venture capital funds, as described in Pratt (1997). First, **small business investment companies** (**SBICs**) are federally chartered corporations established as a result of the Small Business Administration Act of 1958. Since then, SBICs have invested over $14 billion in approximately 80,000 small firms.[3] Historically, these venture capitalists have relied on their unique ability to borrow money from the U.S. Treasury at very attractive rates. SBICs were the only types of VCs that structured their investments as debt rather than equity. This feature seriously hampered their flexibility, but a revision of the law in 1992 has made it possible for SBICs to obtain equity capital from the Treasury in the form of preferred equity interests and also to organize themselves as limited partnerships. Recent evidence suggests that this change, by itself, has not been enough for SBICs to regain venture capital market share.

Second, **financial venture capital funds** are subsidiaries of financial institutions, particularly commercial banks. These are generally set up both to nurture portfolio companies that will ultimately become profitable customers of the corporate parent and to earn high investment returns by leveraging the financial expertise and contacts of existing corporate staff. Though many financial venture capital funds are organized as SBICs, their orientation is sufficiently specialized that they are generally classified separately. Third, **corporate venture capital funds** are subsidiaries or stand-alone firms established by nonfinancial corporations eager to gain access to emerging technologies by making early-stage investments in high-tech firms. Finally, **venture capital limited partnerships** are funds established by professional venture capital firms. These firms act as the general partners organizing, investing, managing, and ultimately liq-

---

[2] The angel capital market is discussed in Freear (1994), Lerner (1998), Freear, Sohl, and Wetzel (2000), and Wong (2001). Additionally, Campbell (2001b) cites a Global Entrepreneurship Monitor 2001 report suggesting that informal investors (angels) provide about $196 billion to start-up and early-stage companies in 29 countries each year.

[3] SBICs are discussed in more depth in Brewer and Genay (1994), Kinn and Zaff (1997), and Birnbaum (1999). A wealth of information about SBICs may be found at http://www.sba.gov/INV/, the home page of SBIC program. We also wish to thank Mr. Richard Testa, long considered America's premier venture capital lawyer, for taking the time to comment on (and sometimes correct) an earlier draft of this chapter. His insights regarding the growth of the venture capital industry proved especially helpful.

uidating the capital raised from the limited partners. Most limited partnerships have a single-industry focus determined by the expertise of the general partners.

Limited partnerships dominate the venture capital industry, at least partly because they make their investment decisions free from outside influences. The SBICs have been hampered both by their historical reliance on inappropriate funding sources and by the myriad regulations that apply to government-sponsored companies. The financial and corporate funds tend to suffer because their ultimate loyalty rests with their corporate parents, rather than their portfolio companies. Divided loyalties lead to conflicts of interest between financier and entrepreneur and between the corporate funds and other venture capital investors. Further, compensating employees who work in the venture capital groups of financial and nonfinancial corporate funds poses a challenge. Corporate funds can either match the lucrative and highly perfor-mance-based compensation packages offered by venture capital limited partnerships, thereby creating significant internal compensation disparities, or they can offer pay packages similar to those offered to most corporate employees. In the latter case, lim-ited partnerships can "poach" the best employees from corporate venture funds. Finally, corporate funds have histories of only intermittent commitment to venture capital investing. Corporate funds tend to scale back dramatically when business con-ditions sour. For all these reasons, the limited partnerships now control over 75 per-cent of total industry resources, and their sway over fund-raising seems to be increas-ing. Gompers and Lerner (2001) provide a detailed history of the development of the U.S. venture capital industry and describe the key comparative advantages of limited partnerships.

INVESTMENT PATTERNS OF U.S. VENTURE CAPITAL FIRMS

Given the media attention lavished on venture capital in the United States, most people are surprised to learn just how small the industry actually was before 1998. Figure 15.1 plots the total amount of capital invested each year from 1990 through the first quarter of 2002. Annual disbursements naturally differ from total fund-raising, as the total amount of money available for investment is the sum of realized investment returns (from IPOs and mergers of portfolio companies) and new fund

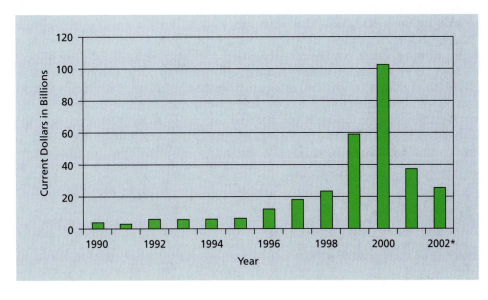

Figure 15.1
Annual Venture Capital Investments in the United States, 1990–2002

Source: National Venture Capital Association (http://www.nvca.com).
* Annualized, based on $6.2 billion invested during the first quarter of 2002.

Table 15.2
Venture Capital Fund-Raising by U.S. Venture Capital Partnerships, 1979–1999

	1979	1983	1987	1991	1995	1999[a]
First closing of funds						
Number of funds	27	147	112	34	84	204
Size (1999 $ in billions)	0.53	6.01	5.93	1.69	4.60	37.46
Sources of funds						
Private pension funds	31%	26%	27%	25%	38%	9%
Public pension funds	[b]	5%	12%	17%	[b]	9%
Corporations	17%	12%	10%	4%	2%	16%
Insurance companies/banks	4%	12%	15%	6%	18%	11%
Endowments	10%	8%	10%	24%	22%	15%
Foreign investors/others	15%	16%	14%	12%	3%	22%
Individuals and family trusts	23%	21%	12%	12%	17%	19%
Independent venture partnerships as a share of total venture capital pool[c]		68%	78%	80%		

Source: Table 1 in Paul Gompers and Josh Lerner, "The Venture Capital Revolution," *Journal of Economic Perspectives* 15 (Spring 2001), pp. 145–168.
[a]In 2000, there were 228 funds raised with committed capital of $67.7 billion.
[b]Public pension funds are included with private pension funds in these years.
[c]This series is defined differently in different years. It is not available for 1979 and after 1994.

inflows from investors. Figure 15.1 reveals that total investments by VCs never exceeded $6 billion until 1996. Total investment spending then surged to an astonishing $102.3 billion (spread over 5,608 companies) in 2000, before declining very sharply thereafter. The average investment of $18.24 million per company during 2000 was over four times larger than the $4.5 million average investment per company in 1995. Even with the dramatic 2-year falloff in venture spending, 2002 was on a pace (as this book was going to press) to register the fourth-highest venture investment year ever.[4]

Whereas the bulk of venture capital funding once came either from corporate sponsors (in the case of financial or corporate funds) or wealthy individuals, institutional investors have become the dominant sources of funding today. As shown in Table 15.2, pension funds alone typically account for 31–42 percent of all new money raised by institutional venture capital firms, though their share in 1999 fell to only 18 percent. Even though few pension funds allocate more than 5 percent of their total assets to private equity funding, their sheer size makes them extremely important investors, and their long-term investment horizons make them ideal partners for venture capital funds. Financial and nonfinancial corporations usually represent the second-largest contributors of capital to venture funds, accounting for 10–30 percent of the total. The corporate share reached 27 percent in 1999. Foundations (endowments) are the third important source of venture capital funding, usually ac-

---

[4.] A number of academic studies have examined how various factors—especially the incidence and levels of personal and corporate taxation—influence the amount of money raised and invested by American venture capital funds each year. Gompers and Lerner (1998a) find that decreases in capital gains tax rates appear to have a positive and important impact on commitments to new venture capital funds. This is actually rather surprising, because the dominant investors in venture capital funds are untaxed pension funds. Gompers and Lerner conclude that the relationship between taxation and venture capital commitments is an induced one because reductions in tax rates cause more entrepreneurs to start companies and thus demand private equity financing.

counting for 10–25 percent of the total. Foreign investors have become increasingly important recently, and (in combination with "other" investors) accounted for 22 percent of 1999's total funding. Individuals and family trusts are the final major group of venture capital investors. These two groups together generally contribute 10–25 percent of the total venture capital funding.

Industrial and Geographic Distribution of Venture Capital Investment

One reason for the success enjoyed by institutional VCs is that they usually invest only in those industries where they have some competitive advantage and where their involvement in portfolio-company management can create real economic value. Table 15.3 lists the industries that received the most venture capital funding in 1998, 2000, and the first quarter of 2002. Typical of the history of venture capital, the majority of investment flowed into information technology industries (communications and computers) during all three periods. Internet-specific investments accounted for a whopping 46.4 percent of the total in year 2000, but for much lower fractions in 1998 and 2002. Reductions in venture capital spending in this sector made room for expanded investments in 2002 in industries such as biotechnology, health care, entertainment, and consumer goods and services.

Another striking regularity in venture capital investment patterns concerns the geographical distribution of portfolio companies. Firms located in California consistently receive more venture backing than firms in any other state. For instance, in the first quarter of 2002, California firms captured 47.1 percent of total funding, more than three times the funding received by firms in New England (13.3%). The money flows into California dwarfed those in other large, populous states such as New York (6.6%) and Texas (5.1%).

Venture Capital Investment by Stage of Company Development

The popular image of VCs holds that they specialize in making investments in start-up or very early-stage companies. This is only partly true. In fact, as Figure 15.2 doc-

Industry	First-Quarter 2002	2000	1998
Computer software & services	17.0%	14.0%	21.6%
Networking & equipment[a]	14.4	46.4	13.4
Biotechnology	12.1	2.7	5.2
Telecommunications	11.6	17.1	17.6
Consumer related	7.2	1.6	6.9
Semiconductor	6.9	5.9	4.2
Medical devices & equipment	6.6	3.5	12.8
Media & entertainment	5.6	—	—
Computer hardware	3.8	2.2	3.1
Industrial/energy	4.5	1.4	2.4
Other products	0.7	5.1	12.7
Total ($ in millions)	$6,228	$102,976	$18,705

Table 15.3
U.S. Venture Capital Investment by Industry: 1998, 2000, and 2002

Full Years 1998 and 2000, Plus First-Quarter 2002

Source: 2002 data from the PricewaterhouseCoopers/Venture Economics/National Venture Capital Association "MoneyTree™" quarterly description of venture capital investment in the United States (http://www.pwcmoneytree.com). Data for earlier years are drawn from the NVCA website (http://www.nvca.com).
[a]This category was called "Internet specific" in 1998 and 2000.

Figure 15.2
U.S. Venture Capital
Investments by Stage of
Company Development,
1997–2002 (full years
1997 and 1999, and first
quarter 2002)

Source: 2002 data from the
PricewaterhouseCoopers/
Venture Economics/National
Venture Capital Association
MoneyTree™ quarterly de-
scription of venture capital
investment in the United States
(http://www.pwcmoneytree
.com). Data for earlier years are
drawn from the NVCA website
(http://www.nvca.com).

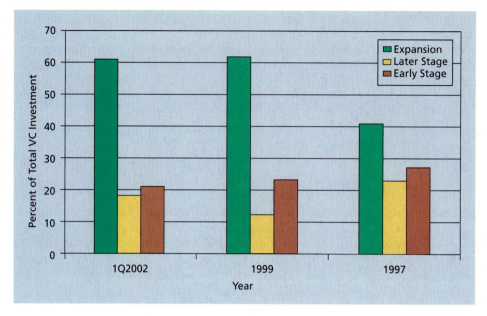

uments, early-stage financing accounted for only 21 percent of total investment in the first quarter of 2002, down from 23 percent in 1999 and 26 percent in 1997. Truly early-stage (start-up and seed-stage) financing represented a mere 1.5 percent in the first quarter of 2002 financing (not shown), and similarly small fractions were allocated in prior years. However, if we broaden the definition of "early stage" to include a fraction of expansion spending, total early-stage investment would probably fall in the range of 35–50 percent of venture capital disbursements each year. Being rational investors, venture capitalists are as leery as anyone else of backing extremely risky new companies, and will do so only if the entrepreneur/founder is well known to the venture capitalists, the venture is extraordinarily promising, or both. Later-stage investments in more mature private companies accounted for 18 percent of total venture capital investment in the first quarter of 2002, 12 percent in 1999, and 23 percent in 1997. These investments represent funding for marketing programs, major production plant expansions, and financing made in preparation for accessing the public capital markets. This has accounted for 12–23 percent of total investment over the past four years.

Although the distribution between early- and later-stage funding varies from year to year, one principle of venture capital funding never changes—the earlier the development stage of the portfolio company, the higher must be the expected return on the venture capitalist's investment. Professional VCs typically demand compound annual investment returns in excess of 50 percent on start-up investments, but they will accept returns of 20–30 percent per year on later-stage deals because the risk is far lower in more-established companies. VCs extract a higher expected return on early-stage investments in part by requiring entrepreneurs to sell them a higher ownership stake in these deals.

Usually, though, there is not a stark choice between early- and later-stage investments. Most VC funds that invest in a company during its early years remain committed to the firm as it develops, and they typically participate in many financing rounds as the portfolio company matures. On average, the prices venture capitalists pay to acquire additional shares in portfolio companies rise in each subsequent round of financing.

ORGANIZATION AND FUNDING OF VENTURE CAPITAL LIMITED PARTNERSHIPS

Most of the top venture capital firms are organized as general partnerships, and many of these are concentrated in California's Silicon Valley south of San Francisco.[5] These firms usually begin the venture financing process by creating a distinct limited partnership fund, typically with a dedicated investment target, such as funding Internet start-ups.

SMART IDEAS VIDEO

Manju Puri, Stanford University

"Venture capital does have a positive role for innovative companies in helping to push their product out quickly."

See the entire interview at **SMARTFinance**

APPLYING THE MODEL

The year 1998 witnessed the successful launch of two megafunds: Warburg, Pincus Equity Partners, L.P.; and Hicks, Muse, Tate, & Furst Equity Fund IV, L.P. These two funds raised $5 billion and $4 billion, respectively. As the Roman numeral after the Hicks, Muse fund name implies, this firm has launched many previous successful funds. Even in the more challenging period of 2000–2001, Gupta (2001) reports that J. P. Morgan Capital Partners started two funds with a combined total value of $13 billion.

Although some venture funds are created by public offerings of limited partnership interests (which can then be freely traded), most are organized and capitalized by private negotiation between the fund's sponsor and a well-established group of institutional investors. To say that a fund is "capitalized" at its inception is something of a misnomer. In practice, the limited partners make capital commitments, which the general partner then draws on over time as the fund becomes fully invested. In addition to organizing the limited partnership, the sponsoring firm acts as the general partner (and has unlimited liability) over the fund's entire life, typically 7 to 10 years. As general partner, the VC is responsible for (1) seeking out investment opportunities and negotiating the terms on which these investments will be made; (2) monitoring the performance of the portfolio companies and providing additional funding and expertise as necessary; (3) finding an attractive exit opportunity, such as an IPO or a merger, that will allow the fund to liquidate its investments; and (4) distributing the realized cash returns from these exit opportunities to the limited partners and then terminating the fund. For its services, the general partner usually receives a percentage claim on the realized return (almost always 20%) as well as an annual management fee equal to 1–3 percent (usually 2.5%) of the fund's total committed capital.

The relationship between VCs and investors is fraught with agency problems. Investors must commit large amounts of money for long-term, illiquid, nontransparent investments in private partnerships over which they can exercise no direct control without forfeiting their limited liability. Venture capitalists have many opportunities to expropriate the limited partners' wealth, including setting up new funds, which exclude the old limited partners, to finance the most promising companies and making side deals with the best portfolio companies. Reputational concerns largely control this problem, but contractual covenants also play a role in limiting agency problems.

Many senior partners at top venture capital firms have become legendary for their skill in finding, nurturing, and bringing to market high-tech companies. Examples include John Doerr of Kleiner Perkins Caufield & Byers, William Hambricht of

[5.] In particular, Sand Hill Road near Stanford University is venture capital's epicenter. This street is home to no fewer than 50 venture capital firms, as well as a large number of accounting, law, and investment banking firms.

Hambricht and Quist, and Sam Rosen of Rosen Partners. These industry leaders have become extraordinarily wealthy, but even "ordinary" venture capitalists did quite well during the 1995–2000 boom. The industry's financial rewards attract numerous would-be VCs, but jobs in the industry are notoriously difficult to obtain, particularly for newly minted MBAs. Partners and associates in venture capital firms often are engineers or other technically trained professionals who themselves worked in high-tech companies before becoming full-time VCs. This experience gives them in-depth knowledge of both the technological and business aspects of the industries in which they invest. It is this expertise, along with capital and contacts, which entrepreneurs look for when they approach a VC for funding. For example, John Doerr of Kleiner Perkins Caufield & Byers has bachelor's and master's degrees in electrical engineering (plus an MBA from Harvard Business School), and worked for Intel Corporation for five years before becoming a venture capitalist.

How Venture Capitalists Structure Their Investments

Although one should be wary of describing anything as unique as a venture capital investment contract as "standard," most agreements between VCs and entrepreneurs share certain characteristics.[6] First and foremost, venture capital contracts allocate risk, return, and ownership rights between the entrepreneur (and other existing owners of a portfolio company) and the fund. The distribution of rights and responsibilities depends on (1) the experience and reputation of the entrepreneur, (2) the attractiveness of the portfolio company as an investment opportunity, (3) the stage of the company's development, (4) the negotiating skills of the contracting parties, and (5) the overall state of the market.[7] If, at a time of fierce competition among VCs, a respected and experienced entrepreneur approaches a fund with an opportunity to invest in an established company with a promising technology, the entrepreneur will secure financing on relatively attractive terms. Gompers and Lerner (2000a) establish a positive link between portfolio-company valuations and heavy cash inflows into the venture capital industry during the periods 1987–1990 and 1992–1995. This impact was greatest in venture capital-intensive regions (especially California and Boston) and for later-stage companies that could profitably employ larger cash infusions. However, if an inexperienced entrepreneur asks for start-up funding at a time when venture capital is scarce (such as the early 1990s), the entrepreneur will have to accept fairly onerous contract terms to attract funding.

Early in the negotiation process, the parties must estimate the portfolio company's value. The company's past R&D efforts, its current and prospective sales revenue, its tangible assets, and the present value of its expected net cash flows all enter into the valuation equation. In large measure the valuation will determine what fraction of the firm the entrepreneur must exchange for venture backing. Next, the parties must

---

[6.] Kaplan and Strömberg (2001) present what is probably the most comprehensive academic analysis of how VCs contract with entrepreneurs to allocate cash flow and control rights between the firm and the VC fund. Other excellent papers on the subject include those by Sahlman (1988, 1990), Testa (1988), Gompers (1995), and Lerner (1995).

[7.] Kaplan and Strömberg (2000) examine the process of venture capital investment screening, and they show that many factors—market size, business strategy, the firm's technology and customer base, and potential competition—influence the investment decision. Kaplan and Strömberg also describe how the allocation of control rights between VC and entrepreneur is determined; Baker and Gompers (2001) examine how board seats are allocated; and Christopher (2001) describes several of the important legal hurdles VCs must confront when evaluating an investment opportunity. Hellmann and Puri (2002) examine how venture capitalists create value by helping professionalize the start-up companies in which they invest. This involves helping companies develop compensation and human resource policies and hire key executives (such as a marketing VP), and intervening to replace poorly performing managers early enough to promote effective change.

agree on the amount of new funding the venture capitalist will provide and the required return on that investment.[8] Naturally, the higher the perceived risk the higher the required return.

Venture capitalists use **staged financing** to minimize their risk exposure. To illustrate how staged financing works, assume that a company needs $25 million in private funding to fully commercialize a promising new technology. Rather than invest the entire amount at once, the venture capitalist initially advances only enough (say, $5 million) to fund the company to its next development stage. Both parties agree to specific performance objectives (e.g., building a working product prototype) as a condition for more rounds of financing. If the company succeeds in reaching those goals, the venture capitalist will provide funding for the next development stage, usually on terms more favorable to the entrepreneur. Staged financing is not only a very efficient way to minimize risk for the venture capitalist, but it also gives the venture fund an extremely valuable option to deny or delay additional funding. This **cancellation option** places the maximum feasible amount of financial risk on the entrepreneur, but in return allows the entrepreneur to obtain funding at a less onerous price than would otherwise be possible. Staged financing also provides tremendous incentives for the entrepreneur to create value because at each new funding stage, the VC provides capital on increasingly attractive terms.

APPLYING THE MODEL

Gompers (1995) provides two classic examples of how staged financing should work in the development of private companies: Apple Computer and Federal Express. Apple received three rounds of private equity funding. In the first round, venture capitalists purchased stock at $0.09 per share, but this rose to $0.28 per share in the second round and then $0.97 per share in the third round. Needless to say, all these investments proved spectacularly profitable when Apple went public at $22.00 per share in 1980. Investors in Federal Express, however, used staged financing with more telling effect during their three rounds of private equity financing. The investors purchased stock for $204.17 per share in the first round, but the firm's early performance was much poorer than anticipated. In the second round, shares were purchased for $7.34 each, but the company's finances continued to deteriorate, so a third financing round, at $0.63 per share, was required. As we know, FedEx eventually became a roaring success and went public at $6.00 per share in 1978, but staged financing allowed venture capitalists to intervene decisively during the firm's problematic early development.

A distinguishing characteristic of venture capital investment contracts is their extensive and sophisticated covenants. These are contract clauses that mandate certain things that the portfolio firm's managers must do (**positive covenants**) and must not do (**negative covenants**). Some of these covenants appear in many standard bond- and loan-financing contracts. For example, venture capital contracts often contain clauses that specify maximum acceptable leverage and dividend payout ratios, require the firm to carry certain types of business insurance, and restrict the firm's ability to acquire other firms or sell assets without prior investor approval. Again,

[8] Entrepreneurs wishing to determine how much capital they should try to obtain from VCs should read the classic Harvard Business School article by Stancill (1987), "How Much Money Does Your New Venture Need?"

Amazon.com provides an illustrative case. The firm's bank required Jeffrey Bezos to personally guarantee all the company's borrowing prior to its IPO. Other covenants, including the following types, occur almost exclusively in private equity investment contracts.

1. Ownership right agreements not only specify the distribution ownership, but also allocate board seats and voting rights to the participating VC. Special voting rights often given to VCs include the right to veto major corporate actions and to remove the management team if the firm fails to meet performance goals. Cole and Sokol (1997) discuss the importance of venture capitalist control rights.

2. Ratchet provisions protect the venture group's ownership rights in the event that the firm sells new equity under duress. Generally, these provisions ensure that the venture capital group's share values adjust so that entrepreneurs bear the penalty of selling low-priced new stock. For example, if the venture fund purchased shares initially for $1 each, and the start-up later sells new stock at $0.50 per share, a "full ratchet" provision mandates that the venture group receives one new share for each old share, thereby protecting the value of the VC's initial stake (a "partial ratchet" only partially protects the venture group). Obviously, it would not take many rounds of financing at reduced prices to completely wipe out a management team's ownership stake.[9]

3. Demand registration rights, participation rights, and **repurchase rights** preserve exit opportunities for VCs. *Demand registration rights* give the venture fund the right to compel the firm to register shares with the SEC for a public offering—at the firm's expense. The venture capital investors in Amazon.com had such a demand registration right, though they never exercised it. *Participation rights* give VCs the option to participate in any private stock sale the firm's managers arrange for themselves. In the event that a portfolio company does not conduct an IPO or sell out to another firm within a specified time period, *repurchase rights* give VCs the option to sell their shares back to the firm.

4. Stock option plans provide incentives for portfolio-company managers in virtually all venture capital deals. As part of these plans, the firm sets aside a large pool of stock to compensate current managers for superior performance and to attract talented new managers as the company grows.

APPLYING THE MODEL

Amazon.com provides an example of using stock options to compensate and motivate managers. At the time of the firm's IPO, no less than 10.8 million shares were reserved under two stock option plans, and over 4 million had already been allocated to the firm's executives.

This listing of covenants is by no means comprehensive. Other common provisions describe the conditions for additional financing and the payoffs to entrepreneurs if the VCs decide to hire new managers. However, the most fascinating and distinguishing feature of venture capital contracts is unquestionably their almost ex-

---

[9.] For a simple discussion of ratchet provisions, see Hoffman and Blakey (1987). The critical importance of the lead venture capitalist being able to retain a proportionate share in multiround financings is described theoretically in Admati and Pfleiderer (1994).

clusive reliance on convertible securities (particularly convertible preferred stock) as the investment vehicle of choice.

Why Venture Capitalists Use Convertible Securities

Most people assume that when VCs invest in a firm, they receive shares of common stock in exchange for their capital. In fact, venture capitalists almost always receive some type of convertible security instead, either convertible debt or, more frequently, convertible preferred stock.[10] There are several reasons for this marked preference. First, venture capitalists would only be able to exercise effective voting control with common stock if they were to purchase a majority of a firm's common shares, which would be extremely expensive and would place far more of the firm's business risk on the venture group than on the entrepreneur. Because convertible debt or preferred stock is a distinct security class, contract terms and covenants specific to that issue are negotiable. Furthermore, because firms can create multiple classes of convertible debt or preferred stock, they can use these securities to construct extremely complex, sophisticated contracting arrangements with different investor groups.[11]

Seniority offers a second reason why venture capitalists generally demand convertible debt or preferred stock rather than common stock. This places the VC ahead of the entrepreneur in the line of claimants on the firm's assets should the firm not succeed. However, preferred stock or subordinated debt leaves the firm the option to issue more senior debt, thereby preserving its borrowing capacity and making it easier for the firm to arrange trade credit or bank loans. The convertible securities held by VCs typically pay a very low dividend, a signal that VCs use these securities for control reasons rather than to generate steady cash flows.

Most important, convertible securities give VCs the right to participate in the upside, as common shareholders do, when portfolio companies thrive. In fact, VCs usually convert to common equity before venture-backed companies execute initial public offerings to lock in their equity stakes and to present an uncluttered balance sheet to prospective investors.

APPLYING THE MODEL

The venture capitalists backing Amazon.com structured their entire investment (in June 1996) as convertible preferred stock, for which they paid $14.05 per share. Two of the firm's directors, who purchased convertible preferred stock in a much smaller subsequent financing round in early 1997, paid $40 per share. ■

The Pricing of Venture Capital Investments

As you might expect, valuing the types of young, rapidly growing companies that venture capital firms finance presents a huge challenge. How do VCs value portfolio companies? The empirical evidence suggests that VCs use a wide variety of valuation methods, and from one deal to the next, valuations can be rather idiosyncratic.

[10.] SBICs have historically been an exception to this rule because their funding patterns dictated they structure their investments as loans. During recent years this has changed because they can now obtain their own funding via a security that is, in effect, preferred stock. Additionally, Wong (2001) shows that angel capitalists generally use only common stock in their investments.

[11.] Numerous theoretical papers have attempted to explain the use of convertibles by venture capitalists. These include papers by Admati and Pfleiderer (1994), Hellmann (1998), Berglöf (1994), and most recently, Bascha and Walz (2001).

Nevertheless, we offer an example to illustrate one common approach.[12] Assume that the president and founder of the start-up company Internet Concepts Corporation (ICC) approaches a technology-oriented venture capital fund for $5 million in new funding to support her firm's rapid growth. After intense negotiations, the parties agree that ICC is currently worth $10 million, and the risk of the firm is such that the venture capitalist is entitled to a 50 percent compound annual (expected) return. To arrive at the $10 million estimate, the VC may compare the portfolio company's sales (or earnings if there are any) to those of similar public companies and apply a pricing multiple. Assume further that both parties agree that ICC should plan to execute an IPO in five years, at which time the firm is expected to have net profits of $4 million and to sell at a price/earnings ratio of 20, which will put the company's value at $80 million. To calculate the value of its stake in the portfolio company as of the IPO date, the VC uses basic future value techniques. The initial investment, A, equals $5 million; the required rate of return, r, is 50 percent; and the time horizon, n, is five years.

$$FV = A(1 + r)^n = \$5,000,000(1.50)^5 = \$5,000,000(7.6) = \$38,000,000$$

(Eq. 15.1)

To determine what fraction of ICC's equity it will receive now, the VC divides the future value of its stake by ICC's expected IPO market valuation:

$$\text{Equity fraction} = FV \div \text{Exp } MV = \$38,000,000 \div \$80,000,000 = 0.475$$

(Eq. 15.2)

This means that the venture capital fund will receive 47.5 percent of ICC's equity in exchange for its $5 million investment. If the VC agrees to accept a lower return, say 40 percent, the VC's expected IPO payoff will be $26.9 million, and the VC would require a 33.6 percent equity stake up front to achieve this return. When the VC requires a higher return, the entrepreneur must relinquish a larger fraction of the firm.

THE PROFITABILITY OF VENTURE CAPITAL INVESTMENTS

The data on venture capital returns is rather sketchy, but it seems clear that investments made by venture capital funds during the middle 1990s earned average compound annual returns of up to 30 percent. Gompers and Lerner (2001) document repeated examples of boom-and-bust investment cycles, in which very high realized returns prompt excessive new capital inflows into venture capital funds, which in turn cause returns to drop sharply over the next harvest cycle. Although the 30 percent annual return was typical for venture capital funds during the late 1970s and early 1980s, Figure 15.3 shows that returns fell short of 30 percent every year from 1984 to 1994. Returns were again at target levels in 1995 and 1996, and then surged in 1999. However, more recent returns following the collapse of the Nasdaq market in March 2000 have been uniformly negative, as Table 15.4 demonstrates. The first column of the table shows the 1-year returns on various types of venture capital investments for 2001, while the other columns list average annual returns over longer horizons ending in 2001. A key question is whether the massive influx of new venture capital that occurred during the 1998–2000 period will have the same negative impact on returns over the next five years.

A strong positive correlation exists between venture returns and returns on small

---

[12.] This example is based on information presented in Schilit and Willig (1996b). Additional discussion of the pricing of VC investments is presented in Morris (1988), Katz (1990), and, in a theoretical context, Hellmann (2002).

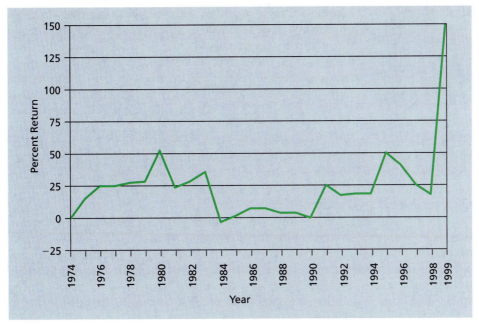

Figure 15.3
Average Annual Rate of Return to Investors in U.S Venture Capital Funds, 1974–1999

Source: Data from Venture Economics as reported in Paul Gompers and Josh Lerner, "The Venture Capital Revolution," *Journal of Economic Perspectives* 15 (Spring 2001), pp. 145–168, fig. 2.
Note: Returns are net of fees and profit sharing.

stock mutual funds, which highlights the importance of a healthy public stock market for new ventures in general and for initial public offerings in particular. Because VCs prefer to exit via an IPO, and because "recycled" returns at least partially flow into new venture investments, any decline in the market's appetite for new issues has an immediate negative impact on the venture capital industry.[13]

EXIT STRATEGIES EMPLOYED BY VENTURE CAPITALISTS

VCs are not long-term equity investors. They seek to add value to a private company and then to harvest their investment. VCs use three principal methods to exit an

Table 15.4
U.S. Venture Capital and Private Equity Returns by Fund Type and Investment Horizons

Fund Type	1 Year	3 Years	5 Years	10 Years	20 Years
Early/seed stage	−33.0%	77.4%	49.4%	32.1%	21.1%
Balanced	−24.3	43.5	32.8	22.7	15.5
Later stage	−20.0	22.5	21.1	24.2	16.9
All venture	**−27.8%**	**49.3%**	**35.9%**	**26.4%**	**17.7%**
All buyouts	−14.5	0.5	5.0	10.8	14.4
Mezzanine	−2.2	7.5	9.2	11.5	11.0
Buyouts and other private equity	−13.4	1.0	5.2	10.9	13.9
All private equity	**−18.5%**	**13.2%**	**14.8%**	**17.3%**	**16.2%**

Source: "Private Equity Performance Continues to Reflect Tough Market Conditions: One-Year Returns Improved Slightly in Q4 2001, but Signs of Recovery Remain Scarce," National Venture Capital Association (June 10, 2002) website (http://www.nvca.com).
Note: Investment horizon returns (average annual pooled *IRR*) as of December 31, 2001.

[13.] The role of venture capitalists in deciding when to take a portfolio company public is detailed in Lerner (1994) and Gompers (1996), and the difficulties encountered by entrepreneur/founders of non-venture-backed firms in trying to arrange an acquisition for their firms are described in Bianchi (1992).

investment: (1) through an initial public offering of shares to outside investors; (2) through a sale of the portfolio company directly to another company; or (3) through selling the company back to the entrepreneur/founders (the **redemption option,** described in Fellers [2001a, 2001b]). IPOs are by far the most profitable and visible option for the venture capitalists. During 1990–2000, IPOs were executed on U.S. capital markets by 5,803 companies and raised $419.5 billion. Figure 15.4, Panels A and B demonstrate the rapid growth in venture-backed IPOs in the 1990s. By 1999, more than half the firms going public enjoyed VC backing. However, venture-backed IPOs accounted for a little less than half of the total IPO proceeds in 1999, suggesting that, on average, venture capital firms focus on smaller companies (or that VC-backed IPOs sell a smaller stake to outsiders in their IPOs).

Perhaps surprising, VCs do not exit immediately at the time of an IPO. Instead, they retain shares for several months or even years and then typically distribute shares back to the limited partners, rather than sell the shares on the open market. The distributions usually occur after a period of sharply rising stock prices, and the average stock-price response to distribution announcements is significantly negative. The studies by Gompers and Lerner (1998b) and Bradley, Jordan, Yi, and Roten (2001) both document this tendency.[14]

Government Support for Venture Capital in the United States

We end our discussion of U.S. venture capital with a few comments on government-sponsored venture capital funding programs. Economic historians document that the federal government has played a key direct or catalytic role in developing many of the most important technologies that underpin modern industrial society—from aerospace engineering to material science to computers (especially computers).[15] Additionally, federally chartered SBICs accounted for two-thirds of all the venture capital funding allocated to U.S. business from the 1950s to 1969 and continued to play an important role even after private partnerships rose to preeminence. Finally, Lerner (1999) documents that one of the most important and visible federal programs, the Small Business Innovation Research (SBIR) grant program, has proven very successful in fostering technological innovation and corporate growth. Firms that received SBIR grants grew significantly faster than a matched set of firms that did not receive grants, suggesting that these grants allowed firms to overcome financing constraints that otherwise would have proven binding. Lerner's finding that the positive effects of SBIR awards were confined to firms based in zip codes with substantial private venture capital activity also suggests that government programs are effective only when they supplement private fund-raising and investment.

Concept Review Questions

3. What is an *angel capitalist,* and how does this type of investor differ from a professional (institutional) venture capitalist?

---

14. According to an NVCA press release on October 16, 2001, the value of cash and stock distributed to limited partners by VCs grew from $1.88 billion during the first quarter of 1999 to an astounding $18.72 billion during the first quarter of 2000, but then fell steadily back to $2.10 billion during the second quarter of 2001.

15. Though Al Gore Jr. took a beating over his claim that he "took the initiative on creating the Internet," it is true that government funding played a role in developing and building the Internet in its early years.

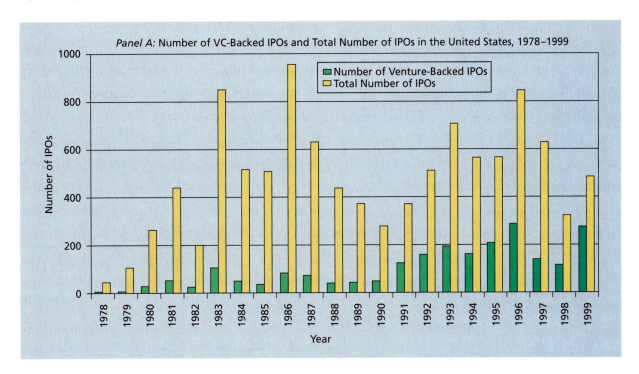

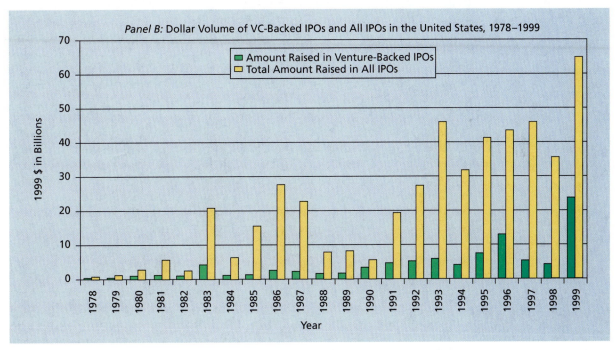

Figure 15.4

Venture-Backed Initial Public Offerings Expressed as a Fraction of All U.S. Initial Public Offerings

Source: Paul Gompers and Josh Lerner, "The Venture Capital Revolution," *Journal of Economic Perspectives* 15 (Spring 2001), pp. 145–168, figs. 3 and 4.

Concept
Review
Questions

4. Why do you think that private limited partnerships have come to dominate the U.S. venture capital industry? Can you think of any weaknesses this organizational form might have as a vehicle for financing entrepreneurial growth companies?

5. Why do venture capitalists almost always use *staged financing* and convertible securities to finance entrepreneurial companies?

6. Entrepreneurs often refer to venture capitalists as "vulture capitalists" due to the amount of equity they demand before investing. Do you think the standard venture capital pricing formula is a justifiable compensation for risk, or is it exploitative?

15.3 INTERNATIONAL MARKETS FOR VENTURE CAPITAL AND PRIVATE EQUITY

Although "classic" venture capital investment by privately financed partnerships has traditionally been a distinctly U.S. phenomenon, private equity financing has long been an established financial specialty in other developed countries, especially in Western Europe. Because Europe is the birthplace both of the industrial revolution and of modern capitalism, it is not surprising that a highly sophisticated method of funneling growth capital to private (often family-owned) businesses evolved there. In fact, private equity fund-raising in Europe compared quite well with that in the United States until 1997 and showed far less annual variability. The chief differences between European and American venture capital lie in (1) the principal sources of funds for venture capital investing, (2) the organization of the venture funds themselves, (3) the development stage of the portfolio companies able to attract venture financing, and (4) the principal method of harvesting venture capital investments. As we will see, these differences are all related and help explain the relative boom in U.S. venture capital compared to that in Europe.[16]

Before proceeding, we should point out a difference in the definition of the term "venture capital" in Europe and the United States. Whereas American commentators tend to refer to all professionally managed, equity-based investments in private, entrepreneurial growth companies as venture capital, European commentators apply the term only to early- and expansion-stage financing. Later-stage investments and funding for management buyouts are called "private equity investment" in Europe. Where necessary, we will maintain this distinction, but in general we will refer to both venture capital and private equity investment simply as "European venture capital."

EUROPEAN VENTURE CAPITAL AND PRIVATE EQUITY FUND-RAISING AND INVESTMENT

As in the United States, venture capital fund-raising and investment in Europe has grown rapidly since the mid-1990s. Figure 15.5 describes the growth in total private equity investment over the period 1989–2001. According to a survey of pan-European private equity and venture capital activity conducted for the European Private Equity & Venture Capital Association (EVCA) by PricewaterhouseCoopers, total investment grew from a stable level of about €5 billion per year during the 1989–1996 period to €25 billion in 1999 and €34.9 billion (invested in some 10,440 companies) in 2000. Disbursements dropped significantly to €24.3 billion during 2001, but this 30 percent decline was far less than the 64 percent decline in U.S. venture capital in-

---

[16.] The discussion in this section draws heavily on Schilit and Willig (1996a), Black and Gilson (1998), Jeng and Wells (2000), and Arundale (2001).

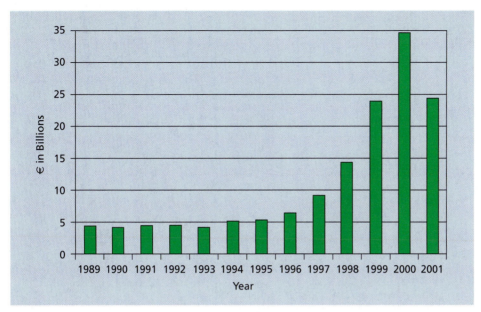

Figure 15.5
European Private Equity
Investment, 1989–2001

Source: Data from Pricewater-
houseCoopers and European
Private Equity and Venture
Capital Association, "2nd
Highest Year for the European
Private Equity Industry," Euro-
pean Private Equity & Venture
Capital Association website
(http://www.evca.com), ac-
cessed May 28, 2002.

vestment between 2000 and 2001. Fund-raising has grown even more dramatically over the past seven years, rising from about €5 billion during 1995 to nearly €48 billion in 2000, and then falling somewhat to €38.2 billion in 2001. Since the early 1980s, a cumulative total of more than €150 billion has been raised for investment in European private equity.

Historically, European venture capital has been funneled to different industries and different types of companies than in the United States, though this has been changing lately. As recently as 1996, less than one-fourth of European venture capital went into high-technology investments. By 2001, however, the fraction allocated to high-tech industries topped 55 percent. Table 15.5 describes the industry breakdown of European private equity investments in technology for the years 1999 and 2000. As in the United States, roughly 80 percent of European high-tech venture capital investment is funneled into computers and communications businesses.

In one important respect, venture capital funding patterns in Europe and the United States have long been similar in that both are highly concentrated geographically. Some 29 percent of year-2001's total investment was targeted at British companies. In second place behind Britain are Germany and France, which each received roughly 15 percent of European venture money in 2001. Italy, with under 9 percent, comes in fourth.

The Changing Sources of Funding for European Venture Capital

The sourcing of European venture capital funds differs from that of their U.S. counterparts primarily in Europe's greater reliance on financial institutions. As shown in Figure 15.6, banks, insurance companies, and other corporate investors accounted for over half (58.8%) of all European venture funding in 2000, whereas pension fund money represents less than a quarter (24.2%) of total fund-raising. Governments account for less than 6 percent of total capital raised.

For a mix of cultural and legal reasons, European venture capital funds are rarely, if ever, organized according to the U.S. model. Instead, funds are generally organized as investment companies under various national laws, and their approach to dealing with portfolio companies is much more akin to the reactive style of U.S. mutual fund

Table 15.5
European Private Equity Investment in Technology by Industry, 1999–2000

Industry	1999		2000	
	Amount	Percentage	Amount	Percentage
Communications: hardware	430	6	585	5
Communications: carriers	912	13	1,590	14
Internet technology	1,092	16	1,843	16
Computer: hardware	375	5	441	4
Computer: software	2,108	31	3,583	31
Computer: services	430	6	636	6
Computer: semiconductors	109	2	379	3
Other electronics related	494	7	977	9
Medical: instruments/ devices	233	3	413	4
Biotechnology	644	10	1,017	9
Total	6,827	100	11,464	100

Source: PriceWaterhouseCoopers, Money for Growth: The European Technology Investment Report 2000 (http://www.pwcmoneytree.com/PDFS/MoneyforGrowth.pdf).
Note: Amounts in € millions for full years 1999 and 2000.

managers than to the proactive style of America's venture capitalists. The relative lack of a vibrant entrepreneurial high-technology sector in Europe also hampers continental VCs' efforts to attract technologically savvy fund managers or entrepreneur/founders who wish to use their expertise to grow new firms.

European Venture Capital Investment by Stage of Company Development

Partly for the reasons previously detailed, European venture capital has historically been less focused on early-stage investments than has America's; as in other areas,

Figure 15.6
European Private Equity Raised by Type of Investor, Year 2000

Source: Pricewaterhouse-Coopers and European Private Equity and Venture Capital Association as reported in Simon Targett, "Institutional Investment: Should Do More," *Financial Times* (June 14, 2001), European Private Equity Survey, p. 5.

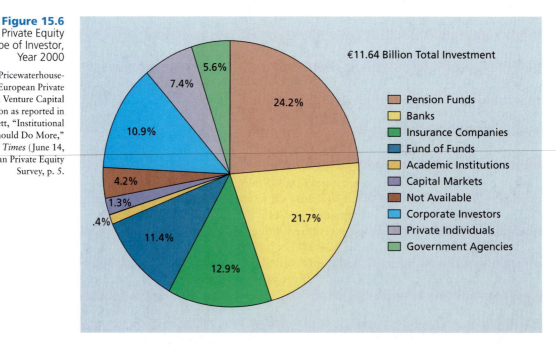

€11.64 Billion Total Investment

- Pension Funds
- Banks
- Insurance Companies
- Fund of Funds
- Academic Institutions
- Capital Markets
- Not Available
- Corporate Investors
- Private Individuals
- Government Agencies

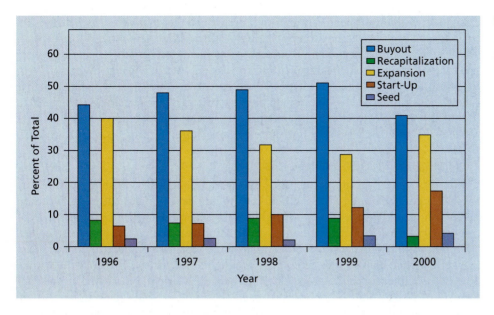

Figure 15.7
Distribution of European
Private Equity Investment
by Stage of Company
Development, 1996–
2000

Source: Katharine Campbell,
"Stock Market Volatility Fails
to Put Off Investors," *Financial
Times* (June 14, 2001a), p. 6.

this is changing fast. The breakdown of European venture capital investment by stage of portfolio-company development over the period 1996–2000 is presented in Figure 15.7. Although buyouts still account for almost 40 percent of European private equity investment, early-stage companies now attract roughly 20 percent of the total. This figure is comparable to recent U.S. levels, and indicates that the risk appetite of European VCs has been increasing steadily. The true test, of course, will be how well this new risk tolerance holds up during the current down cycle in global venture capital investment and returns.

Investment Returns for European Venture Capital Investments

Yet another historical difference between U.S. and European venture capital was in the mostly disappointing returns European private equity investors earned. Figure 15.8

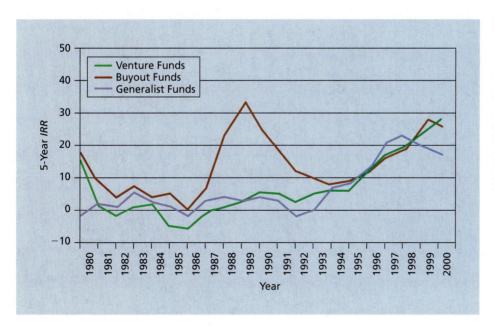

Figure 15.8
Investment Returns to
Categories of European
Private Equity Investment,
1980–2000 (5-year
rolling internal rate of
return)

Source: Pricewaterhouse-
Coopers and European Private
Equity and Venture Capital
Association, "Pan-European
Survey of Performance: From
Inception to 31 December
2000" (http://www.evca.com).

clearly shows that European venture funds performed abysmally over the 1981–1994 period, especially in comparison to the high returns earned by buyout funds. Since 1995, however, European venture fund returns have been steadily rising and were truly stellar during the period from 1997 to year-end 2000. During this period, venture fund returns beat all other types of private equity funds and were much higher than the returns earned by investors in publicly traded European stocks, which had a dismal 2000. Unfortunately, the collapse of Europe's public stock markets after March 2000 augurs very badly for future venture capital returns, as we now discuss.

Exit Strategies of European Venture Capitalists

One of the greatest disappointments of European policymakers wishing to duplicate the success of the United States in high-technology development has been the continent's failure, until very recently, to establish a large, liquid market for the stock of entrepreneurial growth firms. Although several stock markets exist, and these collectively rival U.S. exchanges in total capitalization of listed companies, no European market emerged as a serious alternative to the Nasdaq or the NYSE in the United States as a market for initial public offerings until the German Neuer Markt, the pan-European Easdaq, and other markets such the French Nouveau Marche reached critical mass in the late 1990s. This had a direct impact on the exit strategies that European venture capitalists followed in harvesting their investments in portfolio companies. Whereas IPOs have long been the preferred method of exit for U.S. venture funds, public offerings accounted for only 21 percent of European venture capital divestments in 1996, and comparable fractions in earlier years. The number of European IPOs surged after these markets matured, especially the Neuer Markt, which had attracted over 300 listings by early 2000. Unfortunately, the Neuer Markt collapsed almost as fast as it took off, as Figure 15.9 makes all too clear. By January 2003,

Figure 15.9
The Neuer Markt's Meteoric Rise and Fall

(March 1997–February 2002)

Source: Thomson Financial Datastream, reported in Bertrand Benoit, "Neuer Markt Starts to Feel Squeeze," *Financial Times* (July 11, 2001), p. 19; and Bettina Wassener, "Tarnished Image in Need of Restoration," *Financial Times* Special Survey of Germany (June 12, 2002), p. 2.

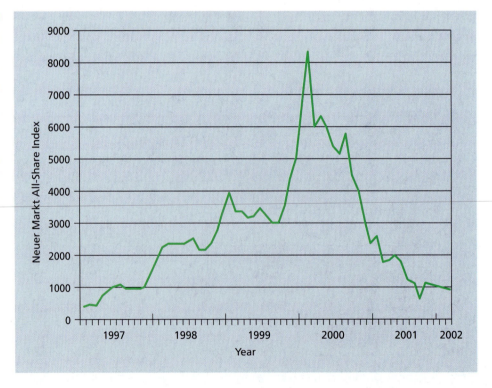

the market's total capitalization had fallen by over 95 percent from its March 2000 peak, amid a series of accounting scandals and great acrimony between entrepreneurs, exchange officials, and investors. The European IPO market effectively closed to all but the most well-established and profitable companies, as only 47 companies went public in Europe during 2001, compared to 249 in 2000. A few European (and a great many Israeli) technology companies have been able to execute IPOs on U.S markets, but this is not a viable option for most entrepreneurial companies.

Public-Sector Support for European Venture Capital

European governments have long taken an activist approach to the promotion and support of venture capital investment. These programs are described in Lerner (2000), in Jeng and Wells (2000), and in most detail in Gompers and Lerner (1997). Unfortunately, both academic research and anecdotal evidence indicate that government efforts to promote a robust entrepreneurial sector would probably be better focused on eliminating regulatory roadblocks, lowering taxes, and providing a more favorable overall business climate than on attempting to directly identify and fund "sunrise" industries. The EVCA explicitly addressed the need for governments to provide a better regulatory environment for entrepreneurship in two recent white papers (see http://www.evca.com). Tellingly, the EVCA called for governments to provide direct financial support only when matched by private financing.

Venture Capital Markets outside the United States and Western Europe

We conclude with an analysis of venture capital financing in markets outside the United States and Western Europe, which includes Canada, Israel, Japan, and all other countries in Asia. Venture capital markets in South America, Africa, Central and Eastern Europe, and the Middle East (outside Israel) are still too small to warrant individual attention, but we do conclude with an overview of venture capital in developing countries generally.

Venture Capital in Canada and Israel

The venture capital industries of Canada and Israel differ dramatically from those in other advanced countries. Canadian government policies have led to a venture capital system that relies heavily on labor unions for funding (see Fineberg 1997). Recent growth in Canada's market (see Christopher 2001) has weakened the union funds' grip on venture capital funding, however, and total investment has grown at a compound annual rate of 60 percent since 1994. In 2000, Canada was the world's fifth-largest recipient of venture capital financing and attracted almost as much investment ($4.3 billion) as Germany, a country three times as populous. Canadian strength in telecommunications technology has been a particular boon to venture capital investment.

In a relative sense, Israel has achieved even greater success, since it was the sixth-largest recipient of venture capital in 2000 and was the world's largest recipient relative to GDP. At least part of Israel's success derives from deliberate policy decisions by the Likud government in the early 1990s, which took concrete steps to commercialize defense-related technology developed with public funding. The influx of trained engineers and scientists from the former Soviet Union also helped, as did the pioneering steps taken by Israeli entrepreneurs to go public in the United States, as this opened a path to public markets others could and did follow.

Venture Capital in Asia

The growth rate of venture capital in Asia has lagged that of Europe and North America over the past decade. There has been steady growth (albeit from a low base) in

COMPARATIVE CORPORATE FINANCE

Does a Nation's Legal System Influence the Size of Its Venture Capital Industry?

This table details how a country's legal system impacts the relative importance of venture capital investment, stock market capitalization, and research and development spending for the 20 countries that received the most venture capital investment during 2000. Family of legal origin refers to which of the four main legal families (English common law, French civil law, German law, and Scandinavian law) the nation bases its commercial code. Expressed as a percentage of GDP, venture capital investment was much higher in countries with legal systems based on English common law (on average, 1.14% of GDP) than in the three types of civil-law countries (on average, 0.31% of GDP), consistent with the "Law and Finance" literature pioneered by La-Porta, López-de-Silanes, Shleifer, and Vishny (1997, 1998, 2000). A similar pattern is observed for stock market capitalization as a percentage of GDP, where the average ratio is 166.4 percent of GDP in common-law countries and 105.0 percent in civil-law countries, but not for R&D spending as a percentage of GDP. This ratio is actually higher in civil-law countries, which suggests that a nation's legal system does not influence the relative amount of national output invested in research, but does influence the propensity to channel research investment through venture capitalists.

Sources: Venture capital financing, PricewaterhouseCoopers, Global Private Equity Report 2001 (http://www.pwcmoneytree.com); GDP and market capitalization are year-2000 values taken from the World Bank database (http://www.worldbank.org) and the World Federation of Exchanges (http://www.world-exchanges.org); R&D spending is from the International Institute for Management Development World Competitiveness Yearbook: 2001 (http://www01.imd.ch/).

Country	Family of Legal Origin	Venture Capital Investment ($US in billions)	Venture Capital Investment (% of GDP)	Stock market Capitalization as a % of GDP	R&D Spending as a % of GDP
Israel	English common law	3.2	3.17	63.6	2.78
Singapore	English common law	1.2	1.41	233.7	1.85
Hong Kong SAR	English common law	2.2	1.38	383.3	0.22
United States	English common law	122.1	1.33	181.8	2.66
Sweden	Scandinavian law/civil	2.1	0.88	156.4	3.69
United Kingdom	English common law	12.2	0.85	203.5	1.79
Canada	English common law	4.3	0.68	126.2	1.58
Netherlands	French civil law	1.8	0.46	176.6	1.93
Taiwan	German law/civil	1.2	0.39	79.9	1.90
France	French civil law	4.9	0.34	103.0	2.21
Argentina	French civil law	0.9	0.32	58.7	0.52
Korea	German law/civil	1.0	0.25	36.5	2.46
Italy	French civil law	2.8	0.24	62.2	1.04
Switzerland	German law/civil	0.6	0.23	268.0	3.12
Germany	German law/civil	4.4	0.21	67.8	2.38
Belgium	French civil law	0.5	0.20	74.4	1.81
Australia	English common law	0.7	0.17	105.9	1.38
Spain	French civil law	1.0	0.17	72.5	0.91
India	English common law	0.5	0.11	33.1	0.51
Japan	German law/civil	2.0	0.05	104.6	3.26
Average, English common-law countries		—	1.14	166.4	1.60
Average, all civil-law countries		—	0.31	105.0	2.10

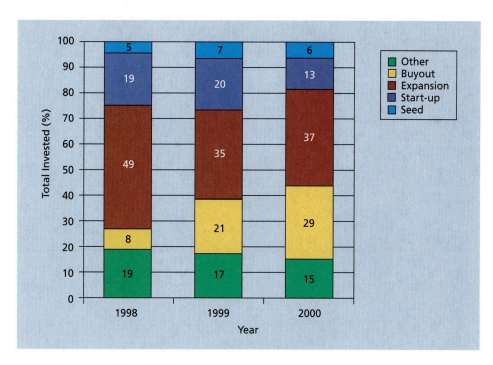

Figure 15.10
Asia-Pacific Private Equity
Investment by Stage of
Investment, 1998–2000

Source: 3i/Pricewaterhouse-
Coopers in Global Private
Equity 2001: A Review of the
Global Private Equity and
Venture Capital Markets
(http://www.pwcmoneytree
.com/PDFS/GPEreport%
202001.pdf)

venture capital funding in much of Asia, but not in Japan. As discussed in Packer (1996) and Hamao, Packer, and Ritter (2000), Japan has a financial specialty referred to as "venture capital," but most of the firms involved are commercial or investment bank subsidiaries that make very few truly entrepreneurial investments. Venture capital shows no real sign of taking root in Japan, and the world's second-largest economy attracted only $2.0 billion (0.05% of GDP) in venture funding in 2000.

Countries such as China lack much of the basic legal and accounting infrastructure needed to support a vibrant venture capital market, and most of Asia suffers from the lack of an efficient IPO market that could serve as an exit mechanism.[17] Figure 15.10 shows how the distribution of Asia-Pacific venture capital investment between early- and later-stage companies evolved over the period from 1998, when investment totaled $4.91 billion, to 2000, when it totaled $9.1 billion.

Venture Capital in Developing Countries

Although up-to-date figures are extremely hard to obtain, the evidence that exists suggests that venture capital fund-raising and investment in developing countries has been growing steadily in recent years, though again from a low base. Chart 1 of Figure 15.11 shows the evolution in the stock of venture capital in developing countries over the 1990–1995 period, and Chart 2 expresses this data in terms of annual flows. Either way, the small totals are discouraging, especially compared to the total values of foreign direct investment that flowed to developing countries over the same period. Aylward (1998) also points out that much of what passes for "venture capital" in developing countries is actually high-risk debt financing. For the foreseeable future, incremental growth from a tiny base is probably all that can be expected for developing-country venture capital.

[17.] China's nascent venture capital market is described in Wei and Yanfu (2002).

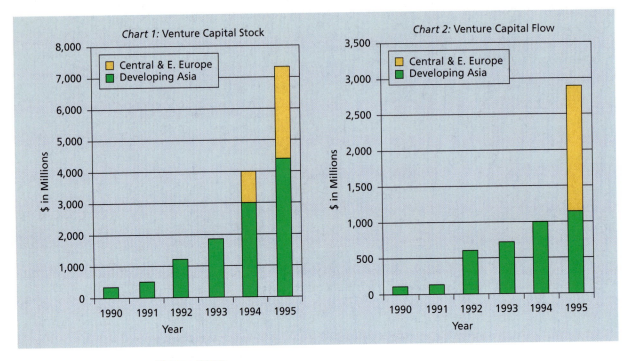

Figure 15.11
Venture Capital Investments in Developing Countries, 1990–1995

Source: Anthony Aylward, "Trends in Venture Capital Finance in Developing Countries," IFC Discussion Paper no. 36, World Bank (Washington D.C., July 1998).

Concept Review Questions

7. Why do you think European governments and stock exchanges are so keen to promote a vibrant entrepreneurial sector? Can you think of any competitive advantages that might accrue to Europe due to its relatively late start in developing IPO markets?

8. What are some of the competitive strengths and weaknesses of venture capital as practiced in Europe, Japan, and Canada compared to that in the United States?

9. How has the European venture capital industry changed over the past five years? Do you think these changes have made it more or less competitive and efficient?

10. What type of growth in venture capital funding and investment have developing countries experienced during recent years? What is their future outlook for venture capital growth?

15.4 SUMMARY

- Entrepreneurial finance requires specialized financial management skills because entrepreneurial growth companies are unlike other private or publicly traded companies. In particular, EGCs must finance much higher asset growth rates than other firms and must tap external financial markets much more frequently.
- In addition to providing risk capital to entrepreneurial growth firms, professional venture capitalists (VCs) provide managerial oversight coupled with technical and business advice, assistance in developing and launching new products, and valuable help recruiting experienced management talent.
- U.S. venture capital investments are highly concentrated both geographically and industrially. Furthermore, the most successful venture capital funds are almost al-

ways organized as limited partnerships and follow distinctive investment strategies (staged investment) using unique financial instruments (convertible preferred stock).

- U.S. venture capitalists endeavor to make intermediate-term (of 3–7 years), high-risk investments in entrepreneurial growth firms, and then exit these investments either by selling the portfolio companies to another firm or (preferably) by executing an initial public offering. During recent years, VCs have, on average, achieved their target compound annual returns of over 30 percent.

- Phenomenal growth in venture capital fund-raising and investment has occurred over the past decade in the United States, Western Europe, and in certain Asian countries, but not in Japan or in most developing countries. The two largest venture capital markets, the United States and Europe, have seen significant convergence in contracting practices, investment patterns, and returns in recent years.

- The funding of European venture capital is moving rapidly toward greater reliance on pension funds (rather than commercial banks), and a much higher fraction of European venture capital investment is being targeted toward early-stage investment than in the past. More of Europe's total funding is also being targeted toward high technology, rather than management buyouts, again mirroring practices in the United States.

- After a long period of relative underperformance, returns on European private equity investment have also increased steadily in recent years. However, the recent collapse of Germany's Neuer Markt has at least temporarily closed what had become the most promising exit route for European venture capitalists.

- Although Canada and Israel have had great success in venture capital funding and investment, growth in venture capital in Asia has lagged that of Europe and North America. Venture capital funding and investment in developing countries has been growing from its low base during recent years.

INTERNET RESOURCES

Note: *For updates to links, please go to the book's website at* http://smart.swcollege.com

http://www.nvca.com—Website of the National Venture Capital Association, which provides a wide range of data and reports about the U.S. venture capital industry, much of it strikingly current

http://www.pwcmoneytree.com—Website of PricewaterhouseCoopers MoneyTree™, which presents details about the company's quarterly and annual venture capital surveys and offers the company's electronic publication, *Global Private Equity Report*, which can be downloaded

http://www.evca.com—Website of the European Venture Capital & Private Equity Association, which presents detailed information about Europe's venture capital industry and provides numerous reports about the European venture capital scene

KEY TERMS

angel capitalists
cancellation option
corporate venture capital funds
demand registration rights
entrepreneurial finance

entrepreneurial growth companies (EGCs)
financial venture capital funds
institutional venture capital funds
negative covenants
ownership right agreements

participation rights   small business investment companies (SBICs)
positive covenants   staged financing
ratchet provisions   stock option plans
redemption option   venture capital
repurchase rights   venture capital limited partnerships

QUESTIONS

15-1. List and describe the key financial differences between entrepreneurial growth companies and large publicly traded firms.

15-2. How does the financing of entrepreneurial growth companies differ from that of most firms in mature industries? How does the concept of "bootstrap finance" relate to this difference?

15-3. What is an *angel capitalist*? How do the financing techniques used by angels differ from those employed by professional venture capitalists?

15-4. Distinguish between the four basic types of venture capital funds. Which type has emerged as the dominant organizational form? Why?

15-5. What are some of the common characteristics of those entrepreneurial growth companies that are able to attract venture capital investment? In which industries and states is the majority of venture capital invested?

15-6. What is meant by early-stage and later-stage venture capital investment? What proportions of venture capital have been allocated between the two in recent years? Which stage requires a higher expected return? Why?

15-7. What are the responsibilities and typical payoff for a general partner in a venture capital limited partnership?

15-8. Define "staged financing." Why is this an efficient risk-minimizing mechanism for venture capitalists?

15-9. Distinguish between *positive covenants* and *negative covenants* in venture capital investment contracts. List and describe some of the more popular covenants found in these contracts.

15-10. What is the most popular form of financing (or security type) required by venture capitalists in return for their investment? Why is this form of financing optimal for both the entrepreneur and the venture capitalist?

15-11. List the major differences between venture capital financing in the United States and Western Europe. What major changes have been occurring recently in the European venture capital industry?

15-12. Why is a vibrant IPO market considered vital to the success of a nation's venture capital industry? What impact is the near collapse of Germany's Neuer Markt likely to have on the European venture capital industry?

15-13. Describe the recent levels of venture capital activity in Canada, Israel, Asia, and developing countries. What is the outlook for each of them?

PROBLEMS

Venture Capital Financing in the United States

15-1. Access the National Venture Capital Association website at http://www.nvca.com, and update Tables 15.3 and 15.4, as well as Figures 15.1 and 15.2, using the most recent data available. What general trends do you see regarding sources of venture capital funding and patterns of investing from this website and its links?

15-2. The venture capital fund Techno Fund II made a $4 million investment in Optical Fibers Corporation five years ago and in return received 1 million shares representing 20 percent of Optical Fibers' equity. Optical Fibers is now planning an initial public offering in which it will sell 1 million newly created shares for $50 per share. Techno has chosen to exercise its demand registration rights and will sell its shares—alongside the newly created shares—in Optical Fibers' IPO. The investment banks underwriting Optical Fibers' IPO will charge a 7 percent underwriting spread, so both the firm and Techno Fund II will receive 93 percent of the $50 per-share offer price. Assuming the IPO is successful, calculate the compound annual return that Techno will have earned on its investment.

15-3. High-Tech Fund III made a $3 million investment in Internet Printing Company (IPC) six years ago and received 2 million shares of series A convertible preferred stock. Each of these shares is convertible into two shares of IPC common stock. Three years later, High-Tech III participated in a second round of financing for IPC and received 3 million shares of series B convertible preferred stock in exchange for a $15 million investment. Each series B share is convertible into one share of IPC common stock. Internet Printing Company is now planning an IPO, but before this the company will convert all its outstanding convertible preferred shares into common stock. After conversion, IPC will have 20 million common shares outstanding and will create another 2 million common shares for sale in the IPO. The underwriter handling IPC's initial offering expects to sell these new shares for $45 each but has prohibited existing shareholders from selling any of their stock in the IPO. The underwriter will keep 7 percent of the offer as an underwriting discount. Assume that the IPO is successful and that IPC shares sell for $60 each immediately after the offering.

   a. Calculate the total number of IPC common shares that High-Tech III will own after the IPO. What fraction of IPC's total outstanding common stock does this represent?

   b. Using the post-issue market price for IPC shares, calculate the (unrealized) compound annual return High-Tech III earned on its original and subsequent investments in IPC stock.

   c. Now assume that the second-round IPC financing had been made under much less favorable conditions and that High-Tech III paid only $1 million instead of $15 million for the 3 million series B shares. Assuming that all the other features of IPC's initial offering described above hold true, calculate the (unrealized) compound annual return High-Tech III earned on this second investment in IPC stock.

15-4. Suppose that 5 out of 10 investments made by a VC fund are a total loss, meaning that the return on each of them is −100 percent. Of the 10 investments, 3 break even, earning a 0 percent return. If the VC fund's expected return equals 50 percent, what rate of return must it earn on the 2 most successful deals to achieve a portfolio return equal to expectations?

15-5. An entrepreneur seeks $4 million from a venture capitalist. They agree that the entrepreneur's venture is currently worth $12 million, and when the company goes public in an IPO in three years, it is expected to have a market capitalization of $70 million. Given the company's stage of development, the VC requires a 40 percent return on investment. What fraction of the firm will the VC receive in exchange for its $4 million investment?

15-6. An entrepreneur seeks $10 million from a VC fund. The entrepreneur and fund managers agree that the entrepreneur's venture is currently worth $25 million and that the company is likely to be ready to go public in five years. At that time, the company is expected to have net income of $7.5 million, and comparable firms are expected to be selling at a price/earnings ratio of 30. Given the company's stage of development, the venture capital fund managers require a 50 percent compound annual return on their investment. What fraction of the firm will the fund receive in exchange for its $10 million investment?

International Markets for Venture Capital and Private Equity

15-7. Access the European Private Equity & Venture Capital Association website at http://www.evca.com, and update Table 15.5 and Figures 15.5 and 15.7, using the most recent data available. What general trends do you see regarding sources of venture capital funding and patterns of investing from this website and its links?

16

Investment Banking and the Public Sale of Equity Securities

OPENING FOCUS

Two European Telecoms Launch Rights Issues to Avert Financial Disaster

It is often said that "the threat of disaster concentrates the mind," which was certainly true for the world's largest telecommunications firms during the bleak period after the steep decline in high-tech stocks in March 2000. After a decade of extremely rapid growth in capital spending, fueled primarily by unprecedented borrowing from banks and bond markets, many telecom companies found themselves teetering on the brink of bankruptcy by the summer of 2001. Slower-than-expected revenue growth, coupled with higher-than-expected costs incurred to roll out "third-generation" cellular telephone networks, had left most of the large European operators with dangerously high debt levels. Without reducing their outstanding debts, firms risked seeing their credit ratings plummet.

In order to avert the prospect of financial meltdown, two of the largest European telecoms—British Telecom (BT) and The Netherlands' KPN—took the highly unusual step of launching immense rights offerings of common stock. BT raised £5.9 billion ($8.5 billion) in June 2001, and KPN issued €5 billion ($4.5 billion) six months later, making these the two largest rights offerings in history. Rights offerings are stock issues sold exclusively to a firm's existing shareholders. Because this strategy keeps all the gains and losses on share issues "within the family," firms usually price rights offerings well below the current market price in order to assure that the offering sells out and the firm raises the funds needed. Both BT and KPN followed this pattern. BT sold its shares, which were selling for 435 pence ($7.54) each at the time of the rights issue, for 300 pence ($5.20) each, while KPN priced its new shares at a smaller (but still significant) 4.5 percent discount to their market price of €5.11 ($4.60) each.

Though both companies saw their stock prices fall sharply when they announced their rights offerings, the rights issues themselves were successful, and both issues met with excess demand (in invest-

ment banking terms, the issues were "oversubscribed"). Coupled with scaled-back investment plans and selected asset sales, these injections of new equity capital revived BT and
KPN, at least temporarily, though both firms' share prices ended 2001 over 75 percent below their all-time highs set less than two years before. Although U.S. telecom firms have
also suffered since March 2000, none have announced plans for a rights issue, because
these have largely disappeared from American finance.

Source: Financial Times, various issues from April 2001 to June 2002.

Although internal financing is the dominant source of funding for corporations
around the world, many firms raise capital externally in any given year. This chapter
and the next examine how corporations tap public and private capital markets. This
chapter focuses on obtaining equity financing and also describes the role that investment banks play in helping firms acquire external capital; Chapter 17 focuses on external debt and lease financing.

Even after managers have decided to raise external capital and to raise equity
rather than debt, they confront many important decisions about how to obtain the
equity capital they need. Managers may or may not enlist the help of an **investment
bank** to sell the firm's securities. If they desire assistance from an investment bank,
managers can negotiate privately with individual banks regarding the terms of the equity sale, or they can solicit competitive bids for the business. Firms can issue shares
to a small group of sophisticated investors in a private placement, they can issue new
shares to existing shareholders through a rights offering, or they can engage in a much
broader public share offering, reaching domestic as well as international investors.

We begin our discussion of these issues by looking at investment banks and the services they offer to equity issuers. Next, we describe the legal rules governing public security sales in the United States, paying special attention to the disclosure requirements imposed on firms raising equity capital. With that background in place, we
examine equity sales conducted by two types of firms: (1) companies issuing equity
for the first time in an initial public offering (IPO), and (2) existing public companies
conducting seasoned equity offerings (SEOs). As you might imagine, the dynamics of
the process are quite different in IPOs and SEOs. Finally, we conclude the chapter with
sections covering private placements and international equity issues.

16.1 INVESTMENT BANKING

AN OVERVIEW OF THE GLOBAL INVESTMENT BANKING INDUSTRY

Investment banks (IBs) play an important role in helping firms raise long-term debt
and equity financing in the world's capital markets. During the past 20 years, and especially since 1990, the global investment banking industry has grown dramatically
in scale and in the variety of services it provides to corporations. Furthermore, with
the recent repeal in the United States of the Glass-Steagall Act, commercial banks formerly excluded from providing investment banking services can now enter that business. Table 16.1 lists the world's 25 largest investment banks, ranked by the total
value of securities underwritten and private placements arranged, syndicated bank
loans arranged, merger and acquisition (M&A) transaction advice provided, and
medium-term notes arranged during the year 2000.

Several very interesting patterns emerge from the table. First, it is clear that investment banks headquartered in the United States dominate the top ranks of global

Table 16.1
Investment Banking Rankings in 2000, Based on Total Value of Securities Issued ($ in billions)

Firm Rank 2000 (1999 in parentheses)	Securities Under-written & Private Placements	Syndicated Bank Loans	M&A Transaction Advice	Medium-Term Notes Arranged	Total Transaction Volume	Percent of Top 25
1. J. P. Morgan Chase (7)	$297	$487	$426	$ 85	$1,295	11.2%
2. Morgan Stanley (3)	344	14	907	18	1,283	11.1
3. Goldman Sachs (1)	303	31	928	6	1,268	11.0
4. Citigroup (4)	360	210	620	46	1,236	10.7
5. Merrill Lynch (2)	493	—	565	105	1,163	10.1
6. Credit Suisse Group (5)	358	60	626	41	1,085	9.4
7. ABN Amro (14)	88	44	47	332	511	4.4
8. Banc of America (10)	120	295	48	20	484	4.2
9. UBS/WDR (12)	161	21	300	—	482	4.2
10. Dresdner KBW (16)	55	24	365	4	449	3.9
11. Lehman Brothers (8)	204	—	181	34	419	3.6
12. Deutsche Bank (11)	209	61	98	41	409	3.6
13. Lazards (15)	—	—	204	—	204	1.8
14. Rothschild (17)	—	—	166	—	166	1.4
15. Barclays (24)	51	64	—	47	162	1.4
16. BNP Paribas (18)	41	23	26	73	162	1.4
17. Bear Stearns (13)	78	—	39	34	151	1.3
18. ING Barings (-)	17	—	120	—	136	1.2
19. RBC Dominion Secur (-)	—	10	93	—	102	0.9
20. Société Générale (-)	17	33	34	—	84	0.7
21. HSBC (22)	34	16	25	—	75	0.7
22. Fleet Boston Corp. (23)	13	37	20	—	71	0.6
23. First Union Corp. (-)	38	23	—	—	62	0.5
24. Commerzbank AG (-)	26	11	—	3	41	0.4
25. CIBC (25)	—	11	27	1	40	0.4
Top 10 Firms	**$2,850**	**$1,353**	**$5,123**	**$838**	**$9,256**	**80.2%**
Top 25 Firms	**$3,497**	**$1,785**	**$6,032**	**$964**	**$11,540**	**100.0%**
Top 10 as % of Top 25	81.5%	83.8%	84.9%	87.0%	80.2%	

Source: Roy C. Smith, "Strategic Directions in Investment Banking—A Retrospective Analysis," *Journal of Applied Corporate Finance* 14 (Spring 2001), pp. 111–123, table 3.
Note: Full credit for each offering is given to the lead underwriter (book runner).

IB firms.[1] The five banks with the highest market share—J. P. Morgan Chase, Morgan Stanley, Goldman Sachs, Citigroup, and Merrill Lynch—are all U.S. based, as are Banc of America (8) and Lehman Brothers (11). Several European banks have broken into the top tier of the global industry in recent years, often by purchasing

[1.] This American preeminence is at least partly a result of the U.S. investment banking industry being deregulated much earlier than Europe's. In particular, the SEC forced U.S. investment banks to end fixed stock trading commissions in May 1975, which prompted both a competitive free-for-all and rapid growth in share trading volume and securities issuance. In contrast, British capital markets were not significantly deregulated until the "Big Bang" reforms were implemented in 1986, and continental European (and Japanese) markets were opened fully only during the 1990s.

one or more U.S. banks. Swiss banks such as Credit Suisse Group and UBS War-burg Dillon Reed (UBS/WDR in Table 16.1) have been especially successful in this regard.

Second, Table 16.1 points out the sheer scale of the global IB industry. The top 10 firms arranged security issues, loans, and mergers worth a staggering $9.26 *trillion* during calendar-year 2000, while the total for the top 25 was $11.54 trillion. For perspective, the world's GDP in 2000 was about $35 trillion. The numbers also reveal a high degree of concentration in the industry. The total transaction volume for the top 10 banks was roughly four times larger than the volume of the investment banks ranked 11 to 25.

Third, different firms appear to specialize in different areas. In particular, IB groups that include a large commercial bank, such as J. P. Morgan Chase, Citigroup, and Banc of America, arrange large volumes of syndicated loans for clients. In contrast, pure investment banks, such as Morgan Stanley, Goldman Sachs, and Merrill Lynch, are more dominant in securities underwriting and M&A transaction advisory work. In part, this pattern derives from the historical separation of U.S. commercial and investment banking activities. Though this degree of separation began to erode as early as 1987, the Gramm-Leach-Bliley Act of 1999, which repealed the Glass-Steagall Act, removed the remaining competitive barriers, and by year-end 2000 several commercial banks had established themselves near the top of the IB industry.

Finally, Table 16.1 shows a high degree of persistence in the industry rankings. The highest-ranked firms in 2000 generally occupied the top rankings in 1999. In 2000, six of these institutions had transactions volume exceeding $1 billion, and these firms are perennial members of investment banking's prestigious **bulge bracket.** Bulge-bracket firms generally occupy the lead or co-lead manager's position in large, new security offerings, meaning that they take primary responsibility for the new offering (even though other banks participate as part of a syndicate), and as a result, they earn higher fees. You can readily identify the lead investment bank in a security offering by looking at the offering *prospectus,* the legal document that describes the terms of the offering. The lead bank's name appears on the front page, usually in larger, bolder print than the names of other participating banks.

KEY INVESTMENT BANKING ACTIVITIES

Investment banks provide a broad range of services to corporations. Table 16.2 breaks out the key sources of revenue for the eight largest U.S.-based investment banks in 2000. The three principal lines of business are *corporate finance, trading,* and *asset management.* Of the three business lines, corporate finance enjoys the highest visibility and includes activities such as security underwriting and M&A advisory work. Corporate finance tends to be the most profitable line of business, especially for more prestigious banks like Goldman Sachs and Morgan Stanley that can charge the highest underwriting and advisory fees. However, corporate finance generates less than one-fourth of the typical IB's revenues, and less than 20 percent for three of the eight banks.

Investment banks earn revenue from trading debt and equity securities in two important ways. First, they act as dealers, facilitating trade between unrelated parties and earning fees in return. Second, they hold inventories of securities and can make or lose money as inventory values fluctuate. Table 16.2 reveals that trading revenues, on average, account for one-quarter of large banks' revenues. Finally, asset management encompasses several different activities, including managing money for individuals with high net worth, operating and advising mutual funds, and managing

Table 16.2
Composition of Investment Banking Revenues of Leading U.S.-Based Investment Banks (IB) in 2000 (% of Revenues)

Firm	Corporate Finance			Trading				Asset Management			Total IB Revenues ($ in millions)
	Under-writing	M&A	Total	Fixed Income	Equities	Principal Investing	Total	Fees	Commis-sions & Other	Total	
J. P. Morgan Chase	13.8%	7.4%	21.2%	22.0%	8.6%	3.4%	34.0%	44.8%	—	44.8%	$20,597
Morgan Stanley	11.6	9.1	20.7	11.4	20.0	0.8	20.8	31.6	15.5	47.1	23,561
Goldman Sachs	16.8	15.6	32.4	18.1	21.0	0.8	21.8	5.7	22.0	27.7	16,590
Citigroup	16.9	—	16.9	14.9	7.2	18.7	25.9	18.7	23.5	42.2	24,161
Merrill Lynch	10.0	5.2	15.2	8.7	13.6	11.8	25.4	21.2	29.6	50.8	26,787
Banc of America	20.7	5.1	25.8	28.3	20.6	—	20.6	18.2	7.2	25.4	5,853
Lehman Brothers	18.5	10.0	28.8	21.2	27.0	—	27.0	—	23.0	23.0	7,707
Bear Stearns	7.4	11.0	18.7	16.1	14.5	10.5	25.0	—	40.2	40.2	5,476
Average			**22.5%**				**25.1%**			**37.7%**	

Source: Roy C. Smith, "Strategic Directions in Investment Banking—A Retrospective Analysis," *Journal of Applied Corporate Finance* 14 (Spring 2001), pp. 111–123, table 4.
Note: All numbers are expressed as a % of that firm's net revenues.

pension funds. As the table shows, revenues from asset management exceed those from the other primary investment banking services.

THE INVESTMENT BANKER'S ROLE IN EQUITY ISSUES

We now turn to the services investment banks provide to issuing companies. The focus is on U.S. practices, but Prowse (1996) and Ljungqvist, Jenkinson, and Wilhelm (2002) document an increasing tendency for security issues around the world to conform to U.S. standards. As usual, we focus on common stock issues, though the procedures for selling bonds (described in Livingston and Miller 2000) and preferred stocks are substantially similar. Investment banks play several different roles throughout the securities offering process, and this section describes the evolution of these roles over the course of an issue. We also describe how issuers compensate IBs for the services they provide.

Though it is possible for firms to issue securities without the assistance of investment bankers, in practice, almost all firms enlist IBs when they issue equity. Broadly speaking, firms can choose an investment banker in one of two ways. The most common approach is a **negotiated offer,** where, as the name implies, the issuing firm negotiates the terms of the offer directly with one investment bank. In the other approach, a **competitively bid offer,** the firm announces the terms of its intended equity sale, and investment banks bid for the business. Though intuition suggests that the firm should obtain a better value when it accepts competitive bids from many banks, the empirical evidence does not unambiguously confirm this prediction.[2] One sign that competitive offers do not necessarily dominate on a cost basis is that the vast majority of equity sales are negotiated rather than competitive offers. If the costs of negotiated deals were much higher, why would so many firms choose that approach? Investment bankers argue that the depth of information they obtain in a negotiated offering raises the probability of a successful outcome for the issuer and that this benefit offsets any additional costs that may result from less competition in the banker-selection process.

Firms issuing securities often enlist the services of more than one investment bank. In these cases, it is typical for one of the banks to be named the **lead underwriter,** while the other participating banks are known as **co-managers.** Chen and Ritter (2000) argue that firms often prefer to issue securities with several co-managers because doing so increases the number of stock analysts that will follow the firm after the offering. Firms believe that a higher analyst following leads to greater liquidity and higher stock values.

Investment bankers sell equity under two types of contracts. In a **best-efforts** arrangement, the investment bank makes no guarantee about the ultimate success of the offering. Instead, it promises to give its best effort to sell the firm's securities at the agreed-upon price, but if there is insufficient demand for the issue, then the firm withdraws the issue from the market. Best-efforts offerings are most common for very small, high-risk companies. The investment bank receives a commission based on the number of shares sold in a best-efforts deal.

In contrast, in a **firm-commitment** offering, the investment bank agrees to **underwrite** the issue, meaning that the bank actually purchases the shares from the firm

---

[2.] Bhagat (1986), Bhagat and Frost (1986), and Hansen and Khanna (1994) examine the choice between competitive and negotiated offerings and find lower costs in negotiated deals. However, competitive offers may only appear to be less costly because the types of firms that use them are different from the types of firms that use negotiated offers. Logue and Tiniç (1999) examine multiple offers by the same firm, AT&T, and find no cost differences in the two offer types.

and resells them to investors. In theory, this arrangement requires the investment bank to bear the risk of inadequate demand for the firm's shares. Bankers mitigate this risk in two ways. First, the lead underwriter forms an **underwriting syndicate** consisting of many investment banks. These banks collectively purchase the firm's shares and market them, thereby spreading the risk exposure across the syndicate. Second, underwriters go to great lengths to determine the demand for a new issue before it comes to market, and they generally set the issue's *offer price* and take possession of the securities no more than a day or two before the issue date. Effectively, the risk that the investment bank might not be able to sell the shares that it underwrites is small.

In firm-commitment offerings, investment banks receive compensation for their services via the **underwriting spread,** the difference between the price at which the banks purchase shares from firms (the **net price**) and the price at which they sell the shares to institutional and individual investors (the **offer price**).[3] In some offerings, the underwriters receive additional compensation in the form of warrants that grant the right to buy shares of the issuing company at a fixed price. Underwriting fees can be quite substantial, especially for firms issuing equity for the first time. Chen and Ritter (2000) report that the vast majority of U.S. initial public offerings have underwriting spreads of exactly 7 percent, though lower spreads are common in very large IPOs. For example, if a firm conducting an IPO wants to sell shares worth $100 million, it will receive $93 million in proceeds from the offer, and the underwriter earns the gross spread of $7 million.

Underwriting spreads vary considerably depending on the type of security being issued. As Table 16.3 indicates, banks charge higher spreads on equity issues than on debt issues. They also charge higher spreads for **unseasoned equity offerings** (i.e., IPOs) than they do for **seasoned equity offerings** (SEOs), equity issues by firms that already have common stock outstanding. In general, the riskier the security being offered, the higher the spread charged by the underwriter. Notice that spreads on non-investment-grade ("junk") bonds exceed those on investment-grade bonds. Similarly, securities that have both debt- and equity-like features, such as convertible bonds or preferred stock, have spreads higher than those of ordinary debt but lower than those of common stock.

Figure 16.1 reveals two additional factors that influence equity underwriting spreads: (1) the percentage spread falls as the risk of the firm decreases and as the firm's size increases; and (2) holding the size and risk of the issuing firm constant, spreads decline as the size of the offer increases, but only up to a point. It is not particularly surprising that spreads should decline as the size of the offer increases because many underwriting costs—organizing and managing the syndicate, soliciting interest from investors, assuring regulatory compliance—are largely fixed. However, Figure 16.1 shows that beyond some point, increasing the size of an offer does increase the issuing firm's cost.

Ljungqvist, Jenkinson, and Wilhelm (2002) show that the spreads on international IPOs are significantly lower than on U.S. initial offers. In part, this reflects differences in underwriting practices across countries. U.S. underwriters typically use a process known as **book building** to assess demand for a company's shares and to set the offer price, in which underwriters ask prospective investors to reveal information

---

[3.] The spread itself is divided into three parts—the **management fee**, the **underwriting fee**, and the **selling concession**—that correspond to the investment banks' responsibilities. The rule of thumb within the investment banking industry is that the spread includes a management fee (about 20 percent), an underwriting fee (about 20 percent), and a selling concession (the remaining 60 percent). However, the proportion of each of the components varies. The spread must be divided because different banks participate as managers, as members of the underwriting syndicate, and as members of the selling group.

Table 16.3
Underwriting Spreads for Different Types of Securities, 2000 versus 1999

Security Type	2000		1999	
	Gross Spread ($ in millions)	Average Fee (%)	Gross Spread ($ in millions)	Average Fee (%)
Debt				
Investment-grade	$1,548	0.304%	$1,987	0.364%
Non-investment-grade[a]	382	1.545	801	2.010
Convertible	990	2.788	481	2.416
Mortgage-backed	23	1.120	4	0.166
Asset-backed	424	0.246	364	0.271
Municipals	29	0.789	67	0.862
Total debt	$3,395	0.455%	$3,703	0.494%
Common stock				
Initial public offerings	$3,971	5.419%	$3,627	5.708%
Seasoned offerings	4,865	3.672	3,696	3.647
Total common stock	$8,871	4.297%	$7,417	4.442%
Preferred stock				
Nonconvertible fixed	$113	1.769%	$541	3.193%
Convertible	244	3.051	303	3.090
Adjustable & other	47	0.949	18	0.829
Total preferred stock	$404	2.090%	$862	2.985%

Source: Britt Tunick and Mairin Burns, "In a Mixed Year, Underwriting Fees Increase, but Suffering Is Widespread," *Investment Dealers' Digest* (February 5, 2001), pp. 16–19.
[a]Commonly called "junk bonds."

Figure 16.1
Predicted Underwriter Spreads for Seasoned Common Stock Offerings

Source: Oya Altinkiliç and Robert S. Hansen, "Are There Economies of Scale in Underwriting Fees? Evidence of Rising External Financing Costs," *Review of Financial Studies* 13 (Spring 2000), pp. 191–218, fig. 3.

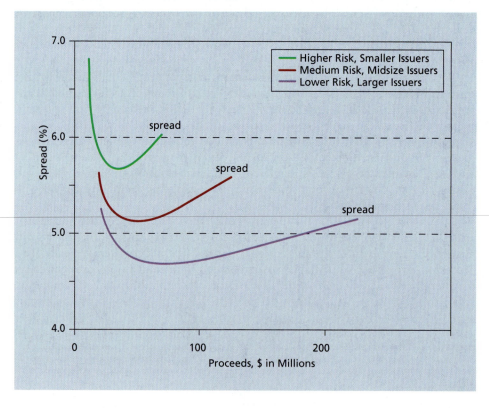

Table 16.4
Gross Spreads on International IPOs: Book Buildings versus Fixed-Price Offers

Country	Book Buildings		Fixed-Price Offerings		t-Test of Difference in Means
	Number of Observations	Gross Spread (mean %)	Number of Observations	Gross Spread (mean %)	
Europe	645	4.43%	370	2.19%	−22.53 **
France	64	4.49			
Germany	164	4.70	10	4.09	−21.56
Italy	53	4.37	2	3.50	−1.15
Netherlands	60	4.46	2	3.55	−0.84
Sweden	25	4.46	2	2.93	−1.69
United Kingdom	83	4.42	333	2.01	−12.76 **
Rest of Western Europe	161	4.17	19	3.66	−1.32
Eastern Europe	35	4.18	2	5.13	0.83
Asia/Pacific	214	4.10%	225	2.21%	−14.41 **
China	60	3.80	27	3.30	−1.40
Hong Kong	42	4.09	79	2.50	−6.34 **
Japan	39	5.38			
Malaysia	2	3.00	40	1.47	−4.22 **
Singapore	5	5.07	50	1.51	−9.58 **
Rest of Asia/Pacific	66	3.57	29	2.65	3.11 *
North & South America	103	5.17%	1	5.00%	
Canada	32	6.34	1	5.00	
Mexico	24	4.75			
Rest of N/S America	47	4.58			
Africa & Middle East	64	6.37%	13	2.19%	−6.07 **
Israel	42	7.44	3	5.17	−2.05 *
South Africa	3	4.67	10	1.30	−5.01 **
Rest of Africa & Middle East	19	4.27			
Total sample	1,025	4.55%	610	2.20%	−28.88 **

Source: Alexander P. Ljungqvist, Tim Jenkinson, and William J. Wilhelm Jr., "Global Integration in Primary Equity Markets: The Role of U.S. Banks and U.S. Investors," *Review of Financial Studies* (2002), forthcoming.
Notes: This table examines the difference in underwriter spreads for 1,635 non-U.S. initial public stock offerings executed via U.S.-style book-building techniques versus those executed via traditional fixed-price underwritings.
**, * Indicates statistical significance at the 1% and 10% levels, respectively.

about their demand for the offering.[4] Through conversations with investors, the underwriter tries to measure the demand curve for a given issue, and the investment bank sets the offer price after gathering all the information it can from investors. In international markets, book building is common, but so is a method called a **fixed-price offer**. In fixed-price offers, underwriters set the final offer price for a new issue weeks in advance. This imposes more risk on the underwriter, and naturally underwriters charge higher spreads as compensation for bearing the additional risk. Table 16.4 lists spreads on international IPOs. The average underwriting spread for fixed-price offers

[4.] Benveniste and Spindt (1989) explain how investment bankers provide investors with an incentive to reveal their demand for a firm's shares. When demand for a new issue is particularly strong, investment bankers do not fully adjust the offer price upward to a market-clearing level. This implies that investors who want to buy shares will be rationed, but it also implies that investors who revealed their interest in the stock will be rewarded when trading begins because they will receive shares that immediately increase in value.

is approximately twice as large as the average spread in deals in which the underwriter uses the book-building approach.

Just what do investment banks do to earn their fees? Investment banks perform a wide variety of services ranging from carrying out the analytical work required to price a new security offering, to assisting the firm with regulatory compliance, marketing the new issues, and developing an orderly market for the firm's securities once they begin trading. The chronology of a typical equity offering provides a useful framework for describing these services.

Services Provided before the Offering

Early in the process of preparing for an equity offering, an investment bank will assist the firm in filing the necessary documents with regulators, starting with the *registration statement*, which provides a wealth of information about the securities being offered as well as the firm selling them. Though preparing this document may sound like a rather trivial undertaking, in fact it is one of the most time-consuming parts of the capital-raising process, especially for IPOs. When a firm files documents with the Securities and Exchange Commission, it must take great pains to be sure that the information provided is timely and accurate, and firms can spend weeks with their bankers putting this document together. We describe the contents of the registration statement more fully in Section 16.2.

While it is preparing the necessary legal documents, the investment bank must also begin to estimate the value of the securities the firm intends to sell. Generally speaking, this task is simpler for debt than for equity, and of course, it is easier to value the equity of a company that already has shares trading on the market than to value the shares in an IPO. Investment banks use a variety of methods to value IPO shares, including discounted cash flow models and market "comparables." In the latter case, an investment bank compares the firm issuing equity to similar publicly traded firms, often estimating the value of the new stock issue by applying a price-to-earnings or price-to-sales multiple to the issuing firm's current or projected financial results.

However, one lesson to be learned from the IPO market over the past few years is that pricing new equity issues is not a purely analytical exercise. Several weeks before the scheduled offering, the firm and its bankers take a whirlwind tour of major U.S. and international cities to solicit demand for the offering from investors. Affectionately called the **road show,** this grueling process usually lasts a week or two, and it gives managers the opportunity to pitch their business plan to prospective investors. The investment banker's goal in this process is to build a book of orders for stock that is greater (often many times greater) than the amount of stock the firm intends to sell. The expressions of interest by investors during the road show are not legally binding purchase agreements, and the investment bank typically does not commit to an offer price at this point but gives investors a range of prices at which they expect to sell the offer. Given the tentative nature of the demand expressed on the road show, the banker seeks to **oversubscribe** the offering to minimize the bank's underwriting risk. Naturally, one way to create excess demand for an offering is to set the offer price below the market-clearing level. As we will see in the next section, the vast majority of IPOs in the United States and other countries are underpriced, meaning that once IPO shares begin trading, they do so at a price that is above the offer price set by the firm and its bankers. When firms conduct seasoned equity offerings, they also tend to sell shares at a slight discount to the market price of the outstanding shares, though underpricing is not as severe in SEOs as in IPOs. As the road show progresses, investment bankers can and do adjust the offer price upward, but they almost always **leave money on the table**—set the offer price below the expected post-issue selling price—in part to reward the investors who reveal their demand for the share issue. Hanley (1993) shows that investment banks only partially adjust the offer price upward in response to favorable demand signals from investors.

SMART PRACTICES VIDEO

Jay Goodgold, Managing Director, Equities Division, Goldman Sachs

"The goal here on the road show is to see the major institutional clients in Boston, New York, Chicago, Denver, Los Angeles, San Francisco, London, Paris, Frankfurt, and Tokyo."

See the entire interview at SMARTFinance

Investment bankers perform additional services designed to ensure that the firm's securities will be attractive to investors. One such service is "cleaning up the balance sheet," essentially consolidating different classes of stock and other forms of financing that are common in firms issuing equity for the first time. In addition, bankers negotiate agreements with the client's managers and directors, stipulating that these corporate insiders will not sell their personal stock holdings immediately after the offering. Finance theory offers an explanation for why bankers use these **lockup agreements,** which restrict insider sales from 30 days to more than a year.

At the time of an equity offering, insiders typically have private information about the firm's prospects. They are motivated to communicate this information to potential investors so the firm's shares will not be undervalued. This is difficult to do, however, because such information is not directly verifiable. Insiders thus face the problem of how to credibly signal what they know.[5] One believable signal is for insiders to retain shares in the firm after the offering, but this will only be a credible signal if the insiders are prohibited from selling in the aftermarket soon after trading begins. Lockup agreements prevent insiders from reneging on their promise to retain shares after trading begins.

Services Provided during and after the Offering

The lead underwriter conducts the security offering, ensuring that on the issue date, participating investors receive their shares, as well as a copy of the final prospectus. The lead underwriter exercises some discretion over the distribution of shares among syndicate members and the **selling group,** investment banks who may assist in selling shares but are not formal members of the syndicate. In oversubscribed offerings, the lead underwriter may exercise a **Green Shoe option** (or *overallotment option*), essentially an option to sell up to an additional 15 percent more shares than originally planned.

Once a firm's securities begin trading, the underwriter may engage in **price stabilization.** The reputation of an underwriter suffers if investors buy shares in an offering, only to find that once trading begins, the share price falls below the offer price. Because investment banks repeatedly approach investors with new share issues, it is very costly for banks if investors lose confidence in the banks' ability to price new issues. Therefore, if a new issue begins to falter in the market, the investment bank may buy shares on its own account, keeping the market price at or slightly above the offer price for an indefinite period. With limited capital, investment banks do not want to take large positions in the shares they underwrite, so the threat of having to stabilize the market gives underwriters an additional incentive to underprice new issues at the outset.

After a share offering is successfully sold, the lead underwriter often serves as the principal **market maker** for trading in the firm's stock, meaning that it continuously quotes bid and ask prices for the new securities. In this role, the lead underwriter will purchase shares from investors wishing to sell, and sell shares to investors wishing to buy, thus "making a market" in the new issue. The lead underwriter also assigns one or more research analysts to cover the issuing firm, and the research reports these ana-

5. Leland and Pyle (1977) suggest that insiders can signal their information through retention of a portion of the firm's ownership. The insiders, who are assumed to be risk averse, would prefer to shift all firm-specific risk to well-diversified investors, but they are willing to retain some risk to signal their private information. According to Leland and Pyle, the more favorable the insiders' information, the larger the number of shares they retain.

Table 16.5
Key Steps in the Initial
Public Offering Process

Major Steps and Main Events	Role of the Underwriter (U/W) in the Main Events
1. Initial step	
Select book-running manager and co-manager	Book-running manager's role includes forming the syndicate and being in charge of the entire process.
Letter of intent	Letter specifies gross spread and Green Shoe (overallotment) option, and protects U/W from unexpected expenses. Doesn't guarantee price or number of shares to be issued.
2. Registration process	
Registration statement and due diligence	After conducting due diligence, U/W files necessary registration statement with SEC.
Red herring	Once registration statement is filed with SEC, it is transformed into a preliminary prospectus (red herring).
3. Marketing	
Distribute prospectus; road show	Red herring is sent to salespeople and institutional investors around the country. Concurrently, company and U/W conduct a road show, and the IB builds a book based on expressed demand—but not legally binding.
4. Pricing and allocation	
Pricing; allocation	Once registration statement has SEC approval, U/W files an acceleration request, asking the SEC to accelerate the date at which the issue becomes effective. Firm and U/W meet the day before the offer to determine price, number of shares, and allocation of shares.
5. Aftermarket activities	
Stabilization; overallotment option	Lead U/W supports the stock price by purchasing shares if price declines. Support can only occur at or below offer price and can continue for only a relatively short period. If stock price goes up, U/W uses overallotment option to cover short position. If price goes down, U/W covers overallotment by buying stock in open market.
Research coverage	Final stage of IPO process begins 25 calendar days after IPO, when the "quiet period" ends. Only after this can U/W and other syndicate members comment on the value of the firm and provide earnings estimates.

Source: Katrina Ellis, Roni Michaely, and Maureen O'Hara, "When the Underwriter is the Market Maker: An Examination of Trading in the IPO Aftermarket," *Journal of Finance* 55 (June 2000), pp. 1039–1074.

lysts write (which naturally tend to be flattering) help generate additional interest in trading the firm's securities. In fact, some firms choose their investment bankers in large measure based on the reputation of the analyst that will cover the stock once it goes public. Table 16.5 summarizes the chronology of an investment bank's activities through the IPO process.

To conclude this section, we want to highlight the systemic conflicts of interest faced by investment bankers. Firms issuing securities, on the one hand, want to obtain the highest possible price for their shares (or bonds). Firms also want favorable coverage from securities analysts employed by their investment bankers. Investors, on the other hand, want to purchase securities at prices low enough to ensure that they will earn a high return on their investments. Investors also value dispassionate, unbiased advice from analysts. Investment bankers must therefore walk a thin line, both in terms of ethics and economics, in pleasing their constituents. Firms issuing securities are wise to remember this. Investment bankers deal with investors, especially institutional investors, on a repeated basis. They must approach this group each time a new offering comes to the market. In contrast, over the life of a firm, there is just one IPO (and perhaps a few SEOs).[6]

SMART ETHICS VIDEO
Jay Ritter, University of Florida
"Lots of buyers were willing to give things to the underwriters in terms of, for instance, generating extra commissions business."

See the entire interview at **SMARTFinance**

Concept Review Questions

1. What are the principal lines of business for top-tier investment banks? How do the business strategies of IBs that are affiliated with large commercial banks differ from those of unaffiliated IBs?

2. What are the major sources of revenue for investment banks?

3. What does the phrase "bulge bracket" mean? What recent regulatory change may create upheaval in the bulge bracket?

4. What services does an investment bank provide before an IPO? After?

16.2 LEGAL RULES GOVERNING PUBLIC SECURITY SALES IN THE UNITED STATES

This section begins by surveying the laws and regulations governing security offerings in the United States. Though we focus on common stock issues, the rules are generally very similar for debt and preferred stock offerings.

Security issues in the United States are regulated at both the state and federal levels. The most important federal law governing the sale of new securities is the **Securities Act of 1933.** The basis for federal regulation of the sale of securities is the concept of **full disclosure,** which means that issuers must reveal all relevant information concerning the company selling the securities and the securities themselves to potential investors. The other major federal law governing securities issues is the **Securities and Exchange Commission Act of 1934.** This act, and its amendments, established the U.S. Securities and Exchange Commission (SEC) and laid out specific procedures for both the public sale of securities and the governance of public companies.[7]

Given the emphasis U.S. securities law places on disclosure, it is no surprise that one of the most important roles investment banks play in the security offering process is performing **due diligence** examinations of potential security issuers. This means that IBs are legally required to search out and disclose all relevant information about

---

[6.] A CEO of a company that conducted an IPO during the 1990s told us, "You have two friends in an IPO: your lawyer and your accountant." Notice that the investment banker didn't make the list.

[7.] Much of the discussion in this section is based on the legal sections of Ritter (1998) and the updated information from his website (http://bear.cba.ufl.edu/ritter/ipodata.htm). Official information can also be accessed from the SEC's website at http://www.sec.gov.

an issuer before selling securities to the public. Investors can sue underwriters if they do not perform adequate due diligence, and of course, the underwriter's reputation suffers as well. Because investors understand that the most prestigious investment bankers have the most to lose from inadequate due diligence, the mere fact that these firms are willing to underwrite an issue provides valuable **certification** that the issuing company is in fact disclosing all material information.

The principal disclosure document for all public security offerings is the **registration statement.** Firms must file this highly detailed document with the SEC before they can solicit investors. Additionally, a final revised version must be approved by the commission before an offering can become **effective,** meaning before any shares can actually be sold to public investors. There are two basic parts to the registration statement: Part I, the **prospectus,** is distributed to all prospective investors; Part II, **supplemental disclosures,** is filed only with the SEC, although investors can obtain a copy from the SEC.

It is not completely accurate to talk about "the" prospectus, because it is not uncommon for the issuing firm to file a half-dozen or more amended prospectuses with the SEC during the registration period preceding an offer. The first, or preliminary prospectus, serves as the principal marketing tool during the period from initial filing with the SEC to the time when the firm responds to the commission's initial findings. The preliminary prospectus is often called a **red herring,** because it has a standard legal disclaimer printed across its cover in red stating that the securities described herein are not (yet) being offered for sale. The red herring lists a range of prices rather than a single price at which the securities may be offered. Usually, the final offer price is set the day before (or even the day of) the offering, and a final prospectus is then distributed with shares sold in the offering.

As the underwriting syndicate responds to SEC feedback, additional prospectuses are printed, until the commission allows the offer to become effective—that is, to proceed to public sale. At that time, a final prospectus is printed that includes the definitive offering price and number of shares being sold. This prospectus is then distributed to initial purchasers of the stock. The actual sale of securities cannot occur until each investor receives a final prospectus. Figure 16.2 presents the title page from the final prospectus of the IPO by Weight Watchers Corporation in November 2001. Credit Suisse First Boston and Goldman, Sachs & Co. were the co-lead underwriters for this offering. The other three IBs included in the title page's bulge bracket were Merrill Lynch & Co., Salomon Smith Barney, and UBS Warburg.

MATERIAL COVERED IN AN OFFERING PROSPECTUS

The prospectus is the primary disclosure document for a security offering. As such, it presents in summary form the most important information described more fully in Part II of the registration statement.[8] The format of the prospectus is both highly standardized and remarkably informative to an experienced observer. The title page presents details about the number of shares being offered and about the underwriting agreement (participants and terms) governing the offering. The next several pages of the prospectus present a thumbnail description of the company and its products, a table detailing the offering and listing how the proceeds will be used, a financial summary of operating results for the past few years, and a simplified balance sheet.

[8.] You can download the prospectus from current and past offerings (going back to the early 1990s) on the SEC's *EDGAR* website (http://www.sec.gov).

17,400,000 Shares

Common Stock

The shares of common stock are being sold by the selling shareholders named in this prospectus. We will not receive any of the proceeds from the shares of common stock sold by the selling shareholders.

Prior to this offering, there has been no public market for our common stock. Our common stock has been authorized for listing on the New York Stock Exchange under the symbol "WTW".

The underwriters have an option to purchase a maximum of 2,610,000 additional shares from certain of the selling shareholders to cover over-allotments of shares.

Investing in our common stock involves risks. See "Risk Factors" beginning on page 8.

	Price to Public	Underwriting Discounts and Commissions	Proceeds to Selling Shareholders
Per Share	$24.00	$1.26	$22.74
Total	$417,600,000	$21,924,000	$395,676,000

Delivery of the shares of common stock will be made on or about November 20, 2001.

Neither the Securities and Exchange Commission nor any state securities commission has approved or disapproved of these securities or determined if this prospectus is truthful or complete. Any representation to the contrary is a criminal offense.

Credit Suisse First Boston   Goldman, Sachs & Co.

Merrill Lynch & Co.

Salomon Smith Barney

UBS Warburg

The date of this prospectus is November 14, 2001.

Figure 16.2
Title Page from Weight Watchers' IPO Prospectus

Source: Weight Watchers International, Inc., Prospectus (November 14, 2001), p. 1.

The main part of the prospectus begins with a more detailed portrait of the company as it currently operates and of its recent history, and then proceeds to a detailed discussion of specific "risk factors" that make the offering especially risky. If a firm's fortunes rest on unproven technology, on key suppliers or customers, or on the talents of key personnel, the firm must disclose these risks. The firm must also disclose whether insiders will control a majority of the votes after the offering.[9] It is often said,

---

9. The risk-factors section often makes for interesting reading. A recent prospectus for a chain of funeral homes listed a decline in the U.S. death rate as an important risk factor. A ski resort's prospectus mentioned that "the success or failure

only partly in jest, that no investor who actually has read a prospectus would ever willingly buy the stock.

Deeper in the prospectus, investors find more detailed information about the issuer's financial condition, its business strategies, and the experience of its management team. The prospectus also reveals key information about how the firm will be governed after the offer. For instance, the prospectus lists the members of the board of directors and any business relationships they have with the corporation. The prospectus discloses the ownership stakes held by corporate officers and directors, both before and after the offer, and describes the compensation packages of the firm's top managers. If the purpose of the offering is to allow an existing shareholder to sell a large block of stock to new investors, the issue is a **secondary offering** and raises no capital for the firm. If the shares offered for sale are newly issued shares, which increase the number of outstanding shares and raise new capital for the firm, the issue is a **primary offering.** If some of the shares come from existing shareholders and some are new, the issue is a **mixed offering.**

The final section of an offering prospectus consists of various appendixes. One of the first of these presents the **cold comfort letter** provided by the firm's auditors, almost invariably one of the major accounting firms. This "letter" is actually a simple statement that the company's financial statements were prepared according to generally accepted accounting principles and accurately reflect all relevant information. Depending on the complexity of a company's business, the cold comfort letter may then be followed by from one to several dozen other appendixes that provide additional details about a firm's operations and/or financial structure. The entire IPO prospectus typically runs 80–160 pages in length.

Securities can be exempt from registration under certain conditions. Securities with a maturity of less than 270 days are exempt, as are intrastate security offerings and securities issued or guaranteed by a bank.[10] In addition, the sale of unregistered securities is allowed in private placements. These are discussed in depth in Section 16.5.

SHELF REGISTRATION (RULE 415)

As an alternative to filing a lengthy registration statement and awaiting SEC approval, firms with more than $150 million in outstanding common stock can use a procedure known as **shelf registration** (**Rule 415**) for the issue. This procedure allows a qualifying company to file a "master registration statement," which is a single document summarizing planned financing covering a 2-year period. Once the SEC approves the issue, it is placed "on the shelf," and the company can sell the new securities to investors out of inventory (off the shelf) as needed any time over the next two years. This has proven to be immensely popular with issuing corporations, which previously had to incur the costs (including costs of delay) of filing separate SEC registrations for each new security issue. In addition to saving time and money, shelf registration allows firms to issue securities in response to changes in market conditions.

The use of shelf registration is especially popular with large firms that frequently need access to the capital markets to raise funds. Although in principle shelf regis-

---

of a new business depends greatly on the ability of its management," and (nearby), "the management has no previous experience in owning and operating a ski resort or any of its amenity services."

[10.] This is the reason that commercial paper (discussed in Chapter 17) invariably has an original maturity of less than 270 days. As it happens, most commercial paper is of much shorter maturity, but the fact that this most important source of short-term financing for top-tier U.S. corporations is specifically design to be an unregulated financial instrument reveals both the importance of security laws and the lengths businesses will go to escape such regulation.

tration allows firms to reduce their reliance on investment bankers, the investment banker continues to be the key link between the firm and the capital markets. Interestingly, academic research documents that underwriting expenses are lower for shelf registrations than for traditional security issues and that firms rarely use shelf registration when they issue equity, whereas debt shelf registrations are quite common. This research result, first documented by Denis (1991), means that firms enjoy a greater benefit from having investment bankers "certify" the value of equity securities, but that certification is less valuable for bonds.

Ongoing Regulatory Requirements for a Publicly Traded Firm

Once a company successfully completes an IPO and lists its shares for trading on an exchange, it becomes subject to all the costs and reporting requirements of a public company. These include cash expenses such as exchange-listing fees and the cost of mailing proxies, annual reports, and other documents to shareholders. Additionally, the law requires public companies to hold general shareholders' meetings at least once each year and to hold special meetings as needed to obtain shareholder approval for certain types of transactions (i.e., approving a merger, authorizing additional shares of stock, or approving new stock option plans). By far, the most costly regulatory constraints on public companies are the disclosure requirements for the firm, its officers and directors, and its principal shareholders. In essence, the company must report any material change in its operations, ownership, or financing. Once a firm "goes public," life becomes very public indeed.

---

5. What is the guiding principle behind most of the important U.S. securities legislation? What role does the security registration play in implementing this philosophy?

6. What is a *red herring?*

7. What is *shelf registration?* Why do you think this has proven to be so popular with issuing firms, and why is it employed so frequently for debt offerings and so infrequently for equity issues?

Concept Review Questions

16.3 THE U.S. MARKET FOR INITIAL PUBLIC OFFERINGS

Given its role in providing capital market access for entrepreneurial growth companies, the U.S. initial public offering market is widely considered a vital economic and financial asset. Indeed, a welcoming IPO market has long been a key building block of America's success in high-technology industries. It is thus not surprising that all the U.S. stock markets compete fiercely for IPO listings. The competition is particularly intense between the two largest, the New York Stock Exchange (NYSE) and the Nasdaq electronic market, which merged with the American Stock Exchange in 1998. Although the number of IPOs (usually a few hundred per year) and the total capital they have raised ($30–$75 billion) each year since the mid-1990s does not seem immense in a $10 trillion economy, IPOs generally represent 30–40 percent of all new common equity raised by U.S. corporations each year. In other words, IPOs collectively raise almost half as much external equity capital each year as do established giants such as IBM, Exxon, and General Motors.

Patterns Observed in the U.S. IPO Market

To the uninitiated, a quick survey of the U.S. IPO market reveals some decidedly odd patterns. For example, it is one of the most highly cyclical securities markets imaginable. As Table 16.6 makes clear, aggregate IPO volume shows a very distinct pattern of boom and bust. Throughout most of the 1990s, the IPO market boomed. In 1999,

Table 16.6
Number of Offerings, First-Day Returns, and Gross Proceeds of U.S. Initial Public Offerings, 1975–2002

Year	Number of Offerings	Average First-day Returns (%)	Gross Proceeds ($ in millions)
1975	12	− 1.5%	$262
1976	26	1.9	214
1977	15	3.6	127
1978	20	11.2	209
1979	39	8.5	312
1980	75	13.9%	$ 934
1981	197	6.2	2,366
1982	83	10.6	1,064
1983	522	9.0	11,323
1984	222	2.6	2,841
1985	216	6.2	5,492
1986	485	5.9	16,349
1987	344	5.6	13,069
1988	129	5.4	4,181
1989	120	7.9	5,402
1990	113	10.4%	$ 4,480
1991	288	11.7	15,771
1992	397	10.0	22,204
1993	507	12.7	29,257
1994	416	9.7	18,300
1995	465	21.0	28,872
1996	666	16.5	42,479
1997	484	13.9	33,218
1998	319	20.0	35,112
1999	490	69.1	65,460
2000	385	55.4%	$65,677
2001	81	13.7	34,368
2002	73	8.3	22,954
1975–79	112	5.7%	$ 1,124
1980–89	2,392	6.8	63,021
1990–99	4,145	20.9	295,153
2000–02	539	42.8	122,999
Total	7,188	17.7%	$482,297

Source: Jay R. Ritter, "Some Factoids about the 2002 IPO Market," downloaded from his website (http://bear.cba.ufl.edu/ritter/ipodata.htm); gross proceeds data are from Securities Data Corporation, and exclude overallotment options but include international portions of issues, if any.

Notes: This table presents summary details about IPOs with an offering price of at least $5 per share sold on U.S stock markets between 1975 and 2002. It excludes American depositary receipts (ADRs), best-efforts offers, unit offers, Regulation A offerings, real estate investment trusts (REITs), partnerships, and closed-end funds. First-day returns are computed as the percentage return from the offering price to the first closing market price.

for example, the market saw 491 transactions take place (almost 2 per business day), raising more than $65 billion. The torrid pace continued during the first part of 2000, but when prices of U.S. stocks tumbled, a chill fell over the market. The number of transactions in 2001 was barely one-sixth of 1999's peak, and only a few dozen companies attempted to go public during 2002. Though this most recent cycle was among the most dramatic in history, the general pattern was by no means unprecedented, following boom-and-bust cycles from the 1960s, 1970s, and 1980s.

Another interesting pattern observed in the IPO market is the tendency for firms going public in a certain industry to "cluster" in time. It is common to see bursts of IPO activity in fairly narrow industry sectors, such as energy, biotechnology, communications, and in the late 1990s, Internet-related companies. Indeed, the latter half of the 1990s saw an incredible boom in both the number of Internet companies going public and the valuations assigned to them by the market. Companies such as Netscape, Yahoo!, Amazon.com, and eBay were able to raise hundreds of millions of dollars in equity despite their relatively short operating histories and nonexistent profits. Investors were so eager to purchase shares in these firms that their stock prices often doubled the first day they began trading.

APPLYING THE MODEL

The short-term stock-price increases for Internet-related IPOs had financial experts scratching their heads in 1999, none more so than the December 9, 1999, debut of VA Linux. The company went public with an offer price of $30 per share, and after one trading day, the stock closed at almost $240 per share. For investors who bought shares at the offer price and sold them as soon as possible, the 1-day return was an astronomical *700 percent*. Investors who held on for the long term did not fare as well. After the IPO, the stock closed above $240 only once, and by January 2003, the company, now renamed VA Software, saw its stock trading at just over $1 per share.

As recently as the early 1980s, investment banks targeted initial offerings almost exclusively at individual investors, more particularly at retail customers of the brokerage firms involved in the underwriting syndicate. Over the past 20 years, however, institutional investors have grown in importance, and now they generally receive 50–75 percent of the shares offered in the typical IPOs, and up to 90 percent or more of the "hot" issues.[11]

A final pattern emerging in the U.S. IPO market is its increasingly international flavor. The largest and most visible of the international IPOs are associated with privatizations of formerly state-owned enterprises. However, both established international companies and non-U.S. entrepreneurial firms are also choosing to make initial stock offerings to U.S. investors, either publicly via a straight IPO or to institutional investors through a **Rule 144A offering**. This special type of offer, which was first approved in April 1990, allows issuing companies to waive some disclosure requirements by selling stock only to sophisticated institutional investors, who may then trade the shares among themselves.

[11.] Academic analyses of the strategic share-allocation decisions made by investment bankers can be found in Hanley and Wilhelm (1995), Booth and Chua (1996), Ljungqvist and Wilhelm (2002), and Aggarwal, Prabhala, and Puri (2002). Ljungqvist and Wilhelm conclude that "discretionary" IPO allocations favoring institutional investors actually work in the best interests of issuing firms. Aggarwal, Prabhala, and Puri document a positive relationship between an IPO's first-day return and the fraction of IPO shares allocated to institutional investors. In other words, institutions receive greater allocations in the "hot" IPOs, those with strong premarket demand.

Advantages and Disadvantages of an IPO

The decision to convert from private to public ownership is not an easy one. The benefits of having publicly traded shares are numerous, but so too are the costs. This section describes the costs and benefits of IPOs for U.S. firms. Interestingly, as we discuss more fully in Section 16.6, Pagano, Panetta, and Zingales (1998) show that the motivations for going public are significantly different for continental European business owners than for their U.S. counterparts.

Benefits of Going Public

Chapter 2 of the accounting firm KPMG Peat Marwick's publication *Going Public: What the CEO Needs to Know* (1998) suggests the following advantages of an IPO to an entrepreneur.

1. New capital for the company. An initial public offering gives the typical private firm access to a larger pool of equity capital than is available from any other source. Whereas venture capitalists can provide perhaps $10–$40 million in funding throughout a company's life as a private firm, an IPO allows that same company to raise many times that amount in one offering. Ljungqvist and Wilhelm (2002) find that the typical U.S. IPO during 1990–2000 raised an average of $110.4 million. An infusion of common equity not only permits the firm to pursue profitable investment opportunities, but also improves the firm's overall financial condition and provides additional borrowing capacity. Furthermore, if the firm's stock performs well, the company will be able to raise additional equity capital in the future.

2. Publicly traded stock for use in acquisitions. Unless a firm has publicly traded stock, the only way it can acquire another company is to pay in cash. After going public, a firm has the option of exchanging its own stock for that of the target firm. Not only does this minimize cash outflow for the acquiring firm, but such a payment method may be free from capital gains tax for the target firm's owners. This tax benefit may reduce the price that an acquirer must pay for a target company.

3. Listed stock for use as a compensation vehicle. Having publicly traded stock allows the company to attract, retain, and provide incentives for talented managers by offering them stock options and other stock-based compensation. Going public also offers liquidity to managers who were awarded options while the firm was private.

4. Personal wealth and liquidity. Entrepreneurship almost always violates finance's basic dictum about diversification: real entrepreneurs generally have most of both their financial wealth and human capital tied up in their companies. Going public allows entrepreneurs to reallocate cash from their businesses and diversify their portfolios. Entrepreneurial families also frequently execute IPOs during times of transition when, for example, the company founder wishes to retire and provide a method of allocating family assets among those heirs who do and do not wish to remain active in the business.

In addition to these benefits, the act of going public generally results in a blaze of media attention, which often helps promote the company's products and services. Being a public company also increases a firm's overall prestige. However, the often massive costs must be weighed against all the obvious benefits of an IPO.

Drawbacks to Going Public

KPMG Peat Marwick's listing also includes the drawbacks of an IPO for a firm's managers.

1. The financial costs of an IPO. Few entrepreneurs are truly prepared for just how costly the process of going public can be in terms of out-of-pocket cash expenses and opportunity costs. Total cash expenses of an IPO, such as printing, accounting, and legal services, frequently approach $1 million, and most of these must be paid even if the offering is postponed or canceled. Additionally, the combined costs associated with the underwriter's discount (usually 7 percent) and initial underpricing of the firm's stock (roughly 15 percent on average) represents a very large transfer of wealth from current owners to the underwriters and to the new stockholders.[12]

2. The managerial costs of an IPO. As costly as an IPO is financially, many entrepreneurs find the unremitting claims made on their time during the IPO planning and execution process to be even more burdensome. Rarely, if ever, can CEOs and other top managers delegate these duties, which grow increasingly intense as the offering date approaches. There are also severe restrictions on what an executive can say or do during the immediate preoffering period. Because the IPO process can take many months (or more) to complete, the cost of going public in terms of managerial distraction is very high. Top executives must also take time to meet with important potential stockholders before the IPO is completed, and forever thereafter.

3. Stock-price emphasis. Owners/managers of private companies frequently operate their firms in ways that balance competing personal and financial interests. This includes seeking profits, but frequently also includes employing family members in high positions and other forms of personal consumption. Once a company goes public, however, external pressures build to maximize the firm's stock price. Furthermore, as managerial shareholdings fall, managers become vulnerable to losing their jobs either through takeover or through dismissal by the board of directors.[13]

4. Life in a fishbowl. Public shareholders have the right to a great deal of information about a firm's internal affairs, and releasing this information to stockholders also implies releasing it to competitors and potential acquirers as well. Managers must disclose, especially in the IPO prospectus, how and in what markets they intend to compete, information that is obviously valuable to competitors. Additionally, managers who are also significant stockholders are subject to binding disclosure requirements and face serious constraints on their ability to buy or sell company stock.

In spite of these drawbacks, we have seen that several hundred management teams each year decide that the benefits of going public outweigh the costs and begin the process of planning for an IPO. In addition to these "standard" IPOs, there are four "special" types of IPOs that warrant additional attention.

Specialized Initial Public Offerings: ECOs, Spin-offs, Reverse LBOs, and Tracking Stocks

The four special types of IPOs are equity carve-outs (ECOs), spin-offs, reverse LBOs, and tracking stocks. As noted in Chapter 13, an equity carve-out occurs when a parent company sells shares of a subsidiary corporation to the public through an initial public offering. The parent company may sell some of the subsidiary shares that it al-

---

[12.] The financial costs of an IPO are documented in Ritter (1987) and Lee, Lochhead, Ritter, and Zhao (1996). Intriguingly, Chen and Ritter (2000) show that the spreads received by underwriters on most midsize IPOs are *exactly* 7 percent, though Altinkiliç and Hansen (2000), Yeoman (2001), and Hansen (2001) contend that this is not necessarily a sign of insufficient competition among underwriters.

[13.] Field and Karpoff (2002) show that managers anticipate their exposure to takeover threat. In their sample of more than 1,000 IPOs, at least 53 percent go public with some form of antitakeover defense in place.

ready owns, or the subsidiary may issue new shares. In any event, the parent company almost always retains a controlling stake in the newly public company.[14]

A **spin-off** occurs when a public parent company "spins off" a subsidiary to the parent's shareholders by distributing shares on a pro rata basis. Thus, after the spin-off, there will be two public companies rather than one. Conceptually, the stock price of the parent should drop by approximately the amount that the market values the shares of the newly public spin-off, though Hite and Owers (1983), Miles and Rosenfeld (1983), and Schipper and Smith (1983) all document significantly positive price reactions for the stock of divesting parent companies at the time of spin-off announcements, perhaps indicating that the market expects that the two independent companies will be managed more effectively than they would have been had they remained together.

APPLYING THE MODEL

Lamont and Thaler (2002) describe one of the most puzzling spin-offs ever. In March 2000, 3Com Corp. sold a 5 percent stake in its subsidiary, Palm Inc., via an equity carve-out. 3Com also announced its intention to spin off the remaining 95 percent of Palm to existing 3Com shareholders, who would receive 1.5 shares of Palm for each share of 3Com they owned. This gave investors two ways to purchase Palm shares. For example, an investor who wanted to buy 150 Palm shares could buy them directly in the carve-out IPO, or the investor could purchase 100 shares of 3Com and wait to receive 150 Palm shares after the spin-off. Of course, in the latter strategy, the investor would ultimately own 150 shares of Palm and 100 shares of 3Com.

What was puzzling about this spin-off was the behavior of 3Com and Palm shares after the carve-out. Conceptually, the stand-alone value of 3Com shares cannot be negative. Therefore, the price of 3Com shares prior to the spin-off should have been *at least* 1.5 times the price of Palm shares in the carve-out (because anyone who owned 1 share of 3Com would ultimately receive an additional 1.5 shares of Palm). In fact, after a single trading day, Palm shares sold for almost 1.2 times more than 3Com shares were worth! In this case, and a few other high-tech spin-offs, it seems that only irrational exuberance can explain the market's response.   ◼

In a **reverse LBO** (or **second IPO**), a formerly public company that has previously gone private through a leveraged buyout goes public again. Reverse LBOs are easier to price than traditional IPOs because information exists about how the market valued the company when it was publicly traded. Muscarella and Vetsuypens (1989) and DeGeorge and Zeckhauser (1993, 1996) study reverse LBOs and find that the LBO partners earn very high returns on these transactions. One reason for this is obvious: only the most successful LBOs can subsequently go public again.

The final type of specialized equity offering, **tracking stocks,** is a very recent innovation. These are equity claims based on (and designed to mirror, or *track*) the earnings of wholly owned subsidiaries of diversified firms. They are hybrid securities, because the tracking stock "firm" is not separated from the parent company in any way,

---

14. Equity carve-outs are examined empirically in Schipper and Smith (1986), Nanda (1991), Slovin, Sushka, and Ferraro (1995), Michaely and Shaw (1995), and most recently in Vijh (1999). These studies generally find that announcements of carve-outs are viewed as good news by investors (the parent's stock experiences a positive abnormal return) and that the long-term returns to buyers of carve-outs are better than those for buyers of other types of common stock offerings. Vijh reports (Table 2) that the mean (median) offering value as a percentage of subsidiary value was 38.2 (32.2) percent for 628 carve-outs during the 1981–1995 period. The average percentage ownership of the subsidiary by the parent after the carve-out was 58.6 (62.5) percent.

but instead remains integrated with the parent legally and operationally. In contrast, both carve-outs and spin-offs result in legally separate firms. AT&T conducted the largest common stock offering in U.S. history when it issued $10.6 billion in AT&T Wireless tracking stock in April 2000. As has been true for most other tracking stock offerings, AT&T's stock rose significantly when it announced the Wireless offering. Unfortunately, both parent and tracking stock performed abysmally during the months after the issue.

THE INVESTMENT PERFORMANCE OF INITIAL PUBLIC OFFERINGS

Are IPOs good investments? The answer seems to depend on the investment horizon of the investor and whether or not the investor can purchase IPO shares at the offer price. If an investor can buy shares at the offer price and **flip** them, selling them on the first trading day, then the returns on IPOs are substantial.[15] If, instead, the investor buys shares in the secondary market and holds them for the long term, the returns are much less rewarding.

Positive Initial Returns for IPO Investors (Underpricing)

Year in and year out, in virtually every country around the world, the very short-term returns on IPOs are surprisingly high. In the United States, the share price in the typical IPO closes roughly 15 percent above the offer price after just one day of trading. Researchers refer to this pattern as **IPO underpricing,** meaning that the offer price in the prospectus is consistently lower than what the market is willing to bear.[16] To capture this **initial return,** an investor must be fortunate enough to receive an allocation of shares from the investment banker and to sell those shares at the first opportunity. Therein lies a problem. Not all investors are allowed to participate in the investment bank's allocations, and bankers discourage those investors who do participate from immediately selling (i.e., flipping) their shares on the open market. For investors who buy IPO shares when they begin trading in the open market in the hope of making a quick profit, the rewards are much smaller, and the risks much greater, than those faced by investors who participate in the initial offering.

APPLYING THE MODEL

On February 19, 2002, shares of the pioneer in Internet payment methods, Paypal Inc. (ticker symbol, PYPL), began trading for the first time. According to the IPO prospectus, Paypal offered its shares for $13.00 to participating investors. At the close of the first day, Paypal shares were worth $18.20, for a 1-day return of 40 percent. However, for investors who could not buy shares from the syndicate and instead bought shares once trading began, the first-day results were not as good. Paypal shares opened the first day of trading at $19.29 before falling 5.7 percent by the day's end.   ■

[15.] Not surprising, underwriters tend to discourage flipping because it raises the odds that they will have to help stabilize the price once trading begins. Siconolfi and McGeehan (1998) describe how investment banks try to identify and punish flippers. Krigman, Shaw, and Womack (1999) offer a different assessment of the economic value of flippers. They find that flipping is both a rational response to perceived pricing errors (caused primarily by issuing firms' unwillingness to lower share offering prices in the face of weak demand) and accurately predicts future returns on newly issued shares.

[16.] The academic literature on IPO underpricing is far too voluminous to cite in depth. Instead, we encourage the interested reader to see the references in the survey and empirical articles by Ibbotson, Sindelar, and Ritter (1994), Loughran, Ritter, and Rydqvist (1994), Lee, Lochhead, Ritter, and Zhao (1996), Ljungqvist and Wilhelm (2001), and Lowry and Schwert (2002).

Average 1-day returns on IPOs of 15 percent present quite a puzzle to financial economists, who in studying these returns have uncovered the following patterns:

1. Large IPOs tend to be less underpriced than smaller offerings. The smaller the offering, the more it is underpriced, and best-efforts offers are more underpriced than firm-commitment issues.

2. Initial returns are higher in "hot-issue markets" than in more normal times. Anyone wishing to make a case that financial markets are prone to irrational exuberance will quickly seize on initial offerings, for the IPO market does appear especially prone to fads. Partly because of the IPO market's relatively small scale, a small change in investor appetite for new issues can have a profound impact on the reception accorded individual offerings. As Ljungqvist and Wilhelm (2001) show, this was most true during the "Internet bubble" of 1999, when average IPO initial returns hit 69 percent, and Internet IPOs were underpriced on average by a stunning 88 percent. During 1999 and the first three quarters of 2000, nearly 200 firms conducting IPOs saw their stock price increase by 100 percent or more on the first trading day. However, the IPO market cooled by the fall of 2000, and from October of that year through the end of 2002, only one IPO doubled in price in its debut.

3. The mean initial return is much higher than the median. Although the "headline" underpricing figures are quite dramatic, only 60–70 percent of all IPOs are substantially underpriced, and the median IPO's initial return is roughly half the average value. The average, in turn, is inflated by a relative handful of extraordinarily popular offerings with initial returns of 50 percent or more.

4. The mean return overstates the actual profits earned by most investors. Rock (1986) argues that IPO investors, especially those who are less sophisticated than the institutions who are the investment banks' best clients, face a classic problem of the **winner's curse.** When an IPO is extremely "hot," both sophisticated and unsophisticated investors will demand shares, and the issue will be very oversubscribed. In these deals, investors will be rationed (with rationing most severe for "ordinary" investors), receiving only a fraction of the shares they would like. As we know, the short-term returns on oversubscribed issues tend to be above average. On the other hand, when an IPO is "cold" and the syndicate has difficulty selling the issue to more-sophisticated clients, ordinary investors will receive all the shares they want. Unfortunately, the short-term returns for these IPOs will be below average. Because they receive small allocations in hot deals and large allocations in cold deals, the unsophisticated players in this market will earn much lower returns than a glance at the average 1-day return for all IPOs might suggest.

5. It is unclear whether venture capital backing or the use of a prestigious underwriter increases or decreases IPO underpricing. At least during the years prior to 1990, venture capital–backed IPOs were, on average, less underpriced than non-venture-backed offers, and issues brought to market by more-prestigious underwriters yielded lower first-day returns than those handled by lesser-known investment bankers. Stated differently, existing owners of venture-backed firms were able to capture more of the postoffer value of their company than could owners of other companies executing IPOs, and the same was true of firms taken public by prestigious underwriters. It is unclear whether this is still true today. Beatty and Welch (1996) show that underwriter prestige and initial return are positively correlated after 1990, though exactly why this has occurred remains a puzzle.

The empirical regularities detailed make clear just how expensive going public tends to be for most companies. Significant underpricing means that money must be

"left on the table" by the owners of a company executing an
IPO, because the initial return is captured by initial purchasers
of the shares rather than by the issuing company. Why IPOs are
underpriced is something of a mystery. Presumably, the firms
issuing stock would prefer to receive a higher price (with less
underpricing) for their shares, and they could choose investment
banks with a track record of less underpricing. Competition

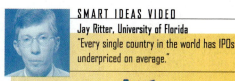

among investment banks on this dimension might reduce underpricing to an economically insignificant level, on average.

Finance theory offers several possible explanations for the underpricing phenomenon. First, given the problem of the winner's curse, firms may have to underprice
shares, on average, to keep relatively unsophisticated players in the market. If the average IPO were not underpriced, then unsophisticated investors would receive large allocations of the IPOs with negative returns and small allocations of those with positive
returns, and would eventually drop out of the market. Second, firms could underprice
their IPOs in an attempt to achieve higher stock valuations later, when they conduct
seasoned offerings. For example, a firm with excellent future prospects might be willing to leave money on the table initially (something a less healthy firm could not afford
to do) to convince investors of just how bright its future looks. If investors recognize
and respond to this signal, then the long-term value of the firm's shares will be higher,
and it can recoup the initial underpricing costs in future equity offerings.

Third, a firm might be willing to underprice its shares to generate excess demand
for the offering. With excess demand, the firm (or its investment bank) could spread
the shares across many different investors, with no single investor holding a large
block. A dispersed ownership structure could benefit the firm if it leads to a more liquid market for the shares and hence a lower cost of capital. Managers might selfishly
prefer more ownership dispersion because investors who own just a few shares are
less likely than those owning large blocks to threaten managers if the firm's stock per-
forms poorly. Fourth, firms may underprice to give investors an incentive to reveal
information they have that helps determine the true value of the firm's stock.

Whatever the case, underpricing is a pervasive phenomenon. However, the long-
run performance of IPOs presents a different puzzle.

Negative Long-Term IPO Returns

Early research on the long-run performance of IPOs was not encouraging for investors. Panel A of Figure 16.3, from Loughran and Ritter (1995), describes how badly
investors who buy IPO shares at the end of the first month of trading, and then hold
these shares for five years thereafter, fare compared to the returns these investors
would have earned by purchasing the shares of comparable, size-matched firms. On
average, investors' net returns are over 40 percent below what they would have
earned after five years on alternative equity investments.

Because these findings challenge the notions that investors are rational and financial
markets efficient, they are quite controversial. More recent research casts doubt on this
long-run underperformance for IPO shares. Studies by Brav and Gompers (1997),
Fama (1998), Brav, Geczy, and Gompers (2000), Eckbo, Masulis, and Norli (2000),
and Gompers and Lerner (2000) conclude that most IPOs do not
yield significant long-run underperformance, provided that IPO
returns are compared to an appropriate benchmark. In particular, Eckbo, Masulis, and Norli (2000) make a compelling case
that much of the observed underperformance can be explained
by leverage effects and risk reductions resulting from the IPO itself. They show that a company's raising new equity capital in an

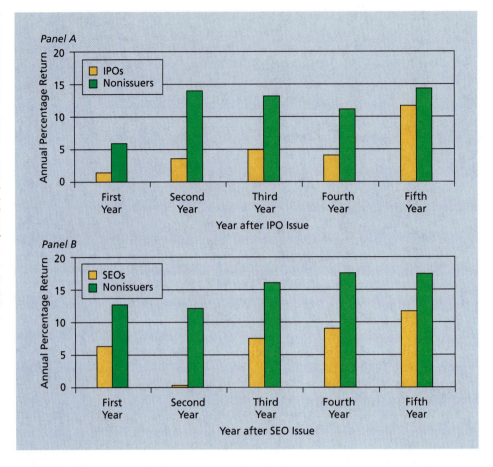

Figure 16.3
The Long-Run Performance of U.S. Initial Public Offerings (IPOs) and Seasoned Equity Offerings (SEOs) versus Matching Firms That Did Not Issue New Equity

These figures describe the average annual raw returns for 4,753 IPOs and their capitalization-matched nonissuing firms (Panel A), and the average annual raw returns for 3,702 SEOs and their capitalization-matched nonissuing firms (Panel B) during the five years after the issue. The sample period covers 1970–1990.

Source: Tim Loughran and Jay R. Ritter, "The New Issues Puzzle," *Journal of Finance* 50 (March 1995), pp. 23–51, fig. 2.

IPO reduces the firm's leverage and its financial risk, so investors will accept a lower required return subsequent to the offering. Given these conflicting findings, we cannot yet draw firm conclusions about the long-run return on IPO shares.

8. What patterns have been observed in the types of firms going public in the United States? Why do you think that certain industries become popular with investors at different times?

9. What are the principal benefits of going public? What are the key drawbacks?

10. Distinguish between an *equity carve-out* and a *spin-off*. How might a spin-off create value for shareholders?

11. What does the term "underpricing" refer to? If the average IPO is underpriced by about 15 percent, how might an unsophisticated investor who regularly invests in IPOs earn an average return less than 15 percent?

12. How does underpricing add to the cost of going public?

16.4 SEASONED EQUITY OFFERINGS IN THE UNITED STATES

Seasoned equity offerings (SEOs) are surprisingly rare for both U.S. and non-U.S. companies. In fact, the typical large U.S. company will not sell new common stock even as frequently as once per decade, though when an SEO is launched, it tends to be much larger than the typical IPO. Seasoned common stock issues must generally follow the same regulatory and underwriting procedures as unseasoned offerings. The company must prepare a registration statement, including a preliminary prospectus, and file it with the SEC. After the SEC approves the registration statement, a final prospectus is printed and the securities can then be sold to investors. Besides its larger average size, a seasoned offering is principally different from an unseasoned offering in that the seasoned securities have an observable market price when the offering is made. Obviously, this makes pricing seasoned offers much easier, and Loderer, Sheehan, and Kadlec (1991) show that SEOs tend to be priced very near the current market price. However, ease of pricing does not mean that investors welcome new equity offering announcements, as we now discuss.

Stock Price Reactions to Seasoned Equity Issue Announcements

One reason corporations issue seasoned equity only very rarely is that stock prices usually fall when firms announce plans to conduct SEOs. On average, the price decline is about 3 percent.[17] In the United States, the average dollar value of this price decline is equal to almost one-third of the dollar value of the issue itself. Clearly, the announcement of seasoned equity issues conveys negative information to investors, though precisely what information is transmitted is not always clear. The message may be that management, which is presumably better informed about a company's true prospects than are outside investors, believes the firm's current stock price is too high. Alternatively, the message may be that the firm's earnings will be lower than expected in the future and management is issuing stock to make up for this internal cash flow shortfall.

There is some evidence that SEOs are bad news for shareholders not only at the time they are announced, but also over longer holding periods of one to five years. Negative long-run returns following seasoned equity offerings are documented in Loughran and Ritter (1995) as shown in Panel B of Figure 16.3, Spiess and Affleck-Graves (1995), and Jegadeesh (2000). As is the case with long-run IPO returns, however, whether or not long-run returns following SEOs are unusually low depends somewhat on the comparison benchmark.

Most equity sales in the United States fall under the category of **general cash offerings**. However, there is a special type of seasoned equity offering that allows the firm's existing owners to buy new shares at a bargain price or to sell that right to other investors. These **rights offerings** are relatively scarce in the United States but are growing in importance internationally.

Rights Offerings

One of the basic tenets of English common law, and thus of U.S. commercial laws derived from it, is that shareholders have first claim on anything of value distributed by a corporation. These **preemptive rights** give common stockholders the right to maintain their proportionate ownership in the corporation by purchasing shares whenever the firm sells new equity.[18] The laws of most American states grant shareholders the preemptive right to participate in new issues, unless this right is removed by shareholder consent. However, the vast majority of publicly traded U.S. companies have removed preemptive rights from their corporate charter, so rights offerings by large

[17.] Myers and Majluf (1984) provide a theoretical explanation for this negative market response to seasoned equity issue announcements based on informational asymmetry between managers and investors: investors interpret SEO announcements as a sign that managers believe that the firm's shares are overvalued.

[18.] For a discussion of the effect of the removal of preemptive rights on shareholder wealth, see Bhagat (1983). In general, removal of rights from corporate charters decreases shareholder wealth.

COMPARATIVE CORPORATE FINANCE

The Widely Varying Importance of Capital Market Finance in Developed Countries

The table below details the total value of new equity and debt security issues on selected national stock and bond markets for the year 2001. The table lists the total value ($US in millions [$mn]) of each type of security issued, the combined value of stock and bond offerings, and the relative importance of this total capital market funding as a percentage of year 2001 GDP (expressed in US dollars). The countries are ranked by year-2001 GDP, though the table does not include countries whose stock exchanges are not members of the World Federation of Exchanges. There are striking differences in the relative importance of capital market finance, even between countries with roughly similar levels of national income.

Sources: Stock and bond issuance data from World Federation of Exchanges (formerly International Federation of Stock Exchanges) website (http://www.world-exchanges.org); GDP data from *World Development Indicators 2001*, World Bank website (http://www.worldbank.org).

| Country | Equity Issues by Domestic Companies | | Private-Sector Bond Issues ($mn) | Total Value of Stock and Bond Offerings ($mn) | Value of Stock and Bond Offerings as % GDP |
	By Already-Listed Companies ($mn)	By Newly Listed Companies ($mn)			
United States: NYSE	$49,290	$28,478	$1,460,465[a]		
Nasdaq	23,981	7,840	NA	$1,570,054	15.76%
Japan	16,917	NA	3,147[a]	20,064	0.42
Germany	2,490[a]	23,343[a]	NA	—	—
United Kingdom	21,049	7,778	120,167	148,994	10.51
France	27,042[b]	10,653[b]	46,027	83,722	6.47
Italy	7,176	3,429	NA	—	—
Canada	7,624	5,967	0	13,591	1.91
Brazil	1,839	242	6,418	8,499	1.43
Mexico	1,244[a]	125[a]	3,158	4,527	0.79
Spain	8,749	17,171	14,589	40,509	7.26
Korea	3,939	108	57,515	61,562	13.47
Australia	5,234	1,796	NA	—	—
Netherlands	25,796[b]	26,463[b]	50,019[b]	102,278	26.77
Argentina	135	NA	8,070	8,205	2.88
Switzerland	NA	2,301	7,214	9,515	3.95
Belgium	59[b]	6,543[b]	NA	—	—
Sweden	472	270	NA	—	—
Turkey	903	0.3	3,233	4,136	2.07

[a] Year 2000 data—2001 unavailable.
[b] Year 2000 data—Amsterdam, Brussels and Paris bourses merged into Euronext in 2001, and the three market totals were reported together for 2001.

American companies are quite rare today.[19] Rights offerings are still quite common in other countries, as this chapter's Opening Focus illustrates.

[19.] The phenomenon of declining U.S. rights offerings is examined in Smith (1977) and Hansen and Pinkerton (1982). The most likely explanation, discussed in Hansen (1988), is that firms announcing rights issues suffer larger price drops than do firms announcing underwritten offers, thereby negating the benefits of lower underwriting fees. Khorana, Wahal, and Zenner (2002) examine rights offerings by closed-end mutual funds, and their findings suggest that managers execute these offerings primarily to enrich themselves at shareholders' expense.

Mechanics of a Rights Offering

When a company makes a rights offering, the board of directors must set a **date of record.** As with dividend record dates, this date determines which shareholders will receive the distributed right. Due to the time needed to make bookkeeping entries when a stock is traded, stocks usually begin trading **ex rights,** without the rights being attached to the stock, two trading days prior to the date of record (just as stocks go *ex dividend*). The issuing firm sends rights to **holders of record,** owners of the firm's shares on the date of record, who may exercise their rights, sell them, or let them expire. Rights are negotiable instruments, and many are traded often enough to be listed on the various securities exchanges. They are exercisable for a specified period, generally not more than a few months, at a **subscription price,** which is set somewhat below the prevailing market price of the firm's stock. The value of a right depends largely on the number of rights needed to purchase a share of stock and the amount by which the rights' subscription price is set below the current market price.

A firm's management must make two basic decisions when preparing for a rights offering. First, management sets the price at which the rights holders can purchase a new share of common stock. The subscription price must be set below the current market price, but how far below depends on several things: management's evaluation of the sensitivity of the market demand to a price change, the degree of dilution of ownership and earnings expected, and the size of the offering.

Once management has determined the subscription price, it must determine the number of rights required to purchase a share of stock. Because the amount of funds to be raised is known in advance, the subscription price can be divided into this value to get the total number of shares that must be sold. Dividing the total number of shares outstanding by the total number of shares to be sold gives management the number of rights required to purchase a share of stock, as illustrated in the following Applying the Model.

APPLYING THE MODEL

Ingram Company, a closely held hand-tool manufacturer, intends to raise $1 million through a rights offering. The firm currently has 160,000 shares outstanding, and these have recently been trading between $53 and $58 per share. The company's investment bank has recommended setting the subscription price for the rights at $50 per share. The bank believes that at this price the offering will be fully subscribed. The firm must therefore sell an additional 20,000 shares ($1,000,000 ÷ $50 per share) to raise $1 million. This means that eight rights (160,000 ÷ 20,000) are needed to purchase a new share at $50. Each right entitles its holder to purchase one-eighth of a share of common stock. ∎

Valuation and Market Behavior of Rights

Theoretically, the value of a right should be the same if the stock is selling with rights (cum rights) or ex rights, meaning that the value of the right is no longer included in the stock's market price. In either case, however, the market value of a right may differ from its theoretical value. Once a rights offering has been declared, shares trade with rights for only a few days. Equation 16.1 is used to find the theoretical value of a right when the stock is trading *with rights, R_W*:

$$R_W = \frac{M_W - S}{N + 1} \qquad \text{(Eq. 16.1)}$$

where R_W = the theoretical value of a right when the stock is selling
                 with rights,

         M_W = market value of the stock with rights,

           S = subscription price of the stock,

           N = number of rights needed to purchase one share of stock.

APPLYING THE MODEL

Ingram Company's stock is selling with rights at a price of $54.50 per share, the subscription price is $50 per share, and eight rights are required to purchase a new share of stock. According to Equation 16.1, the value of a right is $0.50 [($54.50 − $50.00) ÷ (8 + 1)]. A right should therefore be worth $0.50 in the marketplace. ∎

When a share of stock is trading *ex rights,* the share price of the stock is expected to drop by the value of the right. Equation 16.2 is used to find the market value of the stock trading ex rights, M_e. The same notation is used as in Equation 16.1:

$$M_e = M_W - R_W \qquad \text{(Eq. 16.2)}$$

Equation 16.3 gives the theoretical value of a right when the stock is trading ex rights, R_e:

$$R_e = \frac{M_e - S}{N} \qquad \text{(Eq. 16.3)}$$

The use of these equations can be illustrated by returning to the Ingram Company example in the following Applying the Model.

APPLYING THE MODEL

According to Equation 16.2, the market price of the Ingram Company stock selling ex rights is $54 ($54.50 − $0.50). Substituting this value into Equation 16.3 gives the value of a right when the stock is selling ex rights, which is $0.50 [($54.00 − $50.00) ÷8]. The theoretical value of a right when the stock is selling with rights or ex rights is therefore the same.   ∎

As indicated earlier, stock rights are negotiable instruments, often traded on securities exchanges. The market price of a right generally differs from its theoretical value. The extent to which it differs depends on how the firm's stock price is expected to behave during the period when the right is exercisable. By buying rights instead of the stock itself, investors can achieve much higher returns on their money if stock prices rise.

Concept Review Questions

13. What happens to a firm's stock price when the firm announces plans for a seasoned equity offering? What are the long-term returns to investors following an SEO?

14. Why do you think that rights offerings have largely disappeared in the United States?

16.5 PRIVATE PLACEMENTS IN THE UNITED STATES

As noted earlier, a **private placement** involves the sale of securities in a transaction that is exempt from the registration requirements imposed by federal securities law. A private placement occurs when an investment banker arranges for the direct sale of a new security issue to an individual, several individuals, an institutional investor, or a group of institutions. The investment banker is then paid a commission for acting as an intermediary in the transaction. To qualify for a private-placement exemption, the sale of the securities must be restricted to a small group of **accredited investors,** who are individuals or institutions that meet certain income and wealth requirements. The reasoning for the private-placement exemption is that accredited investors are financially sophisticated agents who do not need the protection afforded by the registration process. Typical accredited institutional investors include insurance companies, pension funds, mutual funds, and venture capitalists.

TRADITIONAL PRIVATE PLACEMENTS VERSUS RULE 144A ISSUES

The private-placement exemption is a **transactional exemption,** which means that the securities must be registered before they can be resold or the subsequent sale must also qualify as a private placement. **Rule 144A,** adopted in 1990, provides a private-placement exemption for institutions with assets exceeding $100 million (known as **qualified institutional buyers**) and allows them to freely trade privately placed securities among themselves. The principal reasons for instituting Rule 144A were to increase liquidity and reduce issuing costs in the private-placement market. Another reason was to attract large foreign issuers who were unable or unwilling to conform to U.S. registration requirements for public offerings.

Private placements have several advantages over public offerings. They are less costly in terms of time and money than registering with the SEC, and the issuers do not have to reveal confidential information. Also, because there typically are far fewer investors, the terms of a private placement are easier to renegotiate, if necessary. The disadvantage of private placements is that the securities have no readily available market price, they are less liquid, and there is a smaller group of potential investors than in the public market. The steady, if unspectacular, growth in the total number and value of private placements in the United States is described in Table 16.7. The reader should particularly note two points. First, debt offerings are much more common than equity offerings, though stock issues raise significantly larger amounts on average. Second, note the dominance of Rule 144A as the preferred vehicle for private placements.

---

15. What is a *qualified institutional buyer?* How does this differ from an *accredited investor?*

16. What are the relative advantages and disadvantages of private placements compared to those of public offerings of stock and bond issues?

Concept Review Questions

16.6 INTERNATIONAL COMMON STOCK OFFERINGS

The international market for equity offerings can be broken down into two parts: each nation's market for domestic stock offerings and the international, or cross-border, market for equity offerings. We briefly look at each in turn, beginning with a survey of national markets.

Table 16.7
Private Placements in the United States, 1990–2001

Type of Offering	2001	2000	1999	1998	1995	1990
Overall private placements	$572	$494	$451	$485	$121	$129
	(2,623)	(2,407)	(3,773)	(3,876)	(1,925)	(2,253)
Straight debt	444	356	356	398	43	51
	(1,941)	(1,668)	(3,241)	(3,492)	(718)	(809)
Plain-vanilla equity	114	122	78	90	21	16
	(542)	(547)	(445)	(492)	(309)	(217)
Securitized private placements	137	143	114	103	28	22
	(719)	(606)	(1,273)	(1,044)	(526)	(338)
Yankee private placements	44	68	123	160	39	21
	(232)	(342)	(1,175)	(1,146)	(619)	(338)
Rule 144A by all issuers	490	370	303	391	63	4
	(1,853)	(1,485)	(2,437)	(2,850)	(816)	(38)
Rule 144A by U.S. issuers	385	259	233	282	46	0
	(1,446)	(1,079)	(1,713)	(870)	(617)	
Rule 144A as % of all private placements	85.7%	74.9%	67.2%	80.6%	52.1%	3.1%
Rule 144A by U.S. issuers **as % of all Rule 144A issuers**	78.6%	70.0%	76.6%	72.1%	73.0%	0.0%

Source: The data are taken from late-February or early-March issues of *Investment Dealers' Digest.*
Note: This table details the total value (US$ in billions) and number (in parentheses) of private-placement issues on U.S. capital markets for selected years in the period 1990–2001.

NON-U.S. INITIAL PUBLIC OFFERINGS

Any nation with a well-functioning stock market must have some mechanism for taking private firms public, and the total number of IPOs outside the United States each year usually exceeds the American total by a wide margin. However, far less money is raised in aggregate by private-sector issuers on non-U.S. markets, as these international IPOs are, on average, very much smaller than those on the Nasdaq or NYSE. Yet, many of the same investment anomalies documented in the United States are also observed internationally. First, non-U.S. private-sector IPOs also demonstrate significant first-day returns that are often much higher than for U.S. IPOs. Figure 16.4 summarizes IPO underpricing studies from 38 different countries; all show significant underpricing, and 20 of these countries have mean initial returns greater than the U.S. average.

A second empirical regularity common to both U.S. and international IPOs is that unseasoned international offers also appear to yield negative long-term returns. However, studies of non-U.S. long-run returns are subject to all the methodological problems bedeviling U.S. studies (perhaps even more), so it is unclear whether SEOs truly underperform or not. Third, popular non-U.S. issues also tend to be heavily oversubscribed, and the allocation rules mandated by national law or exchange regulations largely determine who captures the IPO initial returns. Fourth, hot-issue markets are as prevalent internationally as in the United States. Finally, taxation issues (particularly capital gains tax rules) significantly impact how issues are priced and/or which investors the offers target.

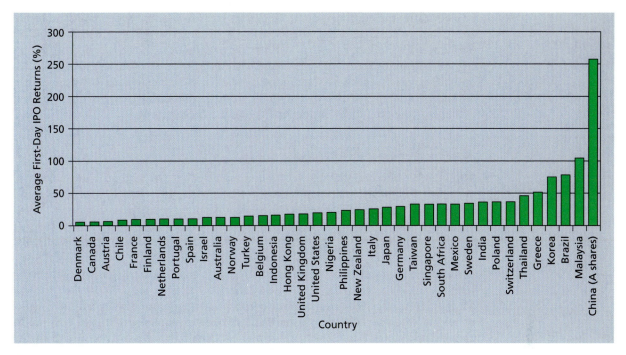

Figure 16.4
Average First-Day Returns on IPOs for 38 Countries

Source: Studies cited in Tim Loughran, Jay R. Ritter, and Kristian Rydqvist, "Initial Public Offerings: International Insights," *Pacific-Basin Finance Journal* 2 (June 1994), pp. 165–199; and updates on Ritter's website (http://bear.cba .ufl.edu/ritter/ipodata.htm).

International IPO markets do, however, differ in important ways from U.S. markets. For example, many governments impose politically inspired mandates on firms wishing to go public, requiring them to allocate minimum fractions of the issue to their employees or to other targeted groups. Furthermore, the net effect of pricing restrictions in many countries is to ensure that IPOs are severely underpriced; this is especially common in countries where shares must be priced on a par value basis and/ or where minimum dividend payouts are mandated. Some governments (including ones as advanced as Japan's) routinely prohibit firms from making IPOs during periods when market conditions are "unsettled" and/or require explicit permission to be obtained before an IPO can be launched. Many countries require that initial offering prices be set far in advance of the issue, which usually means that offerings that actually proceed tend to be highly underpriced. Finally, Pagano, Panetta, and Zingales (1998) show that non-U.S. entrepreneurs often have different motivations for taking firms public than do owner/managers of U.S. private companies. Whereas many U.S. companies go public to acquire the equity capital needed to finance rapid growth, continental European (specifically, Italian) entrepreneurs go public mainly to rebalance their firms' capital structures and to achieve personal liquidity. On a more balanced note, most other countries place fewer restrictions on preoffer marketing and dissemination of information than do U.S. regulators.

One particularly interesting investment banking practice is observed in British Commonwealth countries such as Singapore and (until July 1997) Hong Kong. Menyah, Paudyal, and Inyangete (1995) and Chowdhry and Sherman (1996) show that in these countries, investors must prepay for the shares they request a month or more before the offering itself. Refunds for unallocated shares are then mailed back to the investors after the offering is completed. This gives the issuing firm a powerful incentive to underprice an offering, because doing so ensures that the issue will be massively oversubscribed and that the firm will be able to retain the interest earned on the excess funds held for the month between the subscription and actual issuance dates. Although this may seem a trivial point, many IPOs in these countries are oversubscribed 500 times or more, yielding several million dollars in revenue to the issuing firm and even distorting the money supply of city-states like Singapore.

INTERNATIONAL COMMON STOCK ISSUES

Although the international market for common stock is not, and probably never will be, as large as the international market for debt securities, cross-border trading and issuance of common stock have increased dramatically during the past 15 years. Much of this increase can be accounted for by a growing desire on the part of institutional and individual investors to diversify their investment portfolios internationally. Because foreign stocks currently account for a small fraction of U.S. institutional holdings and those in other developed economies, this total will surely grow rapidly in the years ahead.

Besides issuing stock to investors, corporations have also discovered the benefits of issuing stock outside their home markets. For example, several top U.S. multinational companies have chosen to list their stock in half a dozen or more stock markets. Chaplinsky and Ramchand (2000) show that issuing stock internationally both broadens the ownership base and helps a company integrate itself into the local business scene. A local stock listing increases local business press coverage and also serves as effective corporate advertising. Having locally traded stock can also facilitate corporate acquisitions because shares can then be used as an acceptable method of payment.

American Depositary Receipts and Global Depositary Receipts

Many foreign corporations have discovered the benefits of trading their stock in the United States, though they do so differently than do U.S. companies. The disclosure and reporting requirements mandated by the U.S. Securities and Exchange Commission have historically discouraged all but the largest foreign firms from directly listing their shares on the New York or American Stock Exchanges. For example, in mid-1993, Daimler Benz announced that it would become the first large German company to seek such a listing. Most foreign companies instead tap the U.S. market through **American Depositary Receipts (ADRs)**. These dollar-denominated claims issued by U.S. banks represent ownership of shares of a foreign company's stock held on deposit by the U.S. bank in the issuing firm's home country.[20]

ADRs have proven to be very popular with U.S. investors, at least partly because they allow investors to diversify internationally. However, because the shares are covered by American securities laws and pay dividends in dollars (dividends on the under-

---

[20]. ADRs have been the subject of a significant amount of academic research. Both Jayaraman, Shastri, and Tandon (1993) and Miller (1999) present evidence that listings of ADRs are associated with positive abnormal returns on the underlying shares in their home markets. Muscarella and Vetsuypens (1996) use a sample of "solo splits," or splits of ADR stocks that are not accompanied by splits of the stock in the home-country market, to differentiate between two theoretical explanations for the widely noted increase in share prices around stock splits. They interpret their findings as supportive of the liquidity explanation (splits lower stock prices and thus increase demand for shares by individual investors) over the signaling explanation of the effects of stock-split announcements. Errunza and Miller (2000) show that ADRs lower the cost of capital for their sample of 126 issuing firms from 32 countries. Blass and Yafeh (2001) find that Israeli firms that choose a New York listing over a listing in the home market (Tel Aviv) are younger, more high-tech, and of generally higher quality than their stay-at-home counterparts.

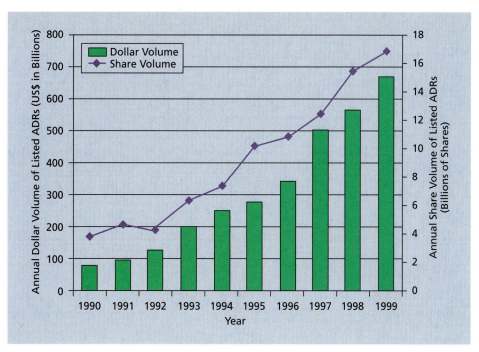

Figure 16.5
Dollar and Share Trading Volume in Public ADR Issues (1990–1999)

Trading volume is compiled for ADRs listed only on the three major U.S. exchanges for 457 listed programs. This figure ignores trading in 901 private Rule 144A issues. Data are compiled from "Depositary Receipts (ADRs and GDRs): 1999 Year-End Market Summary," Bank of New York, Depositary Receipts Division, Worldwide Securities Processing Services, December 31, 1999.

Source: Stephen R. Foerster and G. Andrew Karolyi, "The Long-Run Performance of Global Equity Offerings," *Journal of Financial and Quantitative Analysis* 35 (December 2000), pp. 499–528, fig. 2.

lying shares are converted from the local currency into dollars before being paid out), U.S investors are able to diversify at very low cost. Since an ADR can be converted into ownership of the underlying shares, arbitrage ensures rational dollar valuation of this claim against foreign-currency-denominated stock.[21] Figure 16.5 details the rapid growth in market value and trading volume of ADRs on the three major U.S. stock exchanges over the period 1990–1999.

The shares of over 1,500 foreign companies are traded in the United States in the form of sponsored and unsponsored ADRs. The New York Stock Exchange alone has 464 ADRs from 53 countries listed as of February 2002. A **sponsored ADR** is one for which the issuing (foreign) company absorbs the legal and financial costs of creating and trading the security. In this case, the company will pay a U.S. depositary bank to create an ADR issue. An **unsponsored ADR** is one in which the issuing firm is not involved with the issue at all and may even oppose it. Historically, unsponsored ADRs typically resulted from U.S. investor demand for shares of particular foreign companies. Since 1983, however, the SEC has required that all new ADR programs be sponsored, so relatively few unsponsored ADRs still exist. There are also four different levels of ADR programs, corresponding to different levels of required disclosure and tradability. As described in Karolyi (1998) and Miller (1999), the least costly—in terms of both required disclosure and out-of-pocket expenses—are Level I and Rule 144A offerings, but the shares offered cannot subsequently be traded on one of the major stock exchanges or Nasdaq. Home-country accounting standards are also allowed for these two types of ADR programs. In contrast, Level II and III programs require the use of GAAP and are significantly costlier to arrange, but these shares can be listed for trading on public markets.

[21.] Given the success of ADRs, many large international equity issues use this form even for share **tranches** (portions of the issue) that are destined for sale outside the United States. Large international issues that use this form are often called **Global Depositary Receipts** (**GDRs**) to emphasize their multinational characteristics.

APPLYING THE MODEL

To demonstrate how ADRs are created, assume that Bayerische Motoren Werke, the famous German manufacturer of BMW automobiles, wishes to establish an ADR program for its shares on the New York Stock Exchange. In early February 2002, BMW's shares are trading on the Deutsche Börse (formerly the Frankfurt Stock Exchange) at €42 per share, and the U.S. dollar/euro exchange rate is $0.8620/€. If BMW wishes to establish an ADR program worth about $100 million, the firm might ask Bank of New York (ticker symbol, BK), one of the two leading ADR issuers, to handle the issue and offer to pay all of BK's issuing and listing expenses—including underwriting fees. Assume further that BK believes the ideal price for shares to trade on the NYSE is about $75 per share. BK would implement this ADR program by taking the following steps:

1. Purchase 3 million shares of BMW on the Deutsche Börse at €42/share, paying €126 million. This represents an investment worth $108,612,000 by Bank of New York (€126,000,000 × $0.862/€).
2. Create 1.5 million ADRs for listing on the NYSE, with each ADR representing ownership of two BMW shares.
3. Sell the 1.5 million ADRs to American investors at a price of $72.41 per ADR. This is the dollar price implied by BMW's price in euros, the current $/€ exchange rate, and the fact that each ADR is worth two BMW shares (€42/share × 2 shares/ADR × $0.862/€ = $72.41/ADR).

The total proceeds of this offering are $108,612,000, which is exactly equal to the amount BK paid for the shares originally. Holders of these ADRs have a security that is denominated in dollars, but which perfectly reflects both BMW's share price in euros and fluctuations in the dollar/euro exchange rate.

To demonstrate how ADRs reflect changes in BMW's stock price, assume that BMW's shares increase by €1.00 per share in early-morning trading in Germany. We can compute that the ADRs should rise by $1.72 each (€1.00/share × 2 shares/ADR × $0.862/ €) to $74.13 per share when they begin trading in New York later that day. To demonstrate how ADRs reflect exchange rate movements, assume that BMW's price remains unchanged at €42 per share, but that the euro appreciates from $0.862/€ to $0.8825/€ immediately before trading begins in New York. The ADRs should begin trading at $74.13 per share (€42/share × 2 shares/ADR × $0.8825/€) when the NYSE opens. In other words, either an increase in BMW's stock price from €42.00 to €43.00 per share, holding exchange rates constant, or an appreciation of the euro from $0.862/€ to $0.8825/€ (holding BMW's stock price unchanged) can cause the price of each BMW ADR to rise by $1.72, from $72.41 to $74.13 per ADR.

There have been numerous high-profile ADR offerings in recent years. For example, Deutsche Bank established an American Depositary Receipt program on the New York Stock Exchange on October 1, 2001. Citibank sponsored the company's ADRs, each of which represents five ordinary shares and trades under the symbol TSM. Another example is MATAV, which established an ADR program on the NYSE on November 19, 1997. MATAV, the first Central European company to issue NYSE-listed ADRs, provides local, domestic, and international long-distance telephone service, as well as mobile telephone service, throughout Hungary. Each of the company's ADRs, which trade under the symbol MTA, represents five ordinary shares.

SHARE ISSUE PRIVATIZATIONS

Anyone who examines international share offerings is soon struck by the size and importance of share issue privatizations in non-U.S. stock markets. A government executing a **share issue privatization (SIP)** will sell all or part of its ownership in a state-owned enterprise to private investors via a public share offering. The words *public* and *private* can become confusing in this context; an SIP involves the sale of shares in a state-owned company to *private* investors via a *public* capital market share offering. Since Britain's Thatcher government first popularized privatizations in the early 1980s, there have been roughly 850 privatizing share offerings by almost 100 national governments. These SIPs have raised over $800 billion.[22]

For our purposes, the most important aspect of privatization programs is the transforming role they have played in developing many national stock markets in general, and IPO markets in particular. Share issue privatizations are particularly important for market development because of their size and the way their shares are allocated to potential investors. As Table 16.8 makes clear, SIPs tend to be vastly larger than their private-sector counterparts; in fact, the 10 largest (and 27 of the 29 largest) share offerings in world history have all been privatizations. Almost without exception, SIPs have been the largest share offerings in a country's history, and the first several large privatization IPOs generally yield a dramatic increase in the national stock market's trading volume and liquidity. In addition to size, SIPs differ from private-sector share issues in being almost exclusively secondary offerings. In other words, the proceeds from SIPs go to the government rather than to the firm being privatized. The sole major exception to this rule to date has occurred in China; almost all Chinese SIPs have been primary offerings.

The importance of SIPs in creating new shareholders derives from the way these issues are generally priced and allocated. Governments almost always set offer prices well below their expected open-market value (they deliberately underprice), thereby ensuring great excess demand for shares in the offering. The issuing governments then allocate shares in a way that ensures maximum political benefit. Invariably, governments favor employees and other small domestic investors (who typically have never purchased common stock before) with relatively large share allocations, whereas domestic institutions and foreign investors are allocated far less than they desire. The net result of this strategy is to guarantee that most of the short-term capital gains of privatization IPOs are captured by the many citizen/investors (who vote) rather than by institutional and foreign investors (who do not). Furthermore, the long-run excess returns to investors who purchase privatizing share issues are significantly positive. All these features help promote popular support for privatization and other economic reform measures the government might wish to enact. In all, privatization share

---

[22.] An even more frequently used method of privatization is an asset sale, where a government sells a state-owned firm directly to a private company or to a group of private investors. Asset sales have raised an additional $450 billion over the past two decades, so the cumulative value of proceeds from privatizations now exceeds $1.2 *trillion*. The material in this discussion is drawn primarily from Megginson, Nash, Netter, and Schwartz, (2000), Boutchkova and Megginson (2000), and Jones, Megginson, Nash, and Netter (1999). Additionally, Subrahmanyam and Titman (1999) present a theoretical explanation for the role share offerings (SIPs, as well as private-sector offerings) can play in developing a nation's capital markets.

Table 16.8
Share Issue Privatizations (SIPs), the World's Largest Share Offerings

Date	Company	Country	Amount ($ in millions)	IPO[a]/SEO[b]
Nov 87	Nippon Telegraph & Telephone	Japan	$40,260	SEO
Oct 88	Nippon Telegraph & Telephone	Japan	22,400	SEO
Nov 99	ENEL	Italy	18,900	IPO
Oct 98	NTT DoCoMo	Japan	18,000	IPO
Oct 97	Telecom Italia	Italy	15,500	SEO
Feb 87	Nippon Telegraph & Telephone	Japan	15,097	IPO
Nov 99	Nippon Telegraph & Telephone	Japan	15,000	SEO
Jun 00	Deutsche Telekom	Germany	14,760	SEO
Nov 96	Deutsche Telekom	Germany	13,300	IPO
Oct 87	British Petroleum	United Kingdom	12,430	SEO
Apr 00	*AT&T Wireless (tracking stock)*	*United States*	*10,600*	*IPO*
Nov 98	France Telecom	France	10,500	SEO
Nov 97	Telstra	Australia	10,530	IPO
Oct 99	Telstra	Australia	10,400	SEO
Jun 99	Deutsche Telekom	Germany	10,200	SEO
Dec 90	Regional electricity companies[c]	United Kingdom	9,995	IPO
Dec 91	British Telecom	United Kingdom	9,927	SEO
Jun 00	Telia	Sweden	8,800	IPO
Dec 89	U.K. water authorities[c]	United Kingdom	8,679	IPO
Dec 86	British Gas	United Kingdom	8,012	IPO
Jun 98	Endesa	Spain	8,000	SEO
Jul 97	ENI	Italy	7,800	SEO
Apr 00	*Oracle Japan*	*Japan*	*7,500*	*IPO*
Jul 93	British Telecom	U.K.	7,360	SEO
Oct 93	Japan Railroad East	Japan	7,312	IPO
Dec 98	Nippon Telegraph & Telephone	Japan	7,300	SEO
Oct 97	France Telecom	France	7,080	IPO
Jul 99	Credit Lyonnais	France	6,960	IPO
Feb 94	Elf Acquitaine	France	6,823	SEO
Jun 97	*Halifax Building Society*	*United Kingdom*	*6,813*	*IPO*
Jun 98	ENI	Italy	6,740	SEO
May 94	*Autoliv Sverige*	*Sweden*	*5,818*	*IPO*
Oct 96	ENI	Italy	5,864	SEO
Oct 98	Swisscom	Switzerland	5,600	IPO
Jul 99	*United Parcel Service*	*United States*	*5,500*	*IPO*

Source: William L. Megginson and Jeffry M. Netter, "From State to Market: A Survey of Empirical Studies on Privatization," *Journal of Economic Literature* 39 (June 2001), pp. 321–389.

Notes: This table details the 35 largest share offerings in history (those raising over $5 billion) as of August 15, 2000. The 10 largest (and 30 of the 35 total) issues are offerings of shares in privatized firms. *Private-sector share offerings* are presented in boldface, italicized type; share issue privatizations (SIPs) are presented in regular typeface.

[a] Initial public offering.
[b] Seasoned equity offering.
[c] Indicates a group offering of multiple companies that trade separately after the IPO.

offerings have done as much to promote the development of international stock markets during the last 20 years as any other single factor.

Concept Review Questions

16.7 SUMMARY

- Companies wishing to raise capital externally must make a series of decisions, beginning with whether to issue debt or equity, and whether to employ an investment bank to assist with the securities sale. This chapter focuses on common stock offerings, but the decisions and issuing procedures are very similar for preferred stock and debt securities.

- Firms wishing to raise new common stock equity must decide whether to sell stock to public investors, through a general cash offering, or to rely on sales to existing stockholders in a rights offering. Rights issues are now fairly rare in the United States, though they remain common in other developed countries.

- Common stock can be sold through private placements to accredited investors, or it can be sold to the public if the securities are registered with the SEC. A company's first public offering of common stock is known as its initial public offering or IPO. The average IPO in the United States is underpriced by about 15 percent, and this has held true for several decades. International IPOs are also underpriced. It is unclear whether or not IPOs are poor long-term investments.

- Subsequent offerings of common stock are known as seasoned equity offerings, or SEOs. The announcement of a seasoned equity issue tends to decrease a company's stock price, and there is strong evidence that firms issuing seasoned equity underperform over the long term.

- Investment banks assist companies in selling new securities by underwriting security offerings. Underwriting a security offering involves three tasks: (1) managing the offering, which includes advising the company about the type and amount of securities to sell, (2) underwriting the offering by purchasing the securities from the issuer at a fixed price to shift the price risk from the issuer to the investment bank, and (3) selling the securities to investors.

- The largest share offerings in world history have all been share issue privatizations, or SIPs. Governments have raised over $800 billion since 1981 through these share offerings, and they have transformed stock market capitalization, trading volume, and the number of citizens owning shares in many countries.

INTERNET RESOURCES

Note: *For updates to links, please go to the book's website at* *http://smart.swcollege.com*

http://www.ipo.com —An up-to-date site tracking current and historical IPOs, SEOs, and venture capital financings

http://www. ipomaven.com—A site that contains current information on recent and forthcoming IPOs as well as a variety of other information regarding the IPO market.

http://www.investorhome.com/ipo.htm—A site full of links to other sites with IPO data, research articles, and other information.

KEY TERMS

accredited investors
American Depositary Receipts (ADRs)
best-efforts
book building
bulge bracket
certification
cold comfort letter
co-managers
competitively bid offer
date of record
due diligence
effective
ex rights
final prospectus
firm-commitment
fixed-price offer
flip
full disclosure
general cash offerings
Global Depositary Receipts (GDRs)
Green Shoe option
holders of record
initial return
investment bank
IPO underpricing
lead underwriter
leave money on the table
lockup agreements
management fee
market maker
mixed offering
negotiated offer
net price
offer price
overallotment option
oversubscribe
preemptive rights
preliminary prospectus

price stabilization
primary offering
private placement
prospectus
qualified institutional buyers
red herring
registration statement
reverse LBO
rights offerings
road show
Rule 144A
Rule 144A offering
Rule 415
seasoned equity offerings (SEOs)
second IPO
secondary offering
Securities Act of 1933
Securities and Exchange Commission Act
    of 1934
selling concession
selling group
share issue privatization (SIP)
shelf registration
spin-off
sponsored ADR
subscription price
supplemental disclosures
tracking stocks
tranches
transactional exemption
underwrite
underwriting fee
underwriting spread
underwriting syndicate
unseasoned equity offerings
unsponsored ADR
winner's curse

QUESTIONS

16-1.   What preferences do you think common stock shareholders would have regarding a
company's source of equity financing?

16-2.   Rights offerings are seldom used in the United States to raise equity capital, but they are often used in Europe. How might you explain that fact?

16-3.   What do you think are the most important costs and benefits of becoming a publicly traded firm? If you were asked to advise an entrepreneur whether to take his or her firm public, what are the key questions you would ask before making your recommendation?

16-4.   If you were an investment banker, how would you determine the offering price of an IPO?

16-5.   Are the significantly positive short-run and significantly negative long-run returns earned by IPO shareholders compatible with market efficiency? If not, why not?

16-6.   Why do investment banks require *lockup agreements* when they underwrite security offerings? As a potential investor, what would you think if all the shares in an equity offering were being sold by the company's management and none were new shares being sold by the company itself?

16-7.   List and briefly describe the key services investment banks provide to firms issuing securities before, during, and after the offering.

16-8.   What are *American Depositary Receipts (ADRs),* and why have they proven so popular with U.S. investors?

16-9.   How would you explain the fact that the underwriting spread on IPOs averages about 7 percent of the offering price, whereas the underwriting spread on a seasoned offering of common stock averages less than 5 percent?

16-10.   Discuss the various issues that must be considered in selecting an investment banker for an IPO. Which type of placement is usually preferred by the issuing firm?

16-11.   In terms of IPO investing, what does it mean to "flip" a stock? According to the empirical results regarding short- and long-term returns following equity offerings, is flipping a wise investment strategy?

16-12.   What materials are presented in an IPO prospectus? In general, what result is documented regarding sales of shares by insiders and venture capitalists?

16-13.   How do you explain the highly politicized nature of *share issue privatization (SIP)* pricing and share allocation policies? Are governments maximizing offering proceeds, or are they pursuing primarily political and economic objectives?

PROBLEMS

Investment Banking

16-1.   West Coast Manufacturing Company (WCMC) is executing an initial public offering with the following characteristics. The company will sell 10 million shares at an offer price of $25 per share, the underwriter will charge a 7 percent underwriting fee, and the shares are expected to sell for $32 per share by the end of the first day's trading. Assuming this IPO is executed as expected, answer the following:

   a. Calculate the initial return earned by investors allocated shares in the IPO.
   b. How much will WCMC receive from this offering?
   c. What is the total cost (underwriting fee and underpricing) of this issue to WCMC?

16-2.   Continuing from Problem 16-1, assume that you purchase shares in the West Coast Manufacturing Company at the postoffering market price of $32 per share and hold the shares for one year. You then sell your WCMC shares for $35 per share. WCMC does not pay dividends, and you are not subject to capital gains taxation. During this year, the return on the overall stock market was 11 percent. What net return did you earn on your WCMC share investment? Assess this return in light of the overall market return.

16-3. Norman Internet Service Company (NISC) is interested in selling common stock to raise capital for capacity expansion. The firm has consulted First Tulsa Company, a large underwriting firm, which believes that the stock can be sold for $50 per share. The underwriter's investigation found that its administrative costs will be 2.5 percent of the sale price and its selling costs will be 2.0 percent of the sale price. If the underwriter requires a profit equal to 1 percent of the sale price, how much will the spread have to be in dollars to cover the underwriter's costs and profit?

16-4. The Bloomington Company needs to raise $20 million of new equity capital. Its common stock is currently selling for $42 per share. The investment bankers require an underwriting spread of 7 percent of the offering price, and the company's legal, accounting, and printing expenses associated with the seasoned offering are estimated to be $450,000. How many new shares must the company sell to net $20 million?

16-5. LaJolla Securities Inc. specializes in the underwriting of small companies. The terms of a recent offering were as follows:

Number of shares	2 million
Offering price	$25 per share
Net proceeds	$45 million

LaJolla Securities' expenses associated with the offering were $500,000. Determine LaJolla Securities' profit on the offering if the secondary market price of the shares immediately after the offering began were as follows:

a. $23 per share
b. $25 per share
c. $28 per share

16-6. SMG Corporation sold 20 million shares of common stock in a seasoned offering. The market price of the company's shares immediately before the offering was $14.75. The shares were offered to the public at $14.50, and the underwriting spread was 4 percent. The company's expenses associated with the offering were $7.5 million. How much new cash did the company receive?

The U.S. Market for Initial Public Offerings

16-7. Go to http://www.ipo.com, and find (under IPO Pricings) information about firms that went public in the first few weeks of 2003. Write down the ticker symbols and offer prices for the firms you select; then go to Yahoo! and download daily price quotes since the IPO date. For each firm, calculate the following:

a. The percentage return measured from the offer price to the closing price the first day

b. The percentage return measured from the opening price to the closing price the first day

16-8. Four companies conducted IPOs last month: Hot.Com, Biotech Pipe Dreams Corp., Sleepy Tyme Inc., and Bricks N Mortar International. All four companies went public at an offer price of $10 per share. The first-day performance of each stock (measured as the percentage difference between the IPO offer price and the first-day closing price) appears below:

Company	First-Day Return
Hot.Com	45%
Biotech Pipe Dreams	30%
Sleepy Tyme	5%
Bricks N Mortar	0%

a. If you submitted a bid through your broker for 100 shares of each company, if your orders were filled completely, and if you cashed out of each deal after one day, what was your average return on these investments?

b. Next, suppose that your orders were not all filled completely because of excess demand for "hot" IPOs. Specifically, after ordering 100 shares of each company, you were able to buy only 10 shares of Hot.Com, 20 shares of Biotech Pipe Dreams, 50 shares of Sleepy Tyme, and 100 shares of Bricks N Mortar. Recalculate your average return taking into account that your orders were only partially filled.

Seasoned Equity Offerings in the United States

16-9. Indicate (1) how many shares of stock one right is worth and (2) the number of shares a given stockholder, S, can purchase in each of the cases shown in the following table.

Case	Number of Shares Outstanding	Number of New Shares to Be Issued	Number of Shares Held by Stockholder S
A	500,000	20,000	400
B	2,000,000	50,000	2,500
C	10,000,000	500,000	20,000
D	40,000,000	10,000,000	200,000

16-10. Determine the theoretical value of a right when the stock is selling (1) *with rights* and (2) *ex rights* in each of the cases shown in the following table.

Case	Market Value of Stock with Rights	Subscription Price of Stock	Number of Rights Needed to Purchase One Share of Stock
A	$ 25.00	$ 21.50	5
B	47.00	40.00	4
C	93.50	75.00	6
D	124.50	120.00	3

16-11. Your brother is a stockholder in a corporation that recently declared a rights offering. In need of cash, he has offered to sell you his rights for $0.60 each. The current stock price with rights is $74.50 per share, the subscription price is $72.00 per share, and four rights are needed to purchase one share of common stock.

a. Determine the theoretical value of the rights when the stock is trading *with rights*.
b. Determine the theoretical value of the rights when the stock is trading *ex rights*.
c. Discuss your findings in parts (a) and (b). Is it desirable to accept your brother's offer?

16-12. Northern Manufacturing is interested in raising $1 million of new equity capital through a rights offering. The firm currently has 250,000 shares of common stock outstanding. It expects to set the subscription price at $50 and anticipates that the stock will sell for $55 *with rights*.

a. Calculate the number of new shares the firm must sell to raise the desired amount of funds.
b. How many rights are needed to purchase one share of stock at the subscription price?
c. Sarah Lee holds 24,000 shares of Northern common stock. If she exercises her rights, how many additional shares can she purchase?
d. Determine the theoretical value of a right when the stock is selling (1) *with rights* and (2) *ex rights*.
e. Approximately how much could Sarah sell her rights for immediately after the stock goes ex rights?
f. If the date of record for Northern Manufacturing was Monday, March 15, on what dates would the stock sell (1) *with rights* and (2) *ex rights*?

International Common Stock Offerings

16-13. Assume that Portugal Semiconductor (PSC) wishes to create a sponsored ADR program worth $75 million to trade its shares on the New York Stock Exchange. Assume that PSC is currently selling on the Lisbon Stock Exchange for €11.29 per share, and the current dollar/euro exchange rate is $0.885/€. American Bank and Trust (ABT) is handling the ADR issue for PSC and has advised PSC that the ideal trading price for high-technology shares on the NYSE is about $50 per share (or per ADR).

a. Describe the precise steps ABT must take to create an ADR issue meeting PSC's preferences.

b. Assume that PSC's stock price declines from €11.29 to €10.29 per share. If the exchange rate does not also change, what will happen to PSC's ADR price?

c. If the euro depreciates from $0.885/€ to $0.875/€, but the price of PSC's shares remains unchanged in euros, what will happen to PSC's ADR price?

16-14. Assume that Nippon Computer Manufacturing Company (NCM) wishes to create a sponsored ADR program worth $250 million to trade its shares on Nasdaq. Assume that NCM is currently selling on the Tokyo Stock Exchange for ¥1,550 per share, and the current dollar/yen exchange rate is $0.008089/¥ or, equivalently, ¥123.62/$. Metropolis Bank and Trust (MBT) is handling the ADR issue for NCM and has advised NCM that the ideal trading price for high-technology shares on the Nasdaq is about $20 per share (or per ADR).

a. Describe the precise steps MBT must take to create an ADR issue meeting NCM's preferences.

b. Assume that NCM's stock price rises from ¥1,550 to ¥1650 per share. If the exchange rate does not also change, what will happen to NCM's ADR price?

c. If the yen depreciates from $0.008089/¥ to $0.008050/¥, but the price of NCM's shares remains unchanged in yen, what will happen to NCM's ADR price?

17

Long-Term Debt and Leasing

OPENING FOCUS
Once Floated, WorldCom's Bonds Sink

From the sublime (or at least solvent) to the ridiculous in one year! In May 2001, WorldCom Group, then America's second-largest long-distance phone company, successfully floated the largest bond offering in U.S. history. The $11.9 billion, multicurrency, long-term debt issue carried an investment-grade bond rating (A by one rating agency, BBB by two others), and was underwritten by two of the world's most prestigious investment banks, Salomon Smith Barney and J. P. Morgan Chase. In spite of well-known difficulties facing all telecom firms in 2001, investors welcomed WorldCom's bond issue, which was three times oversubscribed. In fact, WorldCom originally planned to issue only $8 billion and raised the offering size in response to investor demand.

By the summer of 2002, WorldCom's financial and operating problems deepened to the point that bonds issued at par 12 months before sold for 71 cents on the dollar. The firm's bond ratings fell to junk bond levels, and the company's founder and CEO resigned. Nonetheless, in May 2002, WorldCom appeared fundamentally solvent, and many financial analysts still rated the firm's securities as a "buy." One month later, however, WorldCom made the stunning announcement that it improperly recorded almost $4 billion in operating expenses as capital expenditures, meaning that the company had charged only a fraction of the total against earnings. After revising their earnings figures sharply downward, WorldCom fired its longtime chief financial officer and blamed him, along with the company's auditors, for perpetrating the accounting fraud.

The impact of WorldCom's admission was immediate. The company's stock price fell so low (to less than $0.15 per share, from a 1999 high of over $65 per share) that the Nasdaq began delisting proceedings. However, stock prices are supposed to fall sharply when a company encounters financial distress, so this was no real surprise. Much more shocking was the impact on WorldCom's bondholders, who, after all, had purchased investment-grade securities barely one year before. The market value of the bonds issued in May 2001 fell from 71 cents on the dollar to 14 cents almost immediately. These values fell even further in July 2002, when WorldCom defaulted on $4.25 billion in maturing loans, and by the end of July the company was headed for Chapter 11 bankruptcy. Given the size and complexity of WorldCom's debts, and the conflicting interests of the company's bondholders and other creditors (especially its banks), it seemed likely that WorldCom would be embroiled in extended bankruptcy litigation. For the company's bondholders, however, the lesson to be drawn from WorldCom's swift collapse was all too clear: bond ratings are helpful tools for evaluating most public debt offerings by corporations, but a favorable bond rating does not guarantee long-term (or even short-term) financial strength.

Sources: "Bond Sale Sets U.S. Record," Reuters (May 10, 2001); Dena Aubin, "WorldCom Bondholders Propose Debt-Equity Swap," Reuters (July 6, 2002); Vincent Boland and Jenny Wiggins, "WorldCom Bondholders Face Bitter Battle for Cash," *Financial Times* (July 6, 2002); and WorldCom's company website (http://www1.worldcom.com).

In Chapter 16, we examined common stock as a source of corporate financing and the investment banking process by which it is sold. This chapter focuses on two other sources of capital for business: long-term debt and leasing. We examine the key features, costs, advantages, and disadvantages of each of these funding sources, beginning with long-term debt.

17.1 CHARACTERISTICS OF LONG-TERM DEBT FINANCING

Long-term debt is the dominant form of long-term, external financing in all developed economies. On the balance sheet, accountants classify debt as long-term if it matures in more than one year. Firms obtain long-term debt by negotiating with a financial institution for a term loan, or through selling bonds. We discuss each of these in the following sections, as well as *syndicated lending*, which has emerged as one of the most important sources of debt financing for companies located in the 30 member countries of the Organization for Economic Cooperation and Development (OECD)—and especially in the United States. This section first analyzes the choice between public and private debt offerings and then discusses long-term debt covenants and costs.

The Choice between Public and Private Debt Issues

Once a firm's managers decide to employ long-term debt financing, they face a series of practical choices regarding how best to structure the debt. The first, and arguably the most important, decision managers must make is whether to issue debt publicly or privately. In the United States, public long-term debt offerings involve selling securities (bonds and notes) directly to investors, almost always with the help of investment bankers. Firms must register these offerings with the SEC, and most long-term corporate bond offerings take the form of unsecured debentures, as discussed in Section 17.3. Furthermore, the vast majority of U.S. public debt offerings are **fixed-rate** offerings, meaning they have a coupon interest rate that remains constant throughout the issue's life.

Private debt issues take one of two principal forms. **Loans** are private debt agreements arranged between corporate borrowers and financial institutions, especially commercial banks, whereas **private placements** are unregistered security offerings sold directly to *accredited investors*. The best-known and most common form of loan is a *term loan* arranged between a borrower and a single bank. However, the total value of large-denomination, *syndicated* loans funded by multiple banks exceeds that of single-lender term loans by a wide margin. The overwhelming majority of both term loans and syndicated loans are **floating-rate** issues, where the loan is priced at a fixed spread above a base interest rate, usually **LIBOR,** the London Interbank Offered Rate, or the U.S. bank **prime lending rate.** The interest rate paid by issuers of floating-rate debt thus adjusts up and down over time as the base interest rate changes.

Numerous academic researchers have analyzed the factors that influence a firm's choice between issuing debt publicly or privately.[1] Relative costs are obviously important, and higher fixed costs for public issues lead to the straightforward prediction that firms will issue larger offerings publicly and smaller ones privately. However, factors other than simple differences in interest rates also influence the public versus private issue decision. In particular, the value of ongoing creditor monitoring of the borrower seems to be very important, as are the borrower's investment opportunities. In general, private borrowing is preferable for firms where growth options represent more of the firm's value than do tangible assets and for companies with nontransparent production processes, because in these firms creditor monitoring helps to ensure that the firm uses borrowed funds properly.

Debt Covenants

Long-term debt agreements, whether resulting from a term loan or a bond issue, normally include certain *covenants*. These are contractual clauses that place specific operating and financial constraints on the borrower. As noted in Chapter 11, there are two types of covenants: *positive covenants* require the borrower to take a specific action, and *negative covenants* prohibit certain actions. Debt covenants do not normally place a burden on a financially sound business and typically remain in force for the life of the debt agreement.[2]

Covenants allow the lender to monitor and control the borrower's activities to protect itself against the agency problem created by the relationship between owners and lenders. Without these provisions, the borrower could take advantage of the lender by investing in riskier projects without compensating lenders with a higher interest rate on their loans.

Positive Covenants

As noted, positive covenants specify things that a borrower "must do." Some of the most common positive covenants include the following:

1. The borrower is required to maintain satisfactory accounting records in accordance with generally accepted accounting principles (GAAP).
2. The borrower is required periodically to supply audited financial statements that the lender uses to monitor the firm and enforce the debt agreement.
3. The borrower is required to pay taxes and other liabilities when due.
4. The borrower is required to maintain all facilities in good working order, thereby behaving as a going concern.
5. The borrower is required to maintain a minimum level of *net working capital.* Net working capital below the minimum is considered indicative of inadequate liquidity, a common precursor to default.
6. The borrower is required to maintain life insurance policies on certain "key employees" without whom the firm's future would be in doubt. These policies pro-

---

[1] Key early theoretical papers in this literature include those by Diamond (1991) and Rajan (1992). The choice between public and private debt in the United States is examined empirically in Houston and James (1996), Carey (1998), and Krishnaswami, Spindt, and Subramaniam (1999). Anderson and Makhija (1999) perform a similar analysis for Japan.

[2] Debt covenants have been extensively examined in the finance literature beginning with what remains a classic analysis by Smith and Warner (1979). Subsequent papers include those by Press and Weintrop (1990) and El-Gazzar and Pastena (1990).

vide the financial resources to hire qualified people quickly in the event that a key person dies or is disabled.

7. The borrower is often considered to be in default on all debts if it is in default on any debt. This is known as a **cross-default covenant.**

8. Occasionally, a covenant specifically requires the borrower to spend the borrowed funds on a proven financial need.

Negative Covenants

Negative covenants specify what a borrower "must not do." Common negative covenants include the following:

1. Borrowers may not sell accounts receivable to generate cash because doing so could cause a long-run cash shortage if the borrower uses the proceeds to meet current obligations.

2. Long-term lenders commonly impose fixed asset restrictions on the borrower. These constrain the firm with respect to the liquidation, acquisition, and encumbrance of fixed assets because any of these actions could damage the firm's ability to repay its debt.

3. Many debt agreements prohibit borrowing additional long-term debt or require that additional borrowing be subordinated to the original loan. **Subordination** means that all subsequent or more junior creditors agree to wait until all claims of the senior debt are satisfied in full before having their own claims satisfied.

4. Borrowers may not enter into certain types of leases to limit additional fixed-payment obligations.

5. Occasionally, the lender prohibits business combinations by requiring the borrower to agree not to consolidate, merge, or combine in any way with another firm because such an action could significantly change the borrower's business and financial risk.

6. To prevent liquidation of assets through large salary payments, the lender may prohibit or limit salary increases for specified employees.

7. A relatively common provision prohibits the firm's annual cash dividend payments from exceeding 50–70 percent of its net earnings or a specified dollar amount.

In the process of negotiating the terms of long-term debt, the borrower and lender must agree to an acceptable set of covenants. If the borrower violates a covenant, the lender may demand immediate repayment, waive the violation and continue the loan, or waive the violation but alter the terms of the original debt agreement.

Cost of Long-Term Debt

In addition to specifying positive and negative covenants, the long-term debt agreement specifies the interest rate, the timing of interest payments, and the size of principal repayment. The major factors affecting the cost, or interest rate, of long-term debt are loan maturity, loan size, borrower risk, and the basic cost of money.

Loan Maturity

Generally, long-term loans have higher interest rates than short-term loans. Recall from Chapter 4 that the yield curve, which plots the relationship between yield to maturity and time to maturity for bonds having similar risk, typically slopes upward. Factors that can cause an upward-sloping yield curve include (1) the general expectation of higher future inflation or interest rates; (2) lender preferences for shorter-term, more liquid loans; and (3) greater demand for long-term rather than short-term loans relative to the supply of such loans. In a more practical sense, the longer the term, the greater the default risk associated with the loan. To compensate for all these factors, the lender typically charges a higher interest rate on long-term loans.[3]

Loan Size

The size of the loan affects the interest cost of borrowing in an inverse manner. Loan administration costs per dollar borrowed are likely to decrease with increasing loan size. However, the risk to the lender increases, because larger loans result in less diversification. The size of the loan sought by each borrower must therefore be evaluated to determine the net administrative cost and risk trade-off.

Borrower Risk

As noted in Chapter 13, the higher the firm's operating leverage, the greater its business risk. Also, the higher the borrower's debt ratio or the lower its interest coverage ratio, the greater its financial risk. The lender's main concern is with the borrower's ability to fully repay the loan as prescribed in the debt agreement. A lender uses an overall assessment of the borrower's business and financial risk, along with information on past payment patterns, when setting the interest rate on a loan.

Basic Cost of Money

The cost of money is the basis for determining the actual interest rate charged. Generally, the rate on U.S. Treasury securities with equivalent maturities is used as the basic (lowest-risk) cost of money. To determine the actual interest rate to be charged, the lender will add premiums for borrower risk and other factors to this basic cost of money for the given maturity. Alternatively, some lenders determine a prospective borrower's risk class and find the rates charged on loans with similar maturities and terms to firms in the same risk class. Instead of having to determine a risk premium, the lender can use the risk premium prevailing in the marketplace for similar loans.

---

1. What factors should a manager consider when deciding on the amount and type of long-term debt to be used to finance a business?

2. What factors should a manager consider when negotiating the covenants in a long-term debt agreement?

3. How can managers estimate their firms' cost of long-term debt prior to meeting with a lender?

Concept Review Questions

17.2 TERM LOANS

A **term loan** is made by a financial institution to a business and has an initial maturity of more than 1 year, generally 5 to 12 years. Term loans are often made to finance permanent working capital needs, to pay for machinery and equipment, or to liquidate other loans.

[3.] The debt maturity structure choice for publicly traded U.S. firms is analyzed empirically in Barclay and Smith (1995a, 1995b) and Guedes and Opler (1996); Scherr and Hulburt (2001) examine the debt maturity structure of small U.S. firms. International differences in average corporate debt maturity are described and examined empirically in Demirgüç-Kunt and Maksimovic (1999).

Term loans are essentially private placements of debt. However, firms typically negotiate term loans directly with the lender rather than use an investment banker as an intermediary. An advantage of term loans over publicly traded debt is their flexibility. The securities (bonds or notes) in any given public debt issue are usually purchased by many different investors, so it is almost impossible to alter the terms of the borrowing agreement even if new business conditions make such changes desirable. With a term loan, the borrower can negotiate with a single lender for modifications to the borrowing agreement.[4]

Characteristics of Term Loan Agreements

The actual term loan agreement is a formal contract ranging from a few to a few hundred pages. The following items commonly appear in the document: the amount and maturity of the loan, payment dates, interest rate, positive and negative covenants, collateral (if any), purpose of the loan, action to be taken in the event the agreement is violated, and stock purchase warrants. Of these, only payment dates, collateral requirements, and stock purchase warrants require further discussion.

Payment Dates

Term loan agreements usually specify monthly, quarterly, semiannual, or annual loan payments. Generally, these equal payments fully repay the interest and principal over the life of the loan. Occasionally, a term loan agreement will require periodic interest payments over the life of the loan followed by a large lump-sum payment at maturity. This so-called **balloon payment** represents the entire loan principal if the periodic payments represent only interest.

Collateral Requirements

Term lending arrangements may be unsecured or secured. Secured loans have specific assets pledged as **collateral.** The collateral often takes the form of an asset such as machinery and equipment, plant, inventory, pledges of accounts receivable, and pledges of securities. Unsecured loans are obtained without pledging specific assets as collateral. Whether lenders require collateral depends on the lender's evaluation of the borrower's financial condition.[5]

Term lending is often referred to as asset-backed lending; however, term lenders in reality are primarily cash flow lenders. They hope and expect to be repaid out of cash flow, but require collateral both as an alternative source of repayment and as "ransom" to decrease the incentive of borrowing firms to default (because a default-

---

[4.] Companies typically arrange loans with commercial banks as part of a larger, ongoing banking relationship. Large companies often have dozens of these bilateral relationships, but a critical decision for smaller firms is whether to maintain one large banking relationship or several smaller bilateral relationships in order to minimize the risk of not being able to arrange financing during an emergency. Petersen and Rajan (1994) examine this decision for U.S. companies and conclude that fewer, larger relationships are generally preferable to numerous, smaller ones. The primary benefit of a banking relationship for companies comes in the form of larger amounts that they can borrow rather than in cheaper loan rates. Interestingly, Detragiache, Garella, and Guiso (2000) find that Italian companies must pursue exactly the opposite strategy and maintain multiple bilateral banking relationships in order to ensure funding when needed. Finally, Ongena and Smith (2001) show that Norwegian companies frequently terminate their banking relationships as they mature, demonstrating that these firms do not become "locked into" bilateral relationships.

[5.] The use of collateral as backing for a loan has been analyzed theoretically by Stulz and Johnson (1985) and Igawa and Kanatas (1990), and has been examined empirically by Booth (1992). This study supports earlier findings that collateral is associated with higher, rather than lower, interest rates (spreads over a base rate) on secured loans. This implies that collateral allows riskier borrowers to receive credit that would not be granted to them through unsecured lending.

ing borrower would lose the use of valuable corporate assets). Most pledged assets are secured by a **lien,** which is a legal contract specifying under what conditions the lender can take title to the asset if the loan is not repaid, and prohibiting the borrowing firm from selling or disposing of the asset without the lender's consent. The liens serve two purposes: they establish clearly the lender's right to seize and liquidate collateral if the borrower defaults, and they serve notice to subsequent lenders of a prior claim on the asset(s). Some of the more technical aspects of loan default are presented in Chapter 25.

Not all assets make acceptable collateral, of course. For an asset to be useful as collateral, it should (1) be nonperishable, (2) be relatively homogeneous in quality, (3) have a high value relative to its bulk, and (4) have a well-established secondary market where seized assets can be turned into cash without a severe price penalty.

Stock Purchase Warrants

The corporate borrower often gives the lender certain financial perquisites, usually **stock purchase warrants,** in addition to the payment of interest and repayment of principal. Stock purchase warrants are instruments that give their holder the right to purchase a certain number of shares of the firm's common stock at a specified price over a certain period. These are designed to entice institutional lenders to make long-term loans, possibly under relatively favorable terms. Warrants are also frequently used as "sweeteners" for corporate bond issues. We discuss the valuation of stock purchase warrants in detail in Chapter 19.

TERM LENDERS

Students are often surprised to learn about the wide array of sources for term loans. The primary lenders making term loans to businesses are commercial banks, insurance companies, pension funds, regional development companies, the U.S. federal government's Small Business Administration, small business investment companies, commercial finance companies, and equipment manufacturers' financing subsidiaries.

---

4. Suppose that a specialty retail firm takes out a term loan from a bank. Which do you think the bank would prefer to receive as collateral, a claim on the firm's inventory or its receivables?

5. A problem with collateral is that its value is positively correlated with the borrower's ability to repay. Explain.

Concept Review Questions

17.3 CORPORATE BONDS

A *corporate bond* is a debt instrument indicating that a corporation has borrowed a certain amount of money from institutions or individuals and promises to repay it in the future under clearly defined terms. Firms issue bonds with maturities of 10 to 30 years (debt securities with an original maturity of 1 to 10 years are called *notes*) and with a par, or face, value of $1,000. The coupon interest rate on a bond represents the percentage of the bond's par value that the firm will pay to investors each year. In the United States, firms typically pay interest semiannually in two equal coupon payments. Bondholders receive the par value back when the bonds mature.

Table 17.1
Features of Conventional Bonds

Bond Type	Features	Priority of Lender's Claim
Debentures	Unsecured debt issued by creditworthy firms. Most convertible bonds are debentures.	Low priority on par with other general creditors, possibly senior to other subordinated debentures.
Subordinated debentures	Similar to ordinary debentures.	Lower priority than senior debentures.
Income bonds	Pay interest only when earnings are available from which to make such payment. Often associated with firms undergoing restructuring.	Priority equal to that of a general creditor. Missed interest payments do not trigger default.
Mortgage bonds	Secured by real estate or buildings. Can be *open-end* (additional bonds issued against collateral), *limited open-end* (a specified amount of additional bonds can be issued against collateral), or *closed-end*; may contain an *after-acquired clause* (property subsequently acquired becomes part of mortgage collateral).	In default, creditors receive proceeds from sale of mortgaged assets.
Collateral trust bonds	Secured by financial assets held by the issuer. Collateral value generally exceeds bond value.	In default, creditor receives proceeds from sale of financial assets.
Equipment trust certificates	Used to finance transportation equipment. Firm leases equipment from trustee, and after making final lease payment, receives title to the asset.	In default, creditor receives proceeds from sale of equipment.

POPULAR TYPES OF BONDS

Bonds can be classified in a variety of ways. Here we break them into traditional bonds, the basic types that have been around for years, and contemporary, innovative bonds. Table 17.1 summarizes the traditional types of bonds issued by corporations in terms of their key characteristics and priority of lender's claim in the event of default. Note that the first three types, **debentures, subordinated debentures,** and **income bonds,** are unsecured; but the last three, **mortgage bonds, collateral trust bonds,** and **equipment trust certificates,** are secured. As noted, the majority of U.S. corporate bonds are debentures, where the debt is backed by the faith and credit of the issuing corporation itself rather than by specific pledged collateral.[6]

In recent years, corporations have developed a profusion of new debt instruments designed to attract a unique clientele of bond investors whose members pre-

---

[6.] Although not a direct source of financing for individual corporations, the market for **mortgage-backed securities** (**MBS**) has been growing much faster and now represents a market worth a half-trillion dollars per year in the United States alone. MBS offerings are created by pooling large numbers of home mortgage loans and then selling securities backed by these mortgages directly to investors. This market has revolutionized home mortgage lending in the United States because it allows financial institutions to economize on the use of their capital by originating mortgage loans and then selling these to MBS specialists.

Table 17.2
Features of Innovative
Bonds

Bond Type	Characteristics[a]
Zero- (or low-) coupon bonds	Pays no interest and sells at a large discount from par. Investors earn returns in the form of a capital gain. Issuers often call bonds at par value. Issuers receive a tax shield each year as interest accrues.
Junk bonds	Bonds rated lower than Baa by Moody's or lower than BBB by Standard & Poor's. Used to finance growth of young companies and to pay for acquisitions. Junk yields are typically several percentage points higher than investment-grade bond yields.
Floating-rate bonds	Make interest payments that adjust periodically as market rates (such as LIBOR) change. Adjustable interest rate means that these bonds sell close to par.
Extendible notes	Medium-term bonds that at maturity may be redeemed or extended. The interest rate adjusts if the bonds are extended.
Putable bonds	Bonds that grant investors the right to "put" or sell their bonds back to the issuer at a predetermined price (often par value). Holders can exercise their put option after a certain amount of time elapses, or in response to actions taken by the firm (e.g., acquiring another company or issuing new debt).

[a]The claims of lenders (i.e., bondholders) against issuers of each of these types of bonds vary, depending on their other features. Each of these bonds can be unsecured or secured.

sumably would be willing to pay a higher price for a given special feature. A detailed discussion of these innovative offerings is beyond the scope of an overview chapter, but Table 17.2 surveys the characteristics of a few of these contemporary types of bonds.

Legal Aspects of Corporate Bonds

When they issue bonds, corporations raise hundreds of millions of dollars from many unrelated investors. The dispersion in the investor base creates a need for special legal arrangements to protect lenders.

Bond Indenture

A bond **indenture** is a complex and lengthy legal document stating the conditions under which a bond has been issued. It specifies both the rights of the bondholders and the duties of the issuing corporation. In addition to specifying the interest and principal payment dates and containing various positive and negative covenants, the indenture frequently contains *sinking fund requirements* and provisions with respect to a security interest (if the bond is secured).

Sinking Fund Requirements.   We have already described the positive and negative covenants for long-term debt and for bond issues in Section 17.1. However, an additional positive covenant often included in a bond indenture is a **sinking fund** requirement. Its objective is to provide for the systematic retirement of bonds prior to their maturity.[7]

[7.] Dunn and Spatt (1984) examine sinking funds theoretically; Dyl and Joehnk (1979), Ho and Singer (1984), Mitchell (1991), and Wu (1993) examine sinking funds empirically.

To carry out this requirement, the corporation makes semiannual or annual payments to a trustee, who uses these funds to retire bonds by purchasing them in the marketplace. This process is simplified by inclusion of a limited call feature, which permits the issuer to repurchase a fraction of outstanding bonds each year at a stated price. The trustee will exercise this limited call option only when sufficient bonds cannot be purchased in the marketplace or when the market price of the bond is above the call price.

Although U.S. corporations (and non-U.S. companies that can issue bonds in American markets) have the opportunity to issue longer-maturity bonds than those of their international competitors, the actual average maturity of the typical U.S. bond issue is far less than its stated maturity would imply. The reasons for this are the ability of companies to call (and then refinance) bonds and the pervasiveness of mandated sinking funds in long-term U.S. debt security issues. Sinking funds work in such a way that the typical bond issue with, say, $100 million principal amount and a 15-year maturity will probably have only a few million dollars worth of bonds still outstanding when the last bonds are redeemed a decade and a half after issuance. Depending on the terms of the sinking fund, the actual average maturity of this issue (the weighted average years outstanding) will probably be less than 10 years, rather than the 15 years advertised.

Because sinking funds force the corporation to redeem part of each issue early, they reduce the risk of default on an individual issue, for two reasons. First, sinking funds increase the likelihood that investors will become aware of any financial difficulties an issuing firm encounters (by the firm missing a sinking fund payment) early rather than late. This will trigger the demand for effective corrective action, up to and including the removal of the issuing firm's incumbent management team. Second, because at maturity only a fraction of a given bond issue will remain outstanding, the issuing firm's managers will have less incentive to default on the issue and attempt to expropriate bondholder wealth by filing for bankruptcy protection.

Security Interest. The bond indenture is similar to a loan agreement in that any collateral pledged against the bond is specifically identified in the document. Usually, the title to the collateral is attached to the indenture, and the disposition of the collateral in various circumstances is specifically described. The protection of bond collateral is crucial to increasing the safety, and thus enhancing the marketability, of a bond issue.

Trustee

A **trustee** is a third party to a bond indenture and can be an individual, a corporation, or, most often, a commercial bank trust department. The trustee, whose services are paid for by the issuer, acts as a "watchdog" on behalf of the bondholders, making sure that the issuer does not default on its contractual responsibilities. The trustee is empowered to take specified actions on behalf of bondholders if the borrower violates any indenture terms.

METHODS OF ISSUING CORPORATE BONDS

Public issues of corporate bonds in the United States are sold using the general cash offering procedures described in Chapter 16. Corporate issues sold to public investors must be registered with the Securities and Exchange Commission, and large offerings are generally underwritten by an investment banking syndicate. However, there is a tremendous variation in actual offering procedures, and this heterogeneity has increased over time as new debt securities have been developed. In particular, two recent financial and regulatory innovations have transformed U.S. bond-issuance patterns. First, the introduction of *shelf registration* in the early 1980s allowed corporations to register large blocks of debt securities, then sell these in discrete pieces over the subsequent two years as market conditions warranted. As discussed in Chapter 16, shelf registration can be used for both debt and equity offerings, but relatively few issuers use this technique for selling stock. In contrast, most companies that can use shelf registration for debt offerings do so.

The second major innovation occurred in 1990, when the SEC created a new private-placement market by implementing *Rule 144A*, which was described in Chapter 16. This allowed institutional investors to trade nonregistered securities among themselves, and corporate issuers soon found this was a welcoming market for new equity and, especially, debt issues. Because Rule 144A issues offer investors much greater liquidity than do traditional private placements, and yet are less costly than traditional public offerings, U.S. and international corporations now sell securities worth over $400 billion per year using this rule.

General Features of a Bond Issue

Three features commonly observed in a U.S. bond issue are (1) a call feature, (2) a conversion feature, and (3) stock purchase warrants. Each of these features grants an option, either to the issuer or the investor, that has a significant impact on a bond's value.

Call Feature

The call feature is included in most corporate bond issues and gives the issuer the opportunity to repurchase bonds prior to maturity. The call price is the stated price at which bonds may be repurchased. Sometimes the call privilege is exercisable only during a certain period. Typically, the call price exceeds the par value of a bond by an amount equal to one year's interest. For example, a $1,000 bond with a 10 percent coupon interest rate would be callable for around $1,100 [$1,000 + (10% × $1,000)]. The amount by which the call price exceeds the bond's par value is commonly referred to as the *call premium*. This premium compensates bondholders for having the bond called away from them and is the cost to the issuer of calling the bonds.[8]

The call feature is generally advantageous to the issuer because it enables the issuer to retire outstanding debt prior to maturity. Thus, when interest rates fall, an issuer can call an outstanding bond and reissue a new bond at a lower interest rate. When interest rates rise, the call privilege will not be exercised, except possibly to meet sinking fund requirements. Of course, to issue a callable bond, the firm must pay a higher interest rate than that on noncallable bonds of equal risk to compensate bondholders for the risk of having the bonds called away.

Conversion Feature

The conversion feature of **convertible bonds** allows bondholders to change each bond into a stated number of shares of common stock. Bondholders will convert their bonds only when the market price of the stock is greater than the conversion price, hence

---

[8.] For recent examples of the academic literature on the callability of corporate bonds, see Thatcher (1985), Vu (1986), Mitchell (1991), Crabbe and Helwege (1994), and Sarkar (2001).

Table 17.3
Moody's and Standard
& Poor's Bond Ratings

Moody's	Interpretation	Standard & Poor's	Interpretation
Aaa	*Prime quality*	*AAA*	*Bank investment quality*
Aa	*High grade*	*AA*	
A	*Upper medium grade*	*A*	
Baa	*Medium grade*	*BBB*	*Minimum investment grade*
Ba	Lower medium or speculative grade	BB	Speculative
B	Speculative	B	
Caa	Very speculative	CCC	
Ca	Near or in default	CC	
C	Lowest grade	C	Income bond
D	In default	D	In default

Sources: Moody's Investors Services, Inc. and Standard & Poor's Corporation.
Note: Rating grades in italics are considered "*investment grade*"; lesser grades in regular typeface are considered "below investment grade," commonly called *high-yield bonds* or *junk bonds.*

providing a profit for the bondholder. We will discuss the valuation of convertible bonds in detail in Chapter 19.

Stock Purchase Warrants

Like term loans, bonds occasionally have warrants attached as "sweeteners" to make them more attractive to prospective buyers. As we noted earlier, a stock purchase warrant gives its holder the right to purchase a certain number of shares of common stock at a specified price over a certain period of time. We also discuss the valuation of stock purchase warrants in depth in Chapter 19.

Bond Ratings

The risk of publicly traded bond issues is assessed by independent agencies such as Moody's and Standard & Poor's (S&P). Both agencies have 10 major **bond ratings** derived by using financial ratio and cash flow analyses. Table 17.3 summarizes these ratings. Bonds rated Baa or higher by Moody's (BBB by S&P) are known as **investment-grade bonds.** In addition to the rating categories listed in the table, rating agencies may add additional nomenclature to indicate whether a bond is at the high end or low end of a given rating group. For example, Moody's adds numerical modifiers (A1, A2, A3) for high, medium, and low standing, whereas Standard & Poor's uses plus (A+) and minus (A−) signs.

Bonds rated below investment grade are known as **high-yield bonds** or **junk bonds.** As the pejorative name suggests, junk bonds carry a much higher default risk than do investment-grade bonds, but they also offer higher yields. Prior to the late 1970s, such issues were quite rare. Historically, most of the sub-investment-grade bonds trading in the market were **fallen angels,** bonds that received investment-grade ratings when they were first issued but later fell to junk status. During the late 1970s, however, Michael Milken and the investment bank he worked for, Drexel Burnham Lambert, began arranging new junk bond issues for companies such as Turner Broadcasting and MCI. Milken and Drexel also helped corporate raiders issue junk bonds to finance their hostile takeover bids.

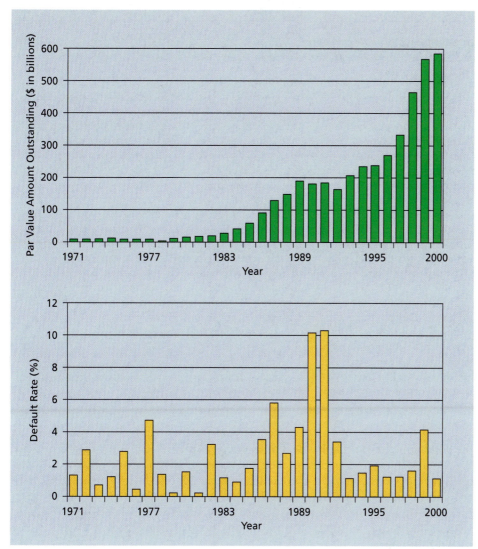

Figure 17.1
Par Value Amounts Outstanding and Default Rates for High-Yield Bonds (Junk Bonds), 1971–2000

Source: Edward I. Altman, "Revisiting the High Yield Bond Market: Mature but Never Dull," *Journal of Applied Corporate Finance* 13 (Spring 2000), pp. 64–74, table 1.
Note: The "default rate" is calculated by dividing the default amount by the par value amount outstanding.

When junk bond default rates rose sharply during the 1990–1991 recession, many commentators wrote off high-yield debt as a viable financing tool. As Figure 17.1 shows, however, the junk bond market not only survived but prospered after the early 1990s. Junk bond investors recognize that they are assuming much of the issuing firm's business risk when they purchase high-yield debt, but they are willing to do so in return for promised yields that approach the returns earned by stockholders.

Because bond ratings reflect the probability of default, there is normally an in-verse relationship between the quality or rating of a bond and the rate of return that it must promise bondholders. High-quality (high-rated) bonds promise lower returns than low-quality (low-rated) bonds. This reflects the lender's risk return trade-off. Of course, a higher *promised* yield may or may not result in a higher *realized* return, because the higher yield reflects a higher expected likelihood that the borrower will default (in whole or in part) on

SMART IDEAS VIDEO
Ed Altman, New York University
"Probably about 75% of the bonds are investment grade; that's BBB or higher."

See the entire interview at **SMARTFinance**

The past two decades have seen a handful of Moslem countries modify their commercial banking laws to make them consistent with the principle of *Syariah,* or the prohibition on the charging of interest on loans. Several other countries have allowed banks to operate under the *Syariah* principle, which is similar to the Catholic Church's injunction against usury (charging interest) during the Middle Ages in Europe. Needless to say, bankers have found this restriction on a core source of revenue to be a serious challenge, but many have been able to comply with the religious intent of the laws by structuring loans as investment partnerships—where the bank's return comes in the form of a share of profits—or by structuring loan payments as fees or dividends rather than interest.

Although Islamic banking has, perhaps unsurprisingly, made few inroads in global markets, it has been relatively successful within the borders of at least some of the countries that have adopted it. But how do you attract international investors to an Islamic bond issue when the same *Syariah*-based restriction on payment of interest applies? The governments of two Moslem countries showed how during July 2002. First, the Malaysian government raised $600 million with the world's first global Islamic bond offering targeted primarily at investors in western Asia and the Middle East. The bond issue carried an investment-grade rating, and investors were promised a return (comparable to dividend payments) equal to 0.95 percentage points above LIBOR, funded by rentals from Malaysian government properties.

The second Islamic bond offering was even more intriguing, because the issuer was the government of Iran, and this was its first international capital market offering since the fundamentalist regime came to power in 1979. The €500 million issue was assigned a B+ bond rating by Fitch and was priced at 425 basis points over the reference rate for interest rate swaps of similar risk. Perhaps most surprising, the issue was targeted at European investors and sold out very quickly.

Sources: Ishun P. Ahmad, "Islamic Bond Investors in for the Long Term," *The New Straits Times Press* [Malaysia] (July 13, 2002); and Arkady Ostrovsky and Bayan Rahman, "Capital Markets: Iran Pays More to Raise €500m," *Financial Times* (July 15, 2002).

the bond sometime during its life. For example, as the U.S. economy sagged in 2001, the default rate on junk bonds reached 9.8 percent, and the loss rate reached 7.8 percent. In other words, almost 1 in 10 junk bonds was in some form of default during the year, and this caused a reduction of 7.8 percent in the returns junk bond investors earned (relative to what they would have earned in the absence of defaults).[9] The next year was no better. In 2002, defaults on junk bonds reached a record $96.9 billion for a 12.8 percent default rate.

After a bond is rated, the rating is not changed unless the likelihood of the company defaulting on the bond issue changes. Perhaps surprising, bond issuers themselves pay the ratings companies to issue ratings on newly issued bonds. The reason for this apparently masochistic behavior is that bonds are essentially unmarketable without a rating. Additionally, having the issuing firm pay for ratings allows the firm to communicate sensitive information privately to the ratings agency. This information can then be usefully reflected in market data without being disclosed to competitors (Kliger and Sarig 2000). Recent empirical research has shown that bond ratings and, especially, ratings changes convey economically relevant information to investors (Dichev and Piotroski 2001).

INTERNATIONAL CORPORATE BOND FINANCING

Companies can sell bonds internationally by tapping the *Eurobond* or *foreign bond* markets. Both of these provide established, creditworthy borrowers the opportunity

[9.] We thank Ed Altman (personal communication) for providing these figures.

to obtain large amounts of long-term debt financing quickly and efficiently, in their choice of currency and with flexible repayment terms. The following sections briefly describe these markets.

Eurobonds

A **Eurobond** is a bond issued by an international borrower and sold to investors in countries with currencies other than the currency in which the bond is denominated. A dollar-denominated bond issued by a U.S. corporation and sold to Western European investors is an example of a Eurobond. The Eurobond market first developed in the early 1960s, when several European and U.S. borrowers discovered that many European investors wanted to hold dollar-denominated, **bearer** bonds. Investors wanted bearer bonds because they would both shelter investment income from taxation—because coupon interest payments were made to the bearer of the bond and names were not reported to tax authorities—and provide protection against exchange rate risk.

Until the mid-1980s, "blue-chip" U.S. corporations were the largest single class of Eurobond issuers, and many of these companies were able to borrow in this market at interest rates below those the U.S. government paid on Treasury bonds (Kim and Stulz 1988). As the market matured, issuers were able to choose the currency in which they borrowed, and European and Japanese borrowers rose to prominence. In more recent years, the Eurobond market has become much more balanced in terms of the mix of borrowers, total issue volume, and currency of denomination. Most Eurobond issues today are, in fact, executed as part of a complicated financial engineering transaction known as a "currency swap," wherein companies headquartered in different countries issue bonds in their home-country currencies and then exchange principal and interest payments with each other. Swaps are described in depth in Chapter 21.

Foreign Bonds

In contrast to a Eurobond, which is issued by an international borrower in a single currency (frequently dollars) in a variety of countries, a **foreign bond** is a bond issued in a host country's financial market, in the host country's currency, by a foreign borrower. A Swiss franc–denominated bond issued in Switzerland by a U.S. company is an example of a foreign bond. Other examples are a dollar-denominated bond issued in the United States by a German company, or a yen-denominated bond issued by an American company in Japan. Many of these issues have colorful names. For example, the two bonds described above would be called Yankee bonds and Samurai bonds, respectively. Similar issues in Britain would be called Bulldog bonds, and issues in Switzerland and the Netherlands would be referred to as Heidi and Rembrandt bonds. The three largest foreign bond markets are Japan, Switzerland, and the United States.

BOND-REFUNDING OPTIONS

A firm that wishes to avoid a large single repayment of principal in the future, or to refund a bond prior to maturity, has two options. Both require foresight and careful analysis on the part of the issuer.

Serial Issues

The borrower can issue **serial bonds,** a certain proportion of which matures each year. When firms issue serial bonds, they attach different interest rates to bonds maturing at different times. Although serial bonds cannot necessarily be retired at the option of the issuer, they do permit the issuer to systematically retire the debt.

Refunding Bonds by Exercising a Call

If interest rates drop following the issuance of a bond, the issuer may wish to **refund** (refinance) the debt with new bonds at the lower interest rate. If a call feature has been included in the issue, the issuer can easily retire it. In an accounting sense, bond refunding will increase earnings per share by lowering interest expense. Of course, the desirability of refunding a bond through exercise of a call is not necessarily obvious, and assessing its long-term consequences requires the use of present value techniques. This bond-refunding decision is another application of the capital budgeting techniques we described in Chapters 7 and 8.

Here the firm must find the net present value (*NPV*) of the bond-refunding cash flows. The initial investment is the incremental after-tax cash outflows associated with calling the old bonds and issuing new bonds, and the annual cash flow savings are the after-tax cash savings that are expected from the reduced debt payments on the new lower-interest bond. These cash flows are the same each year. The resulting cash flow pattern surrounding this decision is "typical": an outflow followed by a series of inflows. The bond refunding decision can be made using the following three-step procedure.

Step 1. Find the initial investment by estimating the incremental after-tax cash outflow required at time 0 to call the old bond, and issue a new bond in its place. Any overlapping interest resulting from the need to pay interest on both the old and new bonds is treated as part of the initial investment.

Step 2. Find the annual cash flow savings, which is the difference between the annual after-tax debt payments with the old and new bonds. This cash flow stream will be an annuity, with a life equal to the maturity of the old bond.

Step 3. Use the after-tax cost of the new debt (as the discount rate) to **find the net present value (*NPV*)** by subtracting the initial investment from the present value of the annual cash flow savings. The annual cash flow savings is a certain cash flow stream that represents the difference between two contractual debt-service streams, the old bond and the new bond. Therefore, the decision is virtually risk-free because it does not increase the firm's financial risk (i.e., degree of indebtedness or ability to service debt). Therefore, the after-tax cost of debt is used as the discount rate because it represents the firm's lowest cost of financing. If the resulting *NPV* is positive, the proposed refunding is recommended; otherwise, it should be rejected.

Application of these bond-refunding decision procedures can be illustrated in the Applying the Model below. However, a few tax-related points must be clarified first.

Call Premiums. The amount by which the call price exceeds the par value of the bond is the **call premium.** It is paid by the issuer to the bondholder to buy back outstanding bonds prior to maturity. The call premium is treated as a tax-deductible expense in the year of the call.

Bond Discounts and Premiums. When bonds are sold at a discount or at a premium, the firm is required to amortize (write off) the discount or premium in equal portions over the life of the bond. The amortized discount is treated as a tax-deductible expenditure, whereas the amortized premium is treated as taxable income. If a bond is retired prior

to maturity, any unamortized portion of a discount or premium is deducted from or added to pretax income at that time.

Flotation or Issuance Costs. Any costs incurred in the process of issuing a bond must be amortized over the life of the bond. The annual write-off is therefore a tax-deductible expenditure. If a bond is retired prior to maturity, any unamortized portion of this cost is deducted from pretax income at that time.

APPLYING THE MODEL

The Samuels Corporation, a manufacturer of industrial pumps, is contemplating calling $30 million of 30-year, $1,000 par value bonds (30,000 bonds) issued five years ago with a coupon interest rate of 14 percent. The bonds have a call price of $1,140 and initially netted proceeds of $29.1 million due to a discount of $30 per bond (30,000 bonds × $970 net per bond). The initial flotation cost was $360,000. The company intends to sell $30 million of 25-year, $1,000 par value bonds with a 12 percent (coupon) interest rate to raise funds for retiring the old bonds. The flotation costs on the new issue are estimated to be $440,000. The firm is currently in the 40 percent tax bracket and estimates its after-tax cost of debt to be 7.2 percent [12% × (1 − 0.40)]. Because the new bonds must first be sold and their proceeds then used to retire the old bonds, the firm expects a 2-month period of overlapping interest during which interest must be paid on both the old and the new bonds.

Step 1. Find the initial investment. To find the initial investment requires a number of calculations.

a. *Call premium.* The call premium per bond is $140 ($1,140 call price − $1,000 par value). Because the total call premium is deductible in the year of the call, its after-tax cost is calculated as follows:

Before tax ($140 × 30,000 bonds)	$4,200,000
Less: Taxes (0.40 × $4,200,000)	1,680,000
After-tax cost of call premium	$2,520,000

b. *Flotation cost of new bond.* This cost was given as $440,000.

c. *Overlapping interest.*[10] The after-tax cost of the overlapping interest on the old bond is treated as part of the initial investment and calculated as follows:

Before tax (0.14 × 2 ÷ 12 × $30,000,000)	$700,000
Less: Taxes (0.40 × $700,000)	280,000
After-tax cost of overlapping interest	$420,000

d. *Unamortized discount on old bond.* The firm was amortizing the $900,000 discount ($30,000,000 par value − $29,100,000 net proceeds from sale) on the old bond over 30 years. Because only 5 of the 30 years' amortization of the discount has been applied, the firm can deduct the remaining 25 years of unamortized discount as a lump sum, thereby reducing taxes by $300,000 (25 ÷ 30 × $900,000 × 0.40).

e. *Unamortized flotation cost of old bond.* The firm was amortizing the $360,000 initial flotation cost on the old bond over 30 years. Because only

---

[10.] Technically, the after-tax amount of overlapping interest could be reduced by the after-tax interest earnings from investment of the average proceeds available from the sale of the new bonds during the interest overlap period. For clarity, any interest earned on the proceeds from sale of the new bonds during the overlap period is ignored.

Table 17.4
Finding the Initial Investment for the Samuels Corporation's Bond-Refunding Decision

a. **Call premium**
   Before tax [($1,140 − $1,000) × 30,000 bonds] $4,200,000
   Less: Taxes (0.40 × $4,200,000)   1,680,000
      After-tax cost of call premium $2,520,000
b. **Plus: Flotation cost of new bond**   440,000
c. **Plus: Overlapping interest**
   Before tax (0.14 × 2 ÷ 12 × $30,000,000) $700,000
   Less: Taxes (0.40 × $700,000)   280,000
      After-tax cost of overlapping interest   420,000
d. **Less: Tax savings from unamortized discount on old bond**
   [25 ÷ 30 × ($30,000,000 − $29,100,000) × 0.40]   300,000
e. **Less: Tax savings from unamortized flotation of old bond**
   (25 ÷ 30 × $360,000 × 0.40)   120,000
      Initial investment $2,960,000

5 of the 30 years' amortization of this cost has been applied, the firm can deduct the remaining 25 years of unamortized flotation cost as a lump sum, thereby reducing taxes by $120,000 (25 ÷ 30 × $360,000 × 0.40).

Summarizing these calculations in Table 17.4, we find the initial investment to be $2,960,000. This means that the Samuels Corporation must pay out $2,960,000 now to implement the proposed bond refunding.

Step 2. Find the cash flow savings. To find the annual cash flow savings requires a number of calculations.

a. *Interest cost of old bond.* The after-tax annual interest cost of the old bond is calculated as follows:

   Before tax (0.14 × $30,000,000) $4,200,000
   Less: Taxes (0.40 × $4,200,000)   1,680,000
   After-tax interest cost $2,520,000

b. *Amortization of discount on old bond.* The firm was amortizing the $900,000 discount ($30,000,000 par value − $29,100,000 net proceeds from sale) on the old bond over 30 years, resulting in an annual write-off of $30,000 ($900,000 ÷ 30). Because it is a tax-deductible noncash charge, the amortization of this discount results in an annual tax savings of $12,000 (0.40 × $30,000).

c. *Amortization of flotation cost on old bond.* The firm was amortizing the $360,000 flotation cost on the old bond over 30 years, resulting in an annual write-off of $12,000 ($360,000 ÷ 30). Because it is a tax-deductible noncash charge, the amortization of the flotation cost results in an annual tax savings of $4,800 (0.40 × $12,000).

d. *Interest cost of new bond.* The after-tax annual interest cost of the new bond is calculated as follows:

Table 17.5
Finding the Annual Cash Flow Savings for the Samuels Corporation's Bond-Refunding Decision

Old Bond

a.	**Interest cost**			
	Before tax (0.14 × $30,000,000)	$4,200,000		
	Less: Taxes (0.40 × $4,200,000)	1,680,000		
	After-tax interest cost		$2,520,000	
b.	**Less: Tax savings from amortization of discount**			
	[($900,000^a ÷ 30) × 0.40]		12,000	
c.	**Less: Tax savings from amortization of flotation cost**			
	[($360,000 ÷ 30) × 0.40]		4,800	
	(1) Annual after-tax debt payment			$2,503,200

New Bond

d.	**Interest cost**			
	Before tax (0.12 × $30,000,000)	$3,600,000		
	Less: Taxes (0.40 × $3,600,000)	1,440,000		
	After-tax interest cost		$2,160,000	
e.	**Less: Tax savings from amortization of flotation cost**			
	[($440,000 ÷ 25) × 0.40]		7,040	
	(2) Annual after-tax debt payment			$2,152,960
	Annual cash flow savings [(1) − (2)]			$ 350,240

^{a}$30,000,000 par value − $29,100,000 net proceeds from sale.

Before tax (0.12 × $30,000,000)	$3,600,000
Less: Taxes (0.40 × $3,600,000)	1,440,000
After-tax interest cost	$2,160,000

e. *Amortization of flotation cost on the new bond.* The firm will amortize the $440,000 flotation cost on the new bond over 25 years, resulting in an annual write-off of $17,600 ($440,000 ÷ 25). Because it is a tax-deductible noncash charge, the amortization of the flotation cost results in an annual tax savings of $7,040 (0.40 × $17,600).

Table 17.5 summarizes these calculations. Combining the first three values (a, b, and c) yields the annual after-tax debt payment for the old bond of $2,503,200. When the values for the new bond (d and e) are combined, the annual after-tax debt payment for the new bond is $2,152,960.

Subtracting the new bond's annual after-tax debt payment from that of the old bond, we find that implementation of the proposed bond refunding will result in an annual cash flow savings of $350,240 ($2,503,200 − $2,152,960).

Step 3. Find the net present value (NPV). Table 17.6 shows the calculations for determining the *NPV* of the proposed bond refunding. The present value of the annual cash flow savings of $350,240 at the 7.2 percent after-tax cost of debt over the 25 years is computed (using Equation 3.7) to be $4,009,056. Subtracting the initial investment of $2,960,000 from the present value of the annual cash flow savings results in a net

Table 17.6
Finding the Net Present
Value of the Samuels
Corporation's Bond-
Refunding Decision

Present value of annual cash flow (from Table 17.5)

$350,240 × PVA$_{7.2\%,\ 25\ years}$

$350,240 × 11.447 = $4,009,056

Less: Initial investment (from Table 17.4)   2,960,000

Net present value (*NPV*) of refunding $1,049,056

Decision: The proposed refunding is recommended because the *NPV* of refunding of
$1,049,056 is greater than $0.

present value of $1,049,056. Because a positive *NPV* results, the proposed bond re-
funding is recommended.

**Concept
Review
Questions**

6. What factors should a manager consider when choosing between a term loan and a bond
issue for funding long-term debt?

7. What factors might influence the choice between a bond issue with a *sinking fund* requirement and a *serial bond* issue?

8. What factors, other than the current interest rate at which new debt could be sold, should
a manager consider when deciding to refund a bond issue?

17.4 SYNDICATED LOANS

A **syndicated loan** is a large-denomination credit arranged by a group (a *syndicate*)
of commercial banks for a single borrower. Although syndicated lending has been a
fixture of U.S. and international finance for over three decades, syndicated loans have
increased dramatically in size, volume, and importance during the last 15 years. During the 1970s and early 1980s, many syndicated loans were arranged for governments in developing countries. These *petrodollar loans* were funded with the (dollar-
denominated) trade surpluses that oil-exporting countries built up following the surge
in oil prices in 1974–1975 and 1980–1982. Oil producers deposited their surpluses
in global banks, which then "recycled" these funds into petrodollar loans. The "Third
World debt crisis" of the early 1980s occurred after developing-country debt loads
hit critical levels and the borrowing countries defaulted on some of their interest and
principal payments.

The majority of syndicated loans were arranged for Western corporate borrowers even during the 1970s and 1980s, and since that time the market has become overwhelmingly corporate. Today, over $2 trillion worth of syndicated loans are arranged
annually, roughly two-thirds of which go to corporate borrowers. The syndicated loan
market appeals to borrowers who need to arrange very large loans quickly. Loans
for top-tier corporate borrowers are floating-rate credits, with very narrow spreads
(10–75 basis points) over LIBOR. Typically, lenders structure these loans as lines
of credit that borrowers can draw down as needed over four to six years. After that
time, the loans generally convert to term credits that firms must repay on a set schedule. One increasingly important use of syndicated lending is as funding for debt-
financed acquisitions by U.S. corporate borrowers, where the ability to borrow large
sums quickly and (relatively) discreetly is especially valuable. Table 17.7 provides details of syndicated loans arranged between January 1980 and April 2000, as well as

Table 17.7
Characteristics of All Syndicated Loans and Various Loan Categories, 1980–2000

Variable of Interest	All Syndi- cated Loans	Project Finance Loans	Corporate Control Loans	General Corporate- Purpose Loans	Capital Structure Loans	Fixed Asset– Based Loans
Number of loans	90,783	4,956	10,795	39,653	25,313	4,680
Total volume, $US in millions	$13,298,457	$634,422	$2,292,431	$4,275,803	$5,289,793	$410,175
Loan size, $US in millions: average	$146	$128	$212	$108	$209	$88
Loan size, $US in millions: median	$50	$52	$59	$39	$65	$50
Average maturity, years	4.8 years	8.6 years	5.1 years	4.5 years	3.9 years	8.1 years
Loans with fixed price (%)	5.9%	13.9%	2.7%	4.9%	3.9%	6.2%
Loans priced vs. LIBOR (%)	69.5%	38.8%	84.6%	66.2%	70.8%	72.5%
Loans to U.S. borrowers (%)	55.8%	13.9%	68.8%	50.3%	74.0%	20.4%
Average spread over LIBOR, basis points (bp)	134 bp	130 bp	195 bp	113 bp	135 bp	86 bp
Average number of syndicate banks	10.7	14.5	11.9	9.4	11.5	9.6
Average country risk score	90.0	74.6	95.4	87.3	94.1	82.7

Source: Data are from the CapitalDATA Loanware database, as employed in Stefanie Kleimeier and William L. Megginson, "Are Project Finance Loans Different from Other Syndicated Credits?" *Journal of Applied Corporate Finance* 13 (Spring 2000), pp. 75–87.

for five loan groupings. *Project finance loans* are limited or nonrecourse lending to vehicle companies, and are typically arranged to finance large infrastructure projects.[11] *Corporate control loans* are arranged to finance corporate acquisitions or leveraged buyouts, and *general corporate-purpose loans* are raised without a specific fund use being designated. *Capital structure loans* are booked for repayment of maturing lines of credit or for recapitalizations, share repurchases, debtor-in-possession financing, standby commercial paper support, or other unspecified purposes. *Fixed asset–based loans* are intended for mortgage lending or funding purchases of aircraft, property, or shipping.

SPECIALIZED SYNDICATED LENDING

Though syndicated loans are used for virtually all types of corporate finance, there are two uses that stand out as so distinct and important that they merit separate treatment: Eurocurrency lending and project finance.

Eurocurrency Lending

The **Eurocurrency loan** market consists of a large number of international banks that stand ready to make floating-rate, hard-currency loans (typically, U.S. dollar–denominated) to international corporate and government borrowers. For example, a British bank that accepts a dollar-denominated deposit in London is creating a *Eurodollar deposit,* and if it then relends the deposit to another bank or corporate borrower, it is making a *Eurodollar loan.* These loans are usually structured as lines of credit on which borrowers can draw. Most large loans (over $500 million) are syndicated, thereby providing a measure of diversification to the lenders.[12] Eurocurrency syndicated loans sometimes exceed $10 billion in size, and loans of $1 billion or more are quite common. Furthermore, in total size, the Eurocurrency market dwarfs all other international corporate financial markets.

Project Finance

Project finance (PF) loans are typically arranged for infrastructure projects—such as toll roads, bridges, power plants, seaports, tunnels, and airports—that require large sums to construct but which, once built, generate significant amounts of free cash flow for many years.[13] Although project finance lending almost always involves the use of syndicated loans, these differ from other types of syndicated credits in two vital ways. First, PF loans are extended to **stand-alone companies** created for the sole purpose of constructing and operating a single project. For example, Esty (1999) shows that the PF loans booked to develop a large oil field in Venezuela were extended to the company, Petrozuata, rather than to either or both of the venture's operating partners—the Venezuelan national oil company, PDVSA, or the American oil company, Conoco. Second, PF loans are almost always limited or nonrecourse credits, backed only by the assets and cash flows of the project, so the sponsors of the project do not guarantee

[11.] The term "vehicle company" does not refer to an auto manufacturer. A vehicle company is a stand-alone company, created solely to own and operate the project being financed.

[12.] Altman and Suggitt (2000) study the default rates in the syndicated loan market, and Megginson, Poulsen, and Sinkey (1995) examine stock market responses to bank announcements that they are participating in syndicated loans to sovereign or corporate borrowers. Recent trends in syndicated lending are described in Jones, Lang, and Nigro (2000).

[13.] The early history of PF lending is described in Kensinger and Martin (1988). Brealey, Cooper, and Habib (1996) discuss how PF lending helps mitigate the agency problems that arise between borrower and lender in standard credit relationships. Finally, Esty (2002) analyzes how PF loans are structured and priced to ensure an adequate return to lenders.

payment of the loan. As described in Kleimeier and Megginson (2000), project finance loans have been employed in many famous recent projects, such as the Eurotunnel under the English Channel, Euro Disneyland in France, the new Athens International Airport, and the Seoul–Pusan High-Speed Rail Project in Korea.

9. What aspect of syndicated lending is most attractive to the lenders?

10. Why are syndicated loans especially useful for financing takeovers?

11. How do project finance loans differ from other types of syndicated loans?

Concept Review Questions

17.5 LEASING

Leasing, like long-term debt, requires the firm to make a series of periodic, tax-deductible payments that may be fixed or variable. You can think of a lease as being comparable to secured long-term debt, because in both cases there is an underlying asset tied to the firm's financial obligation. The **lessee** uses the underlying asset and makes regular payments to the **lessor,** who retains ownership of the asset. Leasing can take a number of forms. Here we discuss the basic types of leases, lease arrangements, the lease contract, the lease-versus-purchase decision, the effects of leasing on future financing, and the advantages and disadvantages of leasing.

Basic Types of Leases

The two basic types of leases available to a business are *operating leases* and *financial leases*. Accountants also use the term *capital leases* to refer to financial leases.

Operating Leases

An **operating lease** is typically a contractual arrangement whereby the lessee agrees to make periodic payments to the lessor, often for five years or less, to obtain an asset's services. The lessee generally receives an option to cancel the lease by paying a cancellation fee. Assets that are leased under operating leases have useful lives that are longer than the lease's term, although as with most assets, the economic usefulness of the assets declines over time. Computer systems are prime examples of assets whose relative efficiency diminishes with new technological developments. The operating lease is a common arrangement for obtaining such systems, as well as for other relatively short-lived assets such as automobiles. When an operating lease expires, the lessee returns the asset to the lessor, who may lease it again or sell it. In some instances, the lease contract will give the lessee the opportunity to purchase the asset. In operating leases, the underlying asset usually has significant market value when the lease ends, and the lessor's original cost generally exceeds the total value of the lessee's payments.

Financial or Capital Leases

A **financial** (or **capital**) **lease** is longer term than an operating lease. Financial leases are noncancelable and therefore obligate the lessee to make payments over a predefined period. Even if the lessee no longer needs the asset, payments must continue until the lease expires. Financial leases are commonly used for leasing land, buildings, and large pieces of equipment. The noncancelable feature of the financial lease makes it quite similar to certain types of long-term debt. As is the case with debt, failure to make the contractual lease payments can result in bankruptcy for the lessee.

Another distinguishing characteristic of the financial lease is that the total payments over the lease period are greater than the lessor's initial cost. In other words, the lessor earns a return by receiving more than the asset's purchase price. Technically, under Financial Accounting Standards Board (FASB) Standard No. 13, "Accounting for Leases," a financial (or capital) lease is defined as having one of the following elements:

1. The lease transfers ownership of the property to the lessee by the end of the lease term.
2. The lease contains an option to purchase the property at a "bargain price." Such an option must be exercisable at a "fair market value" for the lease to be classified as an operating lease.
3. The lease term is equal to 75 percent or more of the estimated economic life of the property (exceptions exist for property leased toward the end of its usable economic life).
4. At the beginning of the lease, the present value of the lease payments is equal to 90 percent or more of the fair market value of the leased property.

The emphasis in this chapter is on financial leases because they result in inescapable long-term financial commitments by the firm.

Lease Arrangements

Lessors use three primary techniques for obtaining assets for leasing. The method selected depends largely on the desires of the prospective lessee. A **direct lease** results when a lessor acquires the assets that are leased to a given lessee. In other words, the lessee did not previously own the assets that it is leasing. In a **sale-leaseback arrangement,** one firm sells an asset to another for cash, then leases the asset from its new owner. You can see the resemblance of this arrangement to a collateralized loan. In such a loan, the lender gives the firm cash up front in exchange for a stream of future payments. If the borrower defaults on those payments, the lender keeps the collateral. In a sale-leaseback, the firm receives cash immediately (giving up ownership of the asset) and effectively repays this loan by leasing back the underlying asset. Sale-leaseback arrangements are therefore attractive to firms that need cash for operations. Leasing arrangements that include one or more third-party lenders are **leveraged leases.** Unlike in direct and sale-leaseback arrangements, the lessor in a leveraged lease acts as an equity participant, supplying only about 20 percent of the cost of the asset, and a lender supplies the balance. In recent years, leveraged leases have become especially popular in structuring leases of very expensive assets.[14]

A lease agreement usually specifies whether or not the lessee is responsible for maintenance of the leased assets. Both operating and financial leases generally include **maintenance clauses** specifying who is to maintain the assets and make insurance and tax payments. Under operating leases these costs are typically the lessor's responsibility, whereas under financial leases, the lessee is typically responsible for these costs. The lessee often has the option to renew a lease at its expiration. **Renewal options** are especially common in operating leases because their term is generally shorter than the

[14.] For a discussion of why manufacturers may prefer to lease rather than sell their products, see Smith and Wakeman (1985) and Waldman (1997).

useful life of the leased assets. **Purchase options** allowing the lessee to purchase the leased asset at maturity occur in both operating and financial leases.[15]

The lessor can be one of a number of parties. In operating lease arrangements, the lessor is quite likely to be the manufacturer's leasing subsidiary or an independent leasing company. Financial leases are frequently handled by independent leasing companies or by the leasing subsidiaries of large financial institutions such as commercial banks and life insurance companies. Life insurance companies are especially active in real estate leasing. Pension funds, like commercial banks, have also been increasing their leasing activities.

THE LEASE CONTRACT

The key items in a lease contract generally include a description of the leased assets, the term or duration of the lease, provisions for its cancellation, lease payment amounts and dates, provisions for maintenance and associated costs, renewal options, purchase options, and other provisions specified in the lease negotiation process. Furthermore, lease contracts spell out the consequences of the violation of any lease provision by either the lessee or the lessor.

THE LEASE-VERSUS-PURCHASE DECISION

The **lease-versus-purchase** (or **lease-versus-buy**) **decision** is one that commonly confronts firms contemplating the acquisition of new fixed assets. The alternatives available are to (1) lease the assets, (2) borrow funds to purchase the assets, or (3) purchase the assets using available liquid resources. Similar financial analysis applies to alternatives 2 and 3. Even if the firm has the liquid resources with which to purchase the assets, the use of these funds is viewed as equivalent to borrowing. Therefore, here we need to compare only the leasing and purchasing alternatives.

The lease-versus-purchase decision involves application of the capital budgeting methods we presented in Chapters 7 and 8. We first determine the relevant cash flows and then apply present value techniques. Although the approach we demonstrate here analyzes and compares the present values of the cash flows for the lease and the purchase, an alternative approach would calculate the net present value of the incremental cash flows. The following steps are involved in the analysis.

Step 1. Find the after-tax cash flow for each year under the lease alternative. This step generally involves a simple tax adjustment of the annual lease payments. In addition, the cost of exercising a purchase option in the final year of the lease term may be included.[16]

Step 2. Find the after-tax cash flows for each year under the purchase alternative. This step involves adjusting the sum of the scheduled loan-payment and maintenance-cost outlay for the tax shields resulting from the tax deductions attributable to maintenance, depreciation, and interest.

[15.] For a discussion on determining the appropriate lease rate for a lease that contains various options, see Grenadier (1995).

[16.] Including the cost of exercising a purchase option in the lease-alternative cash flows ensures that under both the lease and purchase alternatives, the firm owns the asset at the end of the relevant time horizon. The alternative would be to include the cash flows from the sale of the asset in the purchase-alternative cash flows at the end of the lease term. These approaches guarantee avoidance of unequal project lives, which we discussed in Chapter 8. They also make any subsequent cash flows irrelevant because they would either be identical or nonexistent, respectively, under each alternative.

Step 3. Calculate the present value of the cash flows associated with the lease (from Step 1) and purchase (from Step 2) alternatives using the after-tax cost of debt as the discount rate. Although some controversy surrounds the appropriate discount rate, we use the after-tax cost of debt to evaluate the lease-versus-purchase decision because the decision itself involves the choice between two financing alternatives having very low risk. If we were evaluating whether a given machine should be acquired, we would use the appropriate risk-adjusted rate or cost of capital, but in this type of analysis, we are attempting to determine only the better financing technique, leasing or borrowing.

Step 4. Choose the alternative with the lower present value of cash outflows from Step 3. This will be the least costly financing alternative.

The application of each of these steps is demonstrated in the following example.

APPLYING THE MODEL

The Portland Company, a small lumber mill, is contemplating acquiring a new machine tool costing $24,000. Arrangements can be made to lease or purchase the machine. The firm is in the 40 percent tax bracket.

Lease. The firm obtains a 5-year lease requiring annual *beginning*-of-year lease payments of $6,000.[17] The lessor will pay all maintenance costs, and the firm will pay insurance and other costs. The firm exercises its option to purchase the machine for $4,000 at termination of the lease—at the end of year 4 (beginning of year 5).

Purchase. The firm finances the purchase of the machine with a 9 percent, 5-year loan requiring end-of-year installment payments of $6,170.[18] The machine will be depreciated under MACRS using a 5-year recovery period. The firm pays $1,500 per year for a service contract that covers all maintenance costs and also pays insurance and other costs. The firm plans to keep the machine and use it beyond its 5-year recovery period.

Using these data, we can apply the steps presented in the introduction to this model.

Step 1. The annual after-tax cash outflow from the lease payments can be found by multiplying the before-tax payment of $6,000 by 1 minus the tax rate, T_C, of 40 percent.

$$\text{Annual after-tax cash outflow from lease} = \$6,000 \times (1 - T_C)$$
$$= \$6,000 \times (1 - 0.40) = \$3,600$$

Therefore, the lease alternative results in annual cash outflows over the 5-year lease of $3,600, paid at the beginning of each year. In the final year, the $4,000 cost of the purchase option would be added to the $3,600 lease outflow to get a total cash outflow at the end of year 4 (beginning of year 5) of $7,600 ($3,600 + $4,000).

Step 2. The after-tax cash outflow from the purchase alternative is a bit more difficult to find. First, the interest component of each annual loan payment must be deter-

---

[17] Lease payments are generally made at the beginning of the lease period (in this case, a year), and we make that assumption here.

[18] The annual loan payment on the 9 percent, 5-year loan of $24,000 is calculated by using the loan amortization technique that we described in Chapter 3.

Table 17.8
Determining the Interest
and Principal Components
of the Portland Company
Loan Payments

End of Year	Loan Payments (1)	Beginning-of-Year Principal (2)	Payments		End-of-Year Principal [(2) − (4)] (5)
			Interest [0.09 × (2)] (3)	Principal [(1) − (3)] (4)	
1	$6,170	$24,000	$2,160	$4,010	$19,990
2	6,170	19,990	1,799	4,371	15,619
3	6,170	15,619	1,406	4,764	10,855
4	6,170	10,855	977	5,193	5,662
5	6,170	5,662	510	5,660	—[a]

[a]The values in this table have been rounded to the nearest dollar, which results in a slight difference ($2) between the beginning-of-year-5 principal (in column 2) and the year-5 principal payment (in column 4).

mined, because the Internal Revenue Service allows the deduction from income of interest only, not principal, for tax purposes.[19] Table 17.8 presents the calculations required to split the loan payments into their interest and principal components. Columns 3 and 4 show the annual interest and principal paid in each of the five years. Column 1 lists the annual loan payment.

Next, we find the annual depreciation write-off resulting from the $24,000 machine. Using the applicable MACRS 5-year recovery period depreciation percentages from Table 8.1 (on page 267) of 20 percent in year 1, 32 percent in year 2, 19.2 percent in year 3, and 11.52 percent in years 4 and 5 results in the annual depreciation for years 1 through 5 given in column 3 of Table 17.9.[20]

Table 17.9 presents all the calculations required to determine the cash outflows associated with borrowing to purchase the new machine.[21] Column 7 of the table presents the after-tax cash outflows associated with the purchase alternative. A few points should be clarified with respect to the calculations in Table 17.9. The major cash outflows are the total loan payment for each year given in column 1 and the annual maintenance cost, which is a tax-deductible expense, in column 2. The sum of these two outflows is reduced by the tax savings from writing off the maintenance, depreciation, and interest expenses associated with the new machine and its financing, respectively. The resulting cash outflows are the after-tax cash outflows associated with the purchase alternative.

Step 3. The present values of the cash outflows associated with the lease (from Step 1) and purchase (from Step 2) alternatives are calculated in Table 17.10 using the firm's

[19.] When the rate of interest on the loan used to finance the purchase just equals the cost of debt, the present value of the after-tax loan payments (annual principal payments − interest tax shields) discounted at the after-tax cost of debt would just equal the initial loan principal. In such a case, it is unnecessary to amortize the loan to determine the payment amount and the amounts of interest when finding the after-tax cash outflows. The loan payments and interest payments (columns 1 and 3 in Table 17.9) could be ignored, and in their place, the initial loan principal ($24,000) would be shown as an outflow occurring at time 0. To allow for a loan interest rate that is different from the firm's cost of debt and to facilitate understanding, here we isolate the loan payments and interest payments rather than use this computationally more efficient approach.

[20.] The year-6 depreciation is ignored because we are considering the cash flows solely over a 5-year time horizon. Similarly, depreciation on the leased asset when purchased at the end of the lease for $4,000 is ignored. The tax benefits resulting from this depreciation would make the lease alternative even more attractive. Clearly, the analysis would become more precise and more complex if we chose to look beyond the 5-year time horizon, though the basic conclusions would remain unchanged.

[21.] Although other cash outflows such as insurance and operating expenses may be relevant here, they would be the same under the lease and purchase alternatives and therefore would cancel out in the final analysis.

Table 17.9
After-Tax Cash Outflows Associated with Purchasing for Portland Company

End of Year	Loan Payments (1)	Maintenance Costs (2)	Depreciation (3)	Interest[a] (4)	Total Deductions [(2) + (3) + (4)] (5)	Tax Shields [0.40 × (5)] (6)	After-Tax Cash Outflows [(1) + (2) − (6)] (7)
1	$6,170	$1,500	$4,800	$2,160	$ 8,460	$3,384	$4,286
2	6,170	1,500	7,680	1,799	10,979	4,392	3,278
3	6,170	1,500	4,608	1,406	7,514	3,006	4,664
4	6,170	1,500	2,765	977	5,242	2,097	5,573
5	6,170	1,500	2,765	510	4,775	1,910	5,760

[a]From Table 17.8, column 3.

Table 17.10
A Comparison of the Cash Outflows Associated with Leasing versus Purchasing for Portland Company

	Leasing			Purchasing		
End of Year	After-Tax Cash Outflows (1)	Present Value Factors (2)	Present Value of Outflows [(1) × (2)] (3)	After-Tax Cash Outflows[a] (4)	Present Value Factors (5)	Present Value of Outflows [(1) × (2)] (6)
0	$3,600	1.000	$ 3,600	$ 0	1.000	$ 0
1	3,600	0.949	3,416	4,286	0.949	4,066
2	3,600	0.900	3,241	3,278	0.900	2,951
3	3,600	0.854	3,075	4,664	0.854	3,983
4	7,600[b]	0.810	6,158	5,573	0.810	4,514
5	0	0.767	0	5,760	0.767	4,418
		PV of cash outflows	$19,490		PV of cash outflows	$19,932

[a]From column 7 of Table 17.9.
[b]After-tax lease payment outflow of $3,600 plus the $4,000 cost of exercising the purchase option.

5.4 percent after-tax cost of debt [9.0% × (1 − 0.40)]. Applying the appropriate present value interest factors given in columns 2 and 5 to the after-tax cash outflows in columns 1 and 4 results in the present values of lease and purchase cash outflows given in columns 3 and 6, respectively. Column 3 presents the sum of the present values of the cash outflows for the leasing alternative, and column 6, the sum for the purchasing alternative.

Step 4. Because the present value of cash outflows for leasing ($19,490) is lower than that for purchasing ($19,932), the leasing alternative is preferable. Leasing results in an incremental savings of $442 ($19,932 − $19,490) and is therefore the less costly alternative.

The techniques described here for comparing lease and purchase alternatives may be applied in different ways. The approach illustrated by using the Portland Company's data is one of the most straightforward. It is important to recognize that the lower cost of one alternative over the other results from factors such as the differing tax brackets of the lessor and the lessee, different tax treatments for leases versus purchases, and differing risks and borrowing costs for the lessor and the lessee. Therefore, when making a lease-versus-purchase decision, the firm will find that inexpensive borrowing opportunities, high required lessor returns, and a low risk of obsolescence increase the attractiveness of purchasing.[22] Subjective factors must also be included in the decision-making process. Like most financial decisions, the lease-versus-purchase decision requires a certain degree of judgment and/or intuition.

EFFECTS OF LEASING ON FUTURE FINANCING

Because leasing is considered a type of debt funding, it affects a firm's future financing ability. Lease payments are shown as a tax-deductible expense on the firm's income statement. Anyone analyzing the income statement would probably recognize that an asset is being leased, although the actual details of the amount and term of the lease might be unclear. The following sections discuss the lease disclosure requirements established by the Financial Accounting Standards Board (FASB) and the effect of leases on financial ratios.

Lease Disclosure Requirements

Standard No. 13 of the FASB, "Accounting for Leases," requires explicit disclosure of financial (capital) lease obligations on the firm's balance sheet. Such a lease must be shown as a capitalized lease, meaning that the present value of all its payments is included as an asset and corresponding liability on the firm's balance sheet. An operating lease, on the other hand, need not be capitalized, but its basic features must be disclosed in a footnote to the financial statements. Standard No. 13, of course, establishes detailed guidelines to be used in capitalizing leases to reflect them as an asset and corresponding liability on the balance sheet. Subsequent standards have further refined lease capitalization and disclosure procedures. The following Applying the Model provides an example.

[22.] Smith and Wakeman (1985), Krishnan and Moyer (1994), Barclay and Smith (1995b), Grenadier (1995, 1996), and Waldman (1997) examine the lease-versus-purchase decision using U.S. data. Lasfer and Levis (1998) perform a similar analysis using British data, while Beattie, Goodacre, and Thomson (2000) examine the choice between operating and financial leases in Britain. To date, no clear-cut patterns are observed, though firm size, tax status, the relative importance of growth options to firm value, and the likelihood of bankruptcy all seem to play a role. As do most subsequent researchers, Schallheim, Johnson, Lease, and McConnell (1987) find that lease rates are significantly higher than otherwise comparable lending rates, so firms clearly choose leasing for reasons other than lower cost alone.

Davis Company, a manufacturer of printing equipment, is leasing an asset under a 10-year lease requiring annual beginning-of-year payments of $15,000. The lease can be capitalized merely by calculating the present value of the lease payments over the life of the lease. However, the rate at which the payments should be discounted is difficult to determine.[23] If 10 percent is used, the present, or capitalized, value of the lease is found by multiplying the annual lease payment by the present value factor of a 10-year, 10 percent annuity due (Equation 3.8). This value of $101,385 ($15,000 × 6.759) would be shown as an asset and corresponding liability on the firm's balance sheet, which should result in an accurate reflection of the firm's true financial position. ∎

Leasing and Financial Ratios

Because the consequences of missing a financial lease payment are the same as those of missing an interest or principal payment on debt, a financial analyst must view the lease as a long-term financial commitment of the lessee. With FASB Standard No. 13, the inclusion of each financial (capital) lease as an asset and corresponding liability (i.e., long-term debt) provides for a balance sheet that more accurately reflects the firm's financial status. It thereby permits various types of financial ratio analyses to be performed directly on the statement by any interested party.

ADVANTAGES AND DISADVANTAGES OF LEASING

Leasing has a number of commonly cited advantages and disadvantages that should be considered when making a lease-versus-purchase decision. Although not all these advantages and disadvantages hold in every case, it is common for several of them to apply in a given situation.

Advantages

The following are commonly cited advantages of leasing.

1. Leasing allows the lessee, in effect, to depreciate land, which is prohibited if the land were purchased. Because the lessee who leases land is permitted to deduct the total lease payment as an expense for tax purposes, the effect is the same as if the firm had purchased the land and then depreciated it.
2. The use of sale-leaseback arrangements may permit the firm to increase its liquidity by converting an asset into cash, which can then be used as working capital. A firm short of working capital or in a liquidity bind can sell an owned asset to a lessor and lease the asset back for a specified number of years.
3. Leasing provides 100 percent financing. Most loan agreements for the purchase of fixed assets require the borrower to pay a portion of the purchase price as a down payment. Therefore, the borrower is able to borrow (at most) only 90–95 percent of the purchase price of the asset.
4. When a firm becomes bankrupt or is reorganized, the maximum claim of lessors against the corporation is three years of lease payments, and the lessor, of course,

[23] The Financial Accounting Standards Board in Standard No. 13 established certain guidelines for the appropriate discount rate to use when capitalizing leases. Most commonly, the rate that the lessee would have incurred to borrow the funds to buy the asset with a secured loan under terms similar to the lease repayment schedule would be used. This simply represents the before-tax cost of a secured loan.

reclaims the asset. If debt is used to purchase an asset, the creditors have a claim that is equal to the total outstanding loan balance.

5. In a lease arrangement, the firm may avoid the cost of obsolescence if the lessor fails to accurately anticipate the obsolescence of assets and sets the lease payment too low. This is especially true in the case of operating leases, which generally have relatively short lives.

6. A lessee avoids many of the restrictive covenants that are usually included as part of a long-term loan. Requirements with respect to minimum net working capital, subsequent borrowing, business combinations, and so on are not generally found in a lease agreement.

7. In the case of low-cost assets that are infrequently acquired, leasing, especially through operating leases, may provide the firm with needed financing flexibility. That is, the firm does not have to arrange other financing for these assets and can obtain them somewhat conveniently through a lease.

Disadvantages

The following are commonly cited disadvantages of leasing.

1. A lease does not have a stated interest cost. In many leases, the return to the lessor is quite high, so the firm might be better off borrowing to purchase the asset.

2. At the end of the term of the lease agreement, the lessor realizes the salvage value, if any, of an asset. If the lessee had purchased the asset, it could have claimed the asset's salvage value. Of course, in a competitive market, if the lessor expects a higher salvage value, then the lease payments would be lower.

3. Under a lease, the lessee is generally prohibited from making improvements on the leased property or asset without the approval of the lessor. If the property were owned outright, this difficulty would not arise. Of course, lessors generally encourage leasehold improvements when they are expected to enhance the asset's salvage value.

4. If a lessee leases an asset that subsequently becomes obsolete, it still must make lease payments over the remaining term of the lease. This is true even if the asset is unusable.

---

12. Why is it considered important whether a lease is classified as an *operating lease* or as a *financial (or capital) lease*?

13. What factors should be considered when deciding between leasing an asset and borrowing funds to purchase the asset?

Concept Review Questions

17.6 SUMMARY

- Long-term debt and leasing are important sources of capital for businesses. Long-term debt can take the form of term loans or bonds. The characteristics of each can be tailored to meet the needs of both the borrower and the lender.

- The conditions of a term loan are specified in the loan agreement. This agreement specifies the rights and responsibilities of both creditor and borrower, and the agreement typically lists several positive and negative covenants that the borrower must not violate.

- The conditions of a bond issue are specified in the bond indenture and are enforced by a trustee. These legal agreements are highly detailed and not easily modified, because bonds are held by many individual investors. In contrast, privately arranged loan terms can be modified rather easily, because the borrower can negotiate directly with one creditor or a relatively small number of creditors.

- Frequently when interest rates drop, bond issuers make refunding decisions, which involve finding the *NPV* associated with calling outstanding bonds and issuing new lower-interest-coupon bonds to replace the refunded bonds.
- Syndicated loans are large credits arranged by a syndicate of commercial banks for a single borrower. These have been increasing in importance in recent years because very large loans can be arranged quickly and inexpensively and can have very flexible borrowing terms.
- Leasing serves as an alternative to borrowing funds to purchase an asset. Operating leases need not be shown on a firm's balance sheet, whereas capital lease obligations must be shown. Firms often make lease-versus-purchase decisions, which involve choosing the alternative with the lower present value of cash outflows.

INTERNET RESOURCES

Note: *For updates to links, please go to the book's website at* *http://smart.swcollege.com*

http://www.bondsonline.com — Offers a wealth of information on the bond market

http://www.investinginbonds.com — A site with statistics on the Treasury, municipal, and corporate bond markets

KEY TERMS

balloon payment
bearer
bond ratings
call premium
capital lease
collateral
collateral trust bonds
convertible bonds
cross-default covenant
debentures
direct lease
equipment trust certificates
Eurobond
Eurocurrency loan
fallen angels
financial lease
fixed-rate
floating-rate
foreign bond
high-yield bonds
income bonds
indenture
investment-grade bonds
junk bonds
lease-versus-buy decision
lease-versus-purchase decision
leasing

lessee
lessor
leveraged leases
LIBOR
lien
loans
maintenance clauses
mortgage bonds
mortgage-backed securities (MBS)
operating lease
prime lending rate
private placements
project finance (PF) loans
purchase options
refund
renewal options
sale-leaseback arrangement
serial bonds
sinking fund
stand-alone companies
stock purchase warrants
subordinated debentures
subordination
syndicated loan
term loan
trustee

QUESTIONS

17-1.   Comment on the following proposition: Using floating-rate debt eliminates interest rate risk (the risk that interest payment amounts will change in the future) for both the borrower and the lender.

17-2.   What purpose do *covenants* serve in a debt agreement? What factors should a manager consider when negotiating covenants?

17-3.   List and briefly discuss the key features that distinguish long-term debt issues from each other.

17-4.   Define the following: *term loan, balloon payment, collateral,* and *stock purchase warrants.*

17-5.   What is a *debenture?* Why do you think that this is the most common form of corporate bond in the United States, but is much less commonly used elsewhere?

17-6.   How do *sinking funds* reduce default risk?

17-7.   What is a *trustee?* Why do bondholders insist that a trustee be included in all public bond offerings? Why are these less necessary in private debt placements?

17-8.   What impact has adoption of *Rule 144A* had on debt-issuance patterns in the United States?

17-9.   Why are most corporate bonds callable? Who benefits from this feature, and what is the cost of adopting a call provision in a public bond issue?

17-10.   Why do corporations have their debt rated? Compare the role played by rating agencies and a company's outside auditors.

17-11.   What does "investment grade" mean in the context of corporate bond issues? How do these bonds differ from *junk bonds,* and why have the latter proven so popular with investors?

17-12.   What is a *Eurobond?* Why did these bonds come into existence? Why do Eurobond investors like the fact that these are typically "bearer bonds"? What risk does an investor run from holding bearer bonds rather than registered bonds?

17-13.   Explain how uncertainty concerning future interest rates would affect the decision to refund a bond issue.

17-14.   What is a *syndicated loan?* Why have these loans proven so popular with corporate borrowers?

17-15.   What is a *project finance loan?* What role does a vehicle company play in the typical project finance deal?

17-16.   Define the following: *direct lease, sale-leaseback arrangement, leveraged lease,* and *financial (capital) lease.*

17-17.   What elements must be included in a lease in order for it to be considered a financial (capital) lease?

17-18.   Comment on the following statement: A key benefit of leasing is that it allows for the effective depreciation of land.

17-19.   How would the availability of floating-rate debt rather than fixed-rate debt affect the lease-versus-buy decision?

17-20.   What are the key advantages of leasing as compared to borrowing to acquire an asset? What are the key disadvantages of leasing?

PROBLEMS

Corporate Bonds

17-1. The initial proceeds per bond, the size of the issue, the initial maturity of the bond, and the years remaining to maturity are shown in the following table for a number of bonds. In each case, the firm is in the 40 percent tax bracket, and the bond has a $1,000 par value.

Bond	Proceeds per Bond	Size of Issue	Initial Maturity of Bond	Years Remaining to Maturity
A	$ 985	10,000 bonds	20 years	15 years
B	1,025	20,000	25	16
C	1,000	22,500	12	9
D	960	5,000	25	15
E	1,035	10,000	30	16

a. Indicate whether each bond was sold at a discount, at a premium, or at its par value.
b. Determine the total discount or premium for each issue.
c. Determine the annual amount of discount or premium amortized for each bond.
d. Calculate the unamortized discount or premium for each bond.
e. Determine the after-tax cash flow associated with the retirement now of each of these bonds, using the values developed in part (d).

17-2. For each of the callable bond issues in the following table, calculate the after-tax cost of calling the issue. Each bond has a $1,000 par value, and the various issue sizes and call prices are shown in the following table. The firm is in the 40 percent tax bracket.

Bond	Size of Issue	Call Price
A	12,000 bonds	$1,050
B	20,000	1,030
C	30,000	1,015
D	50,000	1,050
E	100,000	1,045
F	500,000	1,060

17-3. The flotation cost, the initial maturity, and the number of years remaining to maturity are shown in the following table for a number of bonds. The firm is in the 40 percent tax bracket.

Bond	Flotation Cost	Initial Maturity of Bond	Years Remaining to Maturity
A	$250,000	30 years	22 years
B	500,000	15	5
C	125,000	20	10
D	750,000	10	1
E	650,000	15	6

a. Calculate the annual amortization of the flotation cost for each bond.
b. Determine the tax savings, if any, expected to result from the unamortized flotation cost if the bond were called today.

17-4. The principal, coupon interest rate, and interest overlap period are shown in the following table for a number of bonds.

Bond	Principal	Coupon Interest Rate	Interest Overlap Period
A	$ 5,000,000	8.0%	3 months
B	40,000,000	7.0	2
C	50,000,000	6.5	3
D	100,000,000	9.0	6
E	20,000,000	5.5	1

a. Calculate the dollar amount of interest that must be paid for each bond during the interest overlap period.

b. Calculate the after-tax cost of overlapping interest for each bond if the firm is in the 40 percent tax bracket.

17-5. Schooner Company is contemplating offering a new $50 million bond issue to replace an outstanding $50 million bond issue. The firm wishes to do this to take advantage of the decline in interest rates that has occurred since the initial bond issuance. The old and new bonds are described in what follows. The firm is in the 40 percent tax bracket.

Old bonds. The outstanding bonds have a $1,000 par value and a 9 percent coupon interest rate. They were issued five years ago with a 20-year maturity. They were initially sold for their par value of $1,000, and the firm incurred $350,000 in flotation costs. They are callable at $1,090.

New bonds. The new bonds would have a $1,000 par value, a 7 percent coupon interest rate, and a 15-year maturity. They could be sold at their par value. The flotation cost of the new bonds would be $500,000. The firm does not expect to have any overlapping interest.

a. Calculate the tax savings that are expected from the unamortized portion or the old bonds' flotation cost.

b. Calculate the annual tax savings from the flotation cost of the new bonds, assuming the 15-year amortization.

c. Calculate the after-tax cost of the call premium that is required to retire the old bonds.

d. Determine the initial investment that is required to call the old bonds and issue the new bonds.

e. Calculate the annual cash flow savings, if any, that are expected from the proposed bond-refunding decision.

f. If the firm has a 4.2 percent after-tax cost of debt, find the net present value (NPV) of the bond-refunding decision. Would you recommend the proposed refunding? Explain your answer.

17-6. High-Gearing Incorporated is considering offering a new $40 million bond issue to replace an outstanding $40 million bond issue. The firm wishes to do this to take advantage of the decline in interest rates that has occurred since the original issue. The two bond issues are described in what follows. The firm is in the 40 percent tax bracket.

Old bonds. The outstanding bonds have a $1,000 par value and a 10 percent coupon interest rate. They were issued five years ago with a 25-year maturity. They were initially sold at a $25 per bond discount, and a $200,000 flotation cost was incurred. They are callable at $1,100.

New bonds. The new bonds would have a 20-year maturity, a par value of $1,000, and a 7.5 percent coupon interest rate. It is expected that these bonds can be sold at par for a flotation cost of $250,000. The firm expects a 3-month period of over-lapping interest while it retires the old bonds.

a. Calculate the initial investment that is required to call the old bonds and issue the new bonds.

b. Calculate the annual cash flow savings, if any, expected from the proposed bond-refunding decision.

c. If the firm uses its after-tax cost of debt of 4.5 percent to evaluate low-risk deci-sions, find the net present value (*NPV*) of the bond-refunding decision. Would you recommend the proposed refunding? Explain your answer.

17-7. Web Tools Company is considering using the proceeds from a new $50 million bond issue to call and retire its outstanding $50 million bond issue. The details of both bond issues are outlined in what follows. The firm is in the 40 percent tax bracket.

Old bonds. The firm's old issue has a coupon interest rate of 10 percent, was is-sued four years ago, and had a 20-year maturity. The bonds sold at a $10 discount from their $1,000 par value, flotation costs were $420,000, and their call price is $1,100.

New bonds. The new bonds are expected to sell at par ($1,000), have a 16-year maturity, and have flotation costs of $520,000. The firm will have a 2-month period of overlapping interest while it retires the old bonds.

a. What is the initial investment that is required to call the old bonds and issue the new bonds?

b. What are the annual cash flow savings, if any, from the proposed bond-refunding decision if (1) the new bonds have an 8 percent coupon interest rate and (2) the new bonds have an 8.5 percent coupon interest rate?

c. Construct a table showing the net present value (*NPV*) of refunding under the two circumstances given in part (b) when (1) the firm has an after-tax cost of debt of 4.8 percent and (2) the firm has an after-tax cost of debt of 5.1 percent.

d. Discuss the set(s) of circumstances (described in part [c]) when refunding would be favorable and when it would not.

e. If the four circumstances summarized in part (d) were equally probable (each had 0.25 probability), would you recommend refunding? Explain your answer.

Leasing

17-8. For each of the loan amounts, interest rates, loan terms, and annual payments shown in the following table, calculate the annual interest paid each year over the term of the loan, assuming that the payments are made at the *end of each year*.

Loan	Amount	Interest Rate	Term	Annual Payment
A	$ 20,000	8%	4 years	$ 6,038
B	35,500	7	6	7,448
C	152,500	9	5	39,207
D	250,000	7.5	10	36,421
E	575,500	6	15	59,204

17-9. Shredding Pines Company wishes to purchase an asset that costs $750,000. The full amount needed to finance the asset can be borrowed at 9 percent interest. The terms of the loan require equal end-of-year payments for the next eight years. Determine the total annual loan payment, and break it into the amount of interest and the amount of principal paid for each year.

17-10. Given the lease payments and terms shown in the following table, determine the yearly after-tax cash outflows for each firm, assuming that lease payments are made at the *beginning of each year* and that the firm is in the 40 percent tax bracket. Assume that no purchase option exists.

Firm	Annual Lease Payment	Term of Lease
A	$ 250,000	5 years
B	160,000	12
C	500,000	8
D	1,000,000	20
E	25,000	6

17-11. GMS Corporation is attempting to determine whether to lease or purchase research equipment. The firm is in the 40 percent tax bracket, and its after-tax cost of debt is currently 6 percent. The terms of the lease and the purchase are as follows:

Lease. Annual beginning-of-year lease payments of $93,500 are required over the 3-year life of the lease. The lessor will pay all maintenance costs; the lessee will pay insurance and other costs. The lessee will exercise its option to purchase the asset for $25,000 paid along with the final lease payment.

Purchase. The $250,000 cost of the research equipment can be financed entirely with a 10 percent loan requiring annual end-of-year payments of $100,529 for three years. The firm in this case will depreciate the equipment under MACRS using a 3-year recovery period. (See Table 8.1 on page 267 for applicable MACRS percentages.) The firm will pay $9,500 per year for a service contract that covers all maintenance costs; the firm will pay insurance and other costs. The firm plans to keep the equipment and use it beyond its 3-year recovery period.

a. Calculate the after-tax cash outflows associated with each alternative.
b. Calculate the present value of each cash outflow stream using the after-tax cost of debt.
c. Which alternative, lease or purchase, would you recommend? Why?

17-12. Eastern Trucking Company needs to expand its facilities. To do so, the firm must acquire a machine costing $80,000. The machine can be leased or purchased. The firm is in the 40 percent tax bracket, and its after-tax cost of debt is 5.4 percent. The terms of the lease and purchase plans are as follows:

Lease. The leasing arrangement requires beginning-of-year payments of $16,900 over five years. The lessor will pay all maintenance costs; the lessee will pay insurance and other costs. The lessee will exercise its option to purchase the asset for $20,000 paid along with the final lease payment.

Purchase. If the firm purchases the machine, its cost of $80,000 will be financed with a 5-year, 9 percent loan requiring equal end-of-year payments of $20,567. The machine will be depreciated under MACRS using a 5-year recovery period. (See Table 8.1 on page 267 for applicable MACRS percentages.) The firm will pay $2,000 per year for a service contract that covers all maintenance costs; the firm will pay insurance and other costs. The firm plans to keep the equipment and use it beyond its 5-year recovery period.

a. Determine the after-tax cash outflows of Eastern Trucking under each alternative.
b. Find the present value of the after-tax cash outflows for each alternative using the after-tax cost of debt.
c. Which alternative, lease or purchase, would you recommend? Why?

17-13. Given the lease payments, terms remaining until the leases expire, and discount rates shown in the following table, calculate the capitalized value of each lease, assuming that lease payments are made annually at the beginning of each year.

Lease	Lease Payment	Remaining Term	Discount Rate
A	$ 40,000	12 years	10%
B	120,000	8	12
C	9,000	18	14
D	16,000	3	9
E	47,000	20	11

Options Basics

OPENING FOCUS
How to Profit from Enron's Demise

If you took a survey of investors asking them what they thought was the worst investment of the year 2001, many would reply, "Enron stock!" It would be hard to argue with that assessment. In January 2001, Enron shares flirted with the $80 mark before starting a long slide that ended in Enron's declaration of bankruptcy on December 2. In the process, Enron shareholders watched over $60 billion of the company's market value evaporate in just a few months, giving Enron the distinction of being the largest bankruptcy in U.S. history to that time. Not surprising, Enron's collapse gave birth to a cottage industry of Enron humor, such as the suggestion that Motorola Inc. should acquire Enron, renaming the combined entity Moron.

But not everyone lost money on Enron. According to Harvard-Watch, a student watchdog group, a Boston hedge fund that managed part of Harvard's endowment made about $50 million for the university by purchasing put options on Enron stock. These options, purchased between April and September, gave Highfields Capital Management the right to sell 3.5 million shares of Enron stock at a fixed price. Needless to say, the opportunity to sell Enron stock at a fixed price, a price set long before Enron's stock became utterly worthless, is a valuable opportunity indeed.

Perhaps more familiar are call options, which grant the right to purchase stock at a fixed price. Call options have become a standard part of the compensation package for everyone from corporate CEOs to newly minted MBAs. Because call options pay off handsomely when the underlying stock price rises, making options an important part of employees' compensation provides incentives for managers to act in shareholders' interest—that is, to take actions that increase the firms' stock prices. So goes the theory, at least. As the relative importance of options in compensation systems has grown, so too have controversies about how large option grants should be, how companies "reprice" options when their stock prices fall, and how the cost of option-based compensation should be treated in the firm's financial reports.

For example, in its October 2001 proxy statement, JDS Uniphase reported that CEO Jozef Straus reaped a profit from exercising his options of more than $150 million. Straus received his option grants during a period in which JDS stock enjoyed remarkable appreciation, but the disclosure of his profits on these options occurred after the firms' stock had fallen more than $150 per share. Investors who wanted to know the impact of these option grants on JDS profits had to do some detective work. JDS reported, in the footnotes to its financial statements, that the cost of its options program increased the firm's net loss by $400 million in 2001.

Source: Justin Pope, "Harvard Activists Group Calls for Harvard to Investigate Enron Ties," *Associated Press* (February 1, 2002).

A bit of folk wisdom says, "Always keep your options open." This implies that choices have value and that having the right to do something is better than being obligated to do it. This chapter shows how to apply that intuition to financial instruments called options. In their most basic forms, **options** allow investors to buy or sell an asset at a fixed price during a given period of time. As the Opening Focus illustrates, having the right (but not the obligation) to buy or sell shares at a fixed price can be extremely valuable, provided the price of the underlying stock moves in the right direction.

Many commentators see options merely as a form of legalized gambling for the rich. We strongly disagree with that perspective. Options exist because they provide real economic benefits that come in many different forms.

First, options do provide incentives for managers to take actions that increase their firms' stock prices, thereby increasing the wealth of shareholders.[1] Abuses may occur when firms award excessive option grants or renegotiate the terms of options agreements after a period of poor stock performance. We see these abuses as a corporate governance problem, not a problem with options per se.

Second, a wide variety of options exist that grant holders the right to buy and sell many different types of assets, not just shares of stock in a single company.[2] Sometimes, trading the option is more cost effective than trading the underlying asset. For example, trading a stock index option, which grants the right to buy or sell a portfolio of stocks such as the S&P 500, enables investors to avoid paying all the transactions costs that would result from trading 500 individual stocks.

Third, firms use options to reduce their exposure to certain types of risk. Firms regularly buy and sell options to shelter their cash flows from movements in exchange rates, interest rates, and commodity prices. In that function, options resemble insurance much more than they resemble gambling.

Fourth, options facilitate the creation of innovative trading strategies. For instance, suppose that an investor is following a pharmaceutical company that has a genetically engineered cancer drug in clinical trials. The company has invested vast resources in this project, so much so that its future depends on the outcome of these trials. If the tests are successful, the company's stock will skyrocket. If not, the firm may go bankrupt. An investor with choices limited to buying or selling the company's stock must decide whether the clinical trials will succeed or fail. As we will see, an investor who can buy and sell options can construct a trading strategy to profit from a large movement in the firm's stock price, regardless of whether that movement is up or down.

[1] For a skeptic's view of this claim, see Lee (2002). Even those who believe that options provide managers with proper incentives disagree on how companies should report the cost of their employee stock option plans in financial statements. Stiglitz (2002) and Malkiel and Baumol (2002) offer contrasting views on this subject.

[2] Though this chapter focuses primarily on options to buy and sell shares of stocks, investors can trade options that grant the right to buy or sell currencies, commodities, fixed-income securities, and many other types of assets at fixed prices.

The growth in options trading, and trading in other exotic financial instruments such as futures contracts, offers some evidence of our claim that options provide real economic benefits to society. As the Comparative Corporate Finance insert explains, the growth in options markets has been a worldwide phenomenon for roughly the past 25 years. In many of the world's largest economies, trading in stock options exceeds the trading volume in the underlying stocks themselves.

One might ask why a chapter on options belongs in a corporate finance textbook. We offer three answers. First, employees of large and small corporations regularly receive options as part of their compensation. It is valuable both for the employees and the employers to understand the value of this component of pay packages. Second, firms often raise capital by issuing securities with embedded options. For example, firms can issue debt that is convertible into shares of common stock at a lower interest rate than ordinary, nonconvertible debt. To evaluate whether the interest savings is worth giving bondholders the opportunity to convert their bonds into shares requires an understanding of option pricing. Third, many capital budgeting projects have optionlike characteristics. As we discussed in Chapters 7–9, the net present value method can generate incorrect accept/reject decisions for projects with downstream options. The best way to develop the ability to recognize which real investment projects have embedded options and which ones do not is to become an expert on ordinary financial options.

We begin this chapter with a brief description of the most common types of stock options and their essential characteristics. Next, we turn our attention to options payoffs, illustrating how options can be used to construct portfolios and unique trading strategies, and gaining insight into how prices of different kinds of options are linked together in the market. The rest of the chapter examines qualitative factors that influence option values and introduces a simple, yet powerful tool for calculating the prices of many different kinds of options.

18.1 OPTIONS VOCABULARY

An option is one of the three main types of **derivative securities,** a class of financial instruments that derive their values from other assets.[3] An option fits this description because its value depends on the price of the underlying stock that the option holder can buy or sell at a fixed price. The asset from which a derivative security obtains its value is called the **underlying asset.** A **call option** grants the right to purchase a share of stock (or some other asset) at a fixed price on or before a certain date. Clearly, a call option increases in value as the underlying stock price increases. The price at which a call option allows an investor to purchase the underlying share is called the **strike price** or the **exercise price.** Call options grant investors the right to purchase a share for a fairly short time period, usually just a few months.[4] The point at which this right expires is called the option's **expiration date.** An **American call option** gives

---

[3.] The other main types of derivatives are futures contracts (and their close cousins, forward contracts) and swaps. A *futures contract* is an agreement between two parties to trade an asset at a fixed price on a specific future date. Unlike an option, a futures contract obligates both parties to fulfill their end of the bargain. A *swap* is an agreement between two parties to exchange streams of cash flows over time. For instance, a currency swap might involve one company paying British pounds to another in exchange for Japanese yen. We discuss other types of derivatives in more detail in Chapter 21.

[4.] Employee stock options, which typically give workers the right to buy stock at a fixed price for up to 10 years, are an important exception to this rule. Some publicly traded options have long expiration dates, too, such as the Long-term Equity AnticiPation Securities (LEAPS) introduced by the American Stock Exchange in 1990.

International Derivatives Trading

Since options began trading in the United States in 1973, the growth in options (and other derivatives) trading has been remarkable, and not only in the United States. In 1978, call options on just 10 stocks began trading on the London Traded Options Market, and that same year the European Options Exchange opened in Amsterdam. Today, equity-linked derivatives such as stock options, stock index options, and index futures contracts trade in roughly 30 countries, including most of the largest economies of North America, Europe, and Asia. Even Brazil, which formed its Bolsa de Mercadorias & Futuros exchange in 1985, now ranks among the world's top-10 equity derivative markets in terms of annual trading volume. Other nations with derivative markets

ranking in the top 10 include the United States, the United Kingdom, Germany, and France.

In many of these markets, trading in equity derivatives exceeds the volume of trading in the underlying stocks. The figure below shows the volume of trading in equity options and equity futures contracts, each relative to trading in stocks, in 13 countries. Using the combined trading volume of options and futures contracts, we see that trading in derivatives is greater than trading in the underlying shares in every country except Canada and Sweden.

Source: Jack C. Francis, William W. Toy, and J. Gregg Whittaker (eds.), *Handbook of Equity Derivatives,* rev. ed. (New York: John Wiley & Sons, 2000).

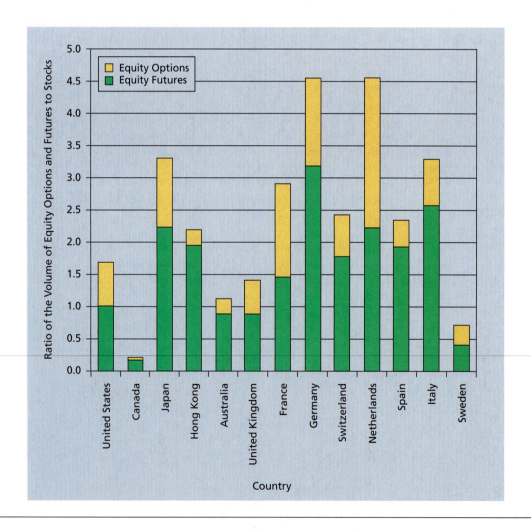

holders the right to purchase stock at a fixed price on or before its expiration date, whereas a **European call option** grants that right only on the expiration date. If we compare the prices of two options that are identical in every respect except that one is American and one is European, the price of the American option should be at least as high as the European option because of the American option's greater flexibility.

A **put option** grants the right to sell a share of stock at a fixed price on or before a certain date. The right to sell stock at a fixed price becomes more and more valuable as the price of the underlying stock decreases. Thus, we have the most basic distinction between put and call options—put options rise in value as the underlying stock price goes down, and call options increase in value as the underlying stock price goes up. Just like call options, put options specify an exercise price at which investors can sell the underlying stock, and they also specify an expiration date at which the right to sell vanishes. Also, put options come in American and European varieties, just as call options do.

The most distinctive feature of options, both puts and calls, can be deduced from the term "option." Investors who own calls and puts have the right to buy or sell shares, but they are not obligated to do so. This feature creates an asymmetry in option payoffs, and that asymmetry is central to understanding how to use options effectively and how to price them, as we will soon see.

An important feature distinguishing calls and puts from other securities, such as stocks and bonds, is that options are not necessarily issued by firms.[5] Rather, an option is a contract between two parties, neither of whom has to have any connection to the company whose stock serves as the underlying asset for the contract. For example, suppose that Tony and Oscar, neither of whom works for General Electric, decide to enter into an options contract. Tony agrees to pay Oscar $5 for the right to purchase one share of General Electric stock for $50 at any time during the next month. As the option buyer, Tony has a **long position** in a call option. He can decide at any point whether he wants to **exercise the option** or not. If he chooses to exercise his option, he will pay Oscar $50 and Oscar will deliver one share of GE stock to Tony. Naturally, Tony will choose to exercise the option only if GE stock is worth more than $50. If GE stock is worth less than $50, Tony will let the option expire worthless and will lose his $5 investment.

On the other side of this transaction, Oscar, as the seller of the option, has a **short position** in a call option.[6] If Tony decides to exercise his option, Oscar's *obligation* is to follow through on his promise to deliver one share of GE for $50. If Oscar does not already own a share of GE stock, he can buy one in the market. Why would Oscar agree to this arrangement? Because he receives the **option premium,** the $5 payment Tony made at the beginning of their agreement. If GE's stock rises above $50, Oscar will lose part or all of the option premium because he must sell Tony an asset for less than it is worth. On the other hand, if GE's stock price does not rise above $50, then Tony will not attempt to buy the asset, and Oscar can keep the $5 option premium.

Options trades do not usually occur in face-to-face transactions between two parties. Instead, options trade either on an **exchange,** such as the Chicago Board Options Exchange (CBOE) in the United States, or on the **over-the-counter market.** Exchanges list options on a limited number of stocks, with a limited set of exercise prices and expiration dates. By limiting the number and variety of listed options, the exchange

---

[5.] This is not to say that firms cannot issue options if they want to. Firms do issue options to employees, and they may also sell options as part of their risk-management activities.

[6.] We may also say that Oscar **writes an option** when he sells the option to Tony.

Table 18.1
Prices of Options on
Intel Stock

Company	Expiration	Strike	Call	Put	
Intel	April	27.5	3.00	0.25	Out-of-the-money puts
30.05	May	27.5	3.50	0.65	In-the-money calls
30.05	July	27.5	4.60	1.50	
30.05	April	30	1.20	0.90	At-the-money puts
30.05	May	30	1.80	1.50	At-the-money calls
30.05	July	30	2.80	2.50	
30.05	April	32.5	0.25	2.60	
30.05	May	32.5	0.75	3.00	
30.05	July	32.5	1.65	3.70	In-the-money puts
30.05	April	35	0.10	4.70	Out-of-the-money calls
30.05	May	35	0.30	4.80	
30.05	July	35	0.90	5.40	

Note: Option quotes retrieved from http://www.cboe.com on April 5, 2002.

expects greater liquidity in the options contracts that are available for trading. Furthermore, an options exchange may serve as a guarantor, fulfilling the terms of an options contract if one party defaults. In contrast, over-the-counter (OTC) options come in a seemingly infinite variety. They are less liquid than exchange-traded options, and traders of OTC options face **counterparty risk,** the risk that the counterparty on specific trade will default on its obligation.

Most investors who trade options never exercise them. An investor who holds an option and wants to convert that holding into cash can do so in several ways. First, one investor can simply sell the option to another investor as long as there is some time remaining before expiration. Second, an investor can receive a **cash settlement** for the option. To illustrate this idea, go back to Tony's call option to buy GE stock for $50. Suppose that the price of GE is $60 per share when the option expires. Rather than have Tony pay Oscar $50 in exchange for one share of GE, Oscar might agree to simply pay Tony $10, the difference between the market price of GE and the option's strike price. Settling in cash eliminates the need for Oscar to buy a share of GE to give to Tony, and the need for Tony to sell that share if he wants to convert his profit into cash. Avoiding these unnecessary trades saves transactions costs.

Table 18.1 shows a set of Intel Corp. (ticker symbol, INTC) option-price quotations taken from the Chicago Board Options Exchange website on April 5, 2002.[7] The first column indicates that the options being quoted are on Intel common stock. The closing price of Intel on the day that these option prices were obtained was $30.05. The second column illustrates the range of expiration dates available for Intel options. The prices illustrated in the table are for options expiring either in April, May, or July. The third column shows the range of option strike prices available, from $27.50 to $35. The fourth and fifth columns give the most recent trading price for calls and puts.[8] For instance, an investor who wanted to buy a call option on Intel

[7.] This table shows only a handful of the options contracts available on Intel stock. We have also chosen to exclude from the table the daily trading volume figures that are usually contained in option-price quotations.

[8.] Two minor institutional details are worth mentioning here. At the CBOE, options expire on the third Saturday of the month. The third Saturday of April in 2002 was April 20, so the April options appearing in this table were set to expire in 15 days. Second, an options contract grants the right to buy or sell 100 shares of the underlying stock, even though the price quotes in the table are on a "per-share" or "per-option" basis. That is, the call price of $3.50 for the May option with a $27.50 strike means that for $350 an investor can purchase the right to buy 100 shares of Intel at $27.50 per

stock, with a strike price of $27.50 and an expiration date in May, would pay $3.50. For a May put with the same strike price, an investor would pay just $0.65.

Options traders say that a call option is **in the money** if the option's strike price is less than the current stock price. For puts, an option is in the money if the strike price exceeds the stock price. Using these definitions, we can say that the call options in the upper three rows of Table 18.1 and the put options in the lower six rows are in the money. Similarly, options traders say that a call option is **out of the money** when the strike price exceeds the current stock price, and puts are out of the money when the strike price falls short of the stock price. Finally, an option is **at the money** when the stock price and the strike price are equal. In Table 18.1, the Intel options with a strike price of $30 are essentially at the money because the stock price is $30.05.

Take one more look at the May call option with a strike price of $27.50. If an investor who owned this option exercised it, he or she could buy Intel stock for $27.50 and resell it at the market price of $30.05, a difference of $2.55. But the current price of this option is $3.50, almost $1 more than the value the investor would obtain by exercising it. In this example, $2.55 is the option's **intrinsic value**.[9] You can think of intrinsic value as measuring the profit an investor makes from exercising the option (ignoring transactions costs as well as the option premium). If an option is out of the money, its intrinsic value is zero. The difference between an option's intrinsic value and its market price, $0.95 for the May call, is the option's **time value**. At the expiration date, the time value equals zero.

Suppose that you purchase the May call with a $30 strike price for $1.80. Suppose also that on the option's expiration date, the price of Intel stock has increased from its current level, $30.05, to $35. That's an increase of 16.6 percent. What would the option be worth at that time? Because the option holder can buy Intel stock at $30 and then immediately resell it for $35, the option should be worth about $5. If the option sells for $5, that's a percentage increase of 178 percent from the $1.80 purchase price! Similarly, if Intel's stock price is just $29 when the option expires, then the option will be worthless. If you purchased the call for $1.80, your return on that investment would be −100 percent, even though Intel's stock fell just $1.05, or −3.5 percent from the date of your purchase.

This example illustrates what may be the most important fact to know about options. *When the price of a stock moves, the dollar change of the stock is generally more than the dollar change of the option price, but the percentage change in the option price is much greater than the percentage change in the stock price.* We have heard students argue that buying a call option is less risky than buying the underlying share because the maximum dollar loss that an investor can experience is much less on the option. That's true only if we compare the $30.05 investment required to buy one share of Intel to the $1.80 required to buy one May Intel call. It is accurate to say that the call investor can lose at most $1.80, while an investor in Intel stock might lose $30.05. But there are two problems with this comparison. First, the likelihood that Intel will go bankrupt and its stock will fall to $0 between April and May is negligible. The likelihood that Intel's stock might dip below $30, resulting in a $0 value for the call option, is much greater. Second, it is better to compare an equal dollar investment in Intel stock and Intel calls rather than compare one stock to one call.

---

share. All the examples in this chapter are constructed as if an investor can trade one option to buy or sell one share. We make that assumption just to keep the numbers simple, but it does not affect any of the main lessons of the chapter.

[9] The intrinsic value of each of the three call options with a strike price of $30 is $0.05. For put options, the intrinsic value equals either $X - S$ or $0, whichever is greater. For example, the intrinsic value of each of the three put options with a strike price of $35 is $4.95 ($35 − $30.05).

An investment of $30.05 would purchase almost 17 Intel call options. Which position do you think is riskier? One share of stock or 17 call options?

1. Explain the difference between the stock price, the *exercise price,* and the *option premium.* Which of these are market prices determined by the forces of supply and demand?

2. Explain the difference between a *long position* and a *short position.* With respect to call options, what is the maximum gain and loss possible for an investor who holds the long position? What is the maximum gain and loss for the investor on the short side of the transaction?

3. Suppose that an investor holds a call option on Nestlé stock. If the investor decides to exercise the option, what will happen to the total shares of common stock outstanding for Nestle?

4. Which of the following would increase the value of a put option: an increase in the stock price, an increase in the strike price, or a lengthening of the expiration period?

18.2 OPTION PAYOFF DIAGRAMS

So far, our discussion of options has been mostly descriptive. Now we turn to the problem of determining an option's market price. Valuing an option is an extraordinarily difficult problem, so difficult in fact that the economists who solved the problem won a Nobel Prize for their efforts. In earlier chapters where we studied the pricing of bonds and stocks, we began by describing their cash flows. We will do the same here, focusing initially on the relatively simple problem of outlining cash flows of options on the expiration date. Eventually, that will help us understand the intuition behind complex option-pricing models.

CALL OPTION PAYOFFS

We define an option's **payoff** as the price an investor would be willing to pay for the option the instant before it expires.[10] An option's payoff is distinct from its price, or premium, because the payoff refers only to the price of the option at a particular instant in time, the expiration date. **Payoff diagrams** are graphs that illustrate an option's payoff as a function of the underlying stock price. They are extremely useful tools for understanding how options behave and how they can be combined to form portfolios with fascinating properties.

Suppose that an investor purchases a call option with a strike price of $75 and an expiration date three months in the future. To acquire this option, the investor pays a premium of $8. When the option expires, what will it be worth? If the underlying stock price is less than $75 on the expiration date, the option will be worthless. No investor would pay anything for the right to buy this stock for $75 when the investor could easily buy it for less in the market. What if the stock price equals $76 on the expiration date? In that case, owning the right to buy the stock at $75 is worth $1, the difference between the stock's market price and the option's exercise price. Ignor-

---

[10.] Alternatively, we could define the payoff as the value an investor would receive, ignoring transactions costs, if he or she exercised the option when it expired. If it did not make sense to exercise the option when it expired, the payoff would be zero.

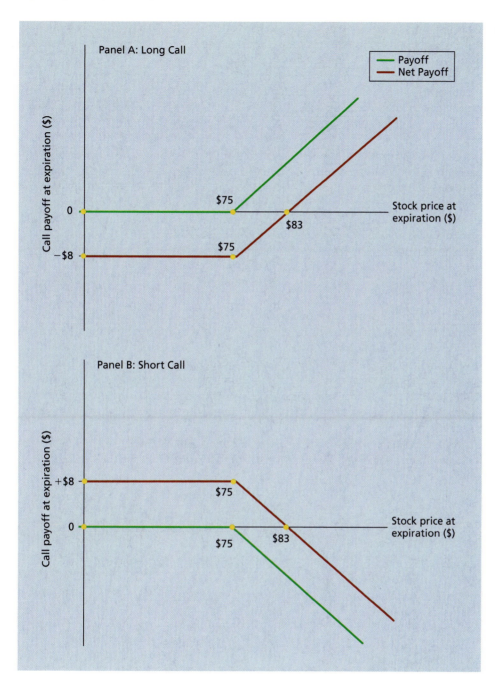

Figure 18.1
Payoff of Call Option at
Expiration

ing transactions costs, an investor who owns the option can buy the stock for $75 and immediately sell it in the market for $76, earning a $1 payoff. In general, the payoff of this option will equal the greater of (1) $0 if the stock price is less than $75 at expiration or (2) the difference between the stock price and $75 if the stock price is more than $75 at expiration. The green line in Panel A of Figure 18.1 shows a payoff diagram for the call option buyer, or the long position. This picture is a classic in finance known as the **hockey-stick diagram.** It shows that the option will at worst be worth $0, and at best, the option's value is unlimited. The red line in the figure represents the investor's **net payoff.** The net-payoff line appears $8 lower than the solid line, reflecting the $8 premium the investor paid to acquire the option. On a net basis, the holder of the call option makes a profit when the price of the stock exceeds $83.[11]

Panel B of Figure 18.1 shows the payoffs from the seller's perspective, or the short position. Options are a zero-sum game, meaning that profits on the long position represent losses on the short side, and vice versa. The green line illustrates that the seller's payoff equals $0 when the stock price is below $75, and that it decreases as the stock price rises above $75. The incentive for the seller to engage in this transaction is the $8 premium. If the option expires out of the money, the seller earns an $8 profit. If the option expires in the money, the seller may realize a net profit or a net loss, depending on how high the stock price is at that time. Whereas the call option buyer enjoys the potential for unlimited gains, the option seller faces exposure to the risk of unlimited losses. Rationally, if $8 is sufficient to induce someone to sell this option and thereby face the potential of huge losses, it must be the case that the seller perceives the probability of a large loss to be relatively low.

PUT OPTION PAYOFFS

Figure 18.2 shows payoffs for put option buyers (long) and sellers (short), again assuming that the strike price of the option is $75 and the option premium equals $8. For an investor holding a put option, the payoff rises as the stock price falls below the option's strike price. However, unlike a call option, a put option has limited potential gains since the price of a stock cannot fall below zero (because the law provides limited liability for a firm's shareholders). The maximum gain on this particular put equals $75 (or $67 on a net basis after subtracting the premium), whereas the maximum loss is, as before, the $8 option premium.

Again, the seller's perspective is just the opposite of the buyer's. The seller earns a maximum net gain of $8 if the option expires worthless because the stock price exceeds $75 on the expiration date, and the seller faces a maximum net loss of $67 if the firm goes bankrupt and its stock becomes worthless.

APPLYING THE MODEL

Jennifer sells a put option on Electro-Lighting Systems Inc. (ELS) stock to Jason. The option's strike price is $65, and it expires in one month. Jason pays Jennifer a premium of $5 for the option. One month later, ELS stock sells for $45 per share. Jason purchases a share of ELS in the open market for $45 and immediately exercises his option to sell it to Jennifer for $65 (or Jennifer and Jason might agree to settle their contract by having Jennifer pay Jason $20). The payoff on Jason's option is $20, or $15 on a net basis. Jennifer loses $20 on the deal, or just $15 taking into account the $5 premium she received up front.

We must now clarify an important point. Thus far, all our discussions about options payoffs have assumed that each option buyer or seller had what traders refer to as a **naked option position.** A naked call option, for example, occurs when an inves-

---

[11.] Notice that when the stock price is above $75 but below $83, it still makes sense for the investor to exercise the option, or to sell it, because it reduces the investor's losses. For example, if the stock price at expiration equals $80, the option payoff is $5, reducing the net loss to -3. The careful reader will notice that we seem to be making a major error by comparing the $8 premium paid up front to the payoff received three months later. At this point, ignoring the time value of money in the graphs is relatively harmless, but rest assured that we will take that into account later when we determine the price of an option.

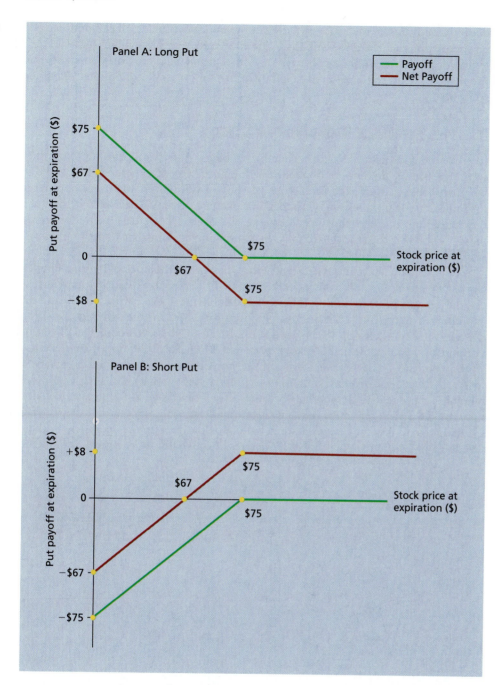

Figure 18.2
Payoff of a Put Option at
Expiration

tor buys or sells an option on a stock without already owning the underlying stock. Similarly, when a trader buys or sells a put option without owning the underlying stock, the trader creates a naked put option. Buying or selling naked options is an act of pure speculation. Investors who buy naked calls believe that the stock price will rise. Investors who sell naked calls believe the opposite. Similarly, buyers of naked puts expect the stock price to fall, and sellers take the opposite view.

But many options trades do not involve this kind of speculation. Investors who own a particular stock may purchase a put option on that stock, not because they expect the stock price to decline, but because they want protection in the event that it does. Executives who own shares of their companies' stock may sell call options, not on speculation that the price will not rise, but because they are willing to give up potential profits on their shares in exchange for current income. To understand this proposition, we need to examine payoff diagrams for portfolios of options and other securities.

PAYOFFS FOR PORTFOLIOS OF OPTIONS AND OTHER SECURITIES

Experienced options traders know that by combining different types of options, they can construct a wide range of portfolios with unusual payoff structures. Think about what happens if an investor simultaneously buys a call option and a put option on the same underlying stock and with the same exercise price. We have seen before that the call option pays off handsomely if the stock price rises, whereas the put option is most profitable if the stock price falls. By combining both into one portfolio, an investor has a position that can make money whether the stock price rises or falls.

Suppose that Cybil cannot decide whether she expects the stock of Internet Phones Corp. (IPC) to rise or fall from its current value of $30. Cybil decides to purchase a call option and a put option on IPC stock, both having a strike price of $30 and an expiration date of April 20. She pays premiums of $4.50 for the call and $3.50 for the put, for a total cost of $8. Figure 18.3 illustrates Cybil's position. The payoff of her portfolio equals $0 if IPC's stock price is $30 on April 20, and if that occurs, Cybil experiences a net loss of $8. But if the stock price is higher or lower than $30 on April 20, at least one of Cybil's options will be in the money. On a net basis, Cybil makes a profit if IPC stock falls below $22 or rises above $38, but she does not have to take a view on which outcome is more likely.

In this example, Cybil is speculating, but not on the direction of IPC stock. Rather, Cybil's gamble is on the volatility of IPC shares. If the shares move a great deal, either

Figure 18.3
Payoff of a Call and a Put

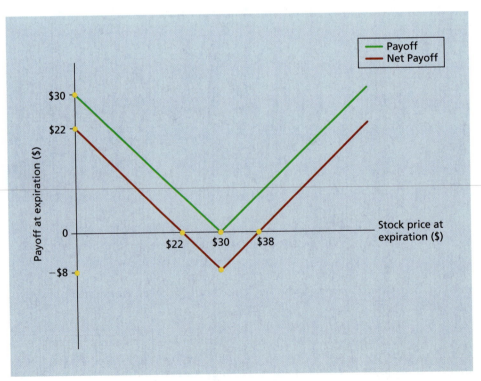

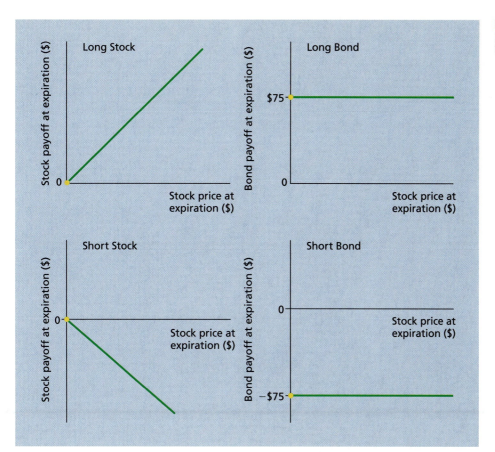

Figure 18.4
Payoff Diagrams for Stocks and Bonds

up or down, she makes a net profit. If the shares have not moved much by April 20, she experiences a net loss. Options traders refer to this type of position as a **long straddle,** a portfolio consisting of long positions in calls and puts on the same stock with the same strike price and expiration date. Naturally, creating a **short straddle** is possible, too. If Cybil believed that IPC stock would not move far from its current value, she could simultaneously sell a put and a call option on IPC stock with a strike price of $30. She would receive $8 in option premiums from this trade, and if IPC stock were priced at $30 on April 20, both of the options she sold would expire worthless. On the other hand, if IPC stock moved up or down from $30, one of the options would be exercised, reducing Cybil's profits from the options sale.

Now let's look at what happens when investors form portfolios by combining options with other securities such as stocks and bonds. To begin, examine Figure 18.4, which displays payoff diagrams for a long position in common stocks and bonds.[12] Remember, a payoff diagram shows the total value of a security (in this case, one share of common stock or one bond) on a specific future date on the y-axis, and the value of a share of stock on that same date on the x-axis. In Figure 18.4, the payoff diagram from holding a share of stock is simply a 45-degree line emanating from the origin because both axes of the graph are plotting the same thing—the value of the stock on a future date.[13]

---

12. In Figure 18.4, we do not plot the net payoff, meaning that the diagram ignores the initial cost of buying stocks or bonds, or the revenue obtained from shorting them.

13. Figure 18.4 also shows the payoff diagram for a short position in stock, and as always, it is just the opposite of the long-payoff diagram. When investors *short-sell* a stock, they borrow the share from another investor, promising to return the

Figure 18.5
Payoff Diagram for
Covered Call Strategy

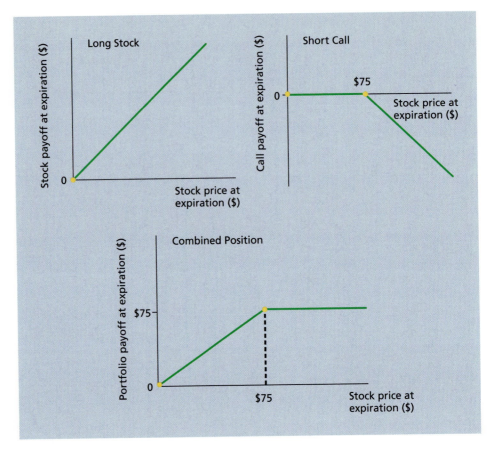

The payoff diagram for the bond requires a little more explanation. The type of bond we have in mind in this example is very special. It is a risk-free, zero-coupon bond with a face value of $75. The bond matures at precisely the same time as the put and call options expire. The payoff for an investor who purchases this bond is simply $75, no matter what the price of the stock underlying the put and call options turns out to be. Thus, the diagram shows a horizontal line at $75 for the long bond's payoff.[14] Again the payoff from shorting the bond can be seen to be the opposite of the long-bond payoff diagram.

Figure 18.5 illustrates **writing covered calls,** a common trading strategy that mixes stock and call options. In this strategy, an investor who owns a share of stock sells a call option on that stock. By selling the call, the investor receives the option premium immediately. However, the trade-off is that if the stock price rises, the holder of the call option will exercise the right to purchase it at the strike price, and the investor will lose the opportunity to benefit from the appreciation in the stock. For example, suppose that Michael owns a share of IBM stock. Michael sells a call option on his share to Kathryn for $6. The option has a strike price of $75. As long as the stock price does not rise above $75, Michael will keep the $6 option premium and will re-

---

share at a future date. Short-selling therefore creates a liability. The magnitude of that liability is just the price of the stock that the short-seller must return on a future date.

[14.] Is it really possible to buy a risk-free bond with a face value of $75? Perhaps not, but an investor could buy 75 Treasury bills, each with a face value of $1,000, resulting in a risk-free bond portfolio with a face value of $75,000. The assumption that investors can buy risk-free bonds with any face value is just a simplification to keep the numbers in our examples manageable.

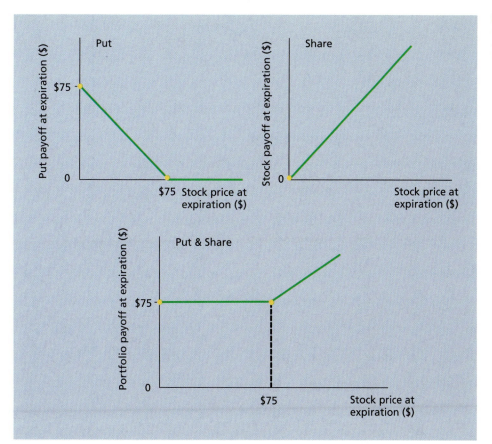

Figure 18.6
Payoff of a Put Option
and a Share of Stock—a
Protective Put

tain ownership of his IBM share. If the price rises above $75, however, Kathryn will call the share away from Michael. He will get $75 in cash from Kathryn, but he will not benefit from appreciation beyond that point.

Consider a portfolio consisting of one share of stock and one put option on that share with a strike price of $75. If, on the expiration date of the option, the stock price equals $75, the put option will be worthless. Therefore, the portfolio's total value will be $75. Notice that the total value of this portfolio cannot drop below $75, even if the stock price does. Imagine that the stock price falls to $50. At that point, the put option's payoff is $25, leaving the combined portfolio value at $75. Simply stated, the put option provides a kind of portfolio insurance, for it guarantees that the share of stock can be sold for at least that amount. However, if the price of the stock rises, the portfolio value will rise right along with it. Though the put option will be worthless, any increase in the stock price beyond $75 increases the portfolio's value as well, as shown in Figure 18.6. This strategy is known as a **protective put.**

Next, evaluate the payoffs of a portfolio consisting of one risk-free, zero-coupon bond with a face value of $75 and one call option with an exercise price of $75. As Figure 18.7 shows, the bond guarantees that an investor holding this portfolio will have a payoff of at least $75. The payoff can be more if the stock price increases above $75, causing the call value to increase.

A careful look at Figures 18.6 and 18.7 reveals a surprising fact. The payoffs of the portfolio containing one share of stock and one put option are exactly the same as the payoffs of the portfolio containing one bond and one call option. Both portfolios offer a minimum return of $75 with considerable upside potential should the

Smart Concepts
See the concept explained step-by-step at
SMARTFinance

Figure 18.7
Payoff of a Call Option
and a Zero-Coupon Bond

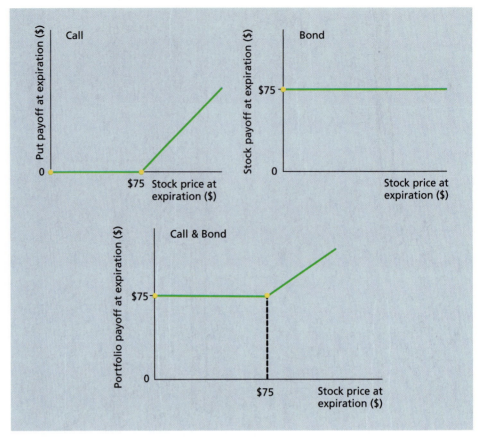

Figure 18.7
Payoff of a Call Option
and a Zero-Coupon Bond

underlying stock price increase. If both of these portfolios offer investors the same cash flows when the options expire, then both portfolios must have the same value today. This **put-call parity** is one of the most fundamental results in option-pricing theory. Put-call parity holds only under a rather restrictive set of assumptions, but it nevertheless has many important practical applications.

Put-Call Parity

Using Put-Call Parity to Find Arbitrage Opportunities

Figures 18.6 and 18.7 illustrate that a portfolio of a stock and a put option offers exactly the same future cash flows as a portfolio of a bond and a call option. To be absolutely certain that the cash flows of these portfolios will be identical at the options' expiration date, the following conditions must be met:

1. The call and put options must be on the same underlying stock.
2. The call and put options must have the same exercise price.
3. The call and put options must share the same expiration date.
4. The underlying stock must not pay a dividend during the life of the options.
5. The call and put options must be European options.
6. The bond must be a risk-free, zero-coupon bond with a face value equal to the strike price of the options and with a maturity date identical to the options' expiration date.

The only points on this list not already mentioned are 4 and 5. For put-call parity to hold, both the call and put options must be European options. Recall that American options can be exercised at any time up to and including the expiration date. In the two portfolios considered in Figures 18.6 and 18.7, if either the call or the put is exercised early, there will be a discrepancy on the expiration date between the portfolios' cash flows. If the cash flows do not match exactly, then put-call parity will not hold. Similarly, if the underlying stock pays a dividend, the portfolio consisting of the stock plus the put option will receive the dividend, but the portfolio containing the call option and the bond will not. Therefore, the cash flows of the two portfolios will not match exactly, and parity will not hold.

If all these conditions are met, we can make the following strong claim. The price of one share of stock, plus the price of one put option on that stock with a strike price of X, must equal the sum of the prices of a call option on the stock (also having a strike price of X) and a risk-free bond with a face value of X. The following is a simple algebraic expression of this idea:

$$S + P = B + C$$

$$S + P = PV(X) + C \qquad \text{(Eq. 18.1)}$$

In these equations, S stands for the current stock price; P and C represent the current premiums on the put and call options, respectively; and B equals the current price of the risk-free, zero-coupon bond. In the second equation, we substitute $PV(\$X)$ for B simply to indicate that if the bond's face value is $\$X$, then the price of that bond will be the present value of $\$X$, discounted at the risk-free rate.

If you blinked, you may have missed the significant intellectual leap we just took. Up to now, all our discussions about options have focused on their payoffs. Remember, we defined an option's payoff as the price someone would pay for it just before it expired. Determining the market value of an option just before it expires is rather trivial, but in Equation 18.1 we are talking about option prices at *any moment in time*, not just on the expiration date. Because the portfolios on the right- and left-hand sides of Equation 18.1 offer investors identical future cash flows, they must have identical market values on the expiration date, one day before expiration, one week before expiration, and at any other moment in time. One implication of this fact is that investors who know the market prices of any three of the securities listed in Equation 18.1 can determine what the market price of the fourth security must be to prevent arbitrage opportunities.

APPLYING THE MODEL

Mototronics Inc. stock currently sells for $28 per share. Put and call options on Mototronics shares are available with a strike price of $30 and an expiration date of one year. The price of the Mototronics call option is $6, and the risk-free rate of interest is 5 percent. What is the appropriate price for the Mototronics put option? Using Equation 18.1 and plugging in the values we know, we can derive a price for the put option:

$$S + P = PV(X) + C$$

$$\$28 + P = \frac{\$30}{(1.05)^1} + \$6$$

$$P = \$6.57$$

How can we be sure that $6.57 is the right price for the put option? Because at any other price, investors would have an arbitrage opportunity, a chance to earn unlimited profits without taking any risk. To see how this would work, suppose that the actual market price of the Mototronics put option is $7 rather than $6.57. At that price, the put option is overvalued, so smart investors will sell it. But doing nothing more than selling the put option is not arbitrage. Arbitrage means simultaneously buying and selling identical assets at different prices to earn a risk-free profit. Therefore, if the first step in the arbitrage is to sell the put for $7, then traders must also buy an identical asset at a lower price. What kind of asset is identical to a put option? Rearranging the put-call parity equation just a little holds the answer:

$$S + P = PV(X) + C$$
$$P = PV(X) + C - S$$

By now, we are aware that put-call parity says that a portfolio containing a share of stock and a put is identical to one containing a bond and a call option. The second equation just shown makes a similar claim. It says that a put option offers cash flows that are identical to those produced by a portfolio containing a bond, a call option, and a short position in the underlying stock.[15] In options lingo, we say that traders can create a **synthetic put option** by purchasing a bond and a call option while simultaneously short-selling the stock.

To exploit the arbitrage opportunity, investors will sell the actual put option for $7. Next, to offset the risk of the first trade, arbitrageurs will purchase a bond and a call option and will short-sell the stock. The immediate consequences of these trades are outlined as follows:

Cash Inflows			Cash Outflows		
Sell put	+$7		Buy bond	$\dfrac{-\$30}{(1.05)^1} = -\$28.57$	
Sell stock	+$28		Buy call	-$6	

Net cash flow = $28 + $7 − $28.57 − $6 = +$0.43

Traders following this strategy pocket $0.43 each time they execute this sequence of trades. Notice that this value equals the difference between the put option's theoretically correct price, $6.57, and its actual price of $7. What remains to be shown is that the profits from this strategy are truly risk-free. Figure 18.8 and Table 18.2 show just that. First, look at the figure. The upper part of the figure shows the payoff from taking a short position in the put option. The lower part shows that by combining a long bond, a long call, and a short stock, an investor creates a portfolio with a payoff identical to a that of a long put option. The short put at the top of the figure and the synthetic long put at the bottom cancel each other out, resulting in a risk-free portfolio.

In the first column of Table 18.2, we list a range of prices that Mototronics stock might reach in one year when these options are expiring. In the next four columns, we list the values of each of the individual positions that arbitrageurs create by following our strategy, given the stock price in the first column. Take a look at the first row of the table where we consider what happens if the value of Mototronics stock in one year is $10. The first trade in our arbitrage strategy was to sell a put option with

---

[15.] In put-call parity math, a negative sign means "sell" rather than "buy." Therefore, the terms on the right side of the equation, $PV(X) + C - S$, mean "buy a bond, buy a call, and sell (or sell short) the stock."

Figure 18.8
Put-Call Parity Arbitrage

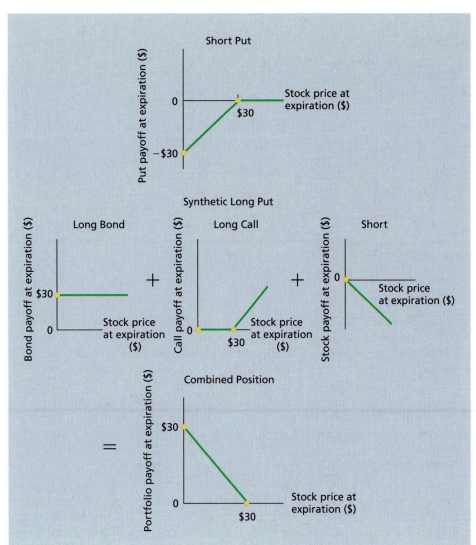

a $30 exercise price. If Mototronics stock is worth $10, then the investor to whom the put option was sold will exercise it, resulting in a loss to the arbitrageur of $20. The second part of the arbitrage strategy was buying a risk-free bond with a face value of $30. Clearly, the value of this holding will be $30 in one year. The third part of the trade was buying a call option with an exercise price of $30. With Mototronics stock at $10, this call will be worthless. The final part of the trade was to short-sell Mototronics stock. At the end of the year, an arbitrageur must return that share to its owner, and doing so will cost the trader $10, the current market price of the stock. Adding all this together, we have the following:

Put option	−$20
Bond	+$30
Call option	$ 0
Short stock	−$10
Total value	$ 0

Table 18.2
Using Arbitrage to Exploit a Mispriced Put

If Mototronics Stock Price Is ($)	Value of (short) Actual Put Is	Value of Long Bond Is	Value of Long Call Is	Value of Short Stock Is	Total Portfolio Value ($)
		Value of Synthetic Put (all values in $)			
10	−20	30	0	−10	−20 + 30 + 0 − 10 = 0
15	−15	30	0	−15	−15 + 30 + 0 − 15 = 0
20	−10	30	0	−20	−10 + 30 + 0 − 20 = 0
25	−5	30	0	−25	−5 + 30 + 0 − 25 = 0
30	0	30	0	−30	0 + 30 + 0 − 30 = 0
35	0	30	5	−35	0 + 30 + 5 − 35 = 0
40	0	30	10	−40	0 + 30 + 10 − 40 = 0

Notes: No matter what value Mototronics stock takes, the value of the actual put that the arbitrageur sold is precisely offset by the value of the synthetic put that the arbitrageur purchased. The arbitrage portfolio consists of short positions in the put option and the stock, and long positions in the bond and the call. The put and call options have an exercise price of $30, and $30 is the bond's face value.

In the last column of Table 18.2, we add up the values of these positions and show that no matter what the price of Mototronics stock turns out to be in one year, the portfolio of securities held by arbitrageurs will be worthless. Holding a portfolio of worthless securities may not seem like much of an investment strategy until you consider that this strategy generated a net cash inflow up front. Arbitrageurs could repeat this strategy over and over again, reaping unlimited profits as long as the prices of the securities they were trading did not change. Of course, the prices will change, quickly eliminating the arbitrage profit.

Corporate Finance Applications of Put-Call Parity

Put-call parity gives us two types of useful information. First, it tells us how the prices of puts, calls, stocks, and bonds should be interrelated. When the prices of these securities become misaligned, an arbitrage opportunity exists. Second, put-call parity tells us how to create synthetic positions. That is, put-call parity shows that it is possible to use combinations of three of the securities to mimic the payoffs of the fourth. In the previous section, we observed that buying a bond and a call option while shorting the underlying stock provided exactly the same payoffs as buying a put option. We can derive the synthetic equivalent of any particular security simply by rearranging the terms in the put-call parity equation. Table 18.3 lists several synthetic positions of interest.

Applications of put-call parity are numerous. Suppose Serex Corporation owns a block of shares of the firm, Meggit Inc. Serex acquired the shares as part of a strategic alliance with Meggit that will end in six months. Serex wants to liquidate these shares to raise money for a new investment. However, due to its ongoing relationship with Meggit, Serex is reluctant to sell the shares immediately, even though Serex managers believe that the firm's investment opportunity may vanish if the company does not act on it quickly. Managers also worry that if the price of Meggit stock falls in the next six months, selling the stock at that time may not raise enough capital, even if the investment opportunity is still available.

Serex has an alternative to an outright sale of its Meggit shares on the open market. Serex can sell the shares synthetically as long as put and call options on Meggit

Table 18.3
Using Put-Call Parity to
Create Synthetic Positions

$S + P = PV(X) + C$	
Actual Position	**Equivalent Synthetic Position**
Long stock (S)	Long bond, long call, short put: $PV(X) + C - P$
Short stock ($-S$)	Short bond, short call, long put: $P - PV(X) - C$
Long call (C)	Long stock, long put, short bond: $S + P - PV(X)$
Long bond $PV(X)$	Long stock, long put, short call: $S + P - C$
Short Put ($-P$)	Long stock, short bond, short call: $S - PV(X) - C$

stock are available. A synthetic sale accomplishes the firm's two main goals of elim-inating exposure to the risk of a decline in the price of the stock and getting cash im-mediately to reinvest elsewhere. Rearrange the put-call parity equation to find the synthetic equivalent of selling stock:

$$S + P = PV(X) + C$$

$$-S = P - PV(X) - C$$

Rather than selling the stock ($-S$), Serex can purchase put options (P), take out a loan ($-PV(X)$), and sell call options ($-C$). By purchasing put options on Meggit shares, Serex obtains protection against the risk of a decline in the stock price (re-member the protective put). By borrowing money, Serex obtains cash today to rein-vest elsewhere. By selling call options, Serex earns premium income that partially off-sets the cost of the puts, but the company also gives up any stock price appreciation (remember the covered call strategy).

Let's put some numbers in this example. Suppose the current market price of Meggit stock is $80. At-the-money call and put options sell for $10.33 and $8, re-spectively. The risk-free rate of interest is 6 percent per year, or just 3 percent per six months. By selling its shares synthetically, Serex will generate an immediate cash inflow of $80 per share:

Buy put $-\$8$ Borrow $PV(\$80) = \dfrac{\$80}{(1.03)^1} = \$77.67$ Sell call $+\$10.33$

Of course this is precisely the same cash inflow Serex would receive from selling one Meggit share. Six months later, if Meggit's stock price has risen above $80, the Meggit shares that Serex owns will be called away at a price of $80. If the stock price has fallen below $80, the put option will enable Serex to sell the shares for $80. Ei-ther way, Serex will part with its shares in return for $80 in cash, with which Serex will repay its loan.

This strategy may be attractive whenever a company wants to divest its holdings of another firm. The motivation to sell synthetically may come from the tax code (i.e., the tax liability of a synthetic sell might be lower than the liability of selling the shares immediately) or from some other barrier such as illiq-uidity of the stock or a minimum required holding period. In-dividual and institutional investors can also use this strategy to sell investments synthetically.

SMART ETHICS VIDEO
John Eck, President of Broadcast
and Network Operations, NBC
"That allowed us to create some doubt around the transaction and allowed us not to have to book the gain up front but to book it as the cash came in."

See the entire interview at **SMARTFinance**

5. What would happen if an investor combined the *protective put* and *covered call* strategies by simultaneously buying a put option with a strike price of $50 and selling a call option with a strike price of $50? You can assume that the investor already owns the underlying stock.

6. Is selling a call the same as buying a put? Explain why or why not.

7. A major corporation is involved in high-profile antitrust litigation with the government. The firm's stock price is somewhat depressed due to the uncertainty of this case. If the company wins, investors expect its stock price to shoot up. If it loses, the stock price will decline even more than it already has. If investors expect a resolution to the case in the near future, what effect do you think it will have on put and call options on the company's stock? (*Hint:* Think about the *long-straddle* investment strategy.)

8. Take another look at the six conditions that must be met for put-call parity to hold. Can you explain why each one of them is necessary?

18.3 QUALITATIVE ANALYSIS OF OPTION PRICING

FACTORS THAT INFLUENCE OPTION VALUES

Before getting into the rather complex quantitative aspects of pricing options, let's see if we can develop some intuition that will help us understand the factors that influence option prices. We begin by taking a closer look at some of the April 5, 2002, price quotations for Intel stock options in Table 18.1. Begin by focusing only on the prices of call and put options that have an exercise price of $32.50. Here are the figures from the table.

Intel	Expiration	Strike	Call	Put
$30.05	April	$32.50	$0.25	$2.60
30.05	May	32.50	0.75	3.00
30.05	July	32.50	1.65	3.70

You should notice a striking pattern here. The prices of both calls and puts rise the longer the time before expiration. To understand why, think about the call option that expires in April. Currently, this option is out of the money because it grants the right to purchase Intel stock for $32.50, but investors can buy Intel in the open market at $30.05. Buying the April call option requires an investment of just $0.25. The option is inexpensive because there is relatively little chance that before the option expires in 15 days, Intel's stock price will increase enough to make exercising the option worthwhile. No investor would exercise this option until Intel stock reached at least $32.51, representing an increase of more than 8 percent from its current price. Investors are not willing to pay more than a few pennies for this option because they doubt that Intel stock will rise that much in 15 days.

However, the price of the July option with a strike price of $32.50 is more than six times greater than the price of the April call. The July option expires in about three and a half months, so investors must think that the odds of an 8 percent increase (or more) in Intel stock over that time period are much higher than the odds of seeing the same move by the third Saturday of April. The same pattern holds for puts. The July put option sells for $1.10 more than the April put option because investors recognize that the chance of a significant drop in Intel stock over a 15-day period is much lower than the chance of a large decrease over the next three and a half months. We can generalize all this as follows: *Holding other factors constant, call and put option prices increase as the time to expiration increases.*[16]

Next, let's examine the prices of all the Intel calls and puts that expire in May. Here are the figures from Table 18.1.

Intel	Expiration	Strike	Call	Put
$30.05	May	$27.50	$3.50	$0.65
30.05	May	30.00	1.80	1.50
30.05	May	32.50	0.75	3.00
30.05	May	35.00	0.30	4.80

Once again, a clear pattern emerges. The prices of call options fall as the strike price increases, and the prices of put options rise as the strike price increases. This relationship is quite intuitive. A call option grants the right to buy stock at a fixed price. That right is more valuable the cheaper the price at which the option holder can buy the stock.[17] Conversely, put options grant the right to sell shares at a fixed price. That right is more valuable the higher the price at which investors can sell.

We can see a similar relationship by looking at what happened to the prices of May Intel options on the next trading day, Monday, April 8, 2002, a day on which Intel stock fell slightly from $30.05 to $29.93.

Intel	Expiration	Strike	Call	Put
$29.93	May	$27.50	$2.85	$1.10
29.93	May	30.00	1.60	1.80
29.93	May	32.50	0.70	3.50
29.93	May	35.00	0.15	no trades

Comparing these prices to those of April 5, we see that the prices of all four call options fell with the decline of Intel shares. The prices of three of the four put options rose (the fourth put did not trade on April 8, so no price is available for that day).[18] Combining the lessons of the last few paragraphs, we can say that *call prices decrease and put prices increase when the difference between the underlying stock price and the exercise price* $(S - X)$ *decreases.*

[16.] There are a few exceptions to this rule. Flip back the calendar to December 2002, and imagine that you own a European put option on Enron stock. Enron's stock trades for pennies a share. If the strike price of your put option is $20, then you can make a profit of almost $20 by exercising your option, if you can exercise it immediately. But what if the option's expiration date is several months away? The potential for further declines in Enron stock, given that it already sells for just a few cents, is negligible, but there is some chance that Enron stock might recover. In this case, you would rather have the right to exercise your option right away, so you would pay more for a European option that expires immediately than you would pay for one that expires a few months in the future.

[17.] After a period of very poor stock performance, firms sometimes "reprice" employee stock options. Repricing typically means that the firm reduces the strike prices of outstanding options earned by employees when the stock price was much higher. Critics argue that if firms simply reset option strike prices after poor performance, then options do little to give managers proper incentives. Carter and Lynch (2001) offer evidence that repricing is necessary to realign the incentives of managers and to retain employees in a highly competitive labor market. Chauvin and Shenoy (2001) suggest another way that managers can lower the strike prices of their options. Managers can selectively disclose bad news just before they receive option grants. Because most firms set the strike price of employee stock options equal to the current market price of the company's stock, executives who release negative information just prior to receiving option grants effectively lower the strike prices of those grants. Chauvin and Shenoy find that in a sample of 783 stock option grants to CEOs, stock returns were unusually low in the 10 days before chief executives received their option packages.

[18.] The careful reader may notice that the magnitude of the price change for many of these options is greater than the $0.12 drop in Intel stock. As we will see in Chapter 19, the dollar change in an option's price is generally less than the dollar change in the underlying asset's price, so the large changes in Intel option prices seem anomalous. The explanation for the apparent anomaly is that the CBOE price quotes are taken from the last trade of the day, and the last option trade of the day may occur at a different time than the last trade in Intel stock. For example, notice that the price of the May call with a strike of $27.50 fell $0.65 from the previous day's price, even though Intel stock fell just $0.12. However, this particular option trade occurred at 10:53 A.M. At that time, Intel's stock price was roughly $29.30, a difference of $0.75 from the previous day's close.

Table 18.4
Option Prices for AOL
Time Warner and Check
Point Software

Company	Expiration	Strike	Call	Put
AOL TW	May	20	3.00	0.65
22.42	May	25	0.55	3.40
22.42	May	30	0.05	5.50
Check Point	May	20	4.00	1.00
22.33	May	25	1.10	3.50
22.33	May	30	0.35	8.60

Note: Option quotes retrieved from http://www.cboe.com on April 5, 2002.

Finally, to isolate the most important, and the most subtle, influence on option prices, take a look at a new set of option prices in Table 18.4. The table shows call and put prices for media giant AOL Time Warner (ticker symbol, AOL) and Internet security software producer Check Point Software Technologies (ticker symbol, CHKP). The first column shows that the stock prices of AOL and Check Point are almost equal to each other, with just $0.09 separating them. Intuition might suggest that because the stock prices are nearly equal, the prices of comparable AOL and Check Point options should be about the same as well. To be more precise, because the price of AOL stock exceeds the price of Check Point shares by $0.09, we might expect AOL call options to be a little more valuable and AOL put options to be a little less valuable than comparable Check Point options. But with such a small difference in the prices of the underlying shares, we do not expect significant differences in the option prices.

Table 18.4 reveals a flaw in this intuition. Comparing AOL and Check Point call options having the same expiration date and exercise price, we see that all the Check Point calls sell for more than the AOL calls. The price discrepancy, both in absolute and relative terms, varies with the options' strike prices, but Check Point calls are clearly more valuable than AOL calls. The same is true of Check Point put options. For example, the May Check Point put with a strike price of $30 sells for $3.10 more than the comparable AOL put. That difference cannot be explained by a mere $0.09 difference in the underlying stock prices. What can explain the difference?

Figure 18.9 contains a clue to the answer. The graph displays the daily percentage price change in AOL and Check Point shares over the 60 trading days ending April 5, 2002. A quick glance at the figure shows that Check Point stock was more volatile than AOL stock over this period. Almost all the daily price changes in AOL stock fell inside the ± 5 percent band. Only about once per month did AOL's stock move up or down by more than 5 percent. In contrast, Check Point's shares experienced a percentage change of 5 percent or more on one out of every four days during this period.[19]

Why should Check Point's higher volatility lead to higher call and put option prices? The answer lies in the asymmetry of option payoffs. When a call option expires, its payoff will be zero for a wide range of stock prices. Whether the stock price falls below the option's strike price by $1, $10, or $100, the payoff will be zero. On the other hand, as the stock price rises above the strike price, the option's payoff increases. A similar relationship holds for puts. The value of a put at expiration will be zero if the stock price is greater than the strike price, and whether the stock price is just above the strike price or far above it does not change the payoff. However, the put option will have a larger payoff the lower the stock price falls, once it falls below

---

[19.] It should not be surprising that Check Point's shares display more volatility than AOL's. AOL is a more diversified firm than Check Point, with significant investments in several different industries. AOL is also a very large firm. For the fiscal year ending December 31, 2001, AOL Time Warner reported revenues exceeding $38.2 billion, whereas Check Point's revenues that same year were a relatively paltry $0.5 billion. Larger firms tend to be less volatile than smaller ones.

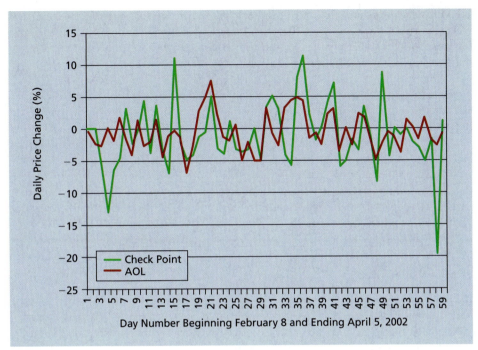

Figure 18.9
Daily Percent Price
Changes for AOL and
Check Point Shares
(60-day period beginning
February 7, 2002, and
ending April 5, 2002)

Note: Only 59 percent changes
are shown because that is the
most that can be obtained from
the 60 observations. The first
day, February 7, 2002, is effectively lost because it represents
day 0.

the strike price. The bottom line is that *call and put option prices increase as the volatility of the underlying stock increases.*

APPLYING THE MODEL

Suppose that you are tracking two stocks, one of which exhibits much more volatility than the other. Call the more volatile stock Extreme Inc. and the less volatile one Steady Corp. At present, shares of both companies sell for about $40. At-the-money call and put options are available on both stocks with an expiration date in three months. Based on the historical volatility of each stock, you estimate a range of prices that you think the shares might attain by the time the options expire. Next to each possible stock price, you write down the option payoff that will occur if the stock actually reaches that price on the expiration date (the strike price is $40 for both options). The following table gives the numbers:

Stock	Potential Prices	Call Payoff	Put Payoff
Extreme Inc.	$15	$ 0	$25
	25	0	15
	35	0	5
	45	5	0
	55	15	0
	65	25	0
Steady Corp.	$30	$ 0	$10
	34	0	6
	38	0	2
	42	2	0
	46	6	0
	50	10	0

The payoffs of calls and puts for both companies are zero exactly half the time. But when the payoffs are not zero, they are much larger for Extreme Inc. than they are for Steady Corp., which makes options on Extreme Inc. shares much more valuable than options on Steady Corp. stock.   ■

Summing up, we now know that option prices increase as time to expiration increases and as the risk of the underlying asset increases. Call option prices decrease the smaller the difference between the stock price and the strike price $(S - X)$, whereas put prices increase as this difference decreases. We are now ready to tie all this together and calculate market price of calls and puts. We conclude this chapter by studying a simple but powerful tool for valuing options, the binomial option-pricing model. In Chapter 19, we will learn about an even more complex approach, one that earned its authors Nobel Prize recognition, known as the Black and Scholes option-pricing model.

Concept Review Questions

9. Throughout most of this book, we have shown that if an asset's risk increases, its price declines. Why is the opposite true for options?

10. Call options increase in value when stock prices rise, and put options increase in value when stock prices fall. How can the same movement in an underlying variable (e.g., an increase in time before expiration, or an increase in volatility) cause both call and put prices to rise at the same time?

18.4 CALCULATING OPTION PRICES

The Binomial Option-Pricing Model

Earlier in this chapter, we studied an important relationship linking the prices of puts, calls, shares, and risk-free bonds. Put-call parity establishes a direct link between the prices of these assets, a link that must hold to prevent arbitrage opportunities. We saw in Section 18.2 that if an option's price gets too high, an arbitrageur can exploit the situation by selling the overpriced option and purchasing an identical synthetic option. A similar logic drives the **binomial option-pricing model.** The binomial model recognizes that investors can combine options (either calls or puts) with shares of the underlying asset to construct a portfolio with a risk-free payoff.[20] Any asset with a risk-free payoff is relatively easy to value—just discount its future cash flows at the risk-free rate. But if we can value a portfolio containing options and shares, then we can also calculate the value of the options simply by subtracting the value of the shares from the value of the portfolio.

We will work through an example that proceeds in three distinct steps showing how to price an option using the binomial method. First, we must find a portfolio of stock and options that generates a risk-free payoff in the future. Second, given that the portfolio offers a risk-free cash payment, we can calculate the present value of that portfolio by discounting its cash flow at the risk-free rate. Third, given the portfolio's present value, we can determine how much of the portfolio's value comes from the stock and how much comes from the option. By subtracting the value of the underlying shares from the value of the portfolio, we obtain the option's market price.

[20]. The seminal work on the binomial model is by Cox, Ross, and Rubenstein (1979).

Figure 18.10
Binomial Option Pricing

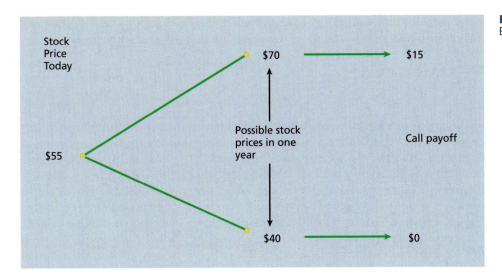

Create a Risk-Free Portfolio

Assume that the shares of Financial Engineers Ltd. currently sell for $55. We want to determine the price of a call option on Financial Engineers stock with an exercise price of $55 and an expiration date in one year. Assume the risk-free rate is 4 percent.

The binomial model begins with an assumption about the volatility of the underlying stock. Specifically, the model assumes that by the time the option expires, the stock will have increased or decreased to a particular dollar value. In this problem, we will assume that one year from now, Financial Engineers' stock price will have risen to $70 or it will have fallen to $40. Figure 18.10 provides a simple diagram of this assumption.[21]

The call option we want to price has a strike price of $55. Therefore, if the underlying stock reaches $70 in one year, the call option will be worth $15. However, if Financial Engineers stock falls to $40, the call option will be worthless.

Here is the crux of the first step. We want to find some combination of Financial Engineers stock and the call option that yields the same payoff whether the stock goes up or down over the next year. In other words, we want to create a risk-free combination of shares and calls. To begin, suppose we purchase one share of stock and h call options. At the moment, we do not know the value of h, but we can solve for it. Because our portfolio objective is to generate the same cash payment one year from now whether our share of stock rises or falls, we can write down the portfolio's payoffs in each possible scenario and then choose h so that the payoffs are equal:

	Cash Flows One Year from Today	
	If the Stock Price Goes Up to $70	**If the Stock Price Drops to $40**
One share of stock is worth	$70	$40
h call options are worth	$15h	$0h
Total portfolio is worth	$70 + $15h	$40 + $0h

[21] How can we possibly know that the price of Financial Engineers stock will be either $70 or $40? Of course, we cannot know that. Almost any price is possible one year in the future. Very soon we will illustrate that this assumption, which seems completely ridiculous now, isn't really necessary in a more complex version of the binomial model. But let's understand the simple version first.

A portfolio containing one share of stock and h call options will have the same cash value in one year if we choose the value of h that solves this equation:

$$\$70 + \$15h = \$40 + \$0h$$
$$h = -2$$

The value of h represents the number of call options in our risk-free portfolio. Because h equals -2, to create a risk-free portfolio, we must *sell two call options* and combine that position with our single share of stock. Why do we sell options to achieve this objective? Remember that the value of a call option rises as the stock price rises. If we own a share of stock and a call option (or several call options) on that stock, the assets in our portfolio will be positively correlated, rising and falling at the same time. Recall from Chapter 5 that the only circumstance in which it is possible to combine two risky assets into a risk-free portfolio occurs when the correlation between the two assets is negative (in fact, -1.0). Therefore, if we buy a share, we must sell call options to create a negative correlation between the assets in our portfolio.

What happens to our portfolio if, in fact, we buy one share and sell two calls? You can see the answer in two ways. First, just plug the value -2 back into the equation we used to solve for h:

$$\$40 = \$40$$

This expression says that the portfolio payoff will be $40 whether the stock price increases or decreases. The other way to see this is to lay out the payoffs of each asset in the portfolio in a table.

	Cash Flows One Year from Today	
	If the Stock Price Goes Up to \$70	**If the Stock Price Drops to \$40**
One share of stock is worth	\$70	\$40
Two short call options are worth	$-\$30$	\$ 0
Total portfolio is worth	\$40	\$40

The first row of the table is self-explanatory. The second row indicates that if we sell two call options and the stock price equals $70 next year, we will owe the holder of the calls $15 per option, or $30 total. On the other hand, if one year from now, the stock price equals $40, the call options we sold will be worthless and we will have no cash outflow. In either case, the total cash inflow from the portfolio will be $40.

Because this portfolio pays $40 in one year no matter what happens, we call it a perfectly hedged portfolio. The value of h is called the **hedge ratio** because it tells us what combination of stocks and calls results in a perfectly hedged position.[22]

Calculating the Present Value of the Portfolio

Because the portfolio consisting of one share of stock and two short call options pays $40 for certain next year, we can say that the portfolio is a type of synthetic, risk-free

---

[22.] The *hedge ratio* can be defined either as the ratio of calls to shares in a perfectly hedged portfolio (the definition we use here) or as the ratio of shares to calls. In this example, the hedge ratio equals either $-2:1$ (using our definition) or $-1:2$, using the alternative definition. Either way, the hedge ratio defines the mix of options and shares that results in a hedged portfolio.

bond. The second step requires us to calculate the present value of the portfolio. Because we already know that the risk-free rate equals 4 percent, we can determine the present value of the portfolio:

$$PV = \frac{\$40}{(1.04)^1} = \$38.46$$

It is crucial at this step to understand the following point. Buying one share of stock and selling two calls yields the same future payoff as buying a risk-free, zero-coupon bond with a face value of $40. Because both of these investments offer $40 at the end of one year with certainty, they should both sell for the same price today. This insight allows us to determine the option's price in the next step.

Determine the Price of the Call Option

If a risk-free bond paying $40 in one year costs $38.46 today, then the net cost of buying one share of Financial Engineers stock and selling two call options must also be $38.46. Why? Because both investment strategies are risk-free and offer the same future cash flows, they must both sell for the same price. Therefore, to determine the price of the option, all we need to do is write down an expression for the cost of our hedged portfolio and set that expression equal to $38.46.

From the information given in the problem, purchasing one share of stock costs $55. Partially offsetting this cost will be the revenue from selling two call options. Denoting the price of the call option with the letter C, we can calculate the total cost of the portfolio as follows:

Total portfolio cost = $55 − 2C = $38.46

Solving for C, *we obtain a call value of $8.27.*

At this point, it is worth reviewing what we have accomplished. We began with an assumption about the future movements of the underlying stock. Next, given the type of option we want to value and its characteristics, we calculated the payoffs of the option for each of the two possible future stock prices. Given those payoffs, we discovered that by buying one share and selling two calls, we could generate a certain payoff of $40 in one year. The present value of that payoff is $38.46, so the net cost of buying the share and selling the calls must also equal $38.46. This implies that we received revenue of $16.54 from selling two calls, or $8.27 each. The following Applying the Model repeats the process to value an identical put option on the same underlying stock.

APPLYING THE MODEL

We begin this problem with the same set of assumptions for Financial Engineers given earlier. Financial Engineers stock sells for $55 but may increase to $70 or decrease to $40 in one year. The risk-free rate equals 4 percent. We want to use the binomial model to calculate the value of a 1-year put option with a strike price of $55. We begin by finding the composition of a perfectly hedged portfolio. As before, begin by writing down the payoffs of a portfolio containing one share of stock and *h* put options:

	Cash Flows One Year from Today	
	If the Stock Price Goes Up to $70	**If the Stock Price Drops to $40**
One share of stock is worth	$70	$40
h put options are worth	0h$	15h$
Total portfolio is worth	$70 + 0h$	$40 + 15h$

Notice that the put option pays $15 when the stock price drops, and it pays nothing when the stock price rises. Set the payoffs in each scenario equal to each other and solve for h:

$$\$70 + \$0h = \$40 + \$15h$$

$$h = 2$$

To create a perfectly hedged portfolio, we must buy one share of stock and two put options. Notice that in this problem, we are buying options rather than selling them. Put values increase when stock values decrease, so it is possible to form a risk-free portfolio containing long positions in both stock and puts because they are negatively correlated.[23] By plugging the value of $h = 2$ back into the equation, we see that an investor who buys one share of stock and two put options essentially creates a synthetic bond with a face value of $70:

$$\$70 + \$0(2) = \$40 + \$15(2)$$

$$\$70 = \$70$$

Given a risk-free rate of 4 percent, the present value today of $70 is $67.31. It would cost $67.31 to buy a 1-year, risk-free bond paying $70, so it must also cost $67.31 to buy the synthetic version of that bond, one share and two puts. Given that the current share price is $55, and letting P stand for the price of the put, we find that the put option is worth $6.15 (rounding to the nearest penny):

$$\text{Cost of 1 share} + 2 \text{ puts} = \$67.31 = \$55 + 2P$$

$$\$12.31 = 2P$$

$$\$6.15 = P$$

Take a moment to look over the two examples of pricing options using the binomial approach. Make a list of the data needed to price these options.

1. The current price of the underlying stock
2. The amount of time remaining before the option expires
3. The strike price of the option

[23.] If the stock underlying a put option has a positive beta, then the put option itself will have a negative beta. In Chapter 6, we learned that the capital asset pricing model predicts that any asset with a negative beta will have an expected return below the risk-free rate. Coval and Shumway (2001) verify that this prediction holds for put options. They estimate that at-the-money put options on the S&P 500 Index earn weekly average returns of -7.7 to -9.5 percent per week. However, the news for the CAPM is only half good. Although put returns fall below the risk-free rate as the CAPM predicts, put returns are much too negative to be entirely consistent with the CAPM.

4. The risk-free rate
5. The possible values of the underlying stock in the future

On this list, the only unknown is the fifth item. You can easily find the other four necessary values simply by looking at current market data.

At this point, we pause to ask one of our all-time favorite exam questions. Look back at Figure 18.10. What assumption are we making there about the probabilities of an up and a down move in Financial Engineers stock? Most people see that the figure shows two possible outcomes and guess that the probabilities must be 50-50. This is not true; at no point in our discussion of the binomial model did we make any assumption about the probabilities of up and down movements in the stock. We don't have to know what those probabilities are to value the option, which is convenient because estimating them could be very difficult.

Why are the probabilities of no concern to us? The first answer is that the market sets the current price of the stock at a level that reflects the odds of future up and down moves. In other words, the probabilities are embedded in the stock price, even though no one can see them directly.

The second answer is that the binomial model prices an option through the principle of "no arbitrage." Because it is always possible to combine a share of stock with options (either calls or puts) into a risk-free portfolio, the binomial model says that the value of that portfolio must be the same as the value of a risk-free bond—otherwise, an arbitrage opportunity would exist because identical assets would be selling at different prices. Because the portfolio containing stock and options offers a risk-free payoff, the probabilities of up and down moves in the stock price do not enter the calculations. An investor holding the hedged portfolio does not need to worry about movements in the stock because they do not affect the portfolio's payoffs.

Almost all students object to the binomial model's assumption that the price of a stock can take just two values in the future. Fair enough. It is certainly true that one year from today, the price of Financial Engineers stock might be $70, $40, or almost any other value. However, it turns out that more complex versions of the binomial do not require analysts to specify just two final prices for the stock. The binomial model can accommodate a wide range of final prices. To see how this works, consider a slight modification to our original problem.

Rather than presume that Financial Engineers stock will rise or fall by $15 over a year's time, suppose that it may rise or fall by $7.50 every six months. That's still a big assumption, but if we make it, we find that the list of potential prices of Financial Engineers stock one year from today has grown from two values to three. Figure 18.11 proves this claim. After one year, the price of the stock might be $40, $55, or $70. Now, let's modify the assumption one more time. Suppose that the price of stock can move up or down $3.75 every three months. Figure 18.11 shows that in this case, the number of possible stock prices one year in the future grows to five.

Given a tree with many branches like the last one in Figure 18.11, we can solve for the value of a call or put option following the same steps we used to value options with a simple two-step tree. Now, imagine a much larger tree, one in which the stock moves up or down every few minutes, or even every few seconds. Each change in the stock price is very small, perhaps a penny or two, but as the tree unfolds and time passes, the number of branches rapidly expands, as does the number of possible values of the stock at the option's expiration date. Looking at the tree's terminal nodes, we see that when the option expires in a year, the price of Financial Engineers stock can take any one of hundreds, or even thousands, of different values, so the complaint about the model's artificial assumption of just two possible stock prices no longer

Figure 18.11
Multistage Binomial Trees

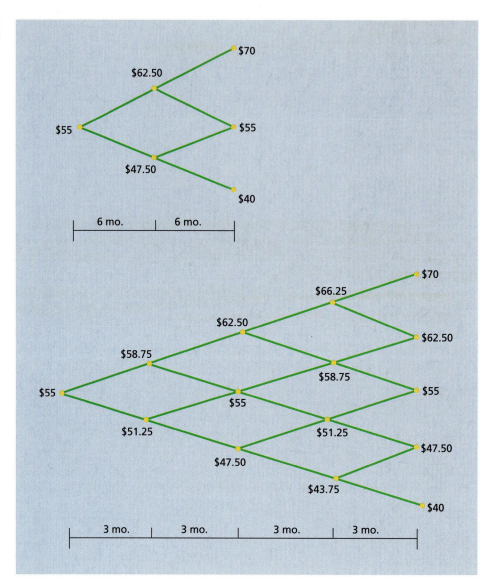

applies. Though extremely tedious, solving for the call value involves working all the way through the tree, applying the same steps over and over again.[24]

The binomial model is an incredibly powerful, flexible tool that analysts can use to price all sorts of options, from ordinary calls and puts, to complex real options embedded in capital investment projects. The genius of the model is in its recognition of the opportunity to use stock and options to mimic the payoffs of risk-free bonds, the easiest of all securities to price. The binomial model has a close cousin that also makes use of the ability to construct risk-free portfolios using stock and options—the risk-neutral method.

[24.] Fortunately, Black and Scholes (1973) and Merton (1973) developed a much more elegant model to solve for option values when the stock price can move in small increments moment by moment. We will study the Black and Scholes model in Chapter 19. For interested students, the final problem in Chapter 18 offers an animated solution for a multistage binomial tree.

THE RISK-NEUTRAL METHOD

In Chapter 5, we argued that most investors are risk averse and require compensation for risk taking. Just briefly, we mentioned the possibility that an investor might be risk neutral, concerned only about the expected return of an investment and indifferent to its risk. What if all investors are risk neutral? If investors do not worry about risk, then in equilibrium, no asset will have to pay a risk premium to survive in the market. The expected return on a share of common stock will be the same as the expected return on a Treasury bill—the risk-free rate.

Clearly, this discussion is purely hypothetical. We live in a world with risk-averse investors, and risky assets do offer risk premiums. However, it is possible to price options starting with the assumption that investors are risk neutral. How can an assumption that we know to be false lead to correct option prices? The answer goes back to arbitrage. Recall that we priced an option by creating a portfolio with a risk-free payoff. Both risk-averse and risk-neutral investors place the same value on a risk-free asset. Therefore, both types of investors would place the same value on the hedged portfolio of options and shares, and both would arrive at the same option price. In other words, because we price options using arbitrage arguments, we can proceed *as if* all investors are risk neutral. Making that assumption we can apply the **risk-neutral method,** which leads to an even simpler approach to calculating option prices, as the following example shows.

Begin with the initial conditions outlined in Figure 18.10. The stock price of Financial Engineers equals $55 now, and it may increase to $70 or fall to $40 in a year. The risk-free rate equals 4 percent. If investors are risk neutral, the expected return on Financial Engineers stock is the same as the risk-free rate. Therefore, as long as Financial Engineers stock does not pay dividends, the expected price of the stock one year from now must be 4 percent more than the current price, or $57.20. Once we know that the expected price in one year is $57.20, we can infer what the probabilities of an up and a down move must be. Let the probability of an up move in the stock be p and the probability of a down move be $1 - p$. We can solve for the probabilities using this expression:[25]

$$\$70p + (1 - p)\$40 = \$57.20$$

$$p = 0.5733$$

$$1 - p = 0.4267$$

If the probabilities of up-and-down moves are 57.33 percent and 42.67 percent respectively, then the expected stock price is $57.20, resulting in an expected 1-year return of 4 percent. Now, let's use those probabilities to calculate the value of the call option. As before, if the stock price reaches $70, then the call with a $55 strike price will be worth $15. The call will be worth nothing if the stock price ends up at $40.

[25.] The trick here is to choose the probabilities of up and down moves so that the expected future price is r% higher than the current price, where r is the risk-free rate. There is a shortcut formula for calculating the probability (p) of an up move in the underlying asset:

$$p = \frac{r^* - d}{u - d}$$

where r^* is 1 plus the risk-free rate, u is 1 plus the percentage increase in the stock price when it goes up, and d is 1 plus the percentage decrease in the stock when it goes down. For instance, in the Financial Engineers problem, the stock may either increase or decrease by $15, which is equal to 27.3 percent of the current market price. Therefore, $r^* = 1.04$, $u = 1.273$, $d = 0.727$, and $p = 0.5733$.

To value the call, just calculate the option's expected cash flow in one year, and discount that at the risk-free rate:

$$\text{Expected cash flow} = p(\$15) + (1-p)(\$0) = 0.5733(\$15) + \$0 = \$8.60$$

$$\text{Call value} = \$8.60 \div 1.04 = \$8.27$$

Notice that $8.27 is precisely the same call value we obtained using the binomial model, which made no assumption about investors' attitudes toward risk. The binomial model works because it is based on the principle that markets do not allow arbitrage opportunities to exist, at least not for long. Therefore, if a combination of stock and options is risk-free, then that combination must sell for the same price as a risk-free bond. If an asset promises a risk-free payoff, risk-averse and risk-neutral investors agree on how it should be valued because neither group requires a risk premium on the asset. Thus, if the binomial model works by creating a risk-free portfolio, it does no harm to assume that investors are risk neutral from the start. Whether investors are risk averse or risk neutral, the binomial model's calculations are the same. That opens the door for us to assume investors are risk neutral, and that assumption gives us a new way to value options.

APPLYING THE MODEL

Assuming investors are risk neutral, let's value the Financial Engineers put option with a strike of $55. If the stock increases to $70, the put is worthless. If the stock falls to $40, the put option pays $15. We already know the probabilities of up-and-down moves from our risk-neutral valuation of the call option, so we will use those probabilities to calculate the expected cash flow from the put. Once we have the expected cash flow, we can discount it at 4 percent to obtain the current market price of the put:

$$\text{Expected cash flow} = p(\$0) + (1-p)\$15 = \$0 + 0.4267(\$15) = \$6.40$$

$$\text{Put price} = \$6.40 \div 1.04 = \$6.15$$

As expected, the put value obtained from risk-neutral valuation matches exactly the price calculated using the binomial model. ∎

Concept Review Questions

11. To value options using the *binomial options-pricing method,* is it necessary to know the expected return on the stock? Why or why not?

12. There is an old saying that nature abhors a vacuum. The financial equivalent is that "markets abhor arbitrage opportunities." Explain the central role this principle plays in the binomial model.

13. Part of the *risk-neutral method* involves calculating the probability of an up or a down move in the underlying stock. Do you think these probabilities correspond to real-world probabilities of up and down moves? Explain.

18.5 SUMMARY

- Options are contracts that grant the buyer the right to buy or sell stock at a fixed price.
- Call options grant the right to purchase shares; put options grant the right to sell shares.
- Options provide a real economic benefit to society and are not simply a form of legalized gambling.
- American options allow investors to exercise their options before the options expire, but European options do not.
- Payoff diagrams show the value of options or portfolios of options on the expiration date. Payoff diagrams are extremely useful in understanding how different options trading strategies work.
- Put-call parity establishes a link between the market prices of calls, puts, shares, and bonds, provided certain conditions hold.
- Put-call parity can be used to calculate the fair value of an option (provided the other prices are known) or to find ways to form synthetic securities.
- Call option prices decrease and put option prices increase as the difference between the underlying stock price and the exercise price decreases.
- Calls and puts both increase in value (usually) when there is more time left before expiration.
- An increase in the volatility of the underlying asset increases the values of calls and puts.
- The binomial option-pricing model and the risk-neutral method permit us to calculate option prices with a minimal set of assumptions.

INTERNET RESOURCES

Note: *For updates to links, please go to the book's website at* http://smart.swcollege.com

http://www.cboe.com — Offers price quotes for many options and provides several tutorials explaining the characteristics of options and how they are traded

---

KEY TERMS

American call option	intrinsic value
at the money	long position
binomial option-pricing model	long straddle
call option	naked option position
cash settlement	net payoff
counterparty risk	options
derivative securities	option premium
European call option	out of the money
exchange	over-the-counter market
exercise price	payoff
exercise the option	payoff diagrams
expiration date	protective put
hedge ratio	put option
hockey-stick diagram	put-call parity
in the money	risk-neutral method

short position   time value
short straddle   underlying asset
strike price   writes an option
synthetic put option   writing covered calls

QUESTIONS

18-1.   Explain why an option is a *derivative security*.

18-2.   Is buying an option more or less risky than buying the underlying stock?

18-3.   What is the difference between an option's price and its payoff?

18-4.   List five factors that influence the prices of calls and puts.

18-5.   What are the economic benefits that options provide?

18-6.   What is the primary advantage of settling options contracts in cash?

18-7.   Suppose that you want to invest in a particular company. What are the pros and cons of buying the company's shares as compared to buying their options?

18-8.   Suppose that you want to make an investment that will be profitable if a company's stock price falls. Contrast the approach of short-selling the company's stock versus buying put options on the stock.

18-9.   Is buying a call the same as selling a put? Explain why or why not.

18-10. Suppose that you own an American call option on Pfizer stock. Pfizer stock has gone up in value considerably since you bought the option, so your investment has been profitable. There is still one month to go before the option expires, but you decide to go ahead and take your profits in cash. Describe two ways that you could accomplish this goal. Which one is likely to leave you with the higher cash payoff?

18-11. Explain why *put-call parity* does not hold for American options.

18-12. Look at the Intel call option prices in Table 18.1. For a given expiration date, call prices increase as the strike price decreases. The strike prices decrease in increments of $2.50. Do the call option prices increase in constant increments? That is, does the call price increase by the same amount as the strike price drops from $35 to $32.50 to $30 and so on? Explain.

18-13. Explain the difference between the *binomial option-pricing model* and the *risk-neutral method* of option pricing.

PROBLEMS

Option Payoff Diagrams

18-1.   Draw payoff diagrams for each of the following portfolios (X = strike price):
   a. Buy a call with $X = \$50$, and sell a call with $X = \$60$.
   b. Buy a bond with a face value of $10, short a put with $X = \$60$, and buy a put with $X = \$50$.
   c. Buy a share of stock, buy a put option with $X = \$50$, sell a call with $X = \$60$, and short a bond (i.e., borrow) with a face value of $50.
   d. What principle do these diagrams illustrate?

18-2. Draw a payoff diagram for the following portfolio (X = strike price): Buy two call options, one with $X = \$20$ and one with $X = \$30$, and sell two call options, both with $X = \$25$.

18-3. Refer to Problem 18-2. Suppose that the options you are buying and selling are the May Check Point calls shown in Table 18.4. Determine the net cost of the option portfolio, and draw a new payoff diagram showing the net payoffs at expiration. Over what range of prices would you make money, and over what range would you lose money? What is your maximum possible loss and gain?

Smart Solutions

See the problem and solution explained step-by-step at SMARTFinance

18-4. Draw a payoff diagram for each of the following portfolios (X = strike price):

  a. Buy a bond with a face value of $80, buy a call with $X = \$80$, and sell a put with $X = \$80$.
  b. Buy a share of stock, buy a put with $X = \$80$, and sell a call with $X = \$80$.
  c. Buy a share of stock, buy a put with $X = \$80$, and sell a bond with a face value of $80.

18-5. Look at the option prices in Table 18.1. For each row of the table, perform the following calculation: (stock price + put price − call price). According to put-call parity, a portfolio containing a share of stock, a put, and a short call has the same payoff as what security? When you perform this calculation for each row of Table 18.1, do your results seem to indicate that the put-call parity holds, at least approximately, or not? Explain. As background information, the annual rate of interest on short-term U.S. Treasury bills was about 1.75 percent at the time the quotes in the table were obtained from the CBOE website.

18-6. Referring to Problem 18-5, if some of the prices in Table 18.1 fail to satisfy put-call parity, provide an explanation for this apparent violation of the "no arbitrage" principle. Put differently, even if prices in the table do not satisfy parity, is it possible that there is still no arbitrage opportunity to exploit?

18-7. Imagine that a stock sells for $33. A call option with a strike price, X, of $35 and an expiration date in six months sells for $4.50. The annual risk-free rate is 5 percent. Calculate the price of a put option that expires in six months and has a strike price of $35.

Smart Solutions

See the problem and solution explained step-by-step at SMARTFinance

18-8. Refer to Problem 18-7. Suppose that the put option described actually sells for $5. Explain in detail how an arbitrageur could exploit this mispricing to earn a risk-free profit.

18-9. Monitoring option prices in the United Kingdom, you notice that call and put prices on the stock of the British exotic pet importer Python Inc. seem to be out of alignment. Specifically, the price of Python stock is £55, and the price of 3-month call and put options on Python stock with exercise prices of £60 are £5.75 and £7.25, respectively. The U.K. risk-free rate of interest is 8 percent (or 2 percent per three months). How can we exploit this arbitrage opportunity?

18-10. Suppose that an American call option is in the money, so the stock price, $S >$ the strike price, X. Demonstrate that the market price of this call (C) cannot be less than the difference between the stock price and the exercise price. That is, explain why this must be true: $C \geq S - X$. (*Hint:* Consider what would happen if $C < S - X$.)

Calculating Option Prices

18-11. A call option expires in three months and has a strike price, $X = \$40$. The underlying stock is worth $42 today. In three months, the stock may increase by $7 or decrease by $6. The risk-free rate is 2 percent per year. Use the binomial option-pricing model to value the call option.

18-12. Refer to Problem 18-11. Use the same set of facts to value a 3-month put option with a strike price, $X = \$40$.

18-13. Given the call and put prices you calculated in Problems 18-11 and 18-12, check to see if put-call parity holds.

18-14. A put option has a strike price of $90. The underlying stock sells for $88, but in four months it could increase to $95 or decrease to $82. The risk-free rate is 3 percent, and the put expires in four months. Use the risk-neutral method to value the put.

18-15. Using the same set of facts from Problem 18-14, use the risk-neutral method to calculate the value of a 3-month call with a strike price, $X = \$90$. After you have determined the call price, check to see if put-call parity holds.

18-16. This problem requires you to use the binomial model to price a complex call option with a variable strike price. Suppose that the current price of a particular stock is $80. The stock pays no dividends and has a beta of 1.2. The strike price of a 6-month call option is $78, but the strike price is not fixed. Specifically, the strike price is indexed to the S&P 500, meaning that if the S&P 500 changes by x percent, then the option's strike price will move in the same direction by x percent. Suppose you believe that the S&P 500 will either rise 20 percent or fall 10 percent in the next six months. If the risk-free rate is 4 percent, what is the value of the call option? (Hint: Use the stock's beta to determine the future values of the stock, which will depend on how the S&P 500 behaves.)

18-17. Explain the following paradox. A put option is a highly volatile security. If the underlying stock has a positive beta, then a put option on that stock will have a negative beta and an expected return below the risk-free rate. How can an equilibrium exist in which a highly risky security such as a put option offers an expected return below a much safer security such as a Treasury bill?

18-18. A stock currently trades for $84. In the next three months it may rise or fall by $5. Similarly, in the three months after that the stock price could increase or decrease by $5. Calculate the price of a 6-month put option with a strike price of $87.50, assuming that the risk-free rate of interest is 1 percent per quarter (roughly 4 percent per year).

18-19. A stock currently trades for $84. In the next three months it may rise or fall by $5. Similarly, in the three months after that the stock price could increase or decrease by $5. Calculate the price of a 6-month call option with a strike price of $87.50, assuming that the risk-free rate of interest is 1 percent per quarter (roughly 4 percent per year.

Smart
Solutions
See the
problem and
solution explained step-by-step at
SMARTFinance

Black and Scholes and Beyond

OPENING FOCUS
Oops! I Bought a Company

To industry experts, the June 2002 announcement that the German media company Bertelsmann would pay almost $3 billion to acquire the 75 percent of Zomba Music Group that it did not already own seemed particularly ill-timed. The previous year had seen the music industry's first sales decline in a decade, and industry experts felt that Zomba's signature acts, such as The Backstreet Boys, had already reached their peak. Even teen idol Britney Spears showed signs of slowing down. Her undeniably successful 2001 self-titled CD sold 750,000 copies in one week, down from the 1.3 million CDs that her previous album, *Oops! . . . I Did It Again,* reached in its first week. Worst of all, Zomba's R&B star, R. Kelly, was facing 21 felony counts of child pornography and a possible prison sentence of up to 15 years. Why would Bertelsmann part with $3 billion in cash to acquire a music company with such an uncertain future?

Bertelsmann, it turns out, had no choice because Clive Calder, head of Zomba Music, had negotiated a put option with Bertelsmann six years earlier when the music business was booming. That option gave Calder the right to sell Zomba outright to Bertelsmann at a fixed price. Ironically, the cash to finance the purchase came from a similar transaction in which Bertelsmann exercised a put option it held to sell its stake in AOL Europe for more than $7 billion. Expressing its displeasure with the forced acquisition of Zomba and other ill-fated investments, Bertelsmann's board of directors fired CEO Thomas Middlehoff in July.

Sources: Raymond Snoddy, "Calder to Cash In on Zomba Sale," *The Times* (London, June 12, 2002); Tim Burt, "Bertelsmann Signals Dramatic Retreat from Internet Ambitions," *Financial Times* (September 2, 2002), p. 1.

From the simple call and put stock options traded on major exchanges, to intricate agreements between business partners, options are everywhere. This chapter continues our discussion of options, starting with the famous option-pricing formula developed by Black and Scholes. Next, we expand our focus to include optionlike securities such as convertible bonds and warrants, before completing our coverage of options with an in-depth analysis of real options—capital investments with characteristics that resemble options.

In 1973, Myron Scholes and Fisher Black published what might fairly be called a trillion-dollar research paper. Their research produced, for the first time, a formula that traders could use to calculate the value of call options, a pathbreaking discovery that had eluded researchers for decades. Black and Scholes did not have to wait long to see if their formula would have an impact in financial markets. That same year, options began trading in the United States on the newly formed Chicago Board Options Exchange (CBOE). Traders on the floor of the exchange used handheld calculators with the Black and Scholes formula programmed in. From that beginning, trading in options exploded over the next three decades, hence the trillion-dollar moniker given to the original research paper.[1]

This chapter begins with an introduction to the Black and Scholes model. This model has much in common with the binomial model we studied in the previous chapter, and it is easier to use. Next, we will discuss how many securities issued by corporations often contain embedded options. Understanding the pros and cons of these securities, either from the buyer's or the seller's perspective, requires some facility with option-pricing concepts. Finally, we will return once more to the topic of real options to see how either the binomial or the Black and Scholes model can be used in a capital budgeting environment.

19.1 THE BLACK AND SCHOLES MODEL

CALCULATING BLACK AND SCHOLES OPTIONS VALUES

When you first encounter it, the **Black and Scholes option-pricing equation** looks rather intimidating. As a matter of fact, the editor at the prestigious academic journal where Black and Scholes published their prize-winning formula originally rejected their paper because he felt it was too technical and not of interest to a wide audience. Although it is true that the derivation of the formula requires a rather high level of mathematics, the intuition behind the equation is fairly straightforward. In fact, the logic of the Black and Scholes model mirrors that of the binomial model.

Black and Scholes began by asking a question. Suppose that investors can buy and sell shares of stock, options on those shares, and risk-free bonds. Does a combination of options and shares exist that provides a risk-free payoff? That should sound familiar, because that is exactly how one begins when pricing an option using the binomial model. However, Black and Scholes's approach to valuing options differs from the binomial method in several important ways.

First, recall from Chapter 18 that the binomial model assumes that over a given period of time, the stock price will move up or down by a known amount. In Figure 18.11, we showed that by shortening the length of the period during which the stock price moves, we increase the number of different prices that the stock might

---

[1] Myron Scholes won the Nobel Prize in economics in 1997 for this achievement, an honor he shared with Robert Merton, another researcher who made seminal contributions to options research. Fisher Black undoubtedly would have been a corecipient of the award, but he died in 1995.

reach by the option's expiration date. Black and Scholes take this approach to its logical extreme. Their model presumes that stock prices can move at every moment in time. If we were to illustrate this assumption by drawing a binomial tree like those in Figure 18.11, the tree would have an infinite number of branches, and on the option's expiration date, the stock price could take on almost any value.

Second, Black and Scholes did not assume that they knew precisely what the up-and-down movements in the stock would be at every instant. They recognized that these movements were essentially random, and therefore unpredictable. Instead, they assumed that the volatility, or standard deviation, of a stock's movements was known. As we will see, the challenge for practitioners using the Black and Scholes model is to find a reliable way to estimate the volatility of the stock underlying an option.

With these assumptions in place, Black and Scholes determined that the price of a European call option (on a non-dividend-paying stock) could be calculated as follows:

$$C = SN(d_1) - Xe^{-rt}N(d_2) \qquad \text{(Eq. 19.1)}$$

$$d_1 = \frac{\ln\left(\dfrac{S}{X}\right) + \left(r + \dfrac{\sigma^2}{2}\right)t}{\sigma\sqrt{t}}$$

$$d_2 = d_1 - \sigma\sqrt{t} \qquad \text{(Eq. 19.2)}$$

Let's dissect this carefully. Most of the terms in the equation we have seen before:

   S = current market price of underlying stock,

   X = strike price of option,

   t = amount of time before option expires (in years),

   r = annual risk-free interest rate,

   σ = annual standard deviation of underlying stock's returns,

   e = 2.718 (approximately),

$N(X)$ = the probability of drawing a value less than or equal to X from the **standard normal distribution.**

Does this list of variables sound familiar? It should, because it is nearly identical to the list of inputs required to use the binomial model. The stock price, S, the strike price, X, the time until expiration, t, and the risk-free rate, r, are all variables that we used before to price options with the binomial method. As mentioned, one difference between this model and the binomial is the assumption that analysts know the standard deviation of a stock's returns, σ. We illustrate a conventional method for estimating this value in an appendix following this chapter, but for now, assume that you have an estimate of volatility from historical data.

What about the term Xe^{-rt}? Recall from our discussion of continuous compounding in Chapter 3 that the term e^{-rt} reflects the present value of \$1 discounted at r percent for t years. Therefore, Xe^{-rt} simply equals the present value of the option's

Figure 19.1
Standard Normal
Distribution

*The expression $N(d_1)$
equals the probability
of drawing a particular
value, d_1, or a lower value
from the standard normal
distribution. In the figure,
$N(d_1)$ is represented by
the shaded portion under
the bell curve. Because
the normal distribution
is symmetric about the
mean, we can write
$N(d_1) = 1 - N(-d_1)$.
Appendix B provides a
table of probabilities for
the standard normal
distribution.*

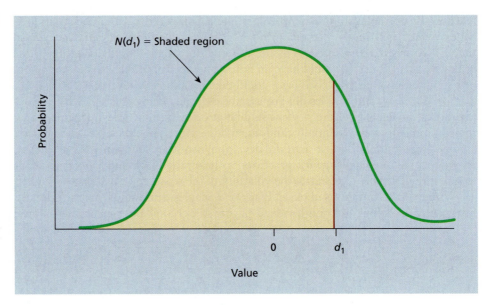

strike price.[2] With this in mind, look again at Equation 19.1. The first term equals the stock price multiplied by a quantity labeled $N(d_1)$. The second term is the present value of the strike price multiplied by a quantity labeled $N(d_2)$. Therefore, we can say that the call option value equals the "adjusted" stock price minus the present value of the "adjusted" strike price, where $N(d_1)$ and $N(d_2)$ represent some kind of adjustment factors. In Chapter 18, we saw that call option values increase as the difference between the stock price and the strike price, $S - X$, increases. The same relationship holds here, although we must now factor in the terms $N(d_1)$ and $N(d_2)$.

In the Black and Scholes equation, d_1 and d_2 are simply numerical values (calculated using Equation 19.2) that depend on the model's inputs: the stock price, the strike price, the interest rate, the time to expiration, and volatility. The expressions $N(d_1)$ and $N(d_2)$ convert the numerical values of d_1 and d_2 into probabilities using the standard normal distribution.[3] Figure 19.1 shows that the value $N(d_1)$ equals the area under the standard normal curve to the left of value d_1. For example, if we calculate the value of d_1 and find that it equals 0, then $N(d_1)$ equals 0.5 because half of the area under the curve falls to the left of zero. The higher the value of d_1, the closer $N(d_1)$ gets to 1.0; and the lower the value of d_1, the closer $N(d_1)$ gets to zero. The same relationship holds between d_2 and $N(d_2)$. Given a particular value of d_1 (or d_2), to calculate $N(d_1)$, you need a table showing the cumulative standard normal probabilities, or you can plug d_1 into the Excel function "=normsdist(d_1)."

A common intuitive interpretation of $N(d_1)$ and $N(d_2)$ is that they represent the risk-adjusted probabilities that the call will expire in the money. Therefore, the following is a verbal description of Equation 19.1: *The call option price equals the stock price minus the present value of the exercise price, adjusted for the probability that*

---

[2] Remember, this expression can be written in two ways:

$$Xe^{-rt} = \frac{X}{e^{rt}}$$

Assuming the continuously compounded risk-free rate of interest equals r and the amount of time before expiration equals t, this is simply the present value of the strike price. See Table A6 in Appendix A for present value factors with continuous discounting.

[3] Recall from statistics that the standard normal distribution has a mean equal to zero and a standard deviation equal to 1.0.

when the option expires, the stock price will exceed the strike price (i.e., the probability that the option expires in the money).

APPLYING THE MODEL

The stock of Cloverdale Food Processors currently sells for $40. A European call option on Cloverdale stock has an expiration date six months in the future and a strike price of $38. The estimate of the annual standard deviation of Cloverdale stock is 45 percent, and the risk-free rate is 6 percent. What is the call worth?

$$d_1 = \frac{\ln\left(\dfrac{40}{38}\right) + \left(0.06 + \dfrac{0.45^2}{2}\right)\dfrac{1}{2}}{0.45\sqrt{\dfrac{1}{2}}} = \frac{(0.0513) + (0.0806)}{0.3182} = 0.4146$$

$$d_2 = d_1 - \sigma\sqrt{t} = 0.4146 - 0.45\sqrt{\frac{1}{2}} = 0.0964$$

$$N(0.4146) = 0.6608 \qquad N(0.0964) = 0.5384$$

$$C = 40(0.6608) - 38(2.718^{-(.06)(0.5)})(0.5384) = \$6.58$$

In Figure 19.2, the solid green line shows how the Black and Scholes value of the Cloverdale call option changes as the price of Cloverdale stock moves up and down.

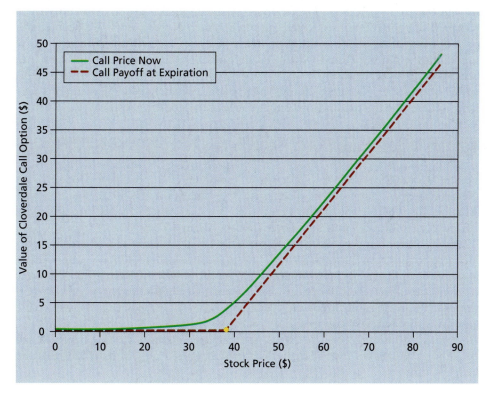

Figure 19.2
Black and Scholes Call Values for Cloverdale

The figure shows the Black and Scholes call price at different stock prices assuming the following:

the call's strike price is $38 ($x = 38$)

the option expires in

6 months $\left(t = \dfrac{1}{2}\right)$

the risk-free rate is 6% ($r = .06$)

the standard deviation of the stock is 45% ($\sigma = 0.45$)

$C = SN(d_1) - Xe^{-rt}N(d_2)$

The red dotted line shows the standard call payoff diagram. When the stock price is very low relative to the strike price, the values $N(d_1)$ and $N(d_2)$ will be very close to zero, and so will the call price. As the stock price approaches the exercise price, the odds that the option will expire in the money increase, as does the call price. Finally, when the stock price exceeds the strike price by a large amount, we can be nearly certain that the option will expire in the money. In that case, $N(d_1)$ and $N(d_2)$ will be close to 1.0, and the call price will (almost) equal the stock price minus the present value of the strike price. Throughout the range of possible stock prices, the solid line is at least as high as the dotted line, and usually it is higher. This means that the option's market price is at least equal to its intrinsic value, and usually it exceeds intrinsic value. However, at the expiration date, the two lines would lie on top of each other.

Take another look at Figure 19.2, this time focusing on the slope of the solid line. That slope measures how much the call price changes as the underlying stock price changes. Options traders refer to this as the **option's delta,** and mathematically the delta equals the value $N(d_1)$ from the Black and Scholes equation. When a call option is far out of the money, the solid line in Figure 19.2 is almost flat, and the option's delta is close to zero. This means that movements in the stock price have very little impact on the option's market value, which is not surprising because the odds are high that the option will expire worthless. Conversely, when the option is deep in the money, the slope of the solid line is almost 1.0, and so is the delta. The call's market price moves almost dollar for dollar with changes in the stock price. This makes sense, too, because if the option is deep in the money, it will almost certainly be exercised. That means the holder of the call option will almost certainly own the stock at some point, so the value of the option should fluctuate in line with the underlying stock.

We can use the concept of an option's delta to make another connection between the Black and Scholes and binomial models. In Chapter 18, we developed a three-step process for using the *binomial model* to value options. The first of the three steps was to find a portfolio of stock and options with a risk-free payoff. We denoted the ratio of the number of options to the number of shares in this perfectly hedged portfolio with the symbol h, and we labeled that number the **hedge ratio.** In Black and Scholes's parlance, the ratio $1 \div N(d_1)$ is equivalent to the hedge ratio from the binomial model. This ratio tells options traders approximately how many options they need to offset the fluctuations of a single share of the underlying stock.

Smart Concepts
See the concept explained step-by-step at

APPLYING THE MODEL

Let's revisit the Cloverdale call option from the previous Applying the Model. Given the parameters in that problem, the market price of the option is $6.58, and the value $N(d_1)$ equals 0.6608. This means that if the price of Cloverdale stock rises (falls) by $1, the price of the call option will rise (fall) by about $0.66.

Suppose that a mutual fund manager owns 100,000 shares of Cloverdale stock. He plans to sell these shares in a week, but he is concerned about a potential decline in the value of the shares between now and then. As a hedging strategy, the manager plans to sell Cloverdale call options. He reasons that because the prices of calls and shares move in the same direction, by holding shares and selling calls, he will create a position that is nearly risk free. But how many Cloverdale calls must he sell?

By taking the reciprocal of $N(d_1)$, the manager discerns that he needs to sell roughly 1.513 calls for each share in his portfolio, or 151,300 total, to construct the hedged position:

$$\frac{1}{N(d_1)} = \frac{1}{0.6608} = 1.513$$

Now, suppose that a week passes and the price of Cloverdale stock has fallen from $40 to $38. This means the manager's stock portfolio has declined in value by $200,000 ($2 per share × 100,000 shares). However, what has happened to the value of the options the manager sold? Use the Black and Scholes equation as before to calculate the option's price, except this time use $38 for the stock price and 0.48 years for the time until expiration (one week less than six months). The new call value is $5.20, so the call price dropped $1.38 during the week. Because the fund manager took a short position in call options, the decline in the call price represents a profit of $1.38 per call or $208,794. That is, the fund manager received $6.58 per call when he sold them, and now a week later he can buy calls at the lower price to close out his position. Notice that the $208,794 net gain on the option trades almost perfectly offsets the $200,000 decline on the manager's Cloverdale stock. In other words, the manager created a hedged portfolio.   ■

The Black and Scholes model was originally conceived to price a European call option on an underlying stock that paid no dividends. Applying the model when the underlying stock pays dividends requires a small adjustment. Holding all else constant, when a firm pays a dividend, the stock price will fall. This effect is largely neutral to shareholders, who experience a decline in their shares but also receive the dividend, but it clearly harms investors holding call options who are not entitled to receive dividends. If investors expect a firm to pay a dividend during the life of a call, they will pay a lower price for the call than if they did not expect any dividends. A simple way to account for this in Equation 19.1 is to reduce the current stock price, S, by the present value of expected dividend payments. That adjustment makes sense because the current price of the stock overstates, by the amount of the dividend, the value of the underlying claim that option investors have the right to purchase.[4]

With a slight modification to Equation 19.1, we can use the Black and Scholes model to value puts rather than calls. To derive a Black and Scholes equation for a put option, we will make use of put-call parity. Remember, put-call parity establishes an equilibrium relationship between the price of a call option, C, a put option, P, the underlying stock, S, and a risk-free bond, $PV(X)$. Put-call parity states the following:

$$S + P = PV(X) + C$$

To put this expression in a form like the Black and Scholes model, replace the term $PV(X)$ with Xe^{-rt}, move the symbol for the stock price to the right-hand side, and replace the symbol for the call price with Equation 19.1. After these steps, we have the following:

$$P = Xe^{-rt} + [SN(d_1) - Xe^{-rt}N(d_2)] - S$$

[4.] Option investors have the right to buy a claim on all the firm's future cash flows, except for the dividend that will be paid before the option expires. Fenn and Liang (2001) find a negative correlation between a firm's dividend payout and the quantity of stock options held by the firm's managers, and a positive correlation between managerial option holdings and the firm's share repurchase activity. It seems that managers are well aware that paying dividends decreases option values while repurchasing shares, if it increases the stock price, increases option values.

Figure 19.3
Black and Scholes
Put Values

*The figure shows the Black
and Scholes put price at
different stock prices assuming the following:*

the call's strike price
is \$38 ($x = 38$)

the option expires in

6 months $\left(t = \dfrac{1}{2} \right)$

the risk-free rate is 6%
($r = .06$)

the standard deviation
of the stock is 45%
($\sigma = 0.45$)

$P = Xe^{-rt} \times$
$[1 - N(d_2) - S(1 - N(d_1))]$

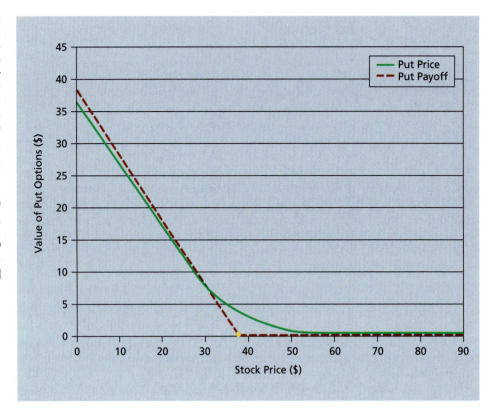

With a little algebraic manipulation, we obtain the following put option formula:

$$P = Xe^{-rt}[1 - N(d_2)] - S[1 - N(d_1)] \qquad \text{(Eq. 19.3)}$$

where d_1 and d_2 have the same definitions as in Equation 19.2. Notice how the terms in this equation have reversed compared to their placement in Equation 19.1. Intuitively, we understand that the terms in the equation switch positions because the circumstances in which a put option is in the money are precisely opposite those that dictate when a call option is in the money. For the same reason, the probabilities $N(d_1)$ and $N(d_2)$ from Equation 19.1 switch in Equation 19.3 to $1 - N(d_1)$ and $1 - N(d_2)$.

The solid green line in Figure 19.3 illustrates how put prices change as the underlying stock price changes. The shape of this line is, in many respects, the mirror image of the line in Figure 19.2 for calls. As the stock price falls, the put value increases; and as the stock price rises, the put value approaches zero.[5] Unlike a call option, a put option does not always sell for more than its intrinsic value. When the stock price is low, the put value falls below intrinsic value (the red dotted line). The interpretation of this phenomenon is as follows. When the stock price is very low, the option

---

[5.] As in Figure 19.2, when the stock price is very low, $N(d_1)$ and $N(d_2)$ are close to zero. Consequently, the terms $1 - N(d_1)$ and $1 - N(d_2)$ in the put pricing equation become very close to 1.0, and the put value approaches the present value of the strike price minus the stock price. At high stock prices, $N(d_1)$ and $N(d_2)$ get close to 1.0, so $1 - N(d_1)$ and $1 - N(d_2)$ approach zero, as does the put value.

holder is almost certain to exercise the option, receiving the strike price in cash. However, because this is a European option, the investor must wait to exercise the option until it expires. The amount by which the option's price falls below its intrinsic value represents the time value of money the investor loses by having to wait until expiration to exercise the option.

One of the most interesting aspects of the Black and Scholes equation is what it does not contain—the expected return on the underlying stock. In other words, it is not necessary to know what return investors expect on the underlying stock to determine the price of an option. This, too, has a parallel in the binomial model. Remember that the binomial model begins with an assumption about up-and-down movements in the underlying stock, but the model does not make any assumption about the probabilities of those up-and-down movements. As long as the current value of the underlying stock can be observed, the probabilities of future up-and-down movements are embedded in the stock price. The binomial and Black and Scholes models both depend on the notion that options and shares can be combined to create a risk-free portfolio, so the future direction of the underlying asset does not enter the pricing mechanics.

VOLATILITY

The Black and Scholes model requires five inputs, four of which can be readily observed in the market. Only the volatility of the underlying stock is uncertain. For companies whose stocks have traded in the public markets for a significant period of time, plenty of historical data exist that analysts can use to estimate volatility, an exercise illustrated in the appendix to this chapter. Even so, what is relevant for option pricing is the volatility of the underlying asset over the life of the option. Estimates of volatility obtained from historical data, even fairly recent data, may or may not be good predictors of the future.

In Chapter 6, we discussed issues that analysts face when they use historical data to estimate a stock's variance or its covariance with other stocks, and those same issues apply here. When the stock of interest trades frequently in a liquid market, analysts can gather a reasonably large sample using daily data. Daily data offer the advantage of using the most recent information available. However, when trading in a stock is thin, daily data can generate misleading signals about a security's true volatility; in that case, using weekly or monthly data to estimate volatility may be preferable.[6]

Pricing an option using Black and Scholes requires an estimate of the underlying stock's volatility. However, if traders can observe the market price of an option directly, they can "invert" the Black and Scholes equation to calculate the level of volatility implied by the option's market price. The value of σ obtained in this manner is called an option's **implied volatility.**

APPLYING THE MODEL

In the previous chapter, we saw that the market price of a May Intel call option with $X = \$27.50$ was $3.50. Suppose that at the time the option was trading at that price, it had 45 days (approximately one-eighth of a year) remaining before expiration. The risk-free rate at that time was 1.75 percent and the price of Intel stock was $30.05.

[6.] Estimating volatility is a thorny issue that has occupied researchers both in academia and in the research departments of investment banks. For a few seminal works in this field, see Cox and Ross (1976), Engle (1982), Bollerslev (1986), and Hull and White (1987).

Given these values, we can use a computer program (or trial and error) to find the value of σ that would generate a Black and Scholes call value of $3.50. In this case, the implied volatility of the May Intel call is 47.4 percent.[7]

Of course, traders cannot use an option's implied volatility to calculate its price because they have to know the price to calculate implied volatility. In other words, traders can use the Black and Scholes equation, along with an estimate of the stock's volatility, to estimate the price of an option; or, if traders know the price of the option, they can use Black and Scholes to find the volatility implied by that price.

Of what practical value is an option's implied volatility if you must first know the option's price to calculate its implied volatility? One application is to use implied volatilities to test the accuracy of the Black and Scholes model. For example, suppose that several call options with different strike prices but the same expiration date trade on the same underlying stock. If we can observe the market prices of these options, then we can determine each option's implied volatility. The Black and Scholes model predicts that the implied volatilities will be identical because all the options share the same underlying asset. If a systematic pattern between an option's strike price and its implied volatility exists, then the Black and Scholes model does not price options correctly at all strike prices.

Early tests of Black and Scholes that used this approach found that options with the same underlying stock indeed had different implied volatilities, which varied with the exercise price.[8] In particular, the implied volatilities of out-of-the-money options seemed much higher than the implied volatilities of at-the-money options. Further tests found that the option prices generated by Black and Scholes were close to actual market prices for at-the-money options, but pricing errors were more substantial for out-of-the-money options.

The existence of a relationship between an option's implied volatility and its strike price affects option-trading practices in several ways. Some traders adopt speculative strategies to try to exploit differences in implied volatility for a single underlying asset. For example, we know that the value of a call option rises with the volatility of the underlying stock. Therefore, one might argue that when two options on the same underlying stock have very different implied volatilities, the option with high implied volatility is overpriced and the option with low implied volatility is underpriced. Traders who hold this belief can take a short position in the first option and a long position in the second to try to profit from any pricing discrepancies. A slightly more sophisticated version of this technique begins by estimating the volatility of an underlying stock by taking a weighted average of the implied volatilities of several options on that stock. The weights might be a function of how close the stock's market price is to the option's strike price, or they might depend on the volume of trading at each strike price. The implied volatilities of some options will naturally be above the weighted average, and others will fall below the average. Traders take speculative long positions in the options with below-average implied volatilities and short positions in those with above-average implied volatilities.

[7] Intel stock usually pays a dividend in May, but in 2002 the dividend amount was just $0.02, small enough to ignore in these calculations.
[8] See Black (1975), MacBeth and Merville (1979), and Emanuel and MacBeth (1982). Researchers found that plotting implied volatility on the y-axis and the strike price on the x-axis resulted in a slightly U-shaped pattern dubbed the "volatility smile."

Why have we invested so much time on valuing ordinary call and put options, given that only a small fraction of business school students become professional options traders? The answer is that options are everywhere, embedded in other corporate securities as well as in capital investment projects. The methods used to price simple call and put options have much wider applications than it may at first appear.

1. What do the Black and Scholes and binomial models have in common? What are their main differences?

2. Examine Figure 19.2. When the stock price is very high, the two lines in the figure are virtually parallel. Why?

3. Look again at Figure 19.2, especially at the portion where the stock price is high. At a given stock price (for example, $70 in the figure), what is the approximate vertical distance between these two lines? In other words, when the call option is deep in the money, what is the difference between the call option's price and its intrinsic value?

4. Using your answer to the previous question as a guide, what happens to the market price of a call option if the risk-free rate increases?

5. Given that options are very risky securities, why do we use the risk-free rate in the Black and Scholes equation?

19.2 OPTIONS EMBEDDED IN OTHER SECURITIES

PLAIN-VANILLA STOCKS AND BONDS

Casual observers of financial markets sometimes argue that bonds are boring compared to the more exotic world of options. After all, what's exciting about an investment that pays a fixed cash flow at regular intervals for a fixed amount of time? In fact, corporate bonds do have something in common with options. When a firm borrows money, it has the option to default on its loans if cash flow is insufficient to repay the debt. The default option explains why corporate bonds must offer higher yields than government bonds.

Suppose that a company has $250 million in equity financing and $250 million in 3-year, zero-coupon bonds with a current market value of $200 million. The company plans to invest $450 million in cash in an asset of some kind, and it hopes that the asset's future cash flows will be sufficient to offer attractive returns to both stockholders and bondholders. However, both bondholders and stockholders know that if the cash flows are not sufficient even to pay bondholders their $250 million at maturity, the firm can walk away from its debts, leaving bondholders to claim whatever cash they can by selling off the firm's remaining assets.

Figure 19.4 shows that the position occupied by bondholders in this example is identical to that of investors holding a combination of risk-free bonds and a short put option. The lower graph in the figure shows a payoff diagram for the firm's bondholders. The underlying asset in this graph is not the value of common stock, as we have grown used to, but the value of the firm's total assets in three years when the bonds mature. When the value of assets is high, bondholders receive the $250 million they were promised and no more. When the value of assets is low, bondholders receive less than $250 million. How much less depends on the value of the remaining assets.

Figure 19.4
Options Embedded in
Ordinary Corporate Bonds

*Corporate bond investors
hold a position that is
equivalent to a portfolio
of risk-free debt and a
short put option. If the
firm's assets are not
sufficient to repay its debt
at maturity, then the firm
puts its assets to the
bondholders.*

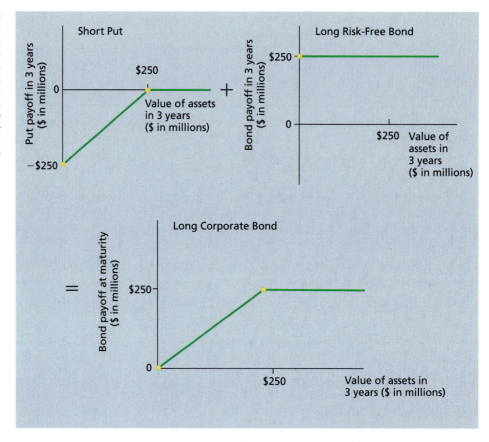

The upper portion of the figure shows the payoffs from a hypothetical portfolio containing a long position in risk-free government bonds with a face value of $250 million and a short position in put options with a strike price of $250 million. As before, the underlying asset for the put option is not the firm's stock, but the firm's assets. Because bondholders are, in effect, selling this put option to the firm, if the firm's assets turn out to be worth less than $250 million, the firm will give the assets to the bondholders for $250 million in cash.[9] The net cash flow to bondholders will equal the $250 million they earn on risk-free bonds, minus any losses they incur on the put option.

In principle, it is possible to quantify the value of the put option that bondholders in effect sell to shareholders. To do so requires an estimate of the volatility of the firm's assets. Depending on what assets the firm invests in, such an estimate may or may not be difficult to obtain. However, there is another way to place a value on the put option. If holding a risky corporate bond is identical to holding a risk-free bond and selling a put option, then we can calculate the put value by simply comparing the market value of the firm's debt to the market value of identical bonds that are risk-free. The difference in prices must equal the put value:

Value of risky debt = value of risk-free debt − put value   **(Eq. 19.4)**

[9.] When firms go bankrupt, bondholders do not usually pay out cash in exchange for the firm's assets. They do something equivalent, however. A bankrupt firm can hand over its assets to lenders, and in exchange, the shareholders of the firm can walk away from their debts. In other words, receiving a cash payment of $250 million is equivalent, in economic terms, to having an outstanding debt of $250 million canceled.

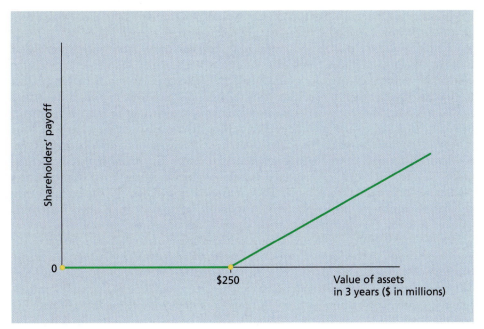

Figure 19.5
Options Embedded in the Stock of a Levered Firm

The shareholders of a levered firm hold a call option. If the firm's assets are worth more than the value of its debts, then shareholders keep the surplus. If not, shareholders receive nothing when the firm defaults.

APPLYING THE MODEL

The market value of this firm's outstanding bonds is $200 million, implying that they offer investors a yield to maturity of 7.72 percent. If the yield to maturity on 3-year government bonds is just 6 percent, the $250 million face value of zero-coupon government bonds would sell today for $250 million ÷ 1.06^3 or $210 million. The $10 million difference equals the value of the put option on the firm's assets—that is, the default option.

Now, let's consider all this from the perspective of shareholders. When the firm borrows $250 million, shareholders know that if the firm cannot repay the loan, they will receive nothing. However, if cash flows are more than sufficient to pay bondholders $250 million, then shareholders receive any excess cash. Figure 19.5 shows a payoff diagram for shareholders. As always, the underlying asset is the value of the firm's assets in three years. Do you recognize this picture? From the shareholders' point of view, they own a claim that is equivalent to a long call option on the underlying assets with a strike price of $250 million.

Figure 19.5 contains some unsettling news for bondholders. Suppose that the objective of this firm's management is to maximize the wealth of shareholders. If holding a share of stock in this company is like holding a call option, then maximizing the share price should be analogous to maximizing the value of a call option. What actions might managers take to maximize the call value? We have seen that a critical factor in determining option values is the volatility of the underlying asset. Managers could increase share prices by increasing the volatility of the firm's assets. Once the firm has outstanding debt, its stock behaves like a call option, so making riskier investments benefits shareholders at the expense of bondholders.

SMART IDEAS VIDEO
Myron Scholes, Stanford University, and Chairman of Oak Hill Platinum Partners
"One of the more recent innovations in the options market that is quite exciting is the development of credit derivatives."

See the entire interview at **SMARTFinance**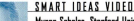

If it seems far-fetched that managers would intentionally take more risk to increase share values, we offer two pieces of evidence that we will hope will persuade you that managers recognize this opportunity. The first piece of evidence is somewhat indirect. When companies enter loan contracts with banks and other lenders, the companies must often agree to abide by a set of loan covenants designed to protect lenders by, among other things, restricting the uses to which firms can apply borrowed funds. If lenders did not worry that firms might borrow to make risky investments (actually, to make riskier investments than they disclosed when they borrowed the money), then there would be no reason for lenders to insist on covenants of this type.

The second piece of evidence is much more direct. In an interesting study, Berger, Ofek, and Yermack (1997) examined the connection between firms' compensation plans and their capital structures. They reasoned as follows. Suppose that a firm chooses to emphasize stock options in the compensation package it offers managers. Managers know that the value of these options depends on several factors, one of which is the volatility of the underlying stock. Therefore, managers who receive a great deal of pay in the form of stock options have the incentive not only to increase the price of the stock, but also to increase its volatility. One way to increase the volatility of equity is to use more debt in the capital structure. Berger, Ofek, and Yermack found a positive correlation between the number of stock options held by a firm's CEO and the firm's debt-to-assets ratio. Though a correlation between option compensation and leverage does not prove that managers increase leverage after receiving stock options, it is at least consistent with that hypothesis. In a similar vein, Rajgopal and Shevlin (2002) find that managers of oil and gas firms with employee stock options take greater exploration risks and engage in less hedging than managers without stock options.

Even plain-vanilla investments such as stocks and corporate bonds have option-like characteristics. Recognizing these characteristics provides unique insights into the forces that influence stock and bond prices, as well as relationships between borrowers and lenders, and between managers and shareholders. Now we turn our attention to other types of corporate securities that have more transparent option features.

WARRANTS

Warrants are securities issued by firms that grant the right to buy shares of stock at a fixed price for a given period of time. Warrants bear a close resemblance to call options, and the same five factors that influence call option values will also affect warrant prices (stock price, risk-free rate, strike price, expiration date, and volatility). However, there are some important differences between warrants and calls.

1. Warrants are issued by firms, whereas call options are contracts between investors who are not necessarily connected to the firm whose stock serves as the underlying asset.
2. When investors exercise warrants, the number of outstanding shares increases, and the issuing firm receives the strike price as a cash inflow. When investors exercise call options, no change in outstanding shares occurs, and the firm receives no cash.
3. Warrants are often issued with expiration dates several years in the future, whereas most options expire in just a few months.
4. Although call and put options trade as stand-alone securities, firms frequently attach warrants to public or privately placed bonds, preferred stock, and sometimes even common stock. When warrants are attached to other securities, they are called **equity kickers**, implying that they give additional upside potential to

COMPARATIVE CORPORATE FINANCE

Derivatives and the Banking Industry

Of great concern for bank regulators the world over is the ever-increasing role that banks play in derivatives markets. After rogue trader Nick Leeson lost more than $1 billion and brought down the venerable U.K. Bearings Bank in the process, regulators worried that bank trading in derivatives might lead to similar fiascos around the world. After all, options and other derivatives are very risky financial instruments, and the potential certainly exists for banks to take big risks through derivatives trading, intentionally or, as in the case of Leeson,

unintentionally. Although we do not want to dismiss these worries entirely, we do believe that banks have a crucial role to play in these markets. The table below lists the top-20 dealers in over-the-counter derivatives (of all types), and it is clear that banks dominate the list.

Source: Garry J. Schinasi, R. Sean Craig, Burkhard Drees, and Charles Kramer, *Modern Banking and OTC Derivatives Markets: The Transformation of Global Finance and Its Implications for Systemic Risk* (Washington, D.C.: International Monetary Fund, 2000).

Derivatives Dealer	Rank in Year 2000	Members of Exchange[a]					
		CME	LIFFE	EUREX	HKFE	TSE	TIFFE
Citigroup	1	x	x	x	x	x	
Goldman Sachs	2	x	x	x	x	x	
Deutsche Bank	3	x	x	x	x	x	
Morgan Stanley	4	x	x	x	x	x	
Warburg Dillon Read	5	x	x	x	x	x	
Merrill Lynch	6	x	x	x	x	x	
J. P. Morgan	7	x	x	x	x	x	
Chase Manhattan	8	x	x	x			x
Credit Suisse First Boston	9	x	x	x	x	x	
Bank of America	10	x	x	x			x
NatWest Group	N/A		x	x			x
Lehman Brothers	12	x	x	x	x	x	
Hong Kong and Shanghai Bank	13	x	x	x	x	x	x
Société Générale	14	x	x	x			
American International	15	x					
Barclays Capital	16	x	x	x	x	x	x
Dresdner Kleinwort Benson	17	x	x	x	x		
BNP-Paribas	18	x	x	x	x	x	
ABN Amro	19	x	x	x	x	x	
Commerzbank	20	x	x	x	x		

[a]CME (Chicago Mercantile Exchange); LIFFE (London International Financial Futures and Options Exchange); EUREX (European Derivatives Market); HKFE (Hong Kong Futures Exchange); TSE (Tokyo Stock Exchange); TIFFE (Tokyo International Financial Futures Exchange)

the security to which they are attached. When firms bundle warrants together with other securities, they may or may not grant investors the right to unbundle them and sell the warrants separately.

For example, on April 12, 2002, UQM Technologies Inc. (ticker symbol, UQM) announced that it had issued 1,160,095 additional shares of common stock for

$4.31 per share. The maker of high-efficiency electric motors also announced that for every five shares that investors purchased, they would receive a warrant allowing them to buy an additional UQM share for $5.73 for the following two years. Clearly, UQM's shares would have to appreciate before the warrants would be worth exercising.

Just a few weeks earlier on March 25, tiny Canadian mining concern Campbell Resources Inc. (Toronto Stock Exchange ticker symbol, CCH) reported that it received C$570,000 upon the exercise of 1,162,791 warrants by Le Fonds d'Investissement REA Inc. Campbell said it planned to use the funds for working-capital requirements during the start-up phase of one of its mines. Le Fonds paid an exercise price of C$0.49 per share, a profitable trade because Campbell shares were trading in Toronto at C$0.65.

In each case, the firm receives capital from warrants, once when they are issued and again if they are exercised. This stands in sharp contrast to the buying, selling, and exercising of call options, which occurs without having any direct cash flow impact on the underlying firms. Nevertheless, the Black and Scholes model can be used to value warrants, provided an adjustment is made to account for the dilution that occurs when firms issue new shares to warrant holders. A simple example will illustrate how to adjust for dilution.

Assume that a small firm has 1,000 shares outstanding worth $10 each. The firm has no debt, so the value of its assets equals the value of its equity, $10,000. Two years ago, when the firm's stock price was just $8, the firm issued 100 shares of common stock to a private investor. Each share had an attached warrant granting the right to purchase one share of stock for $9 for two years. The warrants are about to expire, and the investor intends to exercise them.

What would the investor's payoff be if he held ordinary call options (sold to him by another private investor) rather than warrants? Because the price of the stock is $10 and the strike price is $9, the investor would earn a profit of $1 per share or $100 on the calls. If calls were exercised, the firm would still have 100 shares outstanding worth $10 each. From the firm's point of view, the call exercise would generate neither a cash inflow nor a cash outflow.

In contrast, if the investor exercises his warrants, two changes take place. First, the firm receives cash equal to the strike price ($9) times the number of warrants exercised (100), or a total inflow of $900. This raises the total value of the firm's assets to $10,900. Simultaneously, the firm's outstanding shares increase from 1,000 to 1,100, so the new price per share can be calculated as follows:

New price per share = $10,900 ÷ 1,100 = $9.91

The investor's payoff on the warrants is just $0.91, compared to $1.00 on a comparable call option. Fortunately, it's easy to use the Black and Scholes model to value a call option with characteristics similar to those of a warrant, then multiply the call value times an adjustment factor for dilution. If N_1 represents the number of "old shares" outstanding and N_2 represents the number of new shares issued as a result of the warrants being exercised, then the price of the warrants equals the price of an identical call option, $C, multiplied by the following dilution factor, $\dfrac{N_1}{N_1 + N_2}$:

$$\text{Warrant value} = \$C\left(\frac{N_1}{N_1 + N_2}\right) \qquad \text{(Eq. 19.5)}$$

APPLYING THE MODEL

After issuing new shares of common stock with attached warrants in April 2002, UQM Technologies had 18,829,848 shares of common stock outstanding. We will use the Black and Scholes formula and the adjustment factor in Equation 19.5 to value UQM's warrants. To value the warrants, we must know the price of UQM stock, the expiration date of the warrants, the strike price, and the risk-free rate. We must also have an estimate of UQM's volatility. Here are the relevant figures as of April 12, 2002: stock price = \$4.40; strike price = \$5.73; risk-free rate = 2 percent; expiration = two years; standard deviation = 77 percent.[10]

$$d_1 = \frac{\ln\left(\frac{4.40}{5.73}\right) + \left(0.02 + \frac{0.77^2}{2}\right)2}{0.77\sqrt{2}} = \frac{(-0.264) + (0.633)}{1.089} = 0.339$$

$$d_2 = d_1 - \sigma\sqrt{t} = 0.339 - 0.772 = -0.750$$

$$N(0.339) = 0.633 \qquad N(-0.750) = 0.226$$

$$C = 4.40(0.633) - 5.73(2.718^{-(.02)(2)})(0.226) = \$1.54$$

$$\text{Warrant} = \frac{18,829,848}{18,829,848 + 232,019}(1.54) = \$1.52$$

Investors in the UQM new issue paid \$4.31 in exchange for one share of stock worth \$4.40 and 0.2 warrants worth \$0.30 (0.2 × \$1.54). Thus, investors paid \$4.31 to receive a package of securities worth \$4.70, a discount of 8.3 percent. ■

CONVERTIBLES

A convertible bond grants investors the right to receive payment in the shares of an underlying stock rather than in cash. Usually, the stock that investors have the right to "purchase" in exchange for their bonds is the stock of the firm that issued the bonds. In some cases, however, a firm that owns a large amount of common stock in a different firm will use those shares as the underlying asset for a convertible bond issue. In either case, a **convertible bond** is essentially an ordinary corporate bond with an attached call option or warrant.

In February 2002, the biotech giant, Amgen Inc., announced a sale of 30-year, zero-coupon bonds that would generate proceeds for the company of approximately \$2.5 billion. Amgen's bonds offered investors a yield to maturity of just 1.125 percent, well below the yields on long-term government bonds at the time. How could a biotech firm borrow money at a lower rate than the government? Investors were willing to buy Amgen's bonds despite the low yield because the bonds were convert-

---

[10.] Readers may wonder why we use a stock price of \$4.40 here rather than the \$4.31 at which UQM issued new shares. Although \$4.31 is the price at which UQM issued its shares with attached warrants, the market price of outstanding UQM shares at the time was about \$4.40. Thus, UQM sold its new securities at a discount to market value. We estimated the 77 percent figure for standard deviation based on daily trading data over the preceding three months. See the appendix at the end of the chapter for the calculation.

ible into Amgen common stock. Specifically, each Amgen bond having a face value of $1,000 could be converted into 8.8601 shares of Amgen common stock.

Convertible bonds offer investors the security of a bond and the upside potential of common stock. If Amgen's shares increase in value, the bondholders will redeem their bonds for Amgen shares rather than cash. To see how far Amgen's shares would have to rise before bondholders would want to convert, we must first calculate the market price of Amgen's bonds:

$$\text{Price} = \frac{\$1,000}{(1.01125)^{30}} = \$714.90$$

The **conversion ratio** defines how many Amgen shares bondholders will receive if they convert. In this case, the conversion ratio is 8.8601, so if bondholders chose to convert immediately, they would effectively be paying a **conversion price** for Amgen calculated as follows:

$$\text{Conversion price} = \frac{\$714.90}{8.8601} = \$80.69$$

At the time Amgen issued these bonds, its stock was selling for approximately $57 per share. Holding the price of the bond constant, Amgen's shares would have to rise more than 41 percent before bondholders would want to convert their bonds into Amgen's shares. This 41 percent figure equals the bond's **conversion premium.** At present, it does not make sense for holders of Amgen's convertible bonds to trade them for shares of stock. Nevertheless, we can still ask, what value will bondholders receive if they do convert? If Amgen stock sells for $57 and each bond can be exchanged for 8.8601 shares, the **conversion value** of one bond equals $505.03 (8.8601 × $47). Conversion value is important because it helps define a lower bound on the market value of a convertible bond. For example, suppose that interest rates jump suddenly and the yield on Amgen's bonds goes from 1.125 percent to 2.5 percent. Ignoring the opportunity to convert the bonds, the price would drop as follows:

$$\text{Price} = \frac{\$1,000}{(1.025)^{30}} = \$476.74$$

However, the price of Amgen's bonds cannot dip this low if Amgen's stock remains at $57. If it did drop, investors could exploit an arbitrage opportunity by purchasing one bond for $476.74 and immediately converting it into 8.8601 shares of stock worth $505.03.

In general, we can say that the price of a convertible bond will be, at a minimum, the higher of (1) the value of an identical bond without conversion rights, or (2) the conversion value. Figure 19.6 demonstrates this pattern for a generic convertible bond with a par value of $1,000 and a conversion ratio of 20. The horizontal line represents the present value of the convertible bond's scheduled interest and principal payments, which, for convenience, we assume to be $1,000. The upward-sloping line shows the bond's conversion value at different stock prices, and the curve shows the convertible bond's price. When the stock price is very low, the odds that the bonds will ever be worth converting into shares are low, so the convertible bond sells at a price comparable to that of an ordinary bond. As the share price rises, the value of the conversion option increases.

Most convertible bonds have another feature that complicates matters slightly.

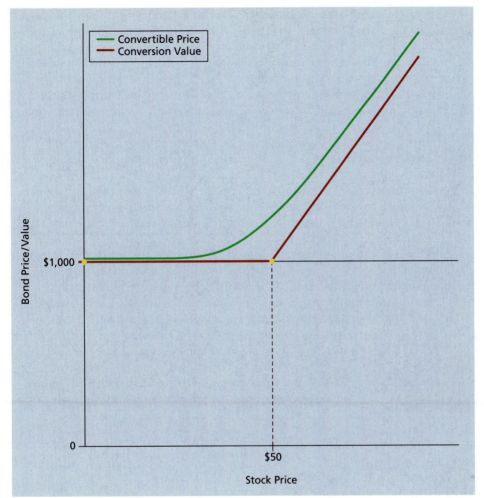

Figure 19.6
The Value of a Convertible Bond

The convertible bond must sell for at least its value as a straight bond, or its conversion value, whichever is greater. If the bond's value is $1,000 and the conversion ratio is 20, then the conversion price equals $50. For each $1 increase in the stock price beyond $50, the bond's conversion value rises by $20.

When firms issue convertibles, they almost always retain the right to call back the bonds. When firms call their outstanding bonds, bondholders can choose, within 30 days of the call, to receive either the call price in cash or a quantity of shares equal to the conversion ratio. Effectively, the call option that firms retain allows them to shorten the conversion option held by bondholders. If a firm calls its bonds, investors will choose cash if the call price exceeds conversion value, and they will choose shares if the opposite is true.

Under what circumstances should a firm call its convertible bonds? If managers are acting in the interests of shareholders, they will never call bonds that are worth less than the call price. Doing so would transfer wealth from shareholders to bondholders. Similarly, if the price of a bond rises above the call price, because the underlying stock has increased in value, then firms should call the bonds. If the firm does not call the bonds, and the stock price continues to increase, when investors ultimately choose to convert their bonds into shares, the firm will be selling stock at a bargain. Again, the result is a transfer of wealth from shareholders to bondholders. Therefore, the optimal policy is to call the bonds when their market value equals the call price.[11]

11. Actually, this would be the optimal call policy if firms could force investors to choose cash or shares immediately upon receiving the call. However, because investors have 30 days to decide whether they want cash or shares, the optimal time

Convertible securities come in many flavors, and each flavor usually has its own colorful acronym. For example, LYONs (liquid-yield option note) are zero-coupon bonds, convertible into the shares of the issuing firm, which are both callable by the issuer and putable by the investors. When a bond is putable, investors have the right to force the issuer to redeem their bonds in cash. DECS (debt exchangeable for common shares) are convertibles that automatically convert to shares at a future date. The conversion ratio of DECS can be variable, such that bondholders must endure the downside risk of the underlying stock, but they do not necessarily enjoy all the upside potential. LYONs, DECS, and other exotic convertibles usually offer investors an interest rate higher than the dividend yield on the underlying stock.[12] Recently, several Internet companies issued a new type of convertible bond named "death spiral" convertibles, as described in Hillion and Vermaelen (2002). These convertible bonds promise lenders a fixed dollar amount of shares, which in turn implies a variable conversion ratio. If the underlying share price falls, the only way to pay lenders a fixed dollar amount of shares is to convert their bonds into more shares. However, as with warrants, convertible bonds create dilution. The name "death spiral" comes from the possibility that as a firm's share price declines and it issues more shares to convertible bondholders, the subsequent dilution will force share prices even lower.

The lesson from this section is that many types of securities issued by corporations have embedded options, and understanding the characteristics of these options is central to pricing the securities with which they are bundled. But an even broader application of option-pricing theory has developed in the last two decades, one that is gaining ground in the corporate world: real options—applying the theoretical apparatus developed for financial options to real investment projects with optionlike qualities.

SMART IDEAS VIDEO
Michael Brennan, UCLA

"It is difficult to overestimate the contribution that this development has had both for financial theory and for financial practice."

See the entire interview at **SMART**Finance

Concept Review Questions

6. Using option-pricing logic, explain why debt covenants often restrict firms from taking out additional loans without the initial lender's consent.

7. Firms wanting to save on borrowing costs should always issue convertible bonds because investors will buy them even though they offer lower yields than ordinary bonds. Comment on this statement.

8. After issuing warrants, what actions might a firm take that would be to the detriment of warrant holders?

19.3 OPTIONS EMBEDDED IN CAPITAL INVESTMENTS—REAL OPTIONS

In Chapters 7 and 9, we learned that the *NPV* rule does not always lead to value-maximizing decisions when firms are considering major investment proposals. The

---

to call may be when the market value of the bonds exceeds the call price slightly. The reason is that if the firm calls the bonds precisely when the market price hits the call price, the stock price might fall during the 30-day decision period. A decline in the stock price would lower the conversion value, and the firm would be forced to redeem the bonds for cash. Allowing the conversion value of the bonds to rise a little beyond the strike price gives the firm a little "slack." See Asquith (1995).

[12.] For a discussion of LYONs, see McConnell and Schwartz (1992).

reason is that the *NPV* approach fails to capture the value of managerial flexibility as the passing of time resolves uncertainty surrounding a particular investment. Managers usually have the option to abandon or to expand an initial investment, and that flexibility often adds to a project's value above and beyond its *NPV*. Smart managers understand this intuitively, but in recent years, tools have emerged that help quantify and refine this intuition.

In this section, we show how to calculate the option value of two capital investment projects. In the first example, which involves oil extraction, we will use the Black and Scholes model to show that oil-drilling rights have value even when it is not economic to drill right away. In the second example, we will use the binomial model to quantify the value to McDonald's Corporation of a pilot investment in a new type of storefront, McTreat Spot.

THE OPTION VALUE OF DRILLING RIGHTS

Let's return to a problem we studied briefly in Chapter 9. A company has the opportunity to bid for drilling rights for one year on a tract of land. The cost of extracting the oil is $18 per barrel, and the current (and expected future) price of oil is $16 per barrel. Because drilling has a negative contribution margin, an *NPV* calculation says that the drilling rights have negative value.

Adding a little more structure to this problem, suppose that the annual standard deviation of the price of oil is 30 percent. Given this volatility, a firm contemplating a bid for the drilling rights can expect that at some point the price of oil may rise to a level that makes drilling profitable. But without knowing when or how high the price of oil may rise, how can the firm quantify the value of the opportunity to drill only when oil prices are sufficiently high?

The right to drill oil is like a call option. By paying the exercise price of $18, the firm has the right to receive one barrel of oil. The option lasts for one year until drilling rights expire. Adding the assumption that the risk-free rate equals 4 percent, we can value this option using the Black and Scholes model:

$$d_1 = \frac{\ln\left(\frac{16}{18}\right) + \left(0.04 + \frac{0.30^2}{2}\right)1}{0.30\sqrt{1}} = \frac{(-0.118) + (0.085)}{0.30} = -0.109$$

$$d_2 = d_1 - \sigma\sqrt{t} = -0.109 - 0.30 = -0.409$$

$$N(-0.109) = 0.456 \qquad N(-0.409) = 0.341$$

$$C = 16(0.456) - 18(2.718^{-(.04)(1)})(0.341) = \$1.40$$

The value of drilling rights equals $1.40 per barrel, so the firm can determine its bid by multiplying this value times the number of barrels expected in the field. If there are fixed costs of drilling above and beyond the $18 extraction costs, bidding makes sense only if the total option value exceeds the fixed costs.

Without question, this problem represents an oversimplification of a real-world drilling-rights problem. For example, the Black and Scholes calculation assumes that the option exercise occurs on a single date one year in the future. In reality, a firm can

decide to pump oil at any time during the year, and it can stop pumping once it has started if the price of oil falls. Modeling this flexibility requires a complex binomial tree, one in which the price of oil moves a little bit each week over the option's life. A complete binomial tree like this will show many different paths that oil prices might take. At each point on each path, the firm must decide whether to begin pumping oil, or if they are already pumping at that point in the tree, whether to stop. Because the binomial valuation approach recognizes that managers have a higher degree of flexibility than contemplated in the Black and Scholes calculation, we expect that a binomial analysis would lead to an option above our current estimate of $1.40 per barrel. Even so, the Black and Scholes model offers a "first cut" at estimating the option value of drilling rights, and it leads the firm to a different conclusion than it would reach from *NPV* analysis alone.

Minicase: Real Options at McDonald's—McTreat Spot[13]

McDonald's Corporation is constantly looking for ways to grow its U.S. business by levering its various hamburger-chain strengths (brand management, inventory and cost control, location development, etc.) into new non-hamburger-store formats. One concept currently (June 2001) under consideration is the McTreat Spot.

The idea behind McTreat Spot is to provide potential customers with convenient places to satisfy their sweet tooth. The current vision of a McTreat Spot is a small kiosk located in high-traffic/high-volume locations like airport concourses and shopping malls, offering ice cream and frozen yogurt products such as sundaes and milkshakes.

There are many uncertainties involved with this new concept. First of all, the company is unsure whether these very small storefronts in high-rent areas can achieve sufficient sales to cover costs and provide a return on capital. Perhaps more important, it is unclear whether customers would like to purchase McDonald's dessert products outside of McDonald's existing stores when faced with specialty-store alternatives (TCBY, Ben & Jerry's, etc.). Finally, as is in all of McDonald's businesses, there is uncertainty about the overall economy; McDonald's management believes that the McTreat Spot enterprise value will be sensitive to the overall state of the economy.

Faced with this uncertainty, McDonald's Corporation has decided to test the new store format in selected shopping malls, the Minneapolis Airport, the Circus-Circus Casino in Las Vegas, and even a few Blockbuster video outlets. Such testing is extraordinarily expensive because each storefront must be uniquely designed and scale economies are not exploitable. In fact, the test stores have negative *NPV*s on their own (i.e., they use more cash than they generate). But the management at McDonald's knows that they have "strategic" value. The question is this: How much is McDonald's willing to spend in the name of "strategy"? In other words, what is the investment value of the McTreat Spot test stores?

Of course, McDonald's does not disclose detailed financial information on individual projects such as this, but we can construct hypothetical values to illustrate how a financial analyst at McDonald's might approach the problem. First, let's consider what would happen if McDonald's were to launch the new concept without testing. Management feels that the potential market is perhaps 1,000 storefronts, and each would cost $750,000 to outfit and get going. This investment is irreversible;

[13.] We thank Richard Shockley for providing this example. Although this example is based on a real project being considered by McDonald's, the numbers in this case are purely hypothetical and are intended only to illustrate how a real options analysis might be applied to the McTreat Spot investment proposal. See Horowitz (2001) and Shockley (2001).

if McDonald's decides to take the big gamble, it would cost $750 million (1,000 × $750,000) up front. Rollout would take two years, and at the end of that rollout period, the value of the business would be readily apparent: either it would be a hit, in which case the *PV* of the free cash flows from operations would be $1.5 billion, or it would be a bust, in which case the *PV* of the free cash flows from operations would be only $500 million. Management is somewhat sanguine about the project and feels it will be a "hit" with probability 0.40 and a bust with probability 0.60. To an analyst evaluating this problem in June 2001, the problem would look like this:

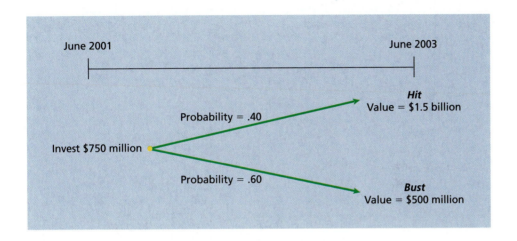

Suppose that McDonald's management assigned a 13 percent discount rate to this project. At that rate, the NPV of an immediate rollout of McTreat Spot is negative in June 2001:

$$NPV = \frac{.4(\$1.5 \text{ billion}) + .6(\$500 \text{ million})}{(1.13)^2} - \$750 \text{ million}$$

$$= \frac{\$900 \text{ million}}{1.277} - \$750 \text{ million}$$

$$= \$704.8 \text{ million} - \$750 \text{ million} = -\$45.2 \text{ million}$$

In other words, immediate rollout is a value-destroying activity for McDonald's shareholders. The present value of cash inflows from entering this business is only $704.8 million, whereas the cost of entering the business is $750 million.

Even though the 2001 *NPV* of the McTreat Spot concept was negative and the *NPV* of any test stores would surely be negative, McDonald's management intuitively understood that the test-store program was very valuable. The reason is that the test stores generate information in addition to cash flow: by doing the testing program for two years, McDonald's can learn the value of a 1,000-store chain *before* investing $750 million. If the test stores indicate that McTreat Spot is a hit, the firm will spend the capital and take the positive-*NPV* business. On the other hand, if the test stores indicate that McTreat Spot is a bust, management will walk away only having spent the cost of the testing program. So the test-store program gives a very different picture:

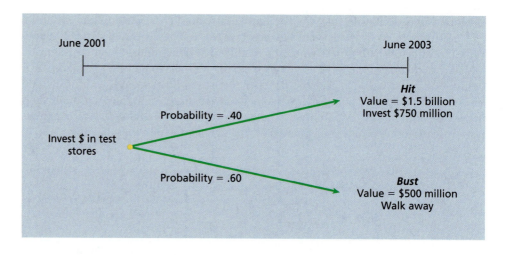

Investing in test stores allows McDonald's to capture the positive *NPV* in the "up" branch of the tree and to walk away without making an additional investment in the "down" branch. This is just like a call option that an investor chooses to exercise if the stock price goes up or to throw away if the stock price goes down. This option, like an ordinary call option, has an underlying asset that determines its value, and it has a strike price that must be paid to acquire the underlying asset. The underlying asset here is the value of the cash inflows from a 1,000-kiosk McTreat chain, and the strike price is the $750 million needed to build all those kiosks. If McDonald's learns that the value of the business is greater than the $750 million cost, the company will exercise its call option by building 1,000 kiosks at a cost of $750 million. That will allow the firm to take the *NPV* of $750 million ($1.5 billion − $750 million) as the payoff in 2003. If McDonald's learns that the value of the business is less than $750 million, it will let the option die unexercised, and the payoff in 2003 will be zero.

Because the test stores create the real option on a 1,000-store chain, we can determine the value of the test-store program itself, which is simply equal to the value of the option it creates plus the *NPV* of its own cash flows. In other words, we can now answer the very difficult question, what is the most McDonald's should spend on the test stores? As long as the option value created by the test stores exceeds their cost (their negative *NPV*), then the test stores actually create value for McDonald's shareholders.

McDonald's can value the option created by the test stores using the binomial model. The key issue is to understand the June 2001 value of the underlying asset. The underlying asset is always what you would get if you exercised the option; in this case, exercise of the option results in McDonald's receiving a 1,000-store McTreat Spot chain. The beginning value of the underlying asset is always the value of what you get if you exercise immediately; in this case, it is the June 2001 estimated value of the McTreat Spot chain (which we have determined to be $704.8 million). Our binomial option problem looks like this:

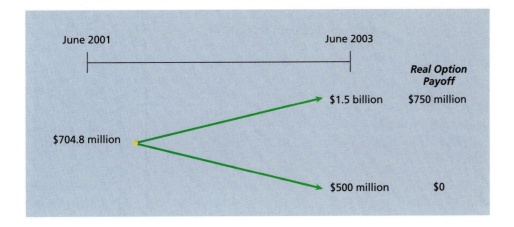

Let's attempt to value this option using the risk-neutral method. Remember, the risk-neutral approach involves choosing the probabilities of the up-and-down moves in the underlying asset such that the expected return from holding the underlying asset equals the risk-free rate (because that's what risk-neutral investors demand). Suppose that the risk-free rate in this problem is 5 percent. At that rate, the value of the underlying asset would grow in two years to the following:

$$\$704.8(1.05)^2 = \$777.0$$

Next, let p represent the probability of an up move and $1 - p$, the probability of a down move. Setting the expected payoff on the underlying asset equal to the risk-free rate, we determine the following ($ in millions):

$$\$1,500p + \$500(1 - p) = \$777$$
$$p = 0.277$$
$$1 - p = 0.723$$

Now, use those probabilities to calculate the expected cash flow in 2003 from the call option. In the up state, the call pays $750, and in the down state, it pays nothing, so the expected cash flow is calculated as follows:

$$\text{Expected cash flow from call option} = \$750p + \$0(1 - p)$$
$$= \$750(0.277) = \$207.8$$

Finally, discount this cash flow for two years at 5 percent to obtain the current price of the call option:

$$\text{Call value today} = \$207.8 \div 1.05^2 = \$188.4$$

In other words, the most McDonald's should be willing to spend on the test stores (given our assumptions) is $188.4 million. As long as the testing program costs less than this (in capital investment as well as negative free cash flow), then testing creates value for the shareholders.

Consider the errors McDonald's might make if it attempts to value this project using decision trees with management's estimate of the up-and-down probabilities of 40 percent and 60 percent, respectively. In the initial decision tree where we calculated the expected *NPV*, ignoring the option to walk away if McTreat Spot was not a hit, McDonald's found a negative *NPV* of −$45.2 million. Focusing on that number alone would be a mistake because it ignores McTreat Spot's option value. What if McDonald's recognized the option value, but priced it using the second decision tree, again with the 40 percent and 60 percent probabilities? Discounting the expected cash flows from that decision tree at 13 percent, the expected *NPV* is calculated as follows:

$$\frac{.4(\$750 \text{ million}) + .6(\$0)}{(1.13)^2} = \$235 \text{ million}$$

That's right—applying management's probabilities to the decision tree of call option payoffs would overvalue the test-store investment by $47.1 million, an error of 25 percent! Why does a decision tree give such an incorrect answer? Because decision trees are not risk adjusted. As discussed previously, the test-store program creates a call option on a full-blown store. One of the things we have learned is that call options are much riskier than the underlying asset on which they are written. Therefore, if the underlying asset here, a fully built McTreat Spot chain, has a risk-adjusted required rate of return of 13 percent, the required rate of return for the *option* on the McTreat Spot chain must be higher. How much higher? We cannot know that without doing the option valuation, but now that we know the correct option value, we can "infer" the proper discount rate by applying management's probabilities of future outcomes and solving for the discount rate that provides the option value:

$$\frac{.4(\$750) + .6(0)}{(1 + r)^2} = \$188.4 \qquad r = 26.2\%$$

In summary, an expected *NPV* calculation undervalues the McTreat project because it ignores the project's option value. However, a decision-tree approach to valuing that option using the 40 percent and 60 percent probabilities overvalues the option. This is a common pattern. *NPV* calculations often understate the value of an investment, but pricing corporate growth options using decision trees leads to overvaluation errors. Analysts must always value real options with the appropriate technology—that is, an option-pricing model such as the binomial or the Black and Scholes.

Concept Review Questions

9. In the oil-drilling example, how should a firm change its bid if it believes the volatility of oil prices will increase? How would the firm change its bid if it valued the drilling rights using *NPV* analysis rather than taking an options perspective on the investment?

10. In the McTreat problem, management believes that the probability of a "hit" is 40 percent. What impact does this belief have on the option valuation of the investment?

19.4 SUMMARY

- Analysts can use the Black and Scholes formula to value a European call on a stock that pays no dividends.
- The Black and Scholes formula requires five inputs: the stock price, the strike price, the risk-free rate, the time to expiration, and the underlying asset's volatility.
- Of the five inputs to the model, only volatility is an unknown that analysts must estimate.
- If analysts can observe the market price of an option, they can use the Black and Scholes equation to solve for the underlying asset's implied volatility.
- When a firm borrows money, both its debt and equity have optionlike characteristics.
- Warrants are similar to call options, though pricing warrants requires an adjustment to the Black and Scholes model to account for dilution.
- Convertible securities combine the characteristics of ordinary bonds with call options.
- Capital investments with optionlike characteristics may be valued using either the binomial or the Black and Scholes model; which valuation approach is appropriate depends on the characteristics of the investment

INTERNET RESOURCES

Note: *For updates to links, please go to the book's website at* http://smart.swcollege.com

http://www.cboe.com — Offers price quotes for many options and provides several tutorials explaining the characteristics of options and how they are traded

http://www.real-options.com — A site with an extensive real options reading list, plus links to news clips and conferences dealing with real options

KEY TERMS

Black and Scholes option-pricing equation	equity kickers
conversion premium	hedge ratio
conversion price	implied volatility
conversion ratio	option's delta
conversion value	standard normal distribution
convertible bond	warrants

QUESTIONS

19-1. In what sense can the terms $N(d_1)$ and $N(d_2)$ in the Black and Scholes model be interpreted as probabilities that a call option will expire in the money?

19-2. How are the values $N(d_1)$ and $N(-d_1)$ related?

19-3. What happens to the value of a call option when the risk-free rate increases, holding everything else constant?

19-4. You observe that the value of a particular put option has increased significantly over the last few days. However, neither the risk-free rate nor the price of the underlying stock has changed. What is the most likely explanation for the change in the value of the put?

19-5. In Section 19.2, we learned that buyers of a corporate bond hold an instrument that is equivalent to a risk-free bond and a short put with the firm's total assets serving as the underlying asset. But the holder of a corporate bond can also be said to hold the following portfolio: (a) the bondholder owns the assets of the firm (the same way that you might say that the bank owns your car until you have paid it off) and (b) the bondholder sold a call option on the firm's underlying assets. Explain how (a) + (b) is equivalent to a corporate bond.

19-6. In Section 19.2, we learned that a shareholder of a levered firm essentially owns a call option on the firm's assets. But we can also view the shareholder's position as the following portfolio: (a) the shareholder owns the firm's assets, (b) the shareholder is short a risk-free bond, and (c) the shareholder owns a put option on the firm's assets with a strike price equal to the risk-free bond's face value. Explain how (a) + (b) + (c) is equivalent to a share of stock in a levered firm.

19-7. In terms of pricing, what are the most important differences between warrants and call options?

19-8. Is the conversion ratio of the Amgen bonds mentioned in section 19.2 constant through time? What about the conversion price?

19-9. What elements of the oil-drilling problem do not fit the Black and Scholes model very well?

19-10. Why is it inappropriate to calculate the expected *NPV* of the McTreat project and use that to base the go or no-go decision?

PROBLEMS

The Black and Scholes Model

19-1. Use the Black and Scholes model to value a call option with the following characteristics: the strike price is $55, the underlying stock's price is $65, the risk-free rate is 4 percent, the time to expiration is six months, and the standard deviation of the underlying asset is 35 percent. What is the value of $N(d_1)$?

19-2. Recalculate the value of the option in the previous problem assuming that the underlying stock sells for $66. By how much does the call price change? Compare this to the value of $N(d_1)$ in the previous problem.

19-3. The following table shows daily closing prices for the common stock of NVIDIA Corp. (ticker symbol, NVDA) and for call options on NVIDIA shares during the last week of June 2002.

Date	Stock	Option
June 28	$17.18	$2.00
June 27	$17.08	$1.95
June 26	$20.07	$3.55
June 25	$21.17	$4.25
June 24	$23.08	$5.55

For each pair of consecutive days, calculate the ratio of the dollar change in the price of the option divided by the dollar change in the price of the stock. Next, calculate the ratio of the percentage change in the option price divided by the percentage change in the stock price. What general patterns emerge from these calculations?

19-4. A particular stock sells for $40 and has a standard deviation of 35 percent. Value a call option on this stock that has three months left before expiration and an exercise price of $55. The risk-free rate is 4 percent.

19-5. Recalculate the value of the call in the previous problem assuming that the stock price is $41. How much did the call value increase? Compare this to the value of $N(d_1)$ in the previous problem.

19-6. Use the Black and Scholes model to value a put option with a strike price of $35 and an expiration date in four months. The underlying stock sells for $40 and has a standard deviation of 55 percent, and the risk-free rate is 6 percent.

19-7. Suppose that the current market price of a stock is $63. The standard deviation of the stock's returns is 35 percent per year, and the risk-free rate is 4 percent. Calculate the value of a 1-year call option with a strike price of $40. What is the value of $N(d_1)$?

19-8. Recalculate the price of the option in Problem 19-7 using the binomial model under the assumption that in one year's time the stock price will move up or down by one standard deviation, or 35 percent (up to $85.05 or down to $40.95). What is the value of the hedge ratio, h, in this problem? Draw a connection between this value and the value of $N(d_1)$ in the previous problem.

19-9. Repeat the calculations in Problems 19-7 and 19-8 assuming that the call's strike price is $80 rather than $40. Once again, compare the values of $N(d_1)$ and h. Comment on what you find.

19-10. A money manager holds 10,000 shares of stock in a particular company and expects to sell them in one week. She is concerned about the possibility that the stock price might fall before she sells, so she decides to buy 10,000 put options. The current market price of the stock is $70, which is also the strike price of the puts. The standard deviation of the underlying stock is 45 percent, and the risk-free rate is 3 percent. The put options expire in four months. One week from today, the manager plans to unwind her position by selling both the shares and the puts at the prevailing market price.

Smart Solutions
See the problem and solution explained step-by-step at
SMARTFinance

  a. What is the aggregate value of the manager's current holdings in this company's stock?
  b. What will she have to pay for 10,000 puts? After purchasing the puts, what is the total market value of her holdings in both stock and puts?
  c. One week later when it is time for her to sell, what will be the market value of her holdings if the stock price has risen to $75? What if the stock price has fallen to $65?
  d. Repeat parts (b) and (c) assuming that the manager bought 20,000 puts rather than 10,000. Comment on how the purchase of twice as many puts affects your answers.

Options Embedded in Other Securities

19-11. Company A owns a large block of shares of Company B. Company A issues bonds that at maturity will be converted into shares of Company B (conversion is mandatory). The number of Company B shares that bondholders will receive at maturity is determined by the following schedule:

Price of Company B (P)	Number of Shares Given to Bondholders
$P < 50$	1 share
$50 \leq P \leq 60$	$\dfrac{1}{P}$ shares
$60 < P$	$\dfrac{5}{6}$ shares

Draw a payoff diagram showing on the y-axis the dollar value of what bondholders receive, and on the x-axis the stock price of Company B. Then, describe how the bonds consist of a portfolio of ordinary bonds and options on Company B's stock.

19-12. Meg and Sons Incorporated has 2 million shares of common stock outstanding, which sell for $40 per share. The company plans to issue $10 million face value in 5-year notes. Each $1,000 par value bond has 20 attached warrants, granting investors the right to purchase Meg and Sons stock for $55 in five years. If the risk-free rate is 5 percent and the standard deviation of Meg and Sons shares is 30 percent, what is the value of the warrants?

19-13. Look again at the Amgen convertible bonds in section 19.2.

a. If the yield to maturity does not change, what will be the price of the bonds one year after they are issued?
b. What will be the conversion price at that time? The conversion premium?

19-14. A company issues 5-year convertible bonds that pay a 6 percent coupon rate and sell at par value, $1,000. The conversion ratio of the bonds is 15.

a. What is the conversion price?
b. If the current stock price for this company is $60, what is the conversion value of the bonds?
c. What is the conversion premium?

Options Embedded in Capital Investments — Real Options

19-15. Recalculate the value of drilling rights from Section 19.3 assuming that the standard deviation of the price of oil is 40 percent rather than 30 percent. Comment on how your conclusion changes when you value this investment using option-pricing logic rather than *NPV*.

19-16. Value the McTreat Spot option described in Section 19.3 using the binomial method rather than the risk-neutral approach. Verify that either approach results in the same option value.

Smart Solutions
See the problem and solution explained step-by-step at
SMARTFinance

APPENDIX 19A: ESTIMATING VOLATILITY FOR THE BLACK AND SCHOLES MODEL

In this appendix, we illustrate how to calculate the standard deviation for a Black and Scholes option valuation. We will use stock-price data for UQM Technologies, whose warrants we priced earlier. The first task is to gather historical trading data for UQM stock. There is no hard-and-fast rule about how much data to gather, or about the frequency with which returns should be measured. As is the case with estimating any parameter with market data, such as a beta, analysts face trade-offs between sample size, data relevance, and the accuracy with which returns can be measured at different frequencies. For instance, if we want our sample to consist of 60 observations, we could choose the last 60 days, weeks, or months. Daily returns probably do a better job of portraying the current state of the company and the market, but daily returns may be subject to measurement problems if the stock does not trade frequently. Weekly or monthly returns solve the measurement problem, but require us to look so far back to gather 60 observations that some data points may no longer reflect the company's current situation. For example, if a company changed its capital structure significantly in the recent past, the stock's current volatility could be quite different from the volatility observed just a few months back.

From Yahoo! we downloaded daily closing prices for UQM stock from January 10 to April 12, 2002, the date that it issued its warrants. The closing prices and corresponding dates appear in columns 1 and 2 of Table 19A.1. Next, we calculate

Table 19A.1
Calculating the Standard Deviation of Returns for UQM Stock

Date (2002)	Closing Price ($)	Price Relative	$\ln(P_t/P_{t-1})$
Apr 12	4.46	1.021	0.020
Apr 11	4.37	1.002	0.002
Apr 10	4.36	1.000	0.000
Apr 9	4.36	1.038	0.037
Apr 8	4.20	0.977	−0.024
Apr 5	4.30	0.998	−0.002
Apr 4	4.31	1.009	0.009
Apr 3	4.27	0.938	−0.064
Apr 2	4.55	1.046	0.045
Apr 1	4.35	0.946	−0.056
Mar 28	4.60	1.000	0.000
Mar 27	4.60	1.022	0.022
Mar 26	4.50	0.978	−0.022
Mar 25	4.60	0.979	−0.022
Mar 22	4.70	1.011	0.011
Mar 21	4.65	0.979	−0.021
Mar 20	4.75	1.011	0.011
Mar 19	4.70	1.033	0.032
Mar 18	4.55	1.000	0.000
Mar 15	4.55	1.007	0.007
Mar 14	4.52	0.976	−0.024
Mar 13	4.63	0.953	−0.048
Mar 12	4.86	0.970	−0.030
Mar 11	5.01	0.936	−0.066
Mar 8	5.35	1.338	0.291
Mar 7	4.00	1.036	0.036
Mar 6	3.86	0.977	−0.023
Mar 5	3.95	0.985	−0.015
Mar 4	4.01	0.990	−0.010
Mar 1	4.05	1.013	0.012
Feb 28	4.00	1.026	0.025
Feb 27	3.90	0.963	−0.038
Feb 26	4.05	1.000	0.000
			(continued)

Table 19A.1
(Continued)

Date (2002)	Closing Price ($)	Price Relative	$\ln(P_t/P_{t-1})$
Feb 25	4.05	1.015	0.015
Feb 22	3.99	0.973	−0.027
Feb 21	4.10	0.976	−0.024
Feb 20	4.20	1.000	0.000
Feb 19	4.20	0.966	−0.035
Feb 15	4.35	1.002	0.002
Feb 14	4.34	1.021	0.021
Feb 13	4.25	0.984	−0.016
Feb 12	4.32	0.995	−0.005
Feb 11	4.34	1.046	0.045
Feb 8	4.15	0.988	−0.012
Feb 7	4.20	0.988	−0.012
Feb 6	4.25	1.000	0.000
Feb 5	4.25	0.955	−0.046
Feb 4	4.45	0.991	−0.009
Feb 1	4.49	0.945	−0.056
Jan 31	4.75	0.990	−0.010
Jan 30	4.80	1.011	0.010
Jan 29	4.75	1.080	0.077
Jan 28	4.40	1.023	0.023
Jan 25	4.30	0.966	−0.034
Jan 24	4.45	1.011	0.011
Jan 23	4.40	1.011	0.011
Jan 22	4.35	0.967	−0.034
Jan 18	4.50	0.978	−0.022
Jan 17	4.60	0.968	−0.032
Jan 16	4.75	1.000	0.000
Jan 15	4.75	0.990	−0.010
Jan 14	4.80	0.896	−0.110
Jan 11	5.36	0.989	−0.011
Jan 10	5.42	NA	NA

0.048 Standard deviation of daily returns (column 4)
0.766 Annualized standard deviation (daily times $\sqrt{250}$)

the price relative on each day, defined as that day's price divided by the price one day earlier:

$$\text{Price relative} = \frac{P_t}{P_{t+1}} = 1 + r_{\text{daily}}$$

Notice that this ratio equals 1 plus the daily return on the stock. To convert this into a continuously compounded return (recall that Black and Scholes assumes continuous compounding), we take the natural logarithm of the price relative. These figures appear in the fourth column of the table. Using this sequence of daily returns, we calculate the standard deviation in the usual way. Finally, to convert our standard deviation from a daily to an annual basis, we multiply it times the square root of the number of trading days in one year, roughly 250.[14] This yields an estimate of annual volatility that we can plug directly into the Black and Scholes equation.

[14] The reason we convert the standard deviation to an annual basis by multiplying by the square root of the number of trading days in a year can be better understood by looking at the conversion for variance. If there are 250 trading days in a year, then the daily variance times 250 equals the annual variance. Take the square root of both sides to get the appropriate conversion factor for standard deviation.

$$\sigma^2_{\text{annual}} = \sigma^2_{\text{daily}}(250)$$

$$\sigma_{\text{annual}} = \sigma_{\text{daily}}\sqrt{250}$$

International Financial Management

OPENING FOCUS
Dollar's Fall Creates Winners and Losers

Shares in the Hong Kong apparel maker, Esprit Holdings Ltd., closed up almost 3.7 percent on Tuesday, July 2, 2002, despite weakness in the broader Hang Seng index of Hong Kong stock levels, which fell 1.3 percent the same day. Analysts pointed to the recent decline in the U.S. dollar (US$) against the euro, among other factors, as the reason for the gain. Just five months earlier, currency traders could exchange $1 for roughly €1.16, but by early July the dollar and the euro traded almost one for one. The sharp decline in the dollar (rise in the euro) benefited Esprit for two reasons. First, since October 1983, the value of the Hong Kong dollar (HK$) had been pegged to the US$ by a mechanism known as a currency board, a system in which Hong Kong monetary authorities stood ready to exchange HK$ for US$ at a fixed exchange rate of HK$7.8 for US$1. Therefore, as the value of the US$ fell against the euro, so did the value of Hong Kong's currency. This allowed Esprit to charge lower euro prices for their clothing in Europe than competing producers, thereby gaining market share, yet still receiving the same HK$ price to cover their costs. Second, almost 70 percent of Esprit's revenues originated in Europe. Put simply, as Esprit sold clothing in European markets, it earned revenues denominated in euros, and the value of those revenues in HK$ terms had been rising along with the euro.

Just three weeks later, shares in the world's fifth-largest insurer, Aegon NV, dropped 28.2 percent in two days on the Amsterdam Stock Exchange after the Dutch company issued a statement that its profits for the year would be 30–35 percent lower than previously anticipated. The reason? The company blamed several factors, but at the top of the list was the decline in the US$, which slid another 1 percent during mid-July. Aegon generated roughly 65 percent of its profits from the United States, in part because of its $10 billion acquisition of Transamerica in 1999. The falling dollar hurt Aegon's bottom line because the company's dollar-denominated business was high volume and Aegon had chosen not to hedge this exposure. Making matters even worse, the company disclosed that it held $200 million in bonds issued by WorldCom, which had filed for bankruptcy just two days earlier.

The lessons here are twofold. First, though the media reports changes in currency values as though they were somehow a symbol of national vigor or lack thereof, currency movements are neither unambiguously good nor unambiguously bad. Rather, major swings in currency values create winners and losers. The decline in the US$ was a boon for Esprit, and for any other company that sold goods in Europe and then converted those revenues back into a depreciating home currency. Conversely, the dollar's value created serious problems for Aegon, and for any other company that earned revenues in US$ and converted them back into an appreciating home currency. Second, because currency fluctuations of this magnitude are by no means unusual, and because of the impact they have on firms' profits, companies often choose to hedge their currency exposures. Understanding the factors that cause currency values to move and the mechanisms by which firms can hedge against those movements is the primary purpose of this chapter.

Sources: "Aegon's Warning Sparks Fears for Other Insurers," *Financial Times* (July 23, 2002); "Esprit Closes Morning Higher on U.S. Strategy Hopes; Euro Exposure," *AFX Asia* (July 2, 2002).

Walk down the aisle of a grocery store, visit a shopping mall, go hunting for a new automobile, or check the outstanding balance of your credit card. In each of these activities, chances are that you will be dealing with products and services provided by **multinational corporations** (**MNCs**), businesses that operate in many countries around the world. In recent decades, international trade in goods and services has expanded dramatically, and so too have the size and scope of MNCs. Although all the financial principles covered in this text thus far apply to MNCs, companies operating across national borders also face unique challenges. Primary among them is coping with exchange rate risk. An **exchange rate** is simply the price of one currency in terms of another, and for the past 30 years, the exchange rates of major currencies have fluctuated daily. These movements create uncertainty for firms that earn revenue and pay operating costs in more than one currency. Currency movements also add to the competitive pressures faced by wholly domestic companies that face competition from foreign firms.

This chapter focuses on the problems and opportunities firms face as a result of globalization, with special emphasis on currency-related issues. First, we explain the rudimentary features of currency markets, including how and why currencies trade and the rules governments impose on trading in their currencies. Second, we describe equilibrium factors that drive currency values, at least for those countries that allow their currency value to float, constantly responding to market forces. Third, we discuss the special risks faced by MNCs and the strategies they employ to manage those risks. We conclude by illustrating some of the long-term and short-term financial decisions confronting MNCs.

20.1 EXCHANGE RATE FUNDAMENTALS

We begin our coverage of exchange rate fundamentals by describing the "rules of the game" as dictated by national governments.

FIXED VERSUS FLOATING EXCHANGE RATES

Since the mid-1970s, the major currencies of the world have had a **floating exchange rate** relationship with respect to the U.S. dollar and to one another, which means that forces of supply and demand continuously move currency values up and down. The opposite of a floating exchange rate regime is a **fixed exchange rate** system. Under a fixed-rate system, governments fix (or *peg*) their currency's value, usually in terms of another currency such as the U.S. dollar. Once a government pegs the currency at a particular value, it must stand ready to pursue economic and financial policies necessary to maintain that value.[1] For example, if demand for the currency increases, the government must stand ready to sell currency so that the increase in demand does not cause the currency to appreciate. Conversely, if demand for the currency falls, then the government must be ready to buy its own currency, thereby supporting the exchange rate. In many countries with fixed exchange rates, governments impose restrictions on the free flow of currencies into and out of the country. Even so, maintaining a currency peg can be quite difficult. For example, in response to mounting economic problems, the government of Argentina allowed the peso, which had been linked to the U.S. dollar, to float freely for the first time in a decade on January 11, 2002. After one day, the peso lost more than 40 percent of its value relative to that of the dollar.

In addition to using purely fixed and purely floating exchange rate systems, countries, usually those that are developing, employ several intermediate or hybrid models. A **managed floating rate system** is a hybrid in which a nation's government loosely "fixes" the value of the national currency in relation to that of another currency, but does not expend the effort and resources that would be required to maintain a completely fixed exchange rate regime. Other countries simply choose to use another nation's currency as their own, and a handful of nations have adopted a **currency board arrangement.** In such an arrangement, the national currency continues to circulate, but every unit of the currency is fully backed by government holdings of another currency—usually the U.S. dollar.

The International Monetary Fund, in its *International Financial Statistics Yearbook 2001,* detailed the exchange rate systems in place for 186 countries as of March 31, 2001. Forty-seven countries had independently floating exchange rates (including most of the OECD countries), 44 had conventional fixed exchange rates (of which 31 were fixed against a single currency and 13 versus a composite), 33 had managed floats, 39 used another currency as their country's legal tender (including the 12 Western European countries using the euro), 8 maintained currency boards (including Hong Kong), and 15 maintained some other type of hybrid system.

In terms of trading volume, the major currencies in international finance today are (in no particular order) the British pound sterling (£), the Swiss franc (SF), the Japanese yen (¥), the Canadian dollar (C$), the U.S. dollar (US$, or simply $), and the euro (€). This final currency was adopted for financial transactions by 11 continental European countries in January 1999, and in early 2002 this became the only currency circulating in these countries—as well as in Greece, which qualified for membership in the **European Monetary Union (EMU)** in 2001.

[1.] The fixed exchange rate system that collapsed in 1973, called the *Bretton Woods system,* was based on the U.S. dollar and had governed international finance since the late 1940s. Under this system, countries established fixed exchange rates (par values) for their currencies versus the dollar, which often did not change for two decades or more.

Exchange Rate Quotes

Figure 20.1 shows exchange rate values quoted in the *Wall Street Journal* on July 24, 2002. Note that the figure states each exchange rate in two ways. The first two columns report the "US$ Equivalent" value of a given currency. The numbers in these columns show the dollar cost of one unit of foreign currency. In row 1, for example, we see that on Tuesday, July 23, one Argentine peso cost $0.2732. One day earlier, one peso cost $0.2762. Because the value of one peso in terms of U.S. currency fell slightly from Monday to Tuesday, we say that the peso **depreciated** against the dollar.

The third and fourth columns of Figure 20.1 present the same information in a slightly different way. These columns show the value of each foreign currency relative to one U.S. dollar. Again, in row 1 we see that on Monday, July 22, it cost 3.62 pesos to purchase one dollar, but on the next day, one dollar was worth a little more, 3.66 pesos. Because the value of one dollar in terms of pesos rose from Monday to Tuesday, we say that the dollar **appreciated** against the peso. Of course, the exchange rate quotes in the first two columns reveal exactly the same information as the quotes in the second two columns. Each of these methods of quoting exchange rates is simply the reciprocal of the other:

$$\frac{dollars}{peso} = \frac{1}{\dfrac{pesos}{dollar}} \qquad \$0.2732/Ps = \frac{1}{Ps\ 3.66/\$}$$

In Figure 20.1, we can also see that many currencies do not float freely against the dollar, because the exchange rates did not move at all from Monday to Tuesday.

Exchange Rates

The New York foreign exchange mid-range rates below apply to trading among banks in amounts of $1 million and more, as quoted at 4 p.m. Eastern time by Reuters and other sources. Retail transactions provide fewer units of foreign currency per dollar.

	U.S. $ EQUIVALENT		CURRENCY PER U.S. $	
Country	Tue.	Mon.	Tue.	Mon.
Argentina (Peso)-y	.2732	.2762	3.6600	3.6200
Australia (Dollar)	.5385	.5468	1.8570	1.8287
Bahrain (Dinar)	2.6525	2.6525	.3770	.3770
Brazil (Real)	.3429	.3444	2.9160	2.9040
Britain (Pound)	1.5587	1.5784	.6416	.6336
1-month forward	1.5558	1.5754	.6428	.6348
3-months forward	1.5503	1.5700	.6450	.6369
6-months forward	1.5414	1.5614	.6488	.6405
Canada (Dollar)	.6307	.6393	1.5855	1.5642
1-month forward	.6302	.6388	1.5868	1.5654
3-months forward	.6291	.6377	1.5896	1.5681
6-months forward	.6275	.6361	1.5937	1.5721
Chile (Peso)	.001433	.001443	698.05	692.85
China (Renminbi)	.1208	.1208	8.2770	8.2770
Colombia (Peso)	.0003913	.0003975	2555.50	2516.00
Czech. Rep. (Koruna)				
Commercial rate	.03265	.03318	30.627	30.136
Denmark (Krone)	.1327	.1355	7.5330	7.3783
Ecuador (US Dollar)	1.0000	1.0000	1.0000	1.0000
Hong Kong (Dollar)	.1282	.1282	7.8000	7.8000
Hungary (Forint)	.004035	.004119	247.81	242.80
India (Rupee)	.02055	.02054	48.670	48.680
Indonesia (Rupiah)	.0001111	.0001134	9005	8818
Israel (Shekel)	.2138	.2156	4.6780	4.6380
Japan (Yen)	.008497	.008598	117.69	116.31
1-month forward	.008511	.008612	117.50	116.12
3-months forward	.008536	.008637	117.14	115.78
6-months forward	.008576	.008678	116.61	115.23
Jordan (Dinar)	1.4184	1.4184	.7050	.7050

	U.S. $ EQUIVALENT		CURRENCY PER U.S. $	
Country	Tue.	Mon.	Tue.	Mon.
Kuwait (Dinar)	3.3212	3.3300	.3011	.3003
Lebanon (Pound)	.0006610	.0006610	1512.88	1512.88
Malaysia (Ringgit)-b	.2632	.2632	3.8000	3.8000
Malta (Lira)	2.3855	2.4166	.4192	.4138
Mexico (Peso)				
Floating rate	.1036	.1036	9.6505	9.6485
New Zealand (Dollar)	.4733	.4793	2.1128	2.0864
Norway (Krone)	.1304	.1333	7.6697	7.5044
Pakistan (Rupee)	.01677	.01677	59.645	59.625
Peru (new Sol)	.2832	.2839	3.5310	3.5225
Philippines (Peso)	.01981	.01985	50.475	50.375
Poland (Zloty)	.2430	.2464	4.1150	4.0590
Russia (Ruble)-a	.03172	.01370	31.530	31.550
Saudi Arabia (Riyal)	.2666	.2666	3.7505	3.7505
Singapore (Dollar)	.5726	.5769	1.7465	1.7335
Slovak Rep. (Koruna)	.02213	.02248	45.186	44.482
South Africa (Rand)	.0990	.1001	10.1035	9.9895
South Korea (Won)	.0008598	.0008654	1163.10	1155.60
Sweden (Krona)	.1041	.1061	9.6030	9.4265
Switzerland (Franc)	.6788	.6921	1.4731	1.4449
1-month forward	.6793	.6926	1.4721	1.4439
3-months forward	.6801	.6934	1.4703	1.4421
6-months forward	.6815	.6949	1.4673	1.4391
Taiwan (Dollar)	.03022	.03046	33.090	32.830
Thailand (Baht)	.02442	.02472	40.945	40.445
Turkey (Lira)	.00000060	.00000060	1677500	1677500
United Arab (Dirham)	.2723	.2723	3.6728	3.6728
Uruguay (Peso)				
Financial	.03774	.04167	26.500	24.000
Venezuela (Bolivar)	.000758	.000763	1318.50	1310.50
SDR	1.3425	1.3454	.7449	.7433
Euro	.9866	1.0078	1.0136	.9923

Special Drawing Rights (SDR) are based on exchange rates for the U.S., British, and Japanese currencies. Source: International Monetary Fund.

a-Russian Central Bank rate. b-Government rate. y-Floating rate.

Figure 20.1
Exchange Rate Quotes

Spot and forward exchange rates for various currencies relative to the U.S. dollar, July 23, 2002.

Source: The *Wall Street Journal*, July 24, 2002.

These currencies include the dinar (Bahrain), the renminbi (China), the riyal (Saudi Arabia), and several others. We can also distinguish between two types of exchange rates. The exchange rate that applies to currency trades that occur immediately is called the **spot exchange rate.** However, in many currencies it is possible to enter a contract today to trade foreign currency at a fixed price at some future date. The price at which that future trade will take place is called the **forward exchange rate.** For example, a U.S. trader wishing to exchange dollars for British pounds could do so on July 23 at the spot exchange rate of $1.5587/£ (or equivalently, £0.6416/$). Alternatively, that trader could enter into an agreement to trade dollars for pounds one month later at the forward rate of $1.5558/£ (or equivalently, £0.6428/$). If the trader chose to transact through a forward contract, no cash would change hands until the date specified by the contract. Though the figure only quotes forward contracts at maturities of one, three, and six months, a much richer set of forward contracts is available in the foreign exchange market.

Just as we compared movements in the spot exchange rate from Monday to Tuesday, we can also examine differences in the spot exchange rate for current transactions and the forward rate for future transactions. For example, look at the rate quotes for Japanese yen. On the spot market, one yen costs $0.008497, but the exchange rate for trades that will take place 180 days later is $0.008576/¥. The yen's cost on the forward market is slightly higher than it is on the spot market. Whenever one currency buys more of another on the forward market than it does on the spot market, traders say that the first currency trades at a **forward premium.** The forward premium is usually expressed as a percentage relative to the spot rate, so for the yen, we can calculate the 180-day forward premium as follows:

$$\frac{F - S}{S} = \frac{\$0.008576/¥ - \$0.008497/¥}{\$0.008497/¥} = 0.0093 \quad \text{or} \quad 0.93\%$$

where F is the symbol for the forward rate and S stands for the spot rate, both quoted in terms of $/¥. Recognizing that the yen's 0.93 percent forward premium refers to a 6-month contract, we could restate the premium in annual terms by multiplying the premium times 2, which would yield an annualized forward premium of 1.86 percent.

If the yen trades at a forward premium relative to the dollar, then the dollar must trade at a **forward discount** relative to the yen, meaning that one dollar buys fewer yen on the forward market than it does on the spot market. Using the same equation, we focus on currency units in terms of ¥/$:

$$\frac{F - S}{S} = \frac{¥116.61/\$ - ¥117.69/\$}{¥117.69/\$} = -0.0092 \quad \text{or} \quad -0.92\%$$

The dollar trades at a −0.92 percent forward discount for a 6-month contract, or about −1.84 percent per year. In other words, the forward discount on the dollar is opposite in sign and similar in magnitude to the forward premium on the yen, though the discount is always smaller in absolute value than the premium. In general, to calculate the annualized forward premium or discount on a currency, based on a forward contract to be executed in N days, use the following equation:

$$\frac{F - S}{S} \times \frac{360}{N}$$

(Eq. 20.1)

APPLYING THE MODEL

Using the exchange rate quotes in Figure 20.1, we can calculate the annualized forward discount (or premium) on the Swiss franc (SF) relative to the $. We will calculate this based on the rate for a 3-month forward contract. The spot rate equals $0.6788/SF, and the 3-month (or 90-day) forward rate equals $0.6801/SF. Notice that the franc buys more dollars on the forward market than it does on the spot market, so it trades at a forward premium. We can determine the annualized premium as follows, given that we are using a 90-day contract:

$$\frac{\$0.6801/SF - \$0.6788/SF}{\$0.6788/SF} \times \frac{360}{90} = 0.0077 \quad \text{or} \quad 0.77\%$$

    The forward discount or premium gives traders information about more than just the price of exchanging currencies at different points in time. The forward premium is tightly linked to differences in interest rates on short-term, low-risk bonds across countries, a relationship that we explore in depth in the next section.

    One last lesson remains to be gleaned from Figure 20.1. In its daily exchange rate table, the *Wall Street Journal* quotes the value of the world's major currencies relative to the U.S. dollar. But what if someone wants to know the exchange rate between British pounds and Canadian dollars? In fact, all the information needed to calculate this exchange rate appears in the figure. We simply need to calculate a **cross exchange rate** by dividing the dollar exchange rate for one currency by the dollar exchange rate for the other currency. For example, using Tuesday's spot rates from the figure, we can determine the £/C$ exchange rate:

$$\frac{\$1.5587/£}{\$0.6307/C\$} = C\$2.4714/£$$

    How can we be sure that one pound buys 2.4714 Canadian dollars simply by taking this ratio? The answer is that if the value of the pound, relative to the Canadian dollar, were different from this number, then currency traders could engage in **triangular arbitrage,** trading currencies simultaneously in different markets to earn a risk-free profit. Because currency markets operate virtually 24 hours per day, and because currency trades take place with lightning speed and with very low transactions costs, arbitrage maintains actual currency values in different markets relatively close to this theoretical ideal.

APPLYING THE MODEL

Suppose that on July 23, 2002, a trader learns that the exchange rate being offered by a bank in London is C$2.5000/£ rather than C$2.4714/£ as calculated previously. What is the arbitrage opportunity? First, note that the figure C$2.5000/£ is "too high" relative to the theoretically correct rate. This means that in London, one pound costs too much in terms of Canadian dollars; in other words, the pound is overvalued, and the Canadian dollar is undervalued. Therefore, a U.S. trader could make a profit by executing the following steps.

1. Convert U.S. dollars to British pounds in New York at the prevailing spot rate. Assume that the trader starts with $1 million, which will convert to £641,600.

2. Simultaneously, the trader sells £641,600 in London (because pounds are over-valued there) at the exchange rate of C$2.5000/£. The trader will then have C$1,604,000.

3. Convert the Canadian dollars back into U.S. currency in New York. Given the spot rate of $0.6307/C$, the trader will receive $1,011,642 in exchange for C$1,604,000.

After making these trades, all of which can occur in the blink of an eye, the trader winds up $11,642 richer, all without taking risk. As long as the exchange rates do not change, the trader can keep making a profit over and over again.   ■

The preceding example shows that a trader can repeatedly make a profit if the exchange rates do not change, but the exchange rates will change, of course, and they will change in a way that brings the market back into equilibrium. Figure 20.2 illustrates what happens as arbitrage takes place. As traders in New York sell U.S. currency in exchange for pounds, the pound appreciates vis-à-vis the U.S. dollar, and the exchange rate will rise from $1.5587/£ to some new higher level. Likewise, as traders in London sell pounds in exchange for Canadian dollars, the pound will depreciate against the Canadian currency and the exchange rate will fall below C$2.5000/£ to a lower level. Finally, as traders reap their profits in New York by selling Canadian and buying U.S. currency, the exchange rate between Canadian and U.S. dollars will rise from C$0.6307/$. Though we cannot say exactly how much each of these exchange rates will move, we can say that collectively they will move enough to reach a new equilibrium in which the cross exchange rate in New York and the exchange rate quoted in London will be virtually identical.

With this basic understanding of foreign exchange rates in place, let us now turn to some important institutional features of the foreign exchange market.

Figure 20.2
Triangular Arbitrage and Foreign Exchange Market Equilibrium

Exchange Rates Available in New York	U.S. $ Equivalent
British £	1.5587
Canadian $	0.6307

Exchange Rate Available in London	£1 = C$2.5000

Market Is Not in Equilibrium Because $\dfrac{1.5587}{0.6307} < 2.5000$

Effects of Arbitragers' Trades

1. Selling US$ and buying £ in New York puts downward pressure on the dollar in that market . . . . . . 0.6307 ↓
2. Selling £ and buying C$ in London puts downward pressure on the pound in London . . . . . . 2.5000 ↓
3. Selling C$ and buying US$ in New York puts upward pressure on the US$ in that market . . . . . . 1.5587 ↑
4. The left-hand side of the equation above gets bigger, while the right-hand side gets smaller, until a new equilibrium is reached

$$\frac{1.5587\uparrow}{0.6307\downarrow} < 2.5000\downarrow \longrightarrow \text{New equilibrium}$$

The Foreign Exchange Market

The foreign exchange (forex) "market" is not actually a physical exchange but a global telecommunications market. In fact, it is the world's largest financial market, with total volume of almost $2 trillion *per day!* The forex market operates continuously during the business week, with trading beginning each calendar day in Tokyo. As the day evolves, trading moves westward as major dealing centers in Singapore, Bahrain (Persian Gulf), continental Europe, London, and finally North America (particularly New York and Toronto) come online. Dealers in all these markets quote buy and sell prices (bid/ask) for currencies versus the U.S. dollar and, to a limited degree, other currencies as well. Prices for all the floating currencies are set by global supply and demand. Trading in fixed-rate currencies is more constrained and regulated and frequently involves a national government (or a state-owned bank) being involved as counterparty on one side of the trade.

The players in the forex market are numerous, as are their motivations for participating in the market. We can break participants in this market into six distinct (but not mutually exclusive) groups: (1) exporters and importers, (2) investors, (3) hedgers, (4) speculators, (5) dealers, and at times, (6) governments.

Businesses that export goods to or import goods from a foreign country need to enter the foreign exchange market to pay bills denominated in foreign currency or to convert foreign currency revenues back into the domestic currency. Along with all the other players in the market, exporters and importers influence currency values. For instance, if Europeans develop a taste for California wines, then European importers will exchange euros (or perhaps pounds, kroner, francs, etc.) for dollars to purchase wine. Other factors held constant, these trades will tend to put upward pressure on the value of the dollar and downward pressure on European currencies.

Investors also trade foreign currency when they seek to buy and sell financial assets in foreign countries. In the summer of 2002, declines in U.S. stocks led some investors to pull out of their American investments and seek investment opportunities elsewhere. Those who did had to sell U.S. dollars and buy the currency of the country in which they wanted to invest, putting downward pressure on the dollar relative to other currencies. In general, the pressures exerted on currencies by investors are much larger than those exerted by exporters and importers because investors account for a larger fraction of currency trading volume. For example, the total value of goods and services traded internationally each year is about $10 trillion, whereas the aggregate value of currency trading is 50 times that, some $500 trillion annually.

Hedgers influence currency values when they take positions to offset the risks of their existing exposures to certain currencies. In contrast, speculators take positions not to reduce risk but to increase it. Speculators sell a currency if they expect it to depreciate and buy if they expect it to appreciate. Some speculators, such as George Soros, have become famous for the enormous profits (or losses) they have earned by taking large positions in certain currencies. When external pressures force a country with a pegged currency to devalue its currency, speculators often take the blame. Whether they deserve blame for causing, accelerating, or exacerbating currency crises or not, speculators can play a useful economic role by taking the opposite side of a transaction from that of hedgers. Speculators help make the foreign currency market more liquid and more efficient.

As in all financial markets, dealers play a crucial role in the foreign exchange business. Most foreign currency trades go through large, international banks in the leading financial centers around the globe: London, New York, Tokyo, and so on. These banks provide a means for buyers and sellers to come together, and as their reward they earn a small fee, the bid-ask spread, on each round-trip buy-and-sell transaction they facilitate.

Finally, governments intervene in financial markets to put upward or downward pressure on currencies as circumstances dictate. Governments that attempt to maintain a fixed exchange rate with the rest of the world must generally intervene more frequently than those that intervene only in times of crisis. As this chapter's Opening Focus illustrates, currency movements create winners and losers, not only across national boundaries but within a given country. For example, a rise in the value of the U.S. dollar makes U.S. exports more expensive and foreign imports cheaper. Remember, an exchange rate is simply a price, the price of trading one currency for another. Though the financial press dramatizes changes in exchange rates by attaching adjectives such as *strong* or *weak* to a given currency, this practice is rather odd when you recognize that they are just talking about a price. For instance, if the price of apples rises and the price of bananas falls, we do not refer to apples as being strong and bananas as being weak! If the price of apples is high, that is good for apple producers and bad for apple consumers. In the same way, a rise in the value of a particular currency benefits some and harms others. Therefore, at least for the major, free-floating currencies, governments are reluctant to intervene because doing so does not unambiguously improve welfare across the board.

Even when governments want to intervene in currency markets, doing so is complicated by the fact that currency values are not set in a vacuum but are linked to other economic variables such as interest rates and inflation. In the next section, we discuss four parity relationships that illustrate the linkages that should hold in equilibrium between exchange rates and other macroeconomic variables.

Concept Review Questions

1. Explain how a rise in the euro might affect a French company exporting wine to the United States, and compare that to the impact on a German firm importing semiconductors from the United States.

2. Holding all other factors constant, how might an increase in interest rates in Britain affect the value of the pound?

3. If someone says, "The exchange rate between dollars and pounds increased today," can you say for sure which currency appreciated and which depreciated? Why or why not?

4. Define spot and forward exchange rates. If a trader expects to buy a foreign currency in one month, can you explain why the trader might prefer to enter into a forward contract today rather than simply wait a month and transact at the spot rate prevailing then?

20.2 THE PARITY CONDITIONS IN INTERNATIONAL FINANCE

In this section, we discuss the major forces that influence the values of all the world's free-floating currencies. Theory suggests that when markets are in equilibrium, spot and forward exchange rates, interest rates, and inflation rates should be linked across countries. Market imperfections, such as trade barriers and transactions costs, may prevent these parity conditions from holding precisely at all times, but they are still powerful determinants of exchange rate values in the long run.

FORWARD—SPOT PARITY

If the spot rate governs foreign exchange transactions in the present and the forward rate equals the price of trading currencies at some point in the future, intuition suggests that the forward rate might be useful in predicting how the spot rate will change over time. For example, suppose that a British firm intends to import U.S. wheat, for which it must pay $1.5 million in one month. The pound currently trades at a forward premium, and the prevailing spot and forward exchange rates are as follows:

Spot = $1.4/£   1-month forward = $1.50/£.

The U.K. firm faces a choice. Either it can lock in the forward rate today, guaranteeing that it will pay £1 million for its wheat ($1.5 million ÷ $1.50/£), or it can wait a month and transact at the spot rate prevailing then. Let us suppose that the U.K. firm in this example is risk neutral. That assumption implies that the firm does not care about exchange rate risk, and it will decide to enter the forward contract only if it believes that trading at the forward rate will be less expensive than trading at the spot rate in 30 days.

This results in a simple decision rule for the U.K. importer. First, it must form a forecast of what the spot exchange rate will be in one month. Let's call that the expected spot rate and denote it with the symbol $E(S)$. We can now determine the U.K. firm's decision rule:

1. Enter the forward contract today if $E(S) < \$1.50/£$.
2. Wait and buy dollars at the spot rate if $E(S) > \$1.50/£$.

For example, assume that the firm's forecast is that the spot rate will not change from its current level of $1.40/£. Given this forecast, the expected cost of purchasing $1.50 million in 30 days is £1,071,429 ($1.5 million ÷ $1.4/£); and given that the firm will need only £1 million if it locks in the forward rate, it does not pay to wait. Conversely, assume that the U.K. firm believes that over the next 30 days, the pound will appreciate to $1.60/£. In that case, the expected cost of paying for the wheat is just £937,500, and the firm should wait. Only if the firm's forecast of the expected spot rate is $1.50/£, equal to the current forward rate, will it be indifferent to whether it locks in the forward contract now or waits 30 days to transact.

If we look at this problem from the perspective of a U.S. firm that must pay in pounds in 30 days to import some good from the United Kingdom, we get just the opposite decision rule. For the (risk-neutral) U.S. firm, entering a forward contract to buy pounds makes sense if the expected spot rate in 30 days is greater than the current forward rate $[E(S) > \$1.50/£]$. Clearly, appreciation in the pound increases the cost of importing from Britain, so if a U.S. firm expects the pound to appreciate above the current forward rate, it will lock in a forward contract immediately. On the other hand, if the U.S. firm expects the spot rate to be less than $1.50/£ in 30 days, it will choose to wait rather than lock in at the forward rate.

Now we broaden the example to include all U.S. and U.K. firms who face a future need to buy foreign currency, and maintain the assumption of risk neutrality. Ideally, U.S. firms who need to buy pounds to import British goods could trade with U.K. firms who must sell pounds and buy dollars to import U.S. goods. However, there is a problem because the circumstances under which firms in each country prefer to trade in the spot market rather than the forward market are mirror images of each other:

1. If $E(S) > F$, the U.K. firms do not want the forward contract, but U.S. firms do.
2. If $E(S) < F$, the U.K. firms want the forward contract, but U.S. firms do not.

Equilibrium will occur in this market only when the forecast of the spot rate is equal to the current forward rate. In that case, U.S. and U.K. firms are indifferent to whether they transact in the spot or the forward market. This yields our first parity condition, known as **forward–spot parity.** It says that the forward rate should be an unbiased predictor of where the spot rate is headed:

$$E(S) = F \hfill \text{(Eq. 20.2)}$$

It would certainly be convenient for currency traders if the forward exchange rate provided a reliable forecast of future spot rates. Unfortunately, most studies suggest that this is not the case. Some researchers have found that, on average, the spot rate moves in the opposite direction than that predicted by the forward rate. Other studies find that whereas the direction of spot rate movements is consistent with the direction predicted by forward rates, the magnitudes are too small. That is, when a currency trades at a forward premium, suggesting the currency will appreciate on the spot market, the currency does appreciate, but not by as much as the forward rate predicted. Finally, virtually all studies of exchange rate movements find a great deal of "noise" or randomness in spot rate movements. Even if spot rates tend to move in the direction predicted by forward rates, they do not do so with a high degree of reliability.

If forward rates do not accurately predict movements in currency values over time, perhaps something else does. Economists have long observed a correlation between currency movements and inflation rate differentials across countries. To illustrate, the figures below report the cumulative inflation that occurred in the United States, Japan, Germany, and France from 1984 to 1996. Beside those figures we show the difference between the U.S. inflation and that which occurred in the other countries, as well as the cumulative change in the values of the yen, the German mark, and the French franc against the dollar over the same period.

Country	Comparative Figures for 1984–1996		
	% Cumulative Inflation	% U.S. Inflation − Foreign	% Change against the $
U.S.	51	NA	NA
Japan	17	+34	+46
Germany	52	−1	−4.5
France	100	−49	−50

Notice the remarkable correspondence between the numbers in the second and third columns. Japan's was the only currency that appreciated against the dollar from 1984 to 1996, and it was the only country on the list with less inflation than the United States. German and U.S. inflation was about equal, and the dollar-mark exchange rate was about the same in 1996 as it was in 1984. French inflation was roughly 50 percentage points higher than U.S. inflation, about equal to the decline in the franc.

These figures suggest that differences in inflation do a good job of explaining currency movements, at least over a long period of time. The second parity relationship reveals why.

PURCHASING POWER PARITY

One of the simplest ideas in economics is that identical goods trading in different markets should sell at the same price, absent any barriers to trade. This **law of one price** has a natural application in international finance. Suppose that a DVD of a hit movie retails in the United States for $20, and the identical DVD can be purchased in Tokyo for ¥2,000. Does the law of one price hold? It depends on the exchange rate. If the spot rate of exchange equals ¥100/$, then the answer is yes. A U.S. consumer can spend $20 to purchase the DVD in the United States or can convert $20 to ¥2,000 and purchase the item in Tokyo. We can generalize this example as follows. Suppose that the price of an item in domestic currency is P_{dom} and the price of the identical item in foreign currency is P_{for}. If the spot exchange rate quoted in foreign currency per domestic is $S^{for/dom}$, then the law of one price holds if the following is true:

$$\frac{P_{for}}{P_{dom}} = S^{for/dom} \qquad \text{(Eq. 20.3)}$$

Naturally, the law of one price extends to any pair of countries, not just the United States and Japan. When Equation 20.3 does not hold, traders may engage in arbitrage to exploit price discrepancies across national boundaries.

APPLYING THE MODEL

Suppose that a pair of Maui Jim sunglasses sells for $200 in the United States and for €180 in Italy. The exchange rate between dollars and euros is €0.95/$. Does the law of one price hold? Apparently not, because the following is true:

$$\frac{180}{200} < 0.95$$

How can arbitrageurs exploit this violation of the law of one price? The previous equation reveals that the price of sunglasses in Italy is too low, or the price in the United States is too high, relative to the current exchange rate. Therefore, suppose that a trader buys sunglasses in Italy for €180 and ships them to the United States. After selling them for $200, the trader can convert back to euros, receiving €190 (C$200 × €0.95/$). The arbitrage profit is €10. As long as the transactions costs of making these trades is less than €10, and as long as there are no other barriers to trade, then the process will continue until the market reaches equilibrium. ■

Now we will add a new wrinkle to the law of one price. Suppose that prices in different countries satisfy Equation 20.3 not just at one moment in time, but all the time. We do not necessarily expect this to be the case for every type of good sold in two countries, but if price discrepancies for similar goods become too large, the forces of arbitrage should push them back into line. Of course, the prices of goods and services change every day due to inflation (or deflation), and there is no reason to expect the inflation rate in one country to be the same as in another. If different countries are subject to different inflation pressures, how can the law of one price hold on an ongoing basis? The answer is that the exchange rate adjusts to maintain equilibrium.

APPLYING THE MODEL

Suppose that the forces of arbitrage have changed the prices of Maui Jim sunglasses in the United States and in Italy so that the law of one price now holds. Specifically, the U.S. price is $195 and the Italian price is €185.25. If the exchange rate is still €0.95/$, then the law of one price holds because the following is true:

$$\frac{€185.25}{\$195} = €0.95/\$$$

Now suppose that the expected rate of inflation in Italy over the next year is 12 percent, but no inflation is expected in the United States. One year from today, Maui Jim sunglasses will still sell for $195 in the United States, but with 12 percent inflation, the price in Italy will rise to €207.48 (€185.25 × 1.12). If these forecasts are correct, then in a year the exchange rate must rise to €1.064/$ for the law of one price to hold:

$$\frac{€207.48}{\$195} = €1.064/\$$$

Remember that this exchange rate is expressed in euros per dollar, so an increase from €0.95/$ to €1.064/$ represents appreciation of the dollar and depreciation of the euro. ∎

Purchasing power parity is an extension of the law of one price. Purchasing power parity says that if the law of one price holds at all times, then differences in expected inflation between two countries are associated with expected changes in currency values. Mathematically, we can express this idea as follows:

$$\frac{E(S^{\text{for/dom}})}{S^{\text{for/dom}}} = \frac{[1 + E(i_{\text{for}})]}{[1 + E(i_{\text{dom}})]} \qquad \text{(Eq. 20.4)}$$

where, as before, the expected spot rate is $E(S)$, the current spot rate is S, the expected rate of inflation in the foreign country is $E(i_{\text{for}})$, and the expected rate of inflation in the domestic country is $E(i_{\text{dom}})$. Notice that the left-hand side of this equation exceeds 1.0 if traders expect the domestic currency to appreciate, and it is less than 1.0 if traders expect the foreign currency to appreciate. Likewise, the right-hand side of the equation exceeds 1.0 when expected inflation is higher abroad than it is at home, and the ratio falls below 1.0 when the opposite is true. Therefore, the equation produces the already familiar prediction that if inflation is higher in one country than another, then the currency of the country with higher inflation will depreciate. The equation also offers the helpful information that traders who want to forecast currency movements should invest resources in forecasting inflation rates.

How accurately does purchasing power parity predict exchange rate movements? As we have already seen, over the long term there is a very high correlation between currency values and inflation rates. Countries with high inflation see their currencies depreciate over time, whereas the opposite happens for countries with lower inflation. This is no accident. If we did not observe this correlation in the data, it would be a signal of gross violations of the law of one price and a sign that arbitrage was not working to bring prices back into line.

But purchasing power parity does not fare as well in the short run. Violations of the law of one price do occur frequently, and many studies suggest that they persist from three to four years on average. Again, arbitrage, or in this case, limits to arbitrage explain why. When goods prices in different countries are out of equilibrium, arbitrageurs must trade the goods, moving them across national borders, to earn a profit. This process cannot occur without investments in time and money, and for certain goods, trade may be impossible due to legal restrictions or the physical impediments to transporting goods. Accordingly, there is no reason to expect goods to flow from one market to the other instantaneously at any moment when the law of one price does not hold. Only if price discrepancies across markets are large enough and persistent enough will arbitrageurs find it profitable to trade. Hence, purchasing power parity does a good job of explaining long-run movements in currencies, but not day-to-day, or even year-to-year, fluctuations.

INTEREST RATE PARITY

Although it is both time-consuming and expensive to move goods across borders, the same cannot generally be said about purely financial transactions. Large institutional investors can buy and sell currencies very rapidly and at low cost, and they can buy and sell financial assets denominated in different currencies just as quickly. Interest rate parity applies the law of one price to financial assets, specifically to risk-free assets denominated in different currencies.

To illustrate, assume that a U.S. institution has $10 million that it wants to invest for 180 days in a risk-free government bill. The current annual interest rate on 180-day U.S. Treasury bills is 2 percent per year (1% for six months), so if the institution chooses this investment, it will have $10.1 million six months later:

$$\$10,000,000\left(1 + \frac{R_{\text{US}}}{2}\right) = \$10,000,000\left(1 + \frac{0.02}{2}\right) = \$10,100,000$$

Alternatively, the institution might choose to convert its $10 million into another currency and invest abroad. However, even if it invests in a risk-free government bill issued by a foreign government, the institution must enter into a forward contract to convert back into dollars when the investment matures. Otherwise, the return on the foreign investment is not risk free and will depend on changes in currency values over the next six months.

For example, suppose that the annual interest rate on a 6-month British government bill is 4.27 percent per year (2.135% for six months). Suppose also that the spot and 6-month forward exchange rates are £0.6416/$ and £0.6488/$, respectively, as given in Figure 20.1. The U.S. institution converts $10 million into £6,416,000 at the spot rate. It invests the pounds for six months at the U.K. interest rate and enters into a forward contract to convert those pounds back into dollars when the U.K. bill matures. At the end of six months, the institution has the following: [2]

$$\$10,000,000(S^{£/\$})\left(1 + \frac{R_{UK}}{2}\right)\left(\frac{1}{F^{£/\$}}\right)$$

$$= \$10,000,000(£0.6416/\$)\left(1 + \frac{0.0427}{2}\right)\left(\frac{1}{£0.6488/\$}\right)$$

$$= \$10,100,157$$

Given the prevailing interest rates on short-term, risk-free U.S. and U.K. bonds, and given current spot and forward exchange rates between dollars and pounds, investors are approximately indifferent to whether they invest in the United States or the United Kingdom. In other words, with respect to short-term, risk-free financial assets, the law of one price holds. This relationship is called **interest rate parity**, which simply means that risk-free investments should offer the same return (after converting currencies) everywhere. As usual, we can express interest rate parity in mathematical terms. Letting R_{for} and R_{dom} represent the risk-free rate on foreign and domestic government debt, we obtain the following equation: [3]

$$\frac{F^{for/dom}}{S^{for/dom}} = \frac{(1 + R_{for})}{(1 + R_{dom})} \qquad \textbf{(Eq. 20.5)}$$

What is the intuitive interpretation of this expression? Observe that if the left-hand side of the equation is greater than 1.0, the domestic currency trades at a forward premium. If domestic investors send money abroad, when they convert back to domestic currency, they will realize an exchange loss because the foreign currency buys less domestic currency than it did at the spot rate. Domestic investors know this, so they require an incentive in the form of a higher foreign interest rate before they will send money abroad. To maintain equilibrium, the right-hand side must also be greater than 1.0, which means that the foreign interest rate must exceed the domestic rate. The bottom line is that when a nation's currency trades at a forward premium (discount), risk-free interest rates in that country should be lower (higher) than they are abroad. [4]

As is the case with purchasing power parity, deviations from interest rate parity create arbitrage opportunities. However, these arbitrage opportunities involve buy-

---

[2.] Notice that in this equation we divide by the forward rate to convert pounds back into dollars. Also, the $157 difference between the payoffs on the U.S. and U.K. investment strategies results from the fact that we only quoted the U.K. interest rate to two decimals. Using a U.K. rate of 4.2668 percent brings the two payoffs within $2 of each other.

[3.] Be careful to match the term of the forward rate to the term of the interest rate in this expression. For example, if you are comparing interest rates on 180-day government bills, you must use a 180-day forward rate. You can see this by going back to the example of the institution with $10 million to invest. If you set the equation representing the institution's U.S. return equal to the equation representing its U.K. return, the following equation results:

$$\frac{F^{£/\$}}{S^{£/\$}} = \frac{1 + \dfrac{R_{UK}}{2}}{1 + \dfrac{R_{US}}{2}}$$

[4.] If interest rates in one country are higher than in another, does that mean that the high-rate country's currencies will depreciate? Though that prediction has obvious intuitive appeal, the opposite seems to occur, on average. See Fama (1984) and more recently, Backus, Foresi, and Telmer (2001).

ing and selling financial assets rather than physical commodities. Naturally, trade in securities can occur rapidly and much less expensively than trade in goods, so the forces of arbitrage are more powerful in maintaining interest rate parity.

APPLYING THE MODEL

Suppose that the 6-month, risk-free rate in the United States is 2 percent and in Canada is 6 percent. The spot exchange rate is C$1.5855/$, and the 180-day forward rate is C$1.5937/$. Interest rate parity does not hold, as shown in the following equation:

$$\frac{C\$1.5937/\$}{C\$1.5855/\$} < \frac{\left(1 + \dfrac{0.06}{2}\right)}{\left(1 + \dfrac{.02}{2}\right)}$$

Because the right-hand side of this equation is "too large" relative to parity, the interest rate in Canada is "too high" or the rate in the U.S. is "too low." The arbitrage opportunity is as follows. An investor borrows money (say $1 million) at 2 percent in the United States, then converts the proceeds into Canadian dollars, and invests them at 6 percent. Six months later, the investor converts the Canadian dollars back into U.S. currency to repay the loan. Anything left over is pure arbitrage profit.

Borrow $1 million in the U.S. at 2 percent for six months → must repay $1,010,000

$1 million → converted at spot rate → C$1,585,500

C$1,585,500 invested for six months at 6 percent →
(C$1,585,500)(1.03) → C$1,633,065

C$1,633,065 converted to US$ at the forward rate → $1,024,700

$1,010,000 needed to repay U.S. loan → leaves $14,700 arbitrage profit ■

The effect of all these transactions, repeated again and again, is to push exchange rates and interest rates back toward parity. As investors borrow in the United States, the U.S. interest rate will rise from 2 percent to a higher level. Similarly, as investors purchase Canadian government bonds, the bond prices will rise and the risk-free rate in Canada will fall. When investors sell U.S. dollars to buy Canadian dollars on the spot market, the spot rate (in terms of Canadian dollars per U.S. dollar) will rise, and just the opposite happens on the forward market as investors sell Canadian dollars to buy U.S. dollars. In terms of the interest rate parity equation, we can see how these forces drive markets to equilibrium:

Smart Concepts
See the concept explained step-by-step at
SMART**Finance**

$$\text{This ratio is increasing} \leftarrow \frac{C\$1.5937/\$ \uparrow}{C\$1.5855/\$ \downarrow} < \frac{\left(1 + \dfrac{0.06 \downarrow}{2}\right)}{\left(1 + \dfrac{.02 \uparrow}{2}\right)} \rightarrow \text{This ratio is decreasing}$$

↓

New equilibrim occurs when inequality becomes an equality

The process illustrated in the preceding example is known as **covered interest arbitrage** because traders attempt to earn arbitrage profits arising from differences in interest rates across countries, and they "cover" their currency exposures with forward contracts. Implicit in this example was the assumption that investors could borrow and lend at the risk-free rate in each country. Not all investors can do this, but large, creditworthy institutions can get very close to this ideal. Moreover, they can execute the trades described in the example at very high speed and at low cost. In the real world, deviations from interest rate parity are small and transitory.

Real Interest Rate Parity (the Fisher Effect)

If nominal rates of return on risk-free investments are equalized around the world, after adjusting for currency translation, perhaps real rates of return are also equalized. **Real interest rate parity** means that investors should earn the same real rate of return on risk-free investments no matter the country in which they choose to invest.[5] Recall from Chapter 5 that the real rate of interest is defined as follows:

$$1 + r_{\text{real}} = \frac{(1 + R)}{[1 + E(i)]}$$

where R_{real} is the real rate of interest, R is the nominal rate, and $E(i)$ is the expected inflation rate. If market forces equalize real rates across national borders, then we can write the following equation:

$$\frac{(1 + R_{\text{for}})}{(1 + R_{\text{dom}})} = \frac{[1 + E(i_{\text{for}})]}{[1 + E(i_{\text{dom}})]}$$

(Eq. 20.6)

This equation says that if real rates are the same in the domestic and the foreign country, then the ratio of (1 plus) nominal interest rates in the two countries must equal the ratio of (1 plus) expected inflation rates. If expected inflation is higher in one country than in another, then the country with higher inflation must offer higher interest rates to give investors the same real return.

APPLYING THE MODEL

Suppose that expected inflation in the United States equals zero and expected inflation in Italy is 12 percent. Suppose also that the 1-year, risk-free rate in the United States is 3 percent. What would the 1-year, risk-free rate have to be in Italy to maintain real interest rate parity?

$$\frac{(1 + R_{\text{Italy}})}{(1 + 0.03)} = \frac{(1 + 0.12)}{(1 + 0)} \qquad R_{\text{Italy}} = 15.36\%$$

As with purchasing power parity, real interest rate parity need not hold at all times, because when deviations from parity occur, limits to arbitrage prevent market

---

[5.] Real interest rate parity is sometimes called the *Fisher effect* after the economist who first recognized the relationship between nominal and real interest rates and the inflation rate.

forces from quickly reaching a new equilibrium. In this case, the limits to arbitrage include the scarcity of risk-free investments that offer fixed real, rather than nominal, returns. In the United States and a few other countries, governments issue bonds with payouts tied to the inflation rate. These bonds offer investors a way to lock in a fixed real rate. In the long run, we expect that real interest rate parity will hold, at least approximately, but that will not necessarily be the case in the short run.

We conclude this section with a quick review of the four parity relationships, highlighting how they are linked together. If we combine Equations 20.2, 20.4, 20.5, and 20.6, we have the following relationships:[6]

$$\frac{E(S)}{S} = \frac{F}{S} = \frac{(1 + R_{\text{for}})}{(1 + R_{\text{dom}})} = \frac{[1 + E(i_{\text{for}})]}{[1 + E(i_{\text{dom}})]} = \frac{E(S)}{S} \qquad \text{(Eq. 20.7)}$$

The first equality simply restates the forward–spot parity relationship. The second equality is the expression for interest rate parity, and the third and fourth equalities define real interest rate parity and purchasing power parity, respectively. Here we see for the first time that if markets are in equilibrium, spot and forward exchange rates, nominal interest rates, and expected inflation rates are all linked internationally. If we want to understand why currency values change, Equation 20.7 gives us a number of clues. The equation also illustrates how difficult it can be for countries to manage their exchange rates. Attempts to push the exchange rate in a particular direction invariably lead to changes in other macroeconomic variables that policymakers may not desire.[7]

The Asset Market Model of Exchange Rates

The four parity conditions provide important insights into the factors that set relative currency values, but they provide an incomplete picture of what will cause exchange rates to change over time, and of how this change will occur. Clearly, all the parity conditions suggest that rising inflation will cause a nation's nominal interest rate to rise and its currency to depreciate, but will this depreciation occur in the spot or the forward market, and will it occur immediately or over time? Moreover, how can we explain the observed tendency of currency traders to react to economic news not covered by the parity conditions—in particular, to news about relative economic growth prospects in two countries?

Before proceeding, we should make a distinction between nominal and real exchange rate changes. Changes in the **nominal exchange rate** are those that exactly mirror changes in relative inflation rates between two countries, whereas changes in the **real exchange rate** measure changes in the purchasing power of a currency. For example, if inflation is 2 percent higher in Europe than in the United States, purchasing power parity predicts that the nominal value of the euro (the dollar) will fall (rise) by about 2 percent, leaving the real exchange rate unchanged. If, in fact, the dollar rises by 3 percent against the euro, then the real value of the dollar has increased.

[6.] Notice that we have divided both sides of Equation 20.2 by the spot rate here. This does no harm to the equality, and it allows us to highlight the connections between forward–spot parity and the other parity relationships.

[7.] In October 1997, market pressure was building for a devaluation of the Hong Kong dollar. Hong Kong's currency board reacted by purchasing vast amounts of Hong Kong currency. One consequence of their activity was that overnight interest rates in Hong Kong briefly reached 280 percent. See Gerlach (2002) for details. A year later, a similar spike occurred in Russian interest rates as the government unsuccessfully attempted to support the ruble.

A model that offers additional insights into the causes of currency movements is the **asset market model of exchange rates.** This model makes a distinction between the demand for a currency as a means of payment (transactions demand) and the demand for currency as a financial asset (as a store of value). It predicts that currency values will be set by investors, who demand a currency in order to invest in that country, rather than by traders, who demand a currency in order to pay for exports or imports.

The asset market model is both flexible and powerful, as it can explain the effect that changes in investor expectations can have on relative currency values. For example, assume that investors receive news suggesting that America's economic growth rate over the next several quarters will be higher than expected. In the absence of comparable new information regarding Europe's growth prospects, international investors will increase their demand for dollars on the foreign exchange market either to make direct investments in U.S. businesses or to make portfolio investments in U.S. capital markets. Other things equal, this increased demand for dollars (or, equivalently, the increased supply of euros), in the face of stable demand for euros, will cause the dollar to appreciate and the €/$ exchange rate to rise. Reputation effects also play a role in the asset market model of exchange rates. If a government establishes a reputation for pursuing sound economic policies, that nation's currency will tend to appreciate as investors come to trust the currency as a store of value.

<table>
<tr><td>

Concept Review Questions

</td><td>

5. Explain the logic behind each of the four parity relationships.

6. Explain the role of arbitrage in maintaining the parity relationships.

7. In what sense is interest rate parity an application of the law of one price?

8. An investor who notices that interest rates are much lower in Japan than in the United States borrows in Japan and invests the proceeds in the United States. This is called uncovered interest arbitrage, but is it really arbitrage? Why or why not?

</td></tr>
</table>

20.3 MANAGING FINANCIAL AND POLITICAL RISK

TRANSACTIONS RISK

Any firm that might experience an adverse change in the value of any of its cash flows as a result of exchange rate movements faces exposure to exchange rate risk. Almost every firm is exposed to exchange rate risk to some degree, even if it operates strictly in one country and has cash flows in only one currency. Such a firm will face exchange rate risk if (1) it produces a good or service that competes with imports in the home market, or (2) it uses as a production input an imported product or service.

Nonetheless, some types of companies face greater exchange rate risk than do others. MNCs obviously face this risk in all aspects of their business, but they also have many opportunities to minimize that risk by, for example, moving production facilities to the countries where their products are sold so that costs and revenues can be in the same currency. The greatest exchange rate exposure occurs when a firm's costs and revenues are largely denominated in different currencies.

As usual, it is easiest to describe the importance of exchange rate risk to an exporter with an example. Assume that the Boeing Co. has just sold an airplane to a Japanese buyer, with the following details. First, Boeing must price the airplane in terms of yen so that it receives payment worth $1 million to cover its U.S. dollar costs and generate an acceptable profit. Second, suppose that Boeing agrees to receive payment for the aircraft in yen. Third, assume that the current yen/dollar exchange rate is ¥100.00/$. Boeing therefore negotiates a price of ¥100 million for the airplane. However, the company is primarily concerned with how many dollars it will collect when payment is made in yen and then converted into dollars on the foreign exchange market.

If Boeing negotiates the terms of this sale at the same time that it receives payment, it does not face any foreign exchange risk. The company will simply exchange ¥100 million for $1 million on the spot market. In reality, Boeing will probably negotiate payment terms months before it expects payment from the Japanese customer. This simple fact creates exchange rate risk, because between the dates when Boeing sets the price in yen for the plane and when it receives payment, the exchange rate can move. Because the contract is denominated in yen, Boeing bears this exchange rate risk, but the risk would not be eliminated by denominating the sales contract in dollars—the risk would simply be shifted to the Japanese buyer.

Suppose that after Boeing agrees to a price, it must wait six months for payment. In that time, the exchange rate changes to ¥110.00/$, meaning that the dollar has appreciated and the yen has depreciated. Boeing will still receive the same ¥100 million, but now the amount is worth just $909,091. Appreciation in the dollar results in Boeing realizing an **exchange rate loss** of $90,909. If the yen appreciates, say to ¥90.00/$, Boeing will receive $1,111,111 and will realize an **exchange rate gain** of $111,111.

This exchange rate risk cannot be eliminated, but it can be **hedged** (transferred to a third party) using financial contracts. Boeing has many hedging options to choose from, including hedging (1) in the forward or futures market, (2) in the currency options market, (3) via swaps, and (4) via money market instruments. Because specific hedging strategies are described in depth in Chapter 21, we will not describe each strategy here. We will demonstrate the use of forward contracts in the following discussion, and we briefly describe other strategies in Table 20.1.

Assume that instead of remaining unhedged, Boeing books the airplane's sale and immediately afterward asks Citibank for a price quote for yen, with delivery to be made in six months. Citibank quotes Boeing a forward price of ¥99/$, which Boeing accepts. Boeing thus *sells yen forward* today, committing itself to deliver ¥100 million and receive $1,010,101 from Citibank exactly six months from now. Once this forward contract is executed, Boeing is no longer exposed to exchange rate risk. The risk has not disappeared; it has simply been transferred from Boeing to Citibank. But why would Citibank be willing to assume this risk?

International banks—and, increasingly, other types of financial institutions—are uniquely positioned to bear exchange rate risk because they can create what amounts to a **natural hedge,** or offsetting risk exposure, as a normal course of their business. This means they are able to easily arrange mirror-image positions with other customers. To see this, consider what type of foreign exchange contract Toyota Motors might demand from Citibank. The exchange rate risk problem for Toyota (one of Japan's biggest exporters) is the opposite of Boeing's: Toyota exports many automobiles from Japan and sells these in the United States. The company receives U.S. dollars as payment, but its costs are in yen, so it would need to *sell dollars forward* (locking in a yen price) in order to cover its costs and make an acceptable profit. Citibank is thus naturally able to buy dollars forward (sell yen) from Toyota and simultaneously sell dollars forward (buy yen) to Boeing, and thus net out the exchange rate exposure on its own books. This is, of course, a simplified example, because Citibank may not have a perfectly offsetting exposure for Boeing's needs, but in that case it would simply execute its own forward contract with another bank—perhaps with Toyota's main bank.

Table 20.1
Exchange Rate Risk Management and Hedging Tools

Tool	Description	Impact on Risk Exposure
Borrowing and lending	Borrow money in currency in which payment is to be received, and lend in home-country currency. Pay off borrowing when payment is made.	Eliminates exchange rate risk as long as there is no risk of default on underlying account receivable.
Forward contracts	If foreign-currency payment is to be received, sell currency forward, locking in a home-country price for foreign currency. If foreign-currency payment must be made, buy currency forward.	Forwards eliminate risk but also eliminate opportunity to profit from favorable changes in currency value. No intermediate cash flows, so can be risky unless counterparty well known.
Futures contracts	Used similarly as forward contracts but involve standardized, exchange-traded financial instruments. Often used for hedging smaller obligations, due to relatively small denomination.	Futures also eliminate both risk and profit opportunity, as futures are an obligation to make or take delivery. Less default risk because exchange traded and marked to market each day.
Options contracts	Call options are rights (not obligations) to sell a standard amount of currency at a fixed price; puts are rights to sell. If a foreign-currency payment is to be received, buy a put option to sell foreign currency; if payment is to be made, buy a call option.	Options uniquely hedge risk of adverse exchange rate movements but preserve potential to profit from favorable exchange rate changes. Downside is that they are very expensive, because premium must be paid for both calls and puts whether exercised or not.
Interest rate swaps	Allow the trading of one interest rate stream (e.g., on a fixed-rate U.S. dollar instrument) for another (e.g., on a floating-rate U.S. dollar instrument).	Permit firms to change the interest rate structure of their assets/liabilities and achieve cost savings due to broader market access.
Currency swaps	Two parties exchange principal amounts of two different currencies initially; they pay each other's interest payments, then reverse principal amounts at a pre-agreed exchange rate at maturity; more complex than interest rate swaps.	All the features of interest rate swaps, plus they allow firms to change the currency structure of their assets/liabilities.

We have discussed how to measure exchange rate risk as it applies to specific transactions and have briefly discussed one method of dealing with it using a forward market hedge. However, this **transactions exposure** is but one of many types of exchange rate risk.

TRANSLATION AND ECONOMIC RISK

For MNCs, there are additional complexities involved with operating internationally if they have affiliates or subsidiaries on the ground in a foreign country. One such complication arises when MNCs translate costs and revenues denominated in foreign currencies to report on their financial statements, which, of course, are denominated in the home currency. This type of risk is called **translation exposure** or **accounting exposure**. In other words, foreign exchange rate fluctuations affect individual accounts in the financial statements. A different, and generally more important, risk element concerns **economic exposure,** which is the overall impact of foreign exchange rate fluctuations on the firm's value.[8] A firm faces economic exposure when exchange rate changes affect its cash flows, even those cash flows not specifically tied to transactions in other currencies. For example, a rise in the value of the dollar against the euro makes European wines less expensive to U.S. consumers, and it makes U.S. wine more expensive for European consumers. A winery operating in the United States, even one that does not sell directly to foreign customers, may realize a decline in cash flows due to competition from suddenly less expensive European vintners.

What can managers do about these risks? Hedging economic exposure is more difficult than hedging transactions exposure, in part because measuring the exposure is more difficult. For instance, a U.S. winery concerned about the declining prices of foreign wines could engage in currency trades that would result in a profit if the dollar appreciates against the euro. In theory, these profits could offset the decline in earnings that occurs when European wines become less expensive, but exactly how large will these losses be for a given change in the exchange rate? Increasingly, MNCs manage their economic exposures both by using sophisticated currency derivatives and by matching costs and revenues in a given currency. For instance, a foreign company exporting to Japan might issue yen-denominated bonds, so-called Samurai bonds, to create a yen-based liability that would partially or fully offset the exposure resulting from yen-based receivables. However, it is important to emphasize that unless the cash inflows and outflows match exactly, some residual yen exposure will remain.

Political Risk

Another important risk facing MNCs is **political risk,** which refers to actions taken by a government that have a negative impact on the value of foreign companies operating in that country, such as raising taxes on a firm's activities or erecting barriers that prevent a firm from repatriating profits back to the home country. In its most extreme form, political risk can mean confiscation of a corporation's assets by a foreign government.

Political risk has two basic dimensions: *macro* and *micro*. **Macro political risk** means that *all* foreign firms in the country will be subject to political risk because of political change, revolution, or the adoption of new policies by a host government. In other words, no individual country or firm is treated differently. An example of macro political risk occurred when communist regimes came to power in China in 1949 and Cuba in 1959–1960. More recently, the near collapse of Indonesia's currency in late 1997 and early 1998, plus the attendant political and economic turmoil elsewhere in Asia, highlights the real and present danger that macro political risk can pose to MNCs and international investors alike.[9] **Micro political risk,** on the other hand, refers to a foreign government targeting punitive action against an individual firm, a specific industry, or companies from a particular foreign country. Examples include the nationalization by a majority of the oil-exporting countries of the assets of the international oil companies in their territories during the 1970s.

[8.] See Pringle and Connolly (1993) or Harris, Nahum, and Shibano (1996) for excellent discussions on these types of exposures and the way firms manage them.

[9.] Twice each year, *Euromoney* magazine publishes a country risk rating index that assigns a number between 0 (extremely risky) and 100 (essentially risk free) to the world's largest developed and developing countries. In the March 2002 index, Luxembourg was the least risky country (with an index value of 99.27), followed by Switzerland (97.41), the United States (95.92), and Norway (95.42). North Korea and Afghanistan were ranked lowest (184 and 185), with index values of 6.30 and 2.04, respectively.

Although political risk can take place in any country, even in the United States, the political instability of many developing countries generally makes the positions of multinational companies most vulnerable there. At the same time, some of the countries in this group have the most promising markets for the goods and services being offered by MNCs. The main question, therefore, is how to engage in operations and foreign investment in such countries and yet avoid or minimize the potential political risk.

There are both positive and negative approaches that MNCs may be able to adopt to cope with political risk. Negative approaches include taking a trade dispute with a host country to the World Trade Organization (described later) or threatening to withhold additional investments from a country unless an MNC's demands are met. Firms may also negotiate agreements with host governments that build in costs that the host government must bear if it breaches the terms of the original agreement. Positive approaches for MNCs include working proactively to develop environmental and labor standards in a country, and generally attempting to become perceived as a domestic company by the host country's citizenry.

EUROPEAN MONETARY UNION AND THE RISE OF REGIONAL TRADING BLOCKS

As a result of the Maastricht Treaty of 1991, 11 of the 15 European Union (EU) nations adopted a single currency, the **euro,** as a continent-wide medium of exchange beginning January 2, 1999. In early 2002, the national currencies of the 12 (now including Greece) countries participating in **monetary union** disappeared and were completely replaced by the euro. At the same time that the European Union is struggling to implement monetary union (which also involved creating a new European Central Bank), the EU must also deal with a wave of new applicants from Eastern Europe and the Mediterranean region. Whatever its final shape, the new community of Europe will offer both challenges and opportunities to a variety of players, including multinational firms. MNCs, especially those based in the United States, will face heightened levels of competition when operating inside the EU.

Another major trading bloc that arose during the 1990s is the Mercosur Group of countries in South America. Beginning in 1991, the nations of Brazil, Argentina, Paraguay, and Uruguay began removing tariffs and other barriers to intraregional trade. The second stage of Mercosur's development began at the end of 1994 and involved the development of a customs union to impose a common tariff on external trade while enforcing uniform and lower tariffs on intragroup trade.[10] To date, Mercosur has been even more successful than its founders had imagined, though the economic collapse of Argentina in early 2002 obviously places Mercosur's near-term viability at risk. The long-term importance of Mercosur will likely depend on whether the U.S. Congress overcomes its reluctance to extend the North American Free Trade Agreement (NAFTA) throughout Latin America. In any case, the Mercosur countries represent well over half of total Latin American GDP, and thus will loom large in the plans of any MNC wishing to access the growth markets of this region.

Although it may seem that the world is splitting into a handful of trading blocs, this is less dangerous than it may appear because many international treaties are in force that guarantee relatively open access to at least the largest economies. The most important such treaty is the **General Agreement on Tariffs and Trade (GATT),** which

---

[10.] An excellent overview of Mercosur is provided in *The Economist* (1996), "Remapping South America: A Survey of Mercosur."

celebrated its fiftieth anniversary in May 1998. The current agreement extends free-trading rules to broad areas of economic activity—such as agriculture, financial services, and intellectual property rights—that had not previously been covered by international treaty and that were thus effectively off-limits to foreign competition. The 1994 revised GATT treaty also established a new international body, the **World Trade Organization** (**WTO**), to police world trading practices and to mediate disputes between member countries. The WTO began operating in January 1995, and one extremely important nation, the People's Republic of China, became a member in 2002.

The Long-Term Success of World Trade and Foreign Direct Investment

Although world trade has recently become a controversial topic, we believe this hostility is misplaced. Trade is by definition a voluntary exchange between two parties (nations, corporations), and several developing countries have achieved dramatic increases in living standards in a generation by adopting open-market policies and promoting trade. Figure 20.3 shows the phenomenal growth in the total value of world trade over the past 35 years.

Some important patterns in merchandise trade flows (both exports and imports) are apparent in Figure 20.3. Clearly, trade has been one of the economic success stories of the past quarter century, and especially since the collapse of the Bretton Woods fixed exchange rate system in 1973. The total value of world trade increased at a compound annual growth rate of slightly more than 8.0 percent over the 1973–2000 period, rising from about $750 billion per year to almost $6.5 trillion. Even after accounting for inflation, this implies that trade among nations has grown much faster than have the underlying economies of the principal trading nations themselves. And, in contrast to the lopsided pattern of direct investment flows, the growth in trade has benefited developing countries far more (proportionally) than it has the developed countries. Developing countries accounted for a minuscule fraction of total exports in 1973, but developing-country exports now account for almost 40 percent of the world's total. It will probably surprise no one that almost all this growth has been achieved by the export-oriented economies of eastern Asia.

Foreign direct investment (**FDI**) is the transfer by a multinational firm of financial, managerial, and technical assets from its home country to a host country. The equity participation on the part of an MNC can be 100 percent (resulting in a wholly owned foreign subsidiary) or less (usually involving a joint-venture project with foreign participants). In contrast to passive, return-oriented **portfolio investments** undertaken by individuals and companies (e.g., internationally diversified mutual funds), FDI involves equity participation, managerial control, and day-to-day operational activities on the part of MNCs. Therefore, FDI projects will be subject not only to business, financial, inflation, and exchange rate risks (as would foreign portfolio investments), but also to the additional element of political risk.

The dramatic growth in the total value of foreign direct investment worldwide over the period 1990–2000 is detailed graphically in Panels A and B of Figure 20.4. The total value of FDI inflows dropped to less than $180 billion during the recession year of 1991, before surging to over $1.2 trillion in 2000.

Figure 20.4 reveals several other points about the patterns observed in modern FDI. The United States attracts the lion's share of total FDI inflows every year—some $225 billion, or over 20 percent of the global total, in recent years. The United Kingdom and China almost always rank second and third, with inflows averaging $75–$100 billion for the U.K. and $40–$60 billion for China during most recent years.

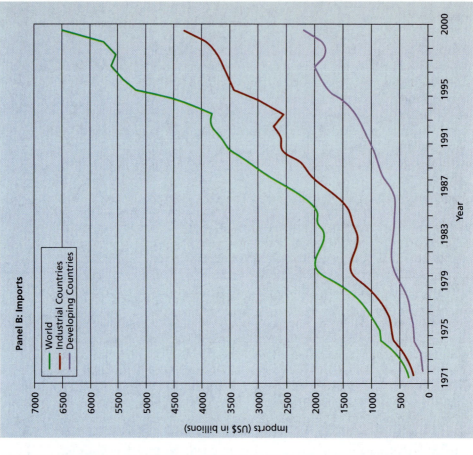

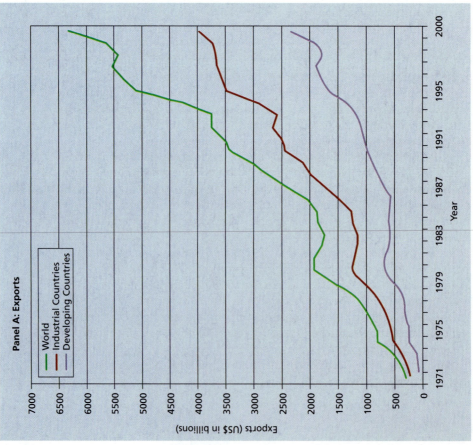

Figure 20.3
The Growth in the Total Value of World Trade in Merchandise, Exports and Imports, 1971–2000

Source: International Financial Statistics Yearbook 2001, International Monetary Fund (Washington, D.C.).

COMPARATIVE CORPORATE FINANCE

What Is Japan's Export-to-GDP Ratio?

Although the "globalization of business" has become so widespread that the phrase has now entered popular culture, the actual importance of international trade nonetheless varies dramatically between countries. One key measure of the importance of trade to an economy is a nation's export-to-GDP ratio, or the total value of that nation's exports during a year divided by the total value of goods and services produced the same year. The table below presents this ratio for several important exporting nations for the year 1999 (data for the United States, Hong Kong, and Singapore are for year 2000). Although the United States is the world's leading exporter in absolute terms, its export-to-GDP ratio is a low 10.8 percent (the U.S. import-to-GDP ratio is usually about two percentage points higher). The large European economies of Germany, France, the United Kingdom, and Italy all have export ratios in the 24–29 percent range, whereas exports represent much larger fractions of the economies of Canada (43.1%), Korea (49.4%), the Netherlands (56.7%), Belgium-Luxembourg (77.3%), and Ireland (111.8%). The export-to-GDP ratios for Hong Kong and Singapore are, respectively, 150.1 percent and an amazing 179.9 percent. But how important are exports to Japan's economy?

Most students (and professors) are astonished to learn that Japan's export-to-GDP ratio is only 10.7 percent, virtually the same as America's. In other words, like the United States, Japan is overwhelmingly a domestic economy. But how can this be? How does a nation renowned for producing and exporting high-quality automobiles, electronic equipment, and industrial gear have such a low export ratio? The answer lies in the very narrow range of products that Japan exports. Whereas the United States, Canada, and many European countries export everything from agricultural products and primary minerals to the highest of high-tech manufactured products, including aircraft and military equipment, Japan exports a relative handful of high-value-added products. In spite of this narrow specialization, Japan perennially runs a large trade surplus—meaning that the value of its goods exports exceeds the value of its imports—with virtually every nation it trades with, especially the United States.

Source: International Financial Statistics Yearbook 2001, International Monetary Fund (Washington, D.C.).

Country	Goods Exports, 2000 (US$ in billions)	Export-to-GDP Ratio, 1999(%)
United States	$774.9	10.8%
Germany	549.2	29.4
Japan	459.5	10.7
France	295.5	26.6
United Kingdom	284.6	27.2
Canada	284.4	43.1
China; PRC mainland	249.1	22.0
Italy	238.7	24.9
Netherlands	208.1	56.7
China; Hong Kong SAR	201.9	150.1
Korea	172.3	49.4
Belgium-Luxembourg	167.0	77.3
Singapore	138.9	179.9
Ireland	73.4	111.8
Euro area (12 countries)	908.2	14.1

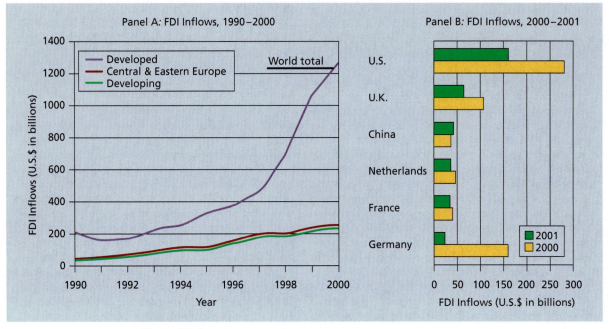

Figure 20.4
Foreign Direct Investment Inflows, 1990–2001 (In US$ Billions)

Source: Panel A: Frances Williams, "Global Foreign Investment Flows 'Set to All by 40%,'" *Financial Times* (September 9, 2001), p. 9; Panel B: *The Economist* (April 6, 2002), p. 89.

It is also undeniably true that the vast majority of all FDI is invested in developed rather than developing countries each year. Perhaps surprising, Britain was the largest single foreign direct investor during 2000, when that nation's companies invested $250 billion abroad. France was the second-largest source of FDI in 2000 ($173 billion), and the United States was third ($139 billion). It is clear that developed nations invest mostly in each other (and China), and most investors are investing in an attempt to better serve other Western consumer markets.

Concept Review Questions

9. Distinguish between transactions, translation, and economic exposure.

10. Describe how a domestic firm might use a forward contract to hedge an economic exposure. Why does uncertainty about the magnitude of the exposure make this difficult?

11. Consider a U.S. firm that has for many years exported to European countries. How does the creation of the euro simplify or complicate the management of transactions exposure for this firm?

20.4 LONG-TERM INVESTMENT DECISIONS

In Chapters 7–9, we emphasized the importance of sound capital budgeting practices for the long-term survival of a corporation. The same lessons covered in those chapters apply to multinational corporations. Whether investing at home or abroad, MNCs should evaluate investments based on their incremental cash flows and should discount those cash flows at a rate that is appropriate given the risk of the investment. However, when a company makes investments denominated in many different currencies, this process becomes a bit more complicated. First, in what currency should the firm express a foreign project's cash flows? Second, how does one calculate the cost of capital for an MNC, or for a given project?

SMART IDEAS VIDEO

Ike Mathur, University of Southern Illinois at Carbondale

"What I find very interesting is that for a long time in international finance we have talked about the first mover advantage."

See the entire interview at SMARTFinance

CAPITAL BUDGETING

Suppose that a U.S. firm is weighing an investment that will generate cash flows in euros. The company's financial analysts have estimated the project's cash flows in euros as follows:

Initial Cost	Year 1	Year 2	Year 3
−€2 million	€900,000	€850,000	€800,000

To calculate the project's *NPV*, the U.S. firm can take either of two approaches. First, it can discount euro-denominated cash flows using a euro-based cost of capital. Having done this, the firm can then convert the resulting *NPV* back to dollars at the spot rate. For example, assume that the risk-free rate in Europe is 5 percent, and the firm estimates that the cost of capital (expressed as a euro rate) for this project is 10 percent (in other words, there is a 5% risk premium associated with the investment). The *NPV*, rounded to the nearest thousand euros, equals €122,000:

$$NPV = -2,000,000 + \frac{900,000}{1.1^1} + \frac{850,000}{1.1^2} + \frac{800,000}{1.1^3} = 122,000$$

Assume that the current spot rate equals $0.95/€. Multiplying this times the *NPV* yields a dollar-based *NPV* of $116,000 (rounded to the nearest thousand dollars).

In this example, we did not make specific year-by-year forecasts of the future spot rates. Doing so is unnecessary because the firm can choose to hedge its currency exposure through a forward contract. Hedging the currency exposure allows the firm to separate the decision to accept or reject the project from projections of where the dollar-to-euro exchange rate might be headed. Of course the firm may have a view on the exchange rate question, but even so, it is wise to first consider the merits of the investment on its own. For instance, suppose that this project has a negative *NPV*, but managers believe that the euro will appreciate over the life of the project, increasing the project's appeal in dollar terms. Given that belief, there is no need for the firm to undertake the project. Instead, it could purchase euros directly, invest them in safe financial assets in Europe, and convert back to dollars several years later. That is, if the firm wants to speculate on currency movements, it need not invest in physical assets to accomplish that objective.

A second approach for evaluating the investment project is to calculate the *NPV* in dollar terms, assuming that the firm hedges the project's cash flows using forward contracts. To begin this calculation, we must know the risk-free rate in the United States. Suppose that this rate is 3 percent. Recognizing that interest rate parity must hold, we can use Equation 20.5 to calculate the 1-year forward rate:

$$\frac{F^{\$/euro}}{S^{\$/euro}} = \frac{(1 + R_{US})}{(1 + R_{euro})} \qquad \frac{F}{0.95} = \frac{1.03}{1.05} \qquad F = \$0.9319/€$$

Similarly, we can calculate the 2-year and 3-year forward rates as follows:

$$\frac{F^{\$/euro}}{S^{\$/euro}} = \frac{(1 + R_{US})^2}{(1 + R_{euro})^2} \qquad F = \$0.9142/€ \qquad \frac{F^{\$/euro}}{S^{\$/euro}} = \frac{(1 + R_{US})^3}{(1 + R_{euro})^3} \qquad F = \$0.8967/€$$

Next, multiply each period's cash flow in euros times the matching spot or forward exchange rate to obtain a sequence of cash flows in dollars (rounded to the nearest thousand dollars):

Currency	Initial Investment	Year 1	Year 2	Year 3
€	2,000,000 × 0.95	900,000 × 0.9319	850,000 × 0.9142	800,000 × 0.8967
$	1,900,000	839,000	777,000	717,000

All that remains is to discount this project's cash flows at an appropriate risk-adjusted U.S. interest rate. But how do we determine that rate? Recall that the European discount rate used to calculate the euro-denominated *NPV* was 10 percent, 5 percent above the European risk-free rate. Intuitively, we might expect that the comparable U.S. rate is 8 percent, representing a 5 percent risk premium over the current risk-free rate in the United States. That intuition is roughly correct. To be precise, use the following formula to solve for the project's required return in U.S. dollar terms:

$$(1 + R) = (1 + 0.10)\frac{(1 + 0.03)}{(1 + 0.05)} \qquad R = 7.9\%$$

This equation takes the project's required return in euro terms, 10 percent, and rescales it to dollar terms by multiplying by the ratio of risk-free interest rates in each country. We can verify that discounting the dollar-denominated cash flows using this rate results in the same *NPV* (again, rounding to the nearest thousand dollars) that we obtained by discounting the cash flows in euros and converting to dollars at the spot rate.

$$NPV = -\$1,900,000 + \frac{\$839,000}{1.079^1} + \frac{\$777,000}{1.079^2} + \frac{\$717,000}{1.079^3} = \$116,000$$

These calculations demonstrate that a company does not have to "take a view" on currency movements when it invests abroad. Whether the company hedges a project's cash flows using forward contracts, or whether it calculates a project's *NPV* in local currency before converting to the home currency at the spot exchange rate, future exchange rate movements need not cloud the capital budgeting decision.

COST OF CAPITAL

In the preceding example, we assumed that the project's cost of capital in Europe was 10 percent, which translated into a dollar-based discount rate of 7.9 percent. But where did the 10 percent come from? We return to the lessons of Chapter 9, namely that the discount rate should reflect the project's risk. One way to assess that risk is to calculate a beta for the investment. However, calculating the beta for an international project raises some questions for which finance as yet has no definitive answer.

For example, suppose that shareholders of the U.S. firm investing in Europe hold mostly U.S. stocks in their portfolios. Perhaps the costs of diversifying internationally are prohibitively expensive for many investors. In that case, when a firm diversifies internationally, it creates value for its shareholders. That stands in sharp contrast to the case when a firm diversifies domestically. Because U.S. investors can diversify their domestic investments at very low cost, they will not realize any benefit if a firm diversifies on their behalf.

If a firm's shareholders cannot diversify internationally, when the firm invests abroad, it should calculate a project's beta by measuring the covariance of similar European investments with the U.S. market, not the European market. The reason is that from the perspective of U.S. investors, the project's systematic risk depends on its covariance with the other assets that U.S. investors already own. A U.S. firm planning to build an electronics manufacturing facility in Germany might compare the returns of existing German electronics firms with returns on a U.S. stock index to estimate a project beta.[11]

In contrast, if the firm's shareholders do hold internationally diversified portfolios, the firm should calculate the project's beta by comparing the covariance of its returns (or returns on similar investments) with returns on a worldwide stock index. This generates the project's "global beta." Next, to estimate the project's required return, the firm should apply the CAPM, multiplying the global market risk premium times the project's beta, and adding the risk-free rate. In all likelihood, because a globally diversified portfolio is less volatile than a portfolio containing only domestic securities, the risk premium on the global market will be less than the domestic risk premium.

APPLYING THE MODEL

A Japanese auto manufacturer decides to build a plant to make cars for the North American market. The firm estimates two project betas. The first calculation takes returns on U.S. auto stocks and calculates their betas relative to those on the Nikkei stock index. Based on these calculations, the Japanese firm decides to apply a beta of 1.1 to the investment. The risk-free rate of interest in Japan is 2 percent, and the market risk premium on the Nikkei index is 8 percent, so the project's required return is calculated as follows:

$$R_{\text{project}} = 2\% + 1.1(8\%) = 10.8\%$$

The second calculation takes the returns on U.S. auto manufacturers and determines their betas relative to those on a world stock index. It turns out that U.S. auto stocks are more highly correlated with the world market than they are with the Nikkei. Combined with the fact that the variance of the world market portfolio is lower than the variance of the Nikkei, this calculation leads to a higher estimate of the project beta, say 1.3. However, offsetting this effect is the fact that the risk premium on the world market portfolio is just 5 percent. Therefore, the second estimate of the project's required return is calculated as follows:

$$R_{\text{project}} = 2\% + 1.3(5\%) = 8.5\%$$ ■

[11.] Of course, the U.S. firm would have to worry about the effects of leverage, unlevering the equity betas of German firms with debt on their balance sheets.

12. Why does discounting the cash flows of a foreign investment using the foreign cost of capital, then converting that to the home currency at the spot rate, yield the same *NPV* as converting the project's cash flows to domestic currency at the forward rate and then discounting them at the domestic cost of capital?

13. What factors determine whether a project's beta will be higher or lower when calculated against a domestic stock index versus a world stock index?

14. Why is it not surprising to find that the risk premium on the world market portfolio is lower than the domestic risk premium?

20.5 SHORT-TERM FINANCIAL DECISIONS

Though the focus in international finance is rightly on long-term investments and economic exposure, managers must also actively measure and manage short-term financial exposures. We have already demonstrated and discussed transactions exposure in the context of exchange rate risk. We conclude by looking at several other issues related to short-term financial decision making in an international context.

CASH MANAGEMENT

In its international cash management, a multinational firm can respond to exchange rate risks by protecting (hedging) its undesirable cash and marketable securities exposures or by making certain adjustments in its operations. Whereas the former approach is more applicable in responding to *accounting exposures,* the latter is better suited against *economic exposures.* Each of these two approaches is examined here.

Hedging Strategies

Hedging strategies are techniques used to offset or protect against risk. In international cash management, these strategies include actions such as borrowing or lending in different currencies; undertaking contracts in the forward, futures, and/or options markets; and also swapping assets/liabilities with other parties. We refer the reader to Section 20.3 and Chapter 21 for detailed examples.

Adjustments in Operations

In responding to exchange rate fluctuations, MNCs can give some protection to international cash flows through appropriate adjustments in assets and liabilities. Two routes are available to a multinational company. The first centers on the operating relationships that a subsidiary of an MNC maintains with *other* firms. Depending on management's expectation of a local currency's position, adjustments in operations would involve the reduction of liabilities if the currency is appreciating or the reduction of financial assets if it is depreciating. For example, if a U.S.-based MNC with a subsidiary in Mexico expects the Mexican currency to *appreciate* in value relative to the U.S. dollar, local customers' accounts receivable would be *increased* and accounts payable would be reduced, if at all possible. If the Mexican currency were, instead, expected to *depreciate,* the local customers' accounts receivable would be *reduced* and accounts payable would be increased.

The second route focuses on the operating relationship a subsidiary has with its parent or with other subsidiaries within the same MNC. In dealing with exchange rate risks, a subsidiary can rely on *intra-MNC accounts*. Specifically, undesirable exchange rate exposures can be corrected to the extent that the subsidiary can take the following steps:

1. In appreciation-prone countries, intra-MNC accounts receivable are collected as soon as possible, and payment of intra-MNC accounts payable is delayed as long as possible.
2. In depreciation-prone countries, intra-MNC accounts receivable are collected as late as possible, and intra-MNC accounts payable are paid as soon as possible.

This technique is known as **leading and lagging,** or simply as "leads and lags." The following example illustrates its potential effectiveness.

APPLYING THE MODEL

Assume that a U.S.-based parent company, American Computer Corporation (ACC), both buys parts from and sells parts to its wholly owned Mexican subsidiary, Tijuana Computer Company (TCC). Assume further that ACC has accounts payable of $10 million that it is scheduled to pay TCC in 30 days, and in turn has accounts receivable of (Mexican peso) MP75.9 million due from TCC within 30 days. Because today's exchange rate is MP7.59/$, the accounts receivable are also worth $10 million. Therefore, parent and subsidiary owe each other equal amounts (though in different currencies), and both are payable in 30 days, but because TCC is a wholly owned subsidiary of ACC, the parent has complete discretion over the timing of these payments.

If ACC believes that the Mexican peso will depreciate from MP7.59/US$ to, say, MP9.00/US$ during the next 30 days, the combined companies can profit by collecting the weak-currency (MP) debt immediately, but delaying payment of the strong-currency (US$) debt for the full 30 days allowed. If parent and subsidiary do this, and the peso depreciates as predicted, the net result is that the MP75.9 million payment from TCC to ACC is made immediately and is safely converted into $10 million at today's exchange rate, whereas the delayed $10 million payment from ACC to TCC will be worth MP90 million (MP9.00/$ × $10,000,000). Thus, the Mexican subsidiary will experience a foreign exchange trading profit of MP14.1 million (MP90,000,000 − MP75,900,000), whereas the U.S. parent receives the full amount ($10 million) due from TCC and therefore is unharmed. Of course, if the dollar is expected to depreciate against the peso, these steps would be reversed.

The example demonstrates that the manipulation of an MNC's consolidated intracompany accounts by one subsidiary generally benefits one subsidiary (or the parent) while leaving the other subsidiary (or the parent) unharmed. The exact degree and direction of the actual manipulations, however, may depend on the tax status of each country. The MNC obviously would want to have the exchange rate losses in the country with the higher tax rate. Finally, changes in intra-MNC accounts can also be subject to restrictions and regulations put forward by the respective host countries of various subsidiaries.

CREDIT AND INVENTORY MANAGEMENT

Multinational firms based in different countries compete for the same global export markets. Therefore, it is essential that they offer attractive credit terms to potential customers. Increasingly, however, the maturity and saturation of developed markets are forcing MNCs to maintain and increase revenues by exporting and selling a higher percentage of their output to developing countries. Given the risks associated with the latter group of buyers, as partly evidenced by the greater volatility of many developing nations' currencies, the MNC must use a variety of tools to protect such revenues. In addition to the use of hedging and various asset and liability adjustments (described earlier), MNCs should seek the backing of their respective governments in both identifying target markets and extending credit. Multinationals based in a number of Western European nations and those based in Japan currently benefit from extensive involvement of government agencies that provide them with the needed service and financial support suggested here. For U.S.-based MNCs, the international positions of government agencies such as the Export-Import Bank currently do not provide a comparable level of support.

In terms of inventory management, MNCs must consider a number of factors related to both economics and politics. In the former category, in addition to maintaining the appropriate level of inventory in various locations around the world, a multinational firm is compelled to deal with exchange rate fluctuations, tariffs, non-tariff barriers, integration schemes such as the EU, and other rules and regulations. Politically, inventories can be subjected to wars, expropriations, blockages, and other forms of government intervention.

Concept Review Questions

15. Assume that a U.S. multinational company has wholly owned subsidiaries in both Britain and Switzerland, which trade with each other and the parent regularly. Further assume that the British pound is expected to appreciate versus the dollar and Swiss franc. How could you profit from this using the technique of "leads and lags"?

16. Assume that your firm has sold a computer to a British company, with delivery and payment (in British pounds) to occur in 30 days. You will receive a fixed payment of £2,000, and the current exchange rate is $1.40/£. What risk do you run by remaining unhedged, and how could you hedge that risk using a forward contract?

20.6 SUMMARY

- Large, globally active firms known as multinational corporations (MNCs) dominate international trade and investment today. MNCs tend to be the most dynamic and successful firms in their industry, and most modern international financial and accounting techniques have been designed to meet their special financial needs.
- Any company that exports a significant amount of goods and services is exposed to exchange rate risk, or the chance that a change in the home currency's value relative to the currency in the customer's market can impose financial losses on the exporter. Importers can face similar risks, though this is less common because sales are usually denominated in the customer's currency. A variety of hedging techniques have been developed to handle this risk—the most commonly used is hedging with a forward contract.
- The total volume of foreign direct investment (FDI) surged during the 1990s and shows no sign of permanently slackening. FDI implies that the investor will exercise operating control of the asset being purchased, which is usually a business firm, a factory, or a significant piece of real estate. Portfolio investment, which is much more passive in nature, has also increased dramatically in recent years. The

recent economic troubles in Asia, Latin America, and Russia have slowed FDI and portfolio investment only slightly, as most of this occurs between developed economies.

• MNCs must pay particularly careful attention to their management of cash, accounts receivable, and other short-term assets, given the potential danger of loss from exchange rate fluctuations. However, MNCs can also use a variety of techniques not only to survive but even to profit from these fluctuations.

INTERNET RESOURCES

Note: *For updates to links, please go to the book's website at* http://smart.swcollege.com

http://www.economist.com/markets/currency/map.cfm —*The Economist* magazine's website; offers a worldwide currency map showing data for each country, including currency name and exchange rate vis-à-vis any other currency, population, capital, and land area; map uses color codes to highlight which nations' currencies have appreciated or depreciated (vis-à-vis any other currency) over the past day, week, month, or year

http://www.bis.org —Bank for International Settlements website; offers interesting publications and data on the international banking industry as well as on derivatives

http://www.oanda.com —A site with enormous coverage of the foreign exchange markets

http://http://news.ft.com/markets —*Financial Times* website; offers a wealth of data on worldwide financial markets

http://www.corporateinformation.com — Offers research on countries and industries with many links for further exploration

http://www.globalmarkets.com —A site by Standard & Poor's that offers information on fixed income, currency, and equity markets around the world

http://www.securities.com —Internet Securities, Inc. website; specializes in providing data and news on emerging markets

http://www.euribor.org —Provides information on the Euribor (Euro Interbank Offered Rate), a rate on loans between prime banks within the European Monetary Union, analogous to LIBOR

http://www.x-rates.com —Allows you to create charts or historical data tables for virtually any of the world's currencies

http://www.euroland.com —Provides data on nine different European stock exchanges

http://www.prsgroup.com — Offers country risk rankings

KEY TERMS

accounting exposure
appreciated
asset market model of exchange rates
covered interest arbitrage
cross exchange rate
currency board arrangement
depreciated
economic exposure
euro

European Monetary Union (EMU)
exchange rate
exchange rate gain
exchange rate loss
fixed exchange rate
floating exchange rate
foreign direct investment (FDI)
forward discount
forward exchange rate

forward premium

forward–spot parity

General Agreement on Tariffs and
    Trade (GATT)

hedged

hedging strategies

interest rate parity

law of one price

leading and lagging

macro political risk

managed floating rate system

micro political risk

monetary union

multinational corporations (MNCs)

natural hedge

nominal exchange rate

political risk

portfolio investments

purchasing power parity

real exchange rate

real interest rate parity

spot exchange rate

transactions exposure

translation exposure

triangular arbitrage

World Trade Organization (WTO)

QUESTIONS

20-1. Define a multinational corporation (MNC). What additional factors must be considered by the manager of an MNC that a manager of a purely domestic firm is not forced to face?

20-2. Who are the major players in foreign currency markets, and what are their motivations for trading?

20-3. Suppose that an exchange rate is quoted in terms of euros per pound. In what direction would this rate move if the euro appreciated against the pound?

20-4. Explain how triangular arbitrage ensures that currency values are essentially the same in different markets around the world at any given moment.

20-5. In what sense is it a misnomer to refer to a currency as weak or strong? Who benefits and who loses if the yen appreciates against the pound?

20-6. What does a spot exchange rate have in common with a forward rate, and how are they different?

20-7. What does it mean to say that a currency trades at a forward premium?

20-8. Explain how the law of one price establishes a relationship between changes in currency values and inflation rates.

20-9. We developed the notion of forward–spot parity by assuming risk-neutral traders. Suppose that managers who make decisions about whether to hedge or not are risk averse. How might this alter the forward–spot parity logic?

20-10. Why does purchasing power parity appear to hold in the long run but not in the short run?

20-11. In terms of risk, is a U.S. investor indifferent about whether to buy a U.S. government bond or a U.K. government bond? Why or why not?

20-12. If the euro trades at a forward premium against the yen, explain why interest rates in Japan would have to be higher than they are in Europe.

20-13. Suppose that the U.S. Federal Reserve suddenly decides to raise interest rates. Trace out the potential impact that this action might have on (1) interest rates abroad, (2) the spot value of the dollar, and (3) the forward value of the dollar.

20-14. Interest rates on risk-free bonds in the United States are about 2 percent, whereas interest rates on Swiss government bonds are 6 percent. Can we conclude that investors around the world will flock to buy Swiss bonds? Why or why not?

20-15. A Japanese investor decides to purchase shares in a company that trades on the London Stock Exchange. The investor's plan is to hold these shares for one year, selling them and converting the proceeds to yen at year's end. During the year, the pound appreciates against the yen. Does this enhance or diminish the investor's return on the stock?

20-16. Suppose that the dollar trades at a forward discount relative to the yen. A U.S. firm must pay a Japanese supplier ¥10 million in three months. A manager in the U.S. firm reasons that because the dollar buys fewer yen on the forward market than it does on the spot market, the firm should not enter a forward hedge to eliminate its exchange rate exposure. Comment on this opinion.

20-17. How is hedging exchange rate exposure using options different from hedging using forward contracts? What does this suggest about the costs of hedging with options rather than forwards?

20-18. What are some strategies for minimizing political risk in a developing country?

PROBLEMS

Exchange Rate Fundamentals

20-1. On April 4, 2002, the Mexican peso (Ps)–U.S. dollar exchange rate was Ps9.0395/$ ($0.1107/Ps). On May 7, 2002, the exchange rate was Ps9.4805/$ ($0.1055/Ps). State which currency appreciated and which depreciated, and then calculate both the percentage appreciation of the currency that rose in value and the percentage depreciation of the currency that declined in value.

20-2. Using the data presented in Figure 20.1, calculate the spot exchange rate between Canadian dollars and British pounds (in pounds per dollar).

20-3. Using the data presented in Figure 20.1, specify whether the following currencies appreciated or depreciated (against the dollar) from Monday to Tuesday: the yen, the Swiss franc, and the Polish zloty. (Focus only on spot rates.)

20-4. Go to http://www.economist.com. Under the "Markets & Data" section, activate the foreign exchange map. On the menu at the far left, choose the U.S. dollar as the base currency.

   a. Click on the "1-month" selection to show the appreciation or depreciation of the world's currencies relative to the dollar. Does it appear that the dollar is appreciating or depreciating against most of the world's currencies, or is the answer mixed?

   b. Next, choose the "1-year" option, and identify two or three countries whose currencies have depreciated the most against the U.S. dollar and two or three whose currencies have appreciated the most. Search the web to try to find out what the most recent inflation figures from those countries are. What lesson does this reveal?

20-5. On April 4, 2002, the *Wall Street Journal* reported the following spot and forward rates for the Japanese yen (¥).

Spot:	$0.007556/¥ (¥132.34/$)
1-month:	$0.007568/¥ (¥132.14/$)
3-month:	$0.007593/¥ (¥131.71/$)

Supply the forward yen premium or discount (specify which it is) for both the 1- and 3-month quotes as an annual percentage rate.

20-6. Using the data presented in Figure 20.1, specify whether the U.S. dollar trades at a forward premium or discount relative to the Canadian dollar, the Japanese yen, and the Swiss franc. Use the 3-month forward rates to determine the answer.

20-7.   Using the data presented in Figure 20.1, determine the forward premium or discount on the Canadian dollar relative to the British pound, the Japanese yen, and the Swiss franc. Use the 6-month forward rates to determine the answer, and express your answer as an annual rate.

20-8.   Assume that you are quoted the following series of exchange rates for the U.S. dollar ($), the Canadian dollar (C$), and the British pound (£):

$0.6000/C$ C$1.6667/$
$1.2500/£   £0.8000/$
C$2.5000/£   £0.4000/C$

Assuming that you have $1 million in cash, how can you take profitable advantage of this series of exchange rates? Show the series of trades that would yield an arbitrage profit, and calculate how much profit you would make.

The Parity Conditions in International Finance

20-9.   Use the data presented in Figure 20.1 to answer Problems 20-9 and 20-10. A particular commodity sells for $5,000 in the United States and ¥600,000 in Japan.
   a. Does the law of one price hold? If not, explain how to profit through arbitrage.
   b. Taking the commodity prices in the United States and Japan as given, at what exchange rate (in terms of yen per dollar) would the law of one price hold?

20-10. If the expected rate of inflation in the United States is 1 percent, the 1-year risk-free interest rate is 2 percent, and the 1-year risk-free rate in Britain is 4 percent, what is the expected inflation rate in Britain?

20-11. Go to http://www.economist.com. Under the "Markets & Data" section, find the link for the "Big Mac index." After exploring this part of the site, explain why the Big Mac index might foreshadow changes in exchange rates. What features of the Big Mac would suggest that Big Macs may not satisfy the law of one price?

20-12. Refer to Problem 20-9. If it costs ¥15,000 to transport the commodity from the United States to Japan, is there still an arbitrage opportunity? At what exchange rate (in yen per dollar) would buying the commodity in the United States and shipping it to sell in Japan become profitable?

20-13. Refer to Problem 20-12. Given shipping costs of ¥15,000, at what exchange rate would it be profitable to buy the commodity in Japan and ship it to the United States to sell? Comment on the general lesson from the last few questions.

Smart Solutions
See the problem and solution explained step-by-step at
SMARTFinance

20-14. Assume that the annual interest rate on a 6-month U.S. Treasury bill is 5 percent, and use the data presented in Figure 20.1 to answer the following:
   a. Calculate the annual interest rate on 6-month bills in Canada and Japan.
   b. Suppose that the annual interest rate on a 6-month bill in Japan is 0.5 percent. Illustrate how to exploit this via covered interest arbitrage.
   c. Suppose that the annual interest rate on a 3-month U.K. government bond is 4 percent. What is the annual interest rate on a 3-month government bond in Switzerland?
   d. Suppose that the actual Swiss interest rate is 0.5 percent. Illustrate how to conduct covered interest arbitrage to exploit this situation.

20-15. Shortly after it was introduced, the euro traded just below parity with the dollar, meaning that one dollar purchased more than one euro. This implies
   a. that U.S. inflation was lower than European inflation
   b. that U.S. interest rates were lower than European rates
   c. that the law of one price does not hold
   d. none of the above

20-16. Assume that the following information is known about the current spot exchange rate between the U.S. dollar and the British pound (£), inflation rates in Britain and the United States, and the real rate of interest—which is assumed to be the same in both countries:

Current spot rate, S = $1.4500/£ (£0.6897/$)

U.S. inflation rate, i_{US} = 1.5 percent per year (0.015)

British inflation rate, i_{UK} = 2.0 percent per year (0.020)

Real rate of interest, R = 2.5 percent per year (0.025)

Based on this data, use the parity conditions of international finance to compute the following:

a. Expected spot rate next year
b. U.S. risk-free rate (on a 1-year bond)
c. British risk-free rate (on a 1-year bond)
d. 1-year forward rate

Finally, show how you can make an arbitrage profit if you are offered the chance to sell or buy pounds forward (for delivery one year from now) at the current spot rate of $1.4500/£ (£0.6897/$). Assuming that you can borrow $1 million or £689,700 at the risk-free interest rate, what would your profit be on this arbitrage transaction?

Managing Financial and Political Risk

20-17. Suppose that the spot exchange rate follows a random walk, which means that the best forecast of the spot rate at some future date is simply its current value. Now suppose that a U.S. firm owes €1 million to a Spanish supplier. If the U.S. firm is risk neutral, describe the circumstances under which the firm will or will not enter into a forward contract to hedge its exposure.

Smart Solutions

See the problem and solution explained step-by-step at

SMARTFinance

20-18. Classic City Exporters (CCE) recently sold a large shipment of sporting equipment to a Swiss company—the goods will be sold in Zurich. The sale was denominated in Swiss francs (SF) and was worth SF500,000. Delivery of the sporting goods and payment by the Swiss buyer are due to occur in six months. The current spot exchange rate is $0.6002/SF (SF1.6661/$), and the 6-month forward rate is $0.6020/SF (SF1.6611/$). What risk would CCE run if it remained unhedged, and how could it hedge that risk with a forward contract? Assuming that the actual exchange rate in six months is $0.5500/SF (SF1.8182/$), compute the profit or loss—and state which it is—CCE would experience if it remains unhedged versus hedging in the forward market.

20-19. A British firm will receive $1 million from a U.S. customer in three months. The firm is considering two strategies to eliminate its foreign exchange exposure. The first strategy is to pledge the $1 million as collateral for a 3-month loan from a U.S. bank at 4 percent interest. The U.K. firm will then convert the proceeds of the loan to pounds at the spot rate. When the loan is due, the firm will pay the $1 million balance due by handing its U.S. receivable over to the bank. This strategy allows the U.K. firm to "monetize" its receivable immediately. The spot exchange rate is 0.6550 pounds per dollar.

The second strategy is to enter a forward contract at an exchange rate of 0.6450 pounds per dollar. This ensures that the U.K. firm will receive £645,000 in three months. If the firm wanted to monetize this payment immediately, it could take out a 3-month loan from a U.K. bank at 8 percent, pledging the proceeds of the forward contract as collateral.

Which of these strategies should the firm follow?

Long-Term Investment Decisions

20-20.   A German company manufactures a specialized piece of manufacturing equipment and leases it to a U.K. enterprise. The lease calls for five end-of-year payments of £1 million. The German firm spent €3.5 million to produce the equipment, which is expected to have no salvage value after five years. The current spot rate is €1.5/£. The risk-free interest rate in Germany is 3 percent, and in the United Kingdom it is 5 percent. The German firm reasons that the appropriate (German) discount rate for this investment is 7 percent. Calculate the *NPV* of this investment in two ways.

    a. First, convert all cash flows to pounds, and discount at an appropriate (U.K.) cost of capital. Convert the resulting *NPV* to euros at the spot rate.

    b. Second, calculate forward rates for each year, convert the pound-denominated cash flows into euros using those rates, and discount at the German cost of capital. Verify that the *NPV* obtained from this approach matches (except perhaps for small rounding errors) that obtained in part (a).

Short-Term Financial Decisions

20-21.   A Canadian firm owes ¥3 million to its Japanese subsidiary. The subsidiary in turn owes the Canadian firm C$45,000. Both payments are due in 30 days, but managers believe that the yen will appreciate against the Canadian dollar over the next 30 days. Specifically, they expect the spot exchange rate to change from ¥70/C$ to ¥60/C$.

    a. If the firm can accelerate one of these payments to the present, which one should it accelerate?

    b. What will be the exchange rate gain from accelerating the payment compared to making the payment in 30 days?

20-22.   A U.S. firm must borrow $1 million to meet operating needs for one year. A U.S. bank offers a 1-year loan at 5 percent interest. A U.K. bank is willing to lend (in pounds) for one year at 7 percent, and a Canadian bank offers a loan at 6 percent (denominated in Canadian dollars). In all cases, the U.S. firm will repay the loan in a lump sum at the end of the year. If it borrows from a foreign lender, the firm will hedge its currency exposure with a forward contract. The current spot and 1-year forward exchange rates are as follows:

Country	Foreign Currency per US$	
	Spot	1-Year Forward
Canada	1.5855	1.6050
United Kingdom	0.6416	0.6550

Which loan should the firm accept?

21

Risk Management and Financial Engineering

OPENING FOCUS

The Fred Hutchinson Cancer Research Center Uses Derivatives to Fight Cancer

The Fred Hutchinson Cancer Research Center in Seattle, Washington, is the world's largest bone-marrow transplant center. In 1991, the center issued $72 million in fixed-rate bonds to finance the construction of research laboratories on the center's new campus. The bond covenants included a 10-year call deferment so the bonds could not be called until January 2001. In addition, the bonds paid an annual coupon between 6.6 percent and 7.4 percent.

By 1999, interest rates on comparable bonds had dropped well below 6 percent, and Randy Main, the CFO for the Hutchinson Center, was concerned that interest rates would increase again before the center was able to refinance (or "refund") the high-coupon-rate bonds. The solution was to enter into an interest rate swap with the investment bank Lehman Brothers. Beginning in January 2001, the center began paying Lehman Brothers a fixed rate of 5.19 percent per year based on a principal of $72 million. In return, Lehman Brothers would pay the center a variable rate of interest. This type of swap is called a *forward swap* because the exchange of interest payments did not begin until January 2001 even though Hutchinson and Lehman entered the agreement in 1999. At the same time the center began exchanging interest payments with Lehman Brothers, the center issued new variable-rate bonds to pay off the old fixed-rate bonds. The center uses the variable-rate cash inflows from the swap to pay the variable-rate coupon payments on the bonds. Both the swap and the new floating-rate bonds will mature in 2029.

The net result of this transaction was that the Hutchinson Center was able to lock in lower fixed-rate borrowing costs. Regardless of what happened to interest rates between 1999 and 2001, the Hutchinson Center was assured that its net borrowing costs would be a fixed rate of 5.19 percent beginning in January 2001. The center estimates that the cost savings from entering into the swap will be about $13 million, money that can be spent on cancer research rather than interest payments.

By entering into the swap agreement, the Hutchinson Center was able to minimize its exposure to the risk of an increase in interest rates between 1999 and 2001. If interest rates declined between 1999 and 2001, however, the Center would not enjoy any reduction in its borrowing costs. The question faced by Randy Main was whether to hedge the center's interest rate risk exposure. Ultimately, Randy Main decided it was better to lock in a reduced borrowing cost rather than risk $13 million on the hope that interest rates would decline.

Source: "Interest Swap Saves Hutch Money," *Seattle Post-Intelligencer* (August 9, 1999), p. C2.

Trading in virtually all types of financial instruments has increased over the past two decades, but no markets have experienced growth rates as explosive as those for the financial instruments used for hedging and risk management. Since the collapse of the Bretton Woods fixed exchange rate regime in 1973, corporations have been exposed to extreme fluctuations in interest rates, in exchange rates, and in the prices of virtually all important raw materials.[1] This increased risk has led to a mushrooming demand for financial instruments and strategies that corporations can use to hedge, or offset, their underlying operating and financial exposures.

This chapter discusses *risk management* and *financial engineering* in the modern corporation. Traditionally, **risk management** has meant the process of identifying firm-specific risk exposures and managing those risk exposures using insurance products. In recent years, however, the risk-management function has expanded to include identifying, measuring, and managing all types of risk exposures, including interest rate, commodity, and currency risk exposures. There are three ways to minimize a firm's risk exposures—diversifying, insuring, and hedging; this chapter focuses on hedging. Derivative securities, including forwards, futures, options, and swaps, are the financial instruments commonly used for hedging and risk management. Figure 21.1 illustrates the growth in the market for these types of products. Currency and interest rate swaps have experienced especially rapid growth.

Though the financial press often portrays derivatives in a negative light, these securities can be an effective means of hedging risk exposures. We will discuss each of these instruments, but we begin with an overview of risk management. Next, we describe each of the major types of derivative securities and discuss how each can be used to manage a firm's risk exposures. Finally, we discuss financial engineering, which is the application of finance principles to design securities and strategies that help firms manage their risk exposures.

21.1 OVERVIEW OF RISK MANAGEMENT

As noted, risk management involves identifying potential events that represent a threat to a firm's cash flows and either minimizing the likelihood of those events or minimizing their impact on the firm's cash flows. Although in the past this process has focused on firm-specific events such as workers' compensation claims, product recalls, product liability claims, and loss from fire or flood, in recent years risk management has come to include the process of identifying, measuring, and managing

---

[1.] The dramatic increase in the volatility of financial assets (including currencies) and the development of markets for risk-management instruments is described in detail in Rawls and Smithson (1989).

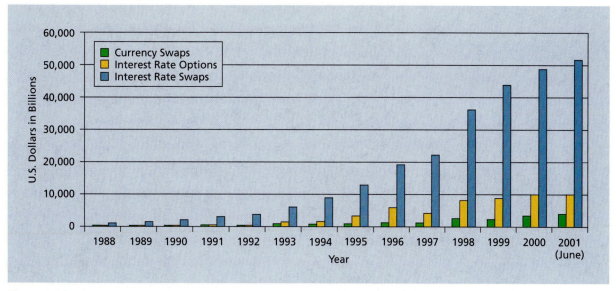

Figure 21.1
Selected Over-the-Counter Derivatives Contracts Outstanding (Year-End Notional Amounts)

Source: International Swaps and Derivatives Association, *ISDA Market Survey,* 1988–1997, and the Bank for International Settlements, *BIS Quarterly Review,* various issues, 1998–2001.

these marketwide sources of exposure. In this section, we provide an overview of this type of risk management.

Risk Factors

If a change in the level of interest rates will adversely affect the cash flows of a company (perhaps by raising its cost of borrowing), that firm is exposed to **interest rate risk.** This is the single most common concern among managers engaged in risk management. Interest rate risk is the risk of suffering losses as a result of unanticipated changes in market rates of interest. The most often cited example of losses caused by interest rate risk is the experience of the savings and loan (S&L) industry in the early 1980s. S&Ls suffered from a mismatch in terms of the maturity of their assets and liabilities because they funded long-term assets (e.g., 30-year, fixed-rate mortgages) with short-term liabilities (e.g., passbook savings deposits and short-term certificates of deposit). When interest rates spiked in the late 1970s and early 1980s, firms in the industry suffered tremendous losses because they were paying high rates on their short-term deposits while continuing to earn low rates on the long-term mortgages in their portfolio.

As illustrated by the S&L industry, interest rate risk is of particular concern to financial firms. However, more and more nonfinancial firms are recognizing that they also are exposed to this type of risk. For example, a retailing firm that funds its seasonal buildup of inventories with floating-rate debt will face higher interest expenses if market rates of interest increase. This is an example of **transaction exposure,** the risk that a change in prices will negatively affect the value of a specific transaction or series of transactions.

Although most corporations focus on the possibility that changes in market rates of interest will increase interest ex-

SMART PRACTICES VIDEO
David Childress, Asset Liability Manager,
Ford Motor Co.
"Interest rate risk really comes down to how assets and liabilities on the balance sheet reprice."

See the entire interview at **SMARTFinance**

COMPARATIVE CORPORATE FINANCE

International Differences in Foreign Exchange Risk Management Emphasis

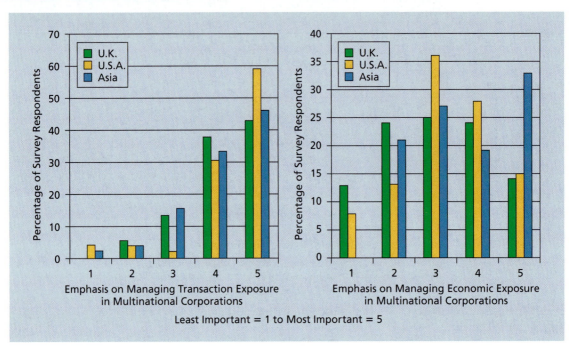

Source: Andrew P. Marshall, "Foreign Exchange Risk Management in UK, USA, and Asia Pacific Multinational Companies," *Journal of Multinational Financial Management* 10 (2000), pp. 185–211.

The two charts summarize the concerns of managers in multinational corporations in the United Kingdom, the United States, and Asia/Pacific countries. Generally, U.S. companies seem to be more concerned with transaction exposures than companies in the U.K. or Asia. Asia/Pacific companies, on the other hand, are more concerned about economic exposure than managers in the U.S. or U.K.

The differences in emphasis can be attributed, in part, to differences in product markets and the location of production facilities. For example, U.S. multinationals often have product markets that are primarily domestic, but their production facilities are commonly in other countries. Consequently, U.S. multinationals tend to focus more on how changes in exchange rates affect their cost structure and less on how changes in exchange rates affect their revenue stream. Asia/Pacific multinationals, on the other hand, often have domestic production facilities and foreign product markets. Therefore, they tend to worry less about the impact of exchange rates on their cost structures and more about the impact of exchange rates on their revenue stream.

penses, changes in interest rates can also affect cash inflows. Some firms have revenue streams that are sensitive to changes in interest rates. For example, a building products manufacturer may experience lower demand when interest rates increase. This is an example of **economic exposure,** the risk that a change in prices will negatively impact the value of all cash flows of a firm. As we will see later in this chapter, there are several ways that corporations can minimize both their transaction and economic exposures to interest rate risk.[2]

[2.] For an intuitive discussion of managing interest rate risk and the building-blocks approach to financial risk management, see Smith, Smithson, and Wilford (1989).

At the same time that currency exchange rates were becoming more volatile, world economies were becoming more integrated. In recent years, currency exchange rates have remained volatile, and the pace of global integration has continued to accelerate. This has given rise to ever increasing exposure to foreign exchange risk, as discussed previously, and in more depth, in Chapter 20.[3] Consider another example of a transaction exposure. A U.S.-based company with manufacturing operations in Canada denominates the products it sells in international markets in the buyer's home currency. Suppose that it books a sale, denominated in euros, to a buyer in Germany, with delivery and payment to occur in three months. If the euro depreciates in value relative to the Canadian dollar (C\$) over the next three months, this company will receive fewer C\$ than expected when it converts the euros received in payment into C\$ to cover its own production costs.

As another example of economic exposure, if this U.S. manufacturing firm faces stiff competition from a Japanese manufacturer and the value of the yen declines, the Japanese firm may be able to reduce the prices it charges in European markets, thereby hurting demand for the products manufactured by the U.S. firm. Again, most firms concentrate on minimizing transaction exposure, but economic exposures are usually much more important. Unfortunately, these exposures are also much harder to hedge, or otherwise manage, because they are systemic.

Although most discussions of risk management focus on interest rate risk and foreign exchange risk, commodity price risk is also very important for many firms. Any firm that uses a commodity as a production input is potentially exposed to losses if the price of the commodity increases. Likewise, the commodity producers are also exposed to the risk that the price of the commodity could decline.[4]

APPLYING THE MODEL

Hershey Foods Corporation illustrates the importance of a successful risk-management strategy. Cocoa is an important input for Hershey. If the price of cocoa increases, Hershey may be able to pass the increase on to consumers in the form of higher prices for Kisses and other confections. However, an increase in the price of Kisses is bound to hurt the demand for them. Consider the consequences of not hedging this risk exposure, especially if competitors such as Nestle and Mars do hedge their exposure by locking in the price they pay for cocoa. Hershey could be faced with having to increase the price of its products in response to an increase in the price of cocoa, while the price of Nestle and Mars products remains the same. Of course, if the price of cocoa declines, Hershey would benefit from the lower price, while Nestle and Mars are committed to paying a higher price.[5]

THE HEDGING DECISION

Although it is clear that the corporate demand for hedging and risk-management products has grown dramatically in recent years, it is less clear why a public com-

---

[3.] For a discussion of foreign exchange risk, see Pringle (1991) and Pringle and Connolly (1993).

[4.] See Haushalter (2000) for an analysis of hedging policies by oil and gas producers.

[5.] Hershey takes its hedging activities so seriously that it has expressed concerns over Financial Accounting Standards Board proposals to require greater disclosure of a firm's activities in derivative markets. Hershey's major competitors, Nestle and Mars, would not be subject to these requirements because Nestle is a Swiss-based firm and Mars is privately held. Hershey is concerned because it believes the new requirements would put it at a competitive disadvantage in terms of its derivative positions. See *Investment Dealers' Digest* (1997).

pany would choose to hedge at all. Risk aversion can explain why individuals and private firms hedge, but this cannot explain why a company that is presumably being run in the interests of a large number of well-diversified shareholders would expend valuable resources to hedge. This section discusses the various potential motivations for hedging and possible hedging strategies.

Motivations for Hedging

The motivations for buying insurance are similar to those for hedging. However, there are some crucial differences. According to Mayers and Smith (1982), by purchasing insurance, a corporation benefits from the insurance company's expertise in terms of its ability to evaluate and price certain types of risks. Therefore, insurance companies have a comparative advantage in bearing these sources of risk. Similarly, insurance companies have the ability to process claims more efficiently and effectively than other corporations. For example, insurance companies have expertise in negotiating, settling, and providing legal representation in liability suits.

Hedging marketwide sources of risk, on the other hand, does not seem to provide any real service other than reduced volatility. In addition, this risk reduction is costly in terms of the resources required to implement an effective risk-management program. There are direct costs associated with hedging—transactions costs of buying and selling forwards, futures, options, and swaps—and indirect costs in the form of managers' time and expertise.

According to modern hedging theory, value-maximizing firms hedge because hedging can increase firm value in several different ways. For most firms, however, the principal reason for hedging is to reduce the likelihood of financial distress. Figure 21.2 illustrates the impact of hedging on the likelihood of financial distress, showing the range of possible cash flows for the firm in a given period and the associated probability distribution. If the firm's cash flows are below point A on the x-axis, the firm experiences financial distress. By hedging, the firm is able to reduce the probability of the firm's cash flows being below point A.

Reducing the likelihood of financial distress benefits the firm by also reducing the likelihood it will experience the costs associated with this distress. Direct costs of distress include out-of-pocket cash expenses that must be paid to third parties (lawyers, auditors, consultants, court personnel, etc.) in the event of bankruptcy or severe financial distress. Many of the indirect costs are contracting costs involving relationships with creditors, suppliers, and employees. For example, a credible promise to

Figure 21.2
Probability Distribution of Possible Cash Flows for a Corporation

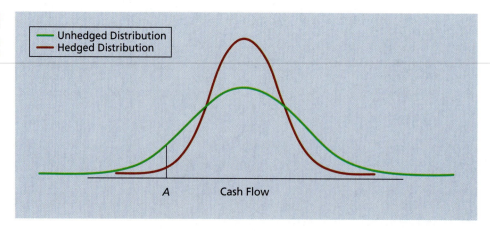

hedge can sometimes entice creditors to lend the firm money on more favorable terms than they would be willing to lend to an unhedged borrower. Similarly, suppliers are more likely to extend trade credit when the likelihood of financial distress is low. In addition to potential cost savings, hedging may increase revenue for firms that sell products with warranties or service contracts. Warranties or service contracts are more likely to be honored, and customers will place a higher value on them, if the firm has a lower likelihood of financial distress. Similarly, if the products will require replacement parts or if there is the possibility of future upgrades, minimizing the likelihood of financial distress can promote sales.

Hedging can also reduce a firm's expected tax liability. If a firm's effective marginal tax rate increases as income increases, hedging can reduce the present value of expected tax liabilities. For example, suppose that a firm thinks its taxable earnings over the coming year will be one of three equally likely levels, depending on the actual realized price of a key input: $0; $10,000; and $20,000. The company will pay $0 taxes if the firm earns $0 income, $1,000 in taxes if the firm earns $10,000, and $3,000 if the firm earns $20,000. Because the company assigns equal probability to each of the three possible outcomes, its expected earnings are $10,000 ($0.333 \times \$0 + 0.333 \times \$10,000 + 0.333 \times \$20,000$), but the expected tax liability is $1,333 ($0.333 \times \$0 + 0.333 \times \$1,000 + 0.333 \times \$3,000$). If the firm hedges by locking in a fixed price for the key input, such that it is assured of $10,000 in earnings, the tax liability will be $1,000. By hedging, the firm reduces its expected tax liability by $333. In addition, hedging can reduce expected tax liabilities by smoothing the profit stream and reducing the likelihood that the firm will pay high taxes in one period while having to forgo (or delay) the benefits of tax shields in another period.[6] Current tax laws limit the extent to which corporations can use losses in one period to offset gains in another period. For this reason, it is in the interest of some corporations to hedge their risk exposures in an effort to avoid losing some of the tax benefits associated with the losses experienced in periods of poor performance.

Closely held firms are more likely to hedge risk exposures because owners of the firm have a greater proportion of their wealth invested in the firm. Because the owners of these firms are less diversified, they generally seek to minimize the risk exposures faced by the firm. Similarly, if the managers of the firm are risk averse, the firm is more likely to pursue strategies that minimize risk exposures. Empirical studies of the relation between ownership structure and hedging activities tend to confirm these expectations. The hedging activities of firms increase as share ownership by managers increases.[7]

Another benefit of hedging is that it makes it easier for the board of directors and outsiders to evaluate the performance of managers. Absent an effective risk-management program, it is difficult to disentangle firm performance due to the manager's performance from firm performance due to external factors. A manager can make his or her performance more observable by minimizing the firm's exposure to external risk factors. For this reason, superior managers may be more inclined to hedge, whereas inferior managers may prefer to disguise their performance behind the firm's unhedged performance.

[6.] Various tax credits and tax loss carryforwards are examples of some of the types of tax shields that may be forfeited in the event that a firm suffers losses. For a discussion of how these tax-preference items affect the incentive to hedge, see Nance, Smith, and Smithson (1993).

[7.] Tufano (1996) finds that hedging activities increase as share ownership by managers increases. However, hedging activities decrease as option holdings by managers increase. Both of these findings are consistent with the argument that managerial incentives affect firms' hedging decisions.

Finally, even though shareholders can hedge the exposures they face as a result of owning shares in a risky firm, there are some circumstances under which it may be less costly for the firm to minimize risk than for the shareholders to hold a diversified portfolio. For some firms, however, the costs of hedging outweigh the benefits. There are substantial fixed costs associated with hedging, including the costs of acquiring the necessary expertise to implement a successful risk-management program, and small firms are therefore less likely to hedge than large firms.[8]

Hedging Strategies

In some circumstances, a firm may not hedge a risk exposure if it is confident that the risk factor will be changing in a positive direction or that it has a comparative advantage in bearing the risk. For example, if a silver-mining company is convinced that the price of silver will increase in the coming months, it may choose not to hedge its exposure to changes in the price of silver. When the price of silver increases, the mining company will benefit from the higher price it will receive for silver. In other circumstances, a firm may overhedge if it is certain that a risk factor will be changing in a negative direction. For example, if the mining company is convinced that the price of silver will decrease in the coming months, it may overhedge by taking a position in a derivative security that will more than offset the reduced price it receives for silver, thereby generating a profit on the price decrease. These examples illustrate that derivatives are an effective means for managers to take a position in a risk factor based on their expectations.[9] It is important to note that if a firm chooses *not* to hedge a risk exposure, or chooses to overhedge, it is **speculating** on changes in the risk factor.

How a firm chooses to hedge a given risk exposure will depend on the costs of the alternative hedging strategies. The firm needs to consider transactions costs, the effectiveness and accuracy of alternative strategies in offsetting underlying risk exposures, and the liquidity and default risks associated with those strategies. Customized hedging strategies, especially those that are financially engineered, are effective and accurate but suffer from greater transactions costs and low liquidity. Off-the-shelf solutions, such as exchange-traded derivative securities, are attractive because of their low transactions costs, high liquidity, and low default risk, but may not effectively and accurately offset the risk exposure.[10]

Derivative Securities

Derivatives are an integral part of a successful risk-management program because they offer an inexpensive means of changing a firm's risk profile. By taking a position in a derivative security that offsets the firm's risk profile, the firm can limit the extent to which firm value is affected by changes in the risk factor. Despite the growth in the markets for derivative securities, it is important to remember that it is not always in the best interests of a firm to hedge its risk exposures. If hedging will not increase firm value, the firm should not hedge.

[8.] See Booth, Smith, and Stolz (1984), Dolde (1993), DeMarzo and Duffie (1995), and Nance, Smith, and Smithson (1993). However, improvements in information technology have made it possible for smaller companies to use sophisticated risk-management techniques (see Moore and Culver 2000).

[9.] For a discussion of the role of selective hedging, see Stulz (1996) and Mello and Parsons (1999).

[10.] For an analysis of the choice of hedging instruments, see Geczy, Minton, and Schrand (1997).

1. Recently, a U.S. senator described the markets for derivative securities as an electronic pyramid scheme. How do you respond?

2. What does it mean to say that by not hedging, a firm is speculating on changes in the risk factor?

3. Why do you think that derivative securities have acquired a questionable reputation?

4. Based on the discussion in this section, should an investment fund manager hedge? If not, why do you think so many of today's money managers choose to hedge?

21.2 FORWARD CONTRACTS

As discussed in Chapter 20, a forward contract involves two parties agreeing today on a price, called the **forward price,** at which the purchaser will buy a specified amount of an asset from the seller at a fixed date sometime in the future. This is in contrast to a cash market transaction in which the buyer and seller conduct their transaction today at the **spot price.** The buyer of a forward contract has a **long position** and has an obligation to pay the forward price for the asset. The seller of a forward contract has a **short position** and has an obligation to sell the asset to the buyer in exchange for the forward price. The future date on which the buyer pays the seller (and the seller delivers the asset to the buyer) is referred to as the **settlement date.** It is important to note that, unlike options, which were discussed in Chapters 18 and 19, forward contracts are obligations, and failure to make or take delivery of the underlying asset represents default. In addition, no cash changes hands in a forward contract until the contract settlement date. For these two reasons, credit risk is a concern in forward contracts, and market participants enter into such contracts only with parties that they know and trust.

Most forward contracts are individually negotiated between corporations and financial intermediaries, but there are active markets for standard denomination and maturity forward contracts on several currencies and raw materials that institutions (including the bank market-makers themselves) can use to hedge their own exposures.

FORWARD PRICES

The forward price is the price that makes the forward contract have zero net present value. The key to determining the fair forward price for a security is being able to form an alternative to the forward contract that has identical cash flows. For example, consider an asset that pays no income (e.g., a discount bond) and does not cost anything to store (e.g., financial assets). Rather than buy the asset six months forward, we could borrow the current price of the asset and buy it today. Six months from now, we would repay the loan plus interest. Whether we buy the asset six months forward or borrow and buy it today, we end up in the same position—owning the asset in six months. Because both strategies have identical cash flows in all circumstances, we can make the argument that the value of both strategies must be the same. This argument is based on **arbitrage,** which involves generating a riskless profit by simultaneously buying the strategy with the low value and selling the strategy with the high value. In a well-functioning market, these opportunities are quickly eliminated.

Therefore, the forward price, F, for an asset that pays no income and does not cost anything to store should be the following:

$$F = S_0(1 + R_f)^n \qquad \text{(Eq. 21.1)}$$

where S_0 = the spot price of the asset at time 0,

         R_f = the risk-free rate of interest at time 0,

         n = number of years until the settlement date of the contract.

If Equation 21.1 does not hold and F is greater than $S_0(1 + R_f)^n$, we can make a riskless profit by simultaneously borrowing an amount equal to S_0, using the borrowed funds to buy the asset, and selling the asset forward. On the settlement date, assuming we are able to borrow at the risk-free rate, we would sell the asset for F by delivering on the forward contract and pay our debt (including interest) of $S_0(1 + R_f)^n$. This arbitrage strategy would generate $F - S_0(1 + R_f)^n > 0$ in riskless profits on the settlement date without requiring any up-front investment.

Alternatively, if F is less than $S_0(1 + R_f)^n$, we would simultaneously short-sell the asset for S_0, lend the proceeds from the short sale at the risk-free rate, and buy the asset forward. On the settlement date, we would collect $S_0(1 + R_f)^n$ from the loan, pay F for the asset, and close out our short-sale position. This arbitrage strategy would generate $S_0(1 + R_f)^n - F > 0$ in riskless profits on the settlement date without requiring any up-front investment.

APPLYING THE MODEL

Helen Clemons is a portfolio manager who plans to buy 1-month Treasury bills in two months with a total face amount of $5 million. The current price for 3-month Treasury bills is $985,149 per $1 million face amount. The current effective annual risk-free rate over the two months is 6.17 percent. The fair forward price is calculated as follows:

$$F = \$985,149(1 + 0.0617)^{2/12} = \$995,029$$

Therefore, the total forward price Helen should pay is $4,975,145 ($995,029 × 5). If this is not the forward rate quoted to her, Helen or another arbitrageur has an opportunity to earn a riskless profit. ■

A similar approach can be used to determine the forward price for an asset that pays income (e.g., a coupon bond) or is costly to store (e.g., commodities). In this case, we must account for the receipt of income and/or the payment of storage cost before the contract matures. We determine the appropriate forward price for these assets as follows:

Smart Concepts
See the concept explained step-by-step at
SMARTFinance

$$F = (S_0 - I + W)(1 + R_f)^n \qquad \text{(Eq. 21.2)}$$

where I = the present value of income to be paid by the asset during the life of the forward contract,

         W = the present value of the cost to store the asset for the life of the forward contract.

APPLYING THE MODEL

Consider a forward contract to purchase a 10-year bond in one year. Currently, an 11-year bond has a coupon rate of 8 percent and a price of $1,100, and will thus make two $40 coupon interest payments over the coming year. The current effective annual risk-free rate of interest over the next year is 5 percent. The fair forward price is calculated as follows:

$$F = \left[\$1,100 - \frac{\$40}{(1 + 0.05)^{0.5}} - \frac{\$40}{(1 + 0.05)} \right](1 + 0.05) = \$1,074.01$$ ■

Of course, we have made a number of assumptions to arrive at Equations 21.1 and 21.2. First, we have assumed that market participants have the ability to borrow and lend at the risk-free rate, but most individual and institutional investors are not able to do so. However, a sufficiently large number of institutional investors can borrow at or near the risk-free rate, such that Equations 21.1 and 21.2 should hold. Second, we have assumed that there are no transactions costs associated with establishing these positions, which will tend to widen the bounds on futures prices. Third, we have assumed that we can use the proceeds from short-selling and that short-selling does not involve any costs. In reality, only institutional investors can use all the proceeds from short-selling, and there are transactions costs associated with short-selling. These costs can be incorporated into the model by discounting the right-hand side of Equations 21.1 and 21.2.

Currency Forward Contracts [11]

Currency forward contracts, which involve exchanging one currency for another at a fixed date in the future, express the forward price as a **forward rate.** Table 21.1 presents selected exchange rates from the Monday, January 7, 2002, *Wall Street Journal* Currency Trading table. The data actually refer to the previous day's trading, Friday, January 4, 2002, as well as the day before, Thursday, January 3, 2002, though we will use Friday's data throughout this discussion. **Spot rates,** which call for immediate delivery, align with the currency name. For example, the spot rate for British pounds (£) on January 4 is $1.4452/£. The 1-month forward rate on the British pound is $1.4426/£.

Figures 21.3 and 21.4 show payoff diagrams for the buyer and seller of a 1-month forward contract on the British pound where the forward rate, which is agreed upon at contract origination, is $1.4426/£. The *x*-axis of these diagrams represents possible spot rates for the British pound on the settlement date. In this example, the settlement date is one month after the origination date, on February 4, 2002. The *y*-axis represents the profit or loss to the parties involved in the transaction. The profit for the buyer is the spot rate for the British pound on the settlement date minus the forward rate. The profit for the seller is the forward rate minus the spot rate on the settlement date. For example, if the spot rate is $1.4900/£ in one month, the profit for the buyer is $0.0474/£ ($1.4900/£ − $1.4426/£). The seller would have a loss of $0.0474/£.[12]

[11.] The theoretical derivation of forward rates is presented in Chapter 20, as are detailed examples of their practical use. We present a much briefer description of their use here as well because forward contracts are such key risk-management tools and because many instructors will choose to cover only one of these two chapters.

[12.] To understand why the profit or loss from a forward position depends on the spot rate at the settlement date, consider the following. If we pay $1.4426/£ on the settlement date and immediately sell the British pounds in the spot market, we will receive $1.4900/£. The net effect of this transaction is a cash inflow of $0.0474/£. On the other hand, if we have the short position, we would be selling British pounds for $0.0474/£ less than they are worth, thus experiencing a loss.

Table 21.1
Selected Exchange Rates,
Friday, January 4, 2002
and Thursday, January 3,
2002

Country	U.S.$ Equivalent		Currency per U.S.$	
	Friday	Thursday	Friday	Thursday
Argentina (peso)	1.0009	1.0009	0.9991	0.9991
Australia (dollar)	0.5205	0.5146	1.9214	1.9434
Britain (pound)	1.4452	1.4384	0.6919	0.6952
1-month forward	1.4426	1.4359	0.6932	0.6964
3-month forward	1.4376	1.4309	0.6956	0.6989
6-month forward	1.4303	1.4239	0.6992	0.7023
Canada (dollar)	0.6266	0.6257	1.5960	1.5982
1-month forward	0.6264	0.6256	1.5963	1.5985
3-month forward	0.6262	0.6254	1.5969	1.5991
6-month forward	0.6263	0.6256	1.5966	1.5985
China (renminbi)	0.1208	0.1208	8.2768	8.2766
Euro	0.8948	0.8995	1.1176	1.1117
France (franc)	0.1364	0.1371	7.3308	7.2929
1-month forward	0.1362	0.1369	7.3400	7.3021
3-month forward	0.1359	0.1366	7.3564	7.3185
6-month forward	0.1356	0.1363	7.3751	7.3372
Germany (mark)	0.4575	0.4599	2.1858	2.1745
1-month forward	0.4569	0.4593	2.1885	2.1772
3-month forward	0.4559	0.4583	2.1934	2.1821
6-month forward	0.4548	0.4571	2.1990	2.1877
Hong Kong (dollar)	0.1282	0.1282	7.7986	7.7980
Japan (yen)	0.007637	0.007594	130.95	131.68
1-month forward	0.007648	0.007606	130.75	131.48
3-month forward	0.007670	0.007628	130.37	131.09
6-month forward	0.007709	0.007666	129.72	130.44
Sweden (Krona)	0.0970	0.0973	10.3125	10.2739
Switzerland (franc)	0.6050	0.6061	1.6529	1.6500
1-month forward	0.6050	0.6061	1.6528	1.6499
3-month forward	0.6051	0.6061	1.6527	1.6498
6-month forward	0.6054	0.6065	1.6517	1.6488
Taiwan (dollar)	0.02278	0.02859	35.015	34.980

Source: Currency Trading, *Wall Street Journal,* (January 7, 2002), p. C11.
Note: The French franc and German mark disappeared in February 2002 and were replaced by the euro. All the other currencies in this table continued to trade after February 2002.

Currency Forward Rates

Determining the fair forward rate in a currency contract is slightly more complicated than for a financial asset that pays no income. Unlike the financial asset discussed previously, currencies generate income in the form of interest earned from investing the currency. However, the principle of how we determine the fair forward price still applies. For example, rather than buy British pounds three months forward, we could borrow $Q_\$$ dollars, convert the dollars to $Q_£$ British pounds at the spot rate, S_0, and lend the pounds. In three months, we would have $Q_£ (1 + R_£)$ British pounds. We would owe $Q_\$(1 + R_\$)$ dollars. Therefore, since this alternative strategy will arrive at the same position as the forward contract, we can determine the forward price for British pounds:

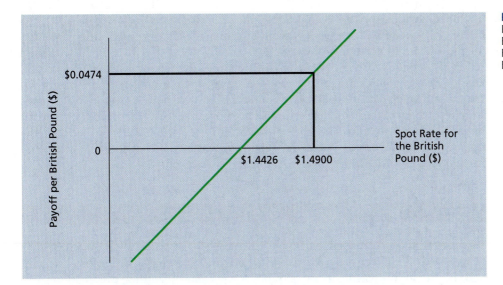

Figure 21.3
Payoff Diagram for the Buyer of a 1-Month Forward Contract on the British Pound

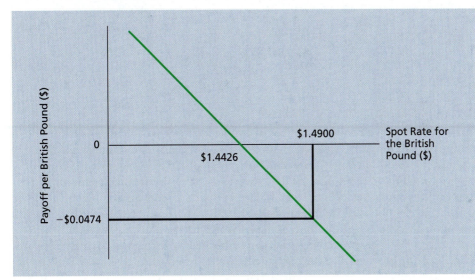

Figure 21.4
Payoff Diagram for the Seller of a 1-Month Forward Contract on the British Pound

$$F_£ = \frac{Q_£(1 + R_£)^n}{Q_\$(1 + R_\$)^n} \quad \text{or} \quad F_£ = S_0\frac{(1 + R_£)^n}{(1 + R_\$)^n} \qquad \text{(Eq. 21.3)}$$

where $F_£$ = the forward price for British pounds, expressed as the number of pounds per dollar, for delivery in n years (where $n = 0.25$ for a 3-month contract, and $n = 0.0833$ for a 1-month contract),

S_0 = the spot price for British pounds, expressed as the number of pounds per dollar, $Q_£/Q_\$$, at time 0,

$R_\$$ = the risk-free rate of interest at time 0 for borrowing/lending in U.S. dollars,

$R_£$ = the risk-free rate of interest at time 0 for borrowing/lending in British pounds,

n = number of years until the settlement date of the contract.

If the forward price violates Equation 21.3 such that $F_£ \neq S_0[(1 + R_£)^n \div (1 + R_\$)^n]$, we could earn a riskless profit by selling the high-priced position and buying the low-priced position. For example, if $F_£ > S_0[(1 + R_£)^n \div (1 + R_\$)^n]$, we would sell British pounds forward at $F_£$, borrow dollars at the rate of $r_\$$, exchange the dollars for British pounds at the spot rate of S_0, and lend the pounds at the rate of $R_£$. On the settlement date of the forward contract, we would collect $Q_£(1 + R_£)^n$ pounds from repayment of the loan, deliver British pounds at the forward rate in exchange for dollars, and use the dollars to repay our debt. If $F_£ > S_0[(1 + R_£)^n \div (1 + R_\$)^n]$, the dollars we would receive from selling pounds forward would be more than we would need to repay our debt, thereby generating a riskless profit.

APPLYING THE MODEL

Suppose that the current spot exchange rate on the Swiss franc (SF) is \$0.5800/SF or SF1.7241/\$. The effective 1-year risk-free rate for borrowing in dollars is 6 percent, and the rate for borrowing in Swiss francs is 5 percent. According to Equation 21.3, the following is the 1-year forward exchange rate on the Swiss franc:

$$F_{SF} = SF1.7241 \frac{(1 + 0.05)}{(1 + 0.06)} = SF1.7079/\$ \quad \text{or} \quad \$0.5855/SF$$

Hedging with Currency Forward Contracts

To see how forward contracts can be used to hedge foreign exchange risk, consider a multinational company's treasurer who expects to receive a 10 million Swiss franc (SF) payment in 90 days. Using the information in Table 21.1, the spot rate is \$0.6050/SF on Friday, January 4, 2002. In 90 days, however, the spot rate may be lower. For example, if the spot rate declines to \$0.5800/SF, then the SF10 million payment will be worth only \$5,800,000 (\$0.5800/SF × SF10,000,000) rather than the \$6,050,000 (\$0.6050/SF × SF10,000,000) it would be worth today.

This type of foreign exchange risk can be hedged by selling the payment forward. The 3-month forward rate for exchanging Swiss francs into dollars is \$0.6051/SF on Friday, January 4, 2002. In three months, after receiving the SF10 million payment, the company will deliver SF10 million to the counterparty in the forward contract and receive in exchange \$6,051,000 (\$0.6051/SF × SF10,000,000), regardless of what the spot rate happens to be at that time. By doing this, the treasurer has hedged the company's foreign exchange risk associated with this payment by locking in the dollar price the company will receive for its foreign currency cash flow.

INTEREST RATE FORWARD CONTRACTS

The underlying asset in an interest rate forward contract is either an interest rate or a debt security. Contracts involving an interest rate as the underlying security are cash settled, which simply means that the underlying security is not transferred from the seller to the buyer. Instead, the buyer and seller exchange the cash value of the contract. Either way, interest rate forward contracts are used to hedge an interest rate risk exposure in much the same way that currency forward contracts are used to hedge a currency risk exposure.

Forward Rate Agreements

A **forward rate agreement** (**FRA**) is an example of a forward contract where the underlying asset is not an asset at all but an interest rate. An *FRA* is an agreement between two parties to exchange cash flows based on a reference interest rate and principal amount at a single point in time in the future. In an *FRA*, the first party will pay the second party if the market rate of interest at a specified future time is greater than the forward rate specified in the contract. If, however, the market rate of interest is less than the forward rate, the second party will pay the first party. The size of the payment will depend on the hypothetical principal amount, called the **notional principal,** and the difference between the market rate of interest and the forward rate. Equation 21.4 shows how to determine the cash flow in an *FRA* (CF_{FRA}). Note that, by convention, this computation uses a 360-day year.

$$CF_{FRA} = \frac{\text{notional principal} \times (r_S - r_F) \times (D/360)}{1 + [r_S \times (D/360)]} \qquad \text{(Eq. 21.4)}$$

where r_S = the reference rate on the contract settlement date (e.g., the 3-month Treasury bill rate),

r_F = the forward rate established at contract origination,

D = the number of days in the contract period.

Hedging with Interest Rate Forward Contracts

To see how *FRA*s can be used to hedge interest rate risk, consider CFE Manufacturing (CFE). The company is planning to borrow $10 million in six months at LIBOR plus 100 basis points and is concerned that LIBOR will increase before the company borrows.[13] To hedge this exposure, CFE and Bankamerica enter into a 6-month *FRA* with a notional principal of $10 million. The terms of the contract are such that CFE will pay Bankamerica if the 3-month LIBOR six months from now is less than the forward rate of 6 percent. If the 3-month LIBOR exceeds 6 percent, Bankamerica must pay CFE. The size of the cash flow is determined by Equation 21.4. For example, if the 3-month LIBOR six months from now is 7 percent, Bankamerica must pay CFE the following:

$$\frac{\$10,000,000 \times (0.07 - 0.06) \times (92/360)}{1 + [0.07 \times (92/360)]} = \$25,106.43$$

However, if the 3-month LIBOR six months from now is 5 percent rather than 7 percent, CFE must pay Bankamerica $25,233.14.

---

5. If Equation 21.2 does not hold, how might an arbitrageur earn a riskless profit?

6. What is the difference in the timing of cash flows in a forward contract and a spot market transaction?

Concept Review Questions

[13.] LIBOR, the London Interbank Offered Rate, is the rate of interest charged for Eurodollar borrowing between banks. Virtually all large bank loans are priced versus LIBOR.

21.3 FUTURES CONTRACTS

Like a forward contract, a **futures contract** involves two parties agreeing today on a price at which the purchaser will buy a given amount of a commodity or financial instrument from the seller at a fixed date sometime in the future. In fact, the contracts are so similar that, for most purposes, we can use the same pricing formulas to price futures contracts that we used for forward contracts.[14] Similarly, we can use the same payoff diagram for futures that we used for forwards.

Although futures and forwards serve the same economic function, there are differences in the characteristics of the two contracts. In contrast to a forward contract, a futures contract is an exchange-traded contract that promises the delivery of a specified volume of a commodity or financial instrument on a standardized date of the month in which the contract expires.[15] For example, gold futures contracts are traded on the New York Mercantile Exchange. The gold futures contract calls for the delivery of 100 troy ounces. Contracts are available for delivery in the current month; the next two months; any February, April, August, and October falling within the next two years; and any June and December falling within the next five years.

Table 21.2
Gold Futures Prices, Friday, January 4, 2002

	Open	High	Low	Settle	Change	Lifetime High	Lifetime Low	Open Interest
Gold (Cmx.Div.NYM)—100 troy oz; $ per troy oz								
Feb-2002	278.70	279.80	277.60	279.20	+0.70	297.50	262.90	66,889
Apr	279.30	280.50	278.30	279.80	+0.70	297.50	267.50	8,470
June	279.60	280.80	279.20	280.40	+0.70	385.00	264.50	9,177
Aug	280.20	280.20	280.20	280.20	+0.70	297.00	272.60	3,275
Dec	281.10	282.40	281.10	281.90	+0.70	385.00	268.10	11,772
Dec-03	288.00	288.00	288.00	288.00	+0.60	359.30	280.00	2,071

Source: Futures Prices, *Wall Street Journal*, (January 7, 2002), p. C13.

Table 21.2 provides data on the prices of gold futures contracts on Friday, January 4, 2002. The first trade of the day, called the **opening futures price,** was $279.60 per troy ounce for delivery in June 2002. The highest price for the day was $280.80/oz. The low for the day was $279.20/oz. The last June 2002 futures price for the day was $280.40/oz. This **closing futures price** is the result of a $0.70/oz increase in the settle price from the previous day, as indicated by the change column. The closing price is also known as the **settlement price** and is used to settle all contracts at the end of each day's trading, in a process called "marking to market" (described below). Also shown are the **lifetime high** and **lifetime low prices** for this contract, which are the highest and lowest settlement prices recorded for this contract since its inception— perhaps several months (or even a year or more) before. The **open interest** represents the number of contracts that are currently outstanding. This number changes every

---

[14.] An intuitive discussion of the pricing of financial futures is provided in French (1989). There are small differences in the pricing of forward and futures contracts. For some purposes, these differences may be important, but for most purposes, the differences are insignificant. For a discussion of these differences, see Cox, Ingersoll, and Ross (1981).

[15.] In practice, delivery can take place on any day during the delivery month for most futures contracts. When a seller decides to deliver, he will notify his broker of his intent to deliver. Two days later, the seller will deliver on the contract.

Table 21.3
Examples of Exchange-Traded Futures Contracts

Contract	Exchange	Face Amount
Grains and oilseeds		
Corn	Chicago Board of Trade	5,000 bushels
Oats	Chicago Board of Trade	5,000 bushels
Wheat	Chicago Board of Trade	5,000 bushels
Canola	Winnipeg Commodity Exchange	20 metric tons
Livestock and meat		
Cattle—feeder	Chicago Mercantile Exchange	50,000 lbs
Cattle—live	Chicago Mercantile Exchange	40,000 lbs
Pork bellies	Chicago Mercantile Exchange	40,000 lbs
Food and fiber		
Cocoa	Coffee, Sugar, & Cocoa Exchange, New York	10 metric tons
Coffee	Coffee, Sugar, & Cocoa Exchange, New York	37,500 lbs
Sugar—world	Coffee, Sugar, & Cocoa Exchange, New York	112,000 lbs
Sugar—domestic	Coffee, Sugar, & Cocoa Exchange, New York	112,000 lbs
Cotton	New York Cotton Exchange	50,000 lbs
Orange juice	New York Cotton Exchange	15,000 lbs
Metals and petroleum		
Copper	Comex, New York Mercantile Exchange	25,000 lbs
Gold	Comex, New York Mercantile Exchange	100 troy oz
Platinum	New York Mercantile Exchange	50 troy oz
Silver	Comex, New York Mercantile Exchange	5,000 troy oz
Crude oil	New York Mercantile Exchange	1,000 bbls
Natural gas	New York Mercantile Exchange	10,000MMBtu
Interest rate		
Treasury bonds	Chicago Board of Trade	$100,000
5-year Treasury notes	Chicago Board of Trade	$100,000
30-day federal funds	Chicago Board of Trade	$5 million
LIBOR	Chicago Mercantile Exchange	$3 million
Eurodollars	Chicago Mercantile Exchange	$1 million
Index		
Dow Jones Industrial Average	Chicago Board of Trade	$10 × average
S&P 500	Chicago Mercantile Exchange	$250 × average
Nikkei 225	Chicago Mercantile Exchange	$5 × average
Currency		
Japanese yen (¥)	Chicago Mercantile Exchange	Y12.5 million
British pound (BP)	Chicago Mercantile Exchange	BP62,500
Swiss franc (SF)	Chicago Mercantile Exchange	SF125,000

Source: Futures Prices, *Wall Street Journal,* (January 7, 2002), p. C13.

day as contracts are bought and sold. If a trader were to take a long position in gold futures contracts at the settle price of $280.40/oz, the total futures price of one contract would be $28,040 ($280.40/oz × 100 troy ounces).

Table 21.3 provides a few examples of the types of available futures contracts and the exchanges on which they are traded. All the contracts traded on these exchanges are standardized with respect to size and delivery date. The economic rationale for designing futures contracts in this way is that it provides a standardized, high-trading-volume (hence low transactions cost) financial instrument that can be used by both individuals and businesses to hedge underlying commercial risks, as well as by speculators wishing to place a highly leveraged bet on the direction of commodity prices. Contract sizes are small enough for individuals to be able to participate in futures markets, and the volume is high enough for businesses to take significant positions by buying or selling multiple contracts.

Although both futures and forwards impose obligations on their holders, the default risk of a futures contract is much lower, for two reasons. First, every major futures exchange operates a clearinghouse that acts as the counterparty to all buyers and sellers. This means that traders need not worry about the creditworthiness of the party they trade with (as forward market traders must), but only about the creditworthiness of the exchange itself. Second, futures contracts feature daily cash settlement of all contracts, called **marking-to-market.** By its very nature, a futures contract is a zero-sum game because whenever the market price of a commodity changes, the underlying value of a long (purchase) or short (sale) position also changes—and one party's gain is the other party's loss. By requiring each contract's loser to pay the winner the net amount of this change each day, futures exchanges eliminate the possibility that large, unrealized losses will build up over time. In a forward contract, on the other hand, there are no cash flows between origination and termination of the contract.

APPLYING THE MODEL

As an example of marking-to-market, consider the gold futures discussed previously. Recall that the settle price for the June 2002 contract was $280.40 per troy ounce. If the settle price on the next business day is $281.00/oz, the person with the long position will receive $0.60/oz (the new futures price minus the original futures price), or a total of $60.00 per contract ($0.60/oz × 100 troy ounces). The person with the short position must pay $0.60/oz. In effect, the new contract with a futures price of $281.00/oz replaces the original contract. The party with the long position is compensated (and the person with the short position must pay) for the increase in the futures price. This type of daily settlement takes place on every trading day until delivery takes place. It is important to note that the party with the long position ultimately ends up paying a total of $280.40/oz, and the party with the short position receives a total of $280.40/oz upon delivery. ■

When taking a position in a futures contract, the investor must deposit a minimum dollar amount called the **initial margin,** which varies by contract, in a **margin account.** The investor deposits gains in or withdraws losses from this account. Each exchange has margin requirements, and brokerage firms may require additional margin above the minimum specified. If losses deplete the margin below the level needed to maintain an open position, the **maintenance margin,** the investor must deposit additional funds in the account to bring the account back to the initial margin. Failure to deposit additional funds before the next day's trading results in the position being closed out by the exchange.

In addition to these distinctions, futures differ from forward contracts in two other important respects. First, futures contracts are designed to have a value (usually around $100,000) that will appeal to a "retail" market of individuals and smaller companies, whereas most actively traded forward contracts have minimum denominations of $1 million or more. This small contract size is rarely a problem for futures traders, however, as those wishing to hedge large exposures can simply purchase multiple contracts. Second, most forward contracts are settled by actual delivery, but this rarely occurs with futures contracts. Instead, futures market hedgers will execute an offsetting trade to close out their position in the futures market whenever they have closed out their underlying commercial risk through delivery in the normal course of business.

The ability to close out a position by taking an offsetting position is referred to as **fungibility.** Fungibility is made possible because the counterparty in a futures contract is the clearinghouse and because futures contracts are settled daily. If an investor were to take a long position in a futures contract and subsequently take a short position in the same contract, the contracts would cancel each other out for two reasons: (1) after marking-to-market, the futures prices of the two contracts would be the same, and (2) the clearinghouse is the counterparty to both contracts. It is important to note that unless buyers or sellers close out their positions, they are required to make or take delivery of the underlying asset.

Hedging with Futures Contracts

Futures contracts are a very effective mechanism for hedging. In addition to futures markets for metals, there are futures markets for foreign currencies, interest rates, stock indexes, and commodities. *Long hedges* involve buying a futures contract to offset an underlying short (sold) position. *Short hedges* involve selling a futures contract to offset an underlying long (purchased) position.

Hedging with Foreign Currency Futures

The multinational company with the SF10million exposure discussed earlier could have chosen to hedge that exposure in the futures market rather than with a forward contract by selling 80 Swiss franc futures contracts (each mandating delivery of SF125,000). Recall that the multinational company will be receiving a payment of 10 million Swiss francs in 90 days. By selling 80 SF futures contracts that expire after the date on which it will receive the SF payments (because futures contracts have fixed delivery periods, they will only rarely exactly match a trader's desired payment date), the company can hedge this exposure using futures rather than forwards. On January 4, 2002, the settle price for March 2002 Swiss franc futures is $0.6057/SF. When the SF payment is received, the company will exchange it for dollars at whatever the spot $/SF exchange rate happens to be at the time, and will simultaneously buy 80 SF futures contracts with the same delivery date as the contracts purchased earlier—thereby offsetting or closing out its futures position. If the dollar value of the Swiss franc declines from $0.6050/SF to, say, $0.50/SF during the 60 days in question, then the company will lose $0.1050/SF, or a total of $1,050,000, on its spot market sale of the SF payment. But this loss will be offset by the profit the company will achieve on its futures position. If the futures price declines from $0.6057/SF to $0.5007/SF, the profit in the futures position will be $0.1050/SF, or a total of $1,050,000, exactly offsetting the loss in the cash market position. If the Swiss franc appreciates rather than depreciates against the dollar, then the company will gain on its cash market transaction and lose on its futures contracts. Either way, hedgers can use a futures contract to hedge an underlying commercial risk without actually having to take physical delivery on the futures contract.

Hedging with Interest Rate Futures

We can use futures contracts to hedge interest rate risk in much the same way that we hedged foreign exchange risk. Consider a corporate treasurer who anticipates borrowing $1 million in five months. The loan will be at 100 basis points over the 3-month LIBOR at the time of borrowing. LIBOR is currently at 5 percent. Eurodollar futures contracts for delivery in six months are trading at a yield of 5.2 percent.[16] By selling one Eurodollar futures contract, the treasurer can effectively lock in a borrowing rate of 6.2 percent (5.2 percent plus 100 basis points) for the three months beginning in six months. As in the currency contract, the treasurer would close out the position in Eurodollar futures and borrow at the same time.

CONCERNS WHEN USING FUTURES CONTRACTS

In the previous examples, we ignored several potential problems associated with using futures markets to hedge. We discuss some of these problems in the following sections.

Basis Risk

The basis in a futures contract is the difference between the futures price and the spot price. **Basis risk** arises from the possibility of unanticipated changes in the basis. As the maturity date approaches, the basis goes to zero. However, if a contract is closed out prior to maturity, as in the previous examples, basis risk can cause gains (losses) in the underlying risky position to differ from the offsetting losses (gains) in the futures position. For example, if the futures price in the example of currency hedging had not changed by exactly the amount as the spot price, the loss in the cash position would have differed from the gain in the futures position.

Cross-Hedging

The underlying securities in the futures contracts were identical to the assets being hedged in the two previous examples. However, the underlying securities in the futures contract and the assets being hedged often have different characteristics, which is called **cross-hedging.** For example, a farmer who uses orange juice futures to hedge his crop of grapefruits is cross-hedging. To minimize basis risk in a cross hedge, we need to determine the relation between changes in the value of the asset being hedged and changes in the value of the asset in the futures contract. It is possible to estimate this relation using historical data. Once we measure the sensitivity of the asset being hedged to changes in the price of the underlying asset in the futures contract, we can use that information to adjust the number of futures contracts to buy or sell in order to achieve an effective hedge.

Tailing the Hedge

Because of the marking-to-market feature of futures contracts, interest is earned on gains to the futures position as they are paid in and interest is lost on losses as they are paid out. This causes gains on a long position in futures to be slightly greater than the losses on a short position in the underlying asset because of the interest earned on the gains. To avoid overhedging, we would want to purchase enough futures contracts to hedge the risk exposure, but not so many that we overhedge. To achieve a

---

[16.] Eurodollar futures contracts are available in the current month, the next month, and every March, June, September, and December in the next 10 years. The Eurodollar futures contracts are based on the 3-month LIBOR.

perfect hedge in the example of currency hedging, we would need to sell slightly fewer than 80 Swiss franc futures contracts. This is called **tailing the hedge.**

Delivery Options

The deliverable instrument in some futures contracts can take a variety of forms. For example, the underlying security in a Treasury bond futures contract is a 20-year Treasury bond. However, the contract allows for the delivery of any Treasury bond that has a maturity date of at least 15 years from the first day of the delivery month. If the bond is callable, it must not be callable for at least 15 years from the first day of the delivery month. When delivery occurs, a conversion factor is used to account for differences in the characteristics of the deliverable instruments. See the Chicago Board of Trade's website (http://www.cbot.com) for information on current conversion factors.

Another delivery option is the timing option. Many futures contracts allow delivery to take place at any time during the delivery month. In fact, several futures contracts allow for delivery to take place several days after the last trading day for a contract. For example, the delivery process for Treasury bond futures contracts is as follows: (1) sometime during the delivery month, the seller notifies the clearinghouse of the intent to deliver on the futures contract; (2) the clearinghouse notifies the party with the oldest long position that delivery will take place in two days; (3) delivery takes place with the seller delivering Treasury bonds to the individual with the long position; and (4) the seller receives the futures price (adjusted by the conversion factors associated with the bonds).

Because delivery rarely takes place in a futures contract, delivery options are not generally a major concern for the manager who is using futures to hedge risk. However, these delivery options do affect futures prices and are important for those market participants who are planning to make or take delivery of the underlying asset in the futures market.

---

7. What is the difference in the cash flows for a forward contract and a futures contract?

8. What features of a futures contract tend to reduce default risk?

9. Describe how tailing a hedge keeps a firm from overhedging.

Concept Review Questions

21.4 OPTIONS AND SWAPS

Options and swaps can also be used to hedge risk exposures. This section discusses both these instruments and describes how they can be used to hedge risk exposures.

Options

As discussed in Chapters 18 and 19, options contracts are pervasive in modern financial systems. There are exchange-traded options contracts on individual common stocks, on stock indexes, on numerous currencies and interest rates, on a bewildering number of industrial and agricultural commodities, and even on futures contracts. Financial institutions custom-design even more options to meet the needs of their customers (these are often called over-the-counter, or OTC options). A call option gives its holder the right to buy a fixed amount of a commodity at a fixed price, on (with a European option) or by (with an American option) a fixed date in the future, whereas a put option entails a similar right to sell that commodity. The valuation of, and pay-off patterns for, options are discussed in depth in Chapters 18 and 19.

For our purposes, the key feature of an option as a hedging tool is that it provides protection against adverse price risk (an investor has the right to exercise the option if price changes make it optimal to do so) without having to forfeit the right to profit if the price on the underlying commodity moves in the investor's favor (in which case, the investor allows the option to expire unexercised).

Hedging with Currency Options

Recall the multinational corporation that is expecting to receive a payment of SF10 million. Earlier, we demonstrated how this foreign exchange risk could be hedged using forwards or futures. We can also hedge this risk using options. For example, the multinational company could have purchased 160 Swiss franc put options (each granting the right to deliver SF62,500) that expire after the date on which it will receive the SF payments (like futures contracts, exchange-traded options have fixed expiration dates and will only rarely exactly match a trader's desired payment date). When the SF payment is received, the company will exchange it for dollars at whatever the spot $/SF exchange rate happens to be at the time, and will simultaneously sell 160 SF put options with the same delivery date as the contracts purchased earlier —thereby offsetting or canceling out its options position. If the dollar value of the Swiss franc has declined from $0.6050/SF to, say, $0.50/SF during the 60 days in question, then the company will lose on its cash market transaction and gain on its options contract. If the Swiss franc appreciates against the dollar, the company will gain on its cash market transaction, and its losses on the options contract will be limited to the premium paid for the option. By using an option to hedge this foreign exchange risk, the multinational corporation minimizes its downside risk without giving up its upside potential. The cost of this hedge is the premium paid for the option.

Hedging with Interest Rate Options

In addition to hedging foreign exchange risk, options are commonly used to hedge interest rate risk. For example, a retailer that has borrowed using a variable-rate loan is probably concerned about interest rates rising. If the loan rate is tied to Treasury bill rates, the firm could hedge this interest rate risk by purchasing a call option on the 13-week T-bill yield. Call options on interest rates are called **interest rate caps.**

The Chicago Board Options Exchange (CBOE) offers options on the 13-week T-bill rate and other, longer-term Treasury rates. See the CBOE's website (http://www.cboe.com) for more information on interest rate options traded on that exchange. The underlying instruments in CBOE interest rate options are yields rather than prices, as in stock options. The underlying values for these options are 10 times the underlying Treasury yields, and the contracts are cash settled at $100 times the difference between the underlying value at option expiration and the strike price. For the retailer, the underlying value would be 10 times the yield to maturity (YTM) on 13-week T-bills. If the retailer paid 1.00 for a July 55 call, the total price of one contract is $100 (1.00 × $100). If the YTM on 13-week T-bills is 6 percent on the option expiration date, the cash settlement will be $500 [(60 − 55) × $100]. The net profit for the hedge will be $400 ($500 settlement − $100 premium). This profit will offset the higher interest costs of the variable-rate loan. If the YTM on 13-week T-bills declines to 5 percent, however, the option will expire worthless, and the retailer will have lost only the $100 premium paid for the option. The advantage of using options to hedge the retailer's interest rate risk is that the retailer retains the potential for lower interest costs if interest rates decline, but is able to offset the potential for higher interest costs if interest rates increase.

Just as an interest rate cap is a call option on interest rates, an **interest rate floor** is a put option on interest rates. Recall from Chapter 18 that a put option represents the right to sell an asset for a specified price within a specified period of time. In the case of interest rate options, which involve cash settlement, a put option will generate a positive payoff for the buyer when the underlying value ($100 times the *YTM*) declines below the strike price.

One common strategy, called an **interest rate collar,** is to buy an interest rate cap and simultaneously sell an interest rate floor. The purpose of this strategy is to use the proceeds from selling the floor to purchase the cap. Of course, by selling the floor, an investor forgoes some upside potential. If our intrepid retailer sold a July 50 put for 0.75 and bought the July 55 call at the same time, the retailer would receive $75 (0.75 × $100) for the put. This would offset all but $25 of the premium paid for the call. The result of this strategy would be the same as just purchasing the cap for all yields above 5.0 percent. Below 5.0 percent, however, gains from the lower interest costs will be offset by losses from selling the put.

SWAPS

In a **swap contract,** two parties agree to exchange payment obligations on two underlying financial liabilities that are equal in principal amount but differ in payment patterns. Investors use swaps to change the characteristics of cash flows, most often to change the characteristics of cash outflows. We will concentrate on the most common types, *interest rate swaps* and *currency swaps*. According to a survey by the Bank for International Settlements (http://www.bis.org), the total notional volume of over-the-counter derivative contracts outstanding totaled more than $95 trillion at the end of 2000, with interest rate swaps accounting for more than half ($48 trillion) of this total. It is important to note that, like forward contracts, swap contracts are over-the-counter instruments and subject to default risk. For this reason, swap market participants enter into contracts only with parties that they know and trust.

Interest Rate Swaps

An **interest rate swap** is the most common type of swap transaction. In a typical interest rate swap, one party will make fixed-rate payments to another party in exchange for floating-rate payments. This is often called a **fixed-for-floating interest rate swap.** As in the *FRA*s discussed earlier, the interest payments on a fixed-for-floating swap will be based on a hypothetical principal amount called the *notional principal*.[17]

Figure 21.5 illustrates the structure of a fixed-for-floating swap. The party making fixed-rate payments, Company A, promises to make fixed-rate payments based on some notional principal amount to a financial intermediary in exchange for floating-rate payments.[18] In this example, as in many swap transactions, an intermediary has arranged the swap and is acting as the counterparty to both contracts. The contract calls for Company A to pay the intermediary 8 percent per year based on a notional principal of $10 million. In return, the intermediary will pay Company A the 6-month LIBOR applied to the same $10 million notional principal amount. In practice, only the **interest differential** is exchanged between the intermediary and Company A.

[17.] A discussion of swap default risk can be found in Sorenson and Bollier (1994). For an intuitive discussion of interest rate swaps, see Bicksler and Chen (1986).

[18.] Empirical evidence, as in Samant (1996), on the use of swaps by nonfinancial firms suggests that fixed-rate payers tend to have greater leverage and more volatile earnings than floating-rate payers. Titman (1992) suggests that when a firm expects its credit quality to improve, it will borrow short-term and use a fixed-for-floating swap to hedge interest rate risk.

Figure 21.5
Typical Structure of a
Fixed-for-Floating Swap

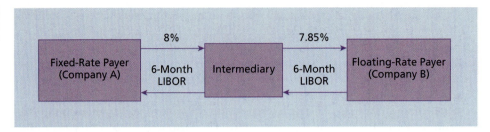

At the same time that the intermediary and company agree to swap interest payments, the intermediary enters into an agreement to pay a fixed rate of interest to the floating-rate payer, Company B, in exchange for a floating rate. In this example, the intermediary agrees to pay Company B 7.85 percent in exchange for the 6-month LIBOR. The intermediary's compensation is the spread between the fixed rate received from Company A and the fixed rate paid to Company B.

Figures 21.6 and 21.7 show payoff diagrams for Company A and Company B in the interest rate swap. The x-axis of these diagrams represents possible spot rates for the 6-month LIBOR at the end of each 6-month period. The y-axis represents the cash flow to the parties involved in the transaction. If the contract calls for semiannual payments, the cash flow for Company A is [$10,000,000 × (LIBOR − 8%) ÷ 2]. The cash flow for Company B is [$10,000,000 × (7.85% − LIBOR) ÷ 2]. If the 6-month LIBOR is 7 percent at the end of the first 6-month period, Company A will pay the intermediary $50,000 [$10,000,000 × (0.07 − 0.08) ÷ 2]. The intermediary will pay Company B $42,500 [$10,000,000 × (0.0785 − 0.07) ÷ 2]. Six months later, if the 6-month LIBOR is 8.5 percent, the intermediary will pay Company A $25,000 [$10,000,000 × (0.085 − 0.08) ÷ 2]. Company B will pay the intermediary $32,500 [$10,000,000 × (0.0785 − 0.085) ÷ 2]. These exchanges will take place every six months until the termination date.

Typically, these interest rate swaps arise because one party wanted to issue fixed-rate debt but chose instead to issue floating-rate debt, either because the fixed-rate market was closed to this issuer or was more costly. By entering a swap agreement,

Figure 21.6
Semiannual Net Cash
Flow for the Fixed-Rate
Payer in a Fixed-for-
Floating Swap with a
Notional Principal of
$10,000,000

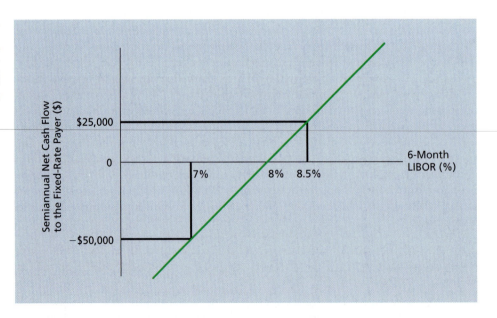

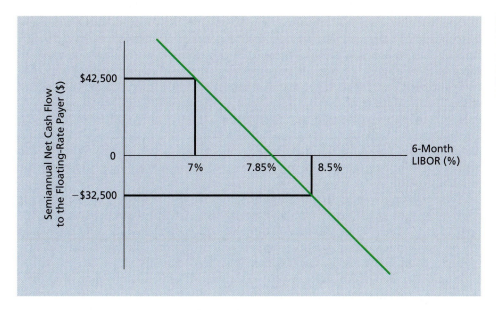

Figure 21.7
Semiannual Net Cash
Flow for the Floating-
Rate Payer in a Fixed-for-
Floating Swap with a
Notional Principal of
$10,000,000

the floating-rate issuer can effectively obtain a fixed-rate payment obligation. By paying a fixed rate and receiving a floating rate, this firm can use the cash inflows in the form of floating-rate payments to make the floating-rate payments on the debt that is outstanding. The net effect of the swap agreement is to offset the floating-rate payments being paid on the floating-rate debt with the floating-rate payments received on the swap. The fixed-rate payments being made on the swap are all that remain. The counterparty in the swap contract (who has better access to fixed-rate debt markets) achieves a preferred floating-rate pattern of payments. As mentioned previously, rather than exchange gross amounts, the two parties will exchange only the net difference between the two payment obligations, the interest differential; therefore, the party that has swapped a fixed-rate payment obligation for one with a floating rate will lose (have to increase payment amounts) if market rates rise and will benefit if market rates fall.

Currency Swaps

The second most common type of swap contract is the **currency swap,** in which two parties exchange payment obligations denominated in different currencies. For example, a U.S. company wishing to invest in Switzerland would prefer to borrow in Swiss francs rather than in dollars. If, however, the company could borrow on more attractive terms in dollars (as is often the case) than in francs, a logical strategy would be to borrow the money needed for investment in dollars, say, by issuing bonds, and then swap payment obligations with a Swiss company seeking dollars for investment in the United States. The Swiss company would issue bonds that are denominated in Swiss francs.

The U.S. company would make periodic Swiss franc payments to the Swiss company. The Swiss company would make periodic dollar payments to the U.S. company. The dollar payments made by the Swiss company would cover the interest and principal payments on the dollar borrowing by the U.S. company, and the Swiss franc payments made by the U.S. company would cover the interest and principal payments on the Swiss franc borrowing by the Swiss company. By engaging in the swap, the U.S. company has transformed its dollar liabilities into Swiss franc liabilities, and the Swiss company has transformed its Swiss franc liabilities into dollar liabilities.

Suppose that the U.S. company issues $7 million in 10-year bonds that have a coupon rate of 8 percent. The Swiss company issues SF10 million in 10-year bonds that also have a coupon rate of 8 percent. In this example, we will assume that the companies have agreed on a fixed exchange rate in the swap contract of $0.70/SF. The two parties will exchange the principal amounts at contract origination. At the end of the first 6-month period, the U.S. company will pay SF400,000 (SF10,000,000 × 0.08 ÷ 2) to the Swiss company in exchange for $280,000 ($7,000,000 × 0.08 ÷ 2). These payments will occur every six months until the termination date. On the termination date, the two parties will exchange principal amounts again to terminate the contract. The principal amounts will then be used to retire the bonds each company originally issued.

Note that unlike interest rate swaps, the notional principal in a currency swap is often exchanged at the origination and termination dates of the contract. If the notional principal were not exchanged at the termination date, the U.S. company would still be faced with a dollar liability when the dollar-denominated bonds mature, and the Swiss company would be faced with a Swiss franc liability.

Another variant of the currency swap is the **fixed-for-floating currency swap.** This is simply a combination of a currency swap and an interest rate swap. In this transaction, the first party pays a fixed rate of interest denominated in one currency to the second party in exchange for a floating rate of interest denominated in another currency. For example, if the U.S. company in the previous example preferred to borrow in Swiss francs at a floating rate of interest and the Swiss company preferred to borrow in dollars at a fixed rate of interest, the two firms could engage in a fixed-for-floating currency swap.

Suppose that the U.S. company was able to borrow $7 million in 10-year bonds with a coupon rate of 8 percent. The Swiss company borrows SF10 million in 10-year bonds with a coupon rate of LIBOR + 100 basis points. As in the currency swap, the two parties will exchange the principal amounts at contract origination. At the end of the first 6-month period, if LIBOR is 6.5 percent, the cost of the loan will be 7.5 percent (0.065 + 0.01). The U.S. company will pay SF375,000 [SF10,000,000 × (0.065 + 0.01) ÷ 2] to the Swiss company in exchange for $280,000 ($7,000,000 × 0.08 ÷ 2). For both parties, the semiannual cash inflows from the swap contract are used to make the interest payments on the bonds that were issued in the cash market. Upon termination of the swap contract, the principal amounts are exchanged again and the bonds are retired.

Concept Review Questions

10. Describe how an interest rate swap is just a portfolio of *FRA*s.

11. Why would any corporation hedge with forwards, futures, or swaps if it can keep its upside potential by hedging with options?

21.5 FINANCIAL ENGINEERING

The key to a successful hedging strategy is the ability to offset the underlying risk exposure. For many firms, however, the underlying risk exposure is unique because the risk exposure is based on an asset whose value is not easily hedged. **Financial engineering,** at least for our purposes here, can be defined as the process of using the principles of financial economics to design and price financial instruments. In particular, financial engineering has meant combining the risk-management building blocks—forwards, futures, options, and swaps—in complex patterns in order to achieve specific risk profiles that benefit corporate issuers or to offer investors unique payoff structures that help complete the capital markets, or both. For example, some firms are not able to use off-the-shelf hedging instruments because those instruments do not have payoff structures that will offset the firm's underlying risk exposures. Similarly, an institutional investor may desire an investment security that has specific payoff structures, but no such security is currently available.

By combining elements of forwards, futures, options, and swaps, however, it is often possible to create a financial instrument that meets the needs of the corporation trying to hedge its risk exposure or that offers the institutional investor an investment opportunity with a unique payoff structure. Modern corporations, and the financial institutions that cater to them, have become extremely adept at this process. For example, Chidambaran, Fernando, and Spindt (2001) describe how Freeport-McMoRan used financial engineering to finance an expansion of its mining facilities in Indonesia. Rather than issue fixed-rate bonds, Freeport-McMoRan issued depository shares that act like bonds with principal and interest payments that are directly tied to the price of gold. This built-in hedge actually enhanced the credit quality of Freeport-McMoRan because of the reduced risk of default.

SMART IDEAS VIDEO
Mitchell Petersen, Northwestern University
"Derivative markets have given investors, as well as managers, a lot more choices."

See the entire interview at **SMARTFinance**

Given that the returns to successful financial innovation can be very high, a great many new financial products are developed every year. Enough of these products succeed that we can identify certain trends that are likely to continue for the foreseeable future. First, longer-maturity risk-management products will continue to be developed. Standard futures, forwards, and options are all short-term contracts, but recent years have seen the introduction of contracts with much longer dates, as well as the development of intermediate- and long-term securities that effectively perform hedging roles. Second, even more complex securities will be developed to hedge multiple interest rate, currency, and input/output pricing risks, particularly in the international arena. Third, new techniques for hedging pricing and underwriting risks in the issuance of new securities will continue to arise as the securitization trend accelerates around the world. Finally, it seems inevitable that new methods of hedging the strategic and currency risks of investing in small, politically unstable or financially underdeveloped countries will emerge in the coming decade as Western capital is committed to the transformation of the formerly socialist or mixed economies of China, India, Russia, and Eastern Europe.

The practice of risk management and financial engineering is evolving, and we have only touched on the basic strategies here. As the markets for derivative securities grow and the practice of risk management develops, it is likely that we will see increasingly complex financially engineered instruments. However, it is important to remember that even the most complex instrument includes elements of the securities we described here.

12. Under what circumstances might a corporation prefer a financially engineered solution for a risk-management problem to an off-the-shelf solution?

Concept Review Questions

21.6 SUMMARY

- Increased volatility in interest rates, currency exchange rates, and commodity prices has led to mushrooming demand for financial instruments that corporations can use to hedge their exposure to these risk factors.

- It is not always in the corporation's best interest to hedge. However, hedging can reduce the likelihood of financial distress, thereby reducing the expected costs of financial distress.

- A forward contract is an over-the-counter instrument that involves two parties agreeing on a price at which the purchaser will buy a specified amount of an asset from the seller at a fixed date sometime in the future. A futures contract is similar to a forward contract but is traded on an organized exchange.

- The fair forward price (or rate) in a forward contract is the price that eliminates the possibility of an arbitrageur generating riskless profits by trading in the forward contract.

- Unlike forward contracts, which are customized instruments, futures are standardized. Several issues to consider when using futures to hedge include basis risk, cross-hedging, tailing the hedge, and delivery options.

- Options offer a corporation the opportunity to hedge its downside risk without giving up its upside potential. However, this comes at a cost in the form of the premium paid for the option. Swap contracts are longer-term hedging instruments that allow corporations to change the characteristics of their periodic cash flows.

- In some cases, a corporation may not be able to hedge its risk exposure using off-the-shelf forwards, futures, options, or swaps. In these cases, the corporation may turn to financial engineering in an effort to create a specialized financial instrument that will hedge the exposure.

INTERNET RESOURCES

Note: *For updates to links, please go to the book's website at* http://smart.swcollege.com

http://www.cbot.com —Website of Chicago Board of Trade (CBOT), the oldest major futures exchange, which lists futures contracts for both commodities (corn, wheat, soybeans, gold) and financial instruments (2-, 5-, 10-, and 30-year Treasury bonds, Eurodollars); The CBOT and its Chicago rival, the Chicago Mercantile Exchange (http://www.cme.com) have retained face-to-face, open-outcry trading in futures "pits," whereas most international futures exchanges are purely electronic markets.

http://www.liffe.com —Website of the London International Financial Futures and Options Exchange (LIFFE), until recently the leading international futures market; remains an important market for trading global interest rate, equity, swap, and commodity contracts; acquired by Euronext during 2002, and now officially called Euronext-LIFFE.

http://www.eurexchange.com —Website of the Eurex futures exchange, which began in December 1996 as a joint venture between the Swiss Exchange and the Deutsche Börse, and within an amazingly short period of time emerged as the leading international futures market; among its more successful products are the German government Bund contract and options on several European stock indexes; Eurex has established a reputation as the world's most technologically advanced futures market.

KEY TERMS

arbitrage	interest rate swap
basis risk	lifetime high price
closing futures price	lifetime low price
cross-hedging	long position
currency forward contracts	maintenance margin
currency swap	margin account
economic exposure	marking-to-market
financial engineering	notional principal
fixed-for-floating currency swap	open interest
fixed-for-floating interest rate swap	opening futures price
forward price	risk management
forward rate	settlement date
forward rate agreement (FRA)	settlement price
fungibility	short position
futures contract	speculating
initial margin	spot price
interest differential	spot rates
interest rate caps	swap contract
interest rate collar	tailing the hedge
interest rate floor	transaction exposure
interest rate risk	

QUESTIONS

21-1. Historically, what types of risk were the focus of most firms' risk-management practices?

21-2. Distinguish between the motivations for purchasing insurance and the motivations for hedging marketwide sources of risk.

21-3. Distinguish between transaction exposure and economic exposure.

21-4. In what way can hedging reduce the risk of financial distress? How might reducing the risk of financial distress increase firm value?

21-5. Explain how hedging can reduce a firm's tax liability.

21-6. Why do closely held firms tend to hedge more than firms with diffuse ownership?

21-7. How can hedging make it easier to evaluate a manager's performance?

21-8. What are the advantages of using exchange-traded derivatives to hedge a risk exposure? What are the advantages of over-the-counter derivatives?

21-9. Conceptually, how do we determine the fair forward price for an asset? What are the necessary assumptions to arrive at a fair forward price?

21-10. Conceptually, what are the differences between Equations 21.1, 21.2, and 21.3? Which equation would you use to determine the fair forward price for an asset that does not earn any income but is costly to store, such as gold or silver? How would you modify the equation?

21-11. Describe the features of a futures contract that make it more liquid than a forward contract.

21-12. Explain the features of a futures contract that make it have less credit risk than a forward contract.

21-13. Why is fungibility an important feature of futures contracts?

21-14. Describe the delivery process for futures contracts. Why does delivery rarely take place in futures contracts?

21-15. Why is a call option on an interest rate called an interest rate cap and a put option called an interest rate floor?

21-16. Explain how a fixed-for-floating swap can be considered a portfolio of forward contracts on 6-month discount bonds.

21-17. Go to the CBOT website (http://www.cbot.com), and determine the contract specifications for soybean meal futures and 10-year U.S. Treasury note futures. Apart from the difference in the type of asset, what is the difference between the two contracts in terms of what qualifies as deliverable grades?

21-18. Go to the CBOT website (http://www.cbot.com), and determine the minimum initial margin requirements for speculators in the contracts traded on that exchange. Which contracts have the smallest margin requirements? Which contracts have the largest requirements? Why do you suppose these contracts have such different margin requirements?

PROBLEMS

Forward Contracts

21-1. Suppose that an investor has agreed to pay $94,339.62 for a 1-year discount bond in one year. Two years from now, the investor will receive the bond's face value of $100,000. The current effective annual risk-free rate of interest is 5.8 percent, and the current spot price for a 2-year discount bond is $88,999.64. Has the investor agreed to pay too much or too little? How might an arbitrageur capitalize on this opportunity?

Smart
Solutions
See the
problem and
solution explained step-by-step at
SMARTFinance

21-2. Company A's stock will pay a dividend of $5 in three months and $6 in six months. The current stock price is $200, and the risk-free rate of interest is 7 percent per year with monthly compounding for all maturities. What is the fair forward price for a 7-month forward contract?

21-3. The current price of gold is $288 per troy ounce. The cost of storing gold is $0.03/oz per month. Assuming an annual risk-free rate of interest of 12 percent compounded monthly, what is the approximate futures price of gold for delivery in four months?

21-4. Following is the current yield to maturity on Treasury bills of various maturities:

Time to Maturity (months)	Yield (%)
1	5.0
3	5.2
6	5.4
9	5.8

Assuming monthly compounding, what should the forward interest rate of a 3-month T-bill be if it is to be delivered at the end of three months? What if it is to be delivered at the end of six months?

21-5.   Using the information in Table 21.1, determine whether the 3-month forward rate on Swiss francs is fair if the annualized yield for risk-free borrowing over the next three months is 8 percent in Switzerland and 5 percent in the United States. If the price is not fair, how could you capitalize on the arbitrage opportunity? What is the potential profit? Assume monthly compounding for borrowing and lending.

21-6.   A U.S. automobile importer is expecting a shipment of custom-made cars from Britain in six months. Upon delivery, the importer will pay for the cars in pounds. Using the information in Table 21.1, suggest a hedging strategy for the importer. Explain the consequences for the spot market transaction and the forward market transaction if the $/£ spot exchange rate increases by 10 percent over the next six months.

21-7.   Suppose that KF Exports enters into a FRA with Interfirst Bank with a notional principal of $50 million and the following terms: In six months, if LIBOR is above 6 percent, KF will pay Interfirst according to the standard FRA formula. On the other hand, if LIBOR is less than 6 percent, Interfirst will pay KF. If LIBOR is 5.5 percent in six months, who pays and how much will the company pay? What if LIBOR is 6.5 percent?

Futures Contracts

21-8.   An investor purchases one gold futures contract for delivery in August 2002. Using the information in Table 21.2, determine the settle price for the contract on Friday, January 4, 2002, according to the Monday, January 7, 2002, *Wall Street Journal*. What is the total futures price for the contract? If the settle price on the next trading day is $282/oz, will the investor have money deposited into his margin account or withdrawn? How much? Suppose that the investor eventually closes out the position by selling at a price of $284/oz. How much is his profit or loss?

21-9.   Consider the following scenarios, determine how to hedge each scenario using bond futures, and comment on whether it would be appropriate to hedge the exposure.

   a. A bond portfolio manager will be paid a large bonus if her $10 million portfolio earns 6 percent in the current fiscal year. She has done very well through the first nine months. However, she is concerned that interest rates might increase over the next few months.

   b. The manager of a company is selling one of its warehouses. The deal will close in two months. The manager plans to buy 6-month Treasury bills when the company receives payment for the warehouse space, but the manager is worried that interest rates might decline in the next two months.

   c. Sam Blackwell plans to retire in a year. Upon retirement, he will be paid a lump sum based on the value of the securities in his defined-contribution retirement plan. Sam's portfolio consists largely of Treasury bonds, and he is worried that interest rates will be increasing in the coming year.

Options and Swaps

21-10.   Chipman Products Company will suffer an increase in borrowing costs if the 13-week Treasury bill rate increases in the next six months. Chipman Products is willing to accept the risk of small changes in the 13-week T-bill rate but wishes to avoid the potential losses associated with large changes. The company plans to hedge its risk exposure using an interest rate collar. If the company buys a call option on the 13-week T-bill rate with a strike price of 60 and sells a put option with a strike price of 50, describe how this strategy will limit the company's exposure to changes in the T-bill rate. The premium on the call is 0.75, and the premium on the put is 0.85. What is the company's profit (or loss) in the option market if the T-bill rate is 4.5 percent in five months? If the T-bill rate is 5.5 percent? If the T-bill rate is 6.5 percent?

21-11. Go to the CBOT website (http://www.cbot.com), and determine the contract specifications for Dow Jones Industrial Average futures. Determine the current futures price for the next available contract month. What would your profit or loss be if you bought one contract today and the Dow Jones Industrial Average increased by 100 points before the last settlement date?

21-12. Company A is based in Switzerland and would like to borrow $10 million at a fixed rate of interest. Because the company is not well known, however, it has not been able to find a willing U.S. lender. However, the company can borrow SF17,825,000 at 11 percent per year for five years. Company B is based in the United States and would like to borrow SF17,825,000 for five years at a fixed rate of interest. It has not been able to find a Swiss lender. However, it has been offered a loan of $10 million at 9 percent per year. Five-year government bonds are yielding 9.5 percent and 8.5 percent in Switzerland and the United States, respectively. Suggest a currency swap that would net the financial intermediary 0.5 percent per year. Be sure to consider default risk in your analysis.

21-13. Citibank and ABM Company enter into a 5-year interest rate swap with a notional principal of $100 million and the following terms: Every year for the next five years, ABM agrees to pay Citibank 6 percent and receive from Citibank LIBOR. Using the following information about LIBOR at the end of each of the next five years, determine the cash flows in the swap.

Year	LIBOR (%)
1	5.0
2	5.5
3	6.2
4	6.0
5	6.4

21-14. Based on the type of swap ABM entered into in the previous problem, what type of liabilities do you think ABM has? Long-term or short-term?

22

Strategic and Operational Financial Planning

OPENING FOCUS

Investors Say "Bravo" for Cable Company Pact with NBC

The ride down had been a long one for Cablevision Systems Corp. stockholders. Shares in the company founded by the father-son team of Chuck and Jimmy Dolan had lost almost 95 percent of their value between January 2001 and August 2002, falling from $90 to $4.95 in that 20-month span. The seventh-largest cable company in the United States, with diverse interests, including ownership in New York's Madison Square Garden, the New York Knicks and New York Rangers professional sports teams, and regional sports cable networks spread across the country, Cablevision had fallen on hard times after borrowing billions to upgrade its cable systems and to acquire assets. On the brink of a liquidity crisis in the fall of 2002, Cablevision tried to find buyers for almost any of its assets to pay down its $7.7 billion debt load.

One such buyer was General Electric's television unit, NBC. On November 5, 2002, the firms announced plans for GE to purchase Cablevision's Bravo network for $1.25 billion. The purchase would give NBC its first entertainment cable channel and would at least give Cablevision more time to work out its financial difficulties, which included a projected $900 million cash shortfall in fiscal-year 2003. Perhaps heartened by the prospect of a recovery, the market boosted Cablevision stock more than 50 percent in the week following the announcement.

The troubles faced by Cablevision Systems Corp. illustrate the importance of corporate financial planning. In their effort to build a media empire, the Dolans did not foresee the decline in the U.S. economy in 2000–2001, and their company was ill prepared to deal with the financial crisis that reached a critical state in 2002. Cablevision faced the prospect of selling at bargain prices many of the assets it had acquired just a few years earlier. Though a well developed financial plan could not have prevented a recession, it might have helped Cablevision develop contingencies that would have enabled the company to ride out the slump without having to divest so many of its prized assets.

Sources: Ronald Grover, "With Friends like Rupert Murdoch . . . ," *Business Week Online* (November 11, 2002); Kim Chipman, "GE's NBC to Buy Bravo from Cablevision," *National Post* (November 5, 2002).

In our experience, almost everyone working in a large corporation encounters two areas of corporate finance on a regular basis. The first area is justification of spending plans, or capital budgeting. Chapters 7 through 9 covered the essential elements of capital budgeting analysis that business professionals in any discipline should know. The second part of corporate finance that touches almost all functional groups in a firm is financial planning. Financial planning encompasses a wide array of activities: setting long-run strategic goals, preparing quarterly and annual budgets, and managing day-to-day fluctuations in cash balances. No one with corporate work experience is completely unfamiliar with budgeting processes, but how budgets and other financial plans are compiled at the corporate level, how they tie together sometimes competing interests within the firm, and how they interact with the firm's strategic objectives can be something of a mystery.

In this chapter and the next, we discuss various elements of a firm's financial planning processes. This chapter emphasizes long-term planning, and Chapter 23 focuses on short-term planning. In both chapters, you will see how firms' financial plans must balance the interests and objectives of different business units and functional areas. For example, in setting long-run strategic and financial goals, a firm must prioritize its desires to increase sales and market share; to increase, decrease, or maintain its exposure to financial risk; to achieve production efficiencies; to attract and retain capable employees; and to distribute cash to shareholders. In almost every instance, making incremental progress on one of these objectives means an incremental sacrifice on one or more of the other goals.

SMART PRACTICES VIDEO

Jackie Sturm, Director of Finance for Technology and Manufacturing, Intel Corp.

"Once the product line business plan is completed, we move into our annual planning process, which is more of a tactical exercise."

See the entire interview at **SMARTFinance**

For better or worse, financial planning, particularly long-term planning, is more art than science—the connection between most financial planning models and the objective of shareholder wealth maximization is tenuous at best. At one level, the advice we would give to a firm constructing a long-term plan is trivial—do whatever is necessary to invest in all positive-*NPV* projects. In practice, a variety of factors make following that advice a major challenge. CFOs usually tell us that they have many more projects with *NPV*s that appear to be positive than they can possibly undertake. Limits on capital, production capacity, human resources, and many other inputs make the planning process more complex than simply accepting all projects that look promising. In this chapter, we concede that the theoretical underpinnings of planning models are weak, and therefore we focus as much as possible on practice. That is, we attempt to describe how firms actually build financial plans rather than argue about how they should plan.

22.1 OVERVIEW OF THE PLANNING PROCESS

A long-term financial plan begins with strategy. Typically, the senior management team conducts an analysis of the markets in which the firm competes. Managers try to identify ways to protect and increase the firm's competitive advantage in those markets. For example, the first priority of a firm that competes by achieving the lowest production cost in an industry might be to determine whether it should make additional investments in manufacturing facilities to achieve even greater production efficiencies. Of course, being the low-cost producer is difficult if the firm's fixed assets are chronically underutilized, so this type of firm will also invest a great deal of time and energy trying to forecast market demand and developing contingency plans if the expected demand does not materialize. If a firm's competitive advantage derives from the value of its brand, it might begin by assessing whether new or expanded marketing programs might increase the value of the brand relative to those of competitors.

Long-term planning requires more than paying close attention to a firm's existing markets. Even more important is the ability to identify and prioritize new market opportunities. Successful long-term planning means asking and answering questions such as the following:

1. In what emerging markets might we have a sustainable competitive advantage?
2. How can we leverage our competitive strengths across existing markets in which we currently do not compete?
3. What threats to our current business exist, and how can we meet those threats?
4. Where in the world should we produce? Where should we sell?
5. Can we deploy resources more efficiently by exiting certain markets and using those resources elsewhere?

As the firm's senior managers develop answers to these questions, they construct a **strategic plan,** a multiyear action plan for the major investments and competitive initiatives that they believe will drive the future success of the enterprise.

Finance plays several roles in this discussion. First, financial managers draw on a broad set of skills to assess the likelihood that a given strategic objective can be achieved. With respect to a major new investment proposal, the first question to ask is probably not "What does it cost?" or "Can we afford it?" Rather, drawing on their experience and knowledge outside the realm of finance, managers should ask, "Does this investment make sense?" or "Is there a good reason to expect this proposal to generate wealth for our shareholders?"

Second, the responsibility to assess whether a strategic action plan is feasible given a firm's existing and prospective sources of funding falls primarily to the finance function. Though some corporate giants, such as Microsoft or Intel, hold such vast amounts of cash that they are nearly unconstrained in terms of their ability to make large, new investments, for most companies financial constraints are more binding. Given a broad set of strategic objectives, financial managers must determine whether the firm's ability to generate cash internally plus its ability to raise cash externally will be sufficient to fund new spending initiatives. As we have seen, firms that pay dividends are extremely reluctant to cut them, so financial analysts generally treat expected dividend payments as a factor that limits a firm's ability to make new investments. Similarly, if fulfilling strategic objectives will require that a firm accept a significant increase in leverage, it is the role of finance to communicate that trade-off to the top management team. We will see in the next section that financial managers have several tools at their disposal that enable them to highlight the trade-offs firms face when setting growth targets.

Third, finance clearly plays an important control function as firms implement their strategic plans. Financial analysts prepare and update cash budgets to make sure that firms do not unknowingly slip into a liquidity crisis. The frequency with which these budgets are constructed and monitored depends on several factors, including the firm's current level of liquidity, its access to external funding sources, and the volatility of demand for its products. At an even more detailed level, analysts monitor individual items in the cash budget, such as changes in inventories, receivables, and payables (our focus in the next chapter). Here, too, financial managers must evaluate trade-offs. For example, a firm's sales force generally prefers that the firm maintain inventories at a level sufficient to ensure that customers do not have to wait for orders to be filled. Managers responsible for production want the firm to hold inventories of raw materials to minimize interruptions in manufacturing. But in both cases, holding higher inventories involves additional costs that may lower the firm's profitability.

Fourth, a major contribution of finance to the strategic planning process involves risk management. When a firm's strategy calls for making new investments in overseas markets (either producing or selling abroad), the firm faces a new set of risk exposures. The finance function is charged with managing these exposures and ensuring, to the extent possible, that the firm takes those risks that it believes it has a comparative advantage in taking and that it hedges risks for which it has no advantage. Similarly, more than in any other functional area, the job of finance is to identify problems that could develop in the future if the firm's strategic plans unfold in unexpected ways. Developing these "problem scenarios" and options for dealing with them when they occur is an important part of finance's risk-management responsibility.

In this chapter, we focus primarily on the second and third roles just described. The next section discusses the financial tools that help managers determine the trade-offs they face when setting growth objectives for the future.

Concept Review Questions

1. A company decides to compete by making a major investment to modernize production facilities. Describe two ways in which meeting this objective might force a firm to sacrifice other objectives.

2. Firm A competes in a market in which the demand for its product and its selling price are highly unpredictable. Firm B competes in a market in which these factors are much more stable. Which firm probably creates and monitors cash budgets more frequently?

22.2   PLANNING FOR GROWTH

SUSTAINABLE GROWTH

Most firms strive to grow over time, and most firms view rapid growth as preferable to slow growth. Of course, rapid growth is not wealth maximizing for all firms at all times, and a great deal of financial research has studied why firms place so much emphasis on growth, even at times to the detriment of shareholders. For the moment, we lay aside the question of whether growth creates or destroys shareholder value. Instead, we want to demonstrate a simple model that highlights the trade-offs that firms must weigh when they choose to grow. These trade-offs depend on several factors, including how rapidly the firm plans to grow, how profitable its existing business is, how much of its earnings it retains and how much it pays out to shareholders, how efficiently it manages its assets, and how much financial leverage it is willing to bear.

First, let us define what we mean by "growth." A firm's growth could be measured by increases in its market value, its asset base, the number of people it employs, or any number of other metrics. For now, let us imagine that a firm establishes a growth target in terms of sales. That is, when we say that a firm plans to grow next

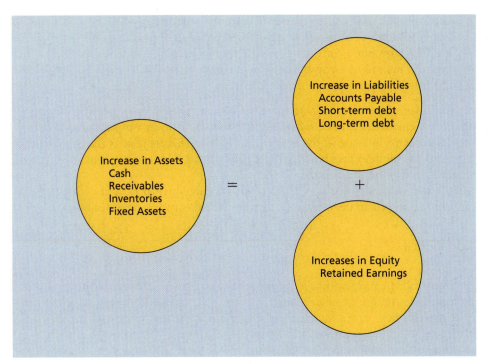

Figure 22.1
Sustainable Growth Equality

As a firm grows, it must invest in new assets to support increased sales volume. The investments in new assets must be financed with some combination of increased liabilities and increased equity.

year by 10 percent, we mean that it hopes to achieve a 10 percent increase in sales. Our experience suggests that most firms define and measure growth targets in terms of sales, so we will adopt that convention as well.

With that definition in mind, think about what growth means for a firm in terms of its balance sheet. An increase in sales probably requires additional investments in assets. Certainly, we would anticipate that increased sales volume would require investments in current assets, such as inventories and receivables; but over time, increases in sales will also require new investments in fixed assets, such as production capacity and office space. As a shortcut, let us assume that a firm's total asset turnover ratio, the ratio of sales divided by total assets, remains constant through time. In other words, any increase in sales will be matched by a comparable percentage increase in assets.

Because the balance sheet equation must hold, increases in liabilities and shareholders' equity must equal the increase in assets. In what forms do we expect increases in liabilities and shareholders' equity to occur? In previous chapters, we learned that most companies issue new common shares very infrequently, so we will rule that out as a potential source of new financing. As with inventories and receivables, accounts payable should increase because higher sales volume means higher purchases. We might also expect to see higher accruals and higher short-term liabilities of other types. Similarly, if a firm's business is profitable, its equity account will increase, even if it does not issue any new stock, by the amount of earnings it retains. Figure 22.1 illustrates that the growth in assets must equal growth in these liability and equity accounts over time.

The **sustainable growth model,** developed by Higgins (1981), takes this balance sheet identity, adds to it a few assumptions, and derives an expression that determines how rapidly a firm can grow while maintaining a balance between its sources (increases in assets) and uses (increases in liabilities and equity) of funds. Specifically, the sustainable growth model assumes the following:

1. The firm will issue no new shares of common stock next year.
2. The firm's total asset turnover ratio, S/A, remains constant.
3. The firm pays out a constant fraction, d, of its earnings as dividends.
4. The firm maintains a constant assets-to-equity ratio, A/E.
5. The firm's net profit margin, m, is constant.

Consider a firm that wants to increase sales next period by g percent. If total assets in the current period equal A and if the asset turnover ratio remains constant, then assets must increase in the next period by gA. This represents the change in the left-hand side of the firm's balance sheet next period. That change must be met with an equal change on the right-hand side.

Given sales this period of S, a net profit margin equal to m, and a dividend payout ratio of d, we can determine the firm's retained earnings next period:

$$S(m)(1 + g)(1 - d)$$

The product of S and m yields net profits in the current year. Multiplying this product times $(1 + g)$ results in next year's profits, and multiplying this result times $(1 - d)$ gives next year's retained earnings. This is the amount by which the equity component of the balance sheet will grow. Next, observe that the ratio of total assets to shareholders' equity equals 1 plus the ratio of total liabilities, L, to shareholders' equity:

$$A = E + L$$

$$\frac{A}{E} = \frac{E + L}{E} = 1 + \frac{L}{E}$$

The assumption that the firm maintains a constant assets-to-equity ratio is therefore equivalent to an assumption that the ratio of liabilities to equity remains constant. Therefore, for each dollar of earnings that the company retains, it can borrow an additional L/E dollars to keep the mix of debt and equity constant. For example, if a firm finances half of its assets with debt and half with equity, then the ratio L/E equals 1.0. If the firm retains \$1 million in earnings in a given year, it can afford to borrow an additional \$1 million to maintain the desired mix of debt and equity. Therefore, the increase in liabilities next year simply equals the product of next year's retained earnings and the ratio of liabilities to equity:

$$S(m)(1 + g)(1 - d)](L/E)$$

Finally, if the increases in assets must match the increases in liabilities and equity, we can write the following:

$$gA = S(m)(1 + g)(1 - d) + [S(m)(1 + g)(1 - d)](L/E)$$
$\uparrow$assets $\uparrow$ret. earnings $\uparrow$liabilities

$$= [S(m)(1 + g)(1 - d)](1 + L/E)$$
$\quad\uparrow$(equity + liabilities)

The insight of the sustainable growth model is that there will be some rate of growth, g^*, that keeps the sources and uses of funds in balance. This *sustainable growth rate* can be calculated as follows:

$$g^* = \frac{m(1-d)\dfrac{A}{E}}{\dfrac{A}{S} - m(1-d)\dfrac{A}{E}}$$

(Eq. 22.1)

Notice how each of the key variables in Equation 22.1 affects the sustainable growth rate. If a firm's profit margin increases, the numerator rises and the denominator falls, so g^* increases. Therefore, generating a higher quantity of profits per dollar of sales provides fuel for a higher growth rate. Similarly, an increase in the ratio of assets-to-equity, which can occur only if the firm is willing to accept higher financial leverage, also increases the sustainable growth rate. Firms willing to borrow more can grow more rapidly. If a firm can increase its total asset turnover ratio, then the ratio of A/S falls and the sustainable growth rate rises. Firms that manage assets more efficiently and generate higher sales volume per dollar of assets can achieve more rapid growth. Finally, a reduction in dividend payouts also tends to increase g^*. When firms retain more earnings, they can finance faster growth.

APPLYING THE MODEL

In 1999, Yahoo! Inc. reported the following financial data:

Sales	$588.6 million
Net income	$61.1 million
Total assets	$1,469.8 million
Total equity	$1,261.3 million
Dividends	$0

From these figures, we can determine that Yahoo!'s net profit margin was 10.38 percent, its assets-to-equity ratio was 1.16, its asset turnover ratio was 0.40 (which implies assets-to-sales of 2.5), and its dividend payout ratio was 0.0. Plugging these values into Equation 22.1 yields a sustainable growth rate of a little over 5 percent. For Yahoo! this meant that the company could increase sales by 5 percent without changing asset turnover, dividend policy, profit margins, or leverage. ■

It is as important to understand what the sustainable growth model *does not* say as it is to grasp what it does say. From the previous calculation, should we assume that Yahoo! managers should set as their firm's growth target an increase in sales of 5 percent, equal to the sustainable growth rate? Not at all. Yahoo! managers should decide what rate of growth maximizes shareholder wealth, and then they should use the sustainable growth model as a planning device to help them prepare for the consequences of their growth plans. For example, suppose that Yahoo! decides that it is best for their shareholders if the firm grows more rapidly than 5 percent. To do so, Yahoo! must alter one or more of the baseline assumptions of the model. Yahoo! could try to find ways to raise its profit margin, to increase its asset turnover, or to increase leverage. Yahoo! does not pay dividends, so it cannot use a dividend cut to increase growth.

APPLYING THE MODEL

In fact, from 1999 to 2000, Yahoo!'s sales increased by roughly 89 percent, almost 18 times the sustainable rate. The sustainable growth model would suggest that to finance this rapid growth, Yahoo! must have achieved some combination of higher profit margins, faster asset turnover, and increased financial leverage. Indeed, by the end of 2000, Yahoo!'s asset turnover ratio had increased by 22 percent (from 0.40 to 0.49), and its assets-to-equity ratio increased by just under 3 percent (from 1.16 to 1.20). These two changes provided the fuel for rapid growth, even though Yahoo!'s profit margin fell roughly 4 percentage points in 2000.   ■

The sustainable growth model gives managers a kind of shorthand projection that ties together growth objectives and financing needs. It provides hints about the levers that managers must pull to achieve growth above the sustainable rate. It also identifies some of the financial benefits of growing more slowly than the sustainable rate. A firm that expects to grow at a rate below g^* can plan to reduce leverage or asset turnover, or it can increase dividends. Again, we emphasize that the model does not say anything about how fast the firm *should* grow.

The sustainable growth concept also highlights tensions that can develop as firms pursue multiple objectives simultaneously. For example, the compensation of the vice president (VP) of marketing may be tied to generating additional sales volume, whereas the CFO's compensation may depend on maintaining the firm's credit rating. We have seen that one way to finance faster growth is to increase leverage, so the goals of increasing sales while maintaining the current degree of leverage may be difficult to achieve simultaneously. For the firm to achieve faster sales growth, the marketing function may indicate that the firm should offer a wider array of products, but doing so may result in lower inventory turns and hence reduced total asset turnover. If the firm is unwilling to increase leverage and if expanding the product line means reducing asset turnover, then meeting the sales target will depend on improving profit margins or cutting dividend payouts.

The primary advantage of the sustainable growth model is its simplicity. However, the financial planning process generally involves more complex projections. These projections are usually embodied in a set of pro forma income statements and balance sheets that firms use to provide a benchmark against which future performance will be judged. Let us now turn to the creation of these statements.

Pro Forma Financial Statements

Periodically, firms produce forecasts of what they expect their balance sheet and income statement to look like a year or two ahead, called **pro forma financial statements.** Occasionally, firms use these statements to communicate their plans to outside investors (such as at the time of an IPO or earnings announcement), but most of the time managers construct these statements for internal planning and control purposes. By making projections of sales volume, profits, fixed asset requirements, working capital needs, and sources of finance, the firm can establish goals to which compensation may be tied, and it can predict any liquidity problems with enough lead time to have additional financing sources available when needed.

The process of creating pro forma financial statements varies from firm to firm, but there are some common elements. For example, most pro forma statements begin with a sales forecast. The sales forecast may be derived in either a "top-down" or "bottom-up" approach. **Top-down** sales forecasts rely heavily on macroeconomic and industry forecasts. Some firms use complex statistical models or subscribe to forecasts produced by firms specializing in econometric modeling. In the top-down approach, senior managers establish a firmwide objective for increased sales. Next, individual divisions or business units receive targets that may not be identical but that collectively aggregate to achieve the firm's overall growth target. Division heads pass down sales targets to product line managers and other smaller-scale units. Again, the sales targets will vary across units within the division, but they must add up to achieve the divisional goal.

Firms that use a **bottom-up** method for forecasting sales begin by talking with customers. Sales personnel try to assess demand in the coming year on a customer-by-customer basis. These figures are added up across sales territories, product lines, and divisions to arrive at the overall sales forecast for the company. Bottom-up forecasting approaches generally do not rely on mathematical and statistical models.

Not surprising, many firms use a blend of these two approaches. For example, a firm may generate a set of assumptions regarding the macroeconomic environment to which all divisions must adhere, but forecasts can still be generated from the customer level and aggregated up. Some firms produce two sets of forecasts, one that uses a statistical approach and another that relies on customer feedback. Senior managers then compare the two forecasts to see how far apart they are before setting a final sales objective.

Starting with the sales forecast, financial analysts construct pro forma balance sheets and income statements using a mix of facts and assumptions. For example, if a firm's strategic plan calls for major investments in fixed assets, the analyst will incorporate those projections in the forecast of the firm's total fixed asset requirements, as well as in the forecast of depreciation expense on the income statement. In the absence of any specific knowledge of capital spending plans, an analyst may assume that total fixed assets will remain at a fixed percentage relative to sales or total assets, and that assumption in turn would drive the depreciation-line item on the income statement.

In a similar fashion, an analyst can make projections for line items that vary with sales volume. For example, by assuming a constant gross profit margin, the analyst can estimate cost of goods sold directly from the sales forecast. When firms construct pro forma statements by extending that logic to all balance sheet and income statement accounts, assuming that all items grow in proportion to sales, they are using the **percentage-of-sales method.** This is a convenient way to construct pro forma statements, and it is usually a good starting point when making financial projections. However, on the balance sheet, items such as receivables, inventory, and payables typically increase with sales, though not always in a linear fashion. For example, a company with $100 billion in sales may not need 100 times as much inventory as a firm with $1 billion in sales.

In constructing pro forma statements, analysts usually leave one line item on the balance sheet as a **plug figure,** and they adjust this account after making all their other projections so that the balance sheet will balance. For example, the analyst may make projections for all asset, liability, and equity accounts except for the cash balance. When the projections are complete, the analyst simply adjusts the cash account to make the balance sheet balance. Alternatively, the analyst might leave a short-term liability account open to serve as the plug figure. The line item representing the amount borrowed on a bank line of credit, for instance, could be used to bring the right-hand and left-hand sides of the balance sheet into equality once the projections are complete.

APPLYING THE MODEL

Table 22.1 shows the 2004 income statement and balance sheet for Zinsmeister Shoe Corporation. We will use this historical information plus some assumptions to generate pro forma financial statements for 2005. Make the following assumptions:

1. Zinsmeister plans to increase sales by 30 percent in 2005.
2. The company's gross profit margin will remain at 35 percent.
3. Operating expenses will equal 10 percent of sales as they did in 2004.
4. Zinsmeister pays 10 percent interest on both its long-term debt and its credit line.
5. Zinsmeister will invest an additional $20 million in fixed assets in 2005, which will increase depreciation expense from $10 million to $15 million in 2005.
6. The company faces a 35 percent tax rate.
7. The company plans to increase cash holdings by $1 million next year.
8. Accounts receivable equal 8.5 percent of sales.
9. Inventories equal 10 percent of sales.
10. Accounts payable equal 12 percent of cost of goods sold.
11. The company will repay an additional $5 million in long-term debt in 2005.
12. The company will pay 50 percent of its net income as a dividend.

From this set of assumptions and the data in Table 22.1, we can construct the pro forma statements for 2005 shown in Table 22.2. First, Zinsmeister's sales increase to $325 million. Cost of goods sold and operating expenses increase 30 percent over the prior year (hitting the percentage-of-sales assumptions above). Interest expense is a

Table 22.1
Financial Statements of Zinsmeister Shoe Corporation for 2004 ($ in thousands)

Zinsmeister Shoe Corporation Balance Sheet as of December 31, 2004			
Assets		**Liabilities and Equity**	
Cash	$ 10,000	Accounts payable	$ 19,500
Accounts receivable	21,250	Credit line	5,000
Inventory	25,000	Current long-term debt	5,000
Current assets	$ 56,250	Current liabilities	$ 29,500
Gross fixed assets	$ 80,000	Long-term debt	$ 20,000
Less: Accumulated depreciation	20,000	Common stock	$ 20,200
Net fixed assets	$ 60,000	Retained earnings	$ 46,550
Total assets	$116,250	Total liabilities and equity	$116,250

Zinsmeister Shoe Corporation Income Statement for the year ended December 31, 2004	
Sales	$250,000
Less: Cost of goods sold	162,500
Gross profit	$ 87,500
Less: Operating expenses	$ 25,000
Less: Interest expense	$ 3,000
Less: Depreciation	$ 10,000
Pretax income	$ 49,500
Less: Taxes	17,325
Net income	$ 32,175

Zinsmeister Shoe Corporation Pro Forma Balance Sheet as of December 31, 2005			
Assets		**Liabilities and Equity**	
Cash	$ 11,000	Accounts payable	$ 25,350
Accounts receivable	27,625	Credit line	3,306
Inventory	32,500	Current long-term debt	5,000
Current assets	$ 71,125	Current liabilities	$ 33,656
Gross fixed assets	$100,000	Long-term debt	$ 15,000
Less: Accumulated depreciation	35,000	Common stock	$ 20,200
Net fixed assets	$ 65,000	Retained earnings	$ 67,269
Total assets	$136,125	Total liabilities and equity	$136,125

Zinsmeister Shoe Corporation Pro Forma Income Statement for the year ended December 31, 2005	
Sales	$325,000
Less: Cost of goods sold	211,250
Gross profit	$113,750
Less: Operating expenses	$ 32,500
Less: Interest expense	$ 2,500
Less: Depreciation	$ 15,000
Pretax income	$ 63,750
Less: Taxes	22,312
Net income	$ 41,438
Dividends	$ 20,719

Table 22.2
Pro Forma Financial Statements for Zinsmeister Shoe Corporation for 2005 ($ in thousands)

tricky item. To begin, assume that Zinsmeister will maintain its $5 million balance on its credit line and will retire the current portion of long-term debt. This means that its total outstanding debt will be $25 million. At 10 percent, interest expense should equal $2.5 million. As we will see, that assumption may change as we continue to build the statements.

Putting these figures together in the pro forma income statement, we see that Zinsmeister earns a net profit of just over $41 million, half of which it pays out to shareholders. Next, build the pro forma balance sheet. Cash is given at $11 million. Accounts receivable and inventory increase with sales as stated, so current assets increase to $71.125 million. With the additional investment in fixed assets of $20 million, less 2004's depreciation expense, net fixed assets grow to $65 million, so total assets equal $136.125 million.

On the right-hand side, accounts payable increase, the current portion of long-term debt remains at $5 million, total long-term debt declines $5 million, and common stock does not change. The retained earnings figure for 2005 equals the 2004 figure plus half of 2005's net income. In this example, we are using the bank line of credit as our plug figure. That is, given all the assumptions so far, the bank line of credit will decline from $5 million to $3.306 million because that is the figure necessary to keep assets in balance with liabilities and equity. However, because the bank line of credit declines, our estimate of interest expense in the income statement is too high. Recall that we predicted interest expense of $2.5 million based on a 10 percent interest rate on total outstanding debt of $25 million. The pro forma balance sheet now shows long-term and short-term debt of just $23.306 million, so interest expense falls to $2.33 million. A decline in interest expense leads to an increase in profits and retained earnings. Higher retained earnings means that the line of credit can be reduced even more, and the cycle repeats. To find the amount of borrowing on the credit line and the corresponding interest expense that rationalizes the balance sheet with the income statement, an analyst would need to use an iterative approach, such as Excel's Solver function. ▪

Nonetheless, the bottom line for Zinsmeister is that its pro forma outlook is quite good. If the company achieves its sales growth target and keeps expenses and working capital accounts in line with historical norms, it can simultaneously invest $20 million in new fixed assets and reduce its outstanding interest-bearing debt. In one sense, that conclusion is hardly surprising. If we take the 2004 data for Zinsmeister and plug it into Equation 22.1, we find that the company's sustainable growth rate is 31.8 percent. Therefore, the firm's target growth rate of 30 percent should leave it with some "financial slack." It is necessary to go through the added steps to build pro forma statements because they provide the firm with a lot more information than the sustainable growth rate does. With the figures in Tables 22.1 and 22.2 programmed into a spreadsheet, analysts could easily study the effects of changes in any of the assumptions on Zinsmeister's ability to pay down debt or perhaps identify a need to increase the credit line balance.

Equation 22.2 presents another shorthand approach for estimating the amount of external financing that a firm will require in the future. The equation states that the external funds required, *EFR*, are a function of three factors. The first term in the equation, $(A \div S)\Delta S$, indicates the additional investment in assets required for a firm if it plans to maintain its asset turnover ratio and increase the dollar volume of sales by ΔS. The second term measures the source of funds available to finance this growth, assuming that the relationship between a firm's sales and its spontaneous liabilities (in this case, simply accounts payable) remains constant. The third term captures the additional financing sources that the firm creates internally through retained earnings:

$$EFR = \frac{A}{S}\Delta S - \frac{AP}{S}\Delta S - mS(1 + g)(1 - d) \qquad \text{(Eq. 22.2)}$$

If we apply this shorthand calculation to Zinsmeister, we can determine its external fund requirements (in thousands of dollars):

$$EFR = \frac{116{,}250}{250{,}000}(75{,}000) - \frac{19{,}500}{250{,}000}(75{,}000)$$

$$- \left(\frac{32{,}175}{250{,}000}\right)250{,}000(1 + 0.30)(1 - 0.5) = 8{,}111$$

Under the assumptions of this model, Zinsmeister will require additional external funding of $8.1 million. In the pro forma projections in Table 22.2, Zinsmeister's total external financing actually declined by $6.7 million.[1] Why the discrepancy? Closer examination of the pro forma statements reveals that several of the assumptions in Equation 22.2 do not hold when we conduct a more complete analysis. For

---

[1] The figure in Table 22.2 includes a $5 million reduction in long-term debt and a $1.7 million reduction in the line of credit. The figure in this equation is still imprecise because the interest expense and outstanding debt figures in Table 22.2 are not fully reconciled.

COMPARATIVE CORPORATE FINANCE

Financial Forecasting at Seagram

In the late 1990s, the Seagram Company, a Canadian beverage and entertainment company, purchased Polygram NV from Royal Phillips Electronics NV for about $10.5 billion. The deal created the world's largest music company with revenues exceeding $6 billion. However, an acquisition of that size was a financial strain for Seagram, which saw its credit rating downgraded from A− to BBB−. Naturally, Seagram's loan spreads increased, its financial ratios grew weaker, and the acquisition of a foreign company exposed Seagram to foreign exchange risk to a degree that it had not previously experienced.

To address these problems, senior managers at Seagram developed a rolling 12-month cash flow forecasting system for all the separate businesses of the firm. Seagram's treasury group developed a standard Excel-based template to capture cash flow data in multiple currencies. Executive Tim Deloso describes the complexity of their spreadsheet model:

Because the system had multi-currency capabilities, separate spreadsheets for each currency were submitted by each business unit. This allowed a Hong Kong dollar-functional spirits company— which imported scotch whiskey from the United Kingdom and cognac from France, yet had intercompany payments to the group headquarters in

U.S. dollars—to capture all cashflow data through four separate currency templates. For the Europe, Middle East, Africa and Asia regions whose treasury activities were managed out of London, this involved 100+ templates for 40+ business units with annual sales and net cashflow movements of $5 billion and $500 million, respectively.

The cash flow forecasting tool had four major objectives. First, Seagram wanted better forecasts to ensure that it would be able to retire a large amount of its outstanding debt over time with free cash flow. Second, with a decline in its credit ratings and increases in the cost of borrowing money, Seagram saw an urgent need for better cash flow numbers to manage liquidity and funding issues. Third, the company believed it was more important than ever for it to manage foreign exchange and interest rate risk exposures, and that could not be done without solid cash flow data. Fourth, the company wanted to release some of the data generated by the system to external stakeholders such as analysts, rating agencies, and banks. By communicating its results externally, Seagram believed that it could quickly improve its credit position and generate value for its shareholders.

Source: Tim Deloso, "Implementing a Strategic Cashflow Forecasting Program," *GT News* (February 15, 2002).

---

instance, from 2004 to 2005, Zinsmeister's ratio of assets to sales is not constant, as the equation assumes; instead, the ratio declines from 0.465 to 0.419. Zinsmeister is increasing sales more rapidly than assets, so its funding needs are actually less than Equation 22.2 assumes. The apparent need for external funding revealed by Equation 22.2 turns into a financial surplus when we build projections on an account-by-account basis as in Table 22.2.

This discussion has presented two important points. First, shorthand approaches such as the sustainable growth model or the equation for determining **external funds required** help managers look ahead to determine whether they should expect a scarcity or a surplus of financial resources given the firm's growth objectives. Second, a more complete picture of a firm's funding requirements can be constructed by building pro forma balance sheets and income statements, leaving one variable on the balance sheet as a plug figure. Managers can use any of these models to avoid unpleasant financial surprises a year or two ahead.

Besides planning for growth that will occur over a period of years, companies also construct financial plans with shorter time horizons. These plans generally focus on temporary cash surpluses or deficits that firms face because of seasonal fluctuations in transactions volume. The next section examines this dimension of financial planning.

**Concept
Review
Questions**

3. Explain the difference between a firm's sustainable growth rate and its optimal growth rate. In what circumstances is a firm's optimal growth rate likely to exceed its sustainable rate, and under what conditions would you expect the opposite to be true?

4. Current asset accounts, especially cash and inventory, usually increase at a rate slightly less than the growth rate in sales. Why? If true, what is the implication of that fact for the sustainable growth model?

22.3 PLANNING AND CONTROL

SHORT-TERM FINANCING STRATEGIES

Several factors cause a firm's sales volume to fluctuate over time. In the previous section, we observed that most firms establish growth as one of their long-term objectives. Therefore, when we look at the sales volume generated by a particular company historically, it is not unusual to observe a distinct upward trend. However, during a single year, many firms experience sharp quarter-to-quarter sales changes due to seasonal factors. Construction-related businesses generate much higher volume in the summer than they do in the winter. In contrast, toy companies experience peak volume in the winter.

Therefore, because sales volume tends to fluctuate around a long-term upward trend, we expect to observe the same pattern when we examine a firm's total assets over time. As sales volume grows, so does the firm's need for fixed and current assets. During the year, a firm's investment in current assets will tend to rise and fall with sales, and this seasonal pattern creates temporary cash surpluses and deficits that the firm must manage.

For example, Panel A of Figure 22.2 plots quarterly sales figures for Hershey Foods from 1992 through the second quarter of 2002. Hershey's fiscal year matches the calendar year, so its quarterly income statements report sales for quarters ending in March, June, September, and December each year. For Hershey, sales usually peak in the third or fourth quarter of each year, whereas sales troughs typically occur in the second quarter. Panel A of Figure 22.2 also reveals a gradual upward trend in Hershey sales, at least from 1992 to 1999. That growth trend leveled off from 2000 to 2002 with the U.S. economic recession.

Panel B of Figure 22.2 plots Hershey's current assets over the same period. The patterns closely match those in Panel A of Figure 22.2. Hershey's current assets show the same seasonal pattern (with a lag of one quarter) and the same upward trend that the company's sales follow. Hershey builds current assets, mostly inventory and receivables, during the third and fourth quarters of each year, and it draws down these items during the first and second quarters.

Because Hershey's current assets fluctuate around a long-term upward trend, we can think of the company's current assets as containing both a temporary and a permanent component. The temporary component reflects the differences between the seasonal peaks and troughs of Hershey's business, and the permanent component represents the minimal investment in current assets that Hershey maintains, even during the quarters when business is slow. Hershey's fixed assets (not shown in the figure) do not exhibit the seasonal pattern that sales and current assets do, but fixed assets do follow the long-term upward trend, essentially following the long-term growth in Hershey's sales.

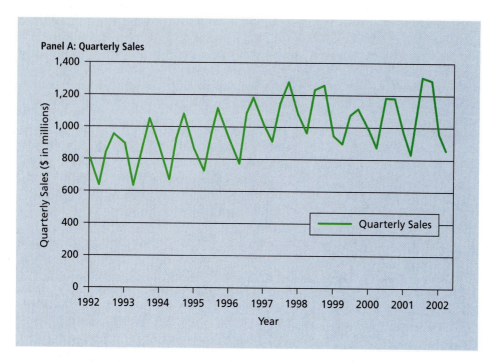

Panel A: Quarterly Sales

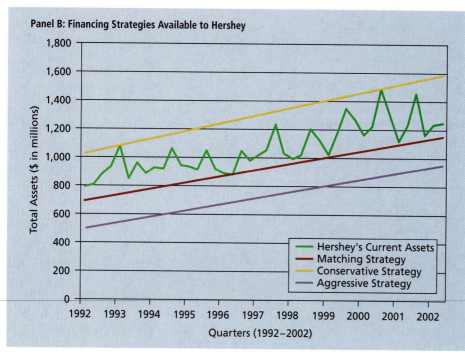

Panel B: Financing Strategies Available to Hershey

Figure 22.2
Quarterly Sales and Assets for Hershey Foods (1992 through the second quarter of 2002)

Panel A shows the seasonal pattern in Hershey's sales, and Panel B shows a similar pattern for current assets. Panel B assumes that Hershey finances all of its fixed assets and a portion of its current assets with long-term financing, with the straight lines representing the amount of current assets covered by Hershey's long-term financing. The purple line represents an aggressive strategy in the sense that Hershey does not secure enough long-term financing to cover the permanent component of the growth in current assets. The yellow line is a conservative strategy because Hershey has sufficient long-term financing to pay for both the permanent upward trend and the seasonal fluctuations in assets. The red line is a matching strategy, a middle-of-the-road approach in which Hershey finances permanent assets (fixed assets plus the permanent component of current assets) with long-term funding sources, and finances temporary or seasonal asset requirements with short-term debt.

What financing strategies might Hershey employ to fund both the long-term trend and the seasonal fluctuations in its business? First, Hershey might adopt a **conservative strategy,** making sure that it has enough long-term financing to cover both its permanent investments in fixed and current assets and the additional investments in current assets that it makes during the third and fourth quarters each year. For example, Hershey might issue long-term bonds to generate enough cash to cover all its

cash needs for several years. If Hershey followed this type of strategy, represented graphically by the yellow line in Panel B of Figure 22.2, it would typically have a cash surplus, drawing down that surplus only when business volume reaches its peak each year. Hershey will invest its excess cash balances in marketable securities. We describe this strategy as conservative because it minimizes the risk that Hershey will experience a liquidity crisis during peak quarters. However, keep in mind that large investments in cash and marketable securities are not likely to make Hershey shareholders rich.[2] Furthermore, because the term structure of interest rates is typically upward sloping, Hershey will generally pay higher interest rates on its long-term debt than it would pay if it were willing to borrow on a short-term basis.

The second strategy that Hershey might adopt is much more aggressive. In this **aggressive strategy,** Hershey relies heavily on short-term borrowing, not only to meet the seasonal peaks each year but also to finance a portion of the long-term growth in sales and assets. In Panel B of Figure 22.2, the aggressive strategy appears as the purple line. The difference between that line and the one representing Hershey's current assets indicates how much short-term debt Hershey has outstanding at any moment in time. During peak quarters, Hershey increases its short-term borrowings, but even during the first and second quarters, when business is relatively slow, Hershey continues to finance at least part of its operations with short-term debt. This implies that Hershey uses short-term financing to fund a portion of its long-term, or permanent, growth in assets. In this strategy, Hershey takes advantage of short-term interest rates, which, as previously noted, are usually lower than long-term rates. However, if short-term rates rise, Hershey will face increased interest expense. Hershey also faces a significant refinancing risk in this strategy. That is, if Hershey's financial condition weakens, it may not be able to roll over short-term debt as it had in the past.

A third strategy that Hershey might follow is known as the **matching strategy,** represented in Panel B of Figure 22.2 by the red line. Firms that follow the matching strategy finance permanent assets (fixed assets plus the permanent component of current assets) with long-term funding sources, and they finance their temporary or seasonal asset requirements with short-term debt. In the figure, notice that Hershey will increase short-term borrowing during peak periods, and it will repay those loans as it draws down its investments in current assets during slow periods. The matching strategy is a middle-of-the-road approach compared to the other alternatives. If Hershey finances its short-term asset requirements with short-term debt, then it will have smaller cash surpluses than under the conservative approach, but its borrowing costs will be lower, on average, because it substitutes less costly short-term debt for long-term debt. Hershey's interest costs will be higher under the matching approach than in the aggressive strategy, but it will face less exposure to refinancing risk, and its interest costs will not fluctuate as much quarter to quarter.

Regardless of which strategy Hershey decides to pursue, the company will pay very careful attention to short-term inflows and outflows of cash. Doing so will allow the company to invest unanticipated cash surpluses and cover unexpected deficits. The primary tool for managing cash flow on a short-term basis is the cash budget.

Smart Concepts

See the concept explained step-by-step at

---

[2] Companies sometimes argue that a large cash reserve is a strategic asset because it enables the firm to make acquisitions quickly as opportunities arise. We agree that, in principle, a cash reserve could have strategic value, but it also enables managers to make value-reducing investments without facing the discipline of raising money in the capital markets. As you will see in Chapter 24, the research evidence suggests that managers of acquiring firms generally do not create wealth for their shareholders.

THE CASH BUDGET

Managers use the tools described in Section 22.2 to make financial projections over horizons of a year or more, but firms also need to monitor their financial performance at higher frequencies. Because it takes cash to operate on a day-to-day basis, firms monitor their cash inflows and outflows very closely, and the primary tool they use to do that monitoring is the cash budget.

A **cash budget** is a statement of the firm's planned inflows and outflows of cash. Firms use the cash budget to ensure that they will have enough cash available to meet short-term financial obligations and that any surplus cash resources can be invested quickly and efficiently. Typically, the cash budget spans a 1-year period, with more frequent breakdowns provided as components of the budget. The CFO of The Finish Line, a specialty retailer, once described his company to us as a "cash and inventory business." What he meant was that running a successful retail enterprise requires very close attention to managing cash flows and inventory holdings. A company like The Finish Line needs to know its exact cash position at the end of every business day. For other firms, monitoring cash positions on a weekly or monthly basis may be sufficient. Besides the volume of cash transactions that a business must process, other factors that determine the frequency with which cash budgets are constructed include the volatility of prices and volume and the importance of seasonal fluctuations.

Running out of cash is an ever-present threat at small and medium-size companies, especially those that are growing rapidly. However, astonishing changes in cash reserves can occur over just a few years, even in large corporations. For example, in December 1999, Boeing Co. reported cash and marketable security holdings in excess of $4.4 billion. Just two years later, that figure had fallen to $0.6 billion. Over the same two years, cash holdings at Phillip Morris, United Parcel Service, and Sears Roebuck fell $4.7 billion, $4.6 billion, and $2.8 billion, respectively. With the possibility of dramatic swings in cash holdings such as these, even large firms have to monitor their cash position closely.

As was the case with pro forma financial statements, the key input required to build a cash budget is the firm's sales forecast. On the basis of the forecast, the financial manager estimates the monthly cash inflows that will result from cash sales and receivable collections. Naturally, a complete cash budget also contains estimates of cash outflows, some of which vary directly with sales and some of which do not. Cash outlays include purchases of raw materials, labor and other production expenses, selling expenses, fixed asset investments, and so on. A cash budget usually presents project inflows first, then projected spending and the net cash inflow or outflow for the period. Depending on the firm's cash balance at the start of the period, the cash budget will either reveal a need for additional financing or demonstrate that the firm will have surplus cash to invest in short-term securities.

SMART PRACTICES VIDEO

Beth Acton, Vice President and Treasurer of Ford Motor Co. (former)

"Because there is a long cycle of developing product from concept to customer, it is critical that we understand what the business implications are for the business planning period."

See the entire interview at **SMARTFinance**

Cash Receipts

Cash receipts include all the firm's cash inflows in a given period. The most common components of cash receipts are cash sales, collections of accounts receivable, and

Table 22.3
Schedule of Projected
Cash Receipts for Farrell
Industries ($ in thousands)

	August	September	October	November	December
Forecast sales	$100	$200	$400	$300	$200
Cash sales (20%)	$20	$ 40	$ 80	$ 60	$ 40
Collection of accounts receivable					
Previous month (50%)		50	100	200	150
Two months prior (30%)			30	60	120
Other cash receipts					30
Total cash receipts			$210	$320	$340

other cash receipts. The collections of accounts receivable are estimated using the payment patterns of the firm's customers.[3]

APPLYING THE MODEL

Consider the cash receipts projections of Farrell Industries, a candy manufacturer, which is developing a cash budget for October, November, and December. Farrell's sales in August and September were $100,000 and $200,000, respectively. Sales of $400,000, $300,000, and $200,000 have been forecast for October, November, and December, respectively. Typically, 80 percent of Farrell's sales are on credit, and 20 percent are cash sales. Farrell collects about half of each month's sales in the next month, and it has to wait two months to collect the remaining 30 percent of sales. Bad debts for Farrell have been negligible. In December, the firm expects to receive a $30,000 dividend from stock it holds in a subsidiary.

Table 22.3 presents the schedule of receipts. The first row shows total sales in each month. Remember, the figures for October–December are projections. The second row lists cash sales in each month, which, by assumption, equal 20 percent of total monthly sales. The third and fourth rows report the expected cash inflows from collecting receivables from the previous two months' sales. The next line reports cash inflows not related to sales, and the final line shows total cash inflows each month.

For example, consider the month of November. Projected sales are $300,000, which implies that expected cash sales equal $60,000. During November, Farrell expects to collect receivables equal to half of October's $400,000 sales, or $200,000. Farrell also expects to collect the 30 percent of September sales still on the books as receivables, or $60,000. No other cash flows are expected in November, so total cash inflows equal $320,000.

Cash Disbursements

Cash disbursements include all outlays of cash by the firm during the period. The most common cash disbursements are cash purchases, fixed asset outlays, payments of accounts payable, wages, interest payments, taxes, and rent and lease payments, but cash disbursements may also include items such as dividends and share repurchases. It is important to remember that depreciation and other noncash expenses are *not* included in the cash budget because they merely represent a scheduled write-off

---

[3.] We discuss payment patterns more fully in the next chapter.

of an earlier cash outflow. Depreciation does have a cash outflow effect through its impact on tax payments.

APPLYING THE MODEL

To demonstrate a schedule of cash disbursements, we continue with Farrell Industries, which has gathered the following data needed for the preparation of a cash disbursements schedule for October, November, and December.

Purchases: The firm's purchases average 70 percent of sales. Of this amount, Farrell pays 10 percent in cash, 70 percent in the month following the purchase, and the remaining 20 percent two months following the purchase. Thus, October purchases are $280,000 (70% × $400,000) with $28,000 (10% × $280,000) paid in cash, $196,000 (70% × $280,000) paid on account in November, and $56,000 (20% × $280,000) paid on account in December.

Rent payments: Rent of $5,000 will be paid each month.

Wages and salaries: The firm's wages and salaries equal 10 percent of monthly sales plus $8,000. Thus, October's wages and salaries will be $48,000 [(10% × $400,000) + $8,000]. The figures for November and December are calculated in the same manner.

Tax payments: Taxes of $25,000 must be paid in December.

Fixed asset outlays: New machinery costing $130,000 will be purchased and paid for in November.

Interest payments: An interest payment of $10,000 is due in December.

Cash dividend payments: Cash dividends of $20,000 will be paid in October.

Principal payments: A $20,000 principal payment is due in December.

Table 22.4 presents the firm's disbursement schedule, based on the preceding data. ∎

Net Cash Flow, Ending Cash, Financing Needs, and Excess Cash

We can calculate the firm's net cash flow by subtracting its cash disbursements from its cash receipts for each period. By adding the beginning cash balance to the firm's net cash flow, we determine the ending cash balance for each period. Like most com-

	August	September	October	November	December
Purchases (70% of sales)	$70	$140	$280	$210	$140
Cash purchases (10%)	$ 7	$ 14	$ 28	$ 21	$ 14
Payments of accounts payable					
~~Previous month (70%)~~		49	98	196	147
Two months prior (20%)			14	28	56
Rent payments			5	5	5
Wages and salaries			48	38	28
Tax payments					25
Fixed asset outlays				130	
Interest payments					10
Cash dividend payments			20		
Principal payments					20
Total cash disbursements			$213	$418	$305

Table 22.4
Schedule of Projected Cash Disbursements for Farrell Industries ($ in thousands)

panies, Farrell does not want its cash balance to dip below some minimum level at any time. Therefore, by subtracting the desired minimum cash balance from the ending cash balance, we arrive at the required total financing or the excess cash balance. If the ending cash balance is less than the desired minimum cash balance, then the firm has a short-term financing need. This need is met using notes payable. If the ending cash balance exceeds the desired minimum cash balance, then the firm has an excess cash balance that it can invest in short-term marketable securities.

APPLYING THE MODEL

Table 22.5 presents the cash budget for Farrell Industries based on the cash receipt and disbursement schedules developed in earlier examples and the following additional information: (1) Farrell's cash balance at the end of September is $50,000, (2) notes payable and marketable securities are $0 at the end of September, and (3) the desired minimum cash balance is $25,000.

For Farrell to maintain its desired minimum ending cash balance of $25,000, it will have notes payable (short-term borrowing) balances of $76,000 in November and $41,000 in December. In October, the firm will have excess cash of $22,000, which it can invest in marketable securities. The required total financing figures in the cash budget refer to *how much will be owed at the end of each month,* but the figures do not represent the monthly change in borrowing. For Farrell, the monthly financial activities are as follows:

October: Invest $22,000 of excess cash.
November: Liquidate $22,000 of excess cash and borrow $76,000. Net cash flow of −$98,000 uses all the available cash reserves ($25,000 minimum cash balance from October + $22,000 excess cash), leaving an ending cash balance of −$51,000. To cover the negative balance ($51,000) and the desired minimum cash balance ($25,000), Farrell must borrow $76,000.
December: Repay $35,000 of amount borrowed. Net cash flows of $35,000 reduced Farrell's end-of-month borrowing needs to $41,000, which is a reduction from November's borrowing needs of $76,000. Thus, Farrell repays $35,000 of the amount borrowed.

Table 22.5
Cash Budget for Farrell Industries ($ in thousands)

	October	November	December
Total cash receipts[a]	$210	$320	$340
Less: Total cash disbursements[b]	213	418	305
Net cash flow	−$ 3	−$ 98	$ 35
Add: Beginning cash	50	47	− 51
Ending cash balance	$ 47	−$ 51	−$ 16
Less: Minimum cash balance	25	25	25
Required total financing (notes payable)[c]		$ 76	$ 41
Excess cash balance (marketable securities)[d]	$ 22		

[a]From Table 22.3.
[b]From Table 22.4.
[c]Values are placed on this line when the ending cash balance is *less than* the desired minimum cash balance. These amounts are typically financed short-term, and therefore are represented by notes payable.
[d]Values are placed on this line when the ending cash balance is *greater than* the desired minimum cash balance. These amounts are typically invested in short-term vehicles and therefore are represented by marketable securities.

The cash budget provides the firm with figures indicating whether a cash short-age (financing need) or a cash surplus (short-term investment opportunity) is expected in each of the months covered by the forecast. Farrell Industries can expect a cash surplus of $22,000 in October, followed by cash shortages of $76,000 in November and $41,000 in December. Each of these values is based on the internal constraint of a minimum cash balance of $25,000.

Because the firm expects to borrow as much as $76,000 during the 3-month period, the financial manager should establish a line of credit to ensure the availability of the necessary funds. The maximum amount of borrowing available on the line of credit should exceed the $76,000 forecast to allow for errors in the forecast.

Because the cash budget provides only month-end totals, it does not ensure that the firm has sufficient credit to cover intramonth financing needs. For example, if a firm's disbursements occur before its receipts during a month, then its intramonth borrowing needs will exceed the monthly totals shown in its cash budget. To assure sufficient credit, the firm may forecast its expected receipts and disbursement on a daily basis and use these estimates along with its cash budget to request adequate credit to cover its maximum expected cash deficit.

Though it is usually the responsibility of the finance group to create a firm's cash budget, the monthly cash surpluses and deficits predicted in the budget are affected by virtually all facets of a firm's operations. For example, changes in receivables collection or payment patterns and changes in inventory turnover can have a dramatic impact on financing needs. Any action that slows collections from customers or accelerates payments to suppliers will increase monthly financial deficits (or reduce surpluses). In that sense, almost any functional area in the firm can affect, or be affected by, the cash budget.

APPLYING THE MODEL

Consider the effect of a change in customer payment patterns on Farrell Industries. In the original example, Farrell Industries had a collection pattern on its accounts receivable as follows: (1) 20 percent cash sales, (2) 50 percent collected one month after sale, and (3) 30 percent collected two months after sale. This pattern resulted in (1) a $22,000 cash surplus in October, (2) $76,000 total borrowing in November, and (3) $41,000 total borrowing in December.

Now assume that Farrell Industries has a slowdown in its collection pattern, perhaps due to the effects of an economic recession. The new pattern is (1) 5 percent cash sales, (2) 40 percent collected after one month, (3) 50 percent collected after two months, and (4) 5 percent uncollectible. This collection pattern changes Farrell's cash receipts to (1) $150,000 in October, (2) $275,000 in November, and (3) $360,000 in December. If Farrell's cash disbursements remain unchanged, the cash budget will show the following: (1) $38,000 total borrowing in October, (2) $181,000 total borrowing in November, and (3) $126,000 total borrowing in December. Comparing these values to the initial collection pattern, it is clear that Farrell's short-term financing requirements have increased.

Two important points were demonstrated in the preceding example. First, changes in a firm's collection or payment pattern alter the timing and magnitude of its financing needs. Second, a slowdown in collections increases the firm's short-term financing needs. Conversely, one would expect a speedup in collections to decrease the firm's financing needs. With regard to payment patterns, a speedup in payments

would likely increase the firm's financing needs, whereas a slowdown in payments would reduce financing needs. The next chapter focuses on the management of working capital accounts such as cash, inventory, receivables, and payables. By managing these items carefully, firms can increase the profitability of their enterprises and lower the need for external financing.

In this chapter, we have emphasized the importance of financial planning and illustrated a few of the most widely used tools of the trade. We want to end with a word of caution. When firms construct financial plans, they clearly hope to meet the plans' goals. But the value of planning is not just in attaining established goals. Rather, its importance derives from the thinking it forces managers to do, not only about what they expect to occur in the future, but what they will do if their expectations are not realized. After all, as the Scottish poet Robert Burns reminds us in "To a Mouse, on Turning Up Her Nest with a Plough,"

SMART PRACTICES VIDEO
Jackie Sturm, Director of Finance for Technology and Manufacturing, Intel Corp.
"I think that one of the things that makes our planning process so elaborate is the opaqueness of our demand situation coupled with the long lead time we have to be able to respond to the market."

See the entire interview at **SMARTFinance**

> The best laid schemes o' mice an' men
> Gang aft a-gley,
> An' lea'e us nought but grief an' pain
> For promis'd joy.

Concept Review Questions

5. Suppose that a firm follows the matching principle. Does this imply that the firm's current assets will equal its current liabilities?

6. Why do firms prepare cash budgets? How do (a) collection patterns and (b) payment patterns impact the cash budget?

7. What does sensitivity analysis add to the cash budgeting process? Why might an intramonth view of the firm's cash flows cause a well-prepared cash budget to fail?

22.4 SUMMARY

- Strategic (long-term) financial plans act as a guide for preparing operating (short-term) financial plans. For most firms, strategic plans are driven by competitive forces that are not always explicitly financial in nature. However, strategic plans have important financial consequences.

- Finance acts as a business partner with other functional units in developing the firm's strategic plan. Once the plan is established, it is the job of finance to ensure that the plan is feasible given the firm's financial resources. Finance also plays a crucial role in monitoring progress vis-à-vis the plan and in managing risks associated with the plan.

- The sustainable growth model is a tool that managers can use to determine the feasibility of a target growth rate under certain conditions. When the growth rate that maximizes shareholder value does not match the sustainable rate, the firm must make adjustments to the model's assumptions, such as altering leverage or dividend policy, to achieve the desired growth rate.

- Pro forma financial statements are projected, or forecast, financial statements, typically based on the historical financial relationships within the firm. The key inputs to pro forma statements are financial statements from the preceding year, the sales forecast for the coming year, and a variety of assumptions. The pro forma

income statement can be prepared by using the percentage-of-sales method, which assumes that all costs are variable or, preferably, by breaking all costs and expenses into fixed and variable components to achieve greater accuracy.

- A cash budget forecasts the short-term cash inflows and outflows of a firm. For a firm with significant seasonal variations in the flow of business, the financial manager typically prepares the cash budget month by month for an entire year. This allows the firm to determine peak borrowing needs and peak short-term investment opportunities, typically over a 1-year period.

- The financial manager often applies sensitivity analysis to the cash budget to assess financing needs under the most adverse situations. Attention must also be given to intramonth cash flows to assure that sufficient credit is available. Changes in collection and payment periods, which change the cash conversion cycle, can significantly impact the magnitude and timing of the firm's cash flows and the resulting financing reflected in its cash budget.

INTERNET RESOURCES

Note: *For updates to links, please go to the book's website at* *http://smart.swcollege.com*

http://www.sba.gov (Small Business Administration)—Provides useful resources for managing small businesses

http://www.toolkit.cch.com—Provides a number of interesting resources, including a cash budgeting spreadsheet template

http://www.journalfp.net—Website of the *Journal of Financial Planning,* a journal devoted to research on corporate planning

http://www.fpanet.org—Website of the Financial Planning Association

http://www.gtnews.com—An excellent site for news regarding cash and treasury management functions

KEY TERMS

aggressive strategy	matching strategy
bottom-up	percentage-of-sales method
cash budget	plug figure
cash disbursements	pro forma financial statements
cash receipts	strategic plan
conservative strategy	sustainable growth model
external funds required	top-down

QUESTIONS

22-1. What is the financial planning process? Define and contrast strategic (long-term) financial plans and operating (short-term) financial plans.

22-2. Describe the roles that financial managers play with regard to strategic planning.

22-3. What does the word *sustainable* mean in "sustainable growth model"?

22-4. In what ways can the sustainable growth model highlight conflicts between a firm's competing objectives?

Smart Solutions
See the problem and solution explained step-by-step at
SMARTFinance

22-5. With reference to Equation 22.1, explain how each of the variables influences the firm's sustainable growth rate.

22-6. If high leverage allows a firm to increase its sustainable growth rate, does that mean that higher leverage is necessarily good for the firm?

22-7. A firm chooses to grow at a rate above its sustainable rate. What changes might we expect to see on the firm's financial statements in the next year?

22-8. A firm chooses to grow at a rate below its sustainable rate. What changes might we expect to see on the firm's financial statements in the next year?

22-9. What is the logic of the percentage-of-sales method for calculating pro forma statements?

22-10. On a year-to-year basis, which balance sheet and income statement items do you think will fluctuate most closely with sales, and which items are not likely to vary as directly with sales volume?

22-11. Describe the differences between top-down and bottom-up sales forecasting methods. Describe advantages and disadvantages of each. Do you think one approach is likely to be more accurate than the other?

22-12. Why does it make sense to let the firm's cash balance or a short-term liability account serve as the plug figure in pro forma projections? Why not use gross fixed assets as the plug?

22-13. Why might pro forma statements and the equation for external funds requirement yield different projections for a firm's financing needs?

22-14. How is a cash budget different from a set of pro forma financial statements? Why do you think that firms typically create cash budgets at higher frequencies than they create pro forma statements?

22-15. Explain how slower inventory turns, slower receivables collections, or faster payments to suppliers would influence the numbers produced by a cash budget.

PROBLEMS

Planning for Growth

22-1. Go to http://yahoo.com or another financial website, and download the most recent two years' balance sheets and income statements for a firm of your choice. Do not choose a firm that issued or retired a significant amount of common stock in either year.

a. Calculate the actual percentage change in sales from two years ago to last year.
b. Using the balance sheet and income statement from two years ago, calculate the firm's sustainable growth rate.
c. If the sustainable growth rate does not equal the actual growth rate in sales, explain how changes in the firm's financial ratios in the second year reflected the firm's decision in the previous year to grow at a rate other than the sustainable rate.

22-2. Eisner Amusement Parks reported the following data in its most recent annual report:

Sales $42.5 million
Net income $3.8 million
Dividends $1.1 million
Assets $50 million

Eisner is financed 100 percent with equity. What is the company's sustainable growth rate? Suppose that Eisner issued bonds to the public and used the proceeds to repur-

chase half of its outstanding shares. This recapitalization would create additional interest expenses of $2 million. Assuming that the company faces a 35 percent tax rate, what impact would this restructuring have on its sustainable growth rate?

22-3. Below are abbreviated financial statements for the last two years for the Norne Energy Corp. All values are expressed in British pounds (£) in billions.

Norne Energy Corp.
Balance Sheet

	2005	2004
Current assets	£2.7	£2.5
Fixed assets	3.5	3.4
Total assets	£6.2	£5.9
Current liabilities	£1.9	£1.8
Long-term debt	2.1	2.2
Shareholders' equity	2.2	1.9
Total liabilities and equity	£6.2	£5.9

Norne Energy Corp.
Income Statement

	2005	2004
Sales	£7.5	£7.1
Net income	0.5	0.4
Dividends	0.2	0.1

a. What was Norne's sustainable growth rate at the end of 2004?
b. How rapidly did Norne actually grow in 2005?
c. What changes in Norne's financial condition from 2004 to 2005 can you trace to the difference between the actual and sustainable growth rates?

22-4. The 2005 sales forecast for Clearwater Development Co. is $150 million. Interest expense will not change in the coming year. Clearwater's 2004 income statement appears below ($ in thousands):

Clearwater Development Co.
Income Statement

Sales	$125,000
Less: Cost of goods sold	80,000
Gross profit	$ 45,000
Less: Operating expenses	$ 30,000
Less: Interest	$ 10,000
Pretax profit	$ 5,000
Less: Taxes (35%)	1,750
Net income	$ 3,250

a. Use the percentage-of-sales method to construct a pro forma income statement for 2005.
b. You learn that 25 percent of the cost of goods sold and operating expense figures for 2004 are fixed costs that will not change in 2005. Reconstruct the pro forma income statement.
c. Compare and contrast the statement prepared in parts (a) and (b). Which statement will likely provide the better estimate of 2005 income? Explain.

22-5. Hill Propane Distributors wants to construct a pro forma balance sheet for 2005. Build the statement using the following data and assumptions:

a. Projected sales for 2005 are $35 million.
b. Hill's gross profit margin is 35 percent.
c. Operating expenses average 10 percent of sales.
d. Depreciation expense last year was $5 million.
e. Hill faces a tax rate of 35 percent.
f. Hill distributes 20 percent of its net income to shareholders as a dividend.
g. Hill wants to maintain a minimum cash balance of $3 million.
h. Accounts receivable equal 8.5 percent of sales.
i. Inventory averages 10 percent of cost of goods sold.
j. Last year's balance sheet lists net fixed assets of $30 million. All these assets are depreciated on a straight-line basis, and none of them will be fully depreciated for at least three years.
k. Hill plans to invest an additional $1 million in fixed assets that it will depreciate over a 5-year life on a straight-line basis.
l. In 2004, Hill reported common stock and retained earnings of $20 million.
m. Accounts payable averages 9 percent of sales.

Will Hill Propane's cash balance at the end of 2005 exceed its minimum requirement of $3 million?

22-6.   The 2004 income statement and balance sheet for T. F. Baker Cosmetics Inc. appear below. The numerical values are in thousands of dollars.

T. F. Baker Cosmetics Inc.
Balance Sheet

Cash	$ 5,000	Accounts payable	$10,000
Accounts receivable	12,500	Short-term bank loan	15,000
Inventory	10,000	Long-term debt	10,000
Current assets	$27,500	Common stock	15,000
Gross fixed assets	$65,000	Retained earnings	12,500
Less: accum. depr.	30,000	Total liabilities and equity	$62,500
Net fixed assets	$35,000		
Total assets	$62,500		

T. F. Baker Cosmetics Inc.
Income Statement

Sales	$150,000
Less: Cost of goods sold	120,000
Gross profit	$ 30,000
Less: Operating expenses	$ 15,000
Less: Depreciation	5,000
Less: Interest expense	2,000
Pretax profit	$ 8,000
Less: Taxes (35%)	2,800
Net income	$ 5,200

At a recent board meeting, the firm decided on the following objectives for 2005:

a. The firm would increase liquidity. For competitive reasons, accounts receivable and inventory balances were expected to continue their historical relationships with sales and cost of goods sold, respectively, but the board felt that the company should double its cash holdings.
b. The firm would accelerate payments to suppliers. This would have two effects. First, by paying more rapidly, the firm would be able to take advantage of early payment discounts, which would increase its gross margin from 20 percent to 22 percent.

Second, by paying earlier, the firm's accounts payable balance, which historically averaged about one-twelfth of cost of goods sold, would decline to 4 percent of cost of goods sold.

c. The firm would expand its warehouse, which would require an investment in fixed assets of $10 million. This would increase projected depreciation expense in 2005 from $5 million to $7 million.

d. The firm would issue no new common stock during the year, and it would initiate a dividend. Dividend payments in 2005 would total $1.2 million.

e. Operating expenses would remain at 10 percent of sales.

f. The firm did not expect to retire any long-term debt, and it was willing to borrow up to the limit of its current credit line with the bank, $20 million. The interest rate on its outstanding debts would average 8 percent.

g. The firm set a sales target for 2005 of $200 million.

Develop a set of pro forma statements to determine whether or not T. F. Baker can simultaneously achieve all these goals.

Planning and Control

22-7. A firm has actual sales of $50,000 in January and $70,000 in February. It expects sales of $90,000 in March and $110,000 in both April and May. Assuming that sales are the only source of cash inflow and that 60 percent of these are cash and the remainder are collected evenly over the following two months, what are the firm's expected cash receipts for March, April, and May?

Smart Solutions
See the problem and solution explained step-by-step at
SMARTFinance

22-8. Batista Fertilizer Corp. had sales of $2 million in March and $2.2 million in April. Expected sales for the next three months are $2.4 million, $2.5 million, and $2.7 million. Batista has a cash balance of $200,000 on May 1 and does not want its balance to dip below that level. Prepare a cash budget for May, June, and July given the following information:

a. Of total sales, 30 percent are for cash, 50 percent are collected in the month after the sale, and 20 percent are collected two months after the sale.

b. Batista has cash receipts from other sources of $100,000 per month.

c. The firm expects to purchase items for $2 million in each of the next three months. All purchases are paid for in cash.

d. Batista has fixed cash expenses of $150,000 per month and variable cash expenses equal to 5 percent of the previous month's sales.

e. Batista will pay a cash dividend of $300,000 in June.

f. The company must make a $250,000 loan payment in June.

g. Batista plans to acquire fixed assets worth $500,000 in July.

h. Batista must make a tax payment of $225,000 in June.

22-9. The actual sales and purchases for McEwing Inc. for September and October 2004, along with its forecast sales and purchases for the November 2004 through April 2005, follow.

Year	Month	Sales	Purchases
2004	September	$310,000	$220,000
2004	October	350,000	250,000
2004	November	270,000	240,000
2004	December	260,000	200,000
2005	January	240,000	180,000
2005	February	280,000	210,000
2005	March	300,000	200,000
2005	April	350,000	190,000

The firm makes 30 percent of all sales for cash and collects 35 percent of its sales in each of the two months following the sale. Other cash inflows are expected to be $22,000 in September and April, $25,000 in January and March, and $37,000 in February. The firm pays cash for 20 percent of its purchases. It pays for 40 percent of its purchases in the following month and for 40 percent of its purchases two months later.

Wages and salaries amount to 15 percent of the preceding month's sales. Lease expenses of $30,000 per month must be paid. Interest payments of $20,000 are due in January and April. A principal payment of $50,000 is also due in April. The firm expects a cash dividend of $30,000 in January and April. Taxes of $120,000 are due in April. The firm also intends to make a $55,000 cash purchase of fixed assets in December.

a. Assuming that the firm has a cash balance of $42,000 at the beginning of November and its desired minimum cash balance is $25,000, prepare a cash budget for November through April.

b. If the firm is requesting a line of credit, how large should the line be? Explain your answer.

22-10. Berlin Inc. expects sales of $300,000 during each of the next three months. It will make monthly purchases of $180,000 during this time. Wages and salaries are $30,000 per month plus 5 percent of sales. The firm expects to make a tax payment of $60,000 in the first month and a $45,000 purchase of fixed assets in the second month and to receive $24,000 in cash from the sale of an asset in the third month. All sales and purchases are for cash. Beginning cash and the minimum cash balance equal zero.

a. Construct a cash budget for the next three months.

b. Berlin is unsure of the level of sales, but all other figures are certain. If the most pessimistic sales figure is $240,000 per month and the most optimistic is $360,000 per month, what are the monthly minimum and maximum ending cash balances that the firm can expect for each month?

c. Discuss how the financial manager can use the data in parts (a) and (b).

23

Short-Term Financial Management*

OPENING FOCUS

Effective Short-Term Financial Management at Dell Computer

Dell Computer Corp. is one of the personal computer industry's biggest success stories. Founded by a 19-year-old college dropout, Michael Dell, in the mid-1980s, Dell has become a leader in the manufacture and distribution of personal computers. Increased demand, lower cost, greater competition, and standardization have transformed the PC market into a commodity business. Dell's competitive advantage comes not from building better computers, but from building them faster and consuming fewer resources in the process. Dell's business model emphasizes minimizing short-term investment, maintaining tight cost controls, generating high sales turnover, and owning few fixed assets.

Dell uses a direct marketing approach in which the company takes orders directly from customers. This allows Dell to build its PCs to demand rather than to an inexact sales forecast. As a result, the customers quickly get what they want. Dell strives to deliver PCs quickly, often in a few days with all of the customer's software preloaded. Also, Dell is not saddled with unwanted inventory, and it does not have to pay a distribution fee to any middlemen, such as retailers.

Dell's manufacturing strategy uses a just-in-time production process that requires the company to hold just 4 days of inventory. In contrast, its main competitor, Compaq (now part of Hewlett-Packard), holds about 23 days of inventory. A network links suppliers to Dell's worldwide manufacturing facilities and provides hourly feedback on inventory levels. This is a huge edge in an industry where the price of chips, drives, and other parts typically declines by 1 percent per week. By taking advantage of the latest prices in components, Dell lowers its production costs, which gives it the enviable choice of either taking a higher profit or undercutting its rivals' prices.

---

* A large part of this chapter was prepared with the assistance of Professor Dubos J. Masson, CCM, Cert CM, of The Resource Alliance and the University of New Orleans. The authors very much appreciate D.J.'s important contribution.

Dell's inventory turnover, on average, is three times faster than the industry average, and its total asset turnover is typically a little less than twice the industry norm.

Besides keeping only 4 days of inventories, Dell collects its receivables in about 27 days and pushes its payables out about 107 days. This means that Dell typically receives payment on the sale of a PC long before it pays suppliers for the component parts, giving the company another significant financial advantage. One sign of this advantage is Dell's high level of liquidity. Dell's cash and marketable securities are three times larger than the industry average. In a sense, this underscores Dell's short-term financial management efforts, which allow the company to respond rapidly to changes in the business environment. Industry competitors typically are cash squeezed and have to be more aggressive in reducing costs and staffing or deferring technology enhancements in order to respond to changes in the business environment.

Sources: Andrew Parks, "How Dell Keeps from Stumbling," *Business Week* (May 14, 2001), pp. 38B–38D; Peter Burrows, "Dell, the Conquerer," *Business Week* (September 24, 2001), pp. 92–102.

SMART IDEAS VIDEO
Raghu Rajan, University of Chicago
"Trade credit is probably the biggest source of finance for most firms."

See the entire interview at **SMARTFinance**

The focus in the preceding chapter was primarily on strategic planning with regard to sustainable growth rates and on operational financial planning using pro forma financial statements and the cash budget. In this chapter, we switch our focus from planning to operations and focus on the firm's short-term, or operating, assets and the funding sources for them. **Operating assets** include cash, marketable securities, accounts receivable, and inventories that are necessary for the day-to-day operation of the firm. Although it is difficult to directly measure their contribution to a firm's profitability, a firm's operating assets are needed to grow a business. For example, effective credit and inventory policies are necessary to grow the business by offering attractive credit terms and maintaining adequate inventory to meet demand quickly with infrequent stockouts. Because investments in operating assets consume the firm's scarce cash resources, they should be efficiently managed and controlled. Similarly, the **short-term financing,** which includes accounts payable, bank loans, commercial paper, international loans, and secured short-term loans, is used by the firm to finance seasonal fluctuations in current asset investments and provide the firm with adequate liquidity to achieve its growth objectives and meet its obligations in a timely manner. Therefore, the objective for managing current assets and liabilities is to be as efficient as possible, which means the firm should minimize unnecessary operating assets and maximize the use of inexpensive short-term financing, typically accounts payable. A number of liquidity and activity ratios introduced in Chapter 2 can be used to gain insight into important aspects of the firm's short-term financial management activities.

SMART PRACTICES VIDEO
Jackie Sturm, Director of Finance for Technology and Manufacturing, Intel Corp.
"Inventory loses value every day you hold it."

See the entire interview at **SMARTFinance**

What evidence can we cite suggesting that firms spend time and effort trying to economize on their investments in current (operating) assets while taking advantage of relatively inexpensive current liabilities (short-term financing)? Table 23.1 reports the median investment, expressed as a percentage of total assets, in current assets and current liabilities for a sample of 200 large U.S. companies in existence from 1981 to 2000. In 1981, current assets accounted for 37.4 percent of total assets for the median firm in this group, but by 2000 that figure had dropped to just 27.8 percent. Over the same period, the importance of current liabilities in financing these firms increased from 22.8 percent in 1981 to 26.7 percent in 2000. Table 23.1 also shows the aggregate investment in current assets and current liabilities for all U.S. manufacturing firms, expressed as a percentage of the aggregate assets of these firms. In 1981,

For a Sample of 200 Large Firms (median)		
Year	Current Assets	Current Liabilities
1981	37.4%	22.8%
2000	27.8%	26.7%

For the Aggregate Manufacturing Corporate Sector			
Year	Current Assets	Current Liabilities	Current Ratio
1981	32.2%	22.6%	1.4
2000	25.4%	21.6%	1.2

Table 23.1
Current Assets and Current Liabilities as a Percentage of Total Assets, 1981 and 2000

Source: Compustat and author's calculations.
Note: This table shows the investments made in current assets and liabilities, expressed as a percentage of total assets, for two groups of firms. The first group is made up of the 200 largest U.S. manufacturing firms with continuous operating histories since 1981. The second group includes all U.S. manufacturing firms listed on Compustat in 1981 and 2000.

current assets accounted for 32.2 percent of aggregate corporate assets, whereas current liabilities made up 22.6 percent of the financing for those assets. By 2000, those figures had changed to 25.4 percent and 21.6 percent, respectively. Put another way, the aggregate *current ratio* of U.S. manufacturing corporations declined from 1.4 in 1981 to 1.2 in 2000. These figures illustrate both the importance of and the advances in short-term financial management by U.S. firms.

A variety of forces prompted firms to find efficiencies in short-term financial management. For example, high inflation in the late 1970s and early 1980s gave firms a tremendous incentive to reduce their investments in non-interest-bearing operating assets. Perhaps even more important, developments in information technology allowed firms to become much more efficient in managing cash, investing short-term cash surpluses, monitoring receivables, managing inventories, managing payables, and establishing and monitoring short-term loans. With better access to information and the ability to move and dispatch funds electronically, firms today can operate with lower levels of operating asset investment.[1]

This chapter focuses on the efficient management of operating assets and short-term financing. We begin with a description of the cash conversion cycle, the goal for managing it, and the actions that can be used to accomplish the goal. Next, we consider the cost trade-offs in short-term financial management and then review the important aspects of accounts receivable management—credit standards, credit terms, collection policy, credit monitoring, and cash application. We next discuss cash management, followed by discussions of collections and accounts payable and disbursements. Finally, we discuss short-term investing and borrowing.

23.1 THE CASH CONVERSION CYCLE

A central concept in short-term financial management is the notion of the operating cycle. A firm's **operating cycle (OC)** measures the time that elapses from the firm's re-

---

[1] A popular professional certification in the field of cash and treasury management is the Certified Cash Manager (CCM) credential offered by the Association for Financial Professionals (http://www.afponline.org). The more than 14,000 CCMs have passed an exam reflecting the required expertise in the field of cash and treasury management, and they have agreed to participate in ongoing professional education to maintain the CCM credential.

ceipt of raw materials to begin production to its collection of cash from the sale of the finished product. As you might expect, operating cycles vary widely by industry. For instance, a bakery, which uses fresh ingredients, keeps finished goods in inventory for only a day or two, and generally sells its products for cash, will have a very short operating cycle. In contrast, semiconductor manufacturers take several months to convert raw materials into finished products, which are sold on credit. The operating cycle for such a firm may extend to six months or longer.

The operating cycle is important because it influences a company's need for internal or external financing. In general, the longer a firm's operating cycle, the greater its need for financing. For example, a bakery might pay its suppliers and its employees using the revenues generated each week, but the semiconductor manufacturer probably cannot persuade suppliers and employees to wait the months it takes to earn cash from chip sales. Therefore, the semiconductor firm has a greater need for financing to operate day to day.

The operating cycle encompasses two major short-term asset categories, inventory and accounts receivable. To calculate the operating cycle, we will use two ratios covered in Chapter 2. First, calculate the average age of inventory (AAI) and the average collection period (ACP). Next, take the sum of these two items to determine the length of the operating cycle. Table 23.2 presents the actual operating cycles for some well-known computer manufacturers and a number of other firms. The raw data for fiscal-year 2001 is given in lines 1 through 5, and the time periods for AAI, ACP, and average payment period (APP) are calculated from the raw data on lines 6 through 8, respectively. Using the AAI and ACP calculated in lines 6 and 7, the OCs are calculated for each firm in line 9. Note that among the five computer manufacturers—IBM, Dell, Gateway, Apple, and Hewlett-Packard—the make-to-order firms, Dell and Gateway, have the shortest operating cycles, closely followed by Apple. IBM and Hewlett-Packard's operating cycles of 152 and 111 days, respectively, are far longer than the 20- to 45-day range of operating cycles for Dell, Gateway, and Apple, probably as a result of their diversified computer businesses. The final four columns show the operating cycles for four noncomputer firms. Clearly, the operating cycle varies greatly across industries as well as across different types of companies within a given industry.

Most firms obtain a significant amount of the financing they need through trade credit, represented by accounts payable. By taking advantage of trade credit, a firm reduces the amount of financing it needs from other sources to make it through the operating cycle. The elapsed time between the points at which a firm pays for raw materials and at which it receives payment for finished goods is called the **cash conversion cycle** (CCC). The difference between the operating cycle and the cash conversion cycle is simply the amount of time that suppliers are willing to extend credit. In other words, to calculate the cash conversion cycle, start with the operating cycle and then subtract the *average payment period* on accounts payable. The formula for the cash conversion cycle follows:

$$CCC = OC - APP = AAI + ACP - APP \qquad \text{(Eq. 23.1)}$$

As Equation 23.1 shows, the cash conversion cycle has three main components: (1) average age of the inventory, (2) average collection period, and (3) average payment period. It also shows that if a firm changes any of these time periods, it changes the amount of time resources are tied up in the day-to-day operation of the firm.

Table 23.2
Operating Cycles (OC) and Cash Conversion Cycles (CCC) for Selected Companies, Fiscal Year 2001

	Computer Companies					Other Companies			
Data ($ in billions)	(IBM) IBM	(DELL) DELL	(GTW) Gateway	(AAPL) Apple	(HPQ) Hewlett- Packard	(ABS) Albertsons	(RL) Polo Ralph Lauren	(GM) GM	(MCD) McDonald's
(1) Sales	87.401	31.168	6.080	5.363	45.226	37.931	2.364	177.260	14.870
(2) Cost of sales	54.084	25.661	5.241	4.128	33.474	27.155	1.217	143.850	10.254
(3) A/P	15.912	7.519	.945	1.518	8.898	2.297	.359	53.513	2.071
(4) A/R	29.420	2.269	.220	.635	6.671	.853	.372	13.283	.882
(5) Inventory	4.304	.278	.120	.011	5.204	3.522	.350	14.558	.106
Time Periods (in days)									
(6) AAI [[5] ÷ [(2) ÷ 365]]	29.05	3.95	8.36	.97	56.74	47.34	104.97	36.94	3.77
(7) ACP [[4] ÷ [(1) ÷ 365]]	122.86	26.57	13.21	43.22	53.84	8.21	57.44	27.35	21.65
(8) APP [[3] ÷ [(2) ÷ 365]][a]	107.39	106.95	65.81	134.22	97.02	30.87	107.67	135.78	73.72
Cycles (in days)									
(9) OC [(6) + (7)]	151.91	30.52	21.57	44.19	110.58	55.55	162.41	64.29	25.42
(10) CCC [(9) − (8)]	44.52	−76.43	−44.24	−90.03	13.56	24.68	54.74	−71.49	−48.30

[a]Note that because "annual purchases" cannot be found in published financial statements, this value is calculated using "cost of sales" (line 2), which is an approach commonly used by external analysts. Because annual purchases are likely to be smaller than the cost of sales, these APPs may be understated.

Again referring to Table 23.2, we can see that the cash conversion cycles for each firm are calculated in line 10 by subtracting the average payment periods in line 8 from the operating cycles calculated in line 9. Reviewing the *CCC* for the computer manufacturers, we see that Dell, Gateway, and Apple have negative *CCC*s, which means that these firms effectively receive cash inflows ahead of having to make the cash outflows needed to generate those inflows. This very desirable *CCC* is in effect a pay-up-front-and-we'll-manufacture-and-ship-the-product-to-you-later type of business. The other top computer manufacturers, IBM and Hewlett-Packard, have positive but relatively short *CCC*s, reflecting very effective current account management. It is interesting to note that two of the other firms, GM and McDonald's, also have negative *CCC*s. Looking at the time periods for their *AAI*, *ACP*, and *APP* in lines 6 through 8, respectively, we can see that their vendors are effectively financing their operations given that their high *APP*s more than cover their time delays in inventory and accounts receivable. Albertsons and Polo Ralph Lauren also have relatively short, positive *CCC*s, primarily due to their somewhat lengthy inventory periods. The cash conversion cycles shown demonstrate both inter- and intraindustry differences in the amount of time firms have their money tied up.

APPLYING THE MODEL

Reese Industries, which has annual sales of $5 billion, a cost of goods sold of 70 percent of sales, and purchases that are 60 percent of cost of goods sold, can be used to demonstrate the cash conversion cycle. Reese has an *AAI* of 70 days, *ACP* of 45 days, and *APP* of 40 days. Also, the 45-day *ACP* can be broken into 37 days until the customer places the payment in the mail and an additional 8 days before the funds are available to the firm in a spendable form. Thus, Reese's operating cycle is 115 days (70 + 45), and its cash conversion cycle is 75 days (70 + 45 − 40). Figure 23.1 presents Reese's operating and cash conversion cycles on a time line.

Reese has invested the following resources in its cash conversion cycle:

   inventory = ($5 billion × 70%) × (70/365) = $671.2 million

+ accounts receivable = ($5 billion) × (45/365) = $616.4 million

− accounts payable = ($5 billion × 70% × 60%) × (40/365)
                    = $230.1 million

= resources invested of $1,057.5 million.

If Reese could reduce from 8 days to 3 days the amount of time it takes to receive, process, and collect payments after they are mailed by the firm's customers, it would reduce its average collection period to 40 days (37 + 3). This would shorten the cash conversion time line by 5 days (8 − 3) and thus reduce the amount of resources Reese has invested in operations. For Reese, a 5-day reduction in the average collection period would reduce the resources invested in the cash conversion cycle by $68.5 million [$5 billion × (5 ÷ 365)]. ■

Simply stated, in order *to positively contribute to the shareholder value-maximization goal, the financial manager should manage the firm's short-term activities in a manner that shortens the cash conversion cycle.* This will allow the firm to op-

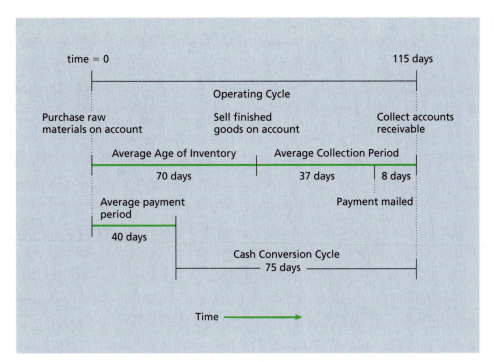

Figure 23.1
Time Line for the Operating and Cash Conversion Cycles for Reese Industries

erate effectively with minimum cash investment. Cash that is not used to fund the cash conversion cycle can be deployed to more-productive long-term investments, can be used to pay down expensive long-term financing, or can be distributed to owners as dividends. A positive cash conversion cycle means that trade credit does not provide enough financing to cover the firm's entire operating cycle. In that case, the firm must seek out other forms of financing, such as bank lines of credit, term loans, and so on. The costs of these financing sources tend to be higher than the costs of trade credit, so the firm benefits by finding ways to shorten its operating cycle or to lengthen its payment period. Actions that accomplish these objectives include the following:

1. *Turn over inventory as quickly as possible* without stockouts that result in lost sales.
2. *Collect accounts receivable as quickly as possible* without losing sales from high-pressure collection techniques.
3. *Pay accounts as slowly as possible* without damaging the firm's credit rating.
4. *Manage mail, processing, and clearing time* to reduce them when collecting from customers and increase them when paying vendors.

Techniques for implementing these four strategies are the focus of the remainder of this chapter.

Concept Review Questions

1. What does the firm's *cash conversion cycle* represent? What is the financial manager's goal with regard to it? Why?

2. How should the firm manage its inventory, accounts receivable, and accounts payable in order to reduce the length of its cash conversion cycle?

23.2 COST TRADE-OFFS IN SHORT-TERM FINANCIAL MANAGEMENT

When attempting to manage the firm's short-term accounts in a manner that minimizes cash while adequately funding the firm's operations, the financial manager must focus on competing costs. Decisions with regard to the optimum levels of both operating assets and short-term financing involve cost trade-offs. For convenience, we will view the current account decision strategies as revenue neutral and therefore examine their cost trade-offs solely with the goal of minimizing total cost. The optimum levels of the key operating assets—cash and marketable securities, accounts receivable, and inventory—involve trade-offs between the cost of holding the operating asset and the cost of maintaining too little of the asset. Figure 23.2 depicts the cost trade-offs and optimum level of a given operating asset. Cost 1 is the holding cost, which increases with larger operating asset account balances, and cost 2 is the cost of holding too little of the operating asset. The total cost is the sum of cost 1 and cost 2 associated with a given account balance for the operating asset. As noted, the optimum balance occurs at the point where total cost is minimized.

The table at the bottom of Figure 23.2 provides more detail on the specific costs for each operating asset. For example, consider cash and marketable securities. As the balance of these accounts increases, the opportunity costs (cost 1) of the funds held in the firm rise. At the same time, the illiquidity and solvency costs (cost 2) fall because the higher the cash and marketable securities balance, the greater the firm's liquidity and the lower its likelihood of becoming insolvent. The optimum balance of cash and marketable securities is therefore the one that minimizes the total of these two competing costs. The cost trade-offs for accounts receivable and inventory can be evaluated similarly using the cost descriptions given in the table and relating them to the two cost functions in the figure. Clearly, in all cases a decrease in the operating asset account balance would have the opposite effect.

The optimum level of short-term financing (accounts payable, accruals, and notes payable) involves the same type of cost trade-offs as demonstrated in Figure 23.2 for operating assets. As noted in the table, as the short-term financing balance increases, the firm faces an increasing cost of reduced liquidity (cost 1). At the same time, the firm's financing costs (cost 2) decline because short-term financing costs are lower than the alternative of using long-term debt and equity financing. Again, the optimum amount of short-term financing is that which minimizes total cost, as shown in the graph in Figure 23.2. A decrease in balance of short-term financing would have the opposite effects on the competing costs.

It should be clear from the preceding discussion that the financial manager's primary focus when managing current accounts is to minimize total cost. Each of these account balances can be evaluated quantitatively using decision models much like the often-cited economic order quantity (EOQ) inventory model, which focuses on determining the inventory order quantity that minimizes total cost. Rather than describe these models, the remainder of the chapter emphasizes effective techniques and strategies for actively managing the current accounts over which the financial manager has direct responsibility.

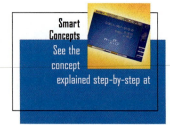

Smart
Concepts
See the
concept
explained step-by-step at

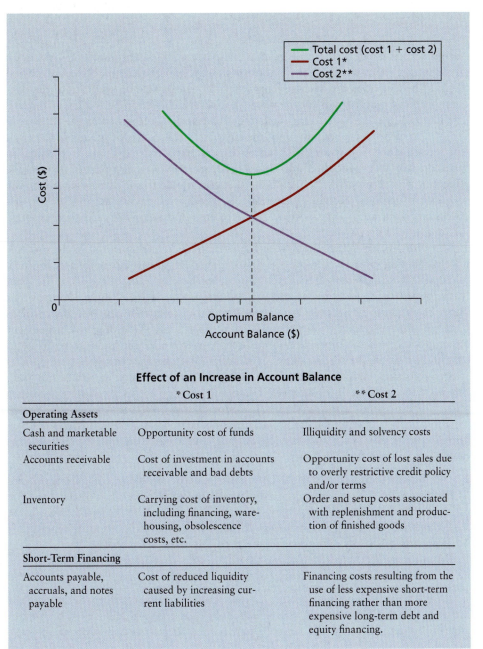

Figure 23.2
Trade-off of Short-Term
Financial Costs

Effect of an Increase in Account Balance

	* Cost 1	** Cost 2
Operating Assets		
Cash and marketable securities	Opportunity cost of funds	Illiquidity and solvency costs
Accounts receivable	Cost of investment in accounts receivable and bad debts	Opportunity cost of lost sales due to overly restrictive credit policy and/or terms
Inventory	Carrying cost of inventory, including financing, warehousing, obsolescence costs, etc.	Order and setup costs associated with replenishment and production of finished goods
Short-Term Financing		
Accounts payable, accruals, and notes payable	Cost of reduced liquidity caused by increasing current liabilities	Financing costs resulting from the use of less expensive short-term financing rather than more expensive long-term debt and equity financing.

**Concept
Review
Questions**

3. What are the general cost trade-offs that the financial manager must consider when managing the firm's operating assets? How do these costs behave as a firm considers reducing its accounts receivable by offering more-restrictive credit terms? How can the optimum balance be determined?

4. What are the general cost trade-offs associated with the firm's level of short-term financing? How do these costs behave when a firm substitutes short-term financing for long-term financing? How would you quantitatively model this decision to find the optimal level of short-term financing?

23.3 ACCOUNTS RECEIVABLE MANAGEMENT

Accounts receivable (A/R) result from a company selling its products or services on credit and are represented in the cash conversion cycle by the **average collection period** (*ACP*). This period is the average length of time from a sale on credit until the payment becomes usable funds for the firm. The average collection period has two parts. The first, and generally the longest, is the credit period, measured as the time from the sale (or customer invoicing) until the customers place their payments in the mail. The second is the time from when the customers place their payments in the mail to when the firm has spendable funds in its bank account. The first part of the average collection period involves managing the credit available to the firm's customers; the second part involves receiving, processing, and collecting payments. This section discusses customer credit, and Section 23.5 presents discussions of receiving, processing, and collecting payments.

As with all current accounts, receivables management requires managers to balance competing interests. On the one hand, managers (generally the cash or treasury managers) would prefer to receive cash payments sooner rather than later, and that leads toward strict credit terms and strict enforcement of those terms. On the other hand, firms can use credit terms as a marketing tool to attract new customers (or to keep current customers from defecting to another firm). This objective argues for easier credit terms and more flexible enforcement. It is also important to understand that in most firms, the credit policy is generally not under the control of the financial (cash or treasury) managers, but rather under the sales or customer service function. For many companies, in order to be competitive, credit terms are a very necessary part of determining the ultimate sales price for their products and services.

Effectively managing the credit and accounts receivable process involves cooperation between sales, customer service, finance, and accounting staffs. The key areas of concern involve the following:

1. Setting and communicating the company's general credit and collections policies
2. Determining who is granted credit and how much credit is allowed for each customer
3. Managing the billing and collection process in a timely and accurate manner
4. Applying payments and updating the accounts receivable ledger
5. Monitoring accounts receivable on both an individual and aggregate basis
6. Following up on overdue accounts and initiating collection procedures, if required

In the typical company, the credit and accounts receivable departments handle most of these tasks, but the cash management or treasury area will usually be responsible for managing the actual receipt of payments. As part of this process, the cash manager will usually also have to collect and organize the remittance data that is sent along with the payments so that the A/R department will be able to determine what invoices have been paid. This *cash application* process will be covered in greater detail later in the chapter.

The first decision a company must make is whether it will offer trade credit at all. There are many reasons for offering credit, including increasing or facilitating sales, meeting terms offered by competitors, attracting new customers, or providing general convenience. In a typical business-to-business environment, a company may have to offer trade credit just to generate sales. This is especially the case for a large company selling to smaller companies, where the smaller company literally needs the credit period to sell merchandise so that it can pay its supplier. The small company would not usually have access to other types of credit, so if the supplier did not offer credit, there would be no sale.

As mentioned earlier, many companies see trade credit and credit terms as simply an extension of the sales price and may use credit terms to motivate customers or compete with other suppliers. In many cases, industry practices may dictate whether credit is offered and what the terms are. In today's financial environment, there are also many opportunities for companies to outsource part or all of the credit and accounts receivable process, including use of credit cards, third-party financing, or **factoring,** which involves the outright sale of receivables to a third-party *factor* at a discount.

Once the decision has been made to offer trade credit, a company must then (1) determine its credit standards (Who gets offered credit and how much?), (2) set its credit terms (How long do customers have to pay, and are any discounts offered for early payment?), (3) develop its collection policy (How should delinquent accounts be handled?), and (4) monitor its accounts receivable on both an individual and aggregate basis (What is the status of each customer and the overall quality of its receivables?). In addition, the firm must have effective cash application procedures in place.

CREDIT STANDARDS

The first, and most important, aspect of accounts receivable management is setting credit standards, which involves application of techniques for determining which customers should receive credit and how much credit should be granted. Although much of the focus is on making sure that a company does not accept substandard customers (i.e., potential defaulters on trade credit), there is also the risk that the standards will be set too high and that potential good customers will be rejected. Accounts receivable default rates for a given company should generally be in line with those of other companies in the same industry if it wants to remain competitive.

In analyzing credit requests and determining the level of credit to be offered, the company can gather information from both internal and external sources, weighing the costs of the information against the additional benefits. The company must also take into account the variable costs of the products it would be selling on credit. For example, a company selling a product with a low variable cost (i.e., magazine subscriptions) will often grant credit to almost anyone without a credit check simply because the loss is low if payment is not made and the potential profits are great. Companies selling products with high variable costs (i.e., heavy-equipment manufacturers) will typically do extensive credit checks before granting credit and shipping merchandise.

The usual internal sources of credit information are the credit application and agreement submitted by the applicant and, if available, the company's own records of that applicant's payment history. External sources typically include financial statements, trade references, banks or other creditors, and credit reporting agencies. Using each of these sources involves the internal costs of analyzing the data, and some sources, such as credit reporting agencies, also have explicit external costs for obtaining the data.

SMART PRACTICES VIDEO
Jon Olson, Vice President of Finance, Intel Corp.
"Because cash is king, we want to make sure that we have a high quality collections organization."

See the entire interview at **SMARTFinance**

It is important to remember that the amount of credit offered (the credit limit) must also be determined. In order to reduce some of the credit decision costs, a company may routinely grant small levels of credit to new customers, allowing the credit limit to rise as the customer proves to be a good credit risk. Two popular approaches to the credit granting process are (1) the five C's of credit and (2) credit scoring.

Five C's of Credit

The **five C's of credit** provide a framework for performing in-depth credit analysis, but it does not provide a specific accept or reject decision. Therefore, application of the five C's requires an analyst experienced in reviewing and granting credit requests. Because of the time and expense involved in applying the five C's, this credit selection method is typically used for high-dollar credit requests. Although application of the five C's does not speed up collection of accounts, it lowers the probability of default. The five C's are defined as follows:

1. *Character* refers to the applicant's record of meeting past obligations. The lender would consider the applicant's past payment history, as well as any pending or resolved legal judgments against the applicant. The question addressed here is whether this applicant will pay its account, if able, within the specified credit terms.

2. *Capacity* is the applicant's ability to repay the requested credit. The lender typically assesses the applicant's capacity by using financial statement analysis focused on cash flows available to service debt obligations.

3. *Capital* refers to the financial strength of the applicant as reflected by its capital structure. The lender frequently uses analysis of the applicant's debt relative to equity and its profitability ratios to assess its capital. The analysis of capital determines if the applicant has sufficient equity to survive a business downturn.

4. *Collateral* is the assets the applicant has available for use in securing the credit. Lenders are more willing to grant credit when the borrower has assets that it can pledge as collateral for the loan. In general, the more valuable and more marketable these assets are, the more credit lenders will extend. However, trade credits are rarely secured loans. Therefore, when deciding whether or not to extend trade credit to a customer, a firm will want to know what assets the borrower has that are currently not pledged as collateral for any other outstanding debt. A lender can review the applicant's balance sheet, asset-value appraisals, and any lien filings to evaluate the available collateral. It is important to understand that collateral is a secondary source of repayment used only in the event of default. Accordingly, the collateral is not the primary consideration in deciding to grant credit but serves to strengthen the creditworthiness of a customer that appears to have sufficient cash flows to meet its obligation.

5. *Conditions* refer to current general and industry-specific economic conditions. It also considers any unique conditions surrounding a specific transaction. For example, a firm that has excess inventory of a given item may be willing to accept a lower price or extend more attractive credit terms in order to sell the item.

Credit Scoring

Credit scoring is a method of credit selection that is commonly used with high-volume–low-dollar credit requests. **Credit scoring** applies statistically derived weights (determined using *discriminant analysis*) for key financial and credit characteristics to predict whether or not a credit applicant with specific scores (assigned either subjectively by an analyst or by a computer using certain decision rules) for each characteristic will pay the requested credit in a timely fashion.[2] It uses a weighted average score derived as the sum of the products of the applicant's score and the associated predetermined weight for each characteristic to determine whether to accept or reject the credit applicant. Simply stated, the procedure results in a score that mea-

---

[2] See Srinivasan, Kim, and Eisenbeis (1987) for a discussion of various analytical methods of credit scoring.

Table 23.3
Credit Scoring of a
Consumer Credit
Application by WEG Oil

Financial and Credit Characteristics	Score (0 to 100) (1)	Predetermined Weight (2)	Weighted Score [(1) × (2)] (3)
Credit references	80	.15	12.00
Home ownership	100	.15	15.00
Income range	75	.25	18.75
Payment history	80	.25	20.00
Years at address	90	.10	9.00
Years on job	85	.10	8.50
		1.00	Credit score 83.25

Note: Column 1: Scores assigned by analyst or computer based on information supplied on credit application. Scores range from 0 (lowest) to 100 (highest). Column 2: Weights based on the company's analysis of the relative importance of each characteristic in predicting whether or not a customer will pay its account in a timely fashion. The weights must add up to 1.00.

Table 23.4
Credit Standards for
WEG Oil

Credit Score	Action
Higher than 75	Extend standard credit terms
65 to 75	Extend limited credit; if account is properly maintained, convert to standard credit terms after one year
Lower than 65	Reject application

sures the applicant's overall credit strength, and the score is used to make the accept or reject decision for granting the applicant credit. Credit scoring is most commonly used by large credit card operations, such as those of banks, oil companies, and department stores.

APPLYING THE MODEL

Credit scoring can be demonstrated using WEG Oil, a major oil company that uses credit scoring to make its consumer credit decisions. Each applicant fills out a credit application. Data from the application are input into an expert system, and a computer generates a final credit score for the applicant, generates a letter indicating whether the application was approved, and issues the credit card. Table 23.3 demonstrates the scoring of a consumer credit application, and Table 23.4 describes WEG's predetermined credit standards. Table 23.3 shows that the applicant has a credit score of 83.25 that will result in its receiving WEG's standard credit terms (referring to Table 23.4). ∎

The purpose of credit scoring is to make a relatively informed credit decision quickly and inexpensively, recognizing that the cost of a single bad scoring decision is small. However, if bad debts from scoring decisions increase, then the scoring system must be reevaluated. As with the five C's of credit, credit scoring does not speed up the collection of accounts. Instead, scoring allows the firm to quickly and inexpensively identify those customers that are likely to pay their accounts within the stated credit terms. The other advantage to using credit scoring is that it is a quantitative approach and can generally be verified as statistically valid for compliance with fair credit regulations.

Changing Credit Standards

As a practical matter, the vast majority of sales by U.S. corporations are made on credit, so it is important to understand how establishing and changing credit standards impact sales, costs, and overall cash flows for a given company. As we discussed earlier, it is vitally important to accurately assess the creditworthiness of individual customers who buy on credit, but this does not mean that a firm should extend credit only to those customers who are certain to repay their debts. Following such an excessively conservative strategy will cost the company many profitable sales, especially if industry practice is to be more generous in extending credit. Instead, the firm should accept a degree of default risk in order to increase sales, but obviously not so much that the additional profit from sales is overwhelmed by the need to invest huge amounts in accounts receivable and absorb bad debts. It is also important to understand that the decision to change credit terms usually rests with the sales or customer service departments, not with the financial manager. The financial manager, however, may be called on to help determine the cash flow and financial impact of a proposed change.

Fortunately, it is fairly straightforward to measure the overall financial impact of either a tightening or a relaxation of credit standards. Any change will likely yield both benefits and costs; the decision whether to change standards will naturally depend on whether or not the benefits exceed the costs. In general, *relaxing credit standards* will yield the benefit of increased unit sales and (assuming each unit is sold at a positive contribution margin) additional profits, but it will also yield higher costs from additional investment in accounts receivable and additional bad debt expense. The *contribution margin* is defined as a product's price per unit minus variable costs per unit and is thus a direct measure of gross profit per unit sold. *Tightening credit standards* will generally yield the benefits of reduced investment in accounts receivable and lower bad debt expense at the cost of lower sales and profits. It is easiest to demonstrate how to calculate the net effect of changing credit standards using an example.

APPLYING THE MODEL

Yeoman Manufacturing Company (YMC) produces and sells a CD organizer to music stores nationwide. YMC charges $20/unit, and all of its sales are on credit, with customers selected for credit on the basis of a scoring process. If these credit standards are left unchanged, YMC expects to sell 120,000 units (un) over the coming year, yielding total sales of $2,400,000 (120,000 units × $20/unit). Variable costs are $12/unit, and YMC has fixed costs of $240,000 per year.

The company is contemplating a relaxation of its credit standards that it expects will have the following effects: a 5 percent increase in sales to 126,000 units; an increase in the average collection period from 30 days (the current level) to 45 days; and an increase in bad debt expense from 1 to 2 percent of sales. YMC plans to keep the product's sale price unchanged at $20/unit, which implies that total sales will increase to $2,520,000 (126,000 units × $20/unit). If the firm's required return on investments of equal risk is 12 percent, should YMC relax its credit standards?

YMC's managers must calculate (1) how much profits will increase from the additional sales that relaxing credit standards are expected to generate, (2) how much the additional investment in accounts receivable will cost, (3) how much the additional bad debt expense will cost, and (4) whether the financial benefits exceed the costs.

1. **Additional profit contribution from sales.** Because we are assuming that a 5 percent increase in sales volume will not cause YMC's fixed costs to increase, we need only account for changes in revenues and variable costs. Specifically, we can compute the marginal increase in profits as the increased unit sales volume times the contribution margin per unit sold, as in Equation 23.2:

$$\text{Marginal profit from increased sales} = \Delta \text{ Sales} \times CM = \Delta \text{ Sales} \times (\text{Price} - VC) \qquad \textbf{(Eq. 23.2)}$$

where Δ Sales = change in unit sales resulting from the change in credit policies,

CM = contribution margin,

Price = price per unit,

VC = variable cost per unit.

Using the assumptions just detailed for YMC, we can use Equation 23.2 to determine that relaxing credit standards as suggested will yield a marginal profit of $48,000:

$$\text{Marginal profit from increased sales} = 6{,}000 \text{ un} \times (\$20/\text{un} - \$12/\text{un}) = 6{,}000 \text{ un} \times (\$8/\text{un})$$

$$= \$48{,}000$$

2. **Cost of the marginal investment in accounts receivable.** To determine the cost of the additional investment in accounts receivable, we must calculate the cost of financing the current level of accounts receivable and compare it to the expected cost under the new credit standards. This is more complicated than it sounds, as we must first calculate how much YMC currently has invested in accounts receivable—based on its current annual sales, variable costs, and accounts receivable turnover—and then repeat this process for the level of sales expected to result from a change in credit standards. The steps required are presented in Equations 23.3, 23.4, and 23.5. Note that we use variable costs in calculating investment in accounts receivable because this is the firm's actual cash expense incurred (and tied up in receivables).

$$\text{Average investment in accounts receivable } (AIAR) = \frac{\text{total variable cost of annual sales}}{\text{turnover of accounts receivable}} \qquad \textbf{(Eq. 23.3)}$$

$$\text{Total variable cost of annual sales } (TVC) = \text{annual unit sales} \times \text{variable cost/unit} \qquad \textbf{(Eq. 23.4)}$$

$$\text{Turnover of accounts receivable } (TOAR) = \frac{365}{\text{average collection period } (ACP)} \qquad \textbf{(Eq. 23.5)}$$

We can use these equations to compute the **average investment in accounts receivable** (**AIAR**) for the current, $AIAR_{\text{CURRENT}}$, and proposed, $AIAR_{\text{PROPOSED}}$, credit standards.

First, we compute the **total variable cost of annual sales** (*TVC*) under the current credit standards, $TVC_{CURRENT}$, and the proposed plan, $TVC_{PROPOSED}$, using Equation 23.4:

$$TVC_{CURRENT} = 120,000 \text{ un} \times \$12/\text{un} = \$1,440,000$$

$$TVC_{PROPOSED} = 126,000 \text{ un} \times \$12/\text{un} = \$1,512,000$$

Next, we note that the average collection period under the current plan, $ACP_{CURRENT}$, is 30 days, but this is expected to rise to 45 days under the proposed plan, $ACP_{PROPOSED}$. This allows us to use Equation 23.5 to compute the **turnover of accounts receivable** (*TOAR*) under the current, $TOAR_{CURRENT}$, and proposed, $TOAR_{PROPOSED}$, credit terms:

$$TOAR_{CURRENT} = \frac{365}{ACP_{CURRENT}} = \frac{365}{30 \text{ days}} = 12.2 \text{ times/year}$$

$$TOAR_{PROPOSED} = \frac{365}{ACP_{PROPOSED}} = \frac{365}{45 \text{ days}} = 8.1 \text{ times/year}$$

These turnover measures suggest that if YMC relaxes its credit standards, the turnover of its accounts receivable will slow down from 12.2 times per year to 8.1 times per year. Clearly, this slowing is attributable to the generally slower paying of the additional credit customers generated by the relaxed credit standards.

We now have all the inputs required to use Equation 23.3 to compute the $AIAR_{CURRENT}$ and $AIAR_{PROPOSED}$:

$$AIAR_{CURRENT} = \frac{TVC_{CURRENT}}{TOAR_{CURRENT}} = \frac{\$1,440,000}{12.2} = \$118,033$$

$$AIAR_{PROPOSED} = \frac{TVC_{PROPOSED}}{TOAR_{PROPOSED}} = \frac{\$1,512,000}{8.1} = \$186,667$$

With these measures, we can now determine the **cost of the marginal investment in accounts receivable**, which is equal to the marginal investment in accounts receivable required to support the proposed change in credit standards multiplied by the required return on investment, r_a:

Cost of marginal investment in accounts receivable = additional investment × required return   (Eq. 23.6)

$$= (AIAR_{PROPOSED} - AIAR_{CURRENT}) \times r_a$$

$$= (\$186,667 - \$118,033) \times 0.12 = \$68,634 \times 0.12$$

$$= \$8,236$$

This value of $8,236 is properly considered a cost of adopting the relaxed credit standards because it represents the opportunity cost of investing an additional $68,634 in accounts receivable rather than investing these funds in another earning asset.

3. **Cost of marginal bad debt expense.** Relaxing YMC's credit standards is expected to increase the firm's bad debt expense by 1 percent, from 1 percent to 2 percent of sales. The cost of this is calculated quite easily by subtracting the current level of bad

debt expense, $BDE_{CURRENT}$ (computed as the bad debt expense rate, $\%BDE_{CURRENT}$, times the current annual sales level, $Sales_{CURRENT}$), from the expected level of bad debt expense under the proposed new credit standards, $BDE_{PROPOSED}$ (computed similarly using the annual sales level, $Sales_{PROPOSED}$, and bad debt expense rate, $\%BDE_{PROPOSED}$, under the proposed new credit standards). Equations 23.7 and 23.8 demonstrate the calculations required:

$$
\begin{aligned}
\text{Bad debt expense } (BDE) &= \text{annual sales (Sales)} \\
&\quad \times \text{bad debt expense rate } (\%BDE) \qquad \text{(Eq. 23.7)} \\
BDE_{PROPOSED} &= (Sales_{PROPOSED}) \times (\%BDE_{PROPOSED}) \\
&= \$2,520,000 \times 0.02 = \$50,400 \\
BDE_{CURRENT} &= (Sales_{CURRENT}) \times (\%BDE_{CURRENT}) \\
&= \$2,400,000 \times 0.01 = \$24,000
\end{aligned}
$$

$$
\begin{aligned}
\text{Cost of marginal bad debts} &= BDE_{PROPOSED} - BDE_{CURRENT} \qquad \text{(Eq. 23.8)} \\
&= \$50,400 - \$24,000 = \$26,400
\end{aligned}
$$

4. **Net profit for the credit decision.** Now that we have calculated the individual financial benefits and costs of changing YMC's credit standards, we can use Equation 23.9 to compute the overall net profit for the credit decision:

$$
\begin{aligned}
\text{Net profit for the credit decision} &= \text{Marginal profit from increased sales} - \text{Cost of marginal investment in accounts receivable} - \text{Cost of marginal bad debts} \\
&= \$48,000 - \$8,236 - \$26,400 = \underline{\$13,364}
\end{aligned}
$$

$$\text{(Eq. 23.9)}$$

Because relaxing YMC's credit standards is expected to yield $13,364 in increased profit, the firm should implement the proposed change. The profit from additional sales will more than offset the total cost of additional investment in accounts receivable and the increased bad debt expense. ■

CREDIT TERMS

Credit terms are the terms of sale for customers. Terms of *net 30* mean the customer has 30 days from the beginning of the credit period (typically *end of month* [EOM] or *date of invoice*) to pay the full invoice amount. Some firms offer cash discounts with terms, such as *2/10 net 30*. These terms mean the customer can take a 2 percent discount from the invoice amount if the payment is made within 10 days, or the customer can pay the full amount of the invoice within 30 days.

A firm's regular credit terms are strongly influenced by the nature of its business.[3] For example, a firm selling perishable items will have very short credit terms because

[3] See Ng, Smith, and Smith (1999) for a discussion of the determinants of credit terms. Smith (1987) analyzes trade credit based on information asymmetry. Petersen and Rajan (1997) also discuss theories concerning trade credit. Adams, Wyatt, and Kim (1992) conduct a contingent claims analysis of trade credit, and Scherr (1996) examines optimal trade credit limits. For a thorough discussion of accounts receivable policies, see Dyl (1977) and Gitman and Sachdeva (1981).

its items have little long-term collateral value. These types of firms will typically offer short terms, where the buyer has 7–10 days to make payment. A firm in a seasonal business may tailor its terms to fit the industry cycles with terms known as *seasonal dating*. Most managers want their company's regular credit terms to be consistent with its industry's standards because if its terms are more restrictive than those of its competitors, it will lose business; if its terms are less restrictive than those of its competitors, it will attract customers of poor quality that probably could not pay under the standard industry term.

A popular method used by the firm to lower its investment in accounts receivable is to include a **cash discount** in the credit terms. The cash discount provides a cash incentive for customers to pay sooner. The discount, by speeding collections, will decrease the firm's investment in accounts receivable, which is the objective, but it will also decrease the per-unit profit because the customer pays less than the full invoice amount. Additionally, initiating a cash discount should reduce bad debts, because customers will pay sooner, and increase sales volume, because the customers that take the cash discount pay a lower price for the product. Accordingly, firms considering offering a cash discount must perform a cost-benefit analysis to determine if a cash discount is profitable enough to be included in their credit terms.

APPLYING THE MODEL

Consider Masson Industries, which has an average collection period of 45 days—37 days until the customers place their payments in the mail and a further 8 days to receive, process, and collect payments. Masson is considering changing its credit terms from *net 30* to *2/10 net 30*. The change should reduce the amount of time between the sale and the customer's mailing payments.

Masson currently sells 1,200 units of its product for $2,500 per unit. Its variable cost per unit is $2,000. Masson estimates that 70 percent of its customers will take the 2 percent discount, offering the discount will increase sales by 50 units per year, and offering the discount will not alter its bad debt percentage for this product. Masson's opportunity cost of funds invested in accounts receivable is 13.5 percent per year. Should Masson offer the proposed cash discount? The cost-benefit analysis, presented in Table 23.5, shows that the *net cost* of the cash discount is $2,846. Thus, *Masson should not implement the proposed cash discount.*   ■

COLLECTION POLICY

A company must determine what its collection policy will be and how it will be implemented. As in the case of the credit standards and terms, the approach to collections may be a function of the industry and the competitive environment. For many delinquent accounts, a reminder, form letter, telephone call, or visit may facilitate customer payment. At a minimum, the company should generally suspend further sales until the delinquent account is brought current. When these actions fail to generate customer payment, it may be necessary to negotiate with the customer for past-due amounts and report the customer to credit bureaus. It is possible that the goods were sold with a lien attached, collateral pledged against the account, or additional corporate or personal guarantees given. In these cases, the company should utilize these options for obtaining payment. Generally as a last resort, the account can be turned over to a collection agency or referred to an attorney for direct legal action. Obviously, a cost-benefit analysis should be made at each stage to compare the cost of further collection actions against the cost of simply writing off the account as a bad debt.

Table 23.5
Analysis of Cash
Discounts for Masson
Industries

Marginal profit from increased sales		
[50 units × ($2,500 − $2,000)]		$25,000
Current investment in accounts receivable		
($2,000[a] × 1,200 units) × (45/365)	$295,890	
New investment in accounts receivable		
($2,000[a] × 1,250 units) × (26/365)[b]	178,082	
Reduction in accounts receivable investment	$117,808	
Cost savings from reduced investment		
in accounts receivable		
(.135 × $117,808)[c]		$15,904
Cost of cash discount (.02 × $2,500 × 1,250 × 0.70)		$43,750
Net profit (cost) from proposed cash discount		($ 2,846)

[a]In analyzing the investment in accounts receivable, we use the $2,000 variable cost of the product sold instead of its $2,500 sales price, because the variable cost represents the firm's actual cash expense incurred and tied up in receivables.
[b]The new investment in accounts receivable is tied up for 26 days instead of the 45 days under the original terms. The 26 days is calculated as [(.7 × 10 days + .3 × 37 days) + 8 days] = 26.1 days, which is rounded to 26 days.
[c]Masson's opportunity cost of funds is 13.5% per year.

CREDIT MONITORING

Credit monitoring involves the ongoing review of a firm's accounts receivable to determine if customers are paying according to the stated credit terms. If customers are not paying on time, credit monitoring will alert the firm to the problem. Credit must be monitored on both an individual and an aggregate basis. Individual monitoring is necessary to determine if each customer is paying in a timely manner and to assess if the customer is within its credit limits.

Credit monitoring on an aggregate basis is also important because it indicates the overall quality of the company's accounts receivable. Slow payments are costly to a firm because they increase the average collection period and thus the firm's investment in accounts receivable. If a company is also using its accounts receivable as collateral for a loan, the lending institution will generally exclude any past-due accounts from those used as backup for the credit line. Changes in accounts receivable over time could impact the company's overall liquidity and the need for additional financing. Analysis of accounts receivable payment patterns can also be essential for forecasting future cash receipts in the cash budget.

The three most frequently cited techniques for monitoring the overall quality of accounts receivable are (1) average collection period, (2) aging of accounts receivable, and (3) payment pattern monitoring.

Average Collection Period

The *average collection period* (*ACP*), which is also known as *days' sales outstanding*, or *DSO*, is the second component of the cash conversion cycle. As noted in Chapter 2, it represents the average number of days credit sales are outstanding. The average collection period has two components: (1) the time from sale until the customer places the payment in the mail and (2) the time to receive, process, and collect the payment once it has been mailed by the customer. Equation 23.10 gives the formula for determining the average collection period:

$$\text{Average collection period} = \frac{\text{accounts receivable}}{\text{average sales per day}} \qquad \text{(Eq. 23.10)}$$

Assuming that receipt, processing, and collection time is constant, the average collection period tells the firm, on average, when its customers pay their accounts. In applying this formula, the analysts must be sure to be consistent in the use of the sales period and to adjust for known seasonal fluctuations.

APPLYING THE MODEL

P. Scofield Enterprises has an accounts receivable balance of $1.2 million. Sales during the past 90 days were $3.6 million, for an average daily sales figure of $40,000. Dividing $1.2 million by $40,000 yields Scofield's average collection period, 30 days.

However, a diligent analyst at Scofield notices that sales have been increasing recently, with average daily sales over the last 30 days of $45,000 per day. Using this figure in the denominator of Equation 23.10 results in a collection period of 26.7 days.   ■

The average collection period allows the firm to determine if there is a general problem with its accounts receivable, but the *ACP* is also prone to sending misleading signals when daily sales fluctuate. In the example shown in the Applying the Model, suppose that Scofield's credit terms are net 25. Using the most recent month to calculate average daily sales results in an average collection period of 26.7 days, which is right on target given Scofield's credit terms. However, using average daily sales over the past three months yields a higher collection period. Therefore, when using this ratio to assess the performance of the collections department, analysts have to be wary of the impact of sales fluctuations on their calculations.

If a firm believes it has a collections problem, a first step in analyzing the problem is to age the accounts receivable. By aging its accounts receivable, the firm can determine if the problem exists in its accounts receivable in general or is attributable to a few specific accounts or to a given time period.

Aging of Accounts Receivable

The **aging of accounts receivable** results in a schedule that indicates the portions of the total accounts receivable balance that have been outstanding for specified periods of time. Aging requires the firm's accounts receivable to be broken down into groups based on the time of origin. The breakdown is typically made on a month-by-month basis, going back three or four months. The purpose is to allow the firm to pinpoint problems.

If a firm with terms of net 30 has an average collection period (minus receipt, processing, and collection time) of 50 days, the firm will want to age its accounts receivable. If the majority of accounts are two months old, then the firm has a general problem and should review its accounts receivable operations. If the aging shows that most accounts are collected in about 35 days and a few accounts are significantly past due, then the firm should analyze and pursue collection of those specific past-due accounts. If the firm has an abnormally high percentage of outstanding accounts initiated in a given month, it may be attributable to a specific event during that time period, such as hiring a new credit manager or selling a substandard product whose quality is being disputed by customers who are withholding payment. Table 23.6 provides an example of an aging schedule. If the stated credit terms for the company in this example were 60 days, then the aging schedule would tell us that 80 percent of the company's receivables are current and 20 percent are considered past due.

Table 23.6
Sample Aging Schedule
for Accounts Receivable

Age of Accounts	Accounts Receivable	Percentage of Accounts Receivable
0–30 days	$1,200,000	50%
31–60 days	720,000	30
61–90 days	336,000	14
91+ days	144,000	6
Total accounts receivable	$2,400,000	100%

Payment Pattern Monitoring

The average collection period and the aging of accounts receivable are excellent monitoring techniques when sales are relatively constant. However, for cyclical or growing firms, both techniques provide potentially misleading results. For example, the average collection period divides the accounts receivable balance by the average daily sales. If the accounts receivable balance is measured during a cyclical firm's high sales period, then the average collection period is distorted by the cyclical sales peak. Use of the firm's customer payment pattern avoids the problems of cyclical or growing sales when monitoring accounts receivable. The **payment pattern** is the normal timing in which a firm's customers pay their accounts, expressed as the percentage of monthly sales collected in each month following the sale. Every firm has a pattern in which its credit sales are paid. This pattern is not affected by changes in sales levels and therefore should be constant across time. If the payment pattern changes, the firm should review its credit policies.

One approach to determining this pattern is to analyze a company's sales and resulting collections on a monthly basis. That is, for each month's sales, the amount collected in the month of sale and each of the following months must be computed. By tracking these patterns over a period of time, the company can determine the average pattern of its collections using either a spreadsheet or regression analysis. For most companies, these patterns tend to be fairly stable over time, even as sales volumes might be fluctuating.

APPLYING THE MODEL

To demonstrate the payment pattern, consider DJM Manufacturing, which has determined that, on average, 10 percent of credit sales are collected in the month of sale, 60 percent are collected in the month following the sale, and the remaining 30 percent are collected in the second month following the sale. Thus, if sales for the month of January were $200,000, the company would expect to collect $20,000 in January, $120,000 in February, and the remaining $60,000 in March. Table 23.7 shows an example of this approach, which can be extended to develop the cash receipts portion of the cash budget.

CASH APPLICATION

Cash application is the process through which a customer's payment is posted to its account and the outstanding invoices are cleared as paid. In most business-to-business environments, the typical application method is known as *open item*. In this approach, each invoice sent to a customer is recorded in the A/R journal, and received payments must be "matched" to the invoices in order to clear them. This task is com-

Table 23.7
Payment Pattern
Monitoring of Accounts
Receivable

Sales Forecast	Forecasted Collections for DJM Manufacturing				
	January	February	March	April	May
January: $200,000	$20,000	$120,000	$ 60,000		
February: 150,000		15,000	90,000	$ 45,000	
March: 300,000			30,000	180,000	$ 90,000
April: 400,000				40,000	240,000
May: 250,000					25,000
Total projected collections for cash budget			$180,000	$265,000	$355,000

Note: This table is created using the assumption that 10% of each month's sales are collected in the month of sale, 60% are collected in the month following sale, and the remaining 30% are collected in the second month following sale. The forecasted sales for each month are provided in the first column, the remaining columns total up the actual cash flows for each month. In an actual application, the remaining collections from the prior year's last quarter would be included to complete the projected cash flows in January and February.

plicated by the usual practice of paying multiple invoices with a single check and remittance information. Ideally, the remittance information accompanying the check should clearly indicate any adjustments, discounts, or allowances taken related to each invoice in that remittance. Unfortunately, the remittance information is sometimes no more than barely legible copies of the invoices with handwritten notes on the adjustments stapled to the check. One of the critical tasks of the accounts receivable department, therefore, is to figure out what has been paid for so the outstanding invoices can be closed out.

Some types of companies are able to use an alternative approach called *balance forward*. In this type of system, customer payments are applied to outstanding balances, and any unpaid amounts are simply carried forward to the next billing period. Examples are credit card companies and utilities, where the only remittance information needed is the customer's account number, the amount of payment, and the date received. These systems also generally utilize a scannable remittance document, which allows the payment and account information to be captured on an automated basis. This is important in reducing the costs of the cash application process.

Concept Review Questions

5. Why do a firm's regular credit terms typically conform to those of its industry? On what basis other than credit terms should the firm compete?

6. How are the *five C's of credit* used to perform in-depth credit analysis? Why is this framework typically used only on high-dollar credit requests?

7. How is *credit scoring* used in the credit selection process? In what types of situations is it most useful?

8. What are the key variables to consider when evaluating the benefits and costs of changing *credit standards?* How do these variables differ when evaluating the benefits and costs of changing *credit terms?*

9. Why do we include only the variable cost of sales when estimating the average investment in accounts receivable? Why do we apply an opportunity cost to this investment to estimate its cost?

10. Why should a firm actively monitor the accounts receivable of its credit customers? How do each of the following credit monitoring techniques work: (a) average collection period, (b) aging of accounts receivable, and (c) payment pattern monitoring?

23.4 CASH MANAGEMENT

Many companies employ financial specialists known as cash managers. One of the primary roles of these specialists is to manage the cash flow time line related to collection, concentration, and disbursement of funds for the company. More specifically, their job typically starts when a customer (the payer) initiates payment to the company (the payee) in any format (cash, check, or electronic). Because most business-to-business payments are still effected by sending a check in the mail, the collections process usually involves trying to reduce the time related to mail and check-collection delays. The cash manager is also responsible for concentrating cash from remote collection points into a central account and for initiating payments from the company to its suppliers. The final stage of this process usually involves reconciling the company's various bank accounts and managing all the banking relationships. Any delay in timing on either the collections or disbursement side is generally referred to as *float*.

FLOAT

Float refers to funds that have been sent by the payer but are not yet usable funds to the payee. Float is important in the cash conversion cycle because its presence increases both the firm's average collection period and its average payment period. The primary role of the cash manager on the collections side is to minimize this float wherever possible. On the payments side,

SMART IDEAS VIDEO
Rohan Williamson, Georgetown University
"Japanese firms hold about double the amount of cash that U.S. firms hold."

See the entire interview at **SMARTFinance**

trying to maximize float is a common practice that raises an important ethical question: Is it ethical to intentionally pay a supplier late, beyond the term within which a firm agreed to pay? This topic will be discussed in greater detail later in this chapter.

Float must be viewed from either the receiving party's perspective (the payee) or the paying party's perspective (the payer). The following list points out that both mail and processing float are generally the same from both perspectives, but the final component is different. These components are defined as follows:

1. **Mail float** is the time delay between when payment is placed in the mail and when payment is received. This float component can range from one day to as much as five days or more depending on location and other factors.

2. **Processing float** is the time between receipt of the payment and its deposit into the firm's account. In a mail-based system, this involves opening the envelope, separating the check from the remittance advice, preparing the check for deposit, and actual deposit at the company's bank. This float component can range from less than one day to three or more days depending on any processing delays the company may have.

3. **Availability float** is the time between deposit of the check and availability of the funds to the firm. Although this may be related to the actual clearing time of the check, it is ultimately a function of the availability schedule offered by the deposit bank. For most business checks, this ranges from same day up to three business days depending on where the check is drawn.

4. **Clearing float** is the time between deposit of the check and presentation of the check back to the bank on which it is drawn. This component of float is attributable to the time required for a check to clear the banking system and to have funds debited from the payee's account. In today's clearing system for business checks, avail-

ability float and clearing float are generally the same, but there are some exceptions when checks are drawn on small, geographically remote banks.

In addition to managing the collection, concentration, and disbursement of funds, the cash manager will also be responsible for the following areas:

1. *Financial relationships:* Managing relationships with banks and other providers of cash management services
2. *Cash flow forecasting:* Determining future cash flows to predict surpluses or deficits (see Chapter 22)
3. *Investing and borrowing:* Managing the investing of short-term surpluses or the borrowing for short-term deficits
4. *Information management:* Developing and maintaining information systems to gather and analyze cash management data

The cash manager typically resides in the treasury area of a firm along with such functions as external financing and risk management. In smaller companies, accounting or clerical staffs may perform the cash management function. Managing the specific cash management tasks related to collection, concentration, and disbursement of funds will be covered in the following sections.

CASH POSITION MANAGEMENT

On a daily basis, managing the primary cash management tasks related to the collection, concentration, and disbursement of funds for the company is generally referred to as **cash position management.** That is, each day the cash manager must determine the amount of funds to be collected, move balances to the appropriate accounts, and fund the projected disbursements. The cash position can be managed with some degree of accuracy many weeks into the future with proper forecasting of future cash flows. Most of the cash management products and services offered by banks and other financial institutions are related to managing some part of this process.

At the end of the day, the cash manager must determine if the company will have surplus or deficit funds in its checking accounts and how to manage the difference. If the company has a surplus of funds, then the money may be placed in some type of short-term investment, such as interest-bearing accounts at the bank or portfolios of marketable securities. If, however, the firm will have a deficit, then the cash manager must make arrangements either to transfer funds from investment accounts or to draw on a short-term credit agreement with the firm's bank. The management of these short-term investing and borrowing arrangements is often part of the cash manager's responsibilities.

Many companies, especially smaller ones, do not engage in active cash position management, but rather set a **target cash balance** for their checking accounts. The primary approach to determining these target cash balances is based on transactions requirements or a minimum balance set by the bank. The transactions requirement is determined simply by how much cash a firm needs for its day-to-day operations. Firms with a high volume of daily inflows and outflows will find that some balances remain in non-interest-bearing checking accounts, regardless of their forecasting ability. Many banks also establish a minimum balance for checking accounts for their customers. For smaller companies and banks, this minimum balance is designed to provide some level of compensation to the bank for the services it provides. For larger companies, most banks will put the customer on *account analysis,* which determines the value of the balances a firm leaves on deposit and matches that to the value of the services provided by the bank.

A **bank account analysis statement** is a report (usually monthly) provided to a bank's commercial customers that specifies all services provided, including items processed and any charges assessed. It is basically a detailed invoice that lists all checks cleared, account charges, lockbox charges, electronic transactions, and so on. The statement also lists all balances held by the firm at the bank with a computation of the credit earned on those balances. Although the bank is not allowed under current federal regulations to pay actual interest on corporate checking account balances, it can offer an *earnings credit* for these balances that is used to offset charges. Most companies on account analysis will receive some credit for the transaction balances they leave in the account that will only partially offset the service fees. The remainder owed the bank will then be deducted as a service charge for the month in question.

Concept Review Questions

11. What is *float?* What are its four components? What is the difference between *availability float* and *clearing float?*

12. What activities are involved in *cash position management?* How does the cash manager monitor and take actions with regard to the funds' end-of-day account balances?

13. How do smaller firms that do not engage in cash position management typically set their *target balance?* What is typically detailed in a *bank account analysis statement?*

23.5 COLLECTIONS

The primary objective in the collections process is to collect funds from customers and other sources as quickly and efficiently as possible. This process also involves managing the collection and dissemination of information related to the payments, and in some cases, the information may be even more important than the money itself. One key requirement is to make sure that the accounts receivable department has the remittance information needed to properly post payments and update customer files. A secondary requirement is to provide audit trails for the company's internal and external auditors.

As discussed earlier, the primary delay in the collections process is *collection float,* which is a function of the mail float, processing float, and availability float. One of the primary goals in the collection area is to reduce each of these float components as much as possible. Collection float is typically measured in "dollar-days," the number of dollars in the process of collection multiplied by the number of days of float. For example, $10 million of checks with an average of five days of float would represent $50 million dollar-days.

It is also important to understand the various payment practices in the U.S. business environment. In the United States, most business-to-business payments are still made via a check in the mail. The Comparative Corporate Finance insert compares U.S. payments to those in other countries. Many consumer payments are also made via check, whereas retail establishments must handle cash, debit, and credit cards in addition to checks. The U.S. business environment is also characterized by a large number of financial institutions (approximately 20,000 according to recent FDIC statistics) and a lack of true nationwide branch banking.

Speeding up collections reduces customer collection float time and thus reduces the firm's average collection period, which, in turn, reduces the investment the firm must make in its cash conversion cycle. In our earlier example, Reese Industries has

Why Do U.S. Noncash Payment Instruments Differ from Those in Other Countries?

The primary method of payment for both business and consumer transactions in the United States is a check in the mail. This method is unique to the United States and Canada (to a lesser extent). Another unique feature of the U.S. payments system is the large role played by the Federal Reserve (Fed) in operating and maintaining both the paper and electronic payment systems. Most other countries differ from the United States in both method of payment and role of the central bank in the payments system.

The U.S. banking system is notable for the sheer number of financial institutions. According to recent FDIC statistics, there are over 8,000 U.S. commercial banks, compared to a mere handful in most other countries. The large number of banks, along with other financial institutions such as thrifts and credit unions, requires a central authority (such as the Federal Reserve) to be an active participant in the payment clearing system. To this end, the Fed clears the majority of the checks in the United States, runs the high-dollar payment system (Fedwire), and is the operator of most of the automated clearinghouse (ACH) systems. In most other developed countries, these tasks are generally handled by the larger banks or banking associations.

The great volume of checks in the U.S. payments system (estimated at 69 billion in 2000) requires that high levels of automation be employed in the check printing, clearing, and reconciliation processes. This results in checks being an inexpensive payment option. Coupling this with a highly reliable postal system (especially when

compared to that of most other countries) results in about 70 percent of noncash payment transactions being made by check in the United States. There is much lower use of checks in most other countries. The table below provides statistics for the relative importance of noncash payment instruments in various countries. The primary payment instrument in most foreign countries (especially for business-to-business transactions) is an electronic credit transaction, which represents only 3 percent of the U.S. payments by volume. Direct debits (known as a preauthorized debit in the United States) are widely used in many countries for routine consumer payments. Thus, whereas the check may be "in the mail" in the United States, the primary payment method is electronic in most other countries.

Another difference between the U.S. payments and banking system and that of other countries is the lack of nationwide branching in the United States. In most other countries, there are far fewer banks, but they are generally allowed to branch on a nationwide basis. This greatly simplifies the collection and concentration issues discussed in this chapter and also allows for the use of techniques such as *notional pooling*, in which balances from all the accounts of a company's subsidiaries can be "pooled" to reduce bank interest charges. In a pooling arrangement, the funds are not actually moved as they are in U.S.-style concentration but are just pooled on a notional basis to compute net interest earned or owed on all company accounts. Although U.S. banking regulations were recently relaxed to ease the establishment

Relative Importance of Noncash Payment Instruments: Percentage of Total Volume, 1999				
Country	Checks	Card Payments	Credit Transfers	Direct Debits
Belgium	5.8%	28.9%	51.9%	9.4%
Canada	31.5	51.7	9.4	7.5
France (1998)	40.7	18.2	16.4	13.3
Germany	4.0	5.2	50.6	40.2
Italy	25.6	17.6	37.2	10.4
Netherlands	1.0	28.6	41.6	28.9
Sweden	0.3	24.1	67.5	8.1
Switzerland	0.8	27.3	68.4	3.6
United Kingdom	29.0	34.6	17.6	18.9
United States	68.6	26.6	3.2	1.7

Source: Bank for International Settlements, "Statistics on Payment Systems in Group of 10 Countries," 1999 figures.

of multistate branching, no bank currently has (or is planning) full coverage in all states.

Another distinction of the U.S. banking system is the way balances in demand deposit accounts must be managed. In the United States, banking regulations still prohibit the payment of interest on corporate demand deposits or the existence of automatic overdrafts on these accounts. In most other countries, managing corporate demand deposits is greatly simplified, as interest is paid on positive balances and charged on negative balances.

The final distinction is the closeness of the relationship between bankers and their corporate customers. In the United States, banking regulators require an "arm's-length" relationship between bankers and their customers and also prohibit commercial banks from corporate stock ownership, except within their trust departments. In most other countries, banks are allowed to hold equity positions with their commercial customers and may indeed have very close relationships.

---

annual sales of $5 billion and eight days of total collection float (receipt, processing, and collection time). If Reese can reduce its float time to five days, it reduces its investment in the cash conversion cycle by $41.1 million [$5 billion $\times$ (3 days/365 days)]. A number of popular collection systems and techniques can be used to speed up collections.

Types of Collection Systems

The type of collection system a company utilizes is primarily a function of the nature of its business. Many high-volume retail establishments, such as fast-food restaurants or convenience stores, receive the bulk of their payments in cash. Other types of retail operations, such as department and variety stores, will collect most of their payments by credit card, debit card, or check. As already discussed, the typical business-to-business payment mechanism is a check that is mailed in response to an invoice for the products or services. What can complicate this process is that one check is often used to pay multiple invoices, and there may be adjustments or partial payments related to those invoices. This makes the information collected by the cash manager of critical importance to the accounts receivable department. Collection systems must take into account the information-management requirements related to the payment-application process. Some types of time-critical transactions, such as real estate closings or high-dollar payments, may be made via wire transfers with same-day value. Other forms of high-volume, low-dollar payments, especially those of a recurring nature (utility payments, insurance premiums, etc.) may be made through the *automated clearinghouse (ACH)* system, which generally offers next-day settlement with fairly low transaction costs. The important thing to understand is that the type of collection system used by a company is usually a function of both the type of business and the usual methods of payment for that type of business.

Field-Banking System

In a **field-banking system,** most collections are made either over the counter (as at a retail store) or at a collection office (often used by utilities). These systems are characterized by many collection points, each of which may have a depository account at a local bank. The main collection problem in this type of system is moving the funds from the local (often small) banks up to the main accounts at the company's primary bank. Given the lack of nationwide branch banking, many large national retailers find they must maintain hundreds or even thousands of bank relationships as part of their collections system. Typically, the collections in a field-banking system are local checks, cash, debit cards, and credit cards. Although the debit card and credit card processing is usually highly automated and efficient, the checks and cash must be processed and deposited at the local deposit bank. The funds must then be concentrated (see later section) into the company's main account before the money can be used. The backbone of this type of system is information management—that is, the company needs to know where the money is before the company can make use of it. Most large retailers utilize point-of-sale (POS) information systems that allow them to know on a daily basis how much money has been collected, what formats (cash, check, debit card, or credit card) the money was in, and how much was deposited at the local bank. The task of moving this money into a concentration account is discussed in the section on cash concentration.

Mail-Based System

In a **mail-based collection system,** the company typically has one or more collection points that process the incoming mail payments. These processing centers will receive the mail payments, open the envelopes, separate the check from the remittance information, prepare the check for deposit, and send the remittance information to the accounts receivable department for application of payment. Companies such as utilities and credit card processors that utilize standardized, scannable remittance information can often process payments quickly and efficiently using automated equipment. Although many high-volume processors can justify the cost of the equipment needed for automated processing, other companies may find that using a *lockbox* (covered later) is more cost effective. However, recent developments in payment processing equipment have made automated processing available to smaller companies at a reasonable price.

Electronic Systems

Electronic collection systems are still fairly new but are developing rapidly as both businesses and consumers begin to understand the benefits. One of the key developments in this area is **electronic bill presentment and payment (EBPP)**. In EBPP systems, customers are sent bills in an electronic format and then can pay their bills via electronic means. Most of these systems are web based on the Internet and are beginning to gain some acceptance in the marketplace. The most successful of the consumer systems offer a consolidator-type service, where customers can go to one site to view and pay all their bills rather than have to visit the individual biller's sites. Electronic payment systems are only slowly gaining acceptance in the business-to-business environment.

Some of the primary advantages of using a system such as the ACH for business-to-business payments are (1) reduced float to the receiving party, (2) lower cost of both receivables processing for the receiver and payment initiation and reconciliation costs for the payer, and (3) better forecasting for both parties. Though there may be a need for negotiation of payment dates and possible discounts for changed payment timing, companies that have implemented electronic payments report significant overall savings as a result.

Lockbox Systems

A **lockbox system** is a popular technique for speeding up collections because it affects all three components of float. Instead of mailing payments to the company, customers mail payments to a post office box, which is emptied regularly by the firm's bank. The bank processes each payment and deposits the payments in the firm's account. The bank sends (or transmits electronically by computer) deposit slips and enclosures to the firm so the firm can properly credit its customers' accounts. Lockboxes are geographically dispersed to match the locations of the firm's customers. As a result of being near the firm's customers, lockboxes reduce mail time, and often clearing time. They reduce processing time to nearly zero because the bank deposits payments before the firm processes them. Obviously, a lockbox system reduces collection float, but not without a cost; therefore, a firm must perform a cost-benefit analysis to determine if a lockbox system should be implemented. Equation 23.11 presents a simple formula for the cost-benefit analysis of a lockbox system:

$$\text{Net benefit (cost)} = (FVR \times r_a) - LC \qquad \text{(Eq. 23.11)}$$

where FVR = float value reduction in dollars,

   r_a = cost of capital,

   LC = annual operating cost of the lockbox system.

Thus, if the return on the float reduction exceeds the cost of the lockbox system, the firm should implement the lockbox system.

APPLYING THE MODEL

To demonstrate, consider Reese Industries, which has $5 billion in annual sales and eight days of customer collection float in its cash conversion cycle. Reese wants to determine if it should implement a lockbox system that reduces customer collection float to five days. The reduction in float value from decreasing customer float from eight days to five days is $41.1 million [$5 billion × (3 days/365 days)]. Reese has a cost of capital of 13.5 percent per year. Thus, the value to Reese of reducing customer float by three days is $5.5 million ($41.1 million × 0.135). If the annual cost of the lockbox system is less than $5.5 million, it would be beneficial to implement the system.

   Although lockbox systems are commonly used by large firms whose customers are geographically dispersed, smaller firms can also benefit from a lockbox system. The benefit to small firms often comes primarily from transferring the processing of payments to the bank.

   Lockboxes are typically classified as either retail or wholesale. A *retail lockbox* utilizes standardized, scannable remittance documents in order to highly automate the processing of incoming payments. These types of systems are characterized by very high volumes of low-dollar payments, and the key issue is processing these payments at a minimum per-unit cost. Given the low-dollar amounts of the payments, availability float is generally not a big issue. *Wholesale lockboxes,* on the other hand, primarily process high-dollar payments with nonstandard remittance information. The key issues in this type of system are reducing the availability float related to the large checks and forwarding the remittance information to the accounts receivable department for application of payment. The current practice for wholesale lockboxes is to make extensive use of imaging technology to quickly and accurately relay copies of the remittance information back to the A/R department.

CASH CONCENTRATION

In the previous section, lockbox systems were discussed as a means to reduce collection float. With a lockbox system, the firm has deposits in each lockbox bank. **Cash concentration** is the process of bringing the lockbox and other deposits together into one bank, often called the *concentration bank*.

Cash concentration has three main advantages. First, it creates a large pool of funds for use in making short-term cash investments. Because there is a fixed-cost component in the transaction cost associated with making marketable security investments, investing a single pool of funds reduces the firm's transaction costs. The larger investment pool also allows the firm to choose from a larger variety of marketable securities. Second, concentrating the firm's cash in one account improves the tracking and internal control of the firm's cash. Third, having one concentration bank allows the firm to more effectively implement payment strategies that preserve its investable balances for as long as possible.[4]

The configuration of a company's cash concentration system is generally a function of the collection system. That is, a company with a field-banking system will need a way to move money quickly and efficiently from many small deposit banks into its concentration account, whereas a company with several collection centers or lockboxes will look toward using wire transfers to quickly move large balances from a limited number of collection points into its concentration account. The type of disbursement system (discussed in a later section) will also be an important consideration, as these accounts must be funded either by internal transfer or wire transfer.

FUNDS TRANSFER MECHANISMS

There are a variety of mechanisms for transferring cash from the depository banks to the concentration bank. These mechanisms include (1) depository transfer checks, (2) ACH transfers, and (3) wire transfers. The first method is a **depository transfer check (DTC)**, which is an unsigned check drawn on one of the firm's bank accounts and deposited in another of the firm's bank accounts. For cash concentration, a DTC is drawn on each deposit bank account and deposited in the concentration bank account. Once the DTC has cleared the bank on which it is drawn, the actual transfer of funds is completed. Most firms currently provide deposit information by telephone to the concentration bank, which then prepares and deposits into its account the DTC drawn on the collecting bank account. As this is a paper-based item and subject to normal check-clearing delays, most companies now utilize faster, electronic methods to concentrate funds.

The second mechanism is an **automated clearinghouse (ACH) debit transfer**, which is a preauthorized electronic withdrawal from the payer's account and is generally known in the cash management trade as an **electronic depository transfer (EDT)**. An ACH can be thought of as an electronic DTC and is generally slightly cheaper in cost than a paper-based DTC. A computerized clearing facility, the ACH,

---

[4] In the process of transferring deposits between banks, it is possible that balances may exist at two banks simultaneously. These dual balances are created by "slippage" in the clearing system. *Clearing system slippage* is often cited as an advantage of cash concentration. However, it is a rare case where the firm concentrating its cash can take advantage of the slippage, so we therefore ignore slippage in our discussions.

makes a paperless transfer of funds between the payer and payee banks. An ACH settles accounts among participating banks; individual accounts are settled by respective bank balance adjustments. ACH transfers of this type generally clear in one day, offering significant advantages over the paper-based DTC. For cash concentration, an ACH debit is initiated by the concentration bank and sent to each deposit bank, with funds then moving from the deposit bank into the concentration bank. These transfers can be automatically created from deposit information and can then be centrally initiated from the company's headquarters through its concentration bank. A large nationwide retailer can easily concentrate deposits from many small deposit banks into its concentration account by using the daily deposit information gathered from its stores' point-of-sale systems.

The third mechanism is a **wire transfer.** In the United States, the primary wire transfer system, known as *Fedwire,* is run by the Federal Reserve and is available to all depository institutions. A Fedwire transfer is an electronic communication that removes funds from the payer's bank and deposits the funds in the payee's bank on a same-day basis via bookkeeping entries in the financial institution's Federal Reserve account. Wire transfers can eliminate mail float and clearing float and may provide processing float reductions as well. For cash concentration, the firm moves funds using a wire transfer from each deposit account to its concentration account. Wire transfers are a substitute for DTC and ACH transfers, but they are generally much more expensive, with both the sending and receiving banks charging significant fees for the transaction. Wire transfers are usually used only for high-dollar transfers where the investment value of the funds outweighs the cost of the transfer.

It is clear that the firm must balance the benefits and costs of concentrating cash to determine the type and timing of transfers from its lockbox accounts to its concentration account. The transfer mechanism selected should be the one that is most profitable (i.e., profit per period equals earnings on the increased funds' availability minus the cost of the transfer system). For most companies, the general practice is to use wire transfers for large transfers of funds from lockbox deposits and to use EDTs for high volume, low-dollar transfers from small deposit banks.

APPLYING THE MODEL

To demonstrate alternative transfer methods, consider DJM Manufacturing, which has $120,000 in a deposit account that needs to be transferred to its concentration account. The available choices are an EDT with a total cost of $1 or a wire transfer with a total cost of $15. Because this would be a midweek transfer, the funds would be accelerated by one day. (*Note:* A Friday transfer would represent three days of funds' acceleration.) The firm's opportunity cost for these funds is 7 percent.

In this example, the value of moving the funds via wire transfer is the one day of interest that could be earned if the funds arrived in the concentration account today rather than tomorrow. This amount is calculated to be $23.01 ($120,000 × .07/365). Because the differential cost of wire versus an EDT is $14 ($15 − $1), the company should use a wire in this case and would realize a net benefit of $9.01 ($23.01 − $14.00).

We could also determine the minimum amount for which a wire transfer would be beneficial given the opportunity cost and transfer fees. We take the differential cost of a wire ($14.00) and divide by the daily interest rate (.07/365). In this case, it would be $73,000 [$14.00 ÷ (.07/365)]. If we were transferring funds on a Friday and would thus have three days of interest that could be earned, the minimum transfer amount would be one-third of the standard amount, or $24,333 ($73,000 ÷ 3). ■

14. What is the firm's objective with regard to *collection float?* What are the common types of collection systems?

15. What are the benefits of using a *lockbox system?* How does it work? How can the firm assess the economics of a lockbox system?

16. Why do firms employ *cash concentration* techniques? What are some of the popular transfer mechanisms used by firms to move funds from depository banks to their concentration banks?

17. How can the cash manager model the benefits and costs of various funds transfer mechanisms to assess their economics? How can this analysis be used to determine the minimum transfer amount?

23.6 ACCOUNTS PAYABLE AND DISBURSEMENTS

OVERVIEW OF THE ACCOUNTS PAYABLE PROCESS

The final component of the cash conversion cycle is the **average payment period** (**APP**), which has two parts: (1) the time from the purchase of raw materials until the firm places the payment in the mail and (2) payment float time (disbursement float), the time it takes after the firm places its payment in the mail until the supplier has withdrawn funds from the firm's account. Section 23.4 discussed issues related to payment float time. In this section, we discuss the management of the time that elapses between the purchase of raw materials and mailing the payment to the supplier. This activity is **accounts payable management.**

The primary purpose of the accounts payable (A/P) function is to examine all incoming invoices and determine the proper amount to be paid. As part of this process, the cash manager matches the invoice to both the purchase order and receiving information to ensure that the goods/services were ordered by an authorized person and that they were actually received. The accounts payable clerk may make adjustments to the invoiced amount for price or quantity differences. Companies usually pay multiple invoices with a single check. A company has the right to make full use of any credit period offered, but intentionally delaying payments or increasing disbursement float is considered an unethical cash management practice. Once payment has been authorized (sometimes referred to as "vouchering"), the cash manager is often responsible for the actual payment itself, either managing the preparation and mailing of the checks or initiating the electronic transfer of funds.

The other issue involved with managing disbursements is the choice of a centralized or decentralized payables and payments system. In a centralized system, all invoices are sent to a central accounts payable department where payment is authorized and checks or other forms of payment are initiated. Centralized systems offer many advantages, including easier concentration of funds, improved access to cash position information, better control, and reduced transaction and administrative costs. There are, however, several problems with centralized payables, such as slow payment times (which could damage relationships with vendors or cause missed opportunities for cash discounts) and the need to coordinate between central payables and field offices/managers to resolve any disputes. Some companies utilize a more decentralized approach to the payables and disbursement process, wherein payments are authorized and, in some cases, initiated at the local level. Although this approach generally helps to improve relationships with vendors and enhance local management autonomy, it makes it harder to concentrate funds and obtain daily cash position information and increases the chance of unauthorized disbursements.

CASH DISCOUNTS

When suppliers offer *cash discounts* to encourage their customers to pay before the end of the credit period, it may not be in the firm's best financial interest to pay on the last day of the credit period. Accounts payable with cash discounts have stated credit terms, such as *2/10 net 30,* which means the purchaser can take a *2 percent discount* from the invoice amount if the payment is made within *10 days* of the beginning of the credit period; otherwise, it must pay the full amount within *30 days.* Taking the discount is at the discretion of the purchaser.

When a firm is offered extended credit terms that include a cash discount, it has two options: (1) pay the full invoice amount at the end of the credit period or (2) pay the invoice amount less the cash discount at the end of the cash discount period. In either case, the firm purchases the same goods. Thus, the difference between the payment amount without and with taking the cash discount is, in effect, the interest payment made by the firm to its supplier. The firm in need of short-term funds must therefore compare the interest rate charged by its supplier to the best rate charged by purveyors of short-term financing and choose the lowest-cost option. This comparison is important, because if the firm takes the cash discount, it will shorten its average payment period and thus increase the amount of resources it has invested in operating assets, which will require additional nonspontaneous short-term financing. Equation 23.12 presents the formula for calculating the interest rate, $r_{discount}$, associated with not taking the cash discount and paying at the end of the credit period when cash discount terms are offered:

$$r_{discount} = \frac{d}{(1-d)} \times \frac{365}{(CP - DP)} \qquad \textbf{(Eq. 23.12)}$$

where d = percent discount (in decimal form),

   CP = credit period,

   DP = cash discount period.

APPLYING THE MODEL

Assume that a supplier to Masson Industries has changed its terms from net 30 to 2/10 net 30. Masson has a line of credit with a bank, and the current interest rate on the line of credit is 6.75 percent per year. Should Masson take the cash discount or continue to use 30 days of credit from its supplier? The interest rate from the supplier is calculated using Equation 23.12:

$$r_{discount} = \frac{.02}{(1-.02)} \times \frac{365}{(30-10)} = .372 = 37.2\% \text{ per year}$$

Thus, the annualized rate charged by the supplier to those customers not taking the cash discount is 37.2 percent, whereas the bank charges 6.75 percent. Masson should take the cash discount and obtain needed short-term financing by drawing on its bank line of credit.

Disbursement Products and Methods

Zero-Balance Accounts

Zero-balance accounts (**ZBAs**) are disbursement accounts that always have an end-of-day balance of zero. The purpose is to eliminate nonearning cash balances in corporate checking accounts. A ZBA is often used as a disbursement account under a cash concentration system.

A ZBA is designed as follows. Once all of a given day's checks are presented to the firm's ZBA for payment, the bank notifies the firm of the total amount to be drawn, and the firm transfers funds into the account to cover the amount of that day's checks. This leaves an end-of-day balance of $0 (zero dollars). The ZBA allows the firm to keep all operating cash in an interest-earning account, thereby eliminating idle cash balances. Thus, a firm that uses a ZBA in conjunction with a cash concentration system would need two accounts. The firm would concentrate its cash from the lockboxes into an interest-earning account and write checks against its ZBA. The firm would cover the exact dollar amount of checks presented against the ZBA with transfers from the interest-earning account, leaving the end-of-day balance in the ZBA at $0. In many cases, the funding of the ZBA is made automatically and only involves an accounting entry on the part of the bank.

A ZBA is a disbursement management tool that allows the firm to maximize the use of float on each check without altering the float time of its suppliers. The firm accomplishes this by keeping all its cash in an interest-earning account instead of leaving nonearning balances in its checking account to later cover the checks the firm has written. This allows the firm to maximize earnings on its cash balances by capturing the full float time on each check it writes.

We have discussed only ZBAs in this section. However, banks offer a variety of similar products. Another common product that achieves the same goal as a ZBA is a *sweep account,* in which the bank "sweeps" account surpluses into the appropriate interest-earning vehicle and liquidates similar vehicles in order to cover account shortages when they occur. Many banks also offer multitiered ZBAs that may be used by multidivisional companies or to segregate different types of payments (payrolls, dividends, accounts payable, etc.). This type of account allows the cash manager to better control balances and funding of the master account and associated ZBAs, thus reducing excess balances and transfers.

Controlled Disbursement

Controlled disbursement is a bank service that provides early notification of checks that will be presented against a company's account on a given day. For most large cash management banks, the Federal Reserve Bank makes two presentments of checks to be cleared each day. A bank offering controlled disbursement accounts would get advance electronic notification from the Fed several hours prior to the actual presentment of the items. This allows the bank to let its controlled disbursement customers know what will be presented to their accounts as early as possible in the day. This, in turn, allows the customers to determine their cash position and make any necessary investment/borrowing decisions in the morning, before the checks are presented for payment. Controlled disbursement accounts are often set up as ZBAs to allow for automatic funding through a company's concentration account.

Positive Pay

Positive pay is a bank service used to combat the most common types of check fraud. Given the availability of inexpensive computers, scanners, and printers, it is very easy to create excellent copies of corporate checks or change payees or amounts. The risk to a company issuing checks is that the bank might pay fraudulent items and the fraud would not be revealed until the account is reconciled. When using a positive pay service, the company transmits a check-issued file, designating the check number and amount of each item, to the bank when the checks are issued. The bank matches the presented checks against this file and rejects any items that do not match. It is important to note that several courts have ruled that positive pay is a "commercially reasonable" measure to prevent check fraud. This means that a company that does not use this service when available may find itself liable for fraudulent items accepted by its bank.

DEVELOPMENTS IN ACCOUNTS PAYABLE AND DISBURSEMENTS

Integrated Accounts Payable

Integrated accounts payable, also known as *comprehensive accounts payable,* provides a company with outsourcing of its accounts payable or disbursement operations. The outsourcing may be as minor as contracting with a bank to issue checks and perform reconciliations or as major as outsourcing the entire payables function. One of the most typical approaches to A/P outsourcing is to send a bank (or other financial service provider) a data file containing a listing of all payments to be made. The bank will maintain a vendor file for the company and send each vendor payment in accordance with the company's remittance advice preferred format.

Purchasing/Procurement Cards

Many companies are implementing **purchasing** (or **procurement**) **card programs** as a means of reducing the cost of low-dollar indirect purchases. Though companies have been using credit cards for travel and related expenses for many years, they have only recently begun using them to make routine purchases of supplies, equipment, or services. The purchasing cards are issued to designated employees, and both dollar amounts and vendors where they can be used are limited. Companies that have implemented such programs report significant cost savings from streamlining the purchasing process for low-cost items. The other advantage is that the firm can pay the issuer of the purchasing card in a single, large payment that consolidates many small purchases.

Imaging Services

Many disbursement services offered by banks and other vendors incorporate **imaging services** as part of the package. This technology allows both sides of the check, as well as remittance information, to be converted into digital images. The images can then be transmitted via the Internet or easily stored for future reference. Imaging services are especially useful when incorporated with positive pay services.

Fraud Prevention in Disbursements

In recent years, disbursement fraud, especially related to check payments, has increased significantly. Fraudulent checks can be easily created using inexpensive scanners, computers, and laser printers. As a result, fraud prevention and control have become even more important in the accounts payable and disbursement functions. Some of the common fraud prevention measures include the following:

1. Written policies and procedures for creating and disbursing checks
2. Separating duties (approval, signing, and reconciliation)

3. Using safety features on checks (microprinting, watermarks, tamper resistance, etc.)
4. Setting maximum dollar limits and/or requiring multiple signatures
5. Using positive pay services
6. Increasing the use of electronic payment methods

18. What is the primary purpose of the accounts payable function? Describe the procedures used to manage accounts payable. What are the key differences between centralized and decentralized payables and payment systems?

19. When is it advantageous for a company to pay early and take an offered cash discount? Under what circumstance would the firm be advised to always take any offered cash discounts?

20. What is the difference between a *ZBA* and a *controlled disbursement account?* Are they direct substitutes?

21. What are some of the recent developments in the accounts payable and disbursements area? What role does new technology play in fraud prevention in disbursements?

23.7 SHORT-TERM INVESTING AND BORROWING

As a result of determining the company's cash position, the cash manager will generally have either surplus funds to invest or a need for short-term borrowing. This section discusses the options available for these purposes.

SHORT-TERM INVESTING

Making sure that the company has access to liquid assets when and where they are needed is one of the critical tasks for the cash manager. Although the primary form of liquidity will generally be a company's checking or demand deposit accounts at its banks, these accounts usually do not earn interest, and the company should not hold excess balances in these accounts. To earn some type of short-term return, a company will hold some "near-cash" assets in the form of short-term investments. These investments may be either a source of reserve liquidity or a place to maintain temporary surplus funds.[5]

Because the short-term investments are essentially a substitute for cash, liquidity and the preservation of principal should be the primary concerns. Earning a competitive return is also a consideration; however, care must be taken not to place the underlying principal at risk. Remember that the primary purpose of short-term investments is to maintain a pool of liquid assets as a substitute for cash, not to generate profits for the company. To this end, it is important that a company establish policies and guidelines for the management of short-term investments, which should clearly specify the purpose of the investment portfolio and provide recommendations and/or restrictions on acceptable investments and diversification.

Money Market Mutual Funds

Many large companies will manage their own portfolios of short-term investments, but most companies (especially smaller ones) use money market mutual funds as an al-

---

[5.] *Temporary surplus funds* may result from ongoing operations, seasonal performance, sales of large assets, or proceeds from a large securities issue.

ternative. The **money market mutual funds** invest in the same types of short-term instruments that cash managers do and may, in fact, offer even more flexibility and stability than a self-managed fund. Using these types of funds makes sense, especially when the costs of running and managing a short-term portfolio are factored into the analysis.

In most cases, these funds set their net asset value (*NAV*) to a fixed $1 per share in order to preserve the principal value of the fund. As the value of the fund increases, the fund pays investors in additional shares rather than allow the share price to increase. Commercial money market mutual funds are available from independent companies, as well as from most large banks.

Money Market Financial Instruments

Short-term financial instruments are primarily fixed-income securities generally issued in registered form rather than bearer form, yet they are often called "marketable securities." Many of these securities are also issued in discount form, meaning the investor pays less than face value for the security at the time of purchase and receives the face value at maturity. Table 23.8 lists the more common securities used for money market investments.

U.S. Treasuries: U.S. T-bills are the benchmark of money market investments. The U.S. government issues these short-term securities to finance its activities, and they appeal to a wide range of investors, both domestic and foreign. They are backed by the "full faith and credit" of the U.S. government (making them essentially free of default risk) and have a very active secondary market. They are issued in weekly auctions on a discount basis with maturities of less than one year (usually 13 or 26 weeks). T-bills are available in minimum denominations of $1,000 but are generally traded in round lots of $1 million. Other Treasury instruments such as Treasury notes (T-notes) and Treasury bonds (T-bonds) are initially issued as long-term securities but may be suitable for a short-term portfolio as they approach their maturity. All treasury securities are registered and issued in book entry form and are exempt from state income taxes.

Federal agency issues: These instruments have some degree of federal government backing and are issued by either federal agencies or private, shareholder-owned companies known as *government-sponsored enterprises* (*GSEs*). Most of the agencies are securitized investments backed by home mortgages, student loans, or agricultural lending. Two of the agencies (Ginnie Mae and Vinnie Mac) are backed by the "full faith and credit" of the U.S. government, whereas the rest are backed by the implied intervention of the government in the event of a crisis.

Bank financial instruments: U.S. and foreign banks issue short-term certificates of deposit (CDs) as well as time deposits and banker's acceptances. Many banks also offer money market mutual funds and sweep accounts in which their customers can invest short-term cash.

Corporate obligations: The primary corporate obligation in the short-term market is **commercial paper.** Highly rated corporations typically issue this investment, which is structured as an unsecured promissory note with a maturity of less than 270 days. The short maturity allows for issuance without SEC registration, and commercial paper is usually sold to other corporations rather than the general public. Most issues are also backed by credit guarantees from a financial institution and sold on a discount basis, similar to T-bills. The other corporate obligation used for short-term investments is **adjustable rate preferred stock.** These stocks take advantage of the dividend exclusion (of 70 percent or more) for stock in one corporation held by another corporation. In order to make this investment suitable for short-term holdings, the dividend rate paid on the stock is adjusted according to some rate index. This will

Table 23.8
Money Market Financial Instruments

U.S. Treasuries	Interest Basis	Maturity
Treasury bills (T-bills)	Discount	Less than 1 year
Treasury notes (T-notes)	Interest bearing	1–10 years
Treasury bonds (T-bonds)	Interest bearing	10–30 years

Federal Agency Issues	Underlying Assets	Backing
Government National Mortgage Association (Ginnie Mae)	Home mortgages	Full faith and credit
Department of Veterans Affairs (Vinnie Mac)	VA home loans	Full faith and credit
Federal National Mortgage Association (Fannie Mae)	Home mortgages	GSE—Implied federal backing
Federal Home Loan Mortgage Corporation	Home mortgages	GSE—Implied federal backing
SLM Holding Corporation (Sallie Mae)	Student loans	Quasi-GSE—Implied federal backing
Federal Farm Credit Banks Funding Corporation	Agricultural loans	GSE—Implied federal backing
Farm Credit System Insurance Corporation	Insurer of Farm Credit Banks	GSE—Implied federal backing
Central Bank for Cooperatives (CoBank)	Loans to agricultural cooperatives	GSE—Implied federal backing
Federal Agricultural Mortgage Corporation (Farmer Mac)	Agricultural loans, rural real estate, and home mortgages	GSE—Implied federal backing

Bank Financial Instruments	Special Features
Certificates of deposit— CDs (domestic)	Interest-bearing deposits at financial institutions in the U.S.; may be fixed rate or floating rate with maturities from 7 days to several years
Overnight sweep accounts	Interest-bearing accounts used for investing end-of-day surplus funds
Yankee CDs	Dollar-denominated CDs issued by U.S. branches of foreign banks
Eurodollar CDs	Dollar-denominated CDs issued by banks outside the U.S.
Eurodollar time deposits	Nonnegotiable, fixed-rate time deposits issued by banks outside the U.S., with maturities ranging from overnight to several years
Banker's acceptances	Negotiable short-term instruments used for trade finance
Bank notes	Unsecured or subordinated debt of the bank (not insured)

Corporate Obligations	Special Features
Commercial paper	Unsecured promissory notes issued by corporations; maturities from 1 to 270 days; usually sold on a discount basis and backed by a credit guarantee from a bank
Adjustable rate preferred stock	Tax advantaged for corporate holders due to dividend exclusion rule; dividend rate adjusts to maintain stable pricing

Other Short-Term Investments	Special Features
Money market mutual funds	Available directly from funds or through banks
Asset-backed securities	Debt obligations issued by companies that are secured by assets such as receivables, credit card obligations, consumer finance loans, major retailers, and automobile companies
International money market investments	Short-term bills or notes issued by foreign governments, foreign commercial paper, or other types of interest-bearing deposits in foreign currencies
Repurchase agreements (repos)	A collateralized transaction between a securities dealer or bank and an investor; generally backed by Treasuries or agency securities

stabilize the price, even if interest rates change during the 45-day holding period required to qualify for the dividend exclusion.

Yield Calculations for Discount Instruments (T-Bills or Commercial Paper) [6]

The yield for short-term discount instruments such as T-bills and commercial paper is typically calculated using algebraic approximations rather than more precise present value methods. In the case of a discounted investment, the investor pays less than face value at time of purchase, then receives the face value of the investment at maturity. There are generally no interim interest or coupon payments during the course of holding such an investment. Determining the yield of T-bills or commercial paper generally involves a two-step process. In most cases, the rate on the investment is expressed as the discount rate, which is used to compute the "dollar discount" and selling price for the instrument. For example, a 1-year, $100,000 T-bill sold at a 5 percent discount would sell for $95,000 [$100,000 × (1 − 0.05)]. The investor would pay $95,000 today and receive $100,000 in one year at the maturity date. The yield on this investment would be approximately 5.26 percent ($5,000/$95,000). Though the calculations for a shorter-term investment are slightly more complicated, they follow the same basic approach. **Money market yield** (**MMY**) for discount instruments is calculated on a 360-day basis but must be converted to **bond equivalent yield** (**BEY**) to compare discount instruments to interest-bearing investments, such as bank CDs. Examples of the yield calculations are provided in the following example.

APPLYING THE MODEL

We can use the following steps to determine the yield on a 91-day, $1 million T-bill that is selling at a discount of 3.75 percent. Note that the convention in the discount market is to use 360 days when calculating the purchase price and money market yield.

Step 1: **Calculate the purchase price and dollar discount.**

Purchase price = face value − dollar discount

$$\text{Dollar discount} = (\text{face value} \times \text{discount rate}) \times (\text{days to maturity}/360)$$
$$= (\$1,000,000 \times 0.0375) \times (91/360) = \$9,479.17$$

Purchase price = $1,000,000 − $9,479.17 = $990,520.83

Step 2: **Calculate MMY and BEY.**

$$\text{Money Market Yield } (MMY) = (\text{dollar discount}/\text{purchase price})$$
$$\times (360/\text{days to maturity})$$
$$= (\$9,479.17/\$990,520.83) \times (360/91) = \underline{\underline{3.786\%}}$$

$$\text{Bond Equivalent Yield } (BEY) = \text{Money Market Yield } \times (365/360)$$
$$= 3.786\% \times (365/360) = \underline{\underline{3.839\%}}$$

Short-Term Borrowing

For many companies, a primary source of liquidity is access to short-term lines of credit or commercial paper programs to provide needed funds. This is especially

---

[6] The calculations demonstrated in this section are the same ones we introduced in Section 4.2 of Chapter 4. For convenience as well as custom, we present these formulas a bit differently here.

the case for companies in seasonal businesses where large amounts of operating capital may be needed for only a few months of the year. The role of the cash manager in the establishment of short-term borrowing arrangements is to ensure that the company has adequate credit facilities sufficient to meet short-term cash requirements. Obviously, these arrangements should provide maximum flexibility at a minimum cost.

Most short-term borrowing is done on a variable rate basis, with rates quoted in terms of a base rate plus a spread. The spread is essentially an adjustment for the estimated riskiness and overall creditworthiness of the borrower. The base rate and the spread are referred to as the **all-in-rate.** Typical base rates include the prime rate and LIBOR (London Interbank Offered Rate). The **prime rate** is the rate of interest charged by the largest U.S. banks on short-term loans to business borrowers with good credit ratings. *LIBOR* is the rate that the most creditworthy international banks that deal in Eurodollars charge on interbank loans. For bank lines of credit, there may be commitment fees or compensating balance requirements on the lending agreement. These agreements may also be set up on a multiyear, revolving basis and may use current assets such as receivables or inventory as collateral. In any type of bank lending, most of the terms and conditions are determined from negotiations between the borrower and the bank.

The **effective borrowing rate (*EBR*)** on a bank line of credit is generally determined as the total amount of interest and fees paid, divided by the average usable loan amount. This rate is then adjusted for the actual number of days the loan is outstanding. A demonstration of this calculation follows.

APPLYING THE MODEL

We can determine the *effective borrowing rate, EBR,* on a 1-year line of credit with the following characteristics:

CL = total credit line, $500,000
AL = average loan outstanding, $200,000
CF = commitment fee, .35 percent (35 basis points) on the unused portion of the line
IR = interest rate, 2.5 percent over LIBOR (LIBOR is currently 5.75 percent), which equals 8.25 percent
No compensating balances required
Year basis, 365 days

$$EBR = \frac{(IR \times AL) + [CF \times (CL - AL)]}{AL} \times \frac{365}{\text{days loan is outstanding}}$$

$$= \frac{(.0825 \times \$200,000) + [.0035 \times (\$500,000 - \$200,000)]}{\$200,000} \times \frac{365}{365}$$

$$= \frac{(\$16,500) + (\$1,050)}{\$200,000} \times \frac{365}{365} = \frac{\$17,550}{\$200,000} \times 1 = \underline{\underline{8.775\%}}$$

The effective borrowing rate of 8.775 percent is about 50 basis points above the 8.25 percent interest rate as a result of the commitment fee paid on the unused portion of the line.

22. Why are liquidity and preservation of principal the primary concerns in choosing short-term investments? What guidelines should be included in a short-term investment policy?

23. What securities are considered the benchmark for money market investments, and why? What are some of the popular non–U.S. Treasury money market instruments?

24. What are the key base rates used in variable rate short-term borrowing, and how do they factor into the *all-in-rate?* What other charges might be applicable to short-term borrowing? How do they impact the *effective borrowing rate?*

23.8 SUMMARY

- The cash conversion cycle has three main components: (1) the average age of inventory (*AAI*), (2) the average collection period (*ACP*), and (3) the average payment period (*APP*). The operating cycle (*OC*) is the sum of the *AAI* and *ACP*. The cash conversion cycle (*CCC*) is *OC* − *APP*. The length of the cash conversion cycle determines the amount of resources the firm must invest in its operations.

- The focus of the financial manager in managing the firm's short-term activities is to shorten the cash conversion cycle. The basic strategies are to turn inventory quickly; collect accounts receivable quickly; pay accounts slowly; and manage mail, processing, and clearing time.

- When managing the firm's short-term accounts, the financial manager must focus on competing costs. These cost trade-offs apply to managing cash and marketable securities; accounts receivable; inventory; and accounts payable, accruals, and notes payable. The goal is to balance the cost trade-offs in a fashion that minimizes the total cost of each of these accounts.

- The objective for managing accounts receivable is to collect accounts as quickly as possible without losing sales from high-pressure collection techniques. The key aspects of accounts receivable management include credit standards, credit terms, collection policy, and credit monitoring. Cash discounts are a popular feature of credit terms that help speed collections by allowing customers to receive a discount for early payment.

- Two popular approaches to credit selection are the use of the five C's of credit and, for high-volume–low-dollar requests, credit scoring. A cost-benefit analysis of credit standard, credit term, and other accounts receivable changes can be performed to make sure such actions are profitable. Key variables involved in such an analysis include the additional profit contribution from sales, the cost of the marginal investment in accounts receivable, and the cost of marginal bad debts. The three most popular techniques for credit monitoring are the average collection period, aging of accounts receivable, and payment pattern monitoring.

- The cash manger's job is to manage the cash flow time line related to collection, concentration, and disbursement of the company's funds. Float can be viewed from the perspective of either the receiving party or the paying party. Mail float and processing float are viewed the same from both perspectives. The third float component is availability float (to the receiving party) and clearing float (to the paying party). The receiving party's goal is to minimize collection float, whereas the paying party's goal is to maximize disbursement float.

- Cash managers are also responsible for financial relationships, cash flow forecasting, investing and borrowing, and information management. In large firms, they must manage the firm's cash position. In smaller firms, they set target cash balances based on transactions requirements and minimum balances set by their bank.

- In managing collections, the cash manager attempts to reduce collection float using various collection measures, such as field-banking systems, mail-based systems, and electronic systems. Large firms whose customers are geographically dispersed commonly use lockbox systems.

- Firms use cash concentration to bring lockbox and other deposits together into one bank, often a concentration bank. Firms often use depository transfer checks, ACH transfers, and wire transfers to transfer funds from the depository bank to the concentration bank.

- The objective for managing the firm's accounts payable is to pay accounts as slowly as possible without damaging the firm's credit rating. If a supplier offers a cash discount, the firm in need of short-term funds must determine the interest rate associated with not taking the discount and compare it with its lowest-cost, short-term borrowing alternative. If it can borrow elsewhere at a lower cost, the firm should take the discount; otherwise, it should not take it.

- Financial managers use popular disbursement products and methods such as zero-balance accounts (ZBAs), controlled disbursement, and positive pay. Some of the key developments in accounts payable and disbursements are integrated accounts payable, use of purchasing/procurement cards, imaging services, and a number of fraud prevention measures.

- The cash manager will hold near-cash assets in the form of short-term investments to earn a return on temporary excess cash balances. Investment policies and guidelines should be established for management of short-term investments. Smaller companies are likely to invest their short-term surpluses in money market mutual funds. Larger firms will invest in any of a variety of short-term, fixed-income securities, including U.S Treasuries, federal agency issues, bank financial instruments, and corporate obligations.

- Short-term borrowing can be obtained through the issuance of commercial paper, primarily by large firms, and through lines of credit. Most short-term borrowing is done at a rate quoted at a base rate—the prime rate or LIBOR—plus a spread reflecting the borrower's relative riskiness. The effective borrowing rate can be calculated to capture both the interest costs and other fees associated with a short-term loan.

INTERNET RESOURCES

Note: *For updates to links, please go to the book's website at* http://smart.swcollege.com

http://www.bankone.com—A large Chicago-based bank—the sixth-largest U.S. bank—which offers numerous commercial banking services, including cash management and lending

http://www.csfb.com (Credit Suisse First Boston)—Part of the Credit Suisse global banking corporation, which offers numerous cash management, investment, and lending services to its corporate customers

http://www.dunandbradstreet.com—A site that sells mercantile credit reports on virtually thousands of companies; opening a D& B account required for full access

http://www.phoenixhecht.com—A site that contains a variety of cash and treasury management resources, including links to various areas such as payment systems, cash and treasury management, and electronic commerce http://www.wellsfargo.com—The fifth-largest U.S. bank, which offers numerous commercial banking services, including business lending and leasing, cash management and treasury, and institutional investments

KEY TERMS

accounts payable management
adjustable rate preferred stock
aging of accounts receivable
all-in-rate
automated clearinghouse (ACH) debit transfer
availability float
average collection period (*ACP*)
average investment in accounts receivable (*AIAR*)
average payment period (*APP*)
bank account analysis statement
bond equivalent yield (*BEY*)
cash application
cash concentration
cash conversion cycle (*CCC*)
cash discount
cash position management
clearing float
commercial paper
controlled disbursement
cost of the marginal investment in accounts receivable
credit monitoring
credit scoring
credit terms
depository transfer check (DTC)
effective borrowing rate (*EBR*)

electronic bill presentment and payment (EBPP)
electronic depository transfer (EDT)
factoring
field-banking system
five C's of credit
float
imaging services
integrated accounts payable
lockbox system
mail float
mail-based collection system
money market mutual funds
money market yield (*MMY*)
operating assets
operating cycle (*OC*)
payment pattern
positive pay
prime rate
processing float
procurement card programs
purchasing card programs
short-term financing
target cash balance
total variable cost of annual sales (*TVC*)
turnover of accounts receivable (*TOAR*)
wire transfer
zero-balance accounts (ZBAs)

QUESTIONS

23-1. If you randomly chose a sample of firms and then calculated the operating cycle (*OC*) of each firm, what is likely to be the key cause of differences in their operating cycles? What goal should these firms attempt to achieve with regard to their *OCs*? How and why?

23-2. Why would a firm wish to minimize its cash conversion cycle (*CCC*) even though each of its components is important to the operation of the business? What key actions should the firm pursue to achieve this objective?

23-3. What impact would aggressive action aimed at minimizing a firm's cash conversion cycle (*CCC*) have on the following financial ratios: inventory turnover, average collection period, and average payment period? What are the key constraints on aggressive pursuit of these strategies with regard to inventory, accounts receivable, and accounts payable?

23-4. What are some of the key cost trade-offs that the financial manager must focus on when attempting to manage short-term accounts in a manner that minimizes cash? Make a graph describing the general nature of these cost trade-offs and the optimal level of total cost.

23-5.   Assume that the financial manager is considering stretching the firm's accounts payable by paying its vendors at a later date. What are the key cost trade-offs that would be involved when making this stretching decision? How would you quantitatively model this decision?

23-6.   Why would a firm extend credit to its customers given that such an action would lengthen its cash conversion cycle? What key cost trade-offs would be involved in this decision? What typically dictates the actual credit terms the firm extends to its customers?

23-7.   What key areas of concern must the financial manager address to effectively manage the sometimes competing interests of sales, customer service, finance, and accounting staffs? What areas of the firm are most directly involved in handling most of the accounts receivable tasks?

23-8.   How do firms set their credit standards? Can these standards be strictly quantified for use in screening potential credit customers? What procedures are typically used to evaluate credit applicants in light of the firm's credit standards?

23-9.   Why is using the *five C's of credit* the appropriate credit selection procedure for high-dollar credit requests but not appropriate for high-volume–low-dollar requests, such as department store credit cards?

23-10.   What is *credit scoring?* In what types of situations is it most useful? If you were developing a credit scoring model, what factors might be most useful in predicting whether or not a credit customer would pay in a timely manner?

23-11.   What are the key variables to consider when evaluating potential changes in a firm's credit standards? Why are only variable costs of sales included when estimating the firm's average investment in accounts receivable?

23-12.   If you sell an item to a customer for $20, your cost of that item sale is $16, and the customer defaults and does not pay, how much have you actually lost? When quantifying the analysis of potential accounts receivable policy changes, why are the costs of any bad debts recognized at the sale price rather than the cost of the sale?

23-13.   If a firm were contemplating increasing the cash discount it offers its credit customers for early payment, what key variables would need to be considered when quantitatively analyzing this decision? How do the variables used in this analysis differ from those considered when analyzing a potential change in the firm's credit standards?

23-14.   What is *credit monitoring?* How can each of the following techniques be used to monitor accounts receivable?

     a. Average collection period
     b. Aging of accounts receivable
     c. Payment pattern monitoring

23-15.   Why is the analysis of payment patterns a better credit monitoring technique for seasonal firms than the use of aging of accounts receivable? Are payment patterns typically affected by changes in sales levels?

23-16.   What is *float?* What are its four basic components? Which of these components is the same from both a collection and a payment perspective? What is the difference between *availability float* and *clearing float,* and from which perspective—collection or payment—is each relevant?

23-17.   What is *cash position management?* What types of firms set a *target cash balance?* Why? What is the purpose of a bank's requiring the firm to maintain a minimum balance in its checking account? How does this relate to a *bank account analysis statement?*

23-18. What is the firm's goal with regard to cash collections? Describe each of the following types of collection systems:

a. Field-banking system
b. Mail-based system
c. Electronic system

23-19. What is a *lockbox system?* How does it typically work? Briefly describe the economics involved in performing a cost-benefit analysis of such a system.

23-20. Briefly describe each of the following funds transfer mechanisms:

a. Depository transfer check (DTC)
b. Automated clearinghouse (ACH) debit transfer
c. Wire transfer

Why are wire transfers typically used only for high-dollar transfers?

23-21. What is the goal with regard to managing accounts payable as it relates to the cash conversion cycle? Briefly describe the process involved in managing the accounts payable function.

23-22. How can a firm in need of short-term financing decide whether or not to take a cash discount offered by its supplier? How would this decision change in the event the firm has no alternative source of short-term financing? How would it change for a firm that needs no additional short-term financing?

23-23. Briefly describe each of the following disbursement products/methods:

a. Zero-balance accounts (ZBAs)
b. Controlled disbursement
c. Positive pay

How does a ZBA relate to the firm's *target cash balance?*

23-24. What is the firm's goal in short-term investing? How does it use *money market mutual funds?* Describe some of the popular money market financial instruments in each of the following groups:

a. U.S. Treasuries
b. Federal agency issues
c. Bank financial instruments
d. Corporate obligations

23-25. How are the rates on short-term borrowing typically set? What role does either the *prime rate* or *LIBOR* play in this process? What is the *effective borrowing rate?* How does it differ from the stated *all-in-rate?*

PROBLEMS

The Cash Conversion Cycle

23-1. Canadian Products is concerned about managing its operating assets and liabilities efficiently. Inventories have an average age of 110 days, and accounts receivable have an average age of 50 days. Accounts payable are paid approximately 40 days after they arise. The firm has annual sales of $36 million, its cost of goods sold represents 75 percent of sales, and its purchases represent 70 percent of cost of goods sold. Assume a 365-day year.

a. Calculate the firm's operating cycle (OC).

b. Calculate the firm's cash conversion cycle (CCC).

c. Calculate the amount of total resources Canadian Products has invested in its CCC.

d. Discuss how management might be able to reduce the amount of total resources invested in the CCC.

23-2. The cash conversion cycle is an important tool for the financial manager in managing the day-to-day operations of the firm. As an investor, knowing how the firm manages its CCC would provide useful insights about management's effectiveness in managing the firm's resource investment in the CCC. Access Microsoft's annual statement at http://www.microsoft.com, and calculate Microsoft's CCC. Discuss any difficulties you had as an external user of the company's financial statements. Evaluate Microsoft's CCC in light of your calculations.

23-3. A firm is considering five plans that affect several current accounts. Given the five plans and their probable effects on inventory, receivables, and payables, as shown in the following table, which plan would you favor? Explain.

Plan	Average age of inventory (days)	Average collection period (days)	Average payment period (days)
		Change	
A	+35	+20	+10
B	+20	−15	+10
C	−10	+5	0
D	−20	+15	+5
E	+15	−15	+20

23-4. King Manufacturing turns its inventory 9.1 times each year, has an average payment period of 35 days, and has an average collection period of 60 days. The firm's annual sales are $72 million, its cost of goods sold represents 50 percent of sales, and its purchases represent 80 percent of cost of goods sold. Assume a 365-day year.

a. Calculate the firm's operating cycle (OC) and cash conversion cycle (CCC).

b. Calculate the firm's total resources invested in its CCC.

c. Assuming that the firm pays 14 percent to finance its resource investment in its CCC, how much would it save annually by reducing its CCC by 20 days if this reduction were achieved by shortening the average age of inventory by 10 days, shortening the average collection period by 5 days, and lengthening the average payment period by 5 days?

d. If the 20-day reduction in the firm's CCC could be achieved by a 20-day change in only one of the three components of the CCC, which one would you recommend? Explain.

23-5. Bradbury Corporation turns its inventory five times each year, has an average payment period of 25 days, and has an average collection period of 32 days. The firm's annual sales are $3.6 billion, its cost of goods sold represents 80 percent of sales, and its purchases represent 50 percent of cost of goods sold. Assume a 365-day year.

a. Calculate the firm's operating cycle (OC) and cash conversion cycle (CCC).

b. Calculate the total resources invested in the firm's CCC.

c. Assuming that the firm pays 18 percent to finance its resource investment, how much would it increase its annual profits by reducing its CCC by 12 days if this reduction were solely the result of extending its average payment period by 12 days?

d. If the 12-day reduction in the firm's CCC in part (c) could have alternatively been achieved by shortening either the average age of inventory or the average collection period by 12 days, would you have recommended one of those actions rather than the 12-day extension of the average payment period specified in part (c)? Which change would you recommend? Explain.

23-6.   Use the following firms to complete this problem:

Anheuser-Busch Companies, Inc. (BUD)
Coca-Cola Company (KO)
Adolph Coors Company (RKY)
PepsiCo, Inc. (PEP)

Go to http://yahoo.com, click on "Finance," and input the ticker symbol noted in parentheses following each company name above. Next, click on "Financials" and then on "Display Annual Data" to obtain the most recent income statement and balance sheet for each firm. Use the appropriate financial statement data for each firm to respond to the following instructions and questions.

   a. Use the formulas given in the chapter to calculate the following time periods (in days) for each of the firms:

   (1) Average age of inventory (AAI)
   (2) Average collection period (ACP)
   (3) Average payment period (APP)

   b. Use the time periods calculated in part (a) to calculate each firm's operating cycle (OC) and cash conversion cycle (CCC).

   c. Compare, contrast, and evaluate the OC and CCC calculated in part (b) for each of the following combinations:

   (1) The two soft drink companies (KO and PEP)
   (2) The two beer companies (BUD and RKY)

   How would you describe the differences found for each pair of firms?

   d. Compare and contrast the OC and CCC for the two soft drink companies to those of the two beer companies. Explain any differences you observe.

Cost Trade-offs in Short-Term Financial Management

23-7.   Geet Industries is considering installing a just-in-time (JIT) inventory system in order to significantly reduce its in-process inventories. The annual cost of the system is estimated to be $95,000. The financial manager estimates that with this system, the firm's average inventory investment will decline by 40 percent from its current level of $2.05 million. All other costs are expected to be unaffected by this system. The firm can earn 14 percent per year on equal-risk investments.

   a. What is the annual cost savings expected to result from installation of the proposed JIT system?
   b. Should the firm install the system?

23-8.   Sheth and Sons Inc. is considering changing its pay period for its salaried management from paying salaries every two weeks to paying salaries monthly. The firm's CFO, Ken Smart, believes that such an act will free up cash that can be used elsewhere in the business, which currently faces a cash crunch. In order to avoid a strong negative response from the salaried managers, the firm will simultaneously announce a new health plan that will lower the cost contribution of managers without cutting benefits. Ken's analysis indicates that the bimonthly payroll for the salaried managers is $1.8 million and is expected to remain at that level for the foreseeable future. Because the managers will be paid monthly, there will be 2.2 pay periods in a month, which means that the monthly payroll will be about $4.0 million (2.2 × $1.8 million). The annual cost to the firm of the new health plan will be $180,000. Ken believes that because managers' salaries accrue at a constant rate over the pay period, the average salaries over the period can be estimated by dividing the total amount by 2. The firm believes that it can earn 15 percent annually on any funds made available through the accrual of the managers' salaries.

a. How much additional financing will Sheth and Sons obtain as a result of switching the pay period for managers' salaries from every two weeks to monthly?

b. Should the firm implement the proposed change in pay periods?

Accounts Receivable Management

23-9. International Oil Company (IOC) uses credit scoring to evaluate gasoline credit card applications. The following table presents the financial and credit characteristics considered and weights indicating the relative importance of each characteristic in the credit decision. The firm's credit standards are to accept all applicants with credit scores of 80 or higher, to extend limited credit on a probationary basis to applicants with scores higher than 70 and lower than 80, and to reject all applicants with scores below 70.

Financial and Credit Characteristics	Predetermined Weight
Credit references	.25
Education	.10
Home ownership	.10
Income range	.15
Payment history	.30
Years on job	.10

The firm currently needs to process three applications that were recently received and scored by one of its credit analysts. The scores for each of the applicants on each of the financial and credit characteristics are summarized in the following table.

Financial and Credit Characteristics	Applicant		
	X	Y	Z
	Score (0 to 100)		
Credit references	60	90	80
Education	75	80	80
Home ownership	100	90	60
Income range	70	70	80
Payment history	60	85	70
Years on job	50	60	90

a. Use the data presented to find the credit score for each of the applicants.

b. Recommend the appropriate action that the firm should take for each of the three applicants.

Smart Solutions
See the problem and solution explained step-by-step at
SMARTFinance

23-10. Barans Company currently has an average collection period of 55 days and annual sales of $1 billion. Assume a 365-day year.

a. What is the firm's average accounts receivable balance?

b. If the variable cost of each product is 65 percent of sales, what is the *average investment in accounts receivable?*

c. If the equal-risk opportunity cost of the investment in accounts receivable is 12 percent, what is the total annual cost of the resources invested in accounts receivable?

23-11. Melton Electronics currently has an average collection period of 35 days and annual sales of $72 million. Assume a 365-day year.

a. What is the firm's average accounts receivable balance?

b. If the variable cost of each product is 70 percent of sales, what is the firm's *average investment in accounts receivable?*

c. If the equal-risk opportunity cost of the investment in accounts receivable is 16 percent, what is the total annual cost of the resources invested in accounts receivable?

d. If the firm can shorten the average collection period to 30 days by offering a cash discount of 1 percent for early payment, and 60 percent of the customers take this discount, should the firm offer this discount assuming its cost of bad debts will rise by $150,000 per year?

23-12. Davis Manufacturing Industries (DMI) currently produces and sells 20,000 units of a machine tool each year. All sales are on credit, and DMI charges all customers $500 per unit. Variable costs are $350 per unit, and the firm incurs $2 million in fixed costs each year. DMI's top managers are evaluating a proposal from the firm's CFO that the firm relax its credit standards to increase its sales and profits. The CFO believes this change will increase unit sales by 4 percent. Currently, DMI's average collection period is 40 days, and the CFO expects this to increase to 60 days under the new policy. Bad debt expense is also expected to increase from 1 to 2.5 percent of annual sales. The firm's board of directors has set a required return of 15 percent on investments with this level of risk. Assume a 365-day year.

a. What is DMI's *contribution margin?* By how much will profits from increased sales change if DMI adopts the new credit standards?

b. What is DMI's *average investment in accounts receivable* under the current credit standards? Under the proposed credit standards? What is the cost of this additional investment?

c. What is DMI's *cost of marginal bad debt expense* resulting from the relaxation of its credit standards?

d. What is DMI's net profit/loss from adopting the new credit standards? Should DMI relax its credit standards?

23-13. Jeans Manufacturing thinks that it can reduce its currently high credit costs by tightening its credit standards. However, as a result of the planned tightening, the firm believes its annual sales will drop from $38 million to $36 million. On the positive side, the firm expects its average collection period to fall from 58 to 45 days and its bad debts to drop from 2.5 to 1 percent of sales. The firm's variable cost per unit is 70 percent at its sale price, and its required return on investment is 15 percent. Assume a 365-day year. Evaluate the proposed tightening of credit standards, and make a recommendation to the management of Jeans Manufacturing.

23-14. Webb Inc. currently makes all sales on credit and offers no cash discounts. The firm is considering a 2 percent cash discount for payments within 10 days. The firm's current average collection period is 65 days, sales are 400,000 units, selling price is $50 per unit, and variable cost per unit is $40. The firm expects that the changes in credit terms will result in an increase in sales to 410,000 units, that 75 percent of the sales will take the discount, and that the average collection period will fall to 45 days. Bad debts are expected to drop from 1.0 to 0.9 percent of sales. If the firm's required rate of return on equal-risk investments is 25 percent, assuming a 365-day year, should the firm offer the proposed discount?

23-15. Microboard Inc., a major computer chip manufacturer, is considering lengthening its credit period from net 30 days to net 50 days. Currently, the average collection period is 40 days, and the firm's CFO believes that with the proposed new credit period, the average collection period will be 65 days. The firm's sales are currently $900 million, and the CFO believes that with the new credit terms, sales will increase to $980 million. At the current $900 million sales level, the firm's total variable costs are $630 million. The firm's CFO estimated that with the proposed new credit terms, bad debt expenses will increase from the current level of 1.5 percent of sales to 2.0 percent of sales. The CFO also estimates that due to the increased sales volume and accompanying receivables, the firm will have to add additional facilities and personnel to its credit and collections department. The annual costs of the expanded credit operations resulting from the proposed new credit period is estimated to be $10 million. The firm's required return on similar-risk investments is 18 percent. Assume a 365-day year. Evaluate the economics of Microboard's proposed credit-period lengthening, and make a recommendation to the firm's management.

23-16. United Worldwide's accounts receivable totaled $1.75 million on August 31, 2004. A breakdown of these outstanding accounts on the basis of the month in which the credit sale was initially made follows. The firm extends net 30, EOM credit terms to its credit customers.

Month of Credit Sale	Accounts Receivable
August 2004	$ 640,000
July 2004	500,000
June 2004	164,000
May 2004	390,000
April 2004 or before	56,000
Total (August 31, 2004)	$1,750,000

a. Prepare an aging schedule for United Worldwide's August 31, 2004, accounts receivable balance.
b. Using your findings in part (a), evaluate the firm's credit and collection activities.
c. What are some probable causes of the situation discussed in part (b)?

23-17. Big Air Board Company, a global manufacturer and distributor of both surfboards and snowboards, is in a very seasonal business. Although surfboard sales are only mildly seasonal, the snowboard sales are very seasonal, driven by peak demand in the first and fourth calendar quarters of each year. The following table gives the firm's monthly sales for the immediate past quarter (October through December 2004) and its forecast monthly sales for the coming year (calendar-year 2005).

Month	Sales ($ in millions)
Historic	
October 2004	$3.7
November 2004	3.9
December 2004	4.3
Forecast	
January 2005	$3.8
February 2005	2.6
March 2005	2.2
April 2005	1.6
May 2005	1.8
June 2005	1.9
July 2005	2.0
August 2005	2.2
September 2005	2.4
October 2005	4.1
November 2005	4.6
December 2005	5.1

The firm extends 2/10 net 30, EOM credit terms to all customers. It collects 98 percent of its receivables; the other 2 percent is typically written off as bad debts. Big Air Board's historic collection pattern, which is expected to continue through 2005, is 5 percent collected in the month of the sale, 65 percent collected in the first month following the sale, and 28 percent collected in the second month following the sale. Using the data given, calculate the payment pattern of Big Air Board's accounts receivable, and comment on the firm's monthly collections during calendar-year 2005.

Cash Management

23-18. Nickolas Industries has daily cash receipts of $350,000. A recent analysis of the firm's collections indicated that customers' payments are in the mail an average of 2 days. Once received, the payments are processed in 1.5 days. After the payments are deposited, the receipts clear the banking system, on average, in 2.5 days. Assume a 365-day year.

Smart Solutions
See the problem and solution explained step-by-step at SMARTFinance

    a. How much collection float (in days) does the firm have?

    b. If the firm's opportunity cost is 11 percent, would it be economically advisable for the firm to pay an annual fee of $84,000 for a lockbox system that reduces collection float by 2.5 days? Explain why or why not.

23-19. NorthAm Trucking is a long-haul trucking company serving customers all across the continental United States and parts of Canada and Mexico. At present, all billing activities, from preparation to collection, are handled by staff at corporate headquarters in Bloomington, Indiana. Payments are recorded and deposits are made once a day in the firm's bank, Hoosier National. You have been hired to recommend ways to reduce collection float and thereby generate cost savings.

    a. Suggest and explain at least three specific ways that NorthAm could reduce its collection float.

    b. Your preferred recommendation will cut the collection float by four days. NorthAm bills $108 million per year. Assuming evenly distributed collections throughout a 365-day year and an 8 percent cost of short-term financing, what savings could be achieved by implementing the suggestion? If this recommendation will have an annual cost of $100,000, should NorthAm implement it?

Collections

23-20. Qtime Products believes that use of a lockbox system can shorten its accounts receivable collection period by four days. The firm's annual sales, all on credit, are $65 million, billed on a continuous basis. The firm can earn 9 percent on its short-term investments. The cost of the lockbox system is $57,500 per year. Assume a 365-day year.

    a. What amount of cash will be made available for other uses under the lockbox system?

    b. What net benefit (or cost) will the firm receive if it adopts the lockbox system? Should it adopt the proposed lockbox system?

23-21. Wachovia Corporation is a major (superregional) U.S. bank. The Wachovia corporate website is located at http://www.wachovia.com. Among the cash management services available to its business customer are lockboxes. Access Wachovia's cash management and deposit services at http://www.wachovia.com/corp_inst/page/0,,7_ 17,00.html, and determine the lockbox products available from Wachovia. Discuss the differences between the various lockbox products.

23-22. Quick Burger Inc., a national chain of hamburger restaurants, has accumulated a $27,000 balance in one of its regional collection accounts. It wishes to make an efficient, cost-effective transfer of $25,000 of this balance to its corporate concentration account, thus leaving a $2,000 minimum balance in the regional collection account. It has the following options:

Option 1: DTC at a cost of $1 and requiring four days to clear
Option 2: EDT at a cost of $2.50 and requiring one day to clear
Option 3: Wire transfer at a cost of $12 and clearing the same day (zero days to clear)

a. If Quick Burger can earn 6 percent on its short-term investments, assuming a 365-day year, which of the options would you recommend to minimize the transfer cost?

b. Compare Options 2 and 3, and determine the minimum amount that would have to be transferred in order for the wire transfer (Option 3) to be more cost-effective than the EDT (Option 2).

Accounts Payable and Disbursements

23-23. Determine the interest rate associated with not taking the cash discount and paying at the end of the credit period for the following cash discount terms. Assume a 365-day year.

    a. 2/10 net 50
    b. 1/10 net 30
    c. 2/10 net 150
    d. 3/10 net 60
    e. 1/10 net 45
    f. 1/20 net 80

23-24. In Problem 23-23, you calculated the interest rate associated with not taking the discount for various cash discounts. Now you must decide whether or not to take the cash discount by paying within the discount period. To pay early, you will need to borrow from your firm's line of credit at the local bank. The interest rate on the line of credit is the prime rate plus 2.5 percent. You can get the most recent prime rate from the Federal Reserve at http://www.federalreserve.gov/releases/h15/data.htm. Using the current prime rate, determine whether the firm should borrow from the bank or borrow from its suppliers.

23-25. Access Enterprises has four possible suppliers of an important raw material used in its production process, all offering different credit terms. The products offered by each supplier are virtually identical. The following table shows the credit terms offered by these suppliers. Assume a 365-day year.

Supplier	Credit Terms
A	1/10 net 40, EOM
B	2/20 net 90, EOM
C	1/20 net 60, EOM
D	3/10 net 75, EOM

    a. Calculate the interest rate associated with not taking the discount from each supplier.

    b. If the firm needs short-term funds, which are currently available from its commercial bank at 11 percent, and if each of the suppliers is viewed *separately*, which, if any, of the suppliers' cash discounts should the firm not take? Explain why.

    c. What impact, if any, would the fact that the firm could stretch its accounts payable (net period only) by 20 days from supplier A have on your answer in part (b) relative to this supplier?

23-26. Union Company is examining its operating cash management. One of the options the firm is considering is a zero-balance account (ZBA). The ZBA offered to the firm by its bank has monthly charges of $1,500, and the bank estimates that the firm can expect to earn 8 percent on its short-term investments. Determine the minimum average cash balance that would make this ZBA a benefit to the firm. Assume a 360-day year.

23-27. Wachovia Corporation is a major (superregional) U.S. bank. The Wachovia corporate website is located at http://www.wachovia.com. Among the cash management services available to its business customer are various collection and disbursement products. Access Wachovia's cash management and deposit services at http://www

.wachovia.com/ corp_inst/page/0,,7_17,00.html, and determine the disbursement products available from Wachovia. Compare Wachovia's controlled disbursements and sweep accounts to the text definition for a ZBA.

23-28.   Bank of America is the first truly national bank in the United States. Access its corporate website at http://www.bankofamerica.com, and compare Bank of America's disbursement products with the products from Wachovia Corporation discussed in Problem 23-27.

Short-Term Investing and Borrowing

23-29.   Sager Inc. just purchased a 91-day, $1 million T-bill that was selling at a discount of 3.25 percent.

   a. Calculate the dollar discount and purchase price on this T-bill.
   b. Find the *money market yield* (*MMY*) on this T-bill.
   c. Find the *bond equivalent yield* (*BEY*) on this T-bill.
   d. Rework parts (a), (b), and (c) assuming the T-bill was selling at a 3.0 percent discount. What effect does this drop of 25 basis points in the T-bill discount have on its *BEY*?

23-30.   Matthews Manufacturing is negotiating a 1-year credit line with its bank, Worldwide Bank. The amount of the credit line is $6.5 million with an interest rate set at 1.5 percent above the prime rate. A commitment fee of .50 percent (50 basis points) will be charged on the unused portion of the line. No compensating balances are required, and the loan is made on a 365-day basis.

   a. If the prime rate is assumed constant at 4.25 percent during the term of the loan and Matthews' average loan outstanding during the year is $5.0 million, calculate the firm's *effective borrowing rate (EBR)*.
   b. What effect would an increase in the prime rate to 4.75 percent for the entire year have on Matthews' effective borrowing rate calculated in part (a)?
   c. What effect would a decrease in Matthews' average loan outstanding during the year to $4.0 million have on the effective borrowing rate calculated in part (a)?
   d. Using your findings in parts (a), (b), and (c), compare, contrast, and discuss the effects of interest rate changes versus changes in the average loan outstanding on Matthews' effective borrowing rates.

OPENING FOCUS

The Merger of Pharmacia and Upjohn— Why Mergers Fail and How They Succeed

In 1995, pharmaceutical companies Pharmacia of Sweden and Upjohn of the United States announced their $6 billion merger of equals to a warm reception from investors. At announcement, the weighted average excess return of the stocks of the two companies was 7.5 percent, reflecting an expectation of future gains from the merger. Some of these gains were anticipated to arise from the layoffs of 4,000 or more employees. The savings from these layoffs and other synergies, such as consolidating research and development and marketing expenses, were expected to save the merged firm approximately $500 million per year.

In an attempt to make this deal a true merger of equals, the governance structure of the merged firm (Pharmacia-Upjohn) offered equal representation to both firms. The board of directors was equally split between former Pharmacia and Upjohn directors, and there was an agreement that the chairman of the board and chief executive officer (CEO) be separate offices, with one filled by an American and the other, by a European. Thus, John Zabriskie, former Upjohn CEO, and Jan Ekberg, former Pharmacia chairman, maintained their roles in the new firm. As a further compromise, neither the U.S. nor the Swedish headquarters was closed, but a third, central headquarters was established in London.

Shortly after completion of the merger, unexpected problems began to arise. Because management did not account for the greater strength of labor unions and labor laws in Europe, fewer than 1,000 of the expected 4,000 layoffs were made; incompatible information systems between the United States and Europe made reporting systems unreliable; and the new headquarters had substantially increased overhead expenses with no tangible benefit. Culture clashes also began to surface because of differences in American and European business practices and management styles. The problems continued to grow and culminated in Zabriskie's resignation in January 1997 when the European board members rejected his plan for an-

SMARTfinance
Use the learning tools at http://smartfinance.swcollege.com

other merger as a solution to the company's problems. Between the November 1995 merger date and Zabriskie's resignation, the return on Pharmacia-Upjohn's stock had trailed that of the pharmaceutical industry by 25 percent. The merger was a clear failure up to that point.

Fred Hassan was brought in as an outside CEO four months later to turn around the failed merger. Having no prior history with either Pharmacia or Upjohn and as neither an American nor a European, Hassan had no allegiance to either of the former companies. Hassan was a true agent for Pharmacia-Upjohn, and his management decisions reflected this. Noticing that many of the culture problems stemmed from a "Pharmacia versus Up-john" approach to business, Hassan declared that the merger had created a new company that should have its own culture and should not be wed to prior practices or cultural mores of the former companies. Hassan affirmed this idea by infusing further outsiders into his management team, closing the headquarters in Sweden and London, demanding one standard for information systems, concentrating marketing efforts on the high-growth market of the United States, and focusing research efforts on drugs with higher potential. Within 18 months of Hassan's tenure as CEO, Pharmacia-Upjohn had outperformed the pharmaceutical industry by almost 50 percent. Pharmacia-Upjohn became the new industry darling and was strong enough to acquire rival Monsanto in 2000, a deal that would have been unthinkable three years earlier.

As its name implies, **corporate control** refers to the monitoring, supervision, and direction of a corporation or other business organization. The most common change in corporate control results from the combination of two or more business entities into a single organization, as happens in a merger or acquisition. A change in corporate control also occurs with the consolidation of voting power within a small group of investors, as found in going-private transactions such as leveraged buyouts (LBOs) and management buyouts (MBOs). Transfer of ownership of a business unit with a divestiture and the creation of a new corporation through a spin-off are other ways to bring about such a change.

The forces effecting changes in corporate control and the resulting impact on the business community present some of the most interesting and hotly contested debates in the field of finance. For example, the corporate control contest for RJR Nabisco captivated the attention of corporate America in the fall of 1988, spawned a book and a movie about the takeover, and remains a source of debate for academics and politicians over the social benefit of corporate control activities. We address the causes and consequences of changes in corporate control in this chapter, as well as provide real-world examples of the merger/acquisition process and the technical aspects a corporate manager must consider before making decisions regarding corporate control changes.

24.1 OVERVIEW OF CORPORATE CONTROL ACTIVITIES

You have probably heard the expressions "mergers and acquisitions" or "M&A's" and know what the terms mean in general. However, the terminology of corporate control is far more expansive and specific than these generic terms indicate. For instance, the popular press often uses the term "takeover" to conjure up images of an unwelcome bidder commandeering control of a corporation through the techniques of high finance and the means of great sums of money. A **takeover,** however, simply refers to any transaction in which the control of one entity is taken over by another. Thus, a friendly merger negotiated between the boards of directors and shareholders of two independent corporations is a takeover, as is a successful entrepreneur selling out her enterprise to a corporation. The terminology of corporate control can be easily misconstrued and must be clearly defined to prevent such ambiguities. In the following discussion, we will define the many terms and concepts encountered in the corporate control arena.

CORPORATE CONTROL TRANSACTIONS

Changes in corporate control occur through several mechanisms, most notably via acquisitions. An **acquisition** is the purchase of additional resources by a business enterprise. These resources may come from the purchase of new assets, the purchase of some of the assets of another company, or the purchase of another whole business entity, which is known as a merger. **Merger** is itself a general term applied to a transaction in which two or more business organizations combine into a single entity. Oftentimes, however, the term "merger" is reserved for a transaction in which one corporation takes over another upon the approval of both companies' boards of directors and shareholders after a friendly and mutually agreeable set of terms and conditions and a price are negotiated. Payment is in the form of an exchange of common stock. In actuality, there are many different types of mergers, and they (as well as other corporate control activities) can be differentiated according to several criteria. We define mergers by the mode of target integration used by the acquiring firm, by the level of business concentration created by the merger, and by other transaction characteristics for which mergers are commonly known.

Mode of Integration

There are a number of ways to integrate the assets and resources of an acquired firm into the acquiring company (the acquirer). The following discussion describes the various forms of resource integration (or disintegration in the case of sell-offs) that may be used to combine the resources of an acquirer and target (or to shed resources in the case of a sell-off).

Statutory Merger.   A **statutory merger** is a form of target integration in which the acquirer can absorb the target's resources directly with no remaining trace of the target as a separate entity. Many intrastate bank mergers are of this form.

Subsidiary Merger.   Conversely, an acquirer may wish to maintain the identity of the target as either a separate subsidiary or division. A **subsidiary merger** is often the integration vehicle when there is brand value in the name of the target, such as the case of PepsiCo's merger with Pizza Hut in 1977 (can you imagine eating a Pepsi Pizza?). Sometimes, separate "tracking" or "target" shares are issued in the subsidiary's name. These shares can be issued as new common shares in exchange for the target's common shares (former General Motors subsidiaries Electronic Data Systems and Hughes Electronics had their own traded shares of General Motors common stock in Class E and Class H shares, respectively), or a new class of preferred stock may be issued by the bidding firm to replace the common shares of the target as well.

Consolidation.   **Consolidation** is another integrative form used to effect a merger of two publicly traded companies. Under this form, both the acquirer and target disappear as separate corporations and combine to form an entirely new corporation with new common stock. This form of integration is common in mergers of equals where the market values of the acquirer and target are similar. Many of these new corporations adopt a name that is merely a hybrid of the former names, like the 1985 consolidation of Allied Corporation and Signal Companies to become AlliedSignal. But some managers of newly created companies want a "fresh start" with a company name, as in the case of Sandoz and Ciba-Geigy when they merged in 1997 to form Novartis.

Another type of merger that warrants mention, even though it is not a separate integrative form, is the **reverse merger.** In this transaction, the acquirer has a lesser market value than the target. Differences in size can be substantial in a reverse merger but are often the result of a merger of equals where the *control premium* paid by the acquirer causes the market value of the target to exceed that of the acquirer.[1]

LBOs, MBOs, and Dual-Class Recapitalizations.

Changes in corporate control also occur when voting power is concentrated in the hands of one individual or a small group. Going-private transactions are one way to achieve this concentration of control. Just as they sound, **going-private transactions** transform public corporations into private companies through issuance of large amounts of debt used to buy all (or at least a voting majority) of the outstanding shares of the corporation. The acquiring party may be a leveraged-buyout (LBO) firm, such as Kohlberg, Kravis, and Roberts (KKR), which specializes in such deals; the current managers of the corporation (known as a **management buyout** or **MBO**); or even the employees of the corporation itself through an **employee stock ownership plan** (**ESOP**). A prime example of both an LBO and an MBO attempt is the 1988 corporate control contest for RJR Nabisco. H. Ross Johnson, the CEO of RJR Nabisco, led a management team that attempted to take the company private, but was outbid by KKR in a $29 billion LBO.[2] An LBO that returns as a public company is known as a **reverse LBO.**

A **dual-class recapitalization** may also concentrate control. Under this form of organizational restructuring, the parties wishing to concentrate control (usually management) buy all the shares of a newly issued Class B stock, which carries "super" voting rights (100 votes per share, for example). Traditional Class A shareholders generally receive some form of compensation, such as higher dividends, for the dilution of their voting power.

Tender Offers, Acquisitions, and Proxy Fights.

An acquirer can also attain control of a public corporation through a nonnegotiated purchase of the corporation's shares in the open market or through the voting control of other stockholders' shares via proxy. Theoretically, an acquirer can gain control simply through open-market purchases of a target firm's shares, though regulation se-

SMART IDEAS VIDEO
Steve Kaplan, University of Chicago
"The results have been that LBOs have performed well on average."

See the entire interview at **SMARTFinance**

verely restricts this form of "creeping acquisition" in most developed countries. Generally, an acquirer must explicitly bid for control through a tender offer for shares. A **tender offer** is a structured purchase of the target's shares in which the acquirer announces a public offer to buy a minimum number of shares at a specific price. Interested stockholders may then "tender" their shares at the offer price. If at least the minimum number of shares is tendered, then the acquirer buys those shares at the offer price. The acquirer has the option of buying the shares tendered at the offer price or canceling the offer altogether if the minimum number of shares is not tendered.[3] A two-tiered offer results when the acquirer offers to buy a certain number of shares at one price and then more shares at another price. These offers are especially

---

[1.] A control premium is the difference between premerger market value and acquisition value. For example, if ABC Company offered to buy XYZ Company for $25 per share for its 100 million shares outstanding when the stock price was $20, then the control premium is $5 per share, $500 million total, or 25 percent.

[2.] For an insightful and entertaining look at this deal, as well as the LBO/MBO process, see Burroughs and Helyar (1993).

[3.] The U.S. tender offer process is strictly regulated by the Williams Act, an amendment to the Securities and Exchange Act. See the discussion of the Williams Act in Section 24.3 for more details on the regulation of tender offers.

popular in situations where the acquirer wishes to purchase 100 percent of the shares outstanding as quickly as possible and offers to buy 51 percent at a higher price and the remaining 49 percent at a lower price in an attempt to provide an incentive for shareholders to tender their shares early in order to receive the higher price. A **tender-merger** is a merger that occurs after an acquirer secures enough voting control of the target's shares through a tender offer to effect a merger.

Tender offers are often associated with hostile takeovers, but these are the highly publicized minority cases. In fact, a study by Jennings and Mazzeo (1993) shows that target management resisted only 86 of 263 tender offers from 1979 to 1987. Yet, open-market purchases, tender offers, and proxy fights may all be used in combination to launch a "surprise attack" on an unwitting (and often unwilling) target. Individuals or corporations may own up to 5 percent of any corporation's stock before facing the requirement of filing a Schedule 13-d form with the Securities and Exchange Commission (SEC) identifying themselves as a significant stockholder in the company. Thus, an interested potential acquirer could accumulate a substantial number of shares (known as a *foothold*) without the knowledge of the target's management and then follow a number of acquisition strategies. First, the interested acquirer could simply initiate a tender offer to purchase the remaining shares of the target required for voting control and then effect a merger (a tender-merger as mentioned previously). Second, the potential acquirer could approach the target with both a merger offer and the threat of a proxy fight and/or hostile tender offer to gain the remaining shares needed to obtain voting control of the target if the merger offer is refused. This tactic is known as a **bear hug**. Third, the acquirer could also threaten the target with a hostile tender offer and/or proxy fight in order to gain initial or greater access to the board of directors or to sell its shares to the target firm at a premium price.[4] Target firms employ defensive measures such as **antitakeover amendments** to their corporate charters (also known as **shark repellents**), **poison pills,** the pursuit of **white knights** ("friendly" acquirers who will top the price of an unwelcome bidder), MBOs, stock buybacks, payment of greenmail (see Footnote 4), and other defensive tactics.[5] See Table 24.1 for greater detail on antitakeover mechanisms. Obviously, there are many different acquisition strategies and methods for integrating the resources of the acquiring and acquired firms.

SMART IDEAS VIDEO
James Brickley, University of Utah
"Theoretically, antitakeover devices like poison pills might benefit shareholders."

See the entire interview at **SMART**Finance

Divestitures and Spin-offs. Sometimes, managers prefer to transfer control of certain assets and resources through divestitures, spin-offs, split-offs, equity carve-outs, split-ups, or bust-ups. A **divestiture** occurs when the assets and/or resources of a subsidiary or division are sold to another organization. For example, Advanta Corp. sold its credit card operations to Fleet Financial in 1997 for $500 million.

In a **spin-off,** a parent company creates a new company with its own shares by spinning off a division or subsidiary. Existing shareholders receive a pro rata distribution of shares in the new company. This happened when PepsiCo spun off its restaurant operations (Pizza Hut, Taco Bell, and KFC) in 1997 as a new company named Tricon Global Restaurants (with the catchy ticker symbol YUM). A **split-off** is similar to a spin-off in that a parent company creates a newly independent company from a subsidiary, but ownership of the company is transferred to only certain

---

[4.] The latter practice is a type of *targeted share repurchase* known as **greenmail.** This was a widespread practice used by corporate raiders in the 1980s, but is now outlawed in many states and taxed heavily by the Internal Revenue Service.
[5.] *Poison pills* are takeover defenses that can be triggered unilaterally by the target firm's board and effectively make a hostile takeover prohibitively expensive to the potential acquirer. These are typically adopted *without* shareholder approval.

Table 24.1
Commonly Used Antitakeover Measures

Measure	Antitakeover Effect
Fair price amendments	Corporate charter amendments mandating that a "fair price," usually defined as the highest price paid to any shareholder, be paid to all of the target firm's shareholders in the event of a takeover
Golden parachutes	Large termination arrangements made for executives that are activated after a takeover
Greenmail	The payment of a premium price for the shares held by a potential hostile acquirer, but not paid to all stockholders
Just-say-no defense	Refusal to entertain a takeover offer on the grounds that no consideration offered is sufficient to relinquish control
Pac-Man defense	The initiation of a takeover attempt for the hostile acquirer itself
Poison pills	Dilution of the value of shares acquired by a hostile bidder through the offer of additional shares to all other existing shareholders at a discounted price
Poison puts	Deterrent to hostile takeovers through put options attached to bonds that allow the holders to sell their bonds back to the company at a prespecified price in the event of a takeover
Recapitalization	A change in capital structure designed to make the target less attractive
Staggered director elections	Corporate charter amendments designed to make it more difficult for a hostile acquirer to replace the board of directors with persons sympathetic to a takeover
Standstill agreements	Negotiated contracts that prevent a substantial shareholder from acquiring more shares for a defined period of time
Supermajority approvals	Corporate charter amendments that require the approval of large majorities (67% or 80%) for a takeover to occur
White knight defense	The pursuit of a friendly acquirer to take over the company instead of a hostile acquirer
White squire defense	The sale of a substantial number of shares to an entity that is sympathetic to current management but has no intention of acquiring the firm

existing shareholders in exchange for their shares in the parent. *Equity carve-outs* (described more fully in Chapters 13 and 16) bring a cash infusion to the parent through the sale of a partial interest in a subsidiary through a public offering to new stockholders. Split-ups and bust-ups are the ultimate transfers of corporate control. As it sounds, the **split-up** of a corporation is the split-up and sale of all its subsidiaries so that it ceases to exist (except possibly as a holding company with no assets). A **bust-up** is the takeover of a company that is subsequently split up.

Business Concentration

Mergers may also be classified by the relatedness of the business activities of the merging firms. There are several different classification schemes utilized for the business relatedness of the acquiring and acquired firms, but the most commonly applied scheme is the abbreviated classification offered by the Federal Trade Commission (FTC). In the following paragraphs, we define these FTC classifications, as well as others that are used, and introduce their importance to our eventual discussion of antitrust laws.

Horizontal Mergers. In a strict sense, the FTC defines a **horizontal merger** as a combination of competitors within the same geographic market; the Commission defines a **market extension merger** as a combination of firms that produce the same product in different geographic markets. As interstate commerce and technology have rendered geographic market classification less meaningful over time, the common interpretation of a horizontal merger has loosened to become a merger between companies that produce identical or closely related products in any geographic market—a merger of the old horizontal and market extension classifications, if you will. For example, a merger between two electric companies, one in Oregon and the other in Oklahoma, would have once been considered a market extension merger but would now be classified as horizontal.

The classification of mergers is important with regard to the regulatory authority of the FTC and the Department of Justice (DOJ), especially in the case of horizontal mergers. The FTC and DOJ have broad regulatory powers that can be used to prevent any merger that is deemed to be anticompetitive in nature, and the combinations that have the greatest potential to be anticompetitive are horizontal mergers.

APPLYING THE MODEL

The failed 1997 merger attempt of Staples and Office Depot illustrates the legal perils facing companies wishing to execute horizontal mergers. Both companies were discount office supply retailers with some overlapping geographic markets and only one major competitor (OfficeMax). FTC and DOJ regulators opposed the merger on the grounds that it would be anticompetitive. Staples and Office Depot countered with an offer to sell all the Office Depot stores sharing the same market as a Staples store and an OfficeMax, making the merger more of a traditional market extension merger than a "strict" horizontal merger. The companies also sought to have their market more broadly defined as general discount retail (such as Target and Wal-Mart) so that the impact of the merger would not appear so anticompetitive. The companies' tactics failed, as did their attempted merger, reflecting the evolving definition of horizontal and anticompetitive mergers.

Horizontal mergers also have the greatest potential for wealth creation. Firms with similar businesses and assets have the ability to benefit from economies of scale and scope from combining their resources. These mergers also have the greatest *possibility* of realizing cost savings through the reduction or elimination of overlapping resources. **Market power** is another obvious benefit that might arise from a horizontal merger. Increased market power results when competition is too weak (or nonexistent) to prevent the merged company from raising prices in a market at will. Of course, this is exactly the kind of anticompetitiveness that the regulators in the Staples–Office Depot merger sought to prevent.

Vertical Mergers. A **vertical merger** occurs when companies with current or potential buyer-seller relationships combine to create a more integrated company. These mergers are easiest to think of in terms of steps in the production process. Consider the process of producing and selling finished petroleum products. Petroleum exploration and production is followed by transportation, refining, and end-use sales. If a company in the drilling business acquires a company that refines crude oil, then the driller is moving forward in the production process by purchasing the potential buyer of its crude oil. This type of vertical merger is a **forward integration.** Had a refiner and distributor acquired a driller, then the merger would be a **backward integration,** as exemplified by the 1984 merger between Texaco and Getty Oil. Texaco needed Getty's drilling operations and reserves to complement its own refineries and distribution and marketing outlets in order to be a fully integrated oil company.

There are several obvious potential benefits to vertical integration via merger.

One advantage to a vertical merger is that product quality and procurement can be ensured from earlier stages of the production process with backward integration. For instance, a manufacturer of precision surgical devices might wish to ensure the high-quality standards required of an input such as a laser beam by acquiring the company that manufactures the laser beam. Or, a manufacturer with great sensitivity to inventory conversion cycles could more efficiently monitor an orderly inventory flow by acquiring a supplier of raw materials. Another advantage to backward integration is the reduction of input prices. The "middleman" and associated price markup are eliminated.

Forward integration may also offer benefits. Whereas backward integration emphasizes inputs, forward integration focuses on output quality and distribution. Provision of an outlet for a product is an advantage to forward integration. One reason for Disney's merger with Capital Cities/ABC was to gain access to a television network as an outlet for Disney's television entertainment production. Vertical integration can also be used as a marketing tool. Many retail stores and automobile manufacturers have acquired financing subsidiaries to make it easier for a customer to obtain credit to purchase their products (e.g., Ford Motor Credit).

However, there are also disadvantages to vertical mergers. The major disadvantage is the entry into a new line of business. Acquiring managers are likely to have some knowledge of the target firm's business because it is part of the same production process, but similarities do not always imply compatibility. A manager of an automobile manufacturer might find that what works well for manufacturing cars does not work well for renting them, even though both businesses revolve around automobiles (as Chrysler found out with its Thrifty Rent-a-Car unit). Managers might also find that the cost savings from "eliminating the middleman" are not as great as expected. Eliminating the markup might reduce costs for the acquirer, but it also means that the acquired subsidiary is no longer producing profits for the parent company. The acquirer might overlook or underestimate this factor when attempting to value a target. Finally, vertical mergers may also be subject to antitrust regulation, albeit with a smaller probability than with horizontal mergers.

Conglomerate Mergers. The remaining two types of FTC-defined mergers are diversifying in nature. **Product extension mergers,** or related diversification mergers, are combinations of companies with similar but not exact lines of business. **Pure conglomerate mergers,** or unrelated diversification mergers, occur between companies in completely different lines of business.

Product extension mergers, like market extension mergers, are something of a hybrid classification, in this case a cross between vertical and purely conglomerate mergers. These mergers are not vertical because they are not between firms in different stages of the production process, but their business operations are still related. The 1989 merger of Consolidated Freightways and Emery Air Freight provides an example of a related diversification merger. Consolidated was a major provider of surface freight transportation with a minimal presence in airfreight transportation, the sole business of Emery. Consolidated was experienced in the general business of freight transportation, but not the specific business of airfreight transportation. Managers tend to pursue these types of mergers when searching for a higher-growth business that is not entirely new to them.

Pure conglomerate mergers marry two companies that operate in totally unrelated businesses. Popular especially in the 1960s, these mergers have significantly declined in frequency since the 1980s, as discussed in the following empirical results section. Based on the principles of portfolio diversification, the purpose of these

Table 24.2
Level of Business Concentration Resulting from Merger—an Example of Various Classifications

Line of Business	Acquirer			Target			Combined		
	Revenues	%	%^{2}	Revenues	%	%^{2}	Revenues	%	%^{2}
Chemicals	$ 500,000,000	50.0	.2500	$200,000,000	40.0	.1600	$ 700,000,000	46.7	.2180
Oil refining	300,000,000	30.0	.0900	0	0.0	.0000	300,000,000	20.0	.0400
Coal mining	200,000,000	20.0	.0400	0	0.0	.0000	200,000,000	13.3	.0178
Retail drugs	0	0.0	.0000	150,000,000	30.0	.0900	150,000,000	10.0	.0100
Plastics	0	0.0	.0000	150,000,000	30.0	.0900	150,000,000	10.0	.0100
Total	$1,000,000,000	100.0	.3800	$500,000,000	100.0	.3400	$1,500,000,000	100.0	.2958

Note: Abbreviated FTC classification: horizontal
    Business overlap classification: medium overlap
    Change in focus classification: focus-decreasing

mergers is to put together two companies that operate in businesses so different that if some systematic or idiosyncratic event has an adverse effect on one business, then the other business will be minimally (or even positively) impacted. Merging these two firms is expected to make earnings and cash flows less volatile. The 1984 merger of automaker General Motors and computer/business service consulting firm Electronic Data Systems is a prime example of a pure conglomerate merger.

Other Concentration Classifications. The abbreviated (horizontal/vertical/conglomerate) and full (abbreviated plus market and product extension) FTC merger classifications are not always satisfactory for determining the degree of business concentration created by a merger. Compare the following two hypothetical mergers for an illustration of a possible shortcoming of the FTC classification. The first merger pairs two software companies that operate in no other lines of business. The second merger occurs between the companies in Table 24.2. The acquirer in this merger derives 50 percent of its revenue from chemicals, 30 percent from crude-oil refining, and 20 percent from coal-mining operations. Chemicals are also the primary line of business for the target at 40 percent of revenues, followed by 30 percent from retail drugs and 30 percent from plastics. Because the acquirer and target are in the same primary line of business in both mergers, both are classified as horizontal mergers under the abbreviated FTC scheme. But do both mergers have the same level of business concentration? Obviously not—the first merger clearly has more concentration than the second. The need for a finer definition of business concentration in such cases gave rise to the creation of alternative measures, such as degree of overlapping business and change in corporate focus (defined below).

Healy, Palepu, and Ruback (1992; hereafter HPR) introduced the concept of classifying mergers according to the degree of overlapping business operations between the acquirer and target. Reviewing the lines of business of the acquirer and target, the researchers categorized mergers as having high, medium, and low levels of overlapping business. These categories loosely correspond to (respectively) horizontal, vertical, and conglomerate classifications, but more flexibility exists for assessing the concentration of more complex cases such as our merger in Table 24.2. Although considered a horizontal merger under traditional classification, this merger would fall under medium overlap in the HPR categorization rather than high overlap. You can easily see how the flexibility of the HPR classification allows for a truer account of a merger's business concentration.

An even more finely tuned measure of business concentration revolves around the concept of **corporate focus.** A focused firm concentrates its efforts on its core (primary) business, the opposite end of the spectrum from a diversified firm. Comment and Jarrell (1995) popularized the use of a measure known as the **Herfindahl Index (HI)** to demonstrate the relationship between corporate focus and shareholder wealth. The HI is computed as the sum of the squared percentages, in this case the proportion of revenues derived from each line of business. Thus, the HI exaggerates the difference between focused and diversified firms. A completely focused firm has an HI of 1.00 compared to the diversified acquiring firm in our example, which has an HI of 0.38 ($0.5^2 + 0.3^2 + 0.2^2$). A merger (or divestiture) increases focus if the HI of the merged firm is greater than that of the acquiring firm prior to the merger, preserves focus if the HI does not change, and decreases focus if the HI declines. In our hypothetical mergers, the first merger between the software companies preserves corporate focus whereas the second merger between the diversified companies decreases corporate focus, as the HI declines from 0.380 to 0.296.

Transaction Characteristics

We also find corporate control events categorized according to certain defining characteristics of the transactions, including the method of payment used to finance a transaction, the attitude or response of target management to a takeover attempt, and the accounting treatment used when the firms combine.

Method of Payment. Just like any other type of investment, a merger must be financed with capital components—including debt, retained earnings, and newly issued common stock. These components comprise the consideration offered in a transaction and sum to the transaction value, the dollar value of all forms of payment offered to the target for control of the company. Cash on hand from retained earnings and/or generated from an issue of debt is used in financing a cash-only deal, where the target's shareholders receive only cash for their shares in a public company or the target's owner(s) receives cash for the private enterprise. More rarely, the target receives a new issue of debt in exchange for control in a debt-only transaction.

Conversely, stock is the only mode of payment in a stock-swap or **pure stock exchange merger.** The general stock-swap merger involves the issuance of new shares of common stock in exchange for the target's common stock, but payment may come in the form of either preferred stock or subsidiary tracking shares. The number of shares of the surviving firm's common stock that target shareholders receive is determined by the exchange ratio.[6] For instance, an acquirer with a current stock price of $20 that sets an exchange ratio of 0.75 for a target with a current stock price of $12 and 100 million shares outstanding will issue 75 million new shares in exchange for the target's shares. The transaction value of this merger would be $1.5 billion ($20 × 75 million).[7] An individual who owns 100 shares ($1,200) of the target stock would receive acquirer stock worth $1,500 ($20 × 75 shares), a 25 percent control premium.

Mergers may also be financed with a combination of cash and securities, in transactions known as **mixed offerings.** Research by Loughran and Vijh (1997) reveals

---

[6.] The surviving firm is either the acquiring firm or the new firm created in a consolidation.

[7.] This is under the assumption that the acquirer's stock price remains the same—a very optimistic assumption, as we will later see. In most stock-swap mergers, an acceptable range of stock prices and exchange ratios is negotiated from the outset.

that 24.1 percent of U.S. acquisitions are mixed, compared to 33.2 percent for cash-only deals and 42.8 percent for stock-swap mergers. The Disney–Capital Cities/ABC merger is an example of a mixed offering. Capital Cities/ABC shareholders were offered $65 and one share of Disney stock for each of their shares.

Sometimes, target shareholders are also offered a choice for the medium of exchange. For example, target shareholders could be offered the choice of either $30 cash or 1.25 shares of the surviving company's shares for each share that they hold. This way, the shareholders can make the decision of whether the exchange ratio is sufficient for them to remain shareholders in the surviving company or whether they should "take the money and run" with the cash offer.

Attitude of Target Management. Takeover attempts (successful and unsuccessful) are often classified by the degree of resistance offered by the management of the target firm. Uncontested offers are generally referred to as "friendly" deals, whereas resisted offers are termed "hostile" transactions. As it seems that everyone likes a good fight, hostile deals receive a disproportionate share of attention. However, management resisted only 31 percent of the takeover attempts in the Jennings and Mazzeo (1993) study of public targets. Considering the more recent corporate trend of adopting antitakeover measures to thwart hostile bidders and the fact that takeovers of private or closely held firms are friendly by nature, hostile deals represent an increasingly smaller (but highly publicized) percentage of all corporate control activities. Hilton Hotels' bid for ITT in December 1995 illustrates a typical hostile takeover attempt.

APPLYING THE MODEL

ITT Corp. was the surviving corporation created by a split-up of the old International Telephone & Telegraph in December 1995. Manufacturing operations were spun off as ITT Industries, insurance operations were spun off as ITT Hartford, and the hotel and casino operations were retained by ITT Corp. under the direction of CEO Rand Araskog. On January 27, 1997, Hilton Hotels and its CEO, Stephen Bollenbach, initiated an unsolicited $6.5 billion (plus another $4 billion in assumed debt) takeover bid for ITT Corp. and began one of the most colorful and hostile corporate control contests in business history. The hostile nature of the contest carried over to the personal level as well—Bollenbach once referred to Araskog as a "weenie" for rejecting Hilton's bid.

Araskog had long been chastised by investors for his large compensation package and the lagging stock price of the old International Telephone & Telegraph, which was attributed to Araskog's unwillingness to expedite a return to corporate focus. Although he oversaw the focus-increasing split-up of the old corporation in 1995, Araskog disappointed investors in 1996 with the news that earnings at ITT Corp. would still be lower than expected. Bollenbach then seized the opportunity represented by the deflated stock price of ITT to make a takeover bid for the company that he believed to be a poorly managed underperformer. Bollenbach felt that Hilton could more efficiently run the Sheraton hotel chain and Caesar's World casino and the remaining assets of ITT could be sold off to help finance the deal.

Araskog rejected the takeover bid and fought back with a series of antitakeover measures designed to ward off Bollenbach and Hilton. Included in these measures were a lawsuit against Hilton, further sell-offs of noncore assets, postponement of the annual meeting so that Hilton's proposed slate of directors could not be voted in, and a major restructuring plan that would have split ITT into three companies with staggered director terms—further limiting Hilton's ability to gain control. Hilton then

raised its offer to $8.3 billion and sued for an injunction to prevent the proposed split-up of ITT. A federal court granted Hilton's injunction and ruled that ITT could not restructure without shareholder approval at an organized shareholder meeting.

Realizing after the federal court ruling that defeat was likely and the possibility of remaining an independent corporation was growing smaller, Araskog sought and found a white knight to take over ITT—Starwood Lodging, a "paired share" REIT with tax advantages over Hilton with regard to the takeover of ITT's properties. Starwood made an offer of $9.3 billion for the stock of ITT. Hilton countered with a cash and stock offer of $9.8 billion, which was subsequently countered by an all-stock offer of $10.2 billion by Starwood. Refusing to raise its offer, Hilton stated that its lower offer price was actually superior to Starwood's because it offered a sure thing to ITT shareholders—cash. However, on November 12, 1997, ITT shareholders approved the merger with Starwood, and Hilton abandoned its takeover attempt. Araskog's white knight defense proved successful. ■

Accounting Treatment. Prior to June 30, 2001, two financial accounting procedures existed for recording a merger in the United States: the pooling-of-interests and purchase methods. However, with implementation of Financial Accounting Standards Board (FASB) Statement 141 and the near-concurrent (December 31, 2001) Statement 142, there now exists one standard method of accounting for mergers. Under these new standards, target liabilities remain unchanged, but target assets are "written up" to reflect current market values, and the equity of the target is revised upward to incorporate the purchase price paid. These revised values are then carried over to the surviving firm's financial statements. The intangible asset *goodwill* is created if the restated values of the target lead to a situation in which its assets are less than liabilities and equity. This **goodwill** reflects the premium that an acquiring firm is willing to pay in excess of net asset market value in order to capture synergies from the merger—goodwill becomes an intangible asset on the balance sheet. Going forward, the value of this intangible asset must be evaluated to determine if it has been "impaired" due to a decline in fair value relative to carrying value. If the value of goodwill is impaired, then the amount of the impairment is "written down" from the goodwill account on the balance sheet and charged off against earnings. Otherwise, it remains unchanged on the balance sheet indefinitely. Many large write-downs were taken soon after FASB 142 went into effect at the beginning of 2002. JDS Uniphase, AOL Time Warner, and Nortel Networks all took multi-billion-dollar write-downs in 2002 for acquisitions completed in prior years. See the following Applying the Model for a mathematical example of accounting for mergers.[8]

APPLYING THE MODEL

Assume that a target firm has 5 million shares outstanding at a price $10 per share. The acquiring firm offers a 20 percent takeover premium ($12 per share) for a transaction value of equity of $60 million. The acquiring firm wants the R&D capabilities of the target firm and is willing to pay a premium to obtain those capabilities and leverage R&D synergies. The market value of the target's fixed assets is $65 million. Along with the $10 million in current assets, the target has a market value of assets of $75 million. Deducting the $5 million in current liabilities and $25 million in long-term liabilities, the target firm has a net asset value of $45 million. Thus, the acquir-

---

[8.] See also Moehrle and Reynolds-Moehrle (2001) for more detail on merger accounting.

ing firm is willing to pay $15 million ($60 million less $45 million) for intangible assets in the form of R&D.

Current assets	$10,000,000
Restated fixed assets	65,000,000
Less: Liabilities	30,000,000
Net asset value	$45,000,000
Purchase price paid	$60,000,000
Less: Net asset value	45,000,000
Goodwill	$15,000,000

Further assume that the target firm is treated as a separate reporting subsidiary after the merger. Going forward, the firm must value its intangible assets (goodwill) to determine if the value of $15 million on the balance sheet represents a fair value. As long as the firm can demonstrate that the goodwill is fairly valued, then it will remain unaffected on the balance sheet. However, if the value is "impaired," then the value loss must be reported, deducted from the balance sheet, and taken as a write-off against earnings. For example, if the R&D of the subsidiary does not turn out as synergistic as hoped for two years later, then the fair market value and net asset value of the subsidiary will be estimated. If the fair market value is estimated at $70 million and the net asset value at $60 million, then the value of goodwill is only $10 million, a $5 million impairment. This $5 million would be deducted from the balance sheet and taken as an intangible asset write-down on the income statement.

	Acquirer ($ in millions)	Target ($ in millions)	Merged ($ in millions)	
			Subsidiary	Consolidated
Assets				
Current	$ 50	$10	$10	$ 60
Fixed	350	50	65	415
Goodwill	0	0	15	15
Total assets	$400	$60	$90	$490
Liabilities				
Current	$ 50	$ 5	$ 5	$ 55
Long-term	250	25	25	275
Total	$300	$30	$30	$330
Owner's equity	$100	$30	$60	$160
Total liabilities and equity	$400	$60	$90	$490

Concept Review Questions	**1.** Why are acquired resources integrated into a company in so many different forms? What transaction-specific circumstances might lead to a preference of one integrative form over another? **2.** What is the purpose of classifying mergers by degree of business concentration? Why do you think these classifications have changed over time?

24.2 RATIONALE AND MOTIVES FOR MERGERS AND ACQUISITIONS

As we have seen, the primary objective of any corporation's management team should be the maximization of shareholder wealth. Management should undertake a

potential merger or acquisition, like any other investment, as long as its net present value is positive and enhances shareholder value. Mergers may be value enhancing in several ways. However, we know that corporate managers do not always act as proper agents for their shareholders, and agency problems arise when managers engage in non-value-maximizing behavior. In this section, we examine both the value-maximizing and non-value-maximizing motives that lead managers to pursue mergers and acquisitions.

VALUE-MAXIMIZING MOTIVES

Mergers create value when managers seek goals such as increasing operating profit, realizing gains from restructuring poorly managed firms, or creating greater barriers to entry in their industry. These and other value-enhancing objectives can be achieved through mergers and acquisitions that garner access to new geographic markets, increase market power, capitalize on economies of scale, or create value through the sale of underperforming target resources.

Expansion

Geographic expansion (both domestic and international) may enhance shareholder wealth if the market entered is subject to little or no competition. Managers considering expansion must first evaluate two mutually exclusive alternatives: internal versus external expansion. Internal expansion into a new market, also known as **greenfield entry,** involves acquiring and organizing all resources required for each stage of the investment. These stages involve contracting with an engineering firm to build a new plant, hiring new employees to staff the plant, implementing training programs for the new staff, establishing distribution outlets, and so on.

External expansion is the acquisition of a firm with resources already in place. Acquirers pay a control premium to the owners of the acquired firm for relinquishing control, but the payment of this premium ensures that many of the potential problems of greenfield entry are avoided. For instance, external expansion avoids construction delays in the building of a new plant or the inability to adequately staff a new facility. Usually, external expansion is the better option in situations where rapid expansion is desired or when great uncertainty exists about the success of any stage of greenfield entry. International expansion is another good reason to choose external expansion over internal expansion. The business operations, political climate, and social mores differ so greatly between some countries that an acquisition is often the only viable alternative for international expansion.[9]

HealthSouth, an S&P 500 company, is the nation's largest health-care provider of outpatient and rehabilitation services. However, HealthSouth is a relatively new entrant in corporate America. Founded in Birmingham, Alabama, in 1983 by chairman and CEO Richard Scrushy, HealthSouth has grown from its humble beginnings to its current status through an aggressive expansion strategy spurred by more than 30 major mergers or acquisitions.

HealthSouth began an acquisition program in 1985 that targeted its home state

---

[9]. Joint ventures and strategic alliances also allow access to foreign markets through existing resources, but these are partnering relationships in which profits must be shared.

of Alabama as well as the neighboring states of Florida, Georgia, and Tennessee. Capitalizing on the name recognition of some of its high-profile athlete patients (Bo Jackson, for one), HealthSouth sought to expand its operations nationwide—a feat accomplished in 1996 when the company's acquisition program had placed Health-South centers in all 50 states and the District of Columbia. In 1997, the company continued to expand and consolidate—moving into the United Kingdom and also acquiring the company's largest U.S. competitor, Horizon/CMS Healthcare. Scrushy, in order to create a global brand name, seems intent on perpetuating the successful acquisition strategy employed in the past that turned HealthSouth into a national brand name.

Synergy, Market Power, and Strategic Mergers

A **strategic merger** is one that seeks to create a more efficient merged company than the two premerger companies operating independently. This efficiency-enhancing effect is known as **synergy**. Michael Eisner, CEO of Disney, provided the best definition of synergy with his perception of the value created by his company's merger with Capital Cities/ABC: "1 + 1 = 4." There are three types of merger-related synergies—*operational, managerial,* and *financial.*

Synergies. The main sources of **operational synergy** are economies of scale, economies of scope, and resource complementarities. **Economies of scale** result when relative operating costs are reduced because of an increase in size that allows for the reduction or elimination of overlapping resources. For example, the reason given for the elimination of 12,000 positions in the 1995 merger of Chemical Bank and Chase Manhattan Bank was the cost savings generated from the elimination of overlapping jobs. **Economies of scope** are other value-creating benefits of increased size. The ability for a merged firm to launch a national advertising campaign that would not have been feasible for either of the premerger firms is such a benefit. **Resource complementarities** exist when a firm with a particular operating expertise merges with a firm with another operating strength to create a company that has expertise in multiple areas. A good example of such a complementarity is the merger of two pharmaceutical companies, the first a specialist in researching and developing new drugs and the second a master marketer of drug products. Operating synergies are most likely to be achieved in horizontal mergers and least likely to be realized in conglomerate mergers. However, resource complementarities are just as likely to be realized in vertical mergers as horizontal mergers, because vertical combinations pair companies that specialize in different areas.

Managerial synergies, like operating synergies, cause two firms to have greater value when combined than when they are independent. Managerial synergies, however, result in efficiency gains from the combination of management teams. Similar to resource complementarities, managerial synergies arise when management teams with different strengths are paired together. Consider a merger between two retailing firms with differing managerial expertise. The first retailer has a management team that emphasizes revenue growth and excels in recognizing customer trends. The second retailer has a technically oriented management team that excels in cost containment and has perfected inventory control with its superior information systems. A merger between these two firms should benefit from managerial synergies with a joint emphasis on and expertise in revenue growth and cost containment, assuming the two management teams can mesh together smoothly.

Financial synergies occur when a merger results in less-volatile cash flows, lower default risk, and a lower cost of capital. As financial synergies are largely the antici-

pated result of conglomerate mergers, we defer this discussion to the section on the diversification motive for mergers.

Market Power.   Other, more controversial, motives support increasing firm size through mergers and acquisitions. As we have seen, horizontal mergers have the potential to create more-efficient companies through size-related operational synergies. Horizontal mergers may also profit from size in another fashion: increased market power. As horizontal mergers are those that take place between competitors, the number of competitors in an industry will necessarily decline. Presumably, price competition will also decline if the merger creates a dominant firm that has the power to control prices in a market.

Consider the Staples–Office Depot merger attempt previously mentioned. The two largest competitors in an industry with only three true competitors attempted to merge. The regulatory authorities denied this merger on the grounds that the merged company would have the power to control prices in the office supplies market with only one, much smaller, competitor to provide price competition. Regulatory authorities must balance the corporate benefit of increased efficiency against the consumer cost of increased market power when making decisions on allowing a merger to take place—especially a horizontal merger.

Other Strategic Rationales.   Other strategic reasons also motivate managers to pursue mergers. As we mentioned earlier, in vertical mergers, product quality can sometimes be more closely monitored. Another strategic motive is defensive consolidation in a mature or declining industry. As consumer demand declines in an industry, competitors may seek each other out for a merger in order to survive the permanent industry downturn. Not only does the merged firm stand to benefit from economies of scale and scope, but it will also benefit from the reduction of competition. Of course, this does introduce the market power issue for regulators. But recent history has seen regulators adopt a more permissive attitude toward defensive consolidation—for example, the defensive consolidation in the U.S. defense industry (pardon the pun) in the post–Cold War period.

Cash Flow Generation and Financial Mergers

Financial mergers are motivated by the prospect of uncovering hidden value in a target through a major restructuring or the generation of free cash flow from merger-related tax advantages. Many of the hostile deals of the 1980s were junk bond–financed financial mergers aimed at either "busting up" undervalued firms by selling off the assets of the acquired firm for a value greater than the acquisition price or restructuring the acquired firm to increase its corporate focus. A typical financial merger involves a focused acquirer that acquires a diversified firm with some business operations in the acquirer's line of business. The acquirer then sells the noncore businesses and uses the cash flow to pay down the cost of the acquisition.

Tax considerations may also motivate managers to pursue a particular target for a merger. The asymmetrical nature of the U.S. tax code provides an incentive to merge in certain circumstances. Although taxes must always be paid on positive income, negative income (net losses) creates only tax-loss carrybacks and carryforwards that offset taxes paid (on past income) or due on future income; the government does not pay negative taxes (cash payments) to firms suffering net losses.[10] As discussed in more detail in Chapter 25, **tax-loss carryforwards** can be charged

---

[10.] Imagine the Internal Revenue Service paying corporations to lose money.

against future income for up to 15 years. Acquiring a target that has accumulated tax-loss carryforwards could shelter taxable income and redistribute that cash flow to other uses.

As junk bond financing of acquisitions has declined since the 1980s, so has the occurrence of financial mergers. This merger motive was further minimized by a change in the tax code in 1986 that limited the extent to which tax-loss carryforwards could be used after a merger. Financial mergers still occur, but their importance in the market for corporate control has declined significantly.

Non-Value-Maximizing Motives

Unfortunately, not all mergers are motivated for the purpose of maximizing shareholder wealth. Although the motives of managers may not be intentionally value reducing, most revolve around agency problems between managers and shareholders. We discuss these improper motives below.

Agency Problems

Managers will sometimes disguise their attempts to derive personal benefits from creating and managing larger corporations as the need to expand through mergers and acquisitions. Academic research confirms the importance of this motive with findings that merger activity is positively related to growth in sales and assets but not related to increased profits or stock prices. Considering these findings, Dennis Mueller (1969) offered the **managerialism theory of mergers.** According to this theory, poorly monitored managers will pursue mergers to maximize their corporation's asset size because managerial compensation is usually based on firm size, regardless of whether or not these mergers create value for stockholders.

Michael Jensen (1986) further advanced the managerialism theory with his **free cash flow theory of mergers.** Jensen hypothesizes that managers will use free cash flow to invest in mergers that have negative net present values in order to build corporate empires from which the managers will derive personal benefits, including greater compensation. Obviously, investing in negative-NPV projects is not value enhancing for shareholders. Another variation on this theme is the **managerial entrenchment theory of mergers** proposed by Shleifer and Vishny (1989). Like the free cash flow theory, this theory holds that unmonitored managers will try to build corporate empires through the pursuit of negative-NPV mergers. However, the entrenchment theory holds that the motive is to make the management team indispensable to the firm because of its greater size and the team's supposed expertise in managing a large company. All three theories have a common theme: agency problems motivate managers to seek mergers that benefit themselves but not shareholders.

Richard Roll (1986) offers a similar rationale with his **hubris hypothesis of corporate takeovers.** Roll contends that some managers overestimate their own managerial capabilities and pursue takeovers with the belief that they can better manage their takeover target than the target's current management team can. Acquiring managers then overbid for the target and fail to realize the gains expected from the merger in the postmerger period, thereby diminishing shareholder wealth. Thus, the intent of the managers is not incongruent with the best interests of shareholders (the managers think they will create value), but the result is nonetheless value decreasing.

Diversification

As recently as the late 1960s, diversification was actually considered a value-maximizing motive for merger. Over time, however, the capital markets have learned of

Searching for Effective Corporate Governance and Value-Enhancing Mergers

Enron, WorldCom, Adelphia, Global Crossing, Qwest Communications, Tyco. These are but a few of the high-profile corporate bankruptcies or near failures that have destroyed shareholder wealth and shaken investor confidence in the years after the great 1990s bull market. Underlying the much-publicized accounting scandals and extraordinary executive compensation paid out in these American corporate failures is the ultimate factor that led to their demise—ineffective corporate governance. Stockholders, bondholders, employees, journalists, and politicians (of course) are all demanding to know, "Where were the boards of directors who were supposed to be monitoring the managers?" These same groups are demanding reforms to restore confidence in corporate America, and both domestic and international sources are also seeking corporate reforms.

One domestic reform had already taken place before the spate of corporate failures began. Beginning in 2001, the Financial Accounting Standards Board (FASB) enacted Standards 141 and 142 to update and codify merger and acquisition accounting and the goodwill account created in these transactions. However, these two new standards were promulgated too late to prevent the old tricks being used in merger and acquisition accounting in the 1990s. Before the new standards were enacted, firms could manipulate merger and acquisition accounting rules to overstate their true financial performance. When the merger wave waned and the firms could no longer use their overvalued stock to fund acquisitions, the firms' true financial performance was revealed. Even with the new rules in place, Sam DiPiazza, CEO of accounting firm Pricewaterhouse-Coopers, called for even more stringent accounting rules and implementation of international best accounting practices for U.S. corporations.

International proposals for corporate governance reform are also being considered. Governance structures in the United Kingdom and continental Europe are being discussed as possible alternatives to the typical governance structure in place in publicly traded U.S. corporations. In particular, two major British committees issued guidelines for more effective corporate governance during the 1990s. The three basic recommendations of the Cadbury Committee on the Financial Aspects of Corporate Governance (1992) and the Hempel Committee (1998) were that a corporation's chairman of the board and chief executive officer (CEO) always be separate persons, that the board of directors should have a majority of independent directors, and that no corporate insiders should serve on the board's audit committee. The similarity of capital markets in Britain and America appears to make these guidelines implementable as listing policies for either the New York Stock Exchange or Nasdaq.

In many continental European corporations (especially in Germany), management responsibilities are split between two mutually exclusive groups—a management board and a supervisory board consisting of representatives from the government, financial institutions, labor unions, and other interested parties. Corporate managers do not serve on the supervisory board, which is charged with overseeing the management team. However, the continental governance system is much less consistent with the U.S. model than is the British system. First, hostile takeovers are virtually unheard of in continental Europe, whereas these are commonly used as a disciplining device in Great Britain and the United States. Second, unlike U.S. corporations, financial institutions (and oftentimes the government) have substantial ownership stakes in European corporations. On the other hand, the complete separation of a supervisory board and managers offers an appealing alternative for those seeking to reform U.S. corporate governance.

As the search continues for effective corporate governance structures in the United States and abroad, it has become clear that no country or system has perfected a corporate governance structure. Concurrent with the spectacular U.S. corporate failures that occurred during the spring and summer of 2002 were the precipitous declines in shareholder value and CEO ousters witnessed at French conglomerate Vivendi and German telecom giant Deutsche Telekom. In both cases, the firms could not recover from acquisitions that destroyed firm value. Especially disconcerting was the saga of Sir Christopher Gent, CEO of British telecom firm Vodafone. Gent had led Vodafone through the takeover of Mannesman AG, the largest takeover in history at the time. Unfortunately, the merger was ill-advised and led to a significant loss in shareholder wealth, but an increase in Gent's compensation and stock options. While U.S. reformers were looking to the United Kingdom for ideas on more effective corporate governance, British stockholders and institutional investors were complaining of the ineffective corporate governance that had allowed Gent to enhance his own wealth while stockholders continued to lose money. And the search for effective corporate governance goes on.

the failure of corporate diversification strategies, especially those emphasizing unrelated diversification. Given these empirical discoveries, we must now consider that diversification is a non-value-enhancing motive for merger.[11]

As previously discussed, corporate diversification and conglomerate mergers were an experiment in portfolio theory applied to corporations. The basic premise of corporate diversification is that the combination of two businesses with less than perfectly correlated cash flows will create a merged firm with less-volatile cash flows and inherently lower business risk, where bad outcomes in one business can be offset by good outcomes in another business. Diversification supporters contend that these less-volatile cash flows make debt service less risky, lowering default risk and the required return on debt. As described in Lewellen (1971) and Levy and Sarnat (1970), financial synergy is created by this **coinsurance of debt,** as the debt of each combining firm is now insured with cash flows from two businesses. Other proponents of unrelated diversification cite the existence of internal capital markets as another reason to pursue conglomerate mergers. **Internal capital markets** are created when the high cash flows (*cash cow*) businesses of a conglomerate generate enough cash flow to fund the "rising star" businesses. Since this financing is accomplished internally, underwriting costs are avoided and riskier business ventures can be financed with "cheaper" capital generated from more mature and less risky businesses.

Additional research on corporate diversification generated theories describing the flaws in the diversification motive for merger. Realizing that conglomerate mergers are not likely to benefit from any synergies other than financial, researchers such as Higgins and Schall (1975) and Galai and Masulis (1976) showed that the net effect of conglomerate mergers is zero wealth creation and that any wealth gains experienced by bondholders due to financial synergies are merely redistributed from stockholders. Further, internal capital markets fell into disrepute when it became obvious that managerial control over free cash flow created its own—often severe—agency problems. In particular, capital attained and invested without having to pass a market test is often wasted.

In the early 1980s, researchers theorized that managers pursue conglomerate mergers for risk reduction motives that were personal instead of corporate. Managers recognize that less-volatile cash flows result in a lower probability of a substantially poor performance in any single year and the concomitant threat of management dismissal. Therefore, managers are motivated to pursue conglomerate mergers in order to reduce their employment risk, as discussed in Amihud and Lev (1981). Given the failing results of diversified firms, the **managerial risk reduction theory** seems to be quite insightful and implies that the diversification motive, once thought to be beneficial to stockholders, must now be viewed as a value-destroying rationale caused by agency problems.

Concept Review Questions

3. What characteristics surrounding a merger would lead you to conclude that it is motivated by value-maximizing managers rather than non-value-maximizing managers? What actions could directors or stockholders take to prevent non-value-maximizing mergers?

4. If you wanted to expand your operations into a foreign country with nebulous laws and an unstable political climate, would you favor internal or external expansion? Why?

[11.] Section 24.4 presents a summary of the empirical studies that helped turn academics and practitioners against conglomerate mergers.

24.3 HISTORY AND REGULATION OF MERGERS AND ACQUISITIONS IN THE UNITED STATES

Merger activity in the United States has been defined more by waves of concentrated intensity rather than by continuous activity over time. Mitchell and Mulherin (1996) show that these waves tend to be positively related to high growth rates in the overall economy and are also related to "industry shocks," or industrywide events such as deregulation that affect the corporate control activities of whole industries and lead to these merger waves. In this section, we identify the key merger waves in U.S. history and discuss the factors that led to their occurrence, as well as the corporate control regulation that has evolved over time.

THE HISTORY OF MERGER WAVES

The United States has witnessed five major merger waves in its history, most of which have been similar in nature. They begin with a robust stock market, and the types of mergers occurring in each wave reflect the current regulatory environment. Activity is generally concentrated in industries undergoing changes (shocks), and the merger waves tend to end with large declines in the stock market. The following discussion presents an overview of these waves.

The first major merger wave began in 1897 and was largely the result of a growing emphasis on a truly national economy rather than a grouping of regional economies. When interstate commerce became viable with the completion of transcontinental railroads, corporations sought expansion and market power through market extension mergers. The lax regulatory environment of that period also made in-market horizontal mergers popular. Thus, the first merger wave was primarily a market concentration phase in which monopolies were created in the mining and manufacturing industries. Merger activity peaked in 1899 in this wave and ended with the stock market crash of 1904.

Another merger wave began shortly after World War I with a zeal for consolidation equal to that of the first wave. However, the administration of Theodore Roosevelt had strengthened enforcement of antitrust laws in the early 1900s, limiting the ability to create a monopoly through merger in this second wave. Instead, horizontal combinations created oligopolies within industries rather than one dominant monopoly. Heavily concentrated industries, such as mining and manufacturing, turned to vertical mergers in an attempt to benefit from integration, as further consolidation was not possible. Much like the first wave, the second wave was sparked by the desire to create national rather than regional brands. Transportation services improved with the advent of motor vehicles, and the capability of marketing a national brand became a more realistic possibility with the invention and proliferation of the radio. Also like the first wave, the second wave ended with a stock market decline, the infamous 1929 crash.

Conglomerate mergers set the tone for the third merger wave of the 1960s. A combination of two forces led to the preference for diversification over consolidation in this wave. First, the Celler-Kefauver Act of 1950 created a heightened level of antitrust enforcement because it gave the federal government greater ammunition to deny horizontal and vertical mergers. Second, managers began experimenting with the concept of diversification at the firm level. Corporations became portfolios of business units; the diversification across different industries was supposed to reduce the risk of the corporation and the volatility of its cash flows in the same manner as portfolio diversification. These "portfolio" corporations became known as con-

Table 24.3
Ten Largest Corporate
Takeovers, Ranked
by Transaction Value
(as of December 31,
2001)

Acquirer	Target	Transaction Value ($ in billions)	Year
Vodafone AirTouch PLC (UK)	Mannesmann AG (Germany)	$202.8	2000
America Online Inc. (US)	Time Warner Inc. (US)	164.7	2001
Pfizer Inc. (US)	Warner-Lambert Co. (US)	89.2	2000
Exxon Corp. (US)	Mobil Corp. (US)	78.9	1999
Glaxo Wellcome PLC (UK)	Smithkline Beecham (UK)	76.0	2000
Travelers Group Inc. (US)	Citicorp (US)	72.6	1998
SBC Communications Inc. (US)	Ameritech Corp. (US)	62.6	1999
NationsBank Corp. (US)	BankAmerica Corp. (US)	61.6	1998
Vodafone Group PLC (UK)	AirTouch Communications (US)	60.3	1999
Qwest Communications Inc. (US)	U S WEST Inc. (US)	56.3	2000

Source: Mergers & Acquisitions (SDC Publishing).

glomerates. The push for conglomeration was so great during this wave that approximately 70 percent of the mergers that took place in the 1960s were either pure conglomerate or product extension mergers. Conglomerate giants reached their heyday during this era, only to underperform the overall stock market in later years. This wave ended with the stock market decline of 1969.

The most interesting and dramatic merger wave was the one that occurred in the 1980s. Initiated by the more lax regulatory emphasis of the Reagan administration, the fourth merger wave saw a shift back to corporate specialization and witnessed such occurrences as junk bond financing, hostile takeovers, corporate raiders, greenmail, LBOs, MBOs, and poison pills. One distinguishing characteristic of this merger wave is how junk bond financing transformed the corporate control market. Prior to the 1980s, acquirers were usually larger firms with greater access to capital than the targets that they acquired. However, Michael Milken led the investment bank Drexel Burnham Lambert into a new era of junk bond financing that enabled previously minor players, who would not otherwise have had the financial resources, to become acquirers. Junk bond financing made LBOs and MBOs an active market and also led to several hostile bust-up takeovers, where junk bonds were used to acquire a firm, and then the proceeds from the sale of the acquired firm's assets were used to pay down the acquisition debt. Many antitakeover measures were adopted in the 1980s to prevent such hostile takeover attempts. This merger wave differs from previous ones in that it did not end with a major stock market decline. Many finance professionals felt that the wave would end with the stock market crash of 1987, yet many of the largest acquisitions of that decade took place between the time of the stock market crash and the end of the decade (see Table 24.3). Activity did decline at the end of the decade as the proliferation of junk bond financing became a concern (and the ability to obtain such financing waned with the increasing federal scrutiny of the practices of Drexel Burnham Lambert) and as the market players began to digest the magnitude of the $29 billion buyout of RJR Nabisco. This bidding contest culminated in a transaction value almost twice that of the next-largest deal in history at that time.

Friendly stock-swap mergers became the transaction method of choice in the fifth and latest wave of mergers, which began in 1993 and ended with the sharp drop in takeovers during 2001. Following the trend of corporate specialization from the fourth wave, the vast majority of mergers in this wave occurred between companies in the same industry. Federal regulators remained relatively open to horizontal mergers as merger activity in other countries also led to larger (and supposedly more efficient) foreign competitors. The **industry shock theory of takeovers** seems to explain much of the activity in this wave. The industries with heavy merger activity were health care, banking, and telecommunications, each having gone through a recent shock. Managed care affected health care, and deregulation and rapid technological changes transformed the banking and telecommunications industries. Merger activity in this wave surpassed that in all the others, reaching $3.4 trillion in aggregate transaction value in the peak year of 2000. Of this aggregate value, slightly less than $1.8 trillion was generated from deals completed in the United States and about $1.6 billion, from deals outside the United States. The total value of mergers worldwide fell by half to $1.7 trillion in 2001, and as of October 2002, global M&A volume continued to contract sharply.

REGULATION OF CORPORATE CONTROL ACTIVITIES

SMART PRACTICES VIDEO
David Baum, Co-head of M&A for Goldman Sachs in the Americas
"Today cross-border transactions are about a quarter of the overall M&A business."

See the entire interview at **SMARTFinance**

The legal environment affecting mergers evolved from a state of virtually no regulation during the first merger wave to what is currently a relatively complex nexus of interrelated legal issues, including antitrust enforcement, tender offer regulation, and laws regarding the actions of managers and directors and even actions of state and international regulators. This section addresses these legal issues and their ramifications for the decision to merge.

Antitrust Regulation

Antitrust legislation is intended to prevent an anticompetitive business environment. Obviously, mergers—especially horizontal mergers—often represent the most expedient manner to create corporate behemoths with the power to control prices in their markets. For this reason, antitrust enforcement encompasses the prevention of mergers that are deemed to have anticompetitive effects. Antitrust regulation began with the loophole-ridden Sherman Antitrust Act of 1890, was reinforced by the Clayton Act of 1914, and then was further strengthened by the Celler-Kefauver Act of 1950. The level of antitrust enforcement, administered in part by the Department of Justice (DOJ), tends to be related to the philosophy of the governing executive administration. Following passage of the Celler-Kefauver Act, antitrust laws were relatively strictly enforced until the Reagan administration took office and relaxed antitrust enforcement. Aside from a few noted cases, antitrust enforcement has remained more lax since the 1980s.[12] The following sections outline the major aspects of various antitrust laws as well as the guidelines established by the regulatory agencies for determining the anticompetitive potential of a merger.

Antitrust Laws. The Sherman Antitrust Act initiated antitrust regulation in 1890 and has been amended and modified many times since. The last major federal antitrust legislation was enacted in 1976, but the interpretation of antitrust laws is a dynamic process in which regulatory agencies maintain an ongoing dialogue on the application of the laws. Listed in Table 24.4 are the major federal antitrust laws.

Determination of Anticompetitiveness. Much like the business concentration classifications of the Federal Trade Commission (FTC), the measures and determinants of anticom-

---

[12.] Such exceptions include the DOJ's refusal to allow Microsoft and Intuit to merge in 1994 and its continued pursuit of Microsoft for anticompetitive business practices.

Table 24.4
Major U.S. Antitrust Legislation

Legislation (year)	Purpose of Legislation
Sherman Antitrust Act (1890)	Enacted to prevent the formation of trusts (similar to monopolies) and prohibited "every contract, combination, . . . , or conspiracy in the restraint of trade; allowed aggrieved parties or the federal government to sue violators for triple damages[a]
Clayton Act (1914)	Created to strengthen the Sherman Act after a series of Supreme Court rulings rendered Sherman unenforceable due to its broad and ambiguous prohibitions against monopolistic actions; outlawed specific business activities such as price discrimination, tying contracts, concurrent service on competitors' boards of directors, and acquisition of a competitor's stock in order to lessen competition
Federal Trade Commission Act (1914)	Established the Federal Trade Commission (FTC) as a regulatory agency to complement the Justice Department (DOJ) as an antitrust watchdog
Celler-Kefauver Act (1950)	Closed the "Section 7 loophole" of the Clayton Act, which did not prohibit the acquisition of a competitor's assets in order to lessen competition; severely limited the possibility of obtaining approval for a horizontal merger
Hart-Scott-Rodino Act (1976)	Allowed the FTC or DOJ to rule on the permissibility of a merger prior to consummation

[a]In an ironic example of the triple damages awarded under the provisions of the Sherman Act, the United States Football League (USFL) won its antitrust case against the National Football League (NFL) in 1986. However, the damage was determined to be $1, and the USFL folded before the next season—despite its gargantuan $3 award.

petitiveness have evolved over time. The DOJ established the first set of merger guidelines for determining anticompetitiveness in 1968 and modified them in 1982, 1984, and 1992. The following guidelines are those currently utilized by the DOJ and FTC.

The 1982 guidelines introduced the use of the Herfindahl-Hirschman Index (HHI), a variant of the Herfindahl Index defined earlier, to determine market concentration in the same manner that we used the index to measure business concentration earlier in the chapter. The DOJ determines the anticompetitive effect of a merger by evaluating that merger's impact on the HHI of the industry involved. The HHI is calculated as the sum of the squares of each company's percentage of sales within a market (industry). This HHI is then used to establish a range of concentration levels within a market or industry:

>1,800	Highly concentrated
1,000–1,800	Moderately concentrated
< 1,000	Not concentrated

Mergers resulting in an HHI measure in the highly concentrated category are the most likely to be challenged. Consider the example in Table 24.5. The premerger HHI of this industry is 1,450 (moderately concentrated). A merger between Company 7 and Company 8 would reduce the number of competitors in the industry, but the marginal impact of a merger between the two smallest players in the industry would increase the HHI to only 1,500 and would likely not face a challenge. However, a merger between the two largest firms in the industry would result in an HHI of 2,050—moving this industry from moderately to highly concentrated and likely prompting a challenge by the DOJ or FTC.

Realizing the efficiency-enhancing benefits of economies of scale and scope, which come only from increased size, the regulatory authorities developed an alter-

Table 24.5
Determination of
Anticompetitiveness—an
Illustration of the Use of
the Herfindahl-Hirschman
Index (HHI)

Premerger Concentration			Postmerger Concentration					
Firm	Market Share (%)	Market Share Squared	Firm	Market Share (%)	Market Share Squared	Firm	Market Share (%)	Market Share Squared
1	20%	0.0400	1	20%	0.0400	1 + 2	35%	0.1225
2	15	0.0225	2	15	0.0225	3	15	0.0225
3	15	0.0225	3	15	0.0225	4	15	0.0225
4	15	0.0225	4	15	0.0225	5	15	0.0225
5	15	0.0225	5	15	0.0225	6	10	0.0100
6	10	0.0100	6	10	0.0100	7	5	0.0025
7	5	0.0025	7 + 8	10	0.0100	8	5	0.0025
8	5	0.0025						
Sum		0.1450			0.1500			0.2050
HHI		1,450			1,500			2,050
Concentration		Moderate			Moderate			High

native measure to be used in determining the anticompetitiveness of a merger. This alternative is an elasticity measure that offers an advantage over the strict use of the HHI because the elasticity measure does not necessarily deem a merger to be anticompetitive because of fewer competitors in a highly concentrated industry. Instead, an elasticity measure determines if a merged firm will have the market power to control prices in its market. The DOJ uses a "5 percent rule" to measure elasticity: if a 5 percent increase in price results in a greater than 5 percent decline in demand in a market, then that market is elastic. Elastic markets are less likely to be adversely impacted by a merger and also less likely to be strictly governed by the HHI measure.

APPLYING THE MODEL

The failed 1997 merger attempt of Staples and Office Depot exemplifies the role of regulatory agencies in preventing what are deemed to be anticompetitive combinations. On September 4, 1996, Staples and Office Depot announced their intent to merge in a $3.4 billion deal. At the time, Office Depot and Staples were the largest and second-largest office supply superstores, respectively. Of the $14.0 billion in sales in this market, Office Depot had a market share of $6.6 billion, followed by Staples with $4.1 billion, and the only other major competitor, OfficeMax, with sales of $3.3 billion.

As permitted under the Hart-Scott-Rodino Act, the Federal Trade Commission (FTC) reviewed the proposed merger for anticompetitive effects and requested more information from the companies at the end of the initial review period. At the end of the second review, the FTC concluded that the proposed merger would have an anticompetitive impact if allowed to be consummated and rejected the merger proposal. One of the key points given by the FTC in its rejection was the market power that the merged firm would be able to wield in those markets where no stores other than Staples or Office Depot existed (the 5% rule). In order to remedy this obstacle, Staples and Office Depot proposed to sell 63 stores to OfficeMax in the geographic market where both Staples and Office Depot were located. The FTC again rejected the merger and threatened to sue the companies in federal court if they attempted to pursue their merger. The FTC further threatened that if it could not prevent the merger under the Hart-Scott-Rodino Act through its federal lawsuit, then it would continue to pursue the merged firm for antitrust violations.

The managers of both companies continued to fight for their merger, despite the threats of the FTC. When presenting their argument to the federal judge assigned to the case, lawyers for the companies presented the companies' willingness to sell off stores in order to satisfy the FTC and enhance competition and also contended that the FTC had improperly defined their industry when determining the Herfindahl-Hirschman Index. The FTC had limited their industry classification to office supply superstores with three competitors and an HHI of 3,634 (already highly concentrated), which would increase to 6,394 after the merger. Lawyers for the companies, however, stated that the appropriate industry classification should be discount retailers and should include such discount retailers as Wal-Mart and Kmart in addition to office supply stores. The judge in the case disagreed with the companies' lawyers and sided with the FTC in barring the merger from taking place. The managers of Staples and Office Depot announced their intentions to abandon their merger plans shortly thereafter.

Although merger guidelines have evolved over time and now seem to be less hostile toward horizontal combinations, the DOJ and FTC remain active enforcers of antitrust laws. One merely needs to ask the managers of Staples and Office Depot about this active enforcement. As we mentioned in the section on horizontal mergers, the managers of these corporations attempted to take advantage of the elasticity measure in 1997 with their contention that their true competitors were all the discount retailers rather than OfficeMax alone, the only other major discount office supply chain. The managers explained that the merger of their two companies would have a negligible impact on prices in the discount retailing market. Although this latter argument was probably true, the DOJ and FTC did not accept the managers' contention that their market was too narrowly defined and disapproved the merger.

Other Antitrust Considerations. Managers contemplating a merger now face antitrust scrutiny from sources other than U.S. federal regulators. Globalization and proactive state regulators have created more recent obstacles to merger approval. Individual states have become more active participants in the oversight of anticompetitive business practices since the 1990s. State attorneys general from 14 states joined the antitrust lawsuit first lodged against Microsoft by the Justice Department in 1994. Even after the federal government abandoned its case against Microsoft in 2001 in an effort to settle the case out of court, many of the states refused to abandon their status as plaintiffs against Microsoft. Although only the state of California has expressed an open willingness to file suit in opposition to a merger on the grounds of anticompetitiveness, the vigilance of the plaintiff states in the antitrust case against Microsoft indicates that state regulators could become an impediment to future mergers.

International regulatory authorities, especially in Europe, have also become a force to be reckoned with for those companies attempting large-scale mergers. The European Commission (EC) first signaled its more stringent antitrust regulatory authority in 1999, when it vetoed the proposed merger of U.S. communications giants WorldCom and Sprint. The EC expressed concerns about the pricing power that the combined firm could have if the second- and third-largest U.S. communications firms (behind industry leader AT&T) merged to become the first- or second-largest communications firm in many European markets. The managers of both WorldCom and Sprint abandoned their effort to merge after the EC's decision. EC competition commissioner Mario Monti created an international stir in 2001 when he denied the petition to merge filed by General Electric and Honeywell, although the merger had already been approved by U.S. antitrust authorities. Monti's stern defense of his position and denial of the petition on appeal sends a clear message that firms with international operations that are considering a merger must account for antitrust authorities outside the United States, even if the merger is between American firms.

The Williams Act

During the conglomerate merger wave of the 1960s, hostile tender offers became an increasingly frequent and controversial means to facilitate takeovers. The controversy over these tender offers revolved around target shareholders' inability to evaluate the terms of the tender offers in the often short periods of time for which they were open and around the abuses of higher takeover premiums being offered to select shareholders. In response to this controversy, the Williams Act passed in 1967 and was enacted in 1968 as an amendment to the Securities and Exchange Commission Act of 1934. Section 13 of the Williams Act introduced ownership disclosure requirements, and Section 14 created rules for the tender offer process.

Ownership Disclosure Requirements. Section 13-d of the Williams Act now requires public disclosure of ownership levels beyond 5 percent.[13] This section of the act mandates that any individual, group of individuals acting in concert, or firm must file a Schedule 13-d form within 10 days of acquiring a 5 percent or greater stake in a publicly traded company. This disclosure sends a warning signal to the managers and stockholders of a corporation that a potential acquirer might be lurking about and provides background information on that potential acquirer. Stockholders or managers of the corporation may sue for damages if any material misrepresentation (such as initiating a later takeover attempt when the stated purpose of ownership is for investment purposes) is made on the form.[14]

SMART IDEAS VIDEO

Francesca Cornelli, London Business School

"There is an example that shows how crucial risk arbitrage can be to the success of a takeover."

See the entire interview at **SMARTFinance**

Tender Offer Regulation. Whereas Section 13 of the Williams Act forces the disclosure of pertinent information regarding a potential acquirer, Section 14 governs stock acquisitions via tender offers. Prior to passage of the Williams Act, tender offers were largely unregulated open calls to the shareholders of public companies to tender (sell) their shares at offered prices. Tender offers could be completed swiftly and repeated at different offer prices if desired. Section 14 changed this free-form nature of the tender offer market to a much more restrictive and structured process. Any party initiating a tender offer must file a Schedule 14-d-1 form (a tender offer statement). Managers of tender offer targets are then required to file a Schedule 14-d-9 form, which contains their recommendation to shareholders on whether to accept, reject, or refrain from supplying an opinion on the offer.

Section 14 provides structural rules and restrictions on the tender offer process in addition to establishing disclosure requirements. These rules include a minimum tender offer period of 20 days, the right of target shareholders to withdraw shares al-

---

[13.] The threshold was originally 10 percent but was dropped to 5 percent in 1970.

[14.] It is also illegal to "park" shares, which means engaging another individual to buy shares for you in order to avoid disclosure requirements.

ready tendered at any time during the tender offer period, and the requirement that the acquirer accept all shares tendered and that all tendered shares will receive the same price. Again, the intent of these rules, described in Gaughan (1996), is to prevent a "sneak attack" in which target shareholders have no opportunity to evaluate the terms of a tender offer and also to assure fair treatment for all target shareholders who tender their shares.

Other Legal Issues Concerning Corporate Control

Federal securities laws also regulate the actions of managers in corporate control events. The high-profile insider-trading scandals of the 1980s generated a keen interest in these laws. Individual states have also become more interested in promoting corporate control legislation after witnessing business practices that were perceived as detrimental to the welfare of the electorate. In recent years, many states have developed antitakeover and antitrust laws designed to regulate takeovers of corporations located in their states. We describe the major elements of these other federal and state corporate control laws in the following sections.

Laws Affecting Corporate Insiders. A variety of federal securities laws govern the actions of corporate managers and other individuals considered to be corporate insiders during corporate control events. The majority of these laws attempt to prevent informed trading on material nonpublic information (inside information), such as an upcoming takeover attempt known only to the insiders of the acquiring firm. Rule 10-b-5 dictated by the Securities and Exchange Commission outlaws material misrepresentation of information used in the sale or purchase of a security. Trading on inside information about a pending merger is such a material misrepresentation because material information (news of the merger) is being withheld.

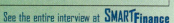

SMART PRACTICES VIDEO
David Baum, Co-head of M&A for Goldman Sachs in the Americas
"When the poison pill was introduced, it changed the landscape related to hostile takeovers."

See the entire interview at **SMARTFinance**

Also, SEC Rule 14-e-3 specifically forbids trading on inside information in tender offers. The Insider Trading Sanctions Act of 1984 strengthened both SEC rules with triple damage awards. Managers are also restricted from issuing misleading information regarding merger negotiations and may be sued if they deny the existence of merger negotiations that are actually taking place.

The SEC has applied the "misappropriation theory" of trading on inside information to extend the prohibitions of Rules 10-b-5 and 14-e-3 to other individuals who trade on inside information but are not corporate insiders. This theory holds that non-insiders who profit from trading on misappropriated inside information are equally guilty of violations of insider-trading rules. The SEC applied the misappropriation theory in a highly publicized case in which it brought suit against a *Wall Street Journal* columnist who traded in the stocks about which he wrote before his column was published. Because he realized the impact of his column on a stock's price, the columnist was charged with trading on material nonpublic information, even though he was not a corporate insider.

Section 16 of the Securities and Exchange Act establishes a monitoring facility for the trading of corporate insiders. Under Section 16-a, insiders must report the sale or purchase of any shares in their affiliated corporation. Section 16-b, the "short swing rule" section, permits a corporation or its shareholders to sue a corporate insider for any profits garnered from buy-sell transactions occurring within a 6-month cycle.

State Laws. Individual states have increasingly regulated corporate control activities over the years. Some states have adopted various antitakeover and anti-bust-up provisions and formed antitrust agencies that restrict corporate control activities in their states beyond the level of federal regulations.

Antitakeover and anti-bust-up provisions include voting initiatives such as supermajority voting, which requires that large majorities (usually 67%) approve a takeover, and control share provisions that require the approval of target shareholders before a potential acquirer may even buy a substantial number of shares in the target firm. Fair price provisions and cash-out statutes are also popular measures that further restrict tender offers. **Fair price provisions** ensure that all target shareholders receive the same offer price in any tender offers initiated by the same acquirer, limiting the ability of acquirers to buy minority shares cheaply with a two-tiered offer. **Cash-out statutes** are "all-or-none" rules that disallow a partial tender offer/acquisition of a company and the ability to control that company with less than 100 percent ownership. Business combination rules prevent the bust-up or other major restructuring of a company that is taken over. These provisions are often used in conjunction with each other, and individual state laws must be reviewed when considering a takeover to determine if these provisions are present, and, if so, what impact their presence will have on the value of the takeover. The formation of state-level antitrust regulatory boards is an even more recent trend in state corporate control regulation. The State of California has filed antitrust lawsuits and merger injunctions. Other states are following California's lead and have become more active antitrust monitors as well.

5. Which industries do you anticipate will experience industry shocks that will spur merger activity in the near future? Do you believe that increasing global competition will further heighten merger activity?

6. How does the dynamic interpretation of antitrust laws affect managers' acquisition strategies? What impact does the involvement of individual states have on the acquisition decision?

Concept Review Questions

24.4 THEORETICAL AND EMPIRICAL RESEARCH ON CORPORATE CONTROL [OPTIONAL]

We have discussed some topics in this chapter that are definitional in nature and others that are theoretical. In this section, we present further theoretical and empirical research that will tie together these topics and give us a broader perspective on corporate control activities and their impact on corporations and their stakeholders. Let us preface this section by stating that the studies summarized in no way encompass all the findings relating to corporate control; we discuss only a few of the major results. We refer you to the comprehensive surveys of Jensen and Ruback (1983), Jarrell, Brickley, and Netter (1988), Shleifer and Vishny (1997b), and Bruner (2002) for further results of interest.

STAKEHOLDER WEALTH EFFECTS AND TRANSACTION CHARACTERISTICS

The consensus result obtained in merger studies is that the common stockholders of target firms in successful takeovers experience large and significant wealth gains. Acquirer returns are not as generalized, and we discuss the theories offered to explain the cross-sectional differences in acquirers' returns. We also explore the wealth effects of various transaction characteristics.

Common Stock Returns

Target Returns. As stated earlier, target-firm stockholders almost always experience substantial wealth gains due to the premium offered for giving up control of their company.[15] The Jensen and Ruback (1983) survey reveals that, on average, target-firm common stockholders receive takeover premiums of 29.1 percent in successful tender offers and 15.9 percent in successful mergers. More-recent studies find that the average takeover premium is 31.8 percent in tender offers and that the average premium has risen over time. Target returns are also higher when there are multiple bidders and when managerial resistance leads to a higher offer, but takeover premiums are lost when resistance is too great and prevents a takeover.[16]

Acquirer Returns. Results concerning the common stock returns of acquiring firms are not as conclusive as those for target shareholders. Studies show that, on average, the common stockholders of acquiring firms experience positive returns in successful tender offers and virtually zero returns in successful mergers. However, in contrast to the rising trend of target returns, a negative trend in acquirer returns occurs over time. This joint trend in target and acquirer returns is primarily attributed to implementation of the Williams Act in 1968. The weighted-average return of acquirers and targets has consistently ranged between 7 percent and 8 percent over time, reflecting a constant anticipated synergistic gain from the combination of the two firms. But the protective provisions of the Williams Act seem to have caused a transfer of this consistent gain from acquirer to target-firm shareholders, as acquirer returns were significantly positive prior to the Williams Act and have become slightly negative since. Jensen and Ruback (1983) and Bradley, Desai, and Kim (1988) also show that shareholders of white knight acquirers almost always lose wealth in corporate control contests.

Mode of Payment. The mode of payment used to finance an acquisition explains much of the cross-sectional variance in acquirers' returns. Multiple studies find higher returns in cash transactions than in stock transactions.[17] These studies also show that the higher returns observed by both acquirers and targets in tender offers relative to negotiated mergers are attributable to the fact that most tender offers are financed by cash, whereas most negotiated mergers are equity financed. Announcement-period target returns are 13 percentage points greater for cash deals, acquirer returns in cash-financed deals are near zero, and those in stock-financed deals are significantly negative. Long-term results are even more startling: common stockholders in cash tender offers outperform those in stock-swap mergers by 123 percent through the fifth postacquisition year.

Researchers have proposed several theories to explain the differential returns between cash and stock offers. The most prominent of these theories revolves around the signaling model first described in Chapter 13. In the context of this model, the mode of payment offered by acquiring firms signals inside information to the capital markets. Managers will finance acquisitions with the cheapest source of capital available. Financing an acquisition with equity signals to the market that equity is a (relatively) cheap source of capital because the acquirer's stock price is overvalued. Receiving this signal, the capital markets will make a downward revision of the value of the acquirer's equity. Other theories concerning the differential returns due to

---

[15.] The rare case where a target shareholder receives a negative takeover premium is known as a *takeunder*.

[16.] See Bradley, Desai, and Kim (1988), Nathan and O'Keefe (1989), and Huang and Walkling (1987).

[17.] See Wansley, Lane, and Yang (1983), Travlos (1987), and Loughran and Vijh (1997).

financing method include the tax and preemptive bidding hypotheses. The *tax hypothesis* postulates that target shareholders must be awarded a capital gains tax premium in cash offers, which is not required in a stock offer. The *preemptive bidding hypothesis* asserts that acquirers wishing to ward off other potential bidders for a target offer a substantial initial takeover premium in the form of cash.

Other Transaction Characteristics. Other transaction characteristics also explain some of the variation in common stock returns. Acquirer returns are positively related to the relative size of the acquirer and the target. Asquith, Bruner, and Mullins (1983) and Jarrell and Poulsen (1989b) show that acquirers that buy relatively larger firms have higher returns than do acquirers that buy smaller targets (less than 10% of the acquirer's size). Researchers contend that this result stems from the greater analysis involved in more-significant acquisitions.

Capital market assessments of operating and managerial performance of both acquirers and targets also explain some of the variation in common stock returns. **Tobin's q,** defined as the market value of a firm's assets divided by their replacement value, serves as a proxy for these capital market assessments. Firms perceived to be well managed or with better long-term prospects have higher q ratios than those that are poorly managed or have poor prospects. A q ratio of greater than one implies that a firm is more valuable as a going concern than as a collection of assets. Multiple studies show that acquisition targets have lower q ratios than nontarget firms, the greatest concentration of hostile takeover activity is in industries with overall low q ratios, and the highest returns in takeovers come from deals between high-q acquirers and low-q targets. This suggests that capital markets reward transactions in which a well-managed company takes over a poorly managed corporation.[18]

Returns to Other Security Holders

Obviously, common stocks are not the only securities affected in corporate control activities. Corporate control events also impact bonds and preferred stocks. Recent empirical research finds that some nonconvertible bondholders experience significant wealth gains, but these gains are driven by the bonds of acquiring firms in nonconglomerate mergers (average gain of 1.9 percent). No financial synergies are realized in conglomerate mergers, and the nonconvertible bondholders in these mergers neither gain nor lose. In general, convertible bond returns are significantly higher than those of nonconvertible bonds. Further research indicates that increased leverage in a merger causes bondholder wealth losses, and also that certain types of restrictive covenants protect bondholder wealth in mergers. No evidence of significant bondholder wealth losses is systematically observed in LBOs, though specific transactions have yielded dramatic bondholder losses. Both convertible and nonconvertible preferred stockholders exhibit significant wealth gains in nonconglomerate mergers.[19]

Impact on Other Stakeholders

Some academics assert that all the wealth gains experienced by common stockholders are not always true value creation in an aggregate social sense and that many of those stockholder gains come at the expense of other corporate and social stakeholders, particularly employees and the federal government (loss of taxes). Empirical evidence indicates that layoffs account for 10–20 percent of hostile takeover premi-

---

[18.] See Hasbrouck (1985), Lang, Stulz, and Walkling (1989), and Servaes (1991).
[19.] See Dennis and McConnell (1986), Maquieira, Megginson, and Nail (1998), Lehn and Poulsen (1989), and Asquith and Wizman (1990) for more detail.

ums, employment increases slightly in friendly mergers while wages decline, and union concessions and reversions of excess pension assets account for a small part of takeover premiums. Aggregate tax savings and other socially negative effects such as capital expenditure and research and development reductions are negligible (see Shleifer and Vishny 1997b).

BUSINESS CONCENTRATION AND ANTITRUST LEGISLATION

As mentioned before, the types of business-concentrating mergers that spur merger activity have changed over time. The following discussion presents empirical results on the relationship between the level of business concentration and firm value and elaborates on the effect of antitrust legislation on managers' decisions to pursue horizontal mergers.

Horizontal Mergers and Antitrust Effects

The Celler-Kefauver Act substantially changed the market for horizontal mergers by outlawing mergers that might have the potential to be anticompetitive. So strong was the enforcement of antitrust regulation after the Celler-Kefauver Act that the Supreme Court sided with the DOJ or the FTC in every case challenging a merger pursuant to passage of the act through 1972 (see Ellert 1976). This strict enforcement pushed many potential acquirers away from horizontal mergers and sparked interest in the academic community about the social costs and benefits of horizontal mergers. Studies show that horizontal mergers do result in wealth gains for merging firms, but these gains come from scale economies and not from collusion by the remaining companies in the industry.[20]

Corporate Diversification and the Return to Focus

The stringent antitrust enforcement imposed after Celler-Kefauver contributed to the preference of interindustry mergers over horizontal mergers. This trend also led to some undesirable consequences for corporate America and was reversed by the return to corporate focus that began in the 1980s. A series of studies documented the failure of corporate diversification strategies and the bust-up of conglomerate firms. The following are results of some of these studies: over half of unrelated acquisitions are eventually divested, the hostile takeovers of the 1980s were a mechanism used to break up the inefficient conglomerates created in previous decades, and asset sales that lead to an increase in focus create wealth for the divesting firm.[21]

The validity of the financial synergy motive for conglomerate mergers has also been questioned. Academics contend that the existence of internal capital markets will lead to investment in lines of business with poor investment opportunities and no economic value added. Indeed, academic research has not documented any financial synergies. Performance measures also prove corporate diversification to be a failure in general. Various studies demonstrate the superior operating performance of mergers that occur between companies with high levels of business overlap relative to those that occur between companies with little overlap in their businesses. Research also shows that diversified firms trade at a significant discount in market value relative to their focused counterparts of around 15 percent, and firms increasing focus experience value gains and those decreasing focus suffer wealth losses. Capital markets have also learned of the failure of diversification and now greet the announcements of di-

---

[20.] See Stillman (1983) and Eckbo (1983).
[21.] See Ravenscraft and Scherer (1987), Stulz (1990), Kaplan and Weisbach (1992), Berger and Ofek (1996), Bhagat, Shleifer, and Vishny (1990), and John and Ofek (1995).

versifying mergers with negative stock-price reactions. Empirical evidence strongly supports the notion that mergers that decrease focus cause a loss in firm value.[22]

MANAGERIAL MOTIVES

Several academic studies have examined the motives of managers engaging in corporate control activities. Most studies focus on motives rooted in agency problems and the level of insider shareholdings. As discussed in earlier chapters, there is a significant positive relationship between the value of a firm and the percentage of equity owned by its managers. As this percentage increases, the interests of the firm's managers and owners converge, agency costs are reduced, and firm value increases. Other research finds that a nonlinear (positive for low levels, then negative for higher levels) relationship exists between managerial ownership and firm value. Regardless of the model examined, empirical results suggest that managers with divergent interests from the shareholders they represent pursue non-value-maximizing mergers.[23] Further research also shows a positive relationship between firm size, sales growth, and executive compensation and the existence of a negative relationship between the level of free cash flow and firm value in poorly managed firms. In aggregate, these findings provide strong empirical support for the idea that agency problems motivate non-value-maximizing mergers.[24]

Many academics contend that the corporate control market is the ideal mechanism for controlling managers with improper motives. In one of the earliest "modern" corporate control papers, H. G. Manne (1965) points out that a manager who is not acting in the best interests of shareholders will cause the company's stock price to drop to a point that makes the market value of equity a relative bargain for control of the firm's assets. Hence, a takeover will ensue and the non-value-maximizing managers will be replaced. Eugene Fama (1980) extends this argument with his idea that managers who are replaced in a takeover face harsh labor markets because they are perceived as managers who do not maximize shareholder wealth.

Fittingly, we end this chapter here as the concept of corporate control activities in the modern corporation has come full circle. On the one hand, mergers and acquisitions may be used by value-maximizing managers to expand their companies and benefit from a synergistic combination of two firms. On the other hand, hostile takeovers may be used to supplant non-value-maximizing managers and mitigate such agency problems. Thus, corporate control activities are a major force in fulfilling the ultimate goal of a corporation—maximizing shareholder wealth.

SMART IDEAS VIDEO
David Denis, Purdue University
"On net the governance mechanisms have evolved to offset the decline in takeover activity."

See the entire interview at **SMARTFinance**

Concept Review Questions

7. Given the empirical results presented in this section, how would you structure a takeover as the CEO of an acquiring firm? Would your perspective change as a stockholder? As a bondholder?

8. As conglomerate mergers and corporate diversification have proven to be failures in general, why would any manager pursue these objectives? Can you think of any cases where corporate diversification has worked successfully? What distinguishes these cases from the norm?

[22.] See Healy, Palepu, and Ruback (1992), Lang and Stulz (1994), Berger and Ofek (1995), Comment and Jarrell (1995), Morck, Shleifer, and Vishny (1990), and Megginson, Morgan, and Nail (2003) for empirical results.

[23.] See Stulz (1988), Morck, Shleifer, and Vishny (1988), Amihud, Lev, and Travlos (1990), and Lewellen, Loderer, and Rosenfeld (1985) for further theoretical and empirical detail.

[24.] See Murphy (1985) and Lang, Stulz, and Walkling (1991).

24.5 SUMMARY

- Mergers and acquisitions are major corporate finance events that, when executed efficiently and with the proper motives, can help managers realize their ultimate goal of maximizing shareholder wealth. Merging firms may be integrated in a number of ways, and the circumstances surrounding the merger determine the means of integration. Transactions may be hostile or friendly; may be financed by cash, stock, debt, or some combination of the three; and may increase, preserve, or decrease the acquirer's level of business concentration.

- Managers have either value-maximizing or non-value-maximizing motives for pursuing mergers. Value-maximizing motives include expansion into new markets, capturing size economies and other synergies, establishing market power, or generating free cash flow to make better investments. Agency problems result in such non-value-maximizing motives as empire building, entrenchment, hubris, and diversification.

- Merger activity occurs in waves spurred by industrywide events such as deregulation. Domestically, we have witnessed five major merger waves: a turn-of-the-twentieth-century wave of horizontal mergers, a 1920s wave of vertical mergers, the 1960s wave of conglomerate mergers, the 1980s wave that deconstructed many of the 1960s conglomerates, and a recent wave of deregulation-based mergers and consolidations made in preparation for an increasingly global economy. Antitrust enforcement at the time affects activity in each of these waves.

- Corporate control activities are regulated by federal, and increasingly, state and international authorities. Federal antitrust legislation has been developed over the course of the century, but its enforcement ebbs and flows with the executive administration in office. The Williams Act established disclosure requirements for ownership in public corporations, as well as regulation of tender offers. Federal securities laws also prohibit corporate insiders from trading on the nonpublic information of a pending takeover.

- Research on corporate control is bountiful. Major empirical findings include the following: target shareholders almost always win, white knights almost always lose, and other acquirers' returns are mixed. The combined value of merging firms also increases, especially in nonconglomerate combinations. The highest announcement-period returns are found in mergers between well-managed acquirers and poorly managed targets. Long-term performance is highest for focus-increasing deals financed with cash and lowest for diversifying mergers financed with stock.

INTERNET RESOURCES

Note: *For updates to links, please go to the book's website at* *http://smart.swcollege.com*

http://www.sec.gov/about/laws.shtml—"The Laws That Govern the Securities Industry" section of the U.S. Securities and Exchange Commission's website; provides a brief overview of the six key laws that the SEC enforces, including those relating to tender offers and M&A regulations

http://europa.eu.int/pol/comp/index_en.htm—The Competition section of the European Union's official website; describes the key legislation setting up this Commission, provides an overview of its enforcement philosophy, and describes key ongoing cases

KEY TERMS

acquisition
antitakeover amendments
antitrust
backward integration
bear hug
bust-up
cash-out statutes
coinsurance of debt
conglomerate mergers
consolidation
corporate control
corporate focus
divestiture
dual-class recapitalization
economies of scale
economies of scope
employee stock ownership plan (ESOP)
fair price provisions
financial synergies
forward integration
free cash flow theory of mergers
going-private transactions
goodwill
greenfield entry
greenmail
Herfindahl Index (HI)
horizontal merger
hubris hypothesis of corporate takeovers
industry shock theory of takeovers
internal capital markets

management buyout (MBO)
managerial synergies
managerialism theory of mergers
market extension merger
market power
merger
mixed offerings
operational synergy
poison pills
product extension mergers
pure conglomerate mergers
pure stock exchange merger
resource complementarities
reverse LBO
reverse merger
shark repellents
spin-off
split-off
split-up
statutory merger
strategic merger
subsidiary merger
synergy
takeover
tax-loss carryforwards
tender offer
tender-merger
Tobin's q
vertical merger
white knights

QUESTIONS

24-1. What is meant by a change in corporate control? List and describe the various ways in which a change of corporate control may occur.

24-2. What is a tender offer, and how can it be used as a mechanism to orchestrate a merger?

24-3. Differentiate between the different levels of business concentration created by mergers. Explain how the changing business environment has caused an evolution in the classification of concentration from the original FTC classification, to the abbreviated FTC classification, and now to the measures of overlap and focus.

24-4. Elaborate on the significance of the mode of payment for the stockholders of the target firm and their continued interest in the surviving firm. Specifically, which form of payment retains the stockholders of the target firm as stockholders in the surviving firm? Which payment form receives preferential tax treatment?

24-5. Relate the industry shock theory of mergers to the history of merger waves. What were the motivating factors for increased merger activity in each of the five major merger waves?

24-6. Under what conditions would external expansion be preferable to internal expansion? What is the ultimate decision criterion for determining the acceptability of any expansion strategy?

24-7. Delineate the value-maximizing motives for mergers. How are these motives interrelated?

24-8. Define the three types of synergy that may result from mergers. What are the sources of these synergies?

24-9. Explain how agency problems may lead to non-value-maximizing motives for mergers. Discuss the various academic theories offered as the rationale for these agency problem–induced motives.

24-10. Describe the relationship between conglomerate mergers and portfolio theory. What is the desired result of merging two unrelated businesses? Has the empirical evidence proven corporate diversification to be successful?

24-11. List the federal laws regulating antitrust and anticompetitive mergers. What are the actions governed by each law? How do the regulatory agencies determine anticompetitiveness?

24-12. What is the purpose of the Williams Act? What are the specific provisions of the act?

24-13. What are the restrictions faced by corporate insiders during corporate control events?

24-14. How have individual states become more active monitors of takeover activity?

24-15. What is the signaling theory of mergers? What is the relationship between signaling and the mode of payment used in acquisitions? Is there a relationship between the mode of payment used in acquisitions and the level of insider shareholdings of acquiring firms?

24-16. Empirically, what are the wealth effects of corporate control activities? Who wins and who loses in corporate control contests? What explanations or theories are offered for the differences in returns of acquiring firms' common stocks? Why are there higher takeover premiums paid in cash transactions than in stock transactions? How do other security holders fare in takeovers?

24-17. Explain the wealth effect of corporate spin-offs. What do the empirical results indicate about the conditions surrounding spin-offs that lead to wealth creation for a corporation?

PROBLEMS

Overview of Corporate Control Activities

24-1. Bulldog Industries is offering as consideration for merger target Blazerco 1.5 shares of their stock for each share of Blazerco. There are 1 million shares of Blazerco outstanding, and its stock price was $50 before the merger offer. Bulldog's preoffer stock price was $40. What is the control premium percentage offered? Now suppose that when the merger is consummated six months later, Bulldog's stock price drops to $30. At that point, what is the control premium percentage and total transaction value?

24-2. You are the director of capital acquisitions for Crimson Software Company. One of the projects you are considering is the acquisition of Geekware, a private software company that produces software for finance professors. Dave Vanzandt, the owner of Geekware, is amenable to the idea of selling his enterprise to Crimson, but he has certain conditions that must be met before selling. The primary condition set forth is a nonnegotiable, all-cash purchase price of $20 million. Your project analysis team estimates that the purchase of Geekware will generate the following marginal cash flow:

Year	Cash Flow
1	$1,000,000
2	3,000,000
3	5,000,000
4	7,500,000
5	7,500,000

Of the $20 million in cash needed for the purchase, $5 million is available from retained earnings, and the remaining $15 million will come from a new debt issue yielding 8 percent. Crimson's tax rate is 40 percent. Should you recommend acquiring Geekware to your CEO?

24-3. Firm A plans to acquire Firm B. The acquisition would result in incremental cash flows for Firm A of $10 million in each of the first five years. Firm A expects to divest Firm B at the end of the fifth year for $100 million. The β for Firm A is 1.1, which is expected to remain unchanged after the acquisition. The risk-free rate, R_f, is 7 percent, and the expected market rate of return, R_m, is 15 percent. Firm A is financed by 80 percent equity and 20 percent debt, and this leverage will also remain unchanged after the acquisition. Firm A pays interest of 10 percent on its debt, which will also remain unchanged after the acquisition.

a. Disregarding taxes, what is the maximum price that Firm A should pay for firm B?

b. Firm A has a stock price of $30 per share and 10 million shares outstanding. If Firm B shareholders are to be paid the maximum price determined in part (a) via a new stock issue, how many new shares will be issued, and what will be the postmerger stock price?

24-4. Charger Incorporated and Sparks Electrical Company are competitors in the business of electrical components distribution. Sparks is the smaller firm and has garnered the attention of the management of Charger, as Sparks has taken away market share from the larger firm by increasing its sales force over the past few years. Charger is considering a takeover offer for Sparks and has asked you to serve on the acquisition valuation team that will turn into the due diligence team if an offer is made and accepted. Given the following information and assumptions, make your recommendation about whether or not the acquisition should be pursued.

Sparks Electrical Company
Condensed Balance Sheet
Previous Year
($ in millions)

	2003
Current assets	$ 12.2
Fixed assets	442.5
Total assets	$454.7
Current liabilities	$ 10.1
Long-term debt	150.0
Total liabilities	$160.1
Shareholder's equity	$294.6
Total liab. and equity	$454.7

Sparks Electrical Company
Condensed Income Statement
Previous Five Years
($ in millions)

	2003	2002	2001	2000	1999
Revenues	$1,626.5	$1,614.1	$1,485.2	$1,380.5	$1,373.4
Less: Cost of goods sold	1,488.1	1,490.9	1,359.5	1,271.4	1,268.0
Gross profit	$ 138.4	$ 123.2	$ 125.7	$ 109.1	$ 105.4
Selling, general, & administrative expenses (SG&A)	$ 41.1	$ 36.8	$ 41.2	$ 35	$ 36.1
Noncash expense (depreciation & amortization)	7.3	6.7	7.1	6.6	6.4
Less: Operating expense	$ 48.4	$ 43.5	$ 48.3	$ 41.6	$ 42.5
Operating profit (EBIT)	$ 90.0	$ 79.7	$ 77.4	$ 67.5	$ 62.9
Less: Interest expense	11.5	12.0	12.0	12.0	12.0
Earnings before taxes (EBT)	$ 78.5	$ 67.7	$ 65.4	$ 55.5	$ 50.9
Less: Taxes paid	24.3	20.8	19.9	16.8	15.3
Net income	$ 54.2	$ 46.9	$ 45.5	$ 38.7	$ 35.6

Assumptions:

- Sparks would become a wholly owned subsidiary of Charger.
- Revenues will continue to grow at 4.3 percent for the next five years and will level off at 4 percent thereafter.
- Cost of goods sold will represent 95 percent of revenue going forward.
- Sales force layoffs will reduce SG&A expenses to $22 million next year with a 2 percent growth rate going forward.
- These layoffs and other restructuring charges are expected to result in expensed restructuring charges of $30 million, $15 million, and $5 million, respectively, over the next three years.
- Noncash expenses are expected to remain around $7 million going forward.
- Interest expenses are expected to remain around $11.5 million going forward.
- A tax rate of 31 percent is assumed going forward.
- Charger's cost of equity is 12 percent.
- Sparks's current market capitalization is $315.7 million.
- Charger will offer Sparks a takeover premium of 20 percent over current market capitalization.

24-5.   Referring to Problem 24-4, assume Sparks has accepted the takeover offer from Charger, and now the new subsidiary must be consolidated within Charger's financial statements. Taking Sparks's most recent balance sheet and a restated market value of assets of $295.6 million, calculate the goodwill that must be booked for this transaction.

24-6.   Referring to Problems 24-4 and 24-5, assume it is now two years after the acquisition of Sparks, and you must perform a goodwill impairment test of the subsidiary. Growth expectations have been lowered to 3 percent going forward. Using the following 5-year projection of cash flows and a 12 percent cost of equity, estimate the horizon value of the subsidiary beyond year 5, the current value of the subsidiary, the current value of goodwill, and any goodwill impairment. Total assets (excluding intangibles) are now $612.5 million, and total liabilities are $175.0 million.

	Cash Flow Projection for Next Five Years				
	2006	2007	2008	2009	2010
Revenues	$1,815.2	$1,869.7	$1,925.7	$1,983.5	$2,043.0
Less: Cost of goods sold @95% of revenue	1,724.4	1,776.2	1,829.5	1,884.3	1,940.9
Gross profit	$ 90.8	$ 93.5	$ 96.2	$ 99.2	$ 102.1
SG&A expense @2% growth rate going forward	$ 23	$ 23.5	$ 23.9	$ 24.4	$ 24.9
Noncash expense (depreciation & amortization)	7.0	7.0	7.0	7.0	7.0
Less: Operating expense	$ 30.0	$ 30.5	$ 30.9	$ 31.4	$ 31.9
Operating profit (*EBIT*)	$ 60.8	$ 63.0	$ 65.3	$ 67.8	$ 70.2
Less: Interest expense	11.5	11.5	11.5	11.5	11.5
Less: Restructuring charges	5.0	0.0	0.0	0.0	0.0
Earnings before taxes (*EBT*)	$ 44.3	$ 51.5	$ 53.8	$ 56.3	$ 58.7
Less: Taxes paid	13.7	16.0	16.7	17.4	18.2
Net income	$ 30.6	$ 35.5	$ 37.1	$ 38.9	$ 40.5
Free cash flow	$ 37.6	$ 42.5	$ 44.1	$ 45.9	$ 47.5

25

Bankruptcy and Financial Distress

OPENING FOCUS
Enron, the Biggest Bankruptcy in U.S. History

It was the biggest bankruptcy in U.S. history to that time. On Sunday, December 2, 2001, Enron Corporation, the world's largest electricity and natural gas trading firm, capped a spectacular fall from the top of the energy world by filing for Chapter 11 bankruptcy reorganization. The company, which ranked as the seventh-largest U.S. firm in terms of revenues, listed assets of over $63 billion, almost double those of the next biggest bankruptcy, the 1987 Texaco failure. The list of creditors attached to Enron's bankruptcy filing is 54 pages long.

Enron stock closed at 26 cents the previous Friday, down from a high of $90.75 in August 2000. The company's rapid collapse was largely of its own making, one observer said. "Enron was a victim of its cowboy mentality. They allowed managers to take incredible risks and to keep the accounting for that stuff off the books." Enron used the value of its rising stock price to finance a variety of corporations and partnerships that magically turned balance sheet losses into gains on the company's income statement. That approach returned to haunt the company in the fall of 2001, when it had to restate earnings back to 1997, eliminating $580 million of reported income.

The company also suffered from a drop in energy prices in 2001 and from throwing billions of dollars into failed ventures. The crisis came on Wednesday, November 28, when credit-rating agencies cut Enron's credit rating to junk bond status, which meant it was required to immediately repay billions of dollars in outstanding loans.

Enron chairman and chief executive Kenneth Lay said the filings, in U.S. Bankruptcy Court in New York, would help the company regain the confidence it had lost. "While uncertainty during the past few weeks has severely impacted the market's confidence in Enron and its trading operations, we are taking the steps announced today to help preserve capital, stabilize our businesses, restore the confidence of our trading counterparties, and enhance our ability to pay our creditors," Lay was quoted as saying. It emerged later that Mr. Lay and other corporate insiders had been selling Enron stock aggressively all year, even as they made repeated, soothing comments about the company's financial health.

The company began belt-tightening measures immediately, including "substantial workforce reductions," primarily in Houston, where it had 7,500 employees. The company also began talking with financial institutions about obtaining debtor-in-possession financing, though these failed when the full scale of Enron's problems—including possible criminal misrepresentation of financial statements—became apparent. A debtor in possession is a Chapter 11 debtor that operates its own business and remains in possession of its assets and property.

Congress held hearings into Enron's collapse in early 2002, and the picture that emerged was of an arrogant, corrupt culture that felt it could do no wrong. It also emerged that Enron's auditing firm, Arthur Andersen, had seemingly been complicit in many of the financial shenanigans—and then began shredding documents once the federal government started to investigate both Enron and Andersen. The Justice Department sued Arthur Andersen for obstruction of justice and won a conviction in June 2002, by which time Andersen had effectively ceased to exist. After winning its case, the Justice Department made clear that Enron and its executives would be among the next targets for prosecution.

Sources: John R. Emshwiller and Rebecca Smith, "Behind Enron's Fall, a Culture of Secrecy Which Cost the Firm Its Investors' Trust," *Wall Street Journal* (December 5, 2001), pp. 1, 16–17; Wendy Zellner and Stephanie Forest, "The Fall of Enron," *Business Week* (December 17, 2001), pp. 30–36; Allan Sloan, "Digging into the Deal That Broke Enron," *Newsweek* (December 17, 2001), pp. 48–49; and Daniel Fisher, "Shell Game," *Forbes* (January 7, 2002), pp. 52–54.

A fundamental concept in economics is that competition forces markets toward a state of long-term equilibrium in which surviving companies produce at minimum average cost. This transition process eliminates firms using obsolete technologies, inefficient firms, and firms producing goods and services that are in excess supply. Consumers benefit because, in the long run, products are manufactured and sold at the lowest possible price. The mechanism through which inefficient firms leave the market is frequently bankruptcy, the legal procedure applied to businesses that fail.

In this chapter, we will examine first how and why firms fail. We then look at U.S. bankruptcy law and the ways that a business that has failed can resolve its difficulties, either voluntarily or involuntarily, through bankruptcy.

25.1 BUSINESS FAILURE FUNDAMENTALS

A **business failure** is an unfortunate circumstance. Although the majority of firms that fail do so within the first year or two of life, other firms grow, mature, and fail much later. The failure of a business can be viewed in a number of ways and can result from one or more causes.

TYPES OF BUSINESS FAILURE

A firm can fail because its returns are negative or low. A firm that consistently reports operating losses will probably experience a decline in market value. If the firm fails to earn a return that is greater than its cost of capital, it can be viewed as having experienced **economic failure.** Negative or low returns, unless remedied, are likely to result eventually in a more serious type of failure.

A second type of failure, **technical insolvency,** occurs when a firm is unable to pay its liabilities as they come due. When a firm is technically insolvent, its assets are still greater than its liabilities, but it is confronted with a **liquidity crisis.** If some of its assets can be converted into cash within a reasonable period, the company may be able to escape complete failure. For example, in February 2001, Amazon.com, the online retailer, had to deny that it was facing a liquidity crisis. "The company has never been in better shape," chief executive Jeff Bezos was quoted as saying. An Amazon supplier said that it had limited the amount of business it does with Amazon. Limiting business with a retailer is a typical first step for a creditor trying to protect itself from loss. Other techniques include shortening the terms under which a creditor will extend credit or even asking for cash in advance.

If a company cannot convert its assets into cash quickly enough, the result is the third and most serious type of failure, **insolvency bankruptcy.** Insolvency occurs when a firm's liabilities exceed the fair market value of its assets. Because the firm's assets equal the sum of its liabilities and stockholders' equity, the only way a firm that has more liabilities than assets can balance its balance sheet is to have a negative stockholders' equity. This means that the claims of creditors cannot be satisfied unless the firm's assets can be liquidated for more than their book value.

Although an insolvent firm is often said to be "bankrupt," **bankruptcy** technically occurs only when a company enters bankruptcy court and effectively surrenders control of the firm to a bankruptcy judge. The failing firm may file for bankruptcy protection itself, or it may be forced into bankruptcy court (under certain conditions, discussed later in this chapter) by its creditors.

Table 25.1 shows the largest bankruptcies in U.S. history through December 2, 2001. The largest U.S. bankruptcy was that of Enron in 2001. Enron's prebankruptcy total assets were over $63 billion. Before Enron, the largest U.S. bankruptcy was that of Texaco in 1987. In June 2002, WorldCom claimed the "crown" of the largest bankruptcy in U.S. history when it filed for protection from its creditors.

MAJOR CAUSES OF BUSINESS FAILURE

The primary cause of business failure is financial distress (as discussed in Chapter 13). This, in turn, is often the result of mismanagement, which accounts for more than 50 percent of all business failures. Numerous specific managerial faults can cause the firm to fail. Overexpansion, poor financial actions, an ineffective sales force, and high production costs can all singly or in combination cause the ultimate failure of the firm. For example, poor financial actions include bad capital budgeting decisions based on unrealistic sales and cost forecasts, failure to identify all relevant cash flows, failure to assess risk properly, inadequate financial evaluation of the firm's strategic plans prior to making financial commitments, inconsistent or inadequate cash flow planning, and failure to control receivables and inventories. Because all major corporate decisions are eventually measured in terms of dollars, the financial manager may play a key role in avoiding or causing a business failure. One of the financial manager's key duties must therefore be to monitor the firm's financial pulse.

Economic activity can contribute to the failure of a firm, especially during economic downturns. The success of some firms runs countercyclical to economic activity, and other firms are unaffected by economic activity. For example, the sale of sewing machines is likely to increase during a recession because people are more willing to make their own clothes and less willing to pay for the labor of others. The sale of boats and other luxury items may decline during a recession, whereas sales of staple items such as electricity are likely to be unaffected. In terms of beta, the measure of nondiversifiable risk, a stock with a negative beta would be associated with a firm whose behavior is generally countercyclical to economic activity.

However, the fortunes of most firms are positively tied to the business cycle, so

Table 25.1
Largest Bankruptcies in U.S. History as of December 2, 2001

Company	Bankruptcy Date	Total Assets, Prebankruptcy
Enron Corp.	December 2, 2001	$63,392,000,000
Texaco, Inc.	April 12, 1987	35,892,000,000
Financial Corp. of America	September 9, 1988	33,864,000,000
Pacific Gas and Electric Co.	April 6, 2001	21,470,000,000
MCorp	March 31, 1989	20,228,000,000
First Executive Corp.	May 13, 1991	15,193,000,000
Gibraltar Financial Corp.	February 8, 1990	15,011,000,000
FINOVA Group, Inc.	March 7, 2001	14,050,000,000
HomeFed Corp.	October 22, 1992	13,885,000,000
Southeast Banking Corporation	September 20, 1991	13,390,000,000
Reliance Group Holdings, Inc.	June 12, 2001	12,598,000,000
Imperial Corp. of America	February 28, 1990	12,263,000,000
Federal-Mogul Corp.	October 1, 2001	10,150,000,000
First City Bancorp. of Texas	October 31, 1992	9,943,000,000
First Capital Holdings	May 30, 1991	9,675,000,000
Baldwin-United	September 26, 1983	9,383,000,000

Source: http://www.bankruptcydata.com (January 3, 2002).

bankruptcy filings always spike upward during economic contractions. If the economy goes into a recession, sales may decrease abruptly, leaving the firm with high fixed costs and insufficient revenues to cover them. In addition, rapid rises in interest rates just prior to a recession can further contribute to cash flow problems and make it more difficult for the firm to obtain and maintain needed financing. If the recession is prolonged, the likelihood of survival decreases even further. A number of major business failures occurring during 2001, such as those of the FINOVA Group and Reliance Group Holdings, resulted from overexpansion and the recessionary economy. On the other hand, the bankruptcy of Pacific Gas and Electric, another massive failure in 2001, was a direct result of policies enacted during a flawed deregulation of California's electricity market during the mid-1990s. Table 25.2 shows the 20 largest public company bankruptcies in 2001 in the United States. Several extremely large bankruptcies also occurred during 2002, including Adelphia, Global Crossing, Qwest Communications, and, of course, WorldCom.

A final cause of business failure is corporate maturity. Firms, like individuals, do not have infinite lives. Like a product, a firm goes through the stages of birth, growth, maturity, and eventual decline. The firm's management should attempt to prolong the growth stage through research, the development of new products, and mergers. Once the firm has matured and has begun to decline, it should seek to be acquired by another firm or liquidate before it fails. Effective management planning should help the firm postpone decline and ultimate failure.

APPLYING THE MODEL

Polaroid is an example of a company that has failed because of corporate maturity. Almost a decade ago, digital photography brought with it distant warnings of the demise of instant photography. Before long, computer chips would capture and store

Table 25.2
Largest Public Company Bankruptcies in 2001

Company	Bankruptcy Date	Total Assets, Prebankruptcy
Enron Corp.	December 2	$63,392,000,000
Pacific Gas and Electric Co.	April 6	21,470,000,000
FINOVA Group, Inc.	March 7	14,050,000,000
Reliance Group Holdings, Inc.	June 12	12,598,000,000
Federal-Mogul Corp.	October 1	10,150,000,000
Comdisco, Inc.	July 16	8,754,000,000
ANC Rental Corp.	November 13	6,349,000,000
360Networks (USA), Inc.	June 26	5,596,000,000
Winstar Communications, Inc.	April 18	4,975,000,000
PSINet, Inc.	May 31	4,492,000,000
Bethlehem Steel Corp.	October 15	4,347,000,000
Laidlaw, Inc.	June 28	4,000,000,000
Exodus Communications, Inc.	September 26	3,894,000,000
USG Corp.	June 25	3,214,000,000
Sunbeam Corp.	February 6	3,132,000,000
Global TeleSystems, Inc.	November 14	2,833,000,000
Hayes Lemmerz International	December 5	2,811,000,000
W. R. Grace & Company	April 2	2,509,000,000
Warnaco Group, Inc.	June 11	2,372,000,000
Arch Wireless, Inc.	December 6	2,309,000,000

Source: http://www.bankruptcydata.com (January 3, 2002).

images and instant, self-developing film would disappear. That prediction came true most recently in the form of Polaroid's insolvency. The company, which dominated the instant photography business for years, filed for Chapter 11 bankruptcy protection (discussed later) on October 12, 2001. The stock price had fallen from nearly $50 per share in 1998 to 28 cents on October 11. Polaroid, it turns out, was unable to change with the times.

The company's troubles date back to the late 1980s when it went deeply into debt to fight off a hostile takeover bid. That was followed by a string of strategic errors, including its failure to anticipate how much digital photography would cut into its instant film business. The company's latest generation of instant cameras has fallen flat because digital cameras for consumers are just as instant and much more versatile. Although the company is trying to reorganize its debts and continue operating, some Wall Street observers predict Polaroid will be forced to liquidate its assets and cease to exist.

Sometimes the cause of a business failure is difficult to anticipate and can happen quite suddenly in response to an economic or political event. For example, ANC Rental Corp., the owner of the Alamo and National car rental chains, filed for Chapter 11 bankruptcy protection on November 13, 2001, as the downturn in the travel sector worsened the company's troubles. ANC claims to have been the hardest-hit car rental company after the September 11 terrorist attacks, mainly because most of its rental offices were at airports. "The drastic decline in travel after September 11 has taken a tremendous toll on our business, and our current capital and expense structure cannot absorb the shortfall," CEO Michael Egan was quoted as saying.

ANC, which listed assets of nearly $6.5 billion, estimates it has more than 1,000 creditors and said funds will be available for distribution to unsecured creditors. Discussions on liquidity options with creditors and other parties are ongoing, and the company said it may mimic the airline industry in seeking financial help from the U.S. government. General Motors, ANC's primary supplier of vehicles, has halted deliveries to the company but expects deliveries to resume eventually.

Concept Review Questions

1. Are the occurrence of operating losses, technical insolvency, and bankruptcy independent, or are they likely to be related?

2. Why do the managers of a business allow its condition to deteriorate to the point where bankruptcy occurs? Why don't the shareholders intervene?

3. Explain how business failures help the economy overall.

25.2 VOLUNTARY SETTLEMENTS

When a firm becomes technically insolvent or bankrupt, it may arrange a **voluntary settlement** or **workout** with its creditors, which enables it to bypass many of the costs involved in legal bankruptcy proceedings. The debtor firm usually initiates the settlement, because such an arrangement may enable it to continue to exist or to be liquidated in a manner that gives the owners the greatest chance of recovering part of their investment. The debtor, possibly with the aid of a key creditor, arranges a meeting between itself and all its creditors. At the meeting, a committee of creditors is selected to investigate and analyze the debtor's situation and recommend a plan of action. The committee discusses its recommendations with both the debtor and the creditors and draws up a plan for sustaining or liquidating the firm.

VOLUNTARY REORGANIZATION

Generally, the rationale for sustaining a firm is that it is reasonable to believe that the firm's recovery is feasible. By sustaining the firm, the creditor can continue to receive business from it. A number of strategies are commonly used to implement a **voluntary reorganization.** An **extension** is an arrangement wherein the firm's creditors are promised payment in full, although not immediately. Usually, when creditors grant an extension, they require the firm to make cash payments for purchases until all past debts have been paid.

A second arrangement, called a **composition,** is a pro rata cash settlement of creditor claims. Instead of receiving full payment for their claims, as in the case of an extension, creditors receive only a partial payment. A uniform percentage of each dollar owed is paid in satisfaction of each creditor's claim.

A third arrangement is **creditor control.** In this case, the creditor committee may decide that the only circumstance in which maintaining the firm is feasible will be replacement of the operating management. The committee may then take control of the firm and operate it until all claims have been settled. Sometimes, a plan involving some combination of extension, composition, and creditor control will result. An example of this would be a settlement whereby the debtor agrees to pay a total of 75 cents on the dollar in three annual installments of 25 cents on the dollar. The creditors also agree to sell additional merchandise to the firm on 30-day terms, if a new management team that is acceptable to them replaces the existing managers.[1]

Voluntary Liquidation

After the credit committee has investigated the situation of the firm, made recommendations, and held talks with the creditors and the debtor, the only acceptable course of action may be liquidation of the firm. **Liquidation** involves winding up the firm's operations, selling off its assets, and distributing the proceeds to creditors. Liquidation can be carried out in two ways, privately or through the legal procedures provided by bankruptcy law. If the debtor firm is willing to accept liquidation, legal procedures may not be required. Generally, avoiding litigation enables the creditors to obtain quicker and higher settlements. However, all the creditors must agree to a private liquidation for it to be feasible.

The objective of the voluntary liquidation process is to recover as much per dollar owed as possible. Under voluntary liquidation, common stockholders, who are the firm's true owners, cannot receive any funds until the claims of all other parties have been satisfied. A common procedure is to have a meeting of the creditors at which they make an **assignment** by passing the power to liquidate the firm's assets to an adjustment bureau, a trade association, or a third party that is designated the *assignee*. The assignee's job is to liquidate the assets, obtaining the best price possible. The assignee is sometimes referred to as **trustee,** because it is entrusted with the title to the company's assets and the responsibility to liquidate them efficiently. Once the trustee has liquidated the assets, it distributes the recovered funds to the creditors and owners (if any funds remain for the owners). The final action in a private liquidation is for the creditors to sign a release attesting to the satisfactory settlement of their claims. If a voluntary settlement for a failed firm cannot be agreed upon, the creditors can force the firm into bankruptcy. Because of bankruptcy proceedings, the firm may be either reorganized or liquidated.

An alternative to liquidation of the firm is for it to be acquired. Merger with a financially sound company may allow the firm suffering from financial distress to return to profitability and continue as a going concern.

Concept Review Questions

4. If you were a supplier and creditor to a company that had undergone a voluntary reorganization, would you continue to do business with the company?

5. If you were a creditor of a company that was undergoing a voluntary reorganization, what would be the advantages and disadvantages from your perspective of handling it as an extension, composition, or creditor control?

6. Why would a firm's shareholders agree to a voluntary liquidation if the business had a negative net worth and they could expect to receive nothing?

25.3 BANKRUPTCY LAW IN THE UNITED STATES

As already stated, bankruptcy in the legal sense occurs when the firm cannot pay its bills or when its liabilities exceed the fair market value of its assets and the firm is

---

[1.] For evidence that transaction costs discourage debt reductions by financially distressed firms when they restructure their debt out of court, see Gilson (1997).

forced into bankruptcy court. In either of these situations, a firm may be declared legally bankrupt. However, creditors generally attempt to avoid forcing a firm into bankruptcy if it appears to have opportunities for future success.

The governing bankruptcy legislation in the United States today is the **Bankruptcy Reform Act of 1978,** which significantly modified earlier bankruptcy legislation. This law contains eight odd-numbered (1 through 15) and one even-numbered (12) chapters. Several of these chapters would apply in the instance of failure; the two key ones are Chapters 7 and 11. We briefly discuss international differences in bankruptcy laws in Chapter 13 (of this book, not of the bankruptcy code).

Chapter 7 of the Bankruptcy Reform Act of 1978 details the procedures to be followed when liquidating a failed firm. This chapter typically comes into play once it has been determined that a fair, equitable, and feasible basis for the reorganization of a failed firm does not exist (although a firm may of its own accord choose not to reorganize and may instead go directly into liquidation). Chapter 7 includes the rules, known as **absolute priority rules** (**APR**), that determine the order in which creditor claims are to be paid. As described in detail in Section 25.5, the APR specify which claimants are to be paid first, and in full, before any payments can be made to more junior claimants.

Chapter 11 outlines the procedures for reorganizing a failed or failing firm, whether its petition is filed voluntarily or involuntarily. If a workable plan for reorganization cannot be developed, the firm will be liquidated under Chapter 7. Table 13.1 shows how the total number of corporate bankruptcies was divided between Chapter 7 and Chapter 11 filings for the period from 1985 to 2000. The table shows that in 2000 there were a total of 1,276,922 bankruptcy filings in the United States. These filings consisted of 36,910 business failures and 1,240,012 nonbusiness (mostly personal) bankruptcies.

When a company files either to reorganize or liquidate in bankruptcy, a collective legal procedure begins by which all claims against the company are resolved. When a firm declares bankruptcy, individual creditors are prevented (stayed) from beginning or continuing with lawsuits against the debtor. Thus, bankruptcy law is substituted for the commercial and tax laws that normally govern firms.

Without a collective procedure, individual creditors would engage in a costly and unproductive race to be first to sue the company for repayment of their own claims. Creditors that sued first would be paid in full until the firm's resources were exhausted, after which other creditors would receive nothing. Both the creditors' duplicative expenses and the costs of the lawsuits themselves would consume assets. Bankruptcy eliminates the benefit of being the first to sue because all claims against the firm are settled simultaneously, and all creditors having the same type of claim receive the same settlement. Although there is still an incentive for creditors to attempt to sue the firm first, the incentive is diminished because a large number of suits will cause the firm to enter bankruptcy voluntarily.

---

7. Why is it necessary to have bankruptcy laws? Why is normal contracting under commercial law insufficient?

8. How does society benefit by allowing firms to declare bankruptcy?

9. Why is it important that bankruptcy law eliminate the incentive for creditors to be the first to sue for repayment of claims?

Concept Review Questions

Companies Can Declare Bankruptcy; Why Not Countries?

On January 6, 2002, Argentina abandoned the decade-old parity between its currency and the U.S. dollar by devaluing the peso. "We are bankrupt," admitted Economy Minister Jorge Remes Lenicov when he announced the devaluation. The government also confirmed that Argentina cannot continue to service its $155 billion of foreign-currency debt, and it declared a moratorium on payments. Because of the default, the price of Argentine bonds fell to about 25 percent of their par value.

Argentina's creditors are bracing themselves for a long fight for their money. The Argentine bondholders formed a committee in November 2001 to communicate some of the large investors' views to the Argentine government. The committee includes investment banks that have begun to pay out on credit-default swaps, derivative securities that guarantee payment should a borrower default. The default swaps total almost $4 billion, and the investment banks now own the bonds returned to them under the terms of the swaps.

The questions for bondholders are how vigorously they should react and how quickly they should call their lawyers. The announcement of a default means that bondholders can now "accelerate" their claims by demanding immediate payment of all principal and interest from the debtor. However, acceleration is unlikely to result in prompt payment because, as the bondholders realize, Argentina has serious problems. Most creditors figure that they will receive more money by negotiation than by confrontation.

In the short term, the moratorium may give Argentina room to maneuver. However, if it ignores its creditors, then difficulties might arise with even the simplest trade finance transactions. In the worst case, creditors could seize Argentine assets abroad, such as ships or aircraft. Also, many of the bond covenants do not contain so-called collective action clauses; therefore, each bondholder is free to litigate individually, a frightening scenario, except for the lawyers.

The question then is, What should Argentina do? Whereas companies can declare bankruptcy and seek protection from their creditors, countries have no such option. They are faced with the bleak choice between bailouts and chaotic defaults. However, that could change. The International Monetary Fund (IMF) has suggested that a country whose debts are "truly unsustainable" should have a mechanism for restructuring them, in the same way that companies can file for bankruptcy protection and reorganize their obligations.

The idea is that a country in financial distress would get temporary legal protection when it stopped making payments on its debt. In return, it would have to promise to negotiate with its creditors in good faith. Lenders would get an incentive to provide new "working capital" by giving new debt seniority over old. Also, small creditors would have to go along with the reorganization plan if enough creditors agreed.

Sovereign bankruptcy is appealing because it might eliminate the need for IMF bailouts while avoiding the legal quagmire of unilateral default. Both creditors and debtors would benefit from clear rules about the procedure for debt restructuring, if the rules balanced the rights of debtors and creditors.

Previous proposals on sovereign bankruptcy have failed, in part, because the details are difficult to work out. Who, for instance, will act as the impartial judge? Also, how do you force a debtor country to negotiate in good faith? After all, countries cannot be threatened with liquidation or a forcible change in "management."

25.4 REORGANIZATION IN BANKRUPTCY

A company's managers typically make the initial decision to attempt to reorganize their firm under the protection of Chapter 11 of the bankruptcy laws. The **reorganization** process in bankruptcy is designed to allow businesses that are in temporary financial distress, but are worth saving, to continue operating while the claims of creditors are settled using a collective procedure.[2] A disadvantage of this procedure is that the managers of the company and not an outside party make the decision to file under Chapter 11. Thus, managers have an incentive to choose the bankruptcy procedure that is best for themselves and for equity holders and not the firm's creditors.

---

[2] Eberhart, Altman, and Aggarwal (1999) describe the stock return performance of firms emerging from Chapter 11. Alderson and Betker (1995) examine the postbankruptcy cash flows of firms emerging from Chapter 11.

This sometimes results in firms being reorganized that are not worth saving because of a lack of economic efficiency. Thus, a problem with reorganization is that even though it may allow some efficient firms to continue operating that would otherwise be liquidated, it is also likely to allow some economically inefficient firms to be saved.[3]

REORGANIZATION PROCEDURES

The procedures for initiation and execution of corporate reorganization under Chapter 11 entail five separate steps: filing, appointment, development and approval of a reorganization plan, acceptance of the plan, and payment of expenses.

Filing

A firm must file a reorganization petition under Chapter 11 in a federal bankruptcy court. There are two basic types of bankruptcy reorganization petitions: voluntary and involuntary. Any firm that is not a municipal or financial institution can voluntarily file a petition for reorganization on its own behalf. Firms sometimes file a voluntary petition to obtain temporary legal protection from creditors or from prolonged litigation. Once they have straightened out their legal or financial affairs, prior to further reorganization or liquidation actions, they will have the petition dismissed. Although such actions are not the intent of the bankruptcy laws, difficulty in enforcing the law has allowed this abuse to occur.

An outside party, usually a creditor, initiates **involuntary reorganization.** An involuntary petition against a firm can be filed if one of three conditions is met:

1. The firm has past-due debts of $5,000 or more.
2. Three or more creditors can prove that they have aggregate unpaid claims of $5,000 against the firm. If the firm has fewer than 12 creditors, any creditor that is owed more than $5,000 can file the petition.
3. The firm is **insolvent,** which means that (a) it is not paying its debts as they come due, (b) within the immediately preceding 120 days a custodian (a third party) was appointed or took possession of the debtor's property, or (c) the fair market value of the firm's assets is less than the stated value of its liabilities.

If the debtor challenges an involuntary petition, a hearing must be held to determine whether the firm is insolvent. If it is, the court enters an "Order for Relief" that formally initiates the process.

Appointment

Upon the filing of a reorganization petition, the filing firm becomes the **debtor in possession (DIP)** of the assets, and its existing management usually remains in control. However, one or more creditors' committees are appointed to represent the interests of creditors.

If the creditors object to the filing firm being the debtor in possession, they can petition the bankruptcy court to appoint a trustee to replace management. However, the incompetence of the existing management, which is strongly suggested by the fact that the firm is in bankruptcy, is not considered a sufficient reason for replacing management. To replace existing management, the creditors usually must present evidence that the management is making preferential transfers to favored creditors or stealing the company's assets.

Because reorganization activities are largely in the hands of the DIP, it is useful

---

[3] See Thorburn (2000) for a description of an alternative procedure used in Sweden in which bankrupt firms are auctioned as going concerns.

to understand the DIP's responsibilities. The DIP's first responsibility is the valuation of the firm to determine whether reorganization is appropriate. To do this, the DIP must estimate both the liquidation value of the business and its value as a going concern. If the DIP finds that its value as a going concern is less than its liquidation value, it will recommend liquidation. If the opposite is true, the DIP will recommend reorganization. If the DIP recommends reorganization of the firm, a plan of reorganization must be drawn up.

Reorganization Plan

After reviewing its situation, the debtor in possession submits a plan of reorganization to the court and files the plan and a disclosure statement summarizing the plan. A hearing is held to determine whether the plan is fair, equitable, and feasible and whether the disclosure statement contains adequate information. The court's approval or disapproval is based on its evaluation of the plan in light of these standards. A plan is considered fair and equitable if it maintains the priorities of the contractual claims of the creditors, preferred stockholders, and common stockholders. The court must also find the reorganization plan *feasible*, meaning that it must be workable. The reorganized corporation must have sufficient working capital, sufficient funds to cover fixed charges, sufficient credit prospects, and sufficient ability to retire or refund debts as proposed by the plan.

The key portion of the reorganization plan generally concerns the firm's capital structure. Because most firms' financial difficulties result from high fixed charges, the company's capital structure is generally recapitalized, or altered, to reduce these charges. Under **recapitalization,** debts are generally exchanged for equity or the maturities of existing debts are extended. The DIP, when recapitalizing the firm, places a great deal of emphasis on building a mix of debt and equity that will allow the firm to meet its debts and provide a reasonable level of earnings for its owners.

Once the optimal capital structure has been determined, the DIP must establish a plan for exchanging outstanding obligations for new securities. The guiding principle is to observe priorities. Senior claims are those with higher legal priority that must be satisfied in full before junior claims (those with lower legal priority). To comply with this principle, senior suppliers of capital must receive a claim on new capital equal to their previous claim. The common stockholders are the last to receive any new securities, and it is not unusual for them to receive nothing. Security holders do not necessarily have to receive the same type of security they held before; often they receive a combination of securities. Once the debtor in possession has determined the new capital structure and distribution of capital, it will submit the reorganization plan and disclosure statement to the court as described.

The DIP is in a strong bargaining position in negotiations over the reorganization plan. During the first four months after the bankruptcy filing—plus any extensions, which are often granted—managers have the exclusive right to propose a plan. Then an extra two months are allowed for voting on management's plan. Only then, and only if no further extensions have been granted, can creditors propose reorganization plans.

Acceptance of the Reorganization Plan

Once approved by the bankruptcy court, the plan and the disclosure statement are given to the firm's creditors and shareholders for their acceptance. Under the Bankruptcy Reform Act, creditors and owners are separated into groups with similar types of claims. Intense bargaining and litigation often occur concerning the construction of the classes of creditors in a reorganization. Creditors that are in substantially the same position are placed in the same class to assure that they receive the same treatment under the reorganization plan. Creditors in different positions are placed in different classes. However, managers sometimes wish to prevent a particular creditor from defeating a reorganization plan. They accomplish this by arguing that the creditor should be part of a larger class in which the creditor's opposition to the plan will be outvoted.

There are two procedures for instituting a reorganization plan: the unanimous consent procedure and the cramdown procedure. Under the **unanimous consent procedure (UCP)**, creditors and equity classes must consent unanimously to the reorganization plan, although not all members of each class are required to consent. The UCP assumes that the company's assets will be worth more if it reorganizes and continues operations than if it liquidates. This difference in value, which under the absolute priority rule (APR) of Chapter 7 would belong entirely to the creditors with senior claims, must be divided up among all the creditors and equity classes by means of a negotiating process, with all classes sharing the difference in value.

A company must be solvent to use the UCP. That is, the value of creditors' claims must be less than the value of the company as a going concern. This implies that the firm's existing equity has some value. If the existing equity is worthless, then the company is considered insolvent, and the UCP cannot be used because equity holders cannot consent to a reorganization plan that eliminates their interest. To make a firm appear solvent, reorganization plans often use inflated valuations of the firm's assets to make them appear to be worth more than the liabilities under the proposed plan.

Reorganization plans using the UCP must be approved by all classes of creditors and by equity as a class. Each class of unsecured creditors must vote for the plan by a two-thirds margin, weighing claims by value, and also by a simple majority, weighing all claims equally. Each secured creditor is a class, and each must vote for the plan if its claims are impaired. (If its claims are not impaired, a secured creditor's consent to the plan is not needed.) Because equity holders must vote for the plan by a two-thirds margin, reorganization plans under the UCP yield a different division of the company's value than would occur under the APR of a Chapter 7 liquidation. Under the UCP, every class, even the equity holders, must receive some value. Under the APR, the equity holders and junior creditors often receive nothing.

Managers can also threaten to transfer the firm's bankruptcy filing from Chapter 11 to Chapter 7 if the creditors do not agree to a plan, a threat that is often effective in prodding unsecured creditors to accept the plan, as they anticipate receiving little or nothing if liquidation occurs. Managers also run the firm during the negotiating process, so secured creditors often fear that the value of their lien assets will decline. Finally, even after their exclusive period for proposing a reorganization plan ends, managers remain in a strong bargaining position. Individual creditors typically are unrepresented except in the largest cases, and severe free-rider problems arise when creditors attempt to form groups and raise funds to take an active part in bargaining.

The **cramdown procedure** is used when a reorganization plan fails to meet the standard for approval by all classes under the UCP or when the firm is clearly insolvent and the existing equity has no value. In a cramdown, if at least one class of creditors has voted for a reorganization plan, the bankruptcy court can approve the plan without the consent of the other classes, as long as each dissenting class is treated fairly and equitably. The fair and equitable standard closely reflects the APR by requiring either that all unsecured creditors receive full payment of their claims over the period of the plan or that all junior classes receive nothing. The cramdown procedure also requires that secured creditors retain their prebankruptcy liens on assets and that they receive periodic cash payments equal to the value of their claims. Cramdowns typically involve higher transaction costs than UCP reorganization plans because the bankruptcy judge often requires asset valuations by outside experts and more court hearings usually occur before the plan is approved.

When no reorganization plan is adopted under either the UCP or cramdown, managers sometimes voluntarily sell the firm as a going concern. In that case, the proceeds of the sale are paid to creditors according to the APR. This liquidating reorganization is similar to a Chapter 7 liquidation, except that the firm is sold as a going concern and is not shut down. Finally, if no progress is being made toward completion of a Chapter 11 reorganization, some creditor usually petitions the bankruptcy judge to order a shift of the firm's bankruptcy filing to a Chapter 7 liquidation.

Payment of Expenses

After the reorganization plan has been approved or disapproved, all parties to the proceedings whose services were beneficial or contributed to the approval or disapproval of the plan file a statement of expenses. If the court finds these claims acceptable, the debtor must pay these expenses within a reasonable period.

APPLYING THE MODEL

Campbell Technologies, a telecommunications equipment manufacturer, has filed Chapter 11 bankruptcy and is seeking to reorganize because it cannot service its debt. The company's current capital structure is as follows:

Debentures (unsecured debt)	$4,000,000
Subordinated debentures	2,000,000
Common stock (100,000 shares)	2,000,000
Total	$8,000,000

The company's book-value leverage is high, with a debt/equity ratio of 3.0 ($6,000,000/ $2,000,000). It has been determined that Campbell Technologies is worth $5 million as a going concern. The company can be reorganized as follows:

Debentures (unsecured debt)	$2,000,000
Subordinated debentures	1,000,000
Common stock (200,000 shares)	2,000,000
Total	$5,000,000

The face value of the debt is cut in half, but the debt holders receive 100,000 shares or half of the company's equity. The debt/equity ratio of Campbell Technologies is now a more reasonable 1.5 ($3,000,000/$2,000,000) and the company's operating profits should be more than sufficient to service the reduced debt burden. ■

Subsidies to Firms That Reorganize

Reorganization is viewed as a means of providing breathing space to viable firms that are in temporary financial distress in order to save jobs and avoid disruption to local communities. In contrast, liquidation is viewed as the process of winding up the operation of firms that are not viable. Therefore, in order to make reorganization attractive to managers and equity holders, Congress has provided a number of subsidies to firms in reorganization. These subsidies come either from the government or from creditors. They give firms in reorganization advantages relative to firms that continue operating outside of bankruptcy and firms that liquidate. The six major subsidies are as follows:

1. When reorganizing firms settle liabilities for less than their face value, the amount of debt forgiveness is deducted as a loss by the creditor but is not immediately treated as taxable income to the reorganizing firm. The debt forgiveness amount becomes taxable when the reorganized firm becomes profitable by reducing either its tax loss carryforward or its depreciation allowances.

2. Firms reorganizing under Chapter 11 have the right to terminate underfunded pension plans, and the U.S. government picks up the uncovered pension costs. For example, three large firms that filed for bankruptcy in the 1980s, LTV, Wheeling-Pittsburgh Steel, and Allis-Chalmers, terminated their pension funds and together transferred almost $3 billion of uncovered pension liabilities to the government.

3. Firms that reorganize retain most of their accrued tax loss carryforwards, which would be lost if they liquidated. These loss carryforwards shelter the firm from paying taxes on corporate profits for a period in the future, if its operations start to be profitable. They also make reorganized firms attractive merger partners for profitable firms, because the profitable firm can use the tax loss carryforward immediately. This subsidy makes reorganization more attractive than liquidation for a failing firm but has no effect on the choice between reorganization and remaining out of bankruptcy.

4. When firms file for bankruptcy, their obligation to pay interest to prebankruptcy creditors, both secured and unsecured, ceases. They do not have to start paying interest again until a reorganization plan is approved, and the unpaid interest does not become a claim against the firm. This subsidy clearly gives managers of failing firms an incentive to file for bankruptcy earlier and to delay proposing a reorganization plan.

5. Firms in reorganization can reject any of their contracts that are not substantially completed. Thus, they can get out of any unprofitable contracts. Although firms are still liable for damages to other parties to rejected contracts, such damage claims are unsecured and likely to receive a low payoff rate. Thus, the cost to the firm of shedding unprofitable contracts is small.

6. Firms in reorganization can reject their collective bargaining labor agreements. Since 1984, however, this step has required the approval of the bankruptcy judge. This has particularly benefited unionized firms in industries that have a mixture of unionized and nonunionized establishments by enabling them to cut all wages to nonunionized levels. A prominent example is Continental Airlines, which, following airline deregulation, filed to reorganize in bankruptcy in 1983. Continental was allowed to cut wages by 50 percent and cut its workforce by 65 percent.

Prepackaged Bankruptcies

Sometimes companies prepare a reorganization plan that is negotiated and voted on by creditors and stockholders before the company actually files for Chapter 11 bankruptcy. This process, known as a **prepackaged bankruptcy,** shortens and simplifies the process, saving the company money, and frequently generating more for the creditors as there is less spent in legal and related fees, less disruption to the company's business, and less damage to its goodwill.

For example, Regal Cinemas, the largest U.S. movie theater chain, simultaneously filed a voluntary petition for Chapter 11 bankruptcy protection and a prepackaged plan of reorganization on October 12, 2001. The reorganization plan gave effective control of the operation of 3,831 movie screens to Denver billionaire Philip Anschutz, who has used the theater industry's misfortunes to gain control of two other chains, United Artists and Edwards. The reorganization plan gives Regal's senior debt holders 100 percent of the reorganized company's stock. As it turns out, Anschutz owns the majority of the senior debt, having bought it for pennies on the dollar from Regal's bankers earlier in the year.

<table>
<tr><td>Concept Review Questions</td><td>10. Under what circumstances would it make sense for a company to reorganize rather than liquidate?

11. Why is the existing management generally allowed to remain in control when a company files for bankruptcy?

12. Why is a cramdown procedure sometimes necessary when a company reorganizes?</td></tr>
</table>

25.5 LIQUIDATION IN BANKRUPTCY

The liquidation of a bankrupt firm usually occurs once the courts have determined that reorganization is not feasible. The managers or creditors of the bankrupt firm must normally file a petition for reorganization. If no petition is filed, if a petition is filed and denied, or if the reorganization plan is denied, the firm must be liquidated. Three important aspects of liquidation in bankruptcy are the procedures, the priority of claims, and the final accounting.

SMART ETHICS VIDEO
Tom Cole, Deutsche Bank, Leveraged Finance Group
"Obviously companies don't want to go bankrupt and obviously investors don't want to lose money."

See the entire interview at **SMARTFinance**

PROCEDURES

When a firm is adjudged bankrupt, the judge may appoint a trustee to perform the many routine duties required in administering the bankruptcy. The trustee takes charge of the property of the bankrupt firm and protects the interest of its creditors. Between 20 and 40 days after the firm has been adjudged bankrupt, the creditors must hold a meeting. The bankruptcy court clerk presides over this meeting, during which the creditors are made aware of the prospects for the liquidation.[4] The trustee is then given the responsibility of liquidating the firm, keeping records, examining creditors' claims, disbursing money, furnishing information as required, and making final reports on the liquidation. In essence, the trustee is responsible for the liquidation of the firm. Occasionally, the court will call subsequent creditor meetings, but only a final meeting for closing the bankruptcy is required.[5]

PRIORITY OF CLAIMS

The trustee has the responsibility to liquidate all the firm's assets and to distribute the proceeds to the holders of provable claims. The courts have established certain procedures for determining the provability of claims, known as the absolute priority rules. The priority of claims, which is specified in Chapter 7 of the Bankruptcy Reform Act, must be maintained by the trustee when distributing the funds from liquidation. It is important to recognize that if in a liquidation any **secured creditors** have specific assets pledged as collateral, they receive the proceeds from the sale of those assets. If these proceeds are inadequate to meet their claim, the secured creditors be-

---

[4] See Pulvino (1999) for a description of the effects of bankruptcy court protection on sales of assets.
[5] For a discussion on the size of liquidation costs, see Alderson and Betker (1995).

come **unsecured** (or **general**) **creditors** for the unrecovered amount because specific collateral no longer exists. These and all other unsecured creditors will divide up, on a pro rata basis, any funds remaining after all prior claims have been satisfied. If the proceeds from the sale of secured assets are in excess of the claims against them, the excess funds become available to meet claims of unsecured creditors.

The complete order of priority of claims is as follows:

1. The expenses of administering the bankruptcy proceedings.
2. Any unpaid interim expenses incurred in the ordinary course of business between filing the bankruptcy petition and the entry of an Order of Relief in an involuntary proceeding. (This step is not applicable in a voluntary bankruptcy.)
3. Wages of not more than $2,000 per worker that have been earned by workers in the 90-day period immediately preceding the commencement of bankruptcy proceedings.
4. Unpaid employee benefit plan contributions that were to be paid in the 180-day period preceding the filing of bankruptcy or the termination of business, whichever occurred first. For any employee, the sum of this claim plus eligible unpaid wages cannot exceed $2,000.
5. Claims of farmers or fishermen in a grain-storage or fish-storage facility, not to exceed $2,000 for each producer.
6. Unsecured customer deposits, not to exceed $900 each, resulting from purchasing or leasing a good or service from the failed firm.
7. Taxes legally due and owed by the bankrupt firm to the federal government, state government, or any other governmental subdivision.
8. Claims of secured creditors, who receive the proceeds from the sale of collateral held, regardless of the priorities described above. If the proceeds from the liquidation of the collateral are insufficient to satisfy the secured creditors' claims, the secured creditors become unsecured creditors for the unpaid amount.
9. Claims of unsecured creditors. The claims of unsecured, or general, creditors and unsatisfied portions of secured creditors' claims are treated equally.
10. Preferred stockholders, who receive an amount up to the par, or stated, value of their preferred stock.
11. Common stockholders, who receive any remaining funds, which are distributed on an equal per-share basis. If different classes of common stock are outstanding, priorities may exist.

In spite of the priorities listed in items 1 through 7, secured creditors have first claim on proceeds from the sale of their collateral. The claims of unsecured creditors, including the unpaid claims of secured creditors, are satisfied next, and, finally, the claims of preferred and common stockholders. Also, some unsecured creditors' claims may be subordinated to those of other unsecured creditors. In the event of liquidation, the subordinated creditors do not receive any cash until the claims to which they are subordinated are paid in full. The following Applying the Model gives a simple example of the application of these priorities by the trustee in bankruptcy liquidation proceedings.

APPLYING THE MODEL

Table 25.3 presents the balance sheet of Oxford Company, a manufacturer of computer drives. The trustee has liquidated the firm's assets, obtaining the largest amounts possible. He obtained $2.1 million for the firm's current assets and $1.8 million for the firm's fixed assets. The total proceeds from the liquidation, therefore,

Table 25.3
Balance Sheet for
Oxford Company

Assets		Liabilities and Stockholders' Equity	
Cash	$ 100,000	Accounts payable	$ 200,000
Accounts receivable	1,200,000	Notes payable—bank	1,500,000
Inventories	3,150,000	Accrued wages[a]	100,000
Total current assets	$4,450,000	Unpaid employee benefits[b]	110,000
Land	$2,000,000	Unsecured customer deposits[c]	90,000
Net plant	1,500,000	Taxes payable	300,000
Net equipment	1,100,000	Total current liabilities	$2,300,000
Total fixed assets	$4,600,000	First mortgage[d]	$1,400,000
Total	$9,050,000	Second mortgage[d]	800,000
		Subordinated debentures[e]	1,000,000
		Total long-term debt	$3,200,000
		Preferred stock (7,000 shares)	$ 700,000
		Common stock (20,000 shares)	$ 200,000
		Paid-in capital in excess of par	300,000
		Retained earnings	$2,350,000
		Total stockholders' equity	$2,850,000
		Total	$9,050,000

[a]This represents wages of $2,000 or less per employee earned within 90 days of filing bankruptcy for the firm's employees.
[b]These unpaid employee benefits were due in the 180-day period preceding the firm's bankruptcy filing, which occurred simultaneously with the termination of its business.
[c]This represents unsecured customer deposits not exceeding $900 each.
[d]The first and second mortgages are on the firm's total fixed assets.
[e]The debentures are subordinated to the bank's note payable.

Table 25.4
Distribution of the
Liquidation Proceeds of
Oxford Company

Proceeds from liquidation	$3,900,000
Expenses of administering bankruptcy and paying bills	$ 500,000
Wages owed workers	100,000
Unpaid employee benefits	110,000
Unsecured customer deposits	90,000
Taxes owed governments	300,000
Funds available for creditors	$2,800,000
First mortgage, paid from $2 million proceeds of fixed asset sale	$1,400,000
Second mortgage, partially paid from the remaining assets	400,000
Funds available for unsecured creditors	$1,000,000

were $3.9 million. It is clear that the firm is legally insolvent because its liabilities of $5.5 million exceed the $3.9 million market value of its assets.

The next step is to distribute the proceeds to the various creditors. The only liability that is not shown on the balance sheet is $500,000 in expenses for administering the bankruptcy proceedings and satisfying unpaid bills incurred between the time of filing the bankruptcy petition and the entry of an Order of Relief. Table 25.4 shows the distribution of the $3.9 million among the firm's creditors and illustrates that once all prior claims on the proceeds to liquidation have been satisfied, the unsecured

Table 25.5
Pro Rata Distribution
of Funds among the
Unsecured Creditors of
Oxford Company

Unsecured Creditors' Claims	Amount	Settlement at 32%[a]	After Subordination
Unpaid balance on second mortgage	$ 400,000[b]	$ 129,032	$ 129,032
Accounts payable	200,000	64,516	64,516
Notes payable—bank	1,500,000	483,871	806,452
Subordinated debentures	1,000,000	322,581	0
Totals	$3,100,000	$1,000,000	$1,000,000

[a]The 32% rate is calculated by dividing the $1 million available for the unsecured creditors by the $3.1 million owed the unsecured creditors. Each is entitled to a pro rata share.

[b]This figure represents the difference between the $800,000 second mortgage and the $400,000 payment on the second mortgage from the proceeds from the sale of the collateral remaining after satisfying the first mortgage.

creditors get the remaining funds. Table 25.5 gives the pro rata distribution of the $1 million among the unsecured creditors. The disposition of funds in the Oxford Company liquidation should be clear from Tables 25.4 and 25.5. Because the claims of the unsecured creditors have not been fully satisfied, the preferred and common shareholders receive nothing.

FINAL ACCOUNTING

The trustee, after liquidating the bankrupt firm's assets and distributing proceeds to satisfy all provable claims in the appropriate order of priority, makes a final accounting to the bankruptcy court and creditors. Once the court approves the final accounting, the liquidation is complete.

For example, Babygear.com filed for liquidation under Chapter 7 of the Bankruptcy Reform Act in December 2001. The company cited a lack of continued funding from investors as the reason for ceasing operations. The two-year-old Internet retailing site had become one of the leading online infant retailers selling furniture, clothes, and toys. The company listed assets of $2.8 million and liabilities of over $10 million. President Preston Bealle stated that Babygear.com could have been profitable within a year, but the company's venture capitalists refused to commit more funds to the business because of the dramatic decline in valuations for Internet retailers.

SMART IDEAS VIDEO
Ed Altman, New York University
"The average time in bankruptcy is around 18 months to two years in the U.S."

See the entire interview at **SMARTFinance**

---

13. What is the purpose of having the absolute priority rule? Why shouldn't the bankruptcy judge be given more discretion?

14. What is the significance of subordinating a claim if a firm is liquidated?

15. Why is the payment of the expenses of administering the bankruptcy proceeding given the highest priority?

Concept
Review
Questions

25.6 PREDICTING BANKRUPTCY

Predicting bankruptcy with some degree of accuracy is possible using Altman's Z score. The **Z score** is the product of a quantitative model that uses a blend of tra-

Table 25.6
Balance Sheet for Poff
Industries

Assets		Liabilities and Stockholders' Equity	
Cash	$ 100,000	Accounts payable	$ 2,000,000
Accounts receivable	1,000,000	Notes payable—bank	1,500,000
Inventories	3,000,000	Total current liabilities	$ 3,500,000
Total current assets	$ 4,100,000	Mortgage	$ 2,000,000
Land	$ 2,000,000	Debentures	3,000,000
Net plant	2,500,000	Total long-term debt	$ 5,000,000
Net equipment	3,000,000	Preferred stock	
Total fixed assets	$ 7,500,000	(100,000 shares)	$ 1,000,000
Total	$11,600,000	Common stock	
		(1,000,000 shares)	1,000,000
		Paid-in capital in excess of par	1,000,000
		Retained earnings	1,100,000
		Total stockholders' equity	$ 3,100,000
		Total	$11,600,000

ditional financial ratios and a statistical technique known as multiple discriminant analysis. The Z score has been found to be about 90 percent accurate in forecasting bankruptcy one year in the future and about 80 percent accurate in forecasting it two years in the future. The model is as follows:

$$Z = 1.2^*X_1 + 1.4^*X_2 + 3.3^*X_3 + 0.6X_4 + 1.0X_5,$$

where X_1 = working capital ÷ total assets,

X_2 = retained earnings ÷ total assets,

X_3 = earnings before interest and taxes ÷ total assets,

X_4 = market value of equity ÷ book value of debt,

X_5 = sales ÷ total assets.

The following are guidelines for classifying businesses: Z score less than 1.8, high probability of failure; Z score between 1.81 and 2.99, unsure; and Z score above 3.0, failure unlikely.

APPLYING THE MODEL

Table 25.6 presents the balance sheet and Table 25.7, the income statement, for Poff Industries, a manufacturer of computer power supplies. The company's stock price currently is $3.50 per share.

The company's Z score can be calculated as follows:

$$1.330 = 1.2^*(0.052) + 1.4^*(0.095) + 3.3^*(0.086) + 0.6^*(0.700) + 1.0^*(0.431)$$

The Z score of 1.330 indicates that the probability that Poff Industries will fail is quite high.

Sales	$5,000,000
Less: Cost of goods sold	3,000,000
Less: Selling and administrative expenses	1,000,000
Earnings before interest and taxes	$1,000,000
Less: Interest	500,000
Earnings before taxes	$ 500,000
Less: Taxes (40%)	200,000
Net income	$ 300,000

Table 25.7
Income Statement for Poff
Industries

16. Why is predicting bankruptcy a useful ability?

17. How are the five factors that determine a Z score related to the financial health of a business?

**Concept
Review
Questions**

25.7 SUMMARY

- A business can fail in two ways. When it cannot pay its liabilities when they come due, the firm is technically insolvent due to a liquidity crisis. When its liabilities exceed the fair market value of its assets, the firm is insolvent. Bankruptcy occurs once a company comes under the authority of a bankruptcy court, which then exercises ultimate control over the firm.

- Mismanagement is the primary cause of business failure. Managerial faults include overexpansion, poor financial actions, an ineffective sales force, and high production costs. Other causes are economic downturns and corporate maturity.

- The financial distress a pending business failure places on a company and its management can have a profound effect on how the firm behaves and how its suppliers and customers perceive it. When a firm is in financial distress, suppliers are reluctant to extend credit and customers are concerned about service and warranties.

- Companies facing financial distress can voluntarily reorganize or liquidate. By acting voluntarily, firms reduce the legal and administrative expenses associated with a formal bankruptcy filing.

- The Bankruptcy Reform Act of 1978 specifies in Chapter 7 how firms are liquidated and in Chapter 11 how firms are reorganized.

- Firms can reorganize under Chapter 11 by means of the unanimous consent procedure or the cramdown procedure. In a reorganization, the terms of the debt can be relaxed by extending the payment term or lowering the interest rate. Also, debt can be exchanged for equity in the firm, thus reducing the amount of cash flow required to service the debt.

- Firms are liquidated under Chapter 7 by means of the absolute priority rule, which ranks the order for paying creditors from the proceeds of the liquidation of the firm's assets.

- The likelihood of bankruptcy can be predicted with a fair degree of accuracy (at least in the short term) using Altman's Z score.

KEY TERMS

absolute priority rules (APR)
assignment
bankruptcy
Bankruptcy Reform Act of 1978
business failure
Chapter 7
Chapter 11
composition
cramdown procedure
creditor control
debtor in possession (DIP)
economic failure
extension
general creditors
insolvency bankruptcy
insolvent

involuntary reorganization
liquidation
liquidity crisis
prepackaged bankruptcy
recapitalization
reorganization
secured creditors
technical insolvency
trustee
unanimous consent procedure (UCP)
unsecured creditors
voluntary reorganization
voluntary settlement
workout
Z score

QUESTIONS

25-1. Discuss why it makes sense to offer subsidies to firms that reorganize rather than liquidate.

25-2. Explain why the option to delay entering bankruptcy has value for corporate managers.

25-3. Why do creditors usually accept a plan for financial rehabilitation rather than demand liquidation of a business?

25-4. A certain number of bankruptcies are good for the economy. Discuss why you agree or disagree with this statement.

25-5. A business should always be liquidated when the liquidation value exceeds the business's value as a going concern. Discuss why you agree or disagree with this statement.

25-6. What are the advantages and disadvantages of a voluntary workout to resolve financial distress? What are the advantages and disadvantages of declaring bankruptcy to resolve financial distress?

25-7. A business can be liquidated for $700,000, or it can be reorganized. Reorganization would require an investment of $400,000. If the company is reorganized, earnings are projected to be $150,000 per year, and the company would trade at a price/earnings ratio of 8.0 times. Should the company be liquidated or reorganized?

25-8. Explain why the priorities for liquidation are determined as they are. Do you agree with the order?

25-9. What is the difference between economic failure and financial distress? Which situation is likely to lead to liquidation, and which is likely to result in reorganization?

25-10. Who would use Altman's Z score to predict bankruptcy? Why would the ability to predict bankruptcy be useful to them?

25-11. What is the purpose of a prepackaged bankruptcy? Would a prepackaged bankruptcy be more likely to be used for a liquidation or a reorganization?

25-12.   Why would some creditors be willing to subordinate their claims to the claims of other creditors?

PROBLEMS

Voluntary Settlements

25-1.   For a firm with outstanding debt of $2.4 million, classify each of the following voluntary settlements as an extension, a composition, or a combination of the two.

   a. Paying all creditors 40 cents on the dollar in exchange for complete discharge of the debt
   b. Paying all creditors in full in three periodic installments
   c. Paying a group of creditors with claims of $1 million in full over two years and immediately paying the remaining creditors 75 cents on the dollar

25-2.   For a firm with outstanding debt of $125,000, classify each of the following voluntary settlements as an extension, a composition, or a combination of the two.

   a. Paying a group of creditors in full in four periodic installments and paying the remaining creditors in full immediately
   b. Paying a group of creditors 80 cents on the dollar immediately and paying the remaining creditors 70 cents on the dollar in two periodic installments
   c. Paying all creditors in full in 270 days

24-3.   For a firm with outstanding debt of $200 million, classify each of the following voluntary settlements as an extension, a composition, or a combination of the two.

   a. Paying a group of creditors in full in three periodic installments and paying the remaining creditors 70 cents on the dollar immediately
   b. Paying a group of creditors 60 cents on the dollar immediately and paying the remaining creditors 80 cents on the dollar in five periodic installments
   c. Paying all creditors 25 cents on the dollar

25-4.   Go to http://www.bankruptcydata.com, and find what were the largest public company bankruptcies during the previous year. Compare the list of the largest bankruptcies in U.S. history presented in Table 25.1 with the current list at http://www.bankruptcydata.com. Have any bankruptcies that occurred after 2001 made the list?

25-5.   Jacobi Supply Company recently ran into financial difficulties that have resulted in the initiation of voluntary settlement procedures. The firm currently has $250,000 in outstanding debts and approximately $100,000 in marketable short-term assets. Indicate, for each of the following plans, whether the plan is an extension, a composition, or a combination of the two. Also indicate the cash payments and timing of the payments required of the firm under each plan.

   a. Each creditor will be paid 40 cents on the dollar immediately, and the debts will be considered fully satisfied.
   b. Each creditor will be paid 40 cents on the dollar in two quarterly installments of 20 cents and 20 cents. The first installment is to be paid in 90 days.
   c. Each creditor will be paid the full amount of its claims in three installments of 50 cents, 25 cents, and 25 cents on the dollar. The installments will be made in 60-day intervals, beginning in 60 days.

25-6.   Heriot Manufacturing Company recently ran into certain financial difficulties that have resulted in the initiation of voluntary settlement procedures. The firm currently has $2 million in outstanding debts and approximately $1.2 million in marketable short-term assets. Indicate, for each of the following plans, whether the plan is an extension, a composition, or a combination of the two. Also indicate the cash payments and timing of the payments required of the firm under each plan.

a. Each creditor will be paid 60 cents on the dollar immediately, and the debts will be considered fully satisfied.

b. Each creditor will be paid 80 cents on the dollar in two quarterly installments of 50 cents and 30 cents. The first installment is to be paid in 90 days.

c. A group of creditors with claims of $600,000 will be immediately paid in full; the rest will be paid 85 cents on the dollar, payable in 90 days.

Liquidation in Bankruptcy

25-7. A firm has $450,000 in funds to distribute to its unsecured creditors. Three possible sets of unsecured creditor claims are presented. Calculate the settlement, if any, to be received by each creditor in each case shown in the following table.

Unsecured Creditors' Claims	Case I	Case II	Case III
Unpaid balance of second mortgage	$300,000	$200,000	$ 500,000
Accounts payable	200,000	100,000	300,000
Notes payable—bank	300,000	100,000	500,000
Unsecured bonds	100,000	200,000	500,000
Total	$900,000	$600,000	$1,800,000

25-8. A firm has $5 million in funds to distribute to its unsecured creditors. Three possible sets of unsecured creditor claims are presented. Calculate the settlement, if any, to be received by each creditor in each case shown in the following table.

Unsecured Creditors' Claims	Case I	Case II	Case III
Unpaid balance of second mortgage	$1,000,000	$2,000,000	$3,000,000
Accounts payable	2,000,000	1,000,000	3,000,000
Notes payable—bank	3,000,000	2,000,000	1,000,000
Unsecured bonds	1,000,000	3,000,000	2,000,000
Total	$7,000,000	$8,000,000	$9,000,000

25-9. Keck Business Forms recently failed and will be liquidated by a court-appointed trustee who will charge $300,000 for her services. The preliquidation balance sheet follows. Assume that the trustee liquidates the assets for $4.8 million, with $2.6 million coming from the sale of current assets and $2.2 million coming from fixed assets. Also assume that the unsecured bonds are subordinate to the notes payable. Prepare a table indicating the amount to be distributed to each claimant. Do the firm's owners receive any funds?

Keck Business Forms
Balance Sheet
as of December 31, 2004

Assets		Liabilities and Stockholders' Equity	
Cash	$ 100,000	Accounts payable	$1,200,000
Marketable securities	50,000	Notes payable—bank	1,100,000
Accounts receivable	1,100,000	Accrued wages[a]	300,000
Inventories	2,400,000	Unpaid employee benefits[b]	200,000
Prepaid expenses	400,000	Unsecured customer deposits[c]	250,000
Total current assets	$4,050,000	Taxes payable	100,000
		Total current liabilities	$3,150,000

(*continued on next page*)

Keck Business Forms
Balance Sheet
as of December 31, 2004
(*continued*)

Assets		Liabilities and Stockholders' Equity	
Land	$1,000,000	First mortgage[d]	$1,500,000
Net plant	2,100,000	Second mortgage[d]	1,000,000
Net equipment	2,300,000	Unsecured bonds	2,000,000
Total fixed assets	$5,400,000	Total long-term debt	$4,500,000
Total	$9,450,000	Preferred stock (5,000 shares)	$ 500,000
		Common stock (10,000 shares)	1,000,000
		Retained earnings	300,000
		Total stockholders' equity	$1,800,000
		Total	$9,450,000

[a]Represents wages of $2,000 or less per employee earned within 90 days of filing bankruptcy for 400 of the firm's employees.
[b]Unpaid employee benefits that were due in the 180-day period preceding the firm's bankruptcy filing, which occurred simultaneously with the termination of its business.
[c]Unsecured customer deposits not exceeding $900 each.
[d]First and second mortgages on the firm's total fixed assets.

Predicting Bankruptcy

25-10. Sosbee Foods has a working capital/total assets ratio of 0.2, a retained earnings/ total assets ratio of 0.1, an earnings before interest and taxes/ total asset ratio of 0.25, a market value of equity/book value of equity ratio of 0.6, and a sales/total assets ratio of 0.8. Calculate and interpret the company's Z score.

25-11. The following balance sheet and income statement are for Weber Industries. The firm's stock currently is priced at $6.00 per share. Calculate and interpret the company's Z score.

Smart Solutions
See the problem and solution explained step-by-step at SMARTFinance

Weber Industries
Balance Sheet
as of December 31, 2004

Assets		Liabilities and Stockholders' Equity	
Cash	$ 400,000	Accounts payable	$ 5,000,000
Accounts receivable	3,000,000	Notes payable—bank	1,000,000
Inventories	4,000,000	Total current liabilities	$ 6,000,000
Total current assets	$ 7,400,000	Mortgage	$ 4,000,000
Land	$ 1,000,000	Debentures	6,000,000
Net plant	5,000,000	Total long-term debt	$10,000,000
Net equipment	8,000,000	Preferred stock (100,000 shares)	$ 1,000,000
Total fixed assets	$14,000,000	Common stock (500,000 shares)	1,000,000
Total	$21,400,000	Paid-in capital in excess of par	2,000,000
		Retained earnings	1,400,000
		Total stockholders' equity	$ 5,400,000
		Total	$21,400,000

Weber Industries
Income Statement
for the Year Ending December 31, 2004

Sales	$6,000,000
Less: Cost of goods sold	3,500,000
Less: Selling and administrative	1,000,000
Earnings before interest and taxes	$1,500,000
Less: Interest	1,100,000
Earnings before taxes	$ 400,000
Less: Taxes (30%)	120,000
Net income	$ 280,000

APPENDIX A: FINANCIAL TABLES

Table A1
Future Value Factors for One Dollar Compounded at r Percent for n Periods

$$FVF_{r\%,n} = (1 + r)^n$$

Period	1%	2%	3%	4%	5%	6%	7%	8%	9%	10%	11%	12%	13%	14%	15%
1	1.010	1.020	1.030	1.040	1.050	1.060	1.070	1.080	1.090	1.100	1.110	1.120	1.130	1.140	1.150
2	1.020	1.040	1.061	1.082	1.103	1.124	1.145	1.166	1.188	1.210	1.232	1.254	1.277	1.300	1.323
3	1.030	1.061	1.093	1.125	1.158	1.191	1.225	1.260	1.295	1.331	1.368	1.405	1.443	1.482	1.521
4	1.041	1.082	1.126	1.170	1.216	1.262	1.311	1.360	1.412	1.464	1.518	1.574	1.630	1.689	1.749
5	1.051	1.104	1.159	1.217	1.276	1.338	1.403	1.469	1.539	1.611	1.685	1.762	1.842	1.925	2.011
6	1.062	1.126	1.194	1.265	1.340	1.419	1.501	1.587	1.677	1.772	1.870	1.974	2.082	2.195	2.313
7	1.072	1.149	1.230	1.316	1.407	1.504	1.606	1.714	1.828	1.949	2.076	2.211	2.353	2.502	2.660
8	1.083	1.172	1.267	1.369	1.477	1.594	1.718	1.851	1.993	2.144	2.305	2.476	2.658	2.853	3.059
9	1.094	1.195	1.305	1.423	1.551	1.689	1.838	1.999	2.172	2.358	2.558	2.773	3.004	3.252	3.518
10	1.105	1.219	1.344	1.480	1.629	1.791	1.967	2.159	2.367	2.594	2.839	3.106	3.395	3.707	4.046
11	1.116	1.243	1.384	1.539	1.710	1.898	2.105	2.332	2.580	2.853	3.152	3.479	3.836	4.226	4.652
12	1.127	1.268	1.426	1.601	1.796	2.012	2.252	2.518	2.813	3.138	3.498	3.896	4.335	4.818	5.350
13	1.138	1.294	1.469	1.665	1.886	2.133	2.410	2.720	3.066	3.452	3.883	4.363	4.898	5.492	6.153
14	1.149	1.319	1.513	1.732	1.980	2.261	2.579	2.937	3.342	3.797	4.310	4.887	5.535	6.261	7.076
15	1.161	1.346	1.558	1.801	2.079	2.397	2.759	3.172	3.642	4.177	4.785	5.474	6.254	7.138	8.137
16	1.173	1.373	1.605	1.873	2.183	2.540	2.952	3.426	3.970	4.595	5.311	6.130	7.067	8.137	9.358
17	1.184	1.400	1.653	1.948	2.292	2.693	3.159	3.700	4.328	5.054	5.895	6.866	7.986	9.276	10.761
18	1.196	1.428	1.702	2.026	2.407	2.854	3.380	3.996	4.717	5.560	6.544	7.690	9.024	10.575	12.375
19	1.208	1.457	1.754	2.107	2.527	3.026	3.617	4.316	5.142	6.116	7.263	8.613	10.197	12.056	14.232
20	1.220	1.486	1.806	2.191	2.653	3.207	3.870	4.661	5.604	6.727	8.062	9.646	11.523	13.743	16.367
21	1.232	1.516	1.860	2.279	2.786	3.400	4.141	5.034	6.109	7.400	8.949	10.804	13.021	15.668	18.822
22	1.245	1.546	1.916	2.370	2.925	3.604	4.430	5.437	6.659	8.140	9.934	12.100	14.714	17.861	21.645
23	1.257	1.577	1.974	2.465	3.072	3.820	4.741	5.871	7.258	8.954	11.026	13.552	16.627	20.362	24.891
24	1.270	1.608	2.033	2.563	3.225	4.049	5.072	6.341	7.911	9.850	12.239	15.179	18.788	23.212	28.625
25	1.282	1.641	2.094	2.666	3.386	4.292	5.427	6.848	8.623	10.835	13.585	17.000	21.231	26.462	32.919
30	1.348	1.811	2.427	3.243	4.322	5.743	7.612	10.063	13.268	17.449	22.892	29.960	39.116	50.950	66.212
35	1.417	2.000	2.814	3.946	5.516	7.686	10.677	14.785	20.414	28.102	38.575	52.800	72.069	98.100	133.176
40	1.489	2.208	3.262	4.801	7.040	10.286	14.974	21.725	31.409	45.259	65.001	93.051	132.782	188.884	267.864
45	1.565	2.438	3.782	5.841	8.985	13.765	21.002	31.920	48.327	72.890	109.530	163.988	244.641	363.679	538.769
50	1.645	2.692	4.384	7.107	11.467	18.420	29.457	46.902	74.358	117.391	184.565	289.002	450.736	700.233	1083.657

Table A1 (continued)

Period	16%	17%	18%	19%	20%	21%	22%	23%	24%	25%	26%	27%
1	1.160	1.170	1.180	1.190	1.200	1.210	1.220	1.230	1.240	1.250	1.260	1.270
2	1.346	1.369	1.392	1.416	1.440	1.464	1.488	1.513	1.538	1.563	1.588	1.613
3	1.561	1.602	1.643	1.685	1.728	1.772	1.816	1.861	1.907	1.953	2.000	2.048
4	1.811	1.874	1.939	2.005	2.074	2.144	2.215	2.289	2.364	2.441	2.520	2.601
5	2.100	2.192	2.288	2.386	2.488	2.594	2.703	2.815	2.932	3.052	3.176	3.304
6	2.436	2.565	2.700	2.840	2.986	3.138	3.297	3.463	3.635	3.815	4.002	4.196
7	2.826	3.001	3.185	3.379	3.583	3.797	4.023	4.259	4.508	4.768	5.042	5.329
8	3.278	3.511	3.759	4.021	4.300	4.595	4.908	5.239	5.590	5.960	6.353	6.768
9	3.803	4.108	4.435	4.785	5.160	5.560	5.987	6.444	6.931	7.451	8.005	8.595
10	4.411	4.807	5.234	5.695	6.192	6.727	7.305	7.926	8.594	9.313	10.086	10.915
11	5.117	5.624	6.176	6.777	7.430	8.140	8.912	9.749	10.657	11.642	12.708	13.862
12	5.936	6.580	7.288	8.064	8.916	9.850	10.872	11.991	13.215	14.552	16.012	17.605
13	6.886	7.699	8.599	9.596	10.699	11.918	13.264	14.749	16.386	18.190	20.175	22.359
14	7.988	9.007	10.147	11.420	12.839	14.421	16.182	18.141	20.319	22.737	25.421	28.396
15	9.266	10.539	11.974	13.590	15.407	17.449	19.742	22.314	25.196	28.422	32.030	36.062
16	10.748	12.330	14.129	16.172	18.488	21.114	24.086	27.446	31.243	35.527	40.358	45.799
17	12.468	14.426	16.672	19.244	22.186	25.548	29.384	33.759	38.741	44.409	50.851	58.165
18	14.463	16.879	19.673	22.901	26.623	30.913	35.849	41.523	48.039	55.511	64.072	73.870
19	16.777	19.748	23.214	27.252	31.948	37.404	43.736	51.074	59.568	69.389	80.731	93.815
20	19.461	23.106	27.393	32.429	38.338	45.259	53.358	62.821	73.864	86.736	101.721	119.145
21	22.574	27.034	32.324	38.591	46.005	54.764	65.096	77.269	91.592	108.420	128.169	151.314
22	26.186	31.629	38.142	45.923	55.206	66.264	79.418	95.041	113.574	135.525	161.492	192.168
23	30.376	37.006	45.008	54.649	66.247	80.180	96.889	116.901	140.831	169.407	203.480	244.054
24	35.236	43.297	53.109	65.032	79.497	97.017	118.205	143.788	174.631	211.758	256.385	309.948
25	40.874	50.658	62.669	77.388	95.396	117.391	144.210	176.859	216.542	264.698	323.045	393.634
30	85.850	111.065	143.371	184.675	237.376	304.482	389.758	497.913	634.820	807.794	1025.927	1300.504
35	180.314	243.503	327.997	440.701	590.668	789.747	1053.402	1401.777	1861.054	2465.190	3258.135	4296.653
40	378.721	533.869	750.378	1051.668	1469.772	2048.400	2847.038	3946.430	5455.913	7523.164	10347.175	14195.439
45	795.444	1170.479	1716.684	2509.651	3657.262	5313.023	7694.712	11110.408	15994.690	22958.874	32860.527	46899.417
50	1670.704	2566.215	3927.357	5988.914	9100.438	13780.612	20796.561	31279.195	46890.435	70064.923	104358.362	154948.026

Table A1 (continued)
Future Value Factors for One Dollar Compounded at r Percent for n Periods

$$FVF_{r\%,n} = (1 + r)^n$$

Period	28%	29%	30%	31%	32%	33%	34%	35%	40%	45%	50%
1	1.280	1.290	1.300	1.310	1.320	1.330	1.340	1.350	1.400	1.450	1.500
2	1.638	1.664	1.690	1.716	1.742	1.769	1.796	1.823	1.960	2.103	2.250
3	2.097	2.147	2.197	2.248	2.300	2.353	2.406	2.460	2.744	3.049	3.375
4	2.684	2.769	2.856	2.945	3.036	3.129	3.224	3.322	3.842	4.421	5.063
5	3.436	3.572	3.713	3.858	4.007	4.162	4.320	4.484	5.378	6.410	7.594
6	4.398	4.608	4.827	5.054	5.290	5.535	5.789	6.053	7.530	9.294	11.391
7	5.629	5.945	6.275	6.621	6.983	7.361	7.758	8.172	10.541	13.476	17.086
8	7.206	7.669	8.157	8.673	9.217	9.791	10.395	11.032	14.758	19.541	25.629
9	9.223	9.893	10.604	11.362	12.166	13.022	13.930	14.894	20.661	28.334	38.443
10	11.806	12.761	13.786	14.884	16.060	17.319	18.666	20.107	28.925	41.085	57.665
11	15.112	16.462	17.922	19.498	21.199	23.034	25.012	27.144	40.496	59.573	86.498
12	19.343	21.236	23.298	25.542	27.983	30.635	33.516	36.644	56.694	86.381	129.746
13	24.759	27.395	30.288	33.460	36.937	40.745	44.912	49.470	79.371	125.252	194.620
14	31.691	35.339	39.374	43.833	48.757	54.190	60.182	66.784	111.120	181.615	291.929
15	40.565	45.587	51.186	57.421	64.359	72.073	80.644	90.158	155.568	263.342	437.894
16	51.923	58.808	66.542	75.221	84.954	95.858	108.063	121.714	217.795	381.846	656.841
17	66.461	75.862	86.504	98.540	112.139	127.491	144.804	164.314	304.913	553.676	985.261
18	85.071	97.862	112.455	129.087	148.024	169.562	194.038	221.824	426.879	802.831	1477.892
19	108.890	126.242	146.192	169.104	195.391	225.518	260.011	299.462	597.630	1164.105	2216.838
20	139.380	162.852	190.050	221.527	257.916	299.939	348.414	404.274	836.683	1687.952	3325.257
21	178.406	210.080	247.065	290.200	340.449	398.919	466.875	545.769	1171.356	2447.530	4987.885
22	228.360	271.003	321.184	380.162	449.393	530.562	625.613	736.789	1639.898	3548.919	7481.828
23	292.300	349.593	417.539	498.012	593.199	705.647	838.321	994.665	2295.857	5145.932	11222.741
24	374.144	450.976	542.801	652.396	783.023	938.511	1123.350	1342.797	3214.200	7461.602	16834.112
25	478.905	581.759	705.641	854.638	1033.590	1248.220	1505.289	1812.776	4499.880	10819.322	25251.168
30	1645.505	2078.219	2619.996	3297.151	4142.075	5194.566	6503.452	8128.550	24201.432	69348.978	191751.059
35	5653.911	7424.032	9727.860	12720.241	16599.217	21617.598	28097.517	36448.688	130161.112	444508.508	*
40	19426.689	26520.909	36118.865	49074.042	66520.767	89963.354	121392.522	163437.135	700037.697	*	*
45	66749.595	94740.782	134106.817	189325.148	266579.595	374389.658	524464.294	732857.577	*	*	*
50	229349.862	338442.984	497929.223	730406.758	*	*	*	*	*	*	*

* Not shown because of space limitations.

Table A2
Present Value Factors for One Dollar Discounted at r Percent for n Periods

$$PVF_{r\%,n} = 1/(1 + r)^n$$

Period	1%	2%	3%	4%	5%	6%	7%	8%	9%	10%	11%	12%	13%	14%	15%
1	0.990	0.980	0.971	0.962	0.952	0.943	0.935	0.926	0.917	0.909	0.901	0.893	0.885	0.877	0.870
2	0.980	0.961	0.943	0.925	0.907	0.890	0.873	0.857	0.842	0.826	0.812	0.797	0.783	0.769	0.756
3	0.971	0.942	0.915	0.889	0.864	0.840	0.816	0.794	0.772	0.751	0.731	0.712	0.693	0.675	0.658
4	0.961	0.924	0.888	0.855	0.823	0.792	0.763	0.735	0.708	0.683	0.659	0.636	0.613	0.592	0.572
5	0.951	0.906	0.863	0.822	0.784	0.747	0.713	0.681	0.650	0.621	0.593	0.567	0.543	0.519	0.497
6	0.942	0.888	0.837	0.790	0.746	0.705	0.666	0.630	0.596	0.564	0.535	0.507	0.480	0.456	0.432
7	0.933	0.871	0.813	0.760	0.711	0.665	0.623	0.583	0.547	0.513	0.482	0.452	0.425	0.400	0.376
8	0.923	0.853	0.789	0.731	0.677	0.627	0.582	0.540	0.502	0.467	0.434	0.404	0.376	0.351	0.327
9	0.914	0.837	0.766	0.703	0.645	0.592	0.544	0.500	0.460	0.424	0.391	0.361	0.333	0.308	0.284
10	0.905	0.820	0.744	0.676	0.614	0.558	0.508	0.463	0.422	0.386	0.352	0.322	0.295	0.270	0.247
11	0.896	0.804	0.722	0.650	0.585	0.527	0.475	0.429	0.388	0.350	0.317	0.287	0.261	0.237	0.215
12	0.887	0.788	0.701	0.625	0.557	0.497	0.444	0.397	0.356	0.319	0.286	0.257	0.231	0.208	0.187
13	0.879	0.773	0.681	0.601	0.530	0.469	0.415	0.368	0.326	0.290	0.258	0.229	0.204	0.182	0.163
14	0.870	0.758	0.661	0.577	0.505	0.442	0.388	0.340	0.299	0.263	0.232	0.205	0.181	0.160	0.141
15	0.861	0.743	0.642	0.555	0.481	0.417	0.362	0.315	0.275	0.239	0.209	0.183	0.160	0.140	0.123
16	0.853	0.728	0.623	0.534	0.458	0.394	0.339	0.292	0.252	0.218	0.188	0.163	0.141	0.123	0.107
17	0.844	0.714	0.605	0.513	0.436	0.371	0.317	0.270	0.231	0.198	0.170	0.146	0.125	0.108	0.093
18	0.836	0.700	0.587	0.494	0.416	0.350	0.296	0.250	0.212	0.180	0.153	0.130	0.111	0.095	0.081
19	0.828	0.686	0.570	0.475	0.396	0.331	0.277	0.232	0.194	0.164	0.138	0.116	0.098	0.083	0.070
20	0.820	0.673	0.554	0.456	0.377	0.312	0.258	0.215	0.178	0.149	0.124	0.104	0.087	0.073	0.061
21	0.811	0.660	0.538	0.439	0.359	0.294	0.242	0.199	0.164	0.135	0.112	0.093	0.077	0.064	0.053
22	0.803	0.647	0.522	0.422	0.342	0.278	0.226	0.184	0.150	0.123	0.101	0.083	0.068	0.056	0.046
23	0.795	0.634	0.507	0.406	0.326	0.262	0.211	0.170	0.138	0.112	0.091	0.074	0.060	0.049	0.040
24	0.788	0.622	0.492	0.390	0.310	0.247	0.197	0.158	0.126	0.102	0.082	0.066	0.053	0.043	0.035
25	0.780	0.610	0.478	0.375	0.295	0.233	0.184	0.146	0.116	0.092	0.074	0.059	0.047	0.038	0.030
30	0.742	0.552	0.412	0.308	0.231	0.174	0.131	0.099	0.075	0.057	0.044	0.033	0.026	0.020	0.015
35	0.706	0.500	0.355	0.253	0.181	0.130	0.094	0.068	0.049	0.036	0.026	0.019	0.014	0.010	0.008
40	0.672	0.453	0.307	0.208	0.142	0.097	0.067	0.046	0.032	0.022	0.015	0.011	0.008	0.005	0.004
45	0.639	0.410	0.264	0.171	0.111	0.073	0.048	0.031	0.021	0.014	0.009	0.006	0.004	0.003	0.002
50	0.608	0.372	0.228	0.141	0.087	0.054	0.034	0.021	0.013	0.009	0.005	0.003	0.002	0.001	0.001

Table A2 (continued)
Present Value Factors for One Dollar Discounted at r Percent for n Periods

$$PVF_{r\%,n} = 1/(1 + r)^n$$

Period	16%	17%	18%	19%	20%	21%	22%	23%	24%	25%	26%	27%
1	0.862	0.855	0.847	0.840	0.833	0.826	0.820	0.813	0.806	0.800	0.794	0.787
2	0.743	0.731	0.718	0.706	0.694	0.683	0.672	0.661	0.650	0.640	0.630	0.620
3	0.641	0.624	0.609	0.593	0.579	0.564	0.551	0.537	0.524	0.512	0.500	0.488
4	0.552	0.534	0.516	0.499	0.482	0.467	0.451	0.437	0.423	0.410	0.397	0.384
5	0.476	0.456	0.437	0.419	0.402	0.386	0.370	0.355	0.341	0.328	0.315	0.303
6	0.410	0.390	0.370	0.352	0.335	0.319	0.303	0.289	0.275	0.262	0.250	0.238
7	0.354	0.333	0.314	0.296	0.279	0.263	0.249	0.235	0.222	0.210	0.198	0.188
8	0.305	0.285	0.266	0.249	0.233	0.218	0.204	0.191	0.179	0.168	0.157	0.148
9	0.263	0.243	0.225	0.209	0.194	0.180	0.167	0.155	0.144	0.134	0.125	0.116
10	0.227	0.208	0.191	0.176	0.162	0.149	0.137	0.126	0.116	0.107	0.099	0.092
11	0.195	0.178	0.162	0.148	0.135	0.123	0.112	0.103	0.094	0.086	0.079	0.072
12	0.168	0.152	0.137	0.124	0.112	0.102	0.092	0.083	0.076	0.069	0.062	0.057
13	0.145	0.130	0.116	0.104	0.093	0.084	0.075	0.068	0.061	0.055	0.050	0.045
14	0.125	0.111	0.099	0.088	0.078	0.069	0.062	0.055	0.049	0.044	0.039	0.035
15	0.108	0.095	0.084	0.074	0.065	0.057	0.051	0.045	0.040	0.035	0.031	0.028
16	0.093	0.081	0.071	0.062	0.054	0.047	0.042	0.036	0.032	0.028	0.025	0.022
17	0.080	0.069	0.060	0.052	0.045	0.039	0.034	0.030	0.026	0.023	0.020	0.017
18	0.069	0.059	0.051	0.044	0.038	0.032	0.028	0.024	0.021	0.018	0.016	0.014
19	0.060	0.051	0.043	0.037	0.031	0.027	0.023	0.020	0.017	0.014	0.012	0.011
20	0.051	0.043	0.037	0.031	0.026	0.022	0.019	0.016	0.014	0.012	0.010	0.008
21	0.044	0.037	0.031	0.026	0.022	0.018	0.015	0.013	0.011	0.009	0.008	0.007
22	0.038	0.032	0.026	0.022	0.018	0.015	0.013	0.011	0.009	0.007	0.006	0.005
23	0.033	0.027	0.022	0.018	0.015	0.012	0.010	0.009	0.007	0.006	0.005	0.004
24	0.028	0.023	0.019	0.015	0.013	0.010	0.008	0.007	0.006	0.005	0.004	0.003
25	0.024	0.020	0.016	0.013	0.010	0.009	0.007	0.006	0.005	0.004	0.003	0.003
30	0.012	0.009	0.007	0.005	0.004	0.003	0.003	0.002	0.002	0.001	0.001	0.001
35	0.006	0.004	0.003	0.002	0.002	0.001	0.001	0.001	0.001	*	*	*
40	0.003	0.002	0.001	0.001	0.001	*	*	*	*	*	*	*
45	0.001	0.001	0.001	*	*	*	*	*	*	*	*	*
50	0.001	*	*	*	*	*	*	*	*	*	*	*

* *PVF* is zero to three decimal places.

Table A2 (continued)

Period	28%	29%	30%	31%	32%	33%	34%	35%	40%	45%	50%
1	0.781	0.775	0.769	0.763	0.758	0.752	0.746	0.741	0.714	0.690	0.667
2	0.610	0.601	0.592	0.583	0.574	0.565	0.557	0.549	0.510	0.476	0.444
3	0.477	0.466	0.455	0.445	0.435	0.425	0.416	0.406	0.364	0.328	0.296
4	0.373	0.361	0.350	0.340	0.329	0.320	0.310	0.301	0.260	0.226	0.198
5	0.291	0.280	0.269	0.259	0.250	0.240	0.231	0.223	0.186	0.156	0.132
6	0.227	0.217	0.207	0.198	0.189	0.181	0.173	0.165	0.133	0.108	0.088
7	0.178	0.168	0.159	0.151	0.143	0.136	0.129	0.122	0.095	0.074	0.059
8	0.139	0.130	0.123	0.115	0.108	0.102	0.096	0.091	0.068	0.051	0.039
9	0.108	0.101	0.094	0.088	0.082	0.077	0.072	0.067	0.048	0.035	0.026
10	0.085	0.078	0.073	0.067	0.062	0.058	0.054	0.050	0.035	0.024	0.017
11	0.066	0.061	0.056	0.051	0.047	0.043	0.040	0.037	0.025	0.017	0.012
12	0.052	0.047	0.043	0.039	0.036	0.033	0.030	0.027	0.018	0.012	0.008
13	0.040	0.037	0.033	0.030	0.027	0.025	0.022	0.020	0.013	0.008	0.005
14	0.032	0.028	0.025	0.023	0.021	0.018	0.017	0.015	0.009	0.006	0.003
15	0.025	0.022	0.020	0.017	0.016	0.014	0.012	0.011	0.006	0.004	0.002
16	0.019	0.017	0.015	0.013	0.012	0.010	0.009	0.008	0.005	0.003	0.002
17	0.015	0.013	0.012	0.010	0.009	0.008	0.007	0.006	0.003	0.002	0.001
18	0.012	0.010	0.009	0.008	0.007	0.006	0.005	0.005	0.002	0.001	0.001
19	0.009	0.008	0.007	0.006	0.005	0.004	0.004	0.003	0.002	0.001	*
20	0.007	0.006	0.005	0.005	0.004	0.003	0.003	0.002	0.001	0.001	*
21	0.006	0.005	0.004	0.003	0.003	0.003	0.002	0.002	0.001	*	*
22	0.004	0.004	0.003	0.003	0.002	0.002	0.002	0.001	0.001	*	*
23	0.003	0.003	0.002	0.002	0.002	0.001	0.001	0.001	*	*	*
24	0.003	0.002	0.002	0.002	0.001	0.001	0.001	0.001	*	*	*
25	0.002	0.002	0.001	0.001	0.001	0.001	0.001	0.001	*	*	*
30	0.001	*	*	*	*	*	*	*	*	*	*
35	*	*	*	*	*	*	*	*	*	*	*
40	*	*	*	*	*	*	*	*	*	*	*
45	*	*	*	*	*	*	*	*	*	*	*
50	*	*	*	*	*	*	*	*	*	*	*

* *PVF is zero to three decimal places.*

Table A3
Future Value Factors for a One-Dollar Ordinary Annuity Compounded at r Percent for n Periods

$$FVFA_{r\%,n} = PMT \times \frac{(1+r)^n - 1}{r}$$

Period	1%	2%	3%	4%	5%	6%	7%	8%	9%	10%	11%	12%	13%	14%	15%
1	1.000	1.000	1.000	1.000	1.000	1.000	1.000	1.000	1.000	1.000	1.000	1.000	1.000	1.000	1.000
2	2.010	2.020	2.030	2.040	2.050	2.060	2.070	2.080	2.090	2.100	2.110	2.120	2.130	2.140	2.150
3	3.030	3.060	3.091	3.122	3.153	3.184	3.215	3.246	3.278	3.310	3.342	3.374	3.407	3.440	3.473
4	4.060	4.122	4.184	4.246	4.310	4.375	4.440	4.506	4.573	4.641	4.710	4.779	4.850	4.921	4.993
5	5.101	5.204	5.309	5.416	5.526	5.637	5.751	5.867	5.985	6.105	6.228	6.353	6.480	6.610	6.742
6	6.152	6.308	6.468	6.633	6.802	6.975	7.153	7.336	7.523	7.716	7.913	8.115	8.323	8.536	8.754
7	7.214	7.434	7.662	7.898	8.142	8.394	8.654	8.923	9.200	9.487	9.783	10.089	10.405	10.730	11.067
8	8.286	8.583	8.892	9.214	9.549	9.897	10.260	10.637	11.028	11.436	11.859	12.300	12.757	13.233	13.727
9	9.369	9.755	10.159	10.583	11.027	11.491	11.978	12.488	13.021	13.579	14.164	14.776	15.416	16.085	16.786
10	10.462	10.950	11.464	12.006	12.578	13.181	13.816	14.487	15.193	15.937	16.722	17.549	18.420	19.337	20.304
11	11.567	12.169	12.808	13.486	14.207	14.972	15.784	16.645	17.560	18.531	19.561	20.655	21.814	23.045	24.349
12	12.683	13.412	14.192	15.026	15.917	16.870	17.888	18.977	20.141	21.384	22.713	24.133	25.650	27.271	29.002
13	13.809	14.680	15.618	16.627	17.713	18.882	20.141	21.495	22.953	24.523	26.212	28.029	29.985	32.089	34.352
14	14.947	15.974	17.086	18.292	19.599	21.015	22.550	24.215	26.019	27.975	30.095	32.393	34.883	37.581	40.505
15	16.097	17.293	18.599	20.024	21.579	23.276	25.129	27.152	29.361	31.772	34.405	37.280	40.417	43.842	47.580
16	17.258	18.639	20.157	21.825	23.657	25.673	27.888	30.324	33.003	35.950	39.190	42.753	46.672	50.980	55.717
17	18.430	20.012	21.762	23.698	25.840	28.213	30.840	33.750	36.974	40.545	44.501	48.884	53.739	59.118	65.075
18	19.615	21.412	23.414	25.645	28.132	30.906	33.999	37.450	41.301	45.599	50.396	55.750	61.725	68.394	75.836
19	20.811	22.841	25.117	27.671	30.539	33.760	37.379	41.446	46.018	51.159	56.939	63.440	70.749	78.969	88.212
20	22.019	24.297	26.870	29.778	33.066	36.786	40.995	45.762	51.160	57.275	64.203	72.052	80.947	91.025	102.444
21	23.239	25.783	28.676	31.969	35.719	39.993	44.865	50.423	56.765	64.002	72.265	81.699	92.470	104.768	118.810
22	24.472	27.299	30.537	34.248	38.505	43.392	49.006	55.457	62.873	71.403	81.214	92.503	105.491	120.436	137.632
23	25.716	28.845	32.453	36.618	41.430	46.996	53.436	60.893	69.532	79.543	91.148	104.603	120.205	138.297	159.276
24	26.973	30.422	34.426	39.083	44.502	50.816	58.177	66.765	76.790	88.497	102.174	118.155	136.831	158.659	184.168
25	28.243	32.030	36.459	41.646	47.727	54.865	63.249	73.106	84.701	98.347	114.413	133.334	155.620	181.871	212.793
30	34.785	40.568	47.575	56.085	66.439	79.058	94.461	113.283	136.308	164.494	199.021	241.333	293.199	356.787	434.745
35	41.660	49.994	60.462	73.652	90.320	111.435	138.237	172.317	215.711	271.024	341.590	431.663	546.681	693.573	881.170
40	48.886	60.402	75.401	95.026	120.800	154.762	199.635	259.057	337.882	442.593	581.826	767.091	1013.704	1342.025	1779.090
45	56.481	71.893	92.720	121.029	159.700	212.744	285.749	386.506	525.859	718.905	986.639	1358.230	1874.165	2590.565	3585.128
50	64.463	84.579	112.797	152.667	209.348	290.336	406.529	573.770	815.084	1163.909	1668.771	2400.018	3459.507	4994.521	7217.716

Table A3 (continued)

Period	16%	17%	18%	19%	20%	21%	22%	23%	24%	25%	26%	27%
1	1.000	1.000	1.000	1.000	1.000	1.000	1.000	1.000	1.000	1.000	1.000	1.000
2	2.160	2.170	2.180	2.190	2.200	2.210	2.220	2.230	2.240	2.250	2.260	2.270
3	3.506	3.539	3.572	3.606	3.640	3.674	3.708	3.743	3.778	3.813	3.848	3.883
4	5.066	5.141	5.215	5.291	5.368	5.446	5.524	5.604	5.684	5.766	5.848	5.931
5	6.877	7.014	7.154	7.297	7.442	7.589	7.740	7.893	8.048	8.207	8.368	8.533
6	8.977	9.207	9.442	9.683	9.930	10.183	10.442	10.708	10.980	11.259	11.544	11.837
7	11.414	11.772	12.142	12.523	12.916	13.321	13.740	14.171	14.615	15.073	15.546	16.032
8	14.240	14.773	15.327	15.902	16.499	17.119	17.762	18.430	19.123	19.842	20.588	21.361
9	17.519	18.285	19.086	19.923	20.799	21.714	22.670	23.669	24.712	25.802	26.940	28.129
10	21.321	22.393	23.521	24.709	25.959	27.274	28.657	30.113	31.643	33.253	34.945	36.723
11	25.733	27.200	28.755	30.404	32.150	34.001	35.962	38.039	40.238	42.566	45.031	47.639
12	30.850	32.824	34.931	37.180	39.581	42.142	44.874	47.788	50.895	54.208	57.739	61.501
13	36.786	39.404	42.219	45.244	48.497	51.991	55.746	59.779	64.110	68.760	73.751	79.107
14	43.672	47.103	50.818	54.841	59.196	63.909	69.010	74.528	80.496	86.949	93.926	101.465
15	51.660	56.110	60.965	66.261	72.035	78.330	85.192	92.669	100.815	109.687	119.347	129.861
16	60.925	66.649	72.939	79.850	87.442	95.780	104.935	114.983	126.011	138.109	151.377	165.924
17	71.673	78.979	87.068	96.022	105.931	116.894	129.020	142.430	157.253	173.636	191.735	211.723
18	84.141	93.406	103.740	115.266	128.117	142.441	158.405	176.188	195.994	218.045	242.585	269.888
19	98.603	110.285	123.414	138.166	154.740	173.354	194.254	217.712	244.033	273.556	306.658	343.758
20	115.380	130.033	146.628	165.418	186.688	210.758	237.989	268.785	303.601	342.945	387.389	437.573
21	134.841	153.139	174.021	197.847	225.026	256.018	291.347	331.606	377.465	429.681	489.110	556.717
22	157.415	180.172	206.345	236.438	271.031	310.781	356.443	408.875	469.056	538.101	617.278	708.031
23	183.601	211.801	244.487	282.362	326.237	377.045	435.861	503.917	582.630	673.626	778.771	900.199
24	213.978	248.808	289.494	337.010	392.484	457.225	532.750	620.817	723.461	843.033	982.251	1144.253
25	249.214	292.105	342.603	402.042	471.981	554.242	650.955	764.605	898.092	1054.791	1238.636	1454.201
30	530.312	647.439	790.948	966.712	1181.882	1445.151	1767.081	2160.491	2640.916	3227.174	3942.026	4812.977
35	1120.713	1426.491	1816.652	2314.214	2948.341	3755.938	4783.645	6090.334	7750.225	9856.761	12527.442	15909.824
40	2360.757	3134.522	4163.213	5529.829	7343.858	9749.525	12936.535	17154.046	22728.803	30088.655	39792.982	52571.998
45	4965.274	6879.291	9531.577	13203.424	18281.310	25295.346	34971.419	48301.775	66640.376	91831.496	126382.798	173697.840
50	10435.649	15089.502	21813.094	31515.336	45497.191	65617.202	94525.279	135992.154	195372.644	280255.693	401374.471	573877.874

Table A3 (continued)

Future Value Factors for a One-Dollar Ordinary Annuity Compounded at r Percent for n Periods

$$FVFA_{r\%,n} = PMT \times \frac{(1 + r)^n - 1}{r}$$

Period	28%	29%	30%	31%	32%	33%	34%	35%	40%	45%	50%
1	1.000	1.000	1.000	1.000	1.000	1.000	1.000	1.000	1.000	1.000	1.000
2	2.280	2.290	2.300	2.310	2.320	2.330	2.340	2.350	2.400	2.450	2.500
3	3.918	3.954	3.990	4.026	4.062	4.099	4.136	4.173	4.360	4.553	4.750
4	6.016	6.101	6.187	6.274	6.362	6.452	6.542	6.633	7.104	7.601	8.125
5	8.700	8.870	9.043	9.219	9.398	9.581	9.766	9.954	10.946	12.022	13.188
6	12.136	12.442	12.756	13.077	13.406	13.742	14.086	14.438	16.324	18.431	20.781
7	16.534	17.051	17.583	18.131	18.696	19.277	19.876	20.492	23.853	27.725	32.172
8	22.163	22.995	23.858	24.752	25.678	26.638	27.633	28.664	34.395	41.202	49.258
9	29.369	30.664	32.015	33.425	34.895	36.429	38.029	39.696	49.153	60.743	74.887
10	38.593	40.556	42.619	44.786	47.062	49.451	51.958	54.590	69.814	89.077	113.330
11	50.398	53.318	56.405	59.670	63.122	66.769	70.624	74.697	98.739	130.162	170.995
12	65.510	69.780	74.327	79.168	84.320	89.803	95.637	101.841	139.235	189.735	257.493
13	84.853	91.016	97.625	104.710	112.303	120.439	129.153	138.485	195.929	276.115	387.239
14	109.612	118.411	127.913	138.170	149.240	161.183	174.065	187.954	275.300	401.367	581.859
15	141.303	153.750	167.286	182.003	197.997	215.374	234.247	254.738	386.420	582.982	873.788
16	181.868	199.337	218.472	239.423	262.356	287.447	314.891	344.897	541.988	846.324	1311.682
17	233.791	258.145	285.014	314.645	347.309	383.305	422.954	466.611	759.784	1228.170	1968.523
18	300.252	334.007	371.518	413.185	459.449	510.795	567.758	630.925	1064.697	1781.846	2953.784
19	385.323	431.870	483.973	542.272	607.472	680.358	761.796	852.748	1491.576	2584.677	4431.676
20	494.213	558.112	630.165	711.376	802.863	905.876	1021.807	1152.210	2089.206	3748.782	6648.513
21	633.593	720.964	820.215	932.903	1060.779	1205.814	1370.221	1556.484	2925.889	5436.734	9973.770
22	811.999	931.044	1067.280	1223.103	1401.229	1604.733	1837.096	2102.253	4097.245	7884.264	14961.655
23	1040.358	1202.047	1388.464	1603.264	1850.622	2135.295	2462.709	2839.042	5737.142	11433.182	22443.483
24	1332.659	1551.640	1806.003	2101.276	2443.821	2840.943	3301.030	3833.706	8032.999	16579.115	33666.224
25	1706.803	2002.616	2348.803	2753.672	3226.844	3779.454	4424.380	5176.504	11247.199	24040.716	50500.337
30	5873.231	7162.824	8729.985	10632.746	12940.859	15738.077	19124.859	23221.570	60501.081	154106.618	383500.118
35	20188.966	25596.664	32422.868	41029.810	51869.427	65504.842	82636.815	104136.251	325400.279	987794.463	*
40	69377.460	91447.963	120392.883	158300.134	207874.272	272613.194	357033.889	466960.385	*	*	*
45	238387.839	326688.902	447019.389	610723.057	833058.110	*	*	*	*	*	*
50	819103.077	*	*	*	*	*	*	*	*	*	*

* Not shown because of space limitations.

Table A4
Present Value Factors for a One-Dollar Ordinary Annuity Discounted at r Percent for n Periods

$$PVFA_{r\%,n} = \frac{PMT}{r} \times \left[1 - \frac{1}{(1+r)^n} \right]$$

Period	1%	2%	3%	4%	5%	6%	7%	8%	9%	10%	11%	12%	13%	14%	15%
1	0.990	0.980	0.971	0.962	0.952	0.943	0.935	0.926	0.917	0.909	0.901	0.893	0.885	0.877	0.870
2	1.970	1.942	1.913	1.886	1.859	1.833	1.808	1.783	1.759	1.736	1.713	1.690	1.668	1.647	1.626
3	2.941	2.884	2.829	2.775	2.723	2.673	2.624	2.577	2.531	2.487	2.444	2.402	2.361	2.322	2.283
4	3.902	3.808	3.717	3.630	3.546	3.465	3.387	3.312	3.240	3.170	3.102	3.037	2.974	2.914	2.855
5	4.853	4.713	4.580	4.452	4.329	4.212	4.100	3.993	3.890	3.791	3.696	3.605	3.517	3.433	3.352
6	5.795	5.601	5.417	5.242	5.076	4.917	4.767	4.623	4.486	4.355	4.231	4.111	3.998	3.889	3.784
7	6.728	6.472	6.230	6.002	5.786	5.582	5.389	5.206	5.033	4.868	4.712	4.564	4.423	4.288	4.160
8	7.652	7.325	7.020	6.733	6.463	6.210	5.971	5.747	5.535	5.335	5.146	4.968	4.799	4.639	4.487
9	8.566	8.162	7.786	7.435	7.108	6.802	6.515	6.247	5.995	5.759	5.537	5.328	5.132	4.946	4.772
10	9.471	8.983	8.530	8.111	7.722	7.360	7.024	6.710	6.418	6.145	5.889	5.650	5.426	5.216	5.019
11	10.368	9.787	9.253	8.760	8.306	7.887	7.499	7.139	6.805	6.495	6.207	5.938	5.687	5.453	5.234
12	11.255	10.575	9.954	9.385	8.863	8.384	7.943	7.536	7.161	6.814	6.492	6.194	5.918	5.660	5.421
13	12.134	11.348	10.635	9.986	9.394	8.853	8.358	7.904	7.487	7.103	6.750	6.424	6.122	5.842	5.583
14	13.004	12.106	11.296	10.563	9.899	9.295	8.745	8.244	7.786	7.367	6.982	6.628	6.302	6.002	5.724
15	13.865	12.849	11.938	11.118	10.380	9.712	9.108	8.559	8.061	7.606	7.191	6.811	6.462	6.142	5.847
16	14.718	13.578	12.561	11.652	10.838	10.106	9.447	8.851	8.313	7.824	7.379	6.974	6.604	6.265	5.954
17	15.562	14.292	13.166	12.166	11.274	10.477	9.763	9.122	8.544	8.022	7.549	7.120	6.729	6.373	6.047
18	16.398	14.992	13.754	12.659	11.690	10.828	10.059	9.372	8.756	8.201	7.702	7.250	6.840	6.467	6.128
19	17.226	15.678	14.324	13.134	12.085	11.158	10.336	9.604	8.950	8.365	7.839	7.366	6.938	6.550	6.198
20	18.046	16.351	14.877	13.590	12.462	11.470	10.594	9.818	9.129	8.514	7.963	7.469	7.025	6.623	6.259
21	18.857	17.011	15.415	14.029	12.821	11.764	10.836	10.017	9.292	8.649	8.075	7.562	7.102	6.687	6.312
22	19.660	17.658	15.937	14.451	13.163	12.042	11.061	10.201	9.442	8.772	8.176	7.645	7.170	6.743	6.359
23	20.456	18.292	16.444	14.857	13.489	12.303	11.272	10.371	9.580	8.883	8.266	7.718	7.230	6.792	6.399
24	21.243	18.914	16.936	15.247	13.799	12.550	11.469	10.529	9.707	8.985	8.348	7.784	7.283	6.835	6.434
25	22.023	19.523	17.413	15.622	14.094	12.783	11.654	10.675	9.823	9.077	8.422	7.843	7.330	6.873	6.464
30	25.808	22.396	19.600	17.292	15.372	13.765	12.409	11.258	10.274	9.427	8.694	8.055	7.496	7.003	6.566
35	29.409	24.999	21.487	18.665	16.374	14.498	12.948	11.655	10.567	9.644	8.855	8.176	7.586	7.070	6.617
40	32.835	27.355	23.115	19.793	17.159	15.046	13.332	11.925	10.757	9.779	8.951	8.244	7.634	7.105	6.642
45	36.095	29.490	24.519	20.720	17.774	15.456	13.606	12.108	10.881	9.863	9.008	8.283	7.661	7.123	6.654
50	39.196	31.424	25.730	21.482	18.256	15.762	13.801	12.233	10.962	9.915	9.042	8.304	7.675	7.133	6.661

Table A4 (continued)
Present Value Factors for a One-Dollar Ordinary Annuity Discounted at r Percent for n Periods

$$PVFA_{r\%,n} = \frac{PMT}{r} \times \left[1 - \frac{1}{(1+r)^n} \right]$$

Period	16%	17%	18%	19%	20%	21%	22%	23%	24%	25%	26%	27%
1	0.862	0.855	0.847	0.840	0.833	0.826	0.820	0.813	0.806	0.800	0.794	0.787
2	1.605	1.585	1.566	1.547	1.528	1.509	1.492	1.474	1.457	1.440	1.424	1.407
3	2.246	2.210	2.174	2.140	2.106	2.074	2.042	2.011	1.981	1.952	1.923	1.896
4	2.798	2.743	2.690	2.639	2.589	2.540	2.494	2.448	2.404	2.362	2.320	2.280
5	3.274	3.199	3.127	3.058	2.991	2.926	2.864	2.803	2.745	2.689	2.635	2.583
6	3.685	3.589	3.498	3.410	3.326	3.245	3.167	3.092	3.020	2.951	2.885	2.821
7	4.039	3.922	3.812	3.706	3.605	3.508	3.416	3.327	3.242	3.161	3.083	3.009
8	4.344	4.207	4.078	3.954	3.837	3.726	3.619	3.518	3.421	3.329	3.241	3.156
9	4.607	4.451	4.303	4.163	4.031	3.905	3.786	3.673	3.566	3.463	3.366	3.273
10	4.833	4.659	4.494	4.339	4.192	4.054	3.923	3.799	3.682	3.571	3.465	3.364
11	5.029	4.836	4.656	4.486	4.327	4.177	4.035	3.902	3.776	3.656	3.543	3.437
12	5.197	4.988	4.793	4.611	4.439	4.278	4.127	3.985	3.851	3.725	3.606	3.493
13	5.342	5.118	4.910	4.715	4.533	4.362	4.203	4.053	3.912	3.780	3.656	3.538
14	5.468	5.229	5.008	4.802	4.611	4.432	4.265	4.108	3.962	3.824	3.695	3.573
15	5.575	5.324	5.092	4.876	4.675	4.489	4.315	4.153	4.001	3.859	3.726	3.601
16	5.668	5.405	5.162	4.938	4.730	4.536	4.357	4.189	4.033	3.887	3.751	3.623
17	5.749	5.475	5.222	4.990	4.775	4.576	4.391	4.219	4.059	3.910	3.771	3.640
18	5.818	5.534	5.273	5.033	4.812	4.608	4.419	4.243	4.080	3.928	3.786	3.654
19	5.877	5.584	5.316	5.070	4.843	4.635	4.442	4.263	4.097	3.942	3.799	3.664
20	5.929	5.628	5.353	5.101	4.870	4.657	4.460	4.279	4.110	3.954	3.808	3.673
21	5.973	5.665	5.384	5.127	4.891	4.675	4.476	4.292	4.121	3.963	3.816	3.679
22	6.011	5.696	5.410	5.149	4.909	4.690	4.488	4.302	4.130	3.970	3.822	3.684
23	6.044	5.723	5.432	5.167	4.925	4.703	4.499	4.311	4.137	3.976	3.827	3.689
24	6.073	5.746	5.451	5.182	4.937	4.713	4.507	4.318	4.143	3.981	3.831	3.692
25	6.097	5.766	5.467	5.195	4.948	4.721	4.514	4.323	4.147	3.985	3.834	3.694
30	6.177	5.829	5.517	5.235	4.979	4.746	4.534	4.339	4.160	3.995	3.842	3.701
35	6.215	5.858	5.539	5.251	4.992	4.756	4.541	4.345	4.164	3.998	3.845	3.703
40	6.233	5.871	5.548	5.258	4.997	4.760	4.544	4.347	4.166	3.999	3.846	3.703
45	6.242	5.877	5.552	5.261	4.999	4.761	4.545	4.347	4.166	4.000	3.846	3.704
50	6.246	5.880	5.554	5.262	4.999	4.762	4.545	4.348	4.167	4.000	3.846	3.704

Table A4 (continued)

Period	28%	29%	30%	31%	32%	33%	34%	35%	40%	45%	50%
1	0.781	0.775	0.769	0.763	0.758	0.752	0.746	0.741	0.714	0.690	0.667
2	1.392	1.376	1.361	1.346	1.331	1.317	1.303	1.289	1.224	1.165	1.111
3	1.868	1.842	1.816	1.791	1.766	1.742	1.719	1.696	1.589	1.493	1.407
4	2.241	2.203	2.166	2.130	2.096	2.062	2.029	1.997	1.849	1.720	1.605
5	2.532	2.483	2.436	2.390	2.345	2.302	2.260	2.220	2.035	1.876	1.737
6	2.759	2.700	2.643	2.588	2.534	2.483	2.433	2.385	2.168	1.983	1.824
7	2.937	2.868	2.802	2.739	2.677	2.619	2.562	2.508	2.263	2.057	1.883
8	3.076	2.999	2.925	2.854	2.786	2.721	2.658	2.598	2.331	2.109	1.922
9	3.184	3.100	3.019	2.942	2.868	2.798	2.730	2.665	2.379	2.144	1.948
10	3.269	3.178	3.092	3.009	2.930	2.855	2.784	2.715	2.414	2.168	1.965
11	3.335	3.239	3.147	3.060	2.978	2.899	2.824	2.752	2.438	2.185	1.977
12	3.387	3.286	3.190	3.100	3.013	2.931	2.853	2.779	2.456	2.196	1.985
13	3.427	3.322	3.223	3.129	3.040	2.956	2.876	2.799	2.469	2.204	1.990
14	3.459	3.351	3.249	3.152	3.061	2.974	2.892	2.814	2.478	2.210	1.993
15	3.483	3.373	3.268	3.170	3.076	2.988	2.905	2.825	2.484	2.214	1.995
16	3.503	3.390	3.283	3.183	3.088	2.999	2.914	2.834	2.489	2.216	1.997
17	3.518	3.403	3.295	3.193	3.097	3.007	2.921	2.840	2.492	2.218	1.998
18	3.529	3.413	3.304	3.201	3.104	3.012	2.926	2.844	2.494	2.219	1.999
19	3.539	3.421	3.311	3.207	3.109	3.017	2.930	2.848	2.496	2.220	1.999
20	3.546	3.427	3.316	3.211	3.113	3.020	2.933	2.850	2.497	2.221	1.999
21	3.551	3.432	3.320	3.215	3.116	3.023	2.935	2.852	2.498	2.221	1.999
22	3.556	3.436	3.323	3.217	3.118	3.025	2.936	2.853	2.498	2.222	2.000
23	3.559	3.438	3.325	3.219	3.120	3.026	2.938	2.854	2.499	2.222	2.000
24	3.562	3.441	3.327	3.221	3.121	3.027	2.939	2.855	2.499	2.222	2.000
25	3.564	3.442	3.329	3.222	3.122	3.028	2.939	2.856	2.499	2.222	2.000
30	3.569	3.447	3.332	3.225	3.124	3.030	2.941	2.857	2.500	2.222	2.000
35	3.571	3.448	3.333	3.226	3.125	3.030	2.941	2.857	2.500	2.222	2.000
40	3.571	3.448	3.333	3.226	3.125	3.030	2.941	2.857	2.500	2.222	2.000
45	3.571	3.448	3.333	3.226	3.125	3.030	2.941	2.857	2.500	2.222	2.000
50	3.571	3.448	3.333	3.226	3.125	3.030	2.941	2.857	2.500	2.222	2.000

Table A5
Future Value Factor for One Dollar Compounded Continuously at r Percent for n Periods

$$FVF_{r\%,n} = e^{rn}$$

Period	1%	2%	3%	4%	5%	6%	7%	8%	9%	10%	11%	12%	13%	14%	15%
1	1.010	1.020	1.030	1.041	1.051	1.062	1.073	1.083	1.094	1.105	1.116	1.127	1.139	1.150	1.162
2	1.020	1.041	1.062	1.083	1.105	1.127	1.150	1.174	1.197	1.221	1.246	1.271	1.297	1.323	1.350
3	1.030	1.062	1.094	1.127	1.162	1.197	1.234	1.271	1.310	1.350	1.391	1.433	1.477	1.522	1.568
4	1.041	1.083	1.127	1.174	1.221	1.271	1.323	1.377	1.433	1.492	1.553	1.616	1.682	1.751	1.822
5	1.051	1.105	1.162	1.221	1.284	1.350	1.419	1.492	1.568	1.649	1.733	1.822	1.916	2.014	2.117
6	1.062	1.127	1.197	1.271	1.350	1.433	1.522	1.616	1.716	1.822	1.935	2.054	2.181	2.316	2.460
7	1.073	1.150	1.234	1.323	1.419	1.522	1.632	1.751	1.878	2.014	2.160	2.316	2.484	2.664	2.858
8	1.083	1.174	1.271	1.377	1.492	1.616	1.751	1.896	2.054	2.226	2.411	2.612	2.829	3.065	3.320
9	1.094	1.197	1.310	1.433	1.568	1.716	1.878	2.054	2.248	2.460	2.691	2.945	3.222	3.525	3.857
10	1.105	1.221	1.350	1.492	1.649	1.822	2.014	2.226	2.460	2.718	3.004	3.320	3.669	4.055	4.482
11	1.116	1.246	1.391	1.553	1.733	1.935	2.160	2.411	2.691	3.004	3.353	3.743	4.179	4.665	5.207
12	1.127	1.271	1.433	1.616	1.822	2.054	2.316	2.612	2.945	3.320	3.743	4.221	4.759	5.366	6.050
13	1.139	1.297	1.477	1.682	1.916	2.181	2.484	2.829	3.222	3.669	4.179	4.759	5.419	6.172	7.029
14	1.150	1.323	1.522	1.751	2.014	2.316	2.664	3.065	3.525	4.055	4.665	5.366	6.172	7.099	8.166
15	1.162	1.350	1.568	1.822	2.117	2.460	2.858	3.320	3.857	4.482	5.207	6.050	7.029	8.166	9.488
16	1.174	1.377	1.616	1.896	2.226	2.612	3.065	3.597	4.221	4.953	5.812	6.821	8.004	9.393	11.023
17	1.185	1.405	1.665	1.974	2.340	2.773	3.287	3.896	4.618	5.474	6.488	7.691	9.116	10.805	12.807
18	1.197	1.433	1.716	2.054	2.460	2.945	3.525	4.221	5.053	6.050	7.243	8.671	10.381	12.429	14.880
19	1.209	1.462	1.768	2.138	2.586	3.127	3.781	4.572	5.529	6.686	8.085	9.777	11.822	14.296	17.288
20	1.221	1.492	1.822	2.226	2.718	3.320	4.055	4.953	6.050	7.389	9.025	11.023	13.464	16.445	20.086
21	1.234	1.522	1.878	2.316	2.858	3.525	4.349	5.366	6.619	8.166	10.074	12.429	15.333	18.916	23.336
22	1.246	1.553	1.935	2.411	3.004	3.743	4.665	5.812	7.243	9.025	11.246	14.013	17.462	21.758	27.113
23	1.259	1.584	1.994	2.509	3.158	3.975	5.003	6.297	7.925	9.974	12.554	15.800	19.886	25.028	31.500
24	1.271	1.616	2.054	2.612	3.320	4.221	5.366	6.821	8.671	11.023	14.013	17.814	22.646	28.789	36.598
25	1.284	1.649	2.117	2.718	3.490	4.482	5.755	7.389	9.488	12.182	15.643	20.086	25.790	33.115	42.521
30	1.350	1.822	2.460	3.320	4.482	6.050	8.166	11.023	14.880	20.086	27.113	36.598	49.402	66.686	90.017
35	1.419	2.014	2.858	4.055	5.755	8.166	11.588	16.445	23.336	33.115	46.993	66.686	94.632	134.290	190.566
40	1.492	2.226	3.320	4.953	7.389	11.023	16.445	24.533	36.598	54.598	81.451	121.510	181.272	270.426	403.429
45	1.568	2.460	3.857	6.050	9.488	14.880	23.336	36.598	57.397	90.017	141.175	221.406	347.234	544.572	854.059
50	1.649	2.718	4.482	7.389	12.182	20.086	33.115	54.598	90.017	148.413	244.692	403.429	665.142	1096.633	1808.042

Table A5 (*continued*)

Period	16%	17%	18%	19%	20%	21%	22%	23%	24%	25%	26%	27%
1	1.174	1.185	1.197	1.209	1.221	1.234	1.246	1.259	1.271	1.284	1.297	1.310
2	1.377	1.405	1.433	1.462	1.492	1.522	1.553	1.584	1.616	1.649	1.682	1.716
3	1.616	1.665	1.716	1.768	1.822	1.878	1.935	1.994	2.054	2.117	2.181	2.248
4	1.896	1.974	2.054	2.138	2.226	2.316	2.411	2.509	2.612	2.718	2.829	2.945
5	2.226	2.340	2.460	2.586	2.718	2.858	3.004	3.158	3.320	3.490	3.669	3.857
6	2.612	2.773	2.945	3.127	3.320	3.525	3.743	3.975	4.221	4.482	4.759	5.053
7	3.065	3.287	3.525	3.781	4.055	4.349	4.665	5.003	5.366	5.755	6.172	6.619
8	3.597	3.896	4.221	4.572	4.953	5.366	5.812	6.297	6.821	7.389	8.004	8.671
9	4.221	4.618	5.053	5.529	6.050	6.619	7.243	7.925	8.671	9.488	10.381	11.359
10	4.953	5.474	6.050	6.686	7.389	8.166	9.025	9.974	11.023	12.182	13.464	14.880
11	5.812	6.488	7.243	8.085	9.025	10.074	11.246	12.554	14.013	15.643	17.462	19.492
12	6.821	7.691	8.671	9.777	11.023	12.429	14.013	15.800	17.814	20.086	22.646	25.534
13	8.004	9.116	10.381	11.822	13.464	15.333	17.462	19.886	22.646	25.790	29.371	33.448
14	9.393	10.805	12.429	14.296	16.445	18.916	21.758	25.028	28.789	33.115	38.092	43.816
15	11.023	12.807	14.880	17.288	20.086	23.336	27.113	31.500	36.598	42.521	49.402	57.397
16	12.936	15.180	17.814	20.905	24.533	28.789	33.784	39.646	46.525	54.598	64.072	75.189
17	15.180	17.993	21.328	25.280	29.964	35.517	42.098	49.899	59.145	70.105	83.096	98.494
18	17.814	21.328	25.534	30.569	36.598	43.816	52.457	62.803	75.189	90.017	107.770	129.024
19	20.905	25.280	30.569	36.966	44.701	54.055	65.366	79.044	95.583	115.584	139.770	169.017
20	24.533	29.964	36.598	44.701	54.598	66.686	81.451	99.484	121.510	148.413	181.272	221.406
21	28.789	35.517	43.816	54.055	66.686	82.269	101.494	125.211	154.470	190.566	235.097	290.035
22	33.784	42.098	52.457	65.366	81.451	101.494	126.469	157.591	196.370	244.692	304.905	379.935
23	39.646	49.899	62.803	79.044	99.484	125.211	157.591	198.343	249.635	314.191	395.440	497.701
24	46.525	59.145	75.189	95.583	121.510	154.470	196.370	249.635	317.348	403.429	512.859	651.971
25	54.598	70.105	90.017	115.584	148.413	190.566	244.692	314.191	403.429	518.013	665.142	854.059
30	121.510	164.022	221.406	298.867	403.429	544.572	735.095	992.275	1339.431	1808.042	2440.602	3294.468
35	270.426	383.753	544.572	772.784	1096.633	1556.197	2208.348	3133.795	4447.067	6310.688	8955.293	12708.165
40	601.845	897.847	1339.431	1998.196	2980.958	4447.067	6634.244	9897.129	14764.782	22026.466	32859.626	49020.801
45	1339.431	2100.646	3294.468	5166.754	8103.084	12708.165	19930.370	31257.043	49020.801	76879.920	120571.715	189094.090
50	2980.958	4914.769	8103.084	13359.727	22026.466	36315.503	59874.142	98715.771	162754.791	268337.287	442413.392	729416.370

Table A5 (continued)
Future Value Factor for One Dollar Compounded Continuously at r Percent for n Periods

$$FVF_{r\%,n} = e^{rn}$$

Period	28%	29%	30%	31%	32%	33%	34%	35%	40%	45%	50%
1	1.323	1.336	1.350	1.363	1.377	1.391	1.405	1.419	1.492	1.568	1.649
2	1.751	1.786	1.822	1.859	1.896	1.935	1.974	2.014	2.226	2.460	2.718
3	2.316	2.387	2.460	2.535	2.612	2.691	2.773	2.858	3.320	3.857	4.482
4	3.065	3.190	3.320	3.456	3.597	3.743	3.896	4.055	4.953	6.050	7.389
5	4.055	4.263	4.482	4.711	4.953	5.207	5.474	5.755	7.389	9.488	12.182
6	5.366	5.697	6.050	6.424	6.821	7.243	7.691	8.166	11.023	14.880	20.086
7	7.099	7.614	8.166	8.758	9.393	10.074	10.805	11.588	16.445	23.336	33.115
8	9.393	10.176	11.023	11.941	12.936	14.013	15.180	16.445	24.533	36.598	54.598
9	12.429	13.599	14.880	16.281	17.814	19.492	21.328	23.336	36.598	57.397	90.017
10	16.445	18.174	20.086	22.198	24.533	27.113	29.964	33.115	54.598	90.017	148.413
11	21.758	24.288	27.113	30.265	33.784	37.713	42.098	46.993	81.451	141.175	244.692
12	28.789	32.460	36.598	41.264	46.525	52.457	59.145	66.686	121.510	221.406	403.429
13	38.092	43.380	49.402	56.261	64.072	72.966	83.096	94.632	181.272	347.234	665.142
14	50.400	57.974	66.686	76.708	88.235	101.494	116.746	134.290	270.426	544.572	1096.633
15	66.686	77.478	90.017	104.585	121.510	141.175	164.022	190.566	403.429	854.059	1808.042
16	88.235	103.544	121.510	142.594	167.335	196.370	230.442	270.426	601.845	1339.431	2980.958
17	116.746	138.380	164.022	194.416	230.442	273.144	323.759	383.753	897.847	2100.646	4914.769
18	154.470	184.934	221.406	265.072	317.348	379.935	454.865	544.572	1339.431	3294.468	8103.084
19	204.384	247.151	298.867	361.405	437.029	528.477	639.061	772.784	1998.196	5166.754	13359.727
20	270.426	330.300	403.429	492.749	601.845	735.095	897.847	1096.633	2980.958	8103.084	22026.466
21	357.809	441.421	544.572	671.826	828.818	1022.494	1261.428	1556.197	4447.067	12708.165	36315.503
22	473.428	589.928	735.095	915.985	1141.388	1422.257	1772.241	2208.348	6634.244	19930.370	59874.142
23	626.407	788.396	992.275	1248.877	1571.837	1978.314	2489.905	3133.795	9897.129	31257.043	98715.771
24	828.818	1053.634	1339.431	1702.750	2164.620	2751.771	3498.187	4447.067	14764.782	49020.801	162754.791
25	1096.633	1408.105	1808.042	2321.572	2980.958	3827.626	4914.769	6310.688	22026.466	76879.920	268337.287
30	4447.067	6002.912	8103.084	10938.019	14764.782	19930.370	26903.186	36315.503	162754.791	729416.370	*
35	18033.745	25591.102	36315.503	51534.151	73130.442	103777.037	147266.625	208981.289	*	*	*
40	73130.442	109097.799	162754.791	242801.617	362217.450	540364.937	806129.759	*	*	*	*
45	296558.565	465096.412	729416.370	*	*	*	*	*	*	*	*
50	*	*	*	*	*	*	*	*	*	*	*

* Not shown due to space limitations.

Table A6
Present Value Factor for One Dollar Discounted Continuously at r Percent for n Periods

$$PVF_{r\%,n} = e^{-rn}$$

Period	1%	2%	3%	4%	5%	6%	7%	8%	9%	10%	11%	12%	13%	14%	15%
1	0.990	0.980	0.970	0.961	0.951	0.942	0.932	0.923	0.914	0.905	0.896	0.887	0.878	0.869	0.861
2	0.980	0.961	0.942	0.923	0.905	0.887	0.869	0.852	0.835	0.819	0.803	0.787	0.771	0.756	0.741
3	0.970	0.942	0.914	0.887	0.861	0.835	0.811	0.787	0.763	0.741	0.719	0.698	0.677	0.657	0.638
4	0.961	0.923	0.887	0.852	0.819	0.787	0.756	0.726	0.698	0.670	0.644	0.619	0.595	0.571	0.549
5	0.951	0.905	0.861	0.819	0.779	0.741	0.705	0.670	0.638	0.607	0.577	0.549	0.522	0.497	0.472
6	0.942	0.887	0.835	0.787	0.741	0.698	0.657	0.619	0.583	0.549	0.517	0.487	0.458	0.432	0.407
7	0.932	0.869	0.811	0.756	0.705	0.657	0.613	0.571	0.533	0.497	0.463	0.432	0.403	0.375	0.350
8	0.923	0.852	0.787	0.726	0.670	0.619	0.571	0.527	0.487	0.449	0.415	0.383	0.353	0.326	0.301
9	0.914	0.835	0.763	0.698	0.638	0.583	0.533	0.487	0.445	0.407	0.372	0.340	0.310	0.284	0.259
10	0.905	0.819	0.741	0.670	0.607	0.549	0.497	0.449	0.407	0.368	0.333	0.301	0.273	0.247	0.223
11	0.896	0.803	0.719	0.644	0.577	0.517	0.463	0.415	0.372	0.333	0.298	0.267	0.239	0.214	0.192
12	0.887	0.787	0.698	0.619	0.549	0.487	0.432	0.383	0.340	0.301	0.267	0.237	0.210	0.186	0.165
13	0.878	0.771	0.677	0.595	0.522	0.458	0.403	0.353	0.310	0.273	0.239	0.210	0.185	0.162	0.142
14	0.869	0.756	0.657	0.571	0.497	0.432	0.375	0.326	0.284	0.247	0.214	0.186	0.162	0.141	0.122
15	0.861	0.741	0.638	0.549	0.472	0.407	0.350	0.301	0.259	0.223	0.192	0.165	0.142	0.122	0.105
16	0.852	0.726	0.619	0.527	0.449	0.383	0.326	0.278	0.237	0.202	0.172	0.147	0.125	0.106	0.091
17	0.844	0.712	0.600	0.507	0.427	0.361	0.304	0.257	0.217	0.183	0.154	0.130	0.110	0.093	0.078
18	0.835	0.698	0.583	0.487	0.407	0.340	0.284	0.237	0.198	0.165	0.138	0.115	0.096	0.080	0.067
19	0.827	0.684	0.566	0.468	0.387	0.320	0.264	0.219	0.181	0.150	0.124	0.102	0.085	0.070	0.058
20	0.819	0.670	0.549	0.449	0.368	0.301	0.247	0.202	0.165	0.135	0.111	0.091	0.074	0.061	0.050
21	0.811	0.657	0.533	0.432	0.350	0.284	0.230	0.186	0.151	0.122	0.099	0.080	0.065	0.053	0.043
22	0.803	0.644	0.517	0.415	0.333	0.267	0.214	0.172	0.138	0.111	0.089	0.071	0.057	0.046	0.037
23	0.795	0.631	0.502	0.399	0.317	0.252	0.200	0.159	0.126	0.100	0.080	0.063	0.050	0.040	0.032
24	0.787	0.619	0.487	0.383	0.301	0.237	0.186	0.147	0.115	0.091	0.071	0.056	0.044	0.035	0.027
25	0.779	0.607	0.472	0.368	0.287	0.223	0.174	0.135	0.105	0.082	0.064	0.050	0.039	0.030	0.024
30	0.741	0.549	0.407	0.301	0.223	0.165	0.122	0.091	0.067	0.050	0.037	0.027	0.020	0.015	0.011
35	0.705	0.497	0.350	0.247	0.174	0.122	0.086	0.061	0.043	0.030	0.021	0.015	0.011	0.007	0.005
40	0.670	0.449	0.301	0.202	0.135	0.091	0.061	0.041	0.027	0.018	0.012	0.008	0.006	0.004	0.002
45	0.638	0.407	0.259	0.165	0.105	0.067	0.043	0.027	0.017	0.011	0.007	0.005	0.003	0.002	0.001
50	0.607	0.368	0.223	0.135	0.082	0.050	0.030	0.018	0.011	0.007	0.004	0.002	0.002	0.001	0.001

Table A6 (continued)
Present Value Factor for One Dollar Discounted Continuously at r Percent for n Periods

$$PVF_{r\%,n} = e^{-rn}$$

Period	16%	17%	18%	19%	20%	21%	22%	23%	24%	25%	26%	27%
1	0.852	0.844	0.835	0.827	0.819	0.811	0.803	0.795	0.787	0.779	0.771	0.763
2	0.726	0.712	0.698	0.684	0.670	0.657	0.644	0.631	0.619	0.607	0.595	0.583
3	0.619	0.600	0.583	0.566	0.549	0.533	0.517	0.502	0.487	0.472	0.458	0.445
4	0.527	0.507	0.487	0.468	0.449	0.432	0.415	0.399	0.383	0.368	0.353	0.340
5	0.449	0.427	0.407	0.387	0.368	0.350	0.333	0.317	0.301	0.287	0.273	0.259
6	0.383	0.361	0.340	0.320	0.301	0.284	0.267	0.252	0.237	0.223	0.210	0.198
7	0.326	0.304	0.284	0.264	0.247	0.230	0.214	0.200	0.186	0.174	0.162	0.151
8	0.278	0.257	0.237	0.219	0.202	0.186	0.172	0.159	0.147	0.135	0.125	0.115
9	0.237	0.217	0.198	0.181	0.165	0.151	0.138	0.126	0.115	0.105	0.096	0.088
10	0.202	0.183	0.165	0.150	0.135	0.122	0.111	0.100	0.091	0.082	0.074	0.067
11	0.172	0.154	0.138	0.124	0.111	0.099	0.089	0.080	0.071	0.064	0.057	0.051
12	0.147	0.130	0.115	0.102	0.091	0.080	0.071	0.063	0.056	0.050	0.044	0.039
13	0.125	0.110	0.096	0.085	0.074	0.065	0.057	0.050	0.044	0.039	0.034	0.030
14	0.106	0.093	0.080	0.070	0.061	0.053	0.046	0.040	0.035	0.030	0.026	0.023
15	0.091	0.078	0.067	0.058	0.050	0.043	0.037	0.032	0.027	0.024	0.020	0.017
16	0.077	0.066	0.056	0.048	0.041	0.035	0.030	0.025	0.021	0.018	0.016	0.013
17	0.066	0.056	0.047	0.040	0.033	0.028	0.024	0.020	0.017	0.014	0.012	0.010
18	0.056	0.047	0.039	0.033	0.027	0.023	0.019	0.016	0.013	0.011	0.009	0.008
19	0.048	0.040	0.033	0.027	0.022	0.018	0.015	0.013	0.010	0.009	0.007	0.006
20	0.041	0.033	0.027	0.022	0.018	0.015	0.012	0.010	0.008	0.007	0.006	0.005
21	0.035	0.028	0.023	0.018	0.015	0.012	0.010	0.008	0.006	0.005	0.004	0.003
22	0.030	0.024	0.019	0.015	0.012	0.010	0.008	0.006	0.005	0.004	0.003	0.003
23	0.025	0.020	0.016	0.013	0.010	0.008	0.006	0.005	0.004	0.003	0.003	0.002
24	0.021	0.017	0.013	0.010	0.008	0.006	0.005	0.004	0.003	0.002	0.002	0.002
25	0.018	0.014	0.011	0.009	0.007	0.005	0.004	0.003	0.002	0.002	0.002	0.001
30	0.008	0.006	0.005	0.003	0.002	0.002	0.001	0.001	0.001	0.001	0.000	*
35	0.004	0.003	0.002	0.001	0.001	0.001	*	*	*	*	*	*
40	0.002	0.001	0.001	0.001	*	*	*	*	*	*	*	*
45	0.001	*	*	*	*	*	*	*	*	*	*	*
50	*	*	*	*	*	*	*	*	*	*	*	*

*Discount factor is zero to three decimal places.

Table A6 (continued)

Period	28%	29%	30%	31%	32%	33%	34%	35%	40%	45%	50%
1	0.756	0.748	0.741	0.733	0.726	0.719	0.712	0.705	0.670	0.638	0.607
2	0.571	0.560	0.549	0.538	0.527	0.517	0.507	0.497	0.449	0.407	0.368
3	0.432	0.419	0.407	0.395	0.383	0.372	0.361	0.350	0.301	0.259	0.223
4	0.326	0.313	0.301	0.289	0.278	0.267	0.257	0.247	0.202	0.165	0.135
5	0.247	0.235	0.223	0.212	0.202	0.192	0.183	0.174	0.135	0.105	0.082
6	0.186	0.176	0.165	0.156	0.147	0.138	0.130	0.122	0.091	0.067	0.050
7	0.141	0.131	0.122	0.114	0.106	0.099	0.093	0.086	0.061	0.043	0.030
8	0.106	0.098	0.091	0.084	0.077	0.071	0.066	0.061	0.041	0.027	0.018
9	0.080	0.074	0.067	0.061	0.056	0.051	0.047	0.043	0.027	0.017	0.011
10	0.061	0.055	0.050	0.045	0.041	0.037	0.033	0.030	0.018	0.011	0.007
11	0.046	0.041	0.037	0.033	0.030	0.027	0.024	0.021	0.012	0.007	0.004
12	0.035	0.031	0.027	0.024	0.021	0.019	0.017	0.015	0.008	0.005	0.002
13	0.026	0.023	0.020	0.018	0.016	0.014	0.012	0.011	0.006	0.003	0.002
14	0.020	0.017	0.015	0.013	0.011	0.010	0.009	0.007	0.004	0.002	0.001
15	0.015	0.013	0.011	0.010	0.008	0.007	0.006	0.005	0.002	0.001	0.001
16	0.011	0.010	0.008	0.007	0.006	0.005	0.004	0.004	0.002	0.001	*
17	0.009	0.007	0.006	0.005	0.004	0.004	0.003	0.003	0.001	*	*
18	0.006	0.005	0.005	0.004	0.003	0.003	0.002	0.002	0.001	*	*
19	0.005	0.004	0.003	0.003	0.002	0.002	0.002	0.001	0.001	*	*
20	0.004	0.003	0.002	0.002	0.002	0.001	0.001	0.001	*	*	*
21	0.003	0.002	0.002	0.001	0.001	0.001	0.001	0.001	*	*	*
22	0.002	0.002	0.001	0.001	0.001	0.001	0.001	*	*	*	*
23	0.002	0.001	0.001	0.001	0.001	0.001	*	*	*	*	*
24	0.001	0.001	0.001	0.001	*	*	*	*	*	*	*
25	0.001	0.001	0.001	*	*	*	*	*	*	*	*
30	*	*	*	*	*	*	*	*	*	*	*
35	*	*	*	*	*	*	*	*	*	*	*
40	*	*	*	*	*	*	*	*	*	*	*
45	*	*	*	*	*	*	*	*	*	*	*
50	*	*	*	*	*	*	*	*	*	*	*

*Discount factor is zero to three decimal places.

APPENDIX B: CUMULATIVE PROBABILITIES FROM THE STANDARD NORMAL DISTRIBUTION

Appendix B

Cumulative Probability, $N(d)$, of Drawing a Value Less than or Equal to d from the Standard Normal Distribution

d	0	0.01	0.02	0.03	0.04	0.05	0.06	0.07	0.08	0.09
0	0.5000	0.5040	0.5080	0.5120	0.5160	0.5199	0.5239	0.5279	0.5319	0.5359
0.1	0.5398	0.5438	0.5478	0.5517	0.5557	0.5596	0.5636	0.5675	0.5714	0.5753
0.2	0.5793	0.5832	0.5871	0.5910	0.5948	0.5987	0.6026	0.6064	0.6103	0.6141
0.3	0.6179	0.6217	0.6255	0.6293	0.6331	0.6368	0.6406	0.6443	0.6480	0.6517
0.4	0.6554	0.6591	0.6628	0.6664	0.6700	0.6736	0.6772	0.6808	0.6844	0.6879
0.5	0.6915	0.6950	0.6985	0.7019	0.7054	0.7088	0.7123	0.7157	0.7190	0.7224
0.6	0.7257	0.7291	0.7324	0.7357	0.7389	0.7422	0.7454	0.7486	0.7517	0.7549
0.7	0.7580	0.7611	0.7642	0.7673	0.7704	0.7734	0.7764	0.7794	0.7823	0.7852
0.8	0.7881	0.7910	0.7939	0.7967	0.7995	0.8023	0.8051	0.8078	0.8106	0.8133
0.9	0.8159	0.8186	0.8212	0.8238	0.8264	0.8289	0.8315	0.8340	0.8365	0.8389
1	0.8413	0.8438	0.8461	0.8485	0.8508	0.8531	0.8554	0.8577	0.8599	0.8621
1.1	0.8643	0.8665	0.8686	0.8708	0.8729	0.8749	0.8770	0.8790	0.8810	0.8830
1.2	0.8849	0.8869	0.8888	0.8907	0.8925	0.8944	0.8962	0.8980	0.8997	0.9015
1.3	0.9032	0.9049	0.9066	0.9082	0.9099	0.9115	0.9131	0.9147	0.9162	0.9177
1.4	0.9192	0.9207	0.9222	0.9236	0.9251	0.9265	0.9279	0.9292	0.9306	0.9319
1.5	0.9332	0.9345	0.9357	0.9370	0.9382	0.9394	0.9406	0.9418	0.9429	0.9441
1.6	0.9452	0.9463	0.9474	0.9484	0.9495	0.9505	0.9515	0.9525	0.9535	0.9545
1.7	0.9554	0.9564	0.9573	0.9582	0.9591	0.9599	0.9608	0.9616	0.9625	0.9633
1.8	0.9641	0.9649	0.9656	0.9664	0.9671	0.9678	0.9686	0.9693	0.9699	0.9706
1.9	0.9713	0.9719	0.9726	0.9732	0.9738	0.9744	0.9750	0.9756	0.9761	0.9767
2	0.9772	0.9778	0.9783	0.9788	0.9793	0.9798	0.9803	0.9808	0.9812	0.9817
2.1	0.9821	0.9826	0.9830	0.9834	0.9838	0.9842	0.9846	0.9850	0.9854	0.9857
2.2	0.9861	0.9864	0.9868	0.9871	0.9875	0.9878	0.9881	0.9884	0.9887	0.9890
2.3	0.9893	0.9896	0.9898	0.9901	0.9904	0.9906	0.9909	0.9911	0.9913	0.9916
2.4	0.9918	0.9920	0.9922	0.9925	0.9927	0.9929	0.9931	0.9932	0.9934	0.9936
2.5	0.9938	0.9940	0.9941	0.9943	0.9945	0.9946	0.9948	0.9949	0.9951	0.9952

Example: Let $d = 1.15$. There is an 87.49% chance of drawing a value less than or equal to d from the standard normal distribution.

APPENDIX C: KEY FORMULAS

Free Cash Flow

A firm's free cash flow (*FCF*) is derived from operating cash flow (*OCF*) and changes in asset and liability accounts as:

$$FCF = OCF - \Delta FA - (\Delta CA - \Delta A/P - \Delta accruals) \qquad \text{(Eq. 2.3)}$$

Present Value of an Ordinary Annuity

The present value of an *n*-year ordinary annuity of $1 per year is:

$$PV = \frac{PMT}{r} \times \left[1 - \frac{1}{(1 + r)^n} \right] \qquad \text{(Eq. 3.7)}$$

Present Value of a Perpetuity

The present value of a perpetual stream of $1 annual payments is:

$$PV = PMT \times \frac{1}{r} = \frac{PMT}{r} \qquad \text{(Eq. 3.10)}$$

Present Value of a Growing Perpetuity

The present value of a perpetual stream of payments, which grows at an annual rate *g*, is:

$$PV = \frac{CF_1}{r - g} \qquad r > g \qquad \text{(Eq. 3.11)}$$

Effective Annual Interest Rate

The effective annual interest rate (*EAR*) can be derived from the stated rate *r* (given *m* compounding periods) as:

$$EAR = \left(1 + \frac{r}{m} \right)^m - 1 \qquad \text{(Eq. 3.14)}$$

Expected Return on a Portfolio

If the expected returns for individual assets in a portfolio are known, the expected return of an n-asset portfolio (with individual asset weights w_i) can be found as:

$$E(R_p) = w_1 E(R_1) + w_2 E(R_2) + w_3 E(R_3) + \cdots + w_N E(R_N) \qquad \text{(Eq. 5.6)}$$

Measures of Risk

Variance of Returns of a Single Asset

The variance of returns on a single asset i can be derived from a historical return series on N periods as:

$$\text{Variance} = \sigma^2 = \frac{\sum_{t=1}^{N}(R_{it} - \overline{R}_i)^2}{N - 1} \qquad \text{(Eq. 5.4)}$$

Covariance of Returns Between Two Assets

The covariance between the returns on two assets, 1 and 2, is calculated using historical return series over N periods as:

$$\text{Covariance }(R_1, R_2) = \sigma_{12} = \frac{\sum_{t=1}^{N}(R_{1t} - \overline{R}_1)(R_{2t} - \overline{R}_2)}{N - 1} \qquad \text{(Eq. 5.8)}$$

Correlation Coefficient

The correlation coefficient is a normalized measure of co-movement between two assets, and is derived from the covariance (σ_{12}) as:

$$\text{Correlation coefficient} = \rho_{12} = \frac{\sigma_{12}}{\sigma_1 \sigma_2} \qquad \text{(Eq. 5.9)}$$

Variance of a Portfolio of Two Stocks

When two stocks are combined into a portfolio, the variance of the portfolio's return is usually less than a weighted average of the individual variances, and is computed as:

$$\text{Portfolio variance} = \sigma_p^2 = w_1^2 \sigma_1^2 + w_2^2 \sigma_2^2 + 2 w_1 w_2 \rho_{12} \sigma_1 \sigma_2 \qquad \text{(Eq. 5.12)}$$

Beta

A stock's beta is a measure of the degree of co-movement between that stock's return and the overall market's return:

$$\beta_i = \frac{\sigma_{im}}{\sigma_m^2} \qquad \text{(Eq. 5.14)}$$

The Capital Market Line

The CML plots the trade-off between an asset or portfolio's risk and return in terms of expected return and standard deviation of return:

$$E(R_p) = R_f + \left\{ \frac{[E(R_m) - R_f]}{\sigma_m} \right\} \sigma_p \qquad \text{(Eq. 6.1)}$$

The Capital Asset Pricing Model

The CAPM yields a unique expected return for an asset or portfolio as a linear function of that asset's beta (β_i) and the risk-free rate R_f:

$$E(R_i) = R_f + \beta_i[E(R_m) - R_f] \qquad \text{(Eq. 6.2)}$$

Arbitrage Pricing Theory

The APT formula computes an asset's return as a function of two or more systematic return factors ($\overline{R}_j$) and the sensitivity (β_{ij}) of that asset's return to each factor:

$$\overline{R}_i - R_f = \beta_{i1}(\overline{R}_1 - R_f) + \beta_{i2}(\overline{R}_2 - R_f) + \beta_{i3}(\overline{R}_3 - R_f) + \cdots + \beta_{in}(\overline{R}_n - R_f)$$

$$\text{(Eq. 6.3)}$$

The Fama-French Model

The Fama-French asset-pricing model generates expected returns as a function of an asset's sensitivity to a market factor ($R_m - R_f$), a size factor ($R_{\text{small}} - R_{\text{big}}$), and a book-to-market ($R_{\text{high}} - R_{\text{low}}$) factor:

$$R_i - R_f = \alpha + \beta_{i1}(R_m - R_f) + \beta_{i2}(R_{\text{small}} - R_{\text{big}}) + \beta_{i3}(R_{\text{high}} - R_{\text{low}}) \qquad \text{(Eq. 6.4)}$$

Net Present Value

Finance's basic valuation model computes the NPV of a project or an asset, usually by subtracting the sum of a series of discounted cash inflows $\dfrac{CF_i}{(1 + r)^i}$ from a single cash outflow (CF_0):

$$NPV = CF_0 + \frac{CF_1}{(1 + r)^1} + \frac{CF_2}{(1 + r)^2} + \frac{CF_3}{(1 + r)^3} + \cdots + \frac{CF_N}{(1 + r)^N} \qquad \text{(Eq. 7.1)}$$

Weighted Average Cost of Capital [without taxes]

The $WACC$ is a weighted average of the cost of debt and equity financing for a firm, in which the weights are the fractions of debt and equity in the firm's capital structure:

$$WACC = \left(\frac{D}{D + E}\right)r_d + \left(\frac{E}{D + E}\right)r_e \qquad \text{(Eq. 9.3)}$$

Asset Beta [without taxes]

Asset betas are derived from equity betas as:

$$\beta_A = \left(\frac{D}{D + E}\right)\beta_d + \left(\frac{E}{D + E}\right)\beta_e \qquad \text{(Eq. 9.4)}$$

The Weighted Average Cost of Capital [with taxes]

Incorporating corporate taxes allows calculation of a firm's $WACC$ when it must pay taxes at rate T_c on its income:

$$WACC = \left(\frac{D}{D + E}\right)(1 - T_c)r_d + \left(\frac{E}{D + E}\right)r_e \qquad \text{(Eq. 9.6)}$$

Equity Beta [with taxes]

When a firm must pay corporate income taxes, the relationship between asset and equity betas is given by:

$$\beta_E = \beta_A \left[1 + (1 - T_c)\frac{D}{E} \right] \qquad \text{(Eq. 9.7)}$$

M&M Proposition I

Modigliani and Miller's famous Proposition I says that a firm's value (V) is determined by discounting its stream of expected net operating income, and is independent of capital structure:

$$V = (E + D) = \frac{NOI}{r} \qquad \text{(Eq. 12.1)}$$

M&M Proposition II

Proposition II determines the rate at which the expected return on a levered firm's equity (r_l) must increase as debt is substituted for equity in its capital structure:

$$r_l = r + (r - r_d)\frac{D}{E} \qquad \text{(Eq. 12.2)}$$

Value of a Levered Firm [including only corporate taxes]

In the presence of corporate income taxes, the value of a levered firm is equal to the value of an otherwise equivalent unlevered firm plus the value of the interest tax shields on its debt:

$$V_L = V_U + PV \text{ tax shield} = V_U + T_c D = \$650,000 + \$175,000 = \$825,000 \qquad \text{(Eq. 12.5)}$$

Gain From Leverage

In the presence of both corporate and personal taxes, the gain from leverage for a firm is a function of the effective tax rates on corporate profits (T_c), equity income received by investors (T_{ps}) and interest income received by investors (T_{pd}):

$$G_L = \left[1 - \frac{(1 - T_c)(1 - T_{ps})}{(1 - T_{pd})} \right] D \qquad \text{(Eq. 12.6)}$$

Value of a Right and Ex-Rights Price

If N is the number of shares required to purchase one share of stock, the value of a right when a stock is selling with rights (R_W) is found in terms of the market value of the stock with (M_W) and without (M_e) the right and the subscription price (S) of the rights issue:

$$R_W = \frac{M_W - S}{N + 1} \qquad \text{(Eq. 16.1)}$$

$$M_e = M_W - R_W \qquad \text{(Eq. 16.2)}$$

$$R_e = \frac{M_e - S}{N} \qquad \text{(Eq. 16.3)}$$

Put-Call Parity

The put-call parity formula shows the relationship that must hold between the values of the stock price (S), the put (P), the call (C), and the present value of the common exercise $(\$X)$ price of the put and call options in order to prevent arbitrage:

$$S + P = B + C$$

$$S + P = PV(X) + C \qquad \text{(Eq. 18.1)}$$

The Black-Scholes Option Pricing Model

The value of a call option, C, is given as:

$$C = SN(d_1) - Xe^{-rt}N(d_2) \qquad \text{(Eq. 19.1)}$$

where:

$$d_1 = \frac{\ln\left(\dfrac{S}{X}\right) + \left(r + \dfrac{\sigma^2}{2}\right)t}{\sigma\sqrt{t}}$$

$$d_2 = d_1 - \sigma\sqrt{t} \qquad \text{(Eq. 19.2)}$$

S = current market price of underlying stock
X = strike price of option
t = amount of time before option expires (in years)
r = annual risk-free interest rate
σ = annual standard deviation of underlying stock's returns
e = 2.718 (approximately)
$N(X)$ = the probability of drawing a value less than or equal to "X" from the standard normal distribution

The Forward Premium or Discount [exchange rates]

The annualized forward discount or premium of a currency is:

$$\frac{F - S}{S} \times \frac{360}{N} \qquad \text{(Eq. 20.1)}$$

The Parity Conditions of International Finance

Forward–Spot Parity

In equilibrium, the forward rate (F) observed for a currency should be equal to the expected future spot exchange rate, $E(S)$, for that currency:

$$E(S) = F \qquad \text{(Eq. 20.2)}$$

Purchasing Power Parity

PPP expresses a currency's expected future spot exchange rate $[E(S^{\text{for/dom}})]$, relative to today's spot rate $(S^{\text{for/dom}})$, as a function of the relative expected inflation rates in the foreign, $E(i_{\text{for}})$, and domestic, $E(i_{\text{dom}})$, markets:

$$\frac{E(S^{\text{for/dom}})}{S^{\text{for/dom}}} = \frac{[1 + E(i_{\text{for}})]}{[1 + E(i_{\text{dom}})]} \qquad \text{(Eq. 20.4)}$$

Interest Rate Parity

IRP expresses a currency's forward exchange rate ($F^{\text{for/dom}}$), relative to today's spot rate ($S^{\text{for/dom}}$), as a function of the relative interest rates in the foreign (R_{for}) and domestic (R_{dom}) markets:

$$\frac{F^{\text{for/dom}}}{S^{\text{for/dom}}} = \frac{(1 + R_{\text{for}})}{(1 + R_{\text{dom}})}$$

(Eq. 20.5)

Real Interest Parity

The real interest parity relationship expresses interest rate parity in real rather than nominal terms:

$$\frac{(1 + R_{\text{for}})}{(1 + R_{\text{dom}})} = \frac{[1 + E(i_{\text{for}})]}{[1 + E(i_{\text{dom}})]}$$

(Eq. 20.6)

Forward Price of an Asset

Given a risk-free rate of interest R_f, the forward price (F) of an asset or commodity to be delivered n periods in the future can be derived from the current spot price (S_0) as:

$$F = S_0(1 + R_f)^n$$

(Eq. 21.1)

BIBLIOGRAPHY

Ackermann, Carl, Richard McEnally, and David Ravenscraft. 1999. "The Performance of Hedge Funds: Risk, Return, and Incentives." *Journal of Finance* 54 (June), pp. 833–874.

Ackert, Lucy F., and Brian F. Smith. 1993. "Stock Price Volatility, Ordinary Dividends, and Cash Flows to Shareholders." *Journal of Finance* 48 (September), pp. 1147–1160.

Adams, Paul D., Steve B. Wyatt, and Yong H. Kim. "A Contingent Claims Analysis of Trade Credit." *Financial Management* 21 (1992), pp. 95–103.

Adler, Michael, and Bernard Dumas. 1983. "International Portfolio Choice and Corporation Finance: A Synthesis." *Journal of Finance* 38 (July), pp. 925–984.

Admati, Anat R., and Paul Pfleiderer. 1994. "Robust Financial Contracting and the Role of Venture Capitalists." *Journal of Finance* 49 (June), pp. 371–402.

Aggarwal, Reena, Nagpurnanand R. Prabhala, and Manju Puri. 2002. "Institutional Allocation in Initial Public Offerings: Empirical Evidence." *Journal of Finance* 57 (June), pp. 1421–1442.

Agrawal, Anup, Jeffrey F. Jaffe, and Gershon N. Mandelker.1992. "The Post-Merger Performance of Acquiring Firms: A Re-examination of an Anomaly." *Journal of Finance* 47 (September), pp. 1605–1622.

Aharony, Joseph, and Itzhak Swary. 1980. "Quarterly Dividend and Earnings Announcements and Stockholders' Returns: An Empirical Analysis." *Journal of Finance* 35 (March), pp. 1–12.

Akerlof, George. 1970. "The Market for 'Lemons,' Qualitative Uncertainty and the Market Mechanism." *Quarterly Journal of Economics* 84 (August), pp. 488–500.

Alderson, Michael J., and Brian L. Betker. 1995. "Liquidation Costs and Capital Structure." *Journal of Financial Economics* 39 (September), pp. 45–69.

Altinkiliç, Oya, and Robert S. Hansen. 2000. "Are There Economies of Scale in Underwriting Fees? Evidence of Rising External Financing Costs." *Review of Financial Studies* 13 (Spring), pp. 191–218.

Altman, Edward. 1984. "A Further Empirical Investigation of the Bankruptcy Cost Question." *Journal of Finance* 39 (September), pp. 1067–1089.

———. 2000. "Revisiting the High Yield Market: Mature but Never Dull." *Journal of Applied Corporate Finance* 13 (Spring), pp. 64–74.

Altman, Edward I., and Heather J. Suggitt. 2000. "Default Rates in the Syndicated Bank Loan Market: A Mortality Analysis." *Journal of Banking and Finance* 24, pp. 229–253.

Ambarish, Ramasastry, Kose John, and Joseph Williams. 1987. "Efficient Signalling with Dividends and Investments." *Journal of Finance* 42 (June), pp. 321–343.

Amihud, Yakov, and Baruch Lev. 1981. "Risk Reduction as a Managerial Motive for Conglomerate Mergers." *Bell Journal of Economics* 12 (Autumn), pp. 605–617.

Amihud, Yakov, Baruch Lev, and Nikolaos Travlos. 1990. "Corporate Control and the Choice of Investment Financing: The Case of Corporate Acquisitions." *Journal of Finance* 45 (June), pp. 603–616.

Anderson, Christopher W., and Anil K. Makhija. 1999. "Deregulation, Disintermediation and Agency Costs of Debt: Evidence from Japan." *Journal of Financial Economics* 51 (February), pp. 309–339.

Ang, James S. 1993. "On Financial Ethics." *Financial Management* 22 (Autumn), pp. 32–59.

Ang, James S., David W. Blackwell, and William L. Megginson. 1991. "The Effect of Taxes on the Relative Valuation of Dividends and Capital Gains: Evidence from Dual-Class British Investment Trusts." *Journal of Finance* 46 (March), pp. 383–399.

Ang, James, and William L. Megginson. 1990. "A Test of the before-Tax versus after-Tax Equilibrium Models of Corporate Debt." *Research in Finance* 8, pp. 97–118.

Arundale, Keith. 2001. "European Private Equity and Venture Capital—Current State of the Market and Prospects for the Industry." Working paper, PricewaterhouseCoopers UK.

Asquith, Paul. 1983. "Merger Bids, Uncertainty and Stockholder Returns." *Journal of Financial Economics* 11 (April), pp. 51–83.

———. 1995. "Convertible Bonds Are Not Called Late." *Journal of Finance* 50 (September), pp. 1275–1289.

Asquith, Paul, Robert Bruner, and David Mullins. 1983. "The Gains for Bidding Firms from Merger." *Journal of Financial Economics* 11 (April), pp.121–139.

Asquith, Paul and David Mullins, Jr. 1983. "The Impact of Initiating Dividend Payments on Shareholders' Wealth." *Journal of Business* 56 (January), pp. 77–96.

———. 1986. "Equity Issues and Stock Price Dilution." *Journal of Financial Economics* 15 (January/February), pp. 61–89.

Asquith, Paul, and Thierry Wizman. 1990. "Event Risk, Covenants, and Bondholder Returns in Leveraged Buyouts." *Journal of Financial Economics* 27 (September), pp. 195–213.

Aylward, Anthony. 1998. "Trends in Venture Capital Finance in Developing Countries." IFC discussion paper no. 36, World Bank (Washington, D.C.).

Backus, David, Silverio Foresi, Abon Mozumdar, and Liuren Wu. 2001. "Predictable Changes in Yields and Forward Rates." *Journal of Financial Economics* 59 (March), pp. 281–311.

Backus, David K., Silverio Foresi, and Chris I. Telmer. 2001. "Affine Term Structure Models and the Forward Premium Anomaly." *Journal of Finance* 56 (February), pp. 279–304.

Baker, H. Kent, Gail E. Farrelly, and Richard B. Edelman. 1985. "A Survey of Management Views on Dividend Policy." *Financial Management* 14 (Autumn), pp. 78–84.

Baker, Malcolm, and Paul A. Gompers. 2001. "The Determinants of Board Structure at the Initial Public Offering." Working paper, Harvard Business School.

Baker, Malcolm, and Jeffrey Wurgler. 2002. "Market Timing and Capital Structure." *Journal of Finance* 57 (February), pp. 1–32.

Baldwin, Carliss, and Kim B. Clark. 1992. "Capabilities and Capital Investment: New Perspectives on Capital Budgeting." *Journal of Applied Corporate Finance* 15 (Summer), pp. 67–82.

Ball, Ray. 1995. "The Theory of Market Efficiency: Accomplishments and Limitations." *Journal of Applied Corporate Finance* 8 (Spring), pp. 4–17.

Ball, Ray, and Philip Brown. 1968. "An Empirical Investigation of Accounting Income Numbers." *Journal of Accounting Research* 6 (Autumn), pp. 159–178.

Ball, Ray, S. P. Kothari, and Jay Shanken. 1995. "Problems in Measuring Portfolio Performance: An Application to Contrarian Investment Strategies." *Journal of Financial Economics* 38, pp. 79–107.

Banz, Rolf W. 1981. "The Relationship between Return and Market Value of Common Stocks." *Journal of Financial Economics* 9 (March), pp. 3–18.

Barber, Brad, Reuven Lehavy, Maureen McNichols, and Brett Trueman. 2001. "Can Investors Profit from the Prophets? Security Analyst Recommendations and Stock Returns." *Journal of Finance* 56 (April), pp. 531–563.

———. 2002. "Prophets and Losses: Reassessing the Returns to Analysts' Stock Recommendations." Working paper (September).

Barber, Brad M., and Terrance Odean. 2000. "Trading Is Hazardous to Your Wealth." *Journal of Finance* 55 (April), pp. 773–806.

———. "Online Investors: Do the Slow Die First?" *Review of Financial Studies* 15 (Special), pp. 455–487.

Barclay, Michael J. 1987. "Dividends, Taxes, and Common Stock Prices before the Income Tax." *Journal of Financial Economics* 19 (September), pp. 31–44.

Barclay, Michael J., and Clifford W. Smith, Jr. 1995a. "The Maturity Structure of Corporate Debt." *Journal of Finance* 50 (June), pp. 609–631.

———. 1995b. "The Priority Structure of Corporate Liabilities." *Journal of Finance* 50 (July), pp. 899–917.

Barclay, Michael J., Clifford W. Smith, Jr., and Ross L. Watts. 1995. "The Determinants of Corporate Leverage and Dividend Policies." *Journal of Applied Corporate Finance* 17 (Winter), pp. 4–19.

Bascha, Andreas, and Uwe Walz. 2001. "Convertible Securities and Optimal Exit Decisions in Venture Capital." *Journal of Corporate Finance* 7 (September), pp. 285–306.

Baytas, Ahmet, and Nusret Cakici. 1999. "Do Markets Overreact: International Evidence." *Journal of Banking and Finance* 23, pp. 1121–1144.

Beatty, Anne. 1995. "The Cash Flow and Informational Effects of Employee Stock Ownership Plans." *Journal of Financial Economics* 38 (June), pp. 211–240.

Beatty, Randolph P., and Ivo Welch. 1996. "Issuer Expenses and Legal Liability in Initial Public Offerings." *Journal of Law and Economics* 39 (December), pp. 545–602.

Becker, Kent G., Joseph E. Finnerty, and Joseph Friedman. 1995. "Economic News and Equity Market Linkages between the U.S. and U.K." *Journal of Banking and Finance* 19, pp. 1191–1210.

Bell, Leonie, and Tim Jenkinson. 2002. "New Evidence of the Impact of Dividend Taxation on the Identity of the Marginal Investor." *Journal of Finance* 57 (June), pp. 1321–1346.

Benartzi, Shlomo, Roni Michaely, and Richard Thaler. 1997. "Do Changes in Dividends Signal the Future or the Past?" *Journal of Finance* 52 (July), pp. 1007–1035.

Benoit, Bertrand. 2001. "Neuer Markt Starts to Feel Squeeze." *Financial Times* (July 11), p. 19.

Benveniste, Lawrence M., and Paul A. Spindt. 1989. "How Investment Bankers Determine the Offer Price and Allocation for New Issues." *Journal of Financial Economics* 24 (October), pp. 343–361.

Berger, Philip, and Eli Ofek. 1995. "Diversification's Effect on Firm Value." *Journal of Financial Economics* 37 (January), pp. 39–65.

———. 1996. "Bustup Takeovers of Value-Destroying Diversified Firms." *Journal of Finance* 51 (September), pp. 1175–2000.

Berger, Philip G., Eli Ofek, and David L. Yermack. 1997. "Managerial Entrenchment and Capital Structure Decisions." *Journal of Finance* 54 (September), pp. 1411–1438.

Berglöf, Erik. 1994. "A Control Theory of Venture Capital Finance." *Journal of Law, Economics and Organization* 10, pp. 447–471.

Berglöf, Erik, and Enrico Perotti. 1994. "The Governance Structure of the Japanese Keiretsu." *Journal of Financial Economics* 36 (October), pp. 259–284.

Bergstrom, C., and K. Rydqvist. 1990. "The Determinants of Corporate Ownership: An Empirical Study of Swedish Data." *Journal of Banking and Finance* 14, pp. 237–254.

Bernanke, Ben S., and John Y. Campbell. 1988. "Is There a Corporate Debt Crisis?" *Brookings Papers on Economic Activity* 1, pp. 83–125.

Bernard, Victor L., and Jacob K. Thomas. 1990. "Evidence That Stock Prices Do Not Fully Reflect the Implications of Current Earnings for Future Earnings." *Journal of Accounting and Economics* 12 (December), pp. 305–341.

Bernard, Victor, Jacob K. Thomas, and Jeffery S. Abarbanell. 1993. "How Sophisticated Is the Market in Interpreting Earnings News?" *Journal of Applied Corporate Finance* 6 (Summer), pp. 54–63.

Bernardo, Antonio E., and Bhagwan Chowdhry. 2002. "Resources, Real Options, and Corporate Strategy." *Journal of Financial Economics* 63 (February), pp. 211–234.

Bernardo, Antonio E., and Eric L. Talley. 1996. "Investment Policy and Exit-Exchange Offers within Financially Distressed Firms." *Journal of Finance* 51 (July), pp. 871–888.

Bernstein, Peter L. 1999. "Why the Efficient Market Offers Hope to Active Management." *Journal of Applied Corporate Finance* 12 (Summer), 129–136.

Bethel, Jennifer E., and Stuart L. Gillan. (2002). "The Impact of the Institutional and Regulatory Environment on Shareholder Voting." *Financial Management* 31 (Winter).

Bhagat, Sanjai. 1983. "The Effect of Preemptive Right Amendments on Shareholder Wealth." *Journal of Financial Economics* 12 (November), pp. 289–310.

———. 1986. "The Effect of Management's Choice between Negotiated and Competitive Equity Offerings on Shareholder Wealth." *Journal of Financial and Quantitative Analysis* 21 (June), pp. 181–196.

Bhagat, Sanjai, and Peter Frost. 1986. "Issuing Costs to Existing Shareholders in Competitive and Negotiated Underwritten Public Utility Offerings." *Journal of Financial Economics* 15 (January/February), pp. 223–259.

Bhagat, Sanjai, Andrei Shleifer, and Robert Vishny. 1990. "Hostile Takeovers in the 1980s: The Return to Corporate Specialization." *Brookings Papers on Economic Activity,* pp. 1–72.

Bhattacharya, Sudipto. 1979. "Imperfect Information, Dividend Policy, and 'the Bird in the Hand' Fallacy." *Bell Journal of Economics* 10 (Spring), pp. 259–270.

Bhattacharya, Utpal, and Hazem Daouk. 2002. "The World Price of Insider Trading." *Journal of Finance* 57, pp. 75–108.

Bhattacharya, Utpal, Hazem Daouk, Brian Jorgenson, and Carl-Heinrich Kehr. 2000. "When Is an Event Not an Event: The Curious Case of an Emerging Market." *Journal of Financial Economics* 55, pp. 69–101.

Bhide, Amar. 1992. "Bootstrap Finance: The Art of Start-Ups." *Harvard Business Review* (November/December), pp. 109–117.

———.1993. "The Hidden Costs of Stock Market Liquidity." *Journal of Financial Economics* 34 (August), pp. 31–51.

Bianchi, Alessandra. 1992. "Why You Won't Sell Your Business." *Inc.* (August), pp. 58–63.

Bicksler, James, and Andrew H. Chen. 1986. "An Economic Analysis of Interest Rate Swaps." *Journal of Finance* 41 (July), pp. 645–655.

Birnbaum, Jeffrey H. 1999. "Uncle Sam, Venture Capitalist." *Fortune* (May 24), p. 66.

Bjerring, James H., Josef Lakonishok, and Theo Vermaelen. 1983. "Stock Prices and Financial Analysts'

Recommendations." *Journal of Finance* 38 (March), pp. 187–204.

Black, Bernard. 1992. "Institutional Investors and Corporate Governance: The Case for Institutional Voice." *Journal of Applied Corporate Finance* 5 (Fall), pp. 19–32.

Black, Bernard S., and Ronald J. Gilson. 1998. "Venture Capital and the Structure of Capital Markets: Banks versus Capital Markets." *Journal of Financial Economics* 47 (March), pp. 243–277.

Black, Fischer. 1975. "Fact and Fantasy in the Use of Options." *Financial Analysts Journal* 31 (July/August), pp. 36–41, 61–72.

Black, Fischer, Michael C. Jensen, and Myron Scholes. 1972. "The Capital Asset Pricing Model: Some Empirical Tests." In *Studies in the Theory of Capital Markets,* edited by Michael C. Jensen (New York: Praeger).

Black, Fischer, and Myron S. Scholes. 1973. "The Pricing of Options and Corporate Liabilities." *Journal of Political Economy* 81 (May/June), pp. 637–654.

Blass, Asher, and Yishay Yafeh. 2001."Vagabond Shoes Longing to Stray: Why Foreign Firms List in the United States." *Journal of Banking and Finance* 25 (March), pp. 555–572.

Bollerslev, Tim. 1986. "Generalized Conditional Autoregressive Heteroscedasticity." *Journal of Econometrics* 31 (April), pp. 307–327.

Bonser-Neal, Catherine, and Timothy Morley. 1997. "Does the Yield Spread Predict Real Economic Activity: A Multi-Country Analysis." Federal Reserve Bank of Kansas City *Economic Review* (Third Quarter), pp. 37–53.

Booth, James R. 1992. "Contract Costs, Bank Loans, and the Cross-Monitoring Hypothesis." *Journal of Financial Economics* 31 (February), pp. 25–41.

Booth, James R., and Lena Chua. 1996. "Ownership Dispersion, Costly Information, and IPO Underpricing." *Journal of Financial Economics* 41, pp. 291–310.

Booth, James R., Richard L. Smith, and Richard W. Stolz. 1984. "Use of Interest Rate Futures by Financial Institutions." *Journal of Bank Research* 15, pp. 15–20.

Booth, Laurence, Varouj Aivazian, Asli Demirgüç-Kunt, and Vojislav Maksimovic. 2001. "Capital Structures in Developing Countries." *Journal of Finance* 56 (February), pp. 87–130.

Boubakri, Narjess, and Jean-Claude Cosset. 1998. "The Financial and Operating Performance of Newly Privatized Firms: Evidence from Developing Countries." *Journal of Finance* 53 (June), pp. 1081–1110.

Boutchkova, Maria K., and William L. Megginson. 2000. "Privatization and the Rise of Global Capital Markets." *Financial Management* 29 (Winter), pp. 31–76.

Boyd, John H., and Mark Gertler. 1994. "Are Banks Dead? Or Are the Reports Greatly Exaggerated?" Federal Reserve Bank of Minneapolis *Quarterly Review* (Summer), pp. 2–23.

Bradley, Daniel J., Bradford D. Jordan, Ha-Chin Yi, and Ivan C. Roten. 2001. "Venture Capital and IPO Lockup Expiration: An Empirical Analysis." *Journal of Financial Research* 24 (Winter), pp. 465–492.

Bradley, Michael, Anand Desai, and E. Han Kim. 1988. "Synergistic Gains from Corporate Acquisitions and Their Division between the Stockholders of Target and Acquiring Firms." *Journal of Financial Economics* 21 (May), pp. 3–40.

Bradley, Michael, Gregg Jarrell, and E. Han Kim. 1984. "On the Existence of an Optimal Capital Structure: Theory and Evidence." *Journal of Finance* 39 (May), pp. 857–878.

Brav, Alon, Christopher Geczy, and Paul A. Gompers. 2000. "Is the Abnormal Return following Equity Issuances Anomalous?" *Journal of Financial Economics* 56, pp. 209–249.

Brav, Alon, and Paul A. Gompers. 1997. "Myth or Reality? The Long-Run Underperformance of Initial Public Offerings: Evidence from Venture and Non-Venture Capital–Backed Companies." *Journal of Finance* 52 (December), pp. 1791–1821.

Brav, Alon, and J. B. Heaton. 2002. "Competing Theories of Financial Anomalies." *Review of Financial Studies* 15 (Special), pp. 575–606.

Brealey, Richard A., and Michel A. Habib. 1996. "Using Project Finance to Fund Infrastructure Investments." *Journal of Applied Corporate Finance* 9 (Fall), pp. 25–38.

Breeden, Douglas T. 1979. "An Intertemporal Asset Pricing Model with Stochastic Consumption and Investment Opportunities." *Journal of Financial Economics* 7, pp. 265–296.

Brennan, Michael J. 1970. "Taxes, Market Valuation and Corporate Financial Policy." *National Tax Journal* 23 (December), pp. 417–427.

Brennan, Michael J., and Eduardo S. Schwartz. 1985. "Evaluating Natural Resource Investments." *Journal of Business* 58 (April), pp. 135–157.

Brewer, Elijah, III, and Hesna Genay. 1994. "Small Business Investment Companies: Financial Characteristics and Investments." Working paper, Series no. 94-10, Federal Reserve Bank of Chicago.

Brickley, James A. 1983. "Shareholder Wealth, Information Signalling and the Specially Designated Dividend: An Empirical Study." *Journal of Financial Economics* 12 (August), pp. 187–209.

Brinson, Gary P., L. Randolph Hood, and Gilbert L. Beebower. 1986. "Determinants of Portfolio Performance." *Financial Analysts Journal* 50 (July/August), pp. 39–44.

Brock, William, Josef Lakonishok, and Blake LeBaron. 1992. "Simple Technical Trading Rules and the Stochastic Properties of Stock Returns." *Journal of Finance* 47 (December), pp. 1731–1764.

Brown, Stephen J., and Jerold B. Warner. 1980. "Measuring Security Price Performance." *Journal of Financial Economics* 8 (September), pp. 205–258.

———. 1985. "Using Daily Stock Returns in the Case of Event Studies." *Journal of Financial Economics* 14 (March), pp. 205–258.

Bruner, Robert F. 2002. "Does M&A Pay? A Survey of Evidence for the Decision-Maker." *Journal of Applied Finance* 12 (Spring/Summer), pp. 48–68.

Burroughs, Bryan, and John Helyar. 1993. *Barbarians at the Gate: The Fall of RJR Nabisco* (New York: HarperCollins).

Calegari, Michael J. 2000. "The Effect of Tax Accounting Rules on Capital Structure and Discretionary Accruals." *Journal of Accounting and Economics* 30 (August), pp. 1–31.

Campbell, John Y., and John Ammer. 1993. "What Moves the Stock and Bond Markets? A Variance Decomposition for Long-Term Asset Returns." *Journal of Finance* 48 (March), pp. 3–37.

Campbell, Katharine. 2001a. "Stock Market Volatility Fails to Put Off Investors." *Financial Times* (June 14), p. 6.

———. 2001b. "Informal Financing Totals $196bn a Year." *Financial Times* (November 15), p. 31.

Carey, Mark. 1998. "Credit Risk in Private Debt Portfolios." *Journal of Finance* 52 (August), pp. 1363–1387.

Carhart, Mark M. 1997. "On Persistence in Mutual Fund Performance." *Journal of Finance* 52 (March), pp. 57–82.

Carpenter, Jennifer N., and Anthony W. Lynch. 1999. "Survivorship Bias and Attrition Effects in Measures of Performance Persistence." *Journal of Financial Economics* 54 (December), pp. 337–374.

Carter, Mary E., and Luann J. Lynch. 2001. "An Examination of Executive Stock Option Repricing." *Journal of Financial Economics* 61 (August), pp. 207–225.

Carter, Richard B., and Howard E. Van Auken. 1990. "Personal Equity Investment and Small Business Financial Difficulties." *Entrepreneurship Theory and Practice* (Winter), pp. 51–60.

Chambers, Donald R., and Nelson J. Lacey. 1996. "Corporate Ethics and Shareholder Wealth Maximization." *Financial Practice and Education* 6 (Spring/Summer), pp. 93–96.

Chan, Louis K. C., Narasimhan Jegadeesh, and Josef Lakonishok. 1996. "Momentum Strategies." *Journal of Finance* 51 (December), pp. 1681–1713.

Chan, Louis K. D., Jason Karceski, and Josef Lakonishok.

2003. "The Level of Persistence of Growth Rates." *Journal of Finance* (forthcoming).

Chang, Eric C., Joseph W. Cheng, and Ajay Khorana. 2000. "An Examination of Herd Behavior in Equity Markets: An International Perspective." *Journal of Banking and Finance* 24, pp. 1651–1679.

Chaplinsky, Susan, and Latha Ramchand. 2000. "The Impact of Global Equity Offerings." *Journal of Finance* 55 (December), pp. 2767–2789.

Chauvin, Keith W., and Catherine Shenoy. 2001. "Stock Price Decreases Prior to Executive Stock Option Grants." *Journal of Corporate Finance: Contracting, Governance, and Organization* 7 (March), pp. 53–76.

Chen, Hsuan-Chi, and Jay Ritter. 2000. "The Seven Percent Solution." *Journal of Finance* 55 (June), pp. 1105–1131.

Chen, N., R. Roll, and S. A. Ross. 1986. "Economic Forces and the Stock Market: Testing the APT and Alternative Asset Pricing Theories." *Journal of Business* 59 (July), pp. 383–403.

Chidambaran, N. K., Chitru S. Fernando, and Paul A. Spindt. 2001. "Credit Enhancement through Financial Engineering: Freeport McMoRan's Gold-Denominated Depository Share." *Journal of Financial Economics* 60 (May), pp. 487–528.

Chowdhry, Bhagwan, and Ann Sherman. 1996. "International Differences in Oversubscription and Underpricing of IPO." *Journal of Corporate Finance* 2, pp. 359–381.

Christie, William G., and Vikram Nanda. 1994. "Free Cash Flow, Shareholder Value, and the Undistributed Profits Tax of 1936 and 1937." *Journal of Finance* 49 (December), pp. 1727–1754.

Christopher, Alistair. 2001. "VC and the Law: Potential Legal Hurdles Involved in Funding the Next Big Thing." *Venture Capital Journal* (February), pp. 43–45.

Coggin, T. Daniel, Frank J. Fabozzi, and Shafiqur Rahman. 1993. "The Investment Performance of U.S. Equity Pension Fund Managers: An Empirical Investigation." *Journal of Finance* 48 (July), pp. 1039–1055.

Cole, Jonathan E., and Albert L. Sokol. 1997. "Structuring Venture Capital Investments." In *Pratt's Guide to Venture Capital Sources*, edited by Stanley E. Pratt (New York: Securities Data Publishing).

Comment, Robert, and Gregg Jarrell. 1995. "Corporate Focus and Stock Returns." *Journal of Financial Economics* 37 (January), pp. 67–87.

Conrad, Jennifer, and Gautam Kaul. 1988. "Time Variation in Expected Returns." *Journal of Business* 61 (October), pp. 409–425.

———. 1989. "Mean Reversion in Short-Horizon Expected Returns." *Review of Financial Studies* 2, pp. 225–240.

————. 1993. "Long-Term Market Overreaction or Biases in Computed Returns." *Journal of Finance* 48 (March), pp. 39–64.

Cornell, Bradford, and Alan C. Shapiro. 1987. "Corporate Stakeholders and Corporate Finance." *Financial Management* 16 (Spring), pp. 5–14.

Cox, Don R., and David R. Peterson. 1994. "Stock Returns following Large One-Day Declines: Evidence on Short-Term Reversals and Longer-Term Performance." *Journal of Finance* 49 (March), pp. 255–267.

Cox, John C., Jonathon E. Ingersoll, Jr., and Stephen A. Ross. 1981. "The Relation between Forward and Futures Prices." *Journal of Financial Economics* 9 (December), pp. 321–346.

Cox, John C., and Stephen A. Ross. 1976. "The Valuation of Options for Alternative Stochastic Processes." *Journal of Financial Economics* 3 (January/March), pp. 145–166.

Cox, John C., Stephen A. Ross, and Mark Rubinstein. 1979. "Option Pricing: A Simplified Approach." *Journal of Financial Economics* 7 (September), pp. 229–263.

Crabbe, Leland E. and Jean Helwege. 1994. "Alternative Tests of Agency Theories of Callable Corporate Bonds," *Financial Management* 23 (Winter), pp. 3–20.

Cumby, Robert E., and David M. Modest. 1987. "Testing for Market Timing Ability: A Framework for Market Forecast Evaluation." *Journal of Financial Economics* 19 (September), pp. 169–189.

Cusatis, Patrick J., James A. Miles, and J. Randall Woolridge. 1993. "Restructuring through Spinoffs: The Stock Market Evidence." *Journal of Financial Economics* 33, pp. 293–311.

Daniel, Kent, David Hirshleifer, and Avindhar Subrahmanyam. 1998. "Investor Psychology and Under- and Overreactions." *Journal of Finance* 53 (December), pp. 1839–1882.

Dann, Larry. 1981. "Common Stock Repurchases: An Analysis of Returns to Bondholders and Stockholders." *Journal of Financial Economics* 9 (June), pp. 113–138.

Dann, Larry, and Wayne Mikkelson. 1984. "Convertible Debt Issuance, Capital Structure Change and Financing Related Information: Some New Evidence." *Journal of Financial Economics* 13 (June), pp. 157–186.

DeAngelo, Harry, and Linda DeAngelo. 1985. "Managerial Ownership of Voting Rights: A Study of Public Corporations with Dual Classes of Common Stock." *Journal of Financial Economics* 14 (March), pp. 33–69.

————. 1990. "Dividend Policy and Financial Distress: An Empirical Investigation of Troubled NYSE Firms." *Journal of Finance* 45 (December), pp. 1415–1431.

DeAngelo, Harry, Linda DeAngelo, and Douglas J. Skinner. 1992. "Dividends and Losses." *Journal of Finance* 47 (December), pp. 1837–1863.

————. 1996. "Reversal of Fortune: Dividend Signaling and the Disappearance of Sustained Earnings Growth." *Journal of Financial Economics* 40 (March), pp. 341–371.

————. 2000. "Special Dividends and Evolution of Dividend Signalling." *Journal of Financial Economics* 57 (September), pp. 309–354.

DeAngelo, Harry, and Ronald W. Masulis. 1980. "Optimal Capital Structure under Corporate and Personal Taxation." *Journal of Financial Economics* 8 (March), pp. 3–30.

DeBondt, Werner, and Richard Thaler. 1985. "Does the Stock Market Overreact?" *Journal of Finance* 40 (July), pp. 793–805.

DeGeorge, Francois, and Richard Zeckhauser. 1993. "The Reverse LBO Decision and Firm Performance." *Journal of Finance* 48 (September), pp. 1323–1348.

————. 1996. "The Financial Performance of Reverse Leveraged Buyouts." *Journal of Financial Economics* 42 (November), pp. 293–332.

DeLong, Bradford, Andrei Shleifer, Lawrence H. Summers, and Robert J. Waldmann. 1990. "Noise Trader Risk in Financial Markets." *Journal of Political Economy* 98 (August), pp. 703–738.

DeMarzo, Peter M., and Darrell Duffie. 1995. "Corporate Incentives for Hedging and Hedge Accounting." *Review of Financial Studies* 8, pp. 743–771.

De Miguel, Alberto, and Julio Pindado. 2001. "Determinants of Capital Structure: New Evidence from Spanish Panel Data." *Journal of Corporate Finance* 7 (March), pp. 77–99.

Demirgüç-Kunt, Asli, and Vojislav Maksimovic. 1998. "Law, Finance, and Firm Growth." *Journal of Finance* 53 (December), pp. 2107–2139.

————.1999. "Institutions, Financial Markets, and Firm Debt Maturity." *Journal of Financial Economics* 54 (December), pp. 295–336.

Denis, David J. 1991. "Shelf Registration and the Market for Seasoned Equity Offerings." *Journal of Business* 64 (April), pp. 189–212.

Denis, David J., Diane K. Denis, and Atulya Sarin. 1997. "Agency Problems, Equity Ownership, and Corporate Diversification." *Journal of Finance* 52 (March), pp. 135–160.

Dennis, Debra, and John McConnell. 1986. "Corporate Mergers and Security Returns." *Journal of Financial Economics* 16 (June), pp. 143–187.

Desai, Hemang, and Prem C. Jain. 1995. "An Analysis of the Recommendations of the 'Superstar' Money Managers at *Barron's* Annual Roundtable." *Journal of Finance* 50 (September), pp. 1257–1273.

———. 1997. "Long-Run Common Stock Returns following Stock Splits and Reverse Splits." *Journal of Business* 70 (July), pp. 409–433.

Detragiache, Enrica, Paolo Garella, and Luigi Guiso. 2000. "Multiple versus Single Banking Relationships: Theory and Evidence." *Journal of Finance* 55 (June), pp. 1133–1161.

Dewenter, Kathryn, and Vincent Warther. 1998. "Dividends, Asymmetric Information and Agency Conflicts: Evidence from a Comparison of the Dividend Policies of Japanese and US Firms." *Journal of Finance* 53 (June), pp. 879–904.

Dharan, Bala G., and David L. Ikenberry. 1995. "The Long-Run Negative Drift of Post-Listing Stock Returns." *Journal of Finance* 50 (December), pp. 1547–1574.

Dhillon, Upinder, and Herb Johnson. 1991. "Changes in the Standard & Poor's List." *Journal of Business* 64 (January), pp. 75–85.

Diamond, Douglas W. 1991. "Monitoring and Reputation: The Choice between Bank Loans and Directly Placed Debt." *Journal of Political Economy* 99, pp. 689–721.

Dichev, Ilia D., and Joseph D. Piotroski. 2001. "The Long-Run Stock Returns following Bond Ratings Changes." *Journal of Finance* 56 (February), pp. 173–203.

Dimson, Elroy, and Paul R. Marsh. 2002. *Triumph of the Optimists*. (Princeton, NJ: Princeton University Press).

Dolde, Walter. 1993. "The Trajectory of Corporate Financial Risk Management." *Journal of Applied Corporate Finance* 6 (Fall), pp. 33–41.

D'Souza, Juliet, and William L. Megginson. 1999. "The Financial and Operating Performance of Newly Privatized Firms in the 1990s." *Journal of Finance* 54 (August), pp. 1397–1438.

Dunn, Kenneth B., and Chester S. Spatt. 1984. "A Strategic Analysis of Sinking Fund Bonds." *Journal of Financial Economics* 13 (September), pp. 399–424.

Dwyer, Hubert J., and Richard Lynn. 1989. "Small Capitalization Companies: What Does Financial Analysis Tell Us about Them?" *Financial Review* 24, pp. 397–414.

Dyl, Edward A., and Michael D. Joehnek. 1979. "Sinking Funds and the Cost of Corporate Debt." *Journal of Finance* 34 (September), pp. 887–893.

Eades, Kenneth, Patrick Hess, and E. Han Kim. 1984. "On Interpreting Security Returns during the Ex-dividend Day Period." *Journal of Financial Economics* 13 (March), pp. 3–34.

———. 1994. "Time Series Variation in Dividend Pricing." *Journal of Finance* 49 (December), pp. 1617–1638.

Easterbrook, Frank H. 1984. "Two Agency-Cost Explanations of Dividends." *American Economic Review* 74 (September), pp. 650–659.

Easterbrook, Frank H., and Daniel R. Fischel. 1983. "Voting in Corporate Law." *Journal of Law and Economics* 26 (June), pp. 395–427.

Eberhart, Allan, Edward I. Altman, and Reena Aggarwal. 1999. "The Equity Performance of Firms Emerging from Bankruptcy." *Journal of Finance* 54 (October), pp. 1855–1868.

Eckbo, B. Espen. 1983. "Horizontal Mergers, Collusion, and Stockholder Wealth." *Journal of Financial Economics* 11 (April), pp. 241–273.

———. 1986. "Valuation Effects of Corporate Debt Offerings." *Journal of Financial Economics* 15 (January/February), pp. 119–151.

Eckbo, B. Espen, Ronald W. Masulis, and Øyvind Norli. 2000. "Seasoned Public Offerings: Resolution of the 'New Issues Puzzle.'" *Journal of Financial Economics* 56 (May), pp. 251–291.

Economist, The. 1996. "Remapping South America: A Survey of Mercosur" (October 12).

Edelen, Roger M. 1999. "Investor Flows and the Assessed Performance of Open-End Mutual Funds." *Journal of Financial Economics* 53 (September), pp. 439–466.

Ederington, Louis H., and Jae Ha Lee. 1993. "How Markets Process Information: News Releases and Volatility." *Journal of Finance* 48 (September), pp. 1161–1191.

El-Gazzar, Samir, and Victor Pastena. 1990. "Negotiated Accounting Rules in Private Financial Contracts." *Journal of Accounting and Economics* 12 (March), pp. 381–396.

Ellert, James. 1976. "Mergers, Antitrust Law Enforcement, and Stockholder Returns." *Journal of Finance* 31 (May), pp. 715–732.

Ellis, Katrina, Roni Michaely, and Maureen O'Hara. 2000. "When the Underwriter Is the Market Maker: An Examination of Trading in the IPO Aftermarket." *Journal of Finance* 55 (June), pp. 1039–1074.

Elton, Edwin J., and Martin J. Gruber. 1970. "Marginal Stockholder Tax Rates and the Clientele Effect." *Review of Economics and Statistics* 52 (February), pp. 68–74.

Elton, Edwin J., Martin J. Gruber, Sanjiv Das, and Matthew Hlavka. 1993. "Efficiency with Costly Information: A Reinterpretation of Evidence from Managed Portfolios." *Review of Financial Studies* 6, pp. 1–22.

Emanuel, David C., and James D. MacBeth. 1982. "Further Results on the Constant Elasticity of Variance Call Option Pricing Model." *Journal of Financial and Quantitative Analysis* 17 (November), pp. 533–554.

Engle, Robert F. 1982. "Autoregressive Conditional Heteroscedasticity with Estimates of the Variance of

United Kingdom Inflation." *Econometrica* 50 (July), pp. 987–1007.

Errunza, Vihang R., and Darius P. Miller. 2000. "Market Segmentation and the Cost of Capital in International Equity Markets." *Journal of Financial and Quantitative Analysis* 35 (December), pp. 577–600.

Esty, Benjamin C. 1999. "Petrozuata: A Case Study of the Effective Use of Project Finance." *Journal of Applied Corporate Finance* 12 (Fall), pp. 26–42.

———. 2002. "Returns on Project Financed Investments: Theory and Implications." Harvard Business School teaching note 9-202-102 (February).

Fama, Eugene F. 1965. "The Behavior of Stock Market Prices." *Journal of Business* 38 (January), pp. 34–105.

———. 1970. "Efficient Capital Markets: A Review of Theory and Empirical Work." *Journal of Finance* 25 (May), pp. 383–417.

———. 1980. "Agency Problems and the Theory of the Firm." *Journal of Political Economy* 88 (April), pp. 288–307.

———. 1984. "Forward and Spot Exchange Rates." *Journal of Monetary Economics* 14 (November), pp. 319–338.

———. 1991. "Efficient Capital Markets: II." *Journal of Finance* 46 (December), pp. 1575–1617.

———. 1998. "Market Efficiency, Long-Term Returns, and Behavioral Finance." *Journal of Financial Economics* 49, pp. 283–306.

Fama, Eugene F., and Harvey Babiak. 1968. "Dividend Policy: An Empirical Analysis." *Journal of the American Statistical Association* 63 (December), pp. 1132–1161.

Fama, Eugene F., and Marshall E. Blume. 1966. "Filter Rules and Stock-Market Trading." *Journal of Business* 39 (January), pp. 226–241.

Fama, Eugene F., Lawrence Fisher, Michael C. Jensen, and Richard Roll. 1969. "The Adjustment of Stock Prices to New Information." *International Economic Review* 10 (February), pp. 1–21.

Fama, Eugene F., and Kenneth R. French. 1992. "The Cross-Section of Expected Returns." *Journal of Finance* 47 (June), pp. 427–465.

———. 1996. "Multifactor Explanations of Asset Pricing Anomalies." *Journal of Finance* 51 (March), pp. 55–84.

———. 1998. "Taxes, Financing Decisions, and Firm Value." *Journal of Finance* 53 (June), pp. 819–843.

———. 1999. "The Corporate Cost of Capital and the Return on Corporate Investment." *Journal of Finance* 54 (December), pp. 1939–1967.

———. 2001. "Disappearing Dividends: Changing Firm Characteristics or Lower Propensity to Pay?" *Journal of Financial Economics* 60 (April), pp. 3–43.

———. 2002. "The Equity Premium." *Journal of Finance* 57 (April), pp. 637–659.

———. 2002a. "The Equity Premium." *Journal of Finance* 57 (April), pp. 637–659.

———. 2002b. "Testing Trade-off and Pecking Order Predictions about Dividends and Debt." *Review of Financial Studies* 15 (Spring), pp. 1–33.

Fama, Eugene F., and Michael C. Jensen. 1985. "Organizational Forms and Investment Decisions." *Journal of Financial Economics* 14, pp. 101–118.

Fama, Eugene F., and James D. MacBeth. 1973. "Risk, Return, and Equilibrium: Empirical Tests." *Journal of Political Economy* 81 (May–June), pp. 607–636.

Fama, Eugene F., and Merton H. Miller. 1972. *The Theory of Finance* (New York: Holt, Rinehart & Winston).

Fellers, Charles R. 2001a. "Making an Exit: VCs Examine Their Options." *Venture Capital Journal* (May), pp. 40–42.

———. 2001b. "With Companies Faltering, VCs Look at Redemption Exit." *Venture Capital Journal* (June), pp. 34–38.

Fenn, George W., and Nellie Liang. 2001. "Corporate Payout Policy and Managerial Stock Incentives." *Journal of Financial Economics* 60 (April), pp. 45–72.

Fineberg, Seth. 1997. "Canada's Labor Funds Adapt to Tighter Regs." *Venture Capital Journal* (March), pp. 28–30.

Finnerty, John D., and Douglas R. Emery. 2002. "Corporate Securities Innovation: An Update." *Journal of Applied Finance* 12 (Spring/Summer), pp. 21–47.

Fischer, Edwin O., Robert Heinkel, and Josef Zechner. 1989. "Dynamic Capital Structure Choice: Theory and Tests." *Journal of Finance* 44 (March), pp. 19–40.

Fisher, Irving G. 1965. *The Theory of Interest* (1930; reprint, New York, Augustus M. Kelly).

Foerster, Stephen R., and G. Andrew Karolyi. 2000. "The Long-Run Performance of Global Equity Offerings." *Journal of Financial and Quantitative Analysis* 35 (December), pp. 499–528.

Frankel, Jeffrey A. 1991. "The Japanese Cost of Finance: A Survey." *Financial Management* 20 (Spring), pp. 95–127.

Freear, John. 1994. "The Private Investor Market for Venture Capital." *The Financier* 1 (May), pp. 7–15.

Freear, John, Jeffrey E. Sohl, and William E. Wetzel, Jr. 2000. "The Informal Venture Capital Market: Milestones Passed and the Road Ahead." In *Entrepreneurship 2000*, edited by Donald L. Sexton and Raymond W. Smilor (Chicago: Upstart Publishing Company).

French, Kenneth R. 1989. "Pricing Financial Futures Contracts: An Introduction." *Journal of Applied Corporate Finance* 1 (Winter), pp. 59–66.

Fung, William K. H., and Michael F. Theobald. 1984. "Dividends and Debt under Alternative Tax Systems." *Journal of Financial and Quantitative Analysis* 19 (March), pp. 59–72.

Galai, Dan, and Ron Masulis. 1976. "The Option Pricing Model and the Risk Factor of Stock." *Journal of Financial Economics* 3 (January), pp. 53–81.

Garrett, Ian, and Richard Priestley. 2000. "Dividend Behavior and Dividend Signaling." *Journal of Financial and Quantitative Analysis* 35 (June), pp. 173–189.

Gaughan, Patrick. 1996. *Mergers, Acquisitions, and Corporate Restructurings* (New York: John Wiley & Sons).

Gaver, Jennifer J., and Kenneth M. Gaver. 1993. "Additional Evidence on the Association between the Opportunity Set and Corporate Financing, Dividend, and Compensation Policies." *Journal of Accounting and Economics* 16 (January/April/July), pp. 125–160.

Geczy, Christopher, Bernadette A. Minton, and Catherine Schrand. 1997. "Why Firms Use Currency Derivatives." *Journal of Finance* 52 (September), pp. 1323–1354.

Gerlach, Stefan. 2002. "Hong Kong's Currency Board: Modelling the Discretion on the Strong Side." Working paper, Hong Kong Institute for Monetary Research.

Ghosh, Chimnoy, and J. Randall Woolridge. 1988. "An Analysis of Shareholder Reaction to Dividend Cuts and Omissions." *Journal of Financial Research* 11 (Winter), pp. 281–294.

Gibbons, Michael R., and Patrick Hess. 1981. "Day of the Week Effects and Asset Returns." *Journal of Business* 54 (October), pp. 579–596.

Gilson, Stuart C. 1989. "Management Turnover and Financial Distress." *Journal of Financial Economics* 25 (December), pp. 241–262.

———. 1997. "Transactions Costs and Capital Structure Choice: Evidence from Financially Distressed Firms." *Journal of Finance* 52 (March), pp. 161–196.

Gilson, Stuart C., and Michael R. Vetsuypens. 1993. "CEO Compensation in Financially Distressed Firms: An Empirical Analysis." *Journal of Finance* 48 (June), pp. 425–458.

Goetzmann, William N., and Roger G. Ibbotson. 1994. "Do Winners Repeat?" *Journal of Portfolio Management* 20 (Winter), pp. 9–18.

Goetzmann, William N., Zoran Ivkovic, and K. Geert Rouwenhorst. 2001. "Day Trading International Mutual Funds: Evidence and Policy Solutions." *Journal of Financial and Quantitative Analysis* 36 (September), pp. 287–309.

Golder, Stanley C. 1997. "Structuring the Financing." In *Pratt's Guide to Venture Capital Sources,* edited by Stanley E. Pratt (New York: Securities Data Publishing).

Gompers, Paul A. 1995. "Optimal Investment, Moni-

toring, and the Staging of Venture Capital." *Journal of Finance* 50 (December), pp. 1461–1489.

———. 1996. "Grandstanding in the Venture Capital Industry." *Journal of Financial Economics* 42 (September), pp. 133–156.

Gompers, Paul A., and Josh Lerner. 1997. "Ownership and Control in Entrepreneurial Firms: An Examination of Convertible Securities in Venture Capital Investments." Working paper, Harvard Business School.

———. 1998a. "What Drives Venture Capital Fundraising?" *Brookings Papers on Economic Activity—Microeconomics,* pp. 149–192.

———. 1998b. "Venture Capital Distributions: Short-Run and Long-Run Reactions." *Journal of Finance* 53 (December), pp. 2161–2183.

———. 2000a. "Money Chasing Deals? The Impact of Fund Inflows on Private Equity Valuations." *Journal of Financial Economics* 55 (February), pp. 281–325.

———. 2000b. "The Really Long-Run Performance of Initial Public Offerings: The Pre-NASDAQ Evidence." Working paper, Harvard Business School (September).

———. 2001. "The Venture Capital Revolution." *Journal of Economic Perspectives* 15 (Spring), pp. 145–168.

Gorman, Michael, and William A. Sahlman. 1989. "What Do Venture Capitalists Do?" *Journal of Business Venturing* 4, pp. 231–248.

Goyal, Vidhan K., Kenneth Lehn, and Stanko Racic. 2002. "Growth Opportunities and Corporate Debt Policy: The Case of the U.S. Defense Industry." *Journal of Financial Economics* 64 (April), pp. 35–59.

Graham, John R. 1996. "Debt and the Marginal Tax Rate." *Journal of Financial Economics* 41 (May), pp. 41–73.

———. 1999. "Herding among Investment Newsletters: Theory and Evidence." *Journal of Finance* 54 (February), pp. 237–268.

———. 2000. "How Big Are the Tax Benefits of Debt?" *Journal of Finance* 55 (October), pp. 1901–1941.

Graham, John R., and Campbell R. Harvey. 1996. "Market Timing Ability and Volatility Implied in Investment Newsletters' Asset Allocation Recommendations." *Journal of Financial Economics* 42 (November), pp. 397–421.

———. 2001. "The Theory and Practice of Corporate Finance: Evidence from the Field." *Journal of Financial Economics* 60, pp. 187–243.

———. 2002. "Expectations of Equity Risk Premia from a Corporate Finance Perspective." Working paper, Duke University.

Greene, Jason T., and Charles W. Hodges. 2002. "The Dilution Impact of Daily Fund Flows on Open-End Mutual Funds." *Journal of Financial Economics* 65 (July), pp. 131–158.

Greene, Jason, and Scott Smart. 1999. "Liquidity Provision and Noise Trading: Evidence from the Investment Dartboard Column." *Journal of Finance* 54 (October), pp. 1885–1899.

Grenadier, Steven R. 1995. "Valuing Lease Contracts: A Real Options Approach." *Journal of Financial Economics* 38 (July), pp. 297–331.

———. 1996. "Leasing and Credit Risk." *Journal of Financial Economics* 42 (November), pp. 333–364.

Grinblatt, Mark, and Sheridan Titman. 1989. "Mutual Fund Performance: An Analysis of Quarterly Portfolio Holdings." *Journal of Business* 62 (July), pp. 393–416.

Grossman, Sanford J., and Robert J. Shiller. 1981. "The Determinants of the Variability of Stock Market Prices." *American Economic Review* 71 (May), pp. 222–227.

Gruber, Martin J. 1996. "Another Puzzle: The Growth in Actively Managed Mutual Funds." *Journal of Finance* 51 (July), pp. 783–810.

Grullon, Gustavo, and David L. Ikenberry. 2000. "What Do We Know about Stock Repurchases?" *Journal of Applied Corporate Finance* 13 (Spring), pp. 31–49.

Grullon, Gustavo, Roni Michaely, and Bhaskaran Swaminathan. 2002. "Are Dividend Changes a Sign of Firm Maturity?" *Journal of Business* 75 (July), pp. 387–424.

Grundfest, Joseph A. 1990. "Subordination of American Capital." *Journal of Financial Economics* 27 (September), pp. 89–114.

Guay, Wayne, and Jarrad Harford. 2000. "The Cash-Flow Permanence and Information Content of Dividend Increases versus Repurchases." *Journal of Financial Economics* 57 (September), pp. 385–415.

Guedes, Jose, and Tim Opler. 1996. "The Determinants of the Maturity of Corporate Debt Issues." *Journal of Finance* 51 (December), pp. 1809–1833.

Gupta, Udayan. 2001. "Truth in Numbers?" *Venture Capital Journal* (May), p. 35.

Hamada, Robert S. 1972. "The Effect of the Firm's Capital Structure on the Systematic Risk of Common Stocks." *Journal of Finance* 27 (May), pp. 435–452.

Hamada, Robert S., and Myron S. Scholes. 1985. "Taxes and Corporate Financial Management." In *Recent Advances in Corporate Finance*, edited by Edward I. Altman and Marti Subrahmanyan (Homewood, Ill.: Richard D. Irwin).

Hamao, Yasushi, Frank Packer, and Jay Ritter. 2000. "Institutional Affiliation and the Role of Venture Capital: Evidence from Initial Public Offerings in Japan." *Pacific Basin Finance Journal* 8, pp. 529–558.

Hanley, Kathleen W. 1993. "The Underpricing of Initial Public Offerings and the Partial Adjustment Phenomenon." *Journal of Financial Economics* 34 (October), pp. 231–250.

Hanley, Kathleen W., and William J. Wilhelm, Jr. 1995. "Evidence on the Strategic Allocation of Initial Public Offerings." *Journal of Financial Economics* 37 (February), pp. 239–257.

Hansen, Robert S. 1988. "The Demise of the Rights Issue." *Review of Financial Studies* 1, pp. 289–309.

———. 2001. "Do Investment Banks Compete in IPOs?: The Advent of the '7% Plus Contract.'" *Journal of Financial Economics* 59 (March), pp. 313–186.

Hansen, Robert S., and Claire Crutchley. 1990. "Corporate Earnings and Financings: An Empirical Analysis." *Journal of Business* 63 (July), pp. 347–371.

Hansen, Robert S., and Naveen Khanna. 1994. "Why Negotiation with a Single Syndicate May Be Preferred to Making Syndicates Compete: The Problem of Trapped Bidders." *Journal of Business* 67 (July), pp. 423–457.

Hansen, Robert S., and John M. Pinkerton. 1982. "Direct Equity Financing: A Resolution of a Paradox." *Journal of Finance* 37 (June), pp. 651–665.

Harris, Lawrence, and Eitan Gurel. 1984. "Price and Volume Effects Associated with Changes in the S&P 500 List: New Evidence for the Existence of Price Pressures." *Journal of Finance* 41 (September), pp. 815–830.

Harris, Milton, and Artur Raviv. 1991. "The Theory of Capital Structure." *Journal of Finance* 46 (March), pp. 297–355.

Harris, Trevor S., Nahum Melumad, and Toshi Shibano. 1996. "An Argument against Hedging by Matching the Currencies of Costs and Revenues." *Journal of Applied Corporate Finance* 9 (Fall), pp. 90–97.

Harvey, Campbell. 1993. "The Term Structure Forecasts Economic Growth." *Financial Analysts Journal* (May/June), pp. 6–8.

Hasbrouk, Joel. 1985. "The Characteristics of Takeover Targets." *Journal of Banking and Finance* 9 (September), pp. 351–362.

Haugen, Robert A., and Lemma W. Senbet. 1978. "The Insignificance of Bankruptcy Costs in the Theory of Optimal Capital Structure." *Journal of Finance* 33 (May), pp. 383–393.

Haushalter, G. David. 2000. "Financing Policy, Basis Risk, and Corporate Hedging: Evidence from Oil and Gas Producers." *Journal of Finance* 55 (February), pp. 107–152.

Healy, Paul M., and Krishna Palepu. 1988. "Earnings Information Conveyed by Dividend Initiations and Omissions." *Journal of Financial Economics* 21 (September), pp. 149–175.

Healy, Paul, Krishna Palepu, and Richard Ruback. 1992. "Does Corporate Performance Improve after Mergers?" *Journal of Financial Economics* 31 (April), pp. 135–176.

Heath, David C., and Robert A. Jarrow. 1988. "Ex-dividend Stock Price Behavior and Arbitrage Opportunities." *Journal of Business* 61 (January), pp. 95–108.

Heaton, John, and Robert Korajczyk. 2002. "Introduction to *Review of Financial Studies* Conference on Market Frictions and Behavioral Finance." *Review of Financial Studies* 15 (Special), pp. 353–361.

Hellmann, Thomas. 1998. "The Allocation of Control Rights in Venture Capital Contracts." *Rand Journal of Economics* (Spring), pp. 57–76.

———. 2002. "A Theory of Strategic Venture Investing." *Journal of Financial Economics* 64 (May), pp. 285–314.

Hellmann, Thomas, and Manju Puri. 2002. "Venture Capital and the Professionalization of Start-up Firms: Empirical Evidence." *Journal of Finance* 57 (February), pp. 169–197.

Hendricks, Darryll, Jayendu Patel, and Richard Zeckhauser. 1993. "Hot Hands in Mutual Funds: Short-Run Persistence of Relative Performance, 1974–1988." *Journal of Finance* 48 (March), pp. 93–130.

Hentzler, Herbert A. 1992. "The New Era of Eurocapitalism." *Harvard Business Review* (July/August), pp. 57–68.

Higgins, Robert C. 1981. "Sustainable Growth under Inflation." *Financial Management* 10, pp. 36–40.

Higgins, Robert, and Lawrence Schall. 1975. "Corporate Bankruptcy and Conglomerate Merger." *Journal of Finance* 30 (March), pp. 93–113.

Hillion, Pierre, and Theo Vermaelen. 2002. "Death Spiral Convertibles." Working paper, INSEAD (Fontainebleau, France).

Hines, James R., Jr. 1996. "Dividends and Profits: Some Unsubtle Foreign Influences." *Journal of Finance* 51 (June), pp. 661–689.

Hirshleifer, Jack. 1958. "On the Theory of Optimal Investment Decision." *Journal of Political Economy* 66 (August), pp. 329–352.

Hite, Gailen L., and James E. Owers. 1983. "Security Price Reactions around Corporate Spinoff Announcements." *Journal of Financial Economics* 12, pp. 409–436.

Ho, Thomas, and Donald F. Singer. 1984. "The Value of Corporate Debt with a Sinking Fund Provision." *Journal of Business* 57 (September), pp. 315–336.

Hoffman, Harold M., and James Blakey. 1987. "You Can Negotiate with Venture Capitalists." *Harvard Business Review* (March/April), pp. 16–24.

Horowitz, Bruce. 2001. "Disney Orders McDonald's Burger Joint for New Park." *USA Today* (January 15).

Houston, Joel, and Christopher James. 1996. "Bank Information Monopolies and the Mix of Private and Public Debt Claims." *Journal of Finance* 51 (December), pp. 1863–1889.

Hovakimian, Armen, Tim Opler, and Sheridan Titman. 2001. "The Debt-Equity Choice." *Journal of Financial and Quantitative Analysis* 36 (March), pp. 1–24.

Huang, Yen-Sheng, and Ralph Walkling. 1987. "Target Abnormal Returns Associated with Acquisition Announcements: Payment, Acquisition Form, and Managerial Resistance." *Journal of Financial Economics* 19 (December), pp. 329–349.

Hull, John C., and Alan D. White. 1987. "The Pricing of Options on Assets with Stochastic Volatilities." *Journal of Finance* 42 (June), pp. 281–300.

Ibbotson, Roger G. 1975. "Price Performance of Common Stock New Issues." *Journal of Financial Economics* 2 (September), pp. 235–272.

Ibbotson, Roger G., Jody L. Sindelar, and Jay R. Ritter. 1994. "The Market's Problems with the Pricing of Initial Public Offerings." *Journal of Applied Corporate Finance* 7 (Spring), pp. 66–74.

Igawa, Kazuhiro, and George Kanatas. 1990. "Asymmetric Information, Collateral, and Moral Hazard." *Journal of Financial and Quantitative Analysis* 25 (December), pp. 469–490.

Ikenberry, David, and Josef Lakonishok. 1993. "Corporate Governance through the Proxy Contest: Evidence and Implications." *Journal of Business* 66 (July), pp. 405–435.

Ikenberry, David, Josef Lakonishok, and Theo Vermaelen. 1995. "Market Underreaction to Open Market Stock Repurchases." *Journal of Financial Economics* 39 (October), pp. 181–208.

Ikenberry, David L., Graeme Rankine, and Earl K. Stice. 1996. "What Do Stock Splits Really Signal?" *Journal of Financial and Quantitative Analysis* 31 (September), pp. 357–375.

Investment Dealers' Digest. 1997. "Kiss and Tell" (October 27), p. 19.

Ippolito, Richard A. 1989. "Efficiency with Costly Information: A Study of Mutual Fund Performance, 1965–1984." *Quarterly Journal of Economics* 104 (February), pp. 1–23.

Jaffe, Jeffrey F. 1974. "Special Information and Insider Trading." *Journal of Business* 47, pp. 410–428.

Jagannathan, Murali, Clifford P. Stephens, and Michael S. Weisbach. 2000. "Financial Flexibility and the Choice between Dividends and Stock Repurchases." *Journal of Financial Economics* 57 (September), pp. 355–384.

James, Christopher. 1987. "Some Evidence on the Uniqueness of Bank Loans." *Journal of Financial Economics* 19 (December), pp. 217–235.

Jarrell, Gregg, James Brickley, and Jeffry Netter. 1988. "The Market for Corporate Control: The Empirical Evidence since 1980." *Journal of Economic Perspectives* 2 (Winter), pp. 49–68.

Jarrell, Gregg A., and Annette Poulsen. 1989a. "Stock

Trading before the Announcement of Tender Offers: Insider Trading or Market Anticipation?" *Journal of Law, Economics, and Organization* 5, pp. 225–248.

———. 1989b. "Returns to Acquiring Firms in Tender Offers: Evidence from Three Decades." *Financial Management* 18 (Autumn), pp. 12–19.

Jayaraman, Narasimhan, Kuldeep Shastri, and Kishore Tandon. 1993. "The Impact of International Cross Listings on Risk and Returns: The Evidence of American Depositary Receipts." *Journal of Banking and Finance* 17, pp. 91–103.

Jegadeesh, Narasimhan. 1990. "Evidence of the Predictable Behavior of Security Returns." *Journal of Finance* 45 (July), pp. 881–898.

———. 2000. "Long-Term Performance of Seasoned Equity Offerings: Benchmark Errors and Biases in Expectations." *Financial Management* 29 (Autumn), pp. 5–30.

Jegadeesh, Narasimhan, and Sheridan Titman. 1993. "Returns to Buying Winners and Selling Losers: Implications for Stock Market Efficiency." *Journal of Finance* 48 (March), pp. 65–91.

Jeng, L. A., and P. C. Wells. 2000. "The Determinants of Venture Capital Funding: Evidence across Countries." *Journal of Corporate Finance* 6 (September), pp. 241–289.

Jennings, Robert, and Michael Mazzeo. 1993. "Competing Bids, Target Management Resistance, and the Structure of Takeover Bids." *Review of Financial Studies* 6 (Winter), pp. 883–909.

Jensen, Michael C. 1968. "The Performance of Mutual Funds in the Period 1945–1964." *Journal of Finance* 23 (May), pp. 389–416.

———. 1986. "Agency Costs of Free Cash Flow, Corporate Finance and Takeovers." *American Economic Review* 76 (May), pp. 323–329.

———. 1993. "Presidential Address: The Modern Industrial Revolution, Exit, and the Failure of Internal Control Systems." *Journal of Finance* 48 (July), pp. 831–880.

Jensen, Michael C., and George A. Benington. 1970. "Random Walks and Technical Theories: Some Additional Evidence." *Journal of Finance* 25 (May), pp. 156–169.

Jensen, Michael C., and William H. Meckling. 1976. "Theory of the Firm: Managerial Behavior, Agency Costs, and Ownership Structure." *Journal of Financial Economics* 3 (October), pp. 305–360.

Jensen, Michael, and Richard Ruback. 1983. "The Market for Corporate Control: The Scientific Evidence." *Journal of Financial Economics* 11 (April), pp. 5–50.

Jog, Vijay M., and Allan L. Riding. 1986. "Price Effects of Dual-Class Shares." *Financial Analysts Journal* 42 (January/February), pp. 58–67.

John, Kose, and Eli Ofek. 1995. "Asset Sales and In-

crease in Focus." *Journal of Financial Economics* 37 (January), pp. 105–126.

John, Kose, and Larry H. P. Lang. 1991. "Insider Trading around Dividend Announcements: Theory and Evidence." *Journal of Finance* 40 (September), pp. 1361–1389.

John, Kose, and Joseph Williams. 1985. "Dividends, Dilution and Taxes: A Signalling Equilibrium." *Journal of Finance* 40 (September), pp. 1053–1070.

Jones, Jonathan, William W. Lang, and Peter Nigro. 2000. "Recent Trends in Bank Loan Syndications: Evidence for 1995 to 1999." Working paper no. 2000-10, Office of the Comptroller of the Currency.

Jones, Steven L. 1993. "Another Look at Time-Varying Risk and Return in a Long-Horizon Contrarian Strategy." *Journal of Financial Economics* 33, pp. 119–144.

Jones, Steven L., William L. Megginson, Robert C. Nash, and Jeffry M. Netter. 1999. "Share Issue Privatizations as Financial Means to Political and Economic Ends." *Journal of Financial Economics* 53 (August), pp. 217–253.

Kaiser, Kevin M. J. 1996. "European Bankruptcy Laws: Implications for Corporations Facing Financial Distress." *Financial Management* 25 (Autumn), pp. 67–85.

Kalay, Avner. 1982. "Stockholder-Bondholder Conflict and Dividend Constraints." *Journal of Financial Economics* 10 (July), pp. 211–233.

Kalay, Avner, and Marti G. Subrahmanyan. 1984. "The Ex-dividend Day Behavior of Option Prices." *Journal of Business* 57 (January), pp. 113–128.

Kaplan, Steven N., and Bernadette A. Minton. 1994. "Appointments of Outsiders to Japanese Boards: Determinants and Implications for Managers." *Journal of Financial Economics* 36 (October), pp. 225–258.

Kaplan, Steven, and Per Strömberg. 2000. "How Do Venture Capitalists Choose Investments?" Working paper, University of Chicago.

———. 2001. "Financial Contracting Theory Meets the Real World: An Empirical Analysis of Venture Capital Contracts." Working paper, University of Chicago.

Kaplan, Steven, and Michael Weisbach. 1992. "The Success of Acquisitions: Evidence from Divestitures." *Journal of Finance* 47 (March), pp. 107–138.

Karolyi, G. Andrew. 1998. "Sourcing Equity Internationally with Depositary Receipt Offerings: Two Exceptions That Prove the Rule." *Journal of Applied Corporate Finance* 10 (Winter), pp. 90–101.

Katz, David J. 1990. "Solving the Dilemma of Pricing Secondaries." *Venture Capital Journal* (October), pp. 21–33.

Keim, Donald B. 1983. "Size-Related Anomalies and Stock Return Seasonality: Further Empirical Evidence." *Journal of Financial Economics* 12 (June), pp. 13–32.

Kendall, Maurice G. 1953. "The Analysis of Economic Time Series." *Journal of the Royal Statistical Society,* Series A, vol. 96, pp. 11–25.

Kensinger, John, and John D. Martin. 1988. "Project Finance: Raising Money the Old-Fashioned Way." *Journal of Applied Corporate Finance* 1 (Spring), pp. 69–81.

Kester, W. Carl. 1992. "Governance, Contracting, and Investment Horizons: A Look at Japan and Germany." *Journal of Applied Corporate Finance* 5 (Summer), pp. 83–98.

Khorana, Ajay, Sunil Wahal, and Marc Zenner. 2002. "Agency Conflicts in Closed-End Funds: The Case of Rights Offerings." *Journal of Financial and Quantitative Analysis* 37 (June), pp. 177–200.

Kim, Yong Cheol, and Rene M. Stulz. 1988. "The Eurobond Market and Corporate Financial Policy: A Test of the Clientele Hypothesis." *Journal of Financial Economics* 22, pp. 189–206.

Kinn, Bruce A., and Arnold M. Zaff. 1997. "The Benefits of a Revitalized SBIC Program." In *Pratt's Guide to Venture Capital Sources,* edited by Stanley E. Pratt (New York: Securities Data Publishing), pp. 105–107.

Kleidon, Allan W. 1986. "Variance Bounds Tests and Stock Price Valuation Models." *Journal of Political Economy* 94 (October), pp. 953–1001.

Kleimeier, Stefanie, and William L. Megginson. 2000. "Are Project Finance Loans Different from Other Syndicated Credits?" *Journal of Applied Corporate Finance* 12 (Winter), pp. 75–87.

Kliger, Doron, and Oded Sarig. 2000. "The Information Value of Bond Ratings." *Journal of Finance* 55 (December), pp. 2879–2902.

Kogut, Bruce and Nalin Kulatilaka. 1994. "Operating Flexibility, Global Manufacturing and the Option Value of a Multinational Network." *Management Science* 40 (January), pp. 123–139.

Korajczyk, Robert A., Deborah J. Lucas, and Robert L. McDonald. 1991. "The Effect of Information Releases on the Pricing and Timing of Equity Issues." *Review of Financial Studies* 4, pp. 685–708.

Kothari, S. P., and Jay Shanken. 1992. "Stock Return Variation and Expected Dividends: A Time Series Analysis." *Journal of Financial Economics* 31 (April), pp. 177–210.

———. 1993. "Fundamentals Largely Explain Stock Price Volatility." *Journal of Applied Corporate Finance* 6 (Summer), pp. 81–87.

KPMG Peat Marwick. 1998. *Going Public: What the CEO Needs to Know* (KPMG International).

Krigman, Laurie, Wayne H. Shaw, and Kent L. Womack. 1999. "The Persistence of IPO Mispricing and the Predictive Power of Flipping." *Journal of Finance* 54 (June), pp. 1015–1044.

Krishnan, V. Sivarama, and R. Charles Moyer. 1994. "Bankruptcy Costs and the Financial Leasing Decision." *Financial Management* 23 (Summer), pp. 31–42.

Krishnaswami, Sudha, Paul A. Spindt, and Venkat Subramaniam. 1999. "Information Asymmetry, Monitoring, and the Placement Structure of Corporate Debt." *Journal of Financial Economics* 51, pp. 407–434.

Kulatilaka, Nalin. 1993. "The Value of Flexibility: The Case of a Dual-Use Industrial Steam Boiler." *Financial Management* 22 (Autumn), pp. 271–280.

Lakonishok, Josef, and Seymour Smidt. 1988. "Are Seasonal Anomalies Real? A Ninety-Year Perspective." *Review of Financial Studies* 1 (Winter), pp. 403–425.

Lakonishok, Josef, and Theo Vermaelen. 1983. "Tax Reform and Ex-dividend Day Behavior." *Journal of Finance* 38 (September), pp. 1157–1175.

———. 1986. "Tax-Induced Trading around Ex-dividend Days." *Journal of Financial Economics* 16 (July), pp. 287–319.

———. 1990. "Anomalous Price Behavior around Repurchase Tender Offers." *Journal of Finance* 45 (June), pp. 455–477.

Lamont, Owen A., and Christopher Polk. 2001. "The Diversification Discount: Cash Flows versus Returns." *Journal of Finance* 56 (October), pp. 1693–1721.

Lamont, Owen, and Richard H. Thaler. 2002. "Can the Market Add and Subtract? Mispricing in Tech Stock Carve-Outs." Working paper, University of Chicago.

Lang, Larry, Eli Ofek, and René M. Stulz. 1996. "Leverage, Investment, and Firm Growth." *Journal of Financial Economics* 40 (January), pp. 3–29.

Lang, Larry H. P., and René M. Stulz. 1992. "Contagion and Competitive Intra-industry Effects of Bankruptcy Announcements." *Journal of Financial Economics* 32 (August), pp. 45–60.

———. 1994. "Tobin's q, Corporate Diversification, and Firm Performance." *Journal of Political Economy* 102 (December), pp. 1248–1280.

Lang, Larry, René Stulz, and Ralph Walkling. 1989. "Managerial Performance, Tobin's q and the Gains from Successful Tender Offers." *Journal of Financial Economics* 24 (September), pp. 137–154.

———. 1991. "A Test of the Free Cash Flow Hypothesis: The Case of Bidder Returns." *Journal of Financial Economics* 29 (October), pp. 315–335.

La Porta, Rafael, Florencio López-de-Silanes, and Andrei Shleifer. 2000. "Government Ownership of Banks." NBER working paper 7620, National Bureau of Economic Research (Cambridge, Massachusetts).

La Porta, Rafael, Florencio López-de-Silanes, Andrei Shleifer, and Robert W. Vishny. 1997. "Legal Determinants of External Finance." *Journal of Finance* 52 (July), pp. 1131–1150.

———. 1998. "Law and Finance." *Journal of Political Economy* 106, pp. 1113–1150.

———. 2000. "Agency Problems and Dividend Policies around the World." *Journal of Finance* 55 (February), pp. 1–33.

———. 2002. "Investor Protection and Corporate Valuation." *Journal of Finance* 57 (June), pp. 1147–1170.

Lasfer, M. Ameziane. 1997. "On the Motivation for Paying Scrip Dividends." *Financial Management* 26 (Spring), pp. 62–80.

Lasfer, M. Ameziane, and Mario Levis. 1998. 'The Determinants of the Leasing Decision of Small and Large Companies." *European Financial Management* (June), pp. 159–184.

Lavelle, Louis. 2001. "Special Report: Executive Pay." *Business Week* (April 16), pp. 75–80.

———. 2002. "Executive Pay: Special Report." *Business Week* (April 15), pp. 80–100.

Lease, Ronald C., John J. McConnell, and Wayne H. Mikkelson. 1983. "The Market Value of Control in Publicly-Traded Corporations." *Journal of Financial Economics* 11 (April), pp. 439–471.

Lee, Bong-Soo. 1995. "The Response of Stock Prices to Permanent and Temporary Shocks to Dividends." *Journal of Financial and Quantitative Analysis* 30 (March), pp. 1–22.

———. 1996. "Time-Series Implications of Aggregate Dividend Behavior." *Review of Financial Studies* 9 (Summer), pp. 589–618.

Lee, Chun I., Kimberly C. Gleason, and Ike Mathur. 2000. "Efficiency Tests in the French Derivatives Market." *Journal of Banking and Finance* 24, pp. 787–807.

Lee, Dwight R., and James A. Verbrugge. 1996. "The Efficient Market Thrives on Criticism." *Journal of Applied Corporate Finance* 9 (Spring), pp. 35–40.

Lee, Inmoo, Scott Lochhead, Jay Ritter, and Quanshui Zhao. 1996. "The Costs of Raising Capital." *Journal of Financial Research* 19 (Spring), pp. 59–74.

Lee, Susan. 2002. "The Ugly Option." *Wall Street Journal* (April 10).

Lehn, Kenneth, and Annette Poulsen. 1989. "Free Cash Flow and Shareholder Gains in Going Private Transactions." *Journal of Finance* 44 (July), pp. 771–787.

Leland, Hayne E., and David H. Pyle. 1977. "Informational Asymmetries, Financial Structure, and Financial Intermediation." *Journal of Finance* 32, pp. 371–387.

Lerner, Josh. 1994. "Venture Capitalists and the Decision to Go Public." *Journal of Financial Economics* 35 (June), pp. 293–316.

———. 1995. "Venture Capitalists and the Oversight of Private Firms." *Journal of Finance* 50 (March), pp. 301–318.

———. 1998. "Angel Financing and Public Policy: An Overview." *Journal of Banking and Finance* 22 (August), pp. 773–783.

———. 1999. "The Government as Venture Capitalist: The Long-Run Effects of the SBIR Program." *Journal of Business* 72 (July), pp. 285–318.

———. 2000. *Venture Capital and Private Equity: A Casebook* (New York: John Wiley & Sons).

LeRoy, Christian V., and Stephen F. LeRoy. 1991. "Econometric Aspects of the Variance-Bounds Tests: A Survey." *Review of Financial Studies* 4, pp. 753–791.

Levine, Ross. 1997. "Financial Development and Economic Growth: Views and Agenda." *Journal of Economic Literature* 35, pp. 688–726.

Levy, Haim. 1983. "Economic Evaluation of Voting Power of Common Stock." *Journal of Finance* 38 (March), pp. 79–93.

Levy, Haim, and Marshall Sarnat. 1970. "Diversification, Portfolio Analysis, and the Uneasy Case for Conglomerate Mergers." *Journal of Finance* 25 (September), pp. 795–802.

Lewellen, Jonathan. 2002. "Momentum and Autocorrelation in Stock Returns." *Review of Financial Studies* 15 (Special), pp. 533–563.

Lewellen, Wilbur. 1971. "A Pure Financial Rationale for the Conglomerate Merger." *Journal of Finance* 26 (May), pp. 531–537.

Lewellen, Wilbur, Claudio Loderer, and Ahron Rosenfeld. 1985. "Merger Decisions and Executive Stock Ownership in Acquiring Firms." *Journal of Accounting and Economics* 7 (April), pp. 209–231.

Lie, Erik. 2000. "Excess Funds and Agency Problems: An Empirical Study of Incremental Cash Distributions." *Review of Financial Studies* 13 (Spring), pp. 219–248.

Linn, Scott C., and J. Michael Pinegar. 1988. "The Effect of Issuing Preferred Stock on Common and Preferred Stockholder Wealth." *Journal of Financial Economics* 22 (October), pp. 155–184.

Lins, Karl, and Henri Servaes. 1999. "International Evidence on the Value of Corporate Diversification." *Journal of Finance* 54 (December), pp. 2215–2239.

Lintner, John. 1956. "Distribution of Incomes of Corporations among Dividends, Retained Earnings, and Taxes." *American Economic Review* 46 (May), pp. 97–113.

Lipson, Marc L., Carlos P. Macquieira, and William L. Megginson. 1998. "Dividend Initiations and Earnings Surprises." *Financial Management* 27 (Autumn), pp. 36–45.

Livingston, Miles, and Robert E. Miller. 2000. "Investment Banking Reputation and the Underwriting of

Nonconvertible Debt." *Financial Management* 29 (Summer), pp. 21–34.

Ljungqvist, Alexander, Tim Jenkinson, and William J. Wilhelm, Jr. 2002. "Global Integration in Primary Equity Markets: The Role of U.S. Banks and U.S. Investors." *Review of Financial Studies* (forthcoming).

Ljungqvist, Alexander P., and William J. Wilhelm, Jr. 2001. "IPO Pricing in the Dot-Com Bubble: Complacency or Incentives?" Working paper, New York University.

———. 2002. "IPO Allocations: Discriminatory or Discretionary?" *Journal of Financial Economics* 65 (August), pp. 167–201.

Lo, Andrew W., and A. Craig MacKinlay. 1988. "Stock Market Prices Do Not Follow Random Walks: Evidence from a Simple Specification Test." *Review of Financial Studies* 1 (Spring), pp. 41–66.

———. 1990. "When Are Contrarian Profits due to Stock Market Overreaction?" *Review of Financial Studies* 3, pp. 175–205.

Lo, Andrew W., Harry Mamaysky, and Jiang Wang. 2000. "Foundations of Technical Analysis: Computational Algorithms, Statistical Inference, and Empirical Implementation." *Journal of Finance* 55 (August), pp. 1705–1765.

Loderer, Claudio F., Dennis P. Sheehan, and Gregory B. Kadlec. 1991. "The Pricing of Equity Offerings." *Journal of Financial Economics* 29, pp. 35–57.

Logue, Dennis E., and Seha M. Tiniç. 1999. "Optimal Choice of Contracting Methods: Negotiated versus Competitive Underwriting Revisited." *Journal of Financial Economics* 51 (March), pp. 451–471.

Long, Michael, and Ileen Malitz. 1985. "The Investment-Financing Nexus: Some Empirical Evidence." *Midland Corporate Finance Journal* 3 (Spring), pp. 53–59.

Loughran, Tim, and Jay R. Ritter. 1995. "The New Issues Puzzle." *Journal of Finance* 50 (March), pp. 23–51.

———. 2000. "Uniformly Least Powerful Tests of Market Efficiency." *Journal of Financial Economics* 55, pp. 361–389.

Loughran, Tim, Jay R. Ritter, and Kristian Rydqvist. 1994. "Initial Public Offerings: International Insights." *Pacific Basin Finance Journal* 2, pp. 165–199.

Loughran, Tim, and Anand Vijh. 1997. "Do Long-Term Shareholders Benefit from Corporate Acquisitions?" *Journal of Finance* 52 (December), pp. 1765–1790.

Lowry, Michelle, and G. William Schwert. 2002. "IPO Market Cycles: Bubbles or Sequential Learning?" *Journal of Finance* 57 (June), pp. 1171–1200.

Lummer, Scott C., and John J. McConnell. 1989. "Further Evidence on the Bank Lending Process and the Capital Market Responses to Bank Loan Agreements." *Journal of Financial Economics* 25 (November), pp. 99–122.

Lynch, Anthony W., and Richard R. Mendenhall. 1997. "New Evidence on Stock Price Effects Associated with Changes in the S&P 500 Index." *Journal of Business* 70 (July), pp. 351–383.

MacBeth, James D., and Larry J. Merville. 1979. "An Empirical Examination of the Black-Scholes Call Option Pricing Model." *Journal of Finance* 34 (December), pp. 1173–1186.

MacKie-Mason, Jeffrey K. 1990. "Do Taxes Affect Corporate Financing Decisions?" *Journal of Finance* 45 (December), pp. 1471–1493.

Macquieira, Carlos P., William L. Megginson, and Lance A. Nail. 1998. "Wealth Creation versus Wealth Redistributions in Pure Stock Exchange Mergers." *Journal of Financial Economics* 48 (April), pp. 3–33.

Maksimovic, Vojislav, and Sheridan Titman. 1991. "Financial Policy and Reputation for Product Quality." *Review of Financial Studies* 4, pp. 175–200.

Malkiel, Burton G. 1995. "Returns from Investing in Equity Mutual Funds 1971 to 1991." *Journal of Finance* 50 (June), pp. 549–572.

Malkiel, Burton G., and William J. Baumol. 2002. "Stock Options Keep the Economy Afloat." *Wall Street Journal* (April 4), p. A18.

Manne, H. G. 1965. "Mergers and the Market for Corporate Control." *Journal of Political Economy* 73, pp. 110–120.

Markowitz, Harry. 1952. "Portfolio Selection." *Journal of Finance* 7 (March), pp. 77–91.

Marsh, Paul. 1982. "The Choice between Equity and Debt: An Empirical Study." *Journal of Finance* 37 (March), pp. 121–144.

Masulis, Ronald W. 1980. "The Effect of Capital Structure Change on Security Prices: A Study of Exchange Offers." *Journal of Financial Economics* 8 (June), pp. 139–177.

Mayer, Colin. 1990. "Financial Systems, Corporate Finance, and Economic Development." In *Asymmetric Information, Corporate Finance and Investment,* edited by R. Glenn Hubbard (Chicago: University of Chicago Press).

Mayers, David. 1972. "Non-Marketable Assets and the Determination of Capital Market Equilibrium under Uncertainty." In *Studies in the Theory of Capital Markets,* edited by Michael Jensen (New York: Praeger).

Mayers, David, and Clifford Smith. 1982. "On the Corporate Demand for Insurance." *Journal of Business* 55 (April), pp. 281–296.

McConnell, John J., and Chris J. Muscarella. 1985. "Corporate Capital Expenditure Decisions and the Market Value of the Firm." *Journal of Financial Economics* 14 (September), pp. 399–422.

McConnell, John J., and Eduardo S. Schwartz. 1992. "The Origins of LYONs: A Case Study in Financial

Innovation." *Journal of Applied Corporate Finance* 4 (Winter), pp. 82–89.

McLaughlin, Robyn, and Robert A. Taggart, Jr. 1992. "The Opportunity Cost of Excess Capacity." *Financial Management* 21 (Summer), pp. 12–23.

McQueen, Grant. 1992. "Long-Horizon Mean-Reverting Stock Prices Revisited." *Journal of Financial and Quantitative Analysis* 27 (March), pp. 1–18.

Megginson, William L. 1990. "Restricted Voting Stock, Acquisition Premiums and the Market Value of Corporate Control." *Financial Review* 25 (May), pp. 175–198.

Megginson, William L., Angela Morgan, and Lance Nail. 2003. "The Determinants of Positive Long-Term Performance in Strategic Mergers: Corporate Focus and Cash." *Journal of Banking and Finance* (forthcoming).

Megginson, William L., Robert C. Nash, Jeffry Netter, and Adam Schwartz. 2000. "The Long-Term Return to Investors in Share Issue Privatizations." *Financial Management* 29 (Spring), pp. 67–77.

Megginson, William L., Robert C. Nash, and Matthias van Randenborgh. 1994. "The Financial and Operating Performance of Newly-Privatized Firms: An International Empirical Analysis." *Journal of Finance* 49 (June), pp. 403–452.

———. 1996. "The Record on Privatization." *Journal of Applied Corporate Finance* 9 (Spring), pp. 403–452.

Megginson, William L., and Jeffry M. Netter. 2001. "From State to Market: A Survey of Empirical Studies on Privatization." *Journal of Economic Literature* 39 (June), pp. 321–389.

Megginson, William L., Annette B. Poulsen, and Joseph F. Sinkey, Jr. 1995. "Syndicated Loan Announcements and the Market Value of the Banking Firm." *Journal of Money, Credit, and Banking* 27 (May), pp. 457–475.

Megginson, William L., and Kathleen A. Weiss. 1991. "Venture Capital Certification in Initial Public Offerings." *Journal of Finance* 46 (July), pp. 879–903.

Mello, Antonio S., and John E. Parsons. 1999. "Strategic Hedging." *Journal of Applied Corporate Finance* 12 (Fall), pp. 43–54.

Menyah, Kojo, Krishna Paudyal, and Charles G. Inyangete. 1995. "Subscriber Return, Underpricing, and Long-Term Performance of U.K. Privatization Initial Public Offers." *Journal of Economics and Business* 47, pp. 473–495.

Merton, Robert C. 1973a. "An Intertemporal Capital Asset Pricing Model." *Econometrica* 41 (September), pp. 867–887.

———. 1973b. "Theory of Rational Option Pricing." *Bell Journal of Economics* 4 (Spring), pp. 141–183.

Metrick, Andrew. 1999. "Performance Evaluation with Transactions Data: The Stock Selection of Investment Newsletters." *Journal of Finance* 54 (October), pp. 1743–1775.

Meulbroek, Lisa K. 1992. "An Empirical Analysis of Illegal Insider Trading." *Journal of Finance* 47 (December), pp. 1661–1699.

Mian, Shehzad. 2001. "On the Choice and Replacement of Chief Financial Officers." *Journal of Financial Economics* 60, pp. 143–175.

Michaely, Roni, and Franklin Allen. 2002. "Payout Policy." In *Handbook of Economics,* edited by George Constantinides et al. (North-Holland, forthcoming).

Michaely, Roni, and Wayne H. Shaw. 1995. "The Choice of Going Public: Spin-offs and Carve-Outs." *Financial Management* 24 (Autumn), pp. 5–21.

Michaely, Roni, Richard H. Thaler, and Kent L. Womack. 1995. "Price Reactions to Dividend Initiations and Omissions: Overreaction or Drift?" *Journal of Finance* 50 (June), pp. 573–608.

Mikkelson, Wayne H., and M. Megan Partch. 1986. "Valuation Effects of Security Offerings and the Issuance Process." *Journal of Financial Economics* 15 (January/February), pp. 31–60.

Miles, James A., and James D. Rosenfeld. 1983. "The Effect of Voluntary Spin-off Announcements on Shareholder Wealth." *Journal of Finance* (December), pp. 1597–1606.

Miller, Darius P. 1999. "The Market Reaction to International Cross-Listings: Evidence from Depositary Receipts." *Journal of Financial Economics* 51 (January), pp. 103–123.

Miller, Merton H. 1977. "Debt and Taxes." *Journal of Finance* 32 (May), pp. 261–276.

———. 1999. "The History of Finance: An Eyewitness Account." *Journal of Portfolio Management* (Summer), pp. 95–101. Reprint of a speech made to the German Finance Association on September 25, 1998.

Miller, Merton H., and Franco Modigliani. 1961. "Dividend Policy, Growth, and the Valuation of Shares." *Journal of Business* 34 (October), pp. 411–433.

Miller, Merton H., and Kevin Rock. 1985. "Dividend Policy under Asymmetric Information." *Journal of Finance* 40 (September), pp. 1021–1051.

Mitchell, Karlyn. 1991. "The Call, Sinking Fund, and Term to Maturity Features of Corporate Bonds: An Empirical Investigation." *Journal of Financial and Quantitative Analysis* 26 (June), pp. 201–222.

Mitchell, Mark, and Harold Mulherin. 1996. "The Impact of Industry Shocks on Takeover and Restructuring Activity." *Journal of Financial Economics* 41 (June), pp. 93–229.

Mitchell, Mark, and Erik Stafford. 2000. "Managerial Decisions and Long-Term Stock Price Performance." *Journal of Business* 73 (July), pp. 287–320.

Modigliani, Franco, and Merton Miller. 1958. "The Cost of Capital, Corporation Finance, and the Theory of Investment." *American Economic Review* 48 (June), pp. 261–297.

———. 1963. "Corporate Income Taxes and the Cost of Capital." *American Economic Review* 53 (June), pp. 433–443.

Moehrle, Stephen, and Jennifer Reynolds-Moehrle. 2001. "Say Good-Bye to Pooling and Goodwill Amortization." *Journal of Accountancy* 192 (September), pp. 11–20.

Moel, Alberto, and Peter Tufano. 2002. "When Are Real Options Exercised? An Empirical Study of Mine Closings." *Review of Financial Studies* 15 (Spring), pp. 35–64.

Moore, James, Jay Culver, and Bonnie Masterman. 2000. "Risk Management for Middle Market Companies." *Journal of Applied Corporate Finance* 12 (Winter), pp. 112–119.

Morck, Randall, Andrei Shleifer, and Robert Vishny. 1988. "Management Ownership and Market Valuation: An Empirical Analysis." *Journal of Financial Economics* 20 (January), pp. 293–315.

———. 1990. "Do Managerial Objectives Drive Bad Acquisitions?" *Journal of Finance* 45 (March), pp. 31–48.

Morris, Jane Koloski. 1988. "The Pricing of a Venture Capital Investment." In *Pratt's Guide to Venture Capital Sources,* edited by Stanley E. Pratt (New York: Securities Data Publishing), pp. 55–61.

Moskowitz, Tobias J., and Mark Grinblatt. 1999. "Do Industries Explain Momentum?" *Journal of Finance* 54 (August), pp. 1249–1290.

Mossin, Jan. 1966. "Equilibrium in a Capital Asset Market." *Econometrica* 24 (October), pp. 768–783.

Mueller, Dennis. 1969. "A Theory of Conglomerate Mergers." *Quarterly Journal of Economics* 83, pp. 643–659.

Mulherin, J. Harold, and Annette Poulsen. (1998). "Proxy Contests and Corporate Change: Implications for Shareholder Wealth." *Journal of Financial Economics* 47 (March), pp. 279–313.

Murphy, Kevin. 1985. "Corporate Performance and Managerial Remuneration: An Empirical Analysis." *Journal of Accounting and Economics* 7 (April), pp. 11–42.

Muscarella, Chris J., and Michael R. Vetsuypens. 1989. "The Underpricing of 'Second' Initial Public Offerings." *Journal of Financial Research* (Fall), pp. 183–192.

———. 1990. "Efficiency and Organizational Structure: A Study of Reverse LBOs." *Journal of Finance* 45 (December), pp. 1389–1413.

———. 1996. "Stock Splits: Signaling or Liquidity? The Case of ADR 'Solo-Splits.'" *Journal of Financial Economics* 42 (September), pp. 3–26.

Myers, Stewart C. 1977. "The Determinants of Corporate Borrowing." *Journal of Financial Economics* 5 (November), pp. 147–176.

———. 1984. "The Capital Structure Puzzle." *Journal of Finance* 39 (July), pp. 575–592.

———. 1993. "Still Searching for an Optimal Capital Structure." *Journal of Applied Corporate Finance* 6 (Spring), pp. 4–14.

Myers, Stewart C., and Nicholas S. Majluf. 1984. "Corporate Financing and Investment Decisions When Firms Have Information the Investors Do Not Have." *Journal of Financial Economics* 13, pp. 187–221.

Nance, Deana R., Clifford W. Smith, Jr., and Charles W. Smithson. 1993. "On the Determinants of Corporate Hedging." *Journal of Finance* 48 (March), pp. 267–284.

Nanda, Vikram. 1991. "On the Good News in Equity Carve-Outs." *Journal of Finance* 46 (December), pp. 1717–1737.

Nathan, Kevin, and Terrence O'Keefe. 1989. "The Rise in Takeover Premiums: An Exploratory Study." *Journal of Financial Economics* 23 (June), pp. 101–119.

Ng, Chee K., Janet Kiholm Smith, and Richard L. Smith. "Evidence on the Determinants of Credit Terms Used in Interfirm Trade." *Journal of Finance* 54 (June 1999), pp. 1109–1129.

Nichols, N. A. 1994. "Scientific Management at Merck: An Interview with Judy Lewent." *Harvard Business Review* 72 (January/February), p. 91.

Noe, Thomas H., and Michael J. Rebello. 1996. "Asymmetric Information, Managerial Opportunism, Financing, and Payout Policies." *Journal of Finance* 51 (June), pp. 637–660.

Ojah, Kalu, and David Karemera. 1999. "Random Walks and Market Efficiency Tests of Latin American Emerging Equity Markets: A Revisit." *Financial Review* 34 (May), pp. 57–72.

Ongena, Steven, and David C. Smith. 2001. "The Duration of Bank Relationships." *Journal of Financial Economics* 21, pp. 449–475.

Opler, Tim C., and Sheridan Titman. 1994. "Financial Distress and Corporate Performance." *Journal of Finance* 49 (July), pp. 1015–1040.

Packer, Frank. 1996. "Venture Capital, Bank Shareholding, and IPO Underpricing in Japan." In *Empirical Issues in Raising Equity Capital,* edited by Mario Levis (North Holland), pp. 191–214.

Pagano, Marco, Fabio Panetta, and Luigi Zingales. 1998. "Why Do Companies Go Public? An Empirical Analysis." *Journal of Finance* 53 (February), pp. 27–64.

Pástor, Lubos, and Robert F. Stambaugh. 2002. "Mutual Fund Performance and Seemingly Unrelated Assets." *Journal of Financial Economics* 63, pp. 315–349.

Petersen, Mitchell A., and Raghuram G. Rajan. 1994. "The Benefits of Lending Relationships: Evidence from Small Business Data." *Journal of Finance* 49 (March), pp. 3–37.

Phillips, Gordon M. 1995. "Increased Debt and Industry Product Markets: An Empirical Analysis." *Journal of Financial Economics* 37 (February), pp. 189–238.

Poterba, James. 1987. "Tax Policy and Corporate Savings." *Brookings Papers on Economic Activity* 2 (December), pp. 455–515.

Pound, John, and Richard Zeckhauser. 1990. "Clearly Heard on the Street: The Effects of Takeover Rumors on Stock Prices." *Journal of Business* 63 (July), pp. 291–308.

Pratt, Stanley E. 1997. "The Organized Venture Capital Community." In *Pratt's Guide to Venture Capital Sources*, edited by Stanley E. Pratt (New York: Securities Data Publishing), pp. 75–80.

Press, Eric G., and Joseph B. Weintrop. 1990. "Accounting-Based Constraints in Public and Private Debt Agreements: Their Association with Leverage and Impact on Accounting Choice." *Journal of Accounting and Economics* 12 (January), pp. 65–95.

Pringle, John J. 1991. "Managing Foreign Exchange Exposure." *Journal of Applied Corporate Finance* 3 (Winter), pp. 73–82.

Pringle, John J., and Robert A. Connolly. 1993. "The Nature and Causes of Foreign Currency Exposure." *Journal of Applied Corporate Finance* 6 (Fall), pp. 61–72.

Prowse, Michael. 1992. "Is America in Decline?" *Harvard Business Review* (July/August), pp. 34–45.

Prowse, Stephen D. 1990. "Institutional Investment Patterns and Corporate Financial Behavior in the United States and Japan." *Journal of Financial Economics* 27, pp. 43–66.

———. 1996. "Corporate Finance in International Perspective: Legal and Regulatory Influences on Financial System Development." Federal Reserve Bank of Dallas *Economic Review* (Third Quarter), pp. 2–15.

Pulvino, Todd C. 1999. "The Effects of Bankruptcy Court Protection on Asset Sales." *Journal of Financial Economics* 52 (May), pp. 151–186.

Rajan, Raghuram G. 1992. "Insiders and Outsiders: The Choice between Informed and Arm's Length Debt." *Journal of Finance* 49, pp. 1367–1400.

Rajan, Raghuram, Henri Servaes, and Luigi Zingales. 2000. "The Cost of Diversity: The Diversification Discount and Inefficient Investment." *Journal of Finance* 55 (February), pp. 35–80.

Rajan, Raghuram G., and Luigi Zingales. 1995. "What Do We Know about Capital Structure? Some Evidence from International Data." *Journal of Finance* 50 (December), pp. 1421–1460.

Rajgopal, Shivaram, and Terry J. Shevlin. 2002. "Empirical Evidence on the Relation between Stock Option Compensation and Risk Taking." *Journal of Accounting and Economics* 33 (June), pp. 145–171.

Ravenscraft, David, and F. M. Scherer. 1987. *Mergers, Sell-offs, and Economic Efficiency*. (Washington, D.C.: Brookings Institution).

Rawls, S. Waite, III, and Charles W. Smithson. 1989. "The Evolution of Risk Management Products." *Journal of Applied Corporate Finance* 1 (Winter), pp. 18–26.

Richardson, Matthew, and Tom Smith. 1994. "A Unified Approach to Testing for Serial Correlation in Stock Returns." *Journal of Business* 67 (July), pp. 371–399.

Riley, John. 1979. "Informational Equilibrium." *Econometrica* 47 (March), pp. 331–359.

Ritter, Jay R. 1984. "Signaling and the Valuation of Unseasoned New Issues: A Comment." *Journal of Finance* 39, pp. 1231–1237.

———. 1987. "The Costs of Going Public." *Journal of Financial Economics* 19 (December), pp. 269–281.

———. 1991. "The Long-Run Performance of Initial Public Offerings." *Journal of Finance* 46 (March), pp. 3–27.

———. 1996. "How I Helped Make Fischer Black Wealthier." *Financial Management* 24 (Winter), pp. 104–107.

———. 1998. "Initial Public Offerings." In *Handbook of Modern Finance*, edited by Dennis Logue and James Seward (Boston: Warren Gorham & Lamont).

———. 2001. "The Biggest Mistakes That We Teach." Working paper, University of Florida.

Ritter, Jay, and Navin Chopra. 1989. "Portfolio Rebalancing and the Turn-of-the-Year Effect." *Journal of Finance* 44 (March), pp. 149–166.

Roberts, Harry V. 1959. "Stock Market 'Patterns' and Financial Analysis: Methodological Suggestions." *Journal of Finance* 14 (March), pp. 1–10.

Rock, Kevin. 1986. "Why New Issues Are Underpriced." *Journal of Financial Economics* 15 (January/February), pp. 187–212.

Roe, Mark J. 1990. "Political and Legal Restraints on Ownership and Control of Public Companies." *Journal of Financial Economics* 27 (September), pp. 7–41.

———. 1997. "The Political Roots of American Corporate Finance." *Journal of Applied Corporate Finance* 9 (Winter), pp. 8–22.

Roll, Richard. 1977. "A Critique of the Asset Pricing Theory's Tests, Part I: On Past and Potential Testability of the Theory." *Journal of Financial Economics* 4, pp. 129–176.

———. 1986. "The Hubris Hypothesis of Corporate Takeovers." *Journal of Business* 59 (April), pp. 197–217.

———. 1994. "What Every CEO Should Know about Scientific Progress in Economics: What Is Known and What Remains to Be Resolved." *Financial Management* 23 (Summer), pp. 69–75.

Ross, Stephen A. 1976. "The Arbitrage Theory of Capital Asset Pricing." *Journal of Economic Theory* (December), pp. 341–360.

———. 1977a. "The Determination of Financial Structure: The Incentive-Signaling Approach." *Bell Journal of Economics* 8 (Spring), pp. 23–40.

———. 1977b. "Risk, Return, and Arbitrage." In *Risk and Return in Finance I,* edited by Irwin Friend and James L. Bicksler, pp. 189–218 (Cambridge, Mass.: Ballinger).

Rutterford, Janette. 1988. "An International Perspective on the Capital Structure Puzzle." In *New Developments in International Finance,* edited by Joel M. Stern and Donald H. Chew Jr. (New York: Basil Blackwell).

Sahlman, William A. 1988. "Aspects of Financial Contracting in Venture Capital." *Journal of Applied Corporate Finance* 1 (Summer), pp. 23–36.

———. 1990. "The Structure and Governance of Venture Capital Organizations." *Journal of Financial Economics* 27 (September), pp. 473–524.

Samant, Ajay. 1996. "An Empirical Study of Interest Rate Swap Usage by Nonfinancial Corporate Business." *Journal of Financial Services Research* 10 (March), pp. 43–57.

Sarkar, Sudipto. 2001. "Probability of Call and Likelihood of the Call Feature in a Corporate Bond." *Journal of Banking and Finance* 25 (March), pp. 505–533.

Schallheim, James S., Ramon E. Johnson, Ronald C. Lease, and John J. McConnell. 1987. "The Determinants of Yields on Financial Leasing Contracts." *Journal of Financial Economics* 19, pp. 45–68.

Scherr, Frederick C., and Heather M. Hulburt. 2001. "The Maturity Structure of Small Firms." *Financial Management* 30 (Spring), pp. 85–111.

Schilit, W. Keith, and John T. Willig, eds. 1996a. "The Globalization of Venture Capital." In *Fitzroy Dearborn International Directory of Venture Capital Funds,* 2nd ed. (Chicago: Fitzroy Dearborn Publishers), pp. 79–80.

———. 1996b. "Structuring the Venture Capital Deal." In *Fitzroy Dearborn International Directory of Venture Capital Funds,* 2nd ed. (Chicago: Fitzroy Dearborn Publishers), pp. 71–77.

Schipper, Katherine, and Abbie Smith. 1983. "Effects of Recontracting on Shareholder Wealth: The Case of Voluntary Spin-Offs." *Journal of Financial Economics* 12, pp. 437–468.

———. 1986. "A Comparison of Equity Carve-outs and Seasoned Equity Offerings: Share Price Effects and Corporate Restructuring." *Journal of Financial Economics* 15 (January/February), pp. 153–186.

Schwert, G. William. 1996. "Markup Pricing in Mergers and Acquisitions." *Journal of Financial Economics* 41 (June), pp. 153–192.

Scott, James H., Jr. 1977. "Bankruptcy, Secured Debt, and Optimal Capital Structure." *Journal of Finance* 32 (March), pp. 1–19.

Sekely, William S., and J. Markham Collins. 1988. "Cultural Influences on International Capital Structure." *Journal of International Business Studies* (Spring), pp. 87–100.

Servaes, Henri. 1991. "Tobin's q and the Gains from Takeovers." *Journal of Finance* 46 (March), pp. 409–420.

———. 1996. "The Value of Diversification during the Conglomerate Merger Wave." *Journal of Finance* 51 (September), pp. 1201–1225.

Seyhun, H. Nejat. 1986. "Insiders' Profits, Cost of Trading, and Market Efficiency." *Journal of Financial Economics* 16 (June), pp. 189–212.

Seyhun, H. Nejat, and Michael Bradley. 1997. "Corporate Bankruptcy and Insider Trading." *Journal of Business* 70 (April), pp. 189–216.

Shah, Kshitij. 1994. "The Nature of Information Conveyed by Pure Capital Structure Changes." *Journal of Financial Economics* 36 (August), pp. 89–126.

Sharpe, William F. 1964. "Capital Asset Prices: A Theory of Market Equilibrium under Conditions of Risk." *Journal of Finance* 19 (September), pp. 425–442.

———. 1966. "Mutual Fund Performance." *Journal of Business* 39 (January), pp. 119–138.

Shefrin, Hersh. 2002. "Behavioral Corporate Finance." *Journal of Applied Corporate Finance* 14 (Fall), pp. 113–124.

Shiller, Robert J. 1979. "The Volatility of Long-Term Interest Rates and Expectations Models of the Term Structure." *Journal of Political Economy* 87 (December), pp. 1190–1219.

———. 1981. "Do Stock Prices Move Too Much to Be Justified by Subsequent Changes in Dividends?" *American Economic Review* 71 (June), pp. 421–436.

———. 2000. *Irrational Exuberance* (Princeton, NJ: Princeton University Press).

Shin, Hyun-Han, and Young S. Park. 1999. "Financing Constraints and Internal Capital Markets: Evidence from Korean 'Chaebols.'" *Journal of Corporate Finance* 5 (June), pp. 169–191.

Shleifer, Andrei, and Lawrence Summers. 1988. "Breach of Trust in Hostile Takeovers." In *Corporate Takeovers: Causes and Consequences* (Chicago: University Of Chicago Press).

———. 1990. "The Noise Trader Approach to Finance."

Journal of Economic Perspectives 4 (Spring), pp. 19–33.

Shleifer, Andrei, and Robert Vishny. 1989. "Management Entrenchment." *Journal of Financial Economics* 25 (November), pp. 123–139.

———. 1997a. "The Limits to Arbitrage." *Journal of Finance* 52 (March), pp. 35–55.

———. 1997b. "A Survey of Corporate Governance." *Journal of Finance* 52 (June), pp. 736–783.

Shockley, Richard L., Jr. 2001. "McTreat Spots: Creating Options at McDonalds." Teaching case, Indiana University.

Shyam-Sunder, Lakshmi, and Stewart C. Myers. 1999. "Testing the Static Trade-off against Pecking Order Models of Capital Structure." *Journal of Financial Economics* 51 (February), pp. 219–244.

Siconolfi, Michael, and Patrick McGeehan. 1998. "Wall Street Boosts Penalty on IPO 'Flips.'" *Wall Street Journal* (July 31), p. C1.

Slovin, Myron B., Marie E. Sushka, and Steven R. Ferraro. 1995. "A Comparison of the Information Conveyed by Equity Carve-outs, Spin-offs, and Asset Sell-Offs." *Journal of Financial Economics* 37 (January), pp. 89–104.

Smith, Clifford W., Jr. 1977. "Alternative Methods of Raising Capital: Rights versus Underwritten Offerings." *Journal of Financial Economics* 5 (December), pp. 273–307.

———. 1992. "Economics and Ethics: The Case of Salomon Brothers." *Journal of Applied Corporate Finance* 5 (Summer), pp. 23–28.

Smith, Clifford W., Jr., Charles W. Smithson, and D. Sykes Wilford. 1989. "Managing Financial Risk." *Journal of Applied Corporate Finance* 1 (Winter), pp. 27–48.

Smith, Clifford W., Jr., and L. McDonald Wakeman. 1985. "Determinants of Corporate Leasing Policy." *Journal of Finance* 40 (July), pp. 895–908.

Smith, Clifford W., Jr., and Jerold B. Warner. 1979. "On Financial Contracting: An Analysis of Bond Covenants." *Journal of Financial Economics* 7 (June), pp. 117–161.

Smith, Clifford W., Jr., and Ross L. Watts. 1992. "The Investment Opportunity Set and Corporate Financing, Dividend, and Compensation Policies." *Journal of Financial Economics* 32 (December), pp. 263–292.

Smith, Roy C. 2001. "Strategic Directions in Investment Banking—A Retrospective Analysis." *Journal of Applied Corporate Finance* 14 (Spring), pp. 111–123.

Sorensen, Eric H., and Thierry F. Bollier. 1994. "Pricing Swap Default Risk." *Financial Analysts Journal* 50, pp. 23–33.

Spence, Michael. 1973. "Job Market Signalling." *Quarterly Journal of Economics* 87 (August), pp. 355–374.

Spiess, D. Katherine, and John Affleck-Graves. 1995. "Underperformance in Long-Run Stock Returns following Seasoned Equity Offerings." *Journal of Financial Economics* 38 (July), pp. 243–267.

Stancill, James McNeill. 1987. "How Much Money Does Your New Venture Need?" *Harvard Business Review* (May/June), pp. 122–139.

Stickel, Scott. 1985. "The Effect of Value Line Investment Survey Rank Changes on Common Stock Prices." *Journal of Financial Economics* 14 (March), pp. 121–143.

Stiglitz, Joseph E. 2002. "Accounting for Options." *Wall Street Journal* (May 3).

Stillman, Robert. 1983. "Examining Antitrust Policy towards Mergers." *Journal of Financial Economics* 11 (April), pp. 225–240.

Stulz, Rene M. 1988. "Managerial Control of Voting Rights: Financing Policies and the Market for Corporate Control." *Journal of Financial Economics* 20 (January), pp. 25–54.

———. 1990. "Managerial Discretion and Optimal Financing Policies." *Journal of Financial Economics* 26 (July), pp. 1–25.

———. 1996. "Rethinking Risk Management." *Journal of Applied Corporate Finance* 9 (Fall), pp. 8–24.

Stulz, René M., and Herb Johnson. 1985. "An Analysis of Secured Debt." *Journal of Financial Economics* 14 (December), pp. 501–521.

Subrahmanyam, Avanidhar, and Sheridan Titman. 1999. "The Going-Public Decision and the Development of Financial Markets." *Journal of Finance* 54 (June), pp. 1045–1082.

Sullivan, Ryan, Allan Timmerman, and Halbert White. 1999. "Data-Snooping, Technical Trading Rule Performance, and the Bootstrap." *Journal of Finance* 54 (October), pp. 1647–1691.

Taggart, Robert A., Jr. 1985. "Secular Patterns in the Financing of U.S. Corporations." In *Corporate Capital Structures in the United States*, edited by Benjamin M. Friedman (Chicago: University of Chicago Press).

Targett, Simon. 2001. "Institutional Investment: Should Do More." *Financial Times* (June 14), European Private Equity Survey, p. 5.

Testa, Richard J. 1988. "The Legal Process of Venture Capital Investment." In *Pratt's Guide to Venture Capital Sources*, edited by Stanley E. Pratt (New York: Securities Data Publishing), pp. 66–77.

Thaler, Richard H. 2000. "From Homo Economicus to Homo Sapiens." *Journal of Economic Perspectives* 14 (Winter), pp. 133–141.

Thatcher, Janet S. 1985. "The Choice of Call Provisions Terms: Evidence of the Existence of Agency Costs of Debt." *Journal of Finance* 40 (June), pp. 549–561.

Thompson, Samuel C. 2000. "Demystifying the Use of Beta in Determining the Cost of Capital and an Illustration of Its Use in Lazard's Valuation of Conrail." *Journal of Corporation Law* 25, pp. 241–306.

Thorburn, Karin S. 2000. "Bankruptcy Auctions: Costs, Debt Recovery and Firm Survival." *Journal of Financial Economics* 58 (December), pp. 337–368.

Titman, Sheridan. 1984. "The Effect of Capital Structure on a Firm's Liquidation Decision." *Journal of Financial Economics* 13 (March), pp. 137–151.

———. 1992. "Interest Rate Swaps and Corporate Financing Choices." *Journal of Finance* 47 (September), pp. 1503–1516.

Titman, Sheridan, and Roberto Wessels. 1988. "The Determinants of Capital Structure Choice." *Journal of Finance* 43 (March), pp. 1–19.

Travlos, Nickolas G. 1987. "Corporate Takeover Bids, Methods of Payment, and Bidding Firms' Stock Returns." *Journal of Finance* 42 (September), pp. 943–963.

Triantis, Alexander J., and James E. Hodder. 1990. "Valuing Flexibility as a Complex Option." *Journal of Finance* 45 (June), pp. 549–565.

Trigeorgis, Lenos, and Scott P. Mason. 1987. "Valuing Managerial Flexibility." *Midland Corporate Finance Journal* 5 (Spring), pp. 14–21.

Tufano, Peter. 1996. "Who Manages Risk? An Empirical Examination of Risk Management Practices in the Gold Mining Industry." *Journal of Finance* 51 (September), pp. 1097–1137.

Tyebjee, Tyzoon T., and Albert V. Bruno. 1984. "A Model of Venture Capitalist Investment Activity." *Management Science* 30 (September), pp. 1051–1066.

Vermaelen, Theo. 1981. "Common Stock Repurchases and Market Signalling." *Journal of Financial Economics* 9 (June), pp. 139–183.

Vijh, Anand M. 1999. "Long-Term Returns from Equity Carve-Outs." *Journal of Financial Economics* 51 (February), pp. 273–308.

Vu, Joseph D. 1986. "An Examination of the Corporate Call Behavior of Nonconvertible Bonds." *Journal of Financial Economics* 16 (June), pp. 235–265.

Waldman, Michael. 1997. "Eliminating the Market for Secondhand Goods: An Alternative Explanation for Leasing." *Journal of Law and Economics* 40 (April), pp. 61–92.

Walker, Ernest W., and J. William Petty II. 1978. "Financial Differences between Large and Small Firms." *Financial Management* 7 (Winter), pp. 61–68.

Wansley, James, William Lane, and Ho Yang. 1983. "Abnormal Returns to Acquired Firms by Type of Acquisition and Method of Payment." *Financial Management* 12 (Autumn), pp. 16–22.

Warner, Jerold B. 1977. "Bankruptcy Costs: Some Evidence." *Journal of Finance* 32 (May), pp. 337–347.

Warren, Carl S., James M. Reeve, and Philip E. Fess.

2002. *Corporate Financial Accounting.* 7th ed. (Cincinnati, OH: Thomson South-Western).

Wassener, Bettina. 2002. "Tarnished Image in Need of Restoration." *Financial Times* Special Survey of Germany (June 12), p. 2.

Wedig, Gerard J., Mahmud Hassan, and Michael A. Morrisey. 1996. "Tax Exempt Debt and the Capital Structure of Nonprofit Organizations: An Application to Hospitals." *Journal of Finance* 51 (September), pp. 1247–1283.

Wei, Zhang, and Jiang Yanfu. 2002. "The Relationship between Venture Capitalists' Experience and Their Involvement in the VC-Backed Companies." Working paper, Tsinghua University (Beijing, China).

Welch, Ivo. 2000. "Herding among Security Analysts." *Journal of Financial Economics* 58, pp. 369–396.

———. 2001. "The Equity Premium Consensus Forecast Revisited." Working paper, Yale University.

Wermers, Russ. 2000. "Mutual Fund Performance: An Empirical Decomposition into Stock-Picking Talent, Style, Transactions Costs, and Expenses." *Journal of Finance* 55 (August), pp. 1655–1703.

Whited, Toni M. 2001. "Is It Inefficient Investment That Causes the Diversification Discount?" *Journal of Finance* 56 (October), pp. 1667–1691.

Williams, Frances. 2001. "Global Foreign Investment Flows 'Set to All by 40%.'" *Financial Times* (September 9), p. 9.

Williams, Joseph. 1988. "Efficient Signalling with Dividends, Investment, and Stock Repurchases." *Journal of Finance* 43 (July), pp. 737–747.

Womack, Kent L. 1996. "Do Brokerage Analysts' Recommendations Have Investment Value?" *Journal of Finance* 51 (March), pp. 137–166.

Wong, Andrew. 2001. "Angel Finance: The Other Venture Capital." Working paper, University of Chicago.

Wu, Chunchi. 1993. "Information Asymmetry and the Sinking Fund Provision." *Journal of Financial and Quantitative Analysis* 28 (September), pp. 399–416.

Yeoman, John C. 2001. "The Optimal Spread and Offering Price for Underwritten Securities." *Journal of Financial Economics* 62 (October), pp. 169–198.

Zingales, Luigi. 1994. "The Value of the Voting Right: A Study of the Milan Stock Exchange Experience." *Review of Financial Studies* 7, pp. 125–148.

FURTHER READING

Aggarwal, Reena, and Pat Conroy. 2000. "Price Discovery in Initial Public Offerings and the Role of the Lead Underwriter." *Journal of Finance* 55 (December), pp. 2903–2922.

Alderson, Michael J., and Brian L. Betker. 1999. "Assessing Post-Bankruptcy Performance: An Analysis of Reorganized Firms' Cash Flows." *Financial Management* 28 (Summer), pp. 68–82.

Allen, David S., Robert E. Lamy, and G. Rodney Thompson. 1990. "The Shelf Registration of Debt and Self Selection Bias." *Journal of Finance* 45 (March), pp. 275–287.

Altman, Edward I., and Pablo Arman. 2002. "Default and Returns on High Yield Bonds: Analysis through 2001." *Journal of Applied Finance* 12, pp. 98–112.

Ang, James S., Rebel A. Cole, and James Wuh Lin. 2000. "Agency Costs and Ownership Structure." *Journal of Finance* 55 (February), pp. 81–106.

Anstaett, Kurt W., Dennis P. McCrary, and Stephen T. Monahan, Jr. 1988. "Practical Debt Policy Considerations for Growth Companies: A Case Study Approach." *Journal of Applied Corporate Finance* 1 (Summer), pp. 71–78.

Asquith, Paul, and David W. Mullins, Jr. 1986. "Equity Issues and Offering Dilution." *Journal of Financial Economics* 15 (January/February), pp. 61–89.

Bagwell, Laurie Simon. 1991. "Share Repurchase and Takeover Deterrence." *Rand Journal of Economics* 22, pp. 72–88.

Baks, Klaas P., Andrew Metrick, and Jessica Wachter. 2001. "Should Investors Avoid All Actively Managed Mutual Funds? A Study in Bayesian Performance Evaluation." *Journal of Finance* 56 (February), pp. 45–85.

Ball, Ray, and S. P. Kothari. 1989. "Nonstationary Expected Returns: Implications for Tests of Market Efficiency and Serial Correlation in Returns." *Journal of Financial Economics* 25 (November), pp. 51–74.

Barber, Brad M., and John D. Lyon. 1997. "Detecting Long-Run Abnormal Stock Returns: The Empirical Power and Specification of Test Statistics." *Journal of Financial Economics* 43, 341–372.

Barberis, Nicholas. 2000. "Investing for the Long Run When Returns Are Predictable." *Journal of Finance* 55 (February), pp. 225–264.

Barclay, Michael J., and Clifford W. Smith, Jr. 1988. "Corporate Payout Policy: Cash Dividends versus Open Market Repurchases." *Journal of Financial Economics* 22 (October), pp. 61–82.

———. 1999. "The Capital Structure Puzzle: Another Look at the Evidence." *Journal of Applied Corporate Finance* 12 (Spring), pp. 8–20.

Barnish, Keith, Steve Miller, and Michael Rushmore. 1997. "The New Leveraged Loan Syndication Market." *Journal of Applied Corporate Finance* 10 (Spring), pp. 79–88.

Baron, David P. 1982. "A Model of the Demand for Investment Banking Advising and Distributions Services for New Issues." *Journal of Finance* 37 (September), pp. 955–976.

Baron, David P., and Bengt Holmstrom. 1980. "The Investment Banking Contract for New Issues under Asymmetric Information: Delegation and Incentive Problems." *Journal of Finance* 35 (December), pp. 1115–1138.

Barry, Christopher, Chris Muscarella, John Peavy, and Michael Vetsuypens. 1990. "The Role of Venture Capital in the Creation of Public Companies: Evidence from the Going Public Process." *Journal of Financial Economics* 27, pp. 447–471.

Barry, Christopher B., Chris J. Muscarella, and Michael R. Vetsuypens. 1991. "Underwriter Warrants, Underwriter Compensation, and the Costs of Going Public." *Journal of Financial Economics* 29, pp. 113–135.

Benveniste, Lawrence M., Walid Y. Busaba, and William J. Wilhelm, Jr. 1996. "Price Stabilization as a Bonding Mechanism in New Equity Issues." *Journal of Financial Economics* 42 (October), pp. 223–255.

Berens, James L., and Charles J. Cuny. 1995. "The Capital Structure Puzzle Revisited." *Review of Financial Studies* 8 (Winter), pp. 1185–1208.

Berger, Allen, and Gregory Udell. 1995. "Relationship Lending and Lines of Credit in Small Firm Finance. *Journal of Business* 68 (July), pp. 351–381.

Betker, Brian L. 1995. "Management's Incentives, Equity's Bargaining Power, and Deviations from Absolute Priority in Chapter 11 Bankruptcies." *Journal of Business* 68 (April), pp. 161–183.

Black, Bernard. 1992. "Agents Watching Agents." *UCLA Law Review* 39, pp. 811–893.

Black, Fischer. 1972. "Capital Market Equilibrium with Restricted Borrowing." *Journal of Business* 64 (July), pp. 444–455.

Blackwell, David W., and David S. Kidwell. 1988. "An Investigation of Cost Differences between Public Sales and Private Placements of Debt." *Journal of Financial Economics* 22 (December), pp. 253–278.

Blackwell, David W., M. Wayne Marr, and Michael F. Spivey. 1990. "Shelf Registration and the Reduced Due Diligence Argument: Implications of the Underwriter Certification and the Implicit Insurance Hypothesis." *Journal of Financial and Quantitative Analysis* 25 (June), pp. 245–259.

Blackwell, David, and Drew Winters. 1997. "Banking Relationships and the Effect of Monitoring on Loan Pricing." *Journal of Financial Research* 20 (Summer), pp. 275–289.

Blake, David, and Allan Timmerman. 1998. "Mutual Fund Performance: Evidence from the UK." *European Economic Review* 2, pp. 57–77.

Bohren, Øyvind, B. Espen Eckbo, and Dag Michalsen. 1997. "Why Underwrite Rights Offerings? Some New Evidence." *Journal of Financial Economics* 46, pp. 223–261.

Booth, James R., and Richard L. Smith, Jr. 1986. "Capital Raising, Underwriting and the Certification Hypothesis." *Journal of Financial Economics* 15 (January/February), pp. 261–281.

Bower, Nancy L. 1989. "Firm Value and the Choice of Offering Method in Initial Public Offerings." *Journal of Finance* 44 (July), pp. 647–662.

Brophy, David J., and Mark W. Guthner. 1988. "Publicly Traded Venture Capital Funds: Implications for Institutional 'Fund of Funds' Investors." *Journal of Business Venturing* 3 (Summer), pp. 187–206.

Brous, Peter A., Vinay Datar, and Omesh Kini. 2001. "Is the Market Optimistic about the Future Earnings of Seasoned Equity Offering Firms?" *Journal of Financial and Quantitative Analysis* 36 (June), pp. 141–168.

Carter, Richard B., Frederick H. Dark, and Ajai K. Singh. 1998. "Underwriter Reputation, Initial Returns, and the Long-Run Performance of IPO Stocks." *Journal of Finance* 53, pp. 285–311.

Chan, Louis K. C., Narasimhan Jegadeesh, and Josef Lakonishok. 1995. "Evaluating the Performance of Value versus Glamour Stocks: The Impact of Selection Bias." *Journal of Financial Economics* 38 (July), pp. 269–296.

Chemmanur, Thomas J., and Paolo Fulghieri. 1994. "Reputation, Renegotiation, and the Choice between Bank Loans and Publicly Traded Debt." *Review of Financial Studies* 7 (Fall), pp. 475–506.

Chirinko, Robert S., and Anua R. Singha. 2000. "Testing Static Trade-off against Pecking Order Models of Capital Structure: A Critical Comment." *Journal of Financial Economics* 58, pp. 417–425.

Cleary, Sean. 1999. "The Relationship between Firm Investment and Financial Status." *Journal of Finance* 54 (April), pp. 673–692.

Cornell, Bradford, and Alan C. Shapiro. 1988. "Financing Corporate Growth." *Journal of Applied Corporate Finance* 1 (Summer), pp. 6–22.

Cornell, Bradford, and Erik R. Sirri. 1992. "The Reaction of Investors and Stock Prices to Insider Trading." *Journal of Finance* 47 (July), pp. 1031–1060.

Corwin, Shane A., and Jeffrey H. Harris. 2001. "The Initial Listing Decisions of Firms That Go Public." *Financial Management* 30 (Spring), pp. 35–55.

Daniel, Kent, and Sheridan Titman. 1997. "Evidence on the Characteristics of Cross Sectional Variation in Stock Returns." *Journal of Finance* 52 (March), pp. 1–33.

Davidson, Wallace N., III, and Dipa Dutia. 1991. "Debt, Liquidity, and Profitability in Small Firms." *Entrepreneurship Theory and Practice* (Fall), pp. 53–64.

Dechow, Patricia M., and Richard G. Sloan. 1997. "Returns to Contrarian Investment Strategies: Tests of Naive Expectations Hypotheses." *Journal of Financial Economics* 43 (January), pp. 3–27.

DeLong, Bradford, Andrei Shleifer, Lawrence H. Summers, and Robert J. Waldmann. 1990. "Positive Feedback Investment Strategies and Destabilizing Rational Speculation." *Journal of Finance* 45 (June), pp. 379–395.

Diamond, Douglas. 1989. "Reputation Acquisition in Debt Markets." *Journal of Political Economy* 97, pp. 828–862.

Downes, David H., and Robert Heinkel. 1982. "Signaling and the Valuation of Unseasoned New Issues." *Journal of Finance* 37, pp. 1–10.

D'Souza, Julia, and John Jacob. 2000. "Why Firms Issue Targeted Stock." *Journal of Financial Economics* 56 (June), pp. 459–483.

Dunbar, Craig G. 2000. "Factors Affecting Investment Bank Initial Public Offering Market Share." *Journal of Financial Economics* 55, pp. 3–41.

Dyl, Edward A. 1977. "Another Look at the Evaluation of Investment in Accounts Receivable." *Financial Management* 6 (4), pp. 67–70.

Eberhart, Allan C., William T. Moore, and Reena Aggarwal. 1999. "The Equity Performance of Firms Emerging from Bankruptcy." *Journal of Finance* 54 (October), pp. 1855–1868.

Eberhart, Allan C., William T. Moore, and Rodney L. Roenfeldt. 1990. "Security Pricing and Deviations from the Absolute Priority Rule in Bankruptcy Proceedings." *Journal of Finance* 45 (December), pp. 1457–1469.

Fama, Eugene F., and Kenneth R. French. 1988. "Permanent and Temporary Components of Stock Prices." *Journal of Political Economy* 96 (April), pp. 246–273.

———. 1989. "Business Conditions and Expected Returns on Stocks and Bonds." *Journal of Financial Economics* 25 (November), pp. 23–49.

———. 1992. "The Cross-Section of Expected Stock Returns." *Journal of Finance* 47 (June), pp. 427–465.

———. 1995. "Size and Book-to-Market Factors in Earnings and Returns." *Journal of Finance* 50 (March), pp. 131–155.

———. 1996. "Multifactor Explanations of Asset Pricing Anomalies." *Journal of Finance* 51 (March), pp. 55–84.

———. 1997. "Industry Costs of Equity." *Journal of Financial Economics* 43 (February), pp. 153–193.

Fenn, George W. 2000. "Speed of Issuance and the Adequacy of Disclosure in the 144A High-Yield Debt Market." *Journal of Financial Economics* 56 (June), pp. 383–405.

Field, Laura Casares, and Gordon Hanka. 2001. "The Expiration of IPO Share Lock-Ups." *Journal of Finance* 56 (April), pp. 471–500.

Fraser, Jill Andresky. 1998. "How to Finance Anything." *Inc.* (February), pp. 34–42.

Froot, Kenneth A., David S. Scharfstein, and Jeremy C. Stein. 1993. "Risk Management: Coordinating Corporate Investment and Financing Policies." *Journal of Finance* 48 (December), pp. 1629–1658.

Gande, Amar, Manju Puri, and Anthony Saunders. 1999. "Bank Entry, Competition and the Market for Corporate Securities Underwriting." *Journal of Financial Economics* 54, pp. 165–195.

Garvey, Gerald T., and Gordon Hanka. 1999. "Capital Structure and Corporate Control: The Effect of Antitakeover Statutes on Firm Leverage." *Journal of Finance* 54 (April), pp. 519–546.

Gilson, Stuart C., Edith S. Hotchkiss, and Richard S. Ruback. 2000. "Valuation of Bankrupt Firms." *Review of Financial Studies* 13 (Spring), pp. 43–74.

Gitman, Lawrence J., and Kanwal S. Sachdeva. 1981. "Accounts Receivable Decisions in a Capital Budgeting Framework." *Financial Management* 10, pp. 45–49.

Gompers, Paul, and Josh Lerner. 1996. "The Use of Covenants: An Empirical Analysis of Venture Partnership Agreements." *Journal of Law and Economics* 39 (October), pp. 463–498.

———. 1999. "An Analysis of Compensation in the U.S. Venture Capital Partnership." *Journal of Financial Economics* 51 (January), pp. 3–44.

Graham, John R. 2001. "Estimating the Tax Benefits of Debt." *Journal of Applied Corporate Finance* 14 (Spring), pp. 42–54.

Graham, John R., and Clifford W. Smith, Jr. 1999. "Tax Incentives to Hedge." *Journal of Finance* 54 (December), pp. 2241–2262.

Gul, Ferdinand A. 1999. "Growth Opportunities, Capital Structure and Dividend Policies in Japan." *Journal of Corporate Finance* 5 (June), pp. 141–168.

Habib, Michel A., and Alexander P. Ljungqvist. 2001. "Underpricing and Entrepreneurial Wealth Losses in IPOs: Theory and Evidence." *Review of Financial Studies* 14 (Summer), pp. 433–458.

Hampson, Philip, John Parsons, and Charles Blitzer. 1991. "A Case Study in the Design of an Optimal Sharing Rule for a Petroleum Exploration Venture." *Journal of Financial Economics* 30 (November), pp. 45–67.

Hanley, Kathleen W., A. Arun Kumar, and Paul J. Seguin. 1993. "Price Stabilization in the Market for New Issues." *Journal of Financial Economics* 34 (October), pp. 177–197.

Hardymon, G. Felda, Mark J. DeNino, and Malcolm S. Salter. 1983. "When Corporate Venture Capital Doesn't Work." *Harvard Business Review* (May/June), pp. 114–120.

Hellmann, Thomas, and Manju Puri. 2000. "The Interaction between Product Market and Financing Strategy: The Role of Venture Capital." *Review of Financial Studies* 13 (Winter), pp. 959–984.

Hertzel, Michael, and Richard L. Smith. 1993. "Market Discounts and Shareholder Gains for Placing Equity Privately." *Journal of Finance* 48 (June), pp. 459–485.

Higgins, Robert C. 1977. "How Much Growth Can a Firm Afford?" *Financial Management* 6, pp. 7–16.

Hirschey, Mark, Vernon J. Richardson, and Susan Scholz. 2000. "Stock-Price Effects of Internet Buy-Sell Recommendations: *The Motley Fool* Case." *Financial Review* 35 (May), pp. 147–174.

Hirshleifer, David, Avanidhar Subrahmanyam, and Sheridan Titman. 1994. "Security Analysis and Trading Patterns When Some Investors Receive Information before Others." *Journal of Finance* 49 (December), pp. 1665–1698.

Huemer, Jason. 1992. "Public Venture Capital: Huge Market Goes Largely Untapped." *Venture Capital Journal* (February), pp. 38–44.

Hughes, Patricia J. 1986. "Signalling by Direct Disclosure under Asymmetric Information." *Journal of Accounting and Economics* 8 (June), pp. 119–142.

Indro, Daniel C., Robert T. Leach, and Wayne Y. Lee. 1999. "Sources of Gains to Shareholders from Bankruptcy Resolution." *Journal of Banking and Finance* 23 (January), pp. 21–47.

Ingersoll, Jonathan E., Jr., and Stephen A. Ross. 1992. "Waiting to Invest: Investment and Uncertainty." *Journal of Business* 65 (March), pp. 1–29.

Jain, Bharat A., and Omesh Kini. 1994. "The Post-Issue Operating Performance of IPO Firms." *Journal of Finance* 49 (December), pp. 1699–1726.

Jensen, Michael C. 1978. "Some Anomalous Evidence regarding Market Efficiency." *Journal of Financial Economics* 6 (June/September), pp. 95–101.

Johnson, Greg. 2000. "Yankee Bonds and Cross-Border Private Placements: An Update." *Journal of Applied Corporate Finance* 13 (Fall), pp. 80–91.

Kaplan, Steven, and Per Strömberg. 2001. "Venture Capitalists as Principals: Contracting, Screening, and Monitoring." *American Economic Review* 91 (May), pp. 426–430.

Kaplan, Steven N., and Luigi Zingales. 1997. "Do Financing Constraints Explain Why Investment Is Correlated with Cash Flow?" *Quarterly Journal of Economics* 112, pp. 169–215.

Khorana, Ajay. 1996. "Top Management Turnover: An Empirical Investigation of Mutual Fund Managers." *Journal of Financial Economics* 40 (March), pp. 403–427.

Koch, Paul D., and Catherine Shenoy. 1999. "The Information Content of Dividend and Capital Structure Policies." *Financial Management* 28 (Winter), pp. 16–35.

Kothari, S. P., and Jerold B. Warner. 1997. "Measuring Long-Horizon Security Price Performance." *Journal of Financial Economics* 43, pp. 301–340.

Krigman, Laurie, Wayne H. Shaw, and Kent L. Womack. 2001. "Why Do Firms Switch Underwriters?" *Journal of Financial Economics* 60 (May/June), pp. 245–284.

Lamont, Owen. 1997. "Cash Flow and Investment: Evidence from Internal Capital Markets." *Journal of Finance* (February), pp. 83–109.

Lee, Cheng-Few, and Shafiqur Rahman. 1990. "Market Timing, Selectivity, and Mutual Fund Performance: An Empirical Analysis." *Journal of Business* 63 (April), pp. 261–278.

Lee, Peggy M., and Sunil Wahal. 2002. "Venture Capital, Certification and IPOs." Working paper, Emory University.

Lerner, Josh. 1994. "The Syndication of Venture Capital Investments." *Financial Management* 23 (Autumn), pp. 16–27.

Lorie, James H., and Leonard J. Savage. 1955. "Three Problems in Rationing Capital." *Journal of Business* 28 (October), pp. 229–239.

Majd, Saman, and Robert S. Pindyck. 1987. "Time to Build, Option Value and Investment Decisions." *Journal of Financial Economics* 18 (March), pp. 7–28.

Mandelker, Gershon, and Artur Raviv. 1977. "Investment Banking: An Economic Analysis of Optimal Underwriting Contracts." *Journal of Finance* 32 (June), pp. 683–694.

Martin, John D., and J. William Petty. 1983. "An Analysis of the Performance of Publicly Traded Venture Capital Companies." *Journal of Financial and Quantitative Analysis* 18 (September), pp. 401–410.

Masson, Dubos J., ed. 2001. *Essentials of Cash Management*. 7th ed. Bethesda, MD: Association for Financial Professionals.

Masulis, Ronald W., and Ashok N. Korwar. 1986. "Seasoned Equity Offerings: An Empirical Investigation." *Journal of Financial Economics* 15 (January/February), pp. 91–118.

Miffre, Joëlle. 2001. "Efficiency in the Pricing of the FTSE 100 Futures Contract." *European Financial Management* 7, pp. 9–22.

Mikkelson, Wayne H., M. Megan Partch, and Kshitij Shah. 1997. "Ownership and Operating Performance of Companies That Go Public." *Journal of Financial Economics* 44, pp. 281–307.

Mukherjee, Tarun K. 1991. "A Survey of Corporate Leasing Analysis." *Financial Management* 20 (Autumn), pp. 96–107.

Obstfeld, Maurice, and Kenneth Rogoff. 2001. "The Six Major Puzzles in International Macroeconomics: Is There a Common Cause?" In *NBER Macroeconomics Annual 2000,* edited by Ben Bernanke and Kenneth Rogoff, pp. 339–390 (Cambridge, Mass.: MIT Press).

Parrino, Robert, and Michael Weisbach. 1999. "Measuring Investment Distortions Arising from Stockholder-Bondholder Conflicts." *Journal of Financial Economics* 53 (July), pp. 3–42.

Petersen, Mitchell A., and Raghuram G. Rajan. 1994. "The Benefits of Lending Relationships: Evidence from Small Business Data." *Journal of Finance* 49 (March), pp. 3–37.

Pettit, Richard, and Ronald Singer. 1985. "Small Business Finance: A Research Agenda." *Financial Management* 14 (Spring), pp. 47–60.

Peyer, Urs, and Anil Shivdasani. 2001. "Leverage and Internal Capital Markets: Evidence from Leveraged Recapitalizations." *Journal of Financial Economics* 59 (March), pp. 477–515.

Pratt, Stanley E. 1988. "The Organized Venture Capital Community." In *Pratt's Guide to Venture Capital Sources,* edited by Stanley E. Pratt (New York: Securities Data Publishing), pp. 55–61.

Puri, Manju. 1999. "Commercial Banks as Underwriters: Implications for the Going Public Process." *Journal of Financial Economics* 54, pp. 133–163.

Rajan, Raghuram, and Mitchell Petersen. "Trade Credit: Some Theories and Evidence." *Review of Financial Studies* 10 (1997), pp. 661–692.

Rau, P. Raghavendra. 2000. "Investment Bank Market Share, Contingent Fee Payments, and the Performance of Acquiring Firms." *Journal of Financial Economics* 56 (May), pp. 293–324.

Ravid, S. Abraham, and Stefan Sundgren. 1998. "The Comparative Efficiency of Small-Firm Bankruptcies: A Study of the US and Finnish bankruptcy Codes." *Financial Management* 27 (Winter), pp. 28–40.

Reese, William A., Jr. 1998. "Capital Gains Taxation and Stock Market Activity: Evidence from IPOs." *Journal of Finance* 53 (October), pp. 1799–1819.

Rodriguez, Ricardo. 1988. "The Wealth Maximization Ordering Quantity: An Extension." *Financial Review* 23 (May), pp. 227–232.

Rubinstein, Mark E. 1973. "A Mean-Variance Synthesis of Corporate Financial Policy." *Journal of Finance* 28 (March), pp. 167–181.

Safieddine, Assem, and Sheridan Titman. 1999. "Leverage and Corporate Performance: Evidence from Unsuccessful Takeovers." *Journal of Finance* 54 (April), pp. 547–580.

Samuelson, Paul A. 1965. "Proof That Properly Anticipated Prices Fluctuate Randomly." *Industrial Management Review* 6 (Spring), pp. 41–49.

Scherr, Frederick C. "Optimal Trade Credit Limits." *Financial Management* 25 (1996), pp. 71–85.

Schultz, Paul H., and Mir A. Zaman. 1994. "Aftermarket Support and the Underpricing of Initial Public Offerings." *Journal of Financial Economics* 35 (April), pp. 199–219.

Shapiro, Alan C,. and Sheridan Titman. 1986. "An Integrated Approach to Corporate Risk Management."

In *The Revolution in Corporate Finance*, edited by Joel Stern and Donald Chew (Oxford and Cambridge, Mass.: Basil Blackwell).

Sherman, Ann Geunther. 1992. "The Pricing of Best Efforts New Issues." *Journal of Finance* 47 (June), pp. 781–790.

Sirri, Erik R., and Peter Tufano. 1998. "Costly Search and Mutual Fund Flows." *Journal of Finance* 53 (October), pp. 1589–1622.

Slovin, Myron B., Marie E. Sushka, and K. W. L. Lai. 2000. "Alternative Flotation Methods, Adverse Selection, and Ownership Structure: Evidence from Seasoned Equity Issuance in the U.K." *Journal of Financial Economics* 57 (August), pp. 157–190.

Smith, Clifford W., Jr., and René M. Stulz. 1985. "The Determinants of Firms' Hedging Policies." *Journal of Financial and Quantitative Analysis* 20 (December), pp. 391–405.

Smith, Janet Kiholm. "Trade Credit and Informational Asymmetry." *Journal of Finance* 42 (September 1987), pp. 863–872.

Sneddon, Gregory B., and Jay K. Turner. 1997. "Nontraditional Financing Sources." In *Pratt's Guide to Venture Capital Sources,* edited by Stanley E. Pratt (New York: Venture Economics), pp. 91–96.

Srinivasan, Venkat, Yong H. Kim, and R. A. Eisenbeis. "Credit Granting: A Comparative Analysis of Classification Procedures." *Journal of Finance* 42 (July 1987), pp. 665–681.

Stulz, René M. 1984. "Optimal Hedging Policies." *Journal of Financial and Quantitative Analysis* 19 (June), pp. 127–140.

Vuolteenaho, Tuomo. 2002. "What Drives Firm-Level Stock Returns?" *Journal of Finance* 57 (April), pp. 233–264.

Wakita, Shigeru. 2001. "Efficiency of the Dojima Rice Future Market in Tokugawa-Period Japan." *Journal of Banking and Finance* 25 (March), pp. 535–554.

Weiss, Lawrence A. 1990. "Bankruptcy Resolution: Direct Costs and Violations of Absolute Priority of Claims." *Journal of Financial Economics* 27 (October), pp. 285–314.

Welch, Ivo. 1991. "An Empirical Examination of Models of Contract Choice in Initial Public Offerings." *Journal of Financial and Quantitative Analysis* 26 (December), pp. 497–518.

Whited, Toni M. 1992. "Debt, Liquidity Constraints and Corporate Investment: Evidence from Panel Data." *Journal of Finance* 47 (September), pp. 1425–1460.

Zingales, Luigi. 1998. "Survival of the Fittest or the Fattest? Exit and Financing in the Trucking Industry." *Journal of Finance* 53 (June), pp. 905–938.

GLOSSARY

A

absolute priority rules Rules contained in Chapter 7 of the Bankruptcy Reform Act of 1978 that specify the procedure by which secured creditors are paid first, then unsecured creditors, then preferred shareholders, and finally common stockholders.

accounting rate of return Calculation of a hurdle rate by dividing net income by the book value of assets, either on a year-by-year basis or by taking an average over the project's life.

accredited investors Individuals or institutions that meet certain income and wealth requirements.

accrual-based approach Revenues are recorded at the point of sale and costs when they are incurred, not necessarily when a firm receives or pays out cash.

acquisition The purchase of additional resources by a business enterprise.

activity ratio A measure of the speed with which various accounts are converted into sales or cash.

additional paid-in capital Capital in excess of par value.

additional profit contribution from sales The marginal increase in profits, computed as the increased unit sales volume times the contribution margin per unit sold.

adjustable rate preferred stock A corporate obligation used for short-term investments, These stocks take advantage of the dividend exclusion (of 70 percent or more) for stock in one corporation held by another corporation. In order to make this investment suitable for short-term holdings, the dividend rate paid on the stock is adjusted according to some rate index. This will stabilize the price, even if interest rates

change during the 45-day holding period required to qualify for the dividend exclusion.

agency cost theory of financial structure Michael Jensen and William Meckling (1976) observe that when an entrepreneur owns 100 percent of the stock of a company, there is no separation between corporate ownership and control; the entrepreneur bears all the costs, and reaps all the benefits, of her or his actions.

agency cost/contracting model of dividends A theoretical model that explains empirical regularities in dividend payment and share repurchase patterns.

agency costs The costs that arise due to conflicts of interest between shareholders and managers.

agency costs of debt Costs that must be weighed against the benefits of leverage in reducing the agency costs of outside equity.

agency costs of (outside) equity In an efficient market, informed investors only pay a price per share that fully reflects the perks an entrepreneur is expected to consume after the equity sale, so the entrepreneur bears the full costs of her or his actions.

agency problems The conflict between the goals of a firm's owners and managers.

aggressive strategy When a company relies heavily on short-term borrowing, not only to meet the seasonal peaks each year but also to finance a portion of the long-term growth in sales and assets.

aging of accounts receivable A schedule that indicates the portions of the total accounts receivable balance that have been outstanding for specified periods of time.

all-in rate The base rate and the spread.

allocative efficiency Markets channeling resources to their most productive uses.

American call option Gives holders the right to purchase stock at a fixed price on or before the expiration date.

American Depositary Receipts (ADRs) Dollar-denominated claims, issued by U.S. banks, that represent ownership of shares of a foreign company's stock held on deposit by the U.S. bank in the issuing firm's home country.

angel capitalists Wealthy individuals who make private equity investments on an ad hoc basis.

announcement date The day a firm releases the dividend record and payment dates to the public.

annual cash flow savings The difference between the annual after-tax debt payments for old and new bonds.

annual percentage rate The stated annual rate calculated by multiplying the periodic rate by the number of periods in one year.

annual percentage yield The annual rate of interest actually earned reflecting the impact of compounding frequency.

annuity A stream of equal periodic (frequently annual) cash flows over a stated period of time.

annuity due An annuity for which the payments occur at the beginning of each period.

antitakeover amendments Adding defensive measures to corporate charters to avoid a hostile takeover.

antitrust Legislation intended to prevent mergers that are deemed to have anticompetitive effects on the business environment.

appreciated The condition of a currency that has increased in value compared to another currency.

arbitrage The process of buying something in one market at a low price and simultaneously selling it in another market at a higher price to generate an immediate, risk-free profit.

arbitrage pricing theory Begins with the notion that financial markets are frictionless, so that investors can buy or sell short any of a large number of assets that trade in this market.

arbitrageurs Traders who seek to exploit small pricing differences by purchasing an asset when it is undervalued and reselling it when it is overvalued.

arithmetic average return The average annual return over a period of years.

asset beta A measure of the systematic risk of a real asset based on the covariance of the cash flows generated by that asset divided by the variance of cash flows from the market portfolio.

asset market model of exchange rates This model makes a distinction between the demand for a currency as a means of payment (transactions demand) and the demand for currency as a financial asset (as a store of value).

asset substitution An investment that will increase firm value but does not earn a return high enough to fully redeem the maturing bonds.

assets-to-equity A measurement of the proportion of total assets financed by a firm's equity.

assignment An agreement of the creditors by which they pass the power to liquidate the firm's assets to an adjustment bureau, a trade association, or a third party.

at the money Occurs when an option's stock price and strike price are equal.

atomistic Descriptive of capital markets grown large because of investors willing to accept small ownership and creditor positions in public companies.

automated clearinghouse (ACH) debit transfer A preauthorized electronic withdrawal from the payer's account.

availability float The time between deposit of a check and availability of the funds to a firm.

average age of inventory A measure of inventory turnover, calculated by dividing the turnover figure into 365, the number of days in a year.

average collection period The average length of time from a sale on credit until the payment becomes usable funds for a firm. Also called the *average age of accounts receivable.*

average payment period Calculated by dividing the firm's accounts payable balance by its average daily purchases. Also called the *average payment period.*

B

backward integration A merger in which the acquired company provides an earlier step in the production process.

bait and switch To make an unscrupulous promise to accept a safe project but then accept a risky project after securing low-cost financing.

balloon payment A term loan agreement that requires periodic interest payments over the life of the loan followed by a large lump-sum payment at maturity.

bank account analysis statement A regular report (usually monthly) provided to a bank's commercial customers that specifies all services provided, including items processed and any charges assessed.

bankruptcy Occurs only when a company enters bankruptcy court and effectively surrenders control of the firm to a bankruptcy judge.

bankruptcy costs The direct and indirect costs of the bankruptcy process.

Bankruptcy Reform Act of 1978 The governing bankruptcy legislation in the United States today.

basis risk The possibility of unanticipated changes in the difference between the futures price and the spot price.

bear hug The potential acquirer approaches the target with both a merger offer and the threat of a proxy fight and/or hostile tender offer to gain the remaining shares needed to obtain voting control of the target if the merger offer is refused.

bearer bond Bonds that both shelter investment income from taxation and provide protection against exchange rate risk.

behavioral finance Asserts that because traders in financial markets are human beings, they are subject to all the foibles and fads that bedevil human judgment in other spheres of life.

best-effort Sells equity without making any guarantee about the ultimate success of the offering. The bank promises to give its best effort to sell the firm's securities at the agreed-upon price; but if there is insufficient demand for the issue, then the firm withdraws the issue from the market.

beta A standardized measure of the risk of an individual asset, one that captures only the systematic component of its volatility.

biased self-attribution Investors with this trait will interpret the arrival of new private information supporting their existing beliefs as important confirmatory evidence, but will tend to disregard contradictory new evidence as being random noise.

binomial option-pricing model This model recognizes that investors can combine options (either calls or puts) with shares of the underlying asset to construct a portfolio with a risk-free payoff.

Black and Scholes option-pricing equation A stochastic differential equation relating the time to expiration and the strike price of an option, the current price and the volatility of its underlying stock, and the risk-free interest rate.

board of directors Elected by shareholders to be responsible for hiring and firing managers and setting overall corporate policies.

bond equivalent yield The percentage return on zero-coupon bonds calculated as the difference between the par value and the purchase price.

bond ratings Grades assigned based on degree of risk.

bonding mechanism Shareholders are willing to pay a higher price for a firm's shares, because taking on debt validates a manager's willingness to risk losing control of her firm if she fails to perform effectively.

bonds Debt with original maturities of more than seven years.

book building A process in which underwriters ask prospective investors to reveal information about their demand for the offering. Through conversations with investors, the underwriter tries to measure the demand curve for a given issue, and the investment bank sets the offer price after gathering all the information it can from investors.

bottom-up This kind of sales forecast relies on the assessment by sales personnel of demand in the coming year on a customer-by-customer basis.

break-even analysis The study of what is required for a project's profits and losses to balance out.

bulge bracket Consists of firms that generally occupy the lead or co-lead manager's position in large, new security offerings, meaning that they take primary responsibility for the new offering (even though other banks participate as part of a syndicate), and as a result they earn higher fees.

business failure The unfortunate circumstance of a firm's inability to stay in business.

Business Judgment Rule A legal doctrine giving directors broad legal discretion to use their business judgment and protecting boards of directors from shareholder second-guessing in all but obvious cases of abuse.

bust-up The takeover of a company that is subsequently split up.

call option Grants the right to purchase a share of stock (or some other asset) at a fixed price on or before a certain date.

call premium The amount by which the call price exceeds the par value of a bond. Paid by corporations to call bonds after a protection period ends.

callable Bonds that the issuing corporation has the right to force investors to sell back to the firm at the firm's discretion.

cancellation option Option to deny or delay additional funding for a venture fund.

cannibalization Loss of sales of an existing product when a new product is introduced.

capital asset pricing model States that the expected return on a specific asset equals the risk-free rate plus a premium that depends on the asset's beta and the expected risk premium on the market portfolio.

capital budgeting The process of identifying which long-lived investment projects a firm should undertake.

capital budgeting function Selecting the best projects in which to invest the resources of the firm, based on each project's perceived risk and expected return.

capital investment Investments in long-lived assets such as plant, equipment, and advertising.

capital lease A noncancelable contractual arrangement whereby the lessee agrees to make periodic payments to the lessor, typically for more than five years, to obtain an asset's services.

capital market line Under the assumption of homogeneous expectations, the line connecting the market portfolio to the risk-free rate, which quantifies the relationship between the expected return and standard deviation for portfolios consisting of the risk-free asset and the market portfolio.

capital rationing Choosing a combination of projects that maximizes shareholder wealth, given a set of attractive investment opportunities and subject to the constraint of limited funds.

capital spending Investments in long-lived assets such as plant, equipment, and advertising.

capital structure decision Distributing the financial claims on the firm between debt and equity securities in order to maximize the market value of a firm.

capitalizing Predicting what the firm's cash flows will be over time and then determining the present value of that stream today.

card programs Implemented by companies as means of reducing the cost of low-dollar indirect purchases by using credit cards.

cash application The process through which a customer's payment is posted to its account and the outstanding invoices are cleared as paid.

cash budget A statement of a firm's planned inflows and outflows of cash.

cash concentration The process of bringing the lockbox and other deposits together into one bank, often called the *concentration bank*.

cash conversion cycle The elapsed time between the points at which a firm pays for raw materials and at which it receives payment for finished goods.

cash disbursements These include all outlays of cash by a firm in a given period.

cash discount A method of lowering investment in accounts receivable by rewarding prompt payment.

cash flow approach Used by financial professionals to focus attention on current and prospective inflows and outflows of cash.

cash flow from operations Cash inflows and outflows directly related to the production and sale of a firm's products or services. Calculated as net income plus depreciation and other noncash charges.

cash position management The collection, concentration, and disbursement of funds for the company.

cash receipts These include all of a firm's cash inflows in a given period.

cash settlement Investor sale of an option for cash eliminates the need for the seller to buy shares to give to the buyer, together with the need for the buyer to sell shares if he wants to convert his profit into cash.

cash-out statutes Antitrust "all-or-none" rules that disallow a partial tender offer/acquisition of a company and the ability to control that company with less than 100 percent ownership.

certification Assurance that the issuing company is in fact disclosing all material information.

Chapter 7 Section of the Bankruptcy Reform Act of 1978 that details the procedures to be followed when liquidating a failed firm.

Chapter 11 Section of the Bankruptcy Reform Act of 1978 that outlines the procedures for reorganizing a failed or failing firm, whether its petition is filed voluntarily or involuntarily.

chartists Practitioners of technical analysis.

chief executive officer (CEO) Hired by the board of directors to be responsible for managing day-to-day operations and carrying out the policies established by the board.

clearing float The time between deposit of the check and presentation of the check back to the bank on which it is drawn.

closing futures price The price used to settle all contracts at the end of each day's trading.

coinsurance of debt The debt of each combining firm in a merger is insured with cash flows from two businesses.

cold comfort letter A simple statement that a company's financial statements were prepared according to generally accepted accounting principles and accurately reflect all relevant information.

collateral The specific assets pledged to secure a loan.

collateral trust bonds A secured type of bond.

collective action problem When an individual stockholder expends time and resources monitoring managers, bearing the costs of monitoring management while the benefit of his or her activities accrues to all shareholders.

co-managers Banks other than the lead underwriter when a firm enlists the services of more than one investment bank.

commercial paper The primary corporate obligation in the short-term market. Typically structured as an unsecured promissory note with a maturity of less than 270 days and sold to other corporations and individual investors. Most issues are also backed by credit guarantees from a financial institution, are sold on a discount basis, and are held to maturity.

common stock Stockholder's equity.

competitively bid offer The less common approach firms can take in choosing an investment banker: The firm announces the terms of its intended equity sale, and investment banks bid for the business.

composition A pro rata cash settlement of creditor claims.

compound interest Interest earned both on the principal amount and on the interest earned in previous periods.

conservative strategy When a company makes sure that it has enough long-term financing to cover its permanent investments in fixed and current assets as well as the additional investments in current assets that it makes during the third and fourth quarters each year.

consolidation A merger in which both the acquirer and target disappear as separate corporations, combining to form an entirely new corporation with new common stock.

constant growth model Assumes that dividends will grow at a constant rate forever, when calculating the value of a cash flow stream by using the formula for a growing perpetuity.

constant nominal payment policy Based on the payment of a fixed-dollar dividend in each period.

constant payout ratio dividend policy Used by a firm to establish that a certain percentage of earnings is paid to owners in each dividend period.

continuous compounding Interest compounds at literally every moment as time passes.

contribution margin The sale price per unit minus variable cost per unit.

controlled disbursement A bank service that provides early notification of checks that will be presented against a company's account on a given day.

conversion premium Price to which shares would have to rise before bondholders would want to convert their bonds into shares.

conversion ratio Defines how many shares bondholders will receive if they convert.

conversion value The value bondholders receive if they do convert. Conversion value is important because it helps define a lower bound on the market value of a convertible bond.

convertible Corporate bonds that grant an investor the right to exchange the bonds for shares of stock rather than cash.

convertible bond The investor is granted the right to receive payment in shares of an underlying stock rather than in cash.

corporate charter The legal document created at the corporation's inception to govern its operations.

corporate control The monitoring, supervision, and direction of a corporation or other business organization.

corporate finance The science of managing money in a business environment.

corporate focus A focused firm concentrates its efforts on its core (primary) business; the opposite end of the spectrum from a diversified firm.

corporate governance The system that encompasses a nation's body of commercial law, including the institutions, regulations, and practices that influence how, and in whose interest, managers run companies.

corporate governance function Developing an ownership and corporate governance structure for the company which ensures that the managers act ethically and in the interests of the firm's stakeholders, particularly its stockholders.

corporate insider A commercial bank or other financial institution trusted with confidential information concerning a borrowing firm's operations and opportunities.

corporate venture capital funds Subsidiaries or stand-alone firms established by nonfinancial corporations eager to gain access to emerging technologies by making early-stage investments in high-tech firms.

corporation In U.S. law, a separate legal entity with many of the economic rights and responsibilities enjoyed by individuals.

correlation coefficient A unit-free measure of the co-movement of two assets that standardizes the covariance measure by dividing it by the product of the standard deviations of each asset.

cost of marginal bad debt expense Calculated by subtracting the current level of bad debt expense from the expected level of bad debt expense under the proposed new credit standards.

cost of marginal investment in accounts receivable The marginal investment in accounts receivable required to support a proposed change in credit standards multiplied by the required return on investment.

counterparty risk The risk that the counterparty on specific trade will default on its obligation.

coupon A fixed amount of interest that a bond promises to pay investors.

coupon rate The rate derived by dividing the bond's annual coupon payment by its par value.

coupon yield The amount obtained by dividing the bond's coupon by its current market price (which does not always equal its par value).

covariance A statistical concept that provides a way of measuring the co-movements of two random variables.

coverage ratio A debt ratio that focuses more on income statement measures of a firm's ability to generate sufficient cash flow to make scheduled interest and principal payments.

covered interest arbitrage Occurs when traders attempt to earn arbitrage profits arising from differences in interest rates across countries and "cover" their currency exposures with forward contracts.

cramdown procedure Used when a reorganization plan fails to meet the standard for approval by all classes, but at least one class of creditors has voted for a reorganization plan; or when the firm is clearly insolvent and the existing equity has no value.

credit monitoring The ongoing review of a firm's accounts receivable to determine if customers are paying according to the stated credit terms.

credit scoring Applies statistically derived weights for key financial and credit characteristics to predict whether or not a credit applicant with specific scores for each characteristic will pay the requested credit in a timely fashion.

credit terms The terms of sale for customers.

creditor control The creditor committee takes control of the firm and operates it until all claims have been settled.

cross exchange rate Calculated by dividing the dollar exchange rate for one currency by the dollar exchange rate for another currency.

cross-default covenant In which the borrower is often

considered to be in default on all debts if it is in default on any debt.

cross-hedging The underlying securities in a futures contract and the assets being hedged have different characteristics.

cumulative voting system System that gives to each share of common stock a number of votes equal to the total number of directors to be elected.

currency board arrangement In this arrangement, the national currency continues to circulate, but every unit of the currency is fully backed by government holdings of another currency—usually the U.S. dollar.

currency forward contract Exchange of one currency for another at a fixed date in the future.

currency swap A swap contract in which two parties exchange payment obligations denominated in different currencies.

current ratio A measure of a firm's ability to meet its short-term obligations, defined as current assets divided by current liabilities.

date of record The date on which the names of all persons who own shares in a company are recorded as stockholders and thus eligible to receive a dividend.

debentures Unsecured bonds backed only by the general faith and credit of the borrowing company.

debt Borrowed money.

debt beta A measure of the systematic risk of a real debt based on the covariance between return on debt and returns on a diversified portfolio of securities.

debt overhang A situation of financial distress in which a profitable investment opportunity exists where the shareholders would have to finance the investment while all the benefit would accrue to the bondholders.

debt ratio A measurement of the proportion of total assets financed by a firm's creditors.

debt-to-equity ratio A measurement calculated by dividing long-term debt by stockholders' equity.

debtor in possession The firm filing a reorganization petition.

decision tree A visual representation of the choices that managers face over time with regard to a particular investment.

default risk The risk that the corporation selling a bond may not make all scheduled payments.

deferred taxes Reflect the discrepancy between the taxes that firms actually pay and the tax liabilities they report on their public financial statements.

depository transfer A method for transferring cash from the depository banks to the concentration bank. An unsigned check is drawn on one of the firm's bank accounts and deposited in another of the firm's bank accounts.

depreciated The condition of a currency that has decreased in value compared to a different currency.

derivative securities A class of financial instruments that derive their values from other assets.

derivatives Financial instruments (forwards, futures, options, and swaps) that derive their value from another, underlying asset.

direct costs of bankruptcy Out-of-pocket cash expenses directly related to bankruptcy filing and administration.

direct lease A lessor acquires the assets that are leased to a given lessee.

discount The difference between a bond's par value and the purchase price when the price is less than par value.

discounted payback The amount of time it takes for a project's discounted cash flows to recover the initial investment.

discounting Describes the process of calculating present values.

divestiture Assets and/or resources of a subsidiary or division are sold to another organization.

dividend payout ratio The percentage of current earnings available for common stockholders paid out as dividends. Calculated by dividing the firm's cash dividend per share by its earnings per share.

dividend per share The portion of the earnings per share paid to stockholders.

double taxation problem Taxation of corporate income at both the company and the personal levels—the single greatest disadvantage of the corporate form.

dual-class recapitalization Organizational restructuring in which the parties wishing to concentrate control (usually management) buy all the shares of a newly issued Class B stock, which carries "super" voting rights (100 votes per share, for example).

due diligence Examination of potential security issuers in which investment banks are legally required to search out and disclose all relevant information about an issuer before selling securities to the public.

DuPont system An analysis that uses both income and balance sheet information to break the *ROA* and *ROE* ratios into component pieces.

earnings available for common stockholders Net income net of preferred stock dividends.

earnings per share Earnings available for common stockholders divided by the number of shares of common stock outstanding.

economic exposure The overall impact of foreign exchange rate fluctuations on the firm's value. Also, the risk that a change in prices will negatively impact the value of all cash flows of a firm.

economic failure A firm fails to earn a return that is greater than its cost of capital.

economies of scale Relative operating costs are reduced for merged companies because of an increase in size that allows for the reduction or elimination of overlapping resources.

economies of scope Value-creating benefits of increased size for merged companies.

effective Status of an offering before any shares can actually be sold to public investors.

effective annual rate The annual rate of interest actually paid or earned, reflecting the impact of compounding frequency.

effective borrowing rate Generally determined as the total amount of interest and fees paid, divided by the average usable loan amount.

efficient frontier Portfolios that maximize expected returns for any given level of volatility.

efficient markets hypothesis (EMH) Asserts that financial asset prices fully reflect all available information (as formally presented by Eugene Fama in 1970).

efficient portfolio A portfolio that offers the highest expected return among the group of portfolios with equal or less volatility.

efficient set A set of portfolios, determined graphically, that offer the highest available expected returns without adding volatility.

electronic bill presentment and payment Customers are sent bills in an electronic format and can then pay them via electronic means.

electronic depository transfer (EDT) The term used in the cash management trade for a preauthorized electronic withdrawal from the payer's account.

employee stock ownership plan The transformation of a public corporation into a private company by the employees of the corporation itself.

entrepreneurial finance Study involving investment in and financing of entrepreneurial growth companies.

entrepreneurial growth companies Companies typically funded by venture capitalists.

equilibrium interest rate The rate that "clears the market," equating total savings and investment within an economy.

equipment trust certificates A secured type of bond.

equipment trust receipts Loans extended for the purchase of transportation equipment.

equity An ownership interest usually in the form of common or preferred stock.

equity claimant Owner of a corporation's equity securities.

equity kickers Warrants that are attached to other securities.

equity multiplier A measurement of the proportion of total assets financed by a firm's equity.

equity premium puzzle The surprisingly high equity premium in the United States, which seems to imply that investors historically required a high degree of compensation to invest in stocks rather than T-bills.

equivalent annual cost method Calculates the present value of cash flows for each device over its lifetime.

ethics Standards of conduct in business dealings.

euro Currency adopted as a continent-wide medium of exchange by 12 of the 15 European Union (EU) nations as a result of the Maastricht Treaty of 1991.

Eurobond A bond issued by an international borrower and sold to investors in countries with currencies other than that in which the bond is denominated.

Eurobond issue A single-currency bond sold in several countries.

Eurocurrency loan market A large number of international banks that stand ready to make floating-rate, hard-currency loans to international corporate and government borrowers.

European call option Gives holders the right to purchase stock at a fixed price only on the expiration date.

European Monetary Union (EMU) Consists of 12 continental European countries that use the euro for financial transactions.

event study Examination of how stock markets respond to new information releases.

ex dividend A purchaser of a stock does not receive the current dividend.

ex rights Trading stock without rights being attached to it.

excess earnings accumulation tax A tax levied by the IRS on a firm that has accumulated sufficient excess earnings to allow owners to delay paying ordinary income taxes.

exchange rate The price of one currency in terms of another.

exchange rate gain Seller's gain when the dollar depreciates relative to the purchaser's currency.

exchange rate loss Seller's loss when the dollar appreciates relative to the purchaser's currency.

executive compensation Incentives offered to a manager to encourage him or her to act in the best interests of the owners.

exercise the option Purchase of stock in a call option.

expectations theory In equilibrium, investors should expect to earn the same return whether they invest in long-term Treasury bonds or a series of short-term Treasury bonds.

expiration date The date on which the right to purchase an option expires.

extension An arrangement wherein a firm's creditors are promised payment in full, although not immediately.

external funds required The expectation of a scarcity or a surplus of financial resources, given the firm's growth objectives.

extra dividend The additional dividend that a firm pays if earnings are higher than normal in a given period.

F

factoring The outright sale of receivables to a third party at a discount.

fair bet A gamble that offers an expected payoff of zero.

fair price provisions Antitrust rules that ensure that all target shareholders receive the same offer price in any tender offers initiated by the same acquirer, limiting the ability of acquirers to buy minority shares cheaply with a two-tiered offer.

fallen angels Bonds that received investment-grade ratings when first issued but later fell to junk status.

Fama-French model A mathematical expression similar to the arbitrage pricing theory.

feasible set A set of points, determined graphically, representing the expected return and standard deviation for all possible portfolios of two stocks.

field-banking system System characterized by many collection points, each of which may have a depository account at a local bank.

filter rules Investment strategies.

financial deficit More financial capital for investment and investor payments than is retained in profits by a corporation.

financial engineering The process of using the principles of financial economics to design and price financial instruments.

financial intermediary An institution that raises capital by issuing liabilities against itself. Also, a commercial bank or other entity that lends to corporations.

financial lease A noncancelable contractual arrangement whereby the lessee agrees to make periodic payments to the lessor, typically for more than five years, to obtain an asset's services.

financial leverage Using debt to magnify both the risk and expected return on a firm's investments. Also, the result of the presence of debt when firms finance their operations with debt and equity, leading to a higher stock beta.

financial management function Managing the firm's internal cash flows and its mix of debt and equity financing, both to maximize the value of the debt and equity claims on the firm and to ensure that the company can pay off its obligations when they come due.

financial slack Large cash and marketable security holdings or unused debt capacity.

financial synergies A merger results in less-volatile cash flows, lower default risk, and a lower cost of capital.

financial venture capital funds Subsidiaries of financial institutions, particularly commercial banks.

financing flows Result from debt and equity financing transactions.

financing function Raising capital to support a company's operations and investment programs.

firm-commitment A type of offering in which the investment bankers actually purchase the shares from a firm and resell them to investors.

five C's of credit A framework for performing in-depth credit analysis without providing a specific accept or reject decision.

fixed asset turnover A measurement of the efficiency with which a firm uses its fixed assets, calculated by dividing sales by the number of dollars of fixed asset investment.

fixed exchange rate Occurs when governments fix (or *peg*) their currency's value, usually in terms of another currency such as the U.S. dollar. The opposite of a floating exchange rate.

fixed-for-floating currency swap A combination of a currency swap and an interest rate swap.

fixed-for-floating interest rate swap Typically one party will make fixed-rate payments to another party in exchange for floating-rate payments.

fixed-price offer An offer in which the underwriters set the final offer price for a new issue weeks in advance.

fixed-rate Offerings that have a coupon interest rate that remains constant throughout the issue's life.

flip To buy shares at the offer price and sell them on the first trading day.

float Funds that have been sent by the payer but are not yet usable by the payee.

floating rate The interest rate for a loan priced at a fixed spread above a base interest rate, usually LIBOR or the U.S. bank prime lending rate.

floating exchange rate Occurs when forces of supply and demand continuously move currency values up and down.

floating-rate instruments Loan interest rates that periodically change to reflect changes in market interest rates.

foreign bond A bond issued in a host country's financial market, in the host country's currency, by a nonresident corporation.

foreign direct investment (FDI) The transfer by a multinational firm of financial, managerial, and technical assets from its home country to a host country.

forward discount What a currency trades at when it buys less of another currency on the forward market than it does on the spot market.

forward exchange rate The price at which a future foreign currency trade will take place.

forward integration A merger in which the acquired company provides a later step in the production process.

forward premium What a currency trades at when it buys more of another currency on the forward market than it does on the spot market.

forward price In a forward contract, the price agreed

upon by two parties today, at which the purchaser will buy a specified amount of an asset from the seller at a fixed date sometime in the future and which has zero net present value.

forward rate In a currency forward contract, the forward price.

forward rate agreement A forward contract in which the underlying asset is not an asset at all but an interest rate.

forward-spot parity Holds that the forward rate should be an unbiased predictor of where the spot rate is headed.

free cash flow The net amount of cash flow remaining after the firm has met all operating needs and paid for investments, both long-term (fixed) and short-term (current). Represents the cash amount that a firm could distribute to investors after meeting all its other obligations.

free cash flow theory of mergers Michael Jensen (1986) hypothesizes that managers will use free cash flow to invest in mergers that have negative net present values in order to build corporate empires from which the managers will derive personal benefits, including greater compensation.

full disclosure Requires issuers to reveal all relevant information concerning the company selling the securities and the securities themselves to potential investors.

fungibility The ability to close out a position by taking an offsetting position.

future value Calculation of what the value of an investment made today will be worth at a specific future date.

futures contract Involves two parties agreeing today on a price at which the purchaser will buy a given amount of a commodity or financial instrument from the seller at a fixed date sometime in the future.

G

General Agreement on Tariffs and Trade (GATT) An international treaty that facilitates free trade by overseeing taxes on traded goods and working out trade disagreements.

general cash offerings Most equity sales in the United States fall under this category.

general creditors Creditors who have no specific assets pledged as collateral or the proceeds from the sale of whose pledged assets are inadequate to cover the debt.

general partners One or more participants in a limited partnership who operate the business and have unlimited personal liability.

geometric average return The compound annual return over a period of years.

Glass-Steagall Act Congressional act of 1933 mandating the separation of investment and commercial banking.

goes public A corporation offers its shares for sale to the public.

going-private transaction The transformation of a public corporation into a private company through issuance of large amounts of debt used to buy all (or at least a voting majority) of the outstanding shares of the corporation.

goodwill An intangible asset created if the restated values of the target in a merger lead to a situation in which its assets are less than its liabilities and equity.

Gordon growth model The constant growth valuation model named after Myron Gordon, who popularized this formula during the 1960s and 1970s. It views cash flows as an annuity with an infinite life, promising to pay a growing amount at the end of each year.

Gramm-Leach-Bliley Act Congressional act of 1999 that repealed the Glass-Steagall Act.

Green Shoe option An option to sell up to 15 percent more shares than originally planned. Also called an *overallotment option*.

greenfield entry Internal expansion into a new market.

gross profit margin A measurement of the percentage of each sales dollar remaining after a firm has paid for its goods.

grossed up Increased to provide a given after-tax yield.

growing perpetuity An annuity with an infinite life, promising to pay a growing amount at the end of each year.

H

hedge To transfer to a third party.

hedge fund A professionally managed investment fund.

hedge ratio The combination of stocks and options that results in a perfectly hedged portfolio. Also, the ratio of the number of options to the number of shares in a perfectly hedged portfolio.

hedging Offsetting many of the more threatening market risks.

hedging strategies Techniques used to offset or protect against risk.

herd The notion that analysts follow each others' recommendations.

Herfindahl Index A measure popularized by Comment and Jarrell (1995) to demonstrate the relationship between corporate focus and shareholder wealth.

high-yield bonds Bonds rated below investment grade (also known as *junk bonds*).

hockey-stick diagram A payoff diagram for the call option buyer showing the long position over a range of stock prices.

holders of record Owners of a firm's shares on the date of record.

holding company A company that owns a controlling fraction of the stock in another company.

homemade leverage Borrowing on personal account.

homogeneous expectations The assumption that all investors have access to the same information and that their estimates of the inputs needed to solve for the optimal portfolio are identical.

horizontal merger A combination of competitors within the same geographic market.

hostile takeover The acquisition of one firm by another through an open-market bid for a majority of the target's shares if the target firm's senior managers do not support (or, more likely, actively resist) the acquisition.

hubris hypothesis of corporate takeovers Richard Roll (1986) contends that some managers overestimate their own managerial capabilities and pursue takeovers with the belief that they can better manage their takeover target than the target's current management team can.

I

imaging services Disbursement services offered by banks and other vendors to allow both sides of the check, as well as remittance information, to be converted into digital images. The images can then be transmitted via the Internet or easily stored for future reference. Imaging services are especially useful when incorporated with positive pay services.

implied volatility The value of σ obtained by "inverting" the Black and Scholes equation to calculate the level of volatility implied by the option's market price.

in the money Occurs when a call option's strike price is less than the current stock price.

income bonds An unsecured type of bond.

incremental project A hypothetical project with cash flows equal to the difference in cash flows between large-scale and small-scale investments.

indenture A legal document stating the conditions under which a bond has been issued.

indirect bankruptcy costs Expenses or economic losses that result from bankruptcy but are not cash outflows spent on the process itself.

industry shock theory of takeovers Explains much of the activity in the wave of mergers between companies in the same industry.

inefficient portfolios A portfolio that offers a lower expected return than another portfolio with the same standard deviation.

information intermediation Financial service provided to corporations by intermediaries to help assess borrowers and monitor subsequent use of funds borrowed.

informational efficiency The tendency (or lack thereof)

for prices in a market to rapidly and fully incorporate new, relevant information.

initial margin The minimum dollar amount required of an investor when taking a position in a futures contract.

initial public offering (IPO) A corporation offers its shares for sale to the public for the first time; the first public sale of company stock to outside investors.

initial return The gain when an allocation of shares from an investment banker is sold at the first opportunity because the offer price is consistently lower that what the market is willing to bear.

insolvency bankruptcy A firm's liabilities exceed the fair market value of its assets.

insolvent A firm is *insolvent* when (a) it is not paying its debts as they come due; (b) within the immediately preceding 120 days a custodian (a third party) was appointed or took possession of the debtor's property; or (c) the fair market value of its assets is less than the stated value of its liabilities.

institutional venture capital funds Formal business entities with full-time professionals dedicated to seeking out and funding promising ventures.

integrated accounts payable Provides a company with outsourcing of its accounts payable or disbursement operations. The outsourcing may be as minor as contracting with a bank to issue checks and perform reconciliations or as major as outsourcing the entire payables function.

interest differential In an interest rate swap, only the differential is exchanged.

interest rate cap A call option on interest rates.

interest rate collar A strategy involving the purchase of an interest rate cap and the simultaneous sale of an interest rate floor, using the proceeds from selling the floor to purchase the cap.

interest rate floor A put option on interest rates.

interest rate parity Asserts that risk-free investments should offer the same return (after converting currencies) everywhere.

interest rate risk The risk that changes in market interest rates will cause fluctuations in a bond's price. Also, the risk of suffering losses as a result of unanticipated changes in market interest rates.

interest rate swap A swap contract in which two parties exchange payment obligations involving different interest payment schedules.

internal capital markets Created when the high-cash-flow businesses of a conglomerate generate enough cash to fund the riskier business ventures internally.

internal rate of return The compound annual return on a project, given its up-front costs and subsequent cash flows.

international common stock Equity issues sold in more than one country by nonresident corporations.

intrinsic value A measure of the profit an investor makes from exercising an option (ignoring transactions costs as well as the option premium).

inventory turnover A measure of how quickly a firm sells its goods.

investment bank A bank that helps firms acquire external capital.

investment flows Cash flows associated with the purchase or sale of both fixed assets and business equity.

investment-grade bonds Bonds rated Baa or higher by Moody's (BBB by S&P).

involuntary reorganization A reorganization initiated by an outside party, usually a creditor.

IPO underpricing Occurs when the offer price in the prospectus is consistently lower than what the market is willing to bear.

J

joint and several liability Each partner is personally liable for all the debts of the partnership.

joint hypothesis problem When an anomaly appears, while using an asset pricing model to form judgments about the risks and expected returns of two portfolios, it may be the result of market inefficiency or of a deficient model (or both).

junk bonds Bonds rated below investment grade (also known as *high yield bonds*).

L

law of one price The idea that identical goods trading in different markets should sell at the same price, absent any barriers to trade.

leads and lags Adjustments in the collection and payment of intra-MNC accounts in order to correct for the appreciation and depreciation of currency.

lease Comparable to secured long-term debt; a contractual arrangement providing for a series of periodic, tax-deductible payments in return for use of the underlying asset.

lease-versus-purchase decision The alternatives available are to (1) lease the assets, (2) borrow funds to purchase the assets, or (3) purchase the assets using available liquid resources. Even if the firm has the liquid resources with which to purchase the assets, the use of these funds is viewed as equivalent to borrowing.

leave money on the table To set the offer price below the expected post-issue selling price.

lending versus borrowing problem Choice is offered between cash paid out today in exchange for a larger amount of cash in one year, or cash received today with payback of a larger amount later.

lessee The user of the underlying asset who makes regular payments to the lessor.

lessor The owner of the asset who receives regular payments for its use by the lessee.

leveraged leases The lessor acts as an equity participant, supplying only about 20 percent of the cost of the asset, and a lender supplies the balance.

LIBOR The London Interbank Offered Rate.

lien A legal contract specifying under what conditions a lender can take title to an asset if a loan is not repaid, and prohibiting the borrowing firm from selling or disposing of the asset without the lender's consent.

lifetime high prices The highest settlement prices recorded for a contract since its inception.

lifetime low prices The lowest settlement prices recorded for a contract since its inception.

limited partners One or more totally passive participants in a limited partnership, who do not take any active role in the operation of the business and who do not face personal liability for the debts of the business.

limited partnership Most of the participants in the partnership (the limited partners) have the limited liability of corporate shareholders, but their share of the profits from the business is taxed as partnership income.

liquidation Winding up a firm's operations, selling off its assets, and distributing the proceeds to creditors.

liquidity A measure of a firm's ability to satisfy its short-term obligations as they come due.

liquidity crisis A firm is unable to pay its liabilities as they come due because assets cannot be converted into cash within a reasonable period of time.

liquidity preference theory States that the slope of the yield curve is influenced not only by expected interest rate changes, but also by the liquidity premium that investors require on long-term bonds.

loan amortization A borrower makes equal periodic payments over time to fully repay a loan.

loan amortization schedule Used to determine loan amortization payments and the allocation of each payment to interest and principal.

loan covenant Specifications imposed by a bank on a borrower in an attempt to protect the bank's investment.

loans Private debt agreements arranged between corporate borrowers and financial institutions, especially commercial banks.

lockbox system A technique for speeding up collections that is popular because it affects all three components of float. Instead of mailing payments to the company, customers mail payments to a post office box, which is emptied regularly by the firm's bank.

lockup agreement An agreement that bankers negotiate with a client's managers and directors, stipulating that these corporate insiders will not sell their personal stock holdings immediately after the offering.

long position Taking a long position in a security is equivalent to buying the security. In a *forward* or *futures contract,* the long position is obligated to pay the forward or futures price of the asset when the contract expires.

long straddle A portfolio consisting of long positions in calls and puts on the same stock with the same strike price and expiration date.

long-term debt Debt that matures more than one year in the future.

low-regular-and-extra policy Policy of a firm paying a low regular dividend supplemented by an additional cash dividend when earnings warrant it.

M

macro political risk Risk that applies to *all* foreign firms in a country because of political change, revolution, or the adoption of new policies by the host government.

mail float The time delay between when payment is placed in the mail and when payment is received.

mail-based collection system Processing centers receive the mail payments, open the envelopes, separate the check from the remittance information, prepare the check for deposit, and send the remittance information to the accounts receivable department for application of payment.

maintenance clauses Specifying who is to maintain the assets and make insurance and tax payments.

maintenance margin Margin level required to maintain an open position.

majority voting system System that allows each shareholder to cast one vote per share for each open position on the board of directors.

managed floating-rate system A hybrid system in which a nation's government loosely "fixes" the value of the national currency in relation to that of another currency, but does not expend the effort and resources that would be required to maintain a completely fixed exchange rate regime.

management buyout The transformation of a public corporation into a private company by the current managers of the corporation.

managerial entrenchment theory of mergers Shleifer and Vishny (1989) propose that unmonitored managers will try to build corporate empires through the pursuit of negative-*NPV* mergers, with the motive of making the management team indispensable to the firm because of its greater size and the team's supposed expertise in managing a large company.

managerial opportunism hypothesis Asserts that firms attempt to time the market by issuing equity when share values are high and issuing debt when share prices are low.

managerial risk reduction theory Implies that the diversification motive, once thought to be beneficial to stockholders, must now be viewed as a value-destroying rationale caused by agency problems.

managerial synergies Efficiency gains from combining the management teams of merged companies.

managerialism theory of mergers Poorly monitored managers will pursue mergers to maximize their corporation's asset size because managerial compensation is usually based on firm size, regardless of whether or not these mergers create value for stockholders.

margin account The account into which the investor must deposit the initial margin.

marginal tax rate The percentage of taxes owed on an incremental dollar of income.

market capitalization The value of the shares of a company's stock that are owned by the stockholders: the total number of shares issued multiplied by the current price per share.

market extension merger A combination of firms that produce the same product in different geographic markets.

market maker A lead underwriter that continuously quotes bid and ask prices for new securities after a share offering is successfully sold.

market portfolio The portfolio that all investors want to hold as required for equilibrium, which in theory consists of every available asset with each asset weighted by its market value relative to the total market value of all assets.

market power A benefit that might arise from a horizontal merger when competition is too weak (or nonexistent) to prevent the merged company from raising prices in a market at will.

market price of risk Maximized by investors as they search for the optimal risky portfolio.

market/book ratio A measurement that relates the market value of a firm's shares to their book value.

marking-to-market Daily cash settlement of all futures contracts.

matching strategy When a company finances permanent assets (fixed assets plus the permanent component of current assets) with long-term funding sources and finances its temporary or seasonal asset requirements with short-term debt.

maturity The limited life of a bond.

McFadden Act Congressional act of 1927 that prohibited interstate banking.

merchant bank A bank capable of providing a full range of financial services.

merger A transaction in which two or more business organizations combine into a single entity.

micro political risk Refers to a foreign government's targeting punitive action against an individual firm, a specific industry, or companies from a particular foreign country.

minimum variance portfolio A portfolio of A and B that has less volatility than either A or B.

mixed offering An offering in which some of the shares come from existing shareholders and some are new.

Also, a merger financed with a combination of cash and securities.

mixed stream A series of unequal payments reflecting no particular pattern.

modified accelerated cost recovery system Set forth in the Tax Reform Act of 1986 to define the allowable annual depreciation deductions for various classes of assets.

momentum strategies Trading rules based on return continuations.

monetary union The European Union replaced currencies of the 12 member nations with the euro and is creating a new European Central Bank.

money market The market for debt instruments maturing in one year or less.

money market mutual funds Used by many small companies and some large companies to manage their portfolio.

money market yield The yield for short-term discount instruments such as T-bills and commercial paper is typically calculated using algebraic approximations rather than more precise present value methods.

Monte Carlo simulation A sophisticated analysis that provides for calculating the net present value when provided a range or distribution of potential outcomes for each set of assumptions.

mortgage A loan secured by real property.

mortgage bonds A secured type of bond.

multinational corporations (MNCs) Businesses that operate in many countries around the world.

municipal bonds Issued by U.S. state and local governments. Interest on these bonds is exempt from federal income tax.

mutually exclusive projects When several investments exceed the hurdle rate but only a subset of them can be undertaken at any given time.

N

naked option position Results when an investor buys or sells an option on a stock without already owning the underlying stock.

natural hedge Offsetting risk exposure.

negative covenants Restrictions a borrower must accept in order to secure a loan.

negotiated offer The most common approach that firms take in choosing an investment banker: The issuing firm negotiates the terms of the offer directly with one investment bank.

net payoff The share price less the amount paid to acquire the call option.

net present value The present value of a sequence of cash inflows and outflows. Also, a method for valuing capital investments.

net price The price at which banks purchase shares from firms.

net profit margin A measurement of the percentage of each sales dollar remaining after all costs and expenses, including interest, taxes, and preferred stock dividends, have been deducted.

net working capital The difference between a firm's current assets and its current liabilities. Often used as a measure of liquidity.

noise trader theory Theory of asset pricing put forth by Shleifer and Summers (1990). They suggest that markets are populated by two types of investors: rational arbitrageurs and noise traders.

noise traders Those who trade based on beliefs or sentiments that are not fully justified by fundamental news. Also called *liquidity traders*.

nominal cash flows Amounts that reflect an assumed inflation rate.

nominal exchange rate Changes in this rate are those that exactly mirror changes in relative inflation rates between two countries.

nominal return The stated return.

noncash charges Expenses that appear on the income statement but do not involve an actual outlay of cash.

nondebt tax shields hypothesis States that companies with large amounts of depreciation, investment tax credits, R&D expenditures, and other nondebt tax shields should employ less debt financing than otherwise equivalent companies with fewer such shields.

normal distribution The probability of investment outcomes forms a roughly bell-shaped curve that is symmetric about its mean, which makes it easy to determine the probabilities of events that fall within certain ranges and allows full description by just two characteristics, the mean and the variance.

notes Longer-term debt instruments with original maturities of less than seven years.

notional principal The hypothetical principal amount.

 O

observable variables approach An avenue of empirical research that offers hope of yielding interpretable results by estimating which macroeconomic variables significantly influence security prices.

offer price The price at which banks sell a firm's shares to institutional and individual investors.

open interest The number of contracts that are currently outstanding.

opening futures price Price on the first trade of the day.

operating assets Cash, marketable securities, accounts receivable, and inventories that are necessary for the day-to-day operation of a firm.

operating cycle Measurement of the time that elapses from the firm's receipt of raw materials to begin production to its collection of cash from the sale of the finished product.

operating flows Cash inflows and outflows directly related to the production and sale of a firm's products or services.

operating lease A contractual arrangement whereby the lessee agrees to make periodic payments to the lessor, often for five years or less, to obtain an asset's services. The lessee generally receives an option to cancel, and the asset has a useful life longer than the lease.

operating leverage Measures the tendency of the volatility of operating cash flows to increase with fixed operating costs.

operating profit margin A measurement of the percentage of each sales dollar remaining after deducting all costs and expenses other than interest and taxes.

operational efficiency Determines whether markets produce outputs at the lowest possible cost.

operational synergy Economies of scale, economies of scope, and resource complementarities.

opportunity costs Lost cash flows on an alternative investment that the firm or individual decides not to make.

optimal risky portfolio The portfolio that maximizes the return that investors can expect for a given standard deviation.

option Allows an investor to buy or sell an asset at a fixed price during a given period of time.

option premium The purchase price of the option to buy is kept by the seller if the buyer decides not to make the purchase.

option to default A limited liability feature that allows a bankrupt firm to hand creditors the company's assets in bankruptcy court.

option's delta The slope measures how much the call price changes as the underlying stock price changes.

ordinary annuity An annuity for which the payments occur at the end of each period.

out of the money Occurs when a call option's strike price exceeds the current stock price.

overconfidence Investors exhibit this trait when they believe they are better informed about the true state of a company's affairs than is in fact the case.

overreaction The opposite of *underreaction* to corporate news announcements or prior period returns.

overreaction strategies Trading rules based on reversals.

oversubscribe When the investment banker builds a book of orders for stock that is greater (often many times greater) than the amount of stock the firm intends to sell. These orders are not legally binding, and typically the offer price is given as a range of prices at which they expect to sell the offer.

over-the-counter market There are a seemingly infinite variety. They are less liquid than exchange-traded options.

paid-in-capital The number of shares outstanding times the original selling price of the shares, net of the par value.

par value The face value of a bond, which the borrower repays at maturity. Also, an arbitrary value assigned to common stock on a firm's balance sheet.

partnership A proprietorship with two or more owners who have joined together their skills and personal wealth.

payback period The amount of time it takes for a given project's cumulative net cash inflows to recoup the initial investment.

payment date The actual date on which a firm mails the dividend payment to the holders of record.

payment pattern The normal timing in which a firm's customers pay their accounts, expressed as the percentage of monthly sales collected in each month following the sale.

payoff The price an investor would be willing to pay for an option the instant before it expires.

payoff diagrams Graphs that illustrate an option's payoff as a function of the underlying stock price.

pecking order hypothesis A hypothesis developed by Stewart Myers and his coauthors, which assumes that managers are better informed about the investment opportunities faced by their firms than are outside investors (an asymmetric information assumption), and that managers act in the best interests of existing shareholders.

percentage-of-sales method Constructing pro forma statements by assuming that all items grow in proportion to sales.

perpetuity An annuity with an infinite life, promising to pay the same amount at the end of every year forever.

plug figure A line item left on the balance sheet of a pro forma statement. After all other projections are made, this figure can be adjusted so that the balance sheet balances.

poison pills Defensive measures taken to avoid a hostile takeover.

political risk The actions taken by a government that have a negative impact on the value of foreign companies operating in that country.

portfolio investments Passive, return-oriented investments that do not involve equity participation.

positive covenant Requirements a borrower must meet to secure a loan.

positive pay A bank service used to combat the most common types of check fraud. A company transmits a check-issued file, designating the check number and amount of each item, to the bank when the checks are issued. The bank matches the presented checks against this file and rejects any items that do not match.

preemptive rights These hold that shareholders have first claim on anything of value distributed by a corporation.

preferred habitat theory The effect on the yield curve caused by a desire to invest to match liabilities, despite lower expected returns.

preferred stock Stockholder's equity.

premium The difference between a bond's par value and the purchase price when the price is greater than par value.

prepackaged bankruptcy Companies prepare a reorganization plan that is negotiated and voted on by creditors and stockholders before the company actually files for Chapter 11 bankruptcy.

present value Calculation of the value today of a cash flow to be received at a specific date in the future.

president Hired by the board of directors to be responsible for managing day-to-day operations and carrying out the policies established by the board.

price bubbles Occur when investors irrationally bid prices to unsustainable levels. When investors finally realize their errors, prices fall dramatically (and perhaps suddenly).

price stabilization Purchase of shares by an investment bank when a new issue begins to falter in the market, keeping the market price at or slightly above the offer price for an indefinite period.

price/earnings ratio A measurement of a firm's long-term growth prospects by determining the amount investors are willing to pay for each dollar of a firm's earnings.

primary market transaction Sale of securities to investors by a corporation to raise capital for the firm.

primary offering An offering in which the shares offered for sale are newly issued shares, which increases the number of outstanding shares and raises new capital for the firm.

primary security issues Security offerings that raise capital for firms.

prime rate The rate of interest charged by the largest U.S. banks on short-term loans to business borrowers with good credit ratings.

principal The amount of money on which interest is paid.

private placements Unregistered security offerings sold directly to accredited investors.

privatization When a state sells off all or part of its holdings in SOEs to private companies or to individual private investors.

pro forma financial statement A forecast of what a firm expects its balance sheet and income statement to look like a year or two ahead.

probability distribution A distribution that tells us what investment outcomes are possible and associates a probability with each outcome.

procurement Implemented by companies as a means of reducing the cost of low-dollar indirect purchases.

product extension merger A diversification merger that combines companies with similar but not identical lines of business.

profitability index A capital budgeting tool, defined as the ratio of the present value of a project's cash flows, excluding the initial cash outflow (the initial investment), divided by the initial cash outflow.

project beta The asset beta of a specific project.

project finance (PF) loans Loans usually arranged for infrastructure projects such as toll roads, bridges, and power plants.

Proposition I The famous "irrelevance proposition," which imagines that a company is operating in a world of frictionless capital markets, and in a world where there is uncertainty about corporate revenues and earnings.

Proposition II Asserts that the expected return on a levered firm's equity is a linear function of that firm's debt-to-equity ratio.

prospectus The first part of a registration statement; it is distributed to all prospective investors.

protective put By granting the right to sell a share of stock at a fixed price on or before a certain date, a put option provides a kind of portfolio insurance, guaranteeing that the share of stock can be sold for at least that amount.

proxy fight A ploy used by outsiders to attempt to gain control of a firm by soliciting a sufficient number of votes to unseat existing directors.

proxy statement Used by shareholders not attending an annual meeting to give their votes to another party.

public company A corporation whose shares of stock can be freely traded among investors without obtaining the permission of other investors and whose shares are listed for trading in a public security market.

purchase options The lessee may have the option to purchase the leased asset when the lease expires.

purchasing (or procurement) card programs Implemented by companies as a means of reducing the cost of low-dollar indirect purchases.

purchasing power parity An extension of the law of one price. It maintains that if the law of one price holds at all times, then differences in expected inflation between two countries are associated with expected changes in currency values.

pure conglomerate mergers An unrelated diversification merger that occurs between companies in completely different lines of business.

pure play A firm that competes in a single line of business.

pure stock exchange merger A merger in which stock is the only mode of payment.

put option Grants the right to sell a share of stock at a fixed price on or before a certain date.

put-call parity Results when the payoffs of a portfolio containing one share of stock and one put option are exactly the same as the payoffs of a portfolio containing one bond and one call option.

Q

qualified institutional buyers Institutions with assets exceeding $100 million.

quarterly compounding Interest involves four compounding periods within the year and is paid four times a year.

quick (acid-test) ratio Similar to the current ratio except that it excludes inventory, which is usually the least-liquid current asset.

R

random walk A description of the movement of the price of a financial asset over time. When prices follow a *random walk*, future and past prices are statistically unrelated, and the best forecast of the future price is simply the current price.

ratio analysis Calculating and interpreting financial ratios to assess a firm's performance and status.

rational expectations The assumption that even if investors make mistakes when forming assessments concerning expected returns, their errors are not systematic.

real cash flows Amounts that reflect current prices only and do not incorporate upward adjustments for expected inflation.

real exchange rate Measures changes in the purchasing power of a currency.

real interest rate parity Asserts that investors should earn the same real rate of return on risk-free investments no matter the country in which they choose to invest.

real option The right, but not the obligation, to take a future action that changes an investment's value.

real return Approximately, the difference between an investment's stated or nominal return and the inflation rate.

recapitalization Alteration of a company's capital structure to reduce high fixed charges.

red herring Nickname often given to the preliminary prospectus because of the standard legal disclaimer printed across its cover in red, stating that the securities described herein are not (yet) being offered for sale.

redemption option Option for venture capitalists to sell a company back to its entrepreneur or founders.

refund To refinance a debt with new bonds at a lower interest rate.

registration statement The principal disclosure document for all public security offerings.

renewal options In an operating lease, the lessee often has the option to renew a lease at its expiration.

reorganization The process in bankruptcy designed to allow businesses that are in temporary financial distress but are worth saving to continue operating while the claims of creditors are settled using a collective procedure.

residual claimants Investors who have the right to receive cash flows only after all other claimants have been satisfied. Common stockholders are typically the residual claimants of corporations.

resource complementarities A firm with a particular operating expertise merges with a firm with another operating strength to create a company that has expertise in multiple areas.

retained earnings The cumulative total of the earnings that a firm has reinvested since its inception.

return The total gain or loss on an investment over a given period of time.

return on common equity A measurement that captures the return earned on the common stockholders' (owners') investment in a firm.

return on total assets A measurement of the overall effectiveness of management in generating returns to common stockholders with its available assets.

reverse LBO A formerly public company that has previously gone private through a leveraged buyout and then goes public again. Also called *second IPO*.

reverse merger A merger in which the acquirer has a lesser market value than the target.

reverse stock split Occurs when a firm replaces a certain number of outstanding shares with just one new share.

rights offerings A special type of seasoned equity offering that allows the firm's existing owners to buy new shares at a bargain price or to sell that right to other investors.

risk averse A description of the preferences of investors who must be compensated to bear risk or will pay to shed risk.

risk management The process of identifying firm-specific risk exposures and managing those exposures by means of insurance products. Also includes identifying, measuring, and managing all types of risk exposures.

risk neutral Investors who care only about the returns on their investments, totally disregarding risk.

risk premium The difference in annual returns between common stocks and Treasury bills.

risk-management function Managing the firm's exposures to all types of risk, both insurable and uninsurable, in order to maintain the optimum risk-return trade-off and thereby maximize shareholder value.

risk-neutral method A simpler approach to calculating option prices by using arbitrage arguments, in which the assumption is made that investors are risk neutral.

risk-seeking Investors who prefer to take risk and hence will be willing to invest in a risky asset even when its expected return falls below that of a safer alternative.

road show A tour of major U.S. and international cities taken by a firm and its bankers several weeks before a scheduled offering. The tour's goal is to solicit demand for the offering from investors.

Rule 144A Provides a private-placement exemption for qualified institutional buyers and allows them to freely trade privately placed securities among themselves.

Rule 144A offering A special type of offer, first approved in April 1990, that allows issuing companies to waive some disclosure requirements by selling stock only to sophisticated institutional investors, who may then trade the shares among themselves.

S

S corporation An ordinary corporation in which the stockholders have elected to allow shareholders to be taxed as partners while still retaining their limited-liability status as corporate stockholders.

sale-leaseback arrangement One firm sells an asset to another for cash, then leases the asset from its new owner.

scenario analysis A more complex variation on sensitivity analysis that provides for calculating the net present value when a whole set of assumptions changes in a particular way.

seasoned equity offering (SEO) An equity issue by a firm that already has common stock outstanding.

secondary market transactions Trades between investors that generate no new cash flow for the firm.

secondary offering An offering whose purpose is to allow an existing shareholder to sell a large block of stock to new investors. This kind of offering raises no new capital for the firm.

secured creditors Creditors who have specific assets pledged as collateral and who receive the proceeds from the sale of those assets.

secured debt A loan backed by collateral.

secured debt hypothesis Asserts that assets generating tax shields could also be used as collateral for additional debt, so firms rich in tangible assets were able to use higher levels of secured debt.

Securities Act of 1933 The most important federal law governing the sale of new securities.

Securities and Exchange Commission Act of 1934 This act, and its amendments, established the U.S. Securities and Exchange Commission (SEC) and laid out specific procedures for both the public sale of securities and the governance of public companies.

securitization The repackaging of loans and other traditional bank-based credit products into securities that can be sold to public investors.

security market line The line plotted for the equilibrium expected returns of all securities.

selectivity Stock-picking ability; one of two components of managerial investment performance.

selling group Consists of investment banks that may assist in selling shares but are not formal members of the underwriting syndicate.

semiannual compounding Interest involves two compounding periods within the year and is paid twice a year.

semistrong-form efficiency This version of the EMH asserts that asset prices incorporate all publicly available information.

sensitivity analysis A tool that allows exploration of the importance of individual assumptions concerning a project's net present value by determining the impact of changing one variable while holding all others fixed.

separation of investment and financing The principle that corporations worry only about satisfying the impersonal demands of the financial market, not the personal preferences of investors.

serial bonds Bonds of which a certain proportion mature each year.

settlement date The future date on which the buyer pays the seller and the seller delivers the asset to the buyer.

share issue privatization (SIP) A government executing one of these will sell all or part of its ownership in a state-owned enterprise to private investors via a public share offering.

share repurchase program A company announcing this kind of program states that it will buy some of its own shares over a period of time.

shareholder Owner of common and preferred stock of a corporation.

shares authorized The shares of a company's stock that are authorized by the stockholders to be sold by the board of directors without further stockholder approval.

shares issued The shares of a company's stock that are owned by the stockholders.

shark repellents Antitakeover measures added to corporate charters.

shelf registration (Rule 415) A procedure that allows a qualifying company to file a "master registration statement," a single document summarizing planned financing over a two-year period.

short position Taking a *short position* is equivalent to selling the asset. In a forward or futures contract, the short position is obligated to sell the asset to the buyer at the forward or futures price.

short straddle A portfolio consisting of long positions in calls and puts on the same stock with the same strike price and expiration date.

short-selling A transaction in which an investor sells

borrowed assets that must be returned to the lender of the assets at a later date.

short-term debt Debt that matures in one year or less.

short-term financing Accounts payable, bank loans, commercial paper, international loans, and secured short-term loans that are used by a firm to finance seasonal fluctuations in current asset investments and provide adequate liquidity to achieve its growth objectives and meet its obligations in a timely manner.

signal An action that imposes significant costs on the sender in order to credibly convey information to uninformed outsiders, usually investors.

signaling model A capital structure theory that assumes that managers know more about a firm's prospects than investors do.

signaling model of dividends Assumes that managers use dividends to convey positive information to poorly informed shareholders.

simple interest Interest paid only on the initial principal of an investment, not on the interest that accrues in earlier periods.

single-factor model Just one variable explains differences in returns across securities.

sinking fund An additional positive covenant included in a bond indenture, the objective of which is to provide for the systematic retirement of bonds prior to their maturity.

small business investment companies (SBICs) Federally chartered corporations established as a result of the Small Business Administration Act of 1958.

sole proprietorship A business with a single owner.

special dividend The additional dividend that a firm pays if earnings are higher than normal in a given period.

speculating Choosing not to hedge a risk exposure, or choosing to overhedge.

spin-off A parent company creates a new company with its own shares to form a division or subsidiary, and existing shareholders receive a pro rata distribution of shares in the new company.

split-off A parent company creates a new, independent company with its own shares, and ownership of the company is transferred to certain existing shareholders only, in exchange for their shares in the parent.

split-up The division and sale of all of a company's subsidiaries, so that it ceases to exist (except possibly as a holding company with no assets).

sponsored ADR An ADR for which the issuing (foreign) company absorbs the legal and financial costs of creating and trading the security.

spot exchange rate The exchange rate that applies to currency trades that occur immediately.

spot price A cash market transaction in which the buyer and seller conduct their transaction today.

spot rates Rates that call for immediate delivery.

staged financing Used by venture capitalists to minimize risk exposure.

stakeholders Customers, employees, suppliers, and creditors of a firm.

stand-alone companies Companies created for the sole purpose of constructing and operating a single project.

stated annual rate The contractual annual rate charged by a lender or promised by a borrower.

state-owned enterprises (SOEs) Companies owned and operated by the government that conduct business activities in areas outside what many would consider purely governmental affairs.

statutory merger A target integration in which the acquirer can absorb the target's resources directly with no remaining trace of the target as a separate entity.

stock dividend The payment to existing owners of a dividend in the form of stock.

stock options Outright grants of stock to top managers or, more commonly, giving them the right to purchase stock at a fixed price.

stock purchase warrants Instruments that give their holder the right to purchase a certain number of shares of a firm's common stock at a specified price over a certain period.

strategic merger Seeks to create a more efficient merged company than the two premerger companies operating independently.

strategic plan A multiyear action plan for the major investments and competitive initiatives that a firm's senior managers believe will drive the future success of the enterprise.

strike price The price at which a call option allows an investor to purchase the underlying share. Also called the *exercise price*.

strong-form efficiency In markets characterized by this kind of efficiency, asset prices reflect all information, public and private.

subordinated debenture An unsecured type of bond.

subordinated debt Debt claims that are junior to other claims and therefore are entitled to receive interest or principal payments only if the senior debt claims have been paid in full.

subordination Agreement by all subsequent or more-junior creditors to wait until all claims of the senior debt are satisfied in full before having their own claims satisfied.

subscription price The purchase price set for rights at somewhat below the prevailing market price of the firm's stock.

subsidiary merger A merger in which the acquirer maintains the identity of the target as a separate subsidiary or division.

sunk costs Costs that have already been spent and are not recoverable.

supplemental disclosures The second part to a registration statement. It is filed only with the SEC.

sustainable growth model Derives an expression that determines how rapidly a firm can grow while maintaining a balance between its sources (increases in assets) and uses (increases in liabilities and equity) of funds.

swap contract Agreement between two parties to exchange payment obligations on two underlying financial liabilities that are equal in principal amount but differ in payment patterns.

syndicated bank loans Loans funded by a large number of commercial banks, called a *syndicate*.

synergy An efficiency-enhancing effect resulting from a strategic merger.

synthetic put option Traders can create this by purchasing a bond and a call option while simultaneously short-selling the stock.

systematic risk The proportion of risk that cannot be eliminated through diversification.

T

tailing the hedge Purchasing enough futures contracts to hedge risk exposure, but not so many as to cause overhedging.

takeover Any transaction in which the control of one entity is taken over by another.

target cash balance A cash total is set for checking accounts to avoid engaging active cash position management.

target dividend payout ratio Under this policy, the firm attempts to pay out a certain percentage of earnings, but rather than let dividends fluctuate, it pays a stated dollar dividend and adjusts it toward the target payout slowly as proven earnings increases occur.

target leverage zones An operating range of debt ratio within which corporations seem to prefer to operate.

tax-loss carryforwards Negative income (net losses) can be used to offset taxes due on future income.

technical analysis An investing approach in which analysts search for profitable trading strategies based on recurring patterns in stock prices.

technical insolvency A firm is unable to pay its liabilities as they come due, although its assets are still greater than its liabilities.

tender offer The structured purchase of a target's shares in which the acquirer announces a public offer to buy a minimum number of shares at a specific price.

tender-merger A merger that occurs after an acquirer secures enough voting control of the target's shares through a tender offer to effect a merger.

term loan A loan made by a financial institution to a business, with an initial maturity of more than 1 year, generally 5 to 12 years.

term structure of interest rates The relationship between yield to maturity and time to maturity.

terminal value A number intended to reflect the value of a project at a given future point in time.

time line A graphical presentation of values over time.

time value The difference between an option's intrinsic value and its market price.

time value of money The principle of finance that a dollar received today is more valuable than a dollar (euro, pound, franc, or yen) received in the future.

times interest earned ratio Earnings before interest and taxes divided by interest expense; it measures a firm's ability to make contractual interest payments.

timing The ability to time market turns—getting in before upturns and getting out before crashes. One of two components of managerial investment performance.

Tobin's q The market value of a firm's assets divided by their replacement value; it serves as a proxy for these capital market assessments.

top-down This kind of sales forecast relies heavily on macroeconomic and industry forecasts.

total asset turnover A measurement of the efficiency with which a firm uses all its assets to generate sales; calculated by dividing the dollars of sales a firm generates by the dollars of asset investment.

tracking stocks Equity claims based on (and designed to mirror, or *track*) the earnings of wholly owned subsidiaries of diversified firms.

trade-off model A model of capital structure in which managers choose the mix of debt and equity that strikes a balance between the tax advantages of debt and the various costs of using leverage.

transaction exposure The risk that a change in prices will negatively affect the value of a specific transaction or series of transactions.

transactional exemption Requires that securities be registered before they can be resold, or that the subsequent sale must also qualify as a private placement.

transition economy The changing economy of the countries of Eastern Europe and the former Soviet Union.

translation exposure Arises when MNCs translate costs and revenues denominated in foreign currencies to report on their financial statements, which are denominated in the home currency. Also called *accounting exposure*.

treasury stock Common shares that a firm currently holds in reserve.

triangular arbitrage Trading currencies simultaneously in different markets to earn a risk-free profit.

trustee In bankruptcy, someone appointed by a judge to replace a firm's current management team and to oversee liquidation or reorganization.

U

unanimous consent procedure (UCP) A reorganization plan instituted by consent of all creditors and equity classes.

underinvestment A situation of financial distress in which default is likely, yet a very profitable but short-lived investment opportunity exists.

underlying asset The asset from which a derivative security obtains its value.

underpriced Refers to the typical situation in which an IPO offering price is lower than its price at the end of the first day's trading.

underreact When stock prices on average react positively to a dividend initiation, for example, but then an additional positive reaction continues over the next several months.

underreaction strategies Trading rules based on return continuations.

underwrite The investment banker purchases shares from a firm and resells them to investors.

underwriting spread The difference between the net price and the offer price.

underwriting syndicate Consists of many investment banks that collectively purchase the firm's shares and market them, thereby spreading the risk exposure across the syndicate.

unlevered equity beta The figure calculated by removing the effects of leverage on an equity beta.

unseasoned equity offering An IPO.

unsecured creditors Creditors who have no specific assets pledged as collateral, or the proceeds from the sale of whose pledged assets are inadequate to cover the debt.

unsponsored ADR An ADR in which the issuing firm is not involved with the issue at all and may even oppose it.

unsystematic risk The proportion of risk that can be eliminated through diversification.

 V

variable growth model Assumes that the growth rate dividend will vary during different periods of time, when calculating the value of a firm's stock.

variance bounds Refers to the body of literature launched by Shiller (1979) with his observation that long-term interest rates vary far more than they should, given the actual fluctuations in short-term interest rates.

venture capital A professionally managed pool of money raised for the sole purpose of making actively managed direct equity investments in rapidly growing private companies.

venture capital limited partnerships Funds established by professional venture capital firms.

venture capitalists Professional investors who specialize in high-risk/high-return investments in rapidly growing entrepreneurial businesses.

vertical merger Companies with current or potential buyer-seller relationships combine to create a more integrated company.

voluntary reorganization A strategy that sustains a firm so that the creditor can continue to receive business from it.

voluntary settlement A firm that becomes technically insolvent or bankrupt may make an arrangment with its creditors that enables it to bypass many of the costs involved in legal bankruptcy proceedings.

 W

warrants Securities issued by firms that grant the right to buy shares of stock at a fixed price for a given period of time.

weak-form efficiency In markets characterized by this kind of efficiency, asset prices incorporate all information from the historical price record.

wealth tax A capital gains tax at a rate equal to the dividend tax rate. This tax will make investors indifferent to whether they receive taxable dividends or taxable capital gains; but this will happen only if the tax on stock appreciation is levied every period, regardless of whether the shares are sold or not.

weighted average cost of capital (WACC) The after-tax weighted-average required return on all types of securities issued by a firm, in which the weights equal the percentage of each type of financing in a firm's overall capital structure.

white knights "Friendly" acquirers who will top the price of an unwelcome bidder to avoid a hostile takeover.

winner's curse Because they receive small allocations in hot deals and large allocations in cold deals, the unsophisticated players in this market will earn much lower returns.

wire transfer In the United States, the primary wire transfer system, known as *Fedwire,* is run by the Federal Reserve and is available to all depository institutions.

working capital Refers to what is more correctly known as *net working capital.*

workout A firm that becomes technically insolvent or bankrupt may make an arrangment with its creditors that enables it to bypass many of the costs involved in legal bankruptcy proceedings.

World Trade Organization (WTO) An international body that polices world trading practices and mediates disputes between member countries.

writing covered calls A common trading strategy that mixes stock and call options. In this strategy, an investor who owns a share of stock sells a call option on that stock.

 Y

Yankee bonds Bonds sold by foreign corporations to U.S. investors.

Yankee common stock Stock issued by foreign firms in the U.S. market.

yield curve A graph that plots the relationship between yield to maturity and maturity for a group of similar bonds.

yield spread The difference in yield to maturity between two bonds or two classes of bonds with similar maturities.

yield to maturity The discount rate that equates the present value of the bond's cash flows to its market price.

Z

Z score The product of a quantitative model for forecasting bankruptcy that uses a blend of traditional financial ratios and a statistical technique known as *multiple discriminant analysis*. The Z score has been found to be about 90 percent accurate in forecasting bankruptcy one year in the future and about 80 percent accurate in forecasting it two years in the future.

zero growth model The simplest approach to dividend valuation that assumes a constant dividend stream.

zero-balance accounts Disbursement accounts that always have an end-of-day balance of zero. The purpose is to eliminate nonearning cash balances in corporate checking accounts.

zero-coupon bonds Pure discount instruments, such as U.S. Treasury bills, that promise investors a single fixed payment on a specified future date.

NAME INDEX

COMPANY INDEX

SUBJECT INDEX

WELCOME TO SMART FINANCE!

This new textbook includes complimentary access to the **Smart Finance** Web Site (http://smartfinance.swcollege.com). Visit the site and use the online multimedia learning tools to gain a deeper and richer understanding of corporate finance, including:

◇ **Smart Concepts:** Animated concept review tutorials explain key topics within each chapter and allow students to review on their own time, at their own pace.

◇ **Smart Solutions:** Animated problems and solutions from each chapter contain dynamic charts, graphs, and tables to help sharpen problem-solving skills and master quantitative concepts.

◇ **Smart Ideas Video:** View leading academics and researchers explaining important concepts and theories from each chapter.

◇ **Smart Practices Video:** Watch leaders in business and industry highlight how finance theory, as explained in the text, is used in practice on a daily basis.

◇ **Smart Ethics Video:** See the ways in which both academics and business executives believe ethical conduct is crucial to the health of a firm's bottom line.

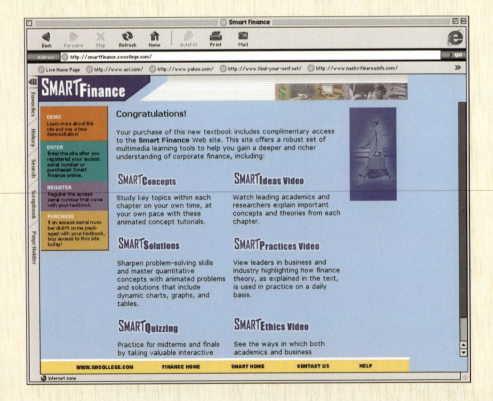